Lecture Notes in Computer Science 2833

Edited by G. Goos, J. Hartmanis, and J. van Leeuwen

Lecture Notes in Computer Science 2883
Edited by G. Goos, J. Hartmanis, and J. van Leeuwen

Springer
Berlin
Heidelberg
New York
Hong Kong
London
Milan
Paris
Tokyo

Francesca Rossi (Ed.)

Principles and Practice of Constraint Programming – CP 2003

9th International Conference, CP 2003
Kinsale, Ireland, September 29 – October 3, 2003
Proceedings

 Springer

Series Editors

Gerhard Goos, Karlsruhe University, Germany
Juris Hartmanis, Cornell University, NY, USA
Jan van Leeuwen, Utrecht University, The Netherlands

Volume Editor

Francesca Rossi
University of Padova
Department of Pure and Applied Mathematics
Via G.B. Belzoni 7, 35131 Padova, Italy
E-mail: frossi@math.unipd.it

Cataloging-in-Publication Data applied for

A catalog record for this book is available from the Library of Congress

Bibliographic information published by Die Deutsche Bibliothek
Die Deutsche Bibliothek lists this publication in the Deutsche Nationalbibliographie;
detailed bibliographic data is available in the Internet at <http://dnb.ddb.de>.

CR Subject Classification (1998): D.1, D.3.2-3, I.2.3-4, F.3.2, F.4.1, I.2.8, J.1

ISSN 0302-9743
ISBN 3-540-20202-1 Springer-Verlag Berlin Heidelberg New York

Springer-Verlag Berlin Heidelberg New York
a member of BertelsmannSpringer Science+Business Media GmbH

http://www.springer.de

© Springer-Verlag Berlin Heidelberg 2003
Printed in Germany

Typesetting: Camera-ready by author, data conversion by Olgun Computergrafik
Printed on acid-free paper   SPIN: 10957295   06/3142   5 4 3 2 1 0

Preface

This volume contains the proceedings of the Ninth International Conference on Principles and Practice of Constraint Programming (CP 2003), held in Kinsale, Ireland, from September 29 to October 3, 2003. Detailed information about the CP 2003 conference can be found at the URL http://www.cs.ucc.ie/cp2003/

The CP conferences are held annually and provide an international forum for the latest results on all aspects of constraint programming. Previous CP conferences were held in Cassis (France) in 1995, in Cambridge (USA) in 1996, in Schloss Hagenberg (Austria) in 1997, in Pisa (Italy) in 1998, in Alexandria (USA) in 1999, in Singapore in 2000, in Paphos (Cyprus) in 2001, and in Ithaca (USA) in 2002.

Like previous CP conferences, CP 2003 again showed the interdisciplinary nature of computing with constraints, and also its usefulness in many problem domains and applications. Constraint programming, with its solvers, languages, theoretical results, and applications, has become a widely recognized paradigm to model and solve successfully many real-life problems, and to reason about problems in many research areas.

This year the research community has shown a very high interest in constraint programming, submitting to CP 2003 a record number of 181 papers, ranging over all aspects of constraint programming, from solvers to languages and from applications to theoretical results. After a reviewing period where each paper was read by three reviewers, and a two-day meeting in Padova (Italy) on June 3–4, 2003, the Program Committee decided to accept 48 papers as full papers, which have been allocated 15 pages in the proceedings. Among these, we selected a best paper: Control Abstraction by Local Search, by Pascal Van Hentenryck and Laurent Michel. We also decided to accept 34 poster papers, which have been allocated 5 pages in the proceedings. Poster papers are not to be thought of as second class papers, but rather as papers describing preliminary work which are, however, very promising and contain very fine and innovative ideas.

This volume also contains the papers of the four invited speakers, who honored the conference with their presentations: Henry Kautz, who told us about recent progress in propositional reasoning and search, Tuomas Sandholm, who proposed automated mechanism design as a new application area, Mark Wallace, who discussed the never-ending debate about languages versus packages, and Toby Walsh, who proposed constraint patterns as a useful modeling tool. Thanks to all of them!

A tradition since CP 2001, CP 2003 included a doctoral program, which allowed Ph.D. students working on constraint programming to come to the conference, to present their work and discuss it with senior researchers, and to listen to tutorials on career and doctoral issues. This volume contains one page for each of the 40 accepted students who don't have a paper on the same subject in the main technical program. I am especially grateful to Michela Milano, who did a wonderful job both in organizing the doctoral program and in raising enough sponsor money to support the participation of 44 students.

CP 2003 also included 10 workshops and 4 advanced tutorials. The tutorials were on preferences (Ronen Brafman and Carmel Domshlak), randomized backtrack search (Carla P. Gomes), dynamic constraint solving (Gérard Verfaillie, Narendra Jussien), and configuration (Daniel Mailharro, Ulrich Junker). Many thanks to all the tutorialists, and also to Christian Bessière who organized all this very smoothly and with a very good resulting workshop and tutorial program.

CP 2003 also included a demo session showing the latest tools in constraint programming. Many thanks to James Little, who organized it very successfully, and also to the 8 groups who responded to the call for demos.

This year for the first time CP was co-located with the ECL^{i}PS^e summer school, held on September 28, 2003. This provided an opportunity for CP 2003 attendees to learn about the basics and also the latest tools available in the ECL^{i}PS^e environment from the developers and designers of the language. Thanks to Mark Wallace who had the idea to co-locate the school with CP 2003.

I would like to thank the whole Program Committee for the time spent with me over email in the 10 months preceding the conference and the two days we physically met for the PC meeting. I especially appreciated the friendly and constructive atmosphere in all the discussions about the submission process and the constructive attitute of all the members towards the numerous problem solving tasks. A special thanks goes to two members of the PC, Peter van Beek and Toby Walsh, who acted as special counselors in difficult situations such as problematic papers or delicate decisions.

I would also like to thank James Bowen, the conference chair, who dealt with all the difficult organizational aspects of the conference, and who managed to convince Science Foundation Ireland to support this conference in a significant way. Many thanks also to Steven Prestwich, the publicity chair.

The PC meeting could not have been organized without the help of my system people and of my Ph.D. student, K. B. Venable. Thanks!

Finally, I would like to thank explicitly all the sponsors: CoLogNET, Cork Constraint Computation Centre, the CP organizing committee, ERCIM, ILOG, the Intelligent Information System Institute at Cornell University, PARC Technologies, Science Foundation Ireland, and SICS. They were all very generous this year, enabling us to support many students and the invited speakers, and also to subsidize the conference fee and many other expenses.

Last but definitely not least, I want to thank the CP organizing committee, who asked me to serve as Program Chair of CP 2003 thus giving me the opportunity to live through a very exciting and learning experience. I hope I met at least some of their expectations for CP 2003.

July 2003   Francesca Rossi

Conference Organization

Conference Chair:	James Bowen, Univ. College Cork, Ireland
Program Chair:	Francesca Rossi, Univ. of Padova, Italy
Doctoral Program Chair:	Michela Milano, Univ. of Bologna, Italy
Workshop/Tutorial Chair:	Christian Bessière, LIRMM, France
Demo Chair:	James Little, Univ. College Cork, Ireland
Publicity Chair:	Steven Prestwich, Univ. College Cork, Ireland

Program Committee

Krzysztof Apt
Fahiem Bacchus
Peter van Beek
Frédéric Benhamou
Christan Bessière
Alexander Bockmayr
James Bowen
Philippe Codognet
Rina Dechter
Boi Faltings
Thom Frühwirth

Carmen Gervet
Carla Gomes
Manuel Hermenegildo
Holger Hoos
Peter Jeavons
Ulrich Junker
Manolis Koubarakis
François Laburthe
Pedro Meseguer
Michela Milano
Jean Charles Régin

Thomas Schiex
Helmut Simonis
Barbara Smith
Peter Stuckey
Michael Trick
Gérard Verfaillie
Toby Walsh
Roland Yap
Makoto Yokoo

CP Organizing Committee

Alan Borning
James Bowen
Alex Brodsky
Jacques Cohen
Alain Colmerauer
Rina Dechter
Eugene Freuder, Chair
Hervé Gallaire

Carla Gomes
Joxan Jaffar
Jean-Pierre Jouannaud
Jean-Louis Lassez
Michael Maher
Ugo Montanari
Anil Nerode
Jean-François Puget

Francesca Rossi
Vijay Saraswat
Gert Smolka
Pascal Van Hentenryck
Ralph Wachter
Toby Walsh
Roland Yap

Sponsors

CoLogNET
Cork Constraint Computation Centre (4C)
CP Organizing Committee
ERCIM
ILOG
The Intelligent Information System Institute at Cornell University
PARC Technologies
Science Foundation Ireland
SICS

Additional Referees

Elvira Albert
Alexis Anglada
Ionut Arun
Francisco Azevedo
Rolf Backofen
Pedro Barahona
Roman Bartak
Bozhena Bidyuk
Stefano Bistarelli
Christian Bliek
Lucas Bordeaux
Alan Borning
Eric Bourreau
Sebastian Brand
Stephane Bressan
Pascal Brisset
Andrei Bulatov
Manuel Carro
Martine Ceberio
Amedeo Cesta
Ee-Chien Chang
Witold Charatonik
Marco Chiarandini
Henning Christiansen
Lau Hoong Chuin
Dave Cohen
Raphael Collet
Martin Cooper
Arnaud Courtois
Joe Culberson
Veronica Dahl
Víctor Dalmau
Romuald Debruyne
Alexander Dekhtyar
Gilles Dequen
Alessandra Di Pierro
Eric Domenjoud
Carmel Domshlak
Lyndon Drake
Irina Dumitrescu
Hani El Sakkout
Martin H. van Emden
Torsten Fahle
Gérard Ferrand

Filippo Focacci
Alan Frisch
Luca di Gaspero
Marco Gavanelli
Hector Geffner
Rosella Gennari
Ian Gent
Yan Georget
Simon de Givry
Frédéric Goualard
Martin Grabmueller
Laurent Granvilliers
Christophe Guettier
Gopal Gupta
Guillaume Hanrot
Warwick Harvey
Martin Henz
Michael Heusch
Katsutoshi Hirayama
Brahim Hnich
Petra Hofstedt
Tad Hogg
Hiroshi Hosobe
W.J. van Hoeve
Frank Hutter
Joxan Jaffar
Christophe Jermann
Bernard Jurkowiak
Narendra Jussien
Olli Kamarainen
Kalev Kask
Henry Kautz
Ed. Kazmierczak
Zeynep Kiziltan
Frédéric Koriche
Arnaud Lallouet
Evelina Lamma
David Larkin
Javier Larrosa
Daniel Leberre
Jimmy Lee
Ho-fung Leung
Olivier Lhomme
C. Likitvivatanavong

Ines Lynce
Michael Maher
Daniel Mailharro
Radu Marinescu
Julio Mariño
Kim Marriott
Robert Matescu
Ian Miguel
Chu Min Li
David Mitchell
Eric Monfroy
Bertrand Neveu
Stefano Novello
Angelo Oddi
Patrice Perny
Thierry Petit
Karen Petrie
Evgueni Petrov
Enrico Pontelli
Nicolas Prcovic
Steven Prestwich
Patrick Prosser
Jean-François Puget
Alessandra Raffaeta
Philippe Refalo
Barry Richards
Tom Richards
Christophe Ringeissen
Georg Ringwelski
Guillaume Rochart
Robert Rodosek
Andrea Roli
Louis-Martin Rousseau
Andrew G.D. Rowley
Michel Rueher
Vassilis Samoladas
Vitor Santos Costa
Frédéric Saubion
Andrea Schaerf
Tommaso Schiavinotto
Joachim Schimpf
Hans Schlenker
Christian Schulte
Meinolf Sellmann

Bart Selman
Andrea Shaerf
Dan Sheridan
Spiros Skiadopoulos
Marcos Silva
Barbara Smith
Kevin Smyth
Francis Sourd
Kostas Stergiou

Martin Sulzmann
Martí Sánchez
Christian Timpe
Dave Tompkins
Carme Torras
Charlotte Truchet
Kristen B. Venable
M.C. Vilarem
Mark Wallace

Richard J. Wallace
Limsoon Wong
Huayue Wu
Neil Yorke-Smith
Tallys Yunes
Yuanlin Zhang

Table of Contents

Poster Papers

Doctoral Abstracts

Ten Challenges *Redux*: Recent Progress in Propositional Reasoning and Search

Henry Kautz[1] and Bart Selman[2]

[1] Department of Computer Science & Engineering
University of Washington
Seattle, WA 98195 USA
kautz@cs.washington.edu
[2] Department of Computer Science
Cornell University
Ithaca, NY 14853 USA
selman@cs.cornell.edu

Abstract. In 1997 we presented ten challenges for research on satisfiability testing [1]. In this paper we review recent progress towards each of these challenges, including our own work on the power of clause learning and randomized restart policies.

1 Introduction

The past few years have seen enormous progress in the performance of Boolean satisfiability (SAT) solvers. Despite the worst-case exponential run time of all known algorithms, SAT solvers are now in routine use for applications such as hardware verification [2] that involve solving hard structured problems with up to a million variables [3, 4]. Each year the International Conference on Theory and Applications of Satisfiability Testing hosts a SAT competition that highlights a new group of "world's fastest" SAT solvers, and presents detailed performance results on a wide range of solvers [5, 6]. In the the 2003 competition, over 30 solvers competed on instances selected from thousands of benchmark problems.

In 1997, we presented ten challenges for research on satisfiability testing [1], on topics that at the time appeared to be ripe for progress. In this paper we revisit these challenges, review progess, and offer some suggestions for future research.

A full review of the literature related to the original challenges, let alone satisfiability testing as a whole, is beyond the scope of this paper. We do highlight several of the main recent developments, but the discussion below is biased towards topics from our own research program in recent years. We welcome pointers to any key papers we may have missed. We plan to keep this document up-to-date with regular revisions posted on the SAT Challenge web page [7].

2 Challenging SAT Instances

Empirical evaluation of sat solvers on benchmark problems (such as those from [8]) has been a effective driving force for progress on both fundamental algo-

F. Rossi (Ed.): CP 2003, LNCS 2833, pp. 1–18, 2003.

rithms and theoretical understanding of the nature of satisfiability. The first two challenges were specific open SAT problems, one random and the other highly structured.

CHALLENGE 1: *Prove that a hard 700 variable random 3-SAT formula is unsatisfiable.*

When we formulated in this challenge in 1997, complete SAT procedures based on DPLL [9] could handle around 300 to 400 variable hard random 3-SAT problems. Progress in recent years had slowed and it was not clear DPLL could be much improved upon for random 3-SAT. In particular, the there was the possibility that the best DPLL methods were obtaining search trees that were close to minimal in terms of the number of backtrack points [10]. Dubois and Dequen [11], however, showed that there was still room for improvement. They introduced a new branching heuristic that exploits so-called "backbone" variables in a SAT problem. A backbone variable of a formula is a variable that is assigned the same truth value in all assignments that satisfy the maximum number of clauses. (For satisfiable formulas, these are simply the satisfying assignments of the formula.) The notion of a backbone variable came out of work on k-SAT using tools from statistical physics, which has provided significant insights into the solution structure of random instances. In particular, it can be shown that a relatively large set of backbone variables suddenly emerges when one passes though the phase transition point for k-SAT ($k \geq 3$) [12]. Using a backbone-guided search heuristic, Dubois and Dequen can solve a 700 variable unsatisfiable, hard random 3-SAT instance in around 25 days of CPU time, thereby approaching practical feasibility.

In the context of this challenge, it should be noted that significant progress has been made in the last decade in terms of our general understanding of the properties of random 3-SAT problems and the associated phase transition phenomenon. A full review of this area would require a separate paper. (See e.g. [13–22].) Many of the developments in the area have been obtained by using tools from statistical physics. This work has recently culminated in a new algorithm for solving satisfiable k-SAT instances near the phase transition point [23]. The method is called survey propagation and involves, in a sense, a sophisticated probabilistic analysis of the problem instance under consideration. An efficient implementation enables the solution of hard random 3-SAT phase transition instances of up to a million variables in about 2 hours of CPU time. For comparsion, the previously most effective procedure for random 3-SAT, WalkSAT [24], can handle instances with around 100,000 variables within this timeframe. The exact scaling properties of survey propagation — and WalksSAT for that matter — are still unknown.

In conclusion, even though we have seen many exciting new results in terms of solving hard random instances, the gap between our ability to handle satisfiable and unsatisfiable instances has actually grown. An interesting question is whether a procedure dramatically different from DPLL can be found for handling unsatisfiable instances.

CHALLENGE 2: *Develop an algorithm that finds a model for the DIMACS 32-bit parity problem.*

The second challenge problem derives from the problem of learning a parity function from examples. This problem is NP-complete and it is argued in [25] that any particular instance is likely to be hard to solve (although average-case NP-completeness has not been formally shown). However, this challenge was solved in 1998 by preprocessing the formula to detect chains of literals that are equivalent considering binary clauses alone, and then applying DPLL after simplification [26][1]. Later [27] showed similar performance by performance equivalency detection at every node in the search tree.

Parity problems are particularly hard for local search methods because such algorithms tend to become trapped at a near-solution such that a small subset of clauses is never satisfied simultaneously. Clause re-weighting schemes [28, 29] try to smooth out the search space by giving higher weight to clauses that are often unsatisfied. A clause weighting scheme based on Langrange multipliers [30] was able to solve the 16-bit versions of the parity learning problems.

3   Challenges for Systematic Search

At the time of our original challenge paper nearly all the best systematic methods for propositional reasoning on clausal formulas were based on creating a resolution proof tree[2]. This includes the depth-first search Davis-Putnam-Loveland-Logemann procedure (DPLL) [33, 34], where the proof tree can be recovered from the trace of the algorithm's execution, but is not explicitly represented in a data structure (the algorithm only maintains a single branch of the proof tree in memory at any one time). Most work on systematic search concentrates on heuristics for variable-ordering and value selection, all in order to the reduce size of the tree.

However, there are known fundamental limitations on the size of the shortest resolution proofs that can be obtained in this manner, even with ideal branching strategies. The study of proof complexity [35] compares inference systems in terms of the sizes of the shortest proofs they sanction. For example, two proof systems are linearly related if there is a linear function $f(n)$ such that for any proof of length n in one system there is a proof of length at most $f(n)$ in the other system. A family of formulas C provides an *exponential separation* between systems S_1 and S_2 if the shortest proofs of formulas in C in system S_1 are exponentially smaller than the corresponding shortest proofs in S_2.

A basic result in proof complexity is that general resolution is exponentially stronger than the DPLL procedure [36, 37]. This is because the trace of DPLL running on an unsatisfiable formula can be converted to a tree-like resolution

---

[1] [26] also described a general preprocessor for identifying conjunctions of nested equivalencies subformulas using linear programming.

[2] Much work in verification has involved non-clausal representations, in particular Boolean Decision Diagrams [31, 32]; but the large body of work on BDD's will not be further discussed here.

proof of the same size, and tree-like proofs must sometimes be exponentially larger than the DAG-like proofs generated by general resolution. Furthermore, it is known that even general resolution requires exponentially long proofs for for certain "intuitively easy" problems [38–40]. The classic example are "pigeon hole" problems that represent the fact that n pigeons cannot fit in $n-1$ holes. Shorter proofs do exist in more powerful proof systems. Examples of proof systems more powerful than resolution include extended resolution, which allows one to introduce new defined variables, and resolution with symmetry-detection, which uses symmetries to eliminate parts of the tree without search. Assuming $NP \neq co - NP$, even the most powerful propositional proof systems would require exponential long proofs worst case — nonetheless, such systems provably dominate resolution in terms of minimum proof size.

Early attempts to mechanize proof systems more powerful than tree-like resolution gave no computational savings, because it is *harder* to find the small proof tree in the new system than to simply crank out a large resolution proof. In essence, the overhead in dealing with the more powerful rules of inference consumes all the potential savings. Our third challenge was to present a practical proof system more powerful than resolution. In reviewing progress in this area we first consider systems more powerful than tree-like (DPLL) resolution, and next ones more powerful than general resolution.

3.1   Beyond DPLL

CHALLENGE 3A: *Demonstrate that a propositional proof system more powerful than tree-like resolution can be made practical for satisfiability testing.*

Two new satisfiability testing algorithms were introduced in 1997, the same year as our challenge paper: rel-sat [41] and SATO [42]. Both were versions of DPLL augmented with "conflict clause learning", a technique that grew out of research in AI on explanation-based approaches to speed-up learning [43–45]. The idea in clause learning is that at each backtrack point the system derives a reason for the inconsistency in the form of a new clause added to the original formula. Rel-sat and SATO were suprisingly powerful, and even able to solve open problems in finite mathematics. Clause learning was further developed for the solvers GRASP [46], Chaff [47, 48] and BerkMin [49], and is currently a key technique in backtracking SAT solvers for applications such as verification.

Marquis-Silva [50] observed that clause learning can be viewed as adding resolvents to a tree-like proof, and Zhang [48] showed how different clause learning schemes could be categorized according to way clauses were derived from cuts in a data structure called a *conflict graph*. The conflict graph records the pattern of *unit propagations* that have been performed at any point in the execution of the algorithm. Each node in the graph is a literal that is currently assumed to be true. The leaves are branch literals and the inner nodes are literals derived by unit propagation. A conflict literal is one that appears both negatively and positively in the graph.

Consider the implication graph at a stage where there is a conflict and fix a conflict graph contained in that implication graph. Pick any cut in the conflict

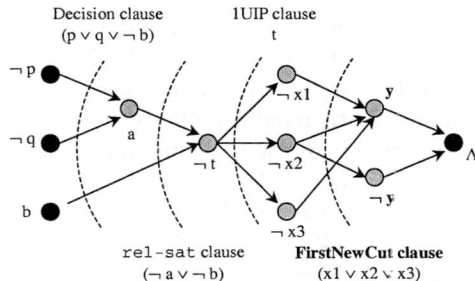

Fig. 1. A conflict graph depicting various learning schemes.

graph that has all decision variables on one side, called the *reason side*, and *false* as well as at least one conflict literal on the other side, called the *conflict side*. All nodes on the reason side that have at least one edge going to the conflict side form a *cause* of the conflict. The negations of the corresponding literals forms the *conflict clause associated with this cut*: that is, a clause that is implied by the original formula. Figure 1 illustrates different possible cuts through a conflict graph, corresponding to different clause learning algorithms.

Although the empirical power of clause learning had been clear for several years, Beame *et al.* [51] provided the first proof of an exponential separation between clause learning and ordinary DPPL. The result was, in fact, even stronger: they showed that there are formulas with short clause learning proofs that require exponentially large *regular resolution* proofs. Regular resolution proofs are DAGS, as in general resolution, but are restricted so that no variable is resolved upon more than once in any path from the root to a leaf. It is easy to see that all tree-like proofs are regular but not vice-versa. They further showed that combining clause learning with *restarts* [52, 53] (where learned clauses are saved between restarts) is equivalent to general resolution. However, the questions of whether clause learning is *strictly stronger* than regular resolution — that is, whether or not there are also formulas with short regular proofs but long clause proofs – and whether clause learning *without* restarts is equivalent to general resolution are open.

Making clause learning work well in practice requires efficient strategies for mananging the large number of learned clauses. The first technique developed for this management problem was relevance-bounded learning [41, 42]. The idea is to discard a learned clause once it is unlikely to be useful later on in the proof. A simple but effective strategy is to throw out clauses of length greater than some fixed k when the search backtracks above the point at which any of the literals in the clause are assigned a value [41]. A second important management technique, called "watched literals", was most fully exploited in Chaff [47]. Watched literals is actually a generic technique for reducing the time needed to tell which clauses have been shortened to length one during the DPPL's unit propagation step. Two literals are arbitrarily chosen in each clause to be "watched". When a literal is set, rather than scanning through all clauses containing the negation of the literal, the algorithm only scans clauses contained *watched* negations of the literal. It is easy to see that this technique still finds all unit clauses, because such a clause is guaranteed to be scanned once it becomes a binary clause. Watched literals allows modern solvers to handle millions of learned clauses with small time overhead (although space can then become problematic).

Clause learning strategies and variable branching strategies have traditionally been studied separately. However, [54] shows that there is great promise in developing branching strategies that explicitly take into account the order in which clauses are learned. They considered a class of formulas known as pebbling formulas [36, 55–57], which can be thought of as representing precedence graphs in dependent task systems and scheduling scenarios. Such formulas require exponential-sized proofs for tree-like resolution, but have polynomial clause-learning proofs. However, it remains difficult to *find* such proofs. [54] preprocesses the formula to extract a *domain-specific* branching sequence — that is, a branching order that can be formally shown to yield small clause learning proofs for formulas encoding pebbling graphs. While ordinary DPLL (with a good branching order) scales to problems with about 60 variables on the pebbling formulas, and clause learning alone scales to 4,000 variables, clause learning with the domain specific ordering handles over 2,000,000 variables. To make this work of practical use we need to develop domain-specific strategies for other common structures that arise in applications such as verification or planning, and automated or semi-automated techniques for recognizing the structures.

3.2 Beyond General Resolution

CHALLENGE 3B: *Demonstrate that a propositional proof system more powerful than general resolution can be made practical for satisfiability testing.*

Currently the most practical extension of general resolution is symmetry detection. The pigeon hole problem is intuitively easy because we immediately see that different pigeons and holes are indistinguishable, so we do not need to actually consider all possible matchings — without loss of generality, attempting to find a particular (say, lexigraphically ordered) matching suffices. [58] showed how to determine if there existed a renaming (permutation) ψ of the variables in a formula that resulted in the same set of clauses, which justified a new rule of inference: from any clause $(a \vee b \vee ...)$, infer $(\psi(a) \vee \psi(b) \vee ...)$. [59] introduced a different way of using symmetries, by strengthening the formula through the addition of clauses that ruled out all but one of the symmetric cases. The drawback of this approach appeared to be the large (quadratic) number of symmetry breaking clauses needed; but [60] showed that a linear sized set of symmetry-breaking predicates was logically equivalent, and led to dramatic speedup on certain structured benchmark problems. Symmetry detection is not, however, a cure-all; [61] showed that any formula that was exponential for resolution could be transformed into one that was still exponential for resolution plus symmetry detection, by adding new literals and clauses that "hid" the symmetry.

As we have noted clause learning alone does not exceed the power of general resolution. However, if instead of cacheing conflicts, one modifies DPLL so that the entire residual formula at each node in the search tree is cached, then the proof complexity of the resulting system can exceed resolution [62] (if the test for a cached formula includes subsumption checking). Furthermore, [63] argues that formula caching is the fastest practical algorithm for *counting* the number of solutions of formula.

CHALLENGE 4: *Demonstrate that integer programming can be made practical for satisfiability testing.*

Over the years, there has been a significant amount of work on the close connection between 0/1 integer programming and SAT (e.g., [64, 65]). A key question is whether techniques developed for integer programming can be of use in SAT solvers. So far, it has been difficult to obtain a concrete computational advantage of integer programming methods on practical SAT instances. The recent work by Warners and van Maaren provides two promising examples of where integer programming and related techniques may have an impact. First, as discussed above, linear programming can be used in a two-phase algorithm for the 32-bit parity formulas [26]. Secondly, by using a semi-definite programming formulation, pigeon hole formulas can be solved efficiently [66]. The challenge remains to incorporate these approaches in more general, practical SAT solvers.

In recent years, we have also seen an interesting development in the opposite direction: use SAT techniques in the design of more efficient solvers for 0/1 integer programming problems. More specifically, one considers pseudo-Boolean encodings, which use Boolean variables and linear inequalities over such variables with integer coefficients. Most interestingly, some of the best solvers for pseudo-Boolean problems are extensions of the best SAT solvers [67–69].

4   Challenges for Stochastic Search

CHALLENGE 5: *Design a practical stochastic local search procedure for proving unsatisfiability.*

Given the success of local search style procedures on satisfiable problem instances, it would be interesting to use a local search strategy for finding "proof objects", *i.e.*, objects that demonstrate the unsatisfiability of an instance. This challenge remains wide open. A key issue is the need to find smaller proof objects. Work on strong backdoor sets, which are small sets of variables that, together with a polytime propagation method, can demonstrate unsatisfiability may lead to some new opportunities in this area [70].

CHALLENGE 6: *Improve stochastic local search on structured problems by efficiently handling variable dependencies.*

DPLL procedures handle variable dependency quite effectively through unit propagation. Local search methods, such as Walksat, handle dependencies through a random walk process, which may require on the order of N^2 flips to travel a dependency chain of N variables [71]. Given the large number of dependent variables in structured instances, the local search methods therefore are often less effective than local search style methods. Note that this is not always the case. For example, in runs on verification benchmarks, Velev [3] showed how the performance of DLM [72] and Walksat [24, 73] is comparable to many of the best DPLL style methods. A series of papers, such as [74–79] among others, has also led to a much improved understanding of local search methods for SAT.

Hirsch [80] introduces a local search procedure, UnitWalk, where variable dependencies are propagated explicitly as part of the search process. The propagation strategy is closed related to the one studied in [81]. UnitWalk is quite effective on certain classes of structured problems but there is still room for improvement. Comparisons with WalkSat shows that neither strategy dominates. This led to QingTing [82], which is a local search solver that dynamically switches between a UnitWalk and a Walksat strategy, depending on the underlying structure of of the problem.

In a different approach to handling dependencies, in [71], redundant clauses are added to the SAT problem instances in a preprocessing phase. The redundant clauses capture long range dependencies between variables. It can be shown, both theoretically and empirically, that such redundant clauses speed up a local search style solver.

Although the challenge problem was formulated specifically in the context of local search methods, techniques for discovering and exploiting various forms of variable dependencies have also been shown to be effective for DPLL style procedures. See, for example, [83–85].

5   Randomized Systematic Search

CHALLENGE 7: *Demonstrate the succesful combination of stochastic search and systematic search techniques, by the creation of a new algorithm that outperforms the best previous examples of both approaches.*

[86, 87] present hybrid approaches, integrating a local search and a DPLL solver. This work provides a promising step towards hybrid solvers, but it remains a challenge to have such solvers outperform non-hybrids on a wide range of benchmark problems.

We implicitly assumed in this challenge, as was common at the time, that stochastic search refers to some form of local search. Systematic, complete methods, such as DPLL, were generally deterministic. A major recent change during the last five years came out of the insight that adding randomization to a complete search method, combined with a restart strategy, can provide a significant computational advance [52]. (Note that explicit randomization is not required. For example, clauses learning between restarts of a DPLL solver, such as used in Chaff, also forces explorations of different parts of the search space on different restarts.)

Randomization and restarts take advantage of the large variations that have been observed between different runs of backtrack search procedures on a given problem instance. In fact, it has been shown that randomized DPLL run time distributions are often — but not always — "heavy-tailed" [88–91]. This means that one observes a mixtures of run times on dramatically different scales. By using rapid restarts, one can take advantage of the occasionally short, successful run [52]. In a recent paper [70], it was shown that such short runs can be explained by the existence of a small set of *backdoor* variables in the problem instance. Once backdoor variables are assigned a value, the polytime propagation and simplication mechanism of the solver under consideration sets the remaining variables without further backtracking. (In case of a unsatisfiable instances, the propagation mechanisms discovers an inconsistancy after propagation.) Practical problem instances can have surprisingly small sets of backdoor variables. We have observed structured instances with tens of thousands of variables with backdoor sets of around a dozen variables. Randomization and restarts, in conjunction with the variable selection heuristics, help the solver discover the backdoor sets. Work on backdoor variables and clause learning, as discussed above, is providing us with a better understanding as to why structured SAT instances with up to a million variables, from, e.g., verification applications, can be solved with current state-of-the-art solvers.

An important related issue is how to decide on a good restart policy. Luby *et al.* [92] described restart policies for general randomized algorithms for two scenarios where runtime itself is the only observable: (i) when each run is a random sample from a known distribution, one can calculate a fixed optimal cutoff; (ii) when there is no knowledge of the distribution, a *universal schedule* mixing short and longer cutoffs comes within a log factor of the minimal run time.

Horvitz *et al.* [93] showed that it is possible to do better than Luby's fixed optimal policy by making observations of a variety of features related to the nature and progress of problem solving during an early portion of the run (referred to as the *observation horizon*) and learning, and then using, a Bayesian model to predict the length of each run. Examples of features of a running SAT solver (satz) included the minimum, maximum, final, and average values of (1) The number of backtracks; (2) The number of unit propagations; (3) Domain-specific measures of the current subproblem (for example, for a coloring problem, the number of nodes that have been colored), as well as the derivatives of such values. Under the assumption that each run is an independent random sample of one runtime distribution (RTD), [94] used observations to discriminate the potentially short runs from the long ones and then adopted different restart cutoffs for the two types of runs.

Ruan *et al.* [95] considered the case where there are k known distributions, and each run is a sample from *one* of the distributions—but the solver is not told *which* distribution. The paper showed how offline dynamic programming can be used to generate the optimal restart policy, and how the policy can be coupled with real-time observations to control restarting. In recent work the same authors [96] generalize this to the case where the k distributions are not specified in advance: instead, the solver first infers how a problem ensemble can be decomposed into a set of sub-ensembles such that each sub-ensemble clusters instances with similar runtime distributions.

The following example from [96] illustrates this approach where instances are clustered by their median runtime. Suppose that the RTD of each instance is a scaled Pareto distribution controlled by a parameter b:

$$P(t) = \begin{cases} b/t^2 & \text{if } t \geq b \\ 0 & \text{if } t < b \end{cases}$$

This is a canonical example of a heavy-tailed distribution. Furthermore, suppose that b is an integer that is uniformly distributed in the range $[11, 100]$ across the problem distribution. The median run time of any particular instance is $2b$, so we expect that median run times of the sampled instances would fall uniformly in the range $[22, 200]$. A binary clustering by the median run times of the samples should give one cluster where the instance medians are in the range $[22, 110]$ (equivalently, $b \in [11, 55]$) and another cluster where the instance medians are in the range $[111, 200]$ (equivalently, $b \in [56, 100]$). Each cluster, or sub-ensemble, yields an *ensemble* run time distribution. The ensemble distribution RTD is the normalized sum of the RTD's of the instances it contains.

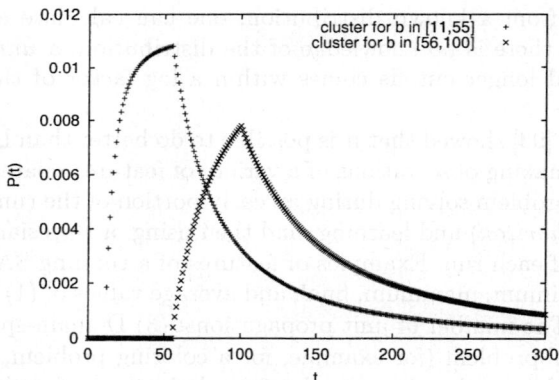

Fig. 2. The sub-ensemble run-time distributions for the example of a family of scaled Pareto distributions.

Fig. 2 shows the sub-ensemble RTD's for this example. The ensemble RTD's are not simple scaled Pareto distributions, because there is a non-zero probability density to the left of the maximum points. One can show (analytically or by computer simulation) that the optimal cutoffs for the two clusters are at 98 and 244 respectively. The dynamic programming procedure mentioned above can then be used to calculate a complete policy—in the case of the example where there are no run-time feature observations, this is a sequence of cutoff values to try on any given instance until solution is reached. In this example, the series of changing cutoff values are 201, 222, 234, 239, 242, 244, 244, ...

On experiments with hard quasigroup completion problems and SAT encodings of planning problems the approach showed a speedup ranging from 57% to 72% over Luby's universal policy. Interestingly, the policy of using fixed cutoff that is optimal under the (false) assumption that all instances in the ensemble are equally difficult fails catastrophically, because some instances are never solved.

6 Challenges for Problem Encodings

CHALLENGE 8: *Characterize the computational properties of different encodings of a real-world problem domain, and/or give general principles that hold over a range of domains.*

There has been a good amount of work on comparing different SAT encodings. For example, [97, 98] consider different translations of constraint satisfaction problems (CSP) into SAT. A central issue in this work is what kinds of encodings preserve local CSP consistency checking in the SAT encoding, where local processing consists mainly of unit-propagation. By exploiting some key ideas from CSPs, such as m-loosenes [99], one can in fact optimize the SAT encodings [100]. Examples of other work in the area are on encoding planning problems [101, 102] and quasi-group completion problems (a multi-coloring task) [103].

This work shows clearly that encodings have a significant impact on the practical solvability of the underlying problems. Some general lessons have been obtained, but there is still a need for more unifying, domain-independent principles.

CHALLENGE 9: *Find encodings of real-world domains which are robust in the sense that "near models" are actually "near solutions".*

In our work on planning [104], we noticed that assignments that satisfy all but a few of the clauses encoding our planning problems often represented action sequences that were very different from valid plans. This means that there can be a significant practical mismatch between a solver that tries to maximize the number of satisfied clauses (which is the standard approach is SAT solvers) and the search for valid plans. In particular, maximizing the number of satisfied clauses does not lead to nearly valid plans. It would seem that it should be possible to design better SAT encodings. This challenge remains open. For some related work, dealing with the robustness of encodings in general, see [105].

CHALLENGE 10: *Develop a generator for problem instances that have computational properties that are more similar to real-world instances.*

The final challenge is in response to the concern that the random k-SAT formulas that dominated benchmarks in 1997 might begin to drive research in the wrong direction [106]. [107] introduced a generation model based on the quasi-group (or Latin square) completion problem (QCP). The task is to determine if a partially colored square can be completed so that no color is repeated in any row or any column. QCP is an NP-complete problem, and random instances exhibit a peak in problem hardness in the area of the phase transition in the percentage of satisfiable instances generated as the ratio of the number of uncolored cells to the total number of cells is varied. The structure implicit in a QCP problem is similar to that found in real-world domains, such as scheduling, bandwidth assignment, and experimental design.

In order to measure the performance of incomplete solvers, it is necessary to have benchmark instances that are known to be satisfiable. This requirement is problematic in domains where incomplete methods can solve larger instances than complete methods: it is not possible to use a complete method to filter out the unsatisfiable instances. [103] described a generation model for quasigroup completion problems that are always guaranteed to be satisfiable. Another interesting approach for generating satisfiable instances is based on a translation of problems from cryptography [108].

Structured problem generators have also been created by linking a random generator for some particular domain to a SAT translator. For example, the Blackbox planning system [109] can be used to convert STRIPS planning problems into CNF formulas. The Blackbox distribution included a simple generator for random logistics planning problems, making it easy to generate random SAT problems that have the underlying structure of a planning problem.

Many SAT benchmarks today are encodings of bounded-model checking verification problems [2, 110]. While hundreds of specific problems are available, it would be useful to be able to randomly generate similar problems by the thousands for testing purposes: we hope to encourage the creation of such a tool.

7   Conclusion

The challenges from our original paper provide a useful framework for discussing some of the exciting progress in satisfiability testing in recent years. We expect further developments on extensions to DPLL and randomized systematic search to continue. Much remains to be done, however, towards the challenges on problem encodings, local search for proofs of unsatisfiability, and hybrid methods.

References

1. Bart Selman, Henry A. Kautz, and David A. McAllester. Ten challenges in propositional reasoning and search. In *Proceedings of the Fifteenth International Joint Conference on Artificial Intelligence (IJCAI'97)*, pages 50–54, 1997.
2. Armin Biere, Alessandro Cimatti, Edmund M. Clarke, and Yunshan Zhu. Symbolic model checking without BDDs. In *Proceedings of the 5th International Conference on Tools and Algorithms for Construction and Analysis of Systems*, pages 193–207, Amsterdam, The Netherlands, March 1999.
3. M. N. Velev and R. E. Bryant. Effective use of boolean satisfiability procedures in the formal verification of superscalar and vliw microprocessors. In *Proc. 38th Design Automation Conference (DAC '01)*, pages 226–231, 2001.
4. P. Bjesse, T. Leonard, and A. Mokkedem. Finding bugs in an alpha microprocessor using satisfiability solvers. In *Proc. 13th Int. Conf. on Computer Aided Verification*, 2001.
5. L. Simon, D. Le Berre, and E. Hirsch. The sat2002 competition, 2002. http://www.satlive.org/SATCompetition/onlinereport.pdf.

6. D. Le Berre and L. Simon. The essentials of the sat'03 competition, 2003. Under review. Draft available at http://www.lri.fr/ simon/contest03/results/.
7. http://www.cs.washington.edu/homes/kautz/challenge/.
8. David S. Johnson and Michael A. Trick, editors. *Cliques, Coloring and Satisfiability: Second DIMACS Implementation Challenge*, volume 26 of *DIMACS Series in Disc. Math. and Theor. Computer Science*. AMS, 1996.
9. M. Davis, G. Logemann, and D. Loveland. A machine program for theorem proving. *Communications of the ACM*, 5:394–397, 1979.
10. C.M. Li and S. Gerard. On the limit of branching rules for hard random unsatisfiable 3-sat. In *Proc. ECAI*, 2000.
11. O. Dubois and G. Dequen. A backbone-search heuristic for efficient solving of hard 3-sat formulae. In *Proc. of the 17th International Joint Conference on Artificial Intelligence (IJCAI '01)*, 2001.
12. R. Monasson, R. Zecchina, S. Kirkpatrick, B. Selman, and L. Troyansky. Determining computational complexity from characteristic phase transitions. *Nature*, 400(8):133–137, 1999.
13. O. Martin, R. Monasson, and R. Zecchina. Statistical mechanics methods and phase transitions in optimization problems. *Theor. Computer Science*, 265, 2001.
14. Phase transitions and algorithmic complexity ipam, July 2002. www.ipam.ucla.edu/programs/ptac2002/ptac2002-schedule.html.
15. Dimitris Achlioptas, Paul Beame, and Michael Molloy. A sharp threshold in proof complexity. In *Proc., 33st Annual ACM Symp. on Theory of Computing*, pages 337–346, Crete, Greece, July 2001.
16. B. Bollobas, C. Borgs, J. T. Chayes, J. Han Kim, and D.B. Wilson. The scaling window of the 2sat transition. *Rand. Struct. Alg.*, 18:301, 2001.
17. Dimitris Achlioptas, Lefteris, M. Kirousis, Evangelos Kranakis, and Danny Krizanc. Rigorous results for (2+p)-sat. *Theor. Comp. Sci.*, 265:109–129, 2001.
18. Olivier Dubois, Rimi Monasson, Bart Selman, and Riccardo Zecchina. Phase transitions in combinatorial problems (special issue). *Theor. Computer Science*, 265, 2001.
19. E. Friedgut. Sharp thresholds of graph properties, and the k-sat problem. *Journal of the American Mathematical Society*, 12:1017–1054, 1999.
20. C. Gomes and B. Selman. Satisfied with physics. (perspective article.). *Science*, 297:784–785, 2002.
21. T. Hogg, B. Huberman, and C. Williams (Eds.). Phase Transitions and Complexity (Special Issue). *Artificial Intelligence*, 81(1–2), 1996.
22. David G. Mitchell, Bart Selman, and Hector J. Levesque. Hard and easy distributions for SAT problems. In *Proc. 10th Natl. Conf. on Artificial Intelligence*, pages 459–465, 1992.
23. Marc Mézard, Giorgio Parisi, and Riccardo Zecchina. Analytic and algorithmic solution of random satisfiability problems. *Science*, 297:812, 2002.
24. B. Selman, H. Kautz, and B. Cohen. Local search strategies for satisfiability testing. In *Dimacs Ser. in Discr. Math. and Theor. Comp. Science*, volume 26, pages 521–532. AMS, 1996.
25. J.M. Crawford, M.J. Kearns, and R.E. Schapire. The minimal disagreement parity problem as a hard satisfiability problem, 1995. unpublished manuscript.
26. J. Warners and H. van Maaren. A two phase algorithm for solving a class of hard satisability problems. *Operations Research Letters*, 23:81–88, 1999.
27. Chu Min Li. Integrating equivalency reasoning into davis-putnam procedure. In *Proceedings of the National Conference on Artificial Intelligence*, pages 291–296, 2000.

28. P. Morris. The breakout method for escaping from local minima. In *Proc. AAAI-93*, pages 40–45, 1993.

29. Bart Selman and Henry Kautz. An empirical study of greedy local search for satisfiability testing. In *Proc. AAAI-93*, pages 46–51, 1993.

30. Z. Wu and B.W. Wah. Trap escaping strategies in discrete lagrangian methods for solving hard satisfiability and maximum satisfiability problems. In *Proc.AAAI-99*, pages 673–678, 1999.

31. J. R. Burch, E. M. Clarke, K. L. McMillan, D. L. Dill, and L. J. Hwang. Symbolic model checking: 10^{20} states and beyond. *Information and Computation*, 98(2):142–170, June 1992.

32. K. L. McMillan. *Symbolic Model Checking*. Kluwer Academic Publishers, 1993.

33. M. Davis and H. Putnam. A computing procedure for quantification theory. *Journal of the ACM*, 7, 1960.

34. M. Davis, G. Logemann, and D. Loveland. A machine program for theorem proving. *Communications of the ACM*, 5:394–397, 1962.

35. Stephen A. Cook and Robert A. Reckhow. The relative efficiency of propositional proof systems. *Journal of Symbolic Logic*, 44(1):36–50, 1977.

36. Maria Luisa Bonet, Juan Luis Esteban, Nicola Galesi, and Jan Johansen. On the relative complexity of resolution refinements and cutting planes proof systems. *SIAM J. Comput.*, 30(5):1462–1484, 2000.

37. Eli Ben-Sasson, Russell Impagliazzo, and Avi Wigderson. Near-optimal separation of treelike and general resolution. Technical Report TR00-005, Elec. Colloq. in Comput. Compl., http://www.eccc.uni-trier.de/eccc/, 2000.

38. A. Haken. The intractability of resolution. *Theoretical Computer Science*, 39:297–308, 1985.

39. V. Chvatal and E. Szemeredi. Many hard examples for resolution. *Journal of the ACM*, 35(4):759–208., 1988.

40. S. Cook and D. Mitchell. Finding hard instances of the satisfiability problem: a survey. In *DIMACS Series in Discr. Math. and Theoretical Comp. Sci.*, volume 35, pages 1–17. 1997.

41. Roberto J. Bayardo Jr. and Robert C. Schrag. Using CST look-back techniques to solve real-world SAT instances. In *Proceedings, AAAI-97: 14th Natl. Conf. on Art. Intel.*, pages 203–208, 1997.

42. Hantao Zhang. SATO: An efficient propositional prover. In *Proceedings of the International Conference on Automated Deduction, LNAI*, volume 1249, pages 272–275, July 1997.

43. R. Stallman and G. Sussman. and forward reasoning and dependency-directed backtracking in a system for computer-aided circuit analysis. *Artificial Intelligence*, 9(2), 1977.

44. J. de Kleer and B. C. Williams. Diagnosing multiple faults. *Artificial Intelligence*, 32(1):97–130, 1987.

45. R. Davis. Diagnostic reasoning based on structure and behavior. *Artificial Intelligence*, 24:347–410, 1984.

46. João P. Marques-Silva and Karem A. Sakallah. GRASP – a new search algorithm for satisfiability. In *Proc. of the International Conference on Computer Aided Design*, pages 220–227, San Jose, CA, November 1996. ACM/IEEE.

47. Matthew W. Moskewicz, Conor F. Madigan, Ying Zhao, Lintao Zhang, and Sharad Malik. Chaff: Engineering an efficient SAT solver. In *Proc. of the 38th Design Automation Conference*, pages 530–535, Las Vegas, NV, June 2001. ACM/IEEE.

48. Lintao Zhang, Conor F. Madigan, Matthew H. Moskewicz, and Sharad Malik. Efficient conflict driven learning in a boolean satisfiability solver. In *Proc. of the International Conference on Computer Aided Design*, pages 279–285, San Jose, CA, November 2001. ACM/IEEE.

49. E. Goldberg and Y. Novikov. Berkmin: A fast and robust sat solver. In *Proceedings of Design Automation and Test in Europe (DATE) 2002*, pages 142–149, 2002.

50. J.P. Marques-Silva. An overview of backtrack search satisfiability algorithms. In *5th International Symposium on Artificial Intelligence and Mathematics*, Fort Lauderdale, Florida, January 1998.

51. Paul Beame, Henry Kautz, and Ashish Sabharwal. Understanding the power of clause learning. In *Proc. of the 18th International Joint Conference on Artificial Intelligence*, Acapulco, Mexico, August 2003.

52. Carla P. Gomes, Bart Selman, and Henry Kautz. Boosting Combinatorial Search Through Randomization. In *Proc. 15th Natl. Conf. on Artificial Intelligence (AAAI-98)*, pages 431–438, 1998.

53. Luis Baptista and Joao P. Marques Silva. Using randomization and learning to solve hard real-world instances of satisfiability. In *Prin. and Prac. of Const. Prog.*, pages 489–494, 2000.

54. Paul Beame, Ashish Agarwal, and Henry Kautz. Using problem structure for efficient clause learning. In *Proceedings of the Sixth International Conference on Theory and Applications of Satisfiability Testing*, 2003.

55. Maria Luisa Bonet and Nicola Galesi. A study of proof search algorithms for resolution and polynomial calculus. In *Proc., 40th Annual Symp. on Found. of Comput. Sci.*, pages 422–432, New York, NY, October 1999. IEEE.

56. E. Ben-Sasson, R. Impagliazzo, and A. Wigderson. Near-optimal separation of treelike and general resolution. Technical Report TR00-005, Electronic Colloquium in Computation Complexity, http://www.eccc.uni-trier.de/eccc/, 2000.

57. Paul Beame, Russell Impagliazzo, Toniann Pitassi, and Nathan Segerlind. Memoization and DPLL: Formula caching proof systems. In *Proc., 18th Annual IEEE Conf. on Comput. Complexity*, Aarhus, Denmark, July 2003. To appear.

58. B. Krishnamurthy. Short proofs for tricky formulas. *Acta Informatica*, 22:253–275, 1985.

59. J. Crawford, M. Ginsberg, E. Luks, and A. Roy. Symmetry-breaking predicates for search problems. In *Proc. Intl. Conf. Principles of Knowledge Representation and Reasoning*, pages 148–159, 1996.

60. F. A. Aloul, I. L. Markov, and K. A. Sakallah. Efficient symmetry breaking for boolean satisfiability. In *Proc. Intl. Joint Conf. on Artificial Intelligence (IJCAI)*, 2003.

61. A. Urquhart. The symmetry rule in propositional logic. *Discrete Applied Mathematics*, 96:177–193, 1999.

62. Paul Beame, Russell Impagliazzo, Toniann Pitassi, and Nathan Segerlind. Memoization and dpll: formula caching proof systems. In *IEEE Conference on Computational Complexity*, 2003.

63. F. Bacchus, S. Dalmao, and T. Pitassi. Dpll with caching: A new algorithm for #sat and bayesian inference, 2003. Technical Report TR03-003, Electronic Cooloquium in Computational Complexity, http://www.ecc.uni-trier.de/eccc/.

64. John Hooker. Resolution vs. cutting plane solution of inference problems: Some computational experience. *Operations Research Letter*, 7:1–7, 1988.

65. A.P. Kamath, N.K. Karmarker, K.G. Ramakrishnan, and M.G.C. Resende. Computational experience with an interior point algorithm on the satisfiability problem. In *Proc. Integer Programming and Combinatorial Optimization*, 1990.

66. J.P. Warners E. de Klerk, H. van Maaren. Relaxations of the satisfiability problem using semidefinite programming, 1999.

67. Joachim Walser. Solving linear pseudo-boolean constraint problems with local search. In *Proc. 14th Natl. Conf. on Artificial Intelligence (AAAI-97)*, 1998.

68. F. Aloul, A. Ramani, I. Markov, and K. Sakallah. Generic ilp versus specialized 0-1 ilp: an update. In *Intl. Conf. on Computer Aided Design (ICCAD)*, 2002.

69. Andrew Parkes. Pb-lib: The pseudo-boolean library, 2003.

70. Ryan Williams, Carla Gomes, and Bart Selman. Backdoors to typical case complexity. In *Proc. of the Eighteenth International Joint Conference on Artificial Intelligence (IJCAI-03)*, 2003.

71. Wei Wei and Bart Selman. Accelerating random walks. In *Proc. 8th Intl. Conf. on the Princ. and Practice of Constraint Programming (CP-2002)*, 2002.

72. B. W. Wah and Y. Shang. A discrete langrangian-based global- search method for solving satisfiability problems. *J. of Global Optim.*, 12, 1998.

73. B. Selman, H. Levesque, and D. Mitchell. Gsat: A new method for solving hard satisfiability problems. In *Proceedings of the Tenth National Conference on Art ificial Intelligence (AAAI-92)*, pages 440–446, San Jose, CA, 1992. AAAI Press.

74. D. Schuurmans and F. Southey. Local search characteristics of incomplete SAT procedures. In *Proceedings of the Seventeenth National Conference on Articial Intelligence (AAAI-2000)*, pages 297–302, 2000.

75. Guilhem Semerjian and Remi Monasson. A study of pure random walk on random satisfiability problems with physical methods. In *Proc. SAT-2003*, 2003.

76. Holger Hoos. On the run-time behaviour of stochastic local search algorithms for SAT. In *Proceedings of AAAI-99*, pages 661–666. AAAI Press, 1999.

77. H. Hoos. Stochastic local search — methods, models, applications. PhD Thesis,TU Darmstadt, 1998.

78. J.A. Boyan and A.W. Moore. Learning evaluation functions for global optimization and Boolean satisfiability. In *Proceedings of the Fifteenth National Conference on Articial Intelligence (AAAI-98)*, pages 3–10, 1998.

79. Jeremy Frank, Peter Cheeseman, and John Stutz. When gravity fails: Local search topology. *Journal of Artificial Intelligence Research*, 7:249–281, 1997.

80. E. A. Hirsch and A. Kojevnikov. Unitwalk: A new sat solver that uses local search guided by unit clause elimination. In *PDMI preprint 9/2001, Steklov Institute of Mathematics at St.Petersburg*, 2001.

81. R. Paturi, P. Pudlak, and F. Zane. Satisfiability coding lemma. In *Proc. of the 38th Annual IEEE Symposium on Foundations of Computer Science, FOCS'97*, pages 566–574, 1997.

82. Xiao Yu Li, Matthias Stallman, and Franc Brglez. Qingting: A local search sat solver using an effective switching strategy and efficient unit propagation. In *Proc. SAT-2003*, 2003.

83. R. I. Brafman. A simplifier for propositional formulas with many binary clauses. In *Proc. IJCAI-2001*, pages 515–520, 2001.

84. F. Bacchus and J. Winter. Effective preprocessing with hyper-resolution and equality reduction. In *Proc. SAT-2003*, 2003.

85. R. Ostrowski, E. Grigoire, B. Mazure, and L. Sais. Recovering and exploiting structural knowledge from cnf formulas. In *Proc. of the Eighth International Conference on Principles and Practice of Constraint Programming (CP'2002), LNCS, Ithaca (N.Y.)*, pages 185–199. Springer, 2002.

86. Djamal Habet, Chu Min Li, Laure Devendeville, and Michel Vasquez. A hybrid approach for sat. In *Proc. of the Eighth International Conference on Principles and Practice of Constraint Programming (CP'2002), LNCS, Ithaca (N.Y.)*, pages 172–184. Springer, 2002.
87. B. Mazure, L. Sais, and E. Gregoire. Boosting complete techniques thanks to local search methods. In *Proc. Math and AI*, 1996.
88. Carla P. Gomes, Bart Selman, Nuno Crato, and Henry Kautz. Heavy-tailed phenomena in satisfiability and constraint satisfaction problems. *J. of Automated Reasoning*, 24(1–2):67–100, 2000.
89. Hubie Chen, Carla Gomes, and Bart Selman. Formal models of heavy-tailed behavior in combinatorial search. In *In Principles and Pratices of Constraint Programming (CP-01)*, 2001.
90. I. Gent and T. Walsh. Easy Problems are Sometimes Hard. *Artificial Intelligence*, 70:335–345, 1993.
91. T. Walsh. Search in a Small World. In *Proceedings of the International Joint Conference on Artificial Intelligence*, Stockholm, Sweden, 1999.
92. M. Luby, A. Sinclair, and D. Zuckerman. Optimal speedup of las vegas algorithms. *Information Process. Letters*, pages 173–180, 1993.
93. Eric Horvitz, Yongshao Ruan, Carla Gomes, Henry Kautz, Bart Selman, and Max Chickering. A Bayesian approach to tackling hard computational problems. In *Proc. 17th Conc. on Uncertainty in Artificial Intelligence (UAI-2001)*, 2001.
94. Henry Kautz, Eric Horvitz, Yongshao Ruan, Bart Selman, and Carla Gomes. Dynamic randomized restarts: Optimal restart policies with observation. AAAI2002, 2002.
95. Yongshao Ruan, Eric Horvitz, and Henry Kautz. Restart policies with dependence among runs: A dynamic programming approach. In *Principles and Practice of Constraint Programming - CP 2002*, 2002.
96. Yongshao Ruan, Eric Horvitz, and Henry Kautz. Hardness-aware restart policies, 2003. under review.
97. Toby Walsh. Reformulating propositional satisfiability as constraint satisfaction. *Lecture Notes in Computer Science*, 1864, 2000.
98. Steven Prestwich. Local search on sat-encoded csps. In *Proc. SAT-2003*, 2003.
99. Peter van Beek and Rina Dechter. Constraint tightness and looseness versus local and global consistency. *JACM*, 44(4):549–566, 1997.
100. Cristian Bessiere, Emmanuel Hebrard, and Toby Walsh. Local consistencies in sat. In *Proc. SAT-2003*, 2003.
101. Henry A. Kautz, David A. McAllester, and Bart Selman. Encoding plans in propositional logic. In *Proc. of the 5th Intl. Conf. on Princ. of Knowl. Repr. and Reasoning*, pages 374–384, Boston, MA, November 1996.
102. Michael Ernst, Todd D. Millstein, and Daniel S. Weld. Automatic SAT-compilation of planning problems. In *IJCAI*, pages 1169–1177, 1997.
103. Dimitris Achlioptas, Carla P. Gomes, Henry A. Kautz, and Bart Selman. Generating satisfiable problem instances. In *AAAI/IAAI*, pages 256–261, 2000.
104. H. Kautz and B. Selman. Pushing the envelope: planning, propositional logic, and stochastic search. In *Proceedings of the 13th AAAI*, pages 1194–2001, 1996.
105. Matthew L. Ginsberg, Andrew J. Parkes, and Amitabha Roy. Supermodels and robustness. In *AAAI/IAAI*, pages 334–339, 1998.
106. D. Johnson. Experimental analysis of algorithms: The good, the bad, and the ugly, 1996. Invited Lecture, *AAAI-96* , Portland, OR. See also http://www.research.att.com/~dsj/papers/exper.ps.

107. C.P. Gomes and B. Selman. Problem Structure in the Presence of Perturbations. In *Proceedings of the Fourteenth National Conference on Artificial Intelligence (AAAI-97)*, pages 221–227, New Providence, RI, 1997. AAAI Press.

108. Fabio Massacci. Using walk-SAT and rel-sat for cryptographic key search. In *Proc. IJCAI-99*, pages 290–295.

109. H.A. Kautz and B. Selman. Unifying SAT-based and graph-based planning. In *Proc. of the 16th International Joint Conference on Artificial Intelligence*, pages 318–325, Stockholm, Sweden, August 1999.

110. Edmund M. Clarke, Armin Biere, Richard Raimi, and Yunshan Zhu. Bounded model checking using satisfiability solving. *Formal Methods in System Design*, 19(1):7–34, 2001.

Automated Mechanism Design:
A New Application Area for Search Algorithms*

Tuomas Sandholm

Computer Science Department
Carnegie Mellon University
Pittsburgh PA 15213
sandholm@cs.cmu.edu

Abstract. *Mechanism design* is the art of designing the rules of the game (aka. *mechanism*) so that a desirable outcome (according to a given objective) is reached despite the fact that each agent acts in his own self-interest. Examples include the design of auctions, voting protocols, and divorce settlement procedures. Mechanisms have traditionally been designed manually for classes of problems. In 2002, Conitzer and Sandholm introduced the *automated mechanism design* approach, where the mechanism is computationally created for the specific problem instance at hand. This approach has several advantages: 1) it can yield better mechanisms than the ones known to date, 2) it applies beyond the problem classes studied manually to date, 3) it can circumvent seminal economic impossibility results, and 4) it shifts the burden of design from man to machine. In this write-up I overview the approach, focusing on problem representations, computational complexity, and initial applications. I also lay out an agenda for future research in this area.

1 Introduction

In multiagent settings, agents generally have conflicting preferences, yet it is crucial to be able to aggregate the preferences, that is, to choose a socially desirable *outcome*, for example a president, resource allocation, or task allocation. This problem prevails among any self-interested agents: humans, companies, *etc.*—and software agents representing such parties.

Preference aggregation mechanisms include voting protocols, auctions, divorce settlement procedures, and collaborative rating systems, to name just a few. Unfortunately, most naive preference aggregation mechanisms suffer from *manipulability*. An agent may have an incentive to misreport its preferences in order to mislead the mechanism into selecting an outcome that is more desirable to the agent than the outcome that would be selected if the agent revealed its preferences truthfully. Manipulation is an undesirable phenomenon because preference aggregation mechanisms are tailored to aggregate preferences in a socially desirable way, and if the agents reveal their preferences insincerely, a

---

* This material is based upon work supported by the National Science Foundation under CAREER Award IRI-9703122, Grant IIS-9800994, ITR IIS-0081246, and ITR IIS-0121678.

F. Rossi (Ed.): CP 2003, LNCS 2833, pp. 19–36, 2003.

socially undesirable outcome may be chosen. Manipulability is a pervasive problem across preference aggregation mechanisms. A seminal negative result, the *Gibbard-Satterthwaite theorem*, shows that under *any* nondictatorial preference aggregation scheme, if there are at least 3 possible outcomes, there are preferences under which an agent is better off reporting untruthfully [25, 47]. (A preference aggregation scheme is called dictatorial if one of the agents dictates the outcome no matter how the others vote.)

Mechanism design is the art of designing the *mechanism* (*i.e.*, rules of the game) so that the agents are motivated to report their preferences truthfully and a desirable (according to a given objective) outcome is chosen. The objective can be, for example, social welfare (*i.e.*, sum of the agents' utilities), seller's revenue, fairness, or some combination of these.

1.1   Manual Mechanism Design

Mechanism design has traditionally been a manual endeavor. The designer uses experience and intuition to hypothesize that a certain rule set is desirable in some ways, and then tries to prove that this is the case. Alternatively, the designer formulates the mechanism design problem mathematically and characterizes desirable mechanisms analytically in that framework. These approaches have yielded a small number of canonical mechanisms over the last 40 years, each of which is designed for a class of settings and a specific objective. The upside of these mechanisms is that they do not rely on (even probabilistic) information about the agents' preferences (*e.g.*, the Vickrey-Clarke-Groves (VCG) mechanism [48, 9, 27]), or they can be easily applied to any probability distribution over the preferences (*e.g.*, the dAGVA mechanism [24, 2], the Myerson auction [39], and the Maskin-Riley multi-unit auction [38]). However, these general mechanisms also have significant downsides:

- The most famous and most broadly applicable general mechanisms, VCG and dAGVA, only maximize social welfare. If the designer is self-interested, as is the case in many electronic commerce settings, these mechanisms do not maximize the designer's objective.
- The general mechanisms that do focus on a self-interested designer are only applicable in very restricted settings. For example, Myerson's expected revenue maximizing auction is for selling a single item, and Maskin and Riley's expected revenue maximizing auction is for selling multiple identical units of an item.
- Even in the restricted settings in which these mechanisms apply, the mechanisms only allow for payment maximization. In practice, the designer may also be interested in the outcome *per se*. For example, an auctioneer may care which bidder receives the item.
- It is often assumed that side payments can be used to tailor the agents' incentives, but this is not always practical. For example, in barter-based electronic marketplaces—such as Recipco, firstbarter.com, BarterOne, and Intagio—side payments are not allowed. Furthermore, among software agents, it might be more desirable to construct mechanisms that do not rely on the ability to

make payments, because many software agents do not have the infrastructure to make payments.

- The most common mechanisms (*e.g.*, VCG, dAGVA, Myerson auction, and the Maskin-Riley auction) assume that the agents have quasilinear preferences. This means that the utility function of each agent $i \in \{1, \ldots, N\}$ can be written as $u_i(o, \pi_1, \ldots, \pi_N) = v_i(o) - \pi_i$, where o is the outcome and π_i is the amount that agent i has to pay. So, very restrictively, it is assumed that 1) the agent's valuation, v_i, of outcomes is independent of money, 2) the agent does not care about other agents' payments, and 3) the agent is risk neutral.

In addition to mechanisms, mechanism design research has yielded impossibility results that state that no mechanism works across a class of settings (for varying definitions of "works" and varying classes). For example, the Gibbard-Satterthwaite theorem, discussed above, states that for the class of general preferences, no mechanism works in the sense that 1) the mechanism's outcome can be any one of at least three candidates, 2) the mechanism is nondictatorial, and 3) every agent's dominant strategy is to reveal his preferences truthfully.

1.2   Automated Mechanism Design

In sharp contrast to manual mechanism design, Conitzer and Sandholm in 2002 introduced a systematic approach—called *automated mechanism design*—where the mechanism is automatically created for the setting and objective at hand [16][1]. This has at least four important advantages:

- It can be used in settings beyond the classes of problems that have been successfully studied in (manual) mechanism design to date.
- It can allow one to circumvent the impossibility results: when the mechanism is designed for the setting (instance) at hand, it does not matter that it would not work on preferences beyond those in that setting (*e.g.*, for a class of settings). Even when the optimal mechanism—created automatically—does not circumvent the impossibility, it always minimizes the pain entailed by impossibility.
- It can yield better mechanisms (in terms of better outcomes and/or stronger nonmanipulability guarantees[2]) than the canonical mechanisms because the mechanism capitalizes on the particulars of the setting (the probabilistic (or other) information that the mechanism designer has about the agents' preferences).

  Given the vast amount of information that parties have about each other today, it is astonishing that the canonical mechanisms (such as first-price

---

[1] Note that automated mechanism design is completely different from *algorithmic mechanism design* [41]. In the latter, the mechanism is designed manually with the goal that *executing* the mechanism is computationally tractable. On the other hand, in automated mechanism design, the mechanism itself is designed automatically.

[2] For example, satisfaction of *ex post* IC and/or IR constraints rather than their *ex interim* variants. These are discussed in Section 2.

reverse auctions), which ignore that information, have prevailed thus far. I foresee an imminent revolution, where future mechanisms will be created automatically. For example, imagine a Fortune 1000 company automatically creating its procurement mechanism based on its statistical knowledge about its suppliers (and potentially also the public prices of the suppliers' inputs, *etc.*). Initial work like this is already being conducted at CombineNet, Inc.
- It shifts the burden of mechanism design from humans to a machine.

2   The Computational Problem

As a first step toward fulfilling the vision of automated mechanism design, we modeled mechanism design as a computational optimization problem [16, 20]. This section reviews that model.

First, the automated mechanism design setting is defined as follows.

Definition 1. *In an* automated mechanism design setting, *we are given*
A finite set of outcomes O;
A finite set of N agents;
For each agent i,

- *a finite set of types Θ_i,*
- *a probability distribution γ_i over Θ_i (in the case of correlated types, there is a single joint distribution γ over $\Theta_1 \times \ldots \times \Theta_N$),*
- *a utility function $u_i : \Theta_i \times O \to \mathbb{R}$ [3];*

An objective function whose expectation the designer wishes to maximize.

There are many possible objective functions the designer might have, for example, social welfare (where the designer seeks to maximize the sum of the agents' utilities), or the minimum utility of any agent (where the designer seeks to maximize the worst utility had by any agent). In both of these cases, the designer is *benevolent*, because the designer, in some sense, is pursuing the agents' collective happiness. On the other hand, a *self-interested* designer cares only about the outcome chosen (that is, the designer does not care how the outcome relates to the agents' preferences, but rather has a fixed preference over the outcomes), and about the net payments made by the agents, which flow to the designer. Specifically, a self-interested designer has an objective function $g(o) + \sum_{i=1}^{N} \pi_i$, where $g : O \to \mathbb{R}$ indicates the designer's own preference over the

---

[3] Though this follows standard game theory notation [37], the fact that the agent has both a utility function and a type is perhaps confusing. It simply means that the agent has a utility function from a finite set of utility functions. If agent is of type 1, then it has the first utility function, an agent of type 2 has the second utility function, and so on. The agent's type is not known to the aggregator. The utility function is common knowledge, but because the agent's type is a parameter in the agent's utility function, the aggregator cannot know what the agent's utility is without knowing the agent's type.

outcomes, and π_i is the payment made by agent i. In the case where $g = 0$ everywhere, the designer is said to be *payment maximizing*. In the case where payments are not possible, g constitutes the objective function by itself.

We now define the kinds of mechanisms under study.

Definition 2. *A deterministic mechanism without payments consists of an outcome selection function* $o : \Theta_1 \times \Theta_2 \times \ldots \times \Theta_N \to O$. *A randomized mechanism without payments consists of a distribution selection function* $p : \Theta_1 \times \Theta_2 \times \ldots \times \Theta_N \to \mathcal{P}(O)$, *where* $\mathcal{P}(O)$ *is the set of probability distributions over* O. *A deterministic mechanism with payments consists of an outcome selection function* $o : \Theta_1 \times \Theta_2 \times \ldots \times \Theta_N \to O$ *and for each agent* i, *a payment selection function* $\pi_i : \Theta_1 \times \Theta_2 \times \ldots \times \Theta_N \to \mathbb{R}$, *where* $\pi_i(\theta_1, \ldots, \theta_N)$ *gives the payment made by agent* i *when the reported types are* $\theta_1, \ldots, \theta_N$. *A randomized mechanism with payments consists of a distribution selection function* $p : \Theta_1 \times \Theta_2 \times \ldots \times \Theta_N \to \mathcal{P}(O)$, *and for each agent* i, *a payment selection function* $\pi_i : \Theta_1 \times \Theta_2 \times \ldots \times \Theta_N \to \mathbb{R}$ [4].

There are two types of constraint on the designer in building the mechanism: individual rationality constraints and incentive compatibility constraints. The following subsections will define them, respectively.

2.1   Individual Rationality (IR) Constraints

The first type of constraint is the following. The utility of each agent has to be at least as great as the agent's fallback utility, that is, the utility that the agent would receive if it did not participate in the mechanism. Otherwise that agent would not participate in the mechanism—and no agent's participation can ever hurt the mechanism designer's objective because at worst, the mechanism can ignore an agent by pretending the agent is not there. (Furthermore, if no such constraint applied, the designer could simply make the agents pay an infinite amount.) This type of constraint is called an *IR (individual rationality)* constraint (aka. participation constraint). There are three different possible IR constraints: *ex ante*, *ex interim*, and *ex post*, depending on what the agent knows about its own type and the others' types when deciding whether to participate in the mechanism. *Ex ante* IR means that the agent would participate if it knew nothing at all (not even its own type). We will not study this concept in this paper. *Ex interim* IR means that the agent would always participate if it knew only its own type, but not those of the others. *Ex post* IR means that the agent would always participate even if it knew everybody's type. We will define the latter two notions of IR formally. First, we need to formalize the concept of the fallback outcome. We assume that each agent's fallback utility is zero for each one of its types. This is without loss of generality because we can add a constant term to an agent's utility function (for a given type), without affecting the decision-making behavior of that expected utility maximizing agent [37].

---

[4] We do not randomize over payments because as long as the agents and the designer are risk neutral with respect to payments, that is, their utility is linear in payments, there is no reason to randomize over payments.

Definition 3. *In any automated mechanism design setting with an IR constraint, there is a* fallback *outcome $o_0 \in O$ where, for any agent i and any type $\theta_i \in \Theta_i$, we have $u_i(\theta_i, o_0) = 0$. (Additionally, in the case of a self-interested designer, $g(o_0) = 0$.)*

We can now to define the notions of individual rationality.

Definition 4. Individual rationality (IR) *is defined as follows.*

– *A deterministic mechanism is* ex interim IR *if for any agent i, and any type $\theta_i \in \Theta_i$, we have $E_{(\theta_1,..,\theta_{i-1},\theta_{i+1},..,\theta_N)|\theta_i}[u_i(\theta_i, o(\theta_1,..,\theta_N)) - \pi_i(\theta_1,..,\theta_N)] \geq 0$.*
  A randomized mechanism is ex interim IR *if for any agent i, and any type $\theta_i \in \Theta_i$, we have $E_{(\theta_1,..,\theta_{i-1},\theta_{i+1},..,\theta_N)|\theta_i} E_{o|\theta_1,..,\theta_n}[u_i(\theta_i, o) - \pi_i(\theta_1,..,\theta_N)] \geq 0$.*
– *A deterministic mechanism is* ex post IR *if for any agent i, and any type vector $(\theta_1,\ldots,\theta_N) \in \Theta_1 \times \ldots \times \Theta_N$, we have $u_i(\theta_i, o(\theta_1,\ldots,\theta_N)) - \pi_i(\theta_1,\ldots,\theta_N) \geq 0$.*
  A randomized mechanism is ex post IR *if for any agent i, and any type vector $(\theta_1,\ldots,\theta_N) \in \Theta_1 \times \ldots \times \Theta_N$, we have $E_{o|\theta_1,..,\theta_n}[u_i(\theta_i, o) - \pi_i(\theta_1,..,\theta_N)] \geq 0$.*

The terms involving payments are left out if payments are not possible.

2.2 Incentive Compatibility (IC) Constraints

The second type of constraint states that the agents should never have an incentive to misreport their type. For this type of constraint, the two most common variants (or *solution concepts*) are *implementation in dominant strategies*, and *implementation in Bayesian Nash equilibrium.*

Definition 5. *Given an automated mechanism design setting, a mechanism is said to* implement its outcome and payment functions in dominant strategies *if truthtelling is always optimal even when the types reported by the other agents are already known. Formally, for any agent i, any type vector $(\theta_1,\ldots,\theta_i,\ldots,\theta_N) \in \Theta_1 \times \ldots \times \Theta_i \times \ldots \times \Theta_N$, and any alternative type report $\hat{\theta}_i \in \Theta_i$, in the case of deterministic mechanisms we have*

$u_i(\theta_i, o(\theta_1,\ldots,\theta_i,\ldots,\theta_N)) - \pi_i(\theta_1,\ldots,\theta_i,\ldots,\theta_N) \geq$
$u_i(\theta_i, o(\theta_1,\ldots,\hat{\theta}_i,\ldots,\theta_N)) - \pi_i(\theta_1,\ldots,\hat{\theta}_i,\ldots,\theta_N).$

In the case of randomized mechanisms we have

$E_{o|\theta_1,..,\theta_i,..,\theta_n}[u_i(\theta_i, o) - \pi_i(\theta_1,\ldots,\theta_i,\ldots,\theta_N)] \geq$
$E_{o|\theta_1,..,\hat{\theta}_i,..,\theta_n}[u_i(\theta_i, o) - \pi_i(\theta_1,\ldots,\hat{\theta}_i,\ldots,\theta_N)].$
The terms involving payments are left out if payments are not possible.

Thus, in dominant strategies implementation, truthtelling is optimal regardless of what the other agents report. If it is optimal only *given* that the other agents are truthful, and given that one does not know the other agents' types, we have implementation in *Bayesian Nash equilibrium.*

Definition 6. *Given an automated mechanism design setting, a mechanism is said to* implement *its outcome and payment functions in Bayesian Nash equilibrium if truthtelling is always optimal to an agent when that agent does not yet know anything about the other agents' types, and the other agents are telling the truth. Formally, for any agent i, any type $\theta_i \in \Theta_i$, and any alternative type report $\hat{\theta}_i \in \Theta_i$, in the case of deterministic mechanisms we have*

$$E_{(\theta_1,\ldots,\theta_{i-1},\theta_{i+1},\ldots,\theta_N)|\theta_i}[u_i(\theta_i, o(\theta_1,\ldots,\theta_i,\ldots,\theta_N)) - \pi_i(\theta_1,\ldots,\theta_i,\ldots,\theta_N)] \geq$$
$$E_{(\theta_1,\ldots,\theta_{i-1},\theta_{i+1},\ldots,\theta_N)|\theta_i}[u_i(\theta_i, o(\theta_1,\ldots,\hat{\theta}_i,\ldots,\theta_N)) - \pi_i(\theta_1,\ldots,\hat{\theta}_i,\ldots,\theta_N)].$$

In the case of randomized mechanisms we have

$$E_{(\theta_1,\ldots,\theta_{i-1},\theta_{i+1},\ldots,\theta_N)|\theta_i}E_{o|\theta_1,\ldots,\theta_i,\ldots,\theta_n}[u_i(\theta_i, o) - \pi_i(\theta_1,\ldots,\theta_i,\ldots,\theta_N)] \geq$$
$$E_{(\theta_1,\ldots,\theta_{i-1},\theta_{i+1},\ldots,\theta_N)|\theta_i}E_{o|\theta_1,\ldots,\hat{\theta}_i,\ldots,\theta_n}[u_i(\theta_i, o) - \pi_i(\theta_1,\ldots,\hat{\theta}_i,\ldots,\theta_N)].$$

The terms involving payments are left out if payments are not possible.

2.3 The Optimization Problem

We can now define the computational problem of automated mechanism design.

Definition 7. *(AUTOMATED-MECHANISM-DESIGN (AMD)) We are given an automated mechanism design setting, an IR notion (ex interim, ex post, or none), and a solution concept (dominant strategies or Bayesian Nash equilibrium). Also, we are told whether payments are possible, and whether randomization is possible. Finally, we are given a target value G. We are asked whether there exists a mechanism of the specified type that satisfies both the IR notion and the solution concept, and gives an expected value of at least G for the objective[5].*

3 Complexity Results

This section discusses the complexity of AMD. An interesting special case is the setting where there is only one agent. In this case, the agent always knows everything there is to know about the other agents' types—because there are no other agents. Since *ex post* and *ex interim* IR only differ on what an agent is assumed to know about other agents' types, the two IR concepts coincide here. Also, because implementation in dominant strategies and implementation in Bayesian Nash equilibrium only differ on what an agent is assumed to know about other agents' types, the two solution concepts coincide here. This observation is a useful tool in proving hardness results: we proved computational hardness in the single-agent setting, which immediately implies hardness for both IR concepts, for both solution concepts, and for any constant number of agents.

Now we are ready to review the hardness results. It turns out that in settings without side payments, such as voting, designing an optimal (*e.g.*, expected social welfare maximizing) deterministic mechanism is $\mathcal{N}P$-complete. This holds whether the designer is benevolent [16, 14] or self-interested [20]. If side payments are allowed, designing a deterministic mechanism is easy if the designer's objective is social welfare (the VCG mechanism suffices), but $\mathcal{N}P$-complete more

---

[5] For studying computational complexity, we phrase AMD as a decision problem, but the corresponding optimization problem is clear.

generally (for example, if the objective is to maximize the expected revenue collected from the bidders [20]—as is the objective in some auctions). All of these hardness results apply even with a uniform prior over types.

Interestingly, if one allows randomized mechanisms, the mechanism design problem becomes solvable in polynomial time using linear programming (LP) (for any constant number of agents) [16, 20][6]. A decision variable in the LP is the probability that a given outcome is chosen given that a certain type revelation vector (each agent reveals a type) occurs. For any constant number of agents, the number of decision variables is polynomial in the number of types and in the number of outcomes. Furthermore, the number of constraints (IC and IR) is polynomial. The LP can then be solved in polynomial time[7].

4   A Tiny Example: Divorce Settlement

We built a basic automated mechanism design system to test the approach in practice. This section illustrates a small example (from [19]). For each setting below, our system found the optimal mechanism. The system used CPLEX, a general-purpose optimization package, to solve the underlying mixed integer/linear program.

Consider a couple getting a divorce. They jointly own a painting and the arbitrator has to decide what happens to the painting. There are 4 options to decide between: (1) the husband gets the painting, (2) the wife gets the painting, (3) the painting remains in joint ownership and is hung in a museum, and (4) the painting is burned. The husband and wife each have two possible types: one that implies not caring for the painting too much (low), and one that implies being strongly attached to the painting (high). (low) is had with probability .8, (high) with .2, by each party. To maximize social welfare, the arbitrator would like to give the painting to whoever cares for it more, but even someone who does not care much for it would prefer having it over not having it, making the arbitrator's job in ascertaining the preferences nontrivial. Specifically, the utility function is (for either party):

```
u(low,get the painting)=2
u(low,other gets the painting)=0
u(low,joint ownership)=1
u(low,burn the painting)=-10 (both consider burning it bad from an art history perspective)

u(high,get the painting)=100
u(high,other gets the painting)=0
u(high,joint ownership)=50
u(high,burn the painting)=-10
```

First, let us assume that side payments are not possible, randomization is not possible, and that implementation in dominant strategies is required. Our system generated the following optimal mechanism for this setting:

---

[6] This holds for any mechanism design objective that is linear in the outcome probabilities.

[7] Randomized automated mechanism design can be solved in polynomial time even if the types are correlated, that is, the agents' types are drawn from a joint distribution, not from separate distributions.

```
           husband_low              husband_high
wife_low   husband gets painting    husband gets painting
wife_high  husband gets painting    husband gets painting
```

So, we cannot do better than always giving the painting to the husband (or always giving it to the wife). (The solver does not look for the "fairest" mechanism because fairness is not part of the objective we specified.) Now let us change the problem slightly, by requiring only implementation in Bayesian Nash equilibrium. For this instance, our system generated the following optimal mechanism:

```
           husband_low          husband_high
wife_low   joint ownership      husband gets painting
wife_high  wife gets painting   painting is burned
```

Thus, when we relax the incentive compatibility constraint to Bayesian Nash equilibrium, we can do better by sometimes burning the painting! The burning of the painting (with which nobody is happy *per se*) is sufficiently helpful in tailoring the incentives that it becomes a key part of the mechanism.

It turns out that we can do better by also allowing for randomization in the mechanism. The optimal randomized mechanism generated by the system is the following:

```
           husband_low                 husband_high
wife_low   .57: husband, .43: wife     1: husband
wife_high  1: wife                      .45: burn; .55: husband
```

The randomization helps because the threat of burning the painting *with some probability* when both report high is enough to obtain the incentive effect that allows us to give the painting to the right party for other type vectors. The mechanism now chooses to randomize over the party that receives the painting rather than awarding joint ownership in the setting where both report low.

We also studied this divorce scenario when the benevolent mechanism designer can use side payments, and when the mechanism designer is self-interested (wants to maximize the amounts paid to him by the divorcees) [19].

5   Initial Applications

The automated mechanism design approach is new, and so far we have only done preliminary experiments. In addition to solving the small divorce scenarios discussed above, our system has yielded the following highlights [19]:

- It reinvented the celebrated Myerson auction [39], which maximizes the seller's expected revenue in a 1-object auction.
- It created expected revenue maximizing combinatorial auctions. This has been a long-standing recognized open research problem in (manual) mechanism design [4, 49]. The general form for such an auction is still unknown, but automated mechanism design created prior-specific optimal mechanisms. (In the manual mechanism design literature, even the problem with only two objects for sale is open; only a case with very special form of complementarity and no substitutability has be en solved [1].)

- It created optimal mechanisms for a public good problem (deciding whether or not to build a bridge). The VCG mechanism could be used in this setting as long as each agent's utility function is quasilinear. However, in the VCG, nonnegative payments are collected from the voters (intuitively, the payments are collected in order to avoid the free rider problem), and those payments have to be burned. According to a seminal impossibility result, this problem plagues *any* mechanism that applies to general quasilinear utility functions, yields a social welfare maximizing decision, and makes truthful reporting of utility functions a dominant strategy [26]. The automated mechanism design approach allowed us to incorporate money burning as a loss in the social welfare objective, and maximize that revised objective. We had automated mechanism design create an optimal mechanism for the bridge building scenario under each variant of the incentive compatibility (IC) constraint discussed above (with the *ex post* IR constraint). In neither variant was money ever burned. Under the *ex interim* IC constraint, the bridge was always built if and only if that was best for the agents. (Under the *ex post* IC constraint this was not always the case.) For the *ex interim* IC constraint, the general-purpose *dAGVA* mechanism could be used to yield the social welfare maximizing choice without burning money [24, 2]. However, a seminal economic impossibility result shows that no mechanism for general quasilinear utility functions yields the social welfare maximizing choice, maintains budget balance, *and satisfies the IR constraint* (even the *ex interim* variant) [40]. As the experiment above showed, automated mechanism design can circumvent this impossibility! It constructed a mechanism that satisfies all these desiderata, and actually the *ex post* (*i.e.*, stronger) variant of the IR constraint.
- It created optimal mechanisms for public goods problems with multiple goods. This is the public goods analog of combinatorial auctions.

6   Structured Preferences

If the agents' utility functions are additively decomposable into independent issues, the input to automated mechanism design can be represented (potentially exponentially) more concisely. (An example of this is a multi-item auction where for each bidder, the value of the bundle of items that she wins is simply the sum of the values that she assigns to the individual items in the bundle.)

In that representation it is $\mathcal{N}P$-complete (even under strong restrictions) to design a mechanism that maximizes one of the following objectives: 1) expected social welfare when payments are not possible, 2) a general objective function even when payments are possible, and 3) expected revenue collected from the agents [21]. However, again, a randomized mechanism can be designed in polynomial time. So, the complexity as a function of the input length is the same in the concise representation as it is in the flat representation. In other words, due to its potentially exponentially shorter input length, the structured representation allows potentially exponentially faster automated mechanism design.

7   Conclusions and Perspective

Mechanism design is the art of designing the rules of the game (aka. *mechanism*) so that a desirable outcome (according to a given objective) is reached despite the fact that each agent acts in his own self-interest. Mechanisms have traditionally been designed manually for classes of problems. In 2002, Conitzer and Sandholm introduced the *automated mechanism design* approach, where the mechanism is computationally created for the specific problem instance at hand. As illustrated in this write-up, this approach has several advantages: 1) it can yield better mechanisms than the ones known to date, 2) it applies beyond the problem classes studied manually to date, 3) it can circumvent seminal economic impossibility results, and 4) it shifts the burden of design from man to machine.

In most variants of the problem, designing a deterministic mechanism is $\mathcal{N}P$-complete (even with just one agent), while a randomized mechanism can be designed in polynomial time using linear programming (for any constant number of agents). Put in perspective, the designer faces uncertainty about the agents' private information, which leads to the need for mechanism design and introduces the associated computational complexity. Interestingly, the designer can remove this complexity *by making the agents face additional uncertainty* (randomization in the mechanism). This comes at no loss, and in some cases at a gain, in the designer's objective because deterministic mechanisms are a subset of randomized ones (the outcome probabilities are 0/1 for each type vector).

Applications overviewed included different types of divorce settlement settings, optimal auctions, optimal combinatorial auctions (a recognized open research problem in manual mechanism design), optimal public goods problems, and optimal combinatorial public goods problems. If the agents' utility functions can be additively decomposed into independent issues, the input to the mechanism design problem can become exponentially shorter, and it turns out that this allows for exponentially faster solving of the design problem.

One potential objection to automatically designed mechanisms is that they can be complex (the mapping from type revelation vectors to outcomes can be long to list), and unintuitive (because they are designed anew for each setting, the agents will likely not have had any previous experience with the mechanism). I would argue that neither of these objections is fundamental: it suffices for each agent to know his best way of *behaving* in the mechanism (which, by the IR and IC constraints, is participating and revealing his type truthfully).

8   Current and Future Research Directions

Automated mechanism design is a brand new area of research, and holds significant promise for enormous theoretical and practical impact. In this section I lay out an agenda for current and future research in this area.

8.1   Real-World Applications

In the short term, the automated mechanism work with greatest practical impact will undoubtedly be the application of the methodology to real-world problems. While we introduced automated mechanism design only recently (in 2002), it is already being adopted in applications. In addition to our own explorations of applications [19] reviewed above, our approach and methodology is being used by others, for example to design auctions [28] and nonmanipulable collaborative rating systems [30]. Promising application areas for the future include other auction settings, voting settings, and a variety of mediation settings.

8.2 Partial Priors and Input Representation

One potential criticism is that in automated mechanism design, the prior distribution of types is used. This runs directly against the *Wilson doctrine* of mechanism design that states that the mechanism should be prior-independent because in many settings the designer does not know the prior. I would argue that in many settings the designer does know a lot about the prior, and it would be silly to ignore it. Consider, for example, a Fortune 1000 company procuring materials from its established supplier base. The company certainly has significant statistical information about the suppliers' capacities and production costs. Secondly, in many settings, good mechanisms *must* use the prior. This is necessary, for example, in revenue-maximizing auctions. Therefore also many of the manually designed mechanisms (*e.g.*, the dAGVA mechanism, the Myerson auction, and the Maskin-Riley auction) do use the prior.

A related potential objection arises from the fact that in some settings the type space can be so large that the input to mechanism design is prohibitive. For example, in a combinatorial auction, the number of bundles is exponential in items, and even if every bundle can have a small number of alternative values (for a given agent), the agent's type space is doubly exponential in items.

To make automated mechanism design practical in these settings, it would be desirable to develop ways to use only partial information about the prior (and the type space), and yet design mechanisms that are provably (or experimentally) close to optimal. Furthermore, could the mechanism design software selectively and incrementally elicit partial information about the input *on an as-needed basis* from the human designer who uses the software—and yet design a (close to) optimal mechanism?

Related research questions include the following. How should the type space be discretized if the actual type space is continuous? Can the discretization be avoided entirely in some settings? Can the input be represented more effectively in some settings? (Section 6 showed that if the agents' utility functions are additively decomposable, the answer to the last question is affirmative.)

8.3 Special-Purpose Algorithms and Characterization Results

While optimal randomized mechanisms are quick to design automatically, optimal deterministic ones tend to be $\mathcal{N}P$-complete to design. CPLEX tends to be able to create optimal deterministic mechanisms with tens of types and tens of outcomes in less than a minute [19]. Future research should improve this scalability through algorithms specially crafted for automated mechanism design.

One interesting approach along that line is to use game-theoretic characterization results (that state features that all mechanisms with certain desirable properties for a class of settings have, *e.g.*, [35, 51]) to prune down the search.

One example along these lines is a general search algorithm for designing deterministic mechanisms for one agent [18]. It tends to outperform CPLEX. Another example is the recent design of a 1-object optimal auction mechanism when the objective is a combination of the bidders' welfare and the seller's expected utility [36]. The main piece of that work is an analytical characterization, but at the end, a binary search algorithm is used to set the key parameter—which depends on the prior and for which an analytical solution does not exist. Yet another example is a recent paper on automated determination of an optimal sequence of take-it-or-leave-it-offers (*e.g.*, by a seller to a set of buyers, one buyer at a time) [46]. It has a simple characterization result that makes modeling of the optimization problem viable, thus enabling computational solving. The latter two examples also serve as examples of techniques that are for a special kind of automated mechanism design setting rather than for the general case.

8.4   Handling Collusion

The mechanism design setting discussed in this write-up so far considers deviations by individual agents. Even if a mechanism is robust against such deviations, a coalition of agents may be better off by reporting their types insincerely. Several solution concepts have been proposed that require robustness against coalitional deviations [3, 7]. Future research should study automated mechanism design under those solution concepts as well.

8.5   Inducing General Mechanisms and Mechanism Design Principles

Another future use of automated mechanism design is to solve for mechanisms for a variety of settings (real or artificially generated), and to see whether new canonical mechanisms (that work across a *class* of settings) and/or mechanism design principles can be inferred.

8.6   Nonstandard Mechanism Types

Perhaps most fundamentally, automated mechanism design could be used while at the same time relaxing some of the core assumptions of mechanism design. In this section I will discuss some important avenues along this line.

Multi-stage Mechanisms. Often in practice only a portion of the type information is needed to determine the outcome. What information is needed from an agent generally depends on what types the other agents have. There has been significant recent work on selective incremental preference elicitation from bidders in combinatorial auctions [10, 12, 11, 29, 52, 8] [8] and from voters in elections [17]. It turns out that in some settings, exponentially less information is communicated in a multi-stage mechanism than in the most communication-efficient single-step mechanism [22].

So, in practice, multi-stage mechanisms may be desirable in order to reduce communication, enhance privacy, and to reduce the agents' effort in settings

---

[8] Ascending (combinatorial) auctions (*e.g.*, [42, 50]) are a special cases of the elicitation model.

where they need to expend effort to determine their own types (for example, in many auctions, a bidder does not know the value of the goods before constructing a plan of what he would do with the goods if he won). Future work includes *automatically* designing multi-stage mechanisms.

Mechanisms with Insincere Equilibrium Play. The mechanism design framework presented in this write-up creates mechanisms in which truthful type reporting is each agent's best strategy. This is justified by a central design principle in mechanism design, the *revelation principle* [37]. It states that anything that can be accomplished with a mechanism where some agents' best strategies involve insincere reporting, can be accomplished with a mechanism where each agent's best strategy is to reveal his type truthfully[9].

However, the revelation principle falls apart in practice when computational complexity is an issue. A recent paper [22] shows that there are settings where 1) the optimal truthful mechanism is $\mathcal{N}P$-complete to execute (for the center, *e.g.*, auctioneer, who is running the mechanism), 2) by moving to insincere mechanisms, one can shift the burden of having to solve the $\mathcal{N}P$-complete problem from the center to one of the agents, 3) the insincere mechanism is equally good as the optimal truthful mechanism in the presence of unlimited computation, and most interestingly, 4) whereas being unable to carry out the complex computation would have hurt the center in achieving his objective in the truthful setting, if the agent is unable to carry out the complex computation, the value of the designer's objective *strictly improves*. This shows that there are at least theoretical settings where it is beneficial to use insincere mechanisms. So, is there an advantage in practical settings? What would such mechanisms look like? Are there principles for constructing them? Could they be automatically designed?

Mechanisms that Take into Account the Agents' Bounded Rationality. Sometimes economic mechanism design falls short: it can hit one of the impossibility results. One way to try to circumvent impossibility results is to relax the incentive compatibility constraint (and hopefully the *other* desirable properties are obtainable). Then, the agents may have incentive to manipulate. A novel way around this is to design mechanisms where *finding* a beneficial insincere type revelation is provably hard computationally. There has been work characterizing the complexity of manipulating known voting protocols [6, 5, 15, 13], and recent work on designing small changes to voting protocols so that manip-

---

[9] The proof is remarkably simple: given any mechanism, we can construct a truth-promoting mechanism whose performance is identical, as follows. We build an interface layer between the agents and the original mechanism. The agents report their types to the interface layer; subsequently, the interface layer inputs into the original mechanism the types *that the agents would have strategically reported* to the original mechanism, if their types were as declared to the interface layer. The resulting outcome is the outcome of the new mechanism. Since the interface layer acts "strategically on each agent's behalf", there is never an incentive to report falsely to the interface layer. The types reported by the interface layer are the strategic types that would have been reported without the interface layer, so the results are exactly as they would have been with the original mechanism.

ulation becomes hard [15, 23]. Future research includes *automatically* designing mechanisms that are provably hard to manipulate.

Another significant issue is that an agent may not know his preferences up front, but can refine them by computing or information gathering. For example, when a trucking company bids for a trucking task, this involves solving (at least) two $\mathcal{N}P$-complete planning problems: the vehicle routing problem with the new task and the problem without it [43, 44]. The difference in the costs of those two local plans is the cost of taking on the new task. Should a bidder evaluate the object he is bidding on if there is a cost to doing so? It turns out that the celebrated Vickrey auction loses its dominant-strategy property if the bidder has the option to evaluate the object or not: Whether or not the bidder should pay the evaluation cost depends on the other bidders' valuations [45].

The issues run even deeper. If a bidder has the opportunity to approximate its valuation to different degrees, how much computing time should the bidder spend on refining its valuation? If there are multiple items for sale, how much computing time should the bidder allocate on different bundles of items? A bidder may even allocate some computing time to evaluate other bidders' valuations (*e.g.*, how much it would cost for a competing trucking company to take on a given set of tasks) so as to be able to bid more strategically; this is called *strategic computing* [33, 32, 31, 34].

To answer these questions, we developed a deliberation control method called a *performance profile tree* for projecting how an anytime algorithm (a black box from the perspective of the deliberation controller) will change the valuation if additional computing is allocated toward refining (or improving) it [33, 32, 31, 34]. Unlike earlier deliberation control methods for anytime algorithms, the performance profile tree is a fully normative model of bounded rationality: it takes into account all the information that an agent can use to make its deliberation control decisions. (This is necessary in the game-theoretic context; otherwise a self-interested agent could take into account some information that the model does not, which could lead to strategic instability and much worse results.)

Using this deliberation control method, the computing actions can be made part of the (auction) game. At every point, each agent can decide on which bundle to allocate its next step of computing as a function of the agent's computing results so far (and in open-cry auction format also the others' bids observed so far). At every point, the agent can also decide to submit bids. One can then solve this model for the Bayesian Nash equilibrium, where each agent's (deliberation and bidding) strategy is a best-response to the others' strategies. This is called a *deliberation equilibrium*. With this model, it has been determined under what conditions strategic computing does (not) occur [33, 32, 31, 34].

Our *performance profile tree* based deliberation control method together with the idea of *deliberation equilibrium* provide a normative model of bounded rationality in multiagent systems, which is needed to determine how computationally constrained self-interested agents would behave in a given mechanism. This allows one to evaluate mechanisms for computationally constrained agents, and hopefully paves the way to designing such mechanisms (automatically). This methodology could also be used to design mechanisms that are computationally hard to manipulate, where hardness is measured not in terms of worst-case complexity, but informed by game-theoretic deliberation control. This methodology could even yield new mechanism design principles. As discussed, the central design principle in mechanism design, the *revelation principle*, ceases to meaningfully hold under computational or communication constraints.

References

1. Mark Armstrong. Optimal multi-object auctions. *Review of Economic Studies*, 67:455–481, 2000.
2. Kenneth Arrow. The property rights doctrine and demand revelation under incomplete information. In M Boskin, editor, *Economics and human welfare*. New York Academic Press, 1979.
3. R Aumann. Acceptable points in general cooperative n-person games. volume IV of *Contributions to the Theory of Games*. Princeton University Press, 1959.
4. Christopher Avery and Terrence Hendershott. Bundling and optimal auctions of multiple products. *Review of Economic Studies*, 67:483–497, 2000.
5. John J. Bartholdi, III and James B. Orlin. Single transferable vote resists strategic voting. *Social Choice and Welfare*, 8(4):341–354, 1991.
6. John J. Bartholdi, III, Craig A. Tovey, and Michael A. Trick. The computational difficulty of manipulating an election. *Social Choice and Welfare*, 6(3):227–241, 1989.
7. B Douglas Bernheim, Bezalel Peleg, and Michael D Whinston. Coalition-proof Nash equilibria: I concepts. *Journal of Economic Theory*, 42(1):1–12, June 1987.
8. Avrim Blum, Jeffrey Jackson, Tuomas Sandholm, and Martin Zinkevich. Preference elicitation and query learning. In *Conference on Learning Theory (COLT)*, Washington, D.C., 2003.
9. E H Clarke. Multipart pricing of public goods. *Public Choice*, 11:17–33, 1971.
10. Wolfram Conen and Tuomas Sandholm. Preference elicitation in combinatorial auctions: Extended abstract. In *Proceedings of the ACM Conference on Electronic Commerce (ACM-EC)*, pages 256–259, Tampa, FL, October 2001. A more detailed description of the algorithmic aspects appeared in the IJCAI-2001 Workshop on Economic Agents, Models, and Mechanisms, pp. 71–80.
11. Wolfram Conen and Tuomas Sandholm. Differential-revelation VCG mechanisms for combinatorial auctions. In *AAMAS-02 workshop on Agent-Mediated Electronic Commerce (AMEC)*, Bologna, Italy, 2002.
12. Wolfram Conen and Tuomas Sandholm. Partial-revelation VCG mechanism for combinatorial auctions. In *Proceedings of the National Conference on Artificial Intelligence (AAAI)*, pages 367–372, Edmonton, Canada, 2002.
13. Vincent Conitzer, Jerome Lang, and Tuomas Sandholm. How many candidates are needed to make elections hard to manipulate? In *Theoretical Aspects of Rationality and Knowledge (TARK IX)*, Bloomington, Indiana, USA, 2003.
14. Vincent Conitzer and Tuomas Sandholm. Automated mechanism design: Complexity results stemming from the single-agent setting, 2002. Draft.
15. Vincent Conitzer and Tuomas Sandholm. Complexity of manipulating elections with few candidates. In *Proceedings of the National Conference on Artificial Intelligence (AAAI)*, pages 314–319, Edmonton, Canada, 2002.
16. Vincent Conitzer and Tuomas Sandholm. Complexity of mechanism design. In *Proceedings of the 18th Annual Conference on Uncertainty in Artificial Intelligence (UAI-02)*, pages 103–110, Edmonton, Canada, 2002.

17. Vincent Conitzer and Tuomas Sandholm. Vote elicitation: Complexity and strategy-proofness. In *Proceedings of the National Conference on Artificial Intelligence (AAAI)*, pages 392–397, Edmonton, Canada, 2002.

18. Vincent Conitzer and Tuomas Sandholm. An algorithm for single-agent deterministic automated mechanism design without payments. In *IJCAI-03 workshop on Distributed Constraint Reasoning (DCR)*, Acapulco, Mexico, 2003.

19. Vincent Conitzer and Tuomas Sandholm. Applications of automated mechanism design. In *UAI-03 workshop on Bayesian Modeling Applications*, Acapulco, Mexico, 2003.

20. Vincent Conitzer and Tuomas Sandholm. Automated mechanism design for a self-interested designer. In *Proceedings of the ACM Conference on Electronic Commerce (ACM-EC)*, pages 232–233, San Diego, CA, 2003. Poster paper. Full-length draft available at www.cs.cmu.edu/~sandholm/.

21. Vincent Conitzer and Tuomas Sandholm. Automated mechanism design with a structured outcome space, 2003.

22. Vincent Conitzer and Tuomas Sandholm. Computational criticisms of the revelation principle. In *AAMAS-03 workshop on Agent-Mediated Electronic Commerce (AMEC)*, Melbourne, Australia, 2003. Poster paper.

23. Vincent Conitzer and Tuomas Sandholm. Universal voting protocol tweaks to make manipulation hard. In *Proceedings of the Eighteenth International Joint Conference on Artificial Intelligence (IJCAI)*, Acapulco, Mexico, 2003.

24. C d'Aspremont and L A Gérard-Varet. Incentives and incomplete information. *Journal of Public Economics*, 11:25–45, 1979.

25. A Gibbard. Manipulation of voting schemes. *Econometrica*, 41:587–602, 1973.

26. J Green and J-J Laffont. *Incentives in Public Decision Making*. Amsterdam: North-Holland, 1979.

27. Theodore Groves. Incentives in teams. *Econometrica*, 41:617–631, 1973.

28. Eric Hsu. Automated mechanism design: Type space and exponential auction. In *AAMAS-03 workshop on Evolutionary Game Theory for Learning in MAS*, Melbourne, Australia, 2003.

29. Benoit Hudson and Tuomas Sandholm. Effectiveness of preference elicitation in combinatorial auctions. In *AAMAS-02 workshop on Agent-Mediated Electronic Commerce (AMEC)*, Bologna, Italy, 2002. Extended version: Carnegie Mellon University, Computer Science Department, CMU-CS-02-124, March. Also: Stanford Institute for Theoretical Economics workshop (SITE-02).

30. Anthony Jameson, Christopher Hackl, and Thomas Kleinbauer. Evaluation of automatically designed mechanisms. In *UAI-03 workshop on Bayesian Modeling Applications*, Acapulco, Mexico, 2003.

31. Kate Larson and Tuomas Sandholm. Bargaining with limited computation: Deliberation equilibrium. *Artificial Intelligence*, 132(2):183–217, 2001. Short early version appeared in the Proceedings of the National Conference on Artificial Intelligence (AAAI), pp. 48–55, Austin, TX, 2000.

32. Kate Larson and Tuomas Sandholm. Computationally limited agents in auctions. In *AGENTS-01 Workshop of Agents for B2B*, pages 27–34, Montreal, Canada, May 2001.

33. Kate Larson and Tuomas Sandholm. Costly valuation computation in auctions. In *Theoretical Aspects of Rationality and Knowledge (TARK VIII)*, pages 169–182, Sienna, Italy, July 2001.

34. Kate Larson and Tuomas Sandholm. An alternating offers bargaining model for computationally limited agents. In *International Conference on Autonomous Agents and Multi-Agent Systems*, Bologna, Italy, July 2002.

35. Ron Lavi, Ahuva Mu'Alem, and Noam Nisan. Towards a Characterization of Truthful Combinatorial Auctions, 2003. Draft, April 8th.
36. Anton Likhodedov and Tuomas Sandholm. Auction mechanism for optimally trading off eficiency and revenue. In *AAMAS workshop on Agent-Mediated Electronic Commerce (AMEC V)*, Melbourne, Australia, 2003.
37. Andreu Mas-Colell, Michael Whinston, and Jerry R. Green. *Microeconomic Theory*. Oxford University Press, 1995.
38. Eric S Maskin and John Riley. Optimal multi-unit auctions. In Frank Hahn, editor, *The Economics of Missing Markets, Information, and Games*, chapter 14, pages 312–335. Clarendon Press, Oxford, 1989.
39. Roger Myerson. Optimal auction design. *Mathematics of Operation Research*, 6:58–73, 1981.
40. Roger Myerson and Mark Satterthwaite. Efficient mechanisms for bilateral exchange. *Journal of Economic Theory*, 28:265–281, 1983.
41. Noam Nisan and Amir Ronen. Algorithmic mechanism design. *Games and Economic Behavior*, 35:166–196, 2001. Early version in STOC-99.
42. David C Parkes and Lyle Ungar. Iterative combinatorial auctions: Theory and practice. In *Proceedings of the National Conference on Artificial Intelligence (AAAI)*, pages 74–81, Austin, TX, August 2000.
43. Tuomas Sandholm. An implementation of the contract net protocol based on marginal cost calculations. In *Proceedings of the National Conference on Artificial Intelligence (AAAI)*, pages 256–262, Washington, D.C., July 1993.
44. Tuomas Sandholm. *Negotiation among Self-Interested Computationally Limited Agents*. PhD thesis, University of Massachusetts, Amherst, 1996. Available at http:// www.cs.cmu.edu/~sandholm/ dissertation.ps.
45. Tuomas Sandholm. Issues in computational Vickrey auctions. *International Journal of Electronic Commerce*, 4(3):107–129, 2000. Special Issue on Applying Intelligent Agents for Electronic Commerce. A short, early version appeared at the Second International Conference on Multi–Agent Systems (ICMAS), pages 299–306, 1996.
46. Tuomas Sandholm and Andrew Gilpin. Sequences of take-it-or-leave-it offers: Near-optimal auctions without full valuation revelation. In *AAMAS workshop on Agent-Mediated Electronic Commerce (AMEC V)*, Melbourne, Australia, 2003.
47. M A Satterthwaite. Strategy-proofness and Arrow's conditions: existence and correspondence theorems for voting procedures and social welfare functions. *Journal of Economic Theory*, 10:187–217, 1975.
48. W Vickrey. Counterspeculation, auctions, and competitive sealed tenders. *Journal of Finance*, 16:8–37, 1961.
49. Rakesh V. Vohra. Research problems in combinatorial auctions. Mimeo, version Oct. 29, 2001.
50. Peter R Wurman and Michael P Wellman. AkBA: A progressive, anonymous-price combinatorial auction. In *Proceedings of the ACM Conference on Electronic Commerce (ACM-EC)*, pages 21–29, Minneapolis, MN, October 2000.
51. Makoto Yokoo. The characterization of strategy/false-name proof combinatorial auction protocols: Price-oriented, rationing-free protocol. In *Proceedings of the Eighteenth International Joint Conference on Artificial Intelligence (IJCAI)*, Acapulco, Mexico, August 2003.
52. Martin Zinkevich, Avrim Blum, and Tuomas Sandholm. On polynomial-time preference elicitation with value queries. In *Proceedings of the ACM Conference on Electronic Commerce (ACM-EC)*, pages 176–185, San Diego, CA, 2003.

Languages versus Packages
for Constraint Problem Solving

Mark Wallace

IC-Parc, Imperial College London, UK

Abstract. One strand of CP research seeks to design a small set of primitives and operators that can be used to build an appropriate algorithm for solving any given combinatorial problem. The aim is to "package" CP, simplifying its use, in contrast to current systems which offer application developers a full constraint programming language. In this talk we examine the risks of this line of research, and argue that our field is still too immature to be ready for "packaging".

1   Introduction

1.1   Usability versus Functionality

Learning a constraint programming language is a major obstacle to the takeup of CP for industrial and other practical applications. Applications developers who wish to take advantage of the technology seek a variety of detours to avoid this obstacle. One approach is to use some familiar system or package to generate constraints which are then passed to CP. Another is to offer CP in a packaged form, where solving methods are simply given as parameter settings.

On the other hand with the rapidly growing variety of real-world CP applications, we are becoming increasingly aware of the limitations of current CP systems for modelling and solving large scale industrial problems. Indeed industrial practitioners of CP find that every time they successfully solve a problem, the client's expectations are raised, and a new larger problem is proposed. Often the new requirement is for a more inclusive application which solves several interconnected problems. These inclusive applications require integrated solutions, which demand even more functionality of the underlying CP systems. A typical example is the extension of a planning system to include a simulator to assess plan quality, and ultimately an extension to perform on-the-day operational control for the delivered application with feedback to the planning module.

The CP community is thus being driven in two directions. Firstly it is driven by usability requirements, in the direction of simpler programming interfaces, and a broader community of applications developers [1, 2]. Secondly it is driven by application needs in the direction of enhanced modelling and solving. Apparently these two directions are diametrically opposed. A simpler interface, which is easier to learn, is only possible if the user has limited control over the underlying functionality. More expressibility and more algorithmic control implies more complexity at the programmer interface.

F. Rossi (Ed.): CP 2003, LNCS 2833, pp. 37–52, 2003.

Weighing up these two alternatives - better usability versus more functionality - the case for usability is very seductive, especially in a research climate where user takeup is a critical measure of research value.

This paper argues the case against concentrating on usability at the current stage in the development of CP. There are two arguments for continuing to emphasise functionality at this stage. We first give an argument *against* focussing on usability as a separate research topic. We then give an argument *for* ensuring that usability tracks functionality.

> Firstly, current usability results may not be a stepping stone into the future. Such results can misguide researchers into standardising on certain interfaces which may not be able to cope with facilities offered in future CP systems. Moreover application developers may be misled by the current interfaces into believing that CP is not suitable for their problems.

A classic example of this was the view held by many CP practitioners for a while that mixed integer programming (MIP) was a technology in competition with CP. This was a consequence of standardisation on FD as *the* constraint solver for CP (despite the fact that a linear solver had earlier been the solver built into the first instance CLP(R) of the CLP Scheme [3]).

> Secondly, by marrying usability research to the ongoing research into CP expressibility and solving power, we produce interfaces to state-of-the-art CP facilities. One consequence is that the new functionality is immediately made available to applications developers, and this exploitation gives important feedback as to its relevance or otherwise.

For instance the value of progress in symmetry breaking can be quickly established by making it available to applications developers, and not hiding it inside research prototypes that can only be used by the original researchers.

Another interesting consequence is that the usability research in itself helps clarify the relationship between separate strands of functionality research, inspiring the researchers to build orthogonal functional components. Using symmetry breaking again as an example, we learn much more about its relation to other techniques, such as linear constraint solving, by building it into generic search routines that also integrate these techniques.

This integration both raises important issues about making the new techniques generic, and it makes the new techniques available to application developers, integrated with the several forms of constraint handling and search needed to solve real life applications. This offers quick turnaround in validating new technology in combination with other innovations.

For these reasons we advocate a research methodology that encourages CP interfaces to move forward hand-in-hand with the emerging functionality. Moreover we advocate a research methodology where different kinds of functionality are developed in the context of a single coherent system, behind a single, changing but coherent, user interface. This ensures that the relationship between these different functionality enhancements are understood as early as possible.

1.2 Contents of This Paper

Many of us in the CP community share a vision of the holy grail as a system that allows the application developer to simply state the problem and leave the computer to automatically solve it in the most efficient way possible. This paper argues that it is to early, now, to aim directly for that final vision. Eventually, yes, but not yet.

The paper does not present any analysis of the expressive power of constraint programming languages as compared with packages. In addressing the title "Languages versus Packages for Constraint Problem Solving", one might argue that a language with recursion is necessary to specify precisely a constraint solving behaviour, and a package whose parameters also had this expressive power should really be termed a "language". One could discuss where CP effort should be invested along the following continuum:

- parameterising
- configuring
- scripting
- programming

We will not enter into any such fine disputation in this paper.

Instead, the remainder of the paper will support the arguments formulated in this introduction. In the next section we examine the use of Mixed Integer Programming (MIP) for solving large combinatorial optimisation problems. The advantages and disadvantages of the MIP approach will be examined and we will consider its consequences on research in this area. Next we will consider the possibility - and possible consequences - of developing generic packages for combinatorial optimisation problems. The following section explores a research area - search in CP - relating the advances made by the research community to the consequent requirements on the interfaces and implementation of search engines. In particular we contrast languages and packages for specifying search behaviour. The discussions are summarised in the conclusion.

2 Mixed Integer Programming (MIP) – Choked by Its Own Success?

In this paper, the argument for languages rather than packages will be presented in the context of a particular area of CP research: CP for combinatorial optimisation. This is, in the shorter term, the most industrially relevant aspect of CP research and it is therefore currently very important. Moreover this is the area with which I am most familiar in my own research. I believe the arguments also hold for other areas of CP research and application, but I only bring examples from the area of combinatorial optimisation (CO).

2.1 MIP Packages

MIP is an approach for modelling and solving CO problems, that has been developed in the Mathematical Programming community over the last half century. It provides restricted modelling power, with only a few constraints, and offers specialised solving methods designed for these constraints. We caricature MIP as a packaged approach. In other words, even though in real life MIP systems offer facilities to invoke external language procedures, we shall use "MIP" as if it was just a package. A number of commercial packages are available that support MIP modelling and solving [4–9], and a wide range of benchmark problems are available that can be run on any MIP package, thus giving an insight into the performance of its solving methods [10].

This state of affairs has many benefits. The interface between the user front end and the underlying solving methods is quite stable and well defined[1]. MIP user front ends and modelling languages can be designed and enhanced independently of any work on the underlying solvers. Application-specific front-ends can be developed which are targeted at specific user communities. Solver performances can be directly compared, independently of their front ends.

2.2 Limitations of MIP

MIP only recognises two constraints, $>=$ and $integer$[2]. It is awkward, but quite fun, mapping any given problem into a combination of the above constraints. One can relatively quickly learn the necessary tricks for representing disjunction, negation and so on. Once one's got the idea, it is amazing how many CO problems one can model and solve using a MIP package.

The English language has a reputation for being easy to learn, but hard to master. MIP is a bit like that. Not only can the MIP model quickly become very large and complicated even for problems which are simple to state, but also the performance of the MIP solver can become unacceptably poor. For non-trivial problems it is extremely hard to design the MIP model which has the best performance. It is even more difficult to recognise for which problems MIP is simply not a suitable approach. The result is that a great deal of time is invested in trying to design efficient MIP models for problems which might or might not be suitable for this approach.

One example is the *coins* problem. What is the minimum number of coins you need in your pocket, in order to be able to buy any item costing up to one Euro? There are 6 coins below one Euro, value 1,2,5,10,20 and 50 cents, and with our coins we need to be able to construct every sum between 1 and 100. The model requires over 600 discrete variables, representing, for each cost between 1 and 100, the number of coins of each denomination used to make up that sum.

---

[1] The interface is only *quite* stable, in the sense that changes are under way. Research is shifting the linear/nonlinear frontier to convex/nonconvex. Ultimately the modelling power and solving methods of future mathematical programming packages, replacing MIP, will probably be based on this new dichotomy.

[2] This is a slight exaggeration, which is intended to simplify rather than mislead.

This problem takes over 30 minutes to solve using MIP, but it is possible to add redundant constraints which tighten the formulation and cut the solving time down to a few seconds [11].

However suppose you now want to design a new set of six coins for the Euro, so as to optimise the solution to the above coins problem. The *currency design* problem is the same as the coins problem, except that now the denominations of the coins are part of the solution and not part of the input. This is not easy, and maybe not possible, to solve efficiently with MIP.

The point is not just that MIP can't be used to solve all CO problems. The really awkward thing is that for a given problem there's no way of knowing whether or not MIP can be made to solve it efficiently.

As an application developer, using a package, one's thinking is within the parameters of the package. If the package isn't solving the problem efficiently, parameter settings can be altered. A package is a box, and very often it's thinking outside the box that is needed for solving the problem!

If one wants to solve the currency design problem, the best advice is probably not to use MIP. This is not intended to be a criticism of MIP, but just a recognition that for certain kinds of problem, of which this is an example, it is best not to be boxed into thinking in terms of MIP. Instead, using domain constraints, quite a simple program can generate an optimal six coin currency in a few seconds. The program, coded in ECLiPSe [12], is listed in the appendix.

3 Generic Packages for Combinatorial Problem Solving

3.1 The Aspiration

If the class of problems to be tackled are CO problems, then one might seek to assemble a set of packages which together encompass problems of this class. Acknowledging that probably *P* is not equal to *NP*, and that there will be problems that cannot be optimally solved in a reasonable amount of time, we can provide amongst our set of packages, incomplete, anytime, solvers that will return nearly optimal or nearly feasible solutions within realistic timescales.

In principle, then, a two-stage process can be followed to solve any problem: first choose the appropriate package and then set the parameters of that package optimally to solve the problem. A neutral problem modelling interface could be provided which allowed the application developer to map a problem down to each of the different available packages by simply setting a parameter to guide the problem mapping software. Indeed there are already several commercial packages of this kind (see for example OptQuest [13], and Nimrod [14]).

Thus we could in effect provide the user with a single generic package for all CO problems. As an aspiration, this is highly motivating. As an immediate objective, it is distorting and may threaten scientific progress in our community!

3.2 The Reality

One of the standard characters in any area of research is the champion of some approach, who is blind to any alternative. His near-relative is the salesman who will sell the same solution to every customer, confidently asserting that his solution will fully meet the needs of the customer.

Suppose a generic package for combinatorial optimisation had been constructed. Suppose, moreover, it proved successful for a relatively wide variety of applications. The risk, particularly in the area of combinatorial optimisation, is that like MIP it could become a victim of its own success. Its protagonists would naturally tend to claim that it met all its objectives.

If the package were a hammer, then all CO problems would be nails. Any problem not easily or efficiently handled by the package would be classed as peculiar, or particularly difficult. Herein lies the risk: instead of recognising deficiencies in the package, there would be a tendency to marginalize the significance of the problem. Since it is of the very nature of CO problems that for any given approach some problem instances will be recalcitrant, then don't blame the approach but blame the problem instead. The danger is that whatever package an applications developer has become accustomed to, (s)he may come to think of it as a generic package for CO problems.

We have taken MIP as the example package in the previous section. The problem we are illustrating here is not a limitation of MIP at all, but a limitation of the thinking induced by packages. As one example, consider the *progressive party* problem [15]. Until Barbara Smith put CP onto the task, the problem owners could have reconciled themselves to the limitations of the MIP-based approach, assuming this was the best one could do for this kind of awkward problem.

We have had similar experiences at IC-Parc and Parc Technologies. For various network scheduling problems the accepted wisdom was that they were too hard to solve optimally. Only when the new combination of CP and MIP was brought to bear, did it become evident that the problems themselves were not so hard, they were only hard to solve using particular kinds of approach.

Linear programming was, and is, a tremendous advance and, enhanced to MIP, it has yielded optimal solutions to some very large CO problems. However, arguably, it has resulted in a certain distortion of the CO research. The effort invested in problems that can be modelled in MIP, such as the TSP [16], has far exceeded the effort invested in industrial problems with awkward side-constraints. The MIP model for such industrial problems typically requires unmanageably large numbers of discrete variables. Consequently real problems are simplified, by dropping or approximating their side-constraints. In this way the research effort remains concentrated on a class of problems which is dictated more by the available technology than by the demands of the real problems themselves.

As a postscript, the arrival of CP on the scene has had quite an impact on MIP research. In particular more work has been invested in *presolving* and search control. Recently MIP has been used to solve the progressive party problem [17], and the lessons from CP have been used to obtain solutions reasonably fast.

The OR and CP research communities are gaining a better and better understanding of the relative advantages of the different technologies, and researchers are exploring new forms of hybridisation to get the best out of their combination.

4   Languages Not Packages – The Case of Search

In this section we discuss the issue of search in CP. This is an active area of research which seems to be highly representative of CP research in general. For these reasons we shall use it as the example research area in comparing languages and packages.

4.1   Search Frameworks

Incremental Labelling. One of the first attempts to categorise the different search algorithms was by Nadel [18]. He named various constraint propagation algorithms as $AC1/5, \ldots AC1/2, AC1, \ldots AC3$. (The range of algorithms continues to grow, though after $AC7$ a new nomenclature was introduced). He then categorised different search algorithms as a combination of tree search (TS) and propagation (see *Nadel's Categories* below).

Table 1. Nadel's Categories

Backtracking	$TS + AC1/5$
Forward Checking	$TS + AC1/4$
Partial Lookahead	$TS + AC1/4 + AC1/3$
Full Lookahead	$TS + AC1/4 + AC1/2$

Later Haralick and Elliott [19] identified the *fail first* heuristic and this was generalised into variable and value choice heuristics. Another orthogonal search facility identified by [19] was "Remember what you have done to avoid making the same mistake". This has been generalised into intelligent backtracking and nogood learning. Finally, within the framework of tree-search, there are different ways of exploring the tree - breadth-first, depth first etc.

In short any given algorithm in the class of search algorithms which label a single variable with a chosen value at each search step, can be specified by four classes of parameters:

– Lookahead
– Variable/Value choice heuristics
– Looking back
– Tree exploration

For brevity we term this class of search algorithms *incremental labelling* algorithms.

The encapsulation of incremental labelling in a package, does serve to simplify and clarify control of search within this framework. Incremental labelling has provided a basis for several packages for performing search. In introducing the package *AISearch* [20] Peter Bouthoorn writes: "the programmer should be able to concentrate on the representation of the problem at hand and need not bother with the implementation of the actual search algorithm". Parameterisable search algorithms are also available from Tudor Hulubei [21], where the search is defined in terms of generic choice operators (called "decomposition" algorithms) and generic lookahead operators (called "filters"). Generic CSP search algorithms are also supplied for teaching support purposes [22]. In a wider framework, a generic package for solving valued CSPs is available from [23], which supports not only tree search but other search methods.

Drawbacks of Packaging. Each of these packages provides, as a package must, a fixed list of alternatives for specifying the search behaviour. The real danger of this approach is not the choice of list, but the thinking that such lists enforce upon language and applications developers.

For example on the assumption that control over looking ahead and looking back are not enough to focus an incremental labelling search, considerable investment has been put into the automatic generation of search heuristics for variable and value choices [24–26]. The risk is that this research effort may have limited practical payoff if only a few large scale industrial problems can be solved by *any* incremental labelling algorithm.

The wider scientific community is developing algorithms every day to solve hard combinatorial problems (see, for example, the Annals of Operations Research, Annals of Mathematics and Artificial Intelligence, Journal of Heuristics, European Journal of Operations Research) and the vast majority do not fit the above framework. Just as an MIP package is probably inappropriate for the currency design problem, so incremental labelling may not be appropriate for large scale industrial problems.

In each of the next four subsections we will consider a particular search functionality and what special requirements it imposes on the underlying language for describing search. The practical importance of these four search functionalities has emerged over recent years. Clearly they only emerged because applications developers were not trapped into a search framework where these functionalities were not available. As the journals listed above illustrate, new search functionalities are appearing continually, so these four are merely a sample.

4.2   Multiple Search Routines

The Issue. For problems whose decision variables are all of the same type, a single global search routine can offer the necessary functionality. However, even simple problems can involve different types of decision variable.

The currency design problem above, for example, has one set of decision variables governing the denominations of the coins, and another set of decision variables specifying how many coins of each denomination must be "kept in the (optimal) pocket". A good search algorithm labels the denominations first, and then the numbers of coins. The extension from one search routine to two, one search being done after the other, is quite simple and obvious.

More challenging are applications where labelling the different types of variables needs to be interleaved. Consider the problem of an ad-hoc sensor network.

The problem involves a set of sensors and a set of targets. A solution is the assignment of a sensor to each target, restricting the number of sensors used, so as to optimise some objective.

The best search algorithm first selects a sensor to be active and then assigns it to an appropriate subset of the targets, before repeating on the remaining sensors and targets. Technically this problem involves two kinds of decision variables: an *on/off* variable for each sensor, and, for each target/sensor pair an *on/off* assignment variable. The search routine labels a sensor variable to *on*, and then labels all the target/sensor variables associated with that sensor.

Let us abstract from the specific problem, calling the variables *type1* and *type2*. In this case the master search routine is the one that labels *type1* variables. After each choice point in the master search routine, a subsidiary search routine is invoked to label an associated subset of the *type2* variables[3].

Language Requirement. Consider a search package designed, however cleverly, for a single global search routine with one type of decision variable. Its adaptation to handle more than one type of decision variable in the currency design problem is easy: the search package must be invoked twice, once on the *denomination* variables and once on the *number* variables.

However this search package cannot be adapted for the ad-hoc sensor network problem because that requires a master search routine which invokes another search routine at every choice point. Instead a language is needed in which it is possible to specify, for any (master) search routine, what search (sub)routine to invoke on which variables after each choice point.

4.3   Computing Heuristics during Search

The Issue. Credit search (CS) [12, p.126] assigns a given portion of the remaining search effort to different subtrees of the current node. Limited Discrepancy Search (LDS) [28] constrains the "distance" between any partial assignment and a given preferred assignment. Both forms of search rely on a value ordering heuristic which associates preferred values with each of the unlabelled decision variables.

Given a fixed value ordering on all the decision variables of a problem, suppose we start at the search leaf node where each variable takes its preferred value. If we design a local search operator which switches a variable to a less preferred value, then LDS corresponds to the exploration of increasing neighbourhoods of the original assignment.

A substantive difference between LDS and local search only emerges when we admit dynamic value ordering heuristic which changes according to the current partial assignment. Typical value ordering heuristics are largely static: the

---

[3] W. Harvey pointed out that a sufficiently sophisticated variable selection procedure, which exploited the association between type2 and type1 variables could be used to achieve the same behaviour as our sensor example. However master/subproblem search routines are a necessary feature of several mathematical programming algorithms like branch and price [27].

only dynamic aspect is to drop values removed from a variable's domain by propagation.

In fact CS and LDS are most useful when problem-specific dynamic value ordering heuristics are exploited - for example using an optimal solution for a linear relaxation of the problem. A significant enhancement of this approach for LDS is to use multiple value ordering heuristics, and only to count a discrepancy if both heuristics agree on the best value for a certain variable, and this variable is assigned a different value [29].

Language Requirement. To support the above functionality the system needs to be able to fire off, at every node in a search tree, one or more problem solvers that solve some different relaxations, or variants, of the current problem and utilises the result to construct search heuristics for the next search step.

4.4   Updating Entailed Information at Search Nodes

The Issue. Consider a constraint satisfaction problem, and a current assignment of values to variables. The satisfaction problem can be handled as an optimisation problem by minimising the amount of "unsatisfaction". This can be measured in two ways. Either a penalty can be associated with each violated constraint [30, 31], or a penalty can be associated with each variable occurring in any violated constraints [32].

For the purposes of this discussion we shall use the first measure, taking GSAT as an example. GSAT uses local search, in which each move is a change in the assignment of one variable. GSAT uses "steepest ascent", at each step choosing a variable and value combination which minimises the remaining "unsatisfaction". Steepest ascent hill climbing is, typically, expensive to implement because of the necessity to find the best amongst the set of neighbours.

For implementing GSAT efficiently it is necessary to maintain a quantity of "red-tape" - redundant information about the current assignment that helps in finding the best neighbour. Accordingly, for each decision variable and for each constraint, the implementation maintains a record of what would happen to that constraint if the variable assignment was changed (either the constraint would become true, or it would stay true, or it would become false). This red-tape is used to efficiently maintain further red-tape (recording the change in the number of satisfied constraints if the variable's assignment were to be changed). In short the change to the variable assignment is propagated to the red-tape, and propagation continues along the red-tape (with apologies for the mixed metaphor).

In the same way the efficient implementation of any local search algorithm requires red tape. The choice of what red tape to maintain depends on the problem constraints, the cost function and the parameters governing the local search routine. For the GSAT example much of the red-tape is needed for the purposes of achieving steepest ascent. Other local search algorithms, such as simulated annealing, would require quite different red-tape.

Language Requirement. What is needed to enable the programmer to have such control is a language such as Localizer [33] which maintains red tape as "invariants".

It is tempting to think that the same red tape could be associated with any problem, e.g. for each variable, constraint and domain value the effect of changing that variable to take that value. However conflict minimisation problems may use a wide variety of cost functions. One could, for example, associate a degree of violation with each constraint, reflecting how badly it is violated. One could also make the red-tape update algorithm constraint-specific. Efficiency is crucial in local search, so this control is absolutely necessary for the algorithm.

4.5   Constraints as Search Node Choices

The Issue. The final issue is the introduction of problem refinement rather than labelling for making choices during search. A search choice may be to assign a value to a variable, or it may be simply to impose an additional constraint on the problem.

One area where constraints are typically used in this way during search is in scheduling applications. Instead of labelling a task start time, a search step is often made by imposing an ordering on two tasks (i.e. imposing a constraint that the end time of one task precedes the start time of the other). A final assignment of task start times can be completed easily when enough of the tasks have been ordered. Note that for scheduling problems, the use of an ordering choice rather than an assignment is common to both tree search algorithms and local search methods, such as Tabu search.

A general approach employing constraints instead of labels during search has been called "probing" [34]. The problem constraints are divided into "easy" constraints and "hard" constraints. For probing the following conditions should hold:

- a conjunction of easy constraints is also an easy constraint
- it is always possible to express a hard constraint as a disjunction of easy constraints.

(Assuming the assignment of a value to a variable is an easy constraint, then any finite constraint can be captured as a disjunction of easy constraints.)

Search is by finding an optimal solution to the current easy constraints, selecting a violated hard constraint (if there is one) and imposing one of the easy constraints in its equivalent disjunction. This defines a complete search tree, whose leaves are easy problems whose optimal solutions also satisfy all the hard constraints of the original problem.

The Language Requirement. To build a probing algorithm it is necessary to give, implicitly or explicitly, the disjunction of easy constraints equivalent to each hard constraint, and specify the solver for the easy constraints. Clearly a programming language is necessary to build any probing algorithm.

4.6   Languages and Packages for Search in CP

For some purposes it suffices to define a search procedure with a few global parameters (in MIP packages, for example , and in the traditional AI world with global procedures such as A*). However for more complex "hybrid" problems the need for more specific ad-hoc search control becomes quickly apparent.

The traditional search control inherited from Prolog was, and is, a very strong influence on search procedures, even for CP systems that are embedded in other languages. The procedure is expressed in terms of a recursion down the tree from root to leaf, with node propagation behaviour and search ordering heuristics expressed as a subprocedure invoked at each recursive call (i.e. node of the tree).

However two concepts have emerged that are hard to shoehorn into the standard recursive procedure: local search; and the separation of search tree specification and (incomplete) search tree exploration. New languages such as Localizer [33] and Salsa [35] have appeared, and new libraries such as ToOLS [36]. A paradigm for search control is emerging where the behaviour is expressed as a complex term whose components are subordinate search procedures and parameters.

The interplay of tree search and local search within a search procedure is becoming better understood, although the handling of multiple types of decision variable in a search procedure is not yet taken seriously (ToOLS currently offers only *sequencing* and *concurrent execution* as ways of combining search procedures).

The current research effort on search control encapsulates the discussion in this paper. Researchers whose CP world has domain variables, define search control languages which simply ignore the challenging requirements of mathematical approaches such as branch and price [27]. Their contribution is important, but we must not let an elegant search control language, applicable only to a limited form of constraint handling, hold back the efforts to develop search control for the full set of CP tools. The new search languages may - perhaps must - be less elegant than the old but this should not prevent their reaching a wide audience.

5   Conclusion

Packages are easy to use, and can help to establish CP across the world in academia and industry. Moreover packages can be extended and adapted to take new concepts and ideas into account. However these extensions are ultimately incoherent and can stifle progress. For example the CSP framework can be extended to accommodate optimisation, uncertainty, and dynamic problems, but for all three extensions together, as encountered in real applications, the framework may be more of a hindrance than a help [37].

The internal combustion engine is, all acknowledge, an old technology which has limited scope to meet the need for energy conservation, but it is so well researched that new young technologies cannot at first compete. Thus the very success of the old technology blights future technology. This is a scenario we should be determined to avoid in CP.

The introduction of CP packages, where functionality is made available at the user interface by parameters, will tend to reduce the flexibility of the interface. Unlike a package, guided by parameters, a language can be extended much more easily to accommodate new concepts and facilities. Moreover the research and development on a single CP language can be shared between many different researchers working on different kinds of functionality. CP language research, accordingly, maps onto the research methodology outlined above.

Our research at IC-Parc is built around the ECLiPSe constraint programming language [12]. The language has provided the flexibility to admit all the features described in this paper. Our research, and those of others in the community, have pushed the language in directions we never expected. The language framework, however, has enabled us to work on modelling features, new solvers, new search methods and new combinations of all these.

In consequence we would advocate CP research to be carried out, as far as possible, within the framework of a coherent CP language or a family of languages.

Acknowledgements

Many thanks to Carmen Gervet, Warwick Harvey and Joachim Schimpf for lots of ideas and feedback on drafts of the paper. The ECLiPSe team, including Joachim, Kish, Warwick, Andy S. and Andy C., are the people who *really* make the case for CP languages, by doing such a great job with ECLiPSe.

An ECLiPSe Program for The Currency Design Problem

```
:- lib(ic).               % For CP solver
:- lib(branch_and_bound). % For CP search

% +N: Number of different coins in the currency
% +Max: Need exact change for anything costing between 1 and Max
% ?Values: Values of the different coins in the currency
%          (in increasing order)
% ?Numbers: The number of each type of coin needed (for the above)
% -Total: The total number of coins needed - this must be minimal
design_currency(N,Max,Values,Numbers,Total) :-
        init_vars(N,Max,Values,Numbers),
        coins_constraints(Max,Values,Numbers,NeedCoinsList),
        redundant_constraints(Values,Numbers),
        Total #= sum(Numbers),
        minimize( search(Values,Numbers,NeedCoinsList), Total ).

init_vars(N,Max,Values,Numbers) :-
        length(Values,N), Values #:: 1..Max,
        length(Numbers,N), Numbers #:: 1..Max.
```

```
coins_constraints(Max,Values,Numbers,NeedCoinsList) :-
    ( for(Amount,0,Max),
      foreach(NeedCoins,NeedCoinsList),
      param(Values,Numbers)
    do
          gen_constraint(Amount,Values,Numbers,NeedCoins)
    ).

gen_constraint(Amount,Values,Numbers,NeedCoins) :-
    ( foreach(Value,Values),
      foreach(HaveCoin,Numbers),
      foreach(NeedCoin,NeedCoins),
      foreach(Product,Products)
    do
          NeedCoin #>= 0,
          NeedCoin #=< HaveCoin,
          Product #= Value*NeedCoin
    ),
    Amount #= sum(Products).

redundant_constraints(Values,Numbers) :-
    ( fromto(Values,[V1|NV],NV,[_]),
      fromto(Numbers,[N|NN],NN,[_])
    do
          NV=[V2|_],
          % If N * V1 >= V2, then you can always replace the
          % Nth V1 coin with an extra V2 coin
          N * V1 #=< V2 - 1
    ).

search(Values,Numbers,NeedCoinsList) :-
    labeling(Values),
    labeling(Numbers),
    ( foreach(NeedCoins,NeedCoinsList) do labeling(NeedCoins) ).

% Euro Coins Problem:
%    ?- design_currency(6,100,[1,2,5,10,20,50],Numbers,Total).
% Currency Design Problem
%    (allow 6 different coins, and exact change up to 100):
%    ?- design_currency(6,100,Values,Numbers,Total).
```

References

1. Cycorp: A finite domain constraint solver optimized to work with opencyc (2002)
   For Cyc see www.opencyc.org and for the package see
   "org.opencyc.constraintsolver".

2. Møller, J., Andersen, H., Hulgaard, H.: (Product configuration over the internet) `citeseer.nj.nec.com/531891.html`.
3. Jaffar, J., Lassez, J.L.: Constraint logic programming. In: Proceedings of the 14th ACM POPL Symposium, Munich, West Germany (1987)
4. ILOG: CPLEX (2002) `www.ilog.com/products/cplex/`.
5. Dash: Xpress-MP (2003) `www.dashoptimization.com/products.html`.
6. GAMS: GAMS: The general algebraic modeling system. (Online documentation at: `www.gams.com`)
7. Paragon Decision Technology B.V.: AIMMS: Advanced integrated multidimensional modeling software. (Online documentation at: `www.aimms.com`)
8. Software, M.: MPL: Mathematical programming language. (Online documentations at: `www.maximal-usa.com/mpl/`)
9. Savelsbergh, M.: MINTO - Mixed INTeger Optimizer. (Online documentations at: `www.isye.gatech.edu/faculty/Martin_Savelsbergh/software/`)
10. Mittelmann, H.: Benchmarks for optimization software (2003) `http://plato.la.asu.edu/bench.html`.
11. Bockmayr, A.: MIP model for the coins problem. Personal Communication (1997)
12. Cheadle, A., Harvey, W., Sadler, A., Schimpf, J., Shen, K., Wallace, M.: ECLiPSe: an introduction (2003) `www.icparc.ic.ac.uk/eclipse/reports/icparc-03-1.pdf`.
13. Glover, F.: (OptQuest: The optimization process) `www.decisioneering.com/spotlight/spotlight14d.html`.
14. Abramson, D.: (Nimrod/O: A software environment for building high performance optimising decision support systems from computational models) `www.csse.monash.edu.au/~davida/nimrodo/`.
15. Smith, B.M., Brailsford, S., Hubbard, P., Williams, H.P.: The Progressive Party Problem: Integer Linear Programming and Constraint Programming Compared. In: CP95: Proceedings 1st International Conference on Principles and Practice of Constraint Programming), Marseilles (1995)
16. Moscato, P.: TSPBIB home page. `www.densis.fee.unicamp.br/~moscato/TSPBIB_home.html` (2000)
17. Kalvelagen, E.: On solving the progressive party problem as a MIP. Technical report, GAMS Development Corp., Washington DC (2002) `www.gams.com/~erwin/ppp.pdf`.
18. Nadel, B.: 9. Symbolic Computation. In: Tree Search and Arc Consistency in Constraint Satisfaction Algorithms. Springer (1988)
19. Haralick, R.M., Elliott, G.L.: Increasing tree search efficiency for constraint satisfaction problems. Artificial Intelligence **14** (1980) 263–313
20. Bouthoorn, P.: (AISearch) `http://sal.kachinatech.com/Z/3/AISEARCH.html`.
21. Hulubei, T.: (The csp library) `www.hulubei.net/tudor/csp/index.html`.
22. Russell, S., Norvig, P.: (CSP problems and solvers) `http://aima.cs.berkeley.edu/python/csp.html#CSP`.
23. de Givry, S.: (VCSP) `www.inra.fr/bia/ftp/T/VCSP/docs/vcsp.txt`.
24. Kask, K., Dechter, R.: A general scheme for automatic generation of search heuristics from specification dependencies. Artificial Intelligence **129** (2001) 91–131
25. Larrosa, J., Meseguer, P.: Generic CSP techniques for the job-shop problem. In: IEA/AIE (Vol. 2). Volume 1416 of Lecture Notes in Computer Science., Springer (1998) 46–55
26. Minton, S.: Automatically configuring constraint satisfaction problems: A case study. Constraints **1** (1996) 7–44

27. Savelsbergh, M.: Branch-and-price: Integer programming with column generation. www.isye.gatech.edu/faculty/Martin_Savelsbergh/publications/eoo.pdf (2002)
28. Harvey, W.D., Ginsberg, M.L.: Limited discrepancy search. In: Proc. IJCAI- Vol. 1, Morgan Kaufmann, 1995 (1995) 607–615
29. Caseau, Y., Laburthe, F., Silverstein, G.: A meta-heuristic factory for vehicle routing problems. In: Proc. Principles and Practice of Constraint Programming. (1999) 144–158
30. Freuder, E., Wallace, R.: Partial constraint satisfaction. Artificial Intelligence **58** (1992)
31. Selman, B., Levesque, H.J., Mitchell, D.: A new method for solving hard satisfiability problems. In: Proceedings of the Tenth National Conference on Artificial Intelligence, AAAI Press (1992) 440–446
32. Minton, S., Johnston, M.D., Philips, A.B., Laird, P.: Minimizing conflicts: a heuristic repair method for constraint satisfaction and scheduling problems. Artificial Intelligence **58** (1992)
33. Michel, L., Van Hentenryck, P.: Localizer. Constraints **5** (2000) 41–82
34. El Sakkout, H., Wallace, M.: Probe backtrack search for minimal perturbation in dynamic scheduling. Constraints **5** (2000) 359–388
35. Laburthe, F., Caseau, Y.: SALSA: A language for search algorithms. Constraints **7** (2002) 255–288
36. de Givry, S., Jeannin, L.: ToOLS: A library for partial and hybrid search methods (2003) Presented at CPAIOR'03, Montreal, www.crt.umontreal.ca/cpaior/article-degivry.pdf.
37. Wallace, M.G.: Search in AI - escaping from the CSP straightjacket. In: Proc. 14th European Conference on Artificial Intelligence, IOS Press (2000) 770–776

Constraint Patterns

Toby Walsh

Cork Constraint Computation Center, University College Cork, Ireland
tw@4c.ucc.ie

Abstract. Constraint models contain a number of common patterns. For example, many constraint models involve an array of decision variables with symmetric rows and/or columns. By documenting such constraint patterns, we can share modelling expertise. Constraint solvers can also be extended to exploit such patterns. For example, we can develop specialized methods like the global lexicographical ordering constraint for breaking such row and column symmetry.

1   Introduction

Many patterns occur in constraint programs. In this paper, I argue that we need to identify, formalize and document these patterns in a similar way to the design patterns identified by the software engineering community. The result will be a systematic and comprehensive methodology for modelling an informal problem. Such a methodology will permit us to tackle the modelling "bottleneck" that hinders the uptake of constraint programming. This is an ambitious project - modelling is not a task which lends itself to a piecemeal approach as even the smallest modelling decision can have far reaching consequences. However, we have made some progress and I describe some of the more interesting constraint patterns which have already been identified. I also discuss the different ways that we can exploit such patterns. For example, one way to exploit common constraint patterns is to extend the constraint language.

2   Design Patterns

Patterns are an approach to design that started in architecture [1], which has since spread to many other areas including software engineering [2]. A pattern describes not only the context of a problem and its solution, but also the rationale behind the solution. Patterns are a valuable mechanism for describing best practice and good design. Patterns therefore have a useful role to play in software engineering. Designing software is hard. Designing good software is even harder. Fortunately, well engineered code exhibits many common patterns that support extensibility, modularity, and performance. By documenting these patterns, we can support and encourage good software engineering.

I can illustrate this by means of an analogy. Consider how you could become an America's Cup match racing helmsman. First, you learn the sailing rules

F. Rossi (Ed.): CP 2003, LNCS 2833, pp. 53–64, 2003.

(e.g. a boat on starboard tack has right of way over a boat on port). Then you learn the basic principles of racing (e.g. when you have the lead, you cover tack to protect that lead). Finally, you study past match races to learn the winning patterns of others (e.g. on a downwind leg, an expert helmsan in a trailing boat often rides an approaching gust, blankets the leading boat's sail, and overtakes on the windward side). Becoming an expert software engineer is little different. First, you learn the rules (e.g. algorithms, and data structures). Then you learn the basic principles (e.g. data abstraction helps code be modular and extensible). Finally, you study expert software engineers to learn valuable patterns (e.g. a good software engineer will often construct iterator methods so that elements of an aggregate object can be accessed without exposing the underlying representation).

Patterns are, by their very nature, not formal objects. They are therefore usually documented in natural language. A pattern descriptions typically includes the following category headings (as well as others that may be more domain specific).

Pattern Name:	A meaningful name for the pattern.
Context:	The circumstances in which the problem the pattern solves occurs.
Problem:	The specific problem that is solved.
Forces:	The often opposing considerations that must be taken into account when choosing a solution.
Solution:	The proposed solution to the problem.
Example:	An example of the problem and its resolution using the proposed solution.

Fig. 1. The typical categories used in specifying a pattern.

3   Constraint Patterns

Why should we identify and document patterns in constraint programming? Constraint programming is programming and so many of the usual software engineering issues arise. However, constraint programming is also about modelling. There are many recurring patterns in good constraint models. These patterns cannot usually be precisely specified as there are many conflicting interactions in a complex problem. Patterns therefore seem a good vehicle for explicitly capturing the knowledge of expert modellers.

What benefits do constraint patterns bring? First, they help tackle the modelling "bottleneck". A library of patterns would be a valuable resource for passing on modelling expertise to neophyte constraint programmers. Second, constraint toolkits can be extended to support commonly occurring patterns. As I argue in Section 4.2, a constraint pattern can motivate the development of a new global constraint or language feature. Third, a longer term goal would be pattern automation. For example, in Sections 4.4 and 4.5, I discuss how we are trying to automate some common constraint patterns.

What drawbacks do constraint patterns have? First, it is hard work to identify and document good patterns. It requires the efforts of a whole community, not just of one individual. Second, patterns do not eliminate all the art of constraint modelling. Many problems also contain an unique feature or an unique combination of features which necessitates a special solution technique that will not be not of a pattern library. Third, patterns are not executable. However, as I argued above, we can look to automate aspects of them.

4 Some Examples

To illustrate what a constraint pattern is, and how it can be useful, I will look at four examples from my own and other people's research.

4.1 Matrix Models

Before I describe the first pattern, I want to define the context for a number of common constraint patterns. A *matrix model* is a constraint program with one or more matrices of decision variables. For example, a natural model of a sports scheduling problem has a 2-d matrix of decision variables, each of which is assigned a value corresponding to the game played in a given week and period [3]. In this case, the matrix is obvious in the solution to the problem: we need a *table* of fixtures. However, as we demonstrate in [4, 5], many problems that are less obviously defined in terms of matrices can be efficiently represented and effectively solved using a matrix model. Sometimes, the matrix model contains multiple matrices of variables. Channelling constraints are then used to link the different matrices together [6–8].

As an example, consider the matrix model given in [4] for the steel mill slab design problem [9]. We have a number of orders, each with a particular weight and colour, to assign to slabs. Slabs come in a number of different sizes. We want to assign orders to slabs and sizes to slabs so that the total weight of orders assigned to a slab does not exceed the slab capacity, and so that each slab contains at most p colours (usually 2). A 2-d matrix of 0/1 decision variables represents which orders are assigned to which slabs. A second matrix of 0/1 decision variables is used to post the colour constraints. Channelling constraints are used to connect this to the order matrix.

In [5], we demonstrated the prevalence of matrix models by surveying the first 31 models in CSPLib. At least 27 of these had natural matrix models, most of them already published. Matrix models are a very natural way to represent relations (e.g. the relation between orders and slabs in the steel mill slab design problem). Matrix models are also a natural way to represent functions (e.g. the function mapping exams to times in an exam timetabling problem). Finally, matrix models are a natural way to represent partitions (e.g. the partitioning of nodes in a graph colouring problem into different colour classes). Another indication of the prevalence of matrix models is the common use of 2-dimension matrices of decision variables in integer linear programming.

Matrices:

$\longrightarrow$ slabs $\longrightarrow$
s_i 4 3 3 3 0 0 0 0 0

$\longrightarrow$ orders $\longrightarrow$
O_{ij} 0 0 0 0 0 0 1 1 1
$\downarrow$ 0 0 0 1 1 1 0 0 0
slabs 0 1 0 0 0 0 0 0 0
$\downarrow$ 1 0 1 0 0 0 0 0 0

$\longrightarrow$ colours
C_{ij} 0 0 0 1
$\downarrow$ 0 0 1 1
slabs 0 1 0 0
$\downarrow$ 1 1 0 0

Constraints:

(row weighted sum) $\forall j \sum_i Weight_i * O_{ij} \le s_j$
(column sum) $\forall i \sum_j O_{ij} = 1$
(row sum) $\forall j \sum_i C_{ij} \le p$
(channelling) $\forall ij \ O_{ij} = 1 \rightarrow C_{Colour_i j} = 1$

Fig. 2. Matrix model for the steel mill slab design problem (taken from [4]).

4.2 Row and Column Symmetry

A common pattern in matrix models is row and column symmetry. For example, the order matrix in the steel mill problem has partial row symmetry since slabs of the same size are indistinguishable and partial column symmetry since orders of the same size and colour are also indistinguishable. We can swap any two slabs of the same size, and any two orders of the same size and colour and obtain an essentially equivalent solution. As a second example, consider generating **Balanced Incomplete Block Designs** or BIBDs (prob028 in CSPLib). A matrix model for this problem uses a 2-d matrix of 0/1 variables, with constraints on the sum of each row and each column, and on the scalar product between rows. This matrix model has complete row and column symmetry since we can permute the rows and columns freely without affecting any of the constraints.

Symmetry in constraint programs is problematic. It increases the search space dramatically. Row and column symmetry is especially problematic as it occurs often and there is a lot of it. For example, an n by m BIBD has $n!m!$ row and column symmetries. Even if are only interested in finding one solution, we may explore many failed and symmetrically equivalent branches. When proving optimality, this can be especially painful. An effective way to break such symmetry is by posting constraints that lexicographically order the rows and columns [10]. We call this **double lex** ordering the matrix. As long as we order the rows and columns in the same direction, (i.e. the rows and columns must both be lexicographically increasing, or must both be lexicographically decreasing), this will leave a solution if one exists. Unfortunately, it does not break all symmetry. Multiple, symmetric solutions can be left after double lex ordering the matrix. Indeed, a paper in this volume [11] proposes an additional ordering constraint, the **all perms** constraint, which can be effectively posted on the rows or columns to eliminate some (but still not all) of the remaining symmetry. To support double lex and all perms ordering constraints, we have developed efficient linear time constraint propagation algorithms [12, 11]. This illustrates how constraint solvers can be extended to support commonly occurring patterns like a global symmetry-breaking constraint. Techniques to eliminate all symmetries exist [13–15], but they appear to be more expensive than they are worth for dealing with row and column symmetries. The symmetries eliminated by double lex ordering and all perms ordering appear to offer a good compromise.

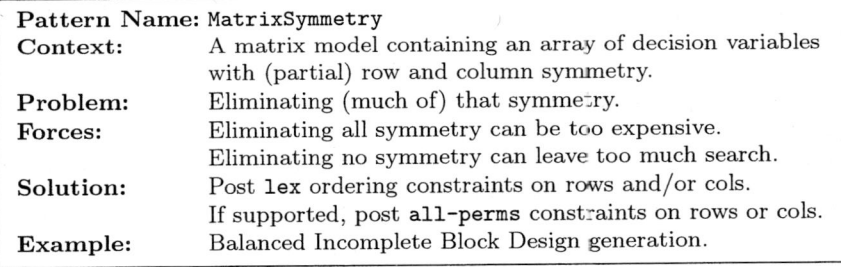

Fig. 3. Constraint pattern for `MatrixSymmetry`.

An alternative to double lex ordering is to post lexicographical ordering constraints on the rows, and multiset ordering constraints on the columns (or vice versa). We have also developed an efficient constraint propagation algorithm for multiset ordering constraints [16]. This volume also contains a paper showing how we can effectively post during search just those symmetry breaking constraints that are not yet broken by the current assignment [17]. These examples illustrate how the solution proposed to a constraint pattern may depend on what is available in our particular solver. Constraint patterns also need to apply to a range of problems. For example, double lex ordering can be applied even to problems like the steel mill slab design problem with *partial* row and column symmetry. In this case, we just order lexicographically those subsets of rows or columns which are indistinguishable.

4.3 Dual Models

The next pattern is documented in a number of papers (e.g. [18, 7, 19]) as well as ILOG's Solver 5.3 User's manual (Volume II). A constraint program defines a set of decision variables, each with an associated domain of values, and a set of constraints defining allowed values for subsets of these variables. The efficiency of a constraint program depends on a good choice for the decision variables, and a careful modelling of the constraints on these variables. Unfortunately, there is often considerable choice even in what to make the variables, and what to make the values. For example, in an exam timetabling problem, the variables could be the exams, and the values could be the times. However, we could take an alternative or dual viewpoint in which the variables are the times, and the values are the exams.

The choice of variables and values is especially evident in permutation problems. In a permutation problem, we have as many values as variables, and each variable takes an unique value. We can therefore easily exchange variables for values. Indeed, it is often beneficial to have both sets of variables with channelling constraints between the primal (or original) model and the dual [18, 7, 19]. Many assignment, scheduling and routing problems are permutation problems. For example, sports tournament scheduling can be modelled as finding a permutation of the games to fit into the time slots, or a permutation of the time slots to fit into the games.

Pattern Name: DualModelling	
Context:	An informal problem specification.
Problem:	Choosing between a primal and an alternative dual viewpoint.
Forces:	Certain constraints can be easier to post on primal.
	Certain constraints can propagate better in primal.
	Certain constraints can be easier to post on dual.
	Certain constraints can propagate better in dual.
Solution:	Consider having a combined model with channelling between the primal and dual variables.
Example:	Balanced Academic Curriculum Problem.

Fig. 4. Constraint pattern for DualModelling.

An alternative or dual viewpoint can be beneficial for a number of reasons. First, we can get different amounts of propagation in a primal, dual or a combined model [7, 19]. Second, certain constraints may be more easily stated (and propagated) on a dual model. If others are more easily stated (and propagated) on the primal, we can decide to use a combined model. Third, branching on the dual variables can be useful. For example, in a permutation problem, dual variables correspond to primal values. Therefore a variable ordering heuristic on dual variables is essentially a value ordering heuristic on the primal model. Variable ordering heuristics like fail first tend to be cheap and effective. On the other hand, value ordering heuristics tend to be neither. Variable ordering on the dual therefore can be an effective means to get value ordering on the primal.

As a concrete example, consider the Balanced Academic Curriculum Problem (prob030 in CSPLib) [20]. The objective is to assign time slots to courses. A natural matrix model is a 2-d array of 0/1 decision variables indicating if a course is given in a particular time slot. Most of the constraints are easy to post using this array of variables (e.g. the constraint that a limited number of courses occur in any time slot is simply a row sum constraint). However, one type of constraint is not easy to post on this array of variables. This is the course prerequisite constraint: every course must occur after all its prerequisites. An easy way to post this constraint is to take an alternative dual viewpoint with a 1-d array of finite-domain variables. Each variable here takes as its value the time slot for a particular course. A prerequisite constraint is now simply ordering constraints between the course variable and each of the course variables associated with its prerequisites. The other constraints are not as easily specified on this 1-d array. It is therefore beneficial to have both arrays and to channel between them [20].

4.4   Auxiliary Variables

The next pattern is documented in [21, 22]. A common method for improving a basic constraint model is to introduce auxiliary variables. Such variables permit propagation to occur between constraints with structure in common. Consider, for example, the problem of finding optimal Golomb rulers (prob006 in CSPLib). A Golomb ruler is a set of m integer valued ticks, such that the distance between any pair of ticks is different from the distance between any other pair. The objective is to find the optimal or shortest such ruler. Such rulers have practical applications in radio astronomy.

A natural model for the Golomb ruler problem has a finite-domain variable, X_i for each tick, and this is assigned the position of the tick on the ruler. To break symmetry between the ticks, we can post constraints of the form $X_i < X_j$ for $i < j$. To ensure that all inter-tick distances are distinct, we can post quaternary constraints of the form: $|X_i - X_j| \neq |X_k - X_l|$. Each such constraint computes two inter-tick differences, and each of these differences appears in a quadratic number of other constraints. A better model introduces auxiliary variables for these differences, D_{ij} and ternary constraints of the form: $D_{ij} = |X_i - X_j|$

Introducing auxiliary variables can be advantageous for several reasons. For example, we can get more propagation through the domains of these auxiliary variables. As a second example, we may be able to post simpler constraints on the auxiliary variables. In the case of the Golomb ruler problem, we can replace the large number of quaternary constraints by a single all-different constraint on the auxiliary variables. We can then use an efficient algorithm for enforcing GAC or BC on such a constraint [23, 24]. In [22], we show that modelling the Golomb ruler with such auxiliary variables increases the amount of constraint propagation and reduces runtimes significantly. More recently, we have developed methods for automatically introducing such auxiliary variables into a constraint model [25, 26].

4.5   Implied Constraints

The next pattern is also described in a number of papers (e.g. [27, 22]), as well as ILOG's Solver 5.3 User's manual (Volume II). A common method for improving a

Pattern Name:	AuxiliaryVars
Context:	A basic model in which two or more constraints repeat expressions.
Problem:	Insufficient propagation between these constraints.
Forces:	Overhead of introducing additional variables.
Solution:	Introduce auxiliary variables for the repeated expressions.
Example:	Golomb ruler problem.

Fig. 5. Constraint pattern for `AuxiliaryVars`.

basic constraint model is to introduce implied constraints. These are constraints which are not logically necessary but which may reduce search. Consider again the problem of finding optimal Golomb rulers. In the last section, we argued for the introduction of auxiliary variables for the inter-tick differences, ternary constraints of the form $D_{ij} = |X_i - X_j|$ and an all-different constraint over D_{ij}. By transitivity, as $X_i < X_j$ for $i < j$, we can infer that $D_{ij} < D_{ik}$ for any $j < k$. This implied constraint is not logically necessary. We obtain the same set of solutions with or without it. However, as shown in [22], its inclusion in the model (along with other implied constraints) reduces search and saves runtime.

Not all implied constraints are useful. Constraint propagation on an implied constraint that is very immediate may do no more pruning than constraint propagation on a basic model. In addition, even if an implied constraint reduces search, it adds overhead to the constraint propagation. In [22], we outline two basic criteria for deciding which implied constraints to add. First, implied constraints either should have specialized, efficient and effective constraint propagation algorithms or should be of small arity. This limits the overheads of adding the implied constraint and helps ensure it will propagate. Second, circumstances in which an implied constraint leads to pruning should be obvious and frequent. The hope is that the implied constraint will reduce search sufficiently to justify the overhead.

One way to develop useful implied constraints is to study the search process. Suppose the constraint solver explores an "obviously" futile part of the search tree. The partial assignments considered by the solver cannot be extended to a complete solution, but they satisfy the constraints in the model. Our challenge then is to identify an implied constraint that would have pruned this branch immediately. We are currently developing methods for inferring useful implied constraints automatically [25, 26]. For example, one of our methods identifies a clique of not-equals constraints (e.g. the constraints $D_{ij} \neq D_{kl}$ in the Golomb ruler problem) and replaces them by an all-different constraint. Another method performs Gaussian-like elimination (e.g. if we introduce an auxiliary variable for a repeated expression, this method eliminates the repeated expression in favour of the auxiliary variable).

5 Related Work

Unfortunately, constraint patterns are rarely described in a general way that permits their immediate use in other applications. One exception is a paper by

Pattern Name:	ImpliedConstraints
Context:	A basic constraint model.
Problem:	Search going down obviously futile branches.
Forces:	Overhead of introducing additional constraints.
	Applicability of the new implied constraints.
Solution:	Introduce implied constraints that prune such branches.
Example:	Golomb ruler problem.

Fig. 6. Constraint pattern for ImpliedConstraints.

Martin Green and David Cohen [28] that identifies a constraint pattern which is useful for modelling a range of assignment problems. The pattern occurs, for example, in the problem of assigning radio frequencies to pilots in a model aircraft tournament. In a straightforward model, in which the pilots are the variables and the values assigned to these variables are the radio frequencies, pilots assigned the same frequency are symmetric. We can therefore swap any two pilots assigned the same frequency and obtain a symmetric solution. To eliminate such symmetries, Green and Cohen propose an alternative viewpoint similar to the swapping of values for variables.

Hans Schlenker and Georg Ringwelski use a design pattern in POOC [29], a platform for object-oriented constraint programming. POOC provides Java wrappers around commercial and academic constraint solvers. Different constraint solvers can thus be easily compared. In addition, Java programmers can rapidly experiment with constraint solving. The wrappers are designed using the object factory design pattern. This defines an interface for creating an object, whilst allowing subclasses to decide which class to instantiate.

6   Conclusions and Future Work

I have argued that we need to identify, formalize and document patterns in constraint models in a similar way to the patterns identified by the software engineering community. A library of such patterns will help tackle the modelling "bottleneck" that hinders the uptake of constraint programming. I have described some of the more interesting constraint patterns which have already been identified. I also discussed the different ways that we can exploit such patterns. For example, one way to exploit common constraint patterns is to extend the constraint language.

There are a number of important directions to follow. First, more patterns need to be collected. As I argued before, this requires the efforts of the whole community, not just of one individual. Second, the patterns outlined here need more detail and generality. Third, the patterns need to be organized into a pattern taxonomy so that they can be accessed easily. See Figure 7 for a possible start to such a taxonomy. Fourth, we need to collect these patterns into a pattern library. I believe such a library would be a significant asset to the constraint programming community. A first attempt at such a library is taking shape at 4c.ucc.ie/patterns/.

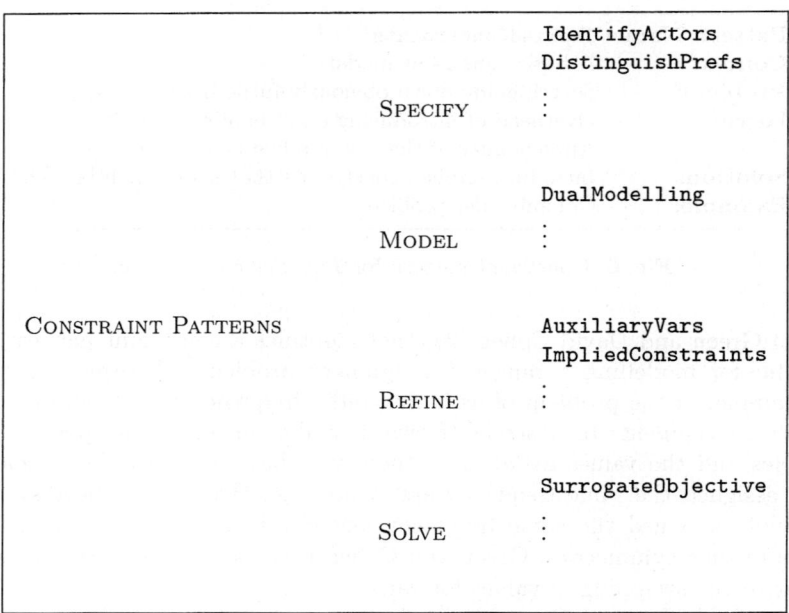

Fig. 7. A sketch of a possible constraint pattern taxonomy.

Acknowledgments

The author is supported by the Science Foundation Ireland. He wishes to thank the members of the 4C lab, the APES research group (especially Barbara Smith), the York AI Group (especially Alan Frisch), the Uppsala ASTRA group, and David Cohen.

References

1. Alexander, C.: A Pattern Language. Oxford University Press, New York (1977)
2. Gamma, E., Helm, R., Johnson, R., Vlissides, J.: Design Patterns: Elements of Reusable Object-Oriented Software. Addison-Wesley (1995)
3. Hentenryck, P.V., Michel, L., Perron, L., Regin, J.C.: Constraint programming in OPL. In Nadathur, G., ed.: Principles and Practice of Declarative Programming, Springer-Verlag (1999) 97–116 Lecture Notes in Computer Science 1702.
4. Fleiner, P., Frisch, A., Hnich, B., Kiziltan, Z., Miguel, I., Walsh, T.: Matrix modelling. Technical Report APES-36-2001, APES group (2001) Available from http://www.dcs.st-and.ac.uk/ apes/reports/apes-36-2001.ps.gz. Presented at Formul'01 Workshop on Modelling and Problem Formulation, CP2001 post-conference workshop.
5. Fleiner, P., Frisch, A., Hnich, B., Kiziltan, Z., Miguel, I., Walsh, T.: Matrix modelling: Exploiting common patterns in constraint programming. In: Proceedings of the International Workshop on Reformulating Constraint Satisfaction Problems. (2002) held alongside CP-2002.

6. Cheng, B., Choi, K., Lee, J., Wu, J.: Increasing constraint propagation by redundant modeling: an experience report. Constraints **4** (1999) 167–192

7. Smith, B.: Modelling a Permutation Problem. In: Proceedings of ECAI'2000 Workshop on Modelling and Solving Problems with Constraints. (2000) Also available as Research Report from http://www.comp.leeds.ac.uk/bms/papers.html.

8. Walsh, T.: Permutation problems and channelling constraints. Technical Report APES-26-2001, APES group (2001) Available from http://www.dcs.st-and.ac.uk/~apes/reports/apes-26-2001.ps.gz. Also in Proceedings of the IJCAI-2001 Workshop on Modelling and Solving Problems with Constraints, 2001.

9. Frisch, A., Miguel, I., Walsh, T.: Modelling a steel mill slab design problem. In: Proceedings of IJCAI-2001 Workshop on Modelling and Solving Problems with Constraints, International Joint Conference on Artificial Intelligence (2001)

10. Fleiner, P., Frisch, A., Hnich, B., Kiziltan, Z., Miguel, I., Pearson, J., Walsh, T.: Breaking row and column symmetry in matrix models. In: 8th International Conference on Principles and Practices of Constraint Programming (CP-2002), Springer (2002)

11. Frisch, A., Jefferson, C., Miguel, I.: Constraints for breaking more row and column symmetries. In Rossi, F., ed.: Proceedings of 9th International Conference on Principles and Practice of Constraint Programming (CP2003), Springer (2003)

12. Frisch, A., Hnich, B., Kiziltan, Z., Miguel, I., Walsh, T.: Global constraints for lexicographic orderings. In: 8th International Conference on Principles and Practices of Constraint Programming (CP-2002), Springer (2002)

13. Crawford, J.: A theoretical analysis of reasoning by symmetry in first-order logic (extended abstract). In: Proceedings of AAAI 1992 Workshop on Tractable Reasoning. (1992) 17–22

14. Gent, I., Smith, B.: Symmetry breaking in constraint programming. In Horn, W., ed.: Proceedings of the 14th European Conference on Artificial Intelligence. (2000) 599–603

15. Fahle, T., Schamberger, S., Sellman, M.: Symmetry breaking. In Walsh, T., ed.: Proceedings of 7th International Conference on Principles and Practice of Constraint Programming (CP2001), Springer (2001) 93–107

16. Frisch, A., Hnich, B., Kiziltan, Z., Miguel, I., Walsh, T.: Multiset ordering constraints. In: Proceedings of 18th IJCAI, International Joint Conference on Artificial Intelligence (2003)

17. Puget, J.F.: Symmetry breaking for matrix models using stabilizers. In Rossi, F., ed.: Proceedings of 9th International Conference on Principles and Practice of Constraint Programming (CP2003), Springer (2003)

18. Cheng, B., Choi, K., Lee, J., Wu, J.: Increasing constraint propagation by redundant modeling: an experience report. Constraints **4** (1999) 167–192

19. Walsh, T.: Permtuation problems and channelling constraints. In: Proceedings of 8th International Conference on Logic for Programming, Artificial Intelligence and Reasoning (LPAR 2001). (2001)

20. Hnich, B., Kiziltan, Z., Walsh, T.: Modelling a balanced academic curriculum problem. In: Proceedings of 4th International Workshop on Integration of AI and OR techniques in Constraint Programming for Combinatorial Optimisation Problems (CP-AI-OR 2002). (2002)

21. Smith, B., Stergiou, K., Walsh, T.: Modelling the golomb ruler problem. In: Proceedings of the IJCAI-99 Workshop on Non-Binary Constraints, International Joint Conference on Artificial Intelligence (1999) Also available as APES report, APES-11-1999 from http://apes.cs.strath.ac.uk/repcrts/apes-11-1999.ps.gz.

22. Smith, B., Stergiou, K., Walsh, T.: Using auxiliary variables and implied constraints to model non-binary problems. In: Proceedings of the 16th National Conference on AI, American Association for Artificial Intelligence (2000) 182–187

23. Régin, J.C.: A filtering algorithm for constraints of difference in CSPs. In: Proceedings of the 12th National Conference on AI, American Association for Artificial Intelligence (1994) 362–367

24. Lopez-Ortiz, A., Quimper, C., Tromp, J., van Beek, P.: A fast and simple algorithm for bounds consistency of the alldifferent constraint. In: Proceedings of the 18th International Conference on AI, International Joint Conference on Artificial Intelligence (2003)

25. Frisch, A., Miguel, I., Walsh, T.: Extensions to proof planning for generating implied constraints. In: Proceedings of 9th Symposium on the Integration of Symbolic Computation and Mechanized Reasoning (Calculemus-01). (2001) 130–141

26. Frisch, A., Miguel, I., Walsh, T.: CGRASS: A system for transforming constraint satisfaction problems. In O'Sullivan, B., ed.: Recent Advances in Constraints. Volume 2627 of Lecture Notes in Artificial Intelligence., Springer (2003) Volume contains selected papers from the ERCIM/CologNet 2002 workshop. The paper is also available as APES-42-2002 Research Report.

27. Proll, L., Smith, B.: Integer linear programming and constraint programming approaches to a template design problem. INFORMS Journal on Computing **10** (1998) 265–275

28. Green, M., Cohen, D.: A CSP design pattern for hard problems. Technical report, Royal Holloway, University of London (2003)

29. Schlenker, H., Ringwelski, G.: Pooc - a platform for object-oriented constraint programming. In O'Sullivan, B., ed.: Recent Advances in Constraints. Volume 2627 of Lecture Notes in Artificial Intelligence., Springer (2003)

Control Abstractions for Local Search

Pascal Van Hentenryck[1] and Laurent Michel[2]

[1] Brown University, Box 1910, Providence, RI 02912
[2] University of Connecticut, Storrs, CT 06269-3155

Abstract. COMET is an object-oriented language supporting a constraint-based architecture for local search through declarative and search components. This paper proposes three novel and lightweight control abstractions for the search component, significantly enhancing the compositionality, modularity, and reuse of COMET programs. These abstractions, which includes events and checkpoints, rely on first-class closures as the enabling technology. They are especially useful for expressing, in a modular way, heuristic and meta-heuristics, unions of heterogeneous neighborhoods, and sequential composition of neighborhoods.

1 Introduction

Historically, most research on modeling and programming tools for combinatorial optimization has focused on systematic search, which is at the core of branch & bound and constraint satisfaction algorithm. It is only recently that more attention has been devoted to programming tools for local search and its variations (e.g., [6, 26, 23, 11, 14, 25]).

COMET [13] is a novel, object-oriented, programming language specifically designed to simplify the implementation of local search algorithms. Comet supports a constraint-based architecture for local search organized around two main components: a declarative component which models the application in terms of constraints and functions, and a search component which specifies the search heuristic and meta-heuristic. Constraints, which are a natural vehicle to express combinatorial optimization problems, are *differentiable objects* in COMET: They maintain a number of properties incrementally and they provide algorithms to evaluate the effect of various operations on these properties. The search component then uses these functionalities to guide the local search using multidimensional, possibly randomized, selectors and other high-level control structures. The architecture enables local search algorithms to be high-level, compositional, and modular. It is possible to add new constraints and to modify or remove existing ones, without having to worry about the global effect of these changes. COMET also separates the modeling and search components, allowing programmers to experiment with different search heuristics and meta-heuristics without affecting the problem modeling. This separation of concerns give COMET some flavor of aspect-oriented programming [9] and feature engineering [24], since constraints represent and maintain properties across a wide range of objects. COMET has been applied to many applications and can be implemented to be

F. Rossi (Ed.): CP 2003, LNCS 2833, pp. 65–80, 2003.

competitive with tailored algorithms, primarily because of its fast incremental algorithms [13].

This paper focuses on the search component and aims at fostering the compositionality, modularity, and genericity of COMET. It introduces three novel control abstractions whose main benefit is to separate, in the source code, components which are usually presented independently in scientific papers. Indeed, most local search descriptions cover the neighborhood, the search heuristic, and the meta-heuristic separately. Yet typical implementations of these algorithms exhibit complex interleavings of these independent aspects and/or require many intermediary classes and/or interfaces. The resulting code is opaque, less extensible, and less reusable. The new control abstractions address these limitations and reduce the distance between high-level descriptions and their implementations.

The first abstraction, *events*, enables programmers to isolate the search heuristic from the meta-heuristic, as well as the algorithm animation from the modeling and search components. The second abstraction, *neighbors*, aims at expressing naturally unions of heterogeneous neighborhoods, which often arise in complex routing and scheduling applications. It allows programmers to separate the neighborhood definition from its exploration, while keeping move evaluation and execution textually close. The third abstraction, *checkpoints*, simplifies the sequential composition of neighborhoods, which is often present in large-scale neighborhood search.

These three control abstractions, not only share the same conceptual motivation, but are also based on a common enabling technology: *first-class closures*. Closures make it possible to separate the definition of a dynamic behaviour from its use, providing a simple and uniform implementation technology for the three control abstractions. Once closures are available, the control abstractions really become lightweight extensions, which is part of their appeal.

The rest of this paper is organized as follows. Section 2 briefly reviews the local search architecture and its implementation in COMET. Section 3 gives a brief overview of closures. Sections 4, 5, and 6 present the new control abstractions and sketches their implementation. Section 7 presents some experimental results showing the viability of the approach. Section 8 concludes the paper.

2   The Constraint-Based Architecture for Local Search

This section is a brief overview of the constraint-based architecture for local search and its implementation in COMET. See [13] for more detail. The architecture consists of a declarative and a search component organized in three layers. The kernel of the architecture is the concept of *invariants* over algebraic and set expressions [14]. Invariants are expressed in terms of incremental variables and specify a relation which must be maintained under modifications to its variables. Once invariants are available, it becomes natural to support the concept of *differentiable objects*, a fundamental abstraction for local search programming. *Differentiable objects maintain a number of properties (using invariants) and can be queried to evaluate the effect of local moves on these properties.* They are

```
1.  range Size = 1..1024;
2.  LocalSolver ls();
3.  UniformDistribution distr(Size);
4.  inc{int} queen[i in Size](ls,Size) := distr.get();
5.  int neg[i in Size] = -i;
6.  int pos[i in Size] = i;

7.  ConstraintSystem S(ls);
8.  S.post(new AllDifferent(queen));
9.  S.post(new AllDifferent(queen,neg));
10. S.post(new AllDifferent(queen,pos));
11. inc{set{int}} conflicts(ls) <- argMax(q in Size) S.violations(queen[q]);
12. m.close();

13. Counter it(ls);
14. while (!S.isTrue()) {
15.    select(q in conflicts)
16.      selectMin(v in Size)(S.getAssignDelta(queen[q],v))
17.        queen[q] := v;
18.    it++;
19. }
```

Fig. 1. The Queens Problem in Comet.

fundamental because many local search algorithms evaluate the effect of various moves before selecting the neighbor to visit. Two important classes of differentiable objects are constraints and functions. A differentiable constraint maintains properties such as its satisfiability, its violation degree, and how much each of its underlying variables contribute to the violations. It can be queried to evaluate the effect of local moves (e.g., assignments and swaps) on these properties. *Differentiable objects also capture combinatorial substructures arising in many applications* and are appealing for two main reasons. On the one hand, they are high-level modeling tools which can be composed naturally to build complex local search algorithms. As such, they bring into local search some of the nice properties of modern constraint satisfaction systems. On the other hand, they are amenable to efficient incremental algorithms that exploit their combinatorial properties. The use of combinatorial constraints is also advocated in [3, 7, 17, 26].

These first two layers, invariants and differentiable objects, constitute the declarative component of the architecture. The third layer of the architecture is the search component which aims at simplifying the implementation of heuristics and meta-heuristics, another critical aspect of local search algorithms. It does not prescribe any specific heuristic or meta-heuristic. Rather, it features high-level constructs and abstractions to simplify the neighborhood exploration and the implementation of meta-heuristics. These includes several multidimensional selectors, abstractions to manipulate solutions, and advanced simulation techniques.

Figure 1 illustrates the architecture, and its implementation in COMET, on the queens problem. The COMET algorithm is based on the min-conflict heuristic [16]. The algorithm starts with an initial random configuration. Then, at each iteration, it chooses the queen violating the largest number of constraints and moves it to a position minimizing its violations. This step is iterated until a solution is found. Since a queen must be placed on every column, the algorithm uses an array `queen` of variables and `queen[i]` denotes the row of the queen placed on column i. Lines 1-6 declare a range, a local solver, a uniform distribution, an array of incremental variables for representing the row of each queen, as well as two arrays of constants. *The modeling component* is given in Lines 7-12. Line 7 declares a constraint system. Lines 8-10 add the three traditional `AllDifferent` constraints, showing how COMET supports "global" combinatorial constraints for local search. Line 11 expresses an invariant which maintains the set of queens with the most violations. Operator `argMax(v in S) E` simply returns the set of values v in S which maximizes E. *The search component* is given in lines 13-19. It iterates lines 15-17 until the constraint system is true, i.e., no constraint is violated. Line 15 selects a most violated queen, while line 16 selects a new value v for the selected queen. The value is selected to minimize the number of violations of the selected queen. To implement this min-conflict heuristic, COMET queries the constraint system, a differential object, to find out the effect of assigning queen q to each row. Line 17 simply executes the move, automatically updating all invariants and constraints. The use of the counter `it` will become clear later in the paper.

Observe that the search and declarative components are clearly separated in the program. It is thus easy to modify one of them (e.g., adding a constraint and/or changing the search heuristic) without affecting the other. Although the two components are physically separated in the program code, they closely collaborate during execution. The declarative component is used to guide the search, while the assignment `queen[q] := v` starts a propagation phase which updates all invariants and constraints. This compositionality and clear separation of concerns are some of the appealing features of the architecture. *This is precisely such properties which this paper tries to foster further.* Note also that the declarative component only specifies the properties of the solutions, as well as the data structures to maintain. It does not specify how to update them, which is the role of the incremental algorithms in the COMET runtime system.

3   Closures in COMET

Closures are the common enabling technology behind all three control abstractions introduced in this paper. A closure is a piece of code together with its environment. Closures are ubiquitous in functional programming languages, where they are first-class citizens. They are rarely supported in object-oriented languages however. To illustrate the use of closures in COMET, consider the following class

```
1.  class DemoClosure {          8.  DemcClosure demo();
2.    DemoClosure() {}            9.  Closure c1 = demo.print(9);
3.    Closure print(int i) {      10. Closure c2 = demo.print(5);
4.      return new closure        11. call(c2);
5.        {cout << i << endl;}    12. call(c1);
6.    }                           13. cal_(c2);
7.  }
```

Method `print` receives an integer i and returns a closure which, when executed, prints i on the standard output. The following snippet shows how to use closures in COMET: the snippet displays 5, 9, and 5 on the standard output. Observe that closures are first-class citizens: They can be stored in data structures, passed as parameters, and returned as results. The two closures created in the example above share the same code (i.e., `cout << i << endl`), but their environments differ. Both contain only one entry (variable i), but they associate the value 9 (closure c1) and the value 5 (closure c2) to this entry. When a closure is created, its environment is saved and, when a closure is executed, the environment is restored before, and popped after, execution of its code. Closures can be rather complex and have environments containing many parameters and local variables, as will become clear later on.

4   Events for Modularity, Compositionality, and Reuse

One of the fundamental benefits of COMET is its ability to separate problem modeling from search. This separation of concerns is made possible by incremental variables, invariants, and differential objects. However, practical applications typically involve other components which would also benefit from such modularity. One such component is algorithm animation, which is valuable early in the development process to visualize the local search behavior. Another component is the meta-heuristic which is often orthogonal and independent from the search heuristic. This section introduces the concept of *publish/subscribe events* in COMET, which make this separation of concerns possible. Informally speaking, classes can publish events, which can be subscribed by event-handlers elsewhere in the code. Methods in the classes can then notify these events, which triggers the event-handler behaviour. We first focus on how to use events for animation and meta-heuristic. We then show how to publish and notify events.

Events for Animation. Consider a graphical animation for the n-queens problem and assume the existence of an `Animation` class handling the graphics and providing a method `updatePosition(int q,int p)` to display the queen on column q on row r. Such an animation is obtained by inserting the snippet

```
forall(q in Size)
    whenever queen[q]@changes(int or,int nr)
        animation.updateQueen(q,nr);
```

just before the search component (between lines 12 and 13). The core of the snippet is an event-handler that specifies that, whenever the value of `queen[q]` changes from or to nr, the code animation.updateQueen(q,nr) must be executed. This event-handler is installed for all queens.

There are a few important points to highlight here. First, the animation code is completely separated from both the modeling and the search components. The glue between the components is the event changes on incremental variables which is *notified* whenever a variable is assigned a new value. The snippet achieves the same effect as calling animation.updateQueen(q,nr) after the assignment of queens, while clearly separating the two aspects and avoiding to clutter the heuristic with animation code. This makes the code more readable and easier to modify and extend. Second, observe that the event-handler behaviour animation.updateQueen(q,nr) is a closure which depends on the value of q in the environment and is created when the event is subscribed to. Closures make the animation code more natural, avoid the definition of intermediary classes, and feature a textual proximity between the event-handler condition (e.g., the queen is assigned a new value) and its behavior (e.g., update the display of the queen). In traditional object-oriented languages, event conditions and behaviors are separated, which complicates reading and requires new class definitions to store the information necessary to execute the behavior. Finally, observe that events are statically and strongly typed: they enable information to be transmitted from the notifier (e.g., the incremental variable) to the event-handler in a safe fashion with no downcasting.

Events are also compositional. Consider, for instance, adding the functionality of coloring the queens differently according to their number of violations. It is sufficient to add the instructions

```
inc{int} violation[q in Size](m) <- S.violations(queen[q]);
forall(q in Size)
    whenever violation[q]@changes(int ov,int nv)
        animation.updateColor(q,nv);
```

This snippet declares an array of incremental variables maintaining the number of violations of each queen, and updates the color of a queen each time its number of violations is updated. Note that the number of violations of a queen may change even when the queen is not moved. Hence, it is not possible to insert the behaviour elsewhere in the program, while remaining incremental, i.e., only considering the queens whose number of violations was modified. This example shows the strengths of events in COMET: they enable elegant animation codes, which would require complex control flows, the creation of intermediary classes, and/or less incrementality in other languages.

Events for Meta-heuristics. Events are also beneficial to separate the search heuristic and the meta-heuristic (e.g., tabu-search). They make it possible to divide the statement into modeling, search, and meta-heuristic components. For illustration purposes, consider upgrading the queen algorithm with a tabu-search strategy, which would make a queen tabu for a number of iterations, each time a queen is moved. The tabu-list management can be almost entirely separated from the search heuristic. For instance, the snippet

```
1.  set{int} tabu();
2.  forall(q in Size)
3.    whenever queen[q]@changes(int o,int n) {
4.        tabu.insert(q);
5.        when it@reaches[it+tLen]()
6.            tabu.remove(q);
7.    }
```

shows a simple management of the tabu list, which we now explain in detail.
The code declares a set tabu to store the tabu queens and features two nested
event-handlers. The outermost event-handler is notified each time a queen is
moved. It inserts the queen in the tabu set and install the second event-handler
(lines 5-6) whose goal is to remove q from the tabu set after tLen iterations,
where tLen is the length of the tabu list. This second handler is interesting in
several ways. First, it features a *key-event*, i.e., an event which is parametrized
by a specific key which is in between brackets in the code. Here the key is an
iteration number and the handler will be notified when the counter it will reach
or exceed the value it+tLen, i.e., the value of the counter when the handler is
installed (subscription time) plus the length of the tabu-list. Second, the handler
uses the when construct, which means that it will be notified only once.

Once this code is in place, the only modification in the search heuristic consists in selecting the queen with the largest number of violations among the
non-tabu queens (instead of among all queens). As a consequence, the "glue"
between the components (i.e., the counter and the tabu-set) is minimal and
the proper behavior is achieved without interleaving the heuristic and the meta
heuristic in the source code. Note that, in complex applications, this glue can be
anticipated in the first place by assuming that moves are always selected from a
restricted set specified by the modeling and/or meta-heuristic components.

Event Specification and Notification. The examples above focused on the event-
handler (the *subscription* part) and showed how the when and whenever are used
to register a behaviour. Since they only used primitive objects, no explicit specification and notification of events (the *publish* part) was necessary. Of course,
COMET makes it possible to define new events. Each class may publish some
events or key-events by declaring them. Its methods are then responsible to notify these events appropriately. To illustrate event specification and notification,
consider a possible implementation of the class Counter in COMET:

```
class Counter {                     Counter::Counter(){_cnt=new inc{int}(0);}
  inc{int} _cnt;                    int Counter::++() {
  Event changes(int ov,int nv);       int old = _cnt++;
  KeyEvent reaches();                  notify changes(old,_cnt);
  Counter();                           notify reaches[_cnt]();
  int ++();                            return _cnt;
}                                   }
```

The class declares an incremental variable _cnt, an event changes with two
parameters, a key-event reaches with no parameter, the constructor and the
operator. The implementation of the operation (on the right part of the snippet)

notifies the **changes** events, passing the old and new values of the incremental variable. It also notifies all the key-events **reaches**, whose keys are smaller or equal to the value of _cnt. These notifications triggers all the event-handlers associated with these events, i.e., it executes the closures which were registered at subscription time by the **when** and **whenever** instructions. In aspect-oriented terms, the **notify** instructions are joint-points and **when** and **whenever** statements are *dynamic* aspects, i.e., aspects associated with instances, not with classes as is typical in aspect-oriented languages.

Implementation of Events. Conceptually, the implementation of events is close to the OBSERVER design pattern. An event is compiled into virtual machine instructions which explicitly use closures as shown below:

```
when x@changes(int o,int n)          aload x
    cout << n << endl;      ⟹       newClosure "cout << n << endl;"
                                     subscribeEvent changes,<o,n>
```

The virtual machine is a JVM-like stack machine and x and the closure are retrieved from the stack in **subscribeEvent**. At the instance level, each event corresponds to a data structure which collects all the subscribers. Upon notification, the appropriate subscribers are executed, i.e., their parameters are properly initialized and their closures are executed.

5 Union of Heterogeneous Neighborhoods

Many complex applications in areas such as scheduling and routing use complex neighborhoods consisting of several heterogeneous moves. For instance, the elegant tabu-search of Dell'Amico and Trubian [5] consists of the union of the subneighborhoods, each of which consisting of several types of moves. Similarly, many advanced vehicle routing algorithms [10, 4, 2] use a variety of moves (e.g., swapping visit orders and relocating customers on other routes), each of which may involve a different number of customers and trucks.

The difficulty in expressing these algorithms come from the temporal disconnection between the move selection and execution. In general, a tabu-search or a greedy local search algorithm first scans the neighborhood to determine the best move, before executing the selected move. However, in these complex applications, the exploration cannot be expressed using a (multidimensional) selector, since the moves are heterogeneous and obtained by iterating over different sets. As a consequence, an implementation would typically create classes to store the information necessary to characterize the different types of moves. Each of these classes would inherit from a common abstract class (or would implement the same interface). During the scanning phase, the algorithm creates instances of these classes to represent selected moves and stores them in a selector whenever appropriate. During the execution phase, the algorithm extracts the selected move and applies its **execute** operation. The drawbacks of this approach are twofold. On the one hand, it requires the definition of a several classes to represent the moves. On the other hand, it fragments the code, separating the *evaluation* of a move from its *execution* in the program source. As a result, the program is less readable and more verbose.

The `neighbor` *Construct.* COMET supports a `neighbor` construct, which relies heavily on closures and eliminates these drawbacks. It makes it possible to specify the move evaluation and execution in one place and avoids unnecessary class definitions. More important, it significantly enhances compositionality and reuse, since the various subneighborhoods do not have to agree on a common interface. They key idea is to view a neighbor as a pair $\langle \delta : int, move : Closure \rangle$ and to have `neighbor` constructs of the form

`neighbor(`δ`,N) M`

where M is a move, δ is its evaluation, and N is a neighbor selector, i.e., a container object to store one or several moves and their evaluations. COMET supports a variety of such selectors and users can define their own, since they all have to implement a common interface. For instance, a typical neighbor selector for tabu-search maintains the best move and its evaluation. The execution of the `neighbor` instruction queries selector N to find out whether it accepts a move of quality δ, in which case the closure of M is submitted to N.

Jobshop Scheduling. We now illustrate how the `neighbor` construct significantly simplifies the implementation of the tabu-search algorithm of Dell'Amico and Trubian (DT) for jobshop scheduling. We first review the basic ideas behind the DT algorithm and then sketch how the neighborhood exploration is expressed in COMET. Algorithm DT uses neighborhood $NC = RNA \cup NB$, where RNA is a neighborhood swapping vertices on a critical path (critical vertices) and NB is a neighborhood where a critical vertex is moved toward the beginning or the end of its critical block. More precisely, RNA considers sequences of the form $\langle p, v, s \rangle$, where v is a critical vertex and p, v, s represent successive tasks on the same machine, and explores all permutations of these three vertices. Neighborhood NB considers a maximal sequence $\langle v_1, \ldots, v_i, \ldots, v_n \rangle$ of critical vertices on the same machine. For each such subsequence and each vertex v_i, it explores the schedule obtained by placing v_i at the beginning or at the end of the block, i.e.,

$$\langle v_i, v_1, \ldots, v_{i-1}, v_{i+1}, \ldots, v_n \rangle \vee \langle v_1, \ldots, v_{i-1}, v_{i+1}, \ldots, v_n, v_i \rangle$$

Since these schedules are not necessarily feasible, NB actually considers the leftmost and rightmost feasible positions for v_i (instead of the first and last position). NB is connected which is an important theoretical property of neighborhoods.

We now show excerpts of the neighborhood implementation in COMET. The top-level methods are as follows:

```
void executeMove() {                 void exploreN(NeighborSelector N)
  MinNeighborSelector N();           {
  exploreN(N);                         exploreRNA(N);
  if (N.hasMove())call(N.getMove());   exploreNB(N);
}                                    }
```

```
1. void exploreNB(NeighborSelector N) {
2.    forall(v in _jobshop.getCriticalVertices()) {
3.        int lm = _jobshop.leftMostFeasible(v);
4.        if (lm > 0) {
5.            int delta = _jobshop.moveBackwardDelta(v,lm);
6.            if (acceptNBLeft(delta,v))
7.                neighbor(delta,N) _jobshop.moveBackward(v,lm);
8.        }
9.        int rm = _jobshop.rightMostFeasible(v);
10.       if (rm > 0) {
11.           int delta = _jobshop.moveForwardDelta(v,rm);
12.           if (acceptNBRight(delta,v))
13.               neighbor(delta,N) _jobshop.moveForward(v,rm);
14.       }
15.   }
16.}
```

Fig. 2. Exploration of Neighborhood *NB* in COMET.

Method executeMove creates a selector, explores the neighborhood, and executes the best move (if any). Method exploreN explores the neighborhood and illustrates the compositionality of the approach: It is easy to add new neighborhoods without modifying existing code, since the subneighborhoods do not have to agree on a common interface or abstract class. The implementation of exploreRNA and exploreNB is of course where the neighbor construct is used. Figure 2 gives the implementation of exploreNB: method exploreRNA is similar in spirit, but somewhat more complex, since it involves 5 different moves, as well as additional conditions to ensure feasibility. Method exploreNB uses the instance variable _jobshop, which is a differentiable object representing the disjunctive graph, a fundamental concept in jobshop scheduling [20]. This differential object maintains the release and tail dates of all vertices, as well as the critical paths, under various operations on the disjunctive graph. The exploreNB method iterates over all critical vertices. For each of them it finds the leftmost feasible insertion point in its critical block (line 3). If such a feasible insertion point exists, it evaluates the move (line 5) and then tests if the move is acceptable (line 6). In the DT algorithm, this involves testing the tabu status, a cycling condition, and the aspiration criterion. If the move is acceptable, the neighbor instruction is executed. The move itself consists of moving vertex v by lm positions backwards. Note that, although the move is specified in the neighbor instruction, it is not executed. Only the best move is executed and this takes place in method executeMove once the entire neighborhood has been explored. The remaining of method exploreNB handles the symmetric forward move.

The neighborhood exploration is particularly elegant (in our opinion). Although a move evaluation and its execution take place at different execution times, the neighbor construct makes it possible to specify them together, significantly enhancing clarity and programming ease. The move evaluation and execution are textually adjacent and the logic underlying the neighborhood is not

made obscure by introducing intermediary classes and methods. Compositionality is another fundamental advantage of the code organization. As mentioned
earlier, new moves can be added easily, without affecting existing code. Equally
or more important perhaps, the approach separates the neighborhood definition
(method `exploreN`) from its use (method `executeMove` in the DT algorithm).
This makes it possible to use the neighborhood exploration in many different
ways without any modification to its code. For instance, a semi-greedy strategy,
which selects one of the k-best moves, only requires to use a semi-greedy selector.
Similarly, method `exploreN` can be used to collect all neighbors which is useful
in intensification strategies based on elite solutions [13].

Implementation of Neighbor. The `neighbor` construct is only syntactic sugar
once closures are available. Indeed, the syntactic form is rewritten as shown
below:

```
forall(v in Size)                     forall(v in Size)
   neighbor(Δ(v),N)      ⟹              δ ← Δ(v)
      M(v);                              if (N.accept(δ))
                                            N.insert(δ,new closure {M(v);});
```

The rewriting uses method `accept` on the selector to determine whether to
accept a move. It also ensures that closures are constructed lazily.

6   Sequential Composition of Neighborhoods

This section discusses the use of checkpoint to express the sequential composition
concisely. Sequential composition is often fundamental in very large neighborhood search, which explores sequences or trees of (possibly heterogeneous) moves
and selects the best encountered neighbor (e.g., [8,1]). This section illustrates
these concepts using variable-depth neighborhood search (VDNS) [8], which was
shown very effective on graph-partitioning and traveling salesman problems.

Variable-Depth Neighborhood Search. VDNS
consists of exploring a sequence of moves and
moving to the state with best evaluation in
the sequence. By exploring sequences which
include degrading moves, VDNS may avoid
being trapped in poor local optima.

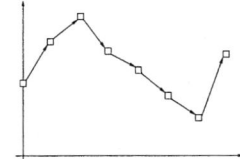

   Consider Figure 3 which plots the quality of a sequence of moves. Each node in
the graph corresponds to a computation state
and two successive nodes are neighbors in the

Fig. 3. A Sequence of Moves.

transition graph of the local search. VDNS explores the whole sequence and then
returns to the best computation state, i.e., the before-last node.

Checkpoints. *Checkpoints* are a simple conceptual abstraction to express VDNS
algorithms. A checkpoint is simply a data structure that implicitly represents the

```
function boolean selectBest(LocalSolver ls,int l,inc{int} f,Closure Move) {
    boolean found = false;
    with checkpoint(ls) {
        Checkpoint chp(ls); int best = f;
        forall(i in 1..l) {
            call(Move);
            if (f < best) {
                found = true; best = f; chp = new Checkpoint(ls);
            }
        }
        chp.restore();
    }
    return found;
}
```

Fig. 4. The implementation of VDNS in COMET.

computation state of a local solver, i.e., the state of all incremental variables and data structures of the solver. Whenever a local solver is in checkpointing mode, checkpoints can be saved and, later, restored in order to reset all incremental variables, constraints, and data structures to their earlier states. Checkpoints are first-class citizens in COMET. They also encapsulate incremental algorithms to avoid saving entire computation states.

Variable-Depth Neighborhood Search in COMET. We now illustrate how to express VDNS in COMET for graph partitioning [8], where moves consists of swapping two vertices, one from each set in the partition. The snippet

```
selectBest(ls,nb/2,cost)
    select(s in BestSwaps) {
        x[s.o] :=: x[s.d]; mark[s.o] := true; mark[s.d] := true;
    }
```

shows the core of the search procedure in COMET. In the snippet, ls is the local solver, nb is the number of vertices, cost is the cost of the partition, bestSwaps is an incremental set of tuples which maintains the best swaps, x is an array of incremental variables specifying which set of the partition a vertex belongs to, and mark is an array of incremental Boolean variables, indicating whether a vertex have been selected in the VDNS sequence already. Note also that a :=: b swaps the values of *a* and *b*. The selectBest function is the cornerstone of the VDNS implementation. It receives four arguments: the local solver, the length of the sequence, the function to minimize (an incremental variable), and a closure representing the move. Here the move consists of selecting a tuple s in BestSwaps and to swap the vertices s.o and s.d. Both vertices are then marked in order to avoid selecting them again in the sequence.

Figure 4 depicts the implementation of function selectBest. It uses the with checkpoint(ls) statement to indicate the use of checkpointing inside the enclosed block. It saves the current state in variable chp using instruction Checkpoint chp(ls). The forall loop explores a sequence of l moves, storing the best computation state in variable `chp`. After this exploration, instruction `chp.restore()` restores the best computation state encountered (possibly the initial state). Note that COMET supports the syntactic rewriting from `f(a`$_1$`,...,a`$_n$`)` S to `f(a`$_1$`,...,a`$_n$`,new closure { S })` when the last argument of function `f` is a closure. The VDNS implementation has a number of interesting features. First, it is entirely generic and reusable: It can be applied to an arbitrary move and separates search heuristic and the meta-heuristic. Second, checkpoints specify *what* to maintain, i.e., the "best" computation states, but not *how* to save or restore it. The implementation uses incremental algorithms to do so, but this is abstracted from programmers. Finally, observe the role of closures for the genericity of the VDNS implementation.

Implementation of Checkpoints. We now discuss the checkpoint implementation. The key to an incremental implementation lies in a representation of computation states as sequences of primitive moves from an initial state (i.e., the state when the checkpoint statement is executed). In other words, a state s is a sequence $\langle m_0, \ldots, m_k \rangle$ where m_i is a primitive move. A primitive move in COMET is a function $f : State \to State$ from computation states to computation states which is invertible, i.e., there exists a function f^{-1} such that $f(f^{-1}(s)) = s$. For instance, a move `x[i]:=j` corresponds to a function $f(s) = s\{x[i]/j\}$ where $s\{y/v\}$ represents the state s where y is assigned the value v. The inverse move is of course $f^{-1}(s) = s\{x[i]/lookup(s^0, x[i])\}$ where s^j is the computation state before executing the move, and *lookup* reads the value of a variable in a computation state. Consider now how to restore a state s_r from a state s_c where

$$s_c = \langle m_0, \ldots, m_n, m'_{n+1}, \ldots, m'_k \rangle$$
$$s_r = \langle m_0, \ldots, m_n, m''_{n+1}, \ldots, m''_l \rangle.$$

The COMET implementation exploits the common prefix of the two states. It undoes the suffix $\langle m'_{n+1}, \ldots, m'_k \rangle$ by using the inverse moves, and then executes the moves $\langle m''_{n+1}, \ldots, m''_l \rangle$. This implementation has several properties. First, its memory requirements are independent of the size of the computation states. Only moves are memorized and the size of a checkpoint c only depends on the length of the sequence from the initial state to c. Second, the runtime requirements are also minimal, since they either reexecute a subsequence executed before or they execute the inverse of such a subsequence. For VDNS, for instance, restoring the best state does not change the asymptotic complexity: in the worst case, restoring the checkpoint involves as much work as exploring the sequence.

The checkpoint implementation is related to techniques underlying generic search strategies (e.g., [19, 15, 22]). However, it does not use backtracking and/or trailing. Rather, it makes heavy use of inverse moves, which is efficient because the invariant propagation algorithm never updates the same incremental variable twice [14] (which is not the case in constraint satisfaction algorithms in general). Our implementation thus combines low memory requirements with incrementality, which is critical for many local search applications.

7   Experimental Results

This section describes some preliminary experimental results to demonstrate the practical viability of the abstractions and of closures. It compares various implementations of the tabu-search algorithm DT (the goal, of course, is not to compare various scheduling algorithms). In particular, it compares the original results [5], a C++ implementation [21], and the COMET implementation. Table 1 presents the results corresponding to Table 3 in [5]. Since DT is actually faster on the LA benchmarks (Table 4 in [5]), these results are representative. In the table, DT is the original implementation on a 33mhz PC, DT* is the scaled times on a 745mhz PC, KS is the C++ implementation on a 440 MHz Sun Ultra, KS* are the scaled times on a 745mhz PC, and CO are the COMET times on a 745mhz PC. Scaling was based on the clock frequency, which is favorable to slower machines (especially for the Sun). The times corresponds to the average over multiple runs (5 for DT, 20 for KS, and 50 for CO). Results for COMET are for the JIT compiler but include garbage collection. The results clearly indicate that COMET can be implemented to be competitive with specialized programs. Note also that the C++ implementation is more than 4,000 lines long, while the COMET program has about 400 lines.

Table 1. Computational Results on the Tabu-Search Algorithm (DT).

	ABZ5	ABZ6	ABZ7	ABZ8	ABZ9	MT10	MT20	ORB1	ORB2	ORB3	ORB4	ORB5
DT	139.5	86.8	320.1	336.1	320.8	155.8	160.1	157.6	136.4	157.3	156.8	140.1
DT*	6.2	3.8	14.2	15.1	14.2	6.9	7.1	7.0	6.0	7.0	6.9	6.2
KS	7.8	8.2	20.7	23.1	20.3	8.7	16.4	9.2	7.8	9.3	8.5	8.1
KS*	4.6	4.8	12.2	13.6	11.9	5.1	9.6	5.4	4.6	5.5	5.0	4.8
CO	5.9	5.7	11.7	9.9	9.0	6.7	9.8	5.6	4.8	5.6	6.3	6.5

8   Conclusion

This paper presented three novel control abstractions for COMET, which significantly enhance the compositionality, modularity, and reuse of COMET. These abstractions may significantly improve conciseness, extensibility, and clarity of the local search implementations. They all rely on first-class closures as the enabling technology and can be implemented efficiently.

One of the most appealing features of COMET is its small number of fundamental concepts, as well as their generality. First-class closures simplify many applications beyond local search (e.g., [12]) and are ubiquitous in functional programming. Events are related to many constructs in the logic and functional communities (e.g., delay mechanisms and reactive functional programming). Invariants (one-way constraints) and constraints are widely recognized as natural vehicles for many applications. These concepts provide significant support for local search, and may significantly reduce the distance between high-level descriptions of the algorithms and their actual implementations. Yet they are nonintrusive and impose minimal "constraints" on programmers, who keeps control of their algorithms and their code organization. An interesting topic for future research is to study how to unify the COMET architecture with the tree-search models proposed in [23, 11], since both approaches have orthogonal strengths.

Acknowledgments

This work was partially supported by NSF ITR Awards DMI-0121495 and ACI-0121497.

References

1. E. Balas and A. Vazacopoulos. Guided local search with shifting bottleneck for job-shop scheduling. Management Science, 44(2), 1998.
2. R. Bent and P. Van Hentenryck. A Two-Stage Hybrid Local Search for the Vehicle Routing Problem with Time Windows. Transportation Science, 2001. (To Appear).
3. C. Codognet and D. Diaz. Yet Another Local Search Method for Constraint Solving. In AAAI Fall Symposium on Using Uncertainty within Computation, Cape Cod, MA., 2001.
4. B. De Backer et al. Solving Vehicle Routing Problems Using Constraint Programming and Metaheuristics. Journal of Heuristics, 6:501–523, 2000.
5. M. Dell'Amico and M. Trubian. Applying Tabu Search to the Job-Shop Scheduling Problem. Annals of Operations Research, 41:231–252, 1993.
6. L. Di Gaspero and A. Schaerf. Writing Local Search Algorithms Using EasyLocal++. in Optimization Software Class Libraries, Kluwer, 2002.
7. P. Galinier and J.-K. Hao. A General Approach for Constraint Solving by Local Search. In CP-AI-OR'00, Paderborn, Germany, March 2000.
8. B. Kernighan and S. Lin. An efficient heuristic procedure for partitioning graphs. Bell System Technical Journal, 49:291–307, 1970.
9. G. Kiczales, J. Lamping, A. Menhdhekar, C. Maeda, C. Lopes, J.-M. Loingtier, and J. Irwin. Aspect-oriented programming. In ECOOP '97.
10. Kindervater, G. and Savelsbergh, M.W. Vehicle routing: Handling edge exchanges. In Local Search in Combinatorial Optimization, Wiley, 1997.
11. F. Laburthe and Y. Caseau. SALSA: A Language for Search Algorithms. In CP'98.
12. D. Manolescu. Workflow Enactment with Continuation and Future Objects. In OOPLSA'02, Seattle, WA, 2002.
13. L. Michel and P. Van Hentenryck. A Constraint-Based Architecture for Local Search. In OOPLSA'02, Seattle, WA, 2002.
14. L. Michel and P. Van Hentenryck. Localizer. Constraints, 5:41–82, 2000.
15. L. Michel and P. Van Hentenryck. A Decomposition-Based Implementation of Search Strategies. ACM Transactions on Computational Logic, 2002. (To Appear).
16. S. Minton, M. Johnston, and A. Philips. Solving Large-Scale Constraint Satisfaction and Scheduling Problems using a Heuristic Repair Method. In AAAI-90.
17. A. Nareyek. Constraint-Based Agents. Springer Verlag, 1998.
18. E. Nowicki and C. Smutnicki. A fast taboo search algorithm for the job shop problem. Management Science, 42(6):797–813, 1996
19. L. Perron. Search Procedures and Parallelism in Constraint Programming. In CP'99, Alexandra, VA, 1999.

20. B. Roy and B. Sussmann. Les problèmes d'ordonnancement avec contraintes disjonctives. Note DS No. 9 bis, SEMA, Paris, France, 1964.
21. K. Schmidt. Using Tabu-search to Solve the Job-Shop Scheduling Problem with Sequence Dependent Setup Times. ScM Thesis, Brown University, 2001.
22. C. Schulte. Comparing trailing and copying for constraint programming. In *ICLP'99*.
23. P. Shaw, B. De Backer, and V. Furnon. Improved local search for CP toolkits. *Annals of Operations Research*, 115:31–50, 2002.
24. C. Turner, A. Fuggetta, L. Lavazza, and A. Wolf. A conceptual basis for feature engineering. *Journal of Systems and Software*, 49(1):3–15, 1999.
25. S. Voss and D. Woodruff. *Optimization Software Class Libraries*. Kluwer, 2002.
26. J. Walser. *Integer Optimization by Local Search*. Springer Verlag, 1998.

Improved Algorithms for Counting Solutions in Constraint Satisfaction Problems

Ola Angelsmark[*] and Peter Jonsson[**]

Department of Computer and Information Science
Linköpings Universitet
S-581 83 Linköping, Sweden
{olaan,petej}@ida.liu.se

Abstract. Counting the number of solutions to CSP instances has vast applications in several areas ranging from statistical physics to artificial intelligence. We provide a new algorithm for counting the number of solutions to binary CSP s which has a time complexity ranging from $\mathcal{O}\left((d/4 \cdot \alpha^4)^n\right)$ to $\mathcal{O}\left((\alpha + \alpha^5 + \lfloor d/4 - 1 \rfloor \cdot \alpha^4)^n\right)$ (where $\alpha \approx 1.2561$) depending on the domain size $d \geq 3$. This is substantially faster than previous algorithms, especially for small d. We also provide an algorithm for counting k-colourings in graphs and its running time ranges from $\mathcal{O}\left(\lfloor \log_2 k \rfloor^n\right)$ to $\mathcal{O}\left(\lfloor \log_2 k + 1 \rfloor^n\right)$ depending on $k \geq 4$. Previously, only an $\mathcal{O}\left(1.8171^n\right)$ time algorithm for counting 3-colourings were known, and we improve this upper bound to $\mathcal{O}\left(1.7879^n\right)$.

1 Introduction

Constraint satisfaction problems (CSPs), first described by Montanari [16], allows for natural descriptions of problems in a wide array of fields, cf. Kumar [14]. The most thoroughly studied problem for CSPs is that of *decidability*, i.e., 'does a given problem have a solution?' but there are a number of alternative questions one can ask, including 'Does variable x have the same value in every solution?' (the *frozen variable problem*) and 'How many solutions are there?' (the *counting problem.*) In this paper we will focus on the latter, usually denoted #CSP.

The #CSP problem has many important applications. A broad range of classical combinatorial problems such as GRAPH RELIABILITY [20] and PERMANENT [19] can be viewed as instances of the #CSP problem. This also holds for many AI problems such as approximate reasoning [17], diagnosis [18] and belief revision [8]. Solving a CSP instance is equivalent to finding a homomorphism between graphs [11], for instance, finding a k-colouring of a graph G is equivalent to finding a homomorphism from G to a complete graph with k vertices. Determining the number of graph homomorphisms from one graph to another has important applications in statistical physics [10] – e.g. computations in the *Potts*

---

[*] Partially supported by CUGS – National Graduate School in Computer Science, Sweden – and the Swedish Research Council (VR) under grant 621-2002-4126.
[**] Partially supported by VR under grant 221-2000-361.

model and the problem of counting q-particle *Widom-Rowlinson* configurations in graphs.

Until quite recently, not much attention has been given to the computational complexity of #CSP. The counting problem belongs to a class known as #P (introduced by Valiant [19, 20]) defined as the class of counting problems computable in nondeterministic polynomial time. Computing the number of solutions to a constraint satisfaction problem is, even if we restrict ourselves to binary CSPs, complete for this class of problems [17]. Lately, however, a number of papers have addressed complexity issues in greater detail [5, 6, 15], and a number of exact algorithms have been developed [1, 3, 7, 9]. Bulatov and Dalmau [5] have formulated a plausible conjecture concerning the complexity of the counting problem: the problem can be solved in polynomial time if and only if the relations under consideration are closed under a *Mal'tsev* operation (and the problem is #P-complete otherwise). Since the set of relations closed under Mal'tsev operations is fairly limited[1], the truth of this conjecture would imply that we are forced to use exponential-time algorithms for solving most naturally arising counting problems.

In this paper we will focus on *exact, deterministic* algorithms for the following two problems: the counting problem for binary CSPs, denoted $\#(d, 2)\text{-CSP}$[2], and the counting problem for k-colourability of graphs, denoted $\#k\text{COL}$. Algorithms for $\#(d, 2)\text{-CSP}$ and $\#3\text{COL}$ have been presented elsewhere [1]. The previously presented algorithm for $\#3\text{COL}$ runs in $\mathcal{O}(1.8171^n)$ time and the running time for the $\#(d, 2)\text{-CSP}$ algorithm is (we omit polynomial factors here and throughout the paper):

- $\mathcal{O}(\alpha^n \cdot (d/2)^n)$, if d is even, and
- $\mathcal{O}(\alpha^n \cdot \lceil (d^2 + d)/4 \rceil^{n/2})$, if d is odd

where $\mathcal{O}(\alpha^n)$ is the time complexity for solving $\#(2, 2)\text{-CSP}$. Running times for a selection of domain sizes can be found in Table 1. Since the running time of this algorithm depends on the running time for solving the $\#(2, 2)\text{-CSP}$ problem, we provide the times both for the $\mathcal{O}(1.3247^n)$ $\#(2, 2)\text{-CSP}$ algorithm originally used [7] and for the improved $\mathcal{O}(1.2561^n)$ algorithm [21].

The old $\#(d, 2)\text{-CSP}$ algorithm has the following general outline:

1. Create $\#(d, 2)\text{-CSP}$ instances 'corresponding' to the original CSP instance.
2. Count the number of solutions to each of these instances.
3. Return the total number of solutions found.

The new algorithm is different in several respects. It creates *weighted* $\#(d, 2)$-CSP instances instead of ordinary $\#(d, 2)\text{-CSP}$ instances – this enables us to use a microstructure-like [12] construction that reduces the number of instances we need to consider. When applied to odd domains, the old algorithm considers pairs

---

[1] For instance, if we only consider domains of size 2, there is a single polynomial class known as the *affine* subclass.

[2] The necessary definitions for the CSP notions used in this paper are found in Section 2.

Table 1. Time complexities for solving $\#(d,2)$-CsP and $\#d$COL.

d	$\#(d,2)$-CsP			$\#d$COL
	Original algorithm	Original algorithm w/improvements	New algorithm	
3	2.2944^n	2.1757^n	1.9819^n	1.7879^n
4	2.6494^n	2.5122^n	2.4895^n	2^n
5	3.7468^n	3.5528^n	3.1270^n	2.7879^n
6	3.9741^n	3.7683^n	3.7456^n	2.7879^n
7	4.9566^n	4.6999^n	4.3831^n	3^n
8	5.2988^n	5.0244^n	4.9789^n	3^n
10	6.6235^n	6.2805^n	6.2350^n	3.7879^n
15	10.2611^n	9.7298^n	9.3619^n	4^n
20	13.2470^n	12.5610^n	12.4471^n	4.7879^n
25	16.9126^n	16.0369^n	15.5740^n	5^n

of variables when constructing the $\#(d,2)$-CsP instances; the technique for doing so is straightforward in principle but inelegant in practice. The new algorithm 'partitions' the domains of the variables into subdomains of sizes between 2 and 5 elements. This leads to a faster and more elegant algorithm but its analysis becomes a bit more complicated. The running time of the algorithm is:

- $\mathcal{O}\left((d/4 \cdot \alpha^4)^n\right) \subseteq \mathcal{O}\left((0.6224d)^n\right)$ if $d \equiv 0 \pmod 4$
- $\mathcal{O}\left((\alpha^5 + \lfloor d/4 - 1\rfloor \cdot \alpha^4)^n\right) \subseteq \mathcal{O}\left((0.6254d)^n\right)$ if $d \equiv 1 \pmod 4$
- $\mathcal{O}\left((\alpha + \lfloor d/4\rfloor \cdot \alpha^4)^n\right) \subseteq \mathcal{O}\left((0.6243d)^n\right)$ if $d \equiv 2 \pmod 4$
- $\mathcal{O}\left((\alpha + \alpha^5 + \lfloor d/4 - 1\rfloor \cdot \alpha^4)^n\right) \subseteq \mathcal{O}\left((0.6262d)^n\right)$ if $d \equiv 3 \pmod 4$

For large domains, the term $d/4 \cdot \alpha^4$ dominates the time complexity, since the number of 4-partitions increase with d. Consequently, the bounds in the list will all approach $\mathcal{O}\left((d/4 \cdot \alpha^4)^n\right) \approx \mathcal{O}\left((0.6224d)^n\right)$ as d grows. The old algorithm approaches $\mathcal{O}\left((0.6280d)^n\right)$ running time and this difference may appear negligible. However, the difference is significant for many domain sizes; for instance, if $d = 5$, the old algorithm runs in $\mathcal{O}\left(3.5528^n\right) = \mathcal{O}\left((0.7106d)^n\right)$ time while the new algorithm runs in $\mathcal{O}\left(3.1271^n\right) = \mathcal{O}\left((0.6255d)^n\right)$ time. Given the modularity of the algorithm, if a faster method for solving the weighted $\#(2,2)$-CsP problem is found, it is easy to 'plug it into' our algorithm, thus improving the time complexity with no extra work.

The second part of this paper contains an algorithm for $\#k$COL, which runs in $\mathcal{O}\left((c_k)^n\right)$ time where

$$c_k = \begin{cases} \lfloor \log_2 k\rfloor & \text{if } k = 2^i \\ \lfloor \log_2 k\rfloor + (\beta - 1) & \text{if } 2^i < k \leq 2^i + 2^{i-1} \\ \lfloor \log_2 k\rfloor + 1 & \text{if } 2^i + 2^{i-1} < k < 2^{i+1} \end{cases}$$

and $\beta \approx 1.7879$. Previously, only an $\mathcal{O}\left(1.8171^n\right)$ time for $\#3$COL was known. The algorithm is once again based on a partitioning technique together with methods for efficiently combining #kCOL algorithms and an $\mathcal{O}(1.7879^n)$ time algorithm for #3COL.

The paper has the following organisation: Section 2 contains the basic definitions needed. Section 3 contains the algorithm for counting solutions to binary CSPs, while Section 4 contains the algorithm for the #kCOL problem. The new algorithm for #3COL is presented in Section 5.

2   Preliminaries

A *(d, l)-constraint satisfaction problem ((d,l)-*CSP*)* is a triple (V, D, C) with V a finite set of variables, D a finite domain of values, with $|D| = d$, and C a set of constraints $\{c_1, c_2, \ldots, c_q\}$. Each constraint $c_i \in C$ is a structure $R(x_{i_1}, \ldots, x_{i_j})$ where $j \leq l$, $x_{i_1}, \ldots, x_{i_j} \in V$ and $R \subseteq D^j$. A *solution* to a CSP instance is a function $f : V \to D$, such that for each constraint $R(x_{i_1}, \ldots, x_{i_j}) \in C$, $(f(x_{i_1}), \ldots, f(x_{i_j})) \in R$. Given a variable v and a set $X \subseteq D$, we let $(v; X)$ denote the unary constraint $v \in X$. Given a (d, l)-CSP instance, the basic computational problem is to decide whether an instance has a solution or not. The corresponding counting problem #(d, l)-CSP is to determine how many solutions the instance has.

We will view $(2, 2)$-CSP instances as instances of 2-SAT for increased readability. A 2-SAT formula is a sentence consisting of the conjunction of a number of clauses, where each clause is of one of the forms $(p \lor q)$, $(\neg p \lor q)$, $(\neg p \lor \neg q)$, (p), $(\neg p)$. The 2-SAT *problem* is to decide whether a given 2-SAT formula is satisfiable or not, and this can be done in linear time [2], whereas the #P-complete #2-SAT *problem* is to decide how many solutions a given formula has. We will use an extended version of the #2-SAT problem.

Definition 1. *(#2-*SAT *with weights)*
*A instance is given as a 2-*SAT *formula F over propositions $X = \{x_1, x_2, \ldots, x_n\}$, and a function $f : X \to \mathbb{N}$ assigning to each proposition an integer weight. Let M be the set of models of F and define $\Pi : M \to \mathbb{N}$ as $\Pi(m) = \sum \{f(x) \mid x$ true in $m\}$. Let $K = \max_{m \in M} \Pi(m)$. A solution to the instance is the number of models that have the total weight K.*

The currently best known algorithm for solving this problem runs in $\mathcal{O}(\alpha^n)$ time [21] where $\alpha \approx 1.2561$.

A *partitioning* $P = \{P_1, \ldots, P_k\}$ of a domain D is a division of D into disjoint subsets s.t. $\bigcup P = D$, and a k-*partition* is an element of P with k elements. Given a partitioning P, let $\sigma(P, i)$ denote the number of i-partitions in P.

The multinomial coefficient

$$\binom{n}{n_1 \cdots n_k} = \frac{n!}{n_1! \cdot \ldots \cdot n_k!}$$

denotes the number of ways of partitioning a set of size n into k sets, each of size n_i (with $n = \sum_{i=1}^{k} n_i$). We will frequently use the *multinomial theorem:* for $x_1, \ldots, x_k \in \mathbb{R}$,

$$\sum_{n_1+\ldots+n_k=n} \binom{n}{n_1 \cdots n_k} \prod_{i=1}^{k} x_i^{n_k} = \left(\sum_{i=1}^{k} x_i\right)^n$$

3 Algorithm for $\#(d,2)$-CSP

The algorithm for $\#(d,2)$-CSP will be presented in three steps: (1) Theorem 1 demonstrates how partitions can be used for solving $\#(d,2)$-CSP; (2) we show how an algorithm for weighted $\#2$-SAT can be used by Theorem 1; and (3) we show how to choose partitionings optimally in Theorem 2.

Before we prove Theorem 1, we need a straightforward lemma:

Lemma 1. *Assume there exists an $\mathcal{O}\left(c^n\right)$ time algorithm for $\#(k,l)$-CSP. Let $\mathcal{I}_k$ denote the set of $\#(d,l)$-CSP instances satisfying the following restriction: for every $(V,D,C) \in \mathcal{I}_k$ and every $v \in V$, there exists a constraint $(v;S)$ in C such that $|S| \leq k$. Then, the $\#$CSP problem restricted to instances in $\mathcal{I}_k$ can be solved in $\mathcal{O}\left(c^n\right)$ time.*

Proof. For each variable in (V,D,C), we know that there are at most k out of d values that it can be assigned. Thus, we can modify the constraints so that every variable picks its values from the set $\{1,\ldots,k\}$. This transformation can obviously be carried out in polynomial time and the resulting instance is an instance of $\#(k,l)$-CSP which can be solved in $\mathcal{O}\left(c^n\right)$ time.

Theorem 1. *Let A be an algorithm for $\#(d,2)$-CSP running in $\mathcal{O}\left(\prod_{i=1}^{d} \alpha_i^{n_i}\right)$ time ($\alpha_i \geq 1$) when applied to an instance containing n_i i-valued variables for $1 \leq i \leq d$. Choose p and a partitioning $P = \{P_1,\ldots,P_k\}$ of $\{1,\ldots,p\}$ such that $|P_i| \leq d$ for every i. Then, there exists an algorithm for $\#(p,2)$-CSP running in $\mathcal{O}\left(\left(\sum_{i=1}^{d} \sigma(P,i)\alpha_i\right)^n\right)$ time.*

Proof. We claim that the algorithm presented in Figure 1 correctly solves the $\#(p,2)$-CSP problem. Let $I = (V,D,C)$ be an arbitrary instance of $\#(p,2)$-CSP and let M be an arbitrary model of I. The members of P are pairwise disjoint so there exists exactly one function from V to P such that $M(v) \in f(v)$ for all $v \in V$. Now, Lemma 1 implies that this model will cause an increase of variable c by one. Consequently, the algorithm will return the total number of models which proves its correctness.

The running time T of the algorithm is bounded by

$$\mathcal{O}\left(\sum_{f \in F} \prod_{v \in V} \alpha_{|f(v)|}\right)$$

where F is the set of total functions from V to P, i.e. the algorithm considers all possible combinations of elements of P and members of V. The performance

```
1   c := 0
2   for every total function f : V → P do
3       I := (V, D, C ∪ {(v_i; f(v_i)) | 1 ≤ i ≤ |V|})
4       compute the number of solutions to I using Lemma 1 and add to c
5   end for
6   return c
```

Fig. 1. Algorithm for $\#(p, 2)$-CSP.

of algorithm A depends only on the domain sizes associated with the variables and this gives us

$$T \in \mathcal{O}\left(\sum_{k_1 + \ldots + k_{|P|} = n} \binom{n}{k_1 \cdots k_{|P|}} \prod_{i=1}^{|P|} \alpha_{|P_i|}^{k_i} \right)$$

where k_i denotes the number of variables whose domain is P_i. By applying the multinomial theorem and using the fact that there are $\sigma(P, i)$ sets of size i in P, we arrive at

$$T \in \mathcal{O}\left(\left(\sum_{i=1}^{|P|} \alpha_{|P_i|} \right)^n \right) = \mathcal{O}\left(\left(\sum_{i=1}^{d} \sigma(P, i)\alpha_i \right)^n \right).$$

$\square$

We will now use Theorem 1 and the algorithm for weighted $\#2$-SAT in order to construct an algorithm for $\#(d, 2)$-CSP.

Given a $\#(d, 2)$-CSP instance $\Theta = (V, D, C)$ containing k_1 1-valued, k_2 2-valued, k_3 3-valued, etc., variables, we can transform it into a weighted $\#2$-SAT instance as follows:

- If $x \in V$ takes its value from a singleton set $\{1\}$, we can remove x in polynomial time by assigning 1 to x and propagate the variable.
- If a variable $x \in V$ takes its value from a two-valued set $\{1, 2\}$, we introduce a proposition x_1 with the interpretation that $x = 1$ if x_1 is true, and $x = 2$ otherwise.
- For a k-valued variable x, we create k propositional variables $x_1, \ldots, x_k$, with the interpretations that $x = i$ if x_i is true, and $x \neq i$ if x_i is false. To ensure that at most one of these can be true in a satisfying assignment, we add clauses

$$\bigwedge_{i \leq j,\ i,j \in \{1,2,\ldots,k\}} (\neg x_i \vee \neg x_j).$$

- Constraints involving only variables with more than 2 possible values can be transformed in a straightforward manner; Given a constraint $xRy \in C$, with x having domain D_x and y having domain D_y, we add the clauses

$$\bigwedge_{a \in D_x, b \in D_y, (a,b) \notin R} (\neg x_a \vee \neg y_b).$$

However, if one of the variables is 2-valued, we need to take into account that its negation also corresponds to an assignment, hence, if $xRy \in C$, $x \in \{1,2\}$ and $y \in D_y$, we add the clauses

$$\bigwedge_{b \in D_y,(0,b) \notin R} (\neg x_0 \vee \neg y_b) \wedge \bigwedge_{b \in D_y,(1,b) \notin R} (x_0 \vee \neg y_b).$$

The case when two variables are 2-valued can be transformed analogously.

Now, we note that there is a slight difference between the two kinds of propositions: A proposition stemming from a 2-valued variable will, regardless of truth-value, give an assignment to the original variable, but this does not hold for the k-valued variables with $k > 2$. To remedy this, we exploit the possibility to give weights to the propositions: we give the weight 0 to each proposition corresponding to a 2-valued variable, and the remaining propositions are assigned the weight 1. A model of the instance will then have the value $\sum_{i \geq 3} k_i$, i.e., the number of k-valued variables, $k > 2$.

After this transformation, we get a 2-SAT formula F with $k_2 + 3k_3 + \ldots$ variables, and applying the algorithm for weighted #2-SAT from [21] will give a running time of $\mathcal{O}\left(1^{k_1} \cdot \alpha^{k_2 + 3k_3 + \cdots}\right) = \mathcal{O}\left(1^{k_1} \cdot \alpha^{k_2} \cdot \alpha^{3k_3} \cdots\right)$, since each 2-valued variable introduces one propositional variable, and each k-valued variable, $k \geq 3$, introduces k propositional variables.

Given a partitioning P of a domain D containing d elements, it follows (by combining the algorithm above and Theorem 1) that we can solve #$(d,2)$-CSP in $\mathcal{O}\left(T(P)^n\right)$ time where

$$T(P) = \sigma(P,1) + \sigma(P,2)\alpha + \sum_{i=3}^{d} \sigma(P,i)\alpha^i.$$

For instance, we can solve #$(d,2)$-CSP in $\mathcal{O}\left(\alpha^{d \cdot n}\right)$ time by using the trivial partitioning $P = \{\{1, \ldots, d\}\}$ but this can be improved by using other partitionings. For example, assume $d = 6$. Using the previous argument, this would give a time complexity of $\mathcal{O}\left(\alpha^{6n}\right) \approx \mathcal{O}\left(3.9278^n\right)$, but if we instead use the partitioning $\{\{1,2\},\{3,4,5,6\}\}$, we arrive at a running time of $\mathcal{O}\left((\alpha + \alpha^4)^n\right) \approx \mathcal{O}\left(3.7455^n\right)$, which is quite an improvement. The obvious question is how to partition the domain to get the optimal running time.

Let $P = \{P_1, \ldots, P_k\}$ be an arbitrary partitioning of a domain D. Since the actual names of the elements in a partition is not important (by Lemma 1), we let the multi-set $[|P_1|, \ldots, |P_k|]$ represent the partitioning P. We will use the following fact repeatedly in the proof: if $T([a_1, \ldots, a_k]) < T([b_1, \ldots, b_m])$, then

$$T([a_1, \ldots, a_k, c_1, \ldots, c_p]) < T([b_1, \ldots, b_m, c_1, \ldots, c_p])$$

for all choices of $c_1, \ldots, c_p$.

Theorem 2. *Let D be a domain of size $d \geq 2$. If $d < 6$, then the partitioning $P = [d]$ is optimal. Otherwise, the following partitionings are optimal:*

- if $d = 4k$, $P = [4, 4, 4, \ldots, 4]$ *(k partitions of size 4)*
- if $d = 4k + 1$, $P = [5, 4, 4, \ldots, 4]$ *(k − 1 of size 4)*
- if $d = 4k + 2$, $P = [2, 4, 4, \ldots, 4]$ *(k of size 4)*
- if $d = 4k + 3$, $P = [2, 5, 4, 4, \ldots, 4]$ *(k − 1 of size 4)*

Proof. Let P be a partition from the list and assume it is suboptimal, i.e., there is a strictly better partition P^* which is optimal. We show that such a P^* does not exist and, consequently, that P is optimal.

Step 1: P^* contains no 1-partitions.
If $d = 2$, then it is obvious that $P^* = [2]$ and P^* contains no 1-partition. We can consequently suppose that $d > 2$. Assume first that $P^* = [1, \ldots, 1]$ (d 1-partitions) and let $P' = [2, 1, \ldots, 1]$ ($d − 1$ 1-partitions). It is easy to see that $T(P') < T(P^*)$ so P^* contains at least one a-partition such that $a > 1$. If a=2, i.e. $P^* = [1, 2, p_1, \ldots, p_k]$, we let $P' = [3, p_1, \ldots, p_k]$ and note that $2.2561 \approx T([1, 2]) > T([3]) \approx 1.9819$ and P^* is not optimal.

Finally, we assume that $P^* = [1, a, p_1, \ldots, p_k]$ for some $a > 2$. We define $P' = [2, a − 1, p_1, \ldots, p_k]$ and show that $T(P') < T(P^*)$ by induction over a. This contradicts the optimality of P^* and proves that P^* does not contain any 1-partitions.

Basis: If $a = 3$, then $2.9819 \approx T([1, 3]) > T([2, 2]) \approx 2.5122$.

Induction: Assume the claim holds for $a = p$. We show that it also holds for $a = p + 1$ by proving that $T([1, p + 1]) > T([2, p])$, i.e. $1 + \alpha^{p+1} > \alpha + \alpha^p$. First observe that $1.3217 \approx \alpha^2 − \alpha + 1 > \alpha \approx 1.2561$. Now, $1 + \alpha^{p+1} = (1 + \alpha^p) \cdot \alpha − (\alpha − 1) > /\text{ind. hyp.}/ > (\alpha + \alpha^{p-1}) \cdot \alpha − \alpha + 1 = \alpha^2 + \alpha^p − \alpha + 1 > /\text{observation}/ > \alpha^p + \alpha$.

Step 2: P is optimal when $1 < d \le 5$.
We note that domains of sizes 2 and 3 should not be partitioned since this implies the introduction of a 1-partition. Furthermore, domains of sizes 4 and 5 should not be partitioned either since $T([4]) < T([2, 2])$ and $T([5]) < T([3, 2])$.

Step 3: P^* contains only a-partitions, $a \in \{2, 4, 5\}$, when $d > 5$.
Assume P^* contains an a-partition and $a > 5$. We begin by inductively proving that $T([a, p_1, \ldots, p_k]) > T([a − 2, 2, p_1, \ldots, p_k])$, i.e. $\alpha^{an} > (\alpha^{a-2} + \alpha^2)^n$. Obviously, this holds when $a = 6$. Assume the assertion holds for every $a < p$. Now, $\alpha^p = \alpha \cdot \alpha^{p-1} > /\text{ind. hyp.}/ > \alpha \cdot (\alpha^{p-3} + \alpha^2) = \alpha^{p-2} + \alpha^3 > \alpha^{p-2} + \alpha^2$. Thus we will always benefit from partitioning a domain if $d > 5$ which implies that the optimal partition P^* will only consist of partitions of sizes 2, 3, 4 and 5.

Assume $P^* = [3, \ldots]$ and note that since $d > 5$, $P^* = [3, a, \ldots]$ where $a \in \{2, 3, 4, 5\}$. It is easy to check that $T([3, 2]) > T([5])$, $T([3, 3]) > T([4, 2])$, $T([3, 4]) > T([5, 2])$ and $T([3, 5]) > T([4, 4])$ so P^* contains no 3-partition.

Step 4: P is optimal when $d > 5$.
We note that P^* cannot contain more than one 2-partition since $T([4]) < T([2, 2])$ and it cannot contain more than one 5-partition since $T([2, 4, 4]) <$

$T([5,5])$. Finally, P^* cannot contain fewer 2 and 5 partitions than P, since otherwise, it would not be a partition of an arbitrary domain. The only alternative is that P^* has the same number of 2- and 5-partitions as P, so $P = P^*$ and P is optimal.   □

Consequently, the resulting algorithm has the following time complexity:

- $\mathcal{O}\left((d/4 \cdot \alpha^4)^n\right) \subseteq \mathcal{O}\left((0.6224d)^n\right)$ if $d \equiv 0 \pmod 4$
- $\mathcal{O}\left((\alpha^5 + \lfloor d/4 - 1 \rfloor \cdot \alpha^4)^n\right) \subseteq \mathcal{O}\left((0.6254d)^n\right)$ if $d \equiv 1 \pmod 4$
- $\mathcal{O}\left((\alpha + \lfloor d/4 \rfloor \cdot \alpha^4)^n\right) \subseteq \mathcal{O}\left((0.6243d)^n\right)$ if $d \equiv 2 \pmod 4$
- $\mathcal{O}\left((\alpha + \alpha^5 + \lfloor d/4 - 1 \rfloor \cdot \alpha^4)^n\right) \subseteq \mathcal{O}\left((0.6262d)^n\right)$ if $d \equiv 3 \pmod 4$

For large domains, the term $d/4 \cdot \alpha^4$ dominates the time complexity, since the number of 4-partitions increase with d. Consequently, the bounds in the list will all approach $\mathcal{O}\left((d/4 \cdot \alpha^4)^n\right) \approx \mathcal{O}\left((0.6222d)^n\right)$ as d grows.

4   Algorithm for #kCOL

We will now present an algorithm for the #$kCOL$ problem. We prefer to present this algorithm using graph-theoretic notation instead of CSP notation since this enables us to use familiar concepts such as induced subgraphs and independent sets. We start with the necessary graph-theoretic preliminaries.

A *graph* G consists of a set $V(G)$ of *vertices*, and a set $E(G)$ of *edges*, where each element of E is an unordered pair of vertices. The *size* of a graph G, denoted $|G|$, is the number of vertices. A *k-colouring* of G is a function $f : V(G) \rightarrow \{1, \ldots, k\}$ such that for all $v, w \in V(G)$, if $C(v) = C(w)$ then $(v, w) \notin E(G)$; that is, no adjacent vertices have the same colour. If G is a graph and $S \subseteq V(G)$, the graph $G|S$ has vertex set S and $E(G|S) = \{(u, v) \in E(G) \mid u, v \in S\}$, is called the *subgraph of G induced by S*. We write $G - S$ to denote the graph $G|(V(G) - S)$.

Theorem 3. *Let $A_1, \ldots, A_m$ be algorithms for $\#k_1COL, \ldots, \#k_mCOL$, respectively, such that algorithm A_i runs in $\mathcal{O}(\alpha_i^n)$ time. Choose p and a partitioning $P = \{P_1, \ldots, P_k\}$ of $\{1, \ldots, p\}$ such that $|P_i| \in \{k_1, \ldots, k_m\}$ for all i. Then, there exists an algorithm for $\#pCOL$ with a time complexity of $\mathcal{O}((((|P| - 1) + \max_{P_i \in P} \alpha_{|P_i|})^n)$.*

Proof. We claim that the algorithm presented in Figure 2 correctly solves the $\#pCOL$ problem. To prove this, arbitrarily choose an instance G of $\#pCOL$, let F be the set of all total functions $V(G) \rightarrow P$ and choose one $f \in F$. We begin by proving that lines 4–8 correctly computes the number of p-colourings satisfying the following condition: variable v can only be coloured by the colours in $f(v)$.

Assume without loss of generality that $P_1 = \{1, \ldots, k\}$ for some $k > 0$. Let $G_1 = G|\{v \in V(G) \mid f(v) = P_1\}$ and $G_{\geq 2} = G|\{v \in V(G) \mid f(v) \neq P_1\}$. We show that $\#pCOL(G) = \#|P_1|COL(G_1) \cdot \#(p - |P_1|)COL(G_2)$. By using this fact inductively, it follows that c' contains the number of solutions relative to f after completion of lines 4-8. To prove this, arbitrarily choose one $|P_1|$-colouring M_1 of G_1 and one $p - |P_1|$-colouring M_2 of G_2. Now, consider the function

$$M(v) = \begin{cases} M_1(v) & \text{if } v \in G_1 \\ M_2(v) + k & \text{otherwise} \end{cases}$$

We prove that M is a p-colouring of G. Arbitrarily choose an edge $(x, y) \in E(G)$. If $x \in G_1$ and $y \notin G_1$, then $M(x) \neq M(y)$ due to the construction of M. Otherwise, x and y are both in G_1 or $G_{\geq 2}$ and the choice of M_1, M_2 guarantees that $M(x) \neq M(y)$. This leads to the following conclusion: any $|P_1|$-colouring of G_1 can be combined with any $p - |P_1|$-colouring of G_2 and $\#pCOL(G) = \#|P_1|COL(G_1) \cdot \#(p - |P_1|)COL(G_2)$.

Finally, it is easy to see that it is correct to add the numbers together as is done in line 9: Let M be an arbitrary p-colouring of G. The fact that P is a partitioning guarantees that there exists exactly one function $f \in F$ such that $M(v) \in f(v)$ for all $v \in V(G)$. Consequently, each model will be counted exactly once (due to the correctness of algorithms $A_1, \ldots, A_m$) and the algorithm is correct.

The running time of the algorithm is bounded by

$$\mathcal{O}\left(\sum_{f \in F} \sum_{P_i \in P} \alpha_{|P_i|}^{|\{v \in V(G); f(v) = P_i\}|} \right) = /\text{reformulation}/$$

$$\mathcal{O}\left(\sum_{n_1 + \ldots + n_{|P|} = n} \binom{n}{n_1 \cdots n_{|P|}} \cdot \left(\sum_{P_i \in P} \alpha_{|P_i|}^{n_i} \right) \right) = /\text{alg. manipulation}/$$

$$\mathcal{O}\left(\sum_{n_1 + \ldots + n_{|P|} = n} \sum_{P_i \in P} \binom{n}{n_1 \cdots n_{|P|}} \cdot \alpha_{|P_i|}^{n_i} \right) = /\text{alg. manipulation}/$$

$$\mathcal{O}\left(\sum_{P_i \in P} \sum_{n_1 + \ldots + n_{|P|} = n} \binom{n}{n_1 \cdots n_{|P|}} \cdot \alpha_{|P_i|}^{n_i} \right) = /\text{multiplication by } 1/$$

$$\mathcal{O}\left(\sum_{P_i \in P} \sum_{n_1 + \ldots + n_{|P|} = n} \binom{n}{n_1 \cdots n_{|P|}} \cdot \alpha_{|P_i|}^{n_i} \cdot \prod_{\substack{j = 1 \\ j \neq i}}^{|P|} 1^{n_j} \right) = /\text{multinomial th.}/$$

$$\mathcal{O}\left(\sum_{P_i \in P} ((|P| - 1) + \alpha_{|P_i|})^n \right) = \mathcal{O}\left((|P| - 1 + \max_{P_i \in P} \alpha_{|P_i|})^n \right)$$

$\square$

```
1   input: undirected graph G
2   c := 0
3   for every total function f : V(G) → P  do
4       c' := 1
5       for Pᵢ ∈ P  do
6           G' := G|{v ∈ V(G) | f(v) = Pᵢ}
7           c' := c' · #|Pᵢ|COL(G')
8       end for
9       c := c + c'
10  end for
11  return c
```

Fig. 2. Algorithm for #pCOL.

We note that #2COL can be solved in polynomial time since the number of 2-colourings of a 2-colourable graph G equals 2^c where c is the number of connected components in G. In the next section, we show that #3COL can be solved in $\mathcal{O}(\beta^n)$ time where $\beta \approx 1.7879$.

Now, from Theorem 3 it follows that as k grows, the number of partitions dominate the time complexity of the algorithm. For example, for $k = 7$, we could use the partition $[3, 2, 2]$ which gives a running time of $\mathcal{O}(3.7879^n)$. If we instead use the partitioning $[3, 4]$ where the #4COL problem is solved using the partition $[2, 2]$, we would get an $\mathcal{O}(((2-1) + (2-1+1))^n) = \mathcal{O}(3^n)$ time algorithm which is significantly faster. Combining the idea of minimising the number of partitions with Theorem 3 and the algorithms for #kCOL, $2 \leq k \leq 3$, yields the following result.

Theorem 4. *There is an algorithm for solving the #kCOL problem in $O((c_k)^n)$ time, where, for some $i \in \mathbb{N}$,*

$$c_k = \begin{cases} \lfloor \log_2 k \rfloor & \text{if } k = 2^i \\ \lfloor \log_2 k \rfloor + (\beta - 1) & \text{if } 2^i < k \leq 2^i + 2^{i-1} \\ \lfloor \log_2 k \rfloor + 1 & \text{if } 2^i + 2^{i-1} < k < 2^{i+1} \end{cases}$$

Proof. We recursively use the partitioning $[\lfloor \frac{k}{2} \rfloor, \lceil \frac{k}{2} \rceil]$ with the algorithms for #2COL and #3COL as base cases. By Theorem 3, the resulting algorithm runs in $\mathcal{O}(c_k^n)$ time where c_k is defined by the recursion $c_2 = 1, c_3 = \beta$ and $c_k = 1 + c_{\lceil k/2 \rceil}$ Using $\beta \approx 1.7879$ from Section 5 and solving this gives the result. It remains to show that this recurrence has the solution stated in the theorem:

First, let $k = 2^i$. By iterating the recursion, we get $c_k = 1 + c_{k/2} = 2 + c_{k/4} = \ldots = (i-1) + c_{k/2^{i-1}} = (i-1) + c_2 = i = \log_2 k$.

Now let $2^i < k \leq 2^i + 2^{i-1}$. For $i = 2$, this amounts to $4 < k \leq 6$, and $\lceil k/2 \rceil = 3$, and, since $c_3 = \beta$ by definition, $c_k = \beta + 1 = \lfloor \log_2 k \rfloor + \beta - 1$. For $i > 2$, $c_{\lceil k/2 \rceil} = \lfloor \log_2 k/2 \rfloor + \beta - 1 = \lfloor \log_2 k \rfloor + \beta - 2$ so $c_k = 1 + c_{\lceil k/2 \rceil} = 1 + \lfloor \log_2 k \rfloor + \beta - 2 = \lfloor \log_2 k \rfloor + \beta - 1$.

Finally, we have $2^i + 2^{i-1} < k < 2^{i+1}$. For $i = 2$, $k = 7$, and $\lceil 7/2 \rceil = 4$, which gives $c_7 = c_4 + 1 = 2 + 1 = \lfloor \log_2 7 \rfloor + 1$. If $2^i + 2^{i-1} < k < 2^{i+1}$,

$2^{i-1} + 2^{i-2} < k/2 \leq 2^i$, and $c_{\lceil k/2 \rceil} = \lfloor \log_2 k/2 \rfloor + 1 = \lfloor \log_2 k \rfloor$ if $\lceil k/2 \rceil < 2^i$. If $\lceil k/2 \rceil = 2^i$, then, as was shown earlier, $c_{\lceil k/2 \rceil} = \lfloor \log_2 k \rfloor$. Consequently, $c_k = 1 + c_{\lceil k/2 \rceil} = 1 + \lfloor \log_2 k \rfloor$. □

5   Algorithm for #3COL

We now present an $\mathcal{O}\,(1.7879^n)$ time algorithm for counting the number of 3-colourings of a graph. We denote the three possible colours R, G and B. An *independent set S* of G is a subset of $V(G)$, such that for every pair $v, w \in S \rightarrow (v, w) \notin E(G)$. The *neighbourhood* of a vertex v is the set of all adjacent vertices, $\{w \mid (v, w) \in E(G)\}$, denoted $Nbd(v)$.

Given a graph G, we associate a variable with each vertex for keeping its colour and we let $G[x := X]$ denote the graph G with the colour of vertex x changed to X.

We define an $R\{G/B\}$ *assignment* of the graph G as a total function $f : V(G) \rightarrow \{R, GB\}$. We say that an $R\{G/B\}$ assignment f is *refineable* to a 3-colouring of G iff for each of the vertices v having colour GB, we can assign $v := G$ or $v := B$ in such a manner that we obtain a 3-colouring of G. We note that having an $R\{G/B\}$ assignment for G which is refineable to a 3-colouring of G, is equivalent to the assignment having the following properties:

P1. the vertices with colour R form an independent set;

P2. the induced subgraph of vertices with colour GB is 2-colourable.

Obviously, these conditions can be checked in polynomial time. We can also count the number of possible refinements of an $R\{G/B\}$ assignment: consider the graph $G' = G|\{v \in V(G) \mid f(v) = GB\}$ and note that the number of refinements equals 2^c where c is the number of connected components in G'. Given an $R\{G/B\}$ assignment f, let $Count_2(G, f)$ denote this number (which is easily computable in polynomial time).

We are now ready to present the algorithm. Let $\phi = (1 + \sqrt{5})/2$ and let $C \approx 0.4711$ be the unique real positive root of the equation $\phi^{1-C} \cdot 2^C = 3^{1-C}$. Begin by identifying an independent set I in G of maximum size using, for instance, Beigel's algorithm [4]. If $|I| \leq C \cdot |G|$, then apply the algorithm in Figure 3. Otherwise, apply the algorithm in Figure 4.

To see that algorithm #3C-1 is correct, we note that the algorithm considers all $R\{G/B\}$-assignments that can be refined to a 3-colouring. In line 3, an uncoloured vertex x with an uncoloured neighbour y is chosen. In the first recursive branch, x is assigned the colour R which implies that y must be coloured GB. In the other branch, x is coloured GB and this choice does not restrict the possible colourings of y. In line 4, the algorithm exhaustively considers all $R\{G/B\}$-assignments of the uncoloured vertices.

The correctness of #3C-2 can proved as follows: For each 3-colouring f of $G - I$, we claim that

```
1   algorithm #3C-1(G)
2   if all v ∈ V(G) are R{G/B}-coloured then
3       return Count₂(G)
4   elsif there exists an uncoloured vertex x with an uncoloured neighbour y then
5       return #3C-1(G[x := R, y := GB])+#3C-1(G[x := GB])
6   else cycle through all R/GB assignments of the uncoloured vertices, apply
            Count₂ on each graph and return the total number of 3-colourings.
7   end if
```

Fig. 3. Algorithm #3C-1.

```
1   algorithm #3C-2(G)
2   c := 0
3   for every 3-colouring f of G − I do
4       c := c + ∏ᵥ∈ᵢ(3 − |{f(w) | w ∈ Nbd(v)}|)
5   end for
6   return c
```

Fig. 4. Algorithm #3C-2.

$$\prod_{v \in I}(3 - |\{f(w) \mid w \in Nbd(v)\}|)$$

is the number of ways f can be extended to a 3-colouring of G. Assume for instance that $v \in I$ has three neighbours x, y, z that are coloured with R, G and B, respectively. Then, $3 - |\{f(w) \mid w \in Nbd(v)\}|$ equals 0 which is correct since f cannot be extended in this case. It is easy to realise that the expression gives the right number of possible colours in all other cases, too. Since I is an independent set, we can simply multiply the numbers of allowed colours in order to count the number of possible extensions of f.

Finally, we consider the time complexity of our algorithm for #3COL. Assume n is the number of vertices in the input graph G. Beigel's [4] algorithm for finding independent sets of maximum size runs in $\mathcal{O}(1.2226^n)$ time. We show below that the worst-case running times of algorithms #3C-1 and #3C-2 are in $\mathcal{O}(1.7879^n)$ which clearly dominates Beigel's algorithm.

Algorithm #3C-1: In the analysis of this algorithm we will encounter recurrences of the form $T(n) \leq \sum_{i=1}^{k} T(n - r_i) + \text{poly}(n)$. They satisfy $T(n) \in \mathcal{O}(\tau(r_1, \ldots, r_k)^n)$ where $\tau(r_1, \ldots, r_k)$ is the largest, real-valued root of the equation $1 - \sum_{i=1}^{k} x^{-r_i} = 0$, see Kullman [13]. This bound does not depend on the polynomial factor poly(n) or the boundary conditions $T(1) = b_1, \ldots, T(k) = b_k$.

If line 4 of the algorithm is not reached, it is straightforward to calculate its running time: lines 2 and 3 satisfy the recursive equation $T(n) \leq T(n - 1) + T(n - 2) + \text{poly}(n)$ and $T(n) \in \mathcal{O}(\phi^n)$ where $\phi = (\sqrt{5} + 1)/2$ is the largest, real-valued root of the equation $1 - x - x^2 = 0$.

We continue by studying line 4 in the algorithm. If this case is reached, the uncoloured vertices form an independent set I' in G. Consequently, $T(n) \in$

$\mathcal{O}\left((2^p \cdot \phi^{(1-p)})^n\right)$ where $p = |I'|/n$. Since I is a maximum independent set in G, it follows that $|I'| \le |I| \le C \cdot n$. Consequently, the worst case of the algorithm appears when $g(p) = 2^p \cdot \phi^{(1-p)}$ is maximised under the constraint $p \le C$. Since $g(p)$ is strictly increasing on $[0, C]$, $g(p)$ is maximised when $p = C$. In this case, the algorithm runs in $\mathcal{O}\left((2^C \cdot \phi^{(1-C)})^n\right) \approx \mathcal{O}(1.7879^n)$ time.

Algorithm #3C-2: We know that $|I| \ge C \cdot n$. Let p satisfy $|I| = p \cdot n$. The number of assignments considered is $3^{n-|I|} = (3^{1-p})^n$. Since the function $g(p) = 3^{(1-p)}$ is strictly decreasing when $p > C$, the largest number of assignments we need to consider appears when p is close to C. In this case, the algorithm runs in $\mathcal{O}\left((3^{1-C})^n\right) \approx \mathcal{O}(1.7879^n)$ time.

Acknowledgments

The authors would like to thank Johan Thapper for providing valuable comments on this paper. Ola Angelsmark is supported in part by CUGS – the National Graduate School in Computer Science, Sweden – and in part by the *Swedish Research Council* (VR) under grant 621-2002-4126. Peter Jonsson is partially supported by VR under grant 221-2000-361.

References

1. O. Angelsmark, P. Jonsson, S. Linusson, and J. Thapper. Determining the number of solutions to a binary CSP instance. In *Proceedings of the 8th International Conference on Principles and Practice of Constraint Programming (CP-2002)*, Sept. 2002.

2. B. Aspvall, M. F. Plass, and R. E. Tarjan. A linear time algorithm for testing the truth of certain quantified Boolean formulas. *Information Processing Letters*, 8(3):121–123, Mar. 1979.

3. R. J. Bayardo Jr. and J. D. Pehoushek. Counting models using connected components. In *Proceedings of the 17th National Conference on Artificial Intelligence and 12th Conference on Innovative Applications of Artificial Intelligence AAAI/IAAI*, pages 157–162, 2000.

4. R. Beigel. Finding maximum independent sets in sparse and general graphs. In *Proceedings of the Tenth Annual ACM-SIAM Symposium on Discrete Algorithms (SODA-1999)*, pages 856–857, 1999.

5. A. Bulatov and V. Dalmau. Towards a dichotomy theorem for the counting constraint satisfaction problem. Technical report, Computing Laboratory, Oxford University, 2003. Available from
web.comlab.ox.ac.uk/oucl/work/andrei.bulatov/counting.ps.

6. N. Creignou and M. Hermann. Complexity of generalized satisfiability counting problems. *Information and Computation*, 125:1–12, 1996.

7. V. Dahllöf, P. Jonsson, and M. Wahlström. Counting satisfying assignments in 2-SAT and 3-SAT. In *Proceedings of the 8th Annual International Computing and Combinatorics Conference (COCOON-2002), Singapore*, pages 535–543, Aug. 2002.

8. A. Darwiche. On the tractable counting of theory models and its applications to truth maintenance and belief revision. *Journal of Applied Non-Classical Logic*, 11(1–2):11–34, 2001.

9. O. Dubois. Counting the number of solutions for instances of satisfiability. *Theoretical Computer Science*, 81(1):49–64, 1991.

10. M. Dyer and C. Greenhill. The complexity of counting graph homomorphisms. *Random Structures and Algorithms*, 17:260–289, 2000.

11. P. G. Jeavons, D. A. Cohen, and J. K. Pearson. Constraints and universal algebra. *Annals of Mathematics and Artificial Intelligence*, 24:51–67, 1998.

12. P. Jégou. Decomposition of domains based on the micro-structure of finite constraint-satisfaction problems. In *Proceedings of the 11th (US) National Conference on Artificial Intelligence (AAAI-93)*, pages 731–736, Washington DC, USA, July 1993. American Association for Artificial Intelligence.

13. O. Kullman. New methods for 3-SAT decision and worst-case analysis. *Theoretical Computer Science*, 223:1–72, 1999.

14. V. Kumar. Algorithms for constraint-satisfaction problems: A survey. *AI Magazine*, 13(1):32–44, Spring 1992.

15. M. L. Littman, T. Pitassi, and R. Impagliazzo. On the complexity of counting satisfying assignments. Unpublished manuscript, 2001.

16. U. Montanari. Networks of constraints: Fundamental properties and applications to picture processing. *Information Sciences*, 7:95–132, 1974.

17. D. Roth. On the hardness of approximate reasoning. *Artificial Intelligence*, 82:273–302, 1996.

18. T. K. Satish Kumar. A model counting characterization of diagnoses. In *Proceedings of the Thirteenth International Workshop on Principles of Diagnosis*, pages 70–76, 2002.

19. L. G. Valiant. The complexity of computing the permanent. *Theoretical Computer Science*, 8(2):189–201, 1979.

20. L. G. Valiant. The complexity of enumeration and reliability problems. *SIAM Journal on Computing*, 8(3):410–421, 1979.

21. M. Wahlström. An algorithm for #2SAT. Technical report, Department of Computer Science, Linköping, Sweden, 2003. In preparation. Preliminary version available from http://www.ida.liu.se/~magwa/research/num2sat.ps.

Boosting Chaff's Performance
by Incorporating CSP Heuristics*

Carlos Ansótegui, Jose Larrubia, and Felip Manyà

Computer Science Department
Universitat de Lleida
Jaume II, 69, E-25001 Lleida, Spain
{carlos,jose,felip}@eup.udl.es

Abstract. Identifying CSP variables in SAT encodings of combinatorial problems allows one to incorporate CSP-like variable selection heuristics into SAT solvers. We show that such heuristics turn out to be more powerful than the best performing state-of-the-art variable selection heuristics for SAT. In particular, we define five novel CSP-like variable selection heuristics for Chaff —one of the most modern, powerful and robust SAT solvers— and provide experimental evidence that Chaff augmented with those heuristics outperforms the original Chaff solver one order of magnitude on difficult SAT-encoded problems like random binary CSPs, pigeon hole, and graph coloring.

1 Introduction

The Artificial Intelligence community has widely investigated the use of Boolean CNF formulas as a constraint programming language to solve NP-complete problems. The approach consists of translating a given problem into Boolean satisfiability (SAT), solving it with a fast SAT solver and mapping the solution back into the original problem. Examples of domains where propositional encodings have been shown effective include hardware verification [24, 25, 32], quasigroup completion [19], planning [20] and scheduling [10]. This led in turn to develop highly optimized complete satisfiability solvers (based on the Davis-Logemann-Loveland algorithm [13, 14]) that incorporate efficient branching heuristics (e.g. Satz [21, 22]), and no-good recording and non-chronological backtracking (e.g. GRASP [30], Relsat [4] and Chaff [25]), as well as incomplete local search solvers like GSAT and WalkSAT [27–29].

A decisive factor that gives rise to large performance improvements in CSP solvers like FC [17] and MAC [11, 26] is that they incorporate powerful variable selection heuristics that take advantage of the domain size of the CSP variables in a given state of the search process. To our best knowledge, and despite its relevance in CSP solver, there is no SAT solver with variable selection heuristics that consider the domain size of CSP variables when solving SAT-encoded

* Research partially supported by project CICYT TIC2001-1577-C03-03 funded by the *Ministerio de Ciencia y Tecnología*.

F. Rossi (Ed.): CP 2003, LNCS 2833, pp. 96–107, 2003.
© Springer-Verlag Berlin Heidelberg 2003

problems that have a more natural representation as CSPs. In that case, CSP variables are *hidden* in SAT encodings: a CSP variable X_i with a domain of size m is usually represented by m Boolean variables plus a set of clauses that ensures that X_i takes exactly one value of its domain. In this paper, we show that we can identify, with a low overhead, sets of Boolean variables that model the same CSP variable, and then design and implement extremely efficient selection variable heuristics for SAT solvers that take into account the domain size of CSP variables. In particular, we define five novel CSP-like variable selection heuristics for Chaff [25] —one of the most modern, powerful and robust SAT solvers— and provide experimental evidence that Chaff augmented with those heuristics outperforms the original Chaff solver one order of magnitude on difficult SAT-encoded problems like random binary CSPs, pigeon hole, and graph coloring.

The paper is structured as follows. In Section 2 we describe how to identify CSP variables in SAT encodings. In Section 3 we introduce Chaff and define five novel variable selection heuristics for Chaff. In Section 4 we describe in detail the experimental investigation we conducted to evaluate the performance of our heuristics on a wide range of SAT-encoded combinatorial problems. Finally, we give some concluding remarks.

2   Detecting CSPs Variables in SAT Encodings

In a SAT encoding, a CSP variable X_i with a domain $D_i = \{1, 2, \ldots, m\}$ is usually represented by m Boolean variables $(x_{i1}, \ldots, x_{im})$ plus a set of clauses that ensures that X_i takes exactly one value of D_i. The intended meaning of x_{ij} is that X_i takes the value j, and the clauses we add are:

- *At-least-one:* $x_{i1} \vee \cdots \vee x_{im}$; there is one of such clauses for each CSP variable. Such clauses ensure that each CSP variable takes at least one value from its domain.
- *At-most-one:* $\neg x_{ij} \vee \neg x_{ik}$; there is one of such binary clause for each pair j, k such that $1 \leq j < k \leq m$. Such clauses ensure that each CSP variable X_i takes no more than one value from its domain.

That pattern is the most commonly found for representing CSP variables in SAT repositories like the SATLIB [18]. Actually, we have found it in all the SAT-encoded instances of combinatorial problems from the SATLIB that have CSP variables with domain size greater than two[1].

We have modified Chaff [2] in such a way that it identifies, during the preprocessing phase, sets of Boolean variables that model the same CSP variable[3]. For

---

[1] Notice that CSP variables with domain size two can be modelled by a Boolean variable.

[2] The version of Chaff used in this paper is zChaff, which is publicly available at http://www.ee.princeton.edu/~chaff/zchaff.php

[3] We have also implemented an option that allows one to enter explicitly to Chaff sets of Boolean variables that model the same CSP variable. Such information is added at the end of the SAT encoding following a particular format.

each CSP variable X_i with a domain size m greater than two, Chaff maintains a data structure that stores the set of Boolean variables $\{x_{i1}, \ldots, x_{im}\}$ that model X_i. In a given state of the search, the current domain size of X_i is the number of free variables in $\{x_{i1}, \ldots, x_{im}\}$. Fortunately, identifying CSP variables in SAT encodings and determining its domain size as the search proceeds can be performed with a very low overhead.

3   Chaff and Our Chaff's Variants

Chaff [25] is one of the most modern, efficient and robust SAT solvers, which won the SAT Competition last year. Chaff implements the well-known Davis-Logemann-Loveland algorithm [13, 14] augmented with restarts, non-chronological backtracking and conflict-driven learning.

The variable selection heuristic of Chaff is called *Variable State Independent Decaying Sum* (vsids), and is described as follows [25]:

1. Each variable in each polarity has a counter, initialized to 0.
2. When a clause is added to the database, the counter associated with each literal in the clause is incremented. Notice that clauses are not only added at the beginning; conflict clauses are learned and added during the search process.
3. The (unassigned) variable and polarity with the highest counter is chosen at each decision.
4. Ties are broken randomly by default, although this is configurable.
5. Periodically, all the counters are divided by a constant. By default such a constant is 2.

As pointed out in [25], this strategy can be viewed as attempting to satisfy the conflict clauses but particularly attempting to satisfy *recent* conflict clauses. Since difficult problems generate many conflicts (and therefore many conflict clauses), the conflict clauses dominate the problems in terms of literal count, so this approach distinguishes itself primarily in how the low pass filtering of the statistics (indicated by step 5 of vsids) favors the information generated by recent conflict clauses.

We have designed and implemented five novel selection variable heuristics for Chaff that take into account the domain size of CSP variables:

- `min-vsids`: it applies the original Chaff heuristic (vsids) only to the Boolean variables that model CSP variables with minimum domain; i.e., it chooses the Boolean variable and polarity with the highest counter among those that model CSP variables with minimum domain. Ties are broken randomly.
- `max-vsids`: is like min-vsids but considering variables with maximum domain.
- `min/vsids`: for each Boolean variable p and polarity, it calculates the ratio of the current domain size of the CSP variable to which p is related to the counter that vsids associates with p. It selects the Boolean variable and polarity with minimum ratio. Ties are broken randomly.

- vsids-min: is like vsids, but ties are broken selecting a variable with minimum domain.
- vsids-max: is like vsids, but ties are broken selecting a variable with maximum domain.

4   Experimental Investigation

We next report the experimental investigation we conducted to evaluate the performance of our heuristics on a wide range of SAT-encoded combinatorial problems. All the experiments were performed with PC's Pentium III with 550 Mhz under Linux.

We considered randomly generated problems as well as problems with structure. As randomly generated problems, we considered SAT-encoded random binary CSPs. We selected them because they include CSP variables (with domain size greater than two) but also because SAT encodings of binary CSPs are an active research area [16, 33]. As problems with structure, we considered a number of combinatorial problems currently available in the SATLIB [18]: Latin squares, all interval series, planning, hanoi, graph coloring, and pigeon hole. We selected such problems because both we identified CSP variables with domain size greater than two in their SAT encodings and because they were not too easy for Chaff.

In all the experiments reported in this section, we compare the original Chaff solver with the best performing heuristics we found for each problem among the novel heuristics we incorporated into Chaff.

4.1   Random Binary CSPs

A constraint satisfaction problem (CSP) consists of a set of variables, each with a domain of values, and a set of constraints. Each constraint is defined over some subset of the original set of variables, and limits the combination of values that the variables in this subset can take. The goal is to find an assignment to the variables such that the assignment satisfies all the constraints. A binary CSP has only binary constraints.

Mappings of binary CSPs into SAT have been investigated by Génisson and Jégou [15], Walsh [33] and Gent [16]. They have proposed three different encodings: *direct, support and log*. We do not consider the log encoding here because it is much worse than the other two on complete solvers.

In the *direct encoding*, we associate a Boolean variable x_{ij} with each value j that can be assigned to the CSP variable X_i. Assuming that X_i has a domain of size m, the direct encoding contains clauses that ensure each CSP variable X_i is given a value: for each i, $x_{i1} \vee \cdots \vee x_{im}$ (called *at-least-one* clauses), and contains clauses that rule out any binary nogoods. For example, if $X_1 = 2$ and $X_3 = 1$ is not allowed, then the clause $\neg x_{12} \vee \neg x_{31}$ (called *conflict* clause) is added. We have also considered the version of the direct encoding that adds clauses that ensure that each CSP variable X_i takes no more than one value: for each i, j, k with $j \neq k$, $\neg x_{ij} \vee \neg x_{ik}$ (called *at-most-one* clauses). We refer to the direct encoding that incorporates such optional clauses as *redundant encoding*.

The experimental results provide evidence that, at least for our benchmark set, the redundant encoding is more efficient than the direct encoding.

In the *support encoding*, analyzed by Gent in [16], the idea is to encode into clauses the *support* for a value instead of encoding conflicts. The support for a value j of a CSP variable X_i across a constraint is the set of values of the other variable in the constraint which allow $X_i = j$. If $v_1, v_2, \ldots, v_k$ are the supporting values of variable X_l for $X_i = j$, we add the clause $\neg x_{ij} \lor x_{lv_1} \lor x_{lv_2} \lor \cdots \lor x_{lv_k}$ (called *support* clause). There is one support clause for each pair of variables X_i, X_l involved in a constraint, and for each value in the domain of X_i. Unlike conflict clauses, we need a similar clause in each direction, one for the pair X_i, X_l and one for X_l, X_i. The support clauses on their own do not provide a correct encoding of CSPs into SAT. To complete an encoding using support clauses we need to add the at-least-one and at-most-one clauses for each CSP variable to ensure that each CSP variable takes exactly one value of its domain.

Our first experiment consists of evaluating our heuristics on SAT-encoded random binary CSPs. We used a publicly available generator of uniform random binary CSPs[4] —designed and implemented by Frost, Bessière, Dechter and Regin— that implements the so-called model B: in the class $\langle n, d, p_1, p_2 \rangle$ with n variables of domain size d, we choose a random subset of exactly $p_1 n(n-1)/2$ constraints (rounded to the nearest integer), each with exactly $p_2 d^2$ conflicts (rounded to the nearest integer); p_1 may be thought of as the *density* of the problem and p_2 as the *tightness* of constraints.

We incorporated into the generator the automatic generation of all the classes of SAT encodings, and created a representative sample of instances of the hard region of the phase transition described in [31] that could be solved within a reasonable time. The sample is formed by 12 sets of 100 instances; the number of variables ranges from 12 to 100, the domain size was selected in such a way that the instances could be solved within a reasonable time, the density was set at values greater than 0.3 in order to avoid sparse constraint problems, and the tightness was derived from the remaining parameters using the equation $p_2 = 1 - d^{\frac{-2}{p_1(n-1)}}$ in order to generate instances of the hard region of the phase transition [31].

The experimental results obtained for all the sets of instances are shown in Table 1. The first column contains the parameters given to the generator of random binary CSPs, the second column is the class of SAT encoding used, the third column is the mean time needed by the original Chaff [5] to solve a set of 100 instances, the fourth column is like the third but with the median time, the fifth column is the ratio of the mean time needed by the original Chaff to solve a set of 100 instances to the time needed by the version of Chaff that incorporates the min-vsids heuristic (i.e., since all the ratios obtained are greater than one, a ratio of r means that the min-vsids heuristic outperforms Chaff by a factor of r), the sixth column is like the fifth but with median times, and the seventh and eighth columns are like the fifth and sixth but for the min/vsids heuristic.

---

[4] http://www.lirmm.fr/~bessiere/generator.html

[5] In our experimental investigation we used the default parameters of Chaff.

Table 1. Experimental results for Random Binary CSPs

parameters $\langle n, d, p_1, p_2 \rangle$	SAT encoding	Chaff (vsids) mean (seconds)	median (seconds)	ratio of vsids to min-vsids mean	median	ratio of vsids to min/vsids mean	median
$\langle 12, 70, 50/66, 3132/4900 \rangle$	direct	4030	4304	27.50	30.23	15.50	18.86
	redundant	1395	1379	13.85	12.68	6.23	6.97
	support	207	192	5.08	4.52	2.75	2.67
$\langle 15, 25, 80/105, 283/625 \rangle$	direct	95	116	13.30	13.76	6.68	8.07
	redundant	53	65	12.32	12.47	7.58	8.42
	support	20	23	7.37	6.77	5.48	5.41
$\langle 15, 30, 80/105, 424/900 \rangle$	direct	488	598	18.53	21.00	7.49	10.36
	redundant	233	261	15.58	15.67	8.97	10.42
	support	73	72	9.51	8.41	7.14	6.09
$\langle 25, 15, 198/300, 65/225 \rangle$	direct	1118	1102	11.32	11.94	5.26	6.15
	redundant	698	620	19.42	18.59	7.57	8.12
	support	508	422	21.46	17.78	9.36	9.74
$\langle 25, 20, 198/300, 126/400 \rangle$	direct	16588	12963	9.13	7.92	4.97	6.52
	redundant	8813	6526	17.78	13.85	8.02	8.07
	support	8820	5836	34.73	23.16	16.93	14.15
$\langle 35, 10, 305/595, 23/100 \rangle$	direct	411	346	7.41	7.24	3.88	3.41
	redundant	243	201	12.45	11.17	4.72	3.97
	support	246	217	15.80	14.99	6.12	6.47
$\langle 35, 15, 305/595, 60/225 \rangle$	direct	67826	40610	4.08	3.35	3.53	3.12
	redundant	49243	28338	13.98	9.09	6.68	5.33
	support	60271	42036	26.23	23.41	12.68	11.84
$\langle 40, 8, 400/780, 12/64 \rangle$	direct	125	109	8.67	7.69	2.83	3.00
	redundant	92	78	18.57	16.08	3.74	3.64
	support	94	82	27.87	17.89	6.89	5.73
$\langle 45, 10, 415/990, 22/100 \rangle$	direct	6217	4492	4.60	4.31	3.39	3.16
	redundant	4253	3206	11.99	11.19	5.35	5.07
	support	5577	4122	20.04	17.06	6.84	6.55
$\langle 70, 5, 880/2415, 3/25 \rangle$	direct	23	19	6.16	6.30	1.77	1.67
	redundant	21	17	13.92	13.41	2.13	2.03
	support	45	32	25.69	21.67	3.52	2.83
$\langle 70, 6, 1050/2415, 4/36 \rangle$	direct	10231	8183	4.55	4.33	2.34	2.20
	redundant	7039	5524	22.45	23.78	3.45	3.23
	support	17341	13983	57.10	58.76	4.47	4.77
$\langle 100, 4, 2000/4950, 1/16 \rangle$	direct	1774	1862	8.81	10.76	1.98	2.10
	redundant	1371	1374	48.18	53.21	2.59	2.89
	support	2492	2375	67.53	72.64	2.57	2.83

Table 1 provides experimental evidence that using heuristics based on selecting a variable with minimum domain outperforms Chaff's original heuristic up to a factor of 70. Even though min/vsids outperforms Chaff in all the instances, min-vsids is superior. Actually, min-vsids is one order of magnitude better than Chaff in most cases. It is also worth to note that, independently of the class of SAT encoding selected, our approach outperforms Chaff.

In his empirical investigation, Gent [16] observed that the support encoding solved with Chaff was superior to the direct encoding in the hard region of the phase transition. We considered a wider sample of instances — which in turn are harder than those considered in [16]— and observed that when the number of nogoods is relatively small the direct encoding outperforms the support encoding, as well as that the redundant encoding is a robust SAT encoding in the hard region of the phase transition.

Figure 1 shows the behaviour of the direct, redundant and support encodings in both the hard and easy regions of the phase transition for different parameter settings; we move from one region to the other by varying the tightness parameter (p_2). For the class $\langle 25, 15, 198/300, p_2 \rangle$, we compare the time needed by Chaff with the time needed by the direct, redundant and support encoding as p_2 increases. For the classes $\langle 12, 70, 50/66, p_2 \rangle$ and $\langle 100, 4, 2000/4950, p_2 \rangle$, we compare Chaff with the best performing encoding in the hard region (cf. Table 1). The bottom right plot shows the behavior of the class $\langle 25, d, 198/300, p_2 \rangle$ on the support encoding as the domain size d is increased. We see clearly that min-vsids scales better than Chaff as the domain size increases. While min-vsids is 11 times faster than Chaff for $d = 10$, min-vsids is 34 times faster than Chaff for $d = 20$. In all the plots, each data point corresponds to the mean time needed to solve 100 instances[6]. Notice that we use a log scale to represent computational cost.

Interestingly, Gent showed in [16] that, with equivalent branching heuristics, the Davis-Putnam algorithm applied to the support encoding explores the same size search tree as the MAC [11, 26] algorithm applied to the original binary CSP encoding. He also found that Chaff outperforms Satz [22] and GRASP [30] on SAT-encoded random binary CSPs. Previously, Walsh [33] showed that the Davis-Putnam algorithm applied to the direct encoding explores the same number of branches as FC [17] applied to the original binary CSP problem, given equivalent branching heuristics. Such results provide a possible explanation to the experiments reported in this section, in the sense that the good performance we obtained could be partly due to the fact that we incorporate into Chaff variable selection heuristics which are similar to those that work well on FC and MAC for random binary CSPs.

4.2   CSP Problems with Structure

We considered a number of combinatorial problems from the SATLIB [18] that are often used in experimental evaluations of SAT solvers: Latin squares, all interval series, planning, hanoi, graph coloring, and pigeon hole. We selected such problems because both we identified CSP variables with domain size greater than two in their SAT encodings and because they were not too easy for Chaff.

Table 2 shows the experimental results obtained for Latin squares, all interval series, planning, and hanoi. For all these problems, the best results were obtained with heuristics that rely on selecting Boolean variables that model CSP variables with minimum domain. There are 22 instances of Latin squares in the SATLIB, but in the table we only give results for the 6 more difficult instances; most of

---

[6] Similar plots are obtained if median time is used.

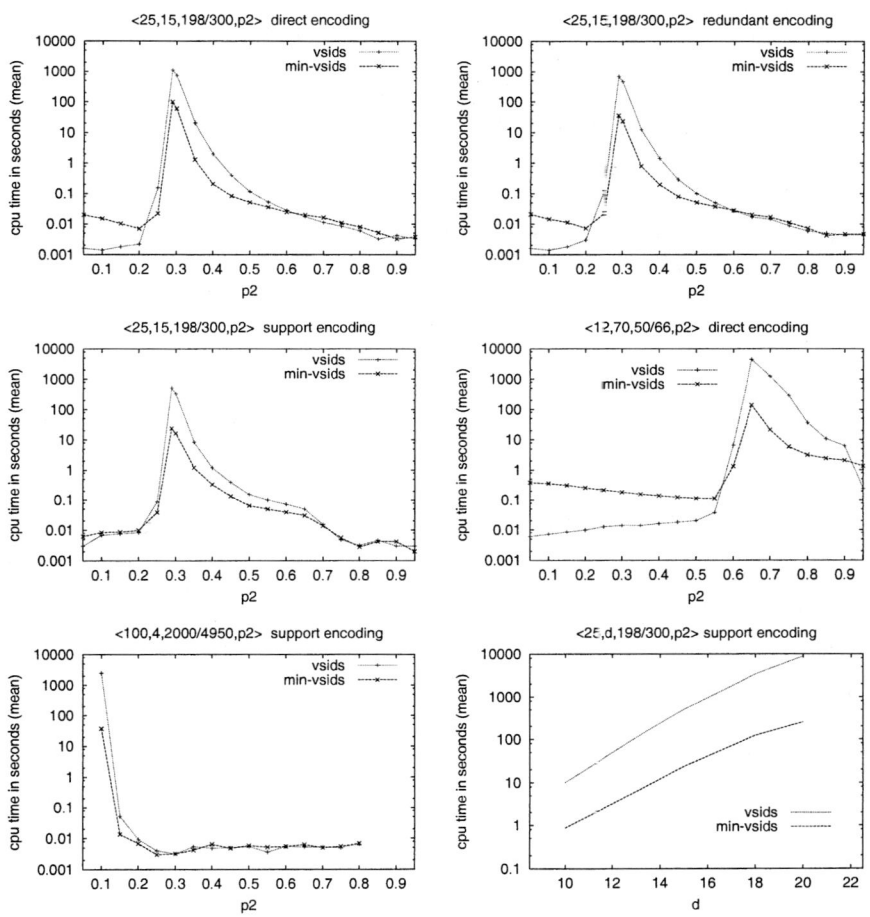

Fig. 1. Experimental results for Random Binary CSPs

the remaining instances were solved in less than one second. A similar situation occurs for planning instances; we only give results for bw_large.c/d. The more difficult instance we found was hanoi5, where vsids-min outperforms Chaff by a factor of 30.

A popular benchmark problem is graph coloring, but the instances available in the SATLIB (morphed and flat graph coloring instances) are solved very quickly by Chaff. We therefore decided to generate hardest flat graph coloring instances using the generator of Culberson [12]. The parameters of the generator are: number of vertices (n), number of colors (k), and edge density (p). We created a sample formed by 6 sets of 100 instances; the number of variables (n) ranges from 50 to 450, the number of colors (k) ranges from 3 to 8 and the edge density (p) ranges from 0.01 to 0.5. The parameter settings were designed to sample across the phase transition following the recommendations given by

Table 2. Experimental results for several problems from the SATLIB: Latin squares, all interval series, planning and hanoi (in the same order they appear in the table)

problem	Chaff (vsids) (seconds)	min-vsids (seconds)	min/vsids (seconds)	vsids-min (seconds)
qg7-12	10	2	2	2
qg6-12	28	11	11	21
qg1-08	37	39	78	97
qg2-08	83	26	52	43
qg5-13	170	22	60	139
qg3-09	222	42	69	229
ais10	3	0.1	1	0.1
ais12	37	1	194	25
bw_large.c	2	2	4	1
bw_large.d	26	95	32	10
hanoi4	1	2	1	6
hanoi5	76043	8955	10661	2484

Table 3. Experimental results for graph coloring

parameters			Chaff (vsids)		min-vsids		min/vsids	
vertices	density	colors	mean	median	mean	median	mean	median
n	p	k	(seconds)	(seconds)	(seconds)	(seconds)	(seconds)	(seconds)
450	0.018	3	1083	305	452	131	372	107
400	0.02	3	355	52	143	40	82	26
200	0.13	5	893	488	19	7	40	10
150	0.14	5	2214	1112	56	31	81	64
60	0.5	8	696	181	1	1	5	1
50	0.5	8	1151	342	3	1	9	2

Culberson[7]. The results obtained are shown in Table 3. Notice that in this case the gains achieve up to two orders of magnitude, and that the performance improvement is better as the number of colors increases.

Like in CSP solvers, we found that heuristics that rely on selecting variables that model CSP variables with minimum domain are usually the best option. Nevertheless, we found that taking into account maximum domains instead of minimum domains was the best option for the pigeon hole problem. As shown in Table 4, max-vsids outperforms Chaff up to one order of magnitude, and exhibits a better scaling behaviour.

5   Conclusions

The results reported in this paper clearly indicate that incorporating CSP-like variable selection heuristics into Chaff leads to a large improvement on performance. Chaff is nowadays considered to be one of the fastest complete SAT

---

[7] http://web.cs.ualberta.ca/~joe/Coloring/Generators/settings.html

Table 4. Experimental results for the pigeon hole problem

holes	Chaff (vsids) (seconds)	max-vsids (seconds)	vsids-max (seconds)
9	3	1	3
10	29	5	26
11	181	21	321
12	1135	93	1115
13	5822	468	4784
14	21350	2028	24352

solvers, which incorporates a lot of technology developed by the SAT and Constraint Programming communities, as well as a careful engineering of all aspects of the search. Taking into account that our approach outperforms Chaff one order of magnitude on most problems, the contributions of this paper open an exciting research avenue in the area of variable selection heuristics for SAT solvers.

We have also incorporated to Satz the techniques described here in order to build a solver for many-valued clausal forms [2]. The experimental results reported in [2] provide evidence that keeping track of information about the origins of the variables in a SAT encoding leads to large performance improvements in a SAT solver that, in contrast to Chaff, relies on look-ahead techniques. We therefore believe that our approach can lead to substantial improvements in most state-of-the-art SAT solvers.

The interest of exploiting information of CSP variable domains in SAT solvers is not limited to variable selection heuristics, it can also have a large impact in the process of learning conflict clauses. For example, given a CSP variable X_i with domain size three that is represented by the Boolean variables x_{i1}, x_{i2}, x_{i3}, if we maintain information of its domain and learn the conflict clause $x_{i1} \lor x_{i2}$, we can then propagate $\neg x_{i3}$. This kind of constraint propagation is not achieved with the existing SAT solvers.

One important lesson that can be learned from the results of this paper is that, when mapping combinatorial problems with finite-domain variables into formalisms with Boolean variables, it is worth to maintain some information about the structure of the original problem. Finally, we would like to point out that this research was inspired by the research on many-valued satisfiability we have developed in the last years (see e.g. [1, 3, 5–9, 23]).

References

1. C. Ansótegui, R. Béjar, A. Cabiscol, C. M. Li, and F. Manyà. Resolution methods for many-valued CNF formulas. In *Fifth International Symposium on the Theory and Applications of Satisfiability Testing, SAT-2002, Cincinnati, USA*, pages 156–163, 2002.
2. C. Ansótegui, J. Larrubia, C. M. Li, and F. Manyà. Mv-Satz: A SAT solver for many-valued clausal forms. In *4th International Conference Journées de L'Informatique Messine, JIM-2003, Metz, France*, 2003.

3. C. Ansótegui, F. Manyà, R. Béjar, and C. Gomes. Solving many-valued SAT encodings with local search. In *Proceedings of the Workshop on Probabilistics Approaches in Search, 18th National Conference on Artificial Intelligence, AAAI-2002, Edmonton, Canada, 2002*, 2002.

4. R. J. Bayardo and R. C. Schrag. Using CSP look-back techniques to solve real-world SAT instances. In *Proceedings of the 14th National Conference on Artificial Intelligence, AAAI'97, Providence/RI, USA*, pages 203–208. AAAI Press, 1997.

5. B. Beckert, R. Hähnle, and F. Manyà. Transformations between signed and classical clause logic. In *Proceedings, International Symposium on Multiple-Valued Logics, ISMVL'99, Freiburg, Germany*, pages 248–255. IEEE Press, Los Alamitos, 1999.

6. B. Beckert, R. Hähnle, and F. Manyà. The SAT problem of signed CNF formulas. In D. Basin, M. D'Agostino, D. Gabbay, S. Matthews, and L. Viganò, editors, *Labelled Deduction*, volume 17 of *Applied Logic Series*, pages 61–82. Kluwer, Dordrecht, 2000.

7. R. Béjar, A. Cabiscol, C. Fernández, F. Manyà, and C. P. Gomes. Capturing structure with satisfiability. In *7th International Conference on Principles and Practice of Constraint Programming, CP-2001,Paphos, Cyprus*, pages 137–152. Springer LNCS 2239, 2001.

8. R. Béjar, R. Hähnle, and F. Manyà. A modular reduction of regular logic to classical logic. In *Proceedings, 31st International Symposium on Multiple-Valued Logics (ISMVL), Warsaw, Poland*, pages 221–226. IEEE CS Press, Los Alamitos, 2001.

9. R. Béjar and F. Manyà. A comparison of systematic and local search algorithms for regular CNF formulas. In *Proceedings of the 5th European Conference on Symbolic and Quantitative Approaches to Reasoning with Uncertainty, ECSQARU'99, London, England*, pages 22–31. Springer LNAI 1638, 1999.

10. R. Béjar and F. Manyà. Solving the round robin problem using propositional logic. In *Proceedings of the 17th National Conference on Artificial Intelligence, AAAI-2000, Austin/TX, USA*, pages 262–266. AAAI Press, 2000.

11. C. Bessière and J. Régin. Refining the basic constraint propagation algorithm. In *Proceedings of IJCAI'01*, pages 309–315, 2001.

12. J. Culberson. Graph coloring page: The flat graph generator. See http://web.cs.ualberta.ca/~joe/Coloring/Generators/flat.html, 1995.

13. M. Davis, G. Logemann, and D. Loveland. A machine program for theorem-proving. *Communications of the ACM*, 5:394–397, 1962.

14. M. Davis and H. Putnam. A computing procedure for quantification theory. *Journal of the ACM*, 7(3):201–215, 1960.

15. R. Génisson and P. Jégou. Davis and Putnam were already checking forward. In *Proceedings of the 12th European Conference on Artificial Intelligence (ECAI), Budapest, Hungary*, pages 180–184, 1996.

16. I. P. Gent. Arc consistency in SAT. In *Proceedings of the 15th European Conference on Artificial Intelligence (ECAI), Lyon, France*, pages –, 2002.

17. R. Haralick and G. Elliot. Increasing tree search efficiency for constraint satisfaction problems. *Artificial Intelligence*, 14:263–313, 1980.

18. H. Hoos. SATLIB: A collection of SAT tools and data. See www.satlib.org, 1999.

19. H. A. Kautz, Y. Ruan, D. Achlioptas, C. P. Gomes, B. Selman, and M. Stickel. Balance and filtering in structured satisfiable problems. In *Proceedings of the International Joint Conference on Artificial Intelligence, IJCAI'01, Seattle/WA, USA*, pages 351–358, 2001.

20. H. A. Kautz and B. Selman. Pushing the envelope: Planning, propositional logic, and stochastic search. In *Proceedings of the 14th National Conference on Artificial Intelligence, AAAI'96, Portland/OR, USA*, pages 1194–1201. AAAI Press, 1996.

21. C. M. Li and Anbulagan. Heuristics based on unit propagation for satisfiability problems. In *Proceedings of the International Joint Conference on Artificial Intelligence, IJCAI'97, Nagoya, Japan*, pages 366–371. Morgan Kaufmann, 1997.

22. C. M. Li and Anbulagan. Look-ahead versus look-back for satisfiability problems. In *Proceedings of the 3rd International Conference on Principles of Constraint Programming, CP'97, Linz, Austria*, pages 341–355. Springer LNCS 1330, 1997.

23. F. Manyà, R. Béjar, and G. Escalada-Imaz. The satisfiability problem in regular CNF-formulas. *Soft Computing: A Fusion of Foundations, Methodologies and Applications*, 2(3):116–123, 1998.

24. J. P. Marques-Silva and L. Guerra. Algorithms for satisfiability in combinational circuits based on backtrack search and recursive learning. In *Proc. of XII Symposium on Integrated Circuits and Systems Design (SBCCI)*, 1999.

25. M. Moskewicz, C. Madigan, Y. Zhao, L. Zhang, and S. Malik. Chaff: Engineering an efficient sat solver. In *39th Design Automation Conference*, 2001.

26. D. Sabin and E. Freuder. Contradicting conventional wisdom in constraint satisfaction. In *Proceedings of ECAI'94*, pages 125–129, 1994.

27. B. Selman and H. A. Kautz. Domain-independent extensions of GSAT: Solving large structured satisfiability problems. In *Proceedings of the International Joint Conference on Artificial Intelligence, IJCAI'93, Chambery, France*, pages 290–295. Morgan Kaufmann, 1993.

28. B. Selman, H. A. Kautz, and B. Cohen. Noise strategies for improving local search. In *Proceedings of the 12th National Conference on Artificial Intelligence, AAAI'94, Seattle/WA, USA*, pages 337–343. AAAI Press, 1994.

29. B. Selman, H. Levesque, and D. Mitchell. A new method for solving hard satisfiability problems. In *Proceedings of the 10th National Conference on Artificial Intelligence, AAAI'92, San Jose/CA, USA*, pages 440–446. AAAI Press, 1992.

30. J. P. M. Silva and K. A. Sakallah. GRASP: A search algorithm for propositional satisfiability. *IEEE Transactions on Computers*, 48(5):506–521, 1999.

31. B. Smith and M. Dyer. Locating the phase transition in binary constraint satisfaction problems. *Artificial Intelligence*, 81:155–181, 1996.

32. M. Velev and R. Bryant. Effective use of boolean satisfiability procedures in the formal verification of superscalar and vliw microprocessors. In *38th Design Automation Conference (DAC '01)*, 2001.

33. T. Walsh. SAT v CSP. In *Proceedings of the 6th International Conference on Principles of Constraint Programming, CP-2000, Singapore*, pages 441–456. Springer LNCS 1894, 2000.

Efficient CNF Encoding
of Boolean Cardinality Constraints

Olivier Bailleux[1] and Yacine Boufkhad[2]

[1] LERSIA, Université de Bourgogne
Avenue Alain Savary, BP 47870
21078 Dijon Cedex
olivier.bailleux@u-bourgogne.fr
[2] LIAFA, Université Paris 7
Case 7014 - 2, place Jussieu F-75251 Paris Cedex 05
Yacine.Boufkhad@liafa.jussieu.fr

Abstract. In this paper, we address the encoding into CNF clauses of Boolean cardinality constraints that arise in many practical applications. The proposed encoding is efficient with respect to unit propagation, which is implemented in almost all complete CNF satisfiability solvers. We prove the practical efficiency of this encoding on some problems arising in discrete tomography that involve many cardinality constraints. This encoding is also used together with a trivial variable elimination in order to re-encode parity learning benchmarks so that a simple Davis and Putnam procedure can solve them.

1 Introduction

Many types of constraints that appear in real world problems have no natural expression in the propositional satisfiability. The cardinality constraint over a set of Boolean variables (i.e., a constraint on the number of variables that can be assigned the value 1) is one of these. The encoding problem that we address is: given a set E of Boolean variables (called input variables) subject to a cardinality constraint requiring that at least μ and at most ρ of them can be equal to 1, build a CNF formula $\Psi(E, \mu, \rho)$ over a set of variables including E such that $\Psi(E, \mu, \rho)$ can be satisfied by a truth assignment if and only if the values assigned to variables in E by this truth assignment satisfy the cardinality constraint. In this paper, we propose an efficient CNF encoding of the cardinality constraint.

While there is no general definition of a good encoding, there are at least some common sense conditions that such an encoding must fulfill. The first one is that the size of the formula must be kept relatively small with respect to E and the second one is that the formula must be adapted to the kind of solver to be used. Our encoding requires $O(n \log(n))$ variables and $O(n^2)$ clauses of length at most 3, where $n = |E|$. This encoding is also efficient in the sense that unit propagation restores the generalized arc consistency on the variables in E.

The straightforward way of encoding of cardinality constraints is based on a bit adder that adds one by one the variables in E, as in [6]. The result of the addition is represented in the usual binary representation of integers, and the Boolean variables that

F. Rossi (Ed.): CP 2003, LNCS 2833, pp. 108–122, 2003.
© Springer-Verlag Berlin Heidelberg 2003

compose it are constrained by some clauses so that the integer they represent is in the prescribed range. While the size of the CNF formula generated by this encoding remains reasonable, its main disadvantage is that a SAT solver based on unit propagation needs to have all the variables in E assigned a value in order to check the cardinality constraint. Even if the constraint is violated by a partial assignment, unit propagation alone does not generate an empty clause. In the encoding described in this paper, the key feature is a unary representation of integer variables that can represent not only the value, if known, of an integer but also the interval where it falls if the Boolean variables in its unary representation are partially assigned. A bit adder based on this representation allows the derivation of the interval where a variable c falls, given the intervals of variables a and b such that $c = a + b$. We obtain a CNF formula where unit propagation derives all the consequences of every assignment with respect to the generalized arc consistency. In particular, it derives an empty clause whenever a partial assignment to the input variables is inconsistent with the cardinality constraint.

In order to subject this encoding to an application where there are these types of constraints, we have tested it on a problem arising in 2-D discrete tomography. The specific problem that we address is the reconstruction of a pattern lying in a 2-D grid, given its projections in four directions. The projection in some direction is the number of points belonging to the pattern in that direction. The reconstruction problem is to find a pattern that complies with the given projections in every direction. This amounts to finding an assignment to the Boolean variables representing the cells of the grid given many cardinality constraints. Each one of these cardinality constraints, represents the fact that the number of cells belonging to the pattern in some direction, is equal to the projection in that direction. This is a good test for our encoding scheme since each variable is involved in four different cardinality constraints. We compared, using some instances of discrete tomography, the performance of our encoding solved by the state of the art SAT solver zchaff [15] versus a commercial constraint solver.

The cardinality constraints also appear in parity learning instances. These benchmarks have been the center of a challenge to solvers. We show that they can be solved easily using a basic DP procedure, by separating them into two parts: an XOR-CNF formula and a formula containing a mixture of cardinality constraint and some XOR-CNF relations.

At this point, one may make some general remarks on the issue of encoding into CNF. The benchmarks that are extensively used to assess the efficiency of SAT algorithms are generally taken as they are. The issue of finding the best encodings or even the pertinence of encoding them into SAT formulas is rarely brought up. In the challenges that are organized for SAT, only two categories of submission are welcomed: solvers and benchmarks. The issue of improving the proposed encodings in ignored. As the most interesting benchmarks are the hardest ones, ignoring the encoding may have this consequence: some intrinsically easy problems may be made hard by an inappropriate encoding, and, as they are hard, they may be considered as interesting benchmarks. If the final goal is the practical solving of hard real world problems and not only to make solvers overcome inappropriate encodings by rediscovering in the CNF formulas some deductions that are obvious in the original problem, then a careful encoding is crucial and must be considered as a third type of contribution beside solvers and benchmarks in the challenges organized for SAT.

The paper is organized as follows. The encoding is described in Section 2, where correctness and efficiency are proved. Then in Section 3 the encoding is applied to the discrete tomography problems after a brief description of these problems. In Section 4, the learning parity instances are revisited in the light of this new encoding of cardinality constraints.

2   Efficient CNF Encoding of Cardinality Constraints

We give first the notations that will be used throughout this paper. The truth values TRUE and FALSE of propositional logic will be denoted 0 and 1. An *instantiation* or a *truth assignment* I of a set V of propositional variables is a function that maps each variable $v \in V$ to a non empty set $I(v) \subseteq \{0,1\}$. A variable v is said to be *fixed* to 0 or *assigned the value* 0 by an instantiation I if $I(v) = \{0\}$, fixed to 1 if $I(v) = \{1\}$, and free if $I(v) = \{0,1\}$. In non-ambiguous contexts, $v = 1$ denotes $I(v) = \{1\}$ and $v = 0$ denotes $I(v) = \{0\}$. An instantiation I of V is said to be *complete* if it fixes all the variables in V. The instantiations that are not complete are said to be *partial*.

For any CNF formula Φ and any instantiation I of a subset of the variables of Φ, $\Phi|_I$ denotes the formula obtained by replacing the variables that are fixed by I with their truth values.

A *unit clause* is a clause that includes only one literal. *Unit propagation* denotes the process that fixes each variable occurring in a unit clause in such a way as to satisfy this clause, up until the empty clause is produced or no unit clause remains.

2.1   The Problem

The goal is to translate a cardinality constraint over a set E of Boolean variables into a CNF formula. The cardinality constraint specifies that the number p of variables fixed to 1 among a set E of Boolean variables is at least μ and at most ρ. The CNF formula $\Psi(E, \mu, \rho)$ is defined on a set $V \supset E$ of propositional variables. The variables in $V \setminus E$ are called *encoding variables*.

The encoding must be *correct* in the sense that for any complete instantiation I of E, $\Psi(E, \mu, \rho)|_I$ is *satisfiable* if and only if I satisfies the cardinality constraint.

The encoding must also be *efficient* in the sense that for any partial instantiation I of E, unit propagation on $\Phi(E, \mu, \rho)|_I$ must restore the generalized arc consistency on the variables in E, specifically:

- if more than ρ variables in E are fixed to 1 or if more than $n - \mu$ variables in E are fixed to 0 then unit propagation produces the empty clause,
- else if ρ variables in E are fixed to 1 then unit propagation fixes to 0 all the other variables in E,
- else if $n - \mu$ variables in E are fixed to 0 then unit propagation fixes to 1 all the other variables in E.

2.2 Encoding Principle

The proposed encoding uses a unary representation of integers. The value of an integer x such that $0 \leq x \leq n$ is represented by 1 x times followed by 0 $n - x$ times. An integer variable v with domain $0..n$ is represented by a set $V = \{v_1, v_2, \ldots, v_n\}$ of n propositional variables. Each possible value of v is encoded as a complete instantiation of V, as described above. If $v = x$, then $v_1 = 1$, $v_2 = 1$, ..., $v_x = 1$ and $v_{x+1} = 0$, ..., $v_n = 0$. A partial instantiation of V is said to be *pre-unary* if for each $v_i = 1$, $v_j = 1$ for any $j < i$ and for each $v_i = 0$, $v_j = 0$ for any j, $i \leq j \leq n$. A unary instantiation is then a complete pre-unary instantiation.

The main advantage of such a representation is that the integer variable can be specified as belonging to an interval. Indeed, the inequality $x \leq v \leq y$ is specified by the partial pre-unary instantiation of V that fixes to 1 any v_i such that $i \leq x$ and fixes to 0 any v_j such that $j \geq y + 1$.

Conversely, any partial pre-unary instantiation I of V is related to an integer interval. The bounds of this interval will be denoted $min(I)$ and $max(I)$. We underline that the classical binary representation of integers does not allow one to specify such membership relations as our representation does.

Example: With $n = 6$, if I is a partial instantiation such that $v_1 = v_2 = 1$, $v_5 = v_6 = 0$, and v_3, v_4 are free, then $min(I) = 2$ and $max(I) = 4$. Then the corresponding integer variable v is such that $2 \leq v \leq 4$.

The number of variables fixed to 1 by an instantiation I will be denoted $N(I)$. When I is the unary representation of an integer, $N(I)$ is then the value of this integer.

The encoding of a cardinality constraint on a set E of variables is done in two parts: a *totalizer* and a *comparator*.

The Totalizer. The totalizer is a CNF formula $\Phi(E)$ defined on 3 sets of variables:

- $E = \{e_1, \ldots, e_n\}$: the set of *input variables*,
- $S = \{s_1, \ldots, s_n\}$: the set of *output variables*,
- a set L of variables called *linking variables*.

These sets of variables can be described by a binary tree built as follows. We start from a isolated node labeled by the integer n and we proceed iteratively: to each terminal node labeled by $m > 1$, we connect two children labeled by $\lfloor m/2 \rfloor$ and $m - \lfloor m/2 \rfloor$, respectively. This procedure produces a binary tree with n leaves labeled by 1. Next, each variable in E is allocated to a leaf in a bijective way. The set S of output variables is allocated to the root node. To each internal node labeled by an integer m, a set of m new variables is allocated which will be used to represent a unary value belonging to $1..m$. The union of the set of variables allocated to the internal nodes is the set L of linking variables.

Example: for $n = 5$, $E = \{e_1, e_2, e_3, e_4, e_5\}$, and $S = \{s_1, s_2, s_3, s_4, s_5\}$ the following tree is obtained:

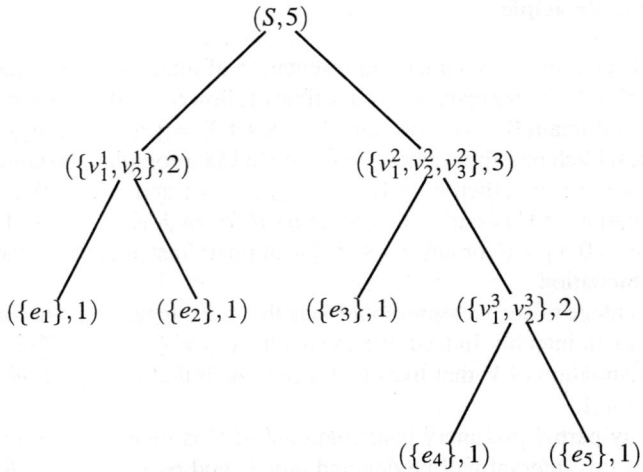

In this example, the set of linking variables is $L = \{v_1^1, v_2^1, v_1^2, v_2^2, v_3^2, v_1^3, v_2^3\}$.

We will now define a set of clauses that ensures that in any complete instantiation of the variables of the totalizer, the set of variables related to any non-leaf node r with children a and b encodes the unary representation of $\alpha + \beta$, where α and β are the integers encoded by the sets of variables related to a and b.

Let r be an internal node related to children a and b. Let $R = \{r_1, \ldots, r_m\}$ be the set of variables related to r, $A = \{a_1, \ldots, a_{m_1}\}$ be the set of variables related to a, and $B = \{b_1, \ldots, b_{m_2}\}$ be the set of variables related to b. The following conjunction of clauses is related to the node r:

$$\bigwedge_{\substack{0 \le \alpha \le m_1 \\ 0 \le \beta \le m_2 \\ 0 \le \sigma \le m \\ \alpha + \beta = \sigma}} (C_1(\alpha, \beta, \sigma) \wedge C_2(\alpha, \beta, \sigma)) \tag{1}$$

with the following notations:

$$a_0 = b_0 = r_0 = 1, a_{m_1+1} = b_{m_2+1} = r_{m+1} = 0$$

$$C_1(\alpha, \beta, \sigma) = (\overline{a_\alpha} \vee \overline{b_\beta} \vee r_\sigma)$$

$$C_2(\alpha, \beta, \sigma) = (a_{\alpha+1} \vee b_{\beta+1} \vee \overline{r_{\sigma+1}})$$

Notice that $C_1(\alpha, \beta, \sigma)$ is the CNF representation of the relation $\sigma \ge \alpha + \beta$ and $C_2(\alpha, \beta, \sigma)$ is the CNF representation of the relation $\sigma \le \alpha + \beta$.

The obtained formula is simplified by removing the clauses including the constant 1 and reducing the clauses including the constant 0. Notice that each clause includes at most three literals.

Lemma 21 (forward propagation) *Let $\Phi(E)$ be a totalizer with n input variables. If p input variables are fixed to 1, q input variables are fixed to 0, and all the other* *variables of the totalizer are free then the partial instantiation I_S of S obtained after unit propagation in $\Phi(E)$ is pre-unary and such that $min(I_S) = p$ and $max(I_S) = n - q$.*

Proof: By induction on the number n of input variables.

For $n = 1$ the totalizer includes only one variable that is either the input and the output variable. The property is then obvious. Now let us consider that the property is true for any $n < v$.

Let $A = \{a_1, a_2, ..., a_{v_A}\}$ denote the set of the $v_A = \lfloor v/2 \rfloor$ variables associated to the first child of the root and $B = \{b_1, b_2, ..., b_{v_A}\}$ denote the set of the $v_B = v - \lfloor v/2 \rfloor$ variables associated to the other child. Considering the leaves of the tree below each child of the root, we get a partition of the input set E into two disjoint subsets E_A and E_B. Let p_A denote the number of variables fixed to 1 in E_A, p_B denote the number of variables fixed to 1 in E_B, q_A denote the number of variables fixed to 0 in E_A and q_B denote the number of variables fixed to 0 in E_B. Clearly, we have $p = p_A + p_B$ and $q = q_A + q_B$. Let I_A and I_B denote the instantiations of A and B obtained after unit propagation in $\Phi(E)$.

It follows from the induction hypothesis that I_A and I_B are pre-unary, $min(I_A) = p_A$, $max(I_A) = v_A - q_A$, $min(I_B) = p_B$, $max(I_B) = v_B - q_B$.

It is easy to see that for every t such that $1 \le t \le p$ there exist t_A, $t_A \le min(I_A)$, and t_B, $t_B \le min(I_B)$ such that $t = t_A + t_B$. Thanks to the clause $\overline{a_{t_A}} \vee \overline{b_{t_B}} \vee s_t$ of the C_1 type associated to the root node, unit propagation fixes to 1 the variable s_t. Consequently, all the variables s_1 to s_p are set to 1. Thanks to the clauses C_2 associated to the root node, we can prove by similar arguments that unit propagation fixes to 0 the variables s_{n-q+1} to s_n.

For the variables s_t such that $p < t \le n - q$, it is easy to see that for every couple (t_A, t_B) such that $t_A + t_B = t$, either $t_A > min(I_A)$ or $t_B > min(I_B)$. Consequently, at least one of the variables a_{t_A} or b_{t_B} is not equal to 1. Then no clause $\overline{a_{t_A}} \vee \overline{b_{t_B}} \vee s_t$ can be reduced to the unit clause s_t. The same arguments applied to the causes C_2 can be used to prove that the clause $\overline{s_t}$ can not be produced. Then the variables s_t such that $p < t \le n - q$ are all free. So I_S is pre-unary, $min(I_S) = p$, and $max(I_S) = n - q$.

Then I_S is the unary representation of the smallest interval containing $N(I_E)$.

Lemma 22 (backward propagation) *Let $\Phi(E)$ be a totalizer with n input variables. If:*

- *p input variables are fixed to 1, q input variables are fixed to 0 $(p+q < n)$, the remaining input variables being free,*
- *and the output variables s_{p+1} to s_{n-q} are all fixed to the same value ε (0 or 1)*

then all the input variables remaining free are instantiated to ε by unit propagation.

Proof: By induction on the number n of input variables.

For $n = 1$ the property is obvious. Now let us consider that the property is true for any $n < v$.

We use the same notations as in the proof of the previous lemma. If we consider solely the assignment to the input variables, the unit propagation assigns to the output variables the values such that $min(I_S) = p$ and $max(I_S) = n - q$. Suppose that s_{p+1} to s_{n-q} variables are assigned the value 0. Let t any integer such that $1 \le t \le n - p$. Clearly, we have $s_{p+t} = s_{p_A+p_B+t} = 0$. If $p_A + t \le v_A$, there is a clause of type C_1 $\overline{a_{p_A+t}} \vee \overline{b_{p_B}} \vee s_{p+t}$.

By unit propagation, this clause assigns the value 0 to a_{p_A+t}. Then every variable a_{p_A+t} such that $p_A + t \leq v_A$ is assigned the value 0. By the same argument we can prove that every variable b_{p_B+t} such that $p_B + t \leq v_B$ is also assigned the value 0. By the induction hypothesis, all the free input variables below the nodes A and B (i.e. all free input variables) are assigned 0.

Similar arguments using the clauses of type C_2 allow the derivation of the conclusion that all the free input variables are assigned 1, if the variables s_{p+1} to s_{n-q} are assigned the value 1.

The Comparator. The comparator is a set of unary clauses that are satisfied if and only if the instantiation of the input variables of the totalizer represents an interval that matches with the cardinality constraint. Then the constraint $\mu \leq N(E_I) \leq \rho$ will be specified as follows:

$$\bigwedge_{1 \leq i \leq \mu} (s_i) \bigwedge_{\rho+1 \leq j \leq n} (\overline{s_j}) \tag{2}$$

We denote by $\Psi(E, \mu, \rho)$, the conjunction of the CNF formula representing the totalizer and the CNF representing the comparator.

2.3   Correctness and Efficiency of the Encoding

The correctness and the efficiency of the proposed CNF encoding of the cardinality constraint follows directly from Lemma 21 and 22.

Theorem 23 *The CNF encoding of a cardinality constraint described in the section 2.2 is correct and efficient.*

Proof

1. **Correctness:** It follows from Lemma 21 that for any complete instantiation of the input variables, unit propagation fixes all the other variables of the totalizer in such a way that the instantiation of the output variables is the unary value of the number of input variables fixed to 1. Then the conjunction of the totalizer and the comparator is satisfiable if and only if the number of input variables fixed to 1 belongs to the interval encoded by the unary clauses of the comparator.

2. **Efficiency:** Let p be the number of input variables fixed to 1, q be the number of input variables fixed to 0 ($p + q < n$), μ be the lower bound and ρ be the upper bound of the interval encoded by the comparator. It follows from lemma 21 that unit propagation fixes s_1 to s_p to 1 and fixes s_{n-q+1} to s_n to 0. In addition, the clauses of the comparator allow unit propagation to fix $s_{\rho+1}$ to s_n to 0 and to fix s_1 to s_μ to 1.

   If $p > \rho$ then unit propagation fixes $s_{\rho+1}$ to 1, which is in conflict with the clause $(\overline{s_{\rho+1}})$ of the comparator, thus the empty clause is produced.

   In the same way, if $q > n - \mu$ then unit propagation fixes s_μ to 0, which is in conflict with the clause (s_μ) of the comparator.

If $p = \rho$ then, because the $n - p$ output variables $s_{\rho+1}$ to s_{n-q} are fixed to 0 by the unit clauses of the comparator, it follows from Lemma 22 that unit propagation fixes the free input variables to 0 .

If $q = n - \mu$ then, because the $n - q$ output variables s_1 to s_μ are fixed to 1 by the unit clauses of the comparator, it follows from Lemma 22 that unit propagation fixes the free input variables to 1.

2.4   Complexity Issues

The binary tree used to specify the totalizer has $\Theta(\log n)$ levels. Each of these levels requires n linking (or output) variables, thus the totalizer includes $\Theta(n \log n)$ encoding variables.

For sake of simplicity, let us consider that n is a power of 2. For each node related to a set of m linking (or output) variables, there are less than $2m^2$ clauses. Let us number the levels from 1 to l, where l is the number of the root level. For any i such that $1 \le i \le l$, the level $l - i$ includes 2^i nodes, each related to $n/2^i$ variables. Then the level $n - i$ includes less than $2^i(2(n/2^i)^2) = 2n^2/2^i$ clauses. So the totalizer includes $O(n^2)$ clauses. Given that the root node of the totalizer requires $\Omega(n^2)$ clauses, and that the comparator requires n clauses, the encoding requires $\Theta(n^2)$ clauses.

Clearly enough, if the cardinality constraint is $\rho \le N(I_E) \le \mu$, all the properties described above remain true if any variable with rank upper than μ is initially fixed to 0. This allows one to simplify the formula, using unit propagation, and then reduce its size. If μ is the same order of magnitude as n, this simplification does not change the size complexity of the encoding.

In the worst case, because unit propagation must fixe all the encoding variables, restoring the generalized arc consistency requires time $\Theta(n \log n)$. This time complexity is not optimal, given that a dedicated algorithm using the rules described section 2.1 can restore the generalized arc consistency of a Boolean cardinality constraint in time $O(n)$.

3   Discrete Tomography Problems

We apply the encoding of the cardinality constraints described in the previous section to a problem arising in discrete tomography. Tomography is a non-destructive method used to examine the interior of solid opaque objects. It consists of sending X-rays at different angles through the object and recording the attenuation at the opposite side. The attenuation reflects the density of the object in a given direction. The problem is then to reconstruct the studied object's image using the attenuation of the X-rays. Tomography is used in many fields ranging from medical imagery to geology and as described in Gardner et al [10] in the determination of the crystalline structure using high resolution transmission electron microscopy. Several mathematical tools have been developed for solving the reconstruction problem in the continuous case. We focus on the reconstruction of 2-D objects given their discrete projections in 4 directions.

This problem have been investigated under various conditions in [17, 4, 19, 9, 13, 1, 21, 3]. Recently Gardner et al [10] proved the NP-Completeness of the problem of testing the existence and the uniqueness of a pattern given its projections in at least 3 directions.

In the 2-D discrete case, the pattern to be reconstructed lies in a grid having n rows and m columns. Each cell of the grid, i.e. a unitary square $[i, i+1] \times [j, j+1]$, is either black, *filled*, if it belongs to the pattern or white, *empty*, if it does not. We will denote the cell located at the intersection of row i and column j by $c_{i,j}$. The i-th row projection and the j-th column projection of the pattern are the numbers of filled cells in the i-the row and the j-th column respectively. The vertical and horizontal projections of a pattern in a grid $n \times m$ are denoted by two vectors $H = (h_1, ..., h_i, ..., h_n) \in \mathbf{N}^n$ and $V = (v_1, ..., v_j, ..., v_m) \in \mathbf{N}^m$, h_i and v_j being the i-th row projection and the j-th column projection respectively. Similarly, the k-th diagonal projection is the number of filled cells among the cells $c_{i,j}$ such that $i + j = k + 1$. The l-th antidiagonal projection is the number of filled cells among the cells $c_{i,j}$ such that $m + i - j = l + 1$. Figure 1 shows the projections of the pattern **6**.

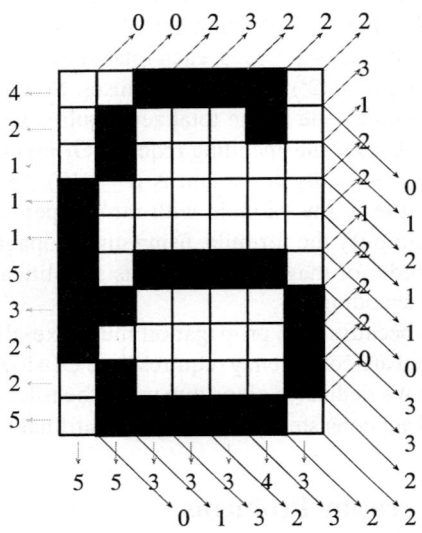

Fig. 1. A pattern representing 6 and its projections, i.e. the number of black cells, in the four directions, yielding the vectors $H = \{4, 3, 1, 1, 1, 5, 3, 2, 2, 5\}$ for the horizontal lines, $V = \{5, 5, 3, 3, 3, 4\}$ for the vertical lines, $S\{0, 0, 2, 3, 2, 2, 2, 3, 1, 2, 2, 1, 2, 2, 2, 0\}$ for the diagonal 45 degrees directions, $T\{0, 1, 2, 1, 1, 0, 3, 3, 2, 2, 2, 3, 2, 3, 1, 0\}$ for the diagonal -45 degrees directions.

We adress specifically this NP-Complete [10] problem:
RECONSTRUCT: Given $m, n \in N$, 4 vectors $H = (h_1, h_2, ..., h_m)$, $V = (v_1, v_2, ..., v_n)$, $S = (s_1, s_2, ..., s_{m+n-1})$ and $T = (t_1, t_2, ..., t_{m+n-1})$, is there a pattern $\mathcal{P}$ falling in a $m \times n$ grid such that the horizontal, vertical, diagonal, and antidiagonal projections are respectively H, V, S and T?
We convert this problem into SAT. Every cell $c_{i,j}$ in the grid is represented by a Boolean variable $x_{i,j}$ such that:

$$x_{i,j} = \begin{cases} 1 \text{ if } c_{i,j} \text{ is filled} \\ 0 \text{ if } c_{i,j} \text{ is empty} \end{cases}$$

An instance $\mathcal{R}(n,m,H,V,S,T)$ of **RECONSTRUCT** is then encoded into a SAT instance $\mathcal{F}(n,m,H,V,S,T)$ that is the conjunction of cardinality constraints in every direction. Namely, $\mathcal{F} = \mathcal{H}(n,m,H) \wedge \mathcal{V}(n,m,V) \wedge S(n,m,S) \wedge \mathcal{T}(n,m,T)$ where:

$$\mathcal{H}(n,m,H) = \bigwedge_{i=1..n} \Psi(\{x_{i,j}, j = 1..m\}, h_i, h_i)$$

$$\mathcal{V}(n,m,V) = \bigwedge_{j=1..m} \Psi(\{x_{i,j}, i = 1..n\}, v_j, v_j)$$

$$S(n,m,S) = \bigwedge_{k=1..m+n-1} \Psi(\{x_{i,j}, i+j = k+1\}, s_k, s_k)$$

$$\mathcal{T}(n,m,T) = \bigwedge_{k=1..m+n-1} \Psi(\{x_{i,j}, m+i-j = k+1\}, t_k, t_k)$$

In order to test the efficiency of encoding this problem into CNF formula, we have used two types of instances, randomly generated instances and hand-crafted instances. The latter are obtained by drawing a pattern as done for Figure 1 and computing the projections in each direction in order to get an instance of **RECONSTRUCT**. Note that by solving the instance obtained, we do not necessarily get the pattern used to generate it. The uniqueness of the the pattern corresponding to some projections can be obtained by augmenting their number, but this is not the purpose of this work. We have also used test instances generated by randomly filling every cell with a prescribed probability p. Not surprisingly, some of our experiments not reported here have shown that the most difficult instances to reconstruct were the instances built using a probability $p = 0.5$.

The few experimental results presented in this section meet two aims. First, verify that the CNF encoding can be competitive with a commercial constraint programming system for solving hand-crafted instances of the discrete tomography problem. Second, address the *scalability* of the CNF encoding on the discrete tomography problem. To this end, we compare the efficiency of solving it with the CNF encoding against the efficiency of solving it using a dedicated solver. All experiments concerning the CNF encoding were done with the "state of the art" SAT solver zchaff [15].

CNF Encoding versus CHIP. This comparison is based on two series of instances derived from the hand-crafted images shown figure 2. Each instance of size $n \times n$ consists of the n first lines and the n first columns of the related image.

Two solving methods are compared for each instance: CHIP V5 [5], the commercial constraint programming system from COSYTEC, and zchaff. The cardinality constraints were translated into the CHIP language by using the ChipAmong constraint [2]. The default heuristic of CHIP was used. Table 1 gives the run times required for solving each instance on a SUN workstation clocked at 450 MHz.

Clearly, thanks to the proposed CNF encoding of the cardinality constraints, our test instances can be solved with zchaff in the same run time as CHIP.

CNF Encoding versus Dedicated Solver. The preceding results show that our CNF encoding of cardinality constraints allows zchaff to outperform the general integer constraint programming system CHIP on some instances of the discrete tomography problem, but these results are restricted to a few test instances. In addition, CHIP is not specialized in solving cardinality constraints over Boolean variables.

Fig. 2. The two patterns: mouse and letters, used in the comparison of CNF encoding plus zchaff versus CHIP.

In order to give an idea of the scalability of the proposed encoding scheme, we will now compare it with a solver dedicated to the discrete tomography problem. To this end, we developed an enumerative solver that maintains generalized arc consistency at each node in the search tree and uses the following heuristic to select the branching variable and value:

For each projection, let P be the number of 1 not yet assigned, V be the number of 0 not yet assigned and U be the number of free variables. Of course $U = V + P$. The weight $w_1(v)w_2(v)$ is assigned to each variable v, where

 - $w_1(v)$ is the sum of the $e^{(P/U)}$ for the four projections related to v,
 - $w_2(v)$ is the sum of the $e^{(V/U)}$ for the four projections related to v.

Table 1. CPU in seconds for solving instances of the discrete tomography problem with CHIP V5 and zchaff.

Instance	CHIP V5	zchaff
mouse-12	0.04	0.09
mouse-14	0.37	0.30
mouse-16	1.60	0.41
mouse-18	2.84	4.45
mouse-20	19.8	35.4
mouse-22	>3600	92.0
letters-12	0.06	0.60
letters-14	1.41	0.66
letters-16	242	66.1
letters-18	>3600	19.8
letters-20	>3600	620

The branching variable v is chosen among those of maximum weight. The first branching value is 1 *iff* $w_2(v) > w_1(v)$.

Figure 2 compares the run times of zchaff and the dedicated solver on a PC running at 2 GHz, for randomly generated instances of the discrete tomography problem. It is not very surprising that the dedicated solver clearly outperforms the association of zchaff and CNF encoding, but, interestingly, the ratio between the two run times does not grow accordingly to the size of the problem. We think that such a result is extremely promising in terms of scalability and tractability of cardinality constraints under CNF encoding.

Table 2. Dedicated solver versus CNF-encoding+zchaff on random patterns (100 instances for each row). The fact that the instances are satisfiable introduces great variations in the ratios. CPU is given in seconds.

Size of the grid	Dedicated solver CPU	Encoding + zchaff CPU	ratio
15×15	0.05	2.7	54
16×16	0.04	10.6	265
17×17	0.07	19	271
18×18	0.11	24	218
19×19	0.15	56	373
20×20	0.33	85	258
21×21	0.27	127	470
22×22	1.42	136	96
23×23	1.8	136	76
24×24	4.1	215	52
25×25	8.6	267	31

4   Parity Learning Instances Revisited

The instances arising from the parity learning problem on 32 bits have been proposed by Crawford [6] for the DIMACS challenge [12]. These instances appeared to be very challenging and none of the algorithms existing at that time were able to solve them. Later, in a paper by Selman & al [18], developing efficient algorithms for these instances is presented as one of the ten challenges in propositional reasoning and search. Following this challenge, two algorithms that solve the par32 instances were published, one by Warners and Van Maaren [20] and the other by Li [14]. The two algorithms do some specific transformations exploiting the special structure of the par32 instances.

In short, we recall only the parity learning problem expression. The reader may refer to [6] for a full and detailed description. We give the sketch of the encoding that we have made for these instances and the experimental results.

Given m sets of subscripts A_i ($1 \le i \le m$) such that $A_i \subseteq \{1, 2, ..., n\}$ and m bits y_1, $y_2,...,y_m$ find n bits, $a_1, a_2, ..., a_n$ such that among the m bits b_i defined as

$$b_i = y_i \oplus a_{k_1} \oplus a_{k_2} \oplus ...$$

where $k_j \in A_i$, at most e are equal to 1.

When $e = 0$ or more generally in the case where all the b_i's are assigned a value, the problem is reduced to find an assignment to an XOR-CNF formula which is known to be polynomial. Even if XOR-SAT is polynomial, a straightforward encoding of the XOR clauses, as it is done in [6], lead to a problem that is difficult for standard SAT solvers. XOR-SAT is polynomial because variable elimination can be done without adding any XOR clause. Indeed, by performing a trivial variable elimination all the a_i's can be eliminated. For example, from $b_i = y_i \oplus a_{k_1} \oplus a_{k_2} \oplus ...$, one can deduce $a_{k_1} = b_i \oplus y_i \oplus a_{k_2} \oplus ...$ and then a_{k_1} can be replaced everywhere by $(b_i \oplus y_i \oplus a_{k_2} \oplus ...)$. When $m > n$ all the a_i's can be eliminated. In general we have $m > n$, which is the case of the most difficult instances of this problem, indeed in [6] m is empirically chosen to be $m = 2n$. We obtain, then, an XOR-CNF formula, formed by the remaining $m - n$ equations, involving only the b_i's subject to the cardinality constraint that at most e of them are equal to 1. We encode then, the XOR-CNF formula using the same method described in [6] and the cardinality constraint using the method of Section 2. We denote the resulting formula by F_C. The n equations giving the a_i's are encoded as usual into a formula F_X.

It is easy to see that given the values of the b_i's, unit propagation on F_X assigns all the a_i's the correct values. Clearly, the satisfiability of the parity learning instance is equivalent to the satisfiability of F_C. The satisfiability of F_C is the hard part. By finding a solution that satisfies F_C, if any, one can derive the correct values of the a_i's by a straightforward unit propagation performed on F_X after assigning to the variables common to F_C and F_X the values they have in this solution.

One may argue that the variable elimination used in the above encoding is partly a solving procedure. An answer this argument is that an analogous preprocessing, simulating this variable elimination done on the XOR equations, can be done by a specific algorithm on the benchmarks as they were encoded by [6]. However while this variable elimination is trivial on the initial problem, discovering it on the encoded formula without knowing the initial problem, is much harder. The algorithm proposed by [20] uses a two phase algorithm as we do by separating the problem into two formulas. However, while they use a sophisticated techniques working on the CNF formulas, we use a trivial method to separate the hard part from the easy one by working directly on the initial problem. This fits with the idea, explained in the introduction, about the importance of not taking the SAT benchmarks as they are but to try to improve their encoding.

We have re-encoded the parity learning instances of the DIMACS benchmark database and we have used, to solve them, a simple Davis and Putnam procedure [8, 7] based on unit propagation and mom's heuristic for variable selection. The results are summarized in table 3, the performances of the basic DP are compared to zchaff and Eqsatz [14]. The latter has been designed for solving these instances. The aim of these experiments is to show that these instances are not intrinsically hard but their apparent hardness comes from their intial encoding.

5   Related Work

The only example of polynomial size CNF encoding of Boolean cardinality constraint that we found in the literature is the one used by Crawford to propositionalize parity

Table 3. The performances of basic DP, Eqsatz and zchaff on the parity learning instances before and after re-encoding them. The performances are given in terms of CPU time in seconds on a Pentium 2Ghz PC under Linux.

Instance of parity learning	Before re encoding			After re encoding		
	Eqsatz	DP	zchaff	Eqsatz	DP	zchaff
par32-1.cnf	308	-	-	42	24	0.9
par32-2.cnf	11	-	-	37	106	205
par32-3.cnf	1241	-	-	2	49	806
par32-4.cnf	190	-	-	60	150	2
par32-5.cnf	2771	-	-	3	1	0.9

learning problem [6]. Like us, Crawford uses a set of clauses that totalizes the number of bits set to 1. But because integers are represented in base two, this totalizer does not allow unit propagation to restore generalized arc consistency.

In fact, encoding constraints into CNF in such a way that unit propagation restores arc-consistency is a very recent research topic. To the best of our knowledge, the first contribution in this field is the paper of Gent [11] on the CNF encoding of binary constraints. The results of Gent are not directly comparable with ours because we do not address the same kind of constraints. It is however interesting to note that, unlike our encoding, Gent's encoding allows unit propagation to restore arc-consistency with an optimal worst case time complexity.

6   Conclusion

In this paper we proposed a new CNF encoding scheme for Boolean cardinality constraints, which allows unit propagation to maintain generalized arc consistency of the encoded constraints. We experimentally showed that, using this encoding method, a SAT solver can address discrete tomography problems and be competitive with a general constraint programming system (Cosytec CHIP), and even with a dedicated solver. We also showed that, associated with a technique of trivial variable elimination, the proposed encoding scheme allows one to drastically improve the efficiency of solving the par32 problem. This problem was hitherto considered as very hard, essentially because of its encoding.

These results confirm that in the area of solving problems under CNF encoding, the encoding scheme is as important as the solver. Then it is very important to define which properties a "good" CNF encoding must verify. The encoding scheme proposed in this paper connects generalized arc consistency in the input problem to unit propagation in the encoded problem. As a research perspective, this could be extended to cardinality constraints on non-binary domains, like the *among* constraint of [2] or the global cardinality constraint of [16].

We think it could be useful to revisit the encoding schemes currently used in the SAT benchmarks and, in a more general way, to propose new tools for efficient CNF encoding of usual global and arithmetic constraints, in the spirit of Gent's work [11] on binary constraints.

References

1. E. BARCUCCI, A. DELLUNGO, M. NIVAT, AND R. PINZANI, *Reconstructing convex polyominoes from horizontal and vertical projections*, Theoret. Comput. Sci., (1996), pp. 321–347.

2. N. BELDICEANU AND E. CONTJEAN, *Introducing global constraints in CHIP*, Mathematical and Computer Modelling, 12 (1994), pp. 97–123.

3. Y. BOUFKHAD, O. DUBOIS, AND M. NIVAT, *Reconstructing (h, v)-convex 2-dimensional patterns of objects from approximate horizontal and vertical projections*, Theoret. Comput. Sci., 290(3) (2003), pp. 1647–1664.

4. S. CHANG, *The reconstruction of binary patterns from their projections*, Comm. ACM, (1971), pp. 21–25.

5. COSYTEC SA, *CHIP C++ Library, Reference Manual, Version 5.4*, October 2001.

6. J. CRAWFORD, *Instances of learning parity function*. http://www.intellektik.informatik.tu-darmstadt.de/SATLIB/Benchmarks/SAT/DIMACS/PARITY/descr.html.

7. M. DAVIS, G. LOGEMANN, AND D. LOVELAND, *A machine program for theorem proving*, Communications of the ACM, 5 (1962), pp. 394–397.

8. M. DAVIS AND H. PUTNAM, *A computing procedure for quantification theory*, Journal of the ACM, 7 (1960), pp. 201–215.

9. A. DELLUNGO, *Polyominoes defined by two vectors*, Theoret. Comput. Sci., 127 (1994), pp. 187–198.

10. R. G. GARDNER, P. GRITZMANN, AND D. PRANGENBERG, *Ont the computational complexity of reconstructing lattice sets from their x-rays*, Discrete Mathematics, (1999), pp. 45–71.

11. I. P. GENT, *Arc consistency in sat*, in Proceedings of the Fifteenth European Conference on Artificial Intelligence (ECAI 2002), 2002.

12. D. JOHNSON AND M. TRICK, eds., *Second DIMACS implementation challenge: cliques, coloring and satisfiability*, vol. 26 of DIMACS Series in Discrete Mathematics and Theoretical Computer Science, American Mathematical Society, 1996.

13. A. KUBA, *The reconstruction of two-directionaly connected binary patterns*, Comput. Graph. Image Process, 27 (1984), pp. 249–265.

14. C. LI, *Integrating equivalency reasoning into davis-putnam procedure*, in AAAI: 17th National Conference on Artificial Intelligence, AAAI / MIT Press, 2000.

15. M. MOSKEWICZ, C. MADIGAN, Y. ZHAO, L. ZHANG, AND S. MALIK, *Chaff: Engineering an efficient sat solver*, in 39th Design Automation Conference, June 2001.

16. J.-C. RÉGIN, *Generalized arc consistency for global cardinality constraint*, in AAAI 96, 1996, pp. 209–215.

17. H. RYSER, *Combinatorial Mathematics*, The Carus Mathematical Monographs, 1963.

18. B. SELMAN, H. A. KAUTZ, AND D. A. MCALLESTER, *Ten challenges in propositional reasoning and search*, in Proceedings of the Fifteenth International Joint Conference on Artificial Intelligence (IJCAI'97), 1997, pp. 50–54.

19. Y. WANG, *Characterization of binary patterns and their projections*, IEEE Trans. Compt., C-24 (1975), pp. 1032–1035.

20. J. WARNERS AND H. VAN MAAREN, *A two phase algorithm for solving a class of hard satisfiability problems*, Op. Res. Lett., 23(3-5) (1999), pp. 81–88.

21. G. WOEGINGER, *The reconstruction of polyominoes from their orthogonal projections*, tech. rep., TU Graz, 1996.

A Two-Stage Hybrid Algorithm
for Pickup and Delivery Vehicle
Routing Problems with Time Windows

Russell Bent and Pascal Van Hentenryck

Brown University, Box 1910 Providence, RI 02912, USA
{rbent,pvh}@cs.brown.edu

Abstract. This paper presents a two-stage hybrid algorithm for pickup and delivery vehicle routing problems with time windows and multiple vehicles (PDPTW). The first stage uses a simple simulated annealing algorithm to decrease the number of routes, while the second stage uses LNS to decrease total travel cost. Experimental results show the effectiveness of the algorithm which has produced many new best solutions on problems with 100, 200, and 600 customers. In particular, it has improved 47% and 76% of the best solutions on the 200 and 600-customer benchmarks, sometimes by as much as 3 vehicles. These results further confirm the benefits of two-stage approaches in vehicle routing. They also answer positively the open issue in the original LNS paper, which advocated the use of LNS for the PDPTW and argue for the robustness of LNS with respect to side-constraints.

1 Introduction

Multiple vehicle routing problems with time windows (VRPTW) have received considerable attention in the last decades. These problems are often approached by meta-heuritics, since problems with as few as 100 customers are currently beyond the scope of state-of-the-art systematic search algorithms. Recent work on the VRPTW has produced significant improvements in solution quality and execution time, often by combining several approaches or heuristics. Comparatively, little research was devoted to pickup and delivery problems with multiple vehicles and time windows (PDPTW) until recently (e.g., [14–16, 21]). Customers in the PDPTW are divided into pickup and delivery pairs. Given such a pair (p, d), a routing must service customers p and d with the same vehicle and must schedule the pickup customer p before the delivery customer d. In standard benchmarks [14], the goal is to minimize the number of used vehicles and, in case of ties, the total travel cost.

The difficulty in pickup and delivery problems, which partly explains why it is less studied than the VRPTW, lies in the side-constraints, which complicate the neighborhoods and invalidate many of the traditional VRPTW moves [18]. However, many practical applications naturally exhibit pickup and delivery constraints in their modeling. This includes dial-a-ride problems, airline scheduling, bus routing, tractor-trailer problems, helicopter support of offshore oil field

F. Rossi (Ed.): CP 2003, LNCS 2833, pp. 123–137, 2003.

platforms, and logistics and maintenance support [16]. *More generally, industrial vehicle routing problems are rarely pure and often feature side-constraints.
Because of its practical relevance and its side-constraints, the PDPTW is a natural model to evaluate the robustness and scalability of various approaches with
respect to side-constraints.*

This paper proposes a two-stage hybrid algorithm for the PDPTW. The
overall structure of the algorithm is motivated by the recognition that minimizing
the objective function directly may not be the most effective way to decrease the
number of routes in vehicle routing problems (e.g., [1, 8]). Indeed, the objective
function often drives the search toward solutions with low travel cost, which may
make it difficult to reach solutions with fewer routes but higher travel cost. To
overcome this limitation, our algorithm divides the search in two steps: (1) the
minimization of the number of routes and (2) the minimization of total travel
cost. This two-step approach makes it possible to design algorithms tailored to
each sub-optimization.

Our algorithm uses two distinct local search procedures to exploit the speci-
ficities of each subproblem. The first step uses a very simple simulated annealing
(SA) algorithm to minimize the number of routes. The SA algorithm only uses
relocation of pairs of customers and one of its key aspects is a lexicographic
evaluation function which minimizes the number of routes (primary criterion),
maximizes the sum of the squares of the route sizes (secondary criterion), and
minimizes travel cost of the routing plan (third criterion). The second criterion
was also used successfully in other applications (e.g., graph coloring [9] and,
more recently, vehicle routing [1]). The second step uses large neighborhood
search (LNS) [19] to minimize total travel cost. It is motivated by our experience that LNS is particularly effective in minimizing total travel cost when
given a solution that minimizes the number of routes, and when the problem is
highly constrained [1]. The use of LNS for pickup and delivery problems was in
fact suggested in the original LNS paper [19], because of its ability to handle
side-constraints gracefully.

Experimental results on difficult PDPTW problems demonstrate the effectiveness of the algorithm. On the standard 100, 200, and 600 customers benchmarks [14], our algorithm produces 2, 25 (47%), and 46 (76%) new best solutions
respectively, while matching or being close to best known solutions on the other
instances. In several 600-customer instances, the algorithm decreases the number of vehicles by as much as 3. These results further confirm the effectiveness
of two-stage approaches in vehicle routing, answers positively the open question
in [19] on the potential of LNS for the PDPTW, and demonstrate the critical
role of the first phase to boost LNS. Similarly, this research confirms that the
structure of LNS makes it relatively easy to incorporate pickup and delivery
constraints in our previous hybrid algorithm [1], validating Shaw's claim on the
robustness of LNS wrt side constraints.

The rest of this paper is organized as follows. Section 2 specifies the PDPTW
and describes the notations. Section 3 gives an overview of the overall algorithm.
Section 4 presents the simulated annealing algorithm, while Section 5 describes

the LNS algorithm for minimizing travel costs. Section 6 presents the experimental results. Section 7 discusses related work and Section 8 concludes the paper.

2   Problem Formulation

This section defines the pickup and delivery vehicle routing problem with time windows (PDPTW) and the various concepts used in this paper.

Customers. The problem is defined in terms of N customers who are represented by the numbers $1, \ldots, N$ and a depot represented by the number 0. The set $\{0, 1, \ldots, N\}$ thus represents all the sites considered in the problem. We use *Customers* to represent the set of customers and *Sites* to represent the set of sites (The distinction between customers and sites simplifies the formalization of the problem and of the algorithm). We use *Customers^p* and *Customers^d* to denote the pickup and delivery customers respectively. The *travel cost* between sites i and j is denoted by c_{ij}. Travel costs satisfy the triangular inequality $c_{ij} + c_{jk} \geq c_{ik}$. The *normalized travel cost* c'_{ij} between sites i and j is defined as

$$c'_{ij} = c_{ij} \ / \ \max_{i,j \in Sites} c_{ij}.$$

Every customer i has a *service time* $s_i \geq 0$. Given a pickup customer i, its delivery counterpart is denoted by $@i$. Every pickup customer has a *demand* $q_i \geq 0$ and its counterpart has demand $q_{@i} = -q_i$.

Vehicles. The PDPTW is defined in terms of m identical vehicles. Each vehicle has a capacity Q.

Routes. A vehicle route, or route for short, starts from the depot, visits a number of customers at most once, and returns to the depot. In other words, a route is a sequence $\langle 0, v_1, \ldots, v_n, 0 \rangle$ or $\langle v_1, \ldots, v_n \rangle$ for short, where all v_i are different. The customers of a route $r = \langle v_1, \ldots, v_n \rangle$, denoted by $cust(r)$, is the set $\{v_1, \ldots, v_n\}$. We also use $route(c)$ to represent the route of customer c. The size of a route, denoted by $|r|$, is the number of customers $|cust(r)|$. The travel cost of a route $r = \langle v_1, \ldots, v_n \rangle$, denoted by $t(r)$, is the cost of visiting all its customers, i.e.,

$$t(r) = c_{0v_1} + c_{v_1 v_2} + \ldots + c_{v_{n-1} v_n} - c_{v_n 0}.$$

if the route is not empty ($n \geq 1$) and is zero otherwise.

Routing Plan. A routing plan is a set of routes $\{r_1, \ldots, r_m\}$ $(m \leq N)$ visiting every customer exactly once, i.e.,

$$\begin{cases} \bigcup_{i=1}^{m} cust(r_i) = Customers \\ cust(r_i) \cap cust(r_j) = \emptyset \ (1 \leq i < j \leq m) \end{cases}$$

Observe that a routing plan assigns a unique successor and predecessor to every customer. These successors and predecessors are sites. The successor and predecessor of customer i in routing plan σ are denoted by $succ(i, \sigma)$ and $pred(i, \sigma)$. For simplicity, our definitions often assume an underlying routing plan σ and we use i^+ and i^- to denote the successor and predecessor of i in σ.

Time Windows. The customers and the depot have time windows. The time window of a site i is specified by an interval $[e_i, l_i]$, where e_i and l_i represent the earliest and latest arrival times respectively. Vehicles must arrive at a site before the end of the time window l_i. They may arrive early but they have to wait until time e_i to begin service. Observe that e_0 represents the time when all vehicles in the routing plan leave the depot and that l_0 represents the time when they must all return to the depot. The *departure time* of customer i, denoted by δ_i, is defined recursively as

$$\begin{cases} \delta_0 = 0 \\ \delta_i = \max(\delta_{i^-} + c_{i^- i}, \ e_i) + s_i \quad (i \in Customers). \end{cases}$$

The earliest service time of customer i, denoted by a_i, is defined as

$$a_i = \max(\delta_{i^-} + c_{i^- i}, \ e_i) \quad (i \in Customers).$$

The earliest arrival time of a route $r = \langle v_1, \ldots, v_n \rangle$, denoted by $a(r)$, is given by $\delta_{v_n} + c_{v_n 0}$ if the route is not empty and is e_0 otherwise. A routing plan satisfies the time window constraint for customer i if $a_i \leq l_i$. A routing plan σ satisfies the time window constraint for the depot if $\forall r \in \sigma : a(r) \leq l_0$.

Capacities. The demand of a route r at customer c, denoted by $q(c)$, is the sum of demands of customers on r up to c, i.e.,

$$q(c) = \sum_{i \in cust(r) \ \& \ \delta_i \leq \delta_c} q_i.$$

The capacity constraint of a customer is satisfied if $q(c) \leq Q$.

Pickup and Deliveries. The pickup and deliveries are represented by *precedence* and *coupling* constraints. The precedence constraint of $c \in Customers^p$ is satisfied if $d_c \leq \delta_{@c}$. Similarly, the coupling constraint of c is satisfied if $route(c) = route(@c)$.

The PDPTW. A solution to the PDPTW is a routing plan $\sigma = \{r_1, \ldots, r_m\}$ satisfying the capacity constraints, time window constraints, and pickup and delivery constraints, i.e.,

$$\begin{cases} q(i) \leq Q & (i \in Customers) \\ a(r_j) \leq l_0 & (1 \leq j \leq m) \\ a_i \leq l_i & (i \in Customers) \\ route(i) = route(@i) & (i \in Customers^p) \\ \delta_i \leq \delta_{@i} & (i \in Customers^p) \end{cases}$$

Function PDPTWOPTIMIZE

1. σ := ROUTEMINIMIZE();
2.   return TRAVELCOSTMINIMIZE(σ);

Fig. 1. The Two-Stage Hybrid Algorithm for Minimizing Routes and Travel Costs.

The size of a routing plan σ, denoted by $|\sigma|$, is the number of non-empty routes in σ, i.e., $\{r \in \sigma \mid cust(r) \neq \emptyset\}$. The PDPTW problem consists of finding a solution σ which minimizes the number of vehicles and, in case of ties, the total travel cost, i.e., a solution σ minimizing the objective function specified by the lexicographic order

$$f(\sigma) = \langle |\sigma|, \sum_{r \in \sigma} t(r) \rangle.$$

3   Overview of the Algorithm

Our algorithm is motivated by the recognition that minimizing the original objective function is not always the most effective way to approach the problem. Indeed, the objective function often drives the search towards solutions with low travel costs. The reduction in the number of routes occurs more as a side-effect of the travel cost minimization than as a primary feature of the search. In addition, focusing on travel cost may make it extremely difficult to reach solutions with fewer routes since it may require considerable degradation of the travel cost component of the objective function. To overcome this limitation, our algorithm separates the optimization into two stages: the minimization of the number of routes and the minimization of travel costs. Each of these two stages is optimized by an algorithm exploiting the underlying structure of the subproblem. (Of course, the second phase may sometimes reduce the number of vehicles as well as a side-effect of reducing travel distance.) The overall algorithm is depicted in Figure 1. The next two sections discuss each suboptimization in detail. Observe that two-stage algorithms has been very successful on the traditional VRPTW, where they have produced many new best solutions recently [1, 8].

4   Minimizing the Number of Routes

The first stage of our algorithm consists of minimizing the number of routes or, equivalently, the number of vehicles used in the routing plan. It uses simulating annealing [11] because of its success in reducing routes on the VRPTW and the overall simplicity of its implementation.

4.1   The Neighborhood

The SA neighborhood is based on a simple pair relocation operator, which is also used in [12, 14, 16]. Given a solution σ, $\mathcal{N}(\sigma)$ denotes the neighborhood of

σ, i.e., the set of feasible solutions that can be reached from σ by using pair relocation, which is defined as follows.

Pair Relocation. For customers i, j, and k, first place i after j, i.e., remove arcs (i^-, i), (i, i^+), (j, j^+) and add arcs (i^-, i^+), (j, i), and (i, j^+). Second, place @i after k, i.e., remove arcs (@i^-, @i), (@i, @i^+), (k, k^+), and add arcs (@i^-, @i^+), $(k, @i)$, and (@$i, k^+)$.

A Random Sub-neighborhood. An interesting feature of our SA algorithm is how it explores the neighborhood. Each iteration focuses on a (random) sub-neighborhood of $\mathcal{N}$ obtained by randomly choosing a customer c from *Customers* and by constructing all the pair relocations using c and @c. The sub-neighborhood is explored exhaustively to determine whether it contains a solution improving the best available routing plan. We denote by $\mathcal{N}(c, \sigma)$ the subset of $\mathcal{N}(\sigma)$ that can be reached by using pair relocation and customers c and @c.

4.2   The Evaluation Function

The evaluation function is another fundamental aspect of our simulated annealing algorithm. As mentioned earlier, the objective function $\langle |\sigma|, \sum_{r \in \sigma} t(r) \rangle$ is not always appropriate, since it may lead the search to solutions with a small travel cost and makes it impossible to remove routes. To overcome this limitation, our simulated algorithm uses a more complex lexicographic ordering

$$e(\sigma) = \langle |\sigma|, -\sum_{r \in \sigma} |r|^2, \sum_{r \in \sigma} t(r) \rangle.$$

especially tailored to minimize the number of routes. The first component is, of course, the number of routes. The second component maximizes $\sum_{r \in \sigma} |r|^2$ which means that it favors solutions containing routes with many customers and routes with few customers over solutions where customers are distributed more evenly among the routes. The intuition is to guide the algorithm into removing customers from some small routes and adding them to larger routes. Components of this type are used on many problems, a typical example being graph coloring [9]. The third component minimizes the travel cost of the routing plan.

4.3   The Simulated Annealing Algorithm

Figure 2 depicts the SA algorithm. The algorithm consists of a number of local searches (lines 2-22), each of which start from the best solution found so far and from the starting temperature. Each local search performs a number of iterations (lines 5-20) and decreases the temperature (line 21). These two steps are repeated until the time limit is exhausted or the temperature has reached its lower bound. Lines 6-19 describe one iteration and are most interesting. Lines 6-8 compute the sub-neighborhood

$$\mathcal{N}(c, \sigma) = \langle \sigma_1, \ldots, \sigma_s \rangle \text{ where } e(\sigma_i) \leq e(\sigma_j) \ (i < j)$$

Function RouteMinimize

```
1.    σ_b := GetInitialSolution();
2.    while (time < timeLimit) {
3.        σ := σ_b;
4.        t := startingTemperature;
5.        while (time < timeLimit & t > temperatureLimit) {
6.            for( i := 1; i ≤ maxIterations; i++) {
7.                c := Random(Customers);
8.                ⟨σ_1,...,σ_s⟩ := N(c,σ) where e(σ_i) ≤ e(σ_j) (i < j);
9.                if e(σ_1) < e(σ_b) then {
10.                   σ_b := σ_1;
11.                   σ := σ_1;
12.               } else {
13.                   r := ⌊random([0,1])^β × s⌋;
14.                   Δ := e(σ) − e(σ_r);
15.                   if Δ ≥ 0 then
16.                       σ := σ_r;
17.                   else if random([0,1]) ≤ e^{Δ/t} then
18.                       σ := σ_r;
19.               }
20.           }
21.           t := α × t;
22.       }
23.   }
24.   return σ_b;
```

Fig. 2. The Simulated Annealing Algorithm to Minimize the Number of Routes.

for a random customer. Lines 9-11 select the solution σ_1 minimizing f in $\mathcal{N}(c,\sigma)$ if it improves the best solution found so far. These lines introduce an aspiration criterion [5] in the simulated annealing algorithm. Lines 13-18 are the core of the algorithm. Line 13 chooses a random element $\sigma_r \in \mathcal{N}(c,\sigma)$ and σ_r is selected as the next routing plan if it does not degrade the current solution (line 15) or with the traditional probability of simulated annealing otherwise (line 17). Observe also line 13 which biases the search towards "good" moves in $\mathcal{N}(c,\sigma)$ when $\beta > 1$.

5   Minimizing the Travel Cost

Our algorithm uses large neighborhood search (LNS) to minimize travel cost. LNS was proposed in [19] for the VRPTW, where it was shown particularly effective on the class 1 problems from the Solomon benchmarks, producing several improvements over the then best published solutions. However, the algorithm performed poorly on the class 2 benchmarks where it could not reduce the number of routes satisfactorily [19] (Our own experimental results confirm the findings of [19] on pickup and delivery problems). By separating the overall optimization in two stages, our algorithm directly addresses this LNS weakness and exploits its strength in minimizing travel cost. The rest of this section describes the LNS algorithm in detail. In general, the algorithm adapts the heuristics and strategies described in [19], although it departs on a number of issues which are critical to scale LNS to large-scale problems.

The Neighborhood and the Evaluation Function. Given a solution σ, the neighborhood of LNS, denoted by $\mathcal{N}_R(\sigma)$, is the set of solutions that can be reached from σ by relocating at most p pairs of customers (where p is a parameter of the implementation). Since LNS also uses subneighborhoods and explores them in a specific order, we use additional notations. In particular, $\mathcal{N}_R(\sigma, S)$ denotes the set of solutions that can be reached from σ by relocating the customers in S. Also, given a partial solution σ with customers $Customers \setminus S$, $\mathcal{N}_I(\sigma, S)$ denotes the solutions that can be obtained by inserting the customers S in σ. Finally, LNS uses the original objective function, which involves the number of routes. This is important since, in some cases, minimizing travel costs makes it possible to decrease the number of routes further.

The Algorithm. At a high level, the LNS algorithm can be seen as a local search where each iteration selects a neighbor σ_c in $\mathcal{N}_R(\sigma_b)$ and accepts the move if $f(\sigma_c) < f(\sigma_b)$. It can be formalized as follows:

```
for(i := 1; i ≤ maxIterations; i++) {
    SELECT  σ_c ∈ N_R(σ_b);
    if  f(σ_c) < f(σ_b) then
        σ_b := σ_c;
}
```

In practice, it is important to refine and extend the above algorithm in three ways. The first modification consists of exploring the neighborhood by increasing number of allowed relocations. The second change generalizes the algorithm to a sequence of local searches. The third modification consists of exploring the subneighborhood $\mathcal{N}_R(\sigma_b, S)$ more exhaustively to find its best solution. The overall algorithm is depicted in Figure 3. Observe line 2 which adds another loop, line 4 which selects a set of customers S of size $2n$, line 5 which selects a best neighbor in $\mathcal{N}_R(\sigma_b, S)$, and line 8 which reinitializes the number of allowed iterations. In fact, the algorithm is now very close to variable neighborhood search [6]. It remains to describe how to select customers and how to implement line 5 in the above algorithm.

Selecting Customers to Relocate. The LNS algorithm adapts the traditional customer selection [19] to the PDPTW. The implementation is depicted in Figure 4. It first selects a customer pair randomly (lines 1-2) and iterates lines 4-7 to remove the $n - 1$ remaining customer pairs. Each such iteration selects a pickup customer from S (the already selected customers) and ranks the remaining pickup customers according to a relatedness criterion (lines 4-5). The new

Function TRAVELCOSTMINIMIZE(σ_b)

```
1.    for(l := 1;l ≤ maxSearches;  l++)
2.      for(n := 1;n ≤ p;  n++)
3.        for(i := 1;i ≤ maxIterations;  i++) {
4.          S := SELECTCUSTOMERS(σ_b,n);
5.          SELECT σ_c ∈ N_R(σ_b,S) SUCH THAT f(σ_c) = min_{σ∈N_R(σ_b,S)} f(σ);
6.          if f(σ_c) < f(σ_b) then {
7.            σ_b := σ_c;
8.            i := 1;
9.          }
```

Fig. 3. The LNS Algorithm to Minimize Travel Cost.

Function SELECTCUSTOMERS(σ, n)

```
1.    c := { RANDOM(Customers^P) };
2.    S := {c,@c};
3.    for(i := 2;i ≤ n;  i++) {
4.      c := RANDOM(S ∩ Customers^P);
5.      ⟨c_0,...,c_{N/2 -i}⟩ := Customers^P \ S SUCH THAT
                          relateness(c,c_i) ≥ relateness(c,c_j)  (i ≤ j);
6.      r := ⌊random([0,1])^β × |Customers^P \ S|⌋;
7.      S := S ∪ {c_r,@c_r};
8.    }
```

Fig. 4. Selecting Customers in the LNS Algorithm.

customer to insert is randomly selected in line 6 and, once again, the algorithm biases the selection toward related neighbors. The relatedness measure is defined as in [19]:

$$relateness(i,j) = \frac{1}{c'_{ij} + v_{ij}}$$

where $v_{ij} = 1$ if $route(i) \neq route(j)$ and is zero otherwise.

The Exploration Algorithm. Our LNS algorithm uses a branch and bound algorithm to explore the selected sub-neighborhood. The algorithm is depicted in Figure 5. If the set of customers to insert is empty, the algorithm checks whether the current solution improves the best solution found so far. Otherwise, it selects the customer pair whose best insertion degrades the objective function the most. The algorithm then explores all the partial solutions obtained by inserting c and @c by increasing order of their travel costs. Also, observe that only the partial solutions whose lower bounds are better than the best solution found so far are explored by the algorithm. The lower bound satisfies the inequality $Bound(\sigma, S) \leq \min_{\sigma' \in N_I(\sigma,S)} f(\sigma')$.

```
Function LDSEXPLORE(σc,S,σb,d,dmax)
```

```
1.    if d ≤ dmax then {
2         if S = ∅ then {
3.            if f(σc) < f(σb) then σb := σc;
4.        } else {
5.            c := arg-maxc∈S minσ∈NI(σ,{c,@c}) f(σ);
6.            Sc := S \ {c, @c};
7.            ⟨σ0,...,σk⟩ := NI(σ,{c, @c}) WHERE f(σi) ≤ f(σj) (i ≤ j);
8.            for(i := 1; i ≤ k; i++) {
9.                if Bound(σi, Sc) < f(σb) then {
10.                   LDSEXPLORE(σi, Sc, σb, d, dmax);
11.                   d := d + 1;
12.               }
13.           }
14.       }
15. }
```

Fig. 5. The Branch and Bound Algorithm with a Limited Discrepancy Strategy.

The bounding function is the cost of a minimum spanning k-tree [4] on the insertion graph with the depot as distinguished vertex, generalizing the well-known 1-tree bound of the traveling salesman problem. The insertion graph vertices are the customers. Given a solution σ over customers $C = \cup_{r \in \sigma} cust(r)$ and a set S of vertices to insert, the insertion graph edges come from three different sets:

1. the edges already in σ;
2. all the edges between customers in S;
3. all the feasible edges connecting a customer from C and a customer from S.

For large-scale problems, finding the best reinsertion is too time-consuming. Our algorithm uses limited discrepancy search (LDS) [7] to explore only a small part of the search tree. More precisely, it only uses one LDS phase which allows up to d discrepancies. Note that the tree is not binary and the heuristic selects the insertion points by increasing lower bounds.

Observe also that the neighborhood $N_I(\sigma, \{c, @c\})$ is of size $O(N^2)$. On large-scale problems or on problems with wide time windows, the computation cost of maintaining this neighborhood during branching can become quite expensive. To overcome this difficulty, our algorithm only maintains the y best feasible insertion points found initially (where y is an implementation parameter). This approximation is critical to scale LNS to large-scale problems.

6   Experimental Results

This section reports preliminary experimental results on the algorithm. All results are given on a 1.2Ghz AMD Athlon Thunderbird K7 processor running

Table 1. 100 Customers.

	Best			SA/LNS				Best			SA/LNS		
	V	TD	Pub	V	TD	Time		V	TD	Pub	V	TD	Time
lc101	10	828.937	LL	10	828.937	0.00	lc201	3	591.557	LL	3	591.557	0.00
lc102	10	828.937	LL	10	828.937	0.00	lc202	3	591.557	LL	3	591.557	0.00
lc103	9	1082.35	SAM	9	**1035.35**	0.02	lc203	3	585.564	LL	3	591.173	0.00
lc104	9	860.011	SAM	9	860.011	0.33	lc204	3	590.599	SAM	3	590.599	4.47
lc105	10	828.937	LL	10	828.937	0.00	lc205	3	588.876	LL	3	588.876	0.00
lc106	10	828.937	LL	10	828.937	0.00	lc206	3	588.493	LL	3	588.493	0.00
lc107	10	828.937	LL	10	828.937	0.01	lc207	3	588.286	LL	3	588.286	0.00
lc108	10	826.439	LL	10	826.439	0.00	lc208	3	588.324	LL	3	588.324	0.00
lc109	9	1027.60	SAM	9	**1000.6**	42.57							
lr101	19	1650.80	LL	19	1650.80	0.00	lr201	4	1253.23	SAM	4	1253.23	0.01
lr102	17	1487.57	LL	17	1487.57	0.01	lr202	3	1197.67	LL	3	1197.67	0.01
lr103	13	1292.68	LL	13	1292.68	0.01	lr203	3	949.396	LL	3	949.396	0.13
lr104	9	1013.39	LL	9	1013.39	0.00	lr204	2	849.05	LL	2	849.05	0.53
lr105	14	1377.11	SAM	14	1377.11	0.00	lr205	3	1054.02	LL	3	1054.02	0.01
lr106	12	1252.62	LL	12	1252.62	0.00	lr206	3	931.625	LL	3	931.625	0.78
lr107	10	1111.31	LL	10	1111.31	0.00	lr207	2	903.053	LL	2	903.056	0.01
lr108	9	968.966	LL	9	968.966	0.00	lr208	2	734.843	LL	2	734.848	0.01
lr109	11	1208.96	SAM	11	1208.96	0.00	lr209	3	930.583	SAM	3	930.586	12.97
lr110	10	1159.35	LL	10	1159.35	0.00	lr210	3	964.224	LL	3	964.224	0.04
lr111	10	1108.90	LL	10	1108.9	0.00	lr211	2	884.294	LL	2	913.837	1.23
lr112	9	1003.77	LL	9	1003.77	0.00							
lrc101	14	1708.70	SAM	14	1708.70	0.00	lrc201	4	1406.94	SAM	4	1406.94	0.14
lrc102	12	1558.07	SAM	12	1558.07	0.00	lrc202	3	1374.27	LL	3	1374.27	0.01
lrc103	11	1258.74	LL	11	1258.74	0.00	lrc203	3	1089.07	LL	3	1089.07	0.01
lrc104	10	1128.40	SAM	10	1128.40	0.01	lrc204	3	818.67	SAM	3	818.663	0.18
lrc105	13	1637.62	SAM	13	1637.62	0.00	lrc205	4	1302.20	LL	4	1302.20	0.05
lrc106	11	1424.73	SAM	11	1424.73	0.00	lrc206	3	1159.03	SAM	3	1159.03	0.01
lrc107	11	1230.14	SAM	11	1230.14	0.00	lrc207	3	1062.05	SAM	3	1062.05	0.05
lrc108	10	1147.43	SAM	10	1147.43	0.00	lrc208	3	852.753	LL	3	852.758	0.11

Linux, using g++ with the -O flag, and double precision floating-point numbers. The results are rounded to six significant digits. Our experimental results use the standard PDPTW benchmarks available at

http://www.sintef.no/static/am/opti/projects/top/vrp/benchmarks.html

See [14] for their descriptions. For prior results, we use the abbreviations LL=[14] and SAM=[21].

Our algorithm was run with a fixed configuration on all benchmarks, which is necessarily suboptimal, in order to demonstrate the robustness of the algorithm across many different problems. Simulated annealing was allowed to run for 5 minutes, with initial temperature of 2000, cooling factor of 0.95, 2500 iterations per temperature, a minimum temperature of 0.01, and $\beta = 10$. LNS was run with a maximum customer pairs removed of 18, 500 attempts for each removal size, 15 as the relatedness determinism, 3 discrepancies, and 15 initial insertion points maintained for each pair removed. LNS is allowed 60 minutes to find a solution (90 minutes for the 600-customer benchmarks) although, in practice, it finds the best solution much quicker in many cases.

Tables 1, 2, and 3 report the experimental results for 100, 200, and 600 customers. The tables compare our algorithm with the best known solutions on these standard benchmarks. For each benchmark, we give the number of vehicles and the travel cost of the best known solution, as well as the best solutions found by our algorithm among 5 runs (10 for the 600-customer instances). We also

Table 2. 200 Customers.

	Best			SA/LNS				Best			SA/LNS		
	V	TD	Pub	V	TD	Time		V	TD	Pub	V	TD	Time
lc1_2_1	20	2704.57	LL	20	2704.57	0.00	lc2_2_1	6	1931.44	SAM	6	1931.44	0.00
lc1_2_2	19	2764.56	LL	19	2764.56	0.05	lc2_2_2	6	1881.40	SAM	6	1881.40	0.09
lc1_2_3	18	2772.18	SAM	**17**	**3134.08**	26.78	lc2_2_3	6	1845.54	SAM	**6**	**1844.33**	2.05
lc1_2_4	17	2708.90	SAM	**17**	**2693.41**	14.29	lc2_2_4	6	1767.12	SAM	6	1778.54	5.63
lc1_2_5	20	2702.05	LL	20	2702.05	0.00	lc2_2_5	6	1891.21	LL	6	1891.21	0.00
lc1_2_6	20	2701.04	LL	20	2701.04	0.00	lc2_2_6	6	1857.78	SAM	6	1857.78	0.05
lc1_2_7	20	2701.04	LL	20	2701.04	0.05	lc2_2_7	6	1850.13	SAM	6	1850.13	0.01
lc1_2_8	20	2689.83	SAM	20	2689.83	0.09	lc2_2_8	6	1824.34	LL	6	1824.34	3.87
lc1_2_9	18	2724.24	LL	18	2724.24	0.36	lc2_2_9	6	1854.21	SAM	6	1854.21	1.32
lc1_2_10	18	2741.56	LL	18	2741.56	1.00	lc2_2_10	6	1817.45	SAM	6	1817.45	0.27
lr1_2_1	20	4819.12	SAM	20	4819.12	2.07	lr2_2_1	5	4073.10	SAM	5	4073.10	1.58
lr1_2_2	18	4228.21	SAM	**17**	**4666.09**	1.86	lr2_2_2	4	3796.16	LL	**4**	**3796.00**	7.36
lr1_2_3	15	3761.52	LL	**15**	**3657.19**	3.53	lr2_2_3	4	3100.03	SAM	4	3100.38	46.49
lr1_2_4	11	2968.57	SAM	**10**	**3146.06**	21.41	lr2_2_4	3	2754.96	SAM	3	2956.15	30.14
lr1_2_5	17	4331.14	SAM	**16**	**4760.18**	5.22	lr2_2_5	4	3438.39	SAM	4	3438.39	2.46
lr1_2_6	15	4068.74	SAM	**14**	**4175.16**	2.03	lr2_2_6	4	3201.54	SAM	4	3208.53	16.74
lr1_2_7	13	3190.75	SAM	**12**	**3851.36**	7.12	lr2_2_7	3	3190.75	LL	3	3337.28	41.52
lr1_2_8	10	2718.23	SAM	**9**	**2871.67**	41.18	lr2_2_8	3	2295.44	SAM	3	2407.66	39.59
lr1_2_9	15	4224.35	SAM	**14**	**4411.54**	37.14	lr2_2_9	4	3198.44	SAM	4	3198.44	1.59
lr1_2_10	12	3654.80	LL	**11**	**3744.95**	4.70	lr2_2_10	3	3447.42	SAM	3	3478.67	44.10
lrc1_2_1	19	3606.06	SAM	19	3606.06	0.06	lrc2_2_1	7	2997.06	SAM	**6**	**3690.10**	10.80
lrc1_2_2	16	3621.30	SAM	**15**	**3681.36**	47.48	lrc2_2_2	6	2674.16	SAM	**6**	**2666.01**	0.41
lrc1_2_3	14	3255.33	SAM	**13**	**3161.75**	27.06	lrc2_2_3	5	2620.85	SAM	**5**	**2523.59**	53.78
lrc1_2_4	10	2890.02	SAM	**10**	**2655.27**	10.67	lrc2_2_4	4	2202.89	SAM	4	2795.7	4.94
lrc1_2_5	16	3750.52	SAM	**16**	**3715.81**	2.20	lrc2_2_5	5	2785.75	SAM	**5**	**2776.93**	2.86
lrc1_2_6	17	3368.66	SAM	17	3368.66	0.97	lrc2_2_6	5	2707.75	SAM	5	2707.96	2.51
lrc1_2_7	16	3326.18	SAM	**15**	**3417.16**	17.17	lrc2_2_7	5	2546.77	SAM	**4**	**3050.03**	16.67
lrc1_2_8	14	3164.50	LL	**14**	**3087.62**	14.99	lrc2_2_8	4	2442.04	SAM	**4**	**2401.84**	40.99
lrc1_2_9	15	3100.88	SAM	**14**	**3129.65**	20.97	lrc2_2_9	4	2209.94	SAM	4	2750.30	23.75
lrc1_2_10	13	2884.71	SAM	**13**	**2833.85**	56.06	lrc2_2_10	4	2059.16	SAM	**3**	**2699.55**	31.46

report the time in minutes taken by LNS to the best solution (the simulating annealing time being fixed). Bold-face entries indicate improvement over the best known solution.

The tables indicate that our algorithm produces very high-quality solutions across the board. For 100 customers, it produces two new best solutions and matches 54 (93%). For 200 customers, it improves 28 (47%) best solutions and matches 24 (40%). For 600 customers, it produces 46 new solutions (77%), while matching 5 more (8%). Since previous work does not report computation times, it is impossible to make comparisons. Most 100-customer instances are solved quickly, spending little time in LNS in almost all instances. On the 200-customer instances, the variation in running time is much larger and can range from a few seconds to almost an hour. The 600-customer instances spend significant amounts of time in LNS. Note that these times are comparable to those of our state-of-the-art VRPTW algorithm [1].

In summary, these preliminary results are extremely encouraging and demonstrate that the approach produces very high-quality results in reasonable times.

7   Discussion and Related Work

This paper originated as an attempt to generalize our hybrid algorithm for the VRPTW to pickup and delivery problems. *The hope was to validate the claim in*

Table 3. 600 Customers.

	Best			SA/LNS				Best			SA/LNS		
	V	TD	Pub	V	TD	Time		V	TD	Pub	V	TD	Time
lc1_6_1	60	14095.6	LL	60	14095.6	0.01	lc2_6_1	19	7977.98	SAM	19	7977.98	0.88
lc1_6_2	59	14164.0	LL	58	14379.5	1.96	lc2_6_2	19	8483.50	SAM	19	8253.67	19.06
lc1_6_3	54	15920.6	SAM	51	14569.3	46.45	lc2_6_3	18	7500.13	SAM	18	7436.50	64.37
lc1_6_4	48	13567.5	SAM	48	13750.6	89.21	lc2_6_4	18	8513.88	LL	18	9479.88	89.99
lc1_6_5	60	14086.3	LL	60	14086.3	0.82	lc2_6_5	19	8596.84	LL	19	8047.37	53.37
lc1_6_6	60	14090.8	LL	60	14090.8	0.51	lc2_6_6	19	8328.40	SAM	19	8237.58	53.36
lc1_6_7	60	14083.8	LL	60	14083.8	0.82	lc2_6_7	19	8704.89	SAM	19	8038.56	48.81
lc1_6_8	59	14670.4	SAM	59	14554.3	11.32	lc2_6_8	18	8147.00	LL	19	7855.38	88.57
lc1_6_9	56	14993.4	LL	55	14648.1	85.44	lc2_6_9	19	8258.20	SAM	19	8304.29	43.55
lc1_6_10	57	15337.7	LL	54	14870.3	59.96	lc2_6_10	18	7963.86	SAM	18	7853.27	55.24
lr1_6_1	59	24149.1	SAM	59	22838.3	53.04	lr2_6_1	12	18842.4	SAM	12	18840.8	23.63
lr1_6_2	46	22854.4	SAM	45	20985.7	55.46	lr2_6_2	11	20243.4	LL	11	22348.2	59.90
lr1_6_3	37	19975.6	LL	37	18685.9	82.16	lr2_6_3	10	17855.1	SAM	10	16657.5	59.69
lr1_6_4	28	14717.3	SAM	28	14199.9	86.05	lr2_6_4	7	14595.6	SAM	7	14223.2	82.71
lr1_6_5	42	21750.6	SAM	40	22188.8	78.88	lr2_6_5	11	15907.5	SAM	10	21250.1	88.26
lr1_6_6	37	20376.7	SAM	35	20406.2	59.73	lr2_6_6	10	19160.3	SAM	9	21722.8	89.44
lr1_6_7	31	16709.3	SAM	28	16963.8	86.42	lr2_6_7	8	16778.0	LL	8	16262.0	59.80
lr1_6_8	21	12978.3	SAM	21	12620.1	88.01	lr2_6_8	8	11671.2	SAM	8	13344.1	38.08
lr1_6_9	37	21821.2	SAM	34	21273.3	88.05	lr2_6_9	10	18791.2	SAM	9	18853.4	58.22
lr1_6_10	30	19120.7	LL	29	18373.9	59.09	lr2_6_10	8	19070.6	SAM	8	18869.2	17.08
lrc1_6_1	54	18251.2	SAM	53	17930.0	24.34	lrc2_6_1	17	13172.6	SAM	17	13111.6	22.16
lrc1_6_2	47	16736.9	SAM	45	16040.3	32.52	lrc2_6_2	15	11537.8	SAM	15	11463.0	55.74
lrc1_6_3	39	15525.2	SAM	36	14407.6	54.82	lrc2_6_3	13	12428.64	SAM	11	15167.3	78.21
lrc1_6_4	27	12138.4	SAM	25	11308.6	89.82	lrc2_6_4	11	8282.80	SAM	8	12512.5	89.42
lrc1_6_5	49	17368.4	SAM	47	16803.9	87.75	lrc2_6_5	15	12401.5	SAM	15	12309.7	46.47
lrc1_6_6	48	17869.8	SAM	45	17126.4	89.60	lrc2_6_6	13	12679.3	SAM	14	12894.1	72.36
lrc1_6_7	42	16020.3	SAM	40	15493.5	59.15	lrc2_6_7	12	12998.4	SAM	12	13851.5	38.01
lrc1_6_8	37	15626.0	LL	36	15352.6	58.93	lrc2_6_8	12	10898.3	SAM	12	11877.8	89.35
lrc1_6_9	37	15342.6	SAM	37	15253.7	71.08	lrc2_6_9	11	11917.2	SAM	11	14810.5	56.60
lrc1_6_10	34	14137.5	SAM	33	13830.5	59.25	lrc2_6_10	10	13165.4	SAM	9	12874.8	73.08

[19] that LNS should handle side-constraints gracefully. The algorithm presented here keeps the two-stage approach of the original algorithm, but it differs in several important ways. First, the SA algorithm was no longer able to use the wealth of moves available for the VRPTW. It is now based on a single move, pair relocation, which is also used in other algorithms for the PDPTW [12, 16]. However, despite its simplicity, the SA algorithm boosts the quality of LNS significantly, since LNS cannot decrease the number of vehicles sufficiently on many benchmarks. The LNS adaptation to the PDPTW was less drastic. The key idea is to select and reinsert pickup and delivery customers in pairs. Additional approximations, i.e., maintaining only a subset of the insertion points, was also necessary to obtain high-quality solutions on large-scale problems and problems with many customers.

Single vehicle pickup and delivery problems were first introduced by [17] in 1980. Small instances of multiple vehicle problems with time windows were introduced and solved optimally in [3]. A good survey of the various models and techniques utilized in early work on pickup and delivery problems can be found in [18]. More recent advances on multiple vehicle problems has focused on meta-heuristics including tabu search and simulated annealing. Tabu search was used in [12, 16] to minimize another objective function, i.e., total schedule duration, in pickup and delivery problems. They use pair relocation as one of their neighborhood operators to move customers between routes. They also introduced pair exchange operators and a single customer relocation within the same route. A tabu search/simulated annealing hybrid was successfully used in [14] to solve the PDPTW. This algorithm was compared in detail in the experimental section. Excellent results were also produced in [21] but the report is not available unfortunately. A squeaky wheel algorithm was also proposed in [15], but it does not seem to be competitive with the two earlier algorithms in solution quality.

8   Conclusion

This paper proposed a two-stage hybrid algorithm for pickup and delivery vehicle routing problems with multiple vehicles and time windows (PDPTW). The algorithm minimizes the number of vehicles using simulated annealing in the first stage, and minimizes travel cost using LNS in the second stage. Experimental results show the effectiveness of the approach which produced many new best solutions on instances with 100, 200, and 600 customers.

More precisely, the results demonstrate that the two-stage approach boosts the solution quality of LNS significantly, that a simple simulated annealing algorithm is excellent in reducing the number of vehicles, and that LNS, with appropriate reductions in its underlying search space, is very effective in optimizing travel cost. The paper also settles positively the open issue in the original LNS paper, which advocated the use of LNS for the PDPTW because of its ability to handle side-constraints gracefully. More generally, these results seem to indicate that a two-step approach, combining SA and LNS, should produce high-quality results for vehicle routing problems with additional side-constraints.

There are many open issues that deserve attention. As research moves to large-scale problems involving several hundreds or thousands of customers, scaling the algorithms raise new interesting challenges that were not systematically studied here. It is indeed unlikely that the same algorithmic configuration would perform effectively on all instances. It would be interesting to study the impact of various decisions on the behaviour of the algorithm and to study how to tune these decisions dynamically during search. It is also clear that a unique algorithm does not exist for all purposes. It would be interesting to study algorithms producing high-quality results for the PDPTW in short times, even if there is some decrease in solution quality and robustness. Finally, it is of great interest to evaluate the approach on complex problems with additional side-constraints. Obviously, progress in that respect will strongly depend on the availability of such complex instances.

Acknowledgments

This work is partly supported by an NDSEG fellowship from (ASEE) and an NSF ITR DMI-0121495 and ACI-0121497 awards.

References

1. Bent, R. and Van Hentenryck, P. A Two-Stage Hybrid Local Search for the Vehicle Routing Problem with Time Windows. *Transportation Science* (to appear).

2. Chiang, W. and Russell, R. Simulated Annealing Metaheuristics for the Vehicle Routing Problem with Time Windows. *Annals of Operations Research*, 63:3–27 (1996).

3. Dumas, Y., Desrosiers, J. and Soumis, F. The Pickup and Delivery Problem with Time Windows *European Journal of Operational Research*, 54:7–22. (1991).

4. Fisher, M., Joernsten, K., and Madsen, O. Vehicle routing with time windows: Two optimization algorithms. *Operations Research*, 45(3):488–492 (1997).

5. Glover, F. Tabu Search. *Orsa Journal of Computing*, 1:190–206 (1989).

6. Hansen, P. and Mladenovic, N. An introduction to variable neighborhood search. In Voss, S., Martello, S., Osman, I. H., and Roucairol, C., editors, *Meta-heuristics, Advances and Trends in Local Search Paradigms for Optimization*, pages 433–458. Kluwer Academic Publishers (1998).

7. Harvey, W. and Ginsberg, M. Limited Discrepancy Search. In *Proceedings of IJCAI-95*, Montreal, Canada (1995).

8. Homberger, J. and Gehring, H. Two Evolutionary Metaheuristics for the Vehicle Routing Problem with Time Windows. *INFOR*, 37:297–318 (1999).

9. Johnson, D., Aragon, C., McGeoch, L., and Schevon, C Optimization by Simulated Annealing: An Experimental Evaluation; Part II, Graph Coloring and Number Partitioning. *Operations Research*, 39(3):378–406 (1991).

10. Kindervater, G. and Savelsbergh, M. Vehicle Routing: Handling Edge Exchanges. In Aarts, E. and Lenstra, J., editors, *Local Search in Combinatorial Optimization*, chapter 10, pages 337–360. John Wiley & Sons Ltd (1997).

11. Kirkpatrick, S., Gelatt, C., and Vecchi, M. Optimization by Simulated Annealing. *Science*, 220:671–680 (1983).

12. Lau, H. and Liang, Z. Pickup and Delivery with Time Windows: Algorithms and Test Case Generations In *Proceedings of the 13th IEEE Conf. on Tools with Artificial Intelligence (ICTAI)*, 333-340 (2001).

13. Lenstra, J. and Rinnooy Kan, A. H. G. Complexity of Vehicle Routing and Scheduling Problems. *Networks*, 11:221–227 (1981).

14. Li, H. and Lim, A. A Metaheuristic for the Pickup and Delivery Problem with Time Windows In *13th IEEE International Conference on Tools with Artificial Intelligence (ICTAI)*, 160–170 (2001).

15. Lim, H., Lim, A., and Rodrigues, B. Solving the Pickup and Delivery Problem with Time Windows Using Squeaky Wheel Optimization with Local Search In *American Conference on Information Systems (AMCIS)*, (2002)

16. Nanry, W. and Barnes, J. Solving the Pickup and Delivery Problem with Time Windows Using Reactive Tabu Search *Transportation Research Part B*, 34:107–121 (2000).

17. Psarafis, H. A Dynamic Programming Solution to the Single Vehicle Many-to-Many Immediate Request Dial-A-Ride Problem *Transportation Science*, 14:130–154 (1980).

18. Savelsbergh, M and Sol, M. The General Pickup and Delivery Problem *Transportation Science*, 29 (1):107–121 (1995).

19. Shaw, P. Using Constraint Programming and Local Search Methods to Solve Vehicle Routing Problems. In *Principles and Practice of Constraint Programming*, pages 417–431 (1998).

20. Solomon, M. Algorithms for the Vehicle Routing and Scheduling Problems with Time Window Constraints. *Operations Research*, 35 (2):254–265 (1987).

21. Unpublished Results SINTEF Applied Mathematics-Department of Optimisation, Technical Report in Progress *http://www.sintef.no/static/am/opti/projects/top/vrp/benchmarks* (2003).

Solving Finite Domain Constraint Hierarchies by Local Consistency and Tree Search*

Stefano Bistarelli[1,2,**], Philippe Codognet[3],
Kin-Chuen Hui[4], and Jimmy Ho Man Lee[4]

[1] Istituto di Informatica e Telematica, CNR, Pisa, Italy
Stefano.Bistarelli@iit.cnr.it
[2] Dipartimento di Scienze
Universitá degli Studi "G. D'annunzio" di Chieti-Pescara, Italy
bista@sci.unich.it
[3] Department of Computer Science
University of Paris 6, France
Philippe.Codognet@lip6.fr
[4] Department of Computer Science and Engineering
The Chinese University of Hong Kong, Hong Kong SAR, China
{kchui,jlee}@cse.cuhk.edu.hk

Abstract. We provide a reformulation of the constraint hierarchies (CHs) framework based on the notion of *error indicators*. Adapting the generalized view of local consistency in semiring-based constraint satisfaction problems (SCSPs), we define *constraint hierarchy k-consistency* (CH-*k*-C) and give a CH-2-C enforcement algorithm. We demonstrate how the CH-2-C algorithm can be seamlessly integrated into the ordinary branch-and-bound algorithm to make it a finite domain CH solver. Experimentation confirms the efficiency and robustness of our proposed solver prototype. Unlike other finite domain CH solvers, our proposed method works for both local and global comparators. In addition, our solver can support arbitrary error functions.

1 Introduction

The Constraint Hierarchy (CH) framework [8] is a general framework for the specification and solutions of over-constrained problems. Originating from research in interactive user-interface applications, the CH framework attracts much effort in the design of efficient solvers in the real number domain [1, 17]. To extend the benefit of the CH framework to also discrete domain applications, such as timetabling and resource allocation, the paper takes a step towards a general and efficient finite domain CH solver, based on consistency techniques and tree search.

Central to the paper is the notion of *constraint hierarchy k-consistency* (CH-*k*-C), defined using error indicators which are structures isomorphic to the structure of a given

---

* We thank the anonymous referees for their constructive comments. The work described in this paper was substantially supported by a grant from the Research Grants Council of the Hong Kong Special Administrative Region (Project no. CUHK4358/02E).

** Part of this research was carried out while the author was visiting the Department of Computer Science and Engineering, The Chinese University of Hong Kong, Hong Kong SAR, China

F. Rossi (Ed.): CP 2003, LNCS 2833, pp. 138–152, 2003.

CH used for storing the error information of the CH problem (similar notion was defined by Bistarelli *et al.* [4]). We give also an algorithm for enforcing CH-2-C of a CH problem. While classical consistency algorithms [19] aim to reduce the size of constraint problems, our CH-2-C algorithm works by explicating error information that is originally implicit in CH problems. We also suggest ways of utilizing such extracted information to help prune non-fruitful computation in a branch-and-bound searching algorithm, which forms the basis of our finite domain CH solver. We have constructed a prototype of the solver, and performed experiments on a set of randomly generated CH problems that confirm the efficiency and robustness of our proposal.

This paper is a revised and extended version of another by the same authors [3].

The rest of the paper is organized as follows. Section 2 provides necessary background definitions. In Section 3, we present an equivalent redefinition of the CH framework using the notion of error indicators and hierarchy problem, which are central in the definition of constraint hierarchy k-consistency and the associated enforcement algorithm in Section 4. In Section 5, we give a constraint hierarchy 2-consistency enforcement algorithm and discuss its complexity. The finite domain CH solver, which has a branch-and-bound backbone, is introduced in Section 6, followed by experimental results in Section 7. Related works are discussed in Section 8 before summarizing the major results and shedding light on possible future direction of research in Section 9.

2   Constraint Hierarchies

Let D be a constraint domain. A *variable* x is an unknown that has an associated *variable domain* $D(x) \subseteq D$, which defines the set of possible values for x. An *n-ary constraint* c is a relation over D^n. A *labeled constraint* c^s is a constraint c with a *strength* $s \in \{0, \ldots, k\}$. The strengths are totally ordered. Constraints with strength $s = 0$ are *required constraints* (or hard constraints) and those with strength $1 \leq s \leq k$ are *non-required constraints* (or soft constraints). The larger the strength, the weaker the constraint is. In addition, each labeled constraint may be associated with a weight w (for use with the global comparators). A *constraint hierarchy* H is a multiset of labeled constraints. The symbol H_i denotes a set of labeled constraints with strength $s = i$. H_0, the *required level*, denotes the set of required constraints which must be satisfied. $H_1, \ldots, H_k$, the *non-required level*, denote the sets of non-required constraints which can be violated but should be satisfied as much as possible. We use an example in Figure 1 to explain CHs in more details. There are three levels in the constraint hierarchy H. There are no required constraints in the required level H_0. However, there are two

$V = \{x, y, z\}$ and $D(x) = D(y) = D(z) = \{1, 2\}$
$H = \{H_0, H_1, H_2, H_3\}$ $H_0 = \emptyset$, $H_1 = \{c_1^1 : x > y, c_2^1 : x = 2\}$, and $H_2 = \{c_1^2 : y = 3, c_2^2 : z < y\}$ $H_3 = \{c_1^3 : z = 1, c_2^3 : x + y + z > 4\}$

Fig. 1. An example of constraint hierarchy.

strong constraints c_1^1 and c_2^1 in H_1, two *medium* constraints c_1^2 and c_2^2 in H_2 and two *weak* constraints c_1^3 and c_2^3 in H_3.

A *valuation* $\theta = \{v_1 \mapsto d_1, \ldots, v_n \mapsto d_n\}$ for a set of variables $\{v_1, \ldots, v_n\}$ assigns to each v_i the value $d_i \in D(v_i)$. Let c be a constraint and θ a valuation. The expression $c\theta$ is the boolean result of applying θ to c. We say that $c\theta$ *holds* if $c\theta$ is *true*. An *error function* $e(c\theta)$ measures how well a constraint c is satisfied by valuation θ. The error function returns non-negative real numbers and must satisfy the property: $e(c\theta) = 0 \Leftrightarrow c\theta$ holds. A *trivial error function* is an error function that gives 0 if $c\theta$ holds and 1 otherwise. The value $e(c\theta)$ returned by an error function is an *error value*. We use $vars(c)$ (or $vars(\theta)$) to denote the set of all variables in constraint c (or valuation θ). The possible valuations for the variables $\{x, y, z\}$ are $\{\theta_1, \theta_2, \theta_3, \theta_4, \theta_5, \theta_6, \theta_7, \theta_8\}$. Figure 2 gives the error values of all valuations in the complete search tree using the trivial error function. The error values of a valuation θ are computed for each constraint $(e(c_1^1\theta), e(c_2^1\theta), e(c_1^2\theta), e(c_2^2\theta), e(c_1^3\theta), e(c_2^3\theta))$. Since, for example, θ_1 satisfies c_1^3 but violates c_1^1, $e(c_1^3\theta_1) = 0$ and $e(c_1^1\theta_1) = 1$ respectively. We can obtain the error values of other valuations similarly. In order to compare values, a number of *comparators* are defined: *locally-better* (l-b), *weighted-sum-better* (w-s-b), *worst-case-better* (w-c-b), and *least-squares-better* (l-s-b). We can use these comparators to define *solutions* of CHs [8].

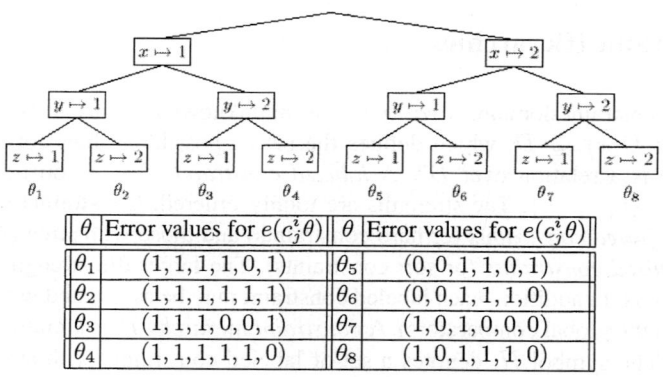

θ	Error values for $e(c_j^i\theta)$	θ	Error values for $e(c_j^i\theta)$
θ_1	$(1,1,1,1,0,1)$	θ_5	$(0,0,1,1,0,1)$
θ_2	$(1,1,1,1,1,1)$	θ_6	$(0,0,1,1,1,0)$
θ_3	$(1,1,1,0,0,1)$	θ_7	$(1,0,1,0,0,0)$
θ_4	$(1,1,1,1,1,0)$	θ_8	$(1,0,1,1,1,0)$

Fig. 2. The possible valuations and their error values.

3   A Reformulation of Constraint Hierarchies

To facilitate subsequent illustration of the CH local consistency concept, we formulate the CH framework [8] (in particular in the definition of comparators and solution set) using error indicators (as defined in [4]).

We denote an error value by ξ, possibly with subscripts. Let $I = \{\xi_1, \ldots, \xi_N\}$ be a poset (partially ordered set), each element ξ_j of which is an *error indicator*. Given a constraint hierarchy $H = \{H_0, \ldots, H_n\}$ where n is the number of non-required levels, and for all $i \in \{0, \ldots, n\}$, $H_i = \{c_1^i, \ldots, c_{k_i}^i\}$ with k_i being the number of constraints in level i. An error indicator ξ_θ of a valuation θ for a set of variables V is a tuple of error values such that $\xi_\theta = \langle\langle\xi_{\theta 1}^0, \ldots, \xi_{\theta k_0}^0\rangle, \ldots, \langle\xi_{\theta 1}^n, \ldots, \xi_{\theta k_n}^n\rangle\rangle$ and

$\forall a \in \{0, \ldots, n\}, \forall b \in \{1, \ldots, k_a\}, \xi_{\theta b}^a = e(c_b^a \theta)$ if $vars(c_b^a) \subset V$ and $\xi_{\theta b}^a = 0$ if $vars(c_b^a) \not\subset V$. Error indicators provide a measure of the "badness" of valuations with respect to H.

To explain the meaning of the error indicator of a valuation, we use the example in Figure 1 with the trivial error function. If $\theta = \{z \mapsto 2\}$, then $\boldsymbol{\xi}_\theta = \langle \langle \rangle, \langle 0, 0 \rangle, \langle 0, 0 \rangle, \langle 1, 0 \rangle \rangle$. If $\theta = \{x \mapsto 1, y \mapsto 2\}$, then $\boldsymbol{\xi}_\theta = \langle \langle \rangle, \langle 1, 1 \rangle, \langle 1, 0 \rangle, \langle 0, 0 \rangle \rangle$. If $\theta = \{x \mapsto 2, z \mapsto 1\}$, then $\boldsymbol{\xi}_\theta = \langle \langle \rangle, \langle 1, 0 \rangle, \langle 1, 0 \rangle, \langle 0, 1 \rangle \rangle$.

The comparator predicate *better* in the original CH formulation is redefined using a *partial order*, denoted by $\prec$. We define $\prec$ to be irreflexive and transitive over I. Hence, it preserves the meaning of *better*. Intuitively, $\boldsymbol{\xi}' \prec \boldsymbol{\xi}''$ means $\boldsymbol{\xi}''$ is "better" than $\boldsymbol{\xi}'$ in I. In general, $\prec$ will not provide a total ordering. For convenience, we define $\preceq$ such that $\forall \boldsymbol{\xi}', \boldsymbol{\xi}'' \in I, \boldsymbol{\xi}' \preceq \boldsymbol{\xi}'' \rightarrow (\boldsymbol{\xi}' \prec \boldsymbol{\xi}'') \vee (\boldsymbol{\xi}' = \boldsymbol{\xi}'')$.

We can redefine *l-b* in the original formulation as a partial order $\prec_{l-b}$ as follows. Given any two valuations θ and σ, and the corresponding error indicators $\boldsymbol{\xi}_\theta$ and $\boldsymbol{\xi}_\sigma$, $\prec_{l-b}$ is defined as:

$$\boldsymbol{\xi}_\theta \prec_{l-b} \boldsymbol{\xi}_\sigma \equiv \exists l > 0 \text{ such that } \forall i \in \{0, \ldots, l-1\},$$
$$\forall j \in \{1, \ldots, k_i\}, \xi_{\theta j}^i = \xi_{\sigma j}^i$$
$$\wedge \exists a \in \{1, \ldots, k_l\}, \xi_{\sigma a}^l < \xi_{\theta a}^l$$
$$\wedge \forall b \in \{1, \ldots, k_l\}, \xi_{\sigma b}^l \leq \xi_{\theta b}^l.$$

The intuitive meaning of $\boldsymbol{\xi}_\theta \prec_{l-b} \boldsymbol{\xi}_\sigma$ is that valuation σ is *locally-better* than valuation θ.

Similarly, we can define *g-b* $\prec_{g-b}$, and its instances *w-s-b* $\prec_{w-s-b}$, *w-c-b* $\prec_{w-c-b}$, and *l-s-b* $\prec_{l-s-b}$ respectively. Given any two valuations θ and σ, and the corresponding error indicators $\boldsymbol{\xi}_\theta$ and $\boldsymbol{\xi}_\sigma$:

$$\boldsymbol{\xi}_\theta \prec_{g-b} \boldsymbol{\xi}_\sigma \equiv \exists l > 0 \text{ such that } \forall i \in \{0, \ldots, l-1\},$$
$$g(\langle \xi_{\theta 1}^i, \ldots, \xi_{\theta k_i}^i \rangle) = g(\langle \xi_{\sigma 1}^i, \ldots, \xi_{\sigma k_i}^i \rangle)$$
$$\wedge g(\langle \xi_{\sigma 1}^l, \ldots, \xi_{\sigma k_l}^l \rangle) < g(\langle \xi_{\theta 1}^l, \ldots, \xi_{\theta k_l}^l \rangle),$$

where g is a *combining function* for error values:

$$\boldsymbol{\xi}_\theta \prec_{w-s-b} \boldsymbol{\xi}_\sigma \equiv \boldsymbol{\xi}_\theta \prec_{g-b} \boldsymbol{\xi}_\sigma, \text{ where } g(\langle \xi_1^i, \ldots, \xi_{k_i}^i \rangle) \equiv \sum_{j \in \{1, \ldots, k_i\}} \xi_j^i,$$
$$\boldsymbol{\xi}_\theta \prec_{w-c-b} \boldsymbol{\xi}_\sigma \equiv \boldsymbol{\xi}_\theta \prec_{g-b} \boldsymbol{\xi}_\sigma, \text{ where } g(\langle \xi_1^i, \ldots, \xi_{k_i}^i \rangle) \equiv \max\{\xi_j^i \mid j \in \{1, \ldots, k_i\}\},$$
$$\boldsymbol{\xi}_\theta \prec_{l-s-b} \boldsymbol{\xi}_\sigma \equiv \boldsymbol{\xi}_\theta \prec_{g-b} \boldsymbol{\xi}_\sigma, \text{ where } g(\langle \xi_1^i, \ldots, \xi_{k_i}^i \rangle) \equiv \sum_{j \in \{1, \ldots, k_i\}} {\xi_j^i}^2.$$

Notice that by definition, all local/global comparators ignore constraints in hierarchy levels greater than or equal to l.

We are now ready to define the solution set S of a CH with variables V by:

$$S_0 = \{\theta \mid vars(\theta) = V, \xi_{\theta i}^0 = 0 \text{ for all } i \in \{1, \ldots, k_0\}\} \text{ and}$$
$$S = \{\theta \in S_0 \mid \forall \sigma \in S_0, \boldsymbol{\xi}_\theta \not\prec \boldsymbol{\xi}_\sigma\}.$$

The following lemma gives the monotonicity of the introduced comparators, which are collectively denoted by $\prec_{better}$ and $\preceq_{better}$ in the rest of the paper.

Lemma 1. *Given any two error indicators ξ' and ξ''. If for all a, b we have $\xi''^a_b \leq \xi'^a_b$, then $\xi' \preceq_{better} \xi''$.*

Notice that the above lemma lets us compare valuation for both local and global comparators (because the $\preceq_{better}$ order implies all the orders induced from any specific comparator) and for arbitrary error functions.

We also introduce the notion of a *hierarchy problem* which is a CH augmented with error information.

Definition 1 (Hierarchy Problem and Error Indicator Store). *A hierarchy problem $P = \langle H, I_H \rangle$ is a constraint problem, where H is a CH with variables V and I_H is a set containing error indicator stores $\xi_{x=d}$ for all variables $x \in V$ and for all $d \in D(x)$. Each $\xi_{x=d}$ is used for keeping an estimate (a lower bound) of the errors of valuations involving $\{x \mapsto d\}$.*

Definition 2 (Solution of a Hierarchy Problem). *A valuation θ is a solution of $P = \langle H, I_H \rangle$ if (1) θ is a solution of H and (2) $\xi_\theta \preceq_{better} \xi_{x=d}$ for all $\xi_{x=d} \in I_H$.*

In other words, solutions of $P = \langle H, I_H \rangle$ are solutions of H which have a "worse" error than the estimates provided in I_H. By the definition, the solutions of H always contain those of $\langle H, I_H \rangle$. Equality holds when the error estimates provided in I_H fails to "filter" out any solutions of H.

Theorem 1. *Consider a CH H and the associated hierarchy problem $P = \langle H, I_H \rangle$, and denote the solution sets of H and P by S_H and S_P respectively.*
  - *$S_P \subseteq S_H$, and*
  - *$S_P = S_H$ if $\xi_\theta \preceq_{better} \xi_{x=d}$ for all $(x \mapsto d) \in \theta$ and $\theta \in S_H$.*

In particular, a hierarchy problem $\langle H, I_H \rangle$ must share the same solution as H if all $\xi_{x=d} \in I_H$ contain only the error value 0 (*i.e.* no error information). This fact is useful in ensuring the correctness of our local consistency algorithm and the completeness of our branch-and-bound solver later.

4   Local Consistency in CHs

The classical notion of *local consistency* [19] characterizes when a constraint problem contains non-fruitful values. The main purpose of detecting local inconsistency is thus to remove the inconsistent values from the variable domains and constraints. Hence, the problem is "simpler" to solve when the problem is smaller. However, we adopt a more general notion of local consistency used for SCSP: *"Applying a local consistency algorithm to a constraint problem means explicitating some implicit constraints, thus possibly discovering inconsistency at a local level"* [5]. We adapt this general notion for CH, and define *constraint hierarchy k-consistency* (CH-k-C).

Before defining CH-k-C, we need two operations, $\mathcal{MAX}$ and $\mathcal{MIN}$, on error indicators. Given a CH H with n non-required levels and any two error indicators, $\xi_\theta, \xi_\sigma \in I$, for H. $\mathcal{MAX}(\xi_\theta, \xi_\sigma)$ is defined as

$$\langle\langle max(\xi_{\theta 1}^0, \xi_{\sigma 1}^0), \ldots, max(\xi_{\theta k_0}^0, \xi_{\sigma k_0}^0)\rangle, \ldots, \langle max(\xi_{\theta 1}^n, \xi_{\sigma 1}^n), \ldots, max(\xi_{\theta k_n}^n, \xi_{\sigma k_n}^n)\rangle\rangle$$

and $\mathcal{MIN}(\xi_\theta, \xi_\sigma)$ is

$$\langle\langle min(\xi_{\theta 1}^0, \xi_{\sigma 1}^0), \dots, min(\xi_{\theta k_0}^0, \xi_{\sigma k_0}^0)\rangle, \dots, \langle min(\xi_{\theta 1}^n, \xi_{\sigma 1}^n), \dots, min(\xi_{\theta k_n}^n, \xi_{\sigma k_n}^n)\rangle\rangle$$

where k_i is the number of constraints in level i of H.

Given two error indicators, $\mathcal{MIN}$ (or $\mathcal{MAX}$) combines the two indicators by taking the best (or the worst). Obviously $\mathcal{MAX}$ and $\mathcal{MIN}$ are commutative and associative. Thus, it makes sense to write $\mathcal{MAX}\{\xi_1, \dots, \xi_K\}$ and $\mathcal{MIN}\{\xi_1, \dots, \xi_K\})$ for any $K > 2$.

Given a CH H with variables V. If $x \in V$ and $d \in D(x)$, we define

$$approx_k(x \mapsto d) =$$
$$\mathcal{MAX}\{\mathcal{MIN}\{\xi_\theta \mid vars(\theta) = \{x\} \cup U, (x \mapsto d) \in \theta\} \mid U \subset V, |U| = k - 1\}$$

for any $1 \leq k \leq |V|$. We call it k-approximation, which provides an estimate of the "badness" of valuations involving the assignment $x \mapsto d$ for all m-ary constraints involving x with $m \leq k$. Since the error indicators of all valuations involving $x \mapsto d$ might not be comparable, we can only give an approximation, and $approx_{|V|}(x \mapsto d)$ gives an error estimate involving all constraints in the problem. However, calculating $approx_{|V|}(x \mapsto d)$ is computationally expensive, and $approx_k(x \mapsto d)$ for some small $k < |V|$ gives a more practical approximation.

Referring to the same example in Section 2,

$$approx_2(y \mapsto 2)$$
$$= \mathcal{MAX}\{\mathcal{MIN}\{\xi_{\{x \mapsto 1, y \mapsto 2\}}, \xi_{\{x \mapsto 2, y \mapsto 2\}}\},$$
$$\mathcal{MIN}\{\xi_{\{y \mapsto 2, z \mapsto 1\}}, \xi_{\{y \mapsto 2, z \mapsto 2\}}\}\}$$
$$= \mathcal{MAX}\{\mathcal{MIN}\{\langle\langle\rangle, \langle 1, 1\rangle, \langle 1, 0\rangle, \langle 0, 0\rangle\rangle, \langle\langle\rangle, \langle 1, 0\rangle, \langle 1, 0\rangle, \langle 0, 0\rangle\rangle\},$$
$$\mathcal{MIN}\{\langle\langle\rangle, \langle 0, 0\rangle, \langle 1, 0\rangle, \langle 0, 0\rangle\rangle, \langle\langle\rangle, \langle 0, 0\rangle, \langle 1, 1\rangle, \langle 1, 0\rangle\rangle\}\}$$
$$= \mathcal{MAX}\{\langle\langle\rangle, \langle 1, 0\rangle, \langle 1, 0\rangle, \langle 0, 0\rangle\rangle, \langle\langle\rangle, \langle 0, 0\rangle, \langle 1, 0\rangle, \langle 0, 0\rangle\rangle\}$$
$$= \langle\langle\rangle, \langle 1, 0\rangle, \langle 1, 0\rangle, \langle 0, 0\rangle\rangle$$

The following theorem states that $approx_k(x \mapsto d)$ is monotonically decreasing in k.

Theorem 2. *If H is a CH with variables V, $x \in V$ and $d \in D(x)$, then $approx_{k_2}(x \mapsto d) \preceq_{better} approx_{k_1}(x \mapsto d), \forall 1 \leq k_1 \leq k_2 \leq |V|$.*

By using Lemma 1 we can show that k-approximations provide upper bounds for the error indicators of complete valuations for any comparators.

Theorem 3. *If H is a CH with variables V, $x \in V$ and $d \in D(x)$, then $\xi_\theta \preceq_{better} approx_{|V|}(x \mapsto d) \preceq_{better} approx_k(x \mapsto d)$ for all $1 \leq k \leq |V|$ and all θ such that $vars(\theta) = V$ and $(x \mapsto d) \in \theta$, where $\preceq_{better}$ represents any locally/globally better comparator.*

Theorem 3 suggests that k-approximations can be used as the basis of the notion of local consistency in CH.

A hierarchy problem $P = \langle H, I_H \rangle$ is *constraint hierarchy k-consistent (CH-k-C)* if the error indicator stores in I_H explicitly indicate the implicit inconsistency information in all m-ary constraints in H where $m \leq k$. Formally, we define CH-k-C as follows.

Definition 3 (CH k-Consistency (CH-k-C)). *Given a hierarchy problem $P = \langle H, I_H \rangle$ with variables V. P is CH-k-C if, for all $\xi_{x=d} \in I_H, \xi_{x=d} \preceq_{better} approx_k(x \mapsto d)$ for some $1 \leq k \leq |V|$.*

The CH-k-C condition of $P = \langle H, I_H \rangle$ imposes that the estimated error information of H placed in the error indicator stores in I_H is *at least* as accurate as that provided by k-approximations. In addition, explicating the error $P = \langle H, I_H \rangle$ using k-approximations makes P CH-k-C without changing the solution space of P.

Theorem 4. *Given a hierarchy problem $P = \langle H, I_H \rangle$ with variables V. If each $\xi'_{x=d} \in I'_H$ is defined as follows:*

$$\xi'_{x=d} = \begin{cases} \xi_{x=d} & \text{if } \xi_{x=d} \preceq_{better} approx_k(x \mapsto d) \\ approx_k(x \mapsto d) & \text{if } approx_k(x \mapsto d) \preceq_{better} \xi_{x=d} \end{cases}$$

where $\xi_{x=d} \in I_H$, then the hierarchy problem $P' = \langle H, I_H \rangle$ is (1) CH-k-C and (2) shares the same solution set as P.

A simple corollary follows directly from Theorems 1 and 4.

Corollary 1. *Given a hierarchy problem $P = \langle H, I_H \rangle$ with variables V, and $P' = \langle H, I_H \rangle$ defined so that each $\xi'_{x=d} \in I'_H$ is:*

$$\xi'_{x=d} = \begin{cases} \xi_{x=d} & \text{if } \xi_{x=d} \preceq_{better} approx_k(x \mapsto d) \\ approx_k(x \mapsto d) & \text{if } approx_k(x \mapsto d) \preceq_{better} \xi_{x=d} \end{cases}$$

where $\xi_{x=d} \in I_H$. Denote the solution sets of H, P, and P' by S_H, S_P, and $S_{P'}$ respectively.

$$S_H = S_P \Leftrightarrow S_H = S_{P'}$$

5   A CH-2-C Enforcement Algorithm

Arc-consistency algorithm is a common and practical technique to detect local inconsistency in classical CSPs [2, 15]. We design and implement an algorithm to enforce CH-2-C. The purpose of the CH-2-C algorithm is to explicate and place in I_H the implicit error information in a CH that is otherwise not visible. Such an algorithm is given in Figure 3. The subroutines **ch1c_pri** and **ch2c_pri**, in Figures 4 and 5 respectively, are responsible for handling unary and binary constraints respectively. The CH-2-C algorithm ensures that all error indicator stores $\xi_{x=d}$ are updated to reach $approx_2(x \mapsto d)$.

Consider a general CH of n_c labeled constraints with n_v number of variables. In addition, the size of the largest variable domain is of n_d. The time complexity of the subroutine **ch1c_pri** is simply of $O(n_d)$, since the only repeating operations, lines 4 to 6 in Figure 4, are placed inside a single loop. These operations are repeated until each element in a variable domain is tested. However, the time complexity of the subroutine **update** (Figure 6) is of $O(n_d{}^2)$. Therefore, in the worst case, the time complexity of the subroutine **ch2c_pri** is of $O(n_d{}^2)$ as shown in Figure 5. Lines 3 to 5 in the pseudocode of the CH-2-C algorithm are the operations for checking constraints as shown in Figure 3.

Algorithm 1: The CH-2-C algorithm.

ch2c(H, V, D, I_H)
begin

1   **for** $l \leftarrow 1$ *to* n **do**
2   **for** $k \leftarrow 1$ *to* $|H_l|$ **do**
3   **let** c be the kth constraint in H_l;
4        $I_H \leftarrow$ **ch1c_pri**(c, l, k, D, I_H);
5        $I_H \leftarrow$ **ch2c_pri**(c, l, k, D, I_H);

6   **return** I_H;
end

Fig. 3. The CH-2-C algorithm.

ch1c_pri(c, l, k, D, I_H)
begin

1   **if** $|vars(c)| = 1$ **then**
2   **let** $\{x\} = vars(c)$;
3   **for** *each* $d \in D(x)$ **do**
4   **let** $\theta = \{x \mapsto d\}$;
5   **let** $\xi = \xi_{x=d} \in I_H$;
6   **if** $\xi_k^l < e(c\theta)$ **then** $\xi_k^l \leftarrow e(c\theta)$;

7   **return** I_H;
end

Fig. 4. A subroutine to check unary constraints.

Since these operations should repeat until all the constraints are considered, the time complexity should be of $O(n_c n_d{}^2)$.

Since an error indicator is a tuple which stores error values of the corresponding constraints, the space complexity for each error indicator is of $O(n_c)$. The memory requirement of the CH-2-C algorithm depends on the number of error indicator stores in I_H. Therefore, we require $n_v n_d$ error indicators. The space complexity of the CH-2-C algorithm is simply of $O(n_v n_d n_c)$ in the worst case.

Notice that some better local consistency algorithms could be defined when considering only a specific comparator (see for instance [4] for specific operators dealing with *l-b*).

6   A Branch-and-Bound Finite Domain CH Solver

The simplest way to find the solution set of a CH is to construct the complete search tree for the problem, so that we can calculate and compare the error values of each valuation.

```
ch2c_pri(c, l, k, D, I_H)
begin
1  │  if |vars(c)| = 2 then
2  │  │   let {x, y} = vars(c);
   │  │   # Update each ξ_{x=d_x} ∈ I_H
3  │  │   I_H ← update(x, y, c, l, k, D, I_H);
   │  │   # Update each ξ_{y=d_y} ∈ I_H
4  │  │   I_H ← update(y, x, c, l, k, D, I_H);
5  │  return I_H;
end
```

Fig. 5. A subroutine to check binary constraints.

```
update(x, y, c, l, k, D, I_H)
begin
1  │  let ξ_{min} be an error value;
2  │  for each d_x ∈ D(x) do
3  │  │   ξ_{min} ← ∞;
4  │  │   for each d_y ∈ D(y) do
5  │  │   │   let θ = {x ↦ d_x, y ↦ d_y};
6  │  │   │   if e(cθ) < ξ_{min} then ξ_{min} ← e(cθ);
7  │  │   let ξ = ξ_{x=d_x} ∈ I_H;
8  │  │   if ξ_k^l < ξ_{min} then ξ_k^l ← ξ_{min};
9  │  return I_H;
end
```

Fig. 6. A subroutine to update error indicator stores.

However, traversing the complete search tree and comparing all the valuations are tedious and time-consuming. We propose to combine the CH-2-C and the branch-and-bound algorithms so as to prune non-fruitful branches of the search tree.

The input to our solver is a hierarchy problem $P = \langle H, I_H \rangle$, in which I_H contains *no* error information. In other words, the error indicator stores in I_H contain only the error value 0. The backbone of our solver is a standard branch-and-bound algorithm, since CH-solving is an optimization problem. A branch-and-bound algorithm always maintains the set of potential best solutions collected so far. The idea is to invoke the CH-2-C algorithm at each node in the search tree, hoping that the overhead in the CH-2-C algorithm can be more than compensated by the pruning that can take place. The correctness and completeness of this step is ensured by Corollary 1, so that maintaining CH-2-C will not change the solution space of the hierarchy problem and the associated CH. At each CH-2-C tree node, before search proceeds down a selected branch corresponding to a

---

Algorithm 2: A Branch-and-bound CH Solver with Pruning.

bb_solv(H, I_H, V, D, S_0, **in out** I_{S_0}, $\prec_{better}$)
begin

     # Any classical arc consistency algorithm

1     $D \leftarrow$ **arc_consistent**(H_0, D);

2   **if** D *contains an empty variable domain* **then**

3   **return** S_0;

4   **else if** D *contains all singleton variable domain* **then**

5   **let** θ be the valuation corresponding to D;

6   **let** ξ_θ be the error indicator corresponding to θ;

7          $\xi_\theta \leftarrow$ **cal_error_values**(H, θ, ξ_θ);

8   **for** *each* $\sigma \in S_0$ **do**

9   **if** $\xi_\sigma \prec_{better} \xi_\theta$ **then**

10                   $S_0 \leftarrow S_0 - \{\sigma\}$; $I_{S_0} \leftarrow I_{S_0} - \{\xi_\sigma\}$;

11   **else if** $\xi_\theta \prec_{better} \xi_\sigma$ **then return** S_0;

12          $S_0 \leftarrow S_0 \cup \{\theta\}$; $I_{S_0} \leftarrow I_{S_0} \cup \{\xi_\theta\}$;

13   **return** S_0;

          for *each* $\xi_{x=d} \in I_H$ **do**

               if $d \notin D(x)$ **then**

                   $I_H \leftarrow I_H - \{\xi_{x=d}\}$;

          $I_H \leftarrow$ **ch2c**(H, V, D, I_H);

14   **choose** variable $x \in V$ for which $|D(x)| \geq 2$;

15     $W \leftarrow D(x)$;

16   **for** *each* $d \in W$ **do**

          if **go**($\xi_{x=d}$, S_0, I_{S_0}, $\prec_{better}$) **then**

17               $S_0 \leftarrow$ **bb_solv**($\{H_0 \wedge x = d, H_1, \ldots, H_n\}$, I_H, V, D, S_0, I_{S_0}, $\prec_{better}$);

18   **return** S_0;

end

Fig. 7. A Branch-and-bound CH Solver with Pruning.

variable assignment, say $x \mapsto d$, the solver tries to verify if $\xi_{x=d}$ in I_H of that tree node is not worse than the error indicator of each potential solution. If that is the case, search proceeds; otherwise, there is no point to explore the selected branch any further, and search is backtracked to try another branch. When a leaf node is reached, we compare the error indicator ξ of the valuation associated with the leaf node against the error indicators of all the collected solutions. If the error indicator of any collected solution is worse than ξ, then the collected solution will be replaced by the current valuation.

    Our CH-2-C algorithm ensures that each error indicator store $\xi_{x=d}$ is $approx_2(x \mapsto d)$. By Theorem 3, the error indicator of every complete valuation involving assignment $x \mapsto d$ must be worse than $approx_2(x \mapsto d)$. If at a search node, $\xi_{x=d}$ is worse than the error indicators of each potential solution collected so far, there is no point to search on since all the possible valuations down that branch must be worse than the potential solutions. The details of our finite domain CH solver is shown in Figure 7, which is a simple adaptation of a basic branch-and-bound solver with the CH-2-C algorithm. The numbered lines give the backbone of the algorithm, while the unnumbered lines are new additions to enable CH-2-C enforcement. The algorithm use as parameters the constraints in H and and the stores in I_H, the variables V and the domain D. It also needs the set of assignments S_0 satisfying constraints in H_0, and the corresponding set of error indicators I_{S_0}. The algorithm is also parametric w.r.t. the type of comparator we want to use ($\prec_{better}$).

Although CH-2-C encompasses also crisp notions of node and arc consistency, we employ classical algorithms [19] for processing the required constraints in H_0 (lines 1) for performance reasons. Lines 5 to 13 deal with the case of a leaf node. Here there is a call to subroutine **cal_error_value** that computes the error $e(c\theta)$ for each θ. The CH-2-C algorithm is invoked between lines 13 and 14. Lines 14 to 17 perform the basic variable instantiation (or searching) recursively. The call to the subroutine **go** determines whether the error indicator store of the variable assignment of the selected branch in I_H of the current node is not worse than the error indicator of each of the collected solutions so far.

7 Experimental Results

We compare the performance of our proposed solver with generate-and-test, basic branch-and-bound, and the reified constraint approach by Lua (the Lua's solver hereafter) [16]. DeltaStar is only a theoretical framework [11], and clp(FD,S) cannot in the current implementation deal with hierarchies. Since both Lua's solver and ours are based on a branch-and-bound backbone, we first implement a solver engine S_g, which searches using ILOG's default *goal* definition, in ILOG Solver 4.4 in a generate-and-test fashion. In order to provide a basic Branch-and-Bound solver (without CH-2-C enforcement) for comparison, we define an alternative ILOG goal to obtain S_b. Our proposed solver S_c is obtained by implementing additional functions and an alternative *goal* definition G_c in S_g. While the input to our solvers is a CH, the input to Lua's solver S_r ("r" stands for "reified constraint") is a CSP with reified constraints for implementing a specific comparator and error function. Our comparison ensures *fairness* since all four solvers share the same backbone.

Our experiments are conducted on Sun Ultra 5/400 workstations with 256MB RAM. We record the execution time taken by S_g, S_b, S_c, and S_r to find the solution set of each problem instance using a particular comparator, denoting these timings t_g, t_b, t_c, and t_r. For each problem instance and comparator, we compute three ratios: t_g/t_c, t_b/t_c, and t_r/t_c. Each number in the following tables corresponds to the average of the same type of ratios for fifteen problem instances in a particular problem set P_i and a particular comparator. The columns on the left compare S_g and S_c, while the ones in the middle compare S_b and S_c, and the ones on the right compare S_r and S_c (only for global comparators). Our 3-part experiments test the effect of *variable domain size*, *number of variables*, and *number of hierarchy levels* on the performance of our proposed solver.

In each part, four sets of CHs: P_1, P_2, P_3, and P_4, each of which contains 15 problem instances, are generaged *randomly*. All problem instances have no hard constraints to make them more "difficult" to solve.

In the first part, the number of variables and the number of hierarchy levels are fixed ($|V| = 5$, $H = \{H_0, H_1, H_2\}$, $|H_0| = 0$, and $|H_1| = |H_2| = 5$) across all instances, while problems in the same set share a specific domain size: P_i has domains of size $10i$ for $i \in \{1, 2, 3, 4\}$.

	t_g/t_c (Mean)				t_b/t_c (Mean)				t_r/t_c (Mean)		
CHs	w-s-b	w-c-b	l-s-b	l-b	w-s-b	w-c-b	l-s-b	l-b	w-s-b	w-c-b	l-s-b
P_1	8	5	7	10	6	4	6	7	5	4	5
P_2	36	15	37	13	18	22	19	9	9	19	9
P_3	267	67	261	171	121	47	123	31	113	42	115
P_4	385	72	342	76	37	35	39	23	17	27	18

In the second part, the variable domain size and the number of hierarchy levels are fixed ($|D(x)| = 5$ for all variables x, $H = \{H_0, H_1, H_2\}$, $|H_0| = 0$, and $|H_1| = |H_2| = 5$) across all instances, while problems in the same set share a specific number of variables: P_i has $2(i + 1)$ variables for $i \in \{1, 2, 3, 4\}$.

	t_g/t_c (Mean)				t_b/t_c (Mean)				t_r/t_c (Mean)		
CHs	w-s-b	w-c-b	l-s-b	l-b	w-s-b	w-c-b	l-s-b	l-b	w-s-b	w-c-b	l-s-b
P_1	1.2	0.9	1.3	1.2	1.2	1.3	1.5	1.4	1.1	1.1	1.4
P_2	6	3	6	5	5	3	5	4	5	3	5
P_3	7	3	7	4	5	4	5	3	4	4	4
P_4	24	8	24	26	3	7	3	5	1.4	6	1.4

In the third part, the number of variables and the variable domain size are fixed ($|V| = 5$, $|D(x)| = 20$ for all variables x, and $|H_0| = 0$) across all instances, while problems in the same set share a specific number of hierarchy levels: P_i has $i + 1$ non-required levels each with 5 constraints for $i \in \{1, 2, 3, 4\}$.

	t_g/t_c (Mean)				t_b/t_c (Mean)				t_r/t_c (Mean)		
CHs	w-s-b	w-c-b	l-s-b	l-b	w-s-b	w-c-b	l-s-b	l-b	w-s-b	w-c-b	l-s-b
P_1	146	108	151	122	44	44	44	32	37	39	39
P_2	209	130	212	116	51	116	50	34	38	104	39
P_3	232	168	219	50	42	121	44	21	31	113	29
P_4	122	154	124	75	58	132	60	26	51	128	52

The CH-2-C algorithm incurs overhead in the branch-and-bound search. For the larger problems in P_2, P_3, and P_4, the extra effort paid by the CH-2-C algorithm at each search node is demonstrated worthwhile. This result is in line with the behavior of embedding classical consistency techniques in basic tree search in solving classical CSPs.

The Lua's solver relies on classical constraint propagation to enforce the semantics and the operations of the comparators via reified constraints. While the approach, based on existing technology, is clever and clean, the pruning power of reified constraints is relatively weak. On the other hand, S_c executes a dedicated algorithm for maintaining

CH-2-C to help pruning and solution filtering, thus attaining a higher efficiency. In particular, S_r performs the worst on the *w-c-b* comparator, since the *error combining constraint* is implemented using the **IlcMax** constraint in ILOG Solver 4.4, which is again weak in propagation.

8 Related Work

Many efficient algorithms have been proposed to solve CHs, such as DeltaBlue [12], SkyBlue [22], DETAIL [18], Indigo [6], Generalized Local Propagation [17], and Ultra-violet [7], apply Local Propagation [24]. Besides, Cassowary and QOCA algorithms [9], adapting the Simplex algorithm [21], can also solve CHs efficiently. However, they are designed for the real number domain. We focus on finite domain CHs solving techniques; we can categorize the techniques into four different approaches.

First, the Incremental Hierarchical Constraint Solver (IHCS) [20] proposes to transform a given constraint hierarchy into a set of *best configurations* (a set of constraints). Therefore, a given CH can be transformed into a set of classical CSPs. However, it can only find *l-b* solutions using the trivial error function. The second approach is to transform CHs into ordinary constraint systems based on *reified constraint propagation* [16]. This approach can only find solutions for *global comparators* (*w-s-b*, *w-c-b*, and *l-s-b*). The third approach exploits the fact that CH is an instance of the SCSP framework [5]. Bistarelli *et al.* [4] show how a c-semiring can be constructed to model all instances of *globally-better*. In addition, only the *w-c-b* can enjoy semiring-based arc-consistency techniques [5] supported in clp(FD,S) [14]. The clp(FD,S) solver, however, limits the size of the semiring to only 32 elements, making it difficult to model any practically sized problems. The last is the refining approach used by DeltaStar [13]. It is a generic finite domain CH solver which can find solutions for arbitrary comparators in theory. However, it recomputes the solution in each recursive step causing significant overhead. Hence, it is used only as a general and theoretical framework for solution, from which efficient algorithms, such as DeltaBlue (only equality constraints) and Cassowary (a very restricted finite domain subsolver), are inspired and designed for some subset of the general problem [11].

This paper is also related to many work in soft constraint processing aiming to show how information gained through local consistency checking during preprocessing can be used to enhance branch-and-bound search using local computations as global bounds. In fact, when dealing with Constraint Hierarchies with only 2 levels, *w-s-b* and *w-l-b* correspond to weighted CSPs and *w-c-b* to fuzzy CSPs. Some work, similar to our, already appear (see for example Weighted CSPs [25], and Valued CSPs[23, 10]). The bounds computed by these works are better then ours when we restrict our computations to only 2-level, and to a specific comparator.

Our results are somewhat more general. We are able to compute bounds for CH with *any number of levels* and *without fixing a priori a comparator*. To reach better bounds we can easily fix a comparator and define a specific $approx_k(x \mapsto d)$ function. Bistarelli *et al.* [4]defined such operators for the specific case of *l-b*.

9   Conclusion

We formally define constraint hierarchy k-consistency (CH-k-C), based on error indicators. Incorporating a CH-2-C enforcement algorithm in a branch-and-bound algorithm, we obtain a general finite domain CH solver, which works for arbitrary comparators. Search space is pruned by utilizing the error information generated by the CH-2-C algorithm. Experiments confirm the efficiency of our research prototype, which brings us one step towards practical finite domain CH solving.

There is room for future research. First, our implementation and even the CH-2-C algorithm are hardly optimized. They have much scope for improvement. Second, we test our solver only on random problems. Experiments on more structured problems and real-life problems are needed. Third, our consistency-based and Lua's reified constraint approaches do not compete. It would be interesting to study if the two methods can be combined to produce more pruning. Fourth, the efficiency of branch-and-bound algorithms can be sensitive to variable and value orderings. It is worthwhile to investigate good ordering heuristics specific to the CH-2-C and the branch-and-bound algorithms. Fifth, the current proposal of our solver guarantees the correctness of local and global comparators. In addition, it is easy to check that our solver can support regional comparator [26], *regionally-better* comparator. The existing comparators, although rigorously and mathematically defined, might be too general for a specific real-life situation. It would be interesting to introduce new comparators that should be of particular relevance to real-life problems and applicable to our solver.

References

1. G.J. Badros, A. Borning, and P.J. Stuckey. The Cassowary linear arithmetic constraint solving algorithm. *ACM Transactions on Computer-Human Interaction*, 8(4):267–306, 2001.
2. C. Bessière, E.C. Freuder, and J.C. Régin. Using inference to reduce arc consistency computation. In *Proceedings of IJCAI95*, pages 592–598, 1995.
3. S. Bistarelli, P. Codognet, H.K.C. Hui, and J.H.M. Lee. Solving finite domain constraint hierarchies by local consistency and tree search. In *(to appear) Proceedings of the Eighteenth International Joint Conference on Artificial Intelligence (2 pages)*, 2003.
4. S. Bistarelli, Y. Georget, and J.H.M. Lee. Capturing (fuzzy) constraint hierarchies in semiring-based constraint satisfaction. Unpublished Manuscript, http://www.sci.unich.it/~bista/drafts/soft-fuzzyCH.pdf, 1999.
5. S. Bistarelli, U. Montanari, and F. Rossi. Semiring-based constraint solving and optimization. *Journal of the ACM*, 44(2):201–236, 1997.
6. A. Borning, R. Anderson, and B. Freeman-Benson. Indigo: A local propagation algorithm for inequality constraints. In *Proceedings of the 1996 ACM Symposium on User Interface Software and Technology*, pages 129–136, 1996.
7. A. Borning and B. Freeman-Benson. Ultraviolet: A constraint satisfaction algorithm for interactive graphics. *Constraints: An International Journal*, 3(1):9–32, 1998.
8. A. Borning, B. Freeman-Benson, and M. Wilson. Constraint hierarchies. *Lisp and Symbolic Computation*, 5(3):223–270, 1992.
9. A. Borning, K. Marriott, P. Stuckey, and Y. Xiao. Solving linear arithmetic constraints for user interface applications. In *Proceedings of the ACM Symposium on User Interface Software and Technology*, pages 87–96, 1997.

10. Martin C. Cooper. Reduction operations in fuzzy or valued constraint satisfaction. *Fuzzy Sets and Systems*, 134(3):311–342, mar 2003.
11. B. Freeman-Benson. Efficiency of DeltaStar. Private Communication, April 2002.
12. B. Freeman-Benson, J. Maloney, and A. Borning. An incremental constraint solver. *Communications of the ACM*, 33(1):54–63, 1990.
13. B. Freeman-Benson, M. Wilson, and A. Borning. DeltaStar: A general algorithm for incremental satisfaction of constraint hierarchies. In *The 11th Annual IEEE Phoenix Conference on Computers and Communications*, pages 561–568, 1992.
14. Y. Georget and P. Codognet. Compiling semiring-based constraints with clp(FD,S). In *Proceedings of the Fourth International Conference on Principles and Practice of Constraint Programming*, 1998.
15. S.A. Grant and B.M. Smith. The phase transition behavior of maintaining arc consistency. In *Proceedings of ECAI96*, pages 175–179, 1996.
16. Martin Henz, Yun Fong Lim, Seet Chong Lua, Xiao Ping Shi, J. Paul Walser, and Roland H. C. Yap. Solving hierarchical constraints over finite domains. In *Sixth International Symposium on Artificial Intelligence and Mathematics*, Fort Lauderdale, Florida, 2000.
17. H. Hosobe, S. Matsuoka, and A. Yonezawa. Generalized local propagation: A framework for solving constraint hierarchies. In *Proceedings of the Second International Conference on Principles and Practice of Constraint Programming*, pages 237–251, 1996.
18. H. Hosobe, K. Miyashita, S. Takahashi, S. Matsuoka, and A. Yonezawa. Locally simultaneous constraint satisfaction. In *Proceedings of PPCP94*, pages 51–62, 1994.
19. A.K. Mackworth. Consistency in networks of relations. *AI Journal*, 8(1):99–118, 1977.
20. F. Menezes, P. Barahona, and P. Codognet. An incremental hierarchical constraint solver. In *First Workshop on Principle and Practice of Constraint Processing*, 1993.
21. J.A. Nelder and R. Mead. A simplex method for function minimization. *The Computer Journal*, 7:308–313, 1965.
22. M. Sannella. The SkyBlue constraint solver and its applications. In V.A. Saraswat and P.V. Hentenryck, editors, *Proceedings of the First Workshop on Principles and Practice of Constraint Programming*. MIT Press, 1994.
23. Thomas Schiex. Arc consistency for soft constraints. In *Proc. 6th International Conference on Principles and Practice of Constraint Programming (CP2000)*, volume 1894, pages 411–424. Springer, 2000.
24. G.L. Steele and G.J. Sussman. Constraints. In *APL conference proceedings part 1*, pages 208–225, 1979.
25. Richard J. Wallace. Directed arc consistency preprocessing. In *Constraint Processing, Selected Papers*, volume 923, pages 121–137. Springer, 1995.
26. M. Wilson and A. Borning. Hierarchical constraint logic programming. *Journal of Logic Programming*, 16:277–318, 1993.

HIBISCUS: A Constraint Programming Application to Staff Scheduling in Health Care

Stéphane Bourdais, Philippe Galinier, and Gilles Pesant

Département de génie informatique
École Polytechnique de Montréal
C.P. 6079, succ. Centre-ville
Montreal, Canada H3C 3A7
{sbs,philipg,pesant}@crt.umontreal.ca

Abstract. This paper presents a constraint programming model and search strategy to formulate and solve staff scheduling problems in health care. This is a well-studied problem for which many different approaches have been developed over the years but it remains a challenge to successfully apply any given instance of a method to the various contexts encountered. We show how the main categories of rules involved may be expressed using global constraints. We describe a modular architecture for heuristic search. The resulting flexible and rather general constraint programming approach is evaluated on benchmark problems from different hospitals and for different types of personnel.

1 Introduction

In many industries and public services work is carried out on a continuous basis, twenty-four hours a day, seven days a week. Health care workers (nurses and doctors) are in such a situation. Managing hospital personnel is a perpetual balancing act between three very important, yet often contradictory, objectives: high quality care provided to patients, good working conditions for the staff, and low costs. The first corresponds to the mission of the health care sector, the second contributes significantly to personnel retention, and the third ensures that we make the best of limited financial resources. Warner [19] recognizes three levels of decision making in managing a nursing staff, and much of it applies equally to doctors:

i. The staffing decision (strategic): dimensioning care units by determining the amount of staff required for each skill.
ii. The scheduling decision (tactical): building the actual schedules that specify when each staff member works and what task is performed, in a scheduling horizon spanning from one week to several months.
iii. The allocation decision (operational): readjusting daily because of unforeseen events such as illness or an increase in demand.

We focus here on the second level and consider the number of care units, the amount of staff and the demand fixed from the first level. Since financial costs

F. Rossi (Ed.): CP 2003, LNCS 2833, pp. 153–167, 2003.
© Springer-Verlag Berlin Heidelberg 2003

are primarily influenced by that first level, the two objectives that remain are the quality of the care provided and working conditions for the staff. Such objectives do not readily lend themselves to formalization. The problem is to some extent fuzzy in the sense that optimality is not easily defined through a formula. In practice, human judgement is required to make a choice from a set of candidate schedules meeting predefined criteria.

There are two main families of solutions in staff scheduling: rotating schedules and personalized schedules. When the personnel is interchangeable, rotating schedules, a repeating pattern of sequences of work and rest days alternating over a few weeks, are particularly well adapted. In effect, everyone has an identical schedule but that is out of phase with the others, thus ensuring fairness among the staff. When members of the personnel have individual restrictions or preferences that must be taken into consideration, such as unavailabilities due to other activities or particular skills, rotating schedules become inappropriate. Personalized schedules for each member of personnel are then preferred. That latter family is typical for doctors and even for nurses.

Staff scheduling is a well-studied problem for which many different approaches have been developed over the years (see for example [6] for a recent survey in the health care sector). In particular, constraint programming has been applied to nurse scheduling. A semi-automated system is described in [1]. A step by step procedure is implemented in [9] for a French hospital, possibly requiring manual adjustments during the scheduling process. Redundant modeling is used in [8] to generate one-week schedules for nurses in a Hong-Kong hospital. Another system written in CHIP is currently used by a French hospital [7]. Finally, [12] combines constraint programming and local search to produce schedules for several German hospitals.

Staff scheduling in health care remains a challenging problem: most of the time it is still solved by hand through a lengthy process, and where automated systems are involved they tend to be strongly linked to a particular context. There are significant differences between hospitals or even between care units of a hospital in the rules governing the schedules, due to government or union regulations but also to local traditions emerging over the years. Nevertheless, the rules encountered fall into a few categories common to all contexts (see Sect. 2).

We make two contributions in this paper. First, we describe a flexible and rather general constraint programming approach to the staff scheduling problem in health care (doctors or nurses), the HIBISCUS software. Though this may not be a new domain of application for constraint programming, we believe its widespread use of global constraints and the different contexts to which it is successfully applied are indeed novel in this area. Second, we propose a modular architecture for heuristic search that combines ranking information on variable/value pairs from the individual constraints present in the model.

In the rest of the paper: Section 2 describes the staff scheduling problem in health care; Section 3 lays down the constraint programming model for HIBIS-CUS; Section 4 develops its search heuristics, including the modular architecture combining information from the constraints; Section 5 presents and discusses the results on real data sets; Section 6 summarizes the contributions and identifies future research directions.

2   Staff Scheduling in Health Care

Scheduling is about assigning resources to tasks (here, staff members to work shifts) in time, while respecting various constraints (here, the rules below). The resulting work schedules consist of sequences of work shifts of several types separated by rest periods. A sample schedule is given at Fig. 4.

2.1   The Rules

We present the main categories of rules for this problem, based on the relevant literature and on our own experience with many hospitals in the Montreal area [6, 11, 2, 10, 18, 4, 5, 17]. Concrete examples of such rules are given in Sect. 3.

Demand (DEM). A sufficient number and variety of shifts must be staffed throughout the scheduling horizon in order to guarantee minimum coverage.

Availability (AVA). A given staff member, according to his qualifications, full/part time status, vacation, and outside responsibilities, is not available at all times. We distinguish *preassignments* (AVA1), *forbidden assignments* (AVA2), and *candidate vacation days* (AVA3) from which a certain number must be selected.

Distribution (DIS). Many rules aim at a fair distribution of shifts among staff members and at balanced individual schedules. We distinguish *individual workloads* (DIS1), constrained to lie in a given range over the whole scheduling horizon or subsets of it to encourage a uniform workload, *balance for a certain type of shift among the staff* (DIS2), either evenly or according to some criterion such as seniority, *distribution of weekends off* (DIS3) across the scheduling horizon for individual staff members, and *relative proportion of certain types of shifts* (DIS4) in individual schedules.

Ergonomics (ERG). This is the largest and most heterogeneous category. Various rules ensure a certain level of quality for the schedules produced and may be specified either globally for the staff or only for certain individuals. We distinguish *patterns of shifts over certain days* (ERG1) such as alternating between two types of shifts on weekends, *length of stretches of shifts of identical type* (ERG2) to avoid working too few or too many days in a row on a certain shift, *patterns of stretches* (ERG3) such as forward rotation (going from day shifts to evening shifts to night shifts to day shifts again), *patterns of stretches of a given length* (ERG4) that ask for at least so many consecutive shifts of a certain type right after shifts of another type, and *preferences and aversions* (ERG5).

Rules regarding demand and availability are always hard. Some distribution and ergonomic rules may be soft.

3   HIBISCUS **Constraint Programming Model**

Let H denote the index set for successive days of the planning horizon, P for staff members, and Q for possible shifts, including **off** and **vacation**. A shift type is a set of shifts sharing a particular property (e.g. morning shifts, work shifts). More generally, a shift type may include any subset of Q. Considering a partition α of Q into m classes, $\alpha = \{Q_1, \cdots, Q_m\}$, the type of a shift q with respect to α, denoted by $t_\alpha(q)$, is the index i such that $q \in Q_i$.

3.1   Variables

For each staff member $i \in P$ and each day $j \in H$, we define an *assignment variable* $X_{ij} \in Q$ that indicates which shift is assigned to i on day j. For short, we use $\mathbf{X}_{i\bullet}$ (respectively $\mathbf{X}_{\bullet j}$) to represent successive assignment variables $\langle X_{i1}, X_{i2}, \ldots, X_{i\,|H|} \rangle$ associated to staff member i (respectively $\langle X_{1j}, X_{2j}, \ldots, X_{|P|j} \rangle$ associated to day j).

In addition to assignment variables, we define as needed some auxiliary variables in order to implement the constraints of the problem. In particular, considering a partition α as before, it is possible to define an auxiliary variable $Y \in \{1, 2, \ldots, m\}$ that indicates the type of an assignment variable X_{ij} as follows: $Y = t_\alpha(X_{ij})$.

3.2   Constraints

Most availability constraints (**AVA**) such as preassignments and forbidden assignments are easily modeled as unary constraints ($X_{ij} = q$ or $X_{ij} \neq q$). We rather focus on the higher arity constraints required. Again, this is a nice application domain for constraint programming because it showcases several of the global constraints developed over the years. We first review those higher arity constraints that are needed, establishing a notation and concentrating on their semantics, filtering capability, and computational complexity. We then go back to the rules presented in Sect. 2 and, using real cases, provide instances together with the way we model them using the following constraints.

SUM Constraints. Consider a vector $\mathbf{U} = \langle U_1, U_2, \ldots, U_n \rangle$ of integer variables and an additional integer variable S. Constraint $\mathrm{SUM}(\mathbf{U}, S)$ guarantees that S is the sum of variables U_i ($1 \leq i \leq n$). The filtering algorithm we use only checks bound consistency and its time complexity is linear in n.

EXTENSION Constraints. Given a vector $\mathbf{U} = \langle U_1, U_2, \ldots, U_n \rangle$ of finite domain variables, constraint $\mathrm{EXTENSION}(\mathbf{U}, \mathcal{T})$ defines in extension the set $\mathcal{T}$ of admissible n-tuples for $\mathbf{U}$. The filtering algorithm that maintains generalized arc-consistency is exponential in n. For that reason, we use this type of constraint only when a small number of variables is involved.

DISTRIBUTION Constraints [15]. Consider vectors $\mathbf{U} = \langle U_1, U_2, \ldots, U_n \rangle$ of finite domain variables, $\mathbf{C} = \langle C_1, C_2, \ldots, C_m \rangle$ of integer variables, and $\mathbf{V} = \langle v_1, v_2, \ldots, v_m \rangle$ of values. Constraint DISTRIBUTION($\mathbf{C}$, $\mathbf{V}$, $\mathbf{U}$) guarantees that each C_j equals the number of variables in $\mathbf{U}$ whose value is v_j. Its filtering algorithm achieves generalized arc consistency and runs in polynomial time. This constraint could be implemented using m ordinary cardinality constraints. However, it is possible to reduce the complexity of filtering by treating simultaneously the m possible values in a global constraint.

SLIDING_DISTRIBUTION Constraints [16]. Consider vector $\mathbf{V} = \langle v_1, v_2, \ldots, v_m \rangle$, vector $\mathbf{U} = \langle U_1, U_2, \ldots, U_n \rangle$ of finite domain variables taking their values in V, and two vectors of m integers $\underline{\lambda}$ and $\overline{\lambda}$. Constraint SLIDING_DISTRIBUTION($\mathbf{U}, V,$ $\underline{\lambda}, \overline{\lambda}, w$) guarantees that in each subsequence of $\mathbf{U}$ of length w, value v_k ($1 \leq k \leq m$) appears between $\underline{\lambda}_k$ and $\overline{\lambda}_k$ times. This constraint is conceptually equivalent to DISTRIBUTION constraints expressed on each position of a sliding window but treating them all at once improves the filtering capability.

STRETCH Constraints [14]. Consider a set $V = \{v_1, v_2, \ldots, v_m\}$ and a sequence $\mathbf{s} = \langle s_1, s_2, \ldots, s_n \rangle$ whose elements belong to V. We call *stretch* of type $v \in V$ in $\mathbf{s}$ any maximal subsequence $\langle s_i, s_{i+1}, \ldots, s_j \rangle$ of elements all equal to v. The length of the stretch equals $j - i + 1$. Consider a vector $\mathbf{U} = \langle U_1, U_2, \ldots, U_n \rangle$ and let $\underline{\lambda}$ and $\overline{\lambda}$ be two vectors of m integers. Constraint STRETCH($\mathbf{U}$, V, $\underline{\lambda}$, $\overline{\lambda}$) guarantees that the length of any stretch of type v_k ($1 \leq k \leq m$) lies between $\underline{\lambda}_k$ and $\overline{\lambda}_k$. The difference with the previous constraint is that we are counting *consecutive* variables of a certain value. The filtering algorithm of the constraint exhibits a running time that is quadratic in m and linear in $\underline{\lambda}$ and $\overline{\lambda}$.

PATTERN Constraints [13]. We call k–pattern any sequence of k elements such that no two successive elements have the same value. Consider a set $V = \{v_1, v_2, \ldots, v_m\}$ and a sequence $\mathbf{s} = \langle s_1, s_2, \ldots, s_n \rangle$ of elements of V. Consider now the sequence $\langle v_{i_1}, v_{i_2}, \ldots, v_{i_\ell} \rangle$ of the types of the successive stretches that appear in $\mathbf{s}$. Let $\mathcal{P}$ be a set of k–patterns. Vector $\mathbf{s}$ satisfies $\mathcal{P}$ if and only if every subsequence of k elements in $\langle v_{i_1}, v_{i_2}, \ldots, v_{i_\ell} \rangle$ belongs to $\mathcal{P}$. For example, let $\mathbf{s} = \langle a, a, b, b, b, a, c, c \rangle$ and $\mathcal{P} = \{(a, b, a), (a, b, c), (b, a, c)\}$. The sequence of the types of the successive stretches that appear in $\mathbf{s}$ is $\langle a, b, a, c \rangle$. Since (a, b, a) and (b, a, c), the two subsequences of three elements in $\langle a, b, a, c \rangle$, both belong to $\mathcal{P}$, $\mathbf{s}$ satisfies $\mathcal{P}$. Constraint PATTERN($\mathbf{U}$, $\mathcal{P}$) guarantees that any assignment for $\mathbf{U}$ satisfies $\mathcal{P}$. The filtering algorithm of constraint PATTERN is low polynomial.

3.3   Instances of the Rules

Demand Constraints (DEM). A demand constraint makes it possible to control the number of staff members that are present at a particular period of a day. A so-called period is simply defined by an interval of time in the day (for example, between noon and 4pm). Observe that staff member i is present at a particular period on day j if and only if shift X_{ij} covers the considered period.

Let us consider the following simplified example where there are five shifts in Q: q_1 from midnight to 8am, q_2 from 8am to 4pm, q_3 from 8am to 8pm, q_4 from 4pm to midnight, and q_5 (off). Therefore, the day is partitioned according to four time periods p_1 =[midnight, 8am], p_2 =[8am, 4pm], p_3 =[4pm, 8pm] and p_4 =[8pm, midnight]. Note that p_1 is covered by shift q_1, p_2 by q_2 and q_3, p_3 by q_3 and q_4, and p_4 by q_4. Consider vectors $\underline{q} = (3,5,6,3)$ and $\overline{q} = (6,8,9,6)$ indicating the minimum and maximum workforce required for each period ($\underline{q}_\ell \leq$ workforce at $p_\ell \leq \overline{q}_\ell$). In order to express the constraint, we first introduce a vector $\mathbf{M} = \langle M_1, \ldots, M_5 \rangle$ of auxiliary variables to represent the number of occurrences of each shift during day j. Then, we state

$$\text{DISTRIBUTION}(\mathbf{M}, Q, \mathbf{X}_{\bullet j}),$$

$$\text{SUM}(\langle M_1 \rangle, S_1), \quad \text{SUM}(\langle M_2, M_3 \rangle, S_2), \quad \text{SUM}(\langle M_3, M_4 \rangle, S_3), \quad \text{SUM}(\langle M_4 \rangle, S_4),$$

$$3 \leq S_1 \leq 6, \quad 5 \leq S_2 \leq 8, \quad 6 \leq S_3 \leq 9, \quad 3 \leq S_4 \leq 6.$$

Workload Constraints (DIS1). A workload constraint is defined by a 5-tuple $(i, j_{\text{beg}}, j_{\text{end}}, \underline{h}, \overline{h})$ and imposes that the number of hours worked by staff member i over the time period (set of successive days) $[j_{\text{beg}}, j_{\text{beg}+1} \cdots j_{\text{end}}]$ lies between $\underline{h}$ and $\overline{h}$.

Let us consider the following example where there are seven shifts in Q: off (that lasts 0 hours); D4 and E4 (4 hours); D6 (6 hours); D8, N and E8 (8 hours). We consider the workload constraint with $(i, j_{\text{beg}}, j_{\text{end}}, \underline{h}, \overline{h}) = (i, 15, 21, 30, 35)$ that requires staff member i to work between 30 and 35 hours over the third week of the horizon (from day 15 to day 21). A straightforward way to express the constraint is to state $30 \leq h(X_{i\,15}) + h(X_{i\,16}) + \cdots + h(X_{i\,21}) \leq 35$, where $h(\mathbf{X})$ represents the duration of the shift assigned to $\mathbf{X}$. Note that, in this case, simple bound consistency would normally be applied.

We use in HIBISCUS the following more powerful way to express the constraint. Let $\alpha_{\text{DIS1}} = \{Q_1, \ldots, Q_p\}$ be the partition of Q into classes of shifts having the same duration and $h_1, \ldots, h_p$ be the durations of shifts in $Q_1, \ldots, Q_p$. In our example, there are four classes and the possible durations of the shifts are 0, 4, 6, and 8. Let $\mathcal{T}$ represent the set of tuples $(m_1 \ldots m_p)$ such that $\underline{h} \leq \sum_{1 \leq k \leq p} h_k m_k \leq \overline{h}$ and $\sum_{1 \leq k \leq p} m_k = j_{\text{end}} - j_{\text{beg}} + 1$. For the example, $\mathcal{T} = \{(m_1, m_2, m_3, m_4) : 30 \leq 0 * m_1 + 4 * m_2 + 6 * m_3 + 8 * m_4 \leq 35$ and $m_1 + m_2 + m_3 + m_4 = 7\} = \{(3,0,0,4),(3,0,1,3),\ldots\}$. We introduce auxiliary variables $\mathbf{Y} = \langle Y_1, \ldots, Y_{j_{\text{end}}-j_{\text{beg}}+1} \rangle$, where $Y_k = t_{\alpha_{\text{DIS1}}}(\mathbf{X}_{ij_{\text{beg}}+k-1})$ $(1 \leq k \leq j_{\text{end}} - j_{\text{beg}} + 1)$ and multiplicity variables $\mathbf{M} = \langle M_1, \ldots, M_p \rangle$, where M_k $(1 \leq k \leq p)$ will count the number of variables in $\{X_{ij_{\text{beg}}}, \ldots, X_{ij_{\text{end}}}\}$ whose assigned value belongs to class Q_k. To express the constraint, we state

$$\text{DISTRIBUTION}(\mathbf{M}, \langle 1, \ldots, p \rangle, \mathbf{Y}), \quad \text{EXTENSION}(\mathbf{M}, \mathcal{T}).$$

Note that this way of expressing the constraint ensures generalized arc consistency. The filtering algorithm is exponential in p but this is not a problem in practice since the number of possible durations never exceeds five in the instances encountered.

In some cases, workloads are expressed not on calendar weeks but on a sliding window of a given number of days. For example in any nine consecutive days, five or six must be worked:

$$\texttt{SLIDING\_DISTRIBUTION}(\mathbf{X}, \langle \textsf{off}, \textsf{day}, \textsf{evening}, \textsf{night} \rangle, \langle 3, 1, 1, 1 \rangle, \langle 4, 9, 9, 9 \rangle, 9).$$

Distribution of Weekends Off (DIS3). Consider a staff member $i \in P$ who may work at most two weekends in a row. Note that to work on a weekend means that the considered staff member performs a work shift on Saturday or Sunday, or even performs a Friday work shift that overlaps Saturday, for example a night shift from 8pm to 4am. We introduce auxiliary variables $\mathbf{W} = \langle \mathsf{W}_1, \mathsf{W}_2, \ldots \rangle$ with $\mathsf{W}_k \in \{\mathsf{y}, \mathsf{n}\}$ indicating whether weekend k is worked at all (y) or not (n) by staff member i. Let $H_k \subset H$ be the set of days that correspond to weekend k and $Q_j \subset Q$ the set of work shifts for day j. We then state

$$\mathsf{W}_k = \mathsf{y} \quad \Leftrightarrow \quad \bigvee_{j \in H_k} \bigvee_{v \in Q_j} (\mathsf{X}_{ij} = v)$$

$$\texttt{STRETCH}(\mathbf{W}, \langle \mathsf{y}, \mathsf{n} \rangle, \langle 1, 1 \rangle, \langle 2, \infty \rangle).$$

Length of Stretches of Shifts of Identical Type (ERG2). Consider a staff member $i \in P$ who may work at least two but at most seven day shifts in a row or evening shifts in a row, and at least three but at most six night shifts in a row. This rule can be expressed as

$$\texttt{STRETCH}(\mathbf{X}_{i\bullet}, \langle \textsf{day}, \textsf{evening}, \textsf{night}, \textsf{off} \rangle, \langle 2, 2, 3, 1 \rangle, \langle 7, 7, 6, \infty \rangle).$$

Consider another rule that says that stretches of night shifts must be at least fourteen days apart. We introduce partition $\alpha_{\textsf{ERG2}} = \{Q_1 = \{\textsf{night}\}, Q_2 = Q \setminus Q_1\}$ and auxiliary variables $\mathbf{Y} = \langle \mathsf{Y}_1, \ldots, \mathsf{Y}_{|H|} \rangle$, where $\mathsf{Y}_k = t_{\alpha_{\textsf{ERG2}}}(\mathsf{X}_{ik})$ ($1 \leq k \leq |H|$). Since class Q_2 includes any shift that may separate two stretches of night shifts, this rule can be expressed as

$$\texttt{STRETCH}(\mathbf{Y}, \langle 1, 2 \rangle, \langle 1, 14 \rangle, \langle \infty, \infty \rangle).$$

Patterns of Stretches (ERG3). Consider a staff member $i \in P$ and the set of shifts $Q = \{\textsf{day}, \textsf{evening}, \textsf{night}, \textsf{off}\}$. In order to impose homogeneous stretches of work and forward rotation (recall from Sect. 2), we introduce the set $\mathcal{P}$ of 3-patterns $\{\textsf{odo}, \textsf{oeo}, \textsf{ono}, \textsf{dod}, \textsf{eoe}, \textsf{non}, \textsf{doe}, \textsf{eon}, \textsf{nod}\}$ (with d=day, e=evening, n=night, and o=off). The first three patterns in $\mathcal{P}$ ensure that the stretches are homogeneous: for example, a day-stretch is preceded and followed by rests and not any other type of work shift. The last six patterns allow us to move from one work stretch to another of the same type or one type forward. We then state

$$\texttt{PATTERN}(\mathbf{X}_{i\bullet}, \mathcal{P}).$$

Patterns of Stretches of a Given Length (ERG4). Any staff member $i \in P$ working three consecutive night shifts must then have at least three days off. Such constraints can be expressed using STRETCH and EXTENSION constraints. Because of space limitations, we can only outline this combination. An auxiliary variable Y_{ij} is linked to each X_{ij}, with a domain containing two values corresponding to night, two others to off, and one to all the other shifts. The first "night" value is reserved to represent stretches of three nights and the first "off" value to represent stretches of three days off. A set of pairs $\mathcal{T}$ is then built to only allow the right transitions from one shift to another. Finally the following constraints are stated:

$$\text{STRETCH}(\mathbf{Y}, \langle 3\text{nights}, 3\text{offs}, \text{night}, \text{off}, \text{others} \rangle, \langle 3, 3, 1, 1, 1 \rangle, \langle 3, 3, 2, \infty, \infty \rangle),$$

$$\text{EXTENSION}(\langle Y_{ij}, Y_{ij+1} \rangle, \mathcal{T}) \quad (1 \leq j \leq |H| - 1).$$

4   HIBISCUS Search Heuristics

This section describes the search heuristics used to complement the model just described. In an initial phase, vacations are taken care of. Vacation days are often preassigned or are otherwise considerably restricted in their location. Consequently they generally have little impact on the search for good solutions and are fixed first.

4.1   Problem Decomposition

Next consider our decision variables X_{ij} arranged in a matrix whose rows correspond to staff members and columns to days of the planning horizon, thus offering a natural graphical representation of a schedule. Note that most of the constraints identified in Sect. 2 link variables horizontally, on individual schedules, while demand constraints (DEM) link them vertically. The many contexts we examined may be partitioned in two classes: those whose vertical constraints are tight (a precise demand as opposed to one lying in a certain range) while the (horizontal) workload constraints (DIS1) are loose (within a range); those whose vertical constraints are loose but whose workload constraints are tight (a set number of hours per week). The former typically corresponds to emergency room physicians and the latter to nurses.

So while the types of constraints encountered may be the same, the relative tightness of some has an impact on which dimension of the problem is harder to solve and hence on which search strategy offers better chances of success. For these two classes, which to our knowledge have always been treated separately in the literature, we use different decomposition strategies but using the same model. They are *decomposition by day* (i.e. column by column) and *decomposition by individual schedule* (i.e. row by row) (see Fig. 1). The decision of which one to use is solely based on which constraints are tight.

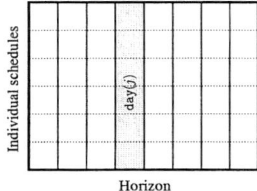 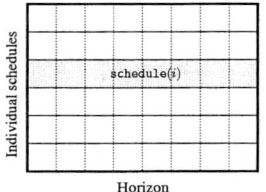

Fig. 1. Two decompositions of the staff scheduling problem.

Either case induces subproblems that must be tackled in a certain order. Days are ordered chronologically to help the satisfaction of horizontal ergonomic constraints and individual schedules are ordered randomly for lack of a significantly better ordering.

4.2   Variable/Value Ordering Heuristic

We describe a simple framework for the definition of heuristics to select variable/value pairs whose main asset is its modular structure following that of the constraint programming model for the problem at hand. To each constraint of the model (hard or soft) we may associate an *incentive heuristic* whose goal is to favor, among uninstantiated variables, value assignments that bring us closer to satisfying that constraint. Each incentive heuristic associates a score to potential assignments and those scores are then combined to dynamically select the next variable/value pair (see Fig. 2).

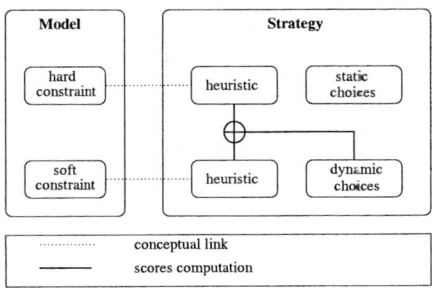

Fig. 2. Modular architecture of the variable/value ordering heuristic.

Incentive heuristic h acts on a subset $\mathbf{X}^h = \{X_1^h, X_2^h, \ldots X_k^h\}$ of the variables of the problem. Given the current domains of those variables, function

$$\phi_h : X_1^h \times D_{X_1^h} \cup \cdots \cup X_k^h \times D_{X_k^h} \to \mathbb{R}$$

assigns numerical scores to variable/value pairs. Let $\mathcal{H}$ denote the set of incentive heuristics present and $\mathbf{X}$ the set of our decision variables X_{ij}. For each potential assignment (X, v) we compute a weighted sum of the individual scores

$$\pi(X, v) = \sum_{h \in \mathcal{H} \,:\, X \in \mathbf{X}^h} \omega_h \cdot \phi_h(X, v).$$

We then select the assignment with the largest $\pi()$ value.

An incentive heuristic can be designed for every type of constraint in the model in order to bring its contribution to the variable/value ordering heuristic. In what follows, we detail one such example and outline another.

Incentive Heuristic for Demand Constraints (DEM). As we saw in Sect. 3.2, demand is broken down for each period of a day. To ease the exposition and without loss of generality, we present the heuristic for the demand on one given period and express it in the slightly more general context of a cardinality constraint. Let $\mathbf{X}$ represent a set of m variables, D_X the current domain of a variable X, T the subset of values of interest, and $\underline{\nu}$ and $\overline{\nu}$ two natural numbers. The number of times variables from $\mathbf{X}$ are assigned a value from T must be at least $\underline{\nu}$ and at most $\overline{\nu}$.

We introduce $\underline{n}$, the number of variables that necessarily take their value in T, and $\overline{n}$, the number of variables that necessarily take their value outside T. These are computed as

$$\underline{n} = |\{X \in X \,:\, D_X \subseteq T\}|$$
$$\overline{n} = |\{X \in X \,:\, T \cap D_X = \emptyset\}|.$$

We also propose $\tilde{n} = \frac{m - \overline{n} + \underline{n}}{2}$ as a rough estimate of the final number of values from T in $\mathbf{X}$.

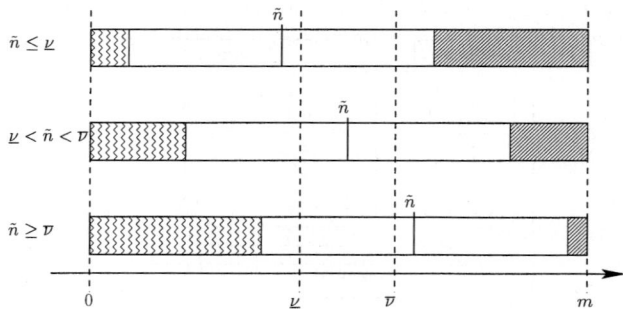

Fig. 3. Three cases of the incentive heuristic for the demand constraint.

Three cases may arise, which we give below with the corresponding score function and which we also illustrate at Fig. 3.

If $\tilde{n} < \underline{\nu}$, we wish to encourage assignments from T:

$$\phi_h(X, v) = \begin{cases} 1 \text{ if } v \in T, \\ 0 \text{ otherwise.} \end{cases}$$

If $\underline{\nu} \leq \tilde{n} \leq \overline{\nu}$, we remain neutral:

Table 1. Instances tested.

Origin	$|P|$	$|H|$	$|Q|$	success rate	avg time	std dev
CHILD	41	42	5	80%	9.5	15.8
BC	54	42	12	70%	8.4	5.1
ERMGH	41	42	4	80%	78.3	192.7
HSC	18	28	8	100%	25.0	53.5

$$\phi_h(\mathbf{X}, v) = 0.$$

If $\tilde{n} > \overline{\nu}$, we wish to discourage assignments from T:

$$\phi_h(\mathbf{X}, v) = \begin{cases} 0 \text{ if } v \in T, \\ 1 \text{ otherwise.} \end{cases}$$

An incentive heuristic for workload constraints (DIS1) can be designed along the same lines since it is a straightforward generalization to weighted cardinality in which weights correspond to the duration of shifts.

5   Experimental Results

The "Optimization of Health Care Management" research team in Montreal has been collecting data from several hospitals in order to create a set of benchmarks on which to evaluate several approaches (column generation, 0-1 linear programming, tabu search, constraint programming) developed by different members of the team over the years. Some initial results have already been obtained and an extensive comparison should soon be possible. In this section, we present some experiments performed on real-world instances from that evolving benchmark: they originate from three hospitals in Montreal.

5.1   Data Sets

Table 1 presents some characteristics of these instances. The first four columns respectively give the name of the instance, the number of staff members, the number of days in the scheduling horizon, and the number of shifts. CHILD and BC are nurse scheduling instances originating from two different units of the same hospital; ERMGH is a nurse scheduling instance from a different hospital; HSC is a physician scheduling instance from still another hospital. A complete description of the instances may be found in [3]. Note that the number of decision variables equals $|P| \cdot |H|$ and the size of all domains equals $|Q|$. Therefore, these instances are quite large.

5.2   Experiments

For the experiments reported here, the search heuristic was kept simple by using a single incentive heuristic at a time, thereby not requiring the setting of weights

ω_h for the combination of different influences. We will eventually investigate the interplay between several incentive heuristics.

For decomposition by individual schedule, recall that the order in which the subproblems are solved is chosen randomly, whereas for decomposition by day, subproblems are solved in chronological order. At this early stage of experimentation with incentive heuristics, chronological variable ordering for the former decomposition and smallest-domain-first variable ordering for the latter perform slightly better than the fully-fledged variable/value ordering heuristic, and so they are used to produce the results reported here. However, the incentive heuristic approach does yield the best results for value ordering and is therefore retained in that capacity. In order to better evaluate the robustness of our algorithm and to offer several candidate solutions to the decision maker, we break ties at random during value ordering.

HIBISCUS was implemented using the ILOG Solver C++ constraint programming library. In our experiments, we performed ten runs of one hour each (on a Sun Ultra-10, 440 MHz). Each run finishes with a success (when a feasible solution is found) or a failure.

Table 1 presents the results obtained. The fifth column gives the success rate based on the ten runs. The sixth and seventh columns respectively give the average computation time and the standard deviation in seconds for the successful runs. In every instance, the success rate is high and the majority of solutions are found within a few seconds.

n°	Mo	Tu	We	Th	Fr	Sa	Su	Mo	Tu	We	Th	Fr	Sa	Su	Mo	Tu	We	Th	Fr	Sa	Su	Mo	Tu	We	Th	Fr	Sa	Su
1	-	-	-	-	-	-	-	D	D	-	-	A	B	H	H	-	B	-	B	A	-	D	-	B	-	-	-	-
2	-	E	E	-	-	-	-	-	-	-	-	-	-	C	H	H	H	-	-	-	-	E	-	D	-	-	-	-
3	-	F	-	B	-	-	-	C	-	B	-	B	A	-	F	-	E	-	-	-	-	F	-	A	-	-	H	
4	-	C	-	A	E	E	E	-	-	-	F	F	-	-	-	-	-	-	-	-	-	-	-	-	-	-	-	
5	-	D	C	C	H	-	H	-	E	E	E	-	-	-	F	D	C	C	-	H	H	-	C	C	C	H	-	-
6	-	A	-	D	-	H	-	-	F	-	D	-	-	-	B	-	-	D	-	-	-	B	-	-	A	-	-	-
7	-	B	-	H	C	D	C	-	B	-	-	A	-	-	-	B	-	F	-	A	B	-	A	H	-	B	-	-
8	-	-	-	-	-	-	-	A	-	C	-	H	H	D	-	D	-	E	E	E	-	-	-	F	F	-	-	
9	F	-	D	-	-	A	B	E	-	H	-	B	-	-	A	-	F	-	F	-	-	H	H	E	-	-	H	-
10	H	H	-	F	B	-	-	H	H	-	A	-	-	-	-	-	-	-	D	-	-	E	-	B	A			
11	E	-	H	-	F	-	-	D	-	C	-	D	C	D	C	-	B	-	-	-	C	-	D	-	-	A	B	
12	D	-	F	-	D	C	D	C	-	F	-	H	-	-	-	-	-	-	B	-	-	H	E	E	E			
13	C	-	B	-	-	B	A	F	-	B	-	-	-	-	E	E	E	-	-	-	F	-	F	-	D	C	D	
14	B	-	-	E	-	-	B	-	-	H	C	D	C	-	A	A	-	B	-	-	E	-	B	-	-	-	-	
15	G	-	G	-	G	-	-	G	-	G	-	-	G	-	G	-	G	-	G	-	G	-	G	-	G	-	-	
16	A	-	A	-	A	-	-	A	-	E	E	E	-	-	-	A	A	-	-	A	-	A	-	C	D	C		
18	-	-	-	-	-	-	-	-	-	-	-	-	-	-	-	-	-	D	C	D	-	-	-	-	-	-	-	
19	-	-	-	-	-	-	-	-	-	-	-	-	-	-	-	-	-	C	D	C	-	-	-	-	-	-	-	

Fig. 4. A sample schedule for HSC. "-" corresponds to off.

5.3   Discussion

Warner [19] proposes a short check-list to compare staff scheduling approaches:

☐ *Coverage* : Are the tasks adequately covered by the schedule provided? Otherwise the hospital must call on additional personnel.

☐ *Quality* : How good are the working conditions of the staff, based on union rules, hospital rules, and individual preferences?

☐ *Stability* : Are individual schedules fairly homogeneous? Then staff members can more easily organize their social and family life.

☐ *Flexibility* : How elegantly does the approach deal with changes from one scheduling horizon to the next (personnel turnover, going from full time to part time, vacation, change of preferences, etc.)?

☐ *Fairness* : Are the tasks equally shared among the staff, while taking into account varying status (seniority, full time vs part time)?

☐ *Cost* : What amount of resources (human, time, computing power) were required to build the schedule?

Coverage is a requirement of the vast majority of the methods proposed, including ours, and therefore it is necessarily achieved. *Quality* and *fairness* depend on how the corresponding rules are handled. Some methods, typically local search but also others, associate penalties to rule violations and try to minimize their weighted combination. We treat most of those rules as (hard) constraints, possibly with some amount of tolerance built in: it is therefore easier to guarantee a certain level of quality and fairness. The danger is that the instance becomes over-constrained and some of the recent work on soft constraints could prove useful. Currently, the search heuristic described in Sect. 4 allows us to add incentives for preferences (ERG5) and to aim for a given target in cases where the constraint has been loosened somewhat by a certain tolerance. Being able to enforce weekly workloads and special rules for weekends off helps in achieving *stability* in the resulting schedules. As for *flexibility*, the fact that schedules have been produced for different hospital contexts, with similar categories of rules but often very distinct instantiations of those rules, shows that our method goes beyond adapting from one scheduling horizon to the next in a given context. Nevertheless, we believe that the weakest part of HIBISCUS is currently its search strategy: it could be made more robust. To its defense, we clearly have not yet explored its full potential in combining incentives. As for *cost*, human cost is very low since no assistance is required and computational cost is also low.

6   Conclusion

This paper presented a constraint programming model and search strategy to formulate and solve staff scheduling problems in health care. HIBISCUS turns out to be quite flexible and able to adapt to many different situations encountered in staff scheduling. This is first due to its global constraints, such as constraints on stretches that make it possible to capture the large number of rules present in this type of application. Another promising feature is the flexible technique proposed in order to introduce search heuristics. We are presently generalizing the introduction of heuristics in HIBISCUS. Again note that, in real life, there is generally no evaluation function to optimize, but simply preferences generally expressed in a fuzzy way, such as: to favour or discourage some particular shifts for a staff member, to balance the types of shifts assigned to a staff member, to balance unpopular shifts between staff members, and so forth. The heuristic approach explored in HIBISCUS seems to be well suited to deal with this kind of soft constraint.

Acknowledgements

The authors would like to thank the other members of the "Optimization of Health Care Management" research team for sharing their insight on the data and the anonymous referees for their constructive comments. This work was partially supported by the Canadian Natural Sciences and Engineering Research Council under grants OGP0218028 and 227247-99.

References

1. S. Abdennadher and H. Schenker. INTERDIP - An Interactive Constraint Based Nurse Scheduler. In *The First International Conference and Exhibition on The Practical Application of Constraint Technologies and Logic Programming - PA-CLP99*, 1999.
2. H. Beaulieu. Planification de l'horaire des médecins dans une salle d'urgence. Master's thesis, Université de Montréal, Canada, 1998.
3. S. Bourdais. Génération automatique d'horaires dans le milieu hospitalier. Master's thesis, École Polytechnique de Montréal, Canada, 2003.
4. I. Buzon and S. D. Lapierre. A Tabu Search Algorithm to Schedule Emergency Room Physicians. Technical report, Centre de Recherche sur les Transports, Montréal, Canada, 1999.
5. I.E.B. Cantera. La confection des horaires de travail des médecins d'urgence résolue à l'aide de la recherche tabou. Master's thesis, Université de Montréal, Canada, 2001.
6. M. W. Carter and S. D. Lapierre. Scheduling Emergency Room Physicians. *Health Care Management Science*, 4:347–360, 2001.
7. P. Chan, K. Heus, and G. Weil. Nurse Scheduling with Global Constraints in CHIP: GYMNASTE. In *Conference on Practical Applications of Constraint Technology*, London, UK, 1998.
8. B.M.W. Cheng, J.H.M. Lee, and J.C.K. Wu. A Constraint-Based Nurse Rostering System Using a Redundant Modeling Approach. In *Eight International Conference on Tools with Artificial Intelligence - TAI 1996*, pages 140–148. IEEE Computer Society Press, 1996.
9. S. J. Darmoni, A. Fajner, N. Mahe, A. Leforestier, M. Vondracek, O. Stelian, and M. Baldenweck. Horoplan: computer-assisted nurse scheduling using contraint-based programming. *Journal of the Society for Health Systems*, 5:41–54, 1995.
10. F. Forget. Confection automatisée des horaires de médecins dans une salle d'urgence. Master's thesis, Université de Montréal, Canada, 2002.
11. P. Labit. IRIS : Amélioration d'une méthode de génération de colonnes pour la confection d'horaires d'infirmières. Master's thesis, École Polytechnique de Montréal, Canada, 2000.
12. H. Meyer and A. Hofe. Nurse rostering as constraint satisfaction with fuzzy constraints and inferred control strategies. In E.C. Freuder and R.J. Wallace, editors, *Constraint Programming and Large Scale Optimisation Problems*, DIMACS Series in Discrete Mathematics and Theoretical Computer Science. 2000.
13. G. Pesant. The Pattern Constraint. In preparation.
14. G. Pesant. A Filtering Algorithm for the Stretch Constraint. In *Principles and Practice of Constraint Programming - CP 2001*, pages 183–195. Springer-Verlag LNCS 2239, 2001.

15. J.-C. Régin. Generalized Arc Consistency for Global Cardinality Constraints. In *Proc. of AAAI-96*, pages 209–215. AAAI Press/MIT Press, 1996.
16. J.-C. Régin and J.-F. Puget. A Filtering Algorithm for Global Sequencing Constraints. In *Principles and Practice of Constraint Programming - CP 1997*, pages 32–46. Springer-Verlag LNCS 1330, 1997.
17. L.-M. Rousseau, G. Pesant, and M. Gendreau. A Hybrid Algorithm to Solve a Physician Rostering Problem. In *Second Workshop on Integration of AI and OR Techniques in Constraint Programming for Combinatorial Optimization Problems*, Paderborn, Germany, 2000.
18. M. Saadie. Planification de l'horaire des médecins dans une salle d'urgence par la programmation par contraintes. Master's thesis, Université de Montréal, Canada, 2003.
19. D. M. Warner. Scheduling Nursing Personnel According to Nursing Preference: A Mathematical Programming Approach. *Operations Research*, 24:842–856, 1976.

Constraint-Based Optimization
with the Minimax Decision Criterion

Craig Boutilier[1], Relu Patrascu[2], Pascal Poupart[1], and Dale Schuurmans[2]

[1] Dept. of Computer Science, University of Toronto, Toronto, ON, M5S 3H5, Canada
cebly,ppoupart@cs.toronto.edu
[2] School of Computer Science, University of Waterloo, Waterloo, ON, N2L 3G1, Canada
rpatrascu,dale@cs.uwaterloo.ca

Abstract. In many situations, a set of hard constraints encodes the feasible configurations of some system or product over which users have preferences. We consider the problem of computing a best feasible solution when the user's utilities are partially known. Assuming bounds on utilities, efficient mixed integer linear programs are devised to compute the solution with minimax regret while exploiting generalized additive structure in a user's utility function.

1 Introduction

The problem of interactive decision making has received a fair amount of attention over the years [10, 17], but recently has seen increasing interest within AI as automated decision aids become more prevalent. As has been argued elsewhere [6, 4], there are many situations in which the set of decisions and their dynamics are fixed, while the *utility functions* of different users vary widely. In such a case, some form of utility elicitation must be undertaken in order to capture user preferences to a sufficient degree to allow an (approximately) optimal decision to be taken. Different approaches to this problem have been proposed, including Bayesian methods that quantify uncertainty about preferences probabilistically [7, 4], and methods that simply pose constraints on the set of possible utility functions and refine these incrementally [17, 5, 16].

These issues arise as well in the context of constraint-based optimization problems. For instance, in a car rental scenario, possible configurations are defined by attributes such as automobile size and class, manufacturer, seating and luggage capacity, etc. Available cars are limited by the configurations offered by manufacturers and stock availability, with hard constraints used to encode infeasible configurations (e.g., no luxury sedans have 4-cylinder engines). Different customers have different preferences for configurations in this restricted decision space [14], and this information must be obtained in an effective way. Typically, categorical preferences are obtained from the customer, and imposed as constraints; but if no feasible solution is found, these constraints are relaxed incrementally.

While interactive preference elicitation has received little attention in the CSP community, optimizing with respect to a given set of preferences over configurations has been studied extensively, with many frameworks proposed for modeling such systems

F. Rossi (Ed.): CP 2003, LNCS 2833, pp. 168–182, 2003.

[15, 3]. Most frameworks can be viewed as adding "soft" constraints that have associated penalties or values that indirectly represent a user's preferences for different configurations. However, modeling preferences as constraints and assuming complete utility information is often problematic. For instance, users may have neither the ability nor the patience to provide full utility information to a system. Furthermore, in many if not most instances, an optimal decision (or some approximation thereof) can be determined with a very partial specification of the user's utility function.

In this paper, we adopt a somewhat different view. We assume a user's preferences are represented directly as a utility function over possible configurations. In the car rental scenario, this utility function can be thought as a measure of the value (not necessarily monetary) of each car from the customer's point of view. Given a utility function and the hard constraints defining the decision space, we have a standard constraint-based optimization problem. However, as argued earlier, it is unrealistic to expect users to express their utility functions with complete precision, nor will we generally require full utility information to make good decisions. Thus we are motivated to consider the problem of "optimizing" in the presence of partial utility information. Specifically, we assume that bounds on utility function parameters are provided, and consider the problem of finding a feasible solution that minimizes *maximum regret* [11] within the space of feasible utility functions. We show that this minimax problem can be formulated and solved using a set of linear integer programs (IPs) and mixed integer programs (MIPs) in the case where utility functions have no structure. In practice, some utility structure is necessary if we expect to solve problems of realistic size. We therefore also consider problems where utility functions can be expressed using a *generalized additive form* [1] (which includes linear functions and graphical models like UCP-nets [5] as special cases). We derive two solution techniques for solving such structured problems: the first gives rise to a MIP with fewer variables combined with an effective constraint generation procedure; the second encodes the entire minimax problem as a single MIP using a cost-network to formulate a compact set of constraints.

Though our emphasis is on solving problems using the minimax regret criterion, we also briefly discuss how preference elicitation relates to this model. Specifically, we describe methods that can be used to refine utility uncertainty in a way that quickly reduces minimax regret. Throughout, our emphasis is on the compact formulation and solution of the constrained optimization problems as mixed integer programs. While these can be solved using a variety of techniques, including branch-and-bound methods with various constraint propagation techniques, we do not consider specialized methods for solving these MIPs (our experiments, for example, use generic MIP solvers). We leave this investigation to future research.

2 Constraint-Based Optimization and Minimax Regret

We begin by describing the basic problem assuming a known utility function to establish background and notation, and then define the minimax regret decision criterion for solving constraint-based decision problems given only incomplete utility information.

2.1   Optimization with Known Utility Functions

We assume a finite set of attributes $\mathbf{X} = \{X_1, X_2, \ldots, X_N\}$ with finite domains. An assignment $\mathbf{x} \in Dom(\mathbf{X})$ is often referred to as a *state*. For simplicity of presentation, we assume these attributes are boolean, but nothing important depends on this. We also have a set of hard constraints $\mathcal{C}$ over these attributes. Each constraint $\mathcal{C}_\ell$, $\ell = 1, \ldots, L$, is defined over a set $\mathbf{X}[\ell] \subset \mathbf{X}$, and thus induces a set of legal configurations of attributes in $\mathbf{X}[\ell]$. We assume that the constraints $\mathcal{C}_\ell$ are represented in some logical form and can be expressed compactly: for example, we might write $X_1 \wedge X_2 \supset \neg X_3$ to denote the legal configurations of X_1, X_2, X_3. We let $Feas(\mathbf{X})$ denote the subset of *feasible states* (i.e., assignments satisfying $\mathcal{C}$).

Suppose we have a known utility function $u : Dom(\mathbf{X}) \to \mathbf{R}$. Our aim is to find an optimal feasible state $\mathbf{x}^*$; i.e., any

$$\mathbf{x}^* \in \arg \max_{\mathbf{x} \in Feas(\mathbf{X})} u(\mathbf{x}).$$

For this reason, we sometimes call feasible states *decisions*. This problem can be formulated in an explicit fashion as a (linear) 0-1 integer program:

$$\max_{\{I_\mathbf{x}, X_i\}} \sum_{\mathbf{x}} u_\mathbf{x} I_\mathbf{x} \text{ subject to } \mathcal{A} \text{ and } \mathcal{C}, \tag{1}$$

where we have:

- variables $I_\mathbf{x}$: for each $\mathbf{x} \in Dom(\mathbf{X})$, $I_\mathbf{x}$ is a boolean variable indicating whether $\mathbf{x}$ is the decision made (i.e., state chosen).
- variables X_i: X_i is a 0-1 variable corresponding to the ith attribute.
- coefficients $u_\mathbf{x}$: for each $\mathbf{x} \in Dom(\mathbf{X})$, constant $u_\mathbf{x}$ denotes the (known) utility of state $\mathbf{x}$.
- constraint set $\mathcal{A}$: for each variable $I_\mathbf{x}$, we impose a constraint that relates it to its corresponding variable assignment. Specifically, for each X_i: if X_i is true in $\mathbf{x}$, we constrain $I_\mathbf{x} \leq X_i$; and if X_i is false in $\mathbf{x}$, we constrain $I_\mathbf{x} \leq 1 - X_i$. We denote by $\mathcal{A}$ these constraints.
- constraint set $\mathcal{C}$: we impose each feasibility constraint $\mathcal{C}_\ell$ on the attributes $X_i \in \mathbf{X}[\ell]$. Logical constraints can be written in a natural way as linear constraints [8].

Note that this formulation assures that, if there is a feasible solution (given the constraints $\mathcal{A}$ and $\mathcal{C}$), then exactly one $I_\mathbf{x}$ will be non-zero.[3]

2.2   Graphical Utility Models

Unfortunately the IP formulation above is not compact since there is one $I_\mathbf{x}$ variable per state and the number of states is exponential in the number of attributes. In such *flat* utility functions, it is not generally possible to formulate the optimization concisely. By contrast, if some structure on the utility function is imposed, say, in the form of a *factored* graphical model, we are then generally able to reduce the number of variables to

---

[3] We assume the utility function is non-negative.

be linear in the number of parameters of the graphical model. We consider here the GAI (generalized additive independence) model [1] because of its generality (encompassing both linear models [13] and UCP-nets [5] as special cases).[4]

Specifically, assume that our utility function can be written as the sum of K local utility functions, or *factors*, over small sets of variables:

$$u(\mathbf{x}) = \sum_{k \leq K} f^k(\mathbf{x}[k]). \tag{2}$$

Here each function f^k depends only on a local family of attributes $\mathbf{X}[k] \subset \mathbf{X}$. We denote by $\mathbf{x}[k]$ the restriction of state $\mathbf{x}$ to the attributes in $\mathbf{X}[k]$. An IP similar to Eq. 1 can be used to solve for the optimal decision in the case of a GAI model:

$$\max_{\{I_{\mathbf{x}[k]}, X_i\}} \sum_{k \leq K} \sum_{\mathbf{x}[k] \in Dom(\mathbf{X}[k])} u_{\mathbf{x}[k]} I_{\mathbf{x}[k]} \text{ subject to } \mathcal{A} \text{ and } \mathcal{C}. \tag{3}$$

Instead of one variable $I_{\mathbf{x}}$ per state, we now have a set of *local state variables* $I_{\mathbf{x}[k]}$ for each family k and each instance $\mathbf{x}[k] \in Dom(\mathbf{X}[k])$. Similarly, we have one associated constant coefficient $u_{\mathbf{x}[k]}$ denoting $f^k(\mathbf{x}[k])$. $I_{\mathbf{x}[k]}$ is true iff the assignment to $\mathbf{X}[k]$ is $\mathbf{x}[k]$. Each $I_{\mathbf{x}[k]}$ is related logically to the attributes $X \in \mathbf{X}[k]$ by constraint set $\mathcal{A}$ as before, and constraint set $\mathcal{C}$ is also imposed as above.

Notice that the number of variables and constraints in this IP (excluding the exogenous feasibility constraints $\mathcal{C}$) is now linear in the number of parameters of the underlying utility model, which will be linear in the number of attributes $|\mathbf{X}|$ if we assume that the size of each utility factor f^k is bounded. This compares favorably with the exponential size of the IP for unfactored utility models in Sec. 2.1.[5]

2.3   Minimax Regret

If the utility function is unknown, then we have a slightly different problem. We cannot maximize expected utility because the utility function is unspecified. However, if we have constraints on the utility function (e.g., in the form of bounds), we can optimize using other criteria. A very natural criterion is *minimax regret* [11,5,16]: prefer the (feasible) assignment $\mathbf{x}$ that obtains minimum max-regret, where max-regret is the largest quantity by which one could "regret" choosing action $\mathbf{x}$ (while allowing the utility function to vary within the bounds).

More formally, let $\mathcal{U}$ denote the set of feasible utility functions, reflecting our partial knowledge of the user's preferences. The set $\mathcal{U}$ may be a finite; but more commonly it will be continuous, defined by bounds (or constraints) on (sets of) utility values $u(\mathbf{x})$ for various states. The *pairwise regret* of state $\mathbf{x}$ with respect to state $\mathbf{x}'$ over feasible utility set $\mathcal{U}$ is defined as

$$R(\mathbf{x}, \mathbf{x}', \mathcal{U}) = \max_{u \in \mathcal{U}} u(\mathbf{x}') - u(\mathbf{x}), \tag{4}$$

---

[4] For example, UCP-nets encompass GAI with some additional restrictions. Hence any algorithm for GAI models automatically applies to UCP-nets, though one might be able to exploit the structure of UCP-nets for *additional* computational gain.

[5] Generally, this IP would be solved using some form of search directly on the X_i variables, in which case there would be no need to explicitly represent $I_{\mathbf{x}[k]}$ (state) variables.

which is the most one could regret choosing $\mathbf{x}$ instead of $\mathbf{x}'$ (e.g., if an adversary could impose any utility function in $\mathcal{U}$). The *maximum regret* of decision $\mathbf{x}$ is:

$$MR(\mathbf{x}, \mathcal{U}) = \max_{\mathbf{x}'} \ R(\mathbf{x}, \mathbf{x}', \mathcal{U}) \tag{5}$$

$$= \max_{\mathbf{x}'} \max_{u \in \mathcal{U}} \ u(\mathbf{x}') - u(\mathbf{x}) \tag{6}$$

The *minimax regret* of feasible utility set $\mathcal{U}$ is:

$$MMR(\mathcal{U}) = \min_{\mathbf{x}} \ MR(\mathbf{x}, \mathcal{U}) \tag{7}$$

$$= \min_{\mathbf{x}} \max_{\mathbf{x}'} \max_{u \in \mathcal{U}} \ u(\mathbf{x}') - u(\mathbf{x}) \tag{8}$$

If the only information we have about a user's utility function is that it lies in the set $\mathcal{U}$, then a decision $\mathbf{x}^*$ that minimizes max-regret—that is, an $\mathbf{x}^*$ such that $MR(\mathbf{x}^*, \mathcal{U}) = MMR(\mathcal{U})$—seems reasonable. Specifically, without distributional information over the set of possible utility functions, choosing (or recommending) a *minimax-optimal* decision $\mathbf{x}^*$ minimizes the worst case loss with respect to possible realizations of the utility function $u \in \mathcal{U}$. Our goal is now to formulate the minimax regret optimization (Eq. 8) in a computationally tractable way.

3   Minimax Regret with Flat Utility Models

If we make no assumptions about the structure of the utility function, Eq. 8 can be interpreted directly as a semi-infinite, quadratic, mixed-integer program (MIP):

$$\min_{\{M_\mathbf{x}, I_\mathbf{x}, X_i\}} \sum_\mathbf{x} M_\mathbf{x} I_\mathbf{x} \text{ subj. to } \begin{cases} M_\mathbf{x} \geq u_{\mathbf{x}'} - u_\mathbf{x} \ \forall \mathbf{x} \in \mathbf{X}, \ \mathbf{x}' \in Feas(\mathbf{X}'), \ u \in \mathcal{U} \\ \mathcal{A} \text{ and } \mathcal{C} \end{cases}$$

where we have:

- variables $M_\mathbf{x}$: for each $\mathbf{x}$, $M_\mathbf{x}$ is a continuous variable denoting the max regret when that state is chosen.
- variables $I_\mathbf{x}$: for each $\mathbf{x}$, $I_\mathbf{x}$ is a boolean variable indicating whether $\mathbf{x}$ is the state chosen.
- coefficients $u_\mathbf{x}$: for each $u \in \mathcal{U}$ and each state $\mathbf{x}$, $u_\mathbf{x}$ denotes the utility of $\mathbf{x}$ given utility function u.
- constraint sets $\mathcal{A}$ and $\mathcal{C}$ (defined as above).

The set of constraints on the $M_\mathbf{x}$ variables is problematic. First, if $\mathcal{U}$ is continuous (the typical case we consider here), then the set of constraints of the form $M_\mathbf{x} \geq u_{\mathbf{x}'} - u_\mathbf{x}$ is also also continuous, since it requires that we "enumerate" all utility values $u_\mathbf{x}$ and $u_{\mathbf{x}'}$ corresponding to any utility function $u \in \mathcal{U}$. Furthermore, it is critical that we restrict our attention to those constraints associated with $\mathbf{x}'$ in the *feasible* set of states (i.e., those satisfying $\mathcal{C}$). Fortunately, we can often tackle this seemingly complex optimization in much simpler stages.

In this paper we consider the case where all utility parameters $u_\mathbf{x}$ are independent and have simple upper and lower bounds (e.g., asking standard gamble queries would provide such bounds [7, 4]). Specifically, we assume an upper bound $u_{\mathbf{x}}\uparrow$ and a lower bound $u_{\mathbf{x}}\downarrow$ on each $u_{\mathbf{x}}$, thus defining the feasible utility set $\mathcal{U}$. These assumptions allow us to compute the minimax regret in three simpler stages, which we now describe.[6]

First, we note that the pairwise regret for an ordered pair of states can be easily computed since each $u_{\mathbf{x}}$ is bounded by an upper and lower bound: $R(\mathbf{x}, \mathbf{x}', \mathcal{U}) = u'_{\mathbf{x}}\uparrow - u_{\mathbf{x}}\downarrow$ if $\mathbf{x} \neq \mathbf{x}'$, and $R(\mathbf{x}, \mathbf{x}', \mathcal{U}) = 0$ if $\mathbf{x} = \mathbf{x}'$. Let $r_{\mathbf{x}, \mathbf{x}'}$ denote this pairwise regret value for each $\mathbf{x}, \mathbf{x}'$, which we now assume has been pre-computed for all pairs.

Second, using Eq. 5, we can also compute the max regret $MR(\mathbf{x}, \mathcal{U})$ of any state $\mathbf{x}$ based on the pre-computed pairwise regret values $r_{\mathbf{x}, \mathbf{x}'}$. Specifically, we can enumerate all feasible states $\mathbf{x}'$, retaining the largest pairwise regret:

$$MR(\mathbf{x}, \mathcal{U}) = \max_{\mathbf{x}' \in Feas(\mathbf{X}')} r_{\mathbf{x}, \mathbf{x}'}. \tag{9}$$

Alternatively, we can search through feasible states "implicitly" with the following IP:

$$MR(\mathbf{x}, \mathcal{U}) = \max_{\{I_{\mathbf{x}'}, X'_i\}} \sum_{\mathbf{x}'} r_{\mathbf{x}, \mathbf{x}'} I_{\mathbf{x}'} \quad \text{subject to } \mathcal{A} \text{ and } \mathcal{C}. \tag{10}$$

Third, letting $m_{\mathbf{x}}$ denote the value of $MR(\mathbf{x}, \mathcal{U})$, we can then compute the minimax regret $MMR(\mathcal{U})$ readily. We simply enumerate all feasible states $\mathbf{x}$ and retain the one with the smallest (precomputed) max regret value $m_{\mathbf{x}}$:

$$MMR(\mathcal{U}) = \min_{\mathbf{x} \in Feas(\mathbf{X})} m_{\mathbf{x}} \tag{11}$$

Again, this enumeration may be done implicitly using the following IP:

$$MMR(\mathcal{U}) = \min_{\{I_{\mathbf{x}}, X_i\}} \sum_{\mathbf{x}} m_{\mathbf{x}} I_{\mathbf{x}} \quad \text{subject to } \mathcal{A} \text{ and } \mathcal{C}. \tag{12}$$

In this flat model case, the two IPs above are not necessarily practical, since they require one indicator variable per state. However, this reformulation does show that the original quadratic MIP with continuous constraints can be solved in stages using finite, linear IPs. More importantly, these intuitions will next be applied to develop an analogous procedure for graphical utility models.[7]

4   Minimax Regret with Graphical Models

The optimization for flat models is interesting in that it allows us to get a good sense of how minimax regret in a constraint-satisfaction setting works. From a practical perspective, however, the above model has little to commend it. By solving IPs with one $I_{\mathbf{x}}$ variable per state, we have lost all of the advantage of using a compact and natural constraint-based approach to problem modeling. As we have seen when optimizing

---

[6] This transformation essentially reduces the *semi-infinite quadratic* MIP to a *finite linear* IP.

[7] Note that this strategy hinges on the fact that we can independently determine upper and lower bounds on the utility value of each state. If utility values are correlated by more complicated constraints, this strategy may not work.

with known utility functions, if there is no *a priori* structure in the utility function, there is very little one can do but enumerate (feasible) states. On the other hand, when the problem structure allows for modeling via factored utility functions the optimization becomes more practical. We now show how much of this practicality remains when our goal is to compute the minimax-optimal state, given uncertainty in a *factored* utility function represented as a graphical model.

Assume a set of factors f^k, $k \leq K$, defined over local families $\mathbf{X}[k]$, as described in Sec. 2.2. The parameters of this utility function are denoted by $u_{\mathbf{x}[k]} = f^k(\mathbf{x}[k])$, where $\mathbf{x}[k]$ ranges over $Dom(\mathbf{X}[k])$. As in the flat-model case, we assume upper and lower bounds on each of these parameters, which we denote by $u_{\mathbf{x}[k]}\uparrow$ and $u_{\mathbf{x}[k]}\downarrow$, respectively. By defining $u(\mathbf{x})$ as in Eq. 2, pairwise regret, max regret and minimax regret are all defined in the same manner outlined in Sec. 2.3. We now show how to compute each of these quantities in turn.

4.1 Computing Pairwise Regret and Max Regret

As in the unfactored case (Sec. 3), it is straightforward to compute the pairwise regret of any pair of states $\mathbf{x}$ and $\mathbf{x}'$. For each factor f^k and assignment pair $\mathbf{x}[k],\mathbf{x}'[k]$, we define the *local pairwise regret*: $r_{\mathbf{x}[k],\mathbf{x}'[k]} = u_{\mathbf{x}'[k]}\uparrow - u_{\mathbf{x}[k]}\downarrow$ when $\mathbf{x}[k] \neq \mathbf{x}'[k]$, and $r_{\mathbf{x}[k],\mathbf{x}'[k]} = 0$ when $\mathbf{x}[k] = \mathbf{x}'[k]$. With factored models, $R(\mathbf{x}, \mathbf{x}', \mathcal{U})$ is the sum of local pairwise regrets:

$$R(\mathbf{x}, \mathbf{x}', \mathcal{U}) = \sum_k r_{\mathbf{x}[k],\mathbf{x}'[k]}. \tag{13}$$

We can compute max regret $MR(\mathbf{x}, \mathcal{U})$ by substituting Eq. 13 into Eq. 5:

$$MR(\mathbf{x}, \mathcal{U}) = \max_{\mathbf{x}' \in Feas(\mathbf{X}')} \sum_k r_{\mathbf{x}[k],\mathbf{x}'[k]} \tag{14}$$

which leads to the following IP formulation:

$$MR(\mathbf{x}, \mathcal{U}) = \max_{\{I_{\mathbf{x}'[k]}, X_i'\}} \sum_k \sum_{\mathbf{x}'[k]} r_{\mathbf{x}[k],\mathbf{x}'[k]} I_{\mathbf{x}'[k]} \text{ subject to } \mathcal{A} \text{ and } \mathcal{C} \tag{15}$$

The above IP differs from its flat counterpart (Eq. 10) in the use of one variable $I_{\mathbf{x}'[k]}$ per utility parameter, and is thus more compact and efficiently solvable.

4.2 Computing Minimax Regret

We can compute minimax regret $MMR(\mathcal{U})$ by substituting Eq. 14 into Eq. 7:

$$MMR(\mathcal{U}) = \min_{\mathbf{x} \in Feas(\mathbf{X})} \max_{\mathbf{x}' \in Feas(\mathbf{X}')} \sum_k r_{\mathbf{x}[k],\mathbf{x}'[k]} \tag{16}$$

which leads to the following MIP formulation:

$$MMR(\mathcal{U}) = \min_{\{I_{\mathbf{x}[k]}, X_i\}} \max_{\mathbf{x}' \in Feas(\mathbf{X}')} \sum_k \sum_{\mathbf{x}[k]} r_{\mathbf{x}[k], \mathbf{x}'[k]} I_{\mathbf{x}[k]} \text{ subject to } \mathcal{A} \text{ and } \mathcal{C} \quad (17)$$

$$= \min_{\{I_{\mathbf{x}[k]}, X_i, M\}} M$$

$$\text{subject to } \begin{cases} M \geq \sum_k \sum_{\mathbf{x}[k]} r_{\mathbf{x}[k], \mathbf{x}'[k]} I_{\mathbf{x}[k]} \ \forall \mathbf{x}' \in Feas(\mathbf{X}') \\ \mathcal{A} \text{ and } \mathcal{C} \end{cases} \quad (18)$$

In Eq. 17, we introduce the variables for the minimization, while in Eq. 18 we transform the minimax program into a min program. The new continuous variable M corresponds to the max regret of any state. In contrast with the flat IP (Eq. 12), this MIP has a number of $I_{\mathbf{x}[k]}$ variables that is linear in the number of utility parameters. However, this MIP is not generally compact because Eq. 18 has one constraint per feasible state $\mathbf{x}'$. Nevertheless, we can get around the potentially large number of constraints in either of two ways.

Constraint Generation The first technique we consider for dealing with the large number of constraints in Eq. 18 is *constraint generation*, a common technique in operations research for solving problems with large numbers of constraints (much like cutting plane and column generation methods). This approach proceeds by repeatedly solving the MIP in Eq. 18, but using only a subset of the constraints on M associated with the feasible states $\mathbf{x}'$. At the first iteration, all constraints on M are ignored. At each iteration, we obtain a solution indicating some decision $\mathbf{x}$ with purported minimax regret; however, since certain unexpressed constraints may be violated, we cannot be content with this solution. Thus, we look for the unexpressed constraint on M that is maximally violated by the current solution. This involves finding a *witness* $\mathbf{x}'$ that maximizes regret w.r.t. the current solution $\mathbf{x}$; that is, a decision $\mathbf{x}'$ (and, implicitly, a utility function) that an adversary would chose to cause a user to regret $\mathbf{x}$ the most.

Recall that finding the feasible $\mathbf{x}'$ that maximizes $R(\mathbf{x}, \mathbf{x}', \mathcal{U})$ involves solving a single IP given by Eq. 15. We then impose the specific constraint associated with witness $\mathbf{x}'$ and re-solve the MIP in Eq. 18 at the next iteration with this additional constraint. It is not hard to see that if no constraint is violated at the current solution $\mathbf{x}$, then $\mathbf{x}$ is the minimax-optimal configuration. The procedure is finite and guaranteed to arrive at the optimal solution. The constraint generation routine is not guaranteed to finish before it has the full set of constraints, but is relatively simple and in practice (as we will see) tends to generate a very small number of constraints. Thus in practice we solve this very large MIP using a series of small MIPs, each with a small number of variables and a set of active constraints that is also, typically, very small.

A Cost Network Formulation A second technique for dealing with the large number of constraints in Eq. 18 is to use a "cost network" to generate a *compact* set of constraints that effectively summarizes this set. This type of approach has been used recently, for example, to solve Markov decision processes [12]. The main benefit of the cost network approach is that, in principle, it allows us to formulate a MIP with a feasible number of constraints.[8]

To formulate a compact constraint system, we first transform the MIP of Eq. 18 into the following equivalent MIP by introducing penalty terms $\rho_{\mathbf{x}[\ell]}$ for each feasibility constraint $\mathcal{C}_\ell$:

$$MMR(\mathcal{U}) = \min_{\{I_{\mathbf{x}[k]}, X_i, M\}} M$$

$$\text{subject to} \begin{cases} M \geq \sum_k \sum_{\mathbf{x}[k]} r_{\mathbf{x}[k], \mathbf{x}'[k]} I_{\mathbf{x}[k]} + \sum_\ell \rho_{\mathbf{x}'[\ell]} & \forall \mathbf{x}' \in Dom(\mathbf{X}') \\ \mathcal{A} \text{ and } \mathcal{C} \end{cases}$$

$$= \min_{\{I_{\mathbf{x}[k]}, X_i, M\}} M$$

$$\text{subject to} \begin{cases} M \geq \sum_k R_{\mathbf{x}'[k]} + \sum_\ell \rho_{\mathbf{x}'[\ell]} & \forall \mathbf{x}' \in Dom(\mathbf{X}') \\ R_{\mathbf{x}'[k]} = \sum_{\mathbf{x}[k]} r_{\mathbf{x}[k], \mathbf{x}'[k]} I_{\mathbf{x}[k]} & \forall k, \mathbf{x}'[k] \in Dom(\mathbf{X}'[k]) \quad (19) \\ \mathcal{A} \text{ and } \mathcal{C} \end{cases}$$

The MIP of Eq. 18 has one constraint on M per feasible state $\mathbf{x}'$, whereas the MIP of Eq. 19 has one constraint per state $\mathbf{x}'$ (whether feasible or not). Therefore, to effectively maintain the feasibility constraints on $\mathbf{x}'$, we add penalty terms $\rho_{\mathbf{x}'[\ell]}$ that essentially make a constraint on M meaningless when its corresponding state $\mathbf{x}'$ is infeasible. This is achieved by defining a local penalty function $\rho^\ell(\mathbf{x}'[\ell])$ for each logical constraint $\mathcal{C}_\ell$ that returns $-\infty$ when $\mathbf{x}'[\ell]$ violates $\mathcal{C}_\ell$ and 0 otherwise.

This transformation has, unfortunately, increased the number of constraints. However, it in fact allows us to rewrite the constraints in a much more compact form, as follows. Instead of enumerating all constraints on M, we analytically construct the constraint that provides the *greatest lower bound*, while simply ignoring the others. This greatest lower bound *GLB* is computed by taking the max of all constraints on M:

$$GLB = \max_{\mathbf{x}'} \sum_k R_{\mathbf{x}'[k]} + \sum_\ell \rho_{\mathbf{x}'[\ell]}$$

$$= \max_{x_1'} \max_{x_2'} \ldots \max_{x_N'} \sum_k R_{\mathbf{x}'[k]} + \sum_\ell \rho_{\mathbf{x}'[\ell]}$$

This maximization can be computed efficiently by using *variable elimination* [9], a well-known form of non-serial dynamic programming [2]. The idea is to distribute the max operator inward over the summations, and then collect the results as new terms which are successively pulled out. Space precludes a detailed presentation of the algorithm—we instead illustrate its workings by means of an example.

To illustrate, consider the following simple example. Suppose we have the attributes X_1, X_2, X_3, X_4, a utility function decomposed into the factors $f^1(x_1, x_2)$, $f^2(x_2, x_3)$,

---

[8] We have observed, however, the constraint generation approach described above is usually faster in practice and much easier to implement, even though it lacks the same worst case run-time guarantees. Indeed, this same fact has been observed in the context of MDPs [18].

$f^3(x_1, x_4)$ and two logical constraints with associated penalty functions $\rho^1(x_1)$ and $\rho^2(x_3, x_4)$. We then obtain

$$GLB = \max_{x_1'} \max_{x_2'} \max_{x_3'} \max_{x_4'} R_{x_1', x_2'} + R_{x_2', x_3'} + R_{x_1', x_4'} + \rho_{x_1'} + \rho_{x_3', x_4'}$$

$$= \max_{x_1'}[\rho_{x_1'} + \max_{x_2'}[R_{x_1', x_2'} + \max_{x_3'}[R_{x_2', x_3'} + \max_{x_4'}[R_{x_1', x_4'} + \rho_{x_3', x_4'}]]]]$$

by distributing the individual max operators inward over the summations. To compute the *GLB*, we successively formulate new terms that summarize the result of completing each max in turn, as follows:

$$\text{Let } A_{x_1', x_3'} = \max_{x_4'} R_{x_1', x_4'} + \rho_{x_3', x_4'}$$

$$\text{Let } A_{x_1', x_2'} = \max_{x_3'} R_{x_2', x_3'} + A_{x_1', x_3'}$$

$$\text{Let } A_{x_1'} = \max_{x_2'} R_{x_1', x_2'} + A_{x_1', x_2'}$$

$$\text{Let } GLB = \max_{x_1'} \rho_{x_1'} + A_{x_1'}$$

Notice that this incremental procedure can be substantially faster than enumerating all states $\mathbf{x}'$. In fact the complexity of each step is only exponential in the local subset of attributes that indexes each auxiliary A variable.

Based on this procedure, we can substitute all the constraints on M in the MIP in Eq. 19 with the following compact set of constraints that analytically encodes the greatest lower bound on M:

$$A_{x_1', x_3'} \geq R_{x_1', x_4'} + \rho_{x_3', x_4'} \quad \forall x_1', x_3', x_4' \in Dom(X_1', X_3', X_4')$$

$$A_{x_1', x_2'} \geq R_{x_2', x_3'} + A_{x_1', x_3'} \quad \forall x_1', x_2', x_3' \in Dom(X_1', X_2', X_3')$$

$$A_{x_1'} \geq R_{x_1', x_2'} + A_{x_1', x_2'} \quad \forall x_1', x_2' \in Dom(X_1', X_2')$$

$$M \geq \rho_{x_1'} + A_{x_1'} \quad \forall x_1' \in Dom(X_1')$$

By encoding constraints in this way, the constraint system specified by the MIP in Eq. 19 can be generally encoded with a small number of variables and constraints. Overall we obtain a MIP where: the number of $I_{\mathbf{x}}$ variables is linear in the number of parameters of the utility function; and the number of auxiliary variables and constraints that are added is locally exponential w.r.t. the largest subset of attributes indexing some auxiliary variable. In practice, since this largest subset is often very small compared to the set of all attributes, the resulting MIP encoding is compact and readily solvable. More precisely, the complexity of this algorithm depends on the order in which the variables in $\mathbf{X}'$ are eliminated, but is exponential in the tree width of the graph induced by the elimination ordering (which is generally only locally exponential) [9].

5   Empirical Results

To test the plausibility of this approach we implemented the solution strategy outlined above and ran a series of experiments to determine whether graphical structure was

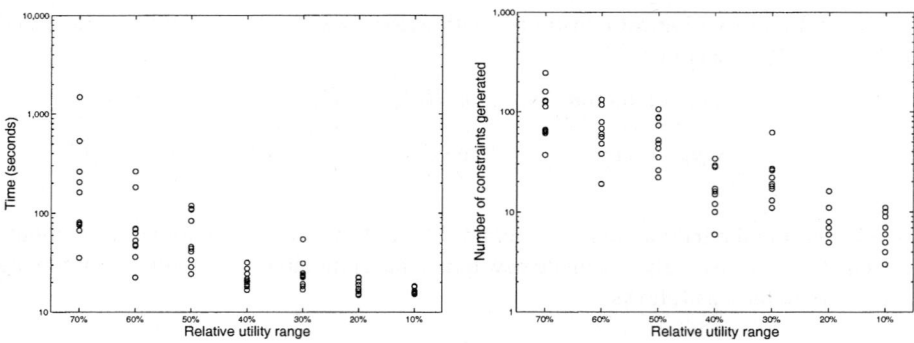

Fig. 1. Car Problem.

sufficient to permit practical solution times. We implemented the constraint generation approach outlined in Sec. 4.2 and used CPLEX as the generic IP solver. Our experiments considered two realistic domains—car rentals and house buying—as well as randomly generated synthetic problems. In each case we imposed a factored graphical structure to reduce the required number of utility parameters (upper and lower bounds).

For the house buying problem, we modeled the domain with 20 (multivalued) variables that specify various attributes of single family dwellings that are normally relevant to making a purchase decision. The variables we used included: square footage, age, size of yard, garage, number of bedrooms, etc. In total, there were 47,775,744 possible configurations of the variables. We then used a factored utility model consisting of 29 local factors, each defined only on one, two or three variables. In total, the number of local utility values (utilities for local configurations) was reduced to 160. Therefore a total of 320 upper and lower bounds had to be specified, a significant reduction over the nearly 10^8 values that would have been required using a unfactored model. The local utility functions represented complementarities and substitutabilities between variables, such as requiring a large yard and a fence to allow a pool, etc.

The rental car problem features 26 multi-valued variables encoding attributes relevant to consumers considering a car rental, such as: automobile size and class, manufacturer, rental agency, seating and luggage capacity, etc. The total number of possible variable configurations is 61,917,360,000. There are 36 local utility factors, each defined on at most five variables. Constraints encode infeasible configurations (e.g., no luxury sedans have 4-cylinder engines).

For both the car and real estate problems, we first computed the configuration with minimax regret given manually chosen bounds on the utility functions. The generation technique of Sec. 4.2 took 40 sec for the car problem and 2 sec for the real estate problem. Interestingly, only 7 constraints were generated in finding the minimax-optimal configuration in both the car and real estate problems (out of the 61,917,360,000 and

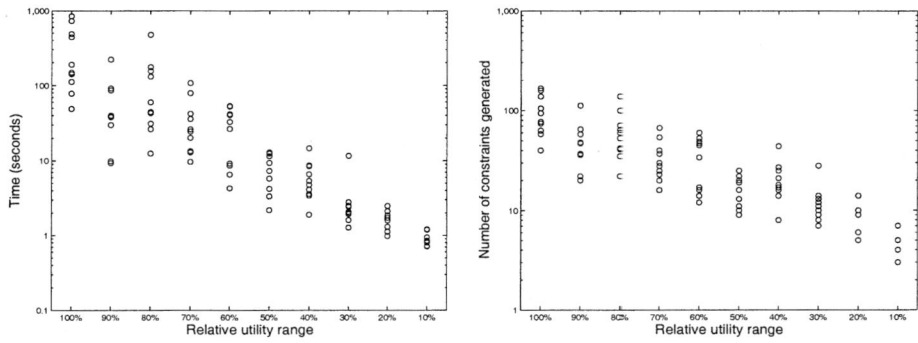

Fig. 2. Real estate problem.

47,775,744 constraints, respectively). The structure exhibited by the utility functions of each problem is largely responsible for this small number of required constraints.

In practice, the minimax regret techniques proposed in this paper would normally be interleaved with some preference elicitation technique. As the bounds on utility parameters get tighter, we would like to know the impact on the running time of our constraint generation algorithm. To that effect, we carried out an experiment where we randomly set bounds, but with varying degrees of tightness. Figures 1 and 2 show how tightening the bounds decreases the running time exponentially, and the number of constraints generated. For this experiment, bounds on utility were generated at random, but the difference between the upper and lower bounds of any utility was capped at a fixed percentage of some predetermined range. Figures 1 and 2 show scatterplots of random problems for varying percentages. As those figures suggest, a significant speed up is obtained as elicitation converges to the true utilities. Intuitively, the optimization required to compute minimax regret benefits from tighter bounds since some configurations emerge as clearly dominant, which in turn requires the generation of fewer constraints.

We carried out a second experiment with synthetic problems. A set of random problems of varying sizes was constructed by randomly setting the utility bounds as well as the variables on which each utility factor depends. Each utility factor depends on at most 3 variables and each variable has at most 5 values. Figure 3 shows the results as we vary the number of variables and factors (the number of factors is always the same as the number of variables). The running time and the number of constraints generated increases exponentially with the size of the problem. Note however that the number of constraints generated is still a tiny fraction of the total number of constraints (if they were all enumerated). For problems with 10 variables, only 8 constraints were necessary (out of 278,864) on average; and for problems of 30 variables, only 47 constraints were necessary (out of 2.8×10^{16}) on average.

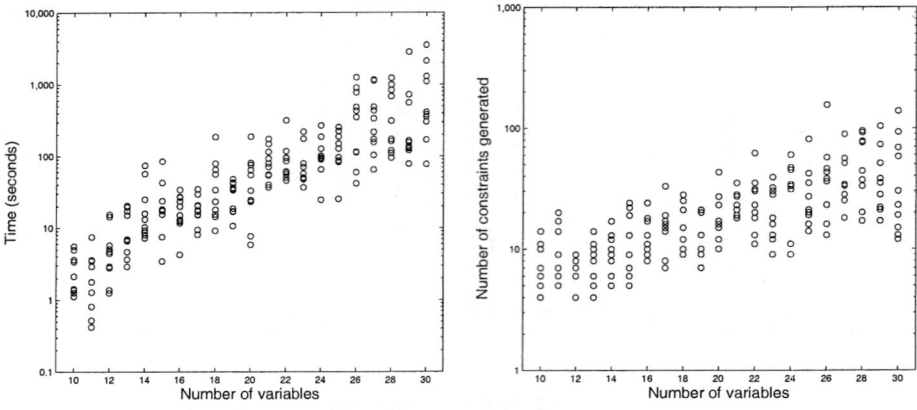

Fig. 3. Artificial random problems – varying sizes

We also tested the impact of elicitation on the efficiency of our constraint generation technique in Figure 4. Here, problems of 30 variables and 30 factors were generated randomly while varying the relative range of the utilities w.r.t. some predetermined range. Each factor has at most 3 variables chosen randomly and each variable can take at most 5 values. Once again, as the bounds get tighter, some configurations emerge as clearly dominant, which allows an exponential reduction in the running time as well as the number of required constraints.

6   Concluding Remarks

We have developed a technique for computing minimax optimal decisions in constraint-based decision problems when a user's utility function is only partially specified in the form of upper and lower bounds on utility parameters. While the corresponding optimizations are potentially complex, we derived methods whereby they could be solved effectively using several IPs and MIPs. Furthermore, we showed how graphical structure in the utility model could be exploited to ensure that the resulting IPs are compact or could be solved using an effective constraint generation procedure.

There are a number of directions in which this work can be extended. Of critical importance is the development of good elicitation strategies that reduce minimax regret quickly. While this work has focused on the computation of minimax-optimal assignments to variables, our current thrust is the incorporation of this approach into querying strategies that can be used to tighten only the most relevant utility parameter bounds. We have devised several elicitation strategies that we hope will work well in practice; but these have yet to be implemented (so their performance still needs to be verified). We briefly describe two of these methods.

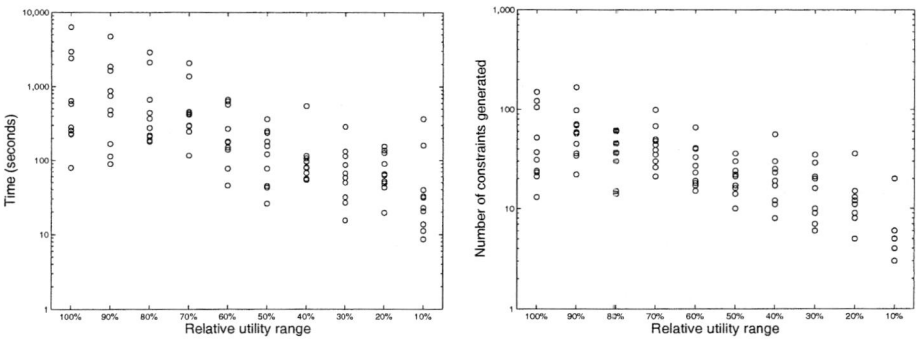

Fig. 4. Artificial random problems – varying relative utility range.

The *optimistic query method* works as follows: at each iteration we compute the *maximax optimal* state x^* (i.e, that with the greatest upper bound on utility). We then query the user about the utility parameters of that factor in such a way that its lower bound on utility is raised to be close (say, within ε) to the upper bound of the state with the second-highest upper bound (which can be computed in a similar way), or its upper bound is reduced to below that of the second state. In either case, we have made progress: in the first case, we have reduced minimax regret to ε; in the second case, we have reduced the regret of every other decision (by an amount equal to the reduction of the upper bound for x^*, less ε).

The *current solution query method* involves computing the minimax optimal state x^* using one of the methods described, as well as its regret-maximizing "witness" x^w (i.e., the state an adversary chooses in order to maximize our regret). We then ask queries about the utility parameters at the both states (e.g., asking a midpoint query about each parameter, thus reducing each interval by half). The intuition behind this approach is that gaining tighter information about the current minimax optimal allocation and its witness is the best way to ensure an improvement in regret level (since these are the parameters that play a role in the active constraints at the current solution).

Apart from elicitation, we are also exploring the use of search and constraint-propagation methods for solving the constraint-optimization problems associated with computing minimax regret. Our goal in this paper was to provide a precise formulation of these computational problems as integer programs, and use off-the-shelf software to solve them. We expect that optimization techniques that are specifically directed toward these problems should prove fruitful. Along these lines, we hope to develop deeper connections to existing work on soft constraints, valued CSPs, etc. Finally, we are quite interested in the possibility of integrating Bayesian methods for reasoning about uncertain utility functions with the constraint-based representation of the decision space.

Acknowledgements This research was supported by the the Institute for Robotics and Intelligent Systems (IRIS) and the Natural Sciences and Engineering Research Council (NSERC). Poupart was supported by a scholarship provided by Precarn Incorporated through IRIS.

References

1. F. Bacchus and A. Grove. Graphical models for preference and utility. In *Proc. 11th Conf. on Uncertainty in AI*, pp.3–10, Montreal, 1995.
2. U. Bertele and F. Brioschi. *Nonserial Dynamic Programming*. Academic, Orlando, 1972.
3. S. Bistarelli, U. Montanari, and F. Rossi. Semiring-based constraint satisfaction and optimization. *Journal of the ACM*, 44(2):201–236, 1997.
4. C. Boutilier. A POMDP formulation of preference elicitation problems. In *Proc. 18th National Conf. on AI*, pp.239–246, Edmonton, 2002.
5. C. Boutilier, F. Bacchus, and R. I. Brafman. UCP-Networks: A directed graphical representation of conditional utilities. In *Proc. 17th Conf. on Uncertainty in AI*, pp.56–64, 2001.
6. U. Chajewska, L. Getoor, J. Norman, and Y. Shahar. Utility elicitation as a classification problem. In *Proc. 14th Conf. on Uncertainty in AI*, pp.79–88, Madison, WI, 1998.
7. U. Chajewska, D. Koller, and R. Parr. Making rational decisions using adaptive utility elicitation. In *Proc. 17th National Conf. on AI*, pp.363–369, Austin, TX, 2000.
8. V. Chandru and J. Hooker. *Optimization Methods for Logical Inference*. Wiley, N.Y., 1999.
9. R. Dechter. Bucket elimination: A unifying framework for probabilistic inference. In *Proc. Twelfth Conf. on Uncertainty in AI*, pp.211–219, Portland, OR, 1996.
10. J. S. Dyer. Interactive goal programming. *Management Science*, 19:62–70, 1972.
11. S. French. *Decision Theory*. Halsted Press, New York, 1986.
12. C. Guestrin, D. Koller, and R. Parr. Max-norm projections for factored MDPs. In *Proc. 17th Intl. Joint Conf. on AI*, pp.673–680, Seattle, 2001.
13. R. L. Keeney and H. Raiffa. *Decisions with Multiple Objectives: Preferences and Value Trade-offs*. Wiley, New York, 1976.
14. D. Sabin and R. Weigel. Product configuration frameworks—a survey. *IEEE Intelligent Systems and their Applications*, 13(4):42–49, 1998.
15. T. Schiex, H. Fargie, and G. Verfaillie. Valued constraint satisfaction problems: Hard and easy problems. In *Proc. 14th Intl. Joint Conf. on AI*, pp.631–637, Montreal, 1995.
16. T. Wang and C. Boutilier. Incremental utility elicitation with the minimax regret decision criterion. In *Proc. 18th Intl. Joint Conf. on AI*, to appear, Acapulco, Mexico, 2003.
17. C. C. White, III, A. P. Sage, and S. Dozono. A model of multiattribute decision making and trade-off weight determination under uncertainty. *IEEE Transactions on Systems, Man and Cybernetics*, 14(2):223–229, 1984.
18. D. Schuurmans, R. Patrascu. Direct value-approximation for factored MDPs. In Advances in Neural Information Processing 14, pp. 1579-1586, MIT Press, Cambridge, MA, 2002.

An Algebraic Approach
to Multi-sorted Constraints

Andrei A. Bulatov and Peter Jeavons

Computing Laboratory, University of Oxford, UK
{Andrei.Bulatov,Peter.Jeavons}@comlab.ox.ac.uk

Abstract. Most previous theoretical study of the complexity of the constraint satisfaction problem has considered a simplified version of the problem in which all variables have the same domain. We show here that this apparently minor simplification can in fact change the complexity of the problem, and hence mask the existence of certain tractable constraint types. In this paper we describe a new algebraic framework which allows us to deal more precisely with problems where different variables may have different domains. Using this new framework we are able to identify new tractable classes of constraints, by combining algorithms devised for the simplified, single domain, problem. We also systematically develop an algebraic structural theory for the general problem, and show that this theory can be used to generalise earlier results about the complexity of certain constraint types.

1   Introduction

There is a striking difference between theoretical studies of the complexity of the Constraint Satisfaction Problem (CSP), and more applied work on this problem: in most theoretical studies constraint satisfaction problems are assumed to have the same domain for all variables (we will call such problems *one-sorted*), while in practice the different variables of a CSP often have different domains (we will call problems of this type *multi-sorted*). This apparently minor simplification can have serious consequences for the analysis of the complexity of different forms of constraint; it can in fact mask the difference between tractability and NP-completeness for certain problems.

Example 1. Consider the following relation of arity 5 containing 17 tuples (shown vertically):

$$\varrho = \begin{pmatrix} 3 & 3 & 1 & 1 & 1 & 1 & 3 & 3 & 3 & 3 & 1 & 1 & 3 & 3 & 1 & 1 & 3 \\ 1 & 3 & 0 & 2 & 1 & 3 & 0 & 2 & 1 & 3 & 0 & 2 & 1 & 3 & 1 & 3 & 3 \\ 2 & 2 & 2 & 2 & 0 & 0 & 0 & 0 & 2 & 2 & 2 & 2 & 2 & 2 & 0 & 0 & 2 \\ c & c & c & c & c & c & c & c & c & c & c & c & a & a & a & a & a \\ b & b & b & b & b & b & b & b & a & a & a & a & b & b & b & b & a \end{pmatrix}$$

F. Rossi (Ed.): CP 2003, LNCS 2833, pp. 183–198, 2003.

If we consider this relation in the usual way as a one-sorted relation over the domain $\{0, 1, 2, 3, a, b, c\}$, then it does not fall into any of the many known (one-sorted) tractable classes[1] [2, 3, 7, 9, 13, 19, 20, 24, 27, 28].

However, if we consider this relation as a *multi-sorted* relation, over the two separate domains $\{0, 1, 2, 3\}$ and $\{a, b, c\}$ (in the sense defined below), then it can easily be shown to be tractable, using the results obtained in this paper (see Example 8). Note that to establish the tractability of a multi-sorted relation it is *not* sufficient simply to show that the projections onto each separate domain are tractable (see Example 5).

This paper is part of a general investigation into how the complexity of the constraint satisfaction problem varies with the forms of constraints which are allowed. Considerable progress has been made in this investigation over the past few years. For example, a complete characterisation of tractable constraint types is now known for both 2-element domains [26] and 3-element domains [1]. In addition, a number of novel efficient algorithms have been developed for solving particular types of CSPs [2, 10, 13, 20].

However, almost all previous work on complexity has focused on the one-sorted CSP; the first goal of this paper is to develop an approach which allows us to study the complexity of multi-sorted constraint satisfaction problems, where different variables have different domains. Using this approach, we show that many of the known algorithms for the one-sorted case can be combined, and hence applied to much broader classes of constraint satisfaction problems.

The second goal of the paper is to further develop the strong links between the study of complexity of the CSP and the mathematical study of finite algebras. These links were introduced and developed for the one-sorted case in [19, 18, 6]. In the multi-sorted case, these links allow one to use even more effectively the powerful mathematical theory developed for classifying the structure of finite algebras [23, 16]. For example, early versions of the results given here have already been successfully applied to obtain new tractable classes [3, 2]. Moreover, the results described in this paper are heavily used in proving a dichotomy theorem for constraint satisfaction problems over a 3-element domain [1].

As an example of the flexibility of the multi-sorted approach developed here, we consider the analysis of constraints which restrict the domain of each individual variable in their scope. By using the link with finite algebras described below, we are able to generalize and strengthen the dichotomy result of [12] classifying all constraints which restrict the domain of each variable to two possible values.

2   The Multi-sorted Constraint Satisfaction Problem

The central notion in the mathematical study of constraints and constraint satisfaction problems is the notion of a *relation*. In this paper we will allow *multi-sorted* relations, that is, relations over an arbitrary collection of sets. These are defined as follows.

---

[1] This was established by using the program *Polyanna* [15] available from http://www.comlab.ox.ac.uk/oucl/research/areas/constraints/software/

Definition 1. *For any collection of sets* $\mathcal{A} = \{A_i \mid i \in I\}$, *and any list of indices* $(i_1, i_2, \ldots, i_m) \in I^m$, *a subset* ϱ *of* $A_{i_1} \times A_{i_2} \times \cdots \times A_{i_m}$, *together with the list* $(i_1, i_2, \ldots, i_m)$, *will be called a* multi-sorted relation *over* $\mathcal{A}$ *with arity* m *and* signature $(i_1, i_2, \ldots, i_m)$. *For any such relation* ϱ, *the signature of* ϱ *will be denoted* $\sigma(\varrho)$.

In the special case where $\mathcal{A}$ contains only a single set A, we shall refer to a relation over $\mathcal{A}$ as a *one-sorted* relation over the set A.

Example 2. Let $\mathcal{A} = \{A_1, A_2\}$, where $A_1 = \{0, 1, 2, 3\}$ and $A_2 = \{a, b, c\}$.

The relation ϱ, defined in Example 1, can be viewed as a multi-sorted relation over $\mathcal{A}$ with arity 5 and signature $(1, 1, 1, 2, 2)$.

Given any set of multi-sorted relations, we can define a corresponding class of multi-sorted constraint satisfaction problems, in the following way.

Definition 2. *Let* Γ *be a set of multi-sorted relations over a collection of sets* $\mathcal{A} = \{A_i \mid i \in I\}$. *The* multi-sorted constraint satisfaction problem over Γ, *denoted* $\mathrm{MCSP}(\Gamma)$, *is defined to be the decision problem with*

INSTANCE: *A quadruple* $(V; \mathcal{A}; \delta; \mathcal{C})$ *where*
  − *V is a set of* variables;
  − δ *is a mapping from* V *to* I, *called the* domain function;
  − $\mathcal{C}$ *is a set of* constraints, *where each constraint* $C \in \mathcal{C}$ *is a pair* $\langle s, \varrho \rangle$, *such that*
    • $s = (v_1, \ldots, v_{m_C})$ *is a tuple of variables of length* m_C, *called the* constraint scope;
    • ϱ *is an element of* Γ *with arity* m_C *and signature* $(\delta(v_1), \ldots, \delta(v_{m_C}))$, *called the* constraint relation.
QUESTION: *Does there exist a* solution, *i.e., a function* φ, *from* V *to* $\bigcup_{A \in \mathcal{A}} A$, *such that, for each variable* $v \in V$, $\varphi(v) \in A_{\delta(v)}$, *and for each constraint* $\langle s, \varrho \rangle \in \mathcal{C}$, *with* $s = (v_1, \ldots, v_m)$, *the tuple* $(\varphi(v_1), \ldots, \varphi(v_m))$ *belongs to* ϱ?

Example 3. Constraint satisfaction problems in which each variable has a distinct set of possible values frequently arise in the study of *databases*, although a rather different vocabulary is normally used, as in the following definition.

Definition 3. *A* relational database *is a finite collection of* tables. *A table consists of a* scheme *and an* instance:

  A scheme *is a finite set of* attributes, *where each attribute has an associated set of possible values, referred to as a* domain.
  An instance *is a finite set of* rows, *where each row is a mapping that associates with each attribute of the scheme a value in its domain.*

A standard problem in the context of relational databases is the CONJUNCTIVE QUERY EVALUATION problem [21, 29]. In this problem we are asked if a *conjunctive query* to a relational database, that is, a query of the form $\exists x_1 \ldots \exists x_k (\varrho_1 \wedge \ldots \wedge \varrho_n)$ where $\varrho_1, \ldots, \varrho_n$ are atomic formulas, has a solution. An instance of a multi-sorted constraint satisfaction problem corresponds to a conjunctive query over a relational database by a simple translation of terms: 'attributes' have to be replaced with 'variables', 'tables' with 'constraint relations', 'scheme' with 'signature', 'instance' with 'constraint relation', and 'rows' with 'tuples'. Hence a conjunctive query is equivalent to a multi-sorted CSP instance whose variables are the variables of the query. For each atomic formula ϱ_i in the query, there is a constraint C such that the scope of C is the list of variables of ϱ_i and the constraint relation of C is the set of models of ϱ_i.

In the special case where Γ is a set of one-sorted relations over a single set A, we shall use the notation $\mathrm{CSP}(\Gamma)$, and refer to this as a *one-sorted* problem class. An instance of $\mathrm{CSP}(\Gamma)$ can be specified by a triple $(V; A; \mathcal{C})$.

Example 4. Consider the GRAPH q-COLORABILITY problem. An instance of this problem consists of a graph G, and the question is whether the vertices of G can be labelled with q colours so that adjacent vertices are assigned different colours.

Each instance G of GRAPH q-COLORABILITY corresponds to an instance $\mathcal{P}_G$ of $\mathrm{CSP}(\{\neq_A\})$, where A is a q-element set and $\neq_A = \{(a, b) \in A^2 \mid a \neq b\}$. The variables of $\mathcal{P}_G$ are the vertices of the graph G, and for each edge $\{v, w\}$ of G, there is a constraint $(\{v, w\}, \neq_A)$ in $\mathcal{P}_G$.

In the remainder of the paper we shall be concerned with distinguishing between those sets of relations which give rise to *tractable* problems (i.e., problems for which there exists a polynomial-time solution algorithm) and those which do not. In order to be able to classify *infinite*, as well as finite, sets of relations, we define the notion of a tractable set of relations in a way that depends on finite subsets only.

Definition 4. *A set of multi-sorted relations, Γ, is said to be* tractable, *if* $\mathrm{MCSP}(\Gamma')$ *is tractable for each finite subset $\Gamma' \subseteq \Gamma$.*

A set of multi-sorted relations, Γ, is said to be NP-complete, *if $\mathrm{MCSP}(\Gamma')$ is NP-complete for some finite subset $\Gamma' \subseteq \Gamma$.*

It might be tempting to assume that the complexity of a set of multi-sorted relations could be determined by considering each of the domains involved separately; in other words, by separating the relations into a number of one-sorted relations, and analysing the complexity of each of these. However, in general this simple approach does not work, as the next example demonstrates.

Example 5. Consider the sets $A_1 = \{0, 1\}$ and $A_2 = \{a, b, c\}$, and the relations

$$\varrho_1 = \begin{pmatrix} 1 & 0 & 0 \\ a & b & c \end{pmatrix}, \qquad \varrho_2 = \begin{pmatrix} 0 & 1 & 0 \\ a & b & c \end{pmatrix}, \qquad \varrho_3 = \begin{pmatrix} 0 & 0 & 1 \\ a & b & c \end{pmatrix}$$

over $\{A_1, A_2\}$, each with signature $(1, 2)$.

If we divide each of these relations into two separate one-sorted relations, then we obtain just the unary relations $\{0, 1\}$ and $\{a, b, c\}$ over the sets A_1 and A_2 respectively. Each of these unary relations individually is clearly tractable.

However, by establishing a reduction from the NP-complete problem ONE-IN-THREE [14], it can be shown that the set of multi-sorted relations $\Gamma = \{\varrho_1, \varrho_2, \varrho_3\}$ is NP-complete.

To obtain the reduction we note that the ONE-IN-THREE problem may be expressed as $\mathrm{CSP}(\{\varrho\})$ where $\varrho = \{(1,0,0),(0,1,0),(0,0,1)\}$. Given any problem instance $\mathcal{P} = (V; \{0,1\}; \{C_1, \ldots, C_q\}) \in \mathrm{CSP}(\{\varrho\})$, we introduce q auxiliary variables $v_1, \ldots, v_q$, distinct from the variables in V, and set $\mathcal{P}' = (V \cup \{v_1, \ldots, v_q\}; \{A_1, A_2\}; \delta; \{C_1^1, C_1^2, C_1^3, C_2^1, \ldots, C_q^3\})$, where $\delta(v) = 1$ if $v \in V$, $\delta(v) = 2$ otherwise, and for each $C_i = \langle(w_1, w_2, w_3), \varrho\rangle$, the new constraints are $C_i^1 = \langle(w_1, v_i), \varrho_1\rangle$, $C_i^2 = \langle(w_2, v_i), \varrho_2\rangle$, and $C_i^3 = \langle(w_3, v_i), \varrho_3\rangle$. It is easy to check that $\mathcal{P}$ and $\mathcal{P}'$ are equivalent.

The next example indicates that a set of constraints which is NP-complete when viewed as one-sorted, can become tractable when viewed as multi-sorted: the tractability is due to the signatures of the relations rather than the tuples they contain.

Example 6. Let A_1 and A_2 be two distinct supersets of a set A_0, and let Γ be the set containing the single binary disequality relation $\neq_{A_0}$, as defined in Example 4, but now considered as a multi-sorted relation over $\{A_1, A_2\}$ with signature $(1, 2)$.

Because of the signature, this constraint can only be imposed between two variables when one of them has domain A_1 and the other has domain A_2. Hence, in this case $\mathrm{MCSP}(\Gamma)$ corresponds to the problem of colouring a *bipartite graph* with $|A_0|$ colours, which is clearly tractable.

It is often desirable to convert a multi-sorted constraint satisfaction problem into a one-sorted problem. The most straightforward way to do this for a given multi-sorted problem instance $(V; \mathcal{A}; \delta; \mathcal{C})$, is to take $B = \bigcup_{A \in \mathcal{A}} A$, and replace each constraint relation with a one-sorted relation over B containing exactly the same tuples.

However, applying this procedure to the disequality relation in Example 6 gives the usual disequality relation over A, which for $|A| > 2$ is NP-complete (see Example 4). Hence, this straightforward conversion method does *not* necessarily preserve the tractability of Γ. To ensure that we do preserve the tractability of Γ, we shall make use of a more sophisticated conversion technique, based on the following definition. Note that in this definition, and throughout the paper, the ith component of a tuple $\bar{a}$ is denoted by $\bar{a}[i]$.

Definition 5. *For any m-ary relation ϱ over $\{A_1, \ldots, A_n\}$ with signature $\sigma(\varrho)$ $= (i_1, \ldots, i_m)$, let $A = A_1 \times A_2 \times \cdots \times A_n$ and define the one-sorted m-ary relation $\chi(\varrho)$ over A as follows:*
$$\chi(\varrho) = \{(\bar{a}_1, \bar{a}_2, \ldots, \bar{a}_m) \in A^m \mid (\bar{a}_1[i_1], \ldots, \bar{a}_m[i_m]) \in \varrho\}.$$
For any set of relations Γ, the set $\{\chi(\varrho) \mid \varrho \in \Gamma\}$ will be denoted $\chi(\Gamma)$.

Note that for any one-sorted relation ϱ, we have $\chi(\varrho) = \varrho$.

Example 7. Let ϱ be the binary disequality relation $\neq_{A_0}$ over $\{A_1, A_2\}$ with signature $(1, 2)$, as in Example 6. In this case $\chi(\varrho)$ is the relation consisting of all pairs $((a, a'), (b, b')) \in (A_1 \times A_2) \times (A_1 \times A_2)$ such that $a, b' \in A_0$ and $a \neq b'$.

Proposition 1. *Let Γ be a set of multi-sorted relations over the finite sets $A_1, \ldots, A_n$. The set Γ is tractable if and only if the corresponding set of one-sorted relations $\chi(\Gamma)$ is tractable.*

Proof: Let $\mathcal{P} = (V; \{A_1, \ldots, A_n\}; \delta; \mathcal{C})$ be an instance of MCSP(Γ) where $\mathcal{C} = \{C_1, C_2, \ldots, C_q\}$ and each $C_i = \langle s_i, \varrho_i \rangle$.

Consider the one-sorted instance $\mathcal{P}' = (V; A; \mathcal{C}')$ where $A = A_1 \times A_2 \times \cdots \times A_n$, $\mathcal{C}' = \{C_1', C_2', \ldots, C_q'\}$, and each $C_i' = \langle s_i, \chi(\varrho_i) \rangle$. Note that every solution to $\mathcal{P}$ can be used to construct a solution for $\mathcal{P}'$ by extending the value assigned to each variable (arbitrarily) to a tuple over A. Conversely, every solution to $\mathcal{P}'$ can be used to obtain a solution for $\mathcal{P}$ by projecting the tuple over A assigned to each variable v onto the co-ordinate given by $\delta(v)$. Hence we have a reduction from MCSP(Γ) to CSP($\chi(\Gamma)$).

Furthermore, every tuple in every constraint relation of $\mathcal{P}$ is replaced by a fixed number of tuples (depending only on the cardinalities of the sets $A_1, \ldots, A_n$ and on the arities of the constraint relations), to obtain the corresponding constraint relation in $\mathcal{P}'$. Hence, for any finite subset of Γ the reduction can be carried out in linear time.

The same arguments can be applied in the reverse direction to obtain a polynomial-time reduction from CSP($\chi(\Gamma)$) to MCSP(Γ). □

3 Polymorphisms and Tractability Results

In earlier papers [19, 18, 6] it has been shown that in the one-sorted case the complexity of CSP(Γ) is determined by certain algebraic properties of the relations in Γ, known as *polymorphisms*. In this section, we first state some of these earlier results on the complexity of the one-sorted case, and then show how they can be extended to the multi-sorted case.

Definition 6. *Let ϱ be a one-sorted relation over a set A, with arity m.*

The operation $f : A^k \to A$ is said to be a polymorphism *of the relation ϱ if, for any tuples $(a_{11}, \ldots, a_{m1}), \ldots, (a_{1k}, \ldots, a_{mk}) \in \varrho$ the tuple $(f(a_{11}, \ldots, a_{1k}), \ldots, f(a_{m1}, \ldots, a_{mk}))$ also belongs to ϱ.*

For any given set of one-sorted relations Γ, the set of all those operations which are polymorphisms of *every* relation in Γ is denoted Pol(Γ).

Theorem 1 ([19, 17]). *Let Γ, Γ_0 be sets of one-sorted relations over a finite set A. If Γ_0 is finite, and Pol(Γ) $\subseteq$ Pol(Γ_0), then there is a polynomial time reduction from CSP(Γ_0) to CSP(Γ).*

Furthermore, certain simple forms of polymorphism have been shown to be sufficient to ensure tractability of the associated one-sorted relations [19, 18].

Definition 7. *– An operation f is called a* constant *operation if there is some fixed $c \in A$ such that $f(x_1, \ldots, x_n) = c$ for all $x_1, \ldots, x_n$.*

- A *binary operation* f *is called a* semilattice operation[2] *if it satisfies the following three identities:* $f(x, f(y, z)) = f(f(x, y), z);$ $f(x, y) = f(y, x);$ $f(x, x) = x.$
- *An n-ary operation f is called a* near-unanimity operation *if* $f(y, x, \ldots, x) = f(x, y, x, \ldots, x) = \cdots = f(x, \ldots, x, y) = x$ *for all* $x, y \in A.$
- *A ternary operation f is called an* affine operation *if* $f(x, y, z) = x - y + z$ *for all* $x, y, z \in A,$ *where* $(A, +, -)$ *is an Abelian group.*

Proposition 2 ([19, 18]). *Let Γ be a set of one-sorted relations over a finite set $A.$*

If $\mathrm{Pol}(\Gamma)$ *contains either a constant operation, or a semilattice operation, or a near-unanimity operation, or an affine operation, then* $\mathrm{CSP}(\Gamma)$ *is tractable.*

To extend the above results to the multi-sorted case, we need to define a suitable extension of the notion of a polymorphism. As we have shown in the previous section (see Example 5), we cannot simply separate out different domains and consider polymorphisms on each one separately; we must ensure that all of the domains are treated in a co-ordinated way. In the following definition, this is achieved by defining different *interpretations* for the same operation applied to different sets.

Definition 8. *Let $\mathcal{A}$ be a collection of sets. An n-ary multi-sorted operation t on $\mathcal{A}$ is defined by a collection of interpretations $\{t^A \mid A \in \mathcal{A}\},$ where each t^A is an n-ary operation on the corresponding set A. The multi-sorted operation t on $\mathcal{A}$ is said to be a* polymorphism *of a multi-sorted relation ϱ over $\mathcal{A}$ with signature $(\delta(1), \ldots, \delta(m))$ if, for any $(a_{11}, \ldots, a_{m1}), \ldots, (a_{1n}, \ldots, a_{mn}) \in \varrho,$ we have*

$$t \begin{pmatrix} a_{11} & \cdots & a_{1n} \\ \vdots & & \vdots \\ a_{m1} & \cdots & a_{mn} \end{pmatrix} = \begin{pmatrix} t^{A_{\delta(1)}}(a_{11}, \ldots, a_{1n}) \\ \vdots \\ t^{A_{\delta(m)}}(a_{m1}, \ldots, a_{mn}) \end{pmatrix} \in \varrho.$$

For any given set of multi-sorted relations Γ, the set of all those multi-sorted operations which are polymorphisms of *every* relation in Γ is denoted $\mathrm{MPol}(\Gamma)$.

The next theorem is the main result of this section. It establishes the remarkable fact that the known one-sorted tractable classes listed in Proposition 2 can be combined in almost arbitrary ways to obtain new multi-sorted tractable classes.

Note that a multi-sorted operation, t, is said to be *idempotent* if all of its interpretations t^A satisfy the identity $t^A(x, x, \ldots, x) = x.$

Theorem 2. *Let Γ be a set of multi-sorted relations over a collection of finite sets $\mathcal{A} = \{A_1, \ldots, A_n\}.$*

If, for each $A_i \in \mathcal{A}$, $\mathrm{MPol}(\Gamma)$ contains a multi-sorted operation f_i such that

- $f_i^{A_i}$ *is a constant operation; or*
- $f_i^{A_i}$ *is a semilattice operation; or*

---

[2] Note that in some earlier papers [19, 17] the term *ACI operation* is used

- $f_i^{A_i}$ is a near-unanimity operation; or
- f_i is idempotent and $f_i^{A_i}$ is an affine operation,

then $\mathrm{MCSP}(\Gamma)$ is tractable.

The proof of Theorem 2 is set out in Propositions 3, 4, and 5.

Before giving these proofs, we need to give a precise definition for the notion of k-consistency, which is widely used in the study of constraint satisfaction problems, but is unfortunately defined in the literature in a number of slightly different ways.

For an n-ary relation ϱ and a set of indices $I = \{i_1, \ldots, i_k\} \subseteq \{1, \ldots, n\}$, the relation $\mathrm{pr}_I \varrho = \{(a_{i_1}, \ldots, a_{i_k}) \mid (a_1, \ldots, a_n) \in \varrho\}$ is called the *projection* of ϱ onto I. (It will sometimes be convenient to abuse this notation by using the variables from a constraint scope as indices of the corresponding constraint relation.)

Definition 9. *Let $\mathcal{P} = (V; \mathcal{A}; \delta; \mathcal{C})$ be an instance of a multi-sorted constraint satisfaction problem. For any subset W of V, the subproblem of $\mathcal{P}$ generated by W, denoted $\mathcal{P}|_W$, is defined to be the problem instance $(W; \mathcal{A}; \delta|_W; \mathcal{C}')$, where the constraints $\mathcal{C}'$ are obtained from the constraints of $\mathcal{P}$ as follows: for each constraint $\langle s, \varrho \rangle \in \mathcal{C}$ of $\mathcal{P}$, choose $s' = s \cap W$ to be a list of those elements of W occurring in s, and set $\langle s', \mathrm{pr}_{s'} \varrho \rangle$ as a constraint of $\mathcal{P}|_W$.*

Definition 10. *For any $k \geq 2$, a constraint satisfaction problem $\mathcal{P}$ is said to be k-consistent if for any subset W containing $k - 1$ variables, and any variable v, any solution to $\mathcal{P}|_W$ can be extended to a solution to $\mathcal{P}|_{W \cup \{v\}}$.*

If $\mathcal{P}$ is i-consistent for $1 \leq i \leq k$, then it is said to be strong k-consistent.

Any constraint satisfaction problem instance $\mathcal{P}$ can be modified to obtain a k-consistent problem instance $\mathcal{P}'$ without changing the set of solutions, by solving all subproblems involving k variables, and then imposing additional constraints on all subsets of $k - 1$ variables that allow only these solutions. This procedure is called 'establishing k-consistency', and $\mathcal{P}'$ is said to be the k-consistent instance associated with $\mathcal{P}$ (see [8] for the one-sorted case).

Definition 11. *A class $\mathbf{C}$ of constraint satisfaction problems is said to be of essential width k if any problem instance $\mathcal{P}$ from $\mathbf{C}$ has a solution if and only if the k-consistent problem associated with $\mathcal{P}$ contains no empty constraint.*

Note that Feder and Vardi [13] introduced a very similar notion of width, which they characterised in terms of Datalog programs.

Every class of problems with finite essential width is tractable, because, for any fixed k, establishing k-consistency takes polynomial time, and recognising the presence of empty constraints can be carried out in linear time.

Proposition 3. *Let Γ be a set of multi-sorted relations over $\mathcal{A} = \{A_1, \ldots, A_n\}$. If, for each $A_i \in \mathcal{A}$, $\mathrm{MPol}(\Gamma)$ contains a multi-sorted operation f_i such that $f_i^{A_i}$ is either a semilattice operation or a near-unanimity operation, then $\mathrm{MCSP}(\Gamma)$ has finite essential width, and is, therefore, tractable.*

A proof of Proposition 3 can be derived from the results of [13, 18, 19].

The next proposition deals with the most involved part of the proof of Theorem 2, because it exploits the subtle interaction between *affine* operations, and the operations considered in Proposition 3, above. To state this proposition, we first need to define certain sets of multi-sorted relations which can be associated with a given set of multi-sorted relations.

Definition 12. *Let Γ be a set of multi-sorted relations over a collection of sets $\mathcal{A}$.*

- *The set of all multi-sorted relations over $\mathcal{A}$ which have the same multi-sorted polymorphisms as Γ will be denoted $\langle \Gamma \rangle$.*
- *For any subset $\mathcal{B}$ of $\mathcal{A}$, the set of all multi-sorted relations in Γ which are multi-sorted relations over $\mathcal{B}$ will be denoted $\Gamma_{\mathcal{B}}$.*

Proposition 4. *Let Γ be a set of multi-sorted relations over $\mathcal{A} = \{A_1, \ldots, A_n\}$. If $\mathrm{MCSP}(\langle \Gamma \rangle_{A_{l+1}, \ldots, A_n})$ is of finite essential width, and for each $A_i \in \mathcal{A}$ with $i \leq l$, $\mathrm{MPol}(\Gamma)$ contains an idempotent multi-sorted operation g_i such that $g_i^{A_i}$ is affine, then $\mathrm{MCSP}(\Gamma)$ is tractable.*

Proof: (sketch) Due to space restrictions, we can only give a very brief outline here of a polynomial-time algorithm for $\mathrm{MCSP}(\Gamma)$.

Let $\mathcal{P}$ be any instance of $\mathrm{MCSP}(\Gamma)$. The variables of $\mathcal{P}$ can be split into two parts, those with domains in $A_1, \ldots, A_l$ (the "affine" part), and those with domains in $A_{l+1}, \ldots, A_n$ (the "finite width" part).

Consider first the affine part. The conditions of Proposition 4 mean, in particular, that, for $i \leq l$, $g_i^{A_i}(x, y, z) = x -_i y +_i z$ where $+_i, -_i$ are the operations of an Abelian group on the base set A_i. It can be shown that in this case $\mathrm{MPol}(\Gamma)$ also contains a single ternary idempotent operation d such that $d^{A_i}(x, y, z) = g_i^{A_i}(x, y, z)$ for $i = 1, 2, \ldots, l$. It follows that $\mathrm{Pol}(\chi(\langle \Gamma \rangle_{A_1, \ldots, A_l}))$ contains an affine operation, and hence, any problem instance from $\mathrm{CSP}(\chi(\langle \Gamma \rangle_{A_1, \ldots, A_l}))$ is solvable in polynomial time, by an algorithm similar to Gaussian elimination. The same is true for the class $\mathrm{MCSP}(\langle \Gamma \rangle_{A_1, \ldots, A_l})$. Moreover, this solution algorithm can be modified to efficiently compute a *basis* of the solution space; in other words, to find a representation for the complete set of solutions which is polynomial in the size of the problem.

Now consider the finite width part. If we restrict $\mathcal{P}$ to these variables, then we need only consider subproblems of size at most k, where k is the essential width of $\mathrm{CSP}(\langle \Gamma \rangle_{A_{l+1}, \ldots, A_n})$. For each solution to such a bounded-size subproblem we can efficiently compute a basis for the possible extensions of that solution to the affine part, as described above. Combining these basis sets, we can find a basis for the complete set of possible solutions to the affine part, and check if it is empty. □

Proposition 5. *Let Γ be a set of multi-sorted relations over $\mathcal{A} = \{A_1, \ldots, A_n\}$. If $\mathrm{MCSP}(\langle \Gamma \rangle_{A_{l+1}, \ldots, A_n})$ is tractable, and for each $A_i \in \mathcal{A}$ with $i \leq l$, $\mathrm{MPol}(\Gamma)$ contains a multi-sorted operation g_i such that $g_i^{A_i}$ is constant, then $\mathrm{MCSP}(\Gamma)$ is tractable.*

Proof: Assume that $\mathrm{MPol}(\Gamma)$ contains a multi-sorted operation g_i, for $i = 1, 2, \ldots, l$, such that $g_i^{A_i}$ is constant. Note that in this case the unary operation $g_i'(x) = g_i(x, \ldots, x)$ also belongs to $\mathrm{MPol}(\Gamma)$. Hence, the operation $g(x) = g_1'(\ldots g_l'(x) \ldots)$ belongs to $\mathrm{MPol}(\Gamma)$ and is constant for all $A_1, \ldots, A_l$. Denote the constant value of g^{A_i} by c_i.

Take a problem instance $\mathcal{P} = (V; \{A_1, \ldots, A_n\}; \delta; \mathcal{C})$ of $\mathrm{MCSP}(\Gamma)$, and set $W = \{v \in V \mid \delta(v) > l\}$. Then the instance $\mathcal{P}|_W$ belongs to $\mathrm{MCSP}(\langle \Gamma \rangle_{A_{l+1}, \ldots, A_n})$, and therefore is tractable, by assumption. Solve $\mathcal{P}|_W$. If it has no solution then neither does $\mathcal{P}$. Otherwise, let φ be a solution. We claim that the mapping $\psi \colon V \to A_1 \cup \ldots \cup A_n$ defined as follows

$$\psi(v) = \begin{cases} c_{\delta(v)}, & \text{if } \delta(v) \leq l, \\ g^{A_{\delta(v)}}(\varphi(v)), & \text{otherwise} \end{cases}$$

is a solution to $\mathcal{P}$.

To establish this, note that for any constraint $C = \langle s, \varrho \rangle \in \mathcal{C}$ there is a tuple $\overline{a} \in \varrho$ such that $\overline{a}[v] = \varphi(v)$ for $v \in s \cap W$. Setting $\overline{b} = g(\overline{a}) \in \varrho$ we get $\overline{b}[v] = c_{\delta(v)} = \psi(v)$ if $\delta(v) \leq l$, and $\overline{b}[v] = g^{A_{\delta(v)}}(\varphi(v)) = \psi(v)$ otherwise. Thus ψ satisfies every constraint in $\mathcal{C}$, and hence is a solution to $\mathcal{P}$.   □

Example 8. Recall the relation ϱ over the sets $A_1 = \{0, 1, 2, 3\}$ and $A_2 = \{a, b, c\}$, defined in Example 1. We can now prove that $\{\varrho\}$ is tractable. To see this, it is sufficient to check that ϱ has two multi-sorted polymorphisms $t(x, y, z)$ and $g(x, y)$, where

- t^{A_1} is the affine operation of the group $\mathbb{Z}_4$, and t^{A_2} is the (ternary) maximum operation on A_2, with respect to the order $a < b < c$ (which is idempotent).
- $g^{A_1}(x, y) = y$, and g^{A_2} is the (binary) maximum operation on A_2, with respect to the order $a < b < c$ (which is a semilattice operation).

Hence we can apply Theorem 2, and conclude that $\mathrm{MCSP}(\{\varrho\})$ is tractable.

4   From Polymorphisms to Algebras

Polymorphisms provide a powerful tool for studying the constraint satisfaction problem. However, as was observed in [6], we get an even more powerful tool if we consider the set of polymorphisms along with the set on which they are defined.

Definition 13. *An* algebra *is an ordered pair $(A; F)$, where A is a nonempty set and F is a family of finitary operations on A. The set A is called the* universe *(or the* base set*), and the operations from F are called* basic. *An algebra is said to be* finite *if its universe is finite.*

The advantage of working explicitly with algebras, rather than just sets of polymorphisms, is that one can exploit the well-developed mathematical theory of algebras. This idea was pursued for the one-sorted case in [6]. Here we briefly summarise the relevant aspects of the one-sorted case. and then consider how the link with algebras can be extended to the multi-sorted case.

First we observe that we can associate any set Γ of one-sorted relations with a corresponding algebra $\mathbb{A}_\Gamma = (A; \text{Pol}\,\Gamma)$. In the reverse direction, we can start with an algebra and obtain a corresponding set of one-sorted relations, in the following way. Given any set of operations, C, on a set A, the set of all relations over A for which all operations from C are polymorphisms is denoted $\text{Inv}(C)$. Hence, given any algebra $(A; F)$, we can define an associated set of one-sorted relations $\text{Inv}(F)$. We will say that an algebra $(A; F)$ is *tractable* if the associated set of one-sorted relations $\text{Inv}(F)$ is tractable.

Using the definitions above, and Theorem 1, we can translate questions about the tractability of a set of one-sorted relations into questions about the tractability of the corresponding algebra.

Corollary 1. *Let Γ be a set of one-sorted relations over a finite set A. The set Γ is tractable if and only if the corresponding algebra $\mathbb{A}_\Gamma$ is tractable.*

It follows from Corollary 1 that all maximal tractable sets of one-sorted relations can be defined by specifying a suitable algebra. Of course, we may need very many operations to define an arbitrary algebra. However, in all known cases, including those listed in Proposition 2 and in papers [1–3, 5, 10, 11], we need very few operations to ensure that an algebra is tractable. Hence the algebraic theory we have sketched here allows a very concise description of all known maximal tractable sets of one-sorted relations, even though each maximal tractable set contains infinitely many relations.

One simple way to extend these ideas to the multi-sorted case is to combine Corollary 1 with Proposition 1, as follows.

Corollary 2. *Let Γ be a set of multi-sorted relations over the collection of finite sets $\{A_1, \ldots, A_n\}$. The set Γ is tractable if and only if the corresponding algebra $\mathbb{A}_{\chi(\Gamma)}$ is tractable.*

However, this simple extension is rather unsatisfactory, because of the potentially large size of the universe of $\mathbb{A}_{\chi(\Gamma)}$. For example, if we have 10 distinct domains each with 20 elements then $\mathbb{A}_{\chi(\Gamma)}$ is an algebra with 20^{10} elements. In the remainder of this section we are going to show that, for any set of multi-sorted relations over $\{A_1, \ldots, A_n\}$, we can define a collection of algebras $\{\mathbb{A}_1, \ldots, \mathbb{A}_n\}$, where the universe of each $\mathbb{A}_i$ is the set A_i, and the complexity of the multi-sorted problem is determined by this collection of smaller algebras. Using these results for the case just mentioned, we may deal with 10 individual 20-element algebras, which is much more convenient, and allows a more complete analysis of the algebraic structure.

To develop this novel theory concerning the tractability of *collections* of algebras we need to introduce a little more standard algebraic terminology. First we note that algebras can be grouped into families which share the same set of basic operations.

Definition 14. *The collection of algebras $\boldsymbol{A} = \{(A_i; F^{A_i}) \mid i \in I\}$ is said to be a collection of* similar *algebras if there exists some fixed set F of multi-sorted* operations over the sets $\{A_i \mid i \in I\}$, such that each set of basic operations F^{A_i} is the set of interpretations of the functions in F on the set A_i. The set F is called the set of basic operations of the collection $\boldsymbol{A}$.

Definition 15. *For any collection of similar algebras* $\boldsymbol{A} = \{(A_i; F^{A_i}) \mid i \in I\}$ *with basic operations* F, *we define* $\mathrm{MInv}(\boldsymbol{A})$ *to be the set* Γ *of all multi-sorted relations over the sets* $\{A_i \mid i \in I\}$ *such that* $\mathrm{MPol}(\Gamma) = F$.

A collection of algebras $\boldsymbol{A}$ will be called tractable if the set of multi-sorted relations $\mathrm{MInv}(\boldsymbol{A})$ is tractable. Similarly, $\boldsymbol{A}$ will be called NP-complete if $\mathrm{MInv}(\boldsymbol{A})$ is NP-complete.

The following theorem shows that, for any set Γ of multi-sorted relations over a finite collection of finite sets, $\mathcal{A}$, there exists a finite algebra $\mathbb{A}$, and a collection $\boldsymbol{A}$ of similar algebras whose universes are the members of $\mathcal{A}$, such that Γ, $\mathbb{A}$, and $\boldsymbol{A}$ are all tractable or intractable simultaneously.

Definition 16. *Let* $\mathbb{A}_1$ *and* $\mathbb{A}_2$ *be similar algebras with universes* A_1, A_2 *and basic operations* F. *A mapping* $\varphi \colon A_1 \to A_2$ *is called a* homomorphism *from* $\mathbb{A}_1$ *to* $\mathbb{A}_2$ *if* $\varphi f^{\mathbb{A}_1}(a_1, \ldots, a_k) = f^{\mathbb{A}_2}(\varphi(a_1), \ldots, \varphi(a_k))$ *for all* $f \in F$ *and all* $a_1, \ldots, a_k \in A_1$, *where* k *is the arity of* f.

If the map φ *is surjective, then* $\mathbb{A}_2$ *is called a* homomorphic image *of* $\mathbb{A}_1$.

Theorem 3. *Let* Γ *be a set of multi-sorted relations over the finite sets* $\{A_1, \ldots, A_n\}$.

The following are equivalent:

(a) Γ *is tractable;*
(b) $\mathbb{A}_{\chi(\widehat{\Gamma})}$ *is tractable, where* $\widehat{\Gamma} = \Gamma \cup \{=_{A_1}, \ldots, =_{A_n}\}$, *and each* $=_{A_i}$ *is the binary equality relation on* A_i;
(c) $\{\mathbb{A}_1, \ldots, \mathbb{A}_n\}$ *is tractable, where each* $\mathbb{A}_i$ *is the image of* $\mathbb{A}_{\chi(\widehat{\Gamma})}$ *under the homomorphism* φ_i *given by* $\varphi_i(\overline{a}) = \overline{a}[i]$.

A corresponding equivalence also holds when "tractable" is replaced by "NP-complete".

Proof: Omitted, see [4]. □

5   Applications to One-Sorted Problems

As well as providing a sound framework for the analysis of the complexity of multi-sorted constraint satisfaction problems, the results developed in this paper have some surprising applications to the one-sorted case. (For example, see [1].)

We will complete this paper by describing an application of the results presented above to the analysis of the complexity of one-sorted constraint satisfaction problems in which the constraints limit each variable to at most two possible values (which may be different for different variables). In other words, we consider sets Γ, containing one-sorted relations, such that for each $\varrho \in \Gamma$, each unary projection $\mathrm{pr}_i\varrho$ contains at most two elements. This problem was previously considered in [12], which established a dichotomy theorem for the complexity of such sets of relations: they are either tractable or NP-complete.

Using the results of this paper we can not only establish this dichotomy, we can also give a precise characterisation of the tractable cases (which are not described in [12]). In fact, we establish the general result that for *any* set, Γ, containing one-sorted relations, the one-sorted problem class $\mathrm{CSP}(\Gamma)$ is polynomial-time equivalent to a certain multi-sorted constraint satisfaction problem, where the domains are the unary projections of the (non-unary) relations in Γ. In the case where all these projections have size at most 2, we can then apply Theorems 2 and 3 to obtain a complete characterisation of all the tractable cases.

Definition 17. *Let Γ be a set of one-sorted relations.*

For any relation $\varrho \in \Gamma$, the set $\Delta(\varrho)$ is defined to be the set of all unary projections of ϱ, and the set $\Delta(\Gamma)$ is defined to be the union of the sets $\Delta(\varrho)$ over all non-unary $\varrho \in \Gamma$.

Definition 18. *Let Γ be a set of one-sorted relations where $\Delta(\Gamma) = \{A_1, \ldots, A_k\}$.*

For any relation $\varrho \in \Gamma$ with arity n, the set Γ_ϱ is defined to be the set of all multi-sorted relations over $\Delta(\Gamma)$ of the form $\varrho \cap (A_{i_1} \times \ldots \times A_{i_n})$ with signature $(i_1, \ldots, i_n)$, for all possible choices of $i_1, \ldots, i_n$.

The set Γ^+ is defined to be the union of the sets Γ_ϱ over all non-unary $\varrho \in \Gamma$.

Proposition 6. *Let Γ be a finite set of one-sorted relations.*

The one-sorted problem $\mathrm{CSP}(\Gamma)$ is polynomial-time equivalent to the multi-sorted problem $\mathrm{MCSP}(\Gamma^+)$.

Proof: First we reduce $\mathrm{CSP}(\Gamma)$ to $\mathrm{MCSP}(\Gamma^+)$. Consider any problem instance $\mathcal{P} = (V; A; \mathcal{C}) \in \mathrm{CSP}(\Gamma)$. Let U be the set of variables constrained by unary constraints only. For any $v \in U$, if the intersection of the unary constraints imposed on v is empty, then $\mathcal{P}$ has no solution. Otherwise, we can assign v with an arbitrary value from this intersection. Hence, we may assume that $U = \varnothing$.

Let $\Delta(\Gamma) = \{A_1, A_2, \ldots, A_k\}$. For each $v \in V$, let $\langle s_v, \varrho_v \rangle \in \mathcal{C}$ be a non-unary constraint whose scope contains v. The set $\mathrm{pr}_v \varrho_v$ is equal to some element $A_i \in \Delta(\Gamma)$; set $\delta(v)$ equal to i. It is not hard to see that $\mathcal{P}$ is equivalent to the multi-sorted problem $\mathcal{P}' = (V; \{A_1, \ldots, A_k\}; \delta; \mathcal{C}')$, where $\mathcal{C}'$ contains the constraint $\langle s, \varrho \cap \prod_{v \in s} A_{\delta(v)} \rangle$ for each $\langle s, \varrho \rangle \in \mathcal{C}$.

To show the converse reduction, we notice that Γ^+ can be viewed as a set of one-sorted relations over the set A. Moreover, every multi-sorted problem instance in $\mathrm{MCSP}(\Gamma^+)$ can be viewed as a one-sorted instance. Hence, we have a trivial reduction from $\mathrm{MCSP}(\Gamma^+)$ to $\mathrm{CSP}(\Gamma^+)$. By using well-known basic properties of polymorphisms (see, for example, [25]), any $f \in \mathrm{Pol}(\Gamma)$ is also a polymorphism of all unary relations A_i, all Cartesian products of the form $A_{i_1} \times \ldots \times A_{i_l}$, and all relations of the form $\varrho \cap (A_{i_1} \times \ldots \times A_{i_l})$, for any $\varrho \in \Gamma$. Hence, $\mathrm{Pol}(\Gamma) \subseteq \mathrm{Pol}(\Gamma^+)$, so $\mathrm{CSP}(\Gamma^+)$ is polynomial-time reducible to $\mathrm{CSP}(\Gamma)$, by Theorem 1. $\square$

Corollary 3. *Let Γ be a set of one-sorted relations over a finite set, such that $|A_i| \leq 2$ for each $A_i \in \Delta(\Gamma)$.*

If, for each $A_i \in \Delta(\Gamma)$ there is an operation $f_i \in \text{MPol}(\Gamma^+)$ such that $f_i^{A_i}$ is either a constant operation, or a semilattice operation, or a near-unanimity operation, or an affine operation, then $\text{CSP}(\Gamma)$ is tractable. Otherwise, it is NP-complete.

Proof: Let $\mathbb{A}_1, \ldots, \mathbb{A}_k$ be the algebras corresponding to Γ^+ as defined in Theorem 3. If the conditions of the corollary hold, then $\Gamma^+ \subseteq \text{MInv}(\mathbb{A}_1, \ldots, \mathbb{A}_k)$ is tractable, by Theorem 2. (The requirement in Theorem 2 for affine operations to be idempotent can be shown to be unnecessary when all sets contain at most 2 elements, by a careful examination of the possible cases.)

Conversely, if for a certain A_i there is no operation with the required properties then, by the dichotomy theorem for one-sorted constraints on a two-element set [26, 6], $\text{MInv}(\{\mathbb{A}_i\}) \subseteq \text{MInv}(\{\mathbb{A}_1, \ldots, \mathbb{A}_k\})$ is NP-complete. Hence, by Theorem 3, Γ^+ is also NP-complete, and therefore Γ is NP-complete, by Proposition 6. □

6   Conclusion

Practical constraint satisfaction problems often involve different domains for different variables. We have shown in this paper that analyzing the complexity of such problems by simply assuming that all these domains are subsets of some single large domain can give a misleading picture of their complexity. To remedy this problem, we have presented a set of algebraic tools that allow one to deal more accurately with such multi-sorted problems.

Using these tools we have been able to show that certain existing polynomial-time algorithms for the one-sorted case can be combined, to give a more powerful polynomial-time algorithm, solving much wider classes of multi-sorted problems.

Finally, we have further investigated the significant link between the study of the constraint satisfaction problem and the study of finite algebras, by extending this link to the multi-sorted case. Elements of this extended algebraic machinery have already proved to be essential tools in the study of the complexity of the conventional one-sorted constraint satisfaction problem. We therefore believe that the theory developed here will lead to a deeper understanding of the structure of both one-sorted and multi-sorted constraint satisfaction problems.

References

1. A.A. Bulatov. A dichotomy theorem for constraints on a three-element set. In *Proceedings 43rd IEEE Symposium on Foundations of Computer Science, FOCS'02*, pages 649–658, Vancouver, Canada, November 2002.
2. A.A. Bulatov. Mal'tsev constraints are tractable. Technical Report PRG-RR-02-05, Computing Laboratory, University of Oxford, Oxford, UK, 2002.

3. A.A. Bulatov and P.G. Jeavons. Tractable constraints closed under a binary operation. Technical Report PRG-TR-12-00, Computing Laboratory, University of Oxford, Oxford, UK, 2000.

4. A.A. Bulatov and P.G. Jeavons. An algebraic approach to multi-sorted constraints. Technical Report PRG-RR-01-18, Computing Laboratory, University of Oxford, Oxford, UK, 2001.

5. A.A. Bulatov, P.G. Jeavons, and A.A. Krokhin. The complexity of maximal constraint languages. In *Proceedings of the 33rd Annual ACM Simposium on Theory of Computing*, pages 667–674, Hersonissos, Crete, Greece, July 2001. ACM Press.

6. A.A. Bulatov, A.A. Krokhin, and P.G. Jeavons. Constraint satisfaction problems and finite algebras. In *Proceedings of 27th International Colloquium on Automata, Languages and Programming—ICALP'00*, volume 1853 of *Lecture Notes in Computer Science*, pages 272–282. Springer-Verlag, 2000.

7. D.A. Cohen, P.G. Jeavons, P. Jonsson, and M. Koubarakis. Building tractable disjunctive constraints. *Journal of the ACM*, 47:826–853, 2000.

8. M.C. Cooper. An optimal k-consistency algorithm. *Art. Intell.*, 41:89–95, 1989.

9. M.C. Cooper, D.A. Cohen, and P.G. Jeavons. Characterising tractable constraints. *Artificial Intelligence*, 65:347–361, 1994.

10. V. Dalmau. A new tractable class of constraint satisfaction problems. In *Proc. 6th International Symposium on Artificial Intelligence and Mathematics*, 2000.

11. V. Dalmau and J. Pearson. Set functions and width 1 problems. In *Proceedings 5th International Conference on Constraint Programming, CP'99*, volume 1713 of *Lecture Notes in Computer Science*, pages 159–173. Springer-Verlag, 1999.

12. T. Feder. Classification of homomorphisms to oriented cycles and of k-partite satisfiability. *SIAM J. of Discrete Math.*, 14(4):471–480. 2001.

13. T. Feder and M.Y. Vardi. The computational structure of monotone monadic SNP and constraint satisfaction: A study through datalog and group theory. *SIAM Journal of Computing*, 28:57–104, 1998.

14. M. Garey and D.S. Johnson. *Computers and Intractability: A Guide to the Theory of NP-Completeness*. Freeman, San Francisco, CA., 1979.

15. R. Gault. Polyanna Technical Manual (version 1.00). Technical Report PRG-RR-01-20, Computing Laboratory, University of Oxford, Oxford, UK, 2001.

16. D. Hobby and R.N. McKenzie. *The Structure of Finite Algebras*, volume 76 of *Contemporary Mathematics*. American Mathematical Society, 1988.

17. P.G. Jeavons. On the algebraic structure of combinatorial problems. *Theoretical Computer Science*, 200:185–204, 1998.

18. P.G. Jeavons, D.A. Cohen, and M.C. Cooper. Constraints, consistency and closure. *Artificial Intelligence*, 101(1-2):251–265, 1998.

19. P.G. Jeavons, D.A. Cohen, and M. Gyssens. Closure properties of constraints. *Journal of the ACM*, 44:527–548, 1997.

20. L. Kirousis. Fast parallel constraint satisfaction. *Artificial Intelligence*, 64:147–160, 1993.

21. Ph.G. Kolaitis and M.Y. Vardi. Conjunctive-query containment and constraint satisfaction. *J. Comput. Syst. Sci.*, 61:302–332, 2000.

22. A.K. Mackworth. Consistency in networks of relations. *Artificial Intelligence*, 8:99–118, 1977.

23. R.N. McKenzie, G.F. McNulty, and W.F. Taylor. *Algebras, Lattices and Varieties*, volume I. Wadsworth and Brooks, California, 1987.

24. U. Montanari. Networks of constraints: Fundamental properties and applications to picture processing. *Information Sciences*, 7:95–132, 1974.

25. R. Pöschel and L.A. Kalužnin. *Funktionen- und Relationenalgebren*. DVW, Berlin, 1979.
26. T.J. Schaefer. The complexity of satisfiability problems. In *Proceedings 10th ACM Symposium on Theory of Computing (STOC'78)*, pages 216–226, 1978.
27. P. van Beek and R. Dechter. On the minimality and decomposability of row-convex constraint networks. *Journal of the ACM*, 42:543–561, 1995.
28. P. van Hentenryck, Y. Deville, and C-M. Teng. A generic arc-consistency algorithm and its specializations. *Artificial Intelligence*, 57:291–321, 1992.
29. M.Y. Vardi. Constraint satisfaction and database theory: a tutorial. In *Proceedings of 19th ACM Symposium on Priciples of Database Systems (PODS'00)*, 2000.

Periodic Constraint Satisfaction Problems: Polynomial-Time Algorithms

Hubie Chen

Department of Computer Science, Cornell University, Ithaca, NY 14853, USA
hubes@cs.cornell.edu

Abstract. We study a generalization of the constraint satisfaction problem (CSP), the *periodic constraint satisfaction problem*. An input instance of the periodic CSP is a finite set of "generating" constraints over a structured variable set that implicitly specifies a larger, possibly infinite set of constraints; the problem is to decide whether or not the larger set of constraints has a satisfying assignment. This model is natural for studying constraint networks consisting of constraints obeying a high degree of regularity or symmetry. Our main contribution is the identification of two broad polynomial-time tractable subclasses of the periodic CSP.

1 Introduction

The *constraint satisfaction problem* (CSP) is a general framework in which many combinatorial search problems can be expressed. An instance of a CSP consists of a network of constraints over a set of variables; the problem is to decide whether or not there is an assignment to the variable set satisfying all of the constraints.

Periodic Constraint Satisfaction Problems. This paper investigates a strict generalization of the CSP, the *periodic constraint satisfaction problem*. In this generalization, the full constraint network – of which satisfiability is to be decided – is specified *implicitly*. An instance of the periodic CSP is a finite set of "generating" constraints over a large, structured variable set, for instance, the set of lattice points in k-dimensional space. A corresponding full set of constraints is obtained by repeating the generating set periodically, and the problem is to decide whether or not the full set of constraints has a satisfying assignment. This model is natural for studying large, possibly infinite constraint networks consisting of constraints obeying a high degree of regularity or symmetry. Such constraint networks arise naturally in many domains, such as scheduling, planning, and hardware design [20, 19].

So that our results may enjoy maximal applicability, we study a very general formulation of the periodic CSP where the underlying variable set of an instance is a group G (that is, the algebraic structure), and the input constraint network is expanded into the full constraint network according to the action of a subgroup of G. This formulation is essentially that studied by Freedman in [12], and

F. Rossi (Ed.): CP 2003, LNCS 2833, pp. 199–213, 2003.
© Springer-Verlag Berlin Heidelberg 2003

encompasses the model studied by Orlin in [21] and subsequently in [20, 19]. Our main contribution is the identification of two broad polynomial-time tractable subclasses of the periodic CSP. (In this context, "polynomial-time" is measured with respect to the input constraint network.) These tractability results encompass the periodic variants of 2-SAT and Horn SAT, and we believe the results to be quite remarkable in light of the fact that the periodic CSP is undecidable in general [12].

Tractability. The *identification of tractable subclasses* is a classic approach to coping with computationally hard problems. There are multiple ways to restrict the CSP in hopes of obtaining such tractable subclasses [22]. One way is to restrict the *constraint language*, or the types of constraints that are permitted in instances. This is the form of restriction which was studied by Schaefer in his now classic dichotomy theorem [23], and since then has been studied in several other contexts [7].

Schaefer's theorem showed that *every* constraint language over a two-element domain gives rise to a CSP subclass which is either in P or is NP-complete. This dichotomy theorem and the many others that have followed [7] are valuable because they identify *all* of the ways tractability can arise from restrictions on the constraint language. In addition, knowledge of intractable subclasses can be quite useful in developing further proofs of intractability. Consequently, much attention has been directed towards extending Schaefer's theorem to constraint languages over *any* finite domain. This has resulted in the identification of many new polynomial-time algorithms for subclasses of the CSP [18, 11, 15, 8, 1, 9, 5, 3, 10], some of which are quite sophisticated, as well as a dichotomy theorem on CSP complexity classifying all constraint languages over a *three*-element domain, due to Bulatov [2].

This paper studies the complexity of the periodic CSP from the standpoint of restricting the constraint language, and hence takes the first steps towards the long-term research goal of establishing a dichotomy theorem on the complexity of the periodic CSP over finite domains.

The Closure Properties Approach. An algebraic approach to studying the relative expressiveness of constraint languages was introduced in [18] and further studied in [14–16, 4, 1, 5, 2, 3, 9]. In this approach, a dual perspective on constraint languages is given by studying the set of functions under which a constraint language is closed, or the *closure properties* of a constraint language. Many of the tractability results cited above demonstrate that closure under an operation of a particular type is sufficient for a constraint language to be tractable, in the context of the CSP. The tractability results for the periodic CSP given in this paper are also phrased in this form: we show that any constraint language closed under a *semilattice* operation or a *dual discriminator* operation gives rise to a tractable subclass of the periodic CSP.

Related Work. Orlin [21] demonstrated the PSPACE-completeness of a number of periodic variants of NP-complete languages, including a problem which he called dynamic satisfiability; in our framework, dynamic satisfiability is obtained as a particular case by setting the group to be $\mathbb{Z}$ (the integers), that is, the lattice points in one-dimensional space.

Marathe, Hunt, and Stearns, in joint work with Radhakrishnan in [20] and Rosenkrantz in [19], studied problems arising from a variety of periodic specifications, focusing on approximation algorithms.

Freedman [12] showed that for group $\mathbb{Z}^2$ and H a subgroup of finite index, the periodic version of 3-SAT is undecidable, while the periodic version of 2-SAT is decidable; however, he gave no running time analysis of his procedure for periodic 2-SAT. He also demonstrated that the periodic version of 3-colorability is undecidable.

2   Preliminaries

This section presents the definitions and notation used throughout the paper. We will assume that the reader has familiarity with basic notions of group theory.

2.1   Constraint Satisfaction Problems

We first introduce the basic terminology of constraint satisfaction problems.

Definition 1. *A* relation *over a set D is a subset of D^k (with $k \geq 1$), and is said to have arity k. For any tuple $t \in D^k$, we denote the ith coordinate of t by $t[i]$. When R is a relation of arity k and $i \in \{1, \ldots, k\}$, let $\pi_i(R)$ denote the relation $\{t[i] : t \in R\}$. A* constraint language *is a finite set of relations which are all over the same set (and may be of different arities).*

Definition 2. *A* constraint *over variable set V and domain D is an expression of the form $R(x_1, \ldots, x_k)$, where R is a relation over D with arity k and $x_1, \ldots, x_k$ are variables in V.*

A collection of constraints yields a *constraint satisfaction problem (CSP)*. Note that we consider only CSPs where all variables have the same domain, although our results are easily generalized to the more general formulation where different variables may have different domains.

Definition 3. *A constraint satisfaction problem (CSP) is a set $\mathcal{C}$ of constraints, each of which is over the same variable set V and domain D; an* assignment *to $\mathcal{C}$ is a function $f : V \to D$. The assignment f* satisfies *a constraint $R(x_1, \ldots, x_k) \in \mathcal{C}$ if $(f(x_1), \ldots, f(x_k)) \in R$, and satisfies $\mathcal{C}$ if it satisfies every constraint $C \in \mathcal{C}$.*

Having defined a CSP and an associated notion of satisfiability, we can now formally define the decision problem for CSPs over a particular constraint language.

Definition 4. *Let Γ be a constraint language over a finite domain D. The* $CSP(\Gamma)$ *decision problem is to decide, given a CSP $\mathcal{C}$ (of finite size) over domain D, where each constraint in $\mathcal{C}$ has relation from Γ, whether or not $\mathcal{C}$ is satisfiable.*

Example 1. Let $D = \{T, F\}$, $V = \{-1, 2, 4, 5\}$, and $R_0 = D^2 \setminus \{(F, F)\}$, $R_1 = D^2 \setminus \{(F, T)\}$, $R_2 = D^2 \setminus \{(T, T)\}$. The CSP $\mathcal{C} = \{R_0(2, 5), R_2(2, 5), R_1(-1, 4)\}$ over V and D is satisfiable, for example, by the assignment $f : V \to D$ such that $f(2) = F$ and $f(x) = T$ for all $x \in V \setminus \{2\}$.

Every instance of the $\mathsf{CSP}(\{R_0, R_1, R_2\})$ problem can be reduced in a simple and assignment-preserving manner to the standard boolean 2-satisfiability problem, and vice-versa. For example, the CSP $\mathcal{C}$ is equivalent to the 2-satisfiability formula $(2 \vee 5) \wedge (\neg 2 \vee \neg 5) \wedge (-1 \vee \neg 4)$. □

We now define formally the periodic constraint satisfaction problem.

Definition 5. *Let Γ be a constraint language over a finite domain D, G be a (possibly infinite) group, and H be a subgroup of G. The PeriodicCSP$(\Gamma; G, H)$ decision problem is to decide, given a CSP $\mathcal{C}$ (of finite size) over variable set G and domain D, where each constraint in $\mathcal{C}$ has relation from Γ, whether or not the (possibly infinite) CSP*

$$H\mathcal{C} \stackrel{\text{def}}{=} \{R(hg_1, \ldots, hg_k) : h \in H, R(g_1, \ldots, g_k) \in \mathcal{C}\}$$

is satisfiable.

The following are examples of periodic CSPs.

Example 2. Let $D = \{T, F\}$, let G be $(\mathbb{Z}, +)$, let H be $(3\mathbb{Z}, +)$, and let $\mathcal{C}$ be the formula

$$\mathcal{C} = \{R_2(2, 5), R_0(2, 5), R'(-1, 4, 3)\}$$

where $R' = D^3 \setminus \{(F, F, F)\}$ and R_0, R_2 are defined as in Example 1.

We have

$$H\mathcal{C} = \ldots \cup \{R_2(-1, 2), R_0(-1, 2), R'(-4, 1, 0)\} \cup$$

$$\{R_2(2, 5), R_0(2, 5), R'(-1, 4, 3)\} \cup \{R_2(5, 8), R_0(5, 8), R'(2, 7, 6)\} \cup \ldots$$

The infinite set of constraints $H\mathcal{C}$ is satisfied by the assignment $f : \mathbb{Z} \to \{T, F\}$ where $f(x)$ is defined to be F if x is congruent to 2 modulo 6, and T otherwise. □

Example 3. Let $D = \{T, F\}$, let G be $(\mathbb{Z}, +)$, let H be $(5\mathbb{Z}, +)$, and let $\mathcal{C}$ be the formula

$$\{R_1(1, 5), N(-4), Y(10), R_2(2, 6)\}$$

where $Y = \{(T)\}$, $N = \{(F)\}$ and R_1, R_2 are defined as in Example 1.

We have

$$H\mathcal{C} = \ldots \cup \{R_1(-4, 0), N(-9), Y(5), R_2(-3, 1)\} \cup$$

$$\{R_1(1, 5), N(-4), Y(10), R_2(2, 6)\} \cup \{R_1(6, 10), N(1), Y(15), R_2(7, 11)\} \cup \ldots$$

It can be seen that the infinite set of constraints $H\mathcal{C}$ contains the constraints $Y(5)$, $R_1(1, 5)$, and $N(1)$. Since no assignment can satisfy these three constraints, we conclude that $H\mathcal{C}$ is unsatisfiable. □

Observe that when $\mathcal{C}$ is an instance of the PeriodicCSP$(\Gamma; G, H)$ problem, the containment $\mathcal{C} \subseteq H\mathcal{C}$ holds, so any satisfying assignment for $H\mathcal{C}$ is also a satisfying assignment for $\mathcal{C}$. Thus, if $H\mathcal{C}$ is satisfiable, then $\mathcal{C}$ is satisfiable. Example 3 demonstrates that the converse does not hold: the example CSP $\mathcal{C}$ is easily seen to be satisfiable – no variable appears in more than one constraint – but $H\mathcal{C}$ is not satisfiable.

2.2   Closure Properties

We now define the notion of the closure properties of a constraint language, which gives a dual perspective (on constraint languages) relevant to considerations of complexity. A number of papers have studied this dual viewpoint [18, 16, 14, 4, 5], and we refer the reader to these papers for more information.

Definition 6. *Let* $\otimes : D^m \to D$ *be a m-ary operation on* D *and let* R *be a k-ary relation over* D. *Suppose* $t_1, \ldots, t_m \in R$. *The expression* $\otimes(t_1, \ldots, t_m)$ *is defined to be a k-tuple via a coordinate-wise action:*

$$\otimes(t_1, \ldots, t_m) \stackrel{\text{def}}{=} (\otimes(t_1[1], \ldots, t_m[1]), \otimes(t_1[2], \ldots, t_m[2]), \ldots, \otimes(t_1[k], \ldots, t_m[k])).$$

The relation $\otimes(R)$ *is defined to be the set* $\{\otimes(t_1, \ldots, t_m) : t_1, \ldots, t_m \in R\}$.

Definition 7. *A relation* R *is closed under* $\otimes$ *if* $\otimes(R) \subseteq R$. *A constraint language* Γ *is closed under* $\otimes$ *if all relations in* Γ *are closed under* $\otimes$. *A constraint* $R(x_1, \ldots, x_k)$ *is said to be closed under* $\otimes$ *if its relation* R *is closed under* $\otimes$. *A set of constraints* $\mathcal{C}$ *is said to be closed under* $\otimes$ *if all constraints in* $\mathcal{C}$ *are closed under* $\otimes$.

3   *H*-Arc Consistency

In this section, we introduce a strengthened version of arc consistency for periodic CSPs, called *H-arc consistency*. Under a mild assumption, an instance of the PeriodicCSP$(\Gamma; G, H)$ problem can be transformed into one that is H-arc consistent in polynomial time; the procedure for doing this will be used as a subroutine in both of the algorithms we give for PeriodicCSP$(\Gamma; G, H)$, in the next two sections.

Definition 8. *Let* D *be a finite set. A CSP* $\mathcal{C}$ *over variable set* V *and domain* D *is arc consistent if for all pairs of constraints* $C_1(v_1, \ldots, v_k)$, $C_2(v'_1, \ldots, v'_l) \in \mathcal{C}$, $v_i = v'_j$ *(with* $1 \le i \le k, 1 \le j \le l$) *implies that* $\pi_i(C_1) = \pi_j(C_2)$.

Definition 9. *Let* D *be a finite set,* G *be a group, and* H *be a subgroup of* G. *A CSP* $\mathcal{C}$ *over variable set* G *and domain* D *is* H-arc consistent *if for all pairs of constraints* $C_1(g_1, \ldots, g_k)$, $C_2(g'_1, \ldots, g'_l) \in \mathcal{C}$, $Hg_i = Hg'_j$ *(with* $1 \le i \le k, 1 \le j \le l$) *implies that* $\pi_i(C_1) = \pi_j(C_2)$.

It is easy to see that H-arc consistency implies arc consistency.

We now identify a computational problem which, when solvable, makes establishing H-arc consistency possible.

Definition 10. *Let G be a group and H be a subgroup of G. The* same coset problem *for (G, H) is to decide, given two group elements $g_1, g_2 \in G$, whether or not $Hg_1 = Hg_2$ (that is, whether g_1 and g_2 are in the same right coset).*

The following is the main theorem of this section, which identifies some key properties of H-arc consistency.

Theorem 1. *Let Γ be a constraint language over domain D, G be a group, and H be a subgroup of G. Suppose $\mathcal{C}$ is an instance of the problem* PeriodicCSP$(\Gamma; G, H)$. *Then there exists a CSP $\mathcal{C}'$ (over variable set G and domain D) with the following four properties:*

1. *$\mathcal{C}'$ is H-arc consistent.*
2. *$H\mathcal{C}'$ has the same satisfying assignments as $H\mathcal{C}$.*
3. *If the same coset problem for (G, H) is decidable in polynomial time, then $\mathcal{C}'$ can be computed in polynomial time from $\mathcal{C}$.*
4. *For any operation $\otimes$ under which Γ is closed, every relation of $\mathcal{C}'$ is closed under $\otimes$.*

Proof. The following algorithm computes $\mathcal{C}'$ from $\mathcal{C}$:

While there are two (not necessarily distinct) constraints

$$C_1(g_1, \ldots, g_k), C_2(g_1', \ldots, g_l') \in \mathcal{C}$$

where g_i and g_j' (for some $1 \leq i \leq k, 1 \leq j \leq l$) are in the same right coset and $\pi_i(C_1) \neq \pi_j(C_2)$, replace the constraints $C_1(g_1, \ldots, g_k), C_2(g_1', \ldots, g_l')$ by $D_1(g_1, \ldots, g_k), D_2(g_1', \ldots, g_l')$, where

$$D_1 = \{t \in C_1 : t[i] \in \pi_j(C_2)\},$$
$$D_2 = \{t \in C_2 : t[j] \in \pi_i(C_1)\}.$$

Let $\mathcal{C}'$ denote the set of constraints after the algorithm terminates.

The loop iterates at most polynomially many times, since there are at most polynomially many pairs g_i and g_j' in the same coset, and a constant number of possibilities for the sets $\pi_i(C_1)$, $\pi_j(C_2)$. The loop condition takes polynomial time to check, assuming that the same coset problem for (G, H) can be solved in polynomial time, so property (3) is satisfied.

By the loop condition, property (1) will be satisfied by the set of constraints which results when the algorithm terminates.

It is straightforward to verify that if C_1 and C_2 are closed under $\otimes$, then D_1 and D_2 are closed under $\otimes$. From this, property (4) follows by induction.

It remains to verify property (2). Suppose the loop terminates after s iterations. Let $\mathcal{C} = \mathcal{C}_0, \mathcal{C}_1, \ldots, \mathcal{C}_s = \mathcal{C}'$ denote the different sets of constraints encountered during the execution of the algorithm.

Any solution to $\mathcal{C}'$ is a solution to $\mathcal{C}$, since when a replacement step is performed, $D_1 \subseteq C_1$ and $D_2 \subseteq C_2$; thus, any solution to $H\mathcal{C}'$ is a solution to $H\mathcal{C}$.

Now let f be a satisfying assignment for $H\mathcal{C}$. We show that if f satisfies $H\mathcal{C}_i$, then f satisfies $H\mathcal{C}_{i+1}$. (By induction, it will follow that f is a satisfying assignment for $H\mathcal{C}'$.) Let $C_1(g_1, \ldots, g_k), C_2(g_1', \ldots, g_l')$ denote the constraints in $\mathcal{C}_i$ that were replaced; g_i and g_j' denote the variables that were identified to be in the same coset; and $D_1(g_1, \ldots, g_k), D_2(g_1', \ldots, g_l')$ denote the new constraints in $\mathcal{C}_{i+1}$. It suffices to show that if f satisfies $C_1(hg_1, \ldots, hg_k)$ and $C_2(hg_1', \ldots, hg_l')$ for all $h \in H$, then f satisfies $D_1(hg_1, \ldots, hg_k)$ and $D_2(hg_1', \ldots, hg_l')$ for all $h \in H$.

Suppose $h \in H$. Since g_i and g_j' are in the same coset, there exists h' such that $g_i = h'g_j'$. Since $C_2(hh'g_1', \ldots, hh'g_l')$ is satisfied by assumption, $f(hg_i) = f(hh'g_j') \in \pi_j(C_2)$. By assumption, $C_1(hg_1, \ldots, hg_k)$ is satisfied by f; since $f(hg_i) \in \pi_j(C_2)$, $D_1(hg_1, \ldots, hg_k)$ is also satisfied by f. (The proof that all constraints $D_2(hg_1', \ldots, hg_l')$ are satisfied is symmetric.) $\square$

4   Semilattice Operations

In this section, we show that instances of the $\mathsf{PeriodicCSP}(\Gamma; G, H)$ problem closed under a semilattice operation are tractable in polynomial time (under a mild assumption on the "computability" of G and H).

Definition 11. *A semilattice operation is a binary operation $\otimes : D^2 \to D$ that is associative, commutative and idempotent. Note that when $\otimes$ is an semilattice operation, we can unambiguously define $\otimes$ on a finite subset of D as follows: for $S = \{s_1, \ldots, s_k\}$, $\otimes(S) = \otimes(s_1, \otimes(s_2, \ldots \otimes (s_{k-1}, s_k)))$.*

In previous work, it was shown that instances of the $\mathsf{CSP}(\Gamma)$ problem closed under a semilattice operation are tractable. Note that Horn clauses are examples of constraints closed under a semilattice operation [18], so this tractability result implies the tractability of Horn SAT.

Theorem 2. *[18] Let Γ be a constraint language. If Γ is closed under a semilattice operation, then $\mathsf{CSP}(\Gamma)$ is decidable in polynomial time.*

We have the following tractability result for the periodic constraint satisfaction problem. Note that this result strictly generalizes Theorem 2; this is seen by setting H to be the subgroup containing only the identity element and G to be any sufficiently large finite group.

Theorem 3. *Let Γ be a constraint language, G be a group, and H be a subgroup of G. If Γ is closed under an semilattice operation and the same coset problem for (G, H) is decidable in polynomial time, then $\mathsf{PeriodicCSP}(\Gamma; G, H)$ is decidable in polynomial time. Moreover, if an instance of $\mathsf{PeriodicCSP}(\Gamma; G, H)$ is satisfiable, it has an H-invariant satisfying assignment.*

By an *H-invariant satisfying assignment*, we mean a satisfying assignment $f : G \to D$ such that for all $g \in G$ and $h \in H$, the equality $f(g) = f(hg)$ holds.
Proof. Suppose that $\otimes$ is an semilattice operation under which Γ is closed. The following is a decision procedure for $\mathsf{PeriodicCSP}(\Gamma; G, H)$: given a problem instance $\mathcal{C}$, apply the H-arc consistency algorithm of Theorem 1 to $\mathcal{C}$, and let $\mathcal{C}'$ denote the resulting CSP. If there is a constraint in $\mathcal{C}'$ such that its associated relation is the empty set, *reject*; otherwise, *accept*.

If the algorithm rejects, then $H\mathcal{C}'$ has no satisfying assignment, since no assignment can satisfy the constraint $C \in \mathcal{C}' \subseteq H\mathcal{C}'$ with the empty set as associated relation. Since $H\mathcal{C}$ and $H\mathcal{C}'$ have the same set of satisfying assignments, $H\mathcal{C}$ is not satisfiable.

If the algorithm accepts, then let $f : G \to D$ be such that for all constraints $C(g_1, \ldots, g_k) \in \mathcal{C}'$, f maps all elements of Hg_i to $\otimes(\pi_i(C))$. This definition is unambiguous because $\mathcal{C}'$ is H-arc consistent. We claim that f is a satisfying assignment for $H\mathcal{C}$; it suffices to show that f satisfies every constraint in $H\mathcal{C}'$.

Let $C(g_1, \ldots, g_k)$ be a constraint in $\mathcal{C}'$, let $t_1, \ldots, t_m$ be the tuples in C and suppose $h \in H$. Observe that $(f(hg_1), \ldots, f(hg_k)) = (f(g_1), \ldots, f(g_k)) = (\otimes(\pi_1(C)), \ldots, \otimes(\pi_k(C))) = \otimes(t_1, \ldots, t_m)$. The tuple $\otimes(t_1, \ldots, t_m)$ is in C since $\mathcal{C}'$ is closed under $\otimes$. Thus $(f(hg_1), \ldots, f(hg_k)) \in C$, and we conclude that f satisfies $C(hg_1, \ldots, hg_k)$. $\square$

This theorem can be readily generalized to constraint languages closed under a *set function*; for the definition of this notion and more information, we refer the reader to [8].

Theorem 4. *Let Γ be a constraint language, G be a group, and H be a subgroup of G. If Γ is closed under a set function and the same coset problem for (G, H) is decidable in polynomial time, then $PeriodicCSP(\Gamma; G, H)$ is decidable in polynomial time. Moreover, if an instance of $PeriodicCSP(\Gamma; G, H)$ is satisfiable, it has an H-invariant satisfying assignment.*

It is easy to see that the same coset problem for group $G = (\mathbb{Z}, +)^k$ and subgroup $H = (d_1\mathbb{Z}, +) \times \cdots \times (d_k\mathbb{Z}, +)$ for any $k \geq 1$ and $d_1, \ldots, d_k \geq 0$ is solvable in polynomial time, yielding the following corollary.

Corollary 1. *Suppose that Γ is a constraint language closed under a set function, G is the group $(\mathbb{Z}, +)^k$ and H is the G-subgroup $(d_1\mathbb{Z}, +) \times \cdots \times (d_k\mathbb{Z}, +)$ for some $k \geq 1$ and $d_1, \ldots, d_k \geq 0$. Then, $PeriodicCSP(\Gamma; G, H)$ is decidable in polynomial time.*

In fact, using an algorithm of [13] it can be shown that the same coset problem is solvable for $(\mathbb{Z}, +)^k$ paired with any subgroup definable by a finite set of equations of the form $w = w'$, where w, w' are elements of $\mathbb{Z}^k$.

5   Dual Discriminator Operations

In this section, we show that instances of the $\mathsf{PeriodicCSP}(\Gamma; G, H)$ problem closed under a dual discriminator operation are tractable in polynomial time.

The tractability result of the previous section required an assumption on the "computability" of G and H; we will need such assumptions for this section's result, as well.

Definition 12. *For any set D, let $\Delta : D^3 \to D$ be the ternary operation defined as $\Delta(x, y, z) = y$ if $y = z$; x otherwise. We call Δ the* dual discriminator *on D.*

As with semilattice operations, closure under dual discriminators was previously shown to ensure tractability in the context of $\mathsf{CSP}(\Gamma)$. This tractability result strictly generalizes the tractability of 2-SAT – it is easily verified that the relations R_0, R_1, and R_2 given by Example 1 are closed under Δ.

Theorem 5. *[17, Theorem 13] Let Γ be a constraint language. If Γ is closed under a dual discriminator operation, then $\mathsf{CSP}(\Gamma)$ is decidable in polynomial time.*

In previous work, a structure theorem was proved on constraints closed under a dual discriminator operation – namely, that any such constraint can be decomposed into binary constraints of a few particular types.

Definition 13. *A* binary constraint *is a constraint which has a relation of arity two. A* complete constraint *is a binary constraint C where the relation of C is equal to $\pi_1(C) \times \pi_2(C)$. A* permutation constraint *is a binary constraint C where the relation of C is equal to $\{(d, \sigma(d)) : d \in \pi_1(C)\}$ for some bijection $\sigma : \pi_1(C) \to \pi_2(C)$. A* two-fan constraint *is a binary constraint $C = R(v, w)$ where the relation R is equal to $(\{x\} \times \pi_2(C)) \cup (\pi_1(C) \times \{y\})$ for some $x, y \in D$. The element x is called the v-fanout, and the element y is called the w-fanout.*

Lemma 1. *[17, Propositions 10 and 12], [6, Lemma 3.4] If C is a constraint over domain D closed under the dual discriminator on D, then C is logically equivalent to a conjunction of complete constraints, permutation constraints, and two-fan constraints.*

In light of Lemma 1, when studying constraints closed under a dual discriminator, we are justified in focusing on the three types of binary constraints given by Definition 13. This observation motivates the following definitions.

Definition 14. *Say that a CSP $\mathcal{C}$ is* implicative *if it is finite, arc consistent, contains only permutation constraints and two-fan constraints, and contains no constraint with empty set as the associated relation.*

Let G be a group and H be a subgroup of G. Say that a CSP $\mathcal{C}$ over variable set G is H-implicative if it is implicative and H-arc consistent.

We give a graph-theoretic characterization of implicative CSPs in the next definition and subsequent lemmas.

Definition 15. *Suppose that the CSP $\mathcal{C}$ is implicative.*
Define the implication graph *of $\mathcal{C}$ to be the directed graph $\mathcal{G}$ where:*

– The vertex set of $\mathcal{G}$ consists of all expressions of the form $(v = d)$ and $(v \neq d)$, with $v \in V$ and $d \in D$.
– The edge set of $\mathcal{G}$ is the union of the set $\{(v = d, v \neq d') : d, d' \in D, v \in V, d \neq d'\}$ and the edge sets of the constraints in $\mathcal{C}$, where we define the edge set of a constraint as follows.
  • If $R(v_1, v_2)$ is a permutation constraint with relation $R = \{(d, \sigma(d)) : d \in \pi_1(C)\}$, define the edge set of C to be the union of the sets

$$\{(v_1 = d, v_2 = \sigma(d)) : d \in \pi_1(C)\} \qquad \{(v_2 \neq \sigma(d), v_1 \neq d) : d \in \pi_1(C)\}$$

$$\{(v_2 = \sigma(d), v_1 = d) : d \in \pi_1(C)\} \qquad \{(v_1 \neq d, v_2 \neq \sigma(d)) : d \in \pi_1(C)\}$$

  • If $R(v_1, v_2)$ is a two-fan constraint with relation $R = (\{x\} \times \pi_2(C)) \cup (\pi_1(C) \times \{y\})$, define the edge set of C to be the union of the sets

$$\{(v_1 = d, v_2 = y) : d \neq x, d \in \pi_1(C)\}$$

$$\{(v_2 \neq y, v_1 \neq d) : d \neq x, d \in \pi_1(C)\}$$

$$\{(v_2 = d, v_1 = x) : d \neq y, d \in \pi_2(C)\}$$

$$\{(v_1 \neq x, v_2 \neq d) : d \neq y, d \in \pi_2(C)\}$$

A feature of the implication graph of a CSP is the following lemma, whose proof is straightforward given the above definition, and omitted.

Lemma 2. *Suppose that $\mathcal{C}$ is an implicative CSP (over variable set V and domain D), and that $f : V \to D$ is a satisfying assignment. For every pair of vertices c, c' in the implication graph of $\mathcal{C}$ such that there is a path from c to c', if f satisfies c, then f satisfies c'.*

We are now able to establish a *sufficient condition* for such an implicative CSP to be satisfiable.

Lemma 3. *Suppose that $\mathcal{C}$ is an implicative CSP. If there is no path in the implication graph of $\mathcal{C}$ from a vertex $v = d$ to the vertex of its "negation" $v \neq d$, then the CSP $\mathcal{C}$ is satisfiable.*

Proof. We prove this by induction on the number of variables of $\mathcal{C}$. We define a partial function f as follows. Pick a variable v and and value $d \in D$, and set $f(v) = d$. For all vertices of the form $v' = d'$ such that there exists a path in the implication graph of $\mathcal{C}$ from $v = d$ to $v' \neq d'$, set $f(v') = d'$. Note that this is well-defined, because if there were paths from $v = d$ to both $v' = d_1$ and $v' = d_2$ (for distinct d_1, d_2), then there would be a path from $v = d$ to $v' \neq d_1$ (as there is an edge from $v' = d_2$ to $v' \neq d_1$). By the symmetry of the graph, there would be a path from $v' = d_1$ to $v \neq d$, implying that there is a path from $v = d$ to $v \neq d$, a contradiction to Lemma 2.

Let $\mathcal{C}'$ be the subset of $\mathcal{C}$ containing those constraints where neither variable has been defined by f.

We claim that any extension f' of f satisfying $\mathcal{C}'$ will satisfy $\mathcal{C}$. It suffices to show that any such extension f' will satisfy $\mathcal{C} \setminus \mathcal{C}'$. For constraints in $\mathcal{C} \setminus \mathcal{C}'$ containing two variables on which f is defined, this is clear from the definition of the implication graph. Any constraint C in $\mathcal{C} \setminus \mathcal{C}'$ containing a variable v on which f is defined and a variable w on which f is not defined must be a two-fan constraint, where $f(v)$ is the v-fanout; consequently, any value of $f(w)$ for which f satisfying $\mathcal{C}'$ will result in f satisfying C, as $\mathcal{C}$ is arc consistent.

The implication graph of $\mathcal{C}'$ is a subgraph of the implication graph of $\mathcal{C}$, so $\mathcal{C}'$ is satisfiable by induction. $\square$

We now give an analog of implication graph (Definition 15) for periodic CSPs. Because one can naively extend Definition 15 to infinite constraint sets by allowing the implication graph to be infinite, it is worth noting that our second notion of implication graph is a *finite* graph, albeit one with edge weights.

Definition 16. (Implication graph of $H\mathcal{C}$) *Let G be a group and H a subgroup of G with finite index. Let S be a subset of G containing exactly one element of G from each right H-coset. Let $r : G \to S$ map a group element g to the element of S which is in the same right coset as g.*

Suppose that $\mathcal{C}$ is an H-implicative CSP over variable set G.

Define the implication graph of $H\mathcal{C}$ *relative to S to be the directed graph $\mathcal{G}$ with edge labels where:*

- *The vertex set of $\mathcal{G}$ consists of all expressions of the form $(g = d)$ and $(g \neq d)$, with $g \in S$ and $d \in D$.*
- *The edge set of $\mathcal{G}$ consists of all edges of the form $r'(e)$, where e is an edge from the implication graph of $\mathcal{C}$ and r' acts on an edge e by mapping the two variables of e under the map r. (For example, $r'(g_1 = d_2, g_2 \neq d_2) \overset{\text{def}}{=} (r(g_1) = d_2, r(g_2) \neq d_2)$.)*
  The label of the edge $r'(e)$ is equal to the group element $r(g_1)g_1^{-1}g_2r(g_2)^{-1}$, where g_1 and g_2 are the two variables of e and the edge is directed from the vertex with variable g_1 to the vertex with variable g_2.

Define the weight *of a path in $\mathcal{G}$ with edges $e_1, \ldots, e_s$ to be the group product $l_1 \cdots l_s$, where l_i is the label of e_i (for all $1 \leq i \leq s$).*

The following lemma is analogous to Lemma 2, and describes how to derive implications concerning satisfying assignments from the implication graph.

Lemma 4. *Suppose that $\mathcal{C}$ is an H-implicative CSP (over variable set G and domain D), and that $f : G \to D$ is a satisfying assignment. For every pair of vertices $g \sim d, g' \sim' d'$ in the implication graph of $H\mathcal{C}$ (with $\sim, \sim' \in \{=, \neq\}$) such that there is a path of weight w from $g \sim d$ to $g' \sim' d'$, if $f(g) \sim d$, then $f(wg') \sim' d'$.*

Next, we present a parallel of Lemma 3 – a sufficient condition for an H-implicative periodic CSP to be satisfiable, based on properties of the implication graph.

Lemma 5. *(Sufficient condition for satisfiability of HC) Let G be a group and H a subgroup of G with finite index. Let S be any subset of G containing exactly one element of G from each right H-coset. Suppose that $\mathcal{C}$ is an H-implicative CSP over variable set G.*

If there is no path with identity weight in the implication graph of $H\mathcal{C}$ (relative to S) from a vertex $v = d$ to the vertex of its "negation" $v \neq d$, then the CSP $H\mathcal{C}$ is satisfiable.

Proof. We show that for any finite subset $\mathcal{C}'$ of $H\mathcal{C}$, there is no path from a vertex $v = d$ to its negation $v \neq d$ in the implication graph of $\mathcal{C}'$. Every such finite subset $\mathcal{C}'$ is then satisfiable by Lemma 3, and that $H\mathcal{C}$ is satisfiable follows by a standard compactness argument.

Suppose there is a path from in the implication graph of a finite subset $\mathcal{C}'$ of $H\mathcal{C}$. Let $e_1, \ldots, e_s$ be the edges of the path, and let $g_1, \ldots, g_{s+1}$ be the elements of G from the vertices on the path. Letting r and r' be defined as in Definition 16, $r'(e_1), \ldots, r'(e_s)$ is a path in the implication graph of $H\mathcal{C}$ with path weight equal to

$$(r(g_1)g_1^{-1}g_2 r(g_2)^{-1})(r(g_2)g_2^{-1}g_3 r(g_3)^{-1}) \cdots (r(g_s)g_s^{-1}g_{s+1} r(g_{s+1})^{-1}).$$

After cancellations, this is equal to $r(g_1)g_1^{-1}g_{s+1}r(g_{s+1})^{-1}$ which is the identity element, because $g_1 = g_{s+1}$. $\square$

We are almost in position to state and prove the tractability result of this section. Before doing so, however, we identify the computability assumptions on a group-subgroup pair (G, H) needed for $\mathsf{PeriodicCSP}(\Gamma; G, H)$ to be tractable.

Definition 17. *Let G be a group and H be a subgroup of G. Say that (G, H) is Δ-helpful if*

- *H is of finite index,*
- *the same coset problem for (G, H) is decidable in polynomial time,*
- *products and inverses can be computed in polynomial time, and*
- *given a directed graph with edge weights from G and two specified vertices w_1, w_2, it can be checked whether or not there is a path from w_1 to w_2 with edge weight equal to the identity of G in polynomial time. (The weight of a path is defined as in Definition 16.)*

The following is our second tractability result – namely, that closure under the dual discriminator implies efficient decidability.

Theorem 6. *Let Γ be a constraint language, G be a group, and H be a subgroup of G. If Γ is closed under the dual discriminator operation Δ and (G, H) is Δ-helpful, then $\mathsf{PeriodicCSP}(\Gamma; G, H)$ is decidable in polynomial time.*

Proof. Fix S to be a subset of G containing exactly one element of G from each right H-coset. Let $r : G \to S$ map a group element g to the element of S which is in the same right coset as g.

Let $\mathcal{C}$ be a PeriodicCSP$(\Gamma; G, H)$ problem instance. By Lemma 1, any constraint from $\mathcal{C}$ is equivalent to a set of binary constraints which can be computed from $\mathcal{C}$ in polynomial time. Thus, we can assume without loss of generality that every relation in Γ is a binary relation.

The following is an algorithm to decide satisfiability of $H\mathcal{C}$.

1. Perform steps (b), (c), and (d) below.
2. While there is a path in the implication graph of $H\mathcal{C}$ from $g = d$ to $g \neq d$ of identity weight (for some $g \in S$ and $d \in D$), do the following:
   (a) For every constraint $R(g_1, g_2)$ where g_i (for either $i = 1$ or 2) is in the same coset as g, replace R with $R' = \{t \in R : t[i] \neq d\}$
   (b) Apply the algorithm of Theorem 1 to $\mathcal{C}$ (replacing $\mathcal{C}$ with the new set of constraints $\mathcal{C}'$)
   (c) If $\mathcal{C}$ contains a constraint with empty relation, *reject*.
   (d) Remove all complete constraints from $\mathcal{C}$.
3. If the loop terminates without rejecting, then *accept.*

Proof of Correctness. When the algorithm of Theorem 1 is applied to $\mathcal{C}$, $\mathcal{C}$ remains Δ-closed. It follows that, after step (b), by Lemma 1, every constraint in $\mathcal{C}$ is either a complete constraint, a permutation constraint, or a two-fan constraint. We will argue that every step of the algorithm preserves satisfiability of $H\mathcal{C}$, implying that if the algorithm rejects in step (c), it does so correctly. Removing complete constraints as in (d) does not affect whether or not $H\mathcal{C}$ is satisfiable, because of the H-consistency of $\mathcal{C}$. Suppose that step (a) of the algorithm is executed; this means that a path of identity weight was found from $g = d$ to $g \neq d$. By Lemma 4, no satisfying assignment of $H\mathcal{C}$ could map g to d, and hence no satisfying assignment could map any element of the coset Hg to d, and so the replacement of step (a) does not change the satisfiability of $H\mathcal{C}$. Moreover, the replacement of step (a) preserves the Δ-closure of $\mathcal{C}$.

If the algorithm accepts, then $H\mathcal{C}$ is satisfiable by Lemma 5.

Polynomiality of Running Time. Observe that the implication graph $\mathcal{G}$ of $H\mathcal{C}$ can be constructed in polynomial time (by the Δ-helpfulness of $H\mathcal{C}$): r can be computed in polynomial time (as the (G, H) same coset problem is decidable in polynomial time), and thus the labels of the edges of $\mathcal{G}$ can be computed in polynomial time (as products and inverses in G can be computed in polynomial time). The loop of step (2) is executed at most a constant number of times, since there are only a constant number of pairs (g, d) with $g \in S$ and $d \in D$. □

Using an algorithm of [13] it can be shown that the pair consisting of the group $G = (\mathbb{Z}, +)^k$ and a subgroup of the form $H = (d_1\mathbb{Z}, +) \times \cdots \times (d_k\mathbb{Z}, +)$ (for any $k \geq 1$ and $d_1, \ldots, d_k \geq 0$) is Δ-helpful; hence, we obtain the following corollary.

Corollary 2. *Suppose that Γ is a constraint language closed under a dual discriminator operation, G is the group $(\mathbb{Z}, +)^k$ and H is the G-subgroup $(d_1\mathbb{Z}, +) \times \cdots \times (d_k\mathbb{Z}, +)$ for some $k \geq 1$ and $d_1, \ldots, d_k \geq 0$. Then, PeriodicCSP$(\Gamma; G, H)$ is decidable in polynomial time.*

6 Conclusions and Future Work

We identified two broad tractable subclasses of the periodic CSP, which were described using the language of closure properties. One prominent and intriguing open question is whether or not the periodic version of CSPs consisting of linear equations over a finite field (equivalently, constraints closed under an affine operation [18]) are tractable, or even decidable. We conjecture that this subclass of the periodic CSP is decidable in polynomial time; demonstrating that such CSPs have "periodic" solutions and that an upper bound on the size of the period is computable might be intermediate steps to resolving this conjecture. As far as the non-periodic, usual CSP is concerned, constraints of the described form are decidable in polynomial time via Gaussian elimination.

Resolution of this conjecture in the positive would provide a full dichotomy theorem for constraint languages over domain size two, by combining the results in this paper with the undecidability result of Freedman [12]. This dichotomy theorem would give a direct correspondence between CSP complexity and periodic CSP complexity (in domain size two), stating that those constraint languages Γ such that $\mathsf{CSP}(\Gamma)$ is tractable give rise to a tractable periodic CSP, while those constraint languages Γ such that $\mathsf{CSP}(\Gamma)$ is NP-complete give rise to an undecidable periodic CSP. In addition, such a resolution would also suggest the conjecture that for all constraint languages Γ, general problems of the form $\mathsf{PeriodicCSP}(\Gamma; (\mathbb{Z}, +)^k, (d_1\mathbb{Z}, +) \times \cdots \times (d_k\mathbb{Z}, +))$ are decidable in polynomial time if and only if $\mathsf{CSP}(\Gamma)$ is. Roughly speaking, this second conjecture states that constraint languages that are tractable in the context of the CSP are well-behaved in that they are also tractable in the context of the periodic CSP! A similar well-behavedness phenomenon seems to take place in the case of the quantified CSP [7], where the tractable constraint languages (in domain size two) are exactly the non-trivial tractable constraint languages in the case of CSP (given by Schaefer's theorem). We believe that further investigation and validation of this phenomenon may prove to be fruitful in understanding the problem structure of CSPs and the variants thereof.

Acknowledgements

The author wishes to thank Jon Kleinberg and Dexter Kozen for helpful discussions.

References

1. Andrei Bulatov and Peter Jeavons. Tractable constraints closed under a binary operation. Technical Report PRG-TR-12-00, Oxford University, 2000.
2. Andrei A. Bulatov. A dichotomy theorem for constraints on a three-element set. In *Proceedings of 43rd IEEE Symposium on Foundations of Computer Science*, pages 649–658, 2002.
3. Andrei A. Bulatov. Malt'sev constraints are tractable. Technical Report PRG-RR-02-05, Oxford University, 2002.

4. Andrei A. Bulatov, Andrei A. Krokhin, and Peter Jeavors. Constraint satisfaction problems and finite algebras. In *Proceedings 27th International Colloquium on Automata, Languages, and Programming – ICALP'00*, volume 1853 of *Lecture Notes In Computer Science*, pages 272–282, 2000.
5. Andrei A. Bulatov, Andrei A. Krokhin, and Peter Jeavons. The complexity of maximal constraint languages. In *ACM Symposium on Theory of Computing*, pages 667–674, 2001.
6. M.C. Cooper, D.A. Cohen, and P.G. Jeavons. Characterising tractable constraints. *Artificial Intelligence*, 65(2):347–361, 1994.
7. Nadia Creignou, Sanjeev Khanna, and Madhu Sudan. *Complexity Classification of Boolean Constraint Satisfaction Problems*. SIAM Monographs on Discrete Mathematics and Applications. Society for Industrial and Applied Mathematics, 2001.
8. V. Dalmau and J. Pearson. Closure functions and width 1 problems. In *Principles and Practice of Constraint Programming—CP'99*, volume 1713 of *Lecture Notes in Computer Science*, pages 159–173. Springer-Verlag, 1999.
9. Victor Dalmau. A new tractable class of constraint satisfaction problems. In *6th International Symposium on Artificial Intelligence and Mathematics*, 2000.
10. Victor Dalmau, Phokion G. Kolaitis, and Moshe Y. Vardi. Constraint satisfaction, bounded treewidth, and finite-variable logics. In *Constraint Programming '02*, Lecture Notes In Computer Science, 2002.
11. Tomás Feder and Moshe Y. Vardi. The computational structure of monotone monadic snp and constraint satisfaction: A study through datalog and group theory. *SIAM J. Comput.*, 28(1):57–104, 1998.
12. Michael Freedman. K-sat on groups and undecidability. In *Proceedings of the ACM Symposium on Theory of Computing (STOC)*, pages 572–576, 1998.
13. Franz Höfting and Egon Wanke. Polynomial algorithms for minimum cost paths in periodic graphs. In *SODA*, pages 493–499, 1993.
14. Peter Jeavons. On the algebraic structure of combinatorial problems. *Theoretical Computer Science*, 200:185–204, 1998.
15. Peter Jeavons, David Cohen, and Martin Cooper. Constraints, consistency, and closure. *Articial Intelligence*, 101(1-2):251–265, 1998.
16. Peter Jeavons, David Cohen, and Justin Pearson. Constraints and universal algebra. *Annals of Mathematics and Artificial Intelligence*, 24(1-4):51–67, 1998.
17. P.G. Jeavons, D.A. Cohen, and M. Gyssens. A unifying framework for tractable constraints. In *Proceedings of 1st International Conference on Principles and Practice of Constraint Programming*, pages 276–291. Springer-Verlag, 1995.
18. P.G. Jeavons, D.A. Cohen, and M. Gyssens. Closure properties of constraints. *Journal of the ACM*, 44:527–548, 1997.
19. M.V. Marathe, H.B. Hunt III, D.J. Rosenkrantz, and R.E. Stearns. Theory of periodically specified problems: Complexity and approximability. In *Proc. 13th IEEE Conference on Computational Complexity*, 1998.
20. M.V. Marathe, H.B. Hunt III, R.E. Stearns, and V. Radhakrishnan. Approximation algorithms for pspace-hard hierarchically and periodically specified problems. *SIAM Journal on Computing*, 27(5):1237–1261, 1998.
21. James Orlin. The complexity of dynamic languages and dynamic optimization problems. In *Proceedings of the ACM Symposium on Theory of Computing (STOC)*, pages 218–227, 1981.
22. Justin K. Pearson and Peter G. Jeavons. A survey of tractable constraint satisfaction problems. Technical report, Royal Holloway, University of London, 1997.
23. Thomas J. Schaefer. The complexity of satisfiability problems. In *Proceedings of the ACM Symposium on Theory of Computing (STOC)*, pages 216–226, 1978.

Box Constraint Collections for Adhoc Constraints*

Chi Kan Cheng[1], Jimmy Ho Man Lee[1], and Peter J. Stuckey[2]

[1] Dept of Comp. Sci. & Eng.
The Chinese University of Hong Kong, Hong Kong SAR
{ckcheng,jlee}@cse.cuhk.edu.hk
[2] Dept. of Comp. Sci. & Soft. Eng.
University of Melbourne, Australia
pjs@cs.mu.oz.au

Abstract. In this paper, we propose a new language-independent representation of adhoc constraints, called a box constraint collection. Using constructive disjunction, this representation achieves domain consistency. We develop an algorithm to automatically generate a box constraint collection for a given adhoc constraint. The result is guaranteed to be complete and correct, and achieve domain consistency. The constructive disjunction propagator for the box constraint collection can be efficiently implemented using indexicals. We give correctness and completeness result for our compilation scheme, and outline optimization techniques. Experiments show that our representation is simple, compact, and propagates efficiently.

1 Introduction

Constraint programming is a promising technique for solving many difficult combinatorial problems. Since real-life constraints can be difficult to describe in symbolic expressions, or provide very weak propagation from their symbolic representation, they are sometimes represented in the form of the sets of solutions or sets of nogoods. This adhoc representation provides strong propagation through generalized arc consistency techniques. However, the adhoc representation is expensive in terms of memory and computation, when the adhoc constraint is large.

There is interest in determining less expensive methods for building propagators for adhoc constraints. The first step in this direction was the automatic generation of propagation rules pioneered by Apt and Monfroy [4]. They represent an adhoc constraint as a set of simple rules of the form $x_1 = v_1 \wedge \ldots \wedge x_n = v_n \rightarrow y \neq a$ such that rule consistency, which is weaker than domain consistency, is achieved. These rules can be extended to $x_1 \in S_1 \wedge \ldots \wedge x_n \in S_n \rightarrow y \neq a$, such that domain consistency is achieved. They propose two algorithms to generate all non-redundant rules for a given adhoc constraint.

Apt and Monfroy's work is extended by Abdennadher and Rigotti [2], who express the propagation rules in CHRs [10] so that user-defined predicates are allowed. They develop

---

* We thank the anonymous referees for their constructive comments. The work described in this paper was substantially supported by a grant from the Research Grants Council of the Hong Kong Special Administrative Region (Project no. CUHK4183/00E).

F. Rossi (Ed.): CP 2003, LNCS 2833, pp. 214–228, 2003.

the PROPMINER algorithm, which generates all non-redundant propagation rules based on the set of user-defined predicates. Constraint handling rules, while expressive, are less efficient than other approaches to implementing constraint solvers.

Indexicals are powerful, and efficient language to define constraint propagation. Dao *et al.* [8] propose a framework and two algorithms to learn indexical operators (a subset of the indexical operators available in GNU Prolog [9]) that achieve bounds-consistency for adhoc constraints. They require that the indexicals must not delete a solution of the original constraint, and at the same time they try to minimize the cases that a nogood is wrongly classified as a solution. Under this formulation, the output indexicals are correct (i.e. they will not remove a solution), but may be incomplete (i.e. they may not detect all nogoods). However, they show that indexicals with good pruning power can often be discovered. Barták [5] gives an efficient filtering algorithm as the basis of the implementation of a binary tabled constraint by clustering the tuples into boxes, but does not discuss how to find the boxes.

In this paper, we propose a new language-independent representation for adhoc constraints, the *box constraint collection*. The idea is to break up an adhoc constraint into pieces and cover these pieces using *box constraints* as tiles. With the aid of constructive disjunction and a suitable choice of forms of constraint to use in the collection, our new representation achieves domain consistency. We can compile this representation using the indexical language provided by SICStus Prolog, to provide efficient propagators for adhoc constraints.

We describe an algorithm, bccFinder, that automatically generates a box constraint collection for an adhoc constraint. The output representation is guaranteed to be complete, correct, and achieve domain consistency. We also suggest a compilation scheme which generates efficient indexicals for box constraint collections, and outline optimization techniques. Experiments confirm the compactness of our representation and efficiency in propagation.

2   Propagation Based Constraint Solving

In this section we give our terminology for constraint satisfaction problems, and propagation based constraint solving.

An *integer valuation* θ is a mapping of variables to integer values, written $\{x_1 \mapsto d_1, \ldots, x_n \mapsto d_n\}$. We extend the valuation θ to map expressions and constraints involving the variables in the natural way. Let *vars* be the function that returns the set of (free) variables appearing in a constraint or valuation.

A *domain* D is a complete mapping from a fixed (countable) set of variables $\mathcal{V}$ to finite sets of integers. A *false domain* D is a domain with $D(x) = \emptyset$ for some x. A domain D_1 is *stronger* than a domain D_2, written $D_1 \sqsubseteq D_2$, if $D_1(x) \subseteq D_2(x)$ for all variables x.

In an abuse of notation, we define a valuation θ to be an element of a (non-false) domain D, written $\theta \in D$, if $\theta(x_i) \in D(x_i)$ for all $x_i \in vars(\theta)$.

We are also interested in the notion of an *initial domain*, denoted by D_{init}. The initial domain gives the initial values possible for each variable.

A *constraint* c over variables $x_1, \ldots, x_n$, written as $c(x_1, \ldots, x_n)$, restricts the values that each variable x_i can take simultaneously. An *adhoc constraint* $c(x_1, \ldots, x_n)$ is

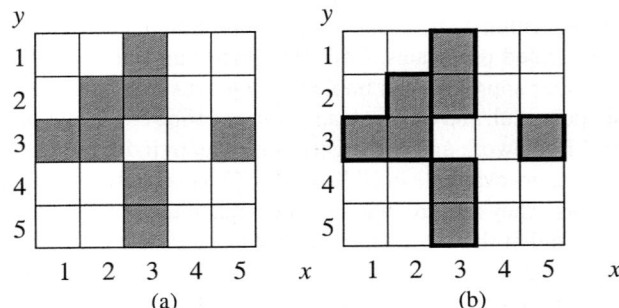

Fig. 1. (a) An adhoc constraint c_{adhoc}, and (b) broken into a box constraint collection.

defined *extensionally* as a set of valuations θ over the variables $x_1, \ldots, x_n$. We say $\theta \in c$ is a *solution* of c. For any valuation θ on variables $x_1, \ldots, x_n$, with $\theta \notin c$, we call θ a *nogood* of c.

Often we define constraints *intensionally* using some well understood mathematical syntax. For an intensionally defined constraint c we have that $\theta \in c$ iff $vars(\theta) = vars(c) \wedge \mathcal{Z} \models_\theta c$, where $\mathcal{Z}$ is the integers. For example the constraint $x_1 = x_2 + 1$ where $D_{init}(x_1) = D_{init}(x_2) = \{1, 2, 3\}$ defines the solution set $\{\{x_1 \mapsto 2, x_2 \mapsto 1\}, \{x_1 \mapsto 3, x_2 \mapsto 2\}\}$.

Two constraints c_1 and c_2 are *equivalent* to each other, denoted by $c_1 \equiv c_2$, if they define the same set of solutions.

A *constraint satisfaction problem* (CSP) [15] consists of a set of constraints $\{c_1, \ldots, c_k\}$ over a set of variables $\{x_1, \ldots, x_n\}$, where each variable x_i can only take values from its domain $D_{init}(x_i)$, a set of integers. Solving a CSP requires finding a value for each variable from its domain so that no constraint is violated, *i.e.* all constraints are satisfied.

We adopt the notion of *propagation solver* from Schulte and Stuckey [14]. A *propagator* f is a monotonically decreasing function from domains to domains. A *propagation solver* for a set of propagators F and current domain D, $solv(F, D)$, repeatedly applies all the propagators in F starting from domain D until there is no further change in resulting domain. We say two sets of propagators F_1 and F_2 are *equivalent* if $solv(F_1, D) = solv(F_2, D)$ for all $D \sqsubseteq D_{init}$.

Define the *generalized arc consistent propagator* (or equivalently the *domain consistent* [14] propagator) for a constraint c as

$$dom(c)(D)(x) = \{\theta(x) \mid \theta \in D \text{ and } \theta \in c(\text{that is } \theta \text{ is a solution of } c)\}$$

3 Box Constraint Collections

Formally, an *adhoc constraint* c over variables $x_1, \ldots, x_n$ is a set of valuations in D_{init} representing the solutions of c. Adhoc constraints are usually implemented as tabled constraints by listing all the solutions or nogoods, incurring space and time overhead.

Example 1. The adhoc constraint c_{adhoc} over x and y for $D_{init}(x) = D_{init}(y) = \{1, 2, 3, 4, 5\}$ shown in Fig. 1(a) can be represented by the set of solutions { $(1, 3)$, $(2, 2)$, $(2, 3)$, $(3, 1)$, $(3, 2)$, $(3, 4)$, $(3, 5)$, $(5, 3)$ } or the set of nogoods { $(1, 1)$, $(1, 2)$, $(1, 4)$, $(1, 5)$, $(2, 1)$, $(2, 4)$, $(2, 5)$, $(4, 1)$, $(4, 2)$, $(4, 3)$, $(4, 4)$, $(4, 5)$, $(5, 1)$, $(5, 2)$, $(5, 4)$, $(5, 5)$ }.

Often we represent a constraint in an adhoc manner because it is difficult (or unwieldy) to describe it using a symbolic expression. However, it may be easier to find symbolic expressions if we examine part of the solution space. Therefore, we propose representing an adhoc constraint c_{adhoc} with a set of simple constraints in DNF. The idea is similar to the use of Karnaugh-Veitch-diagrams [13] for finding prime implicants.

The core idea is to use a disjunction of constraints as "tiles" to cover the solution space of an adhoc constraint. By carefully choosing the shapes of the tiles we can achieve domain consistency using constructive disjunction. Triangles and rectangular boxes are good tile shapes for filling grids.

A *box* $B = \prod_{j=1}^{n} [l_j^B..u_j^B]$ is an n-dimensional hyper-cube, where $[l_j^B..u_j^B]$ is a *interval* of integers l_j^B and u_j^B. If $c(x_1, \ldots, x_n)$ is a constraint on variables $x_1, \ldots, x_n$, then $\bigwedge_{j=1}^{n} l_j^B \leq x_j \leq u_j^B \wedge c(x_1, \ldots, x_n)$ is a *box constraint*, which we write as $B \Rightarrow c$. We restrict the form of constraints c to two *templates*. Either c is *true* and then $B \Rightarrow c$ is simply the box B, or c is of the form $\sum_{j=1}^{n} a_j x_j \leq a_0$, then we call $B \Rightarrow c$ a *triangle*. A *box constraint collection* (BCC) is simply a disjunction of box constraints.

We represent an adhoc constraint c_{adhoc} over variables $x_1, \ldots, x_n$ as a collection of m box constraints

$$c_{adhoc}(x_1, \ldots, x_n) \equiv \bigvee_{i=1}^{m} B_i \Rightarrow c_i(x_1, \ldots, x_n). \tag{1}$$

Example 2. A box constraint collection representation of the adhoc constraint c_{adhoc} shown in Fig. 1(a) is

$$[3..3] \times [4..5] \Rightarrow true \vee [1..2] \times [2..3] \Rightarrow x + y \geq 4$$
$$\vee [5..5] \times [3..3] \Rightarrow true \vee [3..3] \times [1..2] \Rightarrow true$$

The box constraint $[1..2] \times [2..3] \Rightarrow x + y \geq 4$ represents the conjunction $1 \leq x \leq 2 \wedge 2 \leq y \leq 3 \wedge x + y \geq 4$. The BCC representation for c_{adhoc} is shown in Fig. 1(b).

Representing a constraint using a box constraint collection is more compact than a set of solutions. However, disjunctive constraints do not usually propagate as effectively as other representations. But disjunctions of box constraints can be propagated effectively, achieving generalized arc consistency.

Lemma 1. *If each constraint c_i in (1) is implemented by generalized arc consistent propagator $dom(c_i)$, then using constructive disjunction [16] on this representation achieves generalized arc consistency for c_{adhoc}.*

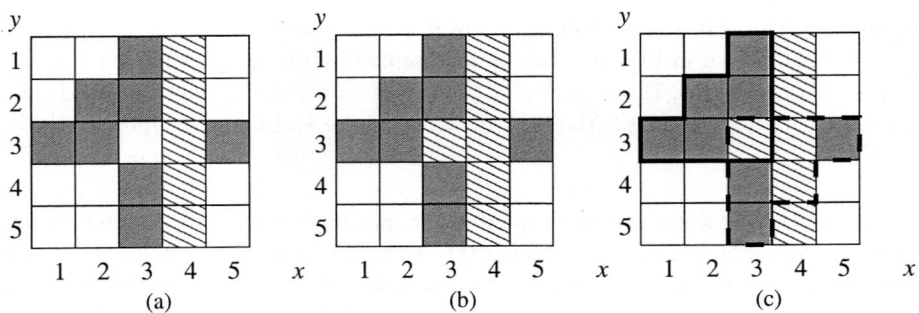

Fig. 2. Freeing the representation by adding "dont care" tuples to c_{adhoc} for (a) $x = 4$ and (b) $x = 3 \wedge y = 3$, and (c) the resulting box constraint collection c_{tri}.

4   Separable Nogoods

We can improve the description of an adhoc constraint by a box constraint collection by determining parts of the constraint which can be represented separately without losing generalized arc consistency of the resulting set of propagators.

Example 3. Consider c_{adhoc} defined in Fig. 1(a). Since $x \neq 4$ is implied by c_{adhoc} we can extract this as a separate constraint, we are then free to model the remainder of c_{adhoc} by filling in some boxes in the $x = 4$ column and this will not change the propagation behavior. Fig. 2(a) shows c_{adhoc} with "dont care" annotations in the $x = 4$ column.

Similarly the remaining nogood (3,3) is such that unless x (y) is assigned to 3, it will not remove the value 3 from the domain of y (x). In this situation, we can represent this nogood with an extra constraint $\neg(x = 3 \wedge y = 3)$ without changing the propagation behavior. Fig. 2(b) shows c_{adhoc} with "dont care" annotation at $x = 3 \wedge y = 3$.

Note that now we can represent c_{adhoc} by the conjunction of constraints $x \neq 4$, $\neg(x = 3 \wedge y = 3)$ and c_{tri} defined as the box constraint collection

$$[1..3] \times [1..3] \Rightarrow x + y \geq 4 \quad \vee \quad [3..5] \times [3..5] \Rightarrow x + y \leq 8$$

We obtain the same propagation behavior. The representation is smaller in terms of the number of box constraints and propagates more efficiently.

These two observations for separability of nogoods in the above example can be formalized as follows.

Lemma 2. *Let c be an adhoc constraint such that $c \to x \neq d$ for some $x \in vars(c)$ and $d \in D_{init}(x)$. Let S be a set of solutions for $vars(c)$ where $x = d$. Then $\{dom(x \neq d), dom(c \cup S)\}$ and $\{dom(c)\}$ are equivalent.*

Lemma 3. *Let c be an adhoc constraint on variables $(x_1, \ldots, x_n)$ with nogood $\theta \notin C$ such that there are no other nogoods $\theta' \notin c$ and $1 \leq i \leq n$ where $\theta(x_i) = \theta'(x_i)$. Then $\{dom((x_1, \ldots, x_n) \neq (\theta(x_1), \ldots, \theta(x_n))), dom(c \cup \{\theta\})\}$ and $\{dom(c)\}$ are equivalent.*

5   Building Box Constraint Collections

In this section, we describe a greedy algorithm, bccFinder, which computes a compact box constraint collection for a given adhoc n-ary constraint c_{adhoc} with solutions *solutions* and nogoods *nogoods*. Before we find the set of box constraints, we remove the set of separable nogoods from c_{adhoc}, by adding extra constraints as discussed in Section 4. This leaves a description of the constraint involving three kinds of tuples: solutions, nogoods, and "dont cares" which may be included or not since they will be removed by other constraints. Then, we repeatedly find box constraints for the remaining uncovered solutions. A valuation θ is *covered* by the constraint c if $\theta \in c$; otherwise, it is *uncovered*. Fig. 3 shows the pseudo-code of bccFinder.

Since we would like to reduce the number of box constraints in the collection, we want each box constraint $B \Rightarrow c$ to cover as many uncovered solutions as possible. Although finding the optimal collection is in practice infeasible, we can find a relatively large box B by greedily growing one, until we cannot find any corresponding c, where c is an instantiation of one of our templates ct. For the code shown, ct is always of the form of $\sum_{j=1}^{n} a_j x_j \leq a_0$ since such constraints are straightforward to find, and have generalized arc consistency propagators which are efficiently computable [14].

To find $B \Rightarrow c$, we randomly pick an uncovered solution and put it into the (unit) box B and initialize C, the constraints on the coefficients a_j, to *true*. As a result, each a_j is unconstrained. Then, we iteratively try to enlarge B in each dimension j. We first reduce the lower bound l_j^B until either the lower bound of x_j is reached, or no enlargement is possible. Then we try to increase the upper bound u_j^B.

Let B' be the enlarged B. The procedure update is called so that for each valuation $\theta \in B' - B$ of the form $\theta \equiv \{x_1 \mapsto d_1, \ldots, x_n \mapsto d_n\}$ we either (a) add the constraint $\sum_{j=1}^{n} a_j d_j \leq a_0$ if $\theta \in solutions$ to ensure θ is included in the box constraint, or (b) add the constraint $\sum_{j=1}^{n} a_j d_j > a_0$ if $\theta \in nogoods$. This update procedure is an exact version of an algorithm by Anthony and Frisch [3] for constraint induction.

If the constraints are satisfiable, there exist values for a_j and we continue expanding the box. If the constraints are unsatisfiable, we first remove all the constraints added in the last expansion and try expanding in a different direction. Eventually every expansion leads to failure (or we have covered the entire space). At this stage we simply choose a value for each a_j that satisfies the current constraints. In our implementation, we solve for a_j's with the SICStus Prolog clp(Q) constraint-solving library [1].

We have created a single box constraint. We add this to our collection, and move all the solutions covered by this box constraint into the "dont care" category. This continues until there are no solutions remaining (which are not "dont care"). We then simplify the resulting collection if possible, by replacing $\sum_{j=1}^{n} a_j x_j \leq a_0$ by *true* if $B \to$ $\sum_{j=1}^{n} a_j x_j \leq a_0$ and removing box constraints which are subsumed by other box constraints.

A box constraint collection with only boxes ($B \Rightarrow true$) can be found similarly, except that B stops expanding along a particular dimension if B' contains at least one nogood.

The box constraint collection being returned is always equivalent to the given adhoc constraint, because when bccFinder terminates, all solutions will be covered, while all nogoods will remain uncovered.

bccFinder(n, $solutions$, $nogoods$)
  $c_B := false$
  $c_S :=$ constraints for separable nogoods
  $separable :=$ nogoods of c_S
  $nogoods := nogoods - separable$
  while ($\exists \theta \in solutions$)
    $B :=$ a unit box equal to θ
    $C := true$
    for $j := 1$ to n
      while ($l_j^B > min(D_{init}(x_j))$)
        $B' := B$ with $l_j^{B'} = l_j^B - 1$
        $C' :=$ update($C, B', B, solutions, nogoods$)
        if (C' is not satisfiable) **break**
        $B := B'$
        $C := C'$
        $solutions := solutions - B$
      endwhile
      while ($u_j^B < max(D_{init}(x_j))$)
        $B' := B$ with $u_j^{B'} = u_j^B + 1$
        $C' :=$ update($C, B', B, solutions, nogoods$)
        if (C' is not satisfiable) **break**
        $B := B'$
        $C := C'$
        $solutions := solutions - B$
      endwhile
    endfor
    let ϕ be a solution of C
    $c_B := c_B \vee (B \Rightarrow \sum_{j=1}^n \phi(a_j)x_j \leq \phi(a_0))$
  endwhile
  simplify c_B
  return $c_B \wedge c_S$

update(C, B', B, $solutions$, $nogoods$)
  for each $\theta \in B' - B$
    if $\theta \in solutions$
      $C := C \wedge \sum_{j=1}^n a_j \theta(x_j) \leq a_0$
    elseif $\theta \in nogoods$
      $C := C \wedge \sum_{j=1}^n a_j \theta(x_j) > a_0$
    endif
  endfor
  if C is satisfiable
    return C
  else return $false$

Fig. 3. Pseudo-code of bccFinder.

The bccFinder algorithm always terminates because each while loop removes at least one valuation (θ) from $solutions$.

Although in worst case clp(Q) takes exponential time to solve for the coefficients of ct, our experiments confirm that our bccFinder algorithm is capable of returning a box constraint collection for an adhoc constraint in a reasonable amount of time.

There are many possible improvements to the simple algorithm shown here. For example we should not examine an expansion where all the valuations in $B' - B$ are in $nogoods$, and we should find large rectangular boxes first before starting the box expansion.

6   Compilation of Box Constraint Collection

In this section, we will explain how a box constraint collection can be compiled into indexicals. The constraint system FD [7, 16] is based on domain constraints and func-

Table 1. The (partial) indexical grammar and its semantics in SICStus Prolog.

Rule	Semantics
$r \to \mathtt{dom}\,(y)$	y_σ
$r \to t_1..t_2$	$\{i \in \mathcal{Z} : t_{1_\sigma} \leq i \leq t_{2_c}\}$
$r \to \{t_1, \ldots, t_n\}$	$\{t_{1_\sigma}, \ldots, t_{n_\sigma}\}$
$r \to r_1\ /\backslash\ r_2$	$r_{1_\sigma} \cap r_{2_\sigma}$
$r \to r_1\ \backslash/\ r_2$	$r_{1_\sigma} \cup r_{2_\sigma}$
$r \to r_1\ ?\ r_2$	$\emptyset$ if $r_{1_\sigma} = \emptyset$; r_{2_σ} otherwise
$t \to \mathtt{integer}$	t
$t \to \mathtt{inf}$	$-\infty$
$t \to \mathtt{sup}$	$+\infty$
$t \to \mathtt{min}\,(y)$	minimum value of y_σ
$t \to \mathtt{max}\,(y)$	maximum value of y_σ
$t \to t_1 + t_2$	$t_{1_\sigma} + t_{2_\sigma}$
$t \to t_1 - t_2$	$t_{1_\sigma} - t_{2_\sigma}$

tional rules called *indexicals*. Indexicals provide an efficient approach to implementing propagators for constraints.

A *domain constraint* is an expression $x \in I$, where I is a finite set of integers. A *store* σ is a set of domain constraints. The expression x_σ denotes the intersection $I_1 \cap \ldots \cap I_n$ for all constraints $x \in I_k$ in σ, where $1 \leq k \leq n$. If σ does not contain a constraint $x \in I$, x_σ is the set $\mathcal{Z}$ of integers. A variable x is *determined in* σ if x_σ is a singleton set.

An *indexical* has the form x in r, where r is a *range* generated by r in Table 1. The *value* of x in r in σ is $x \in r_\sigma$, where r_σ is the value of r in σ, a set of integers. A range may consist of other ranges or terms. A *term* t is generated by t in Table 1. The value of t in σ, t_σ, is an integer. Table 1 summarizes how the values of r_σ and t_σ are computed.

6.1   Basic Compilation

We illustrate the compilation process with the following example.

Example 4. The representation of c_{tri} from Example 3 is a disjunction of two box constraints

$$[1..3] \times [1..3] \Rightarrow x + y \geq 4 \tag{2}$$

$$\vee\ [3..5] \times [3..5] \Rightarrow x + y \leq 8 \tag{3}$$

The indexicals[1] for (2) and (3) are respectively

```
X in ((4-max(Y))..3)        X in (3..(E-min(Y)))
Y in ((4-max(X))..3)        Y in (3..(E-min(X)))
```

---

[1] The syntax of SICStus Prolog, shown in teletype font, requires variables to be in upper case. Upper and lower case variables of the same name should be understood interchangeably.

These maintain generalized arc consistency [14].

We can create an indexical for X for the box constraint collection by combining these indexical rules as follows:

```
Y13 in {0} \/ (dom(Y) /\ (1..3))
Y35 in {6} \/ (dom(Y) /\ (3..5))
X in ((dom(Y) /\ (1..3)) ? ((4-max(Y13))..3)) \/
     ((dom(Y) /\ (3..5)) ? (3..(8-min(Y35)))))
```

$Y13$ records the maximum value of Y in the interval $[1..3]$. The additional value 0 is added to the domain of $Y13$ to ensure it is always non-empty (and thus does not cause failure). We call this additional value a *dummy value* and the constraint between Y and $Y13$ a *confinement constraint*. Similarly $Y35$ records the minimum value of Y in the interval $[3..5]$. The rule for X joins the constraints together, using the $Y13$ or $Y35$ to give the appropriate value of Y for the box of interest.

We can automatically map the indexical expressions for constraints $c_i(x_1, \ldots, x_n)$ to create indexical expression for a disjunction of box constraints $\vee_{i=1}^m B_i \Rightarrow c_i(x_1, \ldots, x_n)$ such that if each indexical for $c_i(x_1, \ldots, x_n)$ maintains generalized arc consistency, then so does this indexical.

Let $B_i = [a_{i1}..b_{i1}] \times \cdots \times [a_{in}..b_{in}]$ then define the indexicals

```
Max_{ij} in {a_{ij}-1} \/ (dom(X_j) /\ (a_{ij}..b_{ij}))
Min_{ij} in {b_{ij}+1} \/ (dom(X_j) /\ (a_{ij}..b_{ij}))
```

Min_{ij} and Max_{ij} are called the *confinement variables* of X_j over B_i. The indexical expression for X_k for a single box constraint $B_i \Rightarrow c_i(x_1, \ldots, x_n)$ is then

```
(dom(X_1) /\ (a_{i1}..b_{i1})) ? ... ? (dom(X_n) /\ (a_{in}..b_{in})) ? (r'_{ik} /\ (a_{ik}..b_{ik}))
```

where r'_{ik} is the indexical r_{ik} for X_k and constraint $c_i(x_1, \ldots, x_n)$ with max(X_j) replaced by max(Max_{ij}), min(X_j) replaced by min(Min_{ij}) and dom(X_j) replaced by dom(X_j) /\ ($a_{ij}..b_{ij}$). We call each dom(X_j) /\ ($a_{ij}..b_{ij}$) a *guard* for r'_{ik}.

The indexical expression for X_k for the disjunction of box constraints $\vee_{i=1}^m B_i \Rightarrow c_i(x_1, \ldots, x_n)$ is obtained by unioning the expressions for each box constraint for X_k.

Theorem 1. *The indexical for box constraint collection*

$$c \equiv \bigvee_{i=1}^m (\bigwedge_{j=1}^n a_{ij} \le x_j \le b_{ij} \wedge c_i(x_1, \ldots, x_n))$$

achieves generalized arc consistency if each indexical for c_i achieves generalized arc consistency.

This guarantees that, by choosing the constraints c_i carefully, the box constraint collection of an adhoc constraint achieves generalized arc consistency.

Adding terms $t \to min(r)$ and $t \to max(r)$ to the indexical language would allow the expression of constructive disjunction of triangles without confinement variables. We conjecture that this would speed up the propagation markedly.

6.2   Optimizing Compilation

The basic compilation generates correct but inefficient indexicals, because there are many redundant operations. We can improve the computation of confinement variable domains, as illustrated by the following example.

Example 5. The confinement indexical

```
Y13 in {0} \/ (dom(Y) /\ (1..3)).
```

is invoked whenever the domain of Y is modified, and performs an expensive intersection operation. If we instead initialize the domain of Y13 to {0} \/ (1..3) then we can replace this intersection. So we replace the single indexical by

```
Y13 in {0} \/ (1..3)
Y13 in {0} \/ dom(Y).
```

Furthermore once dom(Y) and 1..3 are disjoint, the domain of Y13 cannot change. We can add (using SICStus Prologs extended indexicals) a check that removes the second indexical if Y13 in {0}.

Since set operations are expensive, a guard dom(X) /\ (L..U) ? r should be removed or replaced with a more efficient indexical operation whenever possible. We can remove the guard if L..U is the initial domain of X, or r becomes empty for any values in dom(X) outside L..U. In both situations the guard is redundant.

Example 6. Consider the indexical for X in Example 4. If Y13 takes its dummy value 0, then ((4 - max(Y13))..3) is the empty domain. Similarly for the other disjunct. Hence the following indexical is equivalent

```
X in ((4 - max(Y13))..3) \/ (3..(8-min(Y35)))
```

By suitably choosing the dummy values, all guards for indexicals Inf..b and a..Sup can be removed, where a and b are constants and Inf and Sup are terms involving min(Y) and max(Y) of other variables Y.

For the remaining guards, we can replace dom(X) /\ (L..U) with min(X)..U if L is the lower bound of the initial domain of X, because if its domain intersects L..U, the minimum value in its domain must be smaller than U. Similarly, we can replace a guard with L..max(X) if U is the upper bound of its initial domain.

Also, we can remove L..U from r /\ (L..U) if r is always inside the range.

Other optimization techniques include combining indexicals, removing confinement variables and rearranging the execution order of indexicals. However, due to space limitations, they will not be discussed further.

7   Experiments

In this section, we compare the efficiency of two BCC representations (box and triangle) and another approach to representing adhoc constraints in SICStus Prolog. We implement the bccFinder algorithm and conduct the experiments using SICStus Prolog 3.9.1 on

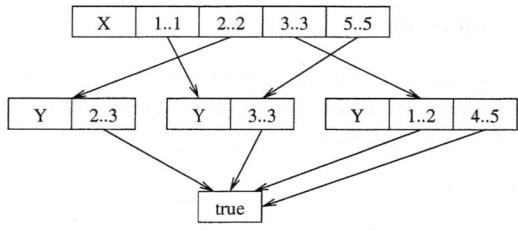

Fig. 4. A DAG representation of c_{adhoc} from Fig. 1.

a Sun Blade 1000 with 2GB of memory (our largest benchmark consumes around only 20MB).

SICStus Prolog introduced in release 3.9.0 a new constraint, `case`, for encoding arbitrary n-ary adhoc constraints. To use the `case` constraint, users must first obtain a directed acyclic graph (DAG) from the list of solutions of the constraint. In the DAG, each node n is either the special leaf node $true$ or includes a variable x_n and a disjoint set of ranges $l_{nj}..u_{nj}$ each with a pointer to the next node n_j. A tuple θ satisfies the relation defined by the graph rooted by node n if n is the leaf node $true$, or there exists j such that $l_{nj} \leq \theta(x_n) \leq u_{nj}$ and θ satisfies the relation defined by graph rooted at n_j [2].

The `case` constraint is a built-in global constraint equipped with an efficient filtering algorithm [6] to traverse the DAG for maintaining generalized arc consistency. In other words, the `case` technology consists of two parts: the DAG representation and the filtering algorithm. It is thus appropriate to compare the space and time tradeoffs of the BCC and the DAG (expanded into a tree[3]) representations when both are compiled into indexicals. We give also the results of using the `case` constraint for reference purposes. We envisage the possibility of an efficient filtering algorithm for maintaining generalized arc consistency of a BCC.

Example 7. A `case` constraint defining c_{adhoc} is given by the DAG show in Fig. 4. The indexical representation of the tree of the DAG is

```
X in ((dom(Y) /\ (2..3)) ? (2..2)) \/
     ((dom(Y) /\ (3..3)) ? ((1..1) \/ (5..5))) \/
     ((dom(Y) /\ ((1..2)\/(4..5))) ? (3..3)),
Y in ((dom(X) /\ (1..1)) ? (3..3)) \/
     ((dom(X) /\ (2..2)) ? (2..3)) \/
     ((dom(X) /\ (3..3)) ? ((1..2) \/ (4..5))) \/
     ((dom(X) /\ (5..5)) ? (3..3)).
```

We compare the propagation efficiency among *box* (indexicals for boxes only), *tri−box* (indexicals for triangles and boxes), *cas* (DAG in the `case` constraint), and

---

[2] Actually the definition is slightly different but effectively equivalent.

[3] The filtering algorithm treats the DAG like a tree. The DAG representation is simply more compact.

Table 2. Performance comparisons on random 3-dimensional convex hull constraints.

N	cas/dag		box		tri-box			W = 10				W = 20			
	B	gen	B	gen	T	B	gen	cas	dag	box	tri-box	cas	dag	box	tri-box
6025	448	1.14	294	27.25	52	18	15.70	37.85	71.12	62.73	35.22	45.05	117.43	111.26	67.28
4754	324	0.70	205	19.74	41	18	13.64	23.07	49.27	41.78	24.89	29.35	81.78	75.18	50.38
7086	385	1.80	287	42.71	57	23	15.62	37.52	60.31	59.98	36.67	37.87	94.20	109.72	75.64
7302	347	1.67	278	57.87	50	18	24.47	18.40	58.97	64.94	34.23	25.69	94.87	113.07	71.48
5598	339	1.18	262	29.20	47	24	14.16	35.76	50.17	56.68	28.97	37.08	88.31	98.60	61.56

Table 3. Performance comparisons on ternary non-linear inequality constraints.

N	cas/dag		box		tri-box			W = 10				W = 20			
	B	gen	B	gen	T	B	gen	cas	dag	box	tri-box	cas	dag	box	tri-box
24591	225	8.48	224	186.81	4	32	101.74	7.99	21.93	25.15	9.70	12.76	36.65	43.67	16.54
20987	489	8.66	309	142.39	7	59	81.37	10.60	41.83	31.20	18.07	16.46	69.05	50.79	31.91
19671	471	8.76	215	122.36	8	47	90.83	11.56	39.86	24.34	17.34	21.46	65.05	44.35	31.92
17886	699	8.30	271	109.50	4	87	65.12	11.51	56.31	27.66	21.77	21.78	94.43	46.47	37.12
21938	499	7.32	238	134.07	15	10	94.38	10.50	44.12	24.94	10.19	17.04	73.34	42.87	21.51

dag (DAG in indexicals). The first three experiments simply test raw propagation. For each variable x in the constraint, we repeat M times picking a subset $S \subseteq D_{init}(x)$ where $|S| = W$, and adding the constraints $x \neq v$ for each $v \in S$. These constraint additions are then removed, and the next set S is selected.

We restrict our attention to benchmarks with structure, such as convex hull and non-linear inequality constraints, since BCC is designed for real-life constraints with meaning and thus reasonable patterns. Our experiment on random constraints show that BCC performs worse than `case` constraints, as expected.

In the first experiment, the adhoc constraint in each problem instance is defined by the convex hull generated by 15 random points chosen from the Cartesian product space of the variable domain 1..30. Table 2 gives the results. N is the number of solutions, B and T are the number of boxes and triangles respectively, and gen is the generation time (in seconds). For cas and dag, we consider each path from root to leaf in the DAG as a box. We use the same DAG for both cas and dag, so that they share the same B and gen. The columns cas, dag, box and $tri-box$ report the execution time (in seconds) of the propagation test when $M = 5000$, and $W = 10$ or $W = 20$.

The second experiment deals with non-linear inequalities of the form $ax^3 + by^3 + cz^3 + dxyz + ex + fy + gz \leq h$, where the integer coefficients a to h are generated randomly from the $[-9..9]$. The initial domain for each variable is 1..30. Results are summarized in Table 3.

We observe from the two experiments that both box and $tri-box$, in particular $tri-box$, use many fewer tiles than cas/dag for covering the same set of solutions. The representation of $tri-box$ is much more compact so that it is always faster than dag and box. The built-in filtering algorithm allows cas to be almost two times more efficient than $tri-box$ in some cases, despite the size disadvantage in representation.

To study further the speed comparison, we conduct the third experiment on structured polyhedrons including dipyramids and sheared rectangular boxes, which are generated

Table 4. Performance comparisons on structured 3-dimensional polyhedron constraints.

N	cas/dag		box		tri-box			W = 10				W = 20			
	B	gen	B	gen	T	B	gen	cas	dag	box	tri-box	cas	dag	box	tri-box
4225	437	1.15	437	39.17	8	0	68.24	34.26	57.39	73.92	4.22	38.44	84.51	112.68	8.56
4858	468	1.30	440	38.85	22	6	48.14	30.53	70.46	87.19	17.44	37.91	113.54	152.76	35.79
4526	240	1.16	30	10.59	28	2	27.26	25.17	30.38	11.69	17.47	30.52	50.48	22.29	34.50
2755	380	0.46	30	5.65	29	5	10.32	33.07	58.63	11.70	24.38	40.23	94.66	24.67	51.53
956	348	0.11	53	1.92	65	12	2.36	23.49	50.80	13.31	44.59	32.51	79.04	26.32	95.87

manually to investigate how the number of triangles and boxes affect the efficiency of BCC. Results are presented in Table 4.

We found that tri-box fares very well against dag, since the representation advantage of tri-box becomes more apparent in polyhedrons with good structures. The size of the cas/dag representation remains in the same order of magnitude as in the previous two experiments. The last three benchmarks exhibit even more regular structure so that they can be covered well also with boxes. In those cases, box is the fastest since the indexicals for implementing boxes lack the overhead of the confinement variables. This dependency on the number of boxes and triangles is more a result of the indexical implementation, but not the representation scheme.

Our last experiment is an application of our method to model induction [12], the outcome of which is a CSP consisting of only adhoc constraints. We study four different formulations (or models) of the Langford's problem (listed as "prob24" in CSPLib [11]): M_1, $M_1{}^*$, $M_1 \cap i(f^{-1}, M_2)$ and $M_1 \cap i(f^{-1}, M_2)^*$. Model M_1 is a hand-crafted model originally with symbolic constraints, but we turn the symbolic constraints into table form. Model $M_1{}^*$ is the same as M_1 except solutions of constraints of the same signature are intersected to form one constraint, which we call *constraint merging*. Model $M_1 \cap i(f^{-1}, M_2)$ is a model constructed from model M_1 plus constraints generated from model induction, while model $M_1 \cap i(f^{-1}, M_2)^*$ is model $M_1 \cap i(f^{-1}, M_2)$ with constraint merging. For more details see [12].

Table 5 summaries the results. The column $inst$ contain the problem instances (in terms of problem size) and $model$ contains the CSP models. Besides giving the number of unary and binary constraints in the u and b columns respectively, we give also the number of *distinct* unary and binary constraints that are learned in columns u_d and b_d. Two constraints are distinct if they have different sets of nogoods. N is the total number of solutions for the problem, while columns cas, dag, box and tri-box give the CPU time in seconds to search for all solutions. Variables are chosen using the first-fail heuristic. It is *important* to note that the search trees of the same problem using different constraint representations are the same since generalized arc consistency is enforced in all cases.

In this application, tri-box is significantly better than even cas for models M_1, $M_1{}^*$, and $M_1 \cap i(f^{-1}, M_2)$. It is because all constraints in the hand-crafted model M_1 are disequality constraints of the form $x \neq y + k$ for different k. Such constraints have a high percentage of connected solutions, allowing the covering of the solutions by only a few triangles and boxes. In $M_1{}^*$ this connectedness and structure are destroyed by constraint merging which removes some solutions from the constraint. In $M_1 \cap$

Table 5. Performance comparisons on different models of Langford's Problem.

$inst$	$model$	u	b	u_d	b_d	N	cas	dag	box	$tri\text{-}box$
(3,9)	M_1	0	369	0	10	6	4.56	4.88	7.86	0.51
	$M_1{*}$	0	351	0	10	6	4.25	4.51	7.21	0.48
	$M_1 \cap i(f^{-1}, M_2)$	9	720	9	361	6	5.85	9.63	12.39	4.34
	$M_1 \cap i(f^{-1}, M_2){*}$	9	351	9	342	6	2.75	6.33	6.97	4.02
(3,10)	M_1	0	455	0	11	10	19.09	20.92	34.12	1.97
	$M_1{*}$	0	435	0	11	10	18.06	19.40	31.41	1.86
	$M_1 \cap i(f^{-1}, M_2)$	10	890	10	446	10	24.49	42.08	54.63	16.62
	$M_1 \cap i(f^{-1}, M_2){*}$	10	435	10	425	10	11.43	28.19	31.46	15.52
(3,11)	M_1	0	550	0	12	0	101.78	110.87	182.27	9.59
	$M_1{*}$	0	528	0	12	0	95.82	102.92	168.50	9.01
	$M_1 \cap i(f^{-1}, M_2)$	11	1078	11	540	0	144.05	241.05	312.26	92.00
	$M_1 \cap i(f^{-1}, M_2){*}$	11	528	11	517	0	60.56	151.29	167.48	82.38

$i(f^{-1}, M_2)$, constraints generated from model induction are not as structured, but model M_1 is still the backbone. The representation advantage of $tri\text{-}box$ degrades for $M_1 \cap i(f^{-1}, M_2)^*$ since the original constraints in M_1 are merged with the unstructured constraints from model induction.

8   Concluding Remarks

We have proposed a new language-independent representation, the box constraint collection, for adhoc constraints. With constructive disjunction, our new representation achieves generalized arc consistency, if all constraints inside the collection do. We have developed a greedy algorithm, **bccFinder**, to compute the box constraint collection of an adhoc constraint. It creates simple and compact representations of adhoc constraints, in a reasonable amount of time. We have shown how to implement box constraint collections as indexicals, and illustrated there efficient propagation on a number of examples. They are significantly more efficient than the DAG representation implemented by indexicals (dag).

Box constraint collections can be implemented in other ways than using indexicals. For binary constraints represented as boxes only (no triangles), Barták [5] gives an efficient arc consistency algorithm. For the more general case, an implementation similar to the `case` constraint seems quite plausible.

We conjecture that the difference in performance between cas and dag is mainly because the cas implementation propagates on all variables simultaneously, while the indexical representation runs each indexical separately. Worse, in the indexical representations (dag, box, and $tri\text{-}box$), when the indexical reduces the domain of x_i because of a change in x_j, then all the indexicals are re-executed since x_i has changed. But this re-execution can never find new information. The re-execution does not occur using `case` (according to our limited understanding). An internal implementation of the BCC constraint (like the `case` constraint) could avoid these overheads, and should lead to similar speedups (dag/cas) over the indexical representation.

We restrict our experiments to binary and ternary adhoc constraints. The BCC idea works for n-ary constraints in general, where $n > 0$. The bccFinder algorithm, however, needs improvement to be practical on higher dimensional constraints. This is an interesting topic for further study.

References

1. *Sicstus Prolog 3.9.1 manual.*
2. S. Abdennadher and C. Rigotti. Automatic generation of propagation rules for finite domains. In *Principles and Practice of Constraint Programming*, pages 18–34, 2000.
3. S. Anthony and A.M. Frisch. Generating numerical literals during refinement. In *ILP97*, pages 61–76, 1997.
4. K.R. Apt and E. Monfroy. Automatic generation of constraint propagation algorithms for small finite domains. In *Principles and Practice of Constraint Programming*, pages 58–72, 1999.
5. R. Barták. Filtering algorithms for tabular constraints. In *Proceedings of Colloqium on Implementation of Constraint and Logic Programming Systems (CICLOPS 2001)*, pages 168–182, 2001.
6. N. Beldiceanu. Global constraints as graph properties on structured networks of elementary constraints of the same type. Technical Report T2000-01, SICS, 2000.
7. B. Carlson and M. Carlsson. Compiling and executing disjunctions of finite domain constraints. In *Int. Conf. on Logic Programming*, pages 117–132, 1995.
8. T.B.H. Dao, A. Lallouet, A. Legtchenko, and L. Martin. Indexical-based solver learning. In *Principles and Practice of Constraint Programming*, pages 541–555, September 2002.
9. D. Diaz and P. Codognet. Design and implementation of the GNU Prolog system. *Journal of Functional and Logic Programming*, 2001(6), 2001.
10. T. Frühwirth. Theory and practice of constraint handling rules. *Journal of Logic Programming*, 37(1–3):95–138, October 1998.
11. I. Gent and T. Walsh. CSPLib: A benchmark library for constraints. In *Principles and Practice of Constraint Programming*, pages 480–481, 1999. Available at http:/www-users.cs.york.ac.uk/ tw/csplib/.
12. Y.C. Law and J.H.M. Lee. Model induction: a new source of csp model redundancy. In *Proceedings of the 18th National Conference on Artificial Intelligence (AAAI-2002)*, pages 57–71, 2002.
13. M. M. Mano and C. R. Kime. *Logic and Computer Design Fundamentals*. Prentice Hall, second edition, 1999.
14. C. Schulte and P.J. Stuckey. When do bounds and domain propagation lead to the same search space. In *3rd Int. Conf. on Principles and Practice of Declarative Programming*, pages 115–126, 2001.
15. E. Tsang. *Foundations of Constraint Satisfaction*. Academic Press, 1993.
16. P. Van Hentenryck, V. Saraswat, and Y. Deville. Design, implementation, and evaluation of the constraint language cc(FD). *Journal of Logic Programming*, 37(1–3):139–164, 1998.

Propagation Redundancy in Redundant Modelling*

Chiu Wo Choi[1], Jimmy Ho Man Lee[1], and Peter J. Stuckey[2]

[1] Department of Computer Science and Engineering
The Chinese University of Hong Kong
Shatin, N.T., Hong Kong SAR, China
{cwchoi,jlee}@cse.cuhk.edu.hk
[2] Deptartment of Computer Science & Software Engineering
University of Melbourne, 3010, Australia
pjs@cs.mu.oz.au

Abstract. Combining mutually redundant models with channelling constraints increases constraint propagation. However, the extra computation efforts of the additional variables and constraints may outweigh the gain of reduction in search space. In fact, many of the constraints in redundant modelling are not only logically redundant but also propagation redundant and hence cannot further reduce search space. We give general theorems for proving propagation redundancy of one constraint with respect to channelling constraints and constraints in the other model. We define a broad form of channelling constraints that are covered by our approach. We illustrate, using problems from CSPLib (http://www.csplib.org/), how detecting and removing propagation redundant constraints can significantly speed up solving behaviour.

1 Introduction

Finding a good model of a constraint satisfaction problem (CSP) is a challenging task. A modeller must specify a set of constraints that capture the definitions of the problem, and the model should also have strong propagation. In other words, the model should be able to quickly reduce the domains of the variables of the problem, *and* the implementation of these propagators should be efficient, *and* the search space should not be too large.

A common technique to increase the propagation is to add redundant constraints, which are logically implied by the constraints of the model. Adding redundant constraints can be beneficial since the constraint solver may extract more information from these redundant constraints. However, not all logically redundant constraints will contribute additional propagation information to the constraint solver. Understanding whether the propagator for a redundant constraint will add useful propagation information is an interesting question. In this paper we show how to determine if a propagator is *propagation redundant* with respect to a set of propagators, and hence will not add useful propagation information.

---

* We thank the anonymous referees for their constructive comments. The work described in this paper was substantially supported by a grant from the Research Grants Council of the Hong Kong Special Administrative Region (Project no. CUHK4183/00E).

F. Rossi (Ed.): CP 2003, LNCS 2833, pp. 229–243, 2003.

An important source of logically redundant constraints arises in redundant modelling [4]. A problem can be modelled differently from two viewpoints using two different sets of variables. By connecting the two different models with channelling constraints, which relates valuations in the two different models, stronger propagation behaviour can be observed. However, the additional variables and constraints impose extra computation overhead. Since each model is complete and only admits the solutions of the problem, each model is logically redundant with respect to the other model plus the channelling constraints. In many cases, some of the constraints are also propagation redundant with respect to the other constraints in the combined model.

Smith [7, 8] has examined the redundant models for a number of individual problems including n-Queens problem, Langford's problem and the social golfers problems. She empirically determined propagation redundancy for constraints in these problems. In this paper we give a theoretical framework which can determine propagation redundancy *a priori*.

Walsh [9] also compares the pruning behaviour of the different notions of consistency over the disequations, channelling constraints, and all-different constraints for permutation problems by introducing the measure of constraint tightness. Propagation redundancy can be seen as a more specific form of constraint tightness, that allows us to give generic approaches to proving better pruning behaviour, in particular about the other constraints in permutation problems.

In order to keep the benefits of redundant modelling without paying all the costs, we give theorems that allow us to show which constraints in a redundant model are not giving extra propagation and can be removed. In order to prove propagation redundancy, we introduce the notion of *propagation rules* which capture each possible propagation by a constraint and *channel functions* which relate these actions from one model to the other. Due to space limitations, we state the lemmas and theorems without proofs[1]. We give experimental results showing the benefits of detecting and removing propagation redundant constraints. An earlier poster [5] examines this problem when combining redundant models with permutation channels. This paper extends the study to cover other forms of channelling constraints.

2   Propagation Based Constraint Solving

In this paper we consider integer and set constraint solving with constraint propagation and tree search. Boolean constraint solving is considered a special case of the integer constraint solving.

Constraints. We consider a typed set of variables $V = V_I \cup V_S$ made up of *integer* variables V_I, for which we use lower case notation such as x and y, and *sets of integers* variables V_S, for which we use upper case notation such as S and T. We use v to denote variables of either kind.

An *valuation* θ is a mapping of integer variables to integer values and set variables to sets of integer values, written $\{x_1 \mapsto d_1, \ldots, x_n \mapsto d_n, S_1 \mapsto A_1, \ldots, S_m \mapsto A_m\}$.

---

[1] A longer version of this paper with the proofs of lemmas and theorems is available at
http://www.cse.cuhk.edu.hk/~cwchoi/cp03long.pdf.

We extend the valuation θ to map expressions or constraints involving the variables in the natural way. Let *vars* be the function that returns the set of variables appearing in an expression, constraint or valuation.

A *primitive constraint* c defines a set of valuations $solns(c)$ each mapping the same set of variables $vars(c)$. We call $solns(c)$ the *solutions* of c. For a primitive constraint c defined by arithmetic expressions we define $solns(c) = \{\theta \mid vars(\theta) = vars(c) \wedge \models_\theta c\}$, that is the set of θ that make the constraint c hold. Primitive constraints can also be defined directly, by giving the set (or table) $solns(c)$.

A *constraint* is a conjunction of primitive constraints, by abuse of notation, we will sometimes treat it as a set of primitive constraints. A constraint c is *logically redundant* with respect to a set of constraints C if $\models C \to c$.

Domains. A *domain* D is a complete mapping from a fixed (countable) set of variables $\mathcal{V}$ to finite sets of integers (for the integer variables in $\mathcal{V}_I$) and to finite sets of finite sets of integers (for the set variables in $\mathcal{V}_S$). A *false domain* D is a domain with $D(v) = \emptyset$ for some v. The *intersection* of two domains D_1 and D_2, denoted $D_1 \sqcap D_2$, is defined by the domain $D_3(v) = D_1(v) \cap D_2(v)$ for all v. A domain D_1 is *stronger* than a domain D_2, written $D_1 \sqsubseteq D_2$, if D_1 is a false domain or $D_1(v) \subseteq D_2(v)$ for all variables v. A domain D_1 is equal to a domain D_2, denoted $D_1 = D_2$, if D_1 and D_2 are both false domains or $D_1(v) = D_2(v)$ for all variables v. We can understand a domain D as a constraint in the obvious way, $D \leftrightarrow \bigwedge_{v \in \mathcal{V}} \bigvee_{d \in D(v)} v = d$.

In an abuse of notation, we define a valuation θ to be an element of a domain D, written $\theta \in D$, if $\theta(v_i) \in D(v_i)$ for all $v_i \in vars(\theta)$.

We will be interested in determining the infimums and supremums of expressions with respect to some domain D. Define the *infimum* and *supremum* of an expression e with respect to a domain D as $\inf_D e = \inf \{\theta(e) \mid \theta \in D\}$ and $\sup_D e = \sup \{\theta(e) \mid \theta \in D\}$.

We will also use *range* notation: $[l .. u]$ denotes the set $\{d \mid l \leq d \leq u\}$ when l and u are integers, while $[L .. U]$ denotes the set of sets of integers $\{A \mid L \subseteq A \subseteq U\}$ when L and U are sets of integers.

We shall be interested in the notion of an *initial domain*, which we denote D_{init}. The initial domain gives the initial values possible for each variable. In effect an initial domain allows us to restrict attention to domains D such that $D \sqsubseteq D_{init}$.

Propagators. A *propagator* f is a monotonically decreasing function from domains to domains, i.e. $D_1 \sqsubseteq D_2$ implies that $f(D_1) \sqsubseteq f(D_2)$, and $f(D) \sqsubseteq D$. A propagator f is *correct* for constraint c iff for all domains D

$$\{\theta \mid \theta \in D\} \cap solns(c) = \{\theta \mid \theta \in f(D)\} \cap solns(c)$$

This is a weak restriction since for example, the identity propagator is correct for all constraints c.

A *propagation solver* for a set of propagators F and current domain D, $solv(F, D)$, repeatedly applies all the propagators in F starting from domain D until there is no further change in resulting domain. In other words, $solv(F, D)$ returns a new domain defined by

$$iter(F, D) = \bigsqcap_{f \in F} f(D) \quad \text{and} \quad solv(F, D) = \text{gfp}(\lambda d.iter(F, d))(D)$$

where gfp denotes the greatest fixpoint w.r.t $\sqsubseteq$ lifted to functions.

Domain Consistency and Set Bounds Consistency. A domain D is *domain consistent*[2] for a constraint c if D is the least domain containing all solutions $\theta \in D$ of c, i.e, there does not exist $D' \sqsubset D$ such that $\theta \in D \wedge \theta \in solns(c) \rightarrow \theta \in D'$.

A set of propagators F maintains *domain consistency* for a constraint c, if $solv(F, D)$ is always domain consistent for c.

Define the *domain consistency propagator* for a constraint c as

$$dom(c)(D)(v) = \{\theta(v) \mid \theta \in D \wedge \theta \in solns(c)\} \text{ where } v \in vars(c)$$
$$dom(c)(D)(v) = D(v) \text{ otherwise}$$

Example 1. Consider the constraint $c \equiv x_1 = 3x_2 + 5x_3$. Suppose domain $D(x_1) = \{2, 3, 4, 5, 6, 7\}$, $D(x_2) = \{0, 1, 2\}$, and $D(x_3) = \{-1, 0, 1, 2\}$. The solutions $\theta \in D$ of c are $\theta_1 = \{x_1 \mapsto 3, x_2 \mapsto 1, x_3 \mapsto 0\}$, $\theta_2 = \{x_1 \mapsto 5, x_2 \mapsto 0, x_3 \mapsto 1\}$, and $\theta_3 = \{x_1 \mapsto 6, x_2 \mapsto 2, x_3 \mapsto 0\}$. Hence, $dom(c)(D) = D'$ where $D'(x_1) = \{3, 5, 6\}$, $D'(x_2) = \{0, 1, 2\}$, and $D'(x_3) = \{0, 1\}$. D' is domain consistent with respect to c.

Domain consistency is prohibitive to compute for constraints involving set variables. For that reason, set bounds propagation is typically used where a domain maps a set variable to a lower bound set of integers and an upper bound set of integers.

We shall enforce this by restricting our attention to domains where the $D(S)$ is a range, that is $D(S) = \{A \mid \inf_D(S) \subseteq A \subseteq \sup_D(S)\}$. This is managed by only using set bounds propagators, which maintain this property.

We can define the domain and set bounds propagators $dsb(c)$ for a constraint c as follows:

$$dsb(c)(D)(v) = [\cap dom(c)(D)(v) \mathinner{..} \cup dom(c)(D)(v)] \text{ where } v \in vars(c) \cap \mathcal{V}_S$$
$$dsb(c)(D)(v) = dom(c)(D)(v) \text{ otherwise}$$

Note that as defined $dsb(c) = dom(c)$ when $vars(c) \subseteq \mathcal{V}_I$. From now on we shall restrict attention to dsb propagators.

3 Propagation Rules

In order to reason effectively about propagation, it will be useful to break down a propagator into the individual propagation steps that it can perform. That is the role of *propagation rules*.

An *atomic constraint* is one of $x_i = d$, $x_i \neq d$, $d \in S_i$ or $d \notin S_i$ where $x_i \in \mathcal{V}_I$, d is an integer, an $S_i \in \mathcal{V}_S$. An atomic constraint represents the basic changes in domain that occur during propagation, the elimination of a value from an integer domain, or the addition of a value to a lower bound, or removal of a value from an upper bound.

---

[2] Equivalently, hyper-arc or generalized arc consistent [3].

Atomic constraints of the form $x_i = d$ are not strictly necessary. They are equivalent to removing all other values from the domain.

A *propagation rule* is of the form $C \rightarrowtail c$ where C is a conjunction of atomic constraints, c is an atomic constraint, and $\not\models C \rightarrow c$. Note our propagation rules when restricted to integer variables are similar to the "membership rules" of [2] except we allow equations on the right hand side.

A propagator f *implements* a propagation rule $C \rightarrowtail c$ if for each $D \sqsubseteq D_{init}$ whenever $\models D \rightarrow C$, then $\models f(D) \rightarrow c$. A propagation rule $C \rightarrowtail c$ defines a propagator (for which we use the same notation) in the obvious way.

$$(C \rightarrowtail c)(D)(v) = \{\theta(v) \mid \theta \in D \wedge \theta \in solns(c)\} \text{ if } vars(c) = \{v\} \text{ and } \models D \rightarrow C$$
$$(C \rightarrowtail c)(D)(v) = D(v) \text{ otherwise}$$

A propagation rule $C_1 \rightarrowtail c_1$ *subsumes* a rule $C_2 \rightarrowtail c_2$ if $\models (D_{init} \wedge C_2) \rightarrow C_1$ and $\models (D_{init} \wedge c_1) \rightarrow c_2$. We can characterize a propagator f in terms of the propagation rules that it implements. Let $rules(f)$ be the set of rules implemented by f. Then $prop(f) \subseteq rules(f)$ are a set of propagation rules such that every $r \in rules(f)$ is subsumed by a rule $r' \in prop(f)$. The set $prop(f)$ can be automatically constructed by the approach of [1].

Example 2. For the propagator $f \equiv dsb(x_1 \neq x_2)$ for $D_{init}(x_1) = D_{init}(x_2) = \{1, 2, 3\}$, $prop(f)$ is

$$\begin{array}{lll} x_1 = 1 \rightarrowtail x_2 \neq 1 & x_1 = 2 \rightarrowtail x_2 \neq 2 & x_1 = 3 \rightarrowtail x_2 \neq 3 \\ x_2 = 1 \rightarrowtail x_1 \neq 1 & x_2 = 2 \rightarrowtail x_1 \neq 2 & x_2 = 3 \rightarrowtail x_1 \neq 3 \end{array}$$

Note that f also implements e.g. $x_1 \neq 1, x_1 \neq 3 \rightarrowtail x_2 \neq 2$, which is subsumed by $x_1 = 2 \rightarrowtail x_2 \neq 2$.

Example 3. For the propagator $f \equiv dsb(S \subseteq T)$ for $D_{init}(S) = D_{init}(T) = \{\emptyset \dots \{1, 2\}\}$. $prop(f)$ is

$$\begin{array}{ll} 1 \in S \rightarrowtail 1 \in T & 2 \in S \rightarrowtail 2 \in T \\ 1 \notin T \rightarrowtail 1 \notin S & 2 \notin T \rightarrowtail 2 \notin S \end{array}$$

A *key result* for domain and set bounds propagators $dsb(c')$, is that the propagation rules implemented are exactly those $C \rightarrowtail c$ where c' implies $C \rightarrow c$.

Lemma 4. $dsb(c')$ *implements* $C \rightarrowtail c$ *iff* $\models (D_{init} \wedge c') \rightarrow (C \rightarrow c)$ □

4   Reasoning about Propagation

In this section we introduce the basic results for reasoning about propagators.

We say a set of propagators F_1 is *stronger* than a set of propagators F_2, written $F_1 \gg F_2$, if $solv(F_1, D) \sqsubseteq solv(F_2, D)$ for all domains $D \sqsubseteq D_{init}$. We say a set of propagators F_1 is *equivalent* to a set of propagators F_2, written $F_1 \approx F_2$, if $solv(F_1, D) = solv(F_2, D)$ for all domains $D \sqsubseteq D_{init}$. A propagator f is made *propagation redundant* by a set of propagators F if $F \gg \{f\}$. It is clear that a constraint c_2 that is logically redundant with respect to constraint c_1 is also propagation redundant with respect to c_1.

Lemma 5. *If $\models D_{init} \wedge c_1 \rightarrow c_2$ then $\{dsb(c_1)\} \gg \{dsb(c_2)\}$.*   □

Typically though a logically redundant constraint c_2 will be made logically redundant by a conjunction of other constraints. It is well known that in general the domain (and set bounds) propagation of a conjunction of constraints is *not* equivalent to applying the domain (and set bounds) propagators individually.

Example 6. Consider the constraint $c_1 \equiv x_1 = 3x_2$, which is equivalent to $c_2 \wedge c_3$ where $c_2 \equiv x_1 \leq 3x_2$ and $c_3 \equiv x_1 \geq 3x_2$. If $D(x_1) = D(x_2) = \{0, 1, 2, 3, 4, 5, 6, 7\}$, then $D_1 = dsb(c_1)(D)$ and $D_2 = solv(\{dsb(c_2), dsb(c_3)\}, D)$ where $D_1(x_1) = \{0, 3, 6\}$ and $D_2(x_1) = \{0, 1, 2, 3, 4, 5, 6\}$. Hence $\{dsb(c_2), dsb(c_3)\} \not\gg \{dsb(c_1)\}$.

But there are cases where propagation of a conjunction is equivalent to propagation on the individual conjuncts.

Lemma 7. *Let c_1 and c_2 be two constraints sharing at most one variable $x \in \mathcal{V}_I$, then $\{dsb(c_1), dsb(c_2)\} \approx \{dsb(c_1 \wedge c_2)\}$.*   □

Note the same result clearly does not hold when the shared variable is a set variable. Consider $c_1 = (S = \{1\} \vee S = \{2, 3\})$ and $c_2 = (S = \{2\} \vee S = \{1, 3\})$, then $solv(\{dsb(c_1), dsb(c_2), D) = D$ where $D(S) = [\emptyset \mathinner{..} \{1, 2, 3\}]$, but $dsb(c_1 \wedge c_2)(D)$ is a false domain.

Propagation rules allow us to break up the consideration of a constraint into individual parts. That is the domain and set bounds propagator of a constraint is equivalent to the union of the propagation rules implemented by the propagator.

Lemma 8. *$\{dsb(c')\} \approx \cup_{C \rightarrowtail c \in prop(dsb(c'))} \{C \rightarrowtail c\}$*   □

5   Redundant Modelling and Channelling Constraints

Redundant modelling [4] models the problem from two different viewpoints. In general, the propagators defined for the two viewpoints act in different ways and discover information at different stages in the search. By joining the two models using channelling constraints, we can get the advantage of both sources of propagation. Of course, each model is logically redundant with respect to the other model plus the channelling constraints. However, in this section, we show cases in which propagation caused by some constraints in one model is subsumed by propagation induced from constraints in the other model through the channelling constraints.

Assume we have one model of the problem M_X using variables X, and another model M_Y using disjoint variables Y. Channelling constraints are used to join these two models together by relating X and Y. There is no real agreement on precisely what channelling constraints may be yet. For the purposes of our theorems we define a channelling constraints as follows.

Let A_X be the atomic constraints for D_{init} on variables X, and A_Y be the atomic constraints for D_{init} on variables Y. A *channel function* $\diamond$ is a bijection from atomic constraints A_X to A_Y.

A *channelling constraint* (or simply *channel*) $C_\Diamond$ is the constraint

$$\bigwedge_{c \in A_X} (c \Leftrightarrow \Diamond(c))$$

The *channel propagator* $F_\Diamond$ is the set of propagation rules inferred from the channel function $\Diamond$.

$$F_\Diamond = \bigcup_{c \in A_X} \{c \longmapsto \Diamond(c), \Diamond(c) \longmapsto c\}$$

Note for channel function $\Diamond$, by definition $\Diamond^{-1}$ is also a channel function, and $C_\Diamond$ and $C_{\Diamond^{-1}}$, as well as $F_\Diamond$ and $F_{\Diamond^{-1}}$, are identical.

We now illustrate how common channels fit into this framework.

Permutation Channels. A common form of redundant modelling is when we consider two viewpoints to a permutation problem. We can view the problem as finding a bipartite matching between two sets of objects of the same size. Assume the two viewpoints have the set of variables $X = \{x_0, \ldots, x_n\}$, and $Y = \{y_0, \ldots, y_n\}$ respectively.

The *permutation channel function* $\bowtie$ is defined as $\bowtie(x_i = j) = (y_j = i)$ and $\bowtie(x_i \neq j) = (y_j \neq i)$. The *permutation channel* $C_\bowtie$ is equivalent to the conjunction of constraints $\bigwedge_{i=0}^{n} \bigwedge_{j=0}^{n} (x_i = j \Leftrightarrow y_j = i)$.

Boolean Channels. Another common redundant modelling is when we give both an integer and Boolean model. Suppose the integer variables are $X = \{x_0, \ldots, x_n\}$, where $D_{init}(x_i) = [0 .. k_i]$, and the Boolean variables are $Z = \{z_{ij} \mid 0 \leq i \leq n, 0 \leq j \leq k_i\}$

The *Boolean channel function* $\triangle$ is defined as $\triangle(x_i = j) = (z_{ij} = 1)$ and $\triangle(x_i \neq j) = (z_{ij} = 0)$. Note that the atomic constraints $z_{ij} \neq 1$ and $z_{ij} \neq 0$ are not needed for Boolean variables since they are equivalent (respectively) to $z_{ij} = 0$ and $z_{ij} = 1$. The *Boolean channel* $C_\triangle$ is equivalent to the conjunction of constraints $\bigwedge_{i=0}^{n} \bigwedge_{j=0}^{k_i} (x_i = j \Leftrightarrow z_{ij} = 1)$.

Set Channels. A common form of redundant modelling is where one model deals with integer variables, and the other with variables over finite sets of integers, and the relation $x_i = j$ holds iff $i \in S_j$. This generalizes the assignment problem to where two or more integer variables can take the same value. Suppose the integer variables are $X = \{x_0, \ldots, x_n\}$, where $D_{init}(x_i) = [0 .. k]$, and the set variables are $\{S_0, \ldots, S_k\}$. The *set channel function* $\{\}$ is defined as $\{\}(x_i = j) = (i \in S_j)$ and $\{\}(x_i \neq j) = (i \notin S_j)$. The *set channel* $C_{\{\}}$ is equivalent to $\bigwedge_{i=0}^{n} \bigwedge_{j=0}^{k} (x_i = j \Leftrightarrow i \in S_j)$.

5.1 Proving Propagation Redundancy Using Channels

We can now prove the fundamental theorem about propagation redundancy through channels. The core result is that a propagation rule that is mapped by a channel function to a rule subsumed by another propagation rule is propagation redundant. We extend channel functions to map conjunctions of constraints in the obvious manner $\Diamond(c_1 \wedge \cdots \wedge c_n) = \Diamond(c_1) \wedge \cdots \wedge \Diamond(c_n)$.

Lemma 9. *Let* $C \rightarrowtail c$ *be a propagation rule on* Y *variables, and* $C' \rightarrowtail c'$ *be a propagation rule on* X *variables. If* $C' \rightarrowtail c'$ *subsumes* $\Diamond^{-1}(C) \rightarrowtail \Diamond^{-1}(c)$ *then* $\{C' \rightarrowtail c'\} \cup F_\Diamond \gg \{C \rightarrowtail c\}$. $\qquad\square$

We can straightforwardly lift this result to talk about propagation rules that are subsumed by the domain and set bounds propagator for a constraint, and then lift to a set of propagation rules implemented by some propagator.

Lemma 10. *Let* $C \rightarrowtail c$ *be a propagation rule on* Y *variables, and* c_X *be a constraint on* X *variables. If* $\models (D_{init} \wedge c_X \wedge \Diamond^{-1}(C)) \rightarrow \Diamond^{-1}(c)$, *then* $\{dsb(c_X)\} \cup F_\Diamond \gg \{C \rightarrowtail c\}$. $\qquad\square$

Corollary 11. *Let* f_Y *be a propagator on* Y *variables, and* c_X *be a constraint on* X *variables. If* $\models (D_{init} \wedge c_X \wedge \Diamond^{-1}(C)) \rightarrow \Diamond^{-1}(c)$ *for all* $C \rightarrowtail c \in prop(f_Y)$, *then* $\{dsb(c_X)\} \cup F_\Diamond \gg \{f_Y\}$. $\qquad\square$

Often a single constraint does not capture all the propagation effects of a constraint on the other side of the permutation model. In that case we may need to find for each particular propagation rule, a constraint on the other side that causes the same propagation to occur.

Theorem 12. *Let* f_Y *be a propagator on* Y *variables. Suppose for each* $r \equiv (C \rightarrowtail c) \in prop(f_Y)$, *there exists constraint* $imp(r)$ *on* X *variables where* $\models (D_{init} \wedge imp(r) \wedge \Diamond^{-1}(C)) \rightarrow \Diamond^{-1}(c)$, *then* $\cup_{r \in prop(f_Y)}\{dsb(imp(r))\} \cup F_\Diamond \gg \{f_Y\}$. $\qquad\square$

The framework just presented is closely related to Brand's approach [10] of identifying redundant rules in the compilation of constraints into rule-based constraint programs [2]. While Brand reasons about redundancy at the rule level, we employ propagation rules as an analysis tool to detect redundancy at the constraint level.

5.2   Restrictive and Unrestrictive Channel Functions

The channels themselves may actually restrict the possible solutions in one or both models involved. We will concentrate on the X model, since the restrictions on the Y model can be seen by examining the inverse channel function.

A channel function $\Diamond$ is *restrictive* (on the variables X) if $\not\models D_{init} \rightarrow \exists Y C_\Diamond$, that is not all valuations on X variables are extensible to solutions of $C_\Diamond$.

Example 13. The $\bowtie$ channel function is restrictive, for example $\{x_1 = 2, x_2 = 2\}$ cannot be extended to be a solution of $C_\bowtie$, since it requires y_2 to take both values 1 and 2. The $\triangle$ channel function is unrestrictive. Any valuation on X variables can be extended to a solution of $C_\triangle$. However $\triangle^{-1}$ is restrictive, for example $\{z_{11} = 1, z_{12} = 1\}$ cannot be extended to a solution of $C_\triangle$ since it requires x_1 to be both 1 and 2.

Restrictive channel function can themselves make constraints propagation redundant.

Smith [7] first observes that the permutation channel makes each of the disequations between variables in either model propagation redundant. Walsh [9] proves this holds for other notions of consistency.

Lemma 14 ([9]). $F_{\bowtie} \gg \{dsb(x_i \neq x_k)\}$ □

Implicit in the Boolean channel is that each integer variable can take only one, and must take one value. This is represented in the Boolean model as the constraint $\sum_{j=0}^{k_i} z_{ij} = 1$. It is enforced by the restrictive channel function $\triangle^{-1}$.

Lemma 15. $F_\triangle \gg \{dsb(\sum_{j=0}^{k_i} z_{ij} = 1)\}$ *for all* $1 \leq i \leq n$.   □

The channel function $\{\}^{-1}$ is restrictive, since each variable $x_i \in X$ can only take a single value j. It means that $S_j \cap S_{j'} = \emptyset$ for all $0 \leq j < j' \leq m$. It is clear that $F_{\{\}}$ makes these constraints propagation redundant.

Lemma 16. $F_{\{\}} \gg \{dsb(S_j \cap S_{j'} = \emptyset)\}$ *for all* $0 \leq j < j' \leq m$.   □

Unrestrictive channel functions do not make any constraints (on X) propagation redundant. Interestingly in this case we can argue about propagation redundancy simply in terms of logical consequence.

Theorem 17. *Let $\Diamond$ be an unrestrictive channel function, let c_Y be a constraint on Y variables, and c_X a constraint on X variables. If $\models (D_{init} \wedge c_X \wedge C_\Diamond) \to c_Y$, then $\{dsb(c_X)\} \cup F_\Diamond \gg \{dsb(c_Y)\}$.*   □

The reason the channel function must be unrestrictive for this result to hold is that the $\models (D_{init} \wedge c_X \wedge C_\Diamond) \to c_Y$ is too weak a condition in the general case.

Example 18. The permutation channel function is restrictive. Now $C \equiv x_0 + x_1 < 2 \wedge C_{\bowtie}$ is such that $\models C \to y_2 = 2$ since the only solutions of C are $\{x_0 \mapsto 0, x_1 \mapsto 1, x_2 \mapsto 2, y_0 \mapsto 0, y_1 \mapsto 1, y_2 \mapsto 2\}$ and $\{x_0 \mapsto 1, x_1 \mapsto 0, x_2 \mapsto 2, y_0 \mapsto 1, y_1 \mapsto 0, y_2 \mapsto 2\}$. But clearly it is not the case that $x_0 + x_1 < 2 \to x_2 = 2$. The problem is that the channel $C_{\bowtie}$ removes solutions of $x_0 + x_1 < 2$ like $\{x_0 \mapsto 0, x_1 \mapsto 0, x_2 \mapsto 0\}$ from consideration.

6   Example Problems

In the following, we give examples where the constraints in redundant modelling are propagation redundant.

6.1   All-Interval Series

The all-interval series problem, listed as "prob007" in CSPLib, from musical composition. The problem is to find a permutation of n numbers from 0 to $n - 1$, such that the differences between adjacent numbers form a permutation from 1 to $n - 1$.

There are two ways to model the problem. The first model, M_X, consists of n variables, $X = \{x_0, \dots, x_{n-1}\}$. Each x_i denotes the number in position i, and $D_{init}(x_i) = \{0, \dots, n-1\}$ for $i \in \{0, \dots, n-1\}$. We introduce auxiliary variables, $\{u_0, \dots, u_{n-2}\}$, that denote the difference between adjacent numbers. The constraints are:

- disequality constraints (IX1): $\forall 0 \leq i < j \leq n - 1$. $x_i \neq x_j$ and $\forall 0 \leq i < j \leq n - 2$. $u_i \neq u_j$.
- interval constraints (IX2): $\forall 0 \leq i \leq n - 2$. $u_i = |x_i - x_{i+1}| - 1$.

The second model, M_Y, also consists of n variables, $Y = \{y_0, \ldots, y_{n-1}\}$. Each y_i denotes the position for the number i, and $D_{init}(y_i) = \{0, \ldots, n-1\}$ for $i \in \{0, \ldots, n-1\}$. The auxilliary variables $\{v_0, \ldots, v_{n-2}\}$ denote the position where the difference value of 1 to $n - 1$ belongs. The constraints are:

- disequality constraints (IY1): $\forall 0 \leq i < j \leq n - 1$. $y_i \neq y_j$ and $\forall 0 \leq i < j \leq n - 2$. $v_i \neq v_j$.
- interval constraints (IY2): The constraints $\forall 0 \leq i < j \leq n - 1$. $(y_i - y_j = 1) \Rightarrow (v_{j-i-1} = y_j)$ and $(y_j - y_i = 1) \Rightarrow (v_{j-i-1} = y_i)$ enforce that if y_i and y_j are adjacent, the position for their difference must be the smaller of them.

In the second model, we observe that only y_0 and y_{n-1} can lead to a difference value of $n - 1$. Therefore, we can add the redundant constraints: (IY3) $(|y_0 - y_{n-1}| = 1) \wedge (v_{n-2} = min(y_0, y_{n-1}))$, to force y_0 and y_{n-1} to be adjacent.

The permutation channels for this problem are more interesting because we have two distinct kinds of variables in each model, each of which is related by a permutation channel. The channels are $x_i = j \Leftrightarrow y_j = i$ and $u_i = j \Leftrightarrow v_j = i$.

Example 19. Consider the constraint $c_Y \equiv (y_i - y_j = 1) \Rightarrow (v_{j-i-1} = y_j)$ of the all-intervals series problem. The propagation rules for $dsb(c_Y)$ have the forms

$$
\begin{aligned}
r1 \quad & y_i = k + 1 \wedge y_j = k \longmapsto v_{j-i-1} = k \\
r2 \quad & v_{j-i-1} \neq k \wedge y_j = k \longmapsto y_i \neq k + 1 \\
r3 \quad & y_i = k + 1 \wedge I \longmapsto y_j \neq k
\end{aligned}
$$

where in $r3$, I is any conjunction of disequations on v_{j-i-1} and y_j, not including $y_j \neq k$ ensuring that $v_{j-i-1} \neq y_j$. We can show for $imp(r1) \equiv imp(r2) \equiv imp(r3) \equiv (u_k = |x_k - x_{k+1}| - 1)$ that $\models (D_{init} \wedge imp(r1) \wedge x_{k+1} = i \wedge x_k = j) \rightarrow (u_k = j - i - 1)$ and $\models (D_{init} \wedge imp(r2) \wedge u_k \neq j - i - 1 \wedge x_k = j) \rightarrow (x_{k+1} \neq i)$. For the remaining propagation rules (r3), it is clear that I must contain $v_{j-i-1} \neq k$ since it does not contain $y_j \neq k$ and it must force the two to be different. We can show that $\models (D_{init} \wedge imp(r3) \wedge u_k \neq j - i - 1 \wedge x_{k+1} = i) \rightarrow (x_k \neq j)$.

Hence the constraint is propagation redundant by Theorem 12. Similarly for the other (IY2) constraints $(y_j - y_i = 1) \Rightarrow (v_{j-i-1} = y_i)$. The disequality constraints (IY1) $y_i \neq y_j$ and $v_i \neq v_j$ are propagation redundant by Lemma 14. The only non-propagation redundant constraints in M_Y is (IY3) $(|y_0 - y_{n-1}| = 1) \wedge (v_{n-2} = min(y_0, y_{n-1}))$.

6.2 n-Queens Problem

In the n-queens problem, the task of which is to place n queens on an $n \times n$ chess board so that no two queens can attack each other.

The first model, M_X, consists of n variables, $X = \{x_0, \ldots, x_{n-1}\}$. Each x_i denotes the column position of the queen on row i, and $D(x_i) = \{0, \ldots, n - 1\}$, for $i \in \{0, \ldots, n - 1\}$. The constraints C_X enforce that no two queens can be on the same:

- column (QX1): $\forall 0 \le i < j \le n - 1.\ x_i \ne x_j$.
- diagonal (QX2): $\forall 0 \le i < j \le n - 1.\ x_i - i \ne x_j - j, x_i + i \ne x_j + j$.

The second model, M_Z, consists of $n \times n$ Boolean variables, $Z = \{z_{00}, \ldots, z_{0(n-1)}, \ldots, z_{(n-1)0}, \ldots, z_{(n-1)(n-1)}\}$. Each z_{ij} denotes whether we have a queen at row i column j or not. The constraints C_Z enforce that no two queens can be on the same:

- row (QZ1): $\forall 0 \le i \le n - 1.\ \sum_{j=0}^{n-1} z_{ij} = 1$.
- column (QZ2): $\forall 0 \le j \le n - 1.\ \sum_{i=0}^{n-1} z_{ij} = 1$.
- main diagonal (QZ3): $\sum_{i=0}^{n-1} z_{ii} \le 1$, and $\sum_{i=0}^{n-1} z_{i(n-1-i)} \le 1$.
- other diagonal (QZ4): $\forall 1 \le k \le n - 1.\ \sum_{j=0}^{n-1-k} z_{j(j+k)} \le 1, \sum_{j=0}^{n-1-k} z_{(j+k)j} \le 1, \sum_{j=0}^{n-1-k} z_{j(n-1-j-k)} \le 1, \sum_{j=0}^{n-1-k} z_{(j+k)(n-1-j)} \le 1$.

We combine the two models using the Boolean channel $x_i = j \Leftrightarrow z_{ij} = 1$.

Example 20. In M_Z, the row constraints (QZ1) $\sum_{j=0}^{n-1} z_{ij} = 1$ are propagation redundant using Lemma 15.

Consider the main diagonal constraint (QZ3) $c_Z \equiv \sum_{i=0}^{n-1} z_{ii} \le 1$. We can show that $c_X \equiv x_1 \ne x_i - i - 1 \wedge \cdots x_{i-1} \ne x_i - 1 \wedge x_{i+1} \ne x_i + 1 \wedge \cdot \cdot x_{n-1} \ne x_i + n - i - 1$ is such that $\models D_{init} \wedge c_X \wedge C_\triangle \to c_Z$. Now $dsb(c_X) \approx dsb(x_1 \ne x_i) \cup \cdots \cup dsb(x_{n-1} \ne x_i)$ by Lemma 7 since they share only one variable x_i. Since $\triangle$ is an unrestrictive channel function, by Theorem 17 we have that $dsb(c_Z)$ is propagation redundant. A similar argument applies to all other diagonal constraints (QZ4).

Note that the column constraints (QZ2) $\sum_{i=0}^{n-1} z_{ij} = 1$ are not propagation redundant, although the constraint $\sum_{i=0}^{n-1} z_{ij} \le 1$ is (using a similar argument to the main diagonal constraints).

6.3 Balanced Academic Curriculum Problem

The problem "prob030" in CSPLib is to design a balanced academic curriculum. Following the description in [6], we can have both the integer model M_X and set model M_S.

Given m courses, and n periods, a, b are the minimum and maximum academic load allowed per period, c, d are the minimum and maximum number of courses allowed per period, t_i specifies the number of credits for course i, and R is a set of pairs $\langle i, j \rangle$ specifying that course i must be taken before course j.

We introduce a set of auxiliary variables l_j, which is shared by both models, to represent the academic load in period j as well as a variable u representing the maximum academic load in any period, i.e. $u = max\{l_j \mid 0 \le j \le n - 1\}$. The objective function simply minimizes u. We also introduce another set of shared auxiliary variables q_j to represent the number of courses assigned to a period.

We have the following constraints that is common to both models (B1): $\forall 0 \le j \le n - 1.\ a \le l_j \le b$ and $c \le q_j \le d$. We also add the following redundant constraints (B2): $\forall 0 \le j \le n - 1.\ (\sum_{j=0}^{n-1} l_j) = (\sum_{i=0}^{m-1} t_i)$ and $(\sum_{j=0}^{n-1} q_j) = m$.

In the integer model, M_X, the variable x_i represents the period to which course i is assigned The constraints for the integer model M_X are:

- (BX1) $\forall 0 \leq j \leq n-1.$ $(\sum_{i=0}^{m-1}((x_i = j) \times t_i)) = l_j$
- (BX2) $\forall 0 \leq j \leq n-1.$ $(\sum_{i=0}^{m-1}(x_i = j)) = q_j$
- (BX3) $\forall \langle i, j \rangle \in R.$ $x_i < x_j$

In the set model the set variables S_j representing the set of courses assigned to period j. The constraints for the set model M_S are:

- (BS1) $\forall 0 \leq i < j \leq n-1.$ $S_i \cap S_j = \emptyset$
- (BS2) $\forall 0 \leq j \leq n-1.$ $(\sum_{i \in S_j} t_i) = l_j$
- (BS3) $\forall 0 \leq j \leq n-1.$ $|S_j| = q_j$
- (BS4) $\forall \langle i, j \rangle \in R. \forall 1 \leq k \leq n-1. \forall 0 \leq k' \leq k.$ $(i \in S_k) \Rightarrow (j \notin S_{k'})$

We can use the set channels to combine the two models, $x_i = j \Leftrightarrow i \in S_j$.

Example 21. The (BS1) constraint $S_i \cap S_j = \emptyset$ is propagation redundant using Lemma 16. For the (BS4) constraint $c_S \equiv (i \in S_k) \Rightarrow (j \notin S_{k'})$ where $k' \leq k$ we can show that $\models (D_{init} \wedge x_i < x_j \wedge C_{\{\}}) \rightarrow c_S$. Hence since $\{\}$ is an unrestrictive channel function by Theorem 17 we have that $dsb(c_S)$ is propagation redundant.

Example 22. In an abuse of notation we use the "pseudo atomic constraint". $x \leq d$ to represent the conjunction $x \neq d+1, \ldots, x \neq \sup_{D_{init}}(x)$ and $x \geq d$ to represent the conjunction $x \neq \inf_{D_{init}}(x), \ldots, x \neq d-1$.

Consider the (BX2) constraint $c_X \equiv (\sum_{i=0}^{m-1}(x_i = j)) = q_j$, the propagation rules $C \rightarrowtail c$ for $dsb(c_X)$ are

$$q_j \leq d \wedge x_{i_1} = j \wedge \cdots \wedge x_{i_d} = j \rightarrowtail x_i \neq j$$
$$x_{i_1} = j \wedge \cdots \wedge x_{i_d} = j \rightarrowtail q_j \geq d$$

for all $I = \{i_1, \ldots, i_d\} \subseteq \{0, \ldots, m-1\}$ and $i \in \{0, \ldots, m-1\} - I$; and

$$q_j \geq d \wedge x_{i_1} \neq j \wedge \cdots \wedge x_{i_{m-d}} \neq j \rightarrowtail x_i = j$$
$$x_{i_1} \neq j \wedge \cdots \wedge x_{i_{m-d}} \neq j \rightarrowtail q_j \leq d$$

for all $I = \{i_1, \ldots, i_{m-d}\} \subseteq \{0, \ldots, m-1\}$ and $i \in \{0, \ldots, m-1\} - I$. Notice that all the atomic constraints involving q_j are mapped to themselves by $\{\}$, since q_j is shared by the two models. The rules are mapped to

$$q_j \leq d \wedge i_1 \in S_j \wedge \cdots \wedge i_d \in S_j \rightarrowtail i \notin S_j$$
$$i_1 \in S_j \wedge \cdots \wedge i_d \in S_j \rightarrowtail q_j \leq d$$
$$q_j \geq d \wedge i_1 \notin S_j \wedge \cdots \wedge i_{m-d} \notin S_j \rightarrowtail i \in S_j$$
$$i_1 \notin S_j \wedge \cdots \wedge i_{m-d} \notin S_j \rightarrowtail q_j \geq d$$

We have that for $c_S \equiv |S_j| = q_j, \models (D_{init} \wedge c_S \wedge \{\}(C)) \rightarrow \{\}(c)$ for all the propagation rules above. Hence, $dsb(c_X)$ is propagation redundant using Corollary 11.

Similar reasoning applies to show that each constraint $(\sum_{i=0}^{m-1}((x_i = j) \times t_i)) = l_j$ of (BX1) is made propagation redundant by (BS2) $(\sum_{i \in S_j} t_i) = l_j$.

7   Experiments

We can take advantage of the reasoning about propagation redundancy to eliminate propagators that are propagation redundant. We then get a model with exactly the same propagation behaviour but with less propagators. This can translate into *faster* propagation[3]. In the following experiments, All the benchmarks were executed using ILOG Solver 4.4 on Sun Ultra 5/400 workstation running Solaris 8.

7.1   All-Interval Series

We compare the different models for solving the all-interval series problem. We search for all solutions in order to fairly compare the propagation strengths and use a first-fail heuristic for variables selection, and least to greatest value selection heuristic.

The models under comparison include the single models: M_X and M_Y, the *full* combined model $M_X + C_{\bowtie} + M_Y$, and an *opt*imized combined model IX2 + $C_{\bowtie}$ + IY3 as discussed in Example 19. Puget and Régin, in their note[4], show that all the solutions can be found more efficiently by replacing (IX1) by (IX1') alldifferent constraints on x and u. The *pr* model uses $IX1' + IX2$. The *pr full* model is the combination of *pr* and M_Y, IX1' + IX2 + $C_{\bowtie}$ + M_Y. The *pr opt* model is the optimized combination of *pr* and M_Y, IX1' + IX2 + $C_{\bowtie}$ + IY3 since the same reasoning applies.

Table 1 gives the results of the comparison. We show the results using three sets of search variables X, Y and $X \cup Y$. Entries with a "—" mean unable to solve the problem after one hour of execution time. Compared with the single models M_X and M_Y, clearly the *full* and *pr full* model reduces the number of fails significantly. The *opt* model maintains the same number of fails as the *full* model and is the fastest for the smaller instance 12. The *pr opt* model maintains the same number of fails as the *pr full* model, and is the fastest for larger instances 13, 14 and 15, as the alldifferent constraints is too expensive for the smaller instance. Note that the optimized models *opt* and *pr opt* can solve the size 15 instance much faster than *pr*, and no other models can solve this instance within the time limit.

7.2   Balanced Academic Curriculum Problem

Table 2 shows the result of finding the optimal solution and proving optimality for some smaller instances derived from the problem instances posted in CSPLib. We use the first-fail heuristic for the search on the integer variables X, and naive enumeration for search on the set variables S. The table entry with value "—" means that Solver cannot solve the problem after one hour of execution time.

The *full* model represents the full combined model between the integer and set model as discussed in Section 6.3, while the *opt* model represents the reduced combined model after removing the redundant propagators as discussed in Example 21 and 22, that is B1 + B2 + BX3 + $C_{\{\}}$ + BS2 + BS3. In [6], the authors reported that it is difficult to find the optimal solution and prove optimality with propagation based solving alone.

---

[3] Note there is no guarantee since e.g. the number of propagation steps may have increased.

[4] Available at http://www.csplib.org/prob/prob007/puget.pdf.

Table 1. Comparing the different models of All-Interval Series Problem

Model	Search Vars	$n = 12$ fails (sec)		$n = 13$ fails (sec)		$n = 14$ fails (sec)		$n = 15$ fails (sec)	
pr	X	38778	(24.32)	156251	(105.26)	674346	(530.47)	3045037	(2328.57)
M_X	X	880112	(260.92)	4914499	(1589.83)	—	—	—	—
full	X	39241	(222.07)	158368	(1048.19)	—	—	—	—
opt	X	39241	(36.34)	158368	(157.84)	685301	(770.57)	—	—
pr full	X	38461	(236.42)	155183	(1088.91)	—	—	—	—
pr opt	X	38461	(42.77)	155183	(188.94)	670045	(910.90)	—	—
M_Y	Y	—	—	—	—	—	—	—	—
full	Y	16280	(70.81)	62949	(303.61)	266130	(1458.74)	—	—
opt	Y	16280	**(6.36)**	62949	(26.00)	266130	(108.54)	1275661	(553.45)
pr full	Y	**12296**	(62.96)	**43681**	(260.90)	**164841**	(1127.64)	—	—
pr opt	Y	**12296**	(7.91)	**43681**	**(25.78)**	**164841**	**(101.42)**	**704097**	**(458.12)**
full	$X \cup Y$	39195	(222.42)	158282	(1065.77)	—	—	—	—
opt	$X \cup Y$	39195	(36.36)	158282	(158.40)	684592	(783.01)	—	—
pr full	$X \cup Y$	38447	(230.65)	155176	(1094.61)	—	—	—	—
pr opt	$X \cup Y$	38447	(42.47)	155176	(198.36)	669950	(898.66)	—	—

Table 2. Comparing the different models for solving the balanced academic curriculum problem

Model	Search Variables	8 Periods fails (sec)	10 Periods fails (sec)	12 Periods fails (sec)
CPLEX	n/a	n/a (1.80)	n/a (2.27)	n/a (20.32)
Hybrid	X	**101** (0.61)	468 (2.20)	58442 (146.47)
Hybrid	Boolean	219 (0.76)	**277** (1.03)	**315** (2.09)
M_X	X	**101** **(0.04)**	468 (0.25)	33602 (11.62)
full	X	**101** (0.24)	470 (1.80)	33530 (192.62)
opt	X	**101** (0.08)	470 (0.68)	33530 (38.54)
M_S	S	— —	— —	— —
full	S	1577 (2.83)	323 (0.81)	882 (4.56)
opt	S	1577 (0.94)	323 **(0.24)**	882 **(0.95)**

However, by adding redundant constraints (B2), we were able to solve all the problem instances with M_X alone. The row *CPLEX* gives the runtime for solving the problem instances with ILOG CPLEX 8.0 using an integer linear programming (ILP) model in [6]. The row *Hybrid* implements the hybrid ILP and CP model described in [6] together with the redundant constraints (B2) using ILOG Hybrid 1.3. Clearly, the *full* model is substantially better in terms of number of fails when compared with the single model (M_X or M_S), The *hybrid* model gives the least number of fails, but suffer from the overhead of invoking two solvers. The *opt* model is more efficient and can solve all the instances in less than 1 second.

8   Conclusion

It is clear that reasoning about propagation redundancy can lead to significantly faster models, that do not increase the search space. Although we have illustrated the use of the theorems herein by hand, the approach can clearly be automated. To use Theorem 12 we can straightforwardly define the propagation rules for many constraints (parametrically in D_{init}) or construct them automatically using the approach of [ ]. Given the propagation rules, we can individually check those that are subsumed by constraints in the other model. If we have a parametric definition, then this check can also be parametric, rather than needing to consider every individual propagation rule. We can use Theorem 17 to prove propagation redundancy without considering propagation rules.

There are clearly many important future directions for this line of work. Modern set bounds propagation solvers (including ILOG Solver 4.4) implement slightly stronger propagators than $dsb(c)$, by including cardinality reasoning. We can model this extra propagation using cardinality variables and propagation rules. For a set constraint c to be propagation redundant we need to prove their redundancy too. For the examples in this paper this is straightforward. We plan to extend the theorems for the general case.

Similarly, many integer constraint solvers use integer bounds propagation. Clearly we can extend the notion of propagation rules to integer bounds propagators using the atomic constraints $x_i \leq d$ and $x_i \geq d$. The only complication arises in formalizing what the bounds propagators are for an individual constraint. Usually bounds propagators do not have a completeness property like Lemma 4.

References

1. S. Abdennadher and C. Rigotti. Automatic generation of rule-based solvers for intentionally defined constraints. *IJAIT* 11(2):283–302, 2002.
2. K. Apt and E. Monfroy. Constraint programming viewed as rule-based programming. *Theory and Practice of Logic Programming*, 1(6):713–750, 2001.
3. C. Bessiére and J. Régin. Arc consistency for general constraint networks: preliminary results. In *IJCAI-97* pages 398–404, 1997.
4. B. Cheng, K. Choi, J. Lee, and J. Wu. Increasing constraint propagation by redundant modelling: an experience report. *Constraints*, 4(2):167–192, 1999.
5. C.W. Choi, J.H.M. Lee, and P. J. Stuckey Propagation Redundancy for Permutation Channels In *IJCAI-03*, to appear.
6. B. Hnich, Z. Kiziltan, and T. Walsh. Modelling a balanced academic curriculum problem. In *CP-AI-OR'02*, pages 121–131, 2002.
7. B. M. Smith. Modelling a permutation problem. Research Report 2000.18, School of Computer Studies, University of Leeds, 2000.
8. B. M. Smith. Dual models in constraint programming. Research Report 2001.02, School of Computer Studies, University of Leeds, 2001.
9. T. Walsh. Permutation problems and channelling constraints. In *LPAR2001*, pages 377–391, 2001.
10. S. Brand. A note on redundant rules in rule-based constraint programming. In *Recent Advances in Constraints*, pages 109 – 120, 2003.

Soft Constraints: Complexity and Multimorphisms

David A. Cohen[1], Martin Cooper[2], Peter Jeavons[3], and Andrei Krokhin[4]

[1] Department of Computer Science, Royal Holloway, University of London, UK
d.cohen@rhul.ac.uk
[2] IRIT, University of Toulouse III, France
cooper@irit.fr
[3] Computing Laboratory, University of Oxford, UK
peter.jeavons@comlab.ox.ac.uk
[4] Department of Computer Science, University of Warwick, UK
andrei.krokhin@dcs.warwick.ac.uk

Abstract. Over the past few years there has been considerable progress in methods to systematically analyse the complexity of classical (crisp) constraint satisfaction problems with specified constraint types. One very powerful theoretical development in this area links the complexity of a set of classical constraints to a corresponding set of algebraic operations, known as polymorphisms.

In this paper we begin a systematic investigation of the complexity of combinatorial optimisation problems expressed using various forms of soft constraints. We extend the notion of a polymorphism by introducing a more general algebraic operation, which we call a multimorphism. We show that a number of maximal tractable sets of soft constraints, both established and novel, can be characterised by the presence of particular multimorphisms.

1 Introduction

In the standard constraint satisfaction framework a *constraint* is usually taken to be a predicate, or relation, specifying the allowed combinations of values for some fixed collection of variables: we will refer to such constraints here as *crisp* constraints. Problems with crisp constraints deal only with *feasibility*: no satisfying solution is considered better than any other.

A number of authors have suggested that the usefulness of the constraint satisfaction framework could be greatly enhanced by extending the definition of a constraint to include also *soft* constraints, which allow different measures of desirability to be associated with different combinations of values [1]. In this extended framework a constraint can be seen as a *function*, mapping each possible combination of values to a measure of desirability or undesirability. Problems with soft constraints deal with *optimisation* as well as feasibility: we seek an assignment of values to all of the variables having the best possible overall combined measure of desirability.

F. Rossi (Ed.): CP 2003, LNCS 2833, pp. 244–258, 2003.

Example 1. Consider an optimisation problem where we have $2n$ variables, $v_1, v_2, \ldots, v_{2n}$, and we wish to assign each variable an integer value in the range $1, 2, \ldots, n$, subject to the following restrictions:

- The value assigned to v_{2n} must be at least twice the value assigned to v_n.
- Each variable v_i should be assigned a value that is as close as possible to $i/2$.
- Each pair of variables v_i, v_{2i} should be assigned a pair of values that are as similar as possible.

To model this situation we might impose constraints as follows:

- A binary constraint on the pair v_n, v_{2n} specified by a function ζ, where $\zeta(x, y) = 0$ if $y \geq 2x$ and ∞ otherwise.
- A unary constraint on each v_i specified by a function ψ_i, where $\psi_i(x) = |x - i/2|^r$ for some $r \geq 1$.
- A binary constraint on each pair v_i, v_{2i} specified by a function δ_r, where $\delta_r(x, y) = |x - y|^r$ for some $r \geq 1$.

We would then seek an assignment to all of the variables which minimises the sum of these constraint functions,

$$\zeta(v_n, v_{2n}) + \sum_{i=1}^{2n} \psi_i(v_i) + \sum_{i=1}^{n} \delta_r(v_i, v_{2i}).$$

The cost of allowing additional flexibility in the specification of constraints, in order to model optimisation criteria as well as feasibility, is generally an increase in computational difficulty. For example, we establish below that the class of problems containing only unary constraints and a soft version of the equality constraint is NP-hard (see Example 5).

On the other hand, for certain types of soft constraint it is possible to solve the associated optimisation problems efficiently. For example, we establish below that optimisation problems of the form described in Example 1 can be solved in polynomial time (see Example 12).

In the case of crisp constraints there has been considerable progress in analyzing the complexity of different types of constraints. This work has led to the identification of a number of classes of constraints which are *tractable*, in the sense that there exists a polynomial time algorithm to determine whether or not any collection of constraints from such a class can be simultaneously satisfied [2, 12, 20, 27]. One powerful result in this area establishes that any tractable class of constraints over a finite domain must be preserved by a non-trivial algebraic operation, known as a *polymorphism* [4, 19, 20].

In the case of soft constraints there has not yet been any detailed investigation of the tractable cases, except for the special case of a two-valued domain [9], and the special case of simple temporal constraints [24]. In this paper we take the first step towards a systematic analysis of the complexity of soft constraints over arbitrary finite domains. To do this we generalise the algebraic ideas used to study crisp constraints, and introduce a new algebraic operation which we call a *multimorphism*. Every soft constraint has an associated set of multimorphisms, and every multimorphism has an associated set of soft constraints. We show that, for several different types of multimorphism, the associated set of soft constraints forms a maximal tractable set. In other words, we show that several maximal tractable classes of soft constraints can be precisely characterised as the set of all soft constraints associated with a particular multimorphism.

The examples given below demonstrate that the framework we introduce here can be used to unify isolated results about tractable problem classes from many different application areas, as well as prompting the discovery of new tractable classes. For example, the notion of a multimorphism can be used to characterise tractable subproblems in all of the following areas: in the case of the SATISFIABILITY problem these include the HORN-SAT and 2-SAT subproblems [15]; in the case of the standard constraint satisfaction problem these include generalisations of HORN-SAT (such as the so-called 'max-closed' constraints [23, 20]), generalisations of 2-SAT (such as the so-called '0/1/all' or 'implicative' constraints [8, 18, 25]) and systems of linear equations [20]; in the case of the optimisation problem MAX-SAT these include the '0-valid' and '2-monotone' constraints [9]; in the case of optimisation problems over sets these include the submodular set functions [17, 26] and bisubmodular set functions [14].

2   Definitions

Several alternative mathematical frameworks for soft constraints have been proposed in the literature, including the very general frameworks of 'semi-ring based constraints' and 'valued constraints' [1]. For simplicity, we shall adopt the valued constraint framework here (although our results can easily be adapted to the semi-ring framework, for appropriate semi-ring structures).

In the valued constraint framework, a constraint is specified by a function which assigns a *cost* to each possible assignment of values. In general, costs may be chosen from any *valuation structure*, satisfying the following definition.

Definition 1. *A **valuation structure**, χ, is a totally ordered set, with a minimum and a maximum element (denoted 0 and ∞), together with a commutative, associative binary **aggregation operator** (denoted $+$), such that for all $\alpha, \beta, \gamma \in \chi$*

$$\alpha + 0 = \alpha \tag{1}$$
$$\alpha + \gamma \geq \beta + \gamma \quad whenever \quad \alpha \geq \beta. \tag{2}$$

For all of the examples given in this paper we shall use the valuation structure $\overline{\mathbb{R}^+}$, consisting of the non-negative real numbers together with infinity, with the usual ordering and the usual addition operation.

Definition 2. *An instance of the valued constraint satisfaction problem, VCSP, is a tuple $\mathcal{P} = \langle V, D, C, \chi \rangle$ where:*

- V is a finite set of **variables**;
- D is a finite set of **values**;
- χ is a valuation structure representing possible **costs**;
- C is a set of **constraints**. Each element of C is a pair $c = \langle \sigma, \phi \rangle$ where σ is a tuple of variables called the **scope** of c, and ϕ is a mapping from $D^{|\sigma|}$ to χ, called the **cost function** of c.

Definition 3. *For any VCSP instance $\mathcal{P} = \langle V, D, C, \chi \rangle$, an **assignment** for $\mathcal{P}$ is a mapping s from V to D. The **cost** of an assignment s, denoted $Cost_{\mathcal{P}}(s)$, is given by the sum (i.e., aggregation) of the costs for the restrictions of s onto each constraint scope, that is,*

$$Cost_{\mathcal{P}}(s) = \sum_{\langle \langle v_1, v_2, \ldots, v_m \rangle, \phi \rangle \in C} \phi(s(v_1), s(v_2), \ldots, s(v_m)).$$

*A **solution** to $\mathcal{P}$ is an assignment with minimal cost, and the question is to find a solution.*

*Example 2 (**Standard CSP**). For any standard constraint satisfaction problem instance $\mathcal{P}$ with crisp constraints, we can define a corresponding valued constraint satisfaction problem instance $\widehat{\mathcal{P}}$ in which the range of the cost functions of all the constraints is the set $\{0, \infty\}$. For each crisp constraint c of $\mathcal{P}$, we define a corresponding soft constraint $\widehat{c}$ of $\widehat{\mathcal{P}}$ with the same scope; the cost function of $\widehat{c}$ maps each tuple allowed by c to 0, and each tuple disallowed by c to ∞.*

In this case the cost of an assignment s for $\widehat{\mathcal{P}}$ equals the minimal possible cost, 0, if and only if s satisfies all of the crisp constraints in $\mathcal{P}$.

*Example 3 (**MAX-CSP**). For any standard constraint satisfaction problem instance $\mathcal{P}$ with crisp constraints, we can define a corresponding valued constraint satisfaction problem instance $\mathcal{P}^{\#}$ in which the range of the cost functions of all the constraints is the set $\{0, 1\}$. For each crisp constraint c of $\mathcal{P}$, we define a corresponding soft constraint $c^{\#}$ of $\mathcal{P}^{\#}$ with the same scope; the cost function of $c^{\#}$ maps each tuple allowed by c to 0, and each tuple disallowed by c to 1.*

In this case the cost of an assignment s for $\mathcal{P}^{\#}$ equals the number of crisp constraints in $\mathcal{P}$ which are violated by s. Hence a solution to $\mathcal{P}^{\#}$ corresponds to an assignment which violates the minimal number of constraints of $\mathcal{P}$.

The problem of finding a solution to a valued constraint satisfaction problem is an NP optimisation problem, that is, it lies in the complexity class NPO (see [9] for a formal definition of this class). It follows from Examples 2 and 3 that the general VCSP is NP-hard. To achieve more tractable versions of VCSP, we will now consider the effect of restricting the forms of cost function allowed in the constraints.

Definition 4. *Let D be a set and χ a valuation structure. A **valued constraint language** over D with costs in χ is defined to be a set of functions, Γ, such that each $\phi \in \Gamma$ is a function from D^m to χ, for some $m \in \mathbb{N}$, where m is called the arity of ϕ.*

The class $\mathrm{VCSP}(\Gamma)$ is defined to be the class of all VCSP instances where the cost functions of all constraints lie in Γ.

For any valued constraint language Γ, if every instance in VCSP(Γ) can be solved in polynomial time then we will say that Γ is **tractable**. On the other hand, if there is a polynomial-time reduction from some NP-complete problem to VCSP(Γ), then we shall say that VCSP(Γ) and Γ are **NP-hard**.

Example 4 (SAT and MAX-SAT). Let Γ be any valued constraint language over D, where $|D| = 2$. In this case VCSP(Γ) is a *Boolean* soft constraint satisfaction problem.

If we restrict Γ even further, by only allowing functions with range $\{0, \infty\}$, as in Example 2, then each VCSP(Γ) corresponds precisely to a standard Boolean crisp constraint satisfaction problem. Such problems are sometimes known as GENERALIZED SATISFIABILITY problems [29, 15]. The complexity of VCSP(Γ) for such restricted sets Γ has been completely characterised, and the six tractable cases have been identified [29, 9].

Alternatively, if we restrict Γ by only allowing functions with range $\{0, 1\}$, as in Example 3, then each VCSP(Γ) corresponds precisely to a standard Boolean maximum satisfiability problem, in which the aim is to satisfy the maximum number of crisp constraints. Such problems are sometimes known as MAX-SAT problems [9]. The complexity of VCSP(Γ) for such restricted sets Γ has been completely characterised, and the three tractable cases have been identified (see Theorem 7.6 of [9]).

We note, in particular, that when Γ contains just the single binary function ϕ_{XOR} defined by

$$\phi_{XOR}(x,y) = \begin{cases} 0 & \text{if } x \neq y \\ 1 & \text{otherwise} \end{cases}$$

then VCSP(Γ) corresponds to the MAX-SAT problem for the exclusive-or predicate, which is known to be NP-hard (see Lemma 7.4 of [9]).

Example 5. Let Γ be a soft constraint language over D, where $|D| \geq 3$, and assume that Γ contains just the set of all unary functions, together with the single binary function ϕ_{EQ} defined by

$$\phi_{EQ}(x,y) = \begin{cases} 0 & \text{if } x = y \\ 1 & \text{otherwise.} \end{cases}$$

Even in this apparently simple case it can be shown [6] that VCSP(Γ) is NP-hard, by reduction from the MINIMUM MULTITERMINAL CUT problem [11].

3   Reductions and Multimorphisms

Let Γ be a valued constraint language, and consider an arbitrary instance $\mathcal{P}$ in VCSP(Γ). If we choose a subset of the variables of $\mathcal{P}$ which is equal to the set of variables in the scope of some constraint of $\mathcal{P}$, then the values taken by those variables are explicitly constrained. What is more, if we choose *any* subset of the variables of $\mathcal{P}$, then the values may still be constrained *implicitly*, due to the combined effect of the constraints of $\mathcal{P}$. The cost function which describes this implicit constraint may or may not be an element of Γ, but can, in a sense, be expressed using elements of Γ.

The next two definitions formalise this idea of a function being *expressible* over a valued constraint language.

Definition 5. *For any* VCSP *instance* $\mathcal{P} = \langle V, D, C, \chi \rangle$, *and any tuple of distinct variables* $W = \langle v_1, \ldots, v_k \rangle$, *the* **cost function for** $\mathcal{P}$ **on** W, *denoted* $\Phi_{\mathcal{P}}^W$, *is defined as follows:*

$$\Phi_{\mathcal{P}}^W(d_1, \ldots, d_k) = \min\{ Cost_{\mathcal{P}}(s) \mid s : V \to D, \langle s(v_1), \ldots, s(v_k) \rangle = \langle d_1, \ldots, d_k \rangle \}$$

Definition 6. *A function* ϕ *is* **expressible** *over a valued constraint language* Γ *if there exists an instance* $\mathcal{P} = \langle V, D, C, \chi \rangle$ *in* VCSP(Γ) *and a list* W *of variables from* V *such that* $\phi = \Phi_{\mathcal{P}}^W$.

The notion of expressibility is a key tool in analysing the complexity of valued constraint languages, as the next result shows.

Proposition 1. *Let* Γ *and* Γ' *be valued constraint languages.*

If Γ' *is finite, and every* $\phi \in \Gamma'$ *is expressible over* Γ, *then* VCSP(Γ') *is polynomial-time reducible to* VCSP(Γ).

Proof. Let $\mathcal{P} = \langle V, D, C, \chi \rangle$ be any instance in VCSP(Γ'), and let $c = \langle \sigma, \phi \rangle$ be a constraint in C. Since ϕ is expressible over Γ, there exists an instance $\mathcal{P}_\phi$ in VCSP(Γ), and a list of variables W of $\mathcal{P}_\phi$, such that $\Phi_{\mathcal{P}_\phi}^W = \phi$. Hence we can replace the constraint c with a copy of $\mathcal{P}_\phi$, where the variables in the scope σ are identified with the list of variables W, and the remaining variables of $\mathcal{P}_\phi$ are disjoint from V, to obtain a new problem instance $\mathcal{P}'$. Note that the solutions to $\mathcal{P}'$, when restricted to V, correspond precisely to the original solutions to $\mathcal{P}$.

By repeating this construction for each constraint c of $\mathcal{P}$, we can obtain an instance $\mathcal{P}''$ of VCSP(Γ). Since Γ' is finite, there is a bound on the size of the instances $\mathcal{P}_\phi$ used in the construction, and so the size of $\mathcal{P}''$ is bounded by a constant multiple of the size of $\mathcal{P}$. Hence we have described a polynomial-time reduction from VCSP(Γ') to VCSP(Γ).

It follows from Proposition 1 that valued constraint languages that are finite and express precisely the same set of functions have the same complexity, up to polynomial-time reduction. Hence to analyse the complexity of a valued constraint language it may be sufficient to determine what functions can be expressed over that language. For example, the next result shows how this idea can be used to establish NP-hardness of a valued constraint language.

Corollary 1. *Let* Γ *be a valued constraint language over* D, *with costs in* $\overline{\mathbb{R}^+}$.

If there exist $d, d' \in D$, *and* $\alpha, \beta \in \overline{\mathbb{R}^+}$, *with* $\alpha < \beta < \infty$, *such that the binary function* ϕ_{XOR+} *given by*

$$\phi_{XOR+}(x, y) = \begin{cases} \alpha & \text{if } x \neq y \,\wedge\, x, y \in \{d, d'\} \\ \beta & \text{if } x = y \,\wedge\, x, y \in \{d, d'\} \\ \infty & \text{otherwise} \end{cases}$$

is expressible over Γ, *then* VCSP(Γ) *is NP-hard.*

Proof. Any instance of VCSP($\{\phi_{XOR+}\}$) must have a solution involving only the two values d and d', since all assignments involving any other values must have costs at least as high. Lemma 7.4 of [9] states that the two-valued problem VCSP($\{\phi_{XOR}\}$) is NP-hard, where ϕ_{XOR} is the Boolean exclusive-or function, as defined in Example 4. Since adding a constant to all cost functions, and scaling all costs by a constant factor, does not affect the difficulty of solving a VCSP instance, we conclude that VCSP($\{\phi_{XOR+}\}$) is also NP-hard.

For crisp constraints, it has been show that the expressive power of a set of relations is determined by certain algebraic invariance properties of those relations, known as *polymorphisms* [4, 20, 22, 21, 28]. The concept of a polymorphism is specific to *relations*, and cannot be applied directly to the *functions* in a valued constraint language. However, we now introduce a more general notion, which we call a *multimorphism*, which does apply directly to functions.

Throughout the rest of the paper, the ith component of a tuple t will be denoted $t[i]$.

Definition 7. *Let D be a set, χ a valuation structure, and $\phi : D^m \rightarrow \chi$ a function.*

We extend the definition of ϕ in the following way: for any positive integer k, and any list of k-tuples, $t_1, t_2, \ldots, t_m$, over D, we define

$$\phi(t_1, t_2, \ldots, t_m) = \sum_{i=1}^{k} \phi(t_1[i], t_2[i], \ldots, t_m[i])$$

*We say that $F : D^k \rightarrow D^k$ is a **multimorphism** of ϕ if, for any list of k-tuples $t_1, t_2 \ldots, t_m$ over D we have*

$$\phi(F(t_1), F(t_2), \ldots, F(t_m)) \leq \phi(t_1, t_2, \ldots, t_m).$$

Example 6. Let $D = \{0, 1, 2, \ldots, |D| - 1\}$ be a subset of the integers, and let $\phi : D^3 \rightarrow \overline{\mathbb{R}^+}$ be the linear function defined by $\phi(x, y, z) = ax + by + cz$, where a, b, c are positive constants.

Consider the function $F : D^2 \rightarrow D^2$ defined by $F(x, y) = \langle \min(x, y), \max(x, y) \rangle$. For any list of pairs, t_1, t_2, t_3, over D we have

$$
\begin{aligned}
&\phi(F(t_1), F(t_2), F(t_3)) \\
&= \quad \phi(\langle \min(t_1[1], t_1[2]), \max(t_1[1], t_1[2]) \rangle, \ldots, \\
&\qquad\qquad \langle \min(t_3[1], t_3[2]), \max(t_3[1], t_3[2]) \rangle) \\
&= \quad \phi(\min(t_1[1], t_1[2]), \min(t_2[1], t_2[2]), \min(t_3[1], t_3[2])) \\
&\qquad + \phi(\max(t_1[1], t_1[2]), \max(t_2[1], t_2[2]), \max(t_3[1], t_3[2])) \\
&= \quad (a \min(t_1[1], t_1[2]) + b \min(t_2[1], t_2[2]) + c \min(t_3[1], t_3[2])) \\
&\qquad + (a \max(t_1[1], t_1[2]) + b \max(t_2[1], t_2[2]) + c \max(t_3[1], t_3[2])) \\
&= \quad a(t_1[1] + t_1[2]) + b(t_2[1] + t_2[2]) + c(t_3[1] + t_3[2]) \\
&= \quad \phi(t_1, t_2, t_3)
\end{aligned}
$$

Hence F is a multimorphism of ϕ.

Example 7. Let R be a relation of arity m, and let ϕ_R be the function defined by

$$\phi_R(x_1, x_2, \ldots, x_m) = \begin{cases} 0 & \text{if } \langle x_1, x_2, \ldots, x_m \rangle \in R \\ \infty & \text{otherwise} \end{cases}$$

There is a close relationship between the *polymorphisms* of the relation R, as defined in [4, 21, 28], and the *multimorphisms* of the function ϕ_R.

For any polymorphism $f : D^k \to D$ of R, it is easy to show that the function $F : D^k \to D^k$ defined by

$$F(x_1, x_2, \ldots, x_k) = \langle f(x_1, x_2, \ldots, x_k), f(x_1, x_2, \ldots, x_k), \ldots, f(x_1, x_2, \ldots, x_k) \rangle$$

is a multimorphism of ϕ_R.

Furthermore, if $F : D^k \to D^k$ is a multimorphism of ϕ_R, then it is straightforward to check from the definitions that each of the k *component* functions, F_i, given by $F_i(x_1, x_2, \ldots, x_k) = F(x_1, x_2, \ldots, x_k)[i]$, is a polymorphism of R.

The following result means that multimorphisms have the key property that they extend to all functions expressible over a given language.

Theorem 1. *Let Γ be a valued constraint language, and F be a multimorphism of every function in Γ.*

If ϕ is expressible over Γ, then F is also a multimorphism of ϕ.

Proof. The proof of this result is a straightforward application of Definition 7 and Definition 6.

In the remainder of the paper we will show that a wide range of tractable optimisation problems are characterised by the presence of certain forms of multimorphism.

Example 8. For any finite set Q, a function ψ defined on subsets of Q is called a **submodular set function** [26] if, for all subsets S and T of Q

$$\psi(S \cup T) + \psi(S \cap T) \leq \psi(S) + \psi(T).$$

The problem of submodular set function minimisation consists in finding a subset S of Q for which $\psi(S)$ is minimal. Such problems arise in a number of different contexts. For example, Cunningham [10] showed that finding the maximum flow in a network can be viewed as a special case of the general problem of submodular function minimisation.

By fixing an arbitrary order for the elements of Q, we can associate each subset S of Q with a tuple t_S of length $|Q|$ over the set $\{0, 1\}$, where $t_S[i] = 1$ if S contains the ith element of Q, and $t_S[i] = 0$ otherwise. Using this association, it is easy to show that a function ψ is a submodular set function if and only if the function ϕ given by $\phi(t_S) = \psi(S)$ has the multimorphism $F : \{0, 1\}^2 \to \{0, 1\}^2$ given by $F(x, y) = \langle \min(x, y), \max(x, y) \rangle$.

It has been known for a long time that real-valued submodular set functions can be minimised in polynomial time using the ellipsoid method [16]. Recently, several different strongly polynomial, combinatorial algorithms have been proposed for this problem [30, 17, 13].

However, the best known polynomial-time bounds for general real-valued submodular set function minimisation are still rather high: the number of oracle calls has been shown to be $O(n^7)$, and the number of fundamental operations has been shown to be $O(n^8)$ [13].

Example 9. For any finite set Q, a function ψ defined on pairs of disjoint subsets of Q is called a **bisubmodular function** [14] if for all pairs (S_1, S_2) and (T_1, T_2) of disjoint subsets of Q

$$\psi(\langle S_1, S_2 \rangle \sqcup \langle T_1, T_2 \rangle) + \psi(\langle S_1, S_2 \rangle \sqcap \langle T_1, T_2 \rangle) \leq \psi(\langle S_1, S_2 \rangle) + \psi(\langle T_1, T_2 \rangle)$$

where

$$\langle S_1, S_2 \rangle \sqcup \langle T_1, T_2 \rangle = \langle (S_1 \cup T_1) \setminus (S_2 \cup T_2), (S_2 \cup T_2) \setminus (S_1 \cup T_1) \rangle$$
$$\langle S_1, S_2 \rangle \sqcap \langle T_1, T_2 \rangle = \langle S_1 \cap T_1, S_2 \cap T_2 \rangle$$

It is known that an integer-valued bisubmodular function ψ can be minimised in $O(n^5 \log M)$ time where M designates the maximum value of the function ψ [14].

By fixing an arbitrary order for the elements of Q, we can associate each pair of disjoint subsets $\langle S_1, S_2 \rangle$ of Q with a tuple $t_{\langle S_1, S_2 \rangle}$ of length $|Q|$ over the set $\{0, 1, 2\}$, where $t_{\langle S_1, S_2 \rangle}[i] = 1$ if S_1 contains the ith element of Q, $t_{\langle S_1, S_2 \rangle}[i] = 2$ if S_2 contains the ith element of Q, and $t_{\langle S_1, S_2 \rangle}[i] = 0$ otherwise. Using this association, it is easy to check that a function ψ is a bisubmodular function if and only if the function ϕ given by $\phi(t_{\langle S_1, S_2 \rangle}) = \psi(\langle S_1, S_2 \rangle)$ has the multimorphism $F : \{0, 1, 2\}^2 \to \{0, 1, 2\}^2$ given by $F(x, y) = \langle min_0(x, y), max_0(x, y) \rangle$, where

$$min_0(x, y) = \begin{cases} \min(x, y) & \text{if } \{x, y\} \neq \{1, 2\} \\ 0 & \text{otherwise} \end{cases}$$

$$max_0(x, y) = \begin{cases} \max(x, y) & \text{if } \{x, y\} \neq \{1, 2\} \\ 0 & \text{otherwise} \end{cases}$$

Hence the bisubmodular functions defined in [14] are also characterised by the presence of a multimorphism.

4 Multimorphisms and Tractable Languages

In this section we will present several tractable valued constraint languages. Some of these are translations of known tractable optimisation problems into the VCSP framework, and others are novel tractable classes. In all cases we are able to give a characterisation of the tractable language in terms of a single multimorphism. Hence, in all cases we have shown that the presence of a particular multimorphism is sufficient to guarantee tractability.

Definition 8. *Given a function $F : D^k \to D^k$, we will write Γ_F to denote the valued constraint language over D with costs in $\overline{\mathbb{R}^+}$, consisting of all functions for which F is a multimorphism.*

4.1 Constant Multimorphisms

The first example we give is a rather straightforward family of tractable languages, characterised by the presence of a single unary multimorphism with a constant value. Although the proof of tractability for this case is trivial, the proof that every language characterised by a constant multimorphism is a *maximal* tractable language is more interesting, and provides a simple example of the techniques we shall use for other cases.

Theorem 2. *Let D be a set, and let $F : D \to D$ be a constant function.*

1. *The set of functions Γ_F is a tractable valued constraint language.*
2. *Any valued constraint language Γ such that $\Gamma \supset \Gamma_F$ is NP-hard.*

Proof. Let d_F be the (constant) value of F.

1. Let ϕ be any function in Γ_F, and let m be the arity of ϕ. Since F is a multimorphism of ϕ, we have, for all $d_1, d_2, \ldots, d_m \in D$,

$$\phi(d_F, d_F, \ldots, d_F) \le \phi(d_1, d_2, \ldots, d_m)$$

   Hence any instance $\mathcal{P}$ in VCSP(Γ_F) has a solution which assigns the value d_F to every variable, so VCSP(Γ_F) is tractable.

2. Now assume that $\Gamma \supset \Gamma_F$, and hence Γ contains a function ϕ of arity m such that F is not a multimorphism of ϕ. Hence there exist $d_1, d_2, \ldots, d_m \in D$ such that $\phi(d_1, d_2, \ldots, d_m) < \phi(d_F, d_F, \ldots, d_F)$.
   If $\phi(d_F, \ldots, d_F) < \infty$, then set $\mu = (\phi(d_F, \ldots, d_F) - \phi(d_1, \ldots, d_m))/2$, otherwise set $\mu = 1$. Choose i_0 such that $d_{i_0} \ne d_F$. Now define the functions δ and ψ as follows:

$$\delta(x_1, \ldots, x_m) = \begin{cases} 0 & \text{if } \langle x_1, \ldots, x_m \rangle \in \{\langle d_1, \ldots, d_m \rangle, \langle d_F, \ldots, d_F \rangle\} \\ \infty & \text{otherwise} \end{cases}$$

$$\psi(x_1, x_2, x_3) = \begin{cases} \mu & \text{if } \langle x_1, x_2, x_3 \rangle \in \{\langle d_{i_0}, d_{i_0}, d_{i_0} \rangle, \langle d_{i_0}, d_F, d_F \rangle\} \\ 0 & \text{otherwise} \end{cases}$$

   Note that $\delta, \psi \in \Gamma_F$.
   We construct the instance $\mathcal{P} \in$ VCSP(Γ) with variables

$$\{X_1, \ldots, X_m, Y_1, \ldots, Y_m, Z_1, \ldots Z_m\}$$

   and constraints

$$\langle \langle X_1, \ldots, X_m \rangle, \phi \rangle, \qquad \langle \langle X_1, \ldots, X_m \rangle, \delta \rangle,$$
$$\langle \langle Y_1, \ldots, Y_m \rangle, \delta \rangle, \qquad \langle \langle Z_1, \ldots, Z_m \rangle, \delta \rangle,$$
$$\langle \langle X_{i_0}, Y_{i_0}, Z_{i_0} \rangle, \psi \rangle$$

   If we set $W = \langle Y_{i_0}, Z_{i_0} \rangle$, then it is straightforward to check that

$$\Phi_{\mathcal{P}}^W(x, y) = \begin{cases} \phi(d_1, d_2, \ldots, d_m) & \text{if } x \ne y \wedge x, y \in \{d_F, d_{i_0}\} \\ \mu + \phi(d_1, d_2, \ldots, d_m) & \text{if } x = y \wedge x, y \in \{d_F, d_{i_0}\} \\ \infty & \text{otherwise} \end{cases}$$

   Hence, by Corollary 1, VCSP(Γ) is NP-hard.

Example 10. Recall from Example 4 that the MAX-SAT optimisation problem has just three maximal tractable classes, which are identified in [9]. Two of these can be characterised by having a constant function as a multimorphism; these are referred to in [9] as '0-valid' relations, and '1-valid' relations.

4.2   Min-max Multimorphisms

The next example we give is a valued constraint language which can be defined on any finite totally ordered set D. This language is characterised by the presence of a single binary multimorphism, which we will call a **min-max** multimorphism. Languages with this multimorphism generalise the class of submodular set functions used in economics and operations research [26] (see Example 8).

Theorem 3. *Let D be a finite totally ordered set, and let $F : D^2 \to D^2$ be the function defined by $F(d, d') = \langle \min(d, d'), \max(d, d') \rangle$.*

1. *The set of finite-valued functions in Γ_F is a tractable valued constraint language.*
2. *Any valued constraint language Γ such that $\Gamma \supset \Gamma_F$ is NP-hard.*

Proof.

1. To establish the tractability of the set of finite-valued functions in Γ_F, we show that this problem can be reduced to the problem of minimising a real-valued submodular set function [26] over a special family of sets known as a ring family [30]. This problem can then be solved in polynomial time using an algorithm due to Schrijver [30]. Details are given in [7].
2. Proof omitted due to space restrictions. See [7] for details.

Example 11. Recall from Example 4 that the MAX-SAT optimisation problem has just three maximal tractable classes, which are identified in [9]. One of these can be characterised by having a min-max multimorphism; this class is referred to in [9] as the class of '2-monotone' relations.

Example 12. It is a simple consequence of the definitions that every *unary* function has a min-max multimorphism.

We have recently shown that a problem instance $\mathcal{P} = (V, D, C, \overline{\mathbb{R}^+})$ involving unary and *binary* functions with a min-max multimorphism, including functions taking infinite values, can be solved in $O(|V|^3|D|^3)$ time [6]. Note that this compares very favourably with the best known complexity bound for optimising submodular set functions of arbitrary arity, as discussed in Example 8.

Let D be the set $\{0, 1, 2, \ldots, |D| - 1\}$, considered as a set of integers. The following *binary* functions all have a min-max multimorphism, and hence any VCSP instance involving constraints with cost functions of these forms can be solved in cubic time.

$$\phi_1(x,y) = \begin{cases} 0 & \text{if } ax \leq by + c \text{ (for positive constants } a, b, c) \\ \infty & \text{otherwise} \end{cases}$$

$$\phi_2(x,y) = ax + by + c \text{ (for positive constants } a, b, c)$$

$$\phi_3(x,y) = \sqrt{x^2 + y^2}$$

$$\phi_4(x,y) = |x - y|^r \text{ (for } r \geq 1)$$

Using these observations we conclude that the discrete optimisation problem described in Example 1 can be solved in cubic time.

Note that some of the functions in Example 12 may appear to be similar to the soft simple temporal constraints with semi-convex cost functions defined and shown to be tractable in [24]. However, there are fundamental differences: the constraints in [24] are defined over an infinite set of values, and their tractability depends crucially on the aggregation operation used for the costs being *idempotent* (i.e., the operation *min*).

4.3 Max-max Multimorphisms

The next example we give is again a valued constraint language which can be defined on any finite totally ordered set D. This language is characterised by the presence of a single binary multimorphism, which we will call a **max-max** multimorphism. Languages with this multimorphism generalise the class of max-closed crisp constraints introduced and shown to be tractable in [23].

Theorem 4. *Let D be a finite totally ordered set, and let $F : D^2 \to D^2$ be the function defined by $F(d, d') = \langle \max(d, d'), \max(d, d') \rangle$.*

1. *The set of functions Γ_F is a tractable valued constraint language.*
2. *Any valued constraint language Γ such that $\Gamma \supset \Gamma_F$ is NP-hard.*

Proof. Omitted due to space restrictions. See [7] for details.

Example 13. The constraint language CHIP incorporates a number of constraint solving techniques for arithmetic and other constraints. In particular it provides a constraint solver for a restricted class of crisp constraints over natural numbers, referred to as *basic constraints* [31]. These basic constraints are of two kinds which are referred to as "domain constraints" and "arithmetic constraints". The domain constraints described in [31] are unary constraints which restrict the value of a variable to some specified finite subset of the natural numbers. The arithmetic constraints described in [31] are unary or binary constraints which have one of the following forms:

$$aX \neq b \qquad aX \leq bY + c$$
$$aX = bY + c \qquad aX \geq bY + c$$

where variables are represented by upper-case letters, and constants by lower case letters, all constants are non-negative, and a is non-zero.

If we represent these crisp constraints as soft constraints where the range of the cost functions is the set $\{0, \infty\}$, as described in Example 2, then it is easy to verify that they all have a max-max multimorphism, and hence form a tractable soft constraint language, by Theorem 4.

Moreover, this tractable language can be extended, as shown in [23], to include functions corresponding to crisp constraints of the following forms, which also have a max-max multimorphism.

$$a_1 X_1 + a_2 X_2 + \ldots + a_r X_r \geq bY + c$$
$$a X_1 X_2 \ldots X_r \geq bY + c$$
$$(a_1 X_1 \geq b_1) \vee (a_2 X_2 \geq b_2) \vee \ldots \vee (a_r X_r \geq b_r) \vee (aY \leq b)$$

Example 14. Let D be an ordered domain and χ a valuation structure. A function $\phi : D^m \to \chi$ is called **antitone** if the value of $\phi(d_1, d_2, \ldots, d_m)$ does not increase when we increase any of the d_i.

All antitone functions have a max-max multimorphism, and hence form a tractable class. More importantly, they may be combined with the crisp constraints described in Example 13 to form a larger tractable class.

For example, let $D = \{0, 1, 2, \ldots, M\}$ be a subset of the integers, and let $\phi : D^2 \to \overline{\mathbb{R}^+}$ be the binary function defined by

$$\phi(x, y) = \begin{cases} (M - x)(M - y) & \text{if } x < y \\ \infty & \text{if } x \geq y \end{cases}$$

This function can be used to express a preference for larger values for x, y provided $x < y$. It is straightforward to check that it has a max-max multimorphism.

4.4   Majority/Minority Multimorphisms

The final example we give is a tractable valued constraint language which can be defined on any finite set D. This language is characterised by the presence of a single ternary multimorphism, which we will call a **majority/minority** multimorphism. Languages with this multimorphism generalise the class of bijective crisp constraints.

Theorem 5. *Let D be a finite set, and let $F : D^3 \to D^3$ be the function defined by $F(x, y, z) = \langle \mathrm{Maj}_1(x, y, z), \mathrm{Maj}_2(x, y, z), \mathrm{Min}_3(x, y, z) \rangle$ where*

$$\mathrm{Maj}_1(x, y, z) = \begin{cases} y & \text{if } y = z \\ x & \text{otherwise.} \end{cases}$$

$$\mathrm{Maj}_2(x, y, z) = \begin{cases} x & \text{if } x = z \\ y & \text{otherwise.} \end{cases}$$

$$\mathrm{Min}_3(x, y, z) = \begin{cases} x & \text{if } y = z \neq x \\ y & \text{if } x = z \neq y \\ z & \text{otherwise.} \end{cases}$$

1. *The set Γ_F is a tractable valued constraint language.*
2. *Any valued constraint language Γ such that $\Gamma \supset \Gamma_F$ is NP-hard.*

Proof. Omitted due to space restrictions. See [7] for details.

5   Conclusions

In this paper we have begun a systematic investigation of the complexity of the optimisation problems resulting from different forms of soft constraint. Since soft constraints are specified by functions, we have introduced an algebraic property of a function, which we call a multimorphism, and shown that in a range of cases the presence of such a property is sufficient to ensure tractability. Indeed, we have shown that the presence of a multimorphism precisely characterises a number of tractable problem classes that appear on the surface to be very different.

Further study is needed to determine whether the notion of a multimorphism exactly captures the expressive power, and hence the complexity, of soft constraints over finite domains. If this is true, then multimorphisms are likely to play a central role in the analysis of complexity for soft constraints, just as the related notion of a polymorphism does in the analysis of complexity for crisp constraints [3–5, 20–22]

References

1. S. Bistarelli, H. Fargier, U. Montanari, F. Rossi, T. Schiex, and G. Verfaillie. Semiring-based CSPs and valued CSPs: Frameworks, properties, and comparison. *Constraints*, 4:199–240, 1999.
2. M. Bjäreland and P. Jonsson. Exploiting bipartiteness to identify yet another tractable subclass of CSP. In J. Jaffar, editor, *Principles and Practice of Constraint Programming—CP'99*, volume 1713 of *Lecture Notes in Computer Science*, pages 118–128. Springer-Verlag, 1999.
3. A.A. Bulatov. A dichotomy theorem for constraints on a three-element set. In *Proceedings 43rd IEEE Symposium on Foundations of Computer Science, FOCS'02*, pages 649–658. IEEE Computer Society, 2002.
4. A.A. Bulatov, A.A. Krokhin, and P.G. Jeavons. Constraint satisfaction problems and finite algebras. In *Proceedings 27th International Colloquium on Automata, Languages and Programming, ICALP'00*, volume 1853 of *Lecture Notes in Computer Science*, pages 272–282. Springer-Verlag, 2000.
5. A.A. Bulatov, A.A. Krokhin, and P.G. Jeavons. The complexity of maximal constraint languages. In *Proceedings 33rd ACM Symposium on Theory of Computing, STOC'01*, pages 667–674, 2001.
6. D. Cohen, M. Cooper, P. Jeavons, and A. Krokhin. A tractable class of soft constraints. Technical Report CSD-TR-02-14, Computer Science Department, Royal Holloway, University of London, Egham, Surrey, UK, December 2002 (short version to appear in *Proceedings of IJCAI'03*).
7. D. Cohen, M. Cooper, P. Jeavons, and A. Krokhin. An investigation of the multimorphisms of tractable and intractable classes of valued constraints. Technical Report CSD-TR-03-03, Computer Science Department, Royal Holloway, University of London, Egham, Surrey, UK, 2003.
8. M.C. Cooper, D.A. Cohen, and P.G. Jeavons. Characterising tractable constraints. *Artificial Intelligence*, 65:347–361, 1994.
9. N. Creignou, S. Khanna, and M. Sudan. *Complexity Classification of Boolean Constraint Satisfaction Problems*, volume 7 of *SIAM Monographs on Discrete Mathematics and Applications*. Society for Industrial and Applied Mathematics, Philadelphia, PA., 2001.

10. W.H. Cunningham. Minimum cuts, modular functions,and matroid polyhedra. *Networks*, 15(2):205–215, 1985.
11. E. Dahlhaus, D.S. Johnson, C.H. Papadimitriou, P.D. Seymour, and M. Yannakakis. The complexity of multiterminal cuts. *SIAM Journal on Computing*, 23(4):864–894, 1994.
12. T. Feder and M.Y. Vardi. The computational structure of monotone monadic SNP and constraint satisfaction: A study through Datalog and group theory. *SIAM Journal of Computing*, 28:57–104, 1998.
13. L. Fleischer and S. Iwata. Improved algorithms for submodular function minimization and submodular flow. In *Proceedings of the 32th Annual ACM Symposium on Theory of Computing*, pages 107–116, 2000.
14. S. Fujishige and S. Iwata. Bisubmodular function minimization. *Lecture Notes in Computer Science*, 2081:160–169, 2001.
15. M. Garey and D.S. Johnson. *Computers and Intractability: A Guide to the Theory of NP-Completeness*. Freeman, San Francisco, CA., 1979.
16. M. Grötschel, L. Lovasz, and A. Schrijver. The ellipsoid method and its consequences in combinatorial optimization. *Combinatorica*, 1:169–198, 1981.
17. S. Iwata, L. Fleischer, and S. Fujishige. A combinatorial strongly polynomial algorithm for minimizing submodular functions. *Journal of the ACM*, 48(4):761–777, 2001.
18. P.G. Jeavons, D.A. Cohen, and M.C. Cooper. Constraints, consistency and closure. *Artificial Intelligence*, 101(1–2):251–265, 1998.
19. P.G. Jeavons, D.A. Cohen, and M. Gyssens. A test for tractability. In *Proceedings 2nd International Conference on Constraint Programming—CP'96*, volume 1118 of *Lecture Notes in Computer Science*, pages 267–281. Springer-Verlag, 1996.
20. P.G. Jeavons, D.A. Cohen, and M. Gyssens. Closure properties of constraints. *Journal of the ACM*, 44:527–548, 1997.
21. P.G. Jeavons, D.A. Cohen, and M. Gyssens. How to determine the expressive power of constraints. *Constraints*, 4:113–131, 1999.
22. P.G. Jeavons, D.A. Cohen, and J.K. Pearson. Constraints and universal algebra. *Annals of Mathematics and Artificial Intelligence*, 24:51–67, 1998.
23. P.G. Jeavons and M.C. Cooper. Tractable constraints on ordered domains. *Artificial Intelligence*, 79(2):327–339, 1995.
24. L. Khatib, P. Morris, R. Morris, and F. Rossi. Temporal constraint reasoning with preferences. In *Proceedings of the 17th International Joint Conference on Artificial Intelligence (IJCAI-01)*, pages 322–327, Seattle, USA, 2001.
25. L. Kirousis. Fast parallel constraint satisfaction. *Artificial Intelligence*, 64:147–160, 1993.
26. G.L. Nemhauser and L.A. Wolsey. *Integer and Combinatorial Optimization*. John Wiley & Sons, 1988.
27. J.K. Pearson and P.G. Jeavons. A survey of tractable constraint satisfaction problems. Technical Report CSD-TR-97-15, Royal Holloway, Univ. of London, 1997.
28. R. Pöschel and L.A. Kalužnin. *Funktionen- und Relationenalgebren*. DVW, Berlin, 1979.
29. T.J. Schaefer. The complexity of satisfiability problems. In *Proceedings 10th ACM Symposium on Theory of Computing, STOC'78*, pages 216–226, 1978.
30. A. Schrijver. A combinatorial algorithm minimizing submodular functions in strongly polynomial time. *JCTB: Journal of Combinatorial Theory, Series B*, 80:346–355, 2000.
31. P. van Hentenryck, Y. Deville, and C-M. Teng. A generic arc-consistency algorithm and its specializations. *Artificial Intelligence*, 57:291–321, 1992.

Constraint Satisfaction Differential Problems

Jorge Cruz and Pedro Barahona

Centro de Inteligência Artificial, DI/FCT/UNL, 2829-516 Caparica, Portugal
{jc,pb}@di.fct.unl.pt

Abstract. System dynamics is often modeled by means of parametric differential equations. Despite their expressive power, they are difficult to reason about and make safe decisions, given their non-linearity and the important effects that the uncertainty on data may cause. Either by traditional numerical simulation or relying on constraint based methods, it is difficult to express a number of constraints on the solution functions (for which there are usually no analytical solutions) and these constraints may only be handled passively, with generate and test techniques. In contrast, the framework we propose not only extends the declarativeness of the constraint based approach but also makes an active use of constraints on the solution functions, which makes it particularly suited for a number of decision making problems, such as those arising in the biomedical applications presented in the paper.

1 Introduction

Many real world problems can be modeled as Continuous Constraint Satisfaction Problems (CCSPs) where variable domains are continuous real intervals and constraints are equalities and inequalities [7]. Constraint reasoning handles the uncertainty of model parameters, by modeling them as numerical variables ranging over given bounds (e.g. intervals of real numbers) and propagates such knowledge through a network of constraints on these variables, in order to decrease the underlying uncertainty (i.e. width of the intervals).

However, parametric differential equations, a general and expressive mathematical tool to model system dynamics (e.g. biomedical systems) are not accommodated in the usual CCSP framework. This is not a major problem only if such systems have analytical solutions, where an explicit representation of the solution functions can be expressed by means of constraints on the parameters, making it possible to take full advantage of constraint reasoning.

The handling of differential equations in the constraint setting has already been addressed [6, 8], but only in the limited setting of Initial Value Problems (IVP), which aim at computing, from a set of differential equations and some initial values, the trajectory of the corresponding solution functions. In contrast with classical numerical approaches that compute numerical approximations of the solutions but do not provide any guarantees on their accuracy, interval methods [11, 14, 13], also known as validated methods, do verify the existence of unique solutions and produce guaranteed error bounds for the solution trajectory along the whole interval of time T.

F. Rossi (Ed.): CP 2003, LNCS 2833, pp. 259–273, 2003.

For such constraints, often required in decision support problems, the validated methods require additional generate and test procedures, where such constraints are used passively. Certain intervals on the parameters are used to generate trajectories, which are subsequently tested, so as to accept or reject such intervals.

In this paper we present a new kind of constraint, a Constraint Satisfaction Differential Problem (CSDP), which represents a differential equation together with additional related information, and we include it in the general CCSP framework extending its expressive power.

Appropriate narrowing functions are defined and used for the propagation of such constraints. Although not discussed in the paper, it is worth mentioning that the effectiveness of the whole approach depends significantly on the type of propagation used in the general CCSP framework. Some examples show the usefulness of imposing global-hull consistency [2–4]), a higher-level consistency criterion built on top of the usual basic criteria (e.g. box-consistency [1] or 2B-consistency [9]).

The paper is organised as follows. After a brief overview of the relevant concepts related with differential equations and their solving procedures, section 2 presents differential equations as CSDPs and their integration in an extended CCSP framework. Section 3 presents a procedure for solving CSDPs. Sections 4 and 5 present two examples in the biomedical area, which show the potential of the formalism developed. The paper ends with a summary of the main conclusions.

2   Constraint Satisfaction Differential Problems

2.1   Ordinary Differential Equations

The behaviour of many systems is naturally modelled by a system of first order Ordinary Differential Equations (ODEs), often parametric. ODEs are equations that involve derivatives w.r.t. a single independent variable, t, usually representing time. An ODE system S, represented in vector notation as

$$\frac{dy}{dt} = f(y, t)$$

determines, for an instantiation of y and t, the evolution of y for an increment of t, and may be regarded as a restriction on the sequence of values that y can take over t. A solution of the above ODE system, for a time interval T, is a function s such that:

$$\forall t \in T : \frac{ds}{dt} = f(s(t), t)$$

Since S does not fully determine the sequence of values of y (but rather a family of such sequences, that is, a family of solutions of S), initial / boundary conditions are usually provided with a complete / partial specification of y at some time point t.

An Initial Value Problem (IVP) is characterised by an ODE system S together with the initial condition $y(t_0) = y_0$. A solution of the IVP w.r.t. an interval of time T $(t_0 \in T)$ is a solution s of S (during T) that satisfies $s(t_0) = y_0$.

Classical numerical approaches for solving IVPs [16] compute numerical approximations of the solutions and do not provide guarantees on their accuracy. A sequence of discrete points $t_0, t_1, \ldots, t_i$ is considered within the interval of time T and for each new point t_{i+1}, the solution $s(t_{i+1})$ is approximated by a value s_{i+1} computed from the approximated values at the previous points.

In contrast, interval methods [11, 14, 13] do verify the existence of unique solutions and produce guaranteed error bounds for the solution trajectory along the whole interval of time T. They use interval arithmetic to calculate each approximation step, explicitly keeping the error term within safe interval bounds.

In most interval approaches, each step between two consecutive points t_i and t_{i+1} generally consists of two phases. The first validates the existence of a unique solution and calculates an *a priori* enclosure of it between the two points. In the second phase, a tighter enclosure of the solution function at point t_{i+1} is obtained through interval arithmetic over a numerical approximation step, with the error term bounded as a result of the enclosure of the previous phase.

Interval Taylor Series (ITS) methods [11, 13] are often used due to its simple error term form. The enclosure for the set of solutions between points t_i and t_{i+1} may be achieved through the application of the Picard-Lindelf operator [14] or an alternative higher order method [13]. The tighter enclosure of the solution function at point t_{i+1} is obtained through an interval extension of the Taylor Series expansion around t_i.

The recent application of constraint techniques for solving IVPs seems to provide competitive results either in the precision of the trajectory enclosure bounds or in the efficiency of the computations [6, 8]. The novelty of the approach is the subdivision of the second phase into a predictor process, for computing an initial enclosure, and a corrector process, for narrowing this enclosure, both based on constraint techniques. However, the goal of these methods is not the integration of differential integration in constraint reasoning. They rather use constraint propagation techniques for improving the traditional methods for solving IVPs.

2.2   Representing ODE Problems with CSDPs

All the information traditionally associated with an ODE problem may be represented as a CSDP. Moreover, the framework allows the specification of additional useful information that cannot be easily handled by classical approaches.

A CSDP is a Constraint Satisfaction Problem (CSP) with a special variable, a special constraint and additional constraints and variables for representing additional restrictions. The special variable (x_{ODE}), whose domain is a set of functions, is associated with an ODE system S for every t within the interval T through the ODE constraint, $ODE_{S,T}(x_{ODE})$. Variable x_{ODE}, denoted solution variable, represents those functions that are solutions of S (during T) and satisfy all the additional restrictions.

Definition 1. (ODE Constraint). *Let S be an n-ary ODE system defined as $\frac{dy}{dt} = f(y,t)$, T a real interval, and F_T the set of all functions from T to $\mathbb{R}^n$. The ODE constraint, denoted $ODE_{S,T}(x_{ODE})$, is defined by means of:*

1. *a unary constraint scope: the solution variable x_{ODE};*
2. *a constraint relation $\rho = \{\langle s \rangle | s \in F_T \wedge \forall t \in T : \frac{ds}{dt} = f(s(t),t)\}$.*

The other variables of the CSDP, denoted restriction variables, are all real valued variables used to model a number of constraints of interest in many applications. These constraints, generally denoted as ODE restrictions, associate some restriction variable with the value of some property of the ODE solutions. Such a property is specified through a function from the set of functions F_T to $\mathbb{R}$.

Definition 2. (ODE Restriction). *Let S be an n-ary ODE system defined as $\frac{dy}{dt} = f(y,t)$, T a real interval, F_T the set of all functions from T to $\mathbb{R}^n$, and r a function from F_T to $\mathbb{R}$. An ODE restriction w.r.t. r is defined by means of:*

1. *a binary constraint scope: the solution variable x_{ODE} and a real variable x;*
2. *a constraint relation $\rho = \{\langle s,v \rangle | s \in F_T \wedge v \in \mathbb{R} \wedge v = r(s)\}$.*

With the above definitions, a CSDP may be formalized as a special CSP.

Definition 3. (CSDP). *Let S be an n-ary ODE system $\frac{dy}{dt} = f(y,t)$, T a real interval, and F_T the set of all functions from T to $\mathbb{R}^n$. A CSDP is a CSP where:*

1. *the set of variables includes the solution variable x_{ODE} and m restriction variables $x_1, \ldots, x_m$;*
2. *the initial domain of the solution variable Dx_{ODE} is F_T and the initial domains of the restriction variables $Dx_1, \ldots, Dx_m$ are real intervals;*
3. *the set of constraints is composed of the ODE constraint $ODE_{S,T}(x_{ODE})$ and a set of ODE restrictions with scope $\langle x_{ODE}, x_i \rangle (1 \leq i \leq m)$.*

In a CSDP, initial and boundary conditions are represented by an appropriate set of constraints denoted Value restrictions. A Value restriction $Value_{j,t}(x)$ associates a variable x with the value of a trajectory component j at a particular time t.

Definition 4. (Value Restriction). *Let S be an n-ary ODE system defined as $\frac{dy}{dt} = f(y,t)$, T a real interval, $t_p \in T$ and $1 \leq j \leq n$. Let F_T be the set of functions from T to $\mathbb{R}^n$, r a function from F_T to $\mathbb{R}$, $s \in F_T$ and s_j the jth component of s. A Value restriction $Value_{j,t_p}(x)$ is an ODE restriction w.r.t. r defined as: $r(s) = s_j(t_p)$.*

Besides initial and boundary conditions, and regarding an ODE solution as a continuous vector function (and each of its components as a continuous real function), several other conditions of interest may be imposed.

Important properties of a continuous function are its maximum and minimum values. Maximum restriction $Maximum_{j,\tau}(x)$ associates x with the maximum value of a trajectory component j within a time interval τ (Minimum restrictions are similar).

Definition 5. (Maximum Restriction). *Let S be an n-ary ODE system defined as $\frac{dy}{dt} = f(y,t)$, $\tau \subseteq T$ real intervals and $1 \leq j \leq n$. Let F_T be the set of functions from T to $\mathbb{R}^n$, r a function from F_T to $\mathbb{R}$, $s \in F_T$ and s_j the jth component of s. A Maximum restriction $Maximum_{j,\tau}(x)$ is an ODE restriction w.r.t. r defined as: $r(s) = s_j(t_p)$ with $t_p \in \tau$ and $\forall_{t \in \tau} s_j(t) \leq s_j(t_p)$.*

Other important ODE restrictions provided in the CSDP framework are Time, Area, First and Last restrictions. A Time restriction $Time_{j,\tau,\geq\theta}(x)$ associates x with the time within time period τ in which the value of a trajectory component j exceeds a threshold θ. Similarly, the Area restriction $Area_{j,\tau,\geq\theta}(x)$ associates x with the area of a trajectory component j, within time period τ, above threshold θ. The First restriction $FirstValue_{j,\tau \geq \theta}(x)$ associates x with the first time within τ in which the value of a trajectory component j exceeds θ. Restrictions $FirstMaximum_{j,\tau}(x)$ and $FirstMinimum_{j,\tau}(x)$ associate x with the first time within τ in which the value of a trajectory component j is respectively a maximum or a minimum. Last restrictions $LastValue_{j,\tau,\geq\theta}(x)$, $LastMaximum_{j,\tau}(x)$ and $LastMinimum_{j,\tau}(x)$ are similar.

Representing an ODE Problem as a CSDP. Consider the ODE system S:

$$\frac{dy_1(t)}{dt} = -0.7y_1(t) \qquad\qquad \frac{dy_2(t)}{dt} = 0.7y_1(t) - \frac{ln(2)}{5}y_2(t) \qquad (1)$$

with a boundary condition $y_1(0) = 1.25$ and an additional restriction requiring the maximum value of y_2 between $t = 1$ and $t = 3$ to lie within interval $[1.1..1.3]$, for which we are interested in the value of y_2 at $t = 6$. Such ODE problem is represented as a CSDP with the following constraints:

1. an ODE constraint $ODE_{S,[0..6]}(x_{ODE})$ associating the solution variable x_{ODE} with the ODE system S for every t within the time interval $[0..6]$;
2. a Value restriction $Value_{1,0}(x_1)$ associating variable x_1 with $y_1(0)$;
3. a Maximum restriction $Maximum_{2,[1..3]}(x_2)$ associating variable x_2 with the maximum value of y_2 within time interval $[1..3]$;
4. a Value restriction $Value_{2,6}(x_3)$ associating variable x_3 with $y_2(6)$;

The initial domains of restriction variables x_1 and x_2 are, respectively, $Dx_1=1.25$ for enforcing the initial condition and $Dx_2=[1.1..1.3]$ for imposing the maximum value requirement. Since x_3 represents an output variable, its initial domain is unbounded. The initial domain of the solution variable x_{ODE} is the set $F_{[0..6]}$ of all functions from $[0..6]$ to $\mathbb{R}^2$. Figure 1 illustrates the problem, showing the CSDP solutions (grey area) and the respective restriction variable domains.

2.3   Integrating CSDP Constraints into Extended CCSPs

The full integration of a CSDP within an extended CCSP is accomplished by sharing the restriction variables of the CSDP. The CSDP is a constraint restraining the possible values of such variables. The CSDP solving procedure is used as a safe narrowing procedure to reduce the domains of the restriction variables.

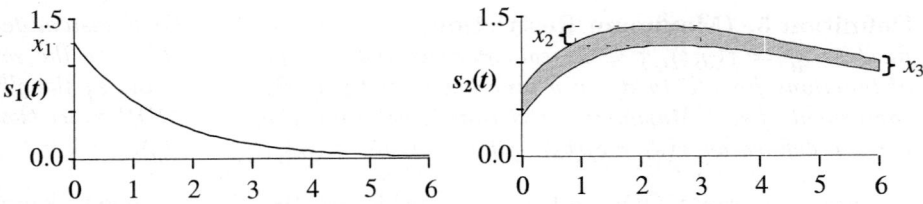

Fig. 1. The CSDP representation of an ODE problem. Its solutions and variables

Definition 6. (CSDP constraint). *A CSDP constraint is a constraint defined as a CSDP where:*

1. *the constraint scope is the set of the CSDP restriction variables;*
2. *the constraint relation is the set of the possible combination values of the restriction variables from the whole set of solutions of the CSDP.*

Definition 7. (Extended CCSP). *An extended CCSP is a CSP where each variable domain is a real interval and each constraint is either an equality constraint, an inequality constraint or a CSDP constraint.*

3   Solving a CSDP

This section presents a procedure to handle a CSDP aiming at pruning the domains of its restriction variables. This is implemented as a function *solveCSDP* which, from a real box representing the domains of the restriction variables, returns a smaller real box discarding some value combinations that can be proved to be inconsistent with the CSDP. As long as the *solveCSDP* function is correct, not eliminating any possible CSDP solution, and contracting, returning a smaller real box, it may be used by the extended CCSP as a correct narrowing function for the CSDP constraint.

The additional narrowing functions associated with the CSDP constraints, together with the usual narrowing functions associated with the numerical constraints, completely characterize the set of narrowing functions of an extended CCSP. This set may be used by a constraint propagation algorithm to prune the domains of the extended CCSP variables.

The solving procedure for CSDPs that we developed maintains a safe enclosure for the set of possible ODE solutions based on validated methods for solving IVPs. This enclosure is used for the representation of the domain of the solution variable and is denoted the ODE trajectory. The quality improvement of such enclosure is combined with the enforcement of the ODE restrictions through constraint propagation on a set of narrowing functions associated with the CSDP.

The next subsection presents the ODE trajectory enclosure. Subsection 3.2 illustrates some of the narrowing functions associated with the CSDP. Subsection 3.3 describes how these narrowing functions are integrated in the constraint propagation algorithm for narrowing the domains of the CSDP variables.

3.1   The ODE Trajectory

An ODE trajectory TR is implemented as a pair of ordered lists $TR=\langle TP, TG\rangle$. List TP defines a sequence of k trajectory time points t_p along the interval of time T (associated with the CSDP) together with corresponding n-ary boxes representing enclosures for the ODE solution values at these points. The first and last time points of such list are the lower and upper bounds of T respectively. List TG defines the sequence of $k-1$ trajectory time gaps (between each pair of consecutive time points, t_{pi} and t_{pi+1}, of the previous list) and the associated n-ary boxes representing enclosures for the ODE solution values between those points. The boxes associated with the elements of these lists are represented as $TP(t_p)$ and $TG([t_{pi}..t_{pi+1}])$ and the intervals associated with their j^{th} component ($1 \leq j \leq n$) as $TP_j(t_p)$ and $TG_j([t_{pi}..t_{pi+1}])$.

Figure 2 shows an ODE trajectory representing a safe enclosure for the set of possible ODE solutions of the CSDP presented in 2.2 (see figure 1). The ODE trajectory is defined through a sequence of seven time points and the time gaps in between. For each component, the intervals associated to each time point and time gap are represented, respectively, as a vertical line and a dashed rectangle.

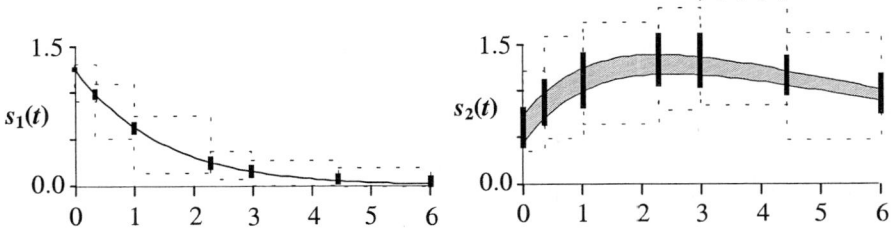

Fig. 2. An ODE trajectory enclosing the ODE solutions of a CSDP

The ODE trajectory of figure 2 represents the set of all functions from $[0..6]$ to $\mathbb{R}^2$ whose components are continuous functions enclosed by the rectangles and crossing the vertical lines. This includes any possible ODE solution and so this ODE trajectory is a safe enclosure for the set of ODE solutions of the CSDP.

During the solving process, the ODE trajectory is modified by the narrowing functions associated with the constraints of the CSDP. Each change of the trajectory is either the narrowing of some box (associated with a time point or gap) or the addition of a new time point (and reformulation of the ordered lists).

3.2   CSDP Narrowing Functions

In any constraint propagation algorithm based on a set of narrowing functions, each such function is a mapping between subsets of the variable domains where the new element is obtained from the original by eliminating some value combinations incompatible with a particular CSP constraint. Thus, applying a narrowing function, the new element cannot be larger (w.r.t. set inclusion) than the original element (boxes are contracted into smaller boxes) and the discarded elements cannot contain solutions of the CSP (the procedure is correct).

In the case of the CSDP narrowing functions, the contracting property is generally attained by preventing the enlargement of any interval domain, either from a restriction variable or from a component of any box of the ODE trajectory. Additionally, the correctness property must be guaranteed for each constraint relation used by the narrowing function for pruning the variable domains.

Associated with the constraint relation of each ODE restriction a pair of narrowing functions is defined: one responsible for reducing the current domain I of the restriction variable given the current ODE trajectory enclosure TR and the other responsible for reducing the uncertainty of TR according to I. In the first case, the correctness property may be achieved by identifying, within TR, the functions that maximise and minimise the values of the restriction variable and guaranteeing that its new domain includes those values. In the second case, this reduction is achieved through the narrowing of one or more boxes of TR and correctness is guaranteed if, considering in isolation each narrowed interval, there are no discarded functions with a value (of the restriction variable) in I.

The following definitions associate narrowing functions with Value and Maximum restrictions (similar ones exist for the other types of ODE restrictions).

Definition 8. (Value Narrowing Functions). *Let $TR=\langle TP, TG \rangle$ be the trajectory enclosure representing the domain of x_{ODE} and I the domain of x. Let TR' be the trajectory enclosure obtained from TR by changing $TP_j(t_p)$ to $TP_j(t_p) \cap I$. The restriction $Value_{j,t_p}(x)$ has associated the narrowing functions:*
1. $NF_1(\langle TR, \ldots, I, \ldots \rangle) = \langle TR, \ldots, TP_j(t_p) \cap I, \ldots \rangle$
2. $NF_2(\langle TR, \ldots, I, \ldots \rangle) = \langle TR', \ldots, I, \ldots \rangle$

Definition 9. (Maximum Narrowing Functions). *Let $TR=\langle TP, TG \rangle$ be the trajectory enclosure representing the domain of x_{ODE} and $I=[i_1..i_2]$ the domain of x. Let a be the maximum of the lower bounds of $TP_j(t_p)$ for any trajectory time point t_p within τ. Let b be the maximum of the upper bounds of $TG_j([t_{pi}..t_{pi+1}])$ for any trajectory time gap $[t_{pi}..t_{pi+1}]$ within τ. Let TR' be the enclosure obtained from TR by changing $TP_j(t_p)$ into $TP_j(t_p) \cap [-\infty..i_2]$ and $TG_j([t_{pi}..t_{pi+1}])$ into $TG_j([t_{pi}..t_{pi+1}]) \cap [-\infty..i_2]$ for every time point t_p and gap $[t_{pi}..t_{pi+1}]$ within τ. The restriction $Maximum_{j,\tau}(x)$ has associated the narrowing functions:*
1. $NF_1(\langle TR, \ldots, I, \ldots \rangle) = \langle TR, \ldots, [a..b] \cap I, \ldots \rangle$
2. $NF_2(\langle TR, \ldots, I, \ldots \rangle) = \langle TR', \ldots, I, \ldots \rangle$

Figure 3 illustrates the narrowing functions for the $Maximum_{2,[1..3]}(x_2)$ restriction of the CSDP presented in 2.2 for the enclosure represented in Figure 2.

All the remaining narrowing functions of a CSDP are associated with the ODE constraint relation and are responsible for reducing the uncertainty of the trajectory enclosure by the successive application of an Interval Taylor Series (ITS) method between consecutive time points.

The narrowing function NF_{link} uses the ITS method to validate (link) some time gap for which the method was never applied in either direction. As a consequence, besides the safe elimination from the ODE trajectory of some functions

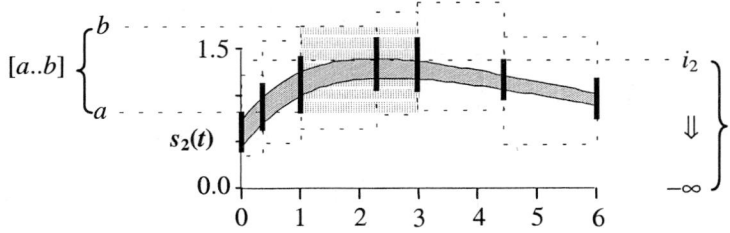

Fig. 3. Narrowing functions associated with a Maximum restriction

incompatible with the ODE constraint, the time gap may become completely or partially validated (in this case, a new time point is inserted and the link narrowing function must be reapplied to completely validate the gap).

The propagate narrowing function $NF_{propagate}$ prunes the ODE trajectory through the reapplication of the ITS method over some time gap, which is chosen to contain the time point with the largest enclosure reduction since the previous application of the ITS method. This heuristics assumes that, when an enclosure for the ODE solutions at some time point is reduced by some narrowing function, the reapplication of the ITS method over the adjacent time gaps may further prune these gaps. Moreover, the repeated application of the interval step method triggered by the reduction of the enclosures propagates this pruning along the ODE trajectory gaps, previously validated with larger starting enclosures.

Additionally, for each ODE restriction, a narrowing function $NF_{improve}$ may also be associated with the ODE constraint to improve the ODE trajectory, thus reducing the restriction variable domain. In general, the narrowing functions responsible for reducing the domain of the restriction variable (except the Value narrowing functions) depend on the time gap enclosures of the ODE trajectory. Therefore, by reducing such time gap enclosures, the restriction variable domain may eventually be narrowed. This is the goal of an improve narrowing function, that is, to reduce some time gap enclosure that later may trigger some other narrowing function associated with an ODE restriction and reduce the domain of a restriction variable. The reduction of the time gap enclosure is achieved through the insertion of a new time point within the gap and the subsequent application of the ITS method linking this point with its adjacent neighbours.

3.3 CSDP Constraint Propagation Algorithm

The constraint propagation algorithm for pruning the domains of the CSDP variables is derived from the propagation algorithm AC3 [10]. The only difference is the imposition of an ordering on the application of the narrowing functions. Since there are no guarantees of monotonicity for the narrowing functions associated with the CSDP constraints, the order of their application may be crucial, not only for the efficiency of the propagation but also for the pruning achieved.

The strategy followed by the algorithm is to propagate as soon as possible any information related with the restriction variables and delay as much as possible the application of the narrowing functions for reducing the ODE trajectory uncertainty. The reason is that whereas the former are easy to deal with and may provide fast domain pruning, the latter may be computationally more expensive as they require the application of the ITS method.

Among the narrowing functions for reducing the ODE trajectory uncertainty, the selection criterion favours the propagate narrowing function that spread as much as possible any domain reduction achieved by any other narrowing function. Moreover, since it does not make sense to try to improve an ODE trajectory that is not completely validated, the link narrowing function is always preferred to any of the improve narrowing functions.

Lack of space prevents us to present at greater detail the algorithm that was developed. These details may be found in [Cru03], together with the proof that the algorithm is correct and terminates.

4   A Differential Model for Drug Design

The gastro-intestinal absorption process subsequent to the oral administration of a therapeutic drug is usually modeled by the two-compartment model [17]:

$$\frac{dx(t)}{dt} = -p_1 x(t) + D(t) \qquad\qquad \frac{dy(t)}{dt} = p_1 x(t) - p_2 y(t) \qquad (2)$$

where x is the concentration of the drug in the gastro-intestinal tract;
         y is the concentration of the drug in the blood stream;
         D is the drug intake regimen; p_1 and p_2 are positive parameters.

The effect of the intake regimen $D(t)$ on the concentrations of the drug in the blood stream during the administration period is determined by the absorption and metabolic parameters, p_1 and p_2. We assume that the drug is taken on a periodic basis (every six hours), providing a unit dosage that is uniformly dissolved into the gastro-intestinal tract during the first half hour. Maintaining such intake regimen, the solution of the ODE system asymptotically converges to a six hours periodic trajectory called the limit cycle, shown in Figure 4 for specific values of the ODE parameters.

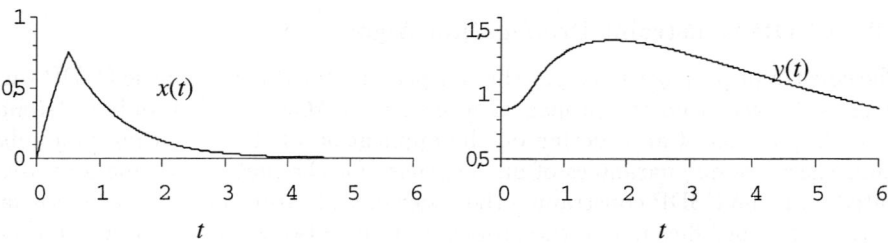

Fig. 4. The periodic limit cycle with p1=1.2 and p2=ln(2)/5

In designing a drug, it is necessary to adjust the ODE parameters to guarantee that the drug concentrations are effective, but causing no side effects. In general, it is sufficient to guarantee some constraints on the drug blood concentrations during the limit cycle, namely, by imposing bounds on its values, on the area under the curve and on the total time it remains above some threshold. Figure 5 shows maximum, minimum, area (≥ 1.0) and time (≥ 1.1) values for the limit cycle of figure 4.

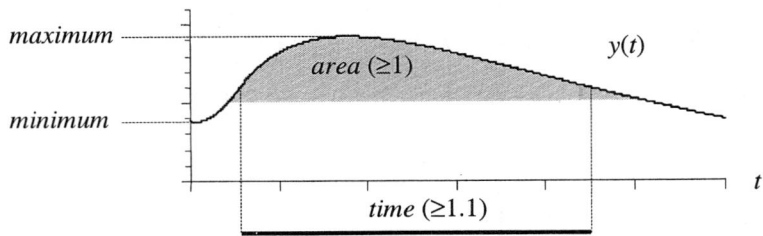

Fig. 5. Maximum, minimum, area and time values at the limit cycle

We show below how the extended CCSP framework can be used for supporting the drug design process. We will focus on the absorption parameter, p_1, which may be adjusted by appropriate time release mechanisms (the metabolic parameter p_2, tends to be characteristic of the drug itself and cannot be easily modified). The tuning of p_1 should satisfy the following requirements during the limit cycle: (i) the concentration in the blood bounded between 0.8 and 1.5; (ii) its area under the curve (and above 1.0) bounded between 1.2 and 1.3; (iii) it cannot exceed 1.1 for more than 4 hours.

4.1   Using the Extended CCSP for Parameter Tuning

The limit cycle and all the requirements may be represented as an extended CCSP. Due to the intake regimen definition $D(t)$, the ODE system has a discontinuity at time $t=0.5$, and is represented by two CSDP constraints in sequence.

The first, P_{S_1}, ranges from the beginning of the limit cycle ($t=0.0$) to time $t=0.5$, and the second P_{S_2}, is associated to the remaining trajectory of the limit cycle (until $t=6.0$). Both CSDP constraints include Value, Maximum Value, Minimum Value, Area and Time restrictions for associating variables with different trajectory properties. Besides variables representing the ODE parameters, the initial trajectory values and the final trajectory values, there are variables representing the maximum and minimum drug concentration values and respective area (≥ 1.0) and time (≥ 1.1) during the time associated with each constraint.

The extended CCSP P connects in sequence the two ODE segments by assigning the same variables to both the final values of P_{S_1} and the initial values of P_{S_2} (parameters p_1 and p_2 are shared by both constraints). Moreover, the 6 hours period is guaranteed by the assignment of the same variables to both the initial values of P_{S_1} and the final values of P_{S_2}. Besides considering all the restriction variables of each ODE segment, new variables for the whole trajectory sum the values in each segment.

CCSP $P = (X, D, C)$ where:

$$X =< x_0, y_0, p_1, p_2, x_{05}, y_{05}, y_{max1}, y_{max2}, y_{min1}, y_{min2},$$
$$y_{a1}, y_{a2}, y_{area}, y_{t1}, y_{t2}, y_{time} >$$
$$D =< Dx_0, Dy_0, Dp_1, Dp_2, Dx_{05}, Dy_{05}, Dy_{max1}, Dy_{max2}, Dy_{min1}, Dy_{min2},$$
$$Dy_{a1}, Dy_{a2}, Dy_{area}, Dy_{t1}, Dy_{t2}, Dy_{time} >$$
$$C = \{ P_{S_1}(x_0, y_0, p_1, p_2, x_{05}, y_{05}, y_{max1}, y_{min1}, y_{a1}, y_{t1}), \ y_{area} = y_{a1} + y_{a2},$$
$$P_{S_2}(x_{05}, y_{05}, p_1, p_2, x_0, y_0, y_{max2}, y_{min2}, y_{a2}, y_{t2}), \ y_{time} = y_{t1} + y_{t2} \}$$

The tuning of drug design may be supported by solving P with the appropriate set of initial domains for its variables. We will assume p_2 to be fixed to a five-hour half live ($Dp_2=[ln(2)/5]$) and p_1 to be adjustable up to about ten-minutes half live ($Dp_1=[0..4]$). The initial value x_0, always very small, is safely bounded in interval $Dx_0=[0.0..0.5]$. Additionally, the following bounds are imposed by the previous drug requirements:

$$Dy_{min1} = [0.8..1.5], \qquad Dy_{max1} = [0.8..1.5], \qquad Dy_{area} = [1.2..1.3],$$
$$Dy_{min2} = [0.8..1.5], \qquad Dy_{max2} = [0.8..1.5], \qquad Dy_{time} = [0.0..4.0].$$

Solving the extended CCSP P (enforcing global hull consistency), with a precision of 10^{-3}, narrows the original p_1 interval to $[1.191, 1.543]$ in less than 3 minutes (the tests were executed in a Pentium 4 at 1.5 GHz with 128 Mb memory). Hence, for p_1 outside this interval the set of requirements cannot be satisfied.

Note the importance of imposing global hull consistency as mentioned above. With a local consistency criteria (either box- or 2B-consistency), no pruning of the above parameter domains is achieved. Enforcing bound-consistency [15] does not achieve the same level of pruning (only prunes the parameter domain to $[1.156..1.580]$ - an increase of 20% in the domain width) in a comparable time.

This may help to adjust p_1 but offers no guarantees on specific choices within the obtained interval. However, guaranteed results may be obtained for particular choices of the p_1 values. Solving P with initial domains $Dx_0 = [0.0..0.5]$, $Dy_0 = [0.8..1.5]$, $Dp_1 = [1.3..1.4]$ and $Dp_2 = [ln(2)/5]$ narrows the remaining unbounded domains to:

$$y_{min1} \in [0.881..0.891], \qquad y_{max1} \in [1.090..1.102], \qquad y_{area} \in [1.282..1.300],$$
$$y_{min2} \in [0.884..0.894], \qquad y_{max2} \in [1.447..1.462], \qquad y_{time} \in [3.908..3.967].$$

Notwithstanding the uncertainty, these results do prove that with p_1 within $[1.3..1.4]$ (an acceptable uncertainty in the manufacturing process), all limit cycle requirements are safely guaranteed. Moreover, they offer some insight on the requirements showing, for instance, the area to be the most critical constraint.

5   The SIR Model of Epidemics

The SIR model [12] is a well-known model of epidemics which divides a population into three classes of individuals and is based of the ODE system:

$$\frac{dS(t)}{dt} = -rS(t)I(t) \qquad \frac{dI(t)}{dt} = rS(t)I(t) - aI(t) \qquad \frac{dR(t)}{dt} = aI(t) \qquad (3)$$

where S are the susceptibles, individuals who can catch the disease;

I are the infectives, individuals who have the disease and can transmit it; R are the removed, individuals who had the disease and are immune/dead; r and a are positive parameters.

The model assumes that the total population is constant $N=S(t)+I(t)+R(t)$ and the incubation period is negligible. Parameter r accounts for the efficiency of the disease transmission (proportional to the frequency of contacts between susceptibles and infectives) and a measures the recovery rate from the infection.

Important questions in epidemic situations are: whether the infection will spread or not; what will be the maximum number of infectives; when will it start to decline; when will it ends; and how many people will catch the disease.

In the following study we will use the extended CCSP framework to answer each of the above questions. We use the data reported in the British Medical Journal (4th March 1978) from an influenza epidemic that occurred in an English boarding school (taken from [12]): a single boy (from a total population of 763) initiated the epidemic and the evolution of the number of infectives is available daily, from day 3 to the end of the epidemic (day 14). The goal of our study is to predict what would happen if a similar disease occurs in a different place, say a small town with a population of about 10000 individuals. Moreover, if there is a vaccine to that disease, what would be the vaccination rate necessary to guarantee that the maximum number of infectives never exceeds some predefined threshold, for example, half of the total population.

5.1   Using an Extended CCSP for Predicting Epidemic Behaviour

The first step for solving the above problem is to characterize an epidemic disease which is similar to the one reported in the boarding school.

The classical approach would be to perform a numerical best fit approximation to compute the parameter values r' and a' that minimize the residual: $\sum_{j=1}^{m} \left(I(t_j) - I_{t_j} \right)^2$ where $I_{t_1}, \ldots, I_{t_m}$ are the infectives observed at times $t_1, \ldots, t_m$, and $I(t_1), \ldots, I(t_m)$ their respective values predicted by the SIR model (3) with $r = r'$ and $a = a'$. In [12] this method is used to compute $r = 0.00218$ and $a = 0.44036$ with a residual of 4221.

An alternative approach, possible in a constraints framework, is to relax the imposition of the "best" fit and merely impose a "good" fit, requiring, for example, that the residual does not exceed 4800.

Such problem can be represented as an extended CCSP P with a CSDP constraint and a numerical constraint. The CSDP constraint P_S, represents the evolution of the susceptibles and infectives (the 1st and 2nd components of the model) during the first 14 days (in the equations the r parameter is multiplied by 0.01 re-scaling it to the interval [0..1]; the best fit value is thus re-scaled to $r=0.218$). This CSDP contains several Value restrictions for associating variables with: the initial values of the susceptible (s_0) and infective (i_0); the parameter values (r and a); and the values of the infective at times $3, \ldots, 14$ ($i_3, \ldots, i_{14}$). The numerical constraint defines the residual (R) from the above variables ($i_3, \ldots, i_{14}$) and the observed values (constants $k_3, \ldots, k_{14}$).

CCSP $P = (X, D, C)$ where:

$$X = \ < s_0, i_0, r, a, i_3, \ldots, i_{14}, R >$$
$$D = \ < Ds_0, Di_0, Dr, Da, Di_3, \ldots, Di_{14}, DR >$$
$$C = \{\ P_S(s_0, i_0, r, a, i_3, \ldots, i_{14}), R = \sum_{j=3}^{14} (i_j - k_j)^2 \}$$

Assuming very wide initial parameter ranges ($Dr=Da=[0..1]$), the "good" fit requirement can be enforced by solving P with the residual initial domain $DR=[0..4800]$ (the values of the susceptible and infective are initialized accordingly to the report: $Ds_0=762$, $Di_0=1$). Solving P (enforcing global hull consistency) with precision 10^{-6}, the parameter ranges are narrowed from $[0..1]$ to:

$r \in [0.213..0.224]$, $a \in [0.423..0.468]$

Once obtained the parameter ranges that may be considered acceptable to characterize epidemic diseases similar to the one observed, the next step is to use them for making predictions in the context of a population of 10000 individuals.

In this case a single CSDP constraint represents the first two components of the model together with ODE restrictions associating variables with the predicted values (besides the Value restrictions to associate variables with the parameter values r and a and the initial values s_0 and i_0). A Maximum restriction represents the infectives maximum value i_{max} and a First restriction represents the time of such maximum t_{max}. A Last restriction represents the duration t_{end} of the epidemics as the last time that the number of infectives exceeds 1. Finally a Value restriction represents the number of people s_{25} that are still susceptible at a time (25) safely after the end of the epidemics.

Solving such problem with the parameters ranging within the previously obtained intervals $Dr=[0.213..0.224]$ and $Da=[0.423..0.468]$, the initial value domains $Ds_0=9999$ and $Di_0=1$, and all the other variable domains unbounded, the results obtained for these domains indicated that:

$i_{max} \in [8939..9064]$ clearly suggesting the spread of a severe epidemics;
$t_{max} \in [0.584..0.666]$ and $t_{end} \in [20.099, 22.405]$ predicting that the maximum will occur during the first 14 to 16 hours, starting then to decline and ending before the 10th hour of day 22;
$s_{25} \in [0..0.001]$ showing that everyone will eventually catch the disease.

If the administration of a vaccine is considered at a rate λ proportional to the number of infectives then, the differential model must be modified into:

$$\frac{dS(t)}{dt} = -rS(t)I(t) - \lambda S(t) \quad \frac{dI(t)}{dt} = rS(t)I(t) - aI(t) \quad \frac{dR(t)}{dt} = aI(t) + \lambda S(t)$$

The requirement that the maximum of infectives cannot exceed half of the population is represented by adding the constraint $i_{max} \le 5000$. Solving this CCSP with the λ initial domain $[0, 1.5]$, its lower bound is raised up to 0.985 indicating that at least such vaccination rate is necessary to satisfy the requirement.

6   Conclusion

This paper extends the Continuous Constraint framework enabling the declarative expression of system dynamics, traditionally modelled by means of parametric differential equations. This is particularly important for decision support applications where one is interested in finding the range of parameters for which some constraints on the solutions of such differential equations are met.

Previous approaches rely on the generation of numerical solutions (either by traditional or constraint based numerical methods) that have to be subsequently tested for the satisfaction of constraints. Given the non-linearity nature of these constraints, a potentially very large number of values (or intervals) for the problem parameters have to be tested passively (possibly with Monte Carlo techniques that only provide probabilistic measures of satisfaction).

The constraint approach proposed in this paper makes an active use of complex constraints, making it more expressive and fully declarative. Although the paper focuses on these features, we intend to assess its efficiency in the future, and explore alternative algorithms to solve CSDPs, namely those that have been proposed to obtain tighter ODE enclosures [6, 8].

Acknowledgements

This work was partly supported by Project Protein (POSI /33794/SRI/2000), funded by the Portuguese Foundation for Sc. and Tech.

References

1. Benhamou, F., McAllester, D., Van Hentenryck, P.: CLP(Intervals) revisited. Logic Programming Symposium, MIT Press (1994) 124-131.
2. Cruz, J., Barahona, P.: Handling Differential Equations with Constraints for Decision Support. Frontiers of Combining Systems, Springer (2000) 105-120.
3. Cruz, J., Barahona, P.: Global Hull Consistency with Local Search for Continuous Constraint Solving. 10th Portuguese Conference on AI.. Springer (2001) 349-362.
4. Cruz, J., Barahona, P.: Maintaining Global Hull Consistency with Local Search for CCSPs. Global Constrained Optimization Constraint Satisfaction, France (2002).
5. Cruz, J.: Constraint Reasoning for Differential Equations. PhD thesis, Univ. Nova Lisboa, Portugal, submitted (2003).
6. Deville, Y., Janssen, M., Van Hentenryck, P.: Consistency Techniques in ODEs. Principles and Practice of Constraint Programming. 162-176, Springer, (1998).
7. Sam-Haroud, D., Faltings, B.V.: Consistency Techniques for Continuous Constraints. Constraints 1(1,2) (1996) 85-118.
8. Janssen, M., Van Hentenryck, P., Deville, Y.: Optimal Pruning in Parametric Differential Equations. Principles Practice of Constraint Programming. Springer (2001).
9. L'homme, O.: Consistency Techniques for Numeric CSPs. IJCAI, (1993) 232-238.
10. Montanari, U.: Networks of Constraints: Fundamental Properties and Applications to Picture Processing. Information Science 7(2) (1974) 95-132.
11. Moore R.E.: Interval Analysis. Prentice-Hall, Englewood Cliffs, NJ (1966).
12. Murray, J. D.: Mathematical Biology, 2nd Edition, Springer (1991)
13. Nedialkov, N.S.: Computing Rigorous Bounds on the Solution of an IVP for an Ordinary Differential Equation. PhD thesis, Univ. of Toronto, Canada (1999).
14. Lohner, R. J.: Einschliebung der Lsung gewhnlicher Anfangs- und Randwertaufgaben und Anwendungen, PhD thesis, Universitt Karlsruhe, 1988.
15. J-F. Puget and P. Van Hentenryck. A Constraint Satisfaction Approach to a Circuit Design Problem. Journal of Global Optimization, MIT Press (1997).
16. Shampine, L.F.: Numerical Solution of ODEs. NY, Chapman and Hall (1994).
17. Spitznagel, E.: Two-Compartment Pharmacokinetic Models. C-ODE-E. Harvey Mudd College, Claremont, CA (1992).

A Wealth of SAT Distributions
with Planted Assignments

Tassos Dimitriou

Athens Information Technology
tassos@ait.gr

Abstract. Evaluation of local search heuristics for constraint satisfaction and satisfiability problems is based on the generation of instances that are guaranteed to be satisfiable. One popular method for creating hard satisfiable instances is the use of *complete* search procedures to filter out unsatisfiable instances. This approach however has two problems; first, the size of instances produced is limited considerably and second, the generated instances are far from being random.

Although one can generate satisfiable instances by reducing certain computational problems to SAT, it is not known how a similar generator can be developed *directly* for k-SAT. In this work we provide a generator for an *optimization* version of k-SAT that has certain useful properties. First, we show how to produce weighted instances of MAX k-SAT where one seeks to maximize the *weight* of satisfied clauses. Second, we provide a nice characterization of the optimal solution; in our model not only we know how the optimal solution looks like but we also prove it is *unique*. Finally, we show that our generator has *tunable complexity*; by appropriately choosing parameters one can control the hardness of the generated instances leading to an easy-hard-easy pattern in the search complexity for good assignments and a new type of phase transition.

1 Introduction

The use of distributions for generating random SAT instances is an important set of benchmark problems for evaluating local search SAT heuristics. Mitchell and Levesque[10], however, have shown that the value of any study whose goal is to evaluate the performance of any SAT algorithm depends upon the proper selection of formula distribution and parameter values. The key property of such "useful" distributions is that they generate instances that appear to be *critically constrained*; at a certain ratio of variables to constraints instances become extremely hard to solve and the average computational cost of finding a solution scales exponentially with the size of the input formula[11, 5]. One important limitation, however, in the applicability of these distributions is the fact that they generate both satisfiable and unsatisfiable instances. Since the unsatisfiable instances must be filtered out with the use of *complete* methods before they can be used in the evaluation of any incomplete SAT heuristic, the size of the problem instances considered unfortunately becomes limited.

F. Rossi (Ed.): CP 2003, LNCS 2833, pp. 274–287, 2003.
© Springer-Verlag Berlin Heidelberg 2003

One way to create a satisfiable distribution of SAT formulas is to start from any assignment (say the all ones assignment) and then create a random formula at the critical region (for the case of 3-SAT this would be when the ratio of clauses to variables is about 4.26). Of course the generated formula doesn't necessarily satisfy the chosen assignment so one would have to delete all unsatisfied clauses first. This method would guarantee that the formula generated is satisfiable. The problem with this approach is that the formula is usually very easy to solve. Local search heuristics easily come up with assignments for such formulas mainly because of the abundance of satisfying assignments around the chosen one. Thus the generated instances are biased and not really on the critical region.

In a similar setting Asahiro, Iwama and Miyano[2] were able to provide hard instances with a single satisfying assignment using a variant of the previous method. Although the AIM approach was an improvement over the previous method, again the generated instances were biased and far from being random. Furthermore, the generator lacked any control parameter that could be used to produce a reasonable phase transition. Other efforts in this area include the translation of cryptographic problems into SAT instances[4, 9]. Although the translated instances are guaranteed to be satisfiable, in practice they are very hard to solve because their solution reduces to a simple exhaustive search of the SAT space (as is usually the case for the cryptographic counterparts). This suggests that these problems are outside the realm of current SAT solvers and cannot be used for their evaluation. Furthermore, the translated instances are neither scalable nor tunable in their hardness.

These drawbacks were remedied in part by Achlioptas et al.[1] where a generator for *satisfiable instances only* was developed. This generator was based on transforming an instance of the quasigroup completion problem (QCP) to a formula that is guaranteed to be satisfiable. The generator starts with a complete Latin square of order N, that is an $N \times N$ table where each entry has one of the N possible colors and where there are no repeated colors in any row or column. Then the colors from a fraction p of the entries get deleted leaving a partial table that is guaranteed to be satisfiable. This instance is then translated to an equivalent Boolean formula which is made k-SAT with the usual introduction of new variables. As demonstrated by Achlioptas et al., this generator has a number of important characteristics. The first is the ability to finely control the hardness of the generated instances by tuning the value of p. The second is the appearance of a new kind of phase transition in the space of problem instances. It is interesting to note however that while the QCP generator can finely control the hardness of the generated instances, Achlioptas et al. ask whether a similar generator can be developed directly for k-SAT.

In this work we introduce a generator for MAX k-WSAT formulas, a *weighted* and *optimization* version of k-SAT. In MAX k-WSAT each clause has a number associated to it, called *weight* or *multiplicity*, which denotes how many copies of the clause appear in the formula. While in MAX k-SAT one is looking for an assignment that maximizes the number of satisfied clauses, in the weighted version of MAX k-SAT the goal is to find an assignment that essentially maximizes the *sum of weights* of the satisfied clauses, since such clauses contribute their multiplicities to the overall number of satisfied clauses. Clearly MAX k-SAT reduces to this problem by making all weights equal to one.

Our generator has a number of important characteristics. The first one is a theoretical result proving that the optimal assignment is *unique*. Since any satisfiability heuristic when feed with an instance from our generator will try to maximize the number/weight of satisfied clauses, this characterization provides algorithm designers with an *a priori* knowledge of the optimal assignment. We call this solution the *hidden* or *planted* assignment. Thus by knowing what to expect, algorithm designers will be able to evaluate better the effectiveness of their algorithms. The second characteristic is the appearance of an easy-hard-easy pattern in the search complexity for good assignments. Traditional phase phenomena usually involve a transition from satisfiable to unsatisfiable instances in the search space. This is not the case here since our generator outputs only instances that can be satisfied in the MAX k-SAT sense. Under the right choice of parameters however, an easy-hard-easy pattern emerges that makes it possible to test algorithms on hard generated instances only. Finally, we were able to link this behavior with a new threshold phenomenon which is related to the uniqueness of the hidden assignment. Below the threshold, there are other solutions that achieve equal total weight and differ from the hidden one in a few variables. Above the threshold however, the hidden assignment becomes the unique optimal solution. Thus there exists a transition from a phase where there are more than one good assignments to a phase where the optimal assignment is unique. The point to be made is that this transition coincides with the hardest to solve problem instances.

2   The Model

We start our exposition by showing how to generate instances of the MAX 2-WSAT problem. Later in Section 4, we will extend our results to instances of MAX k-WSAT. In general, MAX k-WSAT consists of Boolean expressions in Conjunctive Normal Form, i.e. collection of clauses in which every clause consists of exactly k literals and has a positive integer weight associated to it denoting the multiplicity of each clause in the formula. Given an instance of this problem, one is looking for an assignment to the variables that satisfies a set of clauses with maximum total weight. It is clear that MAX 2-WSAT is NP-hard as MAX 2-SAT reduces to it by setting all weights equal to one. In this work we will present a generator for a degenerate version of MAX 2-WSAT, in which *all* weights to the clauses are either β or $\beta + 1$, where β is a fixed integer greater than 0. While this simplification may seem very restrictive at first sight, it is all we need to create a generator of k-SAT instances with useful computational properties. Furthermore, even when $k = 2$ the problem still remains NP-hard.

To generate a formula with the above properties we first start with $2n$ variables, n green and n blue, create the clauses and finally assign weights to them. Here we adopt the view of working with weights directly and not actually creating multiple instances of the same clause as proofs become simpler. Furthermore, as explained in Section 5.1, this leads to faster implementations of heuristics treating WSAT formulas. We call our model $\mathcal{F}_{n,p,\delta}$, where n indicates the number of variables of each color and p, δ are the parameters used to control the maximum total weight achieved by the hidden assignment (Figure 1). The user can choose any values for δ and p provided $p + \delta \leq 1$. The reason for this restriction will become clear in Lemma 1. We do not include the weight β in the definition of the model as this will be set to a specific value later on (Lemma 2).

The model $\mathcal{F}_{n,p,\delta}$ (with super-clauses)

1. Start with $2n$ variables, n green and n blue.
2. **(Create the formula)** For every pair of variables x, y, irrespective of their color and without repetitions, add to the formula the "super-clause" $c(x,y) = (x\bar{y} + \bar{x}y)$.
3. **(Assign the weights)**
   - For all clauses $c(x,y)$, with probability p set the weight $w(x,y)$ of the clause equal to $\beta + 1$, otherwise set it equal to β.
   - For all clauses $c(x,y)$, such that x, y have *different* colors *and* $w(x,y) = \beta$, with probability $\delta(1-p)^{-1} \leq 1$ increase the weight of the clause to $\beta + 1$.

Fig. 1. Description of the generator.

By looking at Figure 1 one should observe that the "clauses" $c(x,y)$ are not really clauses in the ordinary 2-SAT sense. In fact, $c(x,y) = (x + y) \cdot (\bar{x} + \bar{y})$. We chose, however, to work with super-clauses as the results are much easier to describe and the passing to ordinary 2-SAT expressions is again easy. We will denote the two simple clauses of $c(x,y)$ by $c^1_{x,y} = (x + y)$ and $c^2_{x,y} = (\bar{x} + \bar{y})$. It is also clear from the model that the generated formulas are "dense" in that they consist of all possible combinations of the $2n$ variables. Thus it makes no sense to try to satisfy all super-clauses but it makes sense to try to satisfy a suitable subset of those that incurs the maximum possible total weight. We will be able to show later on (Theorem 1) that the best assignment is the one that has the green variables set to true and the blue set to false (or vice versa). However, before we proceed with our main result we need a few definitions and preliminary lemmas.

Definition 1. *A super-clause is called monochromatic if it consists of variables of the same color.*

Definition 2. *An assignment is said to split the variables if exactly n variables are set to true and n are set to false (irrespective of their color).*

We are now ready to prove the first fact that is a simple consequence of the model $\mathcal{F}_{n,p,\delta}$.

Lemma 1. (Monochromatic clauses are lighter on average)
If x, y have the same color then $w(x, y) = \beta+1$ with probability p and β otherwise. If x, y have different colors then $w(x, y) = \beta + 1$ with probability $p + \delta$ and β otherwise.

Proof. The first statement is obvious since by definition monochromatic clauses have weight $\beta+1$ with probability p. To prove the second statement observe that a non-monochromatic clause will have weight $\beta + 1$ if it was initially assigned this weight, or if it had weight β and with probability $\delta(1 - p)^{-1}$ increased its weight. The probability of these two events is $p + (1 - p)\delta(1 - p)^{-1} = p + \delta$.   □

This lemma provides an alternative definition for our model and is used in the proof of the optimality of the hidden assignment. The next lemma is used to reduce the space of good assignments. Since our goal is to be able to generate formulas where assignments are planted, this lemma allows algorithm designers to test their algorithms by knowing what to expect.

Lemma 2 (Look for split assignments). *When the weight β is at least n^2, the best assignments split their variables.*

Proof. Suppose there is an assignment A that achieves total weight W and has $0 < k < n$ variables set to True and $2n - k$ variables set to False. We will show that by choosing β accordingly, there exists a better assignment that achieves greater weight and has its variables split.

Consider the bipartite graph (A, B) formed by putting the true variables on side A and the false on side B. Furthermore, for every pair (x, y) where $x \in A$ and $y \in B$ add the edge from x to y and assign to it the weight of the super-clause $c(x, y)$.

Consider now an arbitrary super-clause $c(x, y) = (x\bar{y} + \bar{x}y)$. This super-clause simply spells the fact that x and y must have *different* truth values in order for $c(x, y)$ to be satisfied and contribute its weight $w(x, y)$ to the total sum. Thus, given the particular assignment A, there can be at most $k(2n - k)$ satisfied super-clauses and the total weight W incurred by A will be equal to the sum of the edges' weights in the bipartite graph. Let there be m edges of weight $\beta + 1$ and the rest with weight β. Then the total weight will be equal to $W = m(\beta + 1) + [k(2n - k) - m]\beta = k(2n - k)\beta + m$, where the m term comes from the edges with weight $\beta + 1$. In any case, $m \leq k(2n - k) < n^2$. Thus,

$$W < k(2n - k)\beta + n^2 = n^2\beta - [(n - k)^2\beta - n^2]. \tag{1}$$

Consider now any assignment A' that have its variables split and let m' be the number of edges of weight $\beta + 1$. By the same argument as before the total weight W' achieved by A' will be at least $W' = n^2\beta + m' \geq n^2\beta$. Since $0 < k < n$, by choosing $\beta = n^2$ we see that the term $[(n - k)^2\beta - n^2]$ in (1) is always positive, thus making the weight W smaller than the weight W' of any assignment with split variables. We conclude that it is always best to look for split assignments.   □

Observe that the previous discussion is valid only if the super-clauses are satisfied as a whole or at least in the NAESAT sense (NAESAT for Not All Equal SAT, is the variant of SAT where we don't allow all literals in a clause to have the same truth value). To pass to ordinary 2-SAT models, since most algorithms are not restricted in their search for assignments, we modify the model by assigning the weight $w(x,y)$ to each of the clauses $c^1_{x,y}$ and $c^2_{x,y}$ of the super-clause. Call this new model $\mathcal{F}'_{n,p,\delta}$. Now, we have to take into account the weight incurred by these clauses even if both literals have the same truth value.

Lemma 3 (Equivalence of the two models). *An assignment A achieves total weight W for a formula f generated according to $\mathcal{F}_{n,p,\delta}$ if and only if it achieves total weight $W + c_f$ when the formula is generated according to $\mathcal{F}'_{n,p,\delta}$, where c_f in a constant that is easily computable and depends only on the particular formula f.*

The proof is very similar to the proof of Lemma 2 and is omitted from this extended abstract. Again we only have to look for split assignments in the new model since by choosing $\beta = n^2$, the best assignments for formulas generated according to $\mathcal{F}'_{n,p,\delta}$ split their variables.

3   Characterizing the Optimal Assignment

In the previous section we showed that the two models are equivalent. Thus from now on we will work only with formulas that consist of super-clauses. To simplify things further we will work only with split assignments since by Lemma 2 we are allowed to do so.

Our goal in this section is to show that for a suitable choice of the parameter δ, the optimal assignment is one that has the green variables set to True and the blue variables set to False (or vice versa).

Definition 3. *We say an assignment has distance k from the optimal one, where $0 \leq k \leq \frac{n}{2}$, if it has split the variables and furthermore it has k blue and $n - k$ green variables set to True.*

Thus in some sense the value of k counts the distance from the planted assignment which has $k = 0$ and as we will show in a while it is the optimal one with high probability.

Theorem 1 (Optimality of hidden assignment). *There is a constant such that for values of $\delta \geq \Omega(\sqrt{(1-p)\ln n/n})$, the assignment which has only the green variables set to true is optimal with high probability.*

Proof. We only give a sketch of the proof here since this result is provided only for completeness. We leave a full proof for the final version of the paper. The first lemma we need is one which shows that assignments of distance k from the hidden one achieve total weight close to their expected values. This is easy to prove since by using Chernoff bounds we can estimate with great accuracy the

---

The model $\mathcal{F}_{n,p,\delta}^k$ (with super-clauses)

1. Start with $2n$ variables, n green and n blue.
2. **(Create the formula)** For every k-tuple of variables $x_1, x_2, \ldots, x_k$, irrespective of their color and without repetitions, add to the formula the "super-clause"

$$c(x_1, x_2, \ldots, x_k) = \neg(x_1 x_2 \cdots x_k + \bar{x}_1 \bar{x}_2 \cdots \bar{x}_k).$$

3. **(Assign the weights)**
   - For all clauses $c(x_1, x_2, \ldots, x_k)$, with probability p set the clause weight $w(x_1, x_2, \ldots, x_k)$ equal to $\beta + 1$, otherwise set it equal to β.
   - For all *non-monochromatic* clauses $c(x_1, x_2, \ldots, x_k)$, such that $w(x_1, x_2, \ldots, x_k) = \beta$, with probability $\delta(p-1)^{-1}$ increase the weight of the clause to $\beta + 1$.

Fig. 2. Generator for k-WSAT formulas.

total weight achieved by the given assignment. An immediate corollary of this result is that no assignment of distance greater than some predefined k_0 achieves better weight than the hidden one.

The second lemma we need is one which proves that any assignment of distance smaller than a predefined value k_1, has a neighboring assignment that achieves even better weight except of course the hidden assignment. This last result suggests that these assignments cannot be optimal. Combining the two lemmas, we get that the hidden assignment is optimal with high probability for the range of δ described in the theorem. $\square$

The optimality theorem characterizes implicitly the values of p for which it is safe to assume that the hidden assignment is optimal with high probability. Since by the definition of the model we know that δ must be less than $1 - p$, it is clear that the theorem will be true for values of p satisfying $1 - p \geq \Omega(\sqrt{(1-p)\ln n}/n)$ or equivalently

$$p \leq 1 - c\frac{\ln n}{n} \tag{2}$$

for some constant c. Thus our approach cannot be used for all formulas, but only for formulas where the monochromatic clauses are not too heavy, as indicated by Equation 2 and Lemma 1.

4   Extension to MAX k-WSAT

To generate MAX k-WSAT instances , $k \geq 3$, we follow the same approach as for the 2-WSAT case. We start again with $2n$ variables, n green and n blue. The only difference now is that clauses consist of exactly k variables. We call our model $\mathcal{F}_{n,p,\delta}^k$, where k indicates that we working with k-WSAT formulas (Figure 2).

As in the 2-WSAT case, the super-clauses are satisfied only when clause variables have different truth values. To pass to ordinary k-SAT formulas observe that $c(x_1, x_2, \ldots, x_k) = (x_1 + x_2 + \cdots + x_k)(\bar{x}_1 + \bar{x}_2 + \cdots + \bar{x}_k)$. We then have to modify the model by assigning the weight $w(x_1, x_2, \ldots, x_k)$ to each of the sub-clauses of the super-clause. A lemma similar in spirit to Lemma 2 shows that again we have to concentrate our search for split assignments by setting $\beta = n^2$.

5 Experimental Results; The Case for $p = \frac{1}{2}$

In this section we present experimental results showing that random instances can be generated by our model in such a way that easy and hard instances can be predictable in advance. Our motivation is to provide developers of local search SAT heuristics with a challenging set of k-SAT instances in which the optimal solution is known beforehand. For ease of exposition we decided to work with formulas satisfying $p = \frac{1}{2}$. Thus monochromatic clauses get weight $\beta + 1$ with probability a half while non-monochromatic clauses get that weight with probability $\frac{1}{2} + \delta$. Although we leave a more detailed experimentation for a final version of this paper we will see that even in this case the formulas generated exhibit some very important properties.

5.1 Locating the Hard Instances

The local search procedure we used for our tests is a modified version of Walk-Sat[13] which we describe below. The main reason for choosing WalkSat is because it is one of the best performing SAT procedures and because we believe that these results on hard instances will be applicable to other SAT heuristics as well. In subsequent work we plan to perform a more thorough analysis using a more representative collection of search methods. To apply WalkSat to formulas with weights on clauses (even if the weights degenerate to the two values β and $\beta + 1$) we need the intuitive modification of the algorithm shown on Table 1. Basically what this table says is replace "number of satisfied clauses" with "weight of satisfied clauses". The rest of the algorithm remains the same. Also observe how the weighted version reduces to the classic WalkSat when all weights are set to one. The reason for this modification is to avoid the extra overhead in running time caused by having multiple copies of the same clause. Since each clause would have to appear at least $\beta = n^2$ times, this would greatly slow down the execution time of any SAT heuristic.

In the experiments that follow we chose to work with MAX 2-WSAT formulas to illustrate the fact that these formulas become extremely difficult to optimize in direct contrast to ordinary 2-SAT formulas, which are solvable in linear time[3]. Although we leave a more detailed analysis of k-WSAT formulas, $k \geq 3$, for the final version of this paper, preliminary work shows that they exhibit similar properties to the 2-WSAT case. In all the figures that follow each sample point was computed after generating 1000 random instances of MAX 2-WSAT.

Table 1. Changes to the basic WalkSat algorithm.

	WalkSat	**Weighted version of WalkSat**
Goal	Maximize *number* of satisfied clauses	Maximize *weight* of satisfied clauses
Strategy	Pick a random unsatisfied clause and flip the variable that results in the smallest decrease in the *number* of satisfied clauses	Pick a random unsatisfied clause and flip the variable that results in the smallest decrease in the *weight* of satisfied clauses

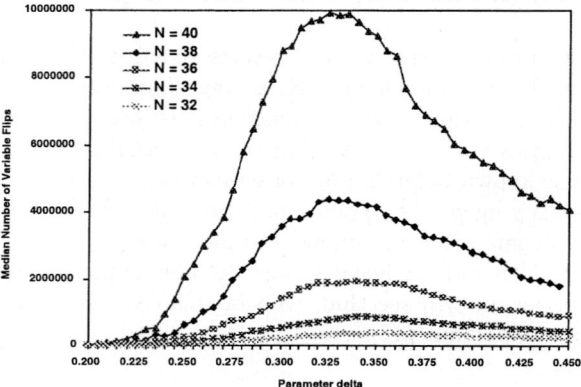

Fig. 3. Median number of total variable flips for random 2-WSAT formulas as a function of the parameter δ.

Figure 3 shows the *median* of the *total number of variable flips* required by WalkSat to locate an assignment that achieves the maximum total weight (as is implied by the hidden assignment) for formulas of size $n = 32, 34, 36, 38$ and 40. As can be seen, an easy-hard-easy pattern emerges which results in an exponential increase in computational cost in the hardest region similar to the behavior of ordinary 3-SAT formulas [11, 5]. This figure also suggests the existence of a *critical region* although we cannot link this behavior with the length of the formulas as all of them have the same number of clauses. We were able, however, to relate this behavior with a phase transition in structural properties of the WSAT instances. It is perhaps worthwhile to comment a little on the shape of the curves in Figure 3. Although the computational cost follows an easy-hard-easy pattern, the second "easy" region where δ is large is no longer very easy compared to the first region where δ is small. This is reminiscent of the behavior of 3-SAT(B), the *bounded decision* versions of 3-SAT defined by Zhang[15], where one is looking for an assignment that violates no more than B constraints. When $B = 0$, one has 3-SAT; when B is the optimal solution cost, one has MAX 3-SAT. Thus, such distributions lie in some sense between the decision problem and its optimization counterpart and like the WSAT instances exhibit easy-hard-"less easy" patterns.

In general, as was shown in [6, 16, 14, 15] and other works, the phase transitions of some NP-complete *decision* problems follow easy-hard-easy patterns and the phase transitions of some NP-hard *optimization* problems follow easy-hard patterns. Thus one may ask, where is the easy-hard behavior of the WSAT formulas? We performed some initial experiments and found that actually WSAT formulas exhibit the behavior of optimization problems, but only when p grows larger than $1/2$. Thus the value of $p = 1/2$ is middle ground and by increasing the value of p one gets a wealth of distributions with higher computational costs and easy-hard patterns.

5.2   Phase Transition

An important characteristic of Figure 3 is that the transition region becomes narrower (occurs for a smaller range of δ) for larger values of n when at the same time the peak shifts to the left as n is increased. Our goal now is to demonstrate a relationship between the hard region and a phase transition in the structural properties of the WSAT formulas.

It is clear that we cannot have a SAT/UNSAT transition as all instances are unsatisfiable. A more profound concept related to phase transitions is the *backbone* ratio of a problem which is the ratio of its variables that take the same values in *all* solutions, i.e. they are *fully constrained*. A phase transition in such a case has the the backbone ratio raise from nearly 0 to nearly 1, with the hardest instances lying around the 50% point. In the case of WSAT formulas, however, we chose not to work with backbones because now solutions are planted and, provided that δ is sufficiently large, solutions are also unique. Thus there is no point in trying to relate the hardness peak with the backbone as there is essentially only one solution and most of the variables have a fixed value. (Furthermore, such results were examined by Zhang[15] on MAX-3SAT formulas.) We were able, however, to relate WSAT's behavior with the probability of uniqueness of the hidden assignment, which is the crucial structural property of WSAT formulas.

In Figure 4(a) we show how the probability that there exist good assignments other than the planted one changes as a function of the parameter δ for $n = 32, 36, 40$. In the same figure we also included the *normalized* cost of WalkSat for locating the hidden assignment (bell shaped curves). Observe now the clear movement to the left and the remarkable correspondence between the hardness peak and the point where the uniqueness probability of the optimal solution is about 65%. The main empirical observation we can draw from this picture is that *the hardest 2-WSAT formulas for WalkSat lie at the point where about 65% of the formulas have the planted solution as the optimal one.* We named the WalkSat algorithm in this conclusion since we expect the location of the peak to depend on the particular heuristic used. Other heuristics may peak at different values but in any case we expect their behavior to be similar to WalkSat's.

In Figure 4(a) there is a clear shift in computational cost as the value of n increases. In Figure 4(b) we observe a similar behavior for the uniqueness probability of the optimal solution for a larger range of values. Observe how

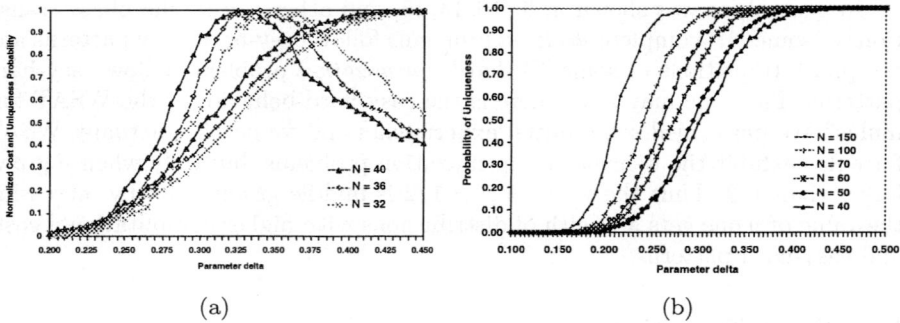

(a)   (b)

Fig. 4. (a) Normalized cost and phase transition. The bell shaped curves correspond to median number of flips normalized to 1 while the sigma shaped curves show the uniqueness probability of the hidden assignment. (b) Phase transition for various values of n.

the threshold function sharpens up for larger values of n, like the satisfiability threshold function for random k-SAT formulas[11]. One difference however is that curves do not cross. Instead the curves are moving to the left, something that is to be expected since the hidden solution is with high probability unique for values of δ larger than $c\sqrt{\ln n/n}$, for some constant c (set $p = 1/2$ in Theorem 1).

All this discussion leads naturally to the question of how one can generate the hardest 2-WSAT formulas. Given some arbitrary value of n how can we determine the value of δ that results in the most difficult to solve instances? The answer is given by *finite-size scaling*[8], in which the horizontal axis is rescaled by a quantity that is a function of n. This has the effect of slowing down the transition for larger values of n and mapping the different curves into a single "universal" curve from which one can derive by working backwards the point where the hardest instances lie.

Figure 5(a) shows the result of rescaling the curves of Figure 4(b). The uniqueness probability is plotted against δ', a rescaled version of δ equal to $\delta' = \delta n^{\epsilon/2}\sqrt{1-\epsilon}$, where $\epsilon = 0.56$. It is perhaps instructive to describe how we derived the rescaling factor $n^{\epsilon/2}\sqrt{1-\epsilon}$. Theorem 1 (with $p = 1/2$) tells us that the planted solution is unique when $\delta = \Omega(\sqrt{\ln n/n})$. This led us to believe that the threshold point will also be a function of this quantity, something like $\delta_0 = c\sqrt{\ln n/n}$, for some (unknown) constant c. If n is to be rescaled and become $n^{1-\epsilon}$, for some ϵ, then the translated point must become $\delta'_0 = c\sqrt{\frac{\ln n^{1-\epsilon}}{n^{1-\epsilon}}}$. By some algebraic manipulation, δ_0 and δ'_0 are related by the equation $\delta'_0 = \delta_0 n^{\epsilon/2}\sqrt{1-\epsilon}$ which, when applied to all values of δ, gives us the universal match shown in Figure 5(a). Finally, Figure 5(b) demonstrates how the computational cost for various values of n collapses into a universal curve. To obtain this, we first normalized the curves Figure 3 and then applied the rescaling described previously. We see clearly that the critical point is when the *rescaled* δ is equal to 0.60 which corresponds to the 65% uniqueness probability in Figure 5(a).

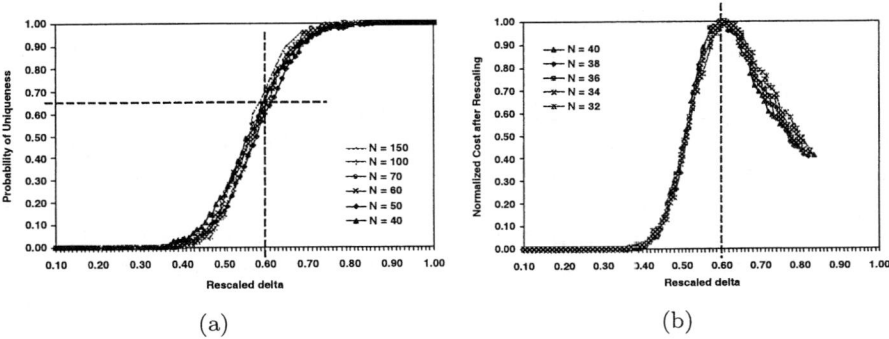

Fig. 5. (a) Phase transition for various values of n after rescaling. (b) Computational cost for various values of n after rescaling.

6   Conclusions and Future Research

In this work we presented a generator for instances of MAX k-WSAT in which every clause has a weight or multiplicity associated with it and the goal is to maximize the total number of satisfied clauses. We showed that our generator produces formulas whose hardness can be finely tuned by a parameter δ that controls the weights of the clauses. Under the right choice of this parameter an easy-hard-easy pattern in the search complexity emerges which is similar to the patterns observed for traditional SAT formulas and complete methods. Furthermore, the distributions examined here seem to be in the middle ground between decision and optimization problems. When p, the other parameter of our generator, is set to $1/2$, the computational cost of finding the optimal solution exhibits an easy-hard-"less easy" pattern which is not typical of optimization problems as should be the case for MAX-WSAT formulas. However, as we hinted in Section 5.1, when the value of p increases, instances should behave more like traditional optimization problems and easy-hard patterns should emerge.

We were able to relate this behavior of WSAT formulas with a new type of phase transition in the structural properties of the generated instances. In particular, we showed how the hardness peak corresponds to a point where there is a transition from formulas which have many optimal assignments to formulas where the optimal assignment is unique. And this is perhaps the most important characteristic of our generator; under the right choice of the parameter δ, not only we know that the optimal solution is unique but we also know that it must assign (a predefined) half of the variables to TRUE and half to FALSE. In conclusion, we believe that our generator will be useful in the analysis and development of future SAT heuristics since by knowing what to expect algorithm designers will better test the effectiveness of their search procedures.

Our work leaves open some ground for further improvements and research. One direction would be to eliminate the weights from the clauses and produce a generator for [MAX] k-SAT instances directly. It seems that the weights are only used to limit the search for split assignments so one may ask if there is a way to do this using no weights. Unfortunately, at this point we don't know how this can be done without losing the structure of the hidden assignment and the a priori knowledge of optimality. Another important question is if the quadratic number of clauses in the case for 2-WSAT (and the $O(n^k)$ number for the general case) can be reduced to linear. Is it possible to generate formulas, even with weights, in which the number of clauses is linear and the hidden assignment is preserved? This would speedup the execution time of algorithms and would further strengthen the hardness results of the generated instances.

Finally, our model is reminiscent of graph theoretic models in which a solution is planted in advance (such as in the clique or coloring problem). The purpose of planting solutions to such problems is to come up with algorithms that are able to recover the planted structure, hoping that these algorithms will behave equally well in real life instances. Our findings for WalkSat do *not* imply that such an algorithm is unlikely to exist for the WSAT model we propose here. In fact Theorem 1 suggests that such a specialized algorithm may exist. Coming up with such an algorithm may pinpoint the important characteristics of the WSAT formulas and may further help in the simplification of them as well as in the evaluation of other SAT search methods.

Acknowledgements

The author wishes to thank Christos Papadimitriou and the anonymous referees for some very useful comments.

References

1. Achlioptas D., Gomes, C., Kautz H. and Selman B. Generating satisfiable problem instances. In *Proc. AAAI-00*, 2000.
2. Asahiro, Y., Iwama, K. and Miyano, E. Random generation of test instances with controlled attributes. In *Second DIMACS Challenge on Cliques, Coloring and Satisfiability*, October 1993.
3. Bengt Aspvall, Micahel F. Plass and Robert E. Tarjan. A linear-time algorithm for testing the truth of certain quantified boolean formulas. *Information Processing Letters*, 8(3):121-123, March 1979.
4. J. Crawford and M. Kearns. Instances for learning the parity function. In [7].
5. I. Gent and T. Walsh. The SAT Phase Transition. In *Proc. ECAI-94*, 105-109.
6. I. Gent and T. Walsh. The TSP Phase Transition. *Artif. Intel.*, 88:349–358, 1996.
7. H. Hoos. SATLIB. A collection of SAT tools and data, 1999. www.informatic.tu-darmstadt.de/AI/SATLIB.
8. Kirkpatrick, S. and Selman, B. Critical behavior in the satisfiability of random Boolean expressions. *Science*, 264, 1297-1301, 1994.
9. Massacci, F. Using WalkSAt and RelSat for cryptographic key search. In *Proc. IJCAI-99*, 199, pp. 290–295.
10. Mitchell, D. and Levesque, H.J. Some pitfalls for experimenters with random SAT. *Artificial Intelligence*, Vol. 81(1-2), 1996, 111-125.
11. Mitchell, D., Selman, B., and Levesque, H.J. Generating hard satisfiability problems. *Artificial Intelligence*, Vol. 81(1-2), 1996.

12. Monasson, R., Zecchina, R., Kirkpatrick, S., Selman, B., and Troyansky, L. Determining computational complexity from characteristic 'phase transitions'. In *Nature*, Vol. 400(8), 1999.

13. B. Selman, H. A. Kautz and B. Cohen. Local search strategies for satisfiability testing. In *Second DIMACS Challenge on Cliques, Coloring and Satisfiability*, 1993.

14. J. Slaney and T. Walsh. Backbones in Optimization and Approximation. In *Proc. IJCAI-01*, 2001.

15. W. Zhang. Phase transitions and backbones of 3-SAT and MAX 3-SAT. In *Proc. CP-2001*.

16. W. Zhang and R. E. Korf. A study of complexity transitions on the asymmetric Travelling Salesman Problem. *Artificial Intelligence*, 81:223–239, 1996.

Redundant Modeling
for the QuasiGroup Completion Problem

Iván Dotú, Alvaro del Val, and Manuel Cebrián

Departamento de Ingeniería Informática
Universidad Autónoma de Madrid
ivan.dotu@ii.uam.es,delval@ii.uam.es,meathook@terra.es

Abstract. The Quasigroup Completion Problem (QCP) is a very challenging benchmark among combinatorial problems, and the focus of much recent interest in the area of constraint programming. [5] reports that QCPs of order 40 could not be solved by pure constraint programming approaches, but could sometimes be solved by hybrid approaches combining constraint programming with mixed integer programming techniques from operations research. In this paper, we show that the pure constraint satisfaction approach can solve many problems of order 45 in the transition phase, which corresponds to the peak of difficulty. Our solution combines a number of known ideas –the use of redundant modeling [3] with primal and dual models of the problem connected by channeling constraints [13] – with some novel aspects, as well as a new and very effective value ordering heuristic.

1 Introduction

The Quasigroup Completion Problem (QCP) is a very challenging benchmark among combinatorial problems, which has been the focus of much recent interest in the area of constraint programming. It has a broad range of practical applications [5]; it has been put forward as a benchmark which can bridge the gap between purely random instances and highly structured problems [6]; and its structure as a multiple permutation problem [13] is common to many other important problems in constraint satisfaction. Thus, solutions that prove effective on QCPs have a good chance of being useful in other problems with similar structure.

In this paper, we present several techniques that together allow us to solve significantly larger QCPs than previously reported in the literature. Specifically, [5] reports that QCPs of order 40 could not be solved by pure constraint programming approaches, but could sometimes be solved by hybrid approaches combining constraint programming with mixed integer programming techniques from operations research. We show that the pure constraint satisfaction approach can solve many problems of order 45 in the transition phase, which corresponds to the peak of difficulty. Our solution builds upon some known ideas, such as the use of redundant modeling [3] with primal and dual models of the problem connected by channeling constraints [13], with some new twists. For example,

F. Rossi (Ed.): CP 2003, LNCS 2833, pp. 288–302, 2003.

we will consider models consisting of only channeling constraints, without any primal or dual constraints, and we demonstrate empirically for the first time the usefulness of channeling constraints linking several pairs of models of a problem, an idea that was considered, but only theoretically, in [15] and [14]. In addition, we present a new value ordering heuristic which proves extremely effective, and that could prove useful for many other problems with multiple models. The idea underlying this heuristic, which originates in the work of [15, 11] for single permutation problems, is that selecting a value for (say) a primal variable is in practice in the presence of channeling constraints also a choice of the dual variables corresponding to that value; therefore we can use *variable* selection heuristics on the dual variables to choose the *value* to assign to the previously chosen primal variable. Finally, we show how redundant constraints can be used to "compile arc consistency into forward checking", that is, to ensure that the latter has as much pruning power as the former but at a much lesser cost in constraint checks.

It is interesting to note that our approach involves only binary constraints, which seems to go against common wisdom about their limitations —when contrasted with the use of non-binary constraints such as alldiff [8]— in solving quasigroup completion problems [9]. It is certainly an interesting issue, which we plan to address in the future, whether the use of alldiff could yield even better results than our approach when coupled with other ideas in this paper[1].

The idea of redundant modeling was first introduced by [3]. The benefits of adding redundant constraints to some given model to improve pruning power were well-known in the literature, but [3] went a step further by considering the redundant combination of full models of a problem, where the models may involve different sets of variables. This combination is achieved by specifying how the various models relate to each other through *channeling constraints*, which provide a mapping among assignments for the different models. The combined model contains the original but redundant models as submodels. The channeling constraints allow the sub-models to cooperate during constraint-solving by propagating constraints among the problems, providing an extra level of pruning and propagation which results in a significant improvement in performance.

Another important modeling idea that we use is that of permutation problems (see e.g. [11, 13]). A constraint satisfaction problem (CSP) is a permutation problem if it has the same number of variables as values, all variables have the same domain and each value can be assigned to a unique variable. Thus, any solution can be seen as assigning a permutation of the values to the variables. In the same manner, a multiple permutation problem has some (possibly overlapping) sets of variables, each of which is a permutation problem. QCP is a paradigmatic example of a multiple permutation problem.

The structure of this paper is as follows. We introduce in Section 2 the quasigroup completion problem (QCP) and present a number of alternative models

---

[1] Besides the obvious computational limitations in running large experimental suites of hard QCP problems, we were limited in this aspect by the unavailability of open source alldiff code.

that can be used to represent it; we then consider in Section 3 various ways of combining these models. Section 4 presents some experimental data to compare the relative merits of the various models, which will lead us to choose one particular model as the best one among those tested. Sections 5 and 6 are the core of the paper, where we apply the new value ordering heuristic to QCPs and then further tune our solution by adding some redundant constraints that allow us to replace the relatively expensive arc consistency with forward checking. Section 7 concludes the paper with some ideas for further research.

2   Models of Quasigroups

A quasigroup is an ordered pair $(Q, \cdot)$, where Q is a set and $\cdot$ is a binary operation on Q such that the equations $a \cdot x = b$ and $y \cdot a = b$ are uniquely solvable for every pair of elements a, b in Q [5]. The order n of the quasigroup is the cardinality of the set Q. A quasigroup can be seen as an $n \times n$ multiplication table which defines a Latin Square, i.e. a matrix which must be filled with "colors" (the elements of the set Q) so that the colors of each row are all distinct, and similarly for columns. Early work on quasigroups focused on quasigroup existence problems, namely the question whether there exist quasigroups with certain properties, solving several significant open mathematical problems [10]. We focus instead on the quasigroup completion problem (QCP), which is the (NP-complete [4]) problem of coloring a partially filled Latin square. QCP share with many real world problems a significant degree of structure, while at the same time allowing the systematic generation of difficult problems by randomly filling the quasigroup with preassigned colors. It is thus ideally suited as a testbed for constraint satisfaction algorithms [6]. Experimental studies of the problem have confirmed its interest for research, by for example helping to discover important patterns in problem difficulty such as heavy-tailed behavior [7].

Among the kind of structure that has been identified in many constraint satisfaction problems, and which is shared by QCPs, is that of permutation problems. These are constraint satisfaction (sub)problems with the same number of variables as values, where a solution is a permutation of the values [13]. Each row and column of a Latin Square defines a permutation problem, thus the QCP is a multiple permutation problem with $2n$ intersecting permutation constraints (n row permutation constraints and n column permutation constraints).

QCPs appear in a number of real world applications such as conflict-free wavelength routing in wide band optical networks, statistical design, and error correcting codes [5].

2.1   Models

Let P be a problem. To model P as a CSP we need to fix a set of variables X, a function F that maps each variable $x_i \in X$ to a domain of possible values, and a set of constraints C defined over the variables in X, so that the set of solutions in the traditional CSP sense corresponds in some exact mathematical sense to the solutions of P, if any. The triple (X, F, C) is then a *model* of P. There is usually more than one model for any given problem, but whichever we choose, we need to ensure that it fully characterizes the problem. Cheng et al. [3] define two models $M_1 = (X_1, F_1, C_1)$ and $M_2 = (X_2, F_2, C_2)$ of a problem P to be *redundant* when the following conditions hold:

1. M_1 and M_2 are models of P respectively, i.e. each of them fully characterizes the set of solutions to P.
2. $X_1 \cap X_2 = \emptyset$.

Redundancy is a double-edged sword: it can help propagation by allowing more values to be pruned at any given point in the search, but it can also hinder it by forcing it to process a larger set of constraints. Fortunately, more fine grained distinctions are possible, as we might choose to combine only parts of various models. We could not speak of combining models if we don't use their respective sets of variables, but it will often be advantageous (as we will see) to drop some of the constraints from one or more models that become redundant when making the combination. If we do this, however, we must be careful to ensure the correctness and completeness of the combined model.

Several models can be defined for QCPs, as described next. While all models have the same logical status, it is common to distinguish between *primal* and *dual* models. The distinction is only a matter of perspective, specially in permutation problems, where variables and values are completely interchangeable.

2.2 Primal Model

The primal model for QCP, as usually defined, takes variables to represent the cells of the Latin Square for a QuasiGroup, and the domains of possible values consist of the colors to be assigned. Thus, the *primal variables* are the set $X = \{x_{ij} \mid 1 \leq i \leq n, 1 \leq j \leq n\}$ where x_{ij} is the the cell in the $i - th$ row and $j - th$ column, and n is the order of the quasigroup, i.e. the number of rows and columns. All variables share a common initial domain, namely $D = \{k \mid 1 \leq k \leq n\}$, where each k represents a color. The *primal constraints* in turn can be divided into row constraints and column constraints. If we choose a binary representation, there are n^2 row constraints of the form $x_{ij} \neq x_{il}$ where $x_{ij}, x_{il} \in X$ and $j \neq l$, which means that two cells in the same row must not have the same color; and n^2 column constraints of the form $x_{ij} \neq x_{lj}$ where $x_{ij}, x_{lj} \in X$ and $i \neq l$, which means that two cells in the same column must not have the same color. Equivalently, we could use just $2n$ *alldiff* constraints [8], one for each row and column. Semantically this makes no difference.

The primal model (or pr model for short) provides a complete characterization of the problem.

2.3 Row Dual Model

There are different ways to formulate dual models for a multiple permutation problem. Here we consider dual models for each of the permutation subproblems

(as opposed to a single dual model of the primal problem), and group them
by row and column, to obtain two complete models of QCPs. In the *row dual
model*, the problem is reformulated as the question of which position (column)
in a given row has a given color. The *row dual variables* are the set $R = \{r_{ik} \mid
1 \leq i \leq n, 1 \leq k \leq n\}$ where r_{ik} is the kth color in the ith row. The domain of
each variable is again the set $D = \{j \mid 1 \leq j \leq n\}$, but now the values represent
columns, i.e. the positions in row i where color k can be placed. The *row dual
constraints* are similar to the primal constraints. There are n^2 constraints of the
form $r_{ik} \neq r_{il}$, where $r_{ik}, r_{il} \in R$ and $l \neq k$, which means that two colors in the
same row must not be assigned to the same column; and n^2 constraints of the
form $r_{ik} \neq r_{jk}$ where $r_{ik}, r_{jk} \in R$ and $i \neq j$, which means that the same color in
different rows must not be assigned to the same column. Alternatively, we could
have *alldiff*$(r_{i1}, \ldots, r_{in})$ for every row i, and *alldiff*$(r_{1k}, \ldots, r_{nk})$ for every color
k.

A simple symmetry argument shows that this model also fully characterizes
the problem.

2.4   Column Dual Model

The second dual model is composed of the set of dual models for each column
permutation constraint, representing the colors in each column. The *column dual
variables* are the set $C = \{c_{jk} \mid 1 \leq j \leq n, 0 \leq k \leq n\}$ where c_{jk} is the kth
color in the jth column. All variables have domain $D = \{i \mid 1 \leq k \leq n\}$, where
i represents the rows where color k can be placed in the jth column. Similar to
the row dual model, we have *column dual constraints* of the form $c_{jk} \neq c_{jl}$ where
$c_{jk}, c_{jl} \in C$ and $k \neq l$, which means that two colors in the same column must
not be assigned to the same row; and of the form $c_{jk} \neq c_{lk}$ where $c_{jk}, c_{lk} \in C$
and $j \neq l$, which means that the same color in different columns must not be
assigned to the same row.

This model also fully characterizes the problem. We refer to the combination
of both dual models as the `dl` model.

3   Combining the Models

A *channeling constraint* for two models $M_1 = (X_1, F_1, C_1)$ and $M_2 = (X_2, F_2, C_2)$
is a constraint relating variables of X_1 and X_2 [3]. We will consider the following
kinds of channeling constraint:

- *Row Channeling Constraints:* Constraints for the n row permutation constraints, linking the primal model with the row dual model:

$$x_{ij} = k \Leftrightarrow r_{ik} = j.$$

- *Column Channeling Constraints:* Corresponding to the n column permutation constraints, they link the primal and the dual column models:

$$x_{ij} = k \Leftrightarrow c_{jk} = i.$$

— *Triangular Channeling Constraints:* These constraints link both dual models, closing a "triangle" among the three models:

$$c_{jk} = i \Leftrightarrow r_{ik} = j.$$

Given two or more redundant, complete models, we can obtain a combined model by simply implementing all the models and linking them by channeling constraints. Thus the full combined model or `pr-dl-ch2-model` resulting from the above models is the model consisting of primal and dual variables and constraints, linked together by row and column channeling constraints[2]. More generally, as long as a combined model includes a complete model of the problem as a submodel, we are free to add any set of variables or constraints from other models, with the only requirement that in order to add a constraint all its variables must belong to the combined model. Thus for example, given the primal variables and constraints, we may choose to add any number of dual and channeling constraints as long as the corresponding variables are also added. For example, we may decide to use only the row dual variables together with the row dual constraints and/or row channeling constraints. Nothing is lost by not including parts of the dual models, since all the necessary information is present in the primal model.

In fact we can take this as far as removing all primal and dual constraints! Walsh [13] shows that arc consistency on the channeling constraints for a permutation problem dominates in pruning power over arc consistency over the binary not-equal constraints. Intuitively, this means that nothing is gained by adding the not-equal constraints once we have the channeling constraints. Note that this doesn't prove the superiority of a model with only channeling constraints over, say, the primal model, as the former also has many more variables and constraints; this issue is empirically examined later. It is important however to show that the model consisting of primal and dual variables, with *only* row and column channeling constraints, but *without* the primal or dual constraints (i.e. alldiff or not-equal) is also a complete model of the problem. We refer to this model as the *bichanneling model* or `ch2`:

Proposition 1. *The bichanneling model is equivalent to the primal model, hence it provides a full characterization of QCPs.*

Proof. If the two models had the same set of variables and associated domains, we could define equivalence just as having the same set of solutions. Since that's not the case here, we need to provide instead a one-to-one mapping between solutions of either model.

Let us say that a primal assignment, or P-assignment for short, is an assignment of values to all the primal variables, and a PD-assignment an assignment to all primal and dual variables.

The proposition can then be phrased more exactly in terms of the following two claims.

---

[2] We don't consider adding the triangular constraints until later.

Claim 1: Any P-assignment A which satisfies the (primal) alldiff constraints can be extended to a PD-assignment B which satisfies the channeling constraints. To extend A to B, we just pick each label $x_{ij} = k$ from A and set $r_{ik} = j$ and $c_{jk} = i$ in B. To see that B is well-defined, note that every r_{ik} gets assigned, since A must use all available colors in order to fill row i in accordance with the primal constraints; and that any given r_{ik} is assigned at most once, since otherwise we would have $x_{ij} = x_{ih}$ for distinct columns j and h, in contradiction with the fact that A satisfies the primal constraints. Similarly for any c_{jk}. Hence B is well-defined, and it satisfies the channeling constraints by construction.

Claim 2: Any PD-assignment B satisfying the row and column channeling constraints, is such that its primal subset A satisfies the primal constraints. Suppose not. Then B assigns the same value k to two primal variables x_{ij} and x_{ih} for $j \neq h$ (or the completely symmetric case where it is row indexes that vary). But since B satisfies the row channeling constraints, B should satisfy $r_{ik} = j$ and $r_{ik} = h$, which is impossible. $\square$

Yet another combined model we will consider later is the *trichanneling model*, or ch3 for short, which adds the triangular channeling constraints to ch2, but still keeps away from the primal and dual constraints. Given the above proposition, ch3 is also a complete model, and redundantly so.

4   Comparing Models

Our initial results on the various models were in fact quite favorable to the bichanneling model. In order to present them, we need to say a few words about the experiments in this paper. First, in order to make our results comparable with others appearing in the literature, all instances were generated using the *lsencode* generator of QCPs, kindly provided to us by Carla Gomes. This generator begins by randomly coloring an empty quasigroup using a local search algorithm, and then randomly decoloring some cells. Hence all problems in our suites have a solution. All instances are of the "balanced" kind, which are known to be the hardest [5]; and most instances correspond to problems with 60% cells preassigned, which is close to the transition phase and corresponds to a peak in problem hardness. Second, all experiments are run with a slightly optimized variant of van Beek's GAC library, which comes as part of the CSP planning system CPLAN [12], and which implements generalized arc consistency (though in our case we only need its binary version, i.e. MAC [1]). As discussed below, neither CBJ nor nogood learning seem to help in QCP, contrary to the experience in many other domains, hence they are disabled in our tests. Also, all experiments use the min-domain variable selection heuristic, which we found to be uniformly the best among the ones we tried (see also [3, 11] and the discussion in Section 5).

In our initial tests, we found that the bichanneling model ch2 could solve many problems that were out of reach for the other models, including many order 35 and some order 40 quasigroups with 60% preassigned cells. Table 1 shows mean time for solved instances and median time for the whole sample,

Table 1. Experimental results for the bichanneling model, MAC, no value ordering.

% preassign →		20%		42%		80%	
order	% solved	mean	median	mean	median	mean	median
30	100%	0.94	0.93	0.43	0.25	0.03	0.02
35	100%	1.99	1.99	0.71	0.53	0.05	0.05
40	100%	4.98	4.98	2.51	1.09	0.08	0.08

	60% preassigned			
order	% solved	timeout	mean (solved)	median (all)
30	18%	100	48.74	100
35	22%	3600	903.07	3600
40	10%	3600	1751.90	3600

Table 2. Comparison of various models using MAC and no value ordering.

pr		pr-dl		pr-dl-ch2		ch2	
time	checks	time	checks	time	checks	time	checks
1.45	1.30	1.93	1.69	1.90	1.69	1	1

both in seconds, and percent of solved instances within the given timeout (also in seconds) for sets of 50 instances of orders 30, 35 and 40, and 20, 42, 60 and 80% preassignment. (These results are also plotted in Figure 1 later.)

Our data confirm the existence of a peak of difficulty around 60% preassignment [5], whereas problems were trivially solvable with all other percentages we tried. Even though the results were promising, specially when compared with other models, they were also disappointing, in that the number of problems that we could solve in the transition phase was rather limited for various dimensions. (Note that in these cases, median time is the same as timeout because less than 50% of instances were solved.) Nevertheless, we decided to pursue further the bichanneling model based on the somewhat anecdotal evidence of its clear superiority over other models. As the following sections show, we succeeded in this goal.

For the sake of a more systematic comparison, we present here a simple comparison of the various models. Due to limited available time, we chose the 29 easiest problems (as measured with the approaches developed later) for order 30 quasigroups with 60% preassignment. These are still relatively difficult problems in the phase transition: the ch2-model took a total of 6624 seconds on the 19 problems (66%) in the sample that were solved with all tested models in less than 1800 seconds, yielding an average of 348.6 seconds per solved problem, and a mean (over the whole sample) of 574.16s. Table 2 shows the result of a comparison between various models on this sample. The table provides the ratios in the accumulated data in time and constraint checks over the solved problems, relative to the performance of ch2. Note that all models tried exactly the same number of assignments in all problems, empirically confirming the fact that arc consistency has identical pruning power in all four models.

We conjecture that these ratios will increase with problem difficulty. But there is little point on belaboring these data, as much better solutions are available, as discussed in the following sections.

5   Variable and Value Ordering

It is well know that the order in which we make our choices as to which variable to instantiate, and with which value, can have a major impact in the efficiency of search. As already pointed out, all the results reported in this paper use the *min-domain* variable ordering heuristic (often denoted dom), which at each search node chooses a variable with the smallest domain to instantiate. The reason for this is simply that we obtained better results with it than with other alternatives we tried. These included more fine-grained heuristics such as dom+degree and dom/degree, yielding further confirmation to previous results by [3] and [11] on simple permutation problems. These other heuristics would often make no difference with respect to dom[3], but when they did it was most often to the worse. (We did not perform a systematic comparison, though.) We also considered a number of variants of the above which took into account the (primal or dual) model to which variables belong, e.g. selecting only among primal variables, or only among primal variables unless some dual variable had a singleton domain, etc. These variants would often significantly underperform the previous ones, so we didn't pursue them further.

[15] introduced a *min-domain value ordering heuristic* for use when dual variables are available during the search. The idea is to choose the value such that the corresponding dual variable has the smallest current domain. To generalize this idea to multiple permutation problems, we need a way to take into account the two dual models. The one that worked best is what we might call the *min-domain-sum value selection heuristic* (or more briefly vdom+, the 'v' standing for value). Once a primal or dual variable is selected, we need to choose a value for it. Since any such value corresponds to one specific variable from each of the two other models, we select the value whose corresponding two variables have a minimal "combined" domain. Specifically, say we have chosen x_{ij}. Then we choose a color k from its currently active domain for which the sum of the current domain sizes of r_{ik} and c_{jk} is minimal among the currently available colors for x_{ij}. Similarly, if the chosen variable is a dual one, say r_{ik}, we choose a column j for this variable as a function of the current domain sizes of the corresponding variables x_{ij} and c_{jk}.

The results when the first combined model was used with the min-domain-sum value ordering heuristic were quite surprising, as it outperformed previous tests in three orders of magnitude in some cases. For example, for the instance

---

[3] This is not much of a surprise, since the degree of a variable (number of constraints in which it is initially involved) cannot discriminate much among variables in a QCP; though this could also depend on details of implementation such as whether constraints are generated for variables that are explicitly or implicitly assigned by the initial coloring.

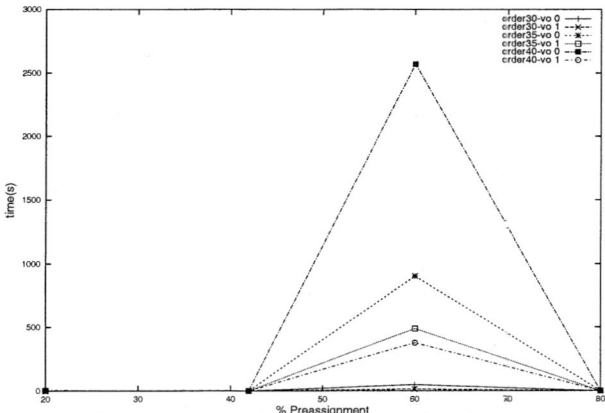

Fig. 1. Mean solution time on QCPs of order 30, 35 and 40 with (vo1) and without (vo0) value ordering.

Table 3. The min-domain value ordering heuristics at the phase transition, using MAC.

order	mean	median	% solved	timeout
30	148.84	174.11	68%	1000
35	533.43	163.48	84%	3600
40	732.94	1010.82	68%	5000
45	1170.81	2971.40	56%	6000

bqwh-35-405-5.pls (balanced instance of order 35 and 60% preassigned cells) it took 2905 secs without value ordering and only 0.40 secs with it. For a more general picture, Figure 1 plots the data of Table 1, obtained with lexicographic value ordering, against the results over the same sample with com+ value ordering.

Encouraged by this performance, we generated a set of 100 balanced instances of orders 30, 35, 40 and 45, with 60% preassignment. Table 3 shows median and mean time in seconds (the latter taken only over solved instances), percent of solved instances and timeouts, in solving these instances with the new variable ordering heuristic.

These results are significantly better than those previously found in the literature, as we can solve over 50% of balanced QCPs of order 45 at the phase transition. Recall that, as pointed out in the introduction, [5], reports that pure constraint programming approaches, even when using specialized forms of arc consistency for non-binary alldiff constraints and a commercial solver, could not solve any problem of order 40 in the phase transition.

We considered other ways of combining domain sizes such as minimizing the product of the corresponding domain sizes (*min-domain-product* or vdom*), and their corresponding maximizing versions, without success. Perhaps there is no deep reason why vdom+ was so clearly superior to vdom*. Maximizing versions were clear underperformers, and there is a reasonable explanation for it. For concreteness, consider choosing a value with the maximal combined domain of the corresponding variables, e.g. a value k for a primal variable x_{ij} such that $domain\text{-}size(r_{ik}) + domain\text{-}size(c_{jk})$ is maximal (over the colors available for x_{ij} at the current stage of search). While large domain sizes are usually indication of less tightness, and thus could be conjectured to capture the idea, often cited in connection with value ordering, of selecting a value which is "more likely to lead to a solution", in this case they have exactly the opposite effect. When $x_{ij} = k$ is the maximal labeling according to this criteria, the domains of r_{ik} and c_{jk} are immediately pruned into singletons. Hence a maximizing choice produces maximal pruning, which is the opposite of what is desired. And conversely, heuristics such as vdom+ choose values that produce the least pruning.

6   Compiling AC to FC with Redundant Constraints

Our next and last step in improving our solution derived from an examination of the pruning behavior of the bichanneling model with arc consistency. Suppose x_{ij} is assigned k at some point during the search. The GAC implementation of CPlan begins by checking arc consistency for constraints with a single uninstantiated variable, i.e. doing forward checking, which forces the domains of r_{ik} and c_{jk} to become the singletons $\{j\}$ and $\{i\}$ respectively, and also prunes, for each $h \neq k$, j from r_{ih}, and i from c_{jh}. Arc consistency will further discover (if not already known at this stage of the search):

- $x_{ih} \neq k$ for any column $h \neq j$, since otherwise $r_{ik} = h \neq j$;
- hence also $c_{hk} \neq i$ for any column $h \neq j$, since otherwise $x_{ih} = k$;
- similarly, $x_{hj} \neq k$ for any row $h \neq i$, since otherwise $r_{ik} = h \neq j$;
- hence also $r_{hk} \neq j$ for any row $h \neq i$, since otherwise $x_{hj} = k$;

It is not difficult to show that GAC cannot prune any more values as a result of an assignment to a primal variable, unless one of the listed prunings reduces a domain to a singleton. All these are useful prunings, but GAC does much more work than needed to obtain them. Each one of the pruned values – one for each $x_{ih}, x_{hj}, c_{hk}, r_{hk}$, potentially $4(n-1)$ pruned values and variables from a single assignment – requires GAC to check all the constraints in which the corresponding variables are involved, namely $2(n-1)$ or $(n-1)$ constraints for, respectively, the primal and dual pruned variables (further, in the CPlan implementation all affected variables have all their values tested, even if at most one will be pruned). This is wasted effort, as no additional pruning is achieved. One can however observe that most of the pruning power can be derived simply by assigning the variables whose domain became singletons (either directly through channeling constraints or indirectly when pruning a single value results in a singleton) and doing forward checking on them. To see that the remaining values pruned by GAC (namely the second and fourth items above) are also pruned by FC with the trichanneling model, observe that $c_{hk} \neq i$ since otherwise $r_{ik} = h \neq j$ using the corresponding triangular channeling constraint, and similarly $r_{hk} \neq j$ since otherwise $c_{jk} = h \neq i$.

Table 4. The ch3 and ch2 models compared, with value ordering.

	ch3-fc			ch2-ac			ratios	
order	acc. time	median	solved	acc. time	median	solved	acc. time	median
30	6445.44	153.04	78%	9557.83	174.11	68%	1.48	1.14
35	29691.18	152.16	86%	45341.22	163.48	85%	1.53	1.07
40	33015.14	637.18	73%	48682.04	1010.82	68%	1.47	1.59
45	38569.95	1650.52	59%	61469.78	2971.40	56%	1.59	1.80

	checks			visits		
order	ch3-fc	ch2-ac	ratio	ch3-fc	ch2-ac	ratio
30	29886	80206	2.68	431	658	0.15
35	114572	279003	2.44	1617	218	0.13
40	205247	445790	2.17	2769	331	0.12
45	108276	321632	2.97	1489	236	0.16

We remark that the same effect can be achieved in different ways, e.g. the bichanneling model supplemented with the dual not-equal constraints also allows forward checking to derive the same consequences.

Table 4 compares the bichanneling model ch2, using only row and column channeling constraints with GAC, versus the trichanneling model ch3 with the three kinds of channeling constraints using only FC, in both cases with the min-domain-sum value ordering. Each sample consists again of 100 balanced instances with 60% preassignment;the accumulated values are over the problems solved by both approaches within the given timeout. The median times are on the other hand over the whole sample. Accumulated times are in seconds while the other accumulated values are in millions of checks and tried assignments respectively.

These tables show that there is a significant improvement in time with the ch3 model using only FC, and this can be traced to the large savings in number of checks. On the other hand, ch3 with FC tries almost one order of magnitude more assignments, which arise from the fact that it must instantiate the variables associated to a given assignment made in the search tree in order to extract the same consequences as AC with ch2; these added tried assignments do not however translate into any more checks or more true backtracking.

The results in this table are not however as straightforward to obtain as the formal result on the equivalent pruning power may suggest. Indeed, our first attempt at implementing ch3 resulted in a slight but noticeable slowdown! On further examination, we realized that this was due to the implementation of the min-domain variable ordering heuristic, which could select many other variables with a singleton domain before the variables associated with the last assignment; as a result, obtaining the same conclusions as AC could be significantly delayed. We solved the problem by keeping a stack of uninstantiated variables with singleton domain, and modifying the min-domain heuristic to pop the most recent variable from that stack whenever it was not empty. This ensures that FC considers those variables that have just become singletons immediately. The solution has nevertheless an ad-hoc flavor, and suggests that for domains such as QCPs, where propagation often forces a value for variables as opposed to merely pruning part of their domain, a more SAT-like propagation may be more indicated; in other words, it is not always sufficient to rely on the min-domain heuristic to propagate in a timely fashion forced values.

Finally, the following figures display a more detailed picture of how ch2 and ch3 compare, showing the time taken to solve all 100 problems in each set, sorted by difficulty, for order 40 and 45 quasigroups at the phase transition. As it can be seen, the ch3 model is almost always superior, but there are some anomalies that are worth investigating further.

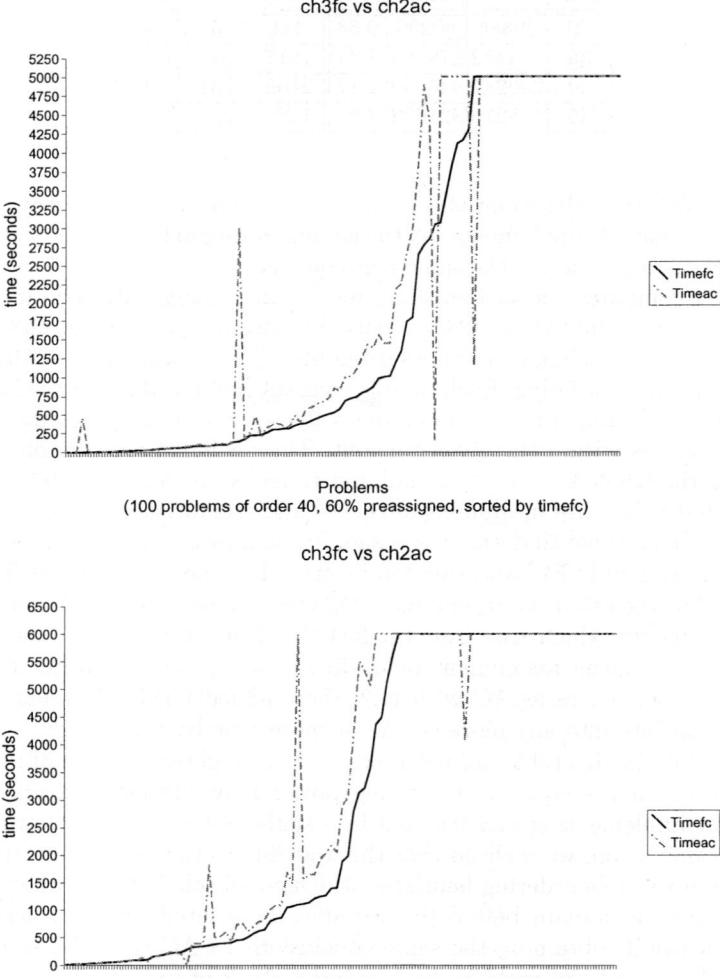

ch3fc vs ch2ac

Problems
(100 problems of order 40, 60% preassigned, sorted by timefc)

ch3fc vs ch2ac

Problems
(100 problems of order 45, 60% preassigned, sorted by timefc)

7 Conclusions and Future Work

In summary, we have shown in this paper that a pure CSP approach can handle quasi-group completion problems significantly larger than was thought possible, using appropriate models, value ordering heuristics, and algorithms, even in the absence of global alldiff constraints. Our solution is arguably much simpler than the hybrid CSP/OR approach developed in [5] yet it seems to clearly outperform it, saving distances for different machines, implementations and execution environments. It would be interesting to see whether the combination of the ideas of this paper with either alldiff constraints or OR techniques could yield further improvements in our ability to solve larger QCPs. For example, we mentioned that the same effect achieved by introducing triangular channeling constraints would be achieved by reintroducing instead the dual not-equal constraints, which in turn could be replaced by dual alldiff constraints.

We have introduced two novel aspects within redundant modeling in multiple permutation problems:

- A novel value ordering heuristic which takes into account the primal and both dual models, and which generalizes for multiple permutation problems ideas introduced in ([15, 11] for simple permutation problems. The speedup produced by this heuristic is quite remarkable, up to three orders of magnitude in some cases.
- The use of channeling constraints linking more than a single pair of models to provide forward checking with the same pruning power as arc consistency at a much smaller cost in constraint checks, and thus in performance, provided that ordering effects are taken into account in the min-domain variable selection heuristic.

Many issues remain to be explored. While we did try a number of alternatives to the presented value ordering heuristics without success, others may be more successful. There are some anomalies in the behavior of the ch3-fc approach vs ch2-ac which could be symptoms of more subtle effects than the ordering effects reported above, and which need to be explored. There is finally the issue of why CBJ and nogood learning did not help in this problem, which may in part suggest that in a sense randomness dominates over structure in QCPs, but which should at any rate be an incentive to develop more effective implementations of these techniques so that at least they do not hurt when they do not help.

References

1. C.Bessiere and J.C.Regin. Mac and combined heuristics: two reason to forsake FC (and CBJ?) on hard problems. In *2nd Int. Conf. on Principles and Practice of Constraint Programming* pp. 61–75, 1996.
2. J.Bitner and E.M.Reingold Backtrack programming techniques. In *Communications of the ACM* 18: 651–655.

3. B.M.W. Cheng, J.H.M. Lee, and J.C.K Wu. Speeding up constraint propagation by redundant modeling. In *2nd Int. Conf. on Principles and Practice of Constraint Programming*, pp. 91–103, 1996.
4. C. Colbourn. The complexity of completing partial latin squares. In *Discrete applied Mathematics*.
5. C. Gomes and D. B. Shmoys. The promise of LP to Boost CSP Techniques for Combinatorial Problems. In *CP-AI-OR'02*, pp. 291–305, 2002.
6. C. Gomes and D. B. Shmoys. Completing Quasigroups or Latin Squares: A Structured Graph Coloring Problem In *Proc. Computational Symposium on Graph Coloring and Extensions*, 2002.
7. C. Gomes, B. Selman, and H. Kautz. Heavy-tailed phenomena in satisfiability and constraint satisfaction problems. In *Journal of Automated Reasoning*, 24:67-100, 2000.
8. J-C. Regin. A filtering algorithm for constraints of difference in CSPs. In *Proc. AAAI'94*, pp. 362–367, 1994.
9. K. Sergiou and T. Walsh. The difference all-difference makes. In *Proc. IJCAI'99*.
10. J. Slaney, M. Fujita and M. Stickel. Automated reasoning and exhaustive search: Quasigroup Existence Problems. In *Computers and Mathematics with Applications*, 29:115–132, 1995.
11. Barbara M. Smith. Modeling a Permutation Problem. In *Proceedings of ECAI'2000 Workshop on Modeling and Solving Problems with Constraints*, 2000.
12. P. van Beek and X. Chen. CPlan: A Constraint Programming Approach to Planning. In *AAAI'99*, pp. 585–590, 1999.
13. T. Walsh. Permutation Problems and Channeling Constraints. In *LPAR-2001*.
14. Barbara M. Smith. Dual Models in Constraint Programming. School Computing Research Report 2001.02, University of Leeds, January 2001.
15. B.M.W. Cheng, K.M.F. Choi, J.H.M. Lee, and J.C.K Wu. Increasing Constraint Propagation by Redundant Modeling: an Experience Report. In *Constraints*, pp. 167–192, Kluwer Academic Publishers,1999.

Open Constraint Optimization

Boi Faltings and Santiago Macho-Gonzalez

Artificial Intelligence Laboratory (LIA)
Swiss Federal Institute of Technology (EPFL)
IN-Ecublens, CH-1015 Ecublens, Switzerland
{boi.faltings,santi.macho}@epfl.ch
http://liawww.epfl.ch/

Abstract. Constraint satisfaction has been applied with great success in *closed-world* scenarios, where all options and constraints are known from the beginning and fixed. With the internet, many of the traditional CSP applications in resource allocation, scheduling and planning pose themselves in *open-world* settings, where options and constraints must be gathered from different agents in a network. We define *open constraint optimization* as a model of such tasks.

Under the assumption that options are discovered in decreasing order of preference, it becomes possible to guarantee optimality even when domains and constraints are not completely known. We propose several algorithms for solving open constraint optimization problems by incrementally gathering options through the network. We report empirical results on their performance on random problems, and analyze how to achieve optimality with a minimal number of queries to the information sources.

1   Constraint Optimization in Distributed Systems

Constraint satisfaction and optimization has been applied with great success to resource allocation, scheduling, planning and configuration. Traditionally, these problems are solved in a *closed-world* setting: all variable domains and constraints are assumed to be completely known, then the problem is solved by a search algorithm.

With increasing use of the internet, many of the problems that constraint programming techniques are good at now pose themselves in a distributed setting. For example, in personnel allocation, it is possible to obtain staff from partner companies. In configuration, it is possible to locate part suppliers through the internet. Furthermore, problems may also involve *agents* with different and possibly conflicting interests, for example when allocating production resources among different factories.

Figure 1 illustrates the context we assume: a set of n agents wish to find an assignment to a set of variables that is optimal with respect to their preferences. A central CSP solver is tasked to find this solution, and queries the agents for their options and preferences using queries more(xi,di). Agents will return their options starting with the one they would most prefer as a solution, and then in

F. Rossi (Ed.): CP 2003, LNCS 2833, pp. 303–317, 2003.
© Springer-Verlag Berlin Heidelberg 2003

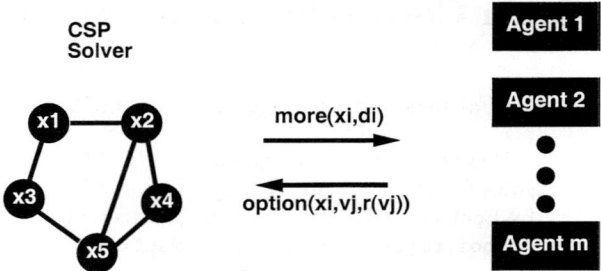

Fig. 1. Context of an open constraint optimization problem. The problem solver uses `more` messages to ask agents for additional values for a variable xi that extend its current domain di. Agents reply with `option` messages that indicate new values vj and their cost r(vj).

non-decreasing order of preference using `option(xi,vj,r(vj))` messages, where `vj` is a new value and `r(vj)` is its cost, a numerical value that reflects the degree of undesirability.

Such a scenario would arise for example when optimizing scheduling and resource allocation in a consortium of enterprises, planning travel using options for transportation and lodging found through search on the internet, or when configuring a product from parts found through electronic catalogs in the internet.

A straightforward way of solving such problems is to ask agents to first report all their values, and then use standard techniques such as branch-and-bound to compute the optimal solution. However, for reasons of privacy, computation or communication effort, agents may not wish to reveal more of their options and preferences than necessary to compute a solution. In this case, it will be better to query for values only as they are required to prove optimality of the solution. In this paper, we propose the framework of *open constraint optimization* as a model of such problems along with general algorithms for solving it.

In comparison with classical constraint optimization, open constraint optimization poses three challenges:

- since the domains and constraints are not completely known, many standard CSP and optimization methods such as consistency or branch-and-bound cannot be directly applied to such a problem. Also, in general it is not clear how to give any optimality guarantee, since the best options may not have been discovered yet.
- besides minimizing computation time, the primary objective is now to minimize the number of values and costs that the agents have to provide. This is important because communication through a network is orders of magnitude slower than computation, because there may be a significant cost involved in getting the extra options, and because agents would prefer to keep this information private.

– when agents are self-interested, there needs to be a mechanism to ensure that agents will report values and costs truthfully, since otherwise the optimization can not produce the correct result.

The first obstacle is that in an open environment, it is in general not possible to prove optimality of any solution, since options that are yet to be discovered may lead to a better solution. However, following an idea of Conen and Sandholm [9] for preference elicitation in auctions, optimality can be ensured if we assume that options are reported in decreasing order of preference. This is a key assumption that we will enforce as part of the definition of open constraint optimization problems. It is also very realistic in real-world settings: usually, agents will want to give their most preferred options first.

We present a model of open constraint optimization problems, show several sound and complete algorithms for solving them, and compare their performance. Provided that agents report information truthfully, our algorithms are sound and complete. We also show that they allow computing the required taxes for a Vickrey-Clark-Grove (VCG) tax mechanism that makes it in each agent's best interest to report information truthfully.

2   Related Work

The most closely related work is that on *interactive constraint satisfaction* ([1]) and *open constraint satisfaction* ([2]) which has addressed the issue of efficiently solving constraint *satisfaction* problems in open, distributed settings. In this paper, we are interested in constraint optimization problems, where the goal is not just to find a solution but also to prove that this solution has the minimal cost. This requires considerably different algorithms.

Open constraint optimization is related to dynamic constraint satisfaction, which allows constraints to be dynamically added and removed. Bessiere ([3]) has shown methods for dynamically adapting consistency computations to such changes. However, dynamic CSP methods require that the set of all possible domain values is known beforehand, and thus do not apply to an open setting. Another major difference is that in open constraint optimization changes are restricted to a monotonic ordering of domains and values, while DCSP allow adding and removing variables in any order.

Another related area is distributed CSP(DisCSP), investigated in particular by Yokoo ([4]) and more recently also other researchers. DisCSP does not require agents to announce the complete variable domains beforehand, so by its formulation it would also allow them to be open. The DisCSP formalism has also been extended to constraint optimization problems, with the most recent result being the ADOPT algorithm [5]. However, search algorithms for solving DisCSP rely on closed-world assumptions over variable domains for initiating backtracks and thus cannot be applied in an open-world context.

3   Assumptions and Notation

3.1   Constraint Optimization Problems

There exists a large variety of formalisms for modeling constraint optimization problems with *soft* constraints. In this paper, we assume that the problems are formulated as discrete weighted constraint optimization problems (WCOP). In a weighted constraint optimization problem, constraints assign each combination of assignments to its variables a cost, and the goal of the optimization is to find an assignment to all variables that minimizes the sum of the costs of all constraints:

Definition 1. *A* discrete *weighted constraint optimization problem (WCOP) is a tuple* $< X, D, C, R >$ *where:*

- $X = \{x_1, .., x_n\}$ *is a set of n variables.*
- $D = \{d_1, .., d_n\}$ *is a set of domains of the variables, each given as a finite set of possible values.*
- $C = \{c_1, .., c_m\}$ *is a set of constraints, where a constraint c_i is given as the list $(x_{i1}, .., x_{ik})$ of variables it involves.*
- $R = \{r_1, .., r_m\}$ *is a set of relations, where a relation r_i is a function $d_{i1} \times .. \times d_{ik} \rightarrow \Re^+$ giving the cost of choosing each combination of values.*

A solution *is a combination of values* $v_1 \in d_1, .., v_n \in d_n$ *such that the sum of the cost of the relations is minimal.*

Note than in a WCOP, any value combination is allowed, but might lead to a very high cost.

As an example, consider the scenario illustrated in Figure 2. A consortium of companies has to decide on three features x_1, x_2 and x_3 of a new product. It considers the options $x_1 \in \{A, B, C\}, x_2 \in \{A, C\}$ and $x_3 \in \{B, C\}$ (but this space may be extended later). The value chosen for each feature carries a certain cost to the consortium such that A has a cost of 0, B a cost of 1 and C a cost of 2. The features have interaction with parts provided by three members S_1, S_2 and S_3, where S_1 influences features x_1 and x_2, S_2 influences x_1 and x_3, and S_3 all three variables. The members make their proposals one variant at a time in strictly non-decreasing order of cost (as would be normal in a negotiation situation). In this example, we assume that they would eventually report the following costs:

$S_1 \Rightarrow r_4 \Rightarrow x_4'$:		$S_2 \Rightarrow r_5 \Rightarrow x_5'$:		$S_3 \Rightarrow r_6 \Rightarrow x_6'$:			
(x_1, x_2)	cost	(x_1, x_3)	cost	(x_1, x_2, x_3)	cost	(x_1, x_2, x_3)	cost
(B,C)	0	(A,C)	0	(A,A,B)	0	(C,A,B)	2
(C,C)	0	(C,C)	0	(B,A,B)	0	(A,C,C)	4
(A,C)	1	(A,B)	1	(A,A,C)	2	(B,C,C)	4
(B,A)	3	(C,B)	3	(A,C,B)	2	(C,A,C)	4
(C,A)	3	(B,C)	3	(B,A,C)	2	(C,C,B)	4
(A,A)	5	(B,B)	5	(B,C,B)	2	(C,C,C)	6

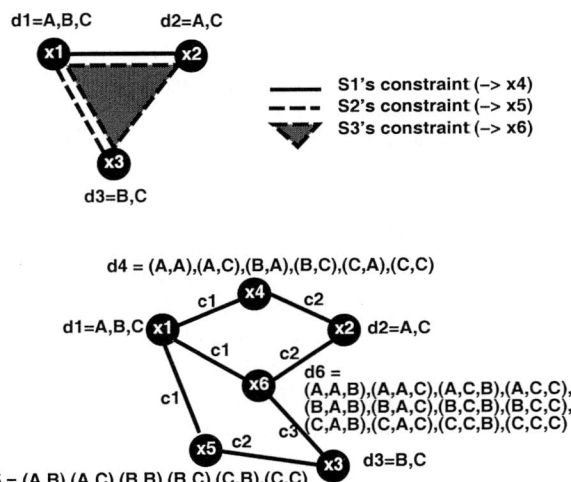

Fig. 2. Constraint optimization problem (top) and its hidden variable encoding (bottom).

The entire problem can thus be modelled as a WCOP as follows:

$X = \{x_1, x_2, x_3\}$
$D = \{(A, B, C), (A, C), (B, C)\}$
$C = \{(x_1), (x_2), (x_3), (x_1, x_2), (x_1, x_3), (x_1, x_2, x_3)\}$
$R = \{r_1, .., r_6\}$ with the valuations given in the text and tables above.

3.2   Hidden Variable Encoding

The WCOP formulation is inconvenient for open settings since we need to distinguish relations and variable domains which may both be discovered incrementally, which considerably encumbers the algorithms. We therefore transform the problem into an equivalent dual one where the constraints are encoded as tuple-valued, "hidden" variables and all constraints are binary relations ensuring that compatible instantiations are chosen for these tuples. As shown in ([6]), this transformation is possible for any constraint satisfaction problem. When we add to this representation the original variables and also link them to the tuples, we obtain the hidden variable encoding ([7]) of the problem.

As observed in [8], the hidden variable encoding generalizes in a straightforward way to weighted constraint optimization problems.

Definition 2. *A* hidden-variable weighted constraint optimization problem *(HWCOP) is a tuple $< X, D, C, R >$ obtained from a WCOP $< X', D', C', R' >$ in the following way:*

- *$X = \{x_1, ..., x_m\}$ corresponds to the constraints C'. We assume that for each variable, there is a unary constraint for each variable giving the costs of its values so that this set also includes all variables of the original problem.*

- $D = \{d_1, ..., d_m\}$ are the domains of the variables in X. They correspond to the domains of the relations of the original WCOP, where we assume that each domain is ordered so that the options with lowest cost come first.
- $C = \{(x_i, x_j, t) | x_i \in x_j\}$ is a set of hard constraints where x_i is a single variable, x_j is a tuple-valued variable containing x_i, and the type t indicates that the constraint is a $c_l, l \in 1..k$ that enforces equality between the individual variable and the l-th element of the tuple.
- $R = R'$ are the cost functions as in the original WCOP.

Figure 2 shows how the example WCOP is transformed into an HWCOP by introducing new variables, x_4, x_5 and x_6, to model the constraints of the three agents. These are linked to the original variables by constraints of type c_1, c_2 and c_3, enforcing equality between the variable and the corresponding element of the tuple. The solutions to the transformed HWCOP are identical to those of the original WCOP as far as the shared variables x_1 to x_3 are concerned.

We further define:

Definition 3. An assignment of an HWCOP is an assignment of a value to each variable and represented as a vector $A = (i_1, .., i_n)$ giving the position of each value in the respective domain. To simplify notation, we denote by $c(v(x_i)) = r_i(v(x_i))$ the cost of the assignment $x_i = v$. The cost of the assignment is the sum of the costs for each variable, i.e. $cost(A) = \sum_{j=1}^{n} c(d_j(i_j(A)))$.

Definition 4. An assignment of a HWCOP is optimal if and only if it is consistent with the constraints and there is no other assignment that has a lower cost. An optimal assignment is a solution to the HWCOP.

We denote by $v^*_{x_1,..,x_k}(x_i)$ the value assigned to x_i in the solution that is optimal for the subproblem $x_1, ..., x_k$ (of which x_i is part); when there are several solutions we choose the lexicographically smallest one.

3.3 Open HWCOP

As stated earlier, we are interested in optimization problems where options are obtained from agents dispersed through a network. We model this as an *open* HWCOP (OHWCOP), where each variable is contributed by an agent and models either a set of options that that agent contributes, or a constraint/preference that the agent wants to impose. Each agent applies the hidden variable encoding locally to the constraints/preferences it has on the joint problem, and communicates to the central solver its variables as well as the constraints that need to be enforced between them and other variables of the combined problem. The constraint solver then solves the problem and finally communicates the solution for each variable to the agents.

We require agents to follow the following rules of the protocol, where violators will be excluded from the optimization:

- agents always return their best values first.
- for each variable, costs are normalized so that the cost of the best tuple is always 0.

and formalize the problem posed to the central solver as:

Definition 5. *An* open hidden-variable weighted constraint optimization problem *(OHWCOP) is a possibly unbounded, partially ordered set* $\{P^0, P^1, ...\}$ *of HWCOP, where* P^i *is defined by a tuple* $< X, D^i, C, R^i >$. *The set is ordered by the relation* $\prec$ *where* $P^i \prec P^j$ *if and only if* $(\forall k \in [1..m]) d^i_k \subseteq d^j_k$, *and* $(\exists k \in [1..m]) d^i_k \subset d^j_k$, *i.e. all domains of* P^j *are at least as large as for* P^i *and at least one is larger.*

Costs are assumed to be stable, i.e. if for some value $v \in d^i_k$, $r^i_k(v) = c$ *then* $r^j_k(v) = c$ *for all* j *such that* $P^i \prec P^j$.

As agents return their best options first, domains are ordered in non-increasing order of cost, i.e. $r^i_k(d^i_k(l-1)) \leq r^i_k(d^i_k(l))$ *for all* $l \leq |d^i_k|$.

A solution to an OHWCOP is an assignment that is a solution to some instance $HWCOP^i$ *and optimal for all higher instances, i.e.* P^j *such that* $P^i \prec P^j$.

The assumption of non-increasing cost is necessary for any form of open constraint optimization:

Proposition 1. *When the assumption that domains are returned in order of non-decreasing cost does not hold, there is no general algorithm for solving OHWCOP that is guaranteed to terminate with the optimal solution without querying the entire domains of all variables.*

Proof. Consider a problem that has a consistent solution with cost 0 involving the values returned last and other consistent assignments with cost > 0 involving other values. Here the optimal solution can only be found after querying all values. Since a general algorithm cannot know whether such a case is present, for any problem that does not have a solution with cost=0 it will have to check all domains completely to guarantee optimality.

4   Solving Open Constraint Optimization Problems

A first approach to solving OHWCOP would be to use standard branch-and-bound search algorithms coupled with a test for whether sufficient values are known to guarantee optimality also with larger domains.

The following proposition shows how far domains have to be known in order to guarantee optimality of the solution. We call an instance that satisfies this proposition *subset domain-sufficient*:

Proposition 2. *The optimal solution to an instance* $HWCOP(i)$ *of an OHWCOP is guaranteed to be optimal for the OHWCOP itself if for any subset of variables* $S = x_{s1}, .., x_{sk}$, *we have:*

$$\sum_{x_{si} \in S} max_{v \in d_{si}} c(v) \geq \sum_{x_i \in X} c(v^*_X(x_i)) - \sum_{x_i \in X-S} c(v^*_{X-S}(x_i))$$

and v^*_{X-S} *is optimal for the subproblem HWCOP involving only variables in* $X - S$.

Proof. Let there be a better solution in an instance $COP(j)$, and let S be the set of variables that have values not in $COP(i)$. Then all the variables $x_{si} \in S$ must have a cost greater than $max_{v \in d_{si}}(c(v))$ for otherwise they would have been in $COP(i)$. But then the cost of this solution would have to be at least:

$$\sum_{x_{si} \in S} max_{v \in d_{si}} c(v) + \sum_{x_i \in X-S} c(v^*_{X-S}(x_i)) \geq \sum_{x_i \in X} c(v^*_X(x_i))$$

so it could not be optimal. Thus, the algorithm achieves optimality in $COP(i)$.

This condition can be used to prove optimality of a solution without knowing the complete domains of all variables by recursively applying it to show optimality of v^*_{X-S} for the remaining sets $X - S$ until this set becomes empty. However, it does not provide an operational criterion for constructing an algorithm that makes a minimal number of queries, since the sequence of sets S that would allow a proof with a minimal number of values cannot be computed without knowing the domains completely. In fact, we can show:

Proposition 3. *There is no general algorithm for solving OHWCOP that is guaranteed to solve all instances with a minimal number of queries.*

Proof. Consider a problem with 3 variables x_1, x_2, x_3 with identical domains $\{a, b\}$ and constraints that require all variables to have equal values. Assume further that x_1 has costs $a/0, b/2$, x_2: $a/1, b/0$ and x_3: $a/0, b/1$. Then the optimal solution a can be found by with querying only the first value for x_3 when variables are taken in the order x_1, x_2, x_3, but requires querying all values when variables are taken in order x_3, x_2, x_1. Since an algorithm cannot distinguish x_1 and x_3 before querying the second value, it could not always choose the optimal order.

It is however possible to show the following, more operational condition, which we call *singleton domain-sufficiency*:

Proposition 4. *The optimal solution to an instance $HWCOP(i)$ of an OHWCOP is guaranteed to be optimal for the OHWCOP itself if the domain of each variable x_k is known up to at least one value whose cost is not smaller than $\overline{c_k}$, where $\overline{c_k}$ is given as:*

$$\overline{c_k} = max_{X' \subseteq X, x_k \in X'} \left(\sum_{x_i \in X'} c(v^*_{X'}(x_i)) - \sum_{x_i \in X' \setminus x_k} c(v^*_{X' \setminus x_k}(x_i)) \right)$$

Proof. Omitted for lack of space.

This condition, slightly stronger than subset domain-sufficiency, can be used to build an algorithm that incrementally queries values only for variables that are not singleton domain-sufficient. However, as the condition has to be checked for each subset of variables, such an algorithm is very inefficient, and for lack of space we don't give it in detail in this paper. We did however implement it and use it as a benchmark later in the paper.

4.1   Basic Incremental Search Algorithm

Another approach is to use best-first algorithms based on A^* that incrementally generate all possible assignments. While this approach can use a lot of memory, it provides a good basis for addressing the problems posed by open domains.

```
Function o-opt(OHWCOP)
Forall x_i, d_i ← more(d_i)
OPEN ← {(1,..,1)}
loop
M ← {a ∈ OPEN|cost(a) = min_{d∈OPEN} cost(d)}
a ← lexicographically smallest element of M
OPEN ← OPEN − {a}
if consistent(a) then
   return a
else
   for j = 1..n do
      b ← (a(1),..,a(j) + 1,..,a(n))
      if b ∉ OPEN then
         OPEN ← OPEN ∪ {b}
         if |d_j| < b(j) then
            d_j ← append(d_j, more(d_j))
```

Algorithm 1: *o-opt: an incremental algorithm for solving OHWCOP.*

Algorithm 1 is inspired by the preference elicitation algorithm of Conen and Sandholm ([9]) for combinatorial auctions and systematically enumerates all possible assignments in the order of increasing weight. Whenever necessary, it moves to a higher HWCOP by extending the domains of one or more variables. The first assignment that is consistent with all constraints is an optimal solution, since all assignments of lower weights have already been searched and found inconsistent, as in the $A*$ algorithm. We can show the following:

Theorem 1. *Algorithm 1 is sound and complete.*

Proof. Soundness is guaranteed by the fact that the algorithm only returns consistent assignments and systematically explores all assignments in strictly nondecreasing order of cost, so that the one returned is also the one with the lowest cost. Completeness is guaranteed by the fact that the algorithm systematically enumerates all assignments.

4.2   Failure-Driven Search

The solution found by Algorithm 1 on our example is the assignment:

$$x_1 = A, x_2 = A, x_3 = B$$

with a total cost of 7. It is interesting to consider what values are queried by the algorithm in order to reach this conclusion. In fact, to establish optimality of this solution, the algorithm will query all values for all variables! And the problem can get much worse: consider a problem with 100 variables where the optimal solution is one where each variable has a cost of 1. The algorithm would, however, query for values up to a cost of 100 for each variable, since a combination of one assignment with a cost of 100 with 99 assignments of cost 0 would have optimal cost. The problem here is that the algorithm generates numerous candidates where the cost of subproblems is far lower than in the optimal solution.

Function **f-o-opt**(OHWCOP)
Forall $x_i, d_i \leftarrow$ **more(d_i)**
$OPEN \leftarrow \{(1,..,1)\}$
loop
$M \leftarrow \{a \in OPEN | cost(a) = min_{d \in OPEN} cost(d)\}$
$a \leftarrow$ lexicographically smallest element of M
$OPEN \leftarrow OPEN - \{a\}$
if $consistent(a)$ **then**
    return a
else
    $c \leftarrow$ first violated constraint in a, i.e. the violated constraint involving an x_k with the smallest k.
    for $j \in vars(c)$ **do**
        $b \leftarrow (a(1),..,a(j)+1,..,a(n))$
        if $b \notin OPEN$ **then**
            if $|d_j| < b(j)$ **then**
                $d_j \leftarrow append(d_j, more(d_j))$
            $OPEN \leftarrow OPEN \cup \{b\}$
end loop

Algorithm 2: *f-o-opt: an failure-driven algorithm for solving OHWCOP.*

Algorithm 2 significantly improves on this based on the observation that it is not necessary to generate all successors to an assignment a:

Proposition 5. *Let $a = (a(1), ..., a(n))$ be an inconsistent assignment and let the pair of variables x_i and x_j such that $d_i(a(i))$ and $d_j(a(j))$ are not consistent with a constraint c between them. Now consider the direct successors $b_k = (a(1), ..., a(k)+1, ..., a(n))$. All direct successors except b_i and b_j are redundant and can be pruned in Algorithm 1 without affecting its sound- and completeness.*

Proof. When $k \neq i, j$ we have that:

- b_k is inconsistent, as it contains the same conflict with c as a.
- all direct or indirect successors to b_k that do not change the values for x_i or x_j are inconsistent, as they still contain the same conflict with c as b_k.
- all direct (indirect) successors to b_k that change the value for x_i or x_j are also a direct (indirect) successor of either b_i or b_j.

where we use the term indirect successor for sequences of direct successor relationships. Thus, all $b_k, k \neq i, j$ cannot be themselves solutions or lead to solutions that would not be generated from b_i and b_j already.

Theorem 2. *Algorithm 2 is sound and complete.*

Proof. Follows from Theorem 1 and Proposition 5.

On the example, Algorithm 2 finds the same solution as Algorithm 1, but queries significantly less values. For example, for variable x_6 it only queries three rather than all 12 values.

Thus, in Algorithm 2, instead of generating all successors to an assignment, we only generate those successors that are involved in the first conflicting constraint. This turns out to have the effect that the algorithm only explores assignments to $x_1, .., x_{k+1}$ once it has found a consistent assignment to $x_1, .., x_k$. This behavior is very similar to that of Russian Doll Search (RDS) ([10]), an algorithm that generates optimal solutions to increasingly large subproblems and uses their costs as bounds for solving larger problems.

A potential problem with Algorithm 2 is that it keeps a complete list $OPEN$ of all currently best nodes, so that memory consumption can become a problem. If necessary, the $OPEN$ list can be incrementally regenerated by a depth-first search process such as $IDA*$ ([11]), limiting memory consumption at the expense of additional computation time. It is straightforward to obtain the same behavior by querying additional values for the variables involved in the first conflict of the candidate tightest to the current cost limit.

Below we consider what guarantees can be given for Algorithm 2 regarding the number of values queried.

4.3   Optimality of the Number of Value Queries

Proposition 2 shows that any algorithm that guarantees optimality of the solution to an OHWCOP must query at least a certain number of values. This bound can be compared to the queries that Algorithm 2 actually makes. For this, we have the following propositions:

Proposition 6. *Algorithm 2 queries at most one value for x_k with cost $\geq c$ until it has examined all assignments to $x_1..x_n$ with total cost $< c + \sum_{j=1}^{k-1} c(v^*_{x_1..x_{k-1}}(x_j))$.*

Proof. Queries for x_k can only result from generating a successor to an assignment a that is consistent up to x_{k-1}, for otherwise, there would be an earlier violated constraint. Now assume that the algorithm had already queried a value for x_k with cost $\geq c$, then since assignment a must have x_k assigned to the highest cost value so far, the cost of assignment a must thus be at least the optimum for $x_1..x_{k-1}$ plus c. For this assignment to reach the head of the OPEN queue, all assignments with lower cost must have already been examined.

Proposition 6 gives us the following bound on the queries per variable:

Proposition 7. *For variable x_k, Algorithm 2 queries values up to a cost threshold that differs from the optimum $\overline{c_k}$ by at most:*

$$\sum_{x_i \in X \backslash x_k} c(v^*_{X \backslash x_k}(x_i)) - \sum_{j=1}^{i-1} c(v^*_{x_1..x_{i-1}}(x_j))$$

Thus, in particular, for x_n it queries the minimally possible number of values.

Proof. When the algorithm terminates, it has examined all assignments with a cost less than that of the solution, i.e. $\sum_{j=1}^{n} c(v^*_X(x_j))$. By Proposition 6, it will thus have queried at most one value for x_k that is beyond the limit:

$$max_k = \sum_{j=1}^{n} c(v^*_X(x_j)) - \sum_{j=1}^{k-1} c(v^*_{x_1..x_{k-1}}(x_j))$$

Subtracting the limit given in Proposition 2 for $S = \{x_k\}$ results in the given relation. Its instantiation for the last variable x_n gives a difference of 0.

   In practice, the empirical results in Figure 3 show that Algorithm 2 is actually very close to optimal.

4.4   Achieving Incentive-Compatibility

Optimization is useless unless the costs are reported truthfully. As already proposed in [12], using the Vickrey-Clark-Groves (VCG) tax mechanism we can make the mechanism *incentive-compatible*, i.e. make it optimal for all agents to tell the truth. In the VCG tax mechanism, each agent pays a tax equal to the difference between the cost of the solution to the optimization problem when it is present and the cost when it is not. More formally, let agent A have imposed the constraints modelled by the set of variables X_A, then the tax, called the Clark tax, is:

$$payment(A) = \sum_{x_k \in X - X_A} c(v^*_X(x_k)) - c(v^*_{X-X_A}(x_k))$$

In the example of Figure 2, the optimal solution is $(x_1, x_2, x_3) = (A, A, B)$ with a cost of 6. Without the constraint x_4, it is still (A, A, B), without x_5, (B, A, B) and without x_6, (A, C, B). Using the notation $C_X(.)$ to denote the cost of a solution to agent X, the tax paid by the agents would be:

	Payment	Value
A	$c_B(AAB) + c_C(AAB) - c_B(AAB) - c_C(AAB)$	$1-1 = 0$
B	$c_A(AAB) + c_C(AAB) - c_A(BAB) - c_C(BAB)$	$5-3 = 2$
C	$c_A(AAB) + c_B(AAB) - c_A(ACB) - c_B(ACB)$	$6-2 = 4$

Note that these taxes reflect the cost of reaching agreement on the variable values; the agents would usually receive other payments for their contributions to the consortium elsewhere.

The following argument shows why this tax makes it optimal for an agent to tell the truth:

- suppose that an agent overstates its costs. In all cases where this influences the solution, this will result in a tax that outweighs the benefit of the manipulated solution.
- suppose that an agent understates its costs. In all cases where this influences the solution, the loss incurred by not having its optimal solution outweighs the savings in tax.

It is important to note that the domains and costs required to compute these payments are the same as those required by Proposition 2. In fact, any algorithm for open constraint optimization that can guarantee optimality is also guaranteed to query all required values and costs for computing the VCG tax payments.

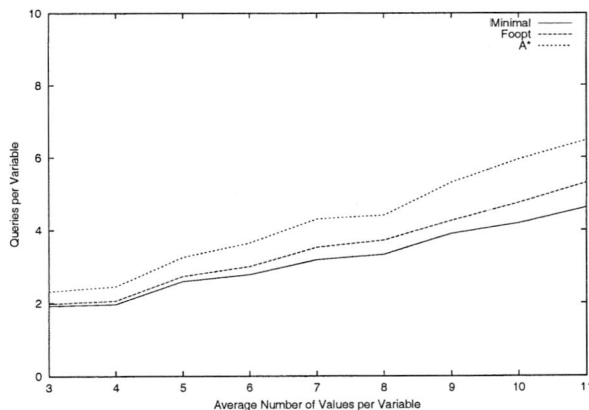

Fig. 3. Comparison of Algorithms 1 (A*) and 2 (foopt) with respect to the average number of values queried in relation to average domain size. Also shown for comparison is a minimal algorithm based on Proposition 4.

5   Empirical Results

Figure 3 compares the number of values queried for the two algorithms on random OHWCOP problems, where the constraint graph was generated randomly and constraints were assigned a random valuation from a uniform distribution between 0 and 1. We can see that both Algorithms 1 and 2 come close to the benchmark performance, with Algorithm 2 being somewhat better. In order to get an idea of what the minimal number of queries is, we also implemented a method that incrementally finds optimal solutions to larger and larger subproblems. It maintains the property of singleton domain-sufficiency as in Proposition 4 and can be shown to query a minimal number of values to maintain this property. It can be seen that Algorithm 2 is almost optimal with respect to that method as well.

In comparison to this performance, the classical method of gathering all values and then solving the problem would query all domain values and can become arbitrarily worse than these algorithms, depending on the looseness of the problem.

Figure 4 compares the number of constraint checks and shows that only Algorithm 2 can be applied to problems of realistic size; in practice it can handle problems of up to 25 variables before constraint checks start to become excessive.

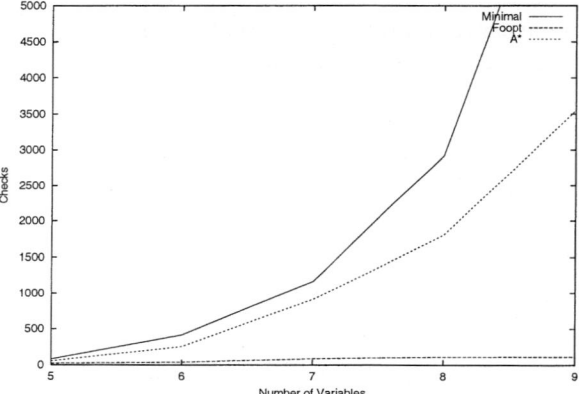

Fig. 4. Comparison of Algorithms 1 (A*) and 2 (foopt) with respect to the number of constraint checks in relation to the number of problem variables. Also shown for comparison is a minimal algorithm based on Proposition 4.

6   Conclusions

Many new and exciting applications in open information systems, in particular the WWW, address problems which CSP techniques are very good at solving. Such applications will appear increasingly with the emergence of web services and the semantic web.

We have presented an extension of the constraint optimization framework that allows solving such systems in an open framework while still guaranteeing optimality of the overall solution. This shows that it is possible to solve optimization problems even without the closed-world assumption, and opens up new possibilites for intelligent systems in open environments.

However, it turns out to be difficult to adapt the depth-first branch-and-bound methods commonly used for constraint optimization to this open framework, as the conditions that are needed to guarantee that they find the optimal solutions are very complex to evaluate. We have shown instead how it is possible to obtain good results by adapting a framework based on best-first search algorithms. By exploiting the local nature of failure in constraint satisfaction problems, we have shown how it is possible to greatly improve the behavior of such an algorithm. However, the size of problems that can be solved efficiently is still far from what can be handled when the closed-world assumption can be made, and we hope to stimulate further research for better algorithms that work in open settings.

Acknowledgements

We like to thank Tuomas Sandholm for interesting discussions and insights.

References

1. Rita Cucchiara, Marco Gavanelli, Evelina Lamma, Paola Mello, Michela Milano, and Massimo Piccardi: "Constraint propagation and value acquisition: why we should do it interactively," *Proceedings of the 16th IJCAI*, Morgan Kaufmann, pp.468-477, 1999
2. B. Faltings and S. Macho-Gonzalez: "Open Constraint Satisfaction," *Proceedings of CP 2002*, LNCS 2470, Springer-Verlag, pp. 356-370, 2002
3. Christian Bessière: "Arc-Consistency in Dynamic Constraint Satisfaction Problems," *Proceedings of the 9th National Conference of the AAAI*, pp. 221-226, 1991
4. Makoto Yokoo: "Algorithms for Distributed Constraint Satisfaction: A Review, *Autonomous Agents and Multi-Agent Systems*, Vol.3, No.2, pp.189–212, 2000
5. Pragnesh Jay Modi, Wei-Min Shen, Milind Tambe, Makoto Yokoo: "An Asynchronous Complete Method for Distributed Constraint Optimization". *Autonomous Agents and Multi-Agent Systems*, September 2003
6. F. Rossi, C. Petrie and V. Dhar: "On the equivalence of constraint satisfaction problems," *Proceedings of ECAI-90*, pp. 550-556, 1990
7. Stergiou, K. and Walsh, T.: "Encodings of Non-Binary Constraint Satisfaction Problems," *Proceedings of tne AAAI '99*, pp. 163-168, 1999
8. Xavier Larrosa, Rina Dechter: "On The Dual Representation of Non-Binary Semiring-Based CSPs" *Workshop 1 (Soft Constraints, of CP 2000*, September, 2000
9. W. Conen, T. Sandholm: "Partial-revelation VCG Mechanism for Combinatorial Auctions," *Proceedings of the AAAI-02*, pp. 367-372, 2002
10. G. Verfaillie, M. Lemaitre, and T. Schiex: "Russian Dcll Search for Solving Constraint Optimization Problems," In Proc. of the 13th National Conference on Artificial Intelligence (AAAI-96), pages 181–187, Portland, OR, USA, 1996
11. R.E. Korf: "Depth-first iterative deepening: an optimal admissible tree search," *Artificial Intelligence* **27**(1), pp. 97-109, 1985
12. E. Ephrati and J. S. Rosenschein: "The Clarke tax as a consensus mechanism among automated agents," *Proceedings of the 9th National Conference on Artificial Intelligence*, pp. 173-178, San Jose, California, July 1991.

Constraints for Breaking More Row and Column Symmetries

Alan M. Frisch, Chris Jefferson, and Ian Miguel

Artificial Intelligence Group
Department of Computer Science
University of York, York, UK
{frisch,caj,ianm}@cs.york.ac.uk

Abstract. Constraint programs containing a matrix of two (or more) dimensions of decision variables often have row and column symmetries: in any assignment to the variables the rows can be swapped and the columns can be swapped without affecting whether or not the assignment is a solution. This introduces an enormous amount of redundancy when searching a space of partial assignments. It has been shown previously that one can remove consistently some of these symmetries by extending such a program with constraints that require the rows and columns to be lexicographically ordered. This paper identifies and studies the properties of a new additional constraint—the first row is less than or equal to all permutations of all other rows—that can be added consistently to break even more symmetries. Two alternative implementations of this stronger symmetry-breaking method are investigated, one of which employs a new algorithm that in time linear in the size of the matrix enforces the constraint that the first row is less than or equal to all permutations of all other rows. It is demonstrated experimentally that our method for breaking more symmetries substantially reduces search effort.

1 Introduction

A common pattern arising in finite domain constraint programs is the matrix of decision variables with two or more dimensions [6]. In two-dimensional matrices it is often the case that some or all of the rows are interchangeable and some or all of the columns are interchangeable. That is, an assignment to the variables in the matrix is a solution if and only if it is still a solution after two of the interchangeable rows are swapped or two of the interchangeable columns are swapped. In a two dimensional matrix this is called *row and column symmetry*. Since this property can also arise in each of many dimensions, more generally it is called *index symmetry*. To simplify our presentation, we assume throughout that we are dealing only with two dimensional matrices in which all rows are interchangeable and all columns are interchangeable.

Symmetry in constraint programs can cause problems for an algorithm that searches a space of partial assignments due to redundancy in the search space. One of the most popular methods for reducing symmetry is to add to the model extra constraints, so-called *symmetry breaking constraints*.

F. Rossi (Ed.): CP 2003, LNCS 2833, pp. 318–332, 2003.

Flener et al [5] studied index symmetry and showed that one can *consistently* add the symmetry-breaking constraint, called lex^2, that both the rows and the columns are lexicographically ordered[1]. This means that for every assignment to the variables that does not satisfy the symmetry-breaking constraint, there is a symmetric assignment that does. They also showed that for certain problems imposing lex^2 can make the difference between solving and failing to solve the problem. Frisch et al [7] introduced an efficient algorithm for maintaining generalised arc-consistency on the constraint that one vector (a row or column of a matrix) is lexicographically less than or equal to another.

Independently, Flener et al [5] and Shlyakhter [14] also showed that lex^2 does not break all row and column symmetries. That is, lex^2 is *incomplete* in that it can be satisfied by two symmetrical assignments. Consider the following two matrices. Both satisfy lex^2, but the second can be obtained from the first by swapping the rows and rotating the columns to the right.

$$\begin{pmatrix} 2 & 2 & 3 \\ 2 & 3 & 1 \end{pmatrix} \qquad \begin{pmatrix} 1 & 2 & 3 \\ 3 & 2 & 2 \end{pmatrix}$$

It is therefore natural to wonder if more symmetry can be broken *effectively* by imposing a symmetry-breaking constraint stronger than lex^2. That is, can we add extra constraints to lex^2 that both break a significant number of the symmetries left by lex^2 and can be propagated efficiently? This paper addresses this question and answers it in the affirmative. In particular, we introduce a new constraint, called *allperm*, that is satisfied by a matrix if and only if the first row is lexicographically less than or equal to all permutations of all other rows. Only the second matrix above satisfies both lex^2 and *allperm*. Section 3 shows that one can consistently impose both lex^2 and *allperm* on a matrix that has symmetric rows and symmetric columns. This is shown to break more symmetries than lex^2 on its own but not to break all symmetries.

The *allperm* constraint can be decomposed into individual lexicographic ordering constraints by adding a constraint for each of the permutations of each row, of which there are a number factorial in the length of the row. This is not an effective way to break symmetry. Instead, we examine other decompositions, leading in Section 6 to an algorithm which implements *allperm* in time linear in the size of the matrix. This algorithm is then tested in Section 8, where it is demonstrated that some problems can be solved much more effectively when symmetries are broken by lex^2 and *allperm* together than by lex^2 on its own.

2   Terminology

We are concerned with finite domain constraint satisfaction problems so every variable is associated with a finite domain of values. An *assignment* maps every variable to a member of its domain. We write $vars(C)$ to denote the variables

---

[1] Though working in a different context, Shlyakhter [14] independently showed the consistency.

constrained by constraint C. We say that a constraint C is *generalised arc consistent* (GAC), written $GAC(C)$, if for every variable $x \in vars(C)$ and every value v in the domain of x, there is an assignment that maps x to v and satisfies C. A finite set of constraints, $\{C_1, \ldots, C_n\}$, is said to be GAC if and only if $C_1 \wedge \cdots \wedge C_n$ is GAC.

A set of constraints S *logically implies* another set of constraints S' if every assignment that satisfies every member of S also satisfies every member of S'. If S and S' logically imply each other, then they are said to be *logically equivalent*.

An $n \times m$ matrix has n columns and m rows. The columns are numbered $1, \ldots, n$ from left to right and the rows are numbered $1, \ldots, m$ from top to bottom. A row of an $n \times m$ matrix can be treated as a vector, $\boldsymbol{x} = \langle x_1, \ldots, x_n \rangle$, by reading it left to right and a column can be treated as a vector, $\boldsymbol{y} = \langle y_1, \ldots, y_m \rangle$, by reading it top to bottom.

This paper focuses on ordering non-empty vectors of equal size, so we shall simplify the presentation by assuming this throughout the paper. One vector, $\boldsymbol{x}$, is defined to be *lexicographically less than or equal to* another, $\boldsymbol{y}$, (written $\boldsymbol{x} \leq_{lex} \boldsymbol{y}$) if $\boldsymbol{x} = \boldsymbol{y}$ or $x_i < y_i$, where i is the smallest index such that $x_i \neq y_i$.

This paper introduces two new orderings on vectors. The first, the anti-multiset ordering, has a definition that mirrors the multiset ordering definition. We write $\sharp\boldsymbol{x}|_v$ to denote the number of occurrences of v in $\boldsymbol{x}$. We define $\boldsymbol{x}$ to be *anti-multiset less than or equal to* $\boldsymbol{y}$, written $\boldsymbol{x} \leq_{\overline{m}} \boldsymbol{y}$, if $\boldsymbol{x} = \boldsymbol{y}$ or $\sharp\boldsymbol{x}|_v > \sharp\boldsymbol{y}|_v$, where v is the smallest value such that $\sharp\boldsymbol{x}|_v \neq \sharp\boldsymbol{y}|_v$. The second ordering is the allperm ordering. We write $\boldsymbol{x} \leq_{ap} \boldsymbol{y}$ if $\boldsymbol{x} \leq_{lex} \boldsymbol{y}'$ for every permutation $\boldsymbol{y}'$ of $\boldsymbol{y}$. It should be noted that this is an abuse of notation as $\leq_{ap}$ is not reflexive (but it is anti-symmetric and transitive).

Using these orderings on vectors, we define some predicates on matrices. Let M be a matrix of values. We write $lex^2(M)$ to mean that the rows of M are lexicographically non-decreasing from top to bottom and the columns are lexicographically non-decreasing from left to right. We write $ams(M)$ to mean that the first row of M is less than or equal to all other rows in the anti-multiset order and, similarly, we write $allperm(M)$ to mean that the first row of M is less than or equal to all other rows in the allperm order.

We also use the symbols $\leq_{lex}$, $\leq_{\overline{m}}$, $\leq_{ap}$, lex^2, ams and $allperm$ to denote constraints that are imposed on vectors or matrices of variables.

3 Basic Properties

In Section 1 we saw an example demonstrating that *allperm* and lex^2 break more symmetries than lex^2 alone. This section shows that imposing both *allperm* and lex^2 on a matrix with row and column symmetry is consistent and is incomplete. We show consistency by examining a complete and consistent set of symmetry-breaking constraints known as the row-wise lex-leader constraints, and incompleteness by example.

One way to break all the index symmetries in a matrix is to impose the row-wise lex-leader constraints, which are a specific case of the more general lex-leader constraints introduced by Crawford et al. [4]. The row-wise lex-leader constraints are derived by considering a matrix of distinct variables and all matrices symmetric to it. Each matrix is converted to a string of variables by scanning the matrix row-wise, left-to-right, top-to-bottom. For example, the 3×2 matrix of variables

$$\begin{pmatrix} A & B & C \\ D & E & F \end{pmatrix}$$

yields the string $ABCDEF$. From these strings we produce a set of constraints asserting that the string from the original matrix—called the *lex-leader*—is lexicographically less than or equal to each of the other strings. Thus, continuing our example, there are 11 other matrices that can be produced by permuting the rows and columns of the above matrix. Each of these yields a string of variables that is constrained to be lexicographically less than or equal to $ABCDEF$; thus 11 constraints, called the row-wise lex-leader constraints, are generated:

(1) $ABCDEF \leq_{lex} ACBDFE$ (2) $ABCDEF \leq_{lex} BACEDF$
(3) $ABCDEF \leq_{lex} BCAEFD$ (4) $ABCDEF \leq_{lex} CBAFED$
(5) $ABCDEF \leq_{lex} CABFDE$ (6) $ABCDEF \leq_{lex} DEFABC$
(7) $ABCDEF \leq_{lex} DFEACB$ (8) $ABCDEF \leq_{lex} EDFBAC$
(9) $ABCDEF \leq_{lex} EFDBCA$ (10) $ABCDEF \leq_{lex} FEDCBA$
(11) $ABCDEF \leq_{lex} FDECAB$

Since the row-wise lex-leader constraints are generated by the method proposed by Crawford et al. [4], we know that they are consistent and complete. However, this does not generally provide an effective way to break row and column symmetries since for an $n \times m$ matrix it yields $n! \cdot m! - 1$ constraints.

It has been shown that the lex^2 constraint is logically implied by the row-wise lex-leader constraints, from which it follows that lex^2 is a consistent symmetry-breaking constraint [14]. We now show a new result—that *allperm* is logically implied by the row-wise lex-leader constraints—from which it follows that the combination of lex^2 and *allperm* is consistent.

We first show by example that the row-wise lex-leader constraints logically imply that the first row is lexicographically less than or equal to a permutation of another row. In particular, using the example matrix above, we show that the row-wise lex-leader constraints imply $ABC \leq_{lex} FED$. First observe that there is a matrix that is symmetric to the above and whose first row is FED (obtained by swapping the two rows and swapping the first and third columns):

$$\begin{pmatrix} F & E & D \\ C & B & A \end{pmatrix}$$

This matrix yields the string $FEDCBA$. Hence, $ABCDEF \leq_{lex} FEDCBA$ is one of the row-wise lex-leader constraints, namely constraint (10) above. And this constraint logically implies $ABC \leq_{lex} FED$.

One can easily generalise this example to a proof that the row-wise lex-leader constraints logically imply every constraint of the form that the first row is lexicographically less than or equal to every permutation of every other row. Hence, we have the following theorem:

Theorem 1. *The row-wise lex-leader constraints for a matrix M of variables logically imply both $lex^2(M)$ and $allperm(M)$. Hence the conjunction of $lex^2(M)$ and $allperm(M)$ is a consistent symmetry-breaking constraint.*

The conjunction of lex^2 and *allperm* is a consistent symmetry-breaking constraint, but it is not complete. To see this observe that the following two matrices can be obtained from each other by permuting rows and columns, yet both satisfy the lex^2 and *allperm* constraints.

$$\begin{pmatrix} 1\ 2\ 3 \\ 3\ 1\ 2 \end{pmatrix} \qquad\qquad \begin{pmatrix} 1\ 2\ 3 \\ 2\ 3\ 1 \end{pmatrix}$$

4   An Alternative Characterisation

This section gives an alternative characterisation of the constraint $lex^2(M) \wedge allperm(M)$.

We start by relating the lexicographic and allperm orderings to the anti-multiset ordering. Let $\boldsymbol{x}{\uparrow}$ denote the vector of values that results from sorting the elements of $\boldsymbol{x}$ from smallest to largest. Notice that $\boldsymbol{x} \leq_{ap} \boldsymbol{y}$ implies $\boldsymbol{x}{\uparrow} \leq_{ap} \boldsymbol{y}$, which implies $\boldsymbol{x} \leq_{\overline{m}} \boldsymbol{y}$. This chain of implications does not hold in the opposite direction, unless $\boldsymbol{x} = \boldsymbol{x}{\uparrow}$.

We now extend these two observations to matrices. From the first observation it follows that that $allperm(M)$ implies $ams(M)$. From the second observation it follows that if the first row of M is non-decreasing, then $ams(M)$ implies $allperm(M)$. Now notice that if the columns of matrix M are lexicographically ordered, then the first row of M is nondecreasing. From this our alternative characterisation follows.

Theorem 2 (Characterisation Theorem). *Let M be a matrix of values. Then (1) $allperm(M)$ implies $ams(M)$, (2) $lex^2(M) \wedge ams(M)$ implies $lex^2(M) \wedge allperm(M)$ and, thus, (3) $lex^2(M) \wedge allperm(M)$ if and only if $lex^2(M) \wedge ams(M)$.*

5   Decomposing the Constraints

There is no known algorithm for maintaining GAC on the conjunction of lex^2 and *allperm* (or, equivalently, the conjunction of lex^2 and *ams*). Furthermore, the complexity of this conjunction suggests that the development of such an algorithm is probably beyond the reach of current capability. Therefore, the best approach is to decompose the constraint into constituents, for each of which a GAC algorithm is known or could be developed. This section examines and compares some decompositions. But first we present a general theorem about decomposition that is particularly useful for our purposes.

5.1   The Decomposition Theorem

The Decomposition Theorem identifies a simple condition under which a conjunction is GAC if each of its conjuncts is GAC.

Let C be a constraint and x be a variable in $vars(C)$. We say that C is *upwardly monotonic* in x if given any assignment that satisfies C, then replacing the value assigned to x with any larger value also satisfies C. We define downwardly monotonic in a similar fashion. A set S of constraints *agree monotonically* if for any two constraints $C_1, C_2 \in S$ and every variable x in $vars(C_1) \cap vars(C_2)$ either C_1 and C_2 are upwardly monotonic in x or both are downwardly monotonic in x.

Theorem 3 (Decomposition Theorem). *Given a finite set, S, of constraints that agree monotonically, $GAC(S)$ if and only if $GAC(C)$ for every $C \in S$.*

Proof. Clearly the "only-if" part holds, so we turn our attention to the "if" part.

Consider an arbitrary value v in domain of a variable x. We know that we can find support for v assigned to x in all constraints it appears in as $GAC(C)$ holds for all $C \in S$. For any constraint which does not refer to x we can choose any variable in the constraint and any value in that variables domain and find support for it.

Without loss of generality we will assume all the monotonic variables are upwardly monotonic. Given a valid assignment for a constraint C which contains the upwardly monotonic variable v then we can increase the value of v and still have a valid assignment for C. Therefore we can take all of the upwardly monotonic variables (except x) in the assignments of all the constraints and increase the values they take to the maximum value in their domain. Now the assignments we have for all the constraints agree on all the variables that appear in more than one constraint. Therefore we have shown $GAC(C)$ for all $C \in S$ implies $GAC(S)$ □

5.2   First Decomposition

The first, and most obvious, decomposition is to break the conjunctions and maintain GAC on the conjuncts. Doing so reduces pruning: $GAC(lex^2(M) \wedge allperm(M))$ is not implied by $GAC(lex^2(M)) \wedge GAC(allperm(M))$. This is demonstrated by considering the 4×2 matrix M of distinct variables where the domains of the eight variables are:

$$\begin{array}{cccc} \{1,2\} & \{1,2\} & \{4\} & \{4\} \\ \{3\} & \{3\} & \{2\} & \{2\} \end{array}$$

Observe that $GAC(lex^2(M)) \wedge GAC(allperm(M))$ but not $GAC(lex^2(M) \wedge allperm(M))$, as no solution assigns 2 to the first variable of the first row. This same example demonstrates that decomposing $GAC(lex^2(M) \wedge ams(M))$ reduces pruning: we have $GAC(lex^2(M))$ and $GAC(ams(M))$ but not $GAC(lex^2(M) \wedge ams(M))$.

Since both decompositions reduce pruning, we would like to know which suffers the greater reduction. From part (1) of the Characterisation Theorem it follows that $GAC(allperm(M))$ implies $GAC(ams(M))$. So $GAC(lex^2(M)) \wedge GAC(allperm(M))$ is at least as strong as $GAC(lex^2(M)) \wedge GAC(ams(M))$. We now give an example to show that it is strictly stronger. Consider M', a 4×2 matrix of distinct variables where the domains of the eight variables are:

$$\begin{array}{cccc}
\{1\} & \{2\} & \{3,4\} & \{3,4\} \\
\{2\} & \{1\} & \{3\} & \{4\}
\end{array}$$

Both $lex^2(M')$ and $ams(M')$ are GAC. However $allperm(M')$ is not; no solution
assigns 4 to the third variable of the first row.

5.3   Further Decomposition

We now turn our attention to the $allperm(M)$ and $ams(M)$ constraints and
show that each can be decomposed without any loss of pruning.

For two vectors of variables x and y that share no variables, the constraints
$x \leq_{lex} y$, $x \leq_{ap} y$ and $x \leq_{\overline{m}} y$ are each downwardly monotonic in the variables
of x and upwardly monotonic in the variables of y.

Let X be a matrix of distinct variables whose rows are $x_1, \ldots, x_n$. Then
we have $GAC(allperm(X))$ if and only if (by the definition of $allperm$)
$GAC(\bigwedge_{2 \leq j \leq n} x_1 \leq_{ap} x_j)$ if and only if (by the Decomposition Theorem)
$\bigwedge_{2 \leq j \leq n} GAC(x_1 \leq_{ap} x_j)$. Similarly, $GAC(ams(X))$ if and only if (by the definition of ams) $GAC(\bigwedge_{2 \leq j \leq n} x_1 \leq_{\overline{m}} x_j)$ if and only if (by the Decomposition
Theorem) $\bigwedge_{2 \leq j \leq n} GAC(x_1 \leq_{\overline{m}} x_j)$.

Thus, without losing any pruning, an algorithm for maintaining GAC on ams
can be implemented by $n - 1$ instances of an algorithm that maintains GAC on
$\leq_{\overline{m}}$. We have obtained an efficient algorithm for maintaining GAC on $\leq_{\overline{m}}$ by
implementing a slight modification to an existing algorithm for maintaining GAC
on $\leq_m$ [8]. The run time of the algorithm is $O(m + d)$ where m is the length
of the vectors and d is the domain size of the variables in the vector. Similarly,
without losing any pruning, an algorithm for maintaining GAC on $allperm$ can
be implemented by $n - 1$ instances of an algorithm that maintains GAC on $\leq_{ap}$.
There is no existing algorithm for maintaining GAC on $\leq_{ap}$, except the factorial
decomposition described in Section 1, so we turn our attention to that task.

6   A GAC Algorithm for *Allperm*

We now prove correct a method of constructing an algorithm that enforces GAC
on $allperm$. We refer throughout to vectors x and y of distinct variables (with
no variables in common). $\max(x_i)$ and $\max(x)$ denote the largest element in the
domain of x_i and the vector of values obtained by replacing each variable in x
with the maximum value in its domain. Similarly for $\min(x_i)$ and $\min(x)$. A
element x_i of x is *bound* if there is only one value in its domain. A *permutation*
of the variables of y is usually denoted by p. We refer to the elements of p either
by their position in p, or by their position in y. $y\uparrow$ is y sorted using the upper
bound of each element. We define $y - y_i$ to be the vector y, with the ith element
removed. If y is a vector of variables and v is a variable, then $v \cdot y$ denotes the
vector that is obtained by placing v at the head of y.

Lemma 1. *$GAC(x \leq_{ap} y)$ implies that for all $y_i \in y$, $GAC(x_1 \leq y_i)$*

Proof. Since the first constraint implies the second, GAC of the first constraint
implies GAC of the second.   □

Theorem 4. *If x_1 is bound to v, some $y_i \in \boldsymbol{y}$ is also bound to v, and for all $y_j \in \boldsymbol{y}$, $min(y_j) \geq v$, then $GAC(\boldsymbol{x} \leq_{ap} \boldsymbol{y})$ if and only if $GAC(\boldsymbol{x} - x_1 \leq_{ap} \boldsymbol{y} - y_i)$.*

Proof. Since for all y_j, $min(y_j) \geq y_i$ then y_i can be taken as the most significant value of the minimum permutation of any assignment to $\boldsymbol{y}$. Consider some assignment to $\boldsymbol{x}$ and $\boldsymbol{y}$. Now, $\boldsymbol{x} \leq_{ap} \boldsymbol{y}$ if and only if $\boldsymbol{x} \leq_{lex} \boldsymbol{y}\uparrow$. Since $x_1 = y_i$, this lexicographic order is unaffected by the presence or otherwise of x_1 and y_i □

We can now perform the first stage of a GAC-enforcing algorithm. First prune x_1 and the y_i by Lemma 1. If the preconditions of Theorem 4 are satisfied, remove one element from each of $\boldsymbol{x}$ and $\boldsymbol{y}$ as shown in the theorem and repeat the process. When $GAC(x_1 \leq y_i)$ for all i and either x_1 is not a singleton or there is no singleton in $\boldsymbol{y}$ equal to x_1, $\boldsymbol{x}$ and $\boldsymbol{y}$ are defined to be "Stage 1 complete".

Theorem 5. *Given "Stage 1 complete" vectors of variables $\boldsymbol{x}$ and $\boldsymbol{y}$, for each permutation $\boldsymbol{p}$ of $\boldsymbol{y}$, $x_1 := max(x_1)$ and $p_1 := min(p_1)$ are the only possible values which can lack support with respect to $\boldsymbol{x} \leq_{lex} \boldsymbol{p}$.*

Proof. From Theorem 4, x_1 and p_1 are not bound and equal and satisfy $GAC(x_1 \leq p_1)$ and hence x_1 and p_1 can be assigned such that $x_1 < p_1$.   □

Lemma 2. *If $\boldsymbol{x} \leq_{ap} \boldsymbol{y}$ is Stage 1 Complete and any element is pruned that lacks support, Stage 1 Completeness is maintained.*

Proof. Enforcing Stage 1 completeness consists of enforcing for all $y_i \in \boldsymbol{y}$, $GAC(x_1 \leq y_i)$ (Lemma 1) and discarding equal bound pairs (Theorem 4). From Theorem 5 only $max(x_1)$ and $min(y_i)$ are candidates for pruning. Pruning in either case cannot produce equal bound pairs nor violate the bounds consistency condition unless an empty domain is produced - in which case we fail.   □

From Theorems 3 and 5, to establish support for the domains of x_1 and each variable y_i in $\boldsymbol{y}$, it is sufficient to consider only the permutations of $\boldsymbol{y}$ of the form $\langle y_1, \ldots \rangle$. We can consider all these permutations simultaneously, as given $\boldsymbol{y}' = \boldsymbol{y} - y_i$, if $\boldsymbol{x} \leq_{lex} y_i \cdot (\boldsymbol{y}'\uparrow)$ is satisfiable, then so are all similar expressions containing other permutations of $\boldsymbol{y}'$,

Given vectors $\boldsymbol{x}$ and $\boldsymbol{y}$ of variables and $\boldsymbol{p} = \boldsymbol{y}\uparrow$ then the pair $(\boldsymbol{x}, \boldsymbol{y})$ is *tail-inconsistent*$_i$ if $\boldsymbol{x}' = \boldsymbol{x} - x_1$ and $\boldsymbol{p}' = \boldsymbol{p} - y_i$ then $\boldsymbol{x}' \leq_{lex} \boldsymbol{p}'$ is unsatisfiable. If $(\boldsymbol{x}, \boldsymbol{y})$ is tail-inconsistent$_i$, the *inconsistency offset* $\eta_{\boldsymbol{x},\boldsymbol{y},i} = j$ is the smallest j such that $min(x'_j) > max(p'_j)$, otherwise $\eta_{\boldsymbol{x},\boldsymbol{y},i} = \infty$. If $\eta_{\boldsymbol{x},\boldsymbol{y},i} < \infty$ there is no valid assignment of $(x) \leq_{ap} \boldsymbol{y}$ with $x_1 = y_i$ so we have to prune the domains of x_1 and y_i to forbid such assignments. After this we will have achieved $GAC(\boldsymbol{x} \leq_{ap} \boldsymbol{y})$ by Theorem 5.

Theorem 6. *Consider two equal length vectors of variables $\boldsymbol{x}$ and $\boldsymbol{y}$. If $\eta_{\boldsymbol{x},\boldsymbol{y},i} = j$ $(j \neq \infty)$, and $\boldsymbol{p} = (\boldsymbol{y} - y_i)\uparrow$ then for all $y_k \in \boldsymbol{y}$ $(max(y_k) \geq max(p_{j+1})$ or $max(y_k) > max(p_j))$ implies $\eta_{\boldsymbol{x},\boldsymbol{y},k} \leq j$*

Proof. Form $(\boldsymbol{y} - \{y_i, y_k\})\uparrow$. Ignoring alternative orderings of variables with equal upper bounds, this permutation is equal to $\boldsymbol{p}$ in at least the first j positions. Now form $(\boldsymbol{y} - y_k)\uparrow$. For the first j positions, $(\boldsymbol{y} - y_k)\uparrow \leq_{lex} \boldsymbol{p}$, since either $max(y_i) > max(p_j)$, or y_i has displaced elements whose upper bound are greater than $max(y_i)$ which can only lexicographically reduce the first j elements.   □

Theorem 7. *Consider vectors of variables x, y and constant i s.t. for all $y_k \in y$, $max(y_i) \geq max(y_k)$. If $\eta_{x,y,i} = j$ ($j \neq \infty$) and $p = (y - y_i)\!\uparrow$ then for all $y_k \in y$, $max(y_k) < max(p_j)$ implies $\eta_{x,y,k} = \infty$*

Proof. (sketch). Form $q = (y - y_k)\!\uparrow$. Without loss of generality assume y_k is the last element of q with upper bound $= max(y_k)$. Since $max(y_k) < max(p_j)$ we know y_k lies in the first $j - 1$ elements of q. As $max(y_i) > max(y_k)$, q agrees with p until the position p_h where y_k occurs, where it will be replaced by a variable with larger upper bound. However as $\eta_{x,y,i} = j$, at this position $max(p_h) = min(x_h)$. As $max(q_h) > min(p_h)$ a consistent instantiation exists.   □

Note that $max(y_i) < max(y_j)$ implies $\eta_{x,y,i} < \eta_{x,y,j}$ so if any k has $\eta_{x,y,k} < \infty$ the y_k with highest upper bound will have. And once we have $\zeta = \eta_{x,y,k}$ we can use theorems 6 and 7 tell us the if every other element is tail inconsistent or not except possibly those with the same upper bound as p_ζ in the minimal permutation which must be tested separately.

6.1   Algorithm Details

The theorems above are embodied in the **GACAP** algorithm below. First, some notes on the structures used. Buckets are objects into which we can place and remove CSP variables. Variables are allocated to buckets according to the largest element in the domain of the variable. When asked to remove an element, a bucket will remove only one, even if it has multiple copies. The function GSNEB returns the smallest non-empty bucket. We *iterate* through a collection of buckets in ascending order.

As described in Section 5.3, an algorithm, **GACAllPerm**, for maintaining GAC on *allperm* on an $n \times m$ matrix can be constructed via $n - 1$ instances of **GACAP**.

6.2   A Worked Example

Consider applying **GACAP** to the pair: $x = \langle \{2, 3\}, \{3, 4\}, \{4, 5\}, \{6\} \rangle$ and $y = \langle \{4, 5\}, \{1, 2, 3\}, \{1, 2\}, \{4, 5\} \rangle$ (where the domains of constituent variables are written as sets). A bucket sort of y is performed first according to the upper bound of each variable. This permutation, denoted p, is used hereafter for clarity. **Stage1** traverses the vectors, using the pointer α to remove from consideration bound equal pairs. Initially, $\alpha = 1$. *MaxPrune*, incrementally set to the maximum of its current value and $min(x_\alpha) - 1$, records the maximum extent to which domain elements can be removed from members of y. This pruning is done in post-processing by **CleanUp** for efficiency reasons (see below). Line 11 sets $max(x_1)$ to the smallest non-empty bucket, as justified by Lemma 1:

$$
\begin{array}{rl}
& \quad\;\; \overset{\alpha}{} \\
x & = \langle \{2, \cancel{3}\}, \; \{3, 4\}, \; \{4, 5\}, \; \{6\} \rangle \\
p & = \langle \{1, 2\}, \; \{1, 2, 3\}, \; \{4, 5\}, \; \{4, 5\} \rangle \\
MaxPrune := & \quad 1
\end{array}
$$

```
 1 Procedure GACAP(vector x, vector y)
 2 GLOBAL:  B := newBucketsort(), α := 1, MaxPrune := min(x₁) − 1, n := length(x)
 3 FOR (yᵢ ∈ y) B.add(yᵢ)
 4 Stage1()
 5 ηPruning()
 6 CleanUp()
```

```
 7 Procedure Stage1()
 8 WHILE (α ≤ n)
 9    MaxPrune := max(MaxPrune, min(xα) − 1)
10    IF (B.GSNEB() ≤ MaxPrune) FAIL
11    xα.setMax(B.GSNEB())
12    IF ¬(xα.isBound() AND B.GSNEB() = xα) RETURN
13    B.remove(B.GSNEB()), α + +
```

```
14 Procedure GetNextNonEqual(iterator,η)
15 WHILE (max(Iterator.current()) = min(xη))
16    IF(η = n) RETURN true
17    η + +, iterator + +
18 RETURN false
```

```
19 Procedure ηPruning()
20 η := α + 1, iterator := MakeIterator(B)
21 IF (GetNextNonEqual(iterator, η)) RETURN
22 checker := max(iterator.current())
23 IF(min(xη) ≤ checker) RETURN
24 FOR (yᵢ ∈ y s.t. max(yᵢ) > checker) yᵢ.setMin(min(xα) + 1)
25 iterator + +
26 IF (GetNextNonEqual(iterator, η)) RETURN
27 IF(min(xη) ≤ max(iterator.current())) RETURN
28 FOR (yᵢ ∈ y s.t. max(yᵢ) = checker) xα.setMax(max(yᵢ) − 1), yᵢ.setMin(min(xα) + 1)
```

```
29 Procedure CleanUp()
30 FOR (yᵢ ∈ y)
31    IF (max(yᵢ) ≤ MaxPrune) yᵢ := max(yᵢ) ELSE yᵢ.setMin(MaxPrune + 1)
```

x_1 and p_1 form a bound equal pair (ignoring elements of p_1 that are removed by **CleanUp**) which is discarded by incrementing α. The same process is repeated:

$$
\begin{aligned}
& \qquad\qquad\qquad\ \alpha \\
x &= \langle \{2, \cancel{3}\},\ \{3, \cancel{4}\},\ \{4, 5\},\ \{6\bar{\ }\} \\
p &= \langle \{1, 2\},\ \{1, 2, 3\},\ \{4, 5\},\ \{4, 5\}\rangle \\
MaxPrune &:= \qquad 2
\end{aligned}
$$

x_2 and p_2 form another bound equal pair. Since no pruning of x_3 is possible and x_3 is not bound, x and p are Stage 1 Complete. η**Pruning** now prunes $\max(x_1)$ and $\min(p_i)$ for $i \geq \alpha$, as necessary. The pointer η is used to traverse the tail of x and p to test if they can be made consistent.

$$
\begin{aligned}
& \qquad\qquad\qquad\ \alpha \qquad\ \eta \\
x &= \langle \{2, \cancel{3}\},\ \{3, \cancel{4}\},\ \{4, 5\},\ \{6\bar{\ }\} \\
p &= \langle \{1, 2\},\ \{1, 2, 3\},\ \{4, 5\},\ \{4, 5\}\rangle \\
MaxPrune &:= \qquad 3
\end{aligned}
$$

If the tail is inconsistent (as here because $\max(p_{\eta-1}) < \min(x_\eta)$) we know how to prune all elements except $p_{\eta-1}$. To check this last variable we remove $p_{\eta-1}$ from p and continue checking for consistency. Finally **CleanUp** traverses p and performs pruning with the value of MaxPrune.

$$
\begin{aligned}
& \qquad\qquad\qquad\ \alpha \qquad\ n \\
x &= \langle \{2, \cancel{3}\},\ \{3, \cancel{4}\},\ \{4, \cancel{5}\},\ \{6\} \rangle \\
p &= \langle \{\cancel{1}, 2\},\ \{\cancel{1}, \cancel{2}, 3\},\ \{\cancel{4}, 5\},\ \{\cancel{4}, 5\}\rangle \\
MaxPrune &:= \qquad 3
\end{aligned}
$$

6.3   Properties

Theorem 8. *The* **GACAP** *algorithm on two vectors of variables* $\boldsymbol{x}$ *and* $\boldsymbol{y}$ *of length* n *runs in time* $O(n + d)$ *where* d *is the maximum size of the domain of the variables in* $\boldsymbol{x}$ *and* $\boldsymbol{y}$.

Proof. (sketch). Sorting $\boldsymbol{y}$ into buckets takes $O(n)$. We traverse $\boldsymbol{x}$ and $\boldsymbol{y}$ examining and/or pruning each element of $\boldsymbol{x}$ and $\boldsymbol{y}$ at most once and also examining (at worst) each of the d buckets, which takes time $O(n + d)$. During **CleanUp** we may prune each element of $\boldsymbol{y}$ once, which is $O(n)$. □

If $d \gg n$ then we use an $O(n \log n)$ algorithm. Instead of sorting $\boldsymbol{y}$ into buckets we sort $\boldsymbol{y}$ from smallest to largest using the upper bound of each domain (in $O(n \log n)$). This alternative algorithm is identical to **GACAP** except instead of iterating through buckets it iterates through this sorted vector.

7   Extensions

The methods used to generate *allperm* from the row-wise lex-leader constraints can also be used to generate useful symmetry-breaking constraints for other symmetry groups. In Molnar's problem (see Section 8.1) we use the result that when a matrix has transpose as well as row and column symmetry then as well as the lex^2 and *allperm* constraints we can also impose consistently $\forall i :$ row 1 $\leq_{ap}$ col i. In a similar example, given an $n \times n$ square matrix with rotation as well as row and column symmetry we can impose the extra symmetry breaking constraints row 1 $\leq_{ap}$ col 1 and row 1 $\leq_{ap}$ col n as well as the usual lex^2 and *allperm*.

Index symmetries in matrices of more than two dimensions can be broken by a generalisation of lex^2 and *allperm*, the latter of which can be implemented by using the **GACAllPerm** algorithm. The *allperm* constraint also can be extended and adapted to the case where only some rows/columns are interchangeable. Finally we note that the **GACAllPerm** algorithm can be extended straightforwardly to cope with vectors of different length.

8   Experimental Results

We tested *allperm* on two benchmark problems in number theory and coding theory. Lack of space prevents the consideration of more domains, but further applications, such as Howell designs [1], difference matrices [13], and balanced generalised weighing matrices [12] can readily be found.

We used ILOG Solver 5.3 with the GAC lexicographic algorithm in [7], an anti-multiset algorithm adapted from the GAC multiset algorithm in [8] (see Section 5.3), and the **GACAllPerm** algorithm from Section 6. lex^2 is approximated using lexicographic ordering constraints on adjacent rows and columns. Recently, it has become possible to enforce GAC on a chain of lexicographic ordering constraints [2]. Currently, the effectiveness of this new constraint is unknown. If proven effective it could be used to improve all models tested here.

8.1   Molnar's Problem

Molnar [11] posed the following problem. Given k, construct two $k \times k$ matrices, M_1 and M_2, of integers such that the determinant of M_1 is one, the determinant of M_2 is ± 1, no entry in M_1 or M_2 is ± 1, and each entry in M_2 is the square of the corresponding entry in M_1.

The solutions to this problem are significant in classifying certain types of topological spaces. Guy [9, Section F28] discusses a variant where 0 entries are also disallowed and both determinants must be 1. Guy's variant is studied here as follows. Given k and an upper bound, u, all solutions are sought (since all solutions are interesting mathematically) where each variable in M_1 is assigned a value between 2 and u. Seeking solutions with positive entries only simplifies what is a difficult problem.

Exchanging two rows or columns of a matrix negates the determinant. Hence, this problem does not have row or column symmetry. However, by relaxing the problem such that the absolute value of the determinant is 1, we *can* apply row and column symmetry breaking. If a solution has a determinant of -1, we exchange a pair of rows/columns. The problem also has transpose symmetry which we will exploit.

We modelled this problem with matrices M_1 and M_2 of decision variables, where each entry of M_2 is constrained to be equal to the square of the corresponding entry of M_1. The determinant of each matrix is expressed as a single, large-arity constraint and bound to a variable *detVar* with domain $\{-1, 1\}$. We considered three models of symmetry breaking:

Model A $lex^2(M_1)$. Since the variables in the bottom row appear most frequently in the definition of the determinant, lex^2 is applied such that this row is least in the lexicographic ordering to agree with the variable ordering described below, ensuring that the column lex constraints are consistent with this choice. Given the transpose symmetry, we also constrain the bottom row to be lexicographically less than or equal to all columns, as discussed in Section 7.

Model B $lex^2(M_1) \wedge ams(M_1)$. In addition, $\leq_{\overline{m}}$ is used to break the transpose symmetry.

Model C $lex^2(M_1) \wedge$ **GACAllPerm**(M_1). **GACAP** is used to break the transpose symmetry.

Experiments are on order 3 and 4 matrices. The variable ordering is by row on M_1, starting at the bottom (most constrained) row. Table 1 summarises the results, which show a clear benefit to using *allperm* to break more symmetry even on the relatively small matrices experimented with here. Furthermore, the improvement increases both with the size of the matrix and the size of the domains. Using **GACAllPerm** provides a ten percent reduction in search effort over anti-multiset on these problems. Since both are linear-time algorithms, there is no reason not to use **GACAllPerm**.

8.2   Error-Correcting Codes

Given an alphabet F, a fixed-length code of a length n is a set C of strings from F^n. Given a code C and a distance function $d(x, y)$ where x and y are elements

Table 1. 256Mb PentiumIII 750MHz. Times in seconds given to 3 significant figures.

Problem order, u	Model A			Model B			Model C		
	Choices	Time	Solutions	Choices	Time	Solutions	Choices	Time	Solutions
3, 3	14	0	-	12	0	-	12	0	-
3, 4	138	0.13	-	114	0.13	-	109	0.13	-
3, 5	742	1.9	-	591	1.6	-	558	1.6	-
3, 6	2,872	18.9	-	2,210	13.8	-	2,067	13.3	-
3, 7	8,695	134	-	6,559	88.4	-	6,172	83.8	-
3, 8	22,948	756	-	17,016	466	-	16,068	440	-
3, 9	53,103	3,470	5	38,979	2,050	3	36,851	1,921	3
3, 10	113,138	13,600	6	82,302	7,800	4	77,793	7,310	4
3, 11	219,383	47,300	7	158,762	26,200	5	150,445	24,800	5
4, 3	139	0.4	-	101	0.4	-	101	0.4	-
4, 4	14,783	155	-	9,267	102	-	8,885	102	-
4, 5	499,836	23,400	19	28,3521	12,500	13	269,373	12,000	13

Table 2. 128Mb PIII 1Ghz. Times given in seconds to 3 significant figures.

Length	Size	Min. Dist.	Model A		Model B		Model C	
			choices	time	choices	time	choices	time
5	6	6	14,931	1.0	12,687	1.0	13,043	1.0
5	7	5	96,942	9.0	34,605	3.5	40,066	4.1
5	8	5	118,712	12.6	51,287	6.0	57,219	6.6
5	9	5	11,311,563	1,230	3,027,982	329	3,040,390	341
6	4	8	1,225	0.1	1,080	0.1	1,081	0.1
6	5	6	1,227,456	80.8	237,005	17.7	276,525	20.2
6	6	6	1,374,943	105	286,010	26.8	338,689	30.6
6	7	6	1,626,743	143	418,624	46.5	484,923	51.8
6	8	6	2,007,190	204	687,130	88.4	763,918	94.9
6	9	6	2,754,911	320	1,322,412	189	1,409,570	196
6	10	6	3,578,967	489	2,033,355	329	2,130,763	338
6	10	6	4,718,395	738	3,058,971	531	3,166,724	561

of C we define the minimum distance of C as the minimum of the distances between all distinct pairs of elements of C.

If $F = \{0, 1, 2, 3\}$ then a commonly used distance function is the *Lee distance*, which is useful in various areas of coding [10] and also indirectly in other areas, such as packing [3]. For two elements, x, y in a code C of length n the Lee distance is defined as $d(x, y) = \sum_{i=1}^{n} min\{|x_i - y_i|, 4 - |x_i - y_i|\}$. This is what we shall use in our experiments.

Following standard practice we represent the code as an $n \times |C|$ matrix, where each row contains one element of the code. The difference constraint is enforced between pairs of rows. This matrix has row and column symmetry: swapping rows simply changes the order in which the elements of the code are represented in the matrix, and the Lee distance is unaffected by swapping columns.

Codes defined over the Lee distance also have value symmetry. Given a code represented by a matrix as defined above, if we take any column and change each value in it by the mapping $(0 \rightarrow 1, 1 \rightarrow 2, 2 \rightarrow 3, 3 \rightarrow 0)$ then the resulting code has the same Lee distance between each pair of rows. Some of this symmetry can be broken by assuming any code has an element consisting of just zeroes. We do this in the experiments below and not not include this element in the matrix of variables we use to solve the problem. In conjunction with this basic model three models of symmetry breaking were tried.

Model A $lex^2(M)$ is enforced using lexicographic ordering constraints on adjacent rows and columns.

Model B $lex^2(M) \wedge ams(M)$.

Model C $lex^2(M) \wedge \mathbf{GACAllPerm}(M)$.

The top-most row and left-first column were constrained to be the smallest under the lexicographic order and the *ams* and *allperm* constraints were placed on the rows. The variables were instantiated in row-wise order starting from the top-most row and the variable ordering used was $(0, 1, 2, 3)$.

The experiment performed was to try to find the code with the largest minimum Lee distance given the length and size of the code.

Table 2 summarises the results. Like Molnar's problem these show that applying extra symmetry breaking constraints to lex^2 can result an improvement of over a 50% reduction in both time and number of fails and the magnitude of these improvements increases with the size of the search. There is a small but measurable difference between models B and C.

9   Future Directions

The question now is whether further constraints can be added to break more symmetry effectively than lex^2 plus *allperm*. There are some obvious possibilities, such as attempting to create an $allperm^2$. However, we have explored and rejected as inconsistent all of the possibilities that seemed straightforward to us. It may be possible to look more deeply at the row-wise lex leader constraints to obtain further symmetry breaking constraints or to consider a different lex-leader from which a stronger set of symmetry breaking constraints might be derived.

Another item of future work is to consider the combination of other types of symmetry with row and column symmetry, such as the transpose symmetry seen in our model for Molnar's problem. The interaction of *allperm* with different variable/value ordering heuristics should also be explored. Our preliminary experimentation suggests that choosing a variable/value ordering that does not conflict with *allperm* is not as straightforward as for lex^2 alone.

10   Conclusion

We have identified an extension to the highly successful lex^2 method of breaking row and column symmetries. In some cases, substantial reductions in search effort are achieved. Furthermore, the efficient implementations here incur negligible overhead. This suggests that when a problem is being modelled using lex^2, where applicable it is always worthwhile adding *allperm*.

Acknowledgements

This research is supported by UK-EPSRC grant number GR/N16129. We thank Warwick Harvey, Brahim Hnich, Zeynep Kiziltan, Toby Walsh and our anonymous reviewers.

References

1. P.J. Schellenberg B.A. Anderson and D.R. Stinson. The existance of Howell designs of even side. In *J. Combin. Theory*, pages 23–55, 1984.
2. M. Carlsson and N. Beldiceanu. Arc-consistency for a chain of lexicographic ordering constraints. Technical Report T2002-18, Swedish Institute of Computer Science, 2002.
3. J.H. Conway and N.J.A. Slone. *Sphere-Packings, Lattices and Groups, 3rd ed.* Springer-Verlag, 1992.
4. James Crawford, Matthew L. Ginsberg, Eugene Luck, and Amitabha Roy. Symmetry-breaking predicates for search problems. In *Proceedings of KR'96: Principles of Knowledge Representation and Reasoning*, pages 148–159, 1996.
5. P. Flener, A.M. Frisch, B. Hnich, Z. Kiziltan, I. Miguel, J. Pearson, and T. Walsh. Breaking row and column symmetries in matrix models. In *Proceedings of the 8th International Conference on Principles and Practice of Constraint Programming*, pages 462–476, 2002.
6. P. Flener, A.M. Frisch, B. Hnich, Z. Kiziltan, I. Miguel, and T. Walsh. Matrix modelling: Exploiting common patterns in constraint programming. In *Proceedings of the International Workshop on Reformulating Constraint Satisfaction Problems*, pages 27–41, 2002.
7. A.M. Frisch, B. Hnich, Z. Kiziltan, I. Miguel, and T. Walsh. Global constraints for lexicographic orderings. In *Proceedings of the 8th International Conference on Principles and Practice of Constraint Programming*, pages 93–108, 2002.
8. A.M. Frisch, I. Miguel, , Z. Kiziltan, B. Hnich, and T. Walsh. Multiset ordering constraints. In *Proceedings of the 18th International Joint Conference on AI*, 2003.
9. R.K. Guy. *Unsolved Problems in Number Theory*. Springer-Verlag, 1994.
10. A.R. Hammons, P.V. Kumar, N.J.A. Slone, and P.Solé. The Z_4-linearity of kerdock, goethals and related codes. *IEEE Trans. Information Theory*, 1993.
11. A.E. Molnar. A matrix problem. *American Mathematical Monthly 81*, pages 383–384, 1974.
12. R.C. Mullin and R.G. Stanton. Group matrices and balanced weighing designs. In *Utilitas Math. 8*, pages 277–301, 1975.
13. G.H.J. van Rees P.J. Schellenberg and S.A. Vanstone. Four pairwise orthogonal latin squares of order 15. In *Ars Combin. 6*, pages 141–150, 1978.
14. Ilya Shlyakhter. Generating effective symmetry-breaking predicates for search problems. *Discrete Applied Mathematics*, 2002.

Generic SBDD
Using Computational Group Theory

Ian P. Gent[1], Warwick Harvey[2], Tom Kelsey[1], and Steve Linton[1]

[1] School of Computer Science, University of St Andrews
St Andrews,Fife, KY16 9SS, UK
{ipg,tom,sal}@dcs.st-and.ac.uk
[2] IC-Parc, Imperial College London
Exhibition Road, London SW7 2AZ, UK
wh@icparc.ic.ac.uk

Abstract. We introduce a novel approach for symmetry breaking by dominance detection (SBDD). The essence of SBDD is to perform 'dominance checks' at each node in a search tree to ensure that no symmetrically equivalent node has been visited before. While a highly effective technique for dealing with symmetry in constraint programs, SBDD forces a major overhead on the programmer, of writing a dominance checker for each new problem to be solved. Our novelty here is an entirely *generic* dominance checker. This in itself is new, as are the algorithms to implement it. It can be used for any symmetry group arising in a constraint program. A constraint programmer using our system merely has to define a small number (typically 2–6) of generating symmetries, and our system detects and breaks all resulting symmetries. Our dominance checker also performs some propagation, again generically, so that values are removed from variables if setting them would lead to a successful dominance check. We have implemented this generic SBDD and report results on its use. Our implementation easily handles problems involving 10^{36} symmetries, with only four permutations needed to direct the dominance checks during search.

1 Introduction

Dealing with symmetries in constraint satisfaction problems has become a popular topic for research in recent years. Main areas of recent study include

1. the modification of backtracking search procedures so that they only return unique solutions, and
2. the use of computational group theory (henceforth CGT) methods to effectively utilise the algebraic structure of symmetries.

The modified search techniques currently broadly fall into two main categories. The first involves adding constraints whenever backtracking occurs, so that symmetric versions of the failed part of the search tree will not be considered in future [1, 11]; these techniques are collectively known as SBDS (Symmetry Breaking During Search). The second category involves performing checks

F. Rossi (Ed.): CP 2003, LNCS 2833, pp. 333–347, 2003.

at nodes in the search tree to see whether they are dominated by the symmetric equivalent of some state already considered [5, 7]; we will collectively refer to these techniques as SBDD (Symmetry Breaking by Dominance Detection). A comparison of SBDS and SBDD, together with a dominance check for a highly symmetric problem, is given in [12].

The SBDD approach as implemented to date (with one exception)[1] involves the coding of a dominance checker. This dominance checker is special purpose, as it must be written for each new problem, or at best for a class of problems such as instances of the "golfers' problem". This checker, as part of the constraint system, has to be written by the constraint programmer, who therefore must use the structure of the problem under consideration to detect dominating search nodes. Yet dominance detection is an algebraic operation, and in particular answers a question in group theory: is this node symmetrically equivalent to a previously visited one? Inevitably, if unconsciously, constraint programmers are being required to act as CGT programmers in order to implement SBDD. The contribution we make is to eliminate this necessity by providing all the algebraic equipment to perform dominance checks automatically given the minimum possible information about the symmetries of the particular problem. These dominance checks either succeed (resulting in a backtrack), or fail supplying a set of assignments, any of which, if added to the current partial assignment of values to variables, would result in the dominance check succeeding – this set is used to reduce the size of domains, thus improving search efficiency, as described in [5, 7].

The explicit use of CGT methods is motivated by the fact that the symmetries of a problem form a group: a tuple $\langle S, \circ \rangle$ where S is a set and $\circ$ is a closed binary operation over S such that:

1. $\circ$ acts associatively: $(a \circ b) \circ c = a \circ (b \circ c)$ for every $a, b, c \in S$;
2. there is a neutral element, e, such that $a \circ e = e \circ a = a$ for every $a \in S$;
3. each element has an inverse: $a \circ a^{-1} = a^{-1} \circ a = e$.

Modern CGT systems are designed to exploit this algebraic structure, and are very efficient: they allow rapid calculations to be done on large groups without the need to iterate over or explicitly represent more than a tiny fraction of the group elements. As well as offering a clear benefit in both time and space, using a CGT approach can make the expression of the symmetries by the programmer much easier: typically only a handful of example symmetries are required to generate the full symmetry group, even for very large groups; we provide examples of this in Section 5.

The main contributions of this paper are twofold. First, we show how to combine a constraint programming system with a CGT system to provide an entirely generic implementation of SBDD. Second, we introduce a novel algorithm for performing the dominance check in a generic manner using techniques from CGT.

---

[1] Although not set in constraint satisfaction terms, *Backtrack Searching in the Presence of Symmetry* [2, 3] contains many SBDD ideas, incidentally predating SBDD itself by a number of years. This work influenced our approach here.

It is instructive to compare this paper with our first application to symmetry breaking using the combination of a CGT system and a constraint programming system, namely our implementation of SBDS reported at CP-02 [9]. The implementation of SBDD using CGT methods raises very different problems from that of SBDS. For SBDS, the task is to compute a set of symmetry breaking constraints. For SBDD, the task is to implement a search algorithm, i.e. the dominance checker. Since the tasks are so different, the implementations themselves are very different. Indeed, a major contribution here is the algorithm for a generic dominance checker, and the resulting CGT program shares no code with the CGT program used for SBDS. Our work here is therefore very novel compared to [9]. The advantage of the current work is that there is no significant space requirement to store the set of constraints, as happens in SBDS. The limiting factor for SBDD is the time taken to search for dominance rather than space. We show that we can deal, in an entirely generic manner, with groups with as many as 10^{36} elements, compared to only a few billion in our implementation of SBDS.

We describe some necessary background on constraint systems and permutation groups in Section 2. We outline SBDD in Section 3, and provide a detailed exposition of the novel algorithm used in our generic implementation in Section 4. Section 5 consists of some experimental results. We discuss our results and highlight future avenues of research in Section 6.

2   Background

We first provide some background material. While we assume familiarity with the basic concepts of constraint satisfaction, we first sketch the problems that arise when a constraint problem contains symmetry. Then, we briefly describe permutation groups and how they can be used in the CGT system GAP, and finally the interface we previously constructed between GAP and ECL^{i}PS^e.

To provide a concrete implementation, we use the constraint logic programming system ECL^{i}PS^e [20] to model the constraint satisfaction problem and to search, while the dominance checks needed for SBDD are performed in a child process, using the world-leading computational group theory system GAP [8]. There is nothing essential about this choice. Barring unforeseen technical problems, we could equally well have used other CGT systems such as Magma, or other constraint systems such as Ilog Solver. GAP and ECL^{i}PS^e are large, mature and widely-used systems. Both systems incorporate libraries and packages for computation in specific areas, together with tools and resources for software development. For our purposes, the GAP permutation group libraries and the ECL^{i}PS^e finite domain libraries are of interest.

ECL^{i}PS^e uses standard finite domain constraints, and, during search, applies constraint propagation techniques developed by the AI community [14]. The standard search method is depth-first, and assigns values to variables at choice points. A complete assignment that satisfies the constraints is a solution.

If no symmetry breaking constraints have been posted before search, then ECL^{i}PS^e will search for and return all solutions, irrespective of any symmetries involved. For example, consider the illustrative problem of finding a list $[A, B, C, D, E, F, G]$ of distinct numbers in $1 \ldots 50$ such that $A^3 + B^3 + C^3 + D^3 = E^3 + F^3 + G^3$. A solution is $[1, 2, 3, 39, 18, 22, 35]$, but this is symmetrically equivalent to those lists with 1, 2, 3, and 39 permuted in any way, and/or 18, 22 and 35 permuted. Our aim is to restrict search to choices which do not lead to one of these other lists. Restricting search to avoid symmetrically equivalent solutions has a larger benefit than avoiding duplicate solutions. Symmetry breaking methods such as SBDD or SBDS also avoid duplicating search from failed nodes. This can have a dramatic effect on time taken, as the same failed search state can reoccur in many symmetric guises, only one of which need be explored.

A permutation is a rearrangement of elements in an ordered list S into a one-to-one correspondence with S itself. The number of permutations on a set of n elements is $n!$. Two permutations can be composed by composing their respective correspondences with S; since all such correspondences are bijective, the composition has an inverse. For example, to construct the resulting composition, one can trace the action of successive permutations. If 1 corresponded to 8 in the first, and 8 corresponded to 3 in the second, then 1 would correspond to 3 in the composition. If we take the identity mapping on S as the required neutral element, composition of permutations forms a group. GAP contains libraries for defining, composing, and manipulating individual permutations, and for computation within permutation groups.

Taking S to be a position indexing of the list $[A, B, C, D, E, F, G]$ described in the previous section, we have $S = [1, 2, 3, 4, 5, 6, 7]$. Permutations in GAP are usually entered and displayed in cycle notation, such as $(1, 2, 3)(5, 7)$ which denotes the correspondence which has as image the list $[2, 3, 1, 4, 7, 6, 5]$. (A human might describe this permutation as '1 goes to 2, 2 goes to 3, 3 goes to 1, 5 and 7 are swapped, 4 and 6 are unchanged.'.)

Given that there are 7! possible permutations on S, which are the permutations which preserve solutions to the $A^3 + B^3 + C^3 + D^3 = E^3 + F^3 + G^3$ problem? This is straightforward in GAP – we simply supply some example permutations, and let GAP compute the resulting permutation group. Swapping A and D and cycling A, B, C and D are solution preserving symmetries, represented by the permutations $(1, 4)$ and $(1, 2, 3, 4)$ respectively. Similarly $(5, 7)$ and $(5, 6, 7)$ denote the swapping of E and G and a cycling of E, F and G. Supplying these 4 permutations to GAP results in permutation group containing 144 elements (3! permutations of E, F and G for each of the 4! permutations of A, B, C and D). In group theoretic terminology this is known as the direct product of the symmetric group on 4 points and the symmetric group on 3 points. In order to use GAP–ECL^{i}PS^e with either the SBDS version given in [9] or the SBDD implementation described in Section 3 of this paper, these 4 permutations are the only information that the constraint logic programmer has to provide to GAP for this problem. GAP can now answer questions such as

- What is the composition of $(1, 4)$ with $(1, 3)(5, 7, 6)$, i.e. the permutation corresponding to performing first $(1, 4)$ and then $(1, 3)(5, 7, 6)$?
  - $(1, 4, 3)(5, 7, 6)$
- Which of our 144 permutations do not move A, C or E?
  - $()$, $(6, 7)$, $(2, 4)$, $(2, 4)(6, 7)$ – this is the point stabiliser of A, C and E.
- To which points is G mapped to by our group elements?
  - $7, 6, 5$ (i.e. G is mapped to E, F and itself) – this is the orbit of G.

Many of the questions passed to GAP by ECL^{i}PS^e during search are answered by (rather more complicated) calculations similar to those given above. It should be noted that, for computational purposes, a symmetry group consists of a generating set of permutations. This set can usually consist of only two elements, but, for our purposes, contains a few examples of known symmetries. The problem of enabling CSP practitioners to express problem symmetries easily is addressed in [13, 15]. No sensible CGT system computes every element of the group; algorithms construct new elements (or subgroups, or coset representatives, etc.) as required.

In [9] we reported on a simple interface between GAP and ECL^{i}PS^e . In GAP–ECL^{i}PS^e all constraint satisfaction modeling and constraint handling is done in ECL^{i}PS^e, as is the choosing of value to variable assignments during search, and any resulting elimination of values from domains by propagation. GAP runs as a sub-process, and is called as and when symmetry breaking information is needed. In effect, ECL^{i}PS^e is the master, and GAP the slave. The key concept that motivates the interface is that the symmetries of a constraint satisfaction problem are permutations on a suitable initial segment of the natural numbers. Since sets of permutations have a well known algebraic structure, and since GAP uses the algebraic structure to enhance and extend computational capability, we use GAP to provide symmetry information to ECL^{i}PS^e during search. We report further details of the interface in [9].

3   Symmetry Breaking by Dominance Detection

In order to deal with symmetry-related questions arising at nodes in the search tree, we define an $M \times N$ array where N is the number of variables in our constraint satisfaction problem, and M is the number of values that the variables can take. The i,j-th element in the array denotes assigning the value i to the variable j, and each element is associated with a unique number (point) from 1 to MN. We then define symmetries in terms of permutations on these $M \times N$ points. It should be noted that

- this allows us to define symmetries on both variables (as in the example above) and values (as in, for example, a graph colouring problem where values representing colours can be interchanged); and
- the algebraic structure is preserved: for the above example we have 144 permutations on 50×7 points, with each permutation corresponding to a unique member of the original group acting on 7 points.

This structure allows us to ask GAP questions regarding the image of (sets of) variable–value assignments under permutations. We write this as p^g, where p is an assignment point and g is an element of a permutation group. We have, for example, $17^{(2,5,17,9,8)} = 9$.

Suppose that we have identified a symmetry group, G, and that we maintain a record in a list S of *fail sets*: sets corresponding to the roots of completed subtrees. Each fail set contains the points from the $M \times N$ array corresponding to the positive decisions made during the search to reach the root of the subtree. Note that we consider decisions, as opposed to domains, as suggested in [12, 18]. As long as we try a positive decision (*Var* = *Val*) before its negative (*Var* $\neq$ *Val*) we are free to ignore the negative decisions [7, 12, 18]. E.g. looking at the $Y = b$ subtree in Figure 1, $Y = b$ has already been fully explored regardless of whether or not $X \neq a$, since the $X = a$ case was covered by the $X = a$ subtree.

Suppose also that *Pointset* denotes the set of points corresponding to variables which have been set to a fixed value in the current search node (either through direct assignment or through propagation). This situation is shown informally in Figure 1, where the circle indicates the current search node and the shaded triangles denote completed subtrees: S contains three single-element sets containing the points corresponding to the assignments $X = a$, $Y = b$ and $Z = c$, and if any variables have been given fixed values as a result of propagating the decisions $X \neq a$, $Y \neq b$ and $Z \neq c$, the corresponding points will appear in *Pointset*.

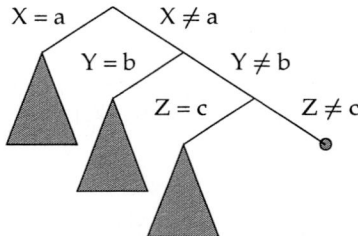

Fig. 1. A partial search tree

We say that our current node is dominated by a completed subtree if there exists a g in G and an s in S such that

$$s^g \subseteq Pointset \quad .$$

If dominance is detected, then it is safe to backtrack, since the current search state is symmetrically equivalent to one considered previously.

In practice, we pass to the dominance checker more information about the current state than just the fixed variables, in order to facilitate domain reduction when dominance is not detected (see Section 4).

```
generic_sbdd(Failset, depth) : −
    choose(Var, Val)
    assert(Var = Val)
    depth := depth + 1
    pt := Point(Var = Val)
    NewFailset := [pt, Failset]
    Doms := [current_domains]
    if consistent(CSP) and askGAP(Doms) = [false, Q] then
        reduce_domains(Q)
        solution_check
        generic_sbdd(NewFailset, depth)
    else
        tellGAP(NewFailset, depth)
        retract(Var = Val)
        assert( not (Var = val))
        Doms := [current_domains]
        if consistent(CSP) and askGap(Doms) = [false, Q] then
            reduce_domains(Q)
            solution_check
            generic_sbdd(Failset, depth)
        else
            backtrack(newdepth)
            generic_sbdd(Failset, newdepth)
        end if
    end if
```

Fig. 2. Pseudo-code for generic SBDD

4   Generic SBDD

Pseudo-code for our generic SBDD implementation is given in Figure 2. The procedure assumes that the search state is at a node at a given depth in the search tree, and that we have a record of the fail set accumulated on the current branch of the search. We first choose a variable–value pair, try the assignment $Var = Val$, and increment the depth counter. The $Var = Val$ choice represents a point, pt, of our value–variable array; we add this to our fail set, as it represents the latest root node of a subtree. We next obtain $Doms$, a list of the domains of all the variables at the current search node (after propagating the $Var = Val$ assignment). Note that $Doms$ implicitly contains $Pointset$, as well as information about which values cannot be assigned to particular variables (either from propagation or from explicit $Var \neq Val$ assertions made on the current branch).

Provided that the CSP is still consistent, we are now ready to ask GAP for a dominance check, details of which are given in Section 4.1. If this check succeeds (i.e. a dominating state was found), we can backtrack in ECL^{i}PS^e as we have already explored an equivalent state. If this check fails (i.e. if no dominating state is found) then we can still benefit by domain reduction. Our dominance checker supplies a set of points that, if any one of the corresponding assignments is made, would result in a successful dominance check. Clearly we should not allow a search which makes any of these assignments, so we remove them from the domains of the variables involved. This not only reduces the sizes of the value domains, but also allows further propagation based on the removals. This is a significant benefit over obtaining a mere yes/no answer to the dominance check.

In this situation, since there was no dominance, we carry on searching by choosing the next variable–value pair, using the updated fail set and depth value. A small, but important, point arises in this situation. The domain reduction after a failed dominance check can lead through propagation to setting all variables and obtaining a complete solution. This solution might turn out to be equivalent to a previously obtained solution. Therefore in this situation we perform a final dominance check to guarantee that all solutions returned are distinct.

When the dominance check succeeds, we retract $Var = Val$ and assert $Var \neq Val$. We tell GAP that our current fail set is the most up to date, and remove pt from it. Now that we are at a different node in the search tree, we can obtain $Doms$ again perform another dominance check. If this check fails, then, as before, we reduce value domain sizes by removing from variable domains any elements we know would have led to dominance if they had been assigned to the variable, check that any solution is not dominated by a previous one, and carry on searching below the $Var \neq Val$ branch.

If, however, the $Var \neq Val$ dominance check succeeds, then we backtrack to the nearest ancestor node where we have yet to consider the negative branch. This point becomes the root of a completed subtree, we update the fail set accordingly, and carry on searching.

4.1 Dominance Check Using Computational Group Theory

We maintain in GAP a record of fail sets, and the depth of their roots. The symmetry group is computed from generators supplied from the ECL^{i}PS^e model of the problem. In fact, the whole group is not usually computed explicitly – a permutation group on n points can have $n!$ elements, leading to a large space overhead unless techniques are used for computing group elements as and when required.

The dominance check is implemented using a tree-like data structure which encodes all of the fail sets currently applicable, while taking maximum advantage of their overlaps. Every possible $Var = Val$ assignment is identified by a point in a symmetry matrix; the symmetry group for a given problem permutes these points, so that every symmetry is defined by a unique permutation.

We can identify disjoint sets of points $A_1, \ldots, A_k$ and $B_0, \ldots, B_k$ such that the fail sets are $A_1 \cup \cdots \cup A_i \cup B_i$ for each i. The right-pointing edges of the tree are labelled with elements of an A_i, the left-pointing ones with elements of a B_i. Each node of the tree can be associated with the sequence of labels on the path to it from the root.

For example, if the current failsets are [52, 79, 72, 51, 64, 57, 50, 53] and [61, 88, 74, 60, 52, 79, 72, 51, 64, 57, 50, 76] and we are asked to check [98, 48, 90, 42, 35, 77, 27, 96, 82, 14, 70, 13, 69, 40, 26, 19, 61, 46, 88, 32, 74, 18, 60, 7, 6, 5, 4, 87, 94, 31, 24, 17, 10, 52, 37, 44, 79, 72, 16, 9, 51, 22, 29, 36, 43, 64, 57, 50], for dominance (this situation arises in the BIBD(7,7,3,3,1) problem described in Section 5.3), then we have $A_1 = \{52, 79, 72, 51, 64, 57, 50\}$, $B_1 = \{53\}$, $A_2 = \{61, 88, 74, 60\}$, $B_2 = \{76\}$.

We perform the dominance check using a recursive search, which descends this tree, entering each node once for every way of mapping the associated sequence of points into the current point list. If we reach a left-pointing leaf, then we have discovered dominance. The implementation of the search uses the standard group theoretic machinery of stabilizer chains, Schreier vectors and transversals, described, for instance in [19].

We can detect relatively easily cases where all but the final element of a fail set can be mapped into *Pointset*, and report them, eventually, back to ECL^{i}PS^e, so that domain deletion can occur. A few other cases can also be detected quickly. It is possible to enhance the search to detect all cases where all but one elements of a fail set can be mapped, but the benefit of the extra propagation never seems to outweigh the cost of the extra search.

Full details and the GAP code used will appear in a forthcoming Technical Report.

Since fail sets and point lists are not, in general, the same size, the more powerful machinery of partition backtrack searching also described in [19] does not appear to be helpful.

A useful optimisation is possible in cases where the points fall into more than one *orbit* under the action of the symmetry group. This arises, for instance, if the symmetries permute the variables and not the values. In this case it may happen that all the points appearing in failsets lie in a subset of the orbits. For instance if all the variables are Boolean, then for some labelling strategies, we will only ever see points corresponding to assignments $Var = true$ appearing in the failsets. In this case, points in other orbits are *irrelevant* in the sense that no symmetry can ever map any point of any failset to them. These points can be ignored in the search, and, more importantly, if no new relevant points have been added to the pointlist since a previous dominance check, the entire check can be omitted.

This implementation produces good performance on moderate-sized examples (up to about 10^{36} symmetries), but the internal search can become bogged down when a subset of some F has a large stabilizer, so that we can find elements of G mapping $f_1, \ldots, f_k$ to $p_1, \ldots, p_k$ in any order, but none of these allow us to map f_{k+1} to anything in *Pointset*. Actually computing the set stabilizers of initial segments of F, while possible, seems to be prohibitively expensive in many cases, but such situations usually arise when the group G preserves a system of imprimitivity (for example the rows and columns of a matrix-structured

problem) and this condition can be recognized cheaply. Exploiting this information will be an important part of future work. Further implementation details
(including source code) are available in [10].

5   Examples

In this section we provide some results of computations using our implemenenta-
tion of generic SBDD in GAP–ECL^{i}PS^e. All the examples were run on a 2.6 GHz
Pentium IV processor with 512 megabytes of memory, and times are reported in
seconds. Where possible we compare the performance of our SBDD implementation with that of our GAP–ECL^{i}PS^e SBDS implementation given in [9], which
provided full symmetry breaking in a few seconds for problems having up to 10^9
symmetries. A major cost in dealing with larger symmetry groups in SBDS is
the communication of information between GAP and ECL^{i}PS^e – the constraints
posted during search are based on large algebraic structures which have to be
returned to ECL^{i}PS^e from GAP. In SBDD, however, we expect to be able to
deal with much larger groups, since inter-process communication consists of the
word *true*, the word *false*, or lists of points of length at most $M \times N$.

5.1   Example: $A^3 + B^3 + C^3 + D^3 = E^3 + F^3 + G^3$

We first consider the illustrative problem given in Section 2. Clearly, breaking
symmetry in this problem is achievable by adding the constraints

$$A \leq B \leq C \leq D \quad \text{and} \quad E \leq F \leq G \quad .$$

We include this example to demonstrate that out implementation breaks all 144
symmetries, with performance comparable to that of SBDS in GAP–ECL^{i}PS^e.
The results for all solutions with domains $1 \ldots 20$ are given in Table 1.

Table 1. Seven cubes problem – comparative results

	SBDD	SBDS	ECL^{i}PS^e
Solutions	265	265	38,160
Backtracks [BT]	38,703	38,483	1.5×10^6
GAP cpu [Gcpu]	1,040	973	n/a
ECL^{i}PS^e cpu [Ecpu]	272	482	4,037
Σ cpu	1,312	1,455	4,037

We see that SBDD and SBDS both eliminate all the symmetries in roughly the
same time, whereas a search which ignores symmetry returns 144×265 solutions.

5.2   Example: Colouring the Vertices of a Dodecahedron

We consider the problem of colouring the vertices of a dodecahedron, the regular polyhedron having 12 pentagonal faces and 20 vertices. This problem has

two useful illustrative features: it involves symmetries in both the variables and values, and obtaining the correct symmetry group is easier than writing a dominance detector for use in SBDD without computational group theory.

The variables $x_1, \ldots, x_{20}$ represent the 20 vertices. The values $c_1, \ldots, c_m$ are the m colours in question. It can be shown that the symmetry group of the dodecahedron is isomorphic to the group of even permutations of five objects, known to group theorists as A_5, which has 60 elements. Since any permutation of a colouring is allowed, the symmetry group of the values is S_m. The total number of symmetries is then $60 \times m!$, acting on $20 \times m$ points. We construct this group in GAP from just four generators:

– the image of the vertices after one rotation of 72° about a face;
– the image of the vertices after one rotation of 120° about a vertex;
– the index of the colours with the first two swapped;
– the index of the colours cycled by one place mod m.

The constraints of the CSP are of the form $x_i \neq x_j$ whenever vertex i is joined by an edge to vertex j. We seek the number of colourings for a given m, such that no colouring is a symmetric equivalent of another.

Table 2. Colouring dodecahedrons – SBDD

GAP–ECL^{i}PS^e (SBDD)							Dominance checks		
Colours	Symms.	Sols.	BT	Gcpu	Ecpu	Σcpu	Success	Fail	Delete
3	360	31	50	0.44	0.07	0.51	71	19	31
4	1440	117902	109502	770.62	109.08	879.70	116396	351720	1176

From Table 2 we see that, for the 3 colour case, 121 dominance checks were made. Of these, 71 stopped further search in a symmetric sub-branch, 19 failed without providing any near misses, and 31 failed and supplied points which could be deleted from current domains as not leading to any new solutions. All 360 symmetries were broken, with the 31 non-isomorphic colourings returned in less than one second.

5.3   Example: Balanced Incomplete Block Designs

We now present results for examples with much larger symmetry groups. Consider the problem of finding $v \times b$ binary matrices such that each row has exactly r ones, each column has exactly k ones, and the scalar product of each pair of distinct rows is λ. This is a computational version of the (v, b, r, k, λ) BIBD problem [4]. We label the $v \times b$ matrix in column order, since $v \leq b$ for all suitable parameters. We assign zeros before ones whenever $k \geq b/2$, otherwise we assign ones before zeros; the heuristic is to use the minimum domain value whenever there are more ones than zeros in each column.

Solutions do not exist for all parameters, and results are useful in areas such as cryptography and coding theory. A solution has $v! \times b!$ symmetric equivalents:

one for each permutation of the rows and/or columns of the matrix. Gent *et al.* [9] reported results with the largest symmetry group having $6! \times 10! \approx 3 \times 10^9$ elements. The results for our generic SBDD implementation are given in Table 3.

Table 3. Balanced incomplete block designs – SBDD

Parameters					GAP–ECL^{i}PS^e (SBDD)					Dominance checks		
v	b	$r\ k\ \lambda$	Symms.	Sols.	BT	Gcpu	Ecpu	Σcpu	Success	Fail	Delete
7	7	3 3 1	10^7	1	2	0.18	0.04	0.22	6	15	10
6	10	5 3 2	10^9	1	2	0.43	0.13	0.56	20	40	31
7	14	6 3 2	10^{14}	4	33	4.63	0.34	4.97	64	146	124
9	12	4 3 1	10^{14}	1	3	1.79	0.10	1.89	9	29	26
11	11	5 5 2	10^{15}	1	65	18.36	0.75	19.11	103	272	177
8	14	7 4 3	10^{15}	4	327	63.04	3.20	66.24	720	1344	727
13	13	4 4 1	10^{19}	1	2	41.92	0.26	42.18	11	38	29
6	20	10 3 4	10^{21}	4	171	53.40	2.19	55.59	381	665	648
7	21	6 2 1	10^{23}	1	2	10.42	0.15	10.57	12	36	31
16	20	5 4 1	10^{31}	1	10	6077.19	0.43	6077.62	22	64	65
13	26	6 3 1	10^{36}	2	425	59338.23	5.81	59344.04	576	1487	968

The first point to note is that, as expected, we can deal with much larger groups than our GAP–ECL^{i}PS^e implementation of SBDS [9]. SBDS was able to deal only with BIBDs in the first two lines of the table. It was up to about four times slower, while an interesting difference was that most cpu time was in ECL^{i}PS^e with GAP dominating time here.

We can see from these results that the absolute number of symmetries of a problem is not necessarily a guide to the difficulty in eliminating them from solutions. The $(8, 14, 7, 3, 4)$ BIBD problem has "only" $\approx 3.5 \times 10^{15}$ symmetries, but is harder to solve than ones with $O(10^{21})$ and $O(10^{23})$ symmetries. As well as the inherent difficulty of the original constraint problem, much depends on the size and nature of structures within the algebraic structure of each symmetry group, which is another reason for utilising a specialised CGT system such as GAP, which is designed to find and exploit these sub-structures. As a general rule, though, it is harder to eliminate solution symmetries from a larger matrix model.

It is also worth noting that the entire symmetry group for any BIBD can be generated from just four permutations: cycling the rows and columns, and swapping the first and last row and the first and last column. These permutations are trivially implemented, and comprise the only information needed by GAP–ECL^{i}PS^e to break all the symmetries of the problem.

The timings obtained are comparable with those presented for the same problems in [6], where lexicographic ordering constraints were use to break the row and column symmetries. The advantage of using SBDD is that all symmetries are broken, whereas a lexicographic solution for the $(6, 20, 10, 3, 4)$ BIBD problem returns 21 solutions. Moreover, while SBDD can work with any variable or value ordering heuristics, a heuristic can interact badly with lexicographic ordering constraints [9].

6   Conclusions

We have presented an implementation of SBDD which

- uses specialist CGT techniques to detect dominance.
- guarantees to return only symmetrically distinct solutions.
- does not require a new dominance checker to be implemented for each new problem – the user only has to supply a small sample of symmetries.
- allows value domains to be reduced at search nodes where no dominance occurs. We do this by removing values of variables which, if set, we know would lead to a successful dominance check.
- eliminates all symmetries in large scale combinatoric problems.

We believe that the use of CGT techniques in SBDD solvers is an important contribution. While there is scope for further optimisation of our techniques, we already have significant advantages over related work. Compared to other implementations of SBDD, we have the key advantage of avoiding the need for a separate dominance check to be implemented, either directly [5] or as a separate constraint satisfaction problem [17]. This is an extremely important step forward in the application of SBDD. Compared to the use of GAP for SBDS [9], we avoid the large space overhead, meaning that – as we reported here – we are able to solve completely problems with groups many orders of magnitude larger. Some techniques, such as [6], do not guarantee to eliminate all symmetries, while we do.

Our implementation is robust: both the ECL^{i}PS^e and GAP searches are deterministic, and will break all the supplied symmetries, since a dominance check is performed at each node visited during search. This robustness may have a negative effect on efficiency. There is evidence that performance can be improved by making full dominance checks at a subset of the visited nodes [5,17], or by using a subset of the full symmetry group of the problem [16]. Both of these approaches depend on the size and structure of the problem being addressed, and we will investigate their applicability to our implementation in the future.

Our work raises a number of questions for further research. First, having implemented both SBDS and SBDD using generic methods, we are in a position to ask whether or not they can be combined in interesting ways to gain the advantages of both. In naïve terms, one can see SBDS as best suited where groups are small, with SBDD effective on larger groups. Yet the symmetries in a constraint problem usually become small as search continues, and it may be possible to implement combined techniques which act like SBDD in some parts of the search tree and like SBDS in other parts. A second question is how far we can integrate SBDS and SBDD with what is perhaps the most commonly used symmetry breaking technique, the use of hand-written symmetry breaking constraints. As these can be very effective, it would be desirable to gain their advantages in terms of simplicity and efficiency, while still having the correctness and uniqueness guarantees of SBDS and SBDD without users having to be expert group theorists.

Acknowledgements

We are very grateful for their helpful comments and other assistance to Iain McDonald, Karen Petrie, Barbara Smith and Toby Walsh. This work is partly supported by EPSRC grant GR/R29666 and by a Royal Society of Edinburgh SEELLD Support Fellowship.

References

1. R. Backofen and S. Will, *Excluding symmetries in constraint-based search*, Proceedings, CP-99, Springer, 1999, LNCS 1713, pp. 73–87.
2. C.A. Brown, L. Finkelstein, and P.W. Purdom, Jr., *Backtrack searching in the presence of symmetry*, Proc. AAECC-6 (T. Mora, ed.), no. 357, Springer-Verlag, 1988, pp. 99–110.
3. C.A. Brown, L. Finkelstein, and P.W. Purdom Jr., *Backtrack searching in the presence of symmetry*, Nordic Journal of Computing **3** (1996), no. 3, 203–219.
4. C.H. Colbourn and J.H. Dinitz (eds.), *The CRC handbook of combinatorial designs*, CRC Press, Rockville, Maryland, USA, 1996.
5. Torsten Fahle, Stefan Schamberger, and Meinolf Sellmann, *Symmetry breaking*, Proc. CP 2001 (T. Walsh, ed.), 2001, pp. 93–107.
6. Pierre Flener, Alan M. Frisch, Brahim Hnich, Zeynap Kızıltan, Ian Miguel, Justin Pearson, and Toby Walsh, *Breaking row and column symmetries in matrix models*, Proceedings of the Eighth International Conference on Principles and Practice of Constraint Programming — CP'2002 (Pascal Van Hentenryck, ed.), Lecture Notes in Computer Science, vol. 2470, Springer-Verlag, 2002, pp. 462–476.
7. Filippo Focacci and Michaela Milano, *Global cut framework for removing symmetries*, Proc. CP 2001 (T. Walsh, ed.), 2001, pp. 77–92.
8. The GAP Group, *GAP - Groups, Algorithms, and Programming, Version 4.2*, 2000, (http://www.gap-system.org).
9. Ian P. Gent, Warwick Harvey, and Tom Kelsey, *Groups and constraints: Symmetry breaking during search*, Proceedings of the Eighth International Conference on Principles and Practice of Constraint Programming — CP'2002 (Pascal Van Hentenryck, ed.), Lecture Notes in Computer Science, vol. 2470, Springer-Verlag, 2002, pp. 415–430.
10. Ian P. Gent, Warwick Harvey, Tom Kelsey, and Steve Linton, *Generic SBDD using computational group theory*, Tech. Report APES-57a-2003, APES Research Group, January 2003, Available from http://www.dcs.st-and.ac.uk/~apes/apesreports.html.
11. I.P. Gent and B.M. Smith, *Symmetry breaking in constraint programming*, Proceedings of ECAI-2000 (W. Horn, ed.), IOS Press, 2000, pp. 599–603.
12. Warwick Harvey, *Symmetry breaking and the social golfer problem*, Proceedings, SymCon-01: Symmetry in Constraints (Pierre Flener and Justin Pearson, eds.), 2001, pp. 9–16.

13. Warwick Harvey, Tom Kelsey, and Karen Petrie, *Symmetry group generation for CSPs*, Tech. Report APES-60-2003, APES Research Group, July 2003, Available from http://www.dcs.st-and.ac.uk/~apes/apesreports.html.

14. Pascal Van Hentenryck, *Constraint satisfaction in logic programming*, Logic Programming Series, MIT Press, Cambridge, MA, 1989.

15. Iain McDonald, *Symmetry breaking systems*, Tech. Report APES-61-2003, APES Research Group, July 2003, Available from http://www.dcs.st-and.ac.uk/~apes/apesreports.html.

16. Iain McDonald and Barbara Smith, *Partial symmetry breaking*, Proceedings of the Eighth International Conference on Principles and Practice of Constraint Programming — CP'2002 (Pascal Van Hentenryck, ed.), Lecture Notes in Computer Science, vol. 2470, Springer-Verlag, 2002, pp. 431–445.

17. J-F. Puget, *Symmetry breaking revisited*, Proceedings of the Eighth International Conference on Principles and Practice of Constraint Programming — CP'2002 (Pascal Van Hentenryck, ed.), Lecture Notes in Computer Science, vol. 2470, Springer-Verlag, 2002, pp. 446–461.

18. Jean-François Puget, *Symmetry breaking revisited*, Proceedings of the Eighth International Conference on Principles and Practice of Constraint Programming — CP'2002 (Pascal Van Hentenryck, ed.), Lecture Notes in Computer Science, vol. 2470, Springer-Verlag, 2002, pp. 446–461.

19. Akos Seress, *Permutation group algorithms*, Cambridge tracts in mathematics, no. 152, Cambridge University Press, 2002.

20. M. G. Wallace, S. Novello, and J. Schimpf, *ECLiPSe : A platform for constraint logic programming*, ICL Systems Journal **12** (1997), no. 1, 159–200.

Using Stochastic Local Search
to Solve Quantified Boolean Formulae

Ian P. Gent[1], Holger H. Hoos[2], Andrew G.D. Rowley[1], and Kevin Smyth[2]

[1] University of St. Andrews, Fife, Scotland
{ipg,agdr}@dcs.st-and.ac.uk
[2] University of British Columbia, Vancouver, Canada
{hoos,ksmyth}@cs.ubc.ca

Abstract. We present a novel approach to solving Quantified Boolean Formulae (QBFs), exploiting the power of stochastic local search methods for SAT. This makes the search process different in some interesting ways from conventional QBF solvers. First, the resulting solver is incomplete, as it can terminate without a definite result. Second, we can take advantage of the high level of optimisations in a conventional stochastic SAT algorithm. Our new solver, WalkQSAT, is structured as two components, one of which controls the QBF search while the other is a slightly adapted version of the classic SAT local search procedure WalkSAT. The WalkSAT component has no knowledge of QBF, and simply solves a sequence of SAT instances passed to it by the QBF component. We compare WalkQSAT with the state-of-the-art QBF solver QuBE-BJ. We show that WalkQSAT can outperform QuBE-BJ on some instances, and is able to solve two instances that QuBE-BJ could not. WalkQSAT often outperforms our own direct QBF solver, suggesting that with more efficient implementation it would be a very competitive solver. WalkQSAT is an inherently incomplete QBF solver, but still solves many unsatisfiable instances as well as satisfiable ones. We also study run-time distributions of WalkQSAT, and investigate the possibility of tuning WalkSAT's heuristics for use in QBFs.

1 Introduction

Stochastic local search (SLS) methods are an area of continuing interest in the satisfiability (SAT) community. While not guaranteed to return a solution (nor to determine unsatisfiability), they can often be more effective than complete methods, as they are not restricted by the need to cover the entire search space systematically. It is natural to wonder if SLS methods can be applied to Quantified Boolean Formulae (QBF) problems. QBF is a generalisation of SAT with applications in areas such as hardware verification, planning, and games. Variables in a QBF instance can be either existentially or universally quantified. Put simply, with details to follow below, a QBF problem is satisfiable if the existential variables can be set to satisfy the instance, in SAT terms, for all possible instantiations of the universal variables.

Unfortunately, the application of SLS methods to QBF is problematic. The most pressing problem is that individual search states are not simply assignments of variables to the two truth values. Instead, the most natural representation of a search state is as a

F. Rossi (Ed.): CP 2003, LNCS 2833, pp. 348–362, 2003.

strategy, defining the values of the existential variables for each possible instantiation of the universals. However this is an infeasibly large object except when there are a very small number of universal variables. Despite the difficulties in applying SLS techniques to QBF solving, there are compelling reasons for doing so. Search in a QBF is a search for many satisfying assignments for a variety of very closely related SAT instances. Not only can SLS methods often perform these searches very fast, they can naturally take advantage of solutions to previous instances as starting points for the current search.

Our incomplete QBF solver, called WalkQSAT, is structured as a collaboration between two components. The first component, the QBF engine. performs a backjumping search based on a successful method from the literature called Conflict and Solution Directed Backjumping (CSBJ) [1]. The second component, the SAT engine, is used as an auxiliary search procedure to find satisfying assignments quickly (details of these components, and how they interact are given later in the paper). We use WalkSAT [2] as the SAT engine for WalkQSAT, although a whole family of QBF algorithms can be designed by using other algorithms for the SAT engine. WalkQSAT has the following properties. If it returns True (T) or False (F) given an instance, that instance is guaranteed to be true or false respectively. If it returns Unknown (U), then the truth or falsity of the instance could not be verified within the given constraints. WalkQSAT is naturally more likely to successfully solve true instances, given that false instances are more likely to contain more states in which WalkSAT will not be able to find a solution, but some false instances can be solved nevertheless. As we will see, WalkQSAT can outperform state-of-the-art solvers on some instances.

This paper introduces for the first time the study of SLS methods for solving QBF instances. Even so, we are in some instances able to outperform the state-of-the-art solver QuBE-BJ. While typically our performance is not as good as QuBE-BJ, we have shown the potential of stochastic local search methods for QBF.

2 Background

A QBF is presented as a Boolean formula in conjunctive normal form (CNF) with a prefix of quantifiers. More formally, a QBF is of the form $\mathbf{Q} = QB$ where the prefix $Q = q_1 x_1 q_2 x_2 \ldots q_n x_n$ is a sequence of pairs of quantifiers $q_i \in \{\forall, \exists\}$ and propositional variables x_i, and B is a propositional formula in CNF. A CNF formula is a conjunction of clauses; each clause is a disjunction of literals, and each literal is a propositional variable in negated or unnegated form. Within the prefix Q every variable in B is quantified exactly once by either an existential or universal quantifier. These variables are then known as existentials and universals respectively.

The satisfiability of the CNF part B of a QBF is defined just as in SAT, i.e. B is satisfied if every clause contains a true literal. However, the QBF is only satisfied if appropriate values can be given to the existentials to allow B to be satisfied for any instantiation of the universals. For this, the order of variables in the prefix is critical. We can define the truth of a QBF recursively. A QBF $\mathbf{Q}$ with an empty prefix is true iff its CNF part B is satisfied. If $\mathbf{Q}$ has a non empty prefix, there are two cases. A QBF $\exists x_1 Q_1$ is true iff either $Q_1[x_1 := T]$ or $Q_1[x_1 := F]$ is true; while a QBF $\forall x_1 Q_1$ is true iff both $Q_1[x_1 := T]$ and $Q_1[x_1 := F]$ are true. For example, a QBF $\forall x_1 \exists x_2 \forall x_3 \exists x_4 B$ is true if and only if for both True (T) and False (F) assignments to x_1, there is an assignment (T or F) to x_2, where for both assignments to x_3 there is an assignment to x_4 for which B is satisfied.

Solving a QBF can be seen as finding a winning strategy in a two player game between universal and existential quantifiers. The variables are the pieces and the assignments the moves. Existential wins if the assignments to the variables leaves a satisfied literal in every clause (i.e. B is satisfiable) and universal if the assignments leave a clause containing all negative literals. The order of the moves are dictated by the order in which the variables appear in the prefix of the QBF. The QBF is satisfiable if the existential player can find a strategy in which she can win no matter what moves the universal player makes; it is unsatisfiable if this is not the case.

2.1 Stochastic Local Search for SAT

Stochastic Local Search (SLS) algorithms for satisfiability (SAT) attempt to solve a given CNF formula B by iteratively changing, or flipping, the value assigned to variables in B such that the number of clauses that remain unsatisfied by the assignment is minimised. The selection of the variable to be flipped in each search step is typically performed using a randomised greedy mechanism. The WalkSAT family [2, 3] comprises some of the most widely studied and best-performing SLS algorithms for SAT; it is based on a randomised greedy local search procedure that flips a variable from an unsatisfied clause in each search step.

SLS-based solvers for SAT are typically incomplete, i.e., they cannot determine the unsatisfiability of a given formula, but may find a satisfying assignment, if it exists, rather efficiently. Thus, applied to an unsatisfiable formula, they will eventually terminate and return Unknown. For satisfiable formulae, True is returned (along with the respective assignment) if a satisfying assignment is found within the given resource limits and Unknown is returned otherwise. The latter particularly happens if the algorithm gets stuck in a local minimum of the underlying evaluation function.

2.2 Backtrack Search for QBFs

Backtrack search attempts to determine the truth of a QBF by assigning truth values to variables and simplifying the formula until it is vacuously true or vacuously false. Then, if false is found, all variables up to and including the last existential variable assigned are unassigned, and the last existential is assigned to the opposite value and the process is repeated. Similarly if true is found, all variables up to and including the last universal are unassigned and the last universal is assigned to the opposite value and the process is repeated. Once a variable has been assigned both True and False, the combination of the results of these two assignments is returned dependant on the quantification of the variable. These can be seen in Figure 1. The point at which the decision is made to assign a variable True or False is known as a branch point.

A QBF is vacuously true if it consists of an empty set of clauses. It is vacuously false if the set of clauses contains either a clause with no literals (empty clause) or a clause with only universal literals (all universal clause). An all universal clause cannot be satisfied since the clause must be true for all assignments to the universals and so

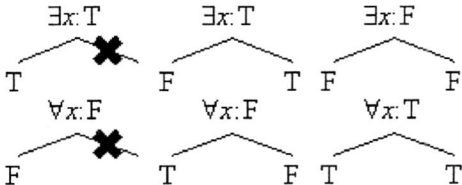

Fig. 1. The possible branching and return values for CSBJ. In the first column the second assignment is not tried since the first assignment yields enough information.

it will be unsatisfied if all the literals are assigned false. (The exception is tautologous clauses, but we remove these during preprocessing.)

If a variable is assigned True, any clause containing the literal of the variable with the positive sign can be removed, and the variable can be removed from any clause containing the literal of the variable with the negative sign. Additionally, the variable can be removed from its quantifier and empty quantifiers can be removed. In a backtrack search, variables are assigned in turn until the QBF is vacuously true or vacuously false. If true (respectively false), the variables are then unassigned until a universal (respectively existential) assignment is undone. This assignment is then reversed and the variables are again assigned until true or false is found and the process is repeated.

A unit clause is a clause that contains only one literal. This literal must be assigned true to eventually get a vacuously true state, otherwise the clause will be empty. A single existential clause is a clause that contains only one existential literal and in which all universal literals are quantified further right in the prefix than the existential. The existential literal must be assigned true because if it is assigned false the clause will become all universal and thus unsatisfied. A pure literal is found when every occurrence of a literal within the set of clauses has the same sign. An existential pure literal can be assigned true. If we reach the vacuously false state then we can be sure that we could have done no better in assigning the literal false, and so backtracking is unnecessary on the variable. A universal pure literal can be assigned false. If we reach the vacuously true state then we can be sure that we would have done no worse in assigning the pure literal true, and so again, no backtracking is required.

Conflict and Solution Directed Backjumping (CSBJ) for QBFs [1] reduces the number of backtracks performed. This is done by calculating either a conflict set or a solution set. A conflict set is a set of existential variables that caused the conflict, i.e. the empty or all universal clause. A solution set is a set of universal variables such that all clauses not satisfied by the current existential assignment are satisfied by at least one of the universal variables. On returning to an existential branch point (in the case of a conflict), or a universal branch point (in the case of a solution), a backtrack need only be performed if the variable assigned at the branch point is in the set. This technique has been shown to be useful in the solving of QBFs [4], in particular on random instances with three or more quantifiers, and on 'real world' instances. The cover set used in solution directed backjumping is not unique [5]. It is important that a small cover set is chosen, to reduce the number of universal backtrack points.

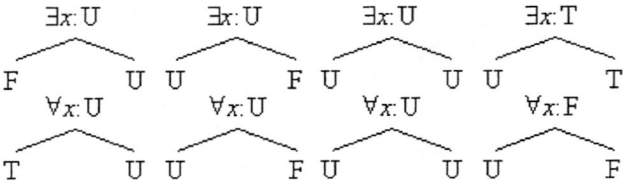

Fig. 2. The additional branching and return values for WalkQSAT. Note how the solver recovers in the last column.

Finally, we mention the Trivial Truth method [6]. This is a method for using a SAT algorithm within a QBF solver. With this technique a counterpart **E** to the QBF **Q** is kept where **E** is the same as **Q**, but with the universals removed. If a solution to **E** can be found, this is also a solution to **Q**. however, if no solution to **E** can be found, nothing has been gained, since **Q** could still be true. If no solution is found, the results are discarded. This SAT search is potentially wasteful since the results of useful search are discarded if the result is false.

3   WalkQSAT

WalkQSAT is in essence an implementation of conflict- and solution-directed backjump-ing (CSBJ) in QBF. However, it uses an auxiliary stochastic SAT solver, WalkSAT, to guide its search. WalkSAT is used to solve the current reduced QBF instance viewed purely as a SAT problem, i.e. treating each universal variable as an existential (unlike trivial truth where the universal variables are removed). This solution is used to set the values of variables in the CSBJ search; when a variable is heuristically chosen in the QBF solver, the value assigned to the variable is the value assigned by WalkSAT in this returned solution. This has two consequences. First, it is possible for WalkSAT to fail to find a solution, either because there is none or because WalkSAT times out. This leads to the inherent incompleteness of WalkQSAT. The second consequence is more positive. Where WalkSAT finds a satisfying assignment, this guarantees that if the same assignments are given to the variables in the QBF search, the vacuously true state will be reached. Thus WalkSAT is being used for more than purely heuristic guidance. From a vacuously true QBF found this way, we continue as CSBJ normally would. That is, we backjump to the most recent universal variable in the solution set. After backjumping, WalkSAT is called to determine the next set of assignments to guarantee a vacuously true state.

It is straightforward to deal with the case that WalkSAT fails to solve an instance. When WalkSAT times out, it returns the value U for unknown. No further attempt is made to solve the corresponding node in the CSBJ search, but Figure 2 shows the additional possibilities and the associated return states allowing for Unknown values at branch points in the QBF search procedure. If an U is returned for the first assignment, WalkQSAT always tries the second assignment, sometimes being able to determine the result. If not, U is passed back.

It might seem that it is impossible for WalkQSAT ever to determine the falsity of a QBF instance, as WalkSAT cannot determine unsatisfiability of SAT instances. However, as any CSBJ algorithm does, WalkQSAT implements single-existential propagation, which can lead to a contradiction. From this a conflict set can be calculated for backjumping, and if the first variable assigned is ever backjumped over, the problem has been proved false. Thus, with QBFs, we encounter a different kind of incompleteness than that of WalkSAT. Specifically: if False is returned, the problem is definitely false; if True is returned, the problem is definitely true; but the solver can still return Unknown if no proof is found. In practice, we found that WalkQSAT was often able to determine falsity of QBF instances. For this, the use of conflict-directed backjumping is a help, as an unknown value returned at a node not in the conflict set does not prevent falsity being proved.

The key issue in design and implementation was to keep WalkSAT and WalkQSAT in step. At any node in its search tree, WalkQSAT needs to get a satisfying assignment to B that is consistent with the values of variables that have been set by branching or propagation at higher levels of the search tree. So we cannot let WalkSAT continue solving the original instance of the QBF viewed as a SAT problem. Instead, we notify WalkSAT each time a variable is assigned, via an interface call *Fix(literal)*. We implemented a variant of WalkSAT in which fixed variables could not be changed. After each variable is set either by branching or propagation, *Fix* is called. This means that whenever WalkQSAT calls WalkSAT, the SAT search is only on variables free at this node in the search tree. When WalkQSAT backtracks over a fixed variable, a corresponding *Release(literal)* call is made. This results in two data structures being maintained to keep the current search state, one of which is a data structure optimised for efficient complete search, while the other is optimised for efficient local search.

One aspect of WalkSAT we found to affect performance was the starting position of its second and later searches. Instead of a random position each time, we found it much more effective to start the search from the last assignment visited during the previous search, except for changes forced by *Fix* calls. This is natural, as often there will be relatively few *Fix* calls between calls to WalkSAT, so a solution at the last node is likely to be a near-solution at the next node. However, since in normal use WalkSAT (for sufficiently high noise settings) is insensitive to whether it is restarted or simply left to run [7,8], it may be surprising that this use of starting position seemed to be necessary. However, this insensitivity to restarts does not hold for very short runs, particularly if these are started very close to a solution.

Figure 3 shows pseudocode for WalkQSAT. This is similar to the pseudocode for QuBE-BJ [1] since WalkQSAT is also a backjumping algorithm. A call to *ChooseLiteral* additionally passes the assignments returned by WalkSAT, and these are used to determine the sign of the literal to be used in the next assignment. The actual literal chosen can be independent of the results of WalkSAT. $InitWr$ calculates the conflict or solution set, given the false (F) or true (T) result respectively. If $InitWr$ is called with the unknown (U) result, it should return the empty set, since backtracking must be performed instead. The function $BackJump$ correctly deals with the case where unknown has been returned, as shown in Figure 2, by immediately backtracking on the last literal assigned, or if the literal has already been backtracked upon, passing back the unknown result.

The variable *last* is used to determine the last action performed by the algorithm. This way, WalkSAT is only called after backjumping has been performed. Other functions have the same meaning as was described in [1], repeated here for completeness:

- **Q** is a global variable storing the QBF in the current state, initially set to the input QBF.
- *Stack* is a global variable storing the search states so far, initially empty.
- T, F, U, UNDEF, SINGLE∃, PURE, L-SPLIT, R-SPLIT, CHOOSE and BACK are constants.
- *Extend(l)* removes $\bar{l}$ from all clauses in which it appears, removes all clauses containing l and pushes l and **Q** onto the stack.
- *Retract()* gets l and **Q** from the top of the stack and undoes all work done by *Extend(l)*.

Note that WalkSAT is only one example of a solver that could be used: any SAT solver can be used as long as it implements the interface defined here, and that it never returns an incorrect value. While in this paper we restrict ourselves to the use of WalkSAT, it will be interesting to see if other SAT solvers can perform well in this framework[1].

The method described here could easily be mistaken for trivial truth, in that a truth assignment is found by WalkSAT. This is not the case however, since trivial truth finds a truth assignment only involving the existentials. WalkSAT finds a truth assignments assuming the universals are existentials. It is this key difference that allows WalkQSAT to get more information from the SAT solver than trivial truth. If trivial truth finds a satisfying assignment, search can be cut off on the current branch. However, if trivial truth fails to find such an assignment, the results of the SAT search are disregarded and search continues. When WalkQSAT finds a satisfying assignment, the results are used to guide search, and are not just discarded. This is clearly different to trivial truth and less wasteful of resources. Another difference with trivial truth is that, if WalkSAT fails to find a satisfying assignment, we stop searching and backtrack, returning Unknown.

4   Experimental Methodology

We explored the performance of WalkQSAT, both in its own terms and against an existing state-of-the-art solver for QBF. To test WalkQSAT experimentally, we need both a good set of benchmark instances, and a good methodology which gives a fair understanding of WalkQSAT with respect to the state of the art. This is particularly important given that there are a number of parameters which can affect WalkQSAT's performance, and that as a randomised procedure it gives different performance on each run. To compare against the state of the art, we compare results with the complete solver QuBE-BJ [1], an implementation of CSBJ. We chose QuBE-BJ because, like WalkQSAT, it is a backjumping algorithm and so makes for a good comparison. We do not know of a solver which is known to be better than QuBE-BJ, so our comparison is with the state of the art. We undertook benchmark tests on both random and structured problems. The latter came from QBFLib (http://www.mrg.dist.unige.it/QBFLIB/), and we used all instances

---

[1] This is why we deal correctly with the possibility of WalkSAT returning F in our pseudocode: while WalkSAT can never return F, other SAT solvers can.

```
function WalkQSAT(QBF Q̂)
    Q:= Q̂;
    Stack := Empty stack;
    last := CHOOSE;
    (res, assignments) := WalkSAT();
    if (res ≠ T) return res;
    do
        res := Simplify();
        if (last = BACK and res = UNDEF)
            (res, assignments) := WalkSAT();
            if (res = T) res := UNDEF;
        if (res = UNDEF)
            l := ChooseLiteral(assignments); last := CHOOSE;
        else
            l := Backjump(res); last := BACK;
        if (l ≠ UNDEF)
            Extend(l); Fix(l);
    while (l ≠ UNDEF);
    return res;

function BackJump(res)
    wr := InitWr(res)
    while (Stack is not empty)
        l := Retract(); Release(l);
        if (l ∈ wr or res = U)
            if (res = F and |l|.type = ∃) or
               (res = T and |l|.type = ∀) or
               (res = U)
                if (|l|.mode = SINGLE∃) or (|l|.mode = R-SPLIT)
                    wr := (wr ∪ |l|.reason)/{l, l̄}
                    if (|l|.result = U) res := |l|.result;
                if (|l|.mode = L-SPLIT)
                    |l|.result = res;
                    |l|.mode = R-SPLIT;
                    |l|.reason := wr;
                    return l;
            else wr := wr/l;
    return UNDEF

function Simplify()
    do
        Q' = Q;
        if (Q is vacuously false) return F
        if (Q is vacuously true) return T
        if (Q contains a single existential literal l)
            |l|.mode := SINGLE∃; Extend(l); Fix(l);
        if (Q contains a pure existential literal l)
            |l|.mode := PURE; Extend(l); Fix(l);
        if (Q contains a pure universal literal l)
            |l|.mode := PURE; Extend(l); Fix(l);
    while (Q' ≠ Q)
    return UNDEF
```

Fig. 3. The WalkQSAT algorithm. This is similar to the pseudocode for QuBE-BJ [1], but with modifications made to account for SAT solver calls, and dealing with Unknown (U) return values. **Q** and *Stack* are global variables.

except the robot problems. For randomised instances, we used Gent and Walsh's Model A [9], because it has been commonly used in previous literature and is well understood. The parameters used were 20 variables per quantifier, 4 quantifier alternations with the universal outermost, 5 variables per clause and a number of clauses from 25 to 450 in steps of 25.

WalkQSAT has a number of parameters that must be set for each run. These affect how the search performed by WalkSAT is carried out. In particular, there is the MaxFlips parameter, which is the number of flips WalkSAT will perform before returning U, and the noise parameter p which affects the level of randomisation vs. hill-climbing. In SAT, MaxFlips is not an important parameter because when using close-to-optimal noise settings, very large MaxFlips settings generally work well [8]. The setting of MaxFlips affects performance in QBF because there is a tradeoff between allowing WalkSAT enough time to solve each instance and spending too much time in wasted searches. Many of the tested subinstances will be unsatisfiable, and extra flips are entirely wasted. The noise parameter is often critical for applications of WalkSAT, and the default value of 0.5 sometimes gives very poor performance. To set these parameters to poor values could give an unduly bad impression of how WalkQSAT performs. On the other hand, to optimise performance on all instances would give an unduly good impression: in practice we cannot optimise parameters when presented with an instance that needs to be solved just once.

To resolve this dilemma, we follow a practice suggested by Hoos [7], of performing a coarse optimisation on a small subset of the instances. To this end, we varied MaxFlips from $1 \times n$ to $50 \times n$, where n is the number of variables in the instance, and noise from 0 to 0.75 on a random instance and an individual structured instance. In neither case did performance seem particularly sensitive to the settings of these parameters. We observed that settings of $10 \times n$ and 0.5 gave good performance in both cases, and we use these values in all experiments we report for WalkQSAT in this paper.

Since WalkQSAT is a randomised procedure, through its use of WalkSAT, data from an individual run could be misleading. Instead we are interested in the entire distribution of data from a number of runs. Throughout this paper we report results on 100 runs of WalkQSAT on each instance we test. The only exceptions are those that QuBE-BJ failed to solve in 20 minutes on a 1GHz PC: for these we tested WalkQSAT in only 25 tries of 20 minutes.

The purpose of this work is to introduce a method for implementing an incomplete solver for QSAT, which has never been done before. We have therefore not investigated different variants of WalkSAT and it is unknown how these will work for QBF solving. It is hypothesised that the variant will not be too important, since the work done by Walk-SAT after the first run appears minimal. For all the experiments, we used the Novelty+ variant of WalkSAT [7]. This variant has been shown to perform very well on many SAT problems, and it is left as further work to examine the performance of other variants in WalkQSAT [7, 8]. All experiments were performed on a cluster of 1 Ghz computers with 512MB RAM running Linux kernel 2.4.7-10 and GNU gcc version 2.96. We used QuBE-BJ version 1.0 (http://www.mrg.dist.unige.it/~qube/Download/download.html). The timeout was 20 minutes (1200 seconds) for all runs.

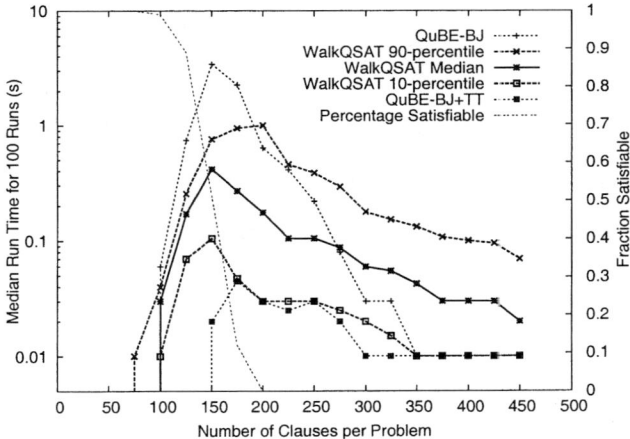

Fig. 4. Phase transition for various algorithms on random problems from Model A (n=20 per quantifier,h=5,outermost quantifier universal,4 quantifier alternations,l=25..450 in steps of 25.

5   Experimental Results

WalkQSAT was compared to QuBE-BJ and QuBE-BJ with trivial truth. Figure 4 shows the phase transition commonly observed for random problems. WalkQSAT performs well here compared to QuBE-BJ but does not often outperform QuBE-BJ with trivial truth, although it often gives the same performance at the 10-percentile range. We conjecture that where WalkQSAT achieves the same performance as QuBE-BJ with trivial truth, it finds the same assignments that trivial truth makes, and so solves the QBF without the use of universals.

This last point can be seen even more clearly in Figure 5 where the 10-percentile errorbar extends to the same run time as QuBE-BJ with trivial truth on some instances. This figure also shows that WalkQSAT can outperform QuBE-BJ without trivial truth, even on false instances, which is a rather surprising result.

Figure 6 shows performance results of WalkQSAT on structured instances. Here, WalkQSAT only performs better than QuBE-BJ near the 10-percentile and only on a few problems. There are some sets of structured instances on which WalkQSAT shows very little variation in run time; this can be seen in the diagonal lines of data points for WalkQSAT for which errorbars are not visible, with corresponding crosses for QuBE-BJ with trivial truth. (these correspond to the CHAIN instances). WalkQSAT can perform better than QuBE-BJ with trivial truth, which illustrates the differences between WalkQSAT and backjumping with trivial truth. WalkQSAT outperforms QuBE-BJ with trivial truth on 168 runs on 13 different instances (i.e. 168 runs out of 1300 runs of WalkQSAT in total), and QuBE-BJ on 340 runs on 20 different instances, out of the 257 structured instances we tested.

As was said previously, where QuBE-BJ and QuBE-BJ with trivial truth did not solve a structured instance before the timeout, WalkQSAT was run on this instance to see if it

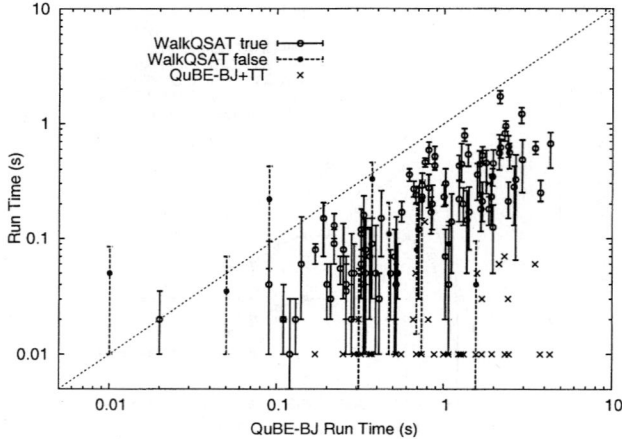

Fig. 5. Run-times for QuBE-BJ vs. WalkQSAT and QuBE-BJ+TT on random model A instances with 125 clauses. The error bars for the WalkQSAT run times indicate the range between the 10 and 90 percentiles of the underlying run-time distributions obtained for the respective instances. The diagonal line indicates equal run-time for QuBE-BJ and the other algorithm; points below (above) this line represent instances on which WalkQSAT or QuBE-BJ+TT, respectively, are faster (slower) than QuBE-BJ.

could solve it. On one problem, TOILET10.1.iv.20 (true), WalkQSAT was able to solve it in 27.37 seconds only once out of 100 runs. On the other 99 runs, WalkQSAT timed-out. On one other problem, szymanski-16-s, QuBE-BJ both with and without trivial truth could not solve the problem due to insufficient memory. On this problem WalkQSAT solved the instance 12 out of 100 times with a median run time of 16.595 seconds.

In order to understand the run-time behaviour of WalkQSAT in more detail, we studied run-time distributions (RTDs) for individual problem instances following the methodology by Hoos and Stützle [8]. Since WalkQSAT, like WalkSAT, is a stochastic algorithm, when applied to the same instance, its run-time will vary stochastically. It is known that for WalkSAT, if sufficiently high noise parameter settings are used, the RTDs are well approximated by exponential distributions [7]. As can be seen in Figures 7 and 8, this is not the case for WalkQSAT. Although considerable variability in run-time can typically be observed, the right tail of the RTDs tends to be much skinnier, indicating that the probability of very long runs (compared to the average or median run-time) is very small. Interestingly, this appears to hold for satisfiable and unsatisfiable, random and structured instances. It implies that, different from several state-of-the art randomised systematic search algorithms for SAT, simple restarting strategies will not improve the performance of the algorithm.

We also note that when measuring only the total number of WalkSAT steps, we obtain run-length distributions that have substantially higher variability. But as can be seen from our RTD results, this large amount of variability present in the WalkSAT runs is reduced, rather than amplified when WalkSAT is used within the CSBJ framework.

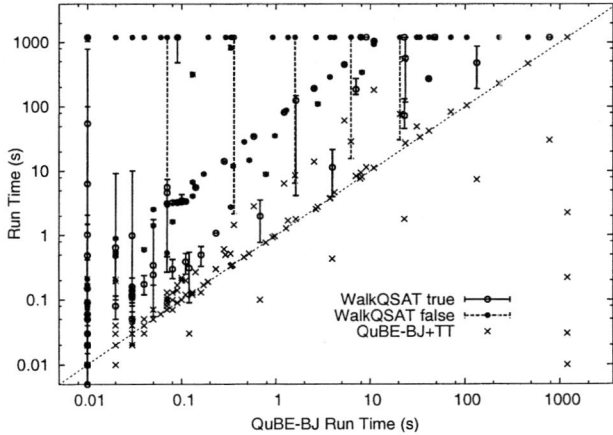

Fig. 6. Performance of WalkQSAT vs. QuBE-BJ and QuBE-BJ+TT on structured QBFLIB instances. See Figure 5 for more details. Where a circle appears without error bars, there is little or no variation in run time over 100 runs.

6   A WalkSAT Heuristic for QBF

The evaluation function of WalkSAT is usually the number of unsatisfied clauses, u. To help reduce the number of universal variables assigned, and so help solution directed backjumping, we alter the evaluation function of WalkSAT to be $\alpha u + \beta e$, where e is the number of satisfied clauses not satisfied by an existential. This gives us two parameters to tune, α and β. Since the important factor is α/β, α is set at 10, and β is varied.

It is found that on Rintanen's impl set of problems from QBFLIB, a value of $\beta > 0$ provides some significant improvements in run time. For example, on impl14, the median run time was 18.1 seconds with $\beta = 0$ and 2.07 seconds with $\beta = 1$. With increasing values of β, the median run time does not vary greatly, e.g. with $\beta = 1000$, the median run time is 2.13 seconds.

Further analysis shows that QuBE-BJ with trivial truth is more effective on these instances than without trivial truth. This is observed in Figure 6 as a set of points that appear below the diagonal representing the impl problems. The reasoning for the effectiveness of β on these problems is therefore likely to be that $\beta > 0$ makes WalkSAT behave more like trivial truth. Whilst this is the case, it has also been observed that $\beta > 0$ on other problems has no detrimental effect; this suggests that it is safe to use a high value of β just in case trivial truth helps on the problem. This is done with the risk that with increasing values of β, the time spent by WalkSAT in optimising the solutions may be better spent elsewhere and may result in WalkSAT not finding a solution at all. Of course, we still do not throw away valuable search as is done in the trivial truth method, but more unknown results may be returned.

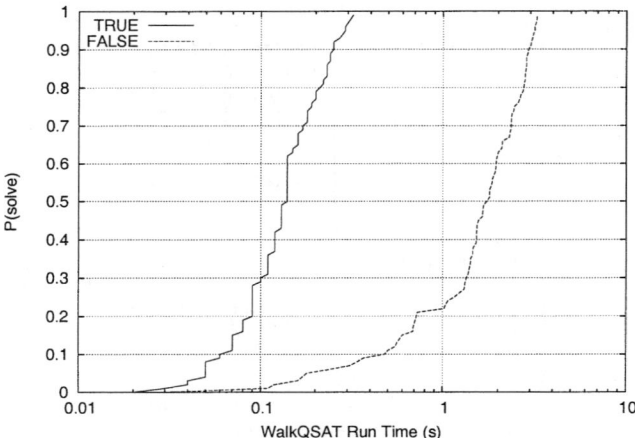

Fig. 7. WalkQSAT run-time distributions for typical satisfiable and unsatisfiable random instances from the phase transition.

7   Related Work

There has been an increase in interest in solving QBFs in recent years, starting with the introduction of a backtracking algorithm [6], followed by its application to planning problems translated to QBF [10]. The next big step was the introduction of backjumping for QBF [1], in particular solution directed backjumping which led to significant improvements in runtime. This gave rise to the next logical step of learning in QBF solvers [5, 11, 12], which provided improvements on some problems, whilst making others worse.

The WalkSAT algorithm family [2, 3, 8] comprises some of the most widely studied and best-performing SLS algorithms for SAT. Novelty$^+$, the WalkSAT variant used in WalkQSAT, was proposed in [7] and is based on the Novelty algorithm from [3].

Some interest in QBF has been on translation of QBF into SAT [13, 14]. This is naturally exponential in space, but the resultant SAT problem can be given to any SAT solver, including WalkSAT and other SLS solvers. To our best knowledge, WalkQSAT is the first QBF solver using SLS, except in this trivial sense.

8   Conclusions and Future Work

In this paper, we have shown the potential of using stochastic local search methods in QBFs. We introduced WalkQSAT, a new QBF solver that combines Conflict and Solution Directed Backjumping (CSBJ) with a Stochastic Local Search procedure. We presented empirical evidence indicating that WalkQSAT, although an inherently incomplete algorithm, in most cases is able to correctly determine the satisfiability of a given QBF, and in many cases correctly determines unsatisfiability. (Like incomplete SLS algorithms

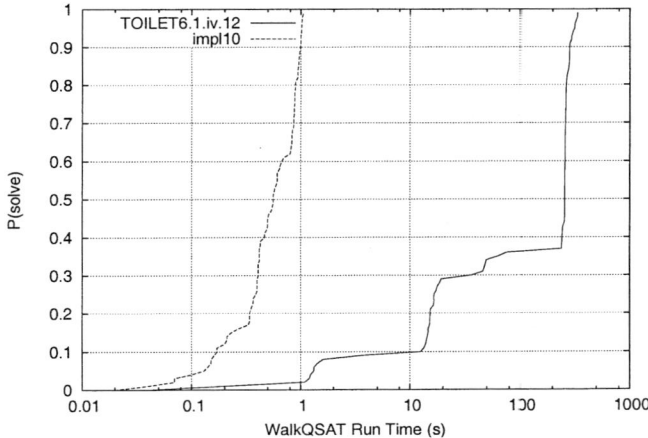

Fig. 8. WalkQSAT run-time distributions for two structured instances.

for SAT and other problems, by design, WalkQSAT never gives an incorrect result, but may return "Unknown".) Although our implementation of WalkQSAT is not optimised for efficiency, it can solve several of the tested benchmark instances faster than QuBE-BJ, a state-of-the-art QBF solver based on CSBJ, and can even solve two instances that QuBE-BJ cannot. Our implementation of WalkQSAT is based on a CSBJ library that is known to be less efficient than QuBE-BJ. Improving this library should help to provide even better results.

A key issue in solution-directed backjumping is obtaining solutions which use only a small number of universal variables, minimizing the size of the solution sets. We have started to facilitate this by providing a modification of the evaluation function of WalkSAT, which improves WalkQSAT's performance on some instances. Furthermore, when WalkQSAT finds a solution quickly, it may be worth continuing the search to see if a better solution can be found, involving fewer universals. This could be seen as a solution-directed version of Schiex's 'stubbornness' for conflict-directed backjumping [15].

Acknowledgements

This work was partly supported by EPSRC grant GR/55382/01 and NSERC Individual Research Grant #238788. The first and third authors are members of the APES research group and thank other members. We thank the anonymous reviewers for their comments.

References

1. Guinchiglia, E., Narizzano, M., Tacchella, A.: Backjumping for quantified Boolean logic satisfiability. In: IJCAI-01. (2001) 275–281
2. Selman, B., Kautz, H.: Domain-independent extensions to GSAT: solving large structured satisfiability problems. In: IJCAI-93. (1993) 290–295

3. McAllester, D., Selman, B., Kautz, H.: Evidence for invariants in local search. In: AAAI'97. (1997) 321–326
 4. Guinchiglia, E., Narizzano, M., Tacchella, A.: An analysis of backjumping and trivial truth in quantified Boolean formulas satisfiability. In: AI*IA-01, Springer (2001) 111–122
 5. Zhang, L., Malik, S.: Towards a symmetric treatment of satisfaction and conflicts in quantified boolean formula evaluation. In: CP-2002, Springer (2002) 200–215
 6. Cadoli, M., Giovanardi, A., Schaerf, M.: An algorithm to evaluate quantified Boolean formulae. In: AAAI-98. (1998) 262–267
 7. Hoos, H.: Stochastic Local Search - Methods, Models, Applications. PhD thesis (1998)
 8. Hoos, H., Stützle, T.: Local search algorithms for SAT: An empirical evaluation. J. of Automated Reasoning **24** (2000) 421–481
 9. Gent, I., Walsh, T.: Beyond NP: the QSAT phase transition. In: AAAI-99. (1999) 648–653
10. Rintanen, J.: Improvements to the evaluation of quantified boolean formulae. In: IJCAI-99. (1999) 1192–1197
11. Guinchiglia, E., Narizzano, M., Tacchella, A.: Learning for quantified boolean logic satisfiability. In: AAAI-2002. (2002) 649–654
12. Letz, R.: Lemma and model caching in decision procedures for quantified boolean formulas. In: TABLEAUX 2002. (2002) 160–175
13. Plaisted, D., Biere, A., Zhu, Y.: A satisfiability procedure for quantified boolean formulae. Discrete Applied Mathematics (2003) To appear.
14. Rintanen, J.: Partial implicit unfolding in the Davis-Putnam procedure for quantified Boolean formulae. In: LPAR-01, Springer (2001) 362–376
15. Schiex, T., Verfaillie, G.: Stubbornness: a possible enhancement for backjumping and no-good recording. In: ECAI-94. (1994) 165–169

Solving Max-SAT as Weighted CSP*

Simon de Givry[1], Javier Larrosa[2], Pedro Meseguer[3], and Thomas Schiex[1]

[1] INRA, Toulouse, France
{degivry,tschiex}@toulouse.inra.fr
[2] Dep. LSI, UPC, Barcelona, Spain
larrosa@lsi.upc.es
[3] IIIA-CSIC, Campus UAB, Bellaterra, Spain
pedro@iiia.csic.es

Abstract. For the last ten years, a significant amount of work in the constraint community has been devoted to the improvement of complete methods for solving soft constraints networks. We wanted to see how recent progress in the weighted CSP (WCSP) field could compete with other approaches in related fields. One of these fields is propositional logic and the well-known Max-SAT problem. In this paper, we show how Max-SAT can be encoded as a weighted constraint network, either directly or using a dual encoding. We then solve Max-SAT instances using state-of-the-art algorithms for weighted Max-CSP, dedicated Max-SAT solvers and the state-of-the-art MIP solver CPLEX. The results show that, despite a limited adaptation to CNF structure, WCSP-solver based methods are competitive with existing methods and can even outperform them, especially on the hardest, most over-constrained problems.

1 Introduction

Since the eighties, both constraint satisfaction and boolean satisfiability have been the topic of intense algorithmic research. In both areas, the main problem is to assign values to variables in such a way that no forbidden combination of values appears in the solution.

Using closely related techniques such as backtrack search, local consistency enforcing (aka constraint propagation), and constraint learning, both areas have produced generic complete solvers which have been applied to a large range of problems. In the SAT domain, one major area of application is electronic design automation (EDA) with problems that range from formal validation to routing.

Quite early in the history of constraint satisfaction, the issue of infeasible problems has been addressed [18, 4, 7]. Most of the recent algorithmic work has focused on the so-called WCSP (weighted constraint satisfaction problem) where the aim is to find an assignment that minimizes the sum of weights associated with the constraints violated by the assignment. Complete algorithms

---

* This research is partially supported by the French-Spanish collaboration PICASSO 05158SM - Integrated Action HF02-69. The second and third authors are also supported by the REPLI project TIC-2002-04470-C03.

F. Rossi (Ed.): CP 2003, LNCS 2833, pp. 363–376, 2003.

that address these problems rely on variants of depth-first branch and bound search using dedicated lower bounds. Since the early algorithms of [6], huge improvements have been obtained using increasingly sophisticated lower bounds. Recently [20, 13, 15], it has been possible to simplify and strengthen the definition of these lower bounds by expressing them as a result of the enforcing of a local consistency property.

In the SAT area, the similar issue of infeasible problems has been considered more recently, leading to increasing interest in the (weighted) Max-SAT problem. In Max-SAT, the problem is to assign values to boolean variables in order to maximize the number of satisfied clauses in a CNF formula. Max-SAT has applications in routing problems [26] and is also closely related to the Max-CUT problem (other applications are described in [10]). When turned into a "yes-no" problem by adding a goal k representing the number of clauses to be satisfied, Max-SAT and even Max-2SAT (where clauses only involve 2 variables) are NP-complete and more precisely MAX-SNP-complete. Both problems have been intensively studied on the theoretical side.

The problem hardness has also been studied empirically in [27]. This phase transition analysis of random Max-3SAT problems shows that using the usual fixed length random SAT model, the Max-3SAT problem does not show an easy/hard/easy pattern as the clauses/variables ratio increases but an easy/hard pattern: the empirical complexity of Max-3SAT increases as this ratio increases.

As usual for solving NP-complete problems, either complete or incomplete algorithms can be used to tackle the problem. There is a long list of incomplete algorithms for Max-SAT. In this paper, we only deal with complete algorithms, that identify provenly optimal solutions in finite time. Two main classes of complete algorithms have been proposed based either on variations on the Davis-Putnam-Logemann-Loveland (DPLL) approach for satisfiability or on 0/1 linear programming models. Along the DPLL line, current solvers use pseudo-boolean formulae to model Max-SAT [2, 25, 5, 1]. A pseudo-boolean (PB) formula is a linear inequality on boolean variables which can model clauses but also more complex constraints such as cardinality constraints [24]. One of the first algorithm in this line is OPBDP [2]. More recently, PBS (Pseudo Boolean Solver) [1] was designed based on the Chaff SAT solver [16].

Also based on the DPLL algorithm, a more theoretical line of research has tried to define complete algorithms that would provide non naive guaranteed worst-case upper bounds on time complexity based on the overall length L of the input formula or the number K of its clauses. While most of this work is essentially theoretical and never reaches the level of actually implementing the algorithms presented, one exception is [9] which implemented a Max-2SAT solver that achieves worst case upper bounds of $O(1.0970^L)$ and $O(1.2035^K)$ [1].

Another natural approach to solve the Max-SAT problem is to model it as a mixed integer linear program (MIP). This linear program can then be solved directly by a dedicated MIP solver such as ILOG CPLEX. Note that dedicated branch and cut algorithms above MINTO have also been defined [3].

---

[1] These theoretical results have been very slightly improved since in [8], but no corresponding implementation is available.

In this paper, we model the Max-SAT problem as a weighted CSP. Because most of the existing work on WCSP has been done on binary WCSP, we consider two possible approaches: *i*) a direct conversion of clauses into constraints, which produces non-binary problems and requires the solver to be adapted to deal with them, and *ii*) a dual (binary) formulation as proposed in [14].

To solve converted Max-SAT instances, we use adapted versions of the WCSP solvers defined in [15] which are depth-first branch and bound algorithms that maintain some level of local consistency during search.

For comparison purposes, we also solve the original Max-SAT problems using two dedicated solvers (OPBDP and PBS), a pure Max-2SAT dedicated solver (`max2sat` by J. Gramm) and a general MIP solver (CPLEX). The results of our experiments show that despite the fact that our generic WCSP code ignores most clauses properties, uses classical CSP data-structures instead of specialized clauses data-structures and relies on simple variable ordering, it can outperform existing pseudo-boolean solvers, commercial MIP solvers and is even competitive with a code restricted to Max-2SAT. The good performances of our algorithm are especially obvious on problems with high clauses/variables ratio which is probably related to the strength of the lower bound induced by (full directional) soft arc consistency. The results we get are consistent with what has been observed in classical CSP when comparing arc consistency maintenance to eg. forward-checking: the overhead for enforcing higher level of consistencies may slow down the algorithm on relatively simple problems but provides both highly increased performances and limited variability in the cpu-times on hard problems.

2 Notation and Definitions

2.1 Sat and (Weighted) Max-SAT

In propositional logic a variable v_i may take values 0 (for false) or 1 (for true). A literal ℓ_i is a variable v_i or its negation $\bar{v}_i$. A clause C_j is a disjunction of literals. A logical formula in conjunctive normal form (CNF) is a conjunction of clauses. Given a logical formula in CNF, the SAT problem considers finding an assignment of the variables that satisfies the formula, or getting a proof that no such assignment exists.

When a logical formula is unsatisfiable, the Max-SAT problem tries to find the assignment that satisfies as many clauses as possible. In the rest of the paper, we assume that each clause C_j is associated with a positive weight w_j. In this case, the weighted Max-SAT problem looks for the assignment that maximizes the sum of weights of satisfied clauses.

2.2 Weighted CSP

A *constraint satisfaction problem* (CSP) is a triple $(\mathcal{X}, \mathcal{D}, \mathcal{C})$, where $\mathcal{X}$ is a set of variables $\{x_1, \ldots, x_n\}$, $\mathcal{D}$ is a collection of domains $\{D_1, \ldots, D_n\}$ and $\mathcal{C}$ is a set of constraints $\{c_1, \ldots, c_e\}$. Each variable $x_i \in \mathcal{X}$ takes values in the finite domain D_i. A constraint c_i is defined over a subset of variables $var(c_i)$, and $rel(c_i) \subset \prod_{j \in var(c_i)} D_j$ specifies the value tuples permitted by c_i. $var(c_i)$ is called the *scope* of the constraint and $|var(c_i)|$ is its *arity*. A tuple t is an ordered set of values assigned to the ordered set of variables $\mathcal{X}_t \subseteq \mathcal{X}$. For a subset B of $\mathcal{X}_t$, the projection of t over B is noted $t \downarrow_B$. A *solution* is a tuple involving all variables that satisfies every constraint.

Following [13], we define Weighted CSP (WCSP) as a specific subclass of valued CSP [21], where constraint costs can take their values in the set $\{0, 1, \ldots, k\}$ and k represents a maximum acceptable cost, $k \in \{1, \ldots, \infty\}$. The combination of two costs is done using bounded addition denoted $\oplus$ and defined as $a \oplus b = \min\{k, a + b\}$.

A WCSP is then a tuple $(k, \mathcal{X}, \mathcal{D}, \mathcal{C})$. $\mathcal{X}$ and $\mathcal{D}$ are variables and domains, as in standard CSP. $\mathcal{C}$ is the set of constraints as cost functions. A constraint c_i assigns costs to assignments to variables $var(c_i)$ (namely, $c_i : \prod_{j \in var(c_i)} D_j \to \{0, \ldots, k\}$). In the rest of the paper, we assume the existence of a unary constraint for every variable and also a zero-arity constraint $c_\varnothing$ (if no such constraint is defined, we can always define *dummy* ones $c_i(a) = 0, \forall a \in D_i$ and $c_\varnothing = 0$).

When a constraint c assigns cost k or above to a tuple t, it means that c forbids t, otherwise t is permitted by c with the corresponding cost. The *cost* of a tuple t, noted $\mathcal{V}(t)$, is the bounded sum over all applicable costs,

$$\mathcal{V}(t) = \bigoplus_{c_i \in \mathcal{C},\ var(c_i) \subseteq \mathcal{X}_t} c_i(t \downarrow_{var(c_i)})$$

Tuple t is *consistent* if $\mathcal{V}(t) < k$. The usual task of interest is to find a complete consistent assignment with minimum cost, which is NP-hard.

3   Modeling and Solving the Max-SAT Problem

3.1   As a Pseudo-Boolean Problem

A *pseudo-boolean* (PB) problem is a special case of CSP where all variables share a bi-valued domain $D = \{0, 1\}$ and constraints are linear inequalities. A PB constraint takes the form,

$$\sum_{i=1}^{n} a_{ij} v_i \quad \begin{matrix} \leq \\ \geq \\ = \end{matrix} \quad b_j, \qquad a_{ij}, b_j \in \mathbf{Z}$$

A Max-SAT instance with r clauses and n variables can be translated into a PB problem as follows. We first introduce r extra variables y_j (one per clause) and replace clause C_j by the relaxed formula $\neg C_j \to y_j$ which forces y_j to 1 when C_j is violated. This formula can directly be represented by a clause and translated to a pseudo-boolean formula denoted $RPB(C_j)$ by replacing each occurrence of $\bar{v}_i$ by $(1 - v_i)$ and the $\vee$ operator by $+$.

There is an extra constraint $\sum_{j=1}^{r} w_j y_j \leq K$, where $K \in [W, \ldots, 0]$ and $W = \sum_{j=1, j \neq m}^{r} w_j$ such that $w_m = \max_j\{w_j\}, j = 1, \ldots, r$. This constraint bounds the maximum violation cost.

As example, the set of clauses $\{\bar{v}_1, \bar{v}_2, v_1 \vee v_2\}$ (all with the same unit weight) generates a PB problem with five variables and four constraints,

$$(1-v_1)+y_1 \geq 1 \qquad (1-v_2)+y_2 \geq 1 \qquad v_1+v_2+y_3 \geq 1 \qquad y_1+y_2+y_3 \leq 2$$

This translation is the most compact encoding we could think of. In their papers, the authors of PBS [1] use a less compact encoding where a stronger formulation $\neg C_j \leftrightarrow y_j$ is used instead of $\neg C_j \rightarrow y_j$. This encoding was also tested with PBS but provided similar results and it is therefore ignored in the rest of this paper.

The PB problem is solved combining DPLL and constraint propagation. *branching.* DPLL is used on the r constraints $RPB(C_j)$ which have a clausal structure. *unsatisfied.* When a y variable becomes instantiated by DPLL, this is propagated through remaining constraints as follows. Assuming that $\{y_1, \ldots, y_p\}$ is the subset of y variables instantiated, if $\sum_{j=1}^{p} w_j y_j > K$ then this constraint is violated. Otherwise, all unassigned y_i such that $w_i > K - \sum_{j=1}^{p} w_j y_j$ must be fixed to 0 (otherwise the constraint would be violated). This propagation may generate new unary clauses, which are again propagated by DPLL, etc. In this way, for a given K the problem is solved or is detected as unsolvable.

To find the minimum weight of unsatisfied clauses K should be minimized. Initially, K takes value W. Then, either a depth-first branch and bound approach (OPBDP) or an iterative approach (PBS) can be used. With iterative resolving, clause learning can naturally speedup the solving process.

3.2   As a Mixed ILP

An *integer linear problem* (ILP) considers the minimization of a linear function of integer variables under linear constraints. Mixed ILP involve continuous and integer variables.

Given a Max-SAT instance with n variables and r clauses, it is translated into a Mixed ILP as follows. We use r extra *continuous* variables y_j, one per clause. Each clause C_j is encoded as the linear constraint $RPB(C_j)$ as in the previous case. Note that integrality constraints on y_i are useless since they only appear in one constraint, where all other variables are integer. The function to minimize is the weighted sum,

$$\min \sum_{j=1}^{r} w_j y_j \qquad (1)$$

As example, the set of clauses $\{\bar{v}_1, \bar{v}_2, v_1 \vee v_2\}$ generates the following ILP,

$$
\begin{array}{llll}
\min & & y_1 + y_2 + y_3 & \\
& 1 - v_1 & + y_1 & \geq 1 \\
& 1 - v_2 & + y_2 & \geq 1 \\
& v_1 + v_2 & + y_3 & \geq 1
\end{array}
$$

where $v_i \in \{0,1\}, i = 1,2, y_j \in [0,1], j = 1,2,3$.

The MIP is solved by computing its linear relaxation, obtained by replacing the integrality requirements by simple bounds, $0 \leq v_i \leq 1, \quad i = 1,\ldots,n$. If the solution of the linear relaxation has integer v variables, it is compared with the best solution found so far. If the solution has fractional v variables, one v_i is chosen for branching, generating two subproblems (one with $v_i = 0$, the other with $v_i = 1$), which are solved by the same method. A number of other sophisticated techniques can be involved in this process [3].

3.3 As a WCSP

Primal Encoding. A weighted Max-SAT instance is directly expressed as a WCSP as follows. WCSP variables are the logical variables of the Max-SAT instance, with the domain $\{0,1\}$. Each clause C_j with weight w_j generates a cost function, which assigns cost 0 to those tuples satisfying C_j, and assigns cost w_j to the only tuple violating C_j. When two cost functions involve the same variables, they can be added together. The WCSP solution, the total assignment with minimum cost, corresponds to the solution of Max-SAT.

The algorithms used to solve the WCSP are specific depth-first branch and bound algorithms. Such algorithms rely on an upper bound ub on the cost of the optimal solution and a lower bound lb on the cost of the optimal extension of the current assignment. The cost of the currently best known solution provides ub. An ad-hoc mechanism provides lb. The current branch is pruned as soon as $lb \geq ub$.

Given the current assignment, we have an associated WCSP subproblem where $S(ub)$ is the valuation structure, $c_\varnothing$ is the current lower bound, and current constraints are the constraints inherited from the parent node projected according with the last assigned variable. To process this subproblem, a given soft local consistency property is enforced at each node. As in the classical CSP case, local consistency enforcing performs local computations that preserve the semantics of the problem, prune infeasible values (whose use would provenly lead to cost greater than or equal to ub) and may increase $c_\varnothing$ (see [19, 13, 15]).

The different levels of local consistencies we have considered are node consistency (NC*), arc consistency (AC*), directional arc consistency (DAC*) and full DAC (FDAC*), for binary problems as defined in [15]. These local consistencies can be enforced in time $O(nd)$ (NC*), $O(n^2d^3)$ (AC*), $O(ed^2)$ (DAC*) and $O(end^3)$ (FDAC*), where e is the number of constraints, n the number of variables and d the maximum domain size.

Among these local consistencies, NC* is the weakest and FDAC* is the strongest. DAC* and AC* are incomparable between them, both are stronger than NC* but weaker than FDAC* [15].

Each form of local consistency defines a solver which maintains the corresponding property. For instance, MFDAC is the branch and bound algorithm that maintains FDAC* during search. Since the Max-SAT translation produces non-binary constraints, we straightforwardly extend the previous local consistencies to the non-binary case as follows: a problem is considered as locally consistent iff it is locally consistent with respect to unary and binary constraints (other constraints are delayed until their arity is reduced by further assignments).

Dual Encoding. An alternative modeling is the dual formulation [14]. There is a variable x_i for each clause C_i. The domain of x_i is the set of possible assignments to the logical variables in C_i. When x_i takes one of its domain values, it represents the fact that the logical variables of C_i have been assigned accordingly. There is a unary constraint on each variable x_i. This constraint assigns cost 0 to each domain value satisfying clause C_i, and assigns cost w_i to the only domain value violating C_i (namely, the assignment which dissatisfies every literal in C_i). There is a binary constraint between every two variables x_i and x_j corresponding to clauses C_i and C_j sharing logical variables. This constraint gives infinite cost to pairs formed by domain values which assign different logical values to the shared logical variables, and cost 0 to every other pair. The solution of the dual problem corresponds to the solution of the primal problem, which produces a solution for Max-SAT. This formulation produces a binary encoding, so that existing WCSP algorithm implementations can be directly applied.

Heuristics. Each time a new variable has to be assigned, the algorithm looks for variables with one feasible value and selects one of them first. If all variables have two values, a variable selection heuristic must be used. Since all domains have the same cardinality, a smallest-domain criterion may not be used.

We denote $T_j = \prod_{i \in var(c_j)} D_i$ the set of tuples valuated by constraint c_j. W_j is the average cost given by c_j, defined as $W_j = \frac{1}{|T_j|} \sum_{t \in T_j} c_j(t)$. We define $Z_i = \sum_{j \in \mathcal{C}, i \in var(c_j)} W_j$. It measures the average cost in which variable x_i is involved.

A natural heuristic would be to select the variable with the highest Z_i, since the assignment of such a variable is likely to produce high costs and, consequently, anticipate pruning. The problem of this heuristic is its computational cost. Unless we can exploit the semantics of the constraints to compute W_j efficiently, its cost is $O(e \times d^r)$ where e is the number of constraints, d is the largest domain size (2 in MaxSAT) and r is the problem arity. We found this heuristic very informative but it was not cost effective. Thus, we made an approximation.

Let Z_i^k be the contribution of k-arity constraints to Z_i. The approximate heuristic selects the variable with highest $Z_i^1 + Z_i^2$, which has cost $O(e_1 d + e_2 d^2)$ with e_1 and e_2 being the number of unary and binary constraints. Only when all variables have $Z_i^1 + Z_i^2$ equal to zero, we discriminate using Z_i^3, which has cost $O(e_3 d^3)$ (this is rarely needed, typically at nodes near to the root). The heuristics is used dynamically, all values are computed at each node according to the current subproblem. Once the variable has been selected, the value with the lowest unary cost is assigned first.

4   Empirical Results

Here we report the results of an empirical evaluation of WCSP techniques compared to state-of-the-art pseudo-boolean and ILP solvers on a set of benchmarks.

4.1   Benchmarks

The benchmarks are composed of:

- unsatisfiable instances of the 2nd DIMACS Implementation Challenge [12]: random 3-SAT instances (*aim* and *dubois*), pigeon hole problem (*hole*), 2-coloring problems (*pret*) and random SAT instances (*jnh*) with variable length clauses (2-14 literals per clause).
- extended *jnh* instances weighted using uniformly distributed integer weights between 1 and 1,000 [17].
- random 2-SAT and 3-SAT instances created by Allen van Gelder *mkcnf* generator [23]. The generation parameters are the clause length l, the number of variables n and the number of clauses r. We generated a set of instances with $(l, n, r) \in \{2, 3\} \times \{40, 80\} \times \{100, 200, \cdots, 3000\}$ [2]. For each parameter configuration, 10 instances were generated. Note that this generator prevents duplicate or opposite literals in clauses but not duplicate clauses.

We assume unit clause weights for all instances, except for the extended *jnh* instances.

We experimented with the 4 types of local consistency (NC*, AC*, DAC* and FDAC*) and 2 problem encodings (primal and dual). Among the 8 alternatives, maintaining FDAC* with the primal encoding was the obvious best choice (it was typically much better than any of the others, and never much worse). For clarity in the analysis, we essentially report results on MFDAC. Our implementation of MFDAC [15] (C code) is compared to four solvers:

- Pseudo-boolean optimization solver OPBDP v1.1 [2] (C++ code).
- Pseudo-boolean solver PBS v0.2 [1] (Sun binary).
- Max-2SAT solver max2sat [9] (Java code), *only* for 2-SAT problems.
- Commercial ILP solver CPLEX v8.1.0 [11] (Sun binary).

We used default configuration parameters for all the solvers, except for PBS which used VSIDS decision heuristic (as advised by the authors) and for CPLEX whose stopping criterion was set to $gub - glb \leq 0.999$ to ensure completeness.

In order to reduce the search effort for all algorithms and put ourselves in a realistic situation, we used *walksat* [22] with default parameters (10 runs of 100000 flips) to compute a first upper bound. This upper bound was injected in all algorithms using either available configuration parameters or by modifying the max2sat code to access an internal parameter. In the case of the DIMACS instances, *walksat* always found the optimum, so the complete solvers had just to prove optimality. In the case of extended *jnh* instances, we used the optimum values from [17]. Because of this preprocessing step, CPLEX focused on optimality proof rather than improving integer solutions (*set mip emphasis 2*). Note that in general, only few Gomory fractional cuts were added by CPLEX. All the experiments, except for CPLEX, ran on a Sun Enterprise 250 (UltraSPARC-II 400MHz, 640 Megabytes at 100 MHz). CPLEX ran on a Sun Blade 1000 (UltraSPARC-III 750MHz, 1 Gigabytes) and a ratio (370/198 from SPEC CPU 2000 results) was applied for time measurements.

---

[2] Only 2000 for 80 variables instances.

Table 1. DIMACS unsatisfiable instances. Time in seconds. A "-" means the problem was not solved in less than 600 seconds.

Name	$|V|$	$|C|$	Opt	MFDAC	OPBDP	PBS	CPLEX
aim-100-1_6-no-1	100	160	1	-	595	0	71
aim-100-1_6-no-2	100	160	1	-	92	0	23
aim-100-1_6-no-3	100	160	1	-	-	0	11
aim-100-1_6-no-4	100	160	1	-	-	0	2
aim-100-2_0-no-1	100	200	1	-	0	0	-
aim-100-2_0-no-2	100	200	1	-	54	0	-
aim-100-2_0-no-3	100	200	1	-	60	0	-
aim-100-2_0-no-4	100	200	1	-	33	0	-
aim-50-1_6-no-1	50	80	1	5	0	0	0
aim-50-1_6-no-2	50	80	1	0	0	0	0
aim-50-1_6-no-3	50	80	1	3	0	0	0
aim-50-1_6-no-4	50	80	1	0	0	0	0
aim-50-2_0-no-1	50	100	1	1	0	0	0
aim-50-2_0-no-2	50	100	1	0	0	0	4
aim-50-2_0-no-3	50	100	1	0	0	0	3
aim-50-2_0-no-4	50	100	1	1	0	0	0
dubois20	60	160	1	407	70	0	-
dubois21	63	168	1	-	145	0	-
dubois22	66	176	1	-	298	0	-
dubois23	69	184	1	-	596	0	-
dubois24	72	192	1	-	-	0	-
dubois25	75	200	1	-	-	0	-
dubois26	78	208	1	-	-	0	-
dubois27	81	216	1	-	-	0	-
dubois28	84	224	1	-	-	0	-
dubois29	87	232	1	-	-	0	-
dubois30	90	240	1	-	-	0	-
hole06	42	133	1	0	1	0	0
hole07	56	204	1	7	27	1	0
hole08	72	297	1	123	-	10	0
hole09	90	415	1	-	-	69	0
pret60_25	60	160	1	532	77	0	-
pret60_40	60	160	1	530	76	0	-
pret60_60	60	160	1	531	77	0	-
pret60_75	60	160	1	530	77	0	-
$|solved|$	35	35	35	16	24	**35**	16
Average	72.1	172.8	1.0	402.0	253.9	**2.4**	329.2

4.2   Results

The results for DIMACS benchmarks are shown in Table 1 and 2. For each instance, the table lists the instance name, the number of variables ($|V|$), the

Table 2. JNH instances with unit clause weights first and with random clause weights next. Time in seconds. A "-" means the problem was not solved in less than 600 seconds.

Name	$|V|$	$|C|$	Opt	MFDAC	OPBDP	PBS	CPLEX	Opt	MFDAC	OPBDP	PBS	CPLEX
jnh04	100	850	1	0	0	0	38	95	2	0	0	112
jnh05	100	850	1	0	0	0	3	183	3	0	0	60
jnh06	100	850	1	0	0	0	39	99	3	0	0	84
jnh08	100	850	2	11	1	13	33	462	11	1	0	157
jnh09	100	850	2	5	1	18	274	333	89	0	2	-
jnh10	100	850	1	0	0	0	5	85	4	1	0	16
jnh11	100	850	1	0	0	0	32	172	26	0	0	439
jnh13	100	850	2	12	1	16	28	109	4	0	0	20
jnh14	100	850	2	10	1	19	170	101	11	0	0	79
jnh15	100	850	2	12	2	20	86	206	9	1	0	89
jnh16	100	850	1	4	8	0	490	6	23	8	0	190
jnh18	100	850	1	0	1	0	31	130	15	2	0	184
jnh19	100	850	2	14	1	40	162	166	12	0	0	97
jnh202	100	800	1	0	0	0	2	68	0	0	0	8
jnh203	100	800	1	0	0	0	13	39	8	0	0	21
jnh208	100	800	1	0	0	0	8	79	7	0	0	35
jnh211	100	800	2	14	0	14	34	259	13	0	0	31
jnh214	100	800	1	0	0	0	7	75	3	0	0	34
jnh215	100	800	1	0	0	0	18	88	15	0	0	46
jnh216	100	800	1	0	1	0	8	12	1	1	0	32
jnh219	100	800	1	0	1	0	34	82	12	1	0	46
jnh302	100	900	4	241	76	-	-	395	17	0	1	114
jnh303	100	900	3	247	37	-	-	351	35	2	1	326
jnh304	100	900	3	31	7	207	150	321	3	0	0	92
jnh305	100	900	3	59	14	-	183	742	65	16	148	-
jnh306	100	900	1	0	2	0	144	16	7	2	0	96
jnh307	100	900	3	25	11	121	130	540	34	1	3	278
jnh308	100	900	2	124	1	17	82	130	3	0	0	60
jnh309	100	900	2	3	0	15	26	276	3	0	0	75
jnh310	100	900	3	69	7	295	173	463	18	3	14	426
solved	30	30	30	**30**	**30**	27	28	30	**30**	**30**	**30**	28
Average	100.0	851.7	1.7	29.4	**6.3**	86.8	120.6	202.8	15.2	**1.9**	5.9	148.7

number of clauses ($|C|$), the optimum (minimization of the clause violation), and the total cpu time in seconds (rounded downwards) for the various solvers. In the case of Table 2, there are two parts corresponding to the original *jnh* instances and the extended *jnh*. In both tables, the last two lines give the number of instances completely solved in less than 600 seconds and the average time for all the instances (if unsolved, 600 is counted). Note that all these problems have an extremely low optimum value, which means that they are near the satisfiability complexity peak. As observed by [27], these instances are hard as SAT instances but easy as Max-SAT instances (the hardest instances have higher clauses to variables ratio which causes high optimum values)

In Table 1, MFDAC was able to solve almost half of the instances while PBS solved them all. We do not report larger instances ($|V| > 100$) where PBS was the only successful algorithm (except for CPLEX on $hole10$). PBS contains several SAT-solver sophistications like conflict diagnosis and clause recording which make it efficient on instances near the transition phase. In comparison, OPBDP is much simpler. But its specific design for SAT (dedicated SAT rules and data structures) makes the difference with MFDAC: OPBDP can visit up to 3 times more nodes per seconds than MFDAC. CPLEX solved the same number of problems than MFDAC and is the best choice for the structured (highly symmetric) pigeon-hole problems[3].

The original unsatisfiable jnh instances are best solved using OPBDP and MFDAC (see table 2, first part) which solved all the instances. MFDAC was 4.6 times slower than OPBDP and explored 6-7 times more nodes than OPBDP. We conjecture that our naive approach for tackling non-binary constraints is responsible of this poor pruning behavior (recall that mean clause length in jnh is equal to 5). PBS is 3 (resp. 14) times slower than MFDAC (resp. OPBDP), mainly due to its bad performances on unsatisfiable instances with 3 or more violated clauses at the optimum. CPLEX was slower than PBS but seems more robust. Adding clause weights boosted all the solvers, except surprisingly for CPLEX ([17] observed exactly the opposite but they were not using an initial bound nor the same configuration parameters as us). OPBDP is still the best choice, but PBS (with equivalences) is now second best and 4.6 times faster than MFDAC.

With randomly-generated Max-kSAT instances and large clauses/variables ratios, MFDAC was by far the best as it is shown in Figure 1. PBS and OPBDP were unable to solve problems with more than 400 clauses. CPLEX exceeded the time limit for Max-2SAT (resp. Max-3SAT) with 40 variables when there are more than 800 (resp. 600) clauses. Considering Max-2SAT (40-variables), MFDAC solved all the 300 instances in less than 156 seconds each. max2sat was second best and solved 220 instances in less than 600 seconds each. At a clauses/variables ratio of only 5 (200/40), we got the following numerical results (mean time in seconds and in parenthesis, mean number of nodes and number of problems completely solved): MFDAC 0s(429nd,10), CPLEX 0.7s(89nd,10), max2sat 1.1s(257nd,10), OPBDP 47.7s(691887nd,10), PBS 582s(1139115nd,1). At a clauses/variables ratio of 10 (400/40), results were: MFDAC 0.1s(4013nd,10), max2sat 15.1s(6002nd,10), CPLEX 24.8s(4839nd,10), OPBDP > 600s(-,0) and PBS > 600s(-,0). For Max-3SAT (40-variables), instances become more difficult, the gap between MFDAC and the other solvers was reduced (CPLEX is 8-9 times slower than MFDAC for a c/v ratio of 10) but the efficiency order between solvers remained the same. With more variables (Max-2SAT 80-variables), CPLEX was faster than MFDAC if there are less than 400 clauses. And with

---

[3] Pigeon-hole problems have very efficient encoding as pseudo-boolean formulae and CPLEX may possibly detect this even if a clausal formulation is used.

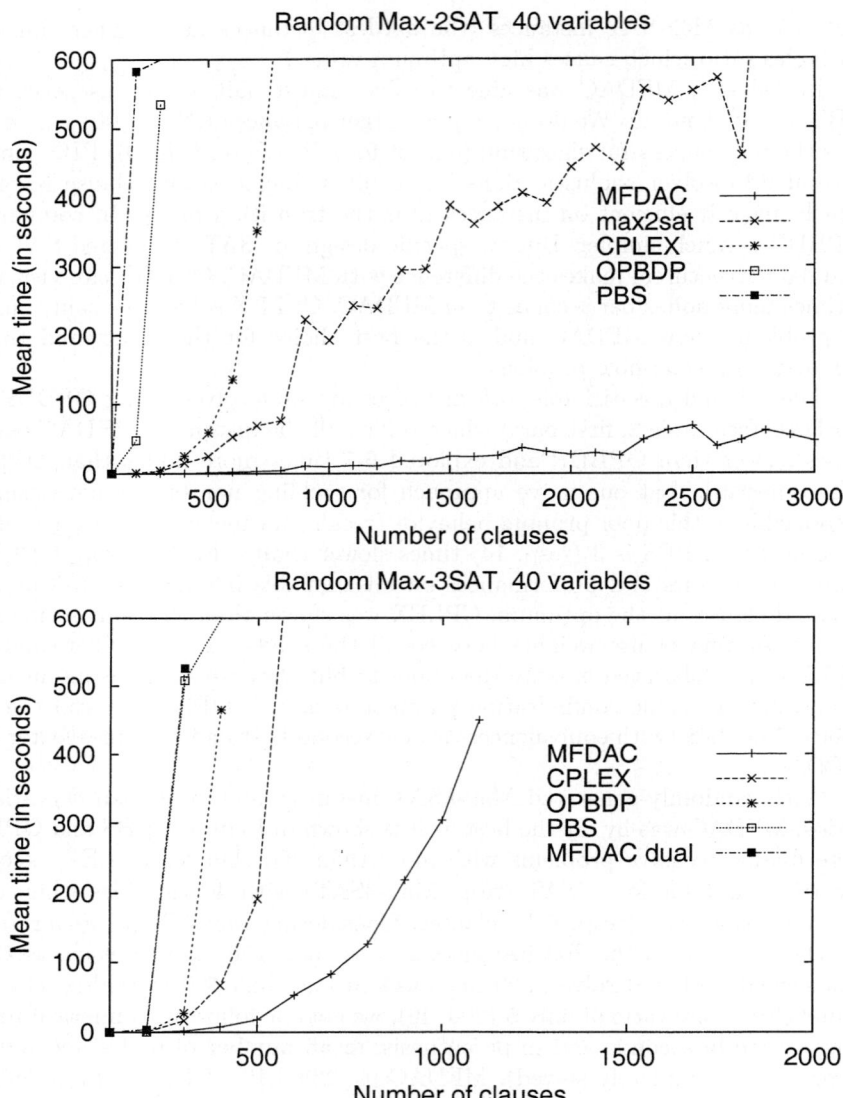

Fig. 1. Randomly-generated Max-2SAT and Max-3SAT instances with 40 variables.

Max-3SAT 80 variables, OPBPD was the winner, and MFDAC second best, for less than 400 clauses. When clauses/variables ratio decreases and when the clause length increases, instances are closer to the satisfiability threshold which is beneficial to SAT-based solvers such as OPDPB. In summary, MFDAC proved its superiority on large clauses/variables ratios. The speed-up obtained was even more important on problems with small length clauses.

5   Conclusion

On the Max-SAT problem, and despite a very limited adaptation of WCSP code to CNF propositional logic formula, we observe that the use of recent local consistency maintenance algorithms defined in [15] allows to reach a level of performance competitive with recent Max-SAT complete solvers and state-of-the art MIP solvers. This is especially true on the hardest problems, with a high clause/variable ratio.

The current MFDAC code used is far from being finely optimized code and is not specifically tuned to Max-SAT problems. For example, it does not specifically exploit the fundamental properties of CNF in propositional logic: the fact that domains are always binary and that dedicated data-structures can be used for CNF representation. The extension of the local consistency to non-binary constraints could also be improved by studying subproblems involving more than 2 variables.

These results show that there is a clear opportunity to study if recent local consistency notions like full directional arc consistency could be adapted to propositional logic and injected in existing Max-SAT solvers. More work is needed to see if these algorithms could be applied to other central combinatorial optimization problems such as Max-CUT or the Maximum Probable Explanation (MPE) problem in Bayesian networks.

Acknowledgements

We would like to thank Michel Correge and Michel Lemaître for letting us use CPLEX, for hosting the associated heavy benchmarking and associated nuisances. We would also like to thank Fadi Aloul and Jens Gramm for making their code available to us.

References

1. ALOUL, F., RAMANI, A., MARKOV, I., AND SAKALLAH, K. Pbs: A backtrack-search pseudo-boolean solver and optimizer. In *Symposium on the Theory and Applications of Satisfiability Testing (SAT)* (Cincinnati, (OH), 2002), pp. 346–353.
2. BARTH, P. A davis-putnam based enumeration algorithm for linear pseudo-boolean optimization. Tech. Rep. MPI-I-95-2-003, Max-Planck Institut Für Informatik, 1995.
3. BORCHERS, B., MITCHELL, J., AND JOY, S. A branch-and-cut algorithm for MAX-SAT and weighted MAX-SAT. In *Satisfiability Problem: Theory and Applications*, D. Du, J. Gu, and P. Pardalos, Eds., vol. 35 of *DIMACS Series in Discrete Mathematics and Theoretical Computer Science*. AMS, 1997, pp. 519–536.
4. BORNING, A., MAHERT, M., MARTINDALE, A., AND WILSON, M. Constraint hierarchies and logic programming. In *Int. conf. on logic programming* (1989), pp. 149–164.
5. DIXON, H., AND GINSBERG, M. Inference methods for a pseudo-boolean satisfiability solver. In *Proceedings of the Eighteenth National Conference on Artificial Intelligence (AAAI-02)* (2002), pp. 635–640.
6. FREUDER, E., AND WALLACE, R. Partial constraint satisfaction. *Artificial Intelligence 58* (Dec. 1992), 21–70.
7. FREUDER, E. C. Partial constraint satisfaction. In *Proc of the 11ᵗʰ IJCAI* (Detroit, MI, 1989), pp. 278–283.

8. GRAMM, J., HIRSCH, E. A., NIEDERMEIER, R., AND ROSSMANITH, P. New worst-case upper bounds for MAX-2-SAT with application to MAX-CUT. Tech. Rep. TR00-037, Electronic Colloquium on Computational Complexity, 2000.

9. GRAMM, J., AND NIEDERMEIER, R. Faster exact solutions for max2Sat. In *Proceedings of the 4th Italian Conference on Algorithms and Complexity* (Rome, Italy, Mar. 2000), G. Bongiovanni, G. Gambosi, and R. Petreschi, Eds., vol. 1767 of *LNCS*, Springer, pp. 174–186.

10. HANSEN, P., AND JAUMARD, B. Algorithms for the maximum satisfiability problem. *Computing 44* (1990), 279–303.

11. ILOG. Cplex solver 8.1.0. www.ilog.com/products/cplex, 2002.

12. JOHNSON, D. S., AND TRICK, M. A., Eds. *Second DIMACS implementation challenge:cliques, coloring and satisfiability*, vol. 26 of *DIMACS Series in Discrete Mathematics and Theoretical Computer Science*. AMS, 1996.

13. LARROSA, J. On arc and node consistency in weighted CSP. In *Proc. AAAI'02* (Edmondton, (CA), 2002).

14. LARROSA, J., AND DECHTER, R. On the dual representation of non-binary semiring-based CSPs. CP'2000 Workshop on Soft Constraints, Oct. 2000.

15. LARROSA, J., AND SCHIEX, T. In the quest of the best form of local consistency for weighted CSP. In *Proc. of the 18th IJCAI* (Acapulco, Mexico, Aug. 2003). see www.inra.fr/bia/T/schiex/Export/ijcai03.pdf.

16. MOSKEWICZ, M., MADIGAN, C., ZHAO, Y., ZHANG, L., AND MALIK, S. Chaff: Engineering an efficient sat solver. In *38th Design Automation Conference (DAC'01)* (June 2001), pp. 530–535.

17. RESENDE, M., PITSOULIS, L., AND PARDALOS, P. Approximate solution of weighted max-SAT problems using GRASP. In *Satisfiability problem: Theory and Applications*, D. Du, J. Gu, and P. Pardalos, Eds., vol. 35 of *DIMACS Series on Discrete Mathematics and Theoretical Computer Science*. AMS, 1997, pp. 393–405.

18. ROSENFELD, A., HUMMEL, R., AND ZUCKER, S. Scene labeling by relaxation operations. *IEEE Trans. on Systems, Man, and Cybernetics 6*, 6 (1976), 173–184.

19. SCHIEX, T. Arc cohérence pour contraintes molles. In *Actes de JNPC'00* (Marseille, June 2000).

20. SCHIEX, T. Arc consistency for soft constraints. In *Principles and Practice of Constraint Programming - CP 2000* (Singapore, Sept. 2000), vol. 1894 of *LNCS*, pp. 411–424.

21. SCHIEX, T., FARGIER, H., AND VERFAILLIE, G. Valued constraint satisfaction problems: hard and easy problems. In *Proc. of the 14th IJCAI* (Montréal, Canada, Aug. 1995), pp. 631–637.

22. SELMAN, B., KAUTZ, H., AND COHEN, B. Noise strategies for improving local search. In *Proc. of AAAI'94* (Seattle, WA, 1994), pp. 337–343.

23. VAN GELDER, A. Cnfgen formula generator. ftp://dimacs.rutgers.edu/pub/challenge/satisfiability/contributed/UCSC/instances, 1993.

24. VAN HENTENRYCK, P., AND DEVILLE, Y. The cardinality operator: A new logical connective for constraint logic programming. In *Proc. of the 8th international conference on logic programming* (Paris, France, June 1991).

25. WHITTEMORE, J., KIM, J., AND SAKALLAH, K. SATIRE: A new incremental satisfiability engine. In *Proceedings of the 38th conference on Design automation* (Las Vegas, NV, June 2001), ACM, pp. 542–545.

26. XU, H., RUTENBAR, R. A., AND SAKALLAH, K. sub-SAT: A formulation for relaxed boolean satisfiability with applications in routing. In *Proc. Int. Symp. on Physical Design* (San Diego (CA), Apr. 2002).

27. ZHANG, W. Phase transitions and backbones of 3-SAT and maximum 3-SAT. In *Proc. of the 7th International Conference on Principles and Practice of Constraint Programming (CP-01)* (Paphos, Cyprus, Nov. 2001), vol. 2239 of *LNCS*, Springer, pp. 153–167.

Constraint Reasoning over Strings

Keith Golden[1] and Wanlin Pang[2]

[1] Computational Science Division, NASA Ames Research Center, Moffett Field, CA 94035
[2] QSS Group Inc., NASA Ames Research Center, Moffett Field, CA 94035

Abstract. This paper discusses an approach to representing and reasoning about constraints over strings. We discuss how string domains can often be concisely represented using regular languages, and how constraints over strings, and domain operations on sets of strings, can be carried out using this representation.

1 Introduction

Constraint satisfaction problems (CSPs) involve finding values for variables subject to constraints that permit or exclude certain combinations of values. Since many tasks in computer science [13,5,22] and many real-world problems [23,14,16,20] can be formulated as CSPs, they have been attracting widespread research and commercial interests for the last two decades. Whereas much work has been done on constraints over finite discrete domains and numerical intervals, there has been little work on constraint reasoning over strings.

Strings appear everywhere, from databases to DNA, and the relationships between the strings and the real-world objects they represent can be formalized as constraints. For example, we are applying constraint-based planning to provide automation in software domains [9,8], domains in which the actions are operations in a software environment, such as moving files, searching for information on the Internet or image processing. One characteristic of nearly all software domains is the ubiquity of strings and constraints. File path names, URLs and the contents of text files and web pages are all represented as text, which often obey specific constraints. For instance, many programs have inputs or outputs in the form of files, whose names follow some canonical form:

- A Java compiler expects the pathname for the source code of "my.package.MyClass" to be "my/package/MyClass.java," and it produces a file "my/package/MyClass.class."
- The pathname of data down-linked from a spacecraft or planetary rover is often in a form like "phase2/sol29/my_instrument/seq0002.jpg," where each component of the pathname refers to some meaningful aspect of the data.

A distinguishing characteristic of software domains and other domains involving strings is that the set of possible strings corresponding to a given name, input or file is either infinite or so large that listing them all would require unacceptable amounts of time and storage. The challenge of effectively representing and reasoning about constraints on strings is to represent infinite string sets without actually requiring infinite space

F. Rossi (Ed.): CP 2003, LNCS 2833, pp. 377–391, 2003.

and to enforce constraints over infinite string sets without exhaustively listing the consistent values. In this paper, we provide such a string representation, based on regular languages, we discuss how common string constraints are defined and handled using this representation, and we show how string constraint problems can be solved.

The remainder of the paper is organized as follows. In Section 2, we review notations of constraint satisfaction problems. In Section 3, we discuss our string domain representation, namely, regular languages. In Section 4, we provide definitions of useful string constraints and describe how they are enforced using this domain representation. In Section 5, we discuss how standard domain operations, such as intersection and equality testing, are handled. In Section 6, we show how the string constraints can be applied to solving some interesting problems. And finally, in Section 7 we conclude by summarizing our contribution.

2   Constraint Satisfaction Problems

A **Constraint Satisfaction Problem (CSP)** is a representation and reasoning framework consisting of variables, domains, and constraints. Formally, it can be defined as a triple $< X, D, C >$ where $X = \{x_1, x_2, \ldots, x_n\}$ is a finite set of variables, $D = \{d(x_1), d(x_2), \ldots, d(x_n)\}$ is a set of domains containing values the variables may take, and $C = \{C_1, C_2, \ldots, C_m\}$ is a set of constraints. Each constraint C_i is defined as a relation R on a subset of variables $V = \{x_i, x_j, \ldots, x_k\}$, called the constraint scope. R may be represented extensionally as a subset of the Cartesian product $d(x_i) \times d(x_j) \times \ldots \times d(x_k)$. A constraint $C_i = (V_i, R_i)$ limits the values the variables in V can take simultaneously to those assignments that satisfy R. Let $V_K = \{x_{k_1}, \ldots, x_{k_l}\}$ be a subset of X. An l-tuple $(x_{k_1}, \ldots, x_{k_l})$ from $d(x_{k_1}) \times \ldots \times d(x_{k_l})$ is called an *instantiation* of variables in V_K. An instantiation is said to be *consistent* if it satisfies all the constraints restricted in V_K. A consistent instantiation of all variables in X is a *solution*. The central reasoning task (or the task of solving a CSP) is to find one or more solutions.

A CSP can be solved by search using, e.g., standard backtracking algorithms [3, 10]. However, for CSPs with infinite domains such as those of interest in this paper, it is not guaranteed that a solution can be found by search alone, because it is infeasible to enumerate all values of infinite variable domains. Instead, the CSPs with infinite domains need to be relaxed by consistency enforcement before or during the search. Enforcing local consistency eliminates inconsistent values from variable domains [15, 2]. In theory, if a given CSP has only one solution, enforcing a certain level of consistency will eventually make every variable domain a singleton domain; if the CSP has more than one solution, or infinitely many solutions, every remaining value in the domain after consistency enforcement will be part of a solution. In practice, an effective constraint solving strategy enforces a certain level of consistency such as generalized arc consistency [17, 18] at each node of the search tree. A key issue is the trade-off between time spent on propagation and the reduction in the search space needed to allow feasible and efficient search. Based on our experience dealing with constraint-based planning in software environments, much depends on how the variable domains are represented and how the constraints are evaluated or executed to enforce consistency. In the next three sections, we focus on our string domain representation and a definition of constraints over string domains. These string constraints are in the constraint library of the constraint reasoning system we implemented and, together with other numerical and boolean constraints, are used to model planning problems.

3 String Domains

We use the same CSP representation both to represent the constraint problem and to search for a solution; the domain $d(x)$ of variable x, representing the set of values that x can take, will, in general, change during the course of search and constraint propagation. Typically, a variable's domain is represented as a list of values. For numeric domains, we can instead represent a domain as an interval, yielding substantial decreases in space and time requirements and making it possible to represent an infinite set of values [11].

In the domains of interest, we frequently want to represent infinite, or very large, sets of strings, such as all possible pathnames matching a given pattern. Representing this set as a list is clearly infeasible, since it is infinite. Intervals are equally inappropriate. While it is possible to represent some sets of strings as intervals, such as all names between "Jones" and "Smith" in the phone book, such intervals are far less useful in practice than are numeric intervals.

However, there is an alternative representation of sets of strings that is far more useful, as evidenced by its ubiquity: regular languages. Regular languages are sets of strings that are accepted by regular expressions or finite automata, which are widely used in string matching, lexical analysis and many other applications. Although there are many languages that are not regular, such as palindromes, regular languages provide a nice tradeoff between expressiveness and tractability. As we will discuss, not only can we enforce generalized arc consistency (GAC) [2] for a wide range of useful string constraints when the domains are represented as regular languages, but we can perform the domain operations necessary for constraint propagation and search.

Regular languages are a much more flexible representation than intervals, in that the set of regular languages is closed under intersection, union and negation, whereas the set of intervals is only closed under intersection. Note that moving to an even more expressive representation would not be an improvement. Neither context-free languages (CFLs) nor deterministic CFLs are closed under intersection, and determining whether a context-sensitive (or more expressive) language is empty is undecidable [12, p 281].

We use two different representations of regular languages: regular expressions and finite automata (FAs). Regular expressions are used as input and are converted to FAs, which are used computationally. A regular expression represents a regular language over an alphabet Σ. In our implementation, Σ is the set of Unicode characters. We use the notation described in Table 1 to describe regular expressions.

The purpose of the notation $\backslash c$ is to "quote" a symbol c that would otherwise be interpreted as a syntax character. For example, $\backslash [$ can be use to refer to the character "[" and $\backslash \backslash$ refers to the character "\".

We represent regular languages internally using FAs, since they are easier to compute with than regular expressions. An FA is a pair $< S, T >$, where S is a set of states and T is a set of labeled transitions between the states. Each transition in T is a triple $< s_1, l, s_2 >$, which we will write $< s_1 \overset{l}{\to} s_2 >$, where s_1 is the starting state of the transition, s_2 is the ending state and $l \in \Sigma$ is the transition label. The input to the FA is a sequence of symbols from Σ. Whenever there are symbols left to read, the FA reads

Table 1. Regular expression syntax

Expression	Accept
[abc]	one of the characters a, b, c
[a − c]	one of the characters in the range $a − c$
~[abc]	any character in Σ except a, b, c
.	any character in Σ
\c	the literal character c
$re_1 re_2$	re_1 followed by re_2
$re_1	re_2$	either re_1 or re_2
$re*$	zero or more repetition of re
$re+$	one or more repetitions of re
$re?$	zero or one occurrences of re
(re)	re (used to override precedence)

the next symbol, c, and follows a transition from the current state whose label is c. If there are multiple transitions labeled c, one is chosen nondeterministically. If there are no transitions labeled c, the FA halts and returns failure. For efficiency, we allow transitions to have sets of labels, represented using the same notation as shown in the first five rows of Table 1 (i.e., one-character regular expressions). For example, we could have a transition $< s_1 \overset{[a-zA-Z]}{\rightarrow} s_2 >$, meaning the transition will be taken if the symbol is any character from the English alphabet. This is logically equivalent to having a separate transition for each symbol. For notational convenience, we also refer to transitions labeled with ε. An ε-transition is always applicable and is followed without reading any characters. An FA has a single *start state*, which is always the first state, $S[0]$, and zero or more *accept states*. To determine whether a string s is in the language accepted by an FA $< S, T >$, we start the FA in $S[0]$ and have it read s until there are no characters left to read. If, at that time, the FA is in an accept state, then s is in the language. Otherwise, it is not. In our visual depiction of FAs, we represent states, transitions, start states and accept states as follows:

A deterministic finite automaton (DFA) is an FA with no epsilon transitions and in which there is exactly one transition out of every state for each label $l \in \Sigma$. An FA that does not satisfy these conditions is a nondeterministic FA (NFA). The minimal DFA representation of a language is a unique, subject to renaming the states [12, p 57]. In the remainder of the paper, we will assume an FA is an NFA unless stated otherwise. NFAs and DFAs have equivalent expressive power, in that both accept the family of regular languages, but NFAs may be exponentially smaller. We call a domain represented using a regular expression or FA a *regular domain*.

Regular expressions and FAs have been used in many application domains involving strings, such as data mining from databases or the Web. For example, in [6], the authors addressed the issue of mining frequent sequences from a database of sequences in the presence of regular expression constraints (see [1] for a detailed discussion on the issue of mining sequential patterns). Regular expression constraints are user-defined sequence patterns that are used to match strings in the database or web during query or search. Our work differs from past work in that we do not simply use regular languages to match fixed strings. Rather, we use them to propagate constraints among string variables, whose domains may be infinite. For example, match is indeed a common constraint in our library. However, the domain of the string to be matched need not be singleton. In addition to match, many other types of string constraints appearing in real-world problems need to be represented. We discuss some common ones in the next section.

There has been some work applying constraint reasoning to strings, but relying on less expressive representations of string domains. [4] reports on a language capable of specifying constraints for searching patterns in bio-sequences, such as the length of a string, the distance between two strings, and the position of a string where a character matches. The sequences (strings of symbols) are represented as lists, and the constraints and the constraint solver are implemented using CLP(FD). [19] discusses CLP(S), CLP extended to deal with strings, and its applications to natural language, images and genetic code processing. In contrast to the work presented here, strings are represented as concatenations of variables and constants, which are strictly less expressive than the regular language representation presented here.

4   Constraints

Constraints are usually defined as mathematical formulations of relationships to be held among objects. For example, $x + y = z$ is a constraint describing an equality relation that holds among three numeric variables x, y, and z. Similarly, for the string variables x, y, and z, we can define a string constraint as $x + y = z$ which represents a concatenation relation; that is, string z is the concatenation of strings x and y. We have implemented a number of string constraints in our constraint reasoning framework, which supports generalized arc consistency (GAC), even on infinite sets of strings. In the following, we give definitions of these constraints, illustrated by how they are enforced using FAs.

4.1   Matches

One of the constraints in the library tests whether a string matches a given regular expression:

matches(string x, regexp re)

Although matches takes two arguments, it is essentially a unary constraint, because it is not enforced unless the domain of re is a singleton, in which case it computes the FA corresponding to the regular expression represented by re and intersects it with the domain of x. Matches subsumes all possible unary constraints over strings expressible in our formalism, so other unary constraints, such as allUpperCase and isAlphaNumeric need not be implemented. Matches is used in type constraints to define the initial domains of variables of given subtypes of string. For example, we can define a Unix filename as any string of non-zero length that does not contain the character '/':

matches($filename$, "~[/]+")

and we can define a time as a string of the form HH:MM:SS:

matches($time$, "((([0 − 1][0 − 9]) | (2[0 − 3])) : [0 − 5][0 − 9] : [0 − 5][0 − 9]")

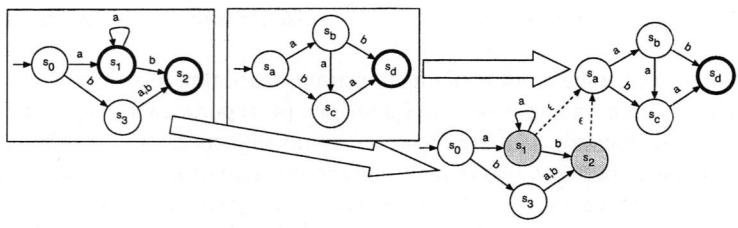

Fig. 1. Concatenation

4.2   Concatenation

One of the most obvious operations on strings is concatenation. The concatenation of two strings, x and y, yields another string, z, which consists of all the characters of x followed by all the characters of y:

concat(z, x, y)

This can be generalized to concatenation of three or more strings in the obvious way. If the domains of x and y are regular, the domain of z will simply be the result of concatenating the FA representations of x and y — that is, adding ε-transitions from the accept states of the FA for x to the start state of the FA for y, as shown in Figure 1, obviously a linear-time operation.

   Less obviously, if the domains of x and z are regular, the domain of y is also regular. To construct an FA for y given FAs for x and z, we in effect traverse the FAs for z and x in parallel, exploring the cross-product of the nodes from the two FAs, starting with the pair of initial states and adding a transition $\{s_n, t_m\} \overset{lab}{\rightarrow} \{s_p, t_q\}$ from every node $\{s_n, t_m\}$ and every label lab such that the transitions $s_n \overset{lab}{\rightarrow} s_p$ and $t_m \overset{lab}{\rightarrow} t_q$ appear in the original FAs (see Figure 2). This is simply the operation that is performed when intersecting two FAs (Section 5.1). Whenever we reach a state $\{s, t\}$, such that s is an accept state in the FA for x, we mark state t. After the traversal is complete, the marked states in the FA for z represent all of the states that can be reached by reading a string accepted by x.

   A new nondeterministic FA (NFA) for y is constructed by copying the FA for z, making the start node a non-start node and making all the marked nodes new start nodes. The complexity of the whole operation is dominated by generating the cross-product FA, so is the same as domain intersection (Section 5.1). A similar procedure can be used to construct an NFA for x, given FAs for y and z.

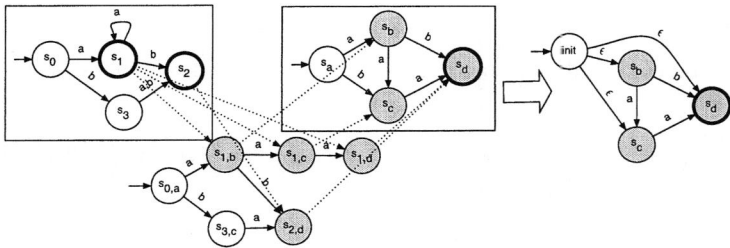

Fig. 2. Given FAs for x (left box) and z (right box), find an FA for y such that z is concatenation of x and y. First, traverse FAs for z and x in parallel, constructing cross-product FA (lower left). Then, identify states that are accept states for x and mark the corresponding states in the FA for z (shaded circles). Construct a new NFA (right) for y by copying the FA for z and making marked nodes start nodes

4.3 Containment

The relation

contains(String a, String b)

means that string b is a substring of a. If the domain of b is a regular language r, then the domain of a is given simply by the regular expression ".*r.*". Given an FA for r, we can create an FA for ".*r.*" in linear time by concatenating the FAs for ".*", r and ".*". If we have some other FA representing the domain of a, we simply intersect that domain with the domain for ".*r.*".

Less obviously, if the domain of a is regular, then so is the domain of b. Given an FA for a, we can construct an NFA for b in linear time by eliminating any dead-end nodes from a (that is, nodes from which it is impossible to reach an accept node), adding a new start state, with ε-transitions to all states, and then making all states in a accept states (Figure 3). Again, we simply intersect this domain with the original domain for b to enforce the constraint.

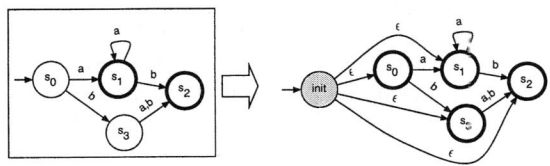

Fig. 3. Given an FA for a regular language r, construct a new FA for all substrings of strings in r

4.4   Length

Constraints on the length of a string can also be represented using FAs:

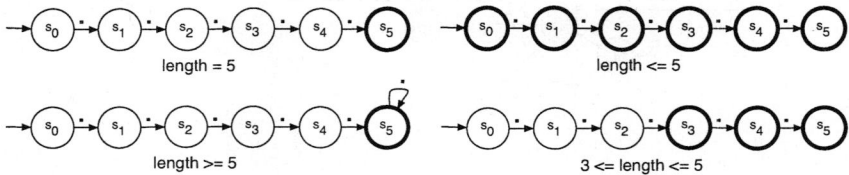

As these examples show, intervals over the length are simple to represent; if we have a constraint of the form length(s, n), and the domain of n is represented as a finite interval, we can enforce the constraint without waiting until n becomes singleton. We simply construct a linear FA whose size is one plus the upper bound of n, and label all of the states whose position exceeds the lower bound as accept states. Similarly, if $d(n) = [x, \infty)$, we construct a linear FA of size $x + 1$ and make the last state an accept state with a self-transition. The time to construct the FA is proportional to either the upper bound of n, or to the lower bound if there is no upper bound.

Conversely, if we have a regular domain representation of s, we can obtain lower and upper bounds for n by determining the shortest and longest paths from the start state to an accept state, a linear-time operation. If there is no upper limit on the size, there will be a loop along a path to an accept state.

4.5   Other Constraints

Many other string constraints are straightforward to represent. To **reverse** all strings in a regular domain, we simply reverse the direction of all the transitions and reverse the status of start and accept states in the FA, a linear time operation. If doing so would result in multiple start states, we create a new, unique start state and add ε-transitions to all would-be start states. To **substitute** one character for another, we can perform the substitution on the labels of the transitions, also linear time. **Subsequences** of strings can be obtained using a combination of **concat** and **length**. For example, to specify the 5-character prefix p of string s, we can write length($p, 5$)∧concat(s, p, r), where r is an unconstrained string.

Another common operation on strings is to specify the character at a given location of the string: characterAt(s, n, c), where c is the character at position n of string s. We will assume than n is a constant (The case where n is a variable can be handled in a similar fashion, but is more complex). We apply the same general idea as the length constraint. In fact, for the character at position n in a string to have any value at all, the string must be at least n characters long, so the characterAt constraint looks like the constraint length $\geq n$, with the addition that the label of the transition leading to the accept state is restricted to the domain of c. Given the domain of s, we could similarly determine the domain of c in $O(n(|\mathcal{S}| + |\mathcal{T}|))$ time, by finding all states reachable in $n - 1$ transitions from the start state, then taking the union of the labels of transitions from which it is possible reach an accept state.

Of the constraints we discussed, matches, concat, contains and reverse are implemented in our constraint library. Implementation of the others is left as future work.

5   Domain Operations

In order to effectively eliminate inconsistent values from regular domains during constraint propagation, we need to be able to perform set operations on the domains, including intersecting two domains, determining whether one is a subset of another and determining whether a domain is empty or singleton. We can perform these operations easily using FAs. It is well known that regular languages are closed under intersection, union and negation [12, p 58-60], and the algorithms for performing these operations on FAs are straightforward.

5.1   Intersection

Since intersection is such an important domain operation, we show the algorithm for intersection below.

intersection

$$
\begin{array}{l}
\textbf{let } \text{init} \leftarrow \{S_1[0], S_2[0]\} \\
\textbf{push } \text{init} \\
\textbf{let } S' \leftarrow \{\text{init}\}, \; T' \leftarrow \{\} \\
\textbf{while}(\text{stack not empty}) \\
\quad \{s_1, s_2\} \leftarrow \textbf{pop}; \\
\quad \text{isAccept}(\{s_1, s_2\}) \leftarrow \text{isAccept}(s_1) \textbf{ and } \text{isAccept}(s_2) \\
\quad \textbf{foreach } \text{lab} \in \Sigma \text{ such that } <s_1 \overset{\text{lab}}{\to} s_x > \in T_1 \textbf{ and } <s_2 \overset{\text{lab}}{\to} s_y > \in T_2 \\
\qquad \text{add } <\{s_1, s_2\} \overset{\text{lab}}{\to} \{s_x, s_y\}> \text{ to } T' \\
\qquad \textbf{if}(\{s_x, s_y\} \notin S') \\
\qquad\quad \text{add } \{s_x, s_y\} \text{ to } S' \\
\qquad\quad \text{push } \{s_x, s_y\} \\
\textbf{return } <S', T'>
\end{array}
$$

The graph is built by exploring reachable states in $S_1 \times S_2$, starting from the pair of initial states. Because of the test in the innermost loop, no state in $S_1 \times S_2$ will be visited more than once. In the idealized case of a DFA in which each transition is represented explicitly, the size of the new FA, and the time to build it, is thus $O(|\Sigma| |S_1| |S_2|)$, independent of the number of transitions in the input FAs. In reality, transitions have *sets* of labels, and the intersections of these sets can result in additional transitions. For example, given transitions in one FA on [a-g] and [h-z], and a transition in the other FA on [d-k], we may end up with transitions in the new FA on [a-c], [d-g], [h-k] and [l-z].

Additionally, an NFA may contain multiple transitions on the same label, so at worst we need to consider all pairs of transitions from the input FAs, giving a space and time complexity of $O(|\mathcal{T}_1||\mathcal{T}_2| + |\mathcal{S}_1||\mathcal{S}_2|)$.

5.2 Negation

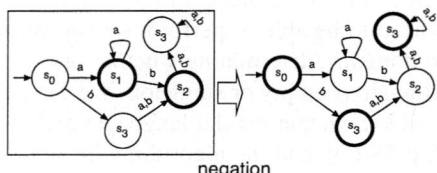

negation

Complementing the accept states of a DFA results in a DFA accepting the complement of the language [12, p 59]. Although complementing the accept states is clearly a linear time operation, converting an NFA to a DFA potentially generates the power set of the NFA, an exponential blowup. Although neither intersection nor negation result in NFAs, some of the constraints defined in Section 4 do.

Given intersection and negation, we can apply the following definitions to compute subset and equality relations between two domains:

$$(fa_1 \subseteq fa_2) \equiv (\neg fa_2 \cap fa_1 = \emptyset)$$
$$(fa_1 = fa_2) \equiv (fa_2 \subseteq fa_1) \wedge (fa_1 \subseteq fa_2)$$
$$(fa_1 - fa_2) \equiv (fa_1 \cap \neg fa_2)$$

5.3 Splitting Domains

Using regular sets as a domain representation, we can propagate constraints very effectively, even when some of the variable domains are infinite. Searching over infinite domains, in contrast, runs the risk of infinite regress, but it can be done by successively splitting the domain into disjoint subsets. Any regular set r can be used to split a domain d, provided neither r nor its complement has an empty intersection with d. The new domains are $d \cap r$ and $d \cap \neg r$. In some applications, a natural choice for sets to split on may present itself. Otherwise, we can easily derive a set r from d by removing transitions from the FA for d. As long as $|d| > 1$, there will be at least one transition leading to an accept state that can be removed without making the language empty (although doing so may require partially unrolling a cycle). r is guaranteed to be a proper subset of d.

5.4 Domain Size

It is important be be able to determine the size of a domain. For example, if the size is 0 (empty), then the constraint network is inconsistent. If the size is 1, then a value for the corresponding variable is determined. Domain size is also useful for variable-ordering heuristics, and knowing whether a domain is finite or infinite is important to avoid searching over infinite domains. Determining the size of a regular domain is less straightforward than determining the size of a set or interval domain, but it can still be done fairly efficiently.

Given a DFA, we can determine the number of strings in the language as follows. We begin by removing all dead-end states from the FA, a linear-time operation. A dead-end state is a state from which it is impossible to reach an accept state. If the initial state is dead-end, then the domain is empty. Once the dead-end states are removed, if the FA contains any loops, then there are infinitely many solutions, because we can follow a loop any number of times and then follow a path to an accept state. We perform a topological sort of the FA, which is linear in the number of arcs. If the sort fails, then there is a loop and thus infinitely many solutions. Otherwise, we traverse the graph in the order dictated by the topological sort, keeping track of the number of paths there are from the initial state to the current state:

$\text{size}(< \mathcal{S}, \mathcal{T} >)$

$$
\begin{bmatrix}
\mathcal{S} \leftarrow \text{topologicalSort}(\mathcal{S}) \\
\text{pathsFromInit}[0] = 1 \\
\textbf{for } i = 0 \textbf{ to } \text{---}\mathcal{S}\text{---} \\
\quad \begin{bmatrix}
\textbf{if } \text{isAccept}(s_i) \textbf{ then } \text{numSolutions} \mathrel{+}= \text{pathsFromInit}[i] \\
\textbf{foreach } \text{transition } < \mathcal{S}[i] \xrightarrow{l} \mathcal{S}[d] > \in \mathcal{T} \\
\quad \begin{bmatrix} \text{pathsFromInit}[d] \mathrel{+}= \text{pathsFromInit}[i] \end{bmatrix}
\end{bmatrix} \\
\textbf{return } \text{numSolutions}
\end{bmatrix}
$$

Let $\mathcal{W}_i \subset \Sigma^*$ be the words that, when read from the initial state, lead to $\mathcal{S}[i]$. To show that the algorithm produces the correct result, we first show that, for all k, before the kth iteration of the **for** loop, pathsFromInit[k] = $|\mathcal{W}_k|$. The proof will be by induction on k.

Base case: Because $\mathcal{S}$ is topologically sorted, $\mathcal{S}[0]$ is the initial state. Before the **for** loop is executed, pathsFromInit[0] = 1 = $|\varepsilon|$ = $|\mathcal{W}_0|$. Now assume, for all $j < k$, that pathsFromInit[j] = $|\mathcal{W}_j|$. Let $\mathcal{S}_k$ be the set of states with transitions to $\mathcal{S}[k]$. Because $\mathcal{S}$ is sorted topologically, $\forall \mathcal{S}[i] \in \mathcal{S}_k$, $i < k$, so all transitions to $\mathcal{S}[k]$ are visited (**foreach** loop) before the kth iteration of the **for** loop. Because the FA is deterministic, no word can be reached by multiple paths, so $|\mathcal{W}_k| = \sum_{\mathcal{S}[i] \in \mathcal{S}_k} |\mathcal{W}_i| \left| \left\{ c \mid < \mathcal{S}[i] \xrightarrow{c} \mathcal{S}[k] > \in \mathcal{T} \right\} \right|$. By assumption, $|\mathcal{W}_i| = \text{pathsFromInit}[i]$, so this is precisely the value stored in pathsFromInit[k] by the kth iteration.

Finally, it suffices to observe that $\text{numSolutions} = \sum_{\{i \mid \text{isAccept}(\mathcal{S}[i])\}} \text{pathsFromInit}[i]$ $= \sum_{\{i \mid \text{isAccept}(\mathcal{S}[i])\}} |\mathcal{W}_i|$, i.e., the number of words accepted by the FA.

6 Examples

6.1 Pathname

In Unix, sets of files are often represented using regular expressions on their pathnames. Correspondingly, regular domains are very useful for representing sets of files in a constraint-based planning problem. In addition to the ability to represent large sets concisely, we can also handle constraints that relate the file's pathname to other attributes of the file. For example, satellite images and other automatically generated data are typically stored in ordinary filesystems, with pathnames based on details of the data, such as the time, subject, source, file format, etc. Suppose we have a remote archive in which satellite images have pathnames of the form:

/downlink/ < year > / < dayOfYear > / < sensor >< gridx >< gridy > . < format >

We can represent this knowledge using a concatenation constraint:

$rpn=$ concat("/downlink/", y, "/", d, "/", s, gx, gy, ".", fmt).

Given only this knowledge, all we know about the remote path names, rpn, is they are characterized by the regular expression "/downlink/.*/.*/.*/.*\..*". However, we may know quite a bit about the other variables, such as how many years the satellite has been in operation, how many days are in a year, the sensors aboard the satellite, the grid coordinate system used to indicate the regions covered by the images, and the available formats. Assuming we are interested in just a subset of the data, we can impose additional constraints on these variables to specify just the files we are interested in. For example, if we want MOD17 data from January 27, 2002 in either HDF or binary format, then the domain of rpn is
"/downlink/2002/27/MOD17[0-9][0-9][0-9][0-9]\.(hdf|bin)"
    String constraints are not just useful for specifying sets of files, but also specifying the effects of file operations. Since the files are on a remote server, we can't access them directly, but we can copy them to a local disk. Suppose we executed the command scp -r server:/downlink/2002 local02 to copy the contents of the directory 2002 to the directory local02. We can describe the effect on the local pathnames, lpn, of the resulting files using the pair of constraints:

1. concat(rpn, "/downlink/2002/", $ldir$)
2. concat(lpn, "local02/", $ldir$)

Since the concat constraint can be used to derive the domain of any variable given the domains of the other two variables, and since we know that the domain of rpn (limited to the files we care about) is
/downlink/2002/27/MOD17[0-9][0-9][0-9][0-9]\.(hdf|bin)
we can enforce the first constraint to obtain the domain of $ldir$:
27/MOD17[0-9][0-9][0-9][0-9]\.(hdf|bin)
We can then apply the second constraint to obtain the domain of lpn:
local02/27/MOD17[0-9][0-9][0-9][0-9]\.(hdf|bin)
If, after copying the files, we discovered that there are only HDF files, we could apply the same constraints in the other direction to conclude that there were no binary files on the server.

6.2   Crossword Puzzle

Another application of string constraints is the *crossword puzzle* problem. Solving crossword puzzles is a popular pastime and also a well-studied problem in computer science. The full problem of solving crossword puzzles, given only the puzzle layout and a list of clues, is a hard problem that involves many aspects of AI [21]. A more commonly addressed problem is generating crossword puzzles, given a fixed board and a list of possible words [7]. This problem becomes a classic constraint satisfaction problem, where the variables of the constraint problem are word slots on the puzzle board in which words can be written, the domains of variables are available words, and the binary constraints on variables enforce the agreement of letters at intersections between slots. Solving the problem reduces to finding a solution to the constraint problem: an assignment of values to the variables such that each variable is assigned a value in its domain and no constraint is violated.

We can use string constraints to formalize the crossword puzzle problem. There is a variable for each slot, each intersection point and each contiguous segment of text within a slot that does not cross an intersection. The variables for word slots take values from all available words, the variables for intersection points take values of letters from the alphabet, and the variables for segments take values of unknown strings of fixed length. Each word slot is constrained to be the concatenation of the segments and intersection points that it contains.

For example, suppose that we have the following crossword puzzle that is taken from *http://yoda.cis.temple.edu:8080/UGAIWWW/lectures95/search/puzzle.html:*

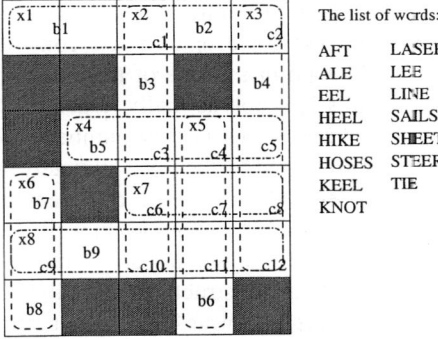

To formalize this puzzle as a CSP with string constraints, we have

- 8 variables for the word slots as marked from x_1 to x_8
- 12 variables for those intersection points marked as c_i
- 9 variables for these segments marked as b_i

We have 8 constraints as follows:

1. $\text{concat}(x_1, b_1, c_1, b_2, c_2)$
2. $\text{concat}(x_2, c_1, b_3, c_3, c_6, c_{10})$
3. $\text{concat}(x_3, c_2, b_4, c_5, c_8, c_{12})$
4. $\text{concat}(x_4, b_5, c_3, c_4, c_5)$
5. $\text{concat}(x_5, c_4, c_7, c_1, b_6)$
6. $\text{concat}(x_6, b_7, c_9, b_8)$
7. $\text{concat}(x_7, c_6, c_7, c_8)$
8. $\text{concat}(x_8, c_9, b_9, c_{10}, c_{11}, c_{12})$

It is worth noting that, although we may have more variables than the traditional CSP formalization, only the x_i variables, that is, those variables representing word slots, need to be searched during the CSP solving. Other variables will be assigned values by propagation. In fact, with the constraint system we implemented to support a constraint-based planner, we can solve the above crossword puzzle example without backtracking.

7   Conclusions

We have discussed an approach to constraint reasoning over strings in which regular languages are used to represent and reason about infinite sets of strings. Regular languages have a number of qualities to recommend them as a domain representation:

- They are closed under intersection, union and negation.
- They can concisely represent infinite sets of strings.
- Many natural string constraints, such as concatenation, containment and length, can be represented in terms of operations on regular languages.
- They are widely used and well understood.

These advantages do come at a price; it can be substantially more costly to represent and reason about regular languages than, say, intervals. All of the set operations and string constraints we have discussed are either linear or quadratic in the size of the FAs representing the string domains. However, as noted, converting an NFA to a DFA may result in an exponential blowup in the size of the FA. Furthermore, even when every operation on the FA results in a polynomially larger FA, the FA can still grow exponentially with the number of operations, i.e., the number of constraints that contain the variable whose domain is represented by the FA. Ultimately, how the FA grows will depend on the nature of the problem at hand. The FA representation can be viewed as a compression of the full sets of strings. It will tend to do well at compressing sets with a lot of symmetry and simple structure, but will not do so well at compressing arbitrary lists of strings, where there is little or no structure to exploit. In the latter cases, the representation will blow up, converging toward an explicit list of the members. The exponential blowup in the representation can be viewed as a failure in the exponential reduction that FAs are capable of providing.

We have implemented a constraint-based planner that uses many of the string constraints discussed here and demonstrated it in software planning domains. Our implementation is complete, but inefficient. Although there are many highly optimized FA packages freely available, they are tailored to string matching, not domain representation, so we wrote our own, with little regard for efficiency. For example, our algorithm for DFA minimization is $O(|T||S|^2)$, even though much faster algorithms are available. Improving the efficiency, and exploring other domains, such as bioinformatics, is the subject of future work.

References

1. R. Agrawal and R. Srikant. Mining sequential patterns. In *Proceedings of the 11th International Conference on Data Engineering*, 1995.

2. C. Bessiere and J. Ch. Arc-consistency for general constraint networks: Preliminary results. In *Proceedings of IJCAI-97*, pages 398–404, Nagoya, Japan, August 1997.

3. J. R. Bitner and E. M. Reingold. Backtrack programming techniques. *Communications of the ACM*, 18(11):651–656, 1975.

4. I. Eidhammer, I. Jonassen, and S. Grindhaug. A constraint based structure description language for biosequences. *Constraints*, 6:173–200, 2001.

5. M. R. Garey and D. S. Johnson. *Computers and Intractability: A Guide to the Theory of NP-Completeness*. Freeman and Co., 1979.

6. M. Garofalakis, R. Rastogi, and K. Shim. SPIRIT:sequential pattern mining with regular expression constraints. In *Proceedings of the 25th VLDB Conference*, 1999.

7. M. Ginsberg, M. Frank, M. Halpin, and M. Torrance. Search lessons learned from crossword puzzles. In *Proceedings AAAI-1990*, pages 210–215, 1990.

8. K. Golden. Automating the processing of earth observation data. In *7th International Symposium on Artificial Intelligence, Robotics and Automation for Space*, 2003.

9. K. Golden and J. Frank. Universal quantification in a constraint-based planner. In *AIPS02*, 2002.

10. S. W. Golomb and L. D. Baumert. Backtrack programming. *Journal of the ACM*, 12(4):516–524, 1965.

11. T. Hickey, M. van Emden, and H. Wu. A unified framework for interval constraints and interval arithmetic. In *Proceedings of CP-1998*, pages 250–264, 1998.

12. J. Hopcraft and J. Ullman. *Introduction to Automata Theory, Languages and Computation*. Addison-Wesley, Philippines, 1979.

13. T. R. Jensen and B. Toft. *Graph Coloring Problems*. Wiley-Interscience, New York, 1995.

14. A. Jónsson and J. Frank. A framework for dynamic constraint reasoning using procedural constraints. In *Proceedings of ECAI-2000*, 2000.

15. A. Mackworth. Consistency in networks of relations. *Artificial Intelligence*, 8(1):99–118, 1977.

16. N. Muscettola. Computing the envolope for stepwise constant resource allocations. In *Proceedings of CP-2002*, 2002.

17. B. A. Nadel. Consistent satisfaction algorithms. *Computational Intelligence*, 5:188–224, 1989.

18. P. Prosser. Hybrid algorithms for the constrain satisfaction problem. *Computational Intelligence*, 9(3):268–299, 1993.

19. A. Rajasekar. Applications in constraint logical programming with strings. In *PPCP-1994*, 1994.

20. F. Rossi, A. Sperduti, K. Venable, L. Khatib, P. Morris, and R. Morris. Learning and solving soft temporal constraints: An experimental study. In *Proceedings of CP-2002*, 2002.

21. N. Shazeer, M. Littman, and G. Keim. Solving crossword puzzles as probabilistic constraint satisfaction. In *Proceedings of AAAI-1999*, 1999.

22. D. L. Waltz. Understanding line drawings of scenes with shadows. In P. H. Winston, editor, *The Psychology of Computer Vision*, pages 19–91. McGraw-Hill, 1975.

23. Monte Zweben and Mark S. Fox. *Intelligent Scheduling*. Morgan Kaufmann Publishers, San Francisco, California, 1994.

Tractability by Approximating
Constraint Languages

Martin J. Green and David A. Cohen

Department of Computer Science
Royal Holloway, University of London, UK

Abstract. A constraint satisfaction problem instance consists of a collection of variables that need to have values assigned to them. The assignments are limited by constraints that force the values taken by certain
collections of variables (the constraint scopes) to satisfy specified properties (the constraint relations).

As the general CSP problem is NP-hard there has been significant effort
devoted to discovering tractable subproblems of the CSP.

The structure of a CSP instance is defined to be the hypergraph formed
by the constraint scopes. Restricting the possible structure of the CSP
instances has been a successful way of identifying tractable subproblems.
The language of a CSP instance is defined to be the set of constraint relations of the instance. Restricting the language allowed for CSP instances
has also yielded many interesting tractable subproblems.

Almost all known tractable subproblems are either structural or relational. In this paper we construct tractable subproblems of the general
CSP that are neither defined by structural nor relational properties.

These new tractable classes are related to tractable languages in much
the same way that general decompositions (cutset, tree-clustering, etc.)
are related to acyclic decompositions. It may well be that our results will
begin to make language based tractability of more practical interest.

We show that our theory allows us to properly extend the binary max-
closed language based tractable class, which is maximal as a tractable
binary constraint language. Our theory also explains the tractability of
the constraint representation of the Stable Marriage Problem which has
not been amenable to existing explanations of tractability. In fact we
provide a uniform explanation for the tractability of the class of max-
closed CSPs and the SMP.

There has been much work done on so called renamable HORN theories
which are a tractable subproblem of SAT. It has been shown that renamable HORN theories are tractably identifiable and solvable. It has also
been shown that finding the largest sub-theory that is renamable HORN
is NP-hard. These results also follow immediately from our theory.

1 Introduction

The Constraint Satisfaction paradigm involves modelling a real-world problem
as a set of variables to which we can assign values from some domain [24]. The

F. Rossi (Ed.): CP 2003, LNCS 2833, pp. 392–406, 2003.

values that can be assigned are limited by constraints. A constraint consists of a list of variables (its scope), and a set of tuples which are the allowed assignments to this list of variables (its relation). A solution is the assignment of a value from the domain to every variable so that all of the constraints are satisfied.

The decision problem for general constraint satisfaction is NP-hard [23]. This motivates the search for subproblems which are tractable. Given some general problem instance we would like to determine if it lies in one of these tractable problem classes and therefore apply a specialised solution technique.

We define the structure of a constraint satisfaction problem instance (CSP) to be the hypergraph whose hyperedges are the scopes of the constraints. The class of CSPs whose structure is acyclic form a tractable subproblem [3]. This structural tractability result has been extended by identifying hypergraphs which are "nearly" acyclic (cycle-cutset [9], hinges [12, 19], tree-clustering [10], hypertrees [17], etc.). The class of instances with such a structure can be tractably reduced to the acyclic case. It is these widely applicable *approximations* to acyclic structure that make structural tractability so useful.

The language of a CSP is defined to be the set of constraint relations of the instance. If we restrict the language of a CSP appropriately we can also obtain a tractable subclass — a so called relational subproblem [20]. Languages that lead to tractable relational subproblems are called tractable languages.

This paper introduces a new study: approximations to tractable language classes. It is hoped that, by generalising these classes, we make them easier to apply to practical problems.

The approximation technique that we apply to CSPs is to identify those that can be reduced to tractable relational subproblems by (independently) permuting the domain values for each variable. We will show that a generic method for determining whether a domain permutation approximation exists for a particular instance corresponds exactly to solving an associated "lifted" problem instance. When the class of lifted problems for a tractable language is itself tractable then we obtain a new large tractable class. The tractable classes of instances that we generate cannot in general be specified by any structural or relational restriction.

Even though identifying domain permutation approximations may be NP-hard this does not reduce its practical applicability. In fact (optimal) structural decompositions are also NP-hard to discover and we have to accept a limitation[1]. However, the extensions of acyclic structure to structural approximations has still been of immense practical value.

Using this new approximation technique we have extended the well-known binary max-closed class of tractable CSPs, which is a maximal binary relational subclass [21].

Our theory also explains the tractability of the constraint representation of the Stable Marriage Problem (SMP) [15].

---

[1] Structural approximations are ranked by a so called width parameter. Smaller widths are better, acyclicity corresponds to width 1. For any fixed k, determining whether a width k or better structural approximation exists is usually the best we can achieve.

We have also explained the tractability of renamable HORN theories [22, 2]. What is more we can explain directly why it is NP-hard to find the largest renamable HORN theory which is a subset of a given set of clauses [11].

1.1   Outline of the Paper

In Section 3 we define the new concept of approximating a tractable language. In Section 4.3 we use the theory to construct novel examples of tractable subproblems of the constraint satisfaction problem. In Section 4.4 we use the new theory to provide an explanation of why arc-consistency is a decision procedure for the constraint representation of the Stable Marriage Problem. In Section 5 we show that the main results from renamable HORN theory may be obtained directly from the theory of approximating tractable languages.

2   Definitions

Definition 1. *A **Constraint Satisfaction Problem instance** (CSP), P, is a triple, $\langle V, D, C \rangle$ where:*

- *V is a set of **variables**.*
- *D is any set, called the **domain** of the instance.*
- *C is a set of **constraints**.*
  Each constraint $c \in C$ is a pair $\langle \sigma, \rho \rangle$ where σ is a list of distinct variables of V and ρ is a $|\sigma|$-ary relation over D.

*A **solution** to P is a mapping $\phi : V \to D$ such that, for each $\langle \sigma, \rho \rangle \in C$, $\phi(\sigma) \in \rho$.*

Informally we may describe V as a set of questions that need to be answered. The domain D is the set of all possible answers that can be given to any of these questions. A constraint is a rationality condition that limits the answers that may be simultaneously assigned to some groups of questions. A solution is then a satisfactory set of answers to all of the questions.

Example 1. The Stable Marriage Problem [13].

We have a set of n men, and a set of n women, and we have to arrange n stable marriages. A pair of marriages can only be stable if no pair of people would prefer to be married to each other than to their spouses. A set of n marriages is called stable if each pair of marriages is stable.

For every man we have his preference ordering which ranks all of the women. Similarly, for each woman we have her preference ordering which ranks the men.

We can express this as a CSP whose variables are the men and whose domain is the set of women. That is we have to choose a woman for each man.

For every pair of men we have a binary constraint. This constraint prevents them from marrying the same woman, and furthermore only allows a successful (stable) marriage.

Since constraints are between every pair of men, it is clear that any solution to this formulation will be a stable marriage. Also, every stable marriage can be found by this formulation since there are no additional constraints imposed. So the solutions are exactly the sets of stable marriages as required.

We will give a formal definition of this class of CSPs, and a straightforward explanation of why this class is easy to solve, in Section 4.4.

2.1   Complexity of Constraint Satisfaction

The decision problem for the general constraint satisfaction problem is:

Definition 2. *Given a CSP, P, does P have a solution?*

It is clear that graph-3 colouring, or indeed 3-SAT, can be reduced to the constraint satisfaction problem. So the decision problem for general CSPs is NP-complete [23].

However there are restrictions to the set of allowed instances that make the constraint satisfaction problem tractable.

In this paper we extend the notion of a tractable subclass of the constraint satisfaction problem by requiring that membership of this class should also be polynomially determined. This is a reasonable restriction, and is in fact one usually adopted by researchers on general satisfiability [11], if we want tractability to correspond to the existence of a good solution method. We are given a CSP and we have first to determine which (tractable) class it belongs to, then to apply the appropriate algorithm.

If we do not make this restriction then we end up with absurd notion that all unsolvable CSPs form a tractable class! The algorithm for solving instances of this class would be easy (just say no), but determining whether an instance is a member of the class is obviously intractable.

Definition 3. *A set S of CSPs is tractable if:*

1. *there exists a uniform polynomial algorithm for determining whether any given CSP is in S;*
2. *there exists a uniform polynomial algorithm for finding a solution to any CSP from S.*

It turns out that there are many tractable subproblems of the constraint satisfaction problem.

Definition 4. *A **hypergraph** H is a pair $\langle V, E \rangle$ where V is a set of vertices and E is a collection of subsets of V, called the **edges** of H.*

*The **structure** of a CSP, P, is the hypergraph whose vertexes are the variables of P and whose hyperedges are the scopes of the constraints of P.*

*A **constraint language** over a domain D is a set of relations over D.*

*The **language** of a CSP, P, is the constraint language defined by the set of relations of the constraints of P. The language of a set of instances is the union of the languages of the instances. For any constraint language Γ we will refer to the set of instances with language contained in Γ as $CSP(\Gamma)$.*

A subproblem S of the general constraint satisfaction problem is called **structural** if it is defined by limiting the structure of the instances of S. A subproblem S is called **relational** if it is defined by limiting the language of the instances of S.

A basic tractable structural subproblem of the constraint satisfaction problem is those instances whose structure is acyclic [3]. However, this class has been extended by considering instances whose structure is "approximately acyclic" in the sense that there is a tractable reduction to an acyclic instance [16]. Such classes have been well-studied and have made the use of tractable structural CSPs applicable to real world examples.

A constraint language is called tractable if the set of instances defined over this language is tractable. There are many known tractable constraint languages [20]. In this paper we derive the first approximation result for tractable languages. This natural extension to the theory of tractability yields large new tractable subproblems. These new subproblems are not in general describable either by limiting the structure, or by restricting the language, of the instances.

Example 2. A propositional **literal** is either a propositional variable (positive) or a negated propositional variable (negative). A **clause** is a disjunct of literals.

Let V^+ and V^- be two infinite disjoint sets of propositional variables. We say that a clause c defined over the variables $V^+ \cup V^-$ is **split-HORN** if the number of disjuncts which are positive variables from V^- plus the number of disjuncts which are negative variables from V^+ is at most 1. Conjuncts of split-HORN clauses may be naturally represented as CSPs over the Boolean domain $\{T, F\}$. For given V^+ and V^- the set of such CSPs is called a **split-HORN problem**.

It is clear that every hypergraph occurs as the structure of a split-HORN instance, so no split-HORN problem is tractable for structural reasons.

There is a well-known dichotomy result for Boolean constraint languages [25]. The language of the instances of any split-HORN problem is NP-hard.

However, we will show the tractability of the split-HORN problem in Section 5 using the theory of approximating constraint languages.

3   Approximating Language: Permuting the Domain

Suppose that we have a tractable constraint language Γ and that P is a CSP not in $\mathrm{CSP}(\Gamma)$. If we can find permutations of the domain (independently) for each variable, that make P into an instance of $\mathrm{CSP}(\Gamma)$, then we can solve the instance P using the algorithm for Γ. We first permute the domains, then apply the algorithm for Γ, then permute the domains back again for any discovered solution.

It is this approximation technique for (tractable) constraint languages that we discuss in this paper.

Definition 5. *A **permutation** of a set D is a bijection from D to D.*

Let $\boldsymbol{\pi} = \langle \pi_1, \ldots, \pi_n \rangle$ be an n-tuple of permutations of D. We apply $\boldsymbol{\pi}$ to n-tuples of values from D in the natural way by applying $\pi_i, i = 1, \ldots, n$ to the ith component. We apply $\boldsymbol{\pi}$ to n-ary relations over D by applying it to each of the allowed tuples.

Let $P = \langle V, D, C \rangle$ be a CSP, and G be a set of permutations of D. A **domain permutation** for P over G is a mapping Π assigning to each variable $v \in V$ a permutation from G.

We define the result, $\Pi(P)$, of applying the domain permutation Π to be the CSP $\langle V, D, C' \rangle$ where

$$C' = \{ \langle \sigma, \Pi(\sigma)(\rho) \rangle | \langle \sigma, \rho \rangle \in C \}$$

The term $\Pi(\sigma)(\rho)$ is the result of applying the $|\sigma|$-tuple of permutations, $\Pi(\sigma)$, to the $|\sigma|$-ary relation ρ.

We now define a subproblem of the constraint satisfaction problem.

Definition 6. *Let Γ be a constraint language, $P = \langle V, D, C \rangle$ a CSP and G a set of permutations of D.*

*If there exists a domain permutation Π for P over G such that $\Pi(P) \in CSP(\Gamma)$ then we say that P is G-**approximately** over Γ.*

*For a given Γ and G the problem of determining whether an instance is G-approximately over Γ is called the **approximation problem** for Γ and G.*

The results of this paper are all applications of the following theorem whose proof is obvious.

Theorem 1. *Let Γ be a tractable language over a domain D, G be a set of permutations of D, and R be a set of instances with a tractable approximation problem for Γ and G. The set of instances of R which are G-approximately over Γ is tractable.*

3.1   The Tractability of Approximation

Suppose that Γ is a constraint language over domain D and that G is a set of permutations of the domain of D. For any given constraint language R over D we may ask whether the approximation problem for Γ and G is tractable for the instances of $CSP(R)$. It turns out that this reduces to finding the tractability of another constraint language dependant on G, R and Γ.

Definition 7. *Let Γ be a constraint language, ρ be an n-ary relation over D, and G be a set of permutations of D. We define the G-lifted relation of ρ for Γ, ρ_Γ^G, to be the following n-ary relation over G:*

$$\rho_\Gamma^G = \{ \langle \pi_1, \ldots, \pi_n \rangle | \langle \pi_1, \ldots, \pi_n \rangle (\rho) \in \Gamma \}$$

Furthermore, for any language R we define the G-lifted relations of R for Γ to be $R_\Gamma^G = \{ \rho_\Gamma^G | \rho \in R \}$.

In other words, for any n-ary relation ρ over D there are some n-tuples of permutations from G which make ρ into a relation of Γ. We call this set of n-tuples over G the G-lifted n-ary relation of ρ for Γ.

We then have the following result.

Proposition 1. *The approximation problem for Γ and G for instances of $CSP(R)$ is tractable iff R_Γ^G is a tractable language.*

Proof. The problem $P = \langle V, D, C \rangle$ of $CSP(R)$ is G-approximately over Γ if and only if there exists some domain permutation Π which, when applied to P results in an instance of $CSP(\Gamma)$.

Now consider some constraint $\langle \sigma, \rho \rangle$ of P. By definition the constraint, $\langle \sigma, \Pi(\sigma)(\rho) \rangle$, has constraint relation in Γ exactly when $\Pi(\sigma)$ is in the relation ρ_Γ^G.

In other words, P is G-approximately over Γ exactly when the CSP P_Γ^G with the same variables as P, domain G and constraints $\{\langle \sigma, \rho_\Gamma^G \rangle | \langle \sigma, \rho \rangle \in C\}$ has a solution.

The result follows immediately.

Example 3. Dechter and van Beek [26] have defined the class of binary **row-convex** relations. They proved that any path-consistent CSP whose relations are row-convex is globally consistent. Furthermore they showed that the approximation problem for row-convex binary relations is tractable, using a result from graph theory. However, since the lifted relations for the row-convex language are all unary the tractability of this approximation problem is trivial.

4   Tractability Results

The general theory has now been presented. This section is concerned with tractability results obtained from this new theory.

It might be hoped that the approximation problem for any *tractable* language is tractable. This is not the case. We show, in Section 4.1 that the approximation problem is not always tractable, even for binary relations. Following on from this we identify several important cases for which the approximation problem is tractable.

4.1   Lifted Tractable Languages Are Not Always Tractable

We first consider the case where Γ is tractable, G is the set of all permutations of the domain D and R is the entire set of relations over D.

We will show that in this case, R_Γ^G is not always tractable, by demonstrating that, for a particular tractable language the lifted binary three valued relations are intractable.

Definition 8. *An n-ary relation, ρ, over $\{1, \ldots, n\}$ is said to be **max-closed** if, whenever $\langle d_1, \ldots, d_n \rangle$, $\langle e_1, \ldots, e_n \rangle$ are in ρ, then so is their pointwise maximum:*

$$\langle \max(d_1, e_1), \ldots, \max(d_n, e_n) \rangle.$$

The class of max-closed relations is tractable [21]. In particular, a polynomial solution technique is to make the entire problem (generalised) arc-consistent [4], and then to choose the largest remaining domain value for each variable.

Definition 9. *A **configuration** of domain values is a pair of 2-sets of domain values.*

*Let ρ be a binary relation over $\{1, \ldots, n\}$. An **impossible cross** for ρ is a configuration $\langle \{a, b\}, \{c, d\} \rangle$, where $a > b$ and $c > d$ such that:*

- $\langle a, d \rangle, \langle b, c \rangle \in \rho$;
- $\langle a, c \rangle \notin \rho$.

We will need the following property of max-closed relations (this is proved as Lemma 6.2 of Jeavons and Cooper [21]).

Proposition 2. *A binary relation ρ is max-closed if and only if it has no impossible crosses.*

4.2   Lifted Binary Relations for Max-closure

We provide here an explanation of a simple process for determining the lifted relations for max-closure for binary three valued relations. We will show in this section that this process can be carried out by solving a six variable two valued CSP for each relation, the so called **permutation CSP**. We generated and solved all such CSPs. We then used a public domain program, Polyanna [14], to determine the complexity of each individual lifted relation, and also every pair of lifted relations. We found that every individual lifted relation is tractable but that there exist intractable pairs.

Consider a binary three valued relation ρ. A pair of permutations Π is a tuple of the lifted relation for ρ exactly when $\Pi(\rho)$ is max-closed. That is, by Proposition 2, when $\Pi(\rho)$ has no impossible crosses. So, to determine whether Π is acceptable we have only to consider its actions on all configurations of ρ. The action of Π on $\langle \{a, b\}, \{c, d\} \rangle$ is determined by whether the order of a and b or the order of c and d are reversed, or not.

There are 16 different possible configurations (of which at most 9 occur in any given relation ρ). Figure 1 shows[2], for four of these configurations, which possible permutations of the domain are allowed. By building a lookup table for all 16 configurations we are able quickly to determine the possible actions on the configurations of any given relation ρ.

A permutation is determined by the list of pairs of domain values whose order is to be swapped.

Definition 10. *We will denote a permutation of the domain $\{1, 2, 3\}$ by a Boolean triple $\langle p_{1,2}, p_{1,3}, p_{2,3} \rangle$ where $p_{1,2}$ is T when the order of 1,2 are swapped, $p_{1,3}$ indicates whether 1 and 3 are swapped, and $p_{2,3}$ indicates whether 2 and 3 are swapped.*

---

[2] We represent binary relations diagrammatically by connecting pairs of domain values when the corresponding tuple is in the relation.

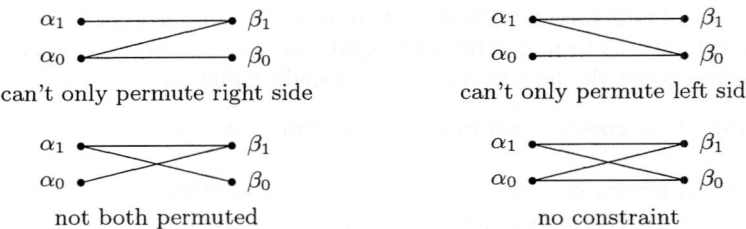

Fig. 1. There are 16 possible configurations between any two arbitrary pairs of domain values, $\alpha_0 < \alpha_1$ and $\beta_0 < \beta_1$. These are used to generate constraints between domain permutations. Four such configurations and the associated constraints are shown here.

However, not all swaps are compatible. If we swap, for example, 1 & 2 and 2 & 3 then we *must* also swap the order of 1 & 3. So, for example, $\langle T, F, T \rangle$ does not represent a permutation.

Definition 11. *Let ρ be a binary three valued relation. We construct the **permutation CSP** for ρ as follows.*

There are six variables, $A_{1,2}, A_{1,3}, A_{2,3}, B_{1,2}, B_{1,3}$, and $B_{2,3}$.

The domain is the set $\{T, F\}$. Variable $A_{c,d}$ is assigned T exactly when c and d are to be swapped in the first column's permutation. Similarly variable $B_{c,d}$ is assigned T exactly when c and d are swapped in the second column's.

There are binary constraints between each of $A_{c,d}$ and $B_{e,f}$ (six constraints) which only allow pairs of permutations that make the $\{c, d\} \times \{e, f\}$ configuration of ρ max-closed.

There are ternary constraints over $\langle A_{1,2}, A_{1,3}, A_{2,3} \rangle$ and $\langle B_{1,2}, B_{1,3}, B_{2,3} \rangle$ whose relation only disallows the non-permutations $\langle F, T, F \rangle$ and $\langle T, F, T \rangle$.

In every case a solution to the permutation CSP represents a pair of permutations of the three element domain. The following result follows immediately from the previous discussion.

Lemma 1. *The solutions to the permutation CSP for ρ precisely represent the tuples (pairs of allowed permutations) of the lifted relation.*

Example 4. An example relation together with its corresponding permutation CSP and the solutions to the permutation CSP are shown in Figure 2.

One possible solution to the permutation CSP is the six-tuple $\langle F, T, T, F, F, T \rangle$. This corresponds to the pair of permutations $\langle F, T, T \rangle$ (move domain element 3 above 1 and 2) and $\langle F, F, T \rangle$ (move domain element 3 above domain element 2). Another solution is the six-tuple $\langle T, T, T, F, F, F \rangle$, corresponding to the permutations $\langle T, T, T \rangle$ (which inverts the domain) and $\langle F, F, F \rangle$ (which leaves the domain unchanged). The results of applying these pairs of permutations are also shown in Figure 2. It is easy to check that the resulting relations are indeed max-closed.

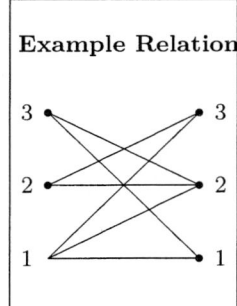 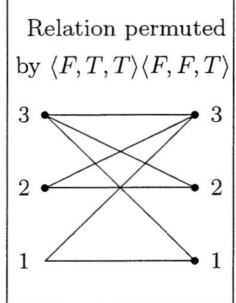 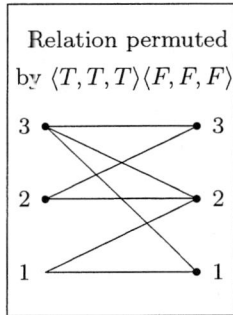

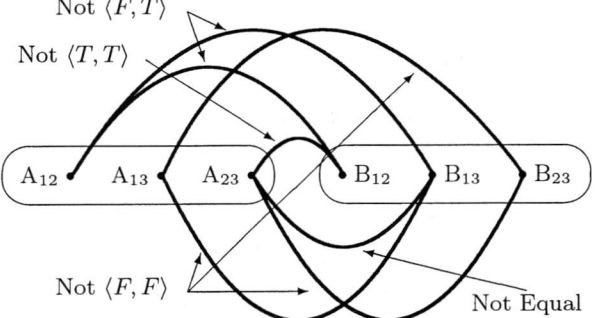

Fig. 2. A binary three valued relation together with its associated permutation CSP. All solutions to the permutation CSP are shown. The results of applying two of the solutions are also shown to demonstrate that the permuted relation is indeed max-closed.

We wrote a dedicated program to generate and solve the permutation CSPs for each of the 512 binary three valued relation. The output of this program was 458 distinct lifted relations.

The tractability of a (finite) constraint language only depends on its so called polymorphisms [20]. Gault has written a program, Polyanna [14], which determines the polymorphisms of an input constraint language. In addition to listing the polymorphisms, Polyanna can classify a constraint language into one of several tractability classes.

We ran each lifted relation through Polyanna. It turned out that the lifted relation for each of the binary three valued relations is tractable.

Polyanna also showed that the entire set of lifted relations forms an NP-complete language[3].

---

[3] Polyanna usually fails to characterise binary NP-complete languages over domains with as many as six elements. In this case we were lucky.

4.3   Novel Classes of Tractable CSPs

In this section we will show that when the set of allowed permutations, G, has size 2, the G-approximation problem for any Γ is tractable for the entire set of binary relations.

We will use this technique to show the tractability of certain classes of CSPs that are not tractable for any relational or structural reason.

Theorem 2. *Let Γ be a constraint language over D, G be a set of two permutations of D, and R be the set of all binary relations, then the G-approximation problem for Γ is tractable.*

Proof. It is enough to note that any lifted relation is binary two valued. It follows that the approximation problem for R may be reduced to the tractable 2-SAT problem.

Example 5. Let D be the ordered domain $\{1, \ldots, k\}$. Let $G = \{\omega, \iota\}$ where $\omega(r) = k - r + 1$, and $\iota(r) = r$.

Recall the binary max-closed language defined in Section 4.1. By Theorem 2 we have that the G-approximation problem for binary max-closed relations is tractable.

The class of tractable instances defined by this approximation certainly includes all CSPs whose language is binary max-closed. In this case the approximation is to apply the permutation ι to each variable.

The class also naturally includes the analogous tractable class of min-closed relations. We approximate these by applying ω to each variable.

In fact there are instances which are neither max-closed nor min-closed. We may obtain such instances from a max-closed instance by arbitrarily applying ω to some subset of the variables.

Since the max-closed binary relations form a maximal class of tractable binary relations (see Theorem 6.5 of Jeavons and Cooper [21]) it is clear that the tractable class of this example is not tractable for any relational reason. Furthermore it includes instances with arbitrary (binary) structure so it is not a structural tractable class.

Example 5 serves as a proof of the following result which shows that this new approximation technique identifies truly novel tractable classes.

Theorem 3. *The set of tractable instances of the constraint satisfaction problem defined by approximating a tractable language is, in general, not definable as either a relational or a structural subproblem.*

4.4   Stable Marriage Problem Instances
Are Approximately Max-closed

An instance of the *Stable Marriage Problem* (recall Example 1) (SMP) consists of n men and n women who are to be married. Each man has a preference list that ranks the women according to which he would prefer to marry. He would prefer to marry those higher in the list than those lower in the list. Similarly each woman has a preference list for the men. The problem is to form a *Marriage* between the men and the women so that each man is married to a woman and every person is in just one marriage. A *Stable Marriage* has no man, m, and woman, w, such that m prefers w to his wife, and w prefers m to her husband.

It is known that the Stable Marriage Problem is tractably solvable. In particular, arc consistency is a decision procedure for the Stable Marriage Problem [15]. Arc-consistency will remove some women from the set of allowed partners for each man. A solution is then for each man to marry his most preferred remaining partner.

4.5 Stable Marriage Problem Instances

An instance of the Stable Marriage Problem is a Constraint Satisfaction Problem instance, $P = \langle V, D, C \rangle$, where:

- $V = \{1, \ldots, n\}$.
- $D = \{1, \ldots, n\}$.
- For each $m \in V$, π_m is a permutation of D, and for each $w \in D$, τ_w is a permutation of V.
  $C = \{c_{s,t} \mid s, t \in V, s < t\}$, where
  $c_{s,t} = \langle \langle s, t \rangle, \rho_{s,t} \rangle$, and

$$\langle p, q \rangle \in \rho_{s,t} \iff p \neq q \,\wedge$$
$$\tau_p(t) > \tau_p(s) \Rightarrow \pi_t(q) > \pi_t(p) \,\wedge$$
$$\tau_q(s) > \tau_q(t) \Rightarrow \pi_s(p) > \pi_s(q)$$

We interpret V as a set of men, and D as a set of women. We interpret $\pi_m(w)$ to be the level of preference (n is the most preferred and 1 the least preferred) that man m has for woman w. Similarly, $\tau_w(m)$ defines the level of preference given to man m by woman w.

We will show that every SMP instance is approximately max-closed. What is more, the required permutations order the domain for each man according to his preferences amongst the women. This completely explains the known solution algorithm. What is more, since the preference orderings are known, we will have shown that the set of SMP instances is an example of the tractability described in this paper.

Definition 12. *Let P be an SMP instance. Consider any pair of marriages and let p be one of the four people involved. We say p is **happy** with respect to this pair of marriages if they prefer their partner to the person (of the same gender) in the other marriage.*

*A pair of marriages is **stable** if there is no unmarried unhappy man and woman.*

Theorem 4. *Let P be an SMP instance and define, for each $m \in V$, $\Pi(m) = \pi_m$. Then $\Pi(P)$ is max-closed.*

This straightforward proof has been omitted for brevity. It is included in a technical report [18].

5   Renamable HORN

There have been many papers published describing the renamable HORN class of problems [22, 1, 2, 6, 7]. It has been shown that recognising, and hence solving, instances of renamable HORN is tractable. Indeed, del Val [11] gives an algorithm which solves both 2-SAT and renamable HORN which he calls "the paradigmic examples of tractable problems in propositional satisfiability".

It has also been shown [5] that identifying a maximal subset of variables for which all clauses are renamable HORN is NP-hard.

Definition 13. *A **HORN-clause** is a clause with at most one positive literal. A set of clauses is **renamable HORN** if there is a replacement of some literals uniformly in all clauses with their negated versions which makes all clauses into HORN clauses.*

We will show in this section that renamable HORN is another simple application of approximate language tractability. In fact we show that for the class of all Boolean relations the lifted relations for HORN is a tractable language. What is more we show that recognising maximal subproblems which are renamable HORN [5] is NP-hard as a simple consequence of our theory.

Proposition 3. *Let c be a clause. Let S_c be the set of variables which must be set to T (all others being set to F) which makes the clause evaluate to F. Then the lifted relation for HORN consists of all those tuples which invert a set of variables κ where the symmetric difference between κ and S_c has size at most 1.*

Proof. Follows directly from the definition of a HORN clause.

We can observe directly from the dichotomy result for the tractability of Boolean constraint languages [25, 20] that the set of lifted relations for all clauses forms a tractable language[4].

Example 6. We can now see that the split-HORN defined in Example 2 is tractable. The instances are all renamable HORN.

Identifying maximum subsets of variables which are renamable HORN now corresponds to solving instances of MAX-SAT for the lifted language. Since the complexity of all Boolean MAX-SAT languages is known [8], we can readily determine that this problem is NP-complete.

---

[4] They are a *Majority closed* language. The relations are all decomposable into binary clauses, so the tractability arises from the tractability of 2-SAT.

6   Conclusion

In this paper we have identified a new class of tractable subproblems of the general constraint satisfaction problem. We have shown that these subproblems are not explained as either structural or language based.

Furthermore we have demonstrated that this theory serves to explain the tractability of the constraint approach to the SMP, since all instances are approximately max-closed. In this sense it unifies two previous classes of CSPs for which arc-consistency is a solution technique.

Lastly, this theory has provided a simple explanation of the tractability of recognising instances of renamable HORN. It even serves to explain why finding maximum subsets of variables which are renamable HORN is NP-hard.

This approximation of relational tractability is both theoretically interesting and may well be practical value.

Acknowledgements

The authors are very grateful to Marc van Dongen [27] who originally derived the SMP example of an approximately max-closed tractable subproblem, though in a different context. His example as an application of approximately tractable theory greatly strengthens our work. We are also grateful to Peter Jeavons who alerted us to the connections between this work and renamable HORN theory, and to the anonymous reviewers who suggested we include Example 3.

References

1. B. Aspvall, M.F. Plass, and R.E. Tarjan. A linear time algorithm for testing the truth of certain quantified Boolean formulas. *Information Processing Letters*, 8:121–123, 1979.
2. Bengt Aspvall. Recognizing disguised NR(1) instances of the satisfiability problem. *Journal of Algorithms*, 1(1):97–103, March 1980. Note.
3. C. Beeri, R. Fagin, D. Maier, and M. Yannakakis. On the desirability of acyclic database schemes. *Journal of the ACM*, 30:479–513, 1983.
4. C. Bessière and J-C. Régin. Arc consistency for general constraint networks: preliminary results. In *Proceedings of IJCAI'97*, pages 398–404, Nagoya, Japan, 1997.
5. Boros. Maximum renamable Horn sub-CNFs. *DAMATH: Discrete Applied Mathematics and Combinatorial Operations Research and Computer Science*, 96, 1999.
6. V. Chandru, C. Coullard, P. Hammer, M. Monta nez, and X Sun. On renamable Horn and generalized Horn functions. *Annals of Mathematics and Artificial Intelligence*, 1:33–48, 1990.
7. V. Chandru and J.N. Hooker. Extended Horn sets in propositional logic. *Journal of the ACM*, 38:205–221, 1991.
8. N. Creignou. A dichotomy theorem for maximum generalized satisfiability problems. *Journal of Computer and System Sciences*, 51:511–522, 1995.
9. R. Dechter and J. Pearl. Network-based heuristics for constraint satisfaction problems. *Artificial Intelligence*, 34(1):1–38, 1988.

10. R. Dechter and J. Pearl. Tree clustering for constraint networks. *Artificial Intelligence*, 38:353–366, 1989.

11. del Val. On 2-SAT and renamable Horn. In *AAAI: 17th National Conference on Artificial Intelligence*. AAAI / MIT Press, 2000.

12. R. Fagin. Degrees of acyclicity for hypergraphs and relational database schemes. *Journal of the ACM*, 30:514–550, 1983.

13. D. Gale and L.S. Shapley. College admissions and stability of marriage. *Amer. Math. Monthly*, 69(1):9–15, 1962.

14. R.L. Gault. Polyanna technical manual (version 1.00). Technical Report RR-01-20, Computing Laboratory, Oxford University, 2001.

15. I.P. Gent, R.W Irving, M.F Manlove, P. Prosser, and B.M. Smith. A constraint programming approach to the stable marriage problem. In *Proceedings of CP 2001: the 7th International Conference on Principles and Practice of Constraint Programming*, volume 2239 of *Lecture Notes in Computer Science*, pages 225–239. Springer-Verlag, 2001.

16. G. Gottlob, L. Leone, and F. Scarcello. Hypertree decompositions: A survey. In *Proceedings 26th International Symposium on Mathematical Foundations of Computer Science, MFCS'01*, volume 2136 of *Lecture Notes in Computer Science*, pages 37–57. Springer-Verlag, 2001.

17. G. Gottlob, L. Leone, and F. Scarcello. Hypertree decomposition and tractable queries. *Journal of Computer and System Sciences*, 64(3):579–627, 2002.

18. M.J. Green and D.A. Cohen. Tractability by approximating constraint languages. Technical Report CSD-TR-03-01, Department of Computer Science, Royal Holloway, University of London, Egham, Surrey, UK, 2003.

19. M. Gyssens, P.G. Jeavons, and D.A. Cohen. Decomposing constraint satisfaction problems using database techniques. *Artificial Intelligence*, 66(1):57–89, 1994.

20. P.G. Jeavons, D.A. Cohen, and M. Gyssens. Closure properties of constraints. *Journal of the ACM*, 44:527–548, 1997.

21. P.G. Jeavons and M.C. Cooper. Tractable constraints on ordered domains. *Artificial Intelligence*, 79(2):327–339, 1995.

22. Harry R. Lewis. Renaming a set of clauses as a Horn set. *JACM*, 25(1):134–135, 1978.

23. A.K. Mackworth. Consistency in networks of relations. *Artificial Intelligence*, 8:99–118, 1977.

24. U. Montanari. Networks of constraints: Fundamental properties and applications to picture processing. *Information Sciences*, 7:95–132, 1974.

25. T.J. Schaefer. The complexity of satisfiability problems. In *Proceedings 10th ACM Symposium on Theory of Computing, STOC'78*, pages 216–226, 1978.

26. P. van Beek and R. Dechter. On the minimality and decomposability of row-convex constraint networks. *Journal of the ACM*, 42:543–561, 1995.

27. M.R.C van Dongen. From local closure properties to a global closure property. Personal communication, 2002. The source of the SMP example.

A Hybrid Constraint Programming and Semidefinite Programming Approach for the Stable Set Problem[*]

Willem Jan van Hoeve

CWI, P.O. Box 94079, 1090 GB Amsterdam, The Netherlands
W.J.van.Hoeve@cwi.nl
http://homepages.cwi.nl/~wjvh/

Abstract. This work presents a hybrid approach to solve the maximum stable set problem, using constraint and semidefinite programming. The approach consists of two steps: subproblem generation and subproblem solution. First we rank the variable domain values, based on the solution of a semidefinite relaxation. Using this ranking we generate the most promising subproblems first, by exploring a search tree using a limited discrepancy strategy. Then the subproblems are being solved using a constraint programming solver. To strengthen the semidefinite relaxation, we propose to infer additional constraints from the discrepancy structure. Computational results show that the semidefinite relaxation is very informative, since solutions of good quality are found in the first subproblems, or optimality is proven immediately.

1 Introduction

This paper describes a hybrid method to solve a classical combinatorial optimization problem, the maximum weighted stable set problem, or *stable set problem*[1] in short. Given a graph with weighted vertices, the stable set problem is to find a subset of vertices of maximum weight, such that no two vertices in this subset are joined by an edge of the graph. In the unweighted case (when all weights are equal to 1), this problem amounts to the maximum cardinality stable set problem, which has been shown to be already NP-hard [24]. Practical applications of the stable set problem are plentiful, they appear in coding theory, computer vision, pattern recognition, and many other areas [4].

We propose a two-phase approach to solve the stable set problem, either with or without proving optimality. The first phase generates subproblems based upon a semidefinite relaxation, the second phase solves the subproblems using constraint programming. Concerning the first phase, given a model for the stable set problem, we solve its semidefinite relaxation. The solution provides us fractional values for the variables of the model. These fractional values are a good

---

[*] An earlier version of this paper appeared as [18].

[1] Alternative names for the stable set problem are vertex packing, coclique or independent set problem.

F. Rossi (Ed.): CP 2003, LNCS 2833, pp. 407–421, 2003.

indication for the optimal (discrete) values of the variables. Hence we divide selected variable domains in two parts: a 'good' subdomain and a 'bad' subdomain. By branching on these subdomains using a limited discrepancy strategy [15], we obtain first a very promising subproblem, and subsequently less promising subproblems.

The second phase consists of the solution of the subproblems. Since they are much smaller than the original problem, we can easily solve them using a constraint programming solver.

As computational results will show, the semidefinite relaxation is quite informative. In several cases we can simply round the solution of the relaxation and obtain a provable optimal solution already. Otherwise, we are likely to find a good solution in one of the first subproblems. Using a limited number of subproblems to investigate, we yield an *incomplete* method producing good solutions. In order to obtain a *complete* search strategy, we need, in principle, to generate and solve all possible subproblems. A good upper bound is necessary to prove optimality earlier. For this reason we investigated the use of 'discrepancy cuts' that can be added to the semidefinite program to strengthen the relaxation and thus prune large parts of the search tree. However, computational results will show that they can not be applied efficiently on the instances we considered.

The outline of the paper is as follows. The next section gives a motivation for the approach proposed in this work. Then, in Section 3 some preliminaries on semidefinite programming are given. In Section 4 we introduce the stable set problem, integer optimization formulations and a semidefinite relaxation. A description of our solution framework is given in Section 5. Section 6 presents the computational results. This is followed by an overview of related literature in Section 7. Finally, in Section 8 we conclude and discuss future directions.

2   Motivation

Combinatorial optimization problems that are NP-hard are often solved with the use of a polynomially solvable relaxation. Let us first motivate why in this paper a semidefinite relaxation is used rather than a (more common) linear relaxation. Indeed, one could argue that linear programs are being solved much faster in general. However, for the stable set problem, linear relaxations are not very tight. Therefore one has to identify and add inequalities that strengthen the relaxation. But it is time-consuming to identify such inequalities, and by enlarging the model the solution process may slow down.

Several papers on approximation theory following [11] have shown the tightness of semidefinite relaxations. However, being tighter, semidefinite programs are more time-consuming to solve than linear programs in practice. Hence one has to trade strength for computation time. For large scale applications, semidefinite relaxations can often be preferred as the relaxation of choice to be used in a branch and bound framework. Moreover, our intention is not to solve a relaxation at every node of the search tree. Instead, we propose to only solve a relaxation at the root node of the first phase (its solution is used to identify the subdomains), and optionally at the root node of a subproblem (in order to strengthen the upper bound). Therefore, we are willing to make the trade-off in favour of the semidefinite relaxation.

Another point of view is the following. Although semidefinite programming has been developing for many years now in the operations research community, no efforts of integration or cooperation with constraint programming have been made to our knowledge. Application of semidefinite programming to problems typical to constraint programming, as was done in the papers on approximation algorithms mentioned in Section 7, is not yet hybrid problem solving. In this paper, however, a first step is being made. The solution of the semidefinite relaxation is used to identify promising subdomains, and also produces a tight upper bound for the constraint programming solver. On the other hand, the solutions found by the constraint programming solver serve as a lower bound inside the semidefinite programming solver.

3   Preliminaries on Semidefinite Programming

In this section we introduce semidefinite programming [28] as an extension of the more common linear programming. Both paradigms can be used to model polynomially solvable relaxations of NP-hard optimization problems.

In linear programming, combinatorial optimization problems are modeled in the following way:

$$\begin{aligned}
\max\ & c^\mathsf{T} x \\
\text{s.t.}\ & a_j^\mathsf{T} x \le b_j\ (j = 1, \ldots, m) \\
& x \ge 0.
\end{aligned} \tag{1}$$

Here $x \in \mathbb{R}^n$ is an n-dimensional vector of decision variables and $c \in \mathbb{R}^n$ a cost vector of dimension n. The m vectors $a_j \in \mathbb{R}^n$ $(j = 1, \ldots, m)$ and the m-dimensional vector $b \in \mathbb{R}^m$ define m linear constraints on x. In other words, this approach models problems using *nonnegative vectors* of variables.

Semidefinite programming makes use of *positive semidefinite matrices* of variables instead of nonnegative vectors. A matrix $X \in \mathbb{R}^{n \times n}$ is said to be positive semidefinite (denoted by $X \succeq 0$) when $y^\mathsf{T} X y \ge 0$ for all vectors $y \in \mathbb{R}^n$. Semidefinite programs have the form

$$\begin{aligned}
\max\ & \operatorname{tr}(CX) \\
\text{s.t.}\ & \operatorname{tr}(A_j X) \le b_j\ (j = 1, \ldots, m) \\
& X \succeq 0.
\end{aligned} \tag{2}$$

Here $\operatorname{tr}(X)$ denotes the *trace* of X, which is the sum of its diagonal elements, i.e. $\operatorname{tr}(X) = \sum_{i=1}^n X_{ii}$. The cost matrix $C \in \mathbb{R}^{n \times n}$ and the constraint matrices $A_j \in \mathbb{R}^{n \times n}$ are supposed to be symmetric. The m reals b_j and the m matrices A_j define again m constraints.

We can view semidefinite programming as an extension of linear programming. Namely, when the matrices C and A_j $(j = 1, \ldots, m)$ are all supposed to be diagonal matrices[2], the resulting semidefinite program is equal to a linear program. In particular, then a semidefinite programming constraint $\operatorname{tr}(A_j X) \leq b_j$ corresponds to the linear programming constraint $a_j^\mathsf{T} x \leq b_j$, where a_j represents the diagonal of A_j.

Applied as a continuous relaxation (i.e. the integrality constraint on the variables is relaxed), semidefinite programming in general produces solutions that are much closer to the integral optimum than linear programming. Intuitively, this can be explained as follows. Demanding positive semidefiniteness of a matrix automatically implies nonnegativity of its diagonal. If this diagonal corresponds (as in the general case described above) to the nonnegative vector of the linear relaxation, the semidefinite relaxation is stronger than a linear relaxation. Unfortunately, it is not a trivial task to otain a good (i.e. efficient) semidefinite program for a given problem.

Theoretically, semidefinite programs have been proved to be polynomially solvable using the so-called ellipsoid method (see for instance [12]). In practice, nowadays fast 'interior point' methods are being used for this purpose (see [3] for an overview). Being a special case of semidefinite programming, linear programs are also polynomially solvable using an ellipsoid or interior point method. However, they are often solved with a special linear programming solver, the simplex method. Although this method can have an exponential running time in theory, in practice it is often faster than an interior point algorithm.

4   The Stable Set Problem

In this section, the stable set problem is formally defined, and formulated in two different ways as an integer optimization problem. From this, a semidefinite programming relaxation is inferred.

4.1   Definition

Consider an undirected weighted graph $G = (V, E)$, where $V = \{1, \ldots, n\}$ is the set of vertices and E a subset of edges $\{(i, j) | i, j \in V, i \neq j\}$ of G, with $|E| = m$. To each vertex $i \in V$ a weight $w_i \in \mathbb{R}$ is assigned (without loss of generality, we can assume all weights to be nonnegative in this case). A *stable set* is a set $S \subseteq V$ such that no two vertices in S are joined by an edge in E. The *stable set problem* is the problem of finding a stable set of maximum total weight in G. This value is called the *stable set number* of G and is denoted by $\alpha(G)$ [3]. The maximum cardinality (or unweighted) stable set problem can be obtained by taking all weights equal to 1.

---

[2] A diagonal matrix is a matrix with nonnegative values on its diagonal entries only.

[3] In the literature $\alpha(G)$ usually denotes the unweighted stable set number. The weighted stable set number is then denoted as $\alpha_w(G)$. In this work, it is not necessary to make this distinction.

4.2   Integer Optimization Formulation

Let us first consider an integer linear programming formulation. We introduce binary variables to indicate whether or not a vertex belongs to the stable set S. So, for n vertices, we have n integer variables x_i indexed by $i \in V$, with initial domains $\{0, 1\}$. In this way, $x_i = 1$ if vertex i is in the stable set S, and $x_i = 0$ otherwise. We can now state the objective function, being the sum of the weights of vertices that are in the stable set S, as $\sum_{i=1}^{n} w_i x_i$. Finally, we define the constraints that restrict two adjacent vertices to be both inside S as $x_i + x_j \leq 1$, for all edges $(i, j) \in E$. Hence the integer linear programming model becomes:

$$\alpha(G) = \max \ \sum_{i=1}^{n} w_i x_i$$
$$\text{s.t. } x_i + x_j \leq 1 \ \forall (i, j) \in E \qquad (3)$$
$$x_i \in \{0, 1\} \ \forall i \in V.$$

Another way of describing the same solution set is presented by the following integer quadratic program

$$\alpha(G) = \max \ \sum_{i=1}^{n} w_i x_i$$
$$\text{s.t. } \ x_i x_j = 0 \ \forall (i, j) \in E \qquad (4)$$
$$x_i^2 = x_i \ \forall i \in V.$$

Note that here the constraint $x_i \in \{0, 1\}$ is replaced by $x_i^2 = x_i$. This quadratic formulation will be used below to infer a semidefinite programming relaxation of the stable set problem.

In fact, both model (3) and model (4) can be used as a constraint programming model. We have chosen the first model, since the quadratic constraints take more time to propagate than the linear constraints, while having the same pruning power.

4.3   Semidefinite Programming Relaxation

The integer quadratic program (4) gives rise to a semidefinite relaxation introduced by Lovász [22] (see Grötschel et al. [12] for a comprehensive treatment). The value of the objective function of this relaxation has been named the *theta number* of a graph G, indicated by $\vartheta(G)$. Let us start again from model (4). As was indicated in Section 3, we want to transform the current model that uses a nonzero vector into a model that uses a positive semidefinite matrix to represent our variables. In the current case, we can construct a matrix $X \in \mathbb{R}^{n \times n}$ by defining $X_{ij} = x_i x_j$. Let us also construct a $n \times n$ cost matrix W with $W_{ii} = w_i$ for $i \in V$ and $W_{ij} = 0$ for all $i \neq j$. Since $X_{ii} = x_i^2 = x_i$, the objective function becomes $\mathrm{tr}(WX)$. The edge constraints are easily transformed as $x_i x_j = 0 \Leftrightarrow X_{ij} = 0$. The first step in the transformation of model (4) can now be made:

$$\max \ \mathrm{tr}(WX)$$
$$\text{s.t. } X_{ij} = 0 \qquad \forall (i, j) \in E$$
$$X_{ij} = x_i x_j \ \forall i, j \in V \qquad (5)$$
$$x_i^2 = x_i \qquad \forall i \in V.$$

This model is still a quadratic program, although reformulated. The problem remains how to model the last, very important, constraint. We need a mapping of the diagonal entries $X_{ii} = x_i^2$ to the vector entries x_i. For this reason, we extend X with another row and column (both indexed by 0) that contain vector x, and define the $(n+1) \times (n+1)$ matrix Y as

$$Y = \begin{pmatrix} 1 & x_1 & \cdots & x_n \\ x_1 & & & \\ \vdots & & X & \\ x_n & & & \end{pmatrix}$$

where the 1 in the leftmost corner of Y is needed to obtain positive semidefiniteness. In this case we can express the required mapping as $Y_{ii} = \frac{1}{2}Y_{i0} + \frac{1}{2}Y_{0i}$ (note that X and Y are symmetric), since then $x_i^2 = Y_{ii} = \frac{1}{2}Y_{i0} + \frac{1}{2}Y_{0i} = x_i$. The final step in the transformation consists of replacing the constraints on X by constraints on Y. In particular, instead of demanding X to be a product of nonnegative vectors, we restrict Y to be a positive semidefinite matrix. Namely, if the vector x represents a stable set, then the matrix Y is positive semidefinite. However, not all positive semidefinite Y matrices represent a stable set, in particular its values can take fractional values.

In order to maintain equal dimension to Y, a row and a column (both indexed by 0) should be added to W, all entries of which containing value 0. Denote the resulting matrix by $\tilde{W}$. The theta number of a graph G can now be described as

$$\begin{aligned} \vartheta(G) = \max \quad & \operatorname{tr}(\tilde{W}Y) \\ \text{s.t. } \quad & Y_{ii} = \tfrac{1}{2}Y_{i0} + \tfrac{1}{2}Y_{0i} \ \forall i \in V \\ & Y_{ij} = 0 \qquad \forall (i,j) \in E \\ & Y \succeq 0. \end{aligned} \qquad (6)$$

By construction, the diagonal value Y_{ii} serves as an indication for the value of variable x_i ($i \in V$) in a maximum stable set. In particular, this program is a relaxation for the stable set problem, i.e. $\vartheta(G) \geq \alpha(G)$. Note that program (6) can easily be rewritten into the general form of program (2). Namely, $Y_{ii} = \frac{1}{2}Y_{i0} + \frac{1}{2}Y_{0i}$ is equal to $\operatorname{tr}(AY)$ where the $(n+1) \times (n+1)$ matrix A consists of all zeroes, except for $A_{ii} = 1$, $A_{i0} = -\frac{1}{2}$ and $A_{0i} = -\frac{1}{2}$, which makes the corresponding b entry equal to 0. Similarly for the edge constraints.

The theta number also arises from other formulations, different from the above, see [12]. In our implementation we have used the formulation that has been shown to be computationally most efficient among those alternatives [13]. Let us introduce that particular formulation (called ϑ_3 in [12]). Again, let $x \in \{0,1\}^n$ be a vector of binary variables representing a stable set. Define the $n \times n$ matrix $X = \xi\xi^\top$ where $\xi_i = \frac{\sqrt{w_i}}{\sqrt{\sum_{j=1}^n w_j x_j}} x_i$. Furthermore, let the $n \times n$ cost matrix U be defined as $U_{ij} = \sqrt{w_i w_j}$ for $i, j \in V$. Observe that in these definitions we exploit the fact that $w_i \geq 0$ for all $i \in V$. The following semidefinite program

$$\vartheta(G) = \max \quad \text{tr}(UX)$$
$$\text{s.t. tr}(X) = 1$$
$$X_{ij} = 0 \; \forall (i,j) \in E \tag{7}$$
$$X \succeq 0$$

gives exactly the theta number of G. When (7) is solved to optimality, the scaled diagonal element $\vartheta(G)X_{ii}$ (a fractional value between 0 and 1) serves as an indication for the value of x_i ($i \in V$) in a maximum stable set (see for instance [13]). Again, it is not difficult to rewrite program (7) into the general form of program (2).

Program (7) uses matrices of dimension n and $m+1$ constraints, while program (6) uses matrices of dimension $n+1$ and $m+n$ constraints. This gives an indication why program (7) is computationally more efficient.

5 Solution Framework

5.1 Overview

The two-phase solution approach proposed here is similar to the one described in [23]. In the first phase subproblems are generated, which are being solved in the second phase. A subproblem consists of a constraint programming model (program (3)) on restricted variable domains. The restricted domain values are selected by a heuristic, in our case the solution to the semidefinite programming relaxation. Each subproblem is solved to optimality using a constraint programming solver. A general overview of the method is presented in Algorithm 1 and explained hereafter.

Let us first explain how we use the solution of the semidefinite program (7) to partition the domain D_i of a variable x_i into D_i^{good} and D_i^{bad} (for $i \in V$). As was stated before, the solution of program (7) assigns fractional values between 0 and 1 to its variables. Naturally, if for a variable x_i the corresponding fractional value $\vartheta(G)X_{ii}$ is close to 1, we regard 1 to be a good value for variable x_i. More specifically, we select the variable x_i with the highest corresponding fractional value $\vartheta(G)X_{ii}$, set $D_i^{\text{good}} = \{1\}$ and $D_i^{\text{bad}} = \{0\}$, and mark it as handled. Then we mark all its neighbours j (with $(i,j) \in E$) as being handled, keeping their original domain $D_j = \{0,1\}$. This procedure is repeated until all variables are handled. For later convenience, we partition V into two distinct sets $V_0 = \{i \in V \mid D_i^{\text{good}} = \{1\}\}$ and $V_1 = V \setminus V_0$. Here V_1 represents the set of neighbours j of V_0, with $D_j = \{0,1\}$.

In a similar way, we can use the solution of the semidefinite relaxation to compute a first feasible integer solution. Namely, follow the same procedure, but now instantiate the selected variable $x_i = 1$ and set its neighbours $x_j = 0$. The objective value of this feasible integer solution is in many cases already equal to the (in case of integer weights downward rounded) solution of the semidefinite relaxation. In that case, we have found an optimal solution and finish. In other cases, we can still use this first solution as a lower bound to be applied during the solution of the subproblem.

Algorithm 1 Solution framework

read problem
set maximum discrepancy
solve semidefinite program (7) → upper bound
round solution of (7) → lower bound
for $i \in V_0$ **do**
    define D_i^{good} and D_i^{bad} using solution of (7)
end for
set discrepancy = 0
while lower bound < upper bound **and** discrepancy ≤ maximum discrepancy **do**
    generate subproblem using LDS branching strategy on D_i^{good} and D_i^{bad}
    solve subproblem → lower bound
    discrepancy = discrepancy + 1
end while

Next, we explain how to generate subproblems using these subdomains. The generation of subproblems makes use of a tree structure of depth $|V_0|$ in which we branch on D_i^{good} versus D_i^{bad}. The tree is traversed using a limited discrepancy strategy (LDS) [15]. LDS visits the nodes of a search tree differently from depth-first search. It tries to follow a given suggestion as good as it can. Branches opposite to the suggestion are regarded as discrepancies and are gradually allowed to be traversed. The first 'run' of LDS doesn't allow any discrepancies, the second allows only one, and so on. This means that for a particular discrepancy k, a path from the root to a leaf is allowed to consist of maximally k right branches. Typically this method is applied until a limited number of discrepancies is reached (say 2 or 3), which yields an incomplete search strategy. In order to be complete, one has to visit all nodes, up to discrepancy d for a binary tree of depth d.

In our case, the suggestion that should be followed are branches of the kind D_i^{good}, while branches D_i^{bad} are regarded as discrepancies. Hence, our first subproblem is the subproblem defined by program (3), with $x_i \in D_i^{\text{good}}$ for all $i \in V_0$. The next $|V_0|$ subproblems have all $x_i \in D_i^{\text{good}}$, except for one $x_k \in D_k^{\text{bad}}$ $(i, k \in V_0)$. The next discrepancy generates $\frac{1}{2}(|V_0|^2 + |V_0|)$ subproblems, each of which contains two variables $x_{k_1} \in D_{k_1}^{\text{bad}}$ and $x_{k_2} \in D_{k_2}^{\text{bad}}$ $(k_1, k_2 \in V_0)$, and so on. Since we expect to obtain a very good solution already in the first subproblems, we will only generate subproblems up to a certain maximum discrepancy. In our experiments the maximum discrepancy is chosen 2 and 4 respectively. Finally, we solve all subproblems to optimality using a constraint programming solver.

Note that the first subproblem, corresponding to discrepancy 0, only contains one solution, namely the one that we obtain in our rounding procedure. By propagation of the edge constraints, all variables $x_j \in D_j = \{0, 1\}$ $(j \in V_1)$ are instantiated automatically to 0. Hence, the subproblem corresponding to discrepancy 0 is obsolete in our current implementation.

5.2   Adding Discrepancy Cuts

In the case one needs to generate and solve subproblems up to a large discrepancy, it is preferable to prove possible suboptimality of a subproblem before entering it, especially when the subproblems are still relatively large. This can be done in several ways.

First, before entering a subproblem, we can identify variables which have a subdomain of size 1, namely those with $i \in V_0$. For those variables, one can add an additional constraint to the semidefinite program (7), enforcing either $x_i = 1$ or $x_i = 0$. Then the semidefinite program can be solved again, and will in general provide a tighter bound, hopefully lower than the current lowerbound, in which case we have proven suboptimality. However, solving the semidefinite program each time before entering a subproblem is very time-consuming and this method will not be very practical.

A better alternative would be to add a specific constraint, a *discrepancy cut*, that is valid for all subproblems of a given discrepancy. Recall that $V_0 = \{i \in V \mid D_i^{\text{good}} = \{1\}\}$. Hence, all subproblems of discrepancy k consist of k variables x_i with $x_i = 0$, and $|V_0| - k$ variables x_i with $x_i = 1$ ($i \in V_0$). This gives rise to two discrepancy cuts, given discrepancy k:

$$\sum_{i \in V_0} x_i = |V_0| - k \tag{8}$$

$$\sum_{i \in V_0} 1 - x_i = k \tag{9}$$

We implemented both of them, and cut (9) gives the best results. Stated in terms of semidefinite program (6), the discrepancy cut looks like $\text{tr}(AY) = |V_0| - k$, with $A_{ii} = 1$ if $i \in V_0$ and $A_{ij} = 0$ otherwise ($i, j \in \{0 \ldots, n\}$). As mentioned before, solving a semidefinite relaxation is relatively expensive, and one should make a tradeoff between its computation time and the gain in time of not solving the subproblems. For the instances we considered, the time needed to solve a semidefinite program is always larger than the time needed to solve all subproblems we would like to proof suboptimal. However, these cuts might be helpful for larger instances.

6   Computational Results

Our experiments are being done on a Pentium 1GHz processor, with 256 Mb RAM. As constraint programming solver we use the ILOG solver library, version 5.1 [19]. As semidefinite programming solver, we use CSDP version 4.1 [5]. The reason for our choices is that both solvers are among the fastest in their field, and because ILOG solver is written in C++, and CSDP is written in C, they can be easily hooked together.

The first instances we consider are randomly generated weighted graphs with n vertices and m edges. The vertex weights are randomly chosen integers from a range of 1 up to n. The edge density is chosen such that the constraint programming solver has difficulties solving them. Namely, the more edge constraints we have, the more propagation can be performed, and the easier the instance is solved by constraint programming. On the other hand, more edge constraints will slow down the semidefinite programming solver, because it is highly sensitive to the size of the semidefinite program to solve.

The name of the instances represent the number of vertices and the edge density, i.e. g75d015 is a graph on 75 vertices with an approximate edge density of 0.15. For these graphs, we have chosen to generate subproblems up to a maximum discrepancy of 4, based upon earlier experience.

We also considered structured instances (1tc.64 up to 1et.256), obtained from problems arising in coding theory [27]. These are unweighted graphs, therefore we have set all weights equal to 1. For these graphs, we generate subproblems up to a discrepancy of 2.

The results of our experiments are given in Table 1. It consists of three parts: the first part describes the instances, the next part gives the results of our approach (*sdp and cp*), the last part concerns the results of a sole constraint programming approach (*cp alone*) applied to program (3).

The columns in this table represent the following. An instance *name* has n vertices and m edges. For the part on our approach, the value of the semidefinite relaxation is ϑ, the rounded solution of the semidefinite relaxation has value *round*, and *best* is the value of the best solution found. This best solution is found in a subproblem generated during discrepancy *best discr*. Note that we generate subproblems up to discrepancy 4 in all cases, as was mentioned in Section 5. The time spent on solving the semidefinite relaxation is denoted by *time sdp*. The time spent on solving all generated subproblems is denoted by *time subp*. These values together form the *total time*. All times are measured in seconds. The number of all backtracking steps made during the search in our approach is collected in *backtracks*. Concerning the sole constraint programming approach, we report the best solution found (*best*), the *total time* spent during search, and the total number of *backtracks*. Note that we have set time limits for the constraint programming solver, to create a fair comparison with our approach. They are 100 seconds for g50d005 up to g150d010, 190 seconds for g150d015 and 324 seconds for the structured instances. Best found solutions that are proven to be optimal are indicated by an asterisk (*).

For the instances in Table 1 we only solved one semidefinite relaxation per problem, namely at the root node. The reason for this is that the time spent during the subproblem search is less than the time spent on computing another relaxation, as reported in the table. Therefore, we cannot gain time by adding discrepancy cuts and computing another semidefinite relaxation.

In general, our method produces better solutions than the constraint programming approach alone. In many cases, the rounded solution of the semidefinite relaxation is already optimal. However, note that there are two instances for which the constraint programming approach gives better solutions. Note also that the structured instances are handled quite well by our approach, while the constraint programming approach produces very low quality solutions for the larger instances.

Table 1. Computational results on randomly generated weighted graphs and structured unweighted graphs. Best found solutions that are proven optimal are marked with an asterisk (*).

instance				sdp and cp							cp alone		
name	n	m	ϑ	round	best	best discr	time sdp	time subp	total time	back-tracks	best	total time	back-tracks
g50d005	50	69	746.00	746	746*	0	0.48	0.00	0.48	0	746*	6.38	160185
g50d010	50	130	568.00	568	568*	0	0.53	0.00	0.53	0	568*	1.54	40878
g50d015	50	191	512.00	512	512*	0	0.71	0.00	0.71	0	512*	0.54	13355
g75d005	75	139	1472.17	1455	1466	1	0.99	3.47	4.46	36492	1077	100.00	2555879
g75d010	75	280	1148.25	1122	1134	3	2.05	1.01	3.06	12964	1074	100.00	2299226
g75d015	75	414	966.76	924	946	4	3.50	0.88	4.38	11136	951*	46.63	1000409
g100d005	100	250	2903.00	2903	2903*	0	3.13	0.00	3.13	0	2415	100.01	1578719
g100d010	100	495	2058.41	1972	2029	4	6.92	7.17	14.09	74252	1850	100.02	1666892
g100d015	100	725	1704.61	1568	1608	4	17.87	4.28	22.15	47222	1644	100.01	1469221
g125d005	125	367	3454.00	3454	3454*	0	7.10	0.00	7.10	0	2656	100.02	1644993
g125d010	125	761	2448.94	2208	2271	4	22.00	13.98	35.98	107610	1668	100.01	1643183
g125d015	125	1110	2033.74	1839	1846	4	59.56	6.15	65.71	53103	1733	100.02	1454377
g150d005	150	549	5043.09	5035	5035	0	15.79	26.89	42.68	135051	3090	100.02	1426234
g150d010	150	1094	3651.38	3281	3423	2	64.83	13.10	77.93	78263	2294	100.02	1462125
g150d015	150	1641	2935.84	2572	2572	0	181.54	4.56	186.10	27306	2224	190.03	2119929
1tc.64	64	192	20.00	20	20*	0	1.05	0.00	1.05	0	19	324.01	10969580
1et.64	64	264	18.85	18	18*	0	0.97	0.00	0.97	0	18*	179.00	5763552
1tc.128	128	512	38.00	38	38*	0	12.03	0.00	12.03	0	19	324.02	9455475
1et.128	128	672	29.33	28	28	0	13.48	0.67	14.15	1929	19	324.02	8562959
1dc.128	128	1471	16.89	16	16*	0	107.71	0.00	107.71	0	13	324.04	6497027
1zc.128	128	2240	20.84	16	18	2	323.53	0.41	323.94	2094	18	324.04	7584769
1tc.256	256	1312	63.43	60	62	2	129.82	8.63	138.45	11588	13	324.03	7284451
1et.256	256	1664	55.14	50	50	0	230.39	5.02	235.41	7184	18	324.04	7656162

A final remark concerns instance 1et.256. In [27], the maximum value of this instance is 48, while we find a solution with value 50. After notification, the author of [27] agreed with our solution.

7   Related Literature

Since the stable set problem is NP-hard, no complete (or exact) algorithm is known that solves the stable set problem in polynomial time. Many other techniques have been proposed, including approximation algorithms, heuristics, or branch and bound structured methods. A survey of different formulations, complete methods and heuristics for the maximum clique problem[4] is given by Pardalos and Xue [25] and, more recently, by Bomze et al. [4]. The maximum clique problem has also been succesfully attacked using constraint programming, by Fahle [7] and Régin [26]. Both papers make use of specialized propagation algorithms for the maximum clique problem.

Although semidefinite programs can be solved in polynomial time theoretically, it lasted until a few years ago until fast solvers for this purpose were implemented. Until then, application inside a branch and bound framework was unrealistic. Still, solving a semidefinite program takes relatively much time, compared to solving a linear program. However, since semidefinite programming solvers are getting faster, semidefinite relaxations become a serious candidate to be used within a branch and bound framework, see for instance the paper by Karisch et al. [20].

A large number of references to papers concerning semidefinite programming are on the web pages of Helmberg [16] and Alizadeh [2]. A general introduction on semidefinite programming applied to combinatorial optimization is given by Goemans and Rendl [10].

Another area that made semidefinite programming useful in practice is that of approximation algorithms. In this field one tries to give a performance guarantee for an algorithm on a particular problem. In particular, the paper [11] by Goemans and Williamson uses a semidefinite relaxation and randomized rounding to prove such a performance guarantee for the maximum cut problem of a graph and satisfiability problems. Following this result numerous papers appeared, also concerning the approximation of satisfiability problems, including [14] and [21].

The solution structure of the current work, namely problem decomposition by branching on promising subdomains, is similar to the method described in [23], which is also present in [8]. In [23] a linear relaxation is used to identify promising values. Moreover, by exploiting the discrepancy structure of the method combined with reduced costs, suboptimality of subproblems can be proved very fast.

Another hybrid approach, using linear programming and constraint programming, has been investigated by Ajili et al. [1] and El Sakkout et al. [6]. A subset of constraints is relaxed as a linear program in such a way that its solution is always integral. The solution to the relaxation serves as a suggestion (a 'probe') for solving the complete program using a constraint programming solver. A probe is used to detect infeasibility, to remove inconsistent domain values and to guide

---

[4] The maximum weighted stable set problem of a graph is equivalent to the maximum weighted clique problem of its complement graph.

the search. During search, many probing steps are being made. This results in a tight cooperation of the linear programming and constraint programming solver.

8   Conclusions and Further Research

We introduced a method that combines semidefinite programming and constraint programming to solve the stable set problem. Our experiments show that constraint programming can indeed benefit greatly from semidefinite programming. On instances that were very difficult to handle for a constraint programming solver, our hybrid method obtained very good results.

The discrepancy cuts we proposed to strengthen the semidefinite relaxation could not be applied efficiently to the instances we considered. However, for larger instances they could be helpful.

Further research in this direction would for instance be to obtain a filtering mechanism similar to the cost-based domain filtering for linear relaxations [9]. In [17], Helmberg describes such a procedure, called variable fixing, for semidefinite relaxations. It would be interesting to see how his method can be applied in a constraint programming framework.

Also, one could consider a different way of selecting promising values from the solution of the semidefinite relaxation. A strategy that incorporates randomized rounding possibly yields better results. This thought is motivated by the use of randomized rounding of semidefinite relaxations in approximation algorithms, as discussed in Section 7.

Finally, this work has much in common with our previous work [23]. The underlying general principle of decomposing a problem into promising subproblems according to a certain heuristic is currently under research.

Acknowledgements

Many thanks to Michela Milano for fruitful discussion and helpful comments while writing this paper. Also thanks to Monique Laurent for constructive remarks.

References

1. F. Ajili and H. El Sakkout. LP probing for piecewise linear optimization in scheduling. In *Third International Workshop on Integration of AI and OR Techniques in Constraint Programming for Combinatorial Optimization Problems (CP-AI-OR'01)*, pages 189–203, 2001.
2. F. Alizadeh. The Semidefinite Programming Page. http://new-rutcor.rutgers.edu/~alizadeh/sdp.html.
3. F. Alizadeh. Interior point methods in semidefinite programming with applications to combinatorial optimization. *SIAM Journal on Optimization*, 5(1):13–51, 1995.
4. I.M. Bomze, M. Budinich, P.M. Pardalos, and M. Pelillo. The Maximum Clique Problem. In D.-Z. Du and P.M. Pardalos, editors, *Handbook of Combinatorial Optimization*, volume 4. Kluwer Academic Publishers, Boston, MA, 1999.

5. B. Borchers. A C Library for Semidefinite Programming. *Optimization Methods and Software*, 11(1):613–623, 1999.
6. H. El Sakkout and M. Wallace. Probe Backtrack Search for Minimal Perturbation in Dynamic Scheduling. *Constraints*, 5(4):359–388, 2000.
7. T. Fahle. Simple and Fast: Improving a Branch-And-Bound Algorithm for Maximum Clique. In *10th Annual European Symposium on Algorithms (ESA 2002)*, volume 2461 of *LNCS*, pages 485–498. Springer Verlag, 2002.
8. F. Focacci. *Solving Combinatorial Optimization Problems in Constraint Programming*. PhD thesis, University of Ferrara, 2001.
9. F. Focacci, A. Lodi, and M. Milano. Cost-based domain filtering. In J. Jaffar, editor, *Fifth International Conference on the Principles and Practice of Constraint Programming (CP'99)*, volume 1713 of *LNCS*, pages 189–203. Springer Verlag, 1999.
10. M. Goemans and F. Rendl. Combinatorial Optimization. In H. Wolkowicz, R. Saigal, and L. Vandenberghe, editors, *Handbook of Semidefinite Programming*, pages 343–360. Kluwer, Dordrecht, 2000.
11. M.X. Goemans and D.P. Williamson. Improved Approximation Algorithms for Maximum Cut and Satisfiability Problems Using Semidefinite Programming. *Journal of the ACM*, 42(6):1115–1145, 1995.
12. M. Grötschel, L. Lovász, and A. Schrijver. *Geometric Algorithms and Combinatorial Optimization*. John Wiley & Sons, New York, 1988.
13. G. Gruber and F. Rendl. Computational experience with stable set relaxations. *SIAM Journal on Optimization*, 13(4):1014–1028, 2003.
14. E. Halperin and U. Zwick. Approximation algorithms for MAX 4-SAT and rounding procedures for semidefinite programs. *Journal of Algorithms*, 40:184–211, 2001.
15. W. D. Harvey and M. L. Ginsberg. Limited Discrepancy Search. In C. S. Mellish, editor, *Proceedings of the Fourteenth International Joint Conference on Artificial Intelligence (IJCAI-95); Vol. 1*, pages 607–615, 1995.
16. C. Helmberg. Semidefinite Programming website.
   http://www-user.tu-chemnitz.de/~helmberg/semidef.html.
17. C. Helmberg. Fixing variables in semidefinite relaxations. *SIAM Journal on Matrix Analysis and Applications*, 21(3):952–969, 2000.
18. W.J. van Hoeve. A hybrid constraint programming and semidefinite programming approach for the stable set problem. In *Fifth International Workshop on Integration of AI and OR Techniques in Constraint Programming for Combinatorial Optimization Problems (CP-AI-OR'03)*, pages 3–16, 2003.
19. ILOG. ILOG Solver 5.1, Reference Manual, 2001.
20. S. E. Karisch, F. Rendl, and J. Clausen. Solving graph bisection problems with semidefinite programming. *INFORMS Journal on Computing*, 12(3):177–191, 2000.
21. H. C. Lau. A new approach for weighted constraint satisfaction. *Constraints*, 7(2):151–165, 2002.
22. L. Lovász. On the Shannon capacity of a graph. *IEEE Transactions on Information Theory*, 25:1–7, 1979.
23. M. Milano and W.J. van Hoeve. Reduced cost-based ranking for generating promising subproblems. In P. van Hentenryck, editor, *Eighth International Conference on the Principles and Practice of Constraint Programming (CP'02)*, volume 2470 of *LNCS*, pages 1–16. Springer Verlag, 2002.
24. C.H. Papadimitriou and K. Steiglitz. *Combinatorial Optimization: Algorithms and Complexity*. Prentice Hall, 1982.

25. P.M. Pardalos and J. Xue. The Maximum Clique Problem. *SIAM Journal of Global Optimization*, 4:301–328, 1994.
26. J.-C. Régin. Solving the Maximum Clique Problem with Constraint Programming. In *Fifth International Workshop on Integration of AI and OR Techniques in Constraint Programming for Combinatorial Optimization Problems (CP-AI-OR'03)*, pages 166–179, 2003.
27. N.J.A. Sloane. Challenge Problems: Independent Sets in Graphs. http://www.research.att.com/~njas/doc/graphs.html.
28. H. Wolkowicz, R. Saigal, and L. Vandenberghe, editors. *Handbook of Semidefinite Programming*, volume 27 of *International series in operations research and management science*. Kluwer, Dordrecht, 2000.

A Constraint-Aided Conceptual Design Environment for Autodesk Inventor*

Alan Holland, Barry O'Callaghan, and Barry O'Sullivan

Cork Constraint Computation Centre
Department of Computer Science, University College Cork, Ireland
{a.holland,b.ocallaghan,b.osullivan}@4c.ucc.ie

Abstract. Engineering conceptual design can be defined as that phase of the product development process during which the designer takes a specification for a product to be designed and generates many broad solutions for it. It is well recognized that few computational tools exist that are capable of supporting the designer work through the conceptual phase of design. However, significant recent developments have been made in solid modeling and 3D computer-aided design. The use of such tools has become a critical element in the more sophisticated product development processes to be found in modern industry. This paper presents a prototype constraint-based computer-aided design (CAD) technology that can be used to support designers working in the early stages of design. The technology has been developed as an add-in application for Autodesk Inventor, a 3D solid-modeling environment. The add-in has, at its core, a constraint filtering system based on generalised arc-consistency processing and backtrack search. We present our current prototype and a detailed demonstration of its functionality. Finally, we describe our current work on a number of additional features for the next prototype, which will be deployed in an industrial context.

1 Introduction

Engineering conceptual design can be regarded as that phase of the engineering design process during which the designer takes a specification for a product to be designed and generates many broad solutions for it. Each of these broad solutions is generally referred to as a *scheme* [7]. It is generally accepted that conceptual design is one of the most critical phases of the product development process. It has been reported that more than 75% of a product's total cost is dictated by decisions made during the conceptual phase of design and that poor conceptual design can never be compensated for at the detailed design stage [10].

To support interactive conceptual design a number of issues must be considered. Firstly, the conceptual design process is initiated by a statement describing the desired properties of the required product. This statement may not be complete and may be modified during design. Secondly, conceptual design is a process in which synthesis of a scheme is a fundamental activity. However, the designer should have the freedom to

---

* This research is funded by Enterprise Ireland, through their Research Innovation Fund (Grant Number RIF-2001-317). The software used for the project, Autodesk Inventor, has been sponsored by cadcoevolution.com, an Irish CAD provider.

F. Rossi (Ed.): CP 2003, LNCS 2833, pp. 422–436, 2003.

approach the process in anyway he wishes. Thirdly, in so far as it is possible, designers should be alerted to any inconsistencies that exist in their designs. Designers may seek explanations for such inconsistencies, or justifications for why certain options are not available to them. Alternatively, designers may wish to be given an explanation detailing how a particular scheme has come about. Fourthly, automated evaluation and comparison of multiple schemes, throughout the design process, is necessary to focus the designer on promising alternatives. Finally, designers prefer to use tools which are familiar to them and, therefore, any additional tools that a designer is expected to use must have a "look-and-feel" similar to those they already use. It was these considerations that set the agenda for the work reported here.

This paper presents a prototype constraint-based computer-aided design (CAD) technology that can be used to support designers working in the early stages of design. We present the current status of our prototype and a detailed demonstration of its functionality. We report on some industrial experiences and describe our current work on a number of additional features for the next prototype, which will be deployed in an industrial context. The CAD technology has, at its core, a constraint filtering system based on generalised arc-consistency processing [3] and backtrack search. Using the technology, the designer can be assisted in developing and evaluating a set of schemes which satisfy the various constraints that are imposed on the design. Explanations and justifications can be generated to aid the designer's understanding of the state of the design problem. Arbitrary constraints can be asserted or retracted by the designer which permits the incorporation of new requirements into the design specification and give the designer freedom to approach the process as he wishes.

The remainder of the paper is organized as follows. Section 2 presents an overview of the relevant literature. Section 3 presents an overview of the theory of conceptual design upon which the work presented in this paper is based. Section 4 presents an overview of the current prototype of our CAD technology for supporting conceptual design. Section 5 outlines our plans for future development and deployment. In Section 6 a number of concluding remarks are made.

2   Related Research

In the design literature three phases of design are generally identified: conceptual design, embodiment design and detailed design [16]. During conceptual design the designer searches for a set of broad solutions to a design problem, each of which satisfies the fundamental requirements of the desired product. The embodiment phase of design is traditionally regarded as the phase during which an initial physical design is developed. This initial physical design involves the determination of component arrangements, initial forms and other part characteristics. The detailed phase of design is traditionally regarded as the phase during which the final physical design is developed.

Constraint-based applications for design have been more commonly applied to the post-conceptual phases of design [11, 12, 21]. The use of constraint processing techniques for supporting configuration design has also been widely reported in the literature [13, 19].

Modern approaches to product development, such as Concurrent Engineering [4], attempt to maximize the degree to which design activities are performed in parallel.

Researchers in the constraint processing community have developed constraint-based technologies that support integrated approaches to product development [5]. Constraint-based approaches to managing conflict in collaborative design systems have also been reported [2, 9, 11]. Using constraints to co-ordinate distributed agents in engineering design has also been reported [17].

Constraint-based approaches to supporting conceptual design have been reported in the literature for quite a number of years [8, 18, 20]. However, most of this research does not address the synthesis problem; the vast majority has focused on constraint propagation and consistency management relating to more numerical design decisions. For example, "Concept Modeler" is based on a set of graph processing algorithms that use bipartite matching and strong component identification for solving systems of equations [20]. The Concept Modeler system allows the designer to construct models of a product using iconic abstractions of machine elements.

Based on the earlier work on Concept Modeler, a system called "Design Sheet" has been developed [18]. This system is essentially an environment for facilitating flexible trade-off studies during conceptual design. It integrates constraint management techniques, symbolic mathematics and robust equation solving capabilities with a flexible environment for developing models and specifying tradeoff studies. The Design Sheet system permits a designer to build a model of a design by entering a set of algebraic constraints. The designer can then use Design Sheet to change the set of independent variables in the algebraic model and perform trade-off studies, optimization and sensitivity analysis.

While not a constraint-based system, the Conceptual Understanding and Prototyping Environment (CUP) is an approach to supporting conceptual design that unites ideas from traditional mechanical design with 3D layouts and knowledge engineering [1]. Of all of the systems reviewed here, CUP is most similar to the approach that we have adopted. However, our technology is entirely constraint-based which gives us the opportunity to exploit the semantics of constraints and use inference as a core technique for navigating the design search space, providing explanations and an immediate declarative approach to modeling the evolving schemes that the designer wishes to explore.

3   The Approach

In this section we will give an overview of the approach to conceptual design that has motivated the design of the CAD system which we will present in Section 4. The model of conceptual design adopted here is based on the well accepted observation that during this phase of design a designer works from an informal set of requirements that the product must satisfy and generates alternative schemes which satisfy them.

Central to the process of scheme generation is an understanding of function and how it can be provided. The process involves the development of a functional decomposition which provides the basis for a realization of physical elements that form a scheme. In addition to determining which physical elements comprise a scheme, the relations between them must also be specified to a sufficient extent to permit the evaluation and comparison of alternative schemes.

In the remainder of this section a brief overview of some of the most important aspects of our approach to conceptual design will be presented. For a more complete discussion of the theory the reader is encouraged to refer to the more detailed literature available [14, 15].

3.1   The Design Specification

The conceptual design process is initiated by the recognition of a need or customer requirement. This need is analyzed and translated into a statement which defines the functionality that the product should provide (referred to as *functional* requirements) and the *physical* requirements that the product must satisfy. This statement is known as a *design specification*.

A design specification will contain both abstract functional requirements as well as concrete physical requirements. The functional requirements define the "purpose" of the desired product at as high a level of abstraction as possible. In addition, two classes of physical requirement can be identified: product requirements and life-cycle requirements. These requirements can be either *categorical requirements* that define constraints between attributes of the product or its life-cycle, or they can be *preferences* related to subsets of these attributes.

Essentially, the design specification comprises a set of constraints which must be satisfied and a set of objective functions with respect to which the desired product must be Pareto optimal [14].

3.2   Conceptual Design Knowledge

In order to successfully synthesize alternative schemes that meet the requirements defined in the design specification, the designer needs considerable knowledge of how function can be provided by physical means. This knowledge exists in a variety of forms; a designer may not only know of particular components, sub-assemblies and technologies that can provide particular functionality, but may be aware of abstract concepts which could also be used. For example, a designer may know that an electric light-bulb can generate heat or, alternatively, that heat can be generated by rubbing two surfaces together. The latter concept is more abstract that the former. In order to effectively support the designer during conceptual design, these alternative types of design knowledge need to be modeled in a formal way. However, a CAD system which supports conceptual design must also be capable of dealing with the designer's "off-the-cuff" ideas and store them for future use if they are deemed useful.

Reasoning about Function. We employ a *function-means map* approach to cataloging how function can be provided by means [6, 14]. In a function-means map two different types of means can be identified: *design principles* and *design entities*. A design principle is a means which is defined in terms of a set of functions that must be provided in order to provide some higher-level functionality. Design principles are abstractions of known approaches to providing function. By utilizing a design principle the designer can decompose higher-level functions without committing to a physical solution too early in the design process. The functions that are required by a design principle collectively replace the function being embodied by that principle. The functions which define a design principle will, generally, have a number of *context relations* defined between them. These context relations describe how the parts in the scheme, which provide these functions, should be configured so that the design principle is used in a valid way. For example, in Figure 1, *principle 1* comprises two functions, *f1* and *f2*, between which a context relation *r1* is defined.

Note that a design principle is not just a model of a known physical design solution, but is an abstraction which can be used to encourage creativity and analogical reasoning during design. An example of this was presented above when defining an abstract concept for generating heat by rubbing two surfaces together.

A design entity, on the other hand, is a physical, tangible means for providing function such as a component or sub-assembly. A design entity is defined by a set of parameters and the constraints that exist between these parameters. For example, an electronic resistor would be modeled as a design entity which is defined by three parameters, resistance, voltage and current, between which Ohm's Law would hold.

Embodiment of Function. As the designer develops a scheme for a product every function in the scheme is embodied by a means. Each means that is available to the designer has an associated *set of behaviors*. Each *behavior* is defined as a set of functions that the means can be used to provide simultaneously. Each behavior associated with a design principle will contain only one function to reflect the fact that it is used to decompose a single function. However, a behavior associated with a design entity may contain many functions to reflect the fact the there are many combinations of functions that the entity can provide at the same time. For example, the bulb design entity mentioned earlier may be able to fulfill the functions *provide light* and *generate heat* simultaneously. However, when a design entity is incorporated into a scheme it is not necessary that every function in this behavior be used in the scheme.

3.3   Scheme Configuration Using Interfaces

Generally, the first means that a designer will select will be a design principle. This design principle will substitute the required (parent) functionality with a set of child functions. Ultimately the designer will embody all leaf-node functions in the functional decomposition with design entities. During this embodiment process, the context relations from the design principles used in the scheme will be used as a basis for defining the interfaces (constraints) between the design entities used in the scheme.

For example, in Figure 1 an example scheme structure is illustrated. The top-level function in this scheme is *f0*. This function is embodied using a design principle called *principle 1*. This design principle introduces two functions, *f1* and *f2* to replace the function *f0*. A context relation, *r1*, is specified between these functions. The function *f1* is embodied by a design principle, *principle 2*, which introduces two further functions, *f3* and *f4* into the scheme. A context relation, *r2*, is specified between these functions. The function *f3* is embodied with the design entity *ent 1*, the function *f4* is embodied with the design entity *ent 2* and the function *f2* is embodied with the design entity *ent 3*. However, between which design entities should the context relations *r1* and *r2* be considered?

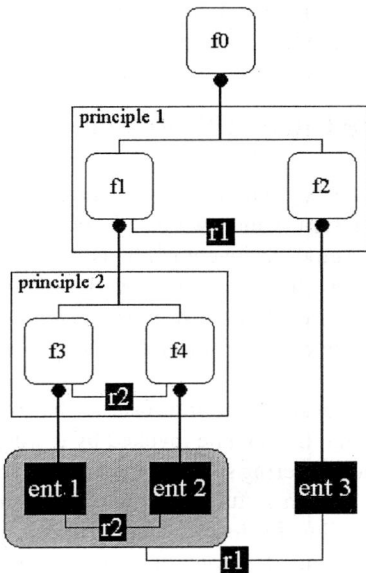

Fig. 1. An example of scheme configuration.

The context relation *r2* must exist between the entities that derive from the functions *f3* and *f4*. The design entities *ent 1* and *ent 2* are used to embody these functions. Thus, the context relation *r2* must be considered between these entities. Since, the design entities *ent 1* and *ent 2* are the means used to provide the functions *f3* and *f4*, these entities can be regarded as being *directly* used to provide these functions.

The context relation *r1* is a little more complex. This context relation must exist between the entities that derive from the functions *f1* and *f2*. The design entity *ent 3* is used to embody the function *f2*. Thus this entity can be regarded as being *directly* used for the function *f2*. The function *f1* is provided by the design principle *principle 2*, whose child functions are in turn embodied by the design entities *ent 1* and *ent 2*. Thus, these design entities can be regarded as being *indirectly* used to provide the function *f1*. Therefore, the context relation *r1* must be considered between the combination of design entities *ent 1* and *ent 2* on the one hand, and *ent 3* on the other hand.

The precise nature of these interfaces cannot be known with certainty until the designer embodies functions with design entities; this is because the link between functions and design entities is generally not known with certainty during the development of the functional decomposition for the scheme. Until the precise nature of a particular interface is known, they are modeled as constraints between design entities which can be used to reason about the product structure; for example, interfaces may represent simple spatial relationships which can inform an evaluation related to the relative position of parts in a product.

The types of interfaces that may be used to synthesize a product structure will be specific to the engineering domain within which the designer is working. Indeed, these interfaces may also be specific to the particular company to which the designer belongs in order to ensure the configurability of the product.

4   An Overview of the Current Prototype

In this section we present the key features of our current prototype CAD technology for supporting conceptual design, which we call ConCAD Expert. The technology is seamlessly integrated with Autodesk Inventor[1]. This particular CAD system has been chosen for a number of reasons. In particular, as well as being one of the most popular 3D solid modeling design environments, Inventor has an architecture similar to most tools of its kind, but has a very rich API through which we can integrate with the host CAD system.

Our technology has been designed to interface to the Inventor (version 5.3) CAD system as an add-in application that can be invoked by the designer at any point. At its core is an interactive constraint filtering system based on generalised arc-consistency [3] and backtrack search. The system is fully interactive, monitoring the consistency of designer decisions and providing feedback when an inconsistency has been detected or the designer has requested justifications or explanations from the system. It was developed using C#, and uses the Autodesk Inventor 5.3 COM API. An XML database has been developed to store the parts available to the CAD system. The XML schema that has been used, represents a part file and the various attributes of each part. We now present many of the features of our prototype in the form of a "walk-through".

Once the conceptual design tool has been invoked, the designer can use a Functional View panel (see left-hand side of Figure 2) to define the functionality and physical constraints that the desired product must satisfy.

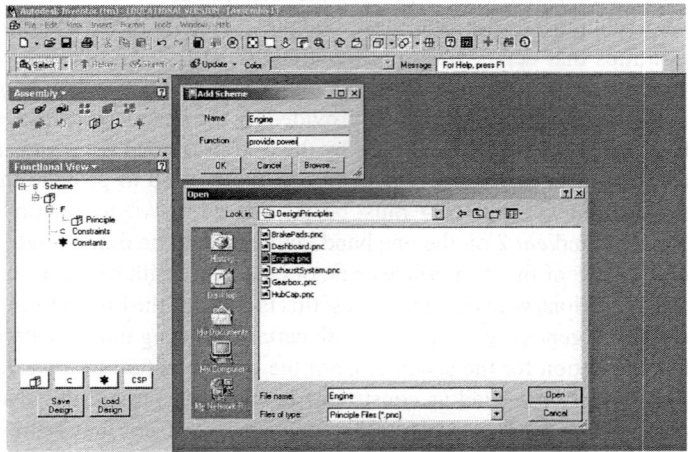

Fig. 2. Beginning a conceptual design session using a design principle.

[1] See: http://www.autodesk.com/inventor

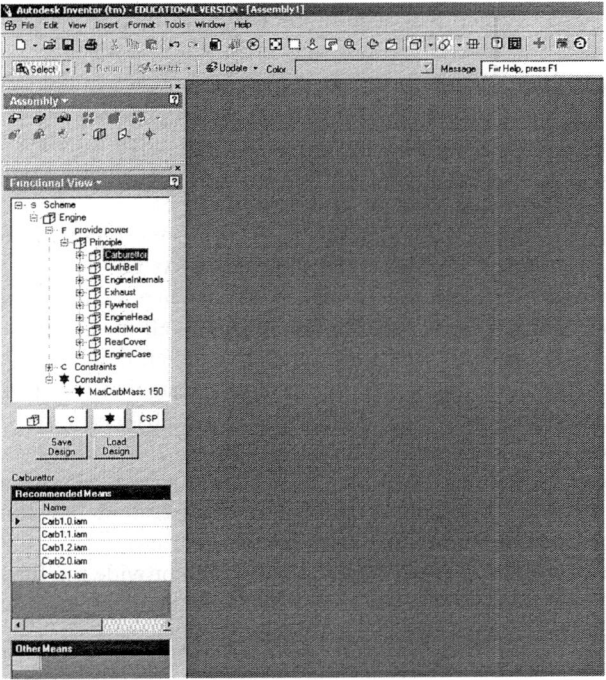

Fig. 3. Viewing recommended means.

Once the ConCAD Expert add-in has been invoked the designer can begin to develop his concept by developing a functional decomposition and mapping functions onto parts which will be loaded into Inventor automatically. In Figure 2 the designer begins to design an engine by incorporating a pre-defined design principle for an internal combustion engine. The result of this action can be seen in Figure 3, where each of the functional elements of an engine can be seen in the Functional View pane. Note that this is an abstract description. Each of the elements in the Functional View pane relates to a design element which is represented as a function. No parts have yet been selected at this point. However, the designer is free to select parts if desired, or can extend the functional description of each element further by incorporating additional design principles into the scheme. Furthermore, the designer can define context relations (constraints) between elements of the functional description, in addition to those that form part of the definition of the engine design principle, if desired. These will define how each of the elements must relate each other in the part model.

At the moment, the designer can select design principles from a predefined database, or can manually define them on-the-fly. Obviously, we would like the conceptual design system to store any new descriptions for use in future projects. At the moment, this must be done by manually including them in the database. However, in the next version of the system the identification and storage of design principles will be done automatically.

In this way the CAD system will acquire the design principles for a particular design domain over time.

At any point in time the designer can view which means in the CAD database are recommended for use in the designer's scheme. Recommended means must not only satisfy the functional requirements defined in the functional decomposition, but must also be consistent with the physical constraints defined explicitly by the designer and implicitly by any other means used in the scheme.

In Figure 3 the designer has asked the CAD system to recommend means for the carburettor element in the functional decomposition. As can be seen on the middle-left side of the figure, five alternative means have been found for this element from which the designer is free to choose. In this example, all means that can provide the required functionality for this element are recommended; otherwise they would have been displayed in the *Other Means* box. A means is no longer recommended if it satisfies the functional constraints, but violates one or more physical constraints.

However, for the purposes of explanation lets assume that before the designer selects one of these means he defines an additional constraint in the CAD system. An interface used to do this is shown in Figure 4. The designer is free to define constraints on any characteristic of the scheme. In this figure, the designer has defined the constraint that ensures that the mass of the means that will be used to provide the functionality of the carburettor will have a mass that is no more than a given maximum value.

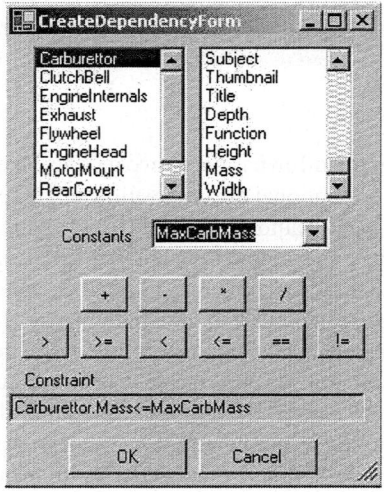

Fig. 4. Specifying additional constraints.

The consequence of this constraint is that some of the means which could have been used as a carburettor have been removed and placed in a list of *Other Means*, which contains those means that are no longer recommended for this situation. This scenario is depicted in the lower left of Figure 5.

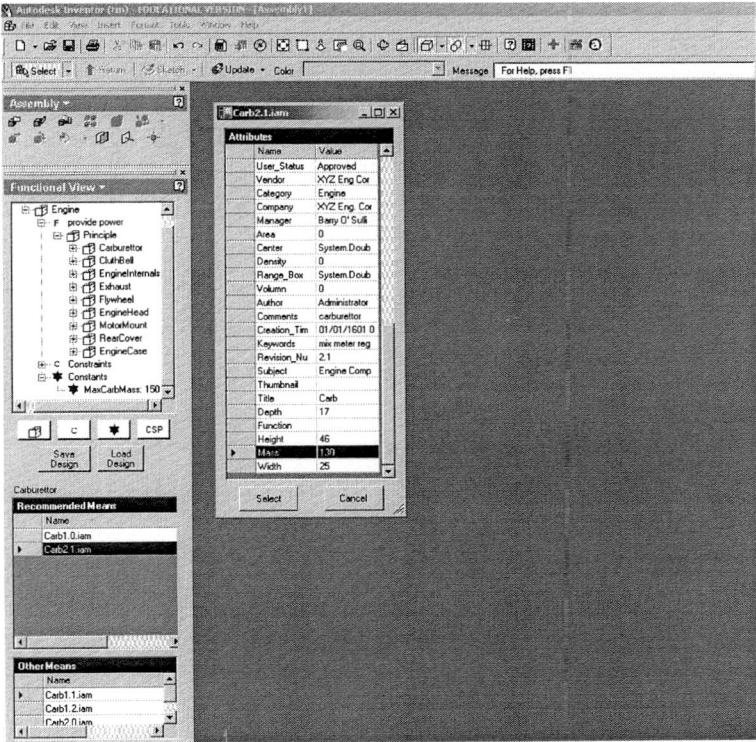

Fig. 5. The effect of the designer's constraint.

Also presented in this figure is a window showing the attributes of a particular means selected by the designer. In this figure the designer has clicked on the recommended part, *Carb2.1.iam*. Note in the attributes window that the mass of the part satisfies the constraint that the maximum mass of the carburettor be no more than 150g.

As the designer makes decisions and interacts with the CAD system, a CSP model describing the characteristics of the desired product is being developed. Part of the constraint model that the designer has developed at this point in our example is presented in Figure 6.

In this figure we can, firstly, see at the top the set of constant definitions. Secondly, we can see the set of variables in our design and their corresponding domains. Finally, we have the set of constraints defined by the design specification for the product, any additional constraints defined by the designer or constraints added to the model which are implied by the designer's decisions.

To illustrate the consequences of constraint addition and domain filtering in our prototype, Figure 7 shows the effect of adding an overall cost constraint to the model. This constraint was entered using the interface presented in Figure 4. We can see from Figure 7 that the list of of recommended means has been reduced further through inference, which in the prototype is based on generalized consistency processing. In this figure the

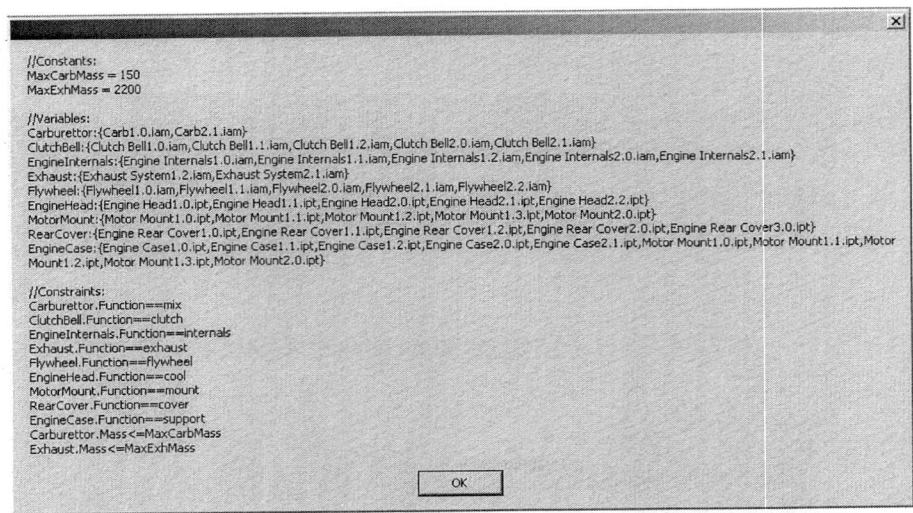

Fig. 6. The CSP can be viewed at any stage during the design process.

designer has asked for an explanation for why the *Carb1.0.iam* is no longer recommended by selecting it from the list. An explanation is given in Figure 8 which specifies the constraints with which the part is inconsistent. Explanations are currently generated directly from the inference algorithm used in the prototype.

Figure 9 presents the extended CSP model of our scheme which includes the designer-specified cost constraint (shown last in the figure). Note how the domains of the more expensive parts were heavily reduced whereas the smaller cheaper parts such as the *mount* were unaffected.

As the designer develops the functional decomposition he can also select parts for providing the necessary functionality. There is no restriction placed on the order that the designer develops a scheme. Figure 10 shows the CAD system interface after the designer has begun to select parts. The constraint model that the CAD system contains at this point not only includes constraints on the functional decomposition and each part, but also constraints on the way parts can be configured. These interface constraints derived from the constraints that the designer specified while developing the functional decomposition for the product, as well as the various design principles that were employed. As the designer develops the scheme further, inference on these constraints will assist the designer make consistent decisions on a valid configuration of these parts.

The designer does not need to fully specify the entire design at this point since that is a detailed design task. All that is required is that the designer specify the scheme to an extent which permits it to be evaluated against the constraints in the design specification and compared against any alternative schemes that have been developed.

5   Next Steps

The CAD technology presented here is being developed for industrial deployment. In anticipation of the release of the tool, we are currently developing the next generation

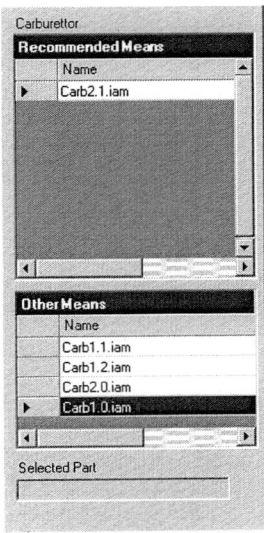

Fig. 7. A constraint was added setting the total Cost below a certain threshold. The Carb1.0.iam assembly violated this constraint because it was too expensive.

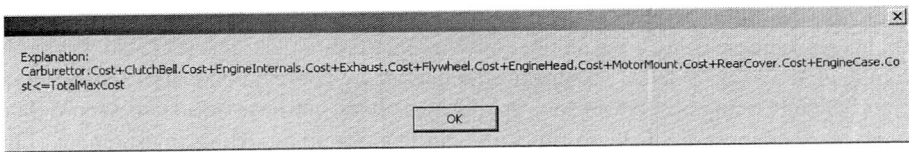

Fig. 8. An explanation showing the cost constraint that the the Carb1.0.iam assembly has violated.

of the CAD system which will have a number of additional capabilities. Some of these are discussed below.

In the current prototype the designer either manually enters the entire functional specification for an artifact, or uses predefined principles. We are currently working on an approach which helps capture new design principles and modifications of existing ones, and store them in the database for future use. In this way, not only will the CAD system be capable of learning from the designer, but will also alleviate a company from having to completely specify a design knowledge-base before the CAD technology is useful. The approach we are adopting is designer-driven. The designer decides what constitutes a sufficiently detailed abstract description of a principle. The system facilitates the designer by storing his concepts, whatever they may be. This feature is critical for real-world deployment; the need to invest heavily in knowledge-base development is a significant disadvantage of many intelligent CAD tools.

In addition to the above, we wish to extend the functional reasoning capabilities of the CAD system in a number of ways. In particular, we are developing a set of standard interface constraints to assist with reasoning about scheme configuration. For

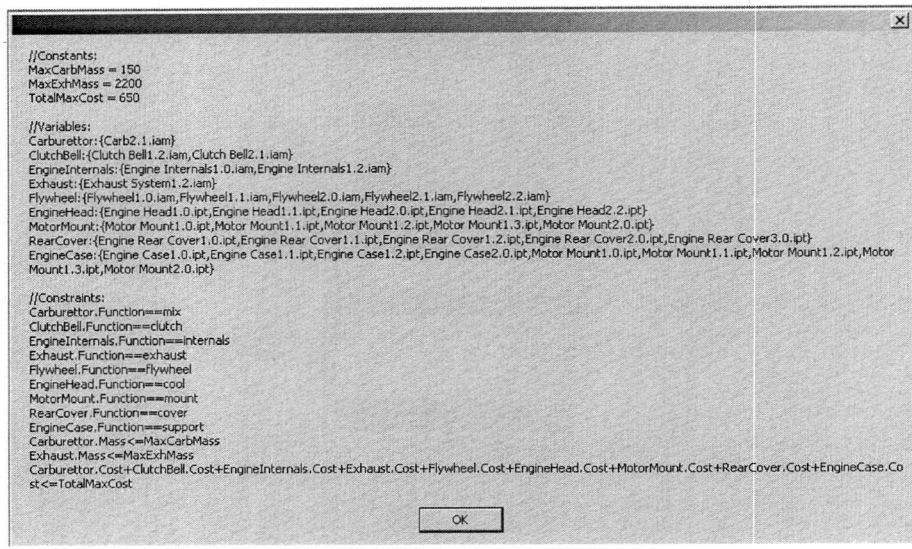

Fig. 9. The CSP after the overall cost constraint was added.

example, the ability to add spatial constraints is important in order to more accurately evaluate schemes. There are a number of other interface constraints that also need to be implemented as primitives, such as mechanical and electrical connections which have some default semantics. At present the designer does not have access to such default interfaces and must define them explicitly within the solid modeling environment of the host CAD system.

At present the functional description of a product is defined textually. We are interested in developing a sketch-based interface for describing the critical functional elements and their relationships. This interface would allow designers to develop their ideas as a marked-up sketch. The mark-up on the sketch would indicate critical elements and the relations between them [22].

Another critical area is explanation generation. We are currently developing novel explanation generation algorithms suited for interactive constraint satisfaction. Improved explanation generation capabilities will also provide us with a basis for providing feedback on comparisons between different design solutions that the designer wishes to consider.

Finally, the approach underlying the CAD technology described here has been evaluated in a number of industrial contexts. In particular, the approach has been evaluated through several case-studies performed in conjunction with industry. Evaluations have been carried out in the fields of discrete electronic design, mechatronics and optical systems. For further details on how the technology has been used in industry, the reader is encouraged to refer to the literature available [14, 15]. In all cases designs of comparable sophistication to those developed by real-world designers and engineers using traditional methods were produced. Further evaluations will be undertaken using the prototypes developed as part of the work reported here.

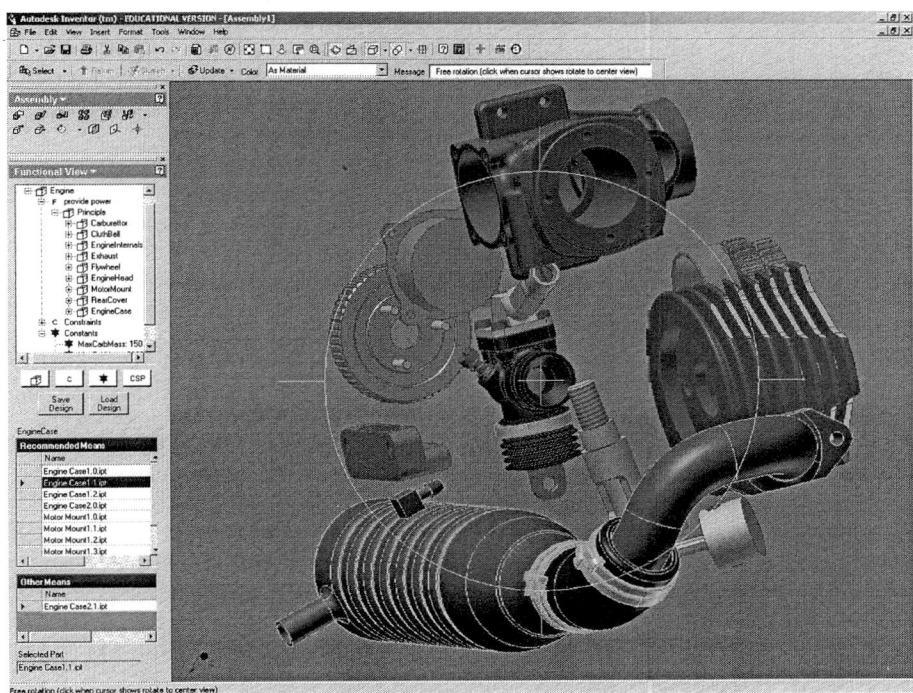

Fig. 10. Developing the scheme's part model in the host CAD system, Autodesk Inventor.

6   Concluding Remarks

Engineering conceptual design can be defined as that phase of the product development process during which the designer takes a specification for a product to be designed and generates many broad solutions to it. It is well recognized that few computational tools exists that are capable of supporting the designer work through the conceptual phase of design. This paper presented a prototype constraint-based computer-aided design (CAD) technology that can be used to support designers working in the early stages of design. We presented the current status of our prototype and a detailed demonstration of its functionality. Finally, we described our current work on a number of additional features for the next prototype, which will be deployed in an industrial context.

References

1. L. Anthony, W.C. Regli, J.E. John, and S.V. Lombeyda. CUP: A computer-aided conceptual design environment for assembly modeling. Technical Report DU-MCS-01005, Department of Mathematics and Computer Science, Drexel University, June 2001.
2. D. Bahler, C. Dupont, and J. Bowen. An axiomatic approach that supports negotiated resolution of design conflicts in Concurrent Engineering. In *Artificial Intelligence in Design*, pages 363–379, 1994. Kluwer Academic Press, Netherlands.

3. C. Bessiere and J.-C. Regin. Arc consistency for general constraint networks: preliminary results. In *Proceedings IJCAI'97*, pages 398–404, 1997.
4. W.P. Birmingham and A. Ward. What is Concurrent Engineering? *Artificial Intelligence for Engineering Design, Analysis and Manufacturing*, 9:67–68, 1995. Guest Editorial in a Special Issue on Concurrent Engineering.
5. J. Bowen and D. Bahler. Frames, quantification, perspectives and negotiation in constraint networks in life-cycle engineering. *Artificial Intelligence in Engineering*, 7:199–226, 1992.
6. J. Buur. *A Theoretical Approach to Mechatronics Design*. PhD thesis, Technical University of Denmark, Lyngby, 1990.
7. M.J. French. *Engineering Design: The Conceptual Stage*. Heinemann, London, 1971.
8. M.D. Gross, S.M. Ervin, J.A. Anderson, and A. Fleisher. Constraints: Knowledge representation in design. *Design Studies*, 9(3):133–143, July 1988.
9. D. Haroud, S. Boulanger, E. Gelle, and I. Smith. Management of conflict for preliminary engineering design tasks. *Artificial Intelligence for Engineering Design, Analysis and Manufacturing*, 9:313–323, 1995.
10. W. Hsu and B. Liu. Conceptual design: Issues and challenges. *Computer-Aided Design*, 32(14):849–850, 2000.
11. C. Lottaz, I.F.C. Smith, Y. Robert-Nicoud, and B.V. Faltings. Constraint-based support for negotiation in collaborative design. *Artificial Intelligence in Engineering*, 14:261–280, 2000.
12. C. Lottaz, R. Stalker, and I. Smith. Constraint solving and preference activation for interactive design. *Artificial Intelligence for Engineering Design, Analysis and Manufacturing*, 12:13–27, 1998.
13. S. Mittal and B. Falkenhainer. Dynamic constraint satisfaction problems. In *AAAI 90*, pages 25–32, July–August 1990.
14. B. O'Sullivan. *Constraint-Aided Conceptual Design*. PhD thesis, Department of Computer Science, University College Cork, Ireland, July 1999. (Also published by Professional Engineering Publishing, 2001, ISBN: 1-86058-335-0).
15. B. O'Sullivan. Interactive Constraint-Aided Conceptual Design. *Journal of Artificial Intelligence for Engineering Design, Analysis and Manufacturing*, 16(4):303–328, 2002.
16. G. Pahl and W. Beitz. *Engineering Design: A systematic approach*. Springer, 1995.
17. C. Petrie, H. Jeon, and M.R. Cutkosky. Combining constraint propagation and backtracking for distributed engineering. In *Workshop on Non-Standard Constraint Processing, ECAI 96*, pages 84–94, August 1996.
18. S. Y. Reddy, K. W. Fertig, and D. E. Smith. Constraint management methodology for conceptual design tradeoff studies. In *Proceedings of the 1996 ASME Design Engineering Technical Conferences and Computers in Engineering Conference*, August 1996. Irvine, California.
19. D. Sabin and R. Weigel. Product configuration frameworks – a survey. *IEEE Intelligent Systems and their applications*, 13(4):42–49, July–August 1998.
20. D. Serrano. *Constraint Management in Conceptual Design*. PhD thesis, MIT, 1987.
21. S. Shimizu and M. Numao. Constraint-based design for 3D shapes. *Artificial Intelligence*, 91:51–69, 1997.
22. T. Stahovich, R. Davis, and H. Shrobe. Generating multiple new designs from a sketch. *Artificial Intelligence*, 104(1–2):211–264, 1998.

Fast Bound Consistency
for the Global Cardinality Constraint

Irit Katriel[*] and Sven Thiel[**]

Max-Planck-Institut für Informatik, Saarbrücken, Germany
{irit,sthiel}@mpi-sb.mpg.de

Abstract. We show an algorithm for bound consistency of *global cardinality constraints*, which runs in time $O(n+n')$ plus the time required to sort the assignment variables by range endpoints, where n is the number of assignment variables and n' is the number of values in the union of their ranges. We thus offer a fast alternative to Régin's arc consistency algorithm [6] which runs in time $O(n^{3/2}n')$ and space $O(n \cdot n')$. Our algorithm can also narrow the bounds for the number of occurrences of each value, which has not been done before.

1 Introduction

The *Global Cardinality Constraint* $GCC(x_1, \cdots, x_n, c_{v_1}, \cdots, c_{v_{n'}})$ is specified on n assignment variables $x_1, \ldots, x_n$ and n' count variables $c_{v_1}, \ldots, c_{v_{n'}}$. The idea is that each assignment variable x_j takes a value in $D = \{v_1, \cdots, v_{n'}\}$ and each value v_i is used exactly c_{v_i} times. With each assignment variable x_j we associate a domain $D_j \subseteq D$, and the domain of a count variable c_{v_i} is an interval $E_i = [L_i, U_i]$. For a tuple $t \in D^n$ and $v \in D$ denote by $occ(v, t)$ the number of occurrences of the value v in t. Then the set S containing all solutions of the constraint is defined as follows:

$$S = \{(w_1, \ldots, w_n; o_1, \ldots, o_{n'}) \mid \forall_j w_j \in D_j \ \wedge \ \forall_i occ(v_i, (w_1, \ldots, w_n)) = o_i \in E_i\}$$

Given a constraint with ranges for the variables, the first question is whether $S \neq \emptyset$, which means that there is an assignment of values to the variables which satisfies the constraint. The *arc consistency* problem for the assignment variables is to reduce the domains of these variables such that D_j is the projection of S onto its jth component. In the *bound consistency* problem we assume $v_1 < \ldots < v_{n'}$ and each D_j is a contiguous interval of values, i.e. $D_j = [\underline{D}_j, \overline{D}_j]$. The problem is to shrink the intervals of both the assignment and the count variables to the minimum sizes such that $S \subseteq D_1 \times \cdots \times D_n \times E_1 \times \cdots \times E_{n'}$. I.e., the domain of the kth variable is bound consistent iff S contains at least one tuple whose kth component equals the smallest (largest) value in the respective domain.

Régin [6] has provided an algorithm that achieves arc consistency for the assignment variables of a GCC, but does not reduce the domains of the count

---

[*] Partially supported by DFG grant SA 933/1-1.
[**] Partially supported by the EU IST Programme, IST-1999-14186 (ALCOM-FT).

F. Rossi (Ed.): CP 2003, LNCS 2833, pp. 437–451, 2003.

variables. He constructs a bipartite graph and computes a maximum flow in it. He then defines the residual graph with respect to this flow, finds the strongly connected components (SCCs) in the residual graph and discards the edges between SCCs that carry no flow. The algorithm runs in time $O(n^{3/2}n')$ and space $O(n \cdot n')$ and is dominated by the complexity of finding a maximum flow using Ford and Fulkerson's algorithm [3].

Mehlhorn and Thiel [5] considered the AllDifferent constraint, which requires that each variable is assigned a different value and is the special case of GCC in which $[L_i, U_i] = [0, 1]$ for all $1 \leq i \leq n'$. They show an algorithm for bound consistency of this restricted case. Though phrased in terms of bipartite matchings, it can also be interpreted as a simplified version of Régin's flow-based algorithm; the maximum flow in this case is a maximum matching in the graph. Their algorithm runs in linear time plus the time required to sort the variables according to the endpoints of their ranges. The improved running time compared to Régin's algorithm is achieved due to the fact that the algorithm exploits the simpler structure of the graph: The assumption that the range of each variable is an interval implies that the bipartite graph is *convex*, which means that the neighborhood of each variable node is a contiguous sequence of value nodes.

For GCC, we show an algorithm of the same flavor that achieves bound consistency for the assignment variables and can also narrow the bounds of the count variables (but in general not to bound consistency). A significant difference between the problems is that in an AllDifferent constraint, only variable nodes must be matched but a value node may or may not be matched. Now, we also have lower bound requirements on the value nodes. We will show, again using matching terminology, that it is still possible to find a maximum flow in the bipartite graph and compute the SCCs in the residual graph in time which is linear in the number of nodes plus the time required for sorting the range endpoints of the assignment variables. This algorithm can be used as a fast and space efficient alternative to Régin's algorithm where bound consistency is enough, or as a preprocessing step to speed up Régin's algorithm where arc consistency is desired. For the full version of this paper, refer to [4]. Source code is available by request from the authors.

2   Preliminaries

2.1   Normalization of the x-Ranges

The x-ranges are called *normalized* if $D = \{1, \cdots, n'\}$. This has the advantage that we can use the values as array indices. Normalization can be achieved by identifying each value v_i with its index i in the sorted order $v_1 \leq \cdots \leq v_n$. To do this we need to compute for every original domain $D_j = [v_{l_j}, v_{h_j}]$ the corresponding normalized domain $D'_j = [l_j, h_j]$. After sorting the endpoints of $D_1, \cdots, D_n$ in ascending order, this can be done in time $O(n + n')$. If the v_i's are integers drawn from the range $[1, n^k]$ for some fixed k, sorting can be done in time $O(n)$. After achieving bound consistency for the normalized domains $D'_1, \ldots, D'_n$, we can easily narrow the original domains to bound consistency.

2.2   A Generalization of Matching

A *matching* in a graph is a subset M of its edges such that each node is adjacent to at most one edge in M. We generalize this notion to capacitated graphs $G = (V, E, C)$ where C is a function that maps every node $\nu \in V$ to an interval $C(\nu) = [L_\nu, U_\nu]$. We call $C(\nu)$ the *capacity requirement* of ν. For a set M of edges and a node ν we denote by $M(\nu)$ the set of all nodes that are adjacent to ν by an edge in M. A *generalized matching* in G is a subset M of its edges such that for each node $\nu \in V$ we have $|M(\nu)| \in [L_\nu, U_\nu]$. We call $M(\nu)$ the set of *matching mates of* ν.

As in [5], we define the *intersection graph* of a GCC, which is in this case a capacitated bipartite graph with n nodes $\{x_1, \cdots, x_n\}$ representing the variables on one side and n' nodes $\{y_1, \cdots, y_{n'}\}$ representing the values in the ranges of the variables on the other side. The capacity ranges of the variable nodes are all $[1, 1]$, indicating that each variable must be assigned exactly one value. For a value node, the capacities are according to the count requirements of the value represented by the node: $\forall_{1 \leq i \leq n'}[L_{y_i}, U_{y_i}] = [L_i, U_i]$, and $\forall_{1 \leq j \leq n}[L_{x_j}, U_{x_j}] = [1, 1]$. The edge (x_j, y_i) exists in the graph if and only if $i \in [\underline{D_j}, \overline{D_j}]$.

Running Example: Throughout the paper, we will illustrate the algorithms with the following example (see Figure 1): $GCC(x_1, \cdots, x_6, c_{v_1}, \cdots, c_{v_4})$ where the assignment variable ranges D_j and the count variable ranges E_i are

E_1	E_2	E_3	E_4
[1,3]	[1,2]	[1,1]	[1,1]

D_1	D_2	D_3	D_4	D_5	D_6
[1,1]	[1,2]	[1,2]	[2,2]	[3,4]	[3,4]

Fig. 1. The intersection graph of the example GCC and a generalized matching in it, marked with bold edges.

Lemma 1. *Let T denote the projection of S onto its first n components. Every generalized matching $M = \{\{x_i, y_{g(i)}\} | 1 \leq i \leq n\}$ corresponds to the tuple $(g(1), \cdots, g(n))$ in T and vice versa.*

Proof. Immediate from the definition of a generalized matching. $\square$

2.3   The Connection to Régin's Algorithm

Régin's algorithm computes a maximum flow in a graph $\vec{H}$ which is similar to our intersection graph with a few differences: It is directed, contains two additional nodes s and t, and the capacity requirements are on the edges and not on the nodes. The edge set of $\vec{H}$ is defined as follows[1]. There is an edge (x_j, y_i) with capacity requirement $[0, 1]$ iff $i \in D_j$. For every y_i there is an edge (y_i, s) with capacity bounds $[L_i, U_i]$, and for every x_j we have the edge (t, x_j) with capacity requirement $[0, 1]$. Régin shows that the constraint has a solution iff the maximum flow from t to s has value n.

His algorithm searches for a flow F of value n. If none exists, it reports failure. Otherwise, it constructs the residual graph $\vec{R}_F$, which allows to determine for each variable the arc consistent values in its domain. $\vec{R}_F$ has the same nodes as $\vec{H}$ (except for t) and the following edges: An edge (x_j, y_i) iff $i \in D_j \wedge F(x_j, y_i) = 0$, an edge (y_i, x_j) iff $i \in D_j \wedge F(x_j, y_i) = 1$, an edge (y_i, s) iff $F(y_i, s) < U_i$, and finally an edge (s, y_i) iff $F(y_i, s) > L_i$. In Corollary 2 in [6], Régin proves that a value i in the domain D_j is consistent for x_j iff $F(x_j, y_i) = 1$ or x_j and y_i belong to the same SCC of $\vec{R}_F$.

A generalized matching M in the intersection graph G corresponds to the flow F_M in $\vec{H}$ such that for each edge (x_j, y_i), $F_M(x_j, y_i) = 1$ if $\{x_j, y_i\} \in M$ and $F_M(x_j, y_i) = 0$ otherwise; $F_M(y_i, s) = |M(y_i)|$ for all i and $F_M(t, x_j) = 1$ for all j. Observe that the total flow from t to s has value n.

As in [5], we augment the residual graph $\vec{R}_{F_M}$ such that we obtain a graph $\vec{G}$ with the following property: A value $i \in D_j$ is arc consistent iff x_j and y_i are in the same SCC of $\vec{G}$. If x_j is matched with y_i in M, $\vec{R}_{F_M}$ contains the edge (y_i, x_j), and in $\vec{G}$ we add the edge (x_j, y_i) in the opposite direction. So if x_j and y_i are matched (equivalently, $F_M(x_j, y_i) = 1$) then they belong to the same SCC of $\vec{G}$. We call $\vec{G}$ the *oriented intersection graph*. Lemma 2 follows easily from the discussion above and Régin's results cited in it:

Lemma 2. *An edge $\{x_j, y_i\}$ in G belongs to a generalized matching iff x_j and y_i are in the same SCC of $\vec{G}$.*

This lemma implies the correctness of the following bound consistency algorithm for the assignment variables:

1. Find a generalized matching in G.
2. Construct $\vec{G}$ and compute its SCCs.
3. Narrow the ranges as much as possible such that they still represent all edges within the SCCs.

We want to point out that our algorithm uses $O(n + n')$ space and does not construct any of these graphs explicitly.

3   Finding a Generalized Matching in the Intersection Graph

The algorithm for finding a generalized matching in a convex graph is given in Figure 2. It makes three passes over the y nodes. In the first two passes it goes

---

[1] The edges in $\vec{H}$ have the opposite direction compared to Régin's graph. We prefer the reversed orientation because it is equivalent and simplifies the following presentation.

from left to right and uses a priority queue P to which x nodes are inserted when they become candidates for matching and in which they are sorted according to the upper endpoints of their domains. That is, the node x that is extracted from P by an *ExtractMin* operation is the one whose domain ends earliest. So any node that remains in P can match the same future y-nodes as x (by convexity), but maybe even more. And hence, it is reasonable to extract x and keep the others.

In the first pass the algorithm ignores the lower bound capacities and finds a generalized matching in the graph $G_{L=0} = (V, E, C_{L=0})$, where $C_{L=0}(y_i) = [0, U_i]$ for all i and $C_{L=0}(x_j) = [1, 1]$ for all j. $G_{L=0}$ is the same as G except that the lower bound capacities of all y nodes are zero. This generalized matching is constructed as follows: The y nodes are traversed from $y_1, \cdots, y_{n'}$. When y_i is reached, all of the x nodes that are connected to y_i, but not to any node with a smaller index, are inserted into the queue; they are now candidates for matching. Then y_i is matched with up to U_i nodes from P (less if P does not contain that many nodes). If, while processing y_i, the algorithm extracts a node from the queue which is not connected to y_i, it reports failure (cf. Lemma 3).

In the second pass, the algorithm makes another traversal of the y nodes in the same order, but this time it ignores the upper bounds and constructs a generalized matching in the graph $G^{U=\infty} = (V, E, C^{U=\infty})$, where $C^{U=\infty}(y_i) = [L_i, \infty]$ for all i and $C^{U=\infty}(x_j) = [1, 1]$ for all j. In this matching, each y node is matched with the minimal number of x nodes such that its lower capacity bound is respected and all x nodes which are not connected to y nodes with higher indices are matched. If the queue becomes empty while the algorithm tries to fulfil the lower capacity bound L_i for node y_i, the algorithm reports failure (see Lemma 6).

The matching found in the first pass is used during the second pass to determine the order in which nodes are inserted into the queue. We will show that if a generalized matching exists, then there also exists a generalized matching such that each y_i is matched only with nodes that were matched in the first pass with nodes from $y_1, \cdots, y_i$ (cf. Lemma 4). Hence, when y_i is reached in the second pass, the nodes that were matched with it in the first pass are inserted into the queue as candidates for matching with it.

The matching found in the second pass may violate the upper capacity bounds in G. The third pass corrects this by traversing the y nodes from $y_{n'}$ to y_1 and shifting these excesses to y nodes with lower indices.

The table below shows the mate of x_j in our running example after each pass of the algorithm.

j	1	2	3	4	5	6
pass 1	1	1	1	2	2	3
pass 2	1	2	2	2	3	4
pass 3	1	1	2	2	3	4

Lemma 3. *If the algorithm reports failure in the first pass, then there is no generalized matching in $G_{L=0}$. And hence, there is also none in G.*

(* Input: (1) Ranges of assignment variables $D_j = [\underline{D}_j, \overline{D}_j]$ for each x_j, $1 \leq j \leq n$ *)
(*   (2) A capacity requirement $[L_i, U_i]$ for each $1 \leq i \leq n'$. *)
(* Output: A generalized matching if it exists, *failure* otherwise. *)

(* 1st pass: find a matching in $G_{L=0}$ (encoded in m) *)
$P \leftarrow [\,]$ (* priority queue containing x nodes sorted according to $\overline{D}$ *)
$j \leftarrow 0$; $U_{n'+1} \leftarrow \infty$
for $i = 1$ to $n' + 1$ **do**
    forall x_h with $\underline{D}_h = i$ **do** $P.Insert\ x_h$
    $u \leftarrow 0$
    while P is not empty and $u < U_i$ **do**
        $j \leftarrow j + 1$; $x_{f(j)} \leftarrow P.ExtractMin$
        $m[f(j)] \leftarrow i$; $u \leftarrow u + 1$
        if $\overline{D}_{f(j)} < i$ **then** report failure
        (* No failure implies $i \in D_{f(j)}$ *)
    end
    $\beta_i \leftarrow j$
endfor

(* 2nd pass: find a matching in $G^{U=\infty}$ and ensure feasibility for G *)
$j \leftarrow 0$; $\alpha_0 \leftarrow 0$
for $i = 1$ to n' **do**
    forall x_h with $m[h] = i$ **do** $P.Insert\ x_h$
    for $\ell = 1$ to L_i **do**
        if P is empty **then** report failure
        $j \leftarrow j + 1$; $x_{g(j)} \leftarrow P.ExtractMin$
        match $y_i \leftrightarrow x_{g(j)}$ (* $m[g(j)] \leq i$ *)
    endfor
    while P is not empty and $P.MinPriority < i + 1$ **do**
        $j \leftarrow j + 1$; $x_{g(j)} \leftarrow P.ExtractMin$
        match $y_i \leftrightarrow x_{g(j)}$ (* $m[g(j)] \leq i$ *)
    end
    $\alpha_i \leftarrow j$
endfor

(* 3rd pass: transform the matching from 2nd pass into a matching in G *)
for $i = n'$ to 1 **do**
    if y_i has currently h mates s.th. $e := h - U_i > 0$ **then**
        for $k = 1$ to e **do**
            choose a current mate x_{j_k} of y_i with $i' := m[j_k] < i$
            match $y_{i'} \leftrightarrow x_{j_k}$ (* y_i looses x_{j_k} *)
        endfor
    endif
endfor

Fig. 2. Algorithm for generalized matching in a convex capacitated bipartite graph.

Proof. Suppose the algorithm reports failure in iteration i after extracting a node x_j (observe that any extraction in iteration $n' + 1$ causes failure.) Then in iteration $i - 1$ it only extracts x nodes that are not connected to y_i, and P contains x_j afterwards. Let i' be the maximum iteration before $i - 1$ such that an x node connected to y_i is extracted or P becomes empty during iteration i'. If no such iteration exists, choose $i' = 0$. Let X denote the x nodes extracted in iterations $i' + 1, \cdots, i - 1$. Since P never becomes empty during these iterations, we have $|X| = \sum_{k=i'+1}^{i-1} U_k$, i.e. X exhausts the capacities of the nodes in $Y = \{y_{i'+1}, \cdots, y_{i-1}\}$.

The nodes in X are not connected to y_i or a y node to its right. We show that there is also no connection to $y_{i'}$ or a y node to its left. Suppose otherwise, i.e. $x_\ell \in X$ is connected to $y_{i''}$ with $i'' \leq i'$. As x_ℓ was inserted to P in iteration i' or earlier and is extracted in a later iteration, P was never empty in iteration i'. By the choice of i', this implies that a node $x_{j'}$ connected to y_i was extracted in iteration i'. As x_l was removed later, it must also be connected to y_i, a contradiction to the choice of i'. Thus all neighbors of the nodes in X are in Y. A similar argument proves that the node x_j, which caused the failure in iteration i, is only connected to nodes in Y.

Since a generalized matching in $G^{U=\infty}$ would have to match the nodes in Y with at least $|X| + 1$ nodes, but can only match them with $|X|$ different nodes, such a matching cannot exist. □

For any matching M and subset $Y \subseteq \{y_1, \cdots, y_{n'}\}$, let $M(Y) = \bigcup_{y \in Y} M(y)$, i.e. $M(Y)$ is the set of all x nodes that are matched with nodes of Y.

Lemma 4. *If there is a generalized matching M' in G, then there is also a generalized matching M with the following property: For all edges $\{x_j, y_i\} \in M$, we have $m[j] \leq i$.*
M can be chosen such that $|M(y_i)| = |M'(y_i)|$ for $i = 1 \cdots, n'$. And hence, it is impossible to match $\{y_1, \cdots, y_i\}$ with more than β_i nodes[2].

Proof. Let M' be a generalized matching in G, and suppose it does not have the desired property. Let i be minimal such that there is an edge $\{x_j, y_i\}$ with $k = m[j] > i$. Not all nodes x_ℓ with $m[\ell] = i$ can be matched with y_i in M', otherwise neither the queue nor the capacity of y_i would have been exhausted after iteration i in the first pass. So there is an edge $\{x_{j'}, y_{i'}\} \in M'$ with $i' \neq i$ and $m[j'] = i$. By the choice of i we have $i' > i$. When $x_{j'}$ was extracted in the first pass, x_j was also in the queue. So we conclude that x_j is also connected to $y_{i'}$. Thus we can swap the mates of x_j and $x_{j'}$ and obtain a new generalized matching M''. M'' does not violate the property for the nodes $y_1, \cdots, y_{i-1}$ and the number of violations at y_i is less than in M'. This shows that we can transform the matching until we eventually obtain a matching M with the desired property. The last statement follows from the fact that $\beta_i = |\{x_j \mid m[j] \leq i\}|$. □

Lemma 5. *If the algorithm does not report failure in iteration i of the second pass, then for any generalized matching M in G we have $|M(\{y_1, \cdots, y_i\})| \geq \alpha_i$.*

---

[2] We will refer to the β_i values in Section 5.

Proof. By induction on i. For $i = 0$ and $i = 1$ the claim is easy to verify. So let us assume that it holds for $i' = 1, \cdots, i-1$ and prove it for i. If the body of the while-loop is not executed, we have $\alpha_i = \alpha_{i-1} + L_i$, and applying the induction for $i' = i - 1$ immediately proves the claim. So suppose that nodes are extracted in the while-loop, which implies that no x that is extracted in iteration i is connected to y_{i+1}. Let i' be the maximum iteration before i such that a node connected to y_{i+1} is removed. If no such iteration exists, choose $i' = 0$. Let X denote the x nodes extracted in the iterations $i' + 1, \ldots, i$, and let $Y = \{y_{i'+1}, \cdots, y_i\}$. A similar argument as in the proof of Lemma 3 shows that the neighbors of any node $x \in X$ are contained in Y. Thus $|M(Y)| \geq |X| = \alpha_i - \alpha_{i'}$. By the induction hypothesis for i', $|M(\{y_1, \cdots, y_i\})| \geq \alpha_{i'} + |M(Y)| = \alpha_i$. $\square$

Lemma 6. *If the algorithm reports failure in the second pass, then there is no generalized matching in G.*

Proof. Suppose that the algorithm reports failure in iteration i, although a generalized matching M exists. By Lemma 4, we can assume that for any edge $\{x_j, y_k\}$ in M we have $m[j] \leq k$. So $y_1, \cdots, y_i$ are matched only with nodes that have been inserted into P so far. From the previous lemma we can conclude that there must be at least $\alpha_{i-1} + L_i$ such nodes. But since the algorithm reports failure, this is not the case, a contradiction to the existance of M. $\square$

Lemma 7. *If the algorithm does not report failure, it constructs a generalized matching in G.*

Proof. If the second pass succeeds, we have a generalized matching in $G^{U=\infty}$, because we fulfil the lower capacity bounds of every y node (cf. the for-loop), and we match every x node with a neighbor on the y side (see the while-loop). So the only problem is the upper capacity bounds of the y nodes. The third pass takes care of these. Observe that this pass sweeps over the y nodes from right to left and distributes the excess mates of a node y_i only to y nodes with lower indices, so that it cannot increase the number of mates of a y node after it was processed. Furthermore, if x_j is matched with y_i at some point in time then $m[j] \leq i$. Since we have equality for at most U_i nodes, we can always select e excessive mates to distribute, if necessary. Suppose a node x_j is removed from y_i and matched with $y_{i'}$ in the third pass, where $i' = m[j]$. From the first pass, it is easy to see that $i' \in D_j$, i.e., x_j and $y_{i'}$ are connected. $\square$

Implementing the Algorithm in Linear Time (for Normalized Domains)

Now we discuss some implementation details of the algorithm. First we show how to implement it in time $O(n' + n \log n)$, and then we refine this implementation to obtain $O(n' + n)$ time. In the first variant we use a binary heap of size n to implement the priority queue P. Then the operations *Insert* and *ExtractMin* take time $O(\log n)$ and *MinPriority* runs in constant time. Before we run the algorithm we sort the x nodes according to their lower range endpoints, which takes time $O(n + n')$ because all domains are in $[1, n']$. This sorting allows us to determine efficiently the nodes that have to be inserted into P in each iteration of the first pass. Recall that the order by which the x nodes are extracted in the first pass determines the order by which they are inserted in the second pass. So the two passes can be implemented in time $O(n' + n \log n)$. The third pass takes linear time. To see this we notice that every x node changes its mate at most once. So we maintain for every y node two seperate lists for the mates that it received in the second and the third pass respectively. Thus we can make sure that we process every x node only once.

In order to shave off the logarithmic factor in the running time, we have to find a faster implementation of the priority queue. As in [5] we simulate the priority queue by creating an instance of the offline-min problem [1, Chapter 4.8], which can be solved in linear time using a special union-find data structure [2]. (The offline-min algorithm needs a sorting of the x's according to their upper interval endpoints, which can be computed in time $O(n + n')$.)

Except for failure detection, the algorithm does not use the mapping f in the first pass at all. So the whole sequence σ of *Insert* and *ExtractMin* operations can be computed without knowing the results of the extractions. Checking if P is empty can be done by counting the number of insertions and comparing it with the number of extractions (which is equal to j). Failure detection can be done after the mapping f has been computed.

We give a brief description of the offline-min algorithm. When it is applied to a sequence σ it determines for every insertion the corresponding extraction. Let $E_1, \cdots, E_n$ be the extract operations in the order in which they occur in σ. The node x_j with minimum priority is the output of the first extraction E_k that follows its insertion. After deleting E_k from σ we process the x with next higher priority, and so on. We implement this with a union-find structure that maintains a partition $\mathcal{P}$ of $E_1, \cdots, E_n$. Every set in $\mathcal{P}$ has the form $\{E_h, E_{h+1}, \cdots, E_k\}$, where all extractions except for E_k have been deleted. Suppose we process x_j and let E_s be the first extraction in the original sequence after the insertion of x_j. Observe that E_s may have been deleted already. To determine the extraction E_k for x_j, we simply have to find the set S in $\mathcal{P}$ containing E_s. Deleting E_k amounts to uniting S with the set of E_{k+1}.

We cannot use the offline-min algorithm directly for the second pass, because we need to know the result of the *MinPriority* operation in the while-loop online. But a slight enhancement will do the job (see Figure 3). We initialize our data structures as above but we only create a set for the mandatory extractions that are made in the for-loop. When we find a tentative extraction E_k for x_j, we verify that E_k occurs in iteration $i \leq \overline{D}_j$. If not, then we know that x_j is extracted by the while-loop in iteration $\overline{D}_j$, and we do not delete E_k. We want to point out that we detect failure if there is a mandatory extraction for which no corresponding insertion is found. Assuming w.l.o.g. that $\sum_{i=1}^{n'} L_i \leq n$, the algorithm runs in time $O(n' + n)$.

$k \leftarrow 1$ (* E_k will always be the next mandatory extraction *)
for $i = 1$ to n' **do**
    forall x_j with $m[j] = i$ **do** $s[j] \leftarrow k$ (* x's inserted in iteration i (before E_k) *)
    for $\ell = 1$ to L_i **do**
        create set $\{E_k\}$ labelled $\mathcal{L}_k^{(i,\ell)}$ (* for mandatory extraction ℓ in iter. i *)
        $k \leftarrow k + 1$
    endfor
endfor
create set $\{E_k\}$ labelled with $\mathcal{L}_k^{(n'+1,0)}$ (* dummy extraction *)
forall x_j sorted in ascending according to $\overline{D}$ **do**
    $S \leftarrow \mathrm{find}(E_{s[j]})$; let $\mathcal{L}_k^{(i,\ell)}$ be its label
    if $i \leq \overline{D}_j$ **then**
        x_j is removed by extraction ℓ in the for-loop of iteration i
        unite S with the set S' containing E_{k+1} and
            label the union with the former label of S'
    else
        x_j is extracted by the while-loop in iteration $\overline{D}_j$
    endif
endfor

Fig. 3. Enhanced offline-min algorithm for the second pass.

4 Finding the SCCs of the Oriented Intersection Graph

As described in Section 1, we construct an oriented graph $\vec{G}$ from the intersection graph and the generalized matching M (see Figure 4). The edges which are not within a strongly connected component of $\vec{G}$ describe inconsistent assignments of values to variables. Mehlhorn and Thiel [5] gave an algorithm that finds the SCCs of a simpler oriented intersection graph in $O(n+n')$ time. Their graph does not contain the additional node s, which violates the convexity property of the graph because there is an edge from s to each node in $\{y_i : |M(y_i)| > L_i\}$, and this set is not necessarily consecutive. We first use their algorithm to compute the SCCs of the graph $\vec{G}\backslash s$. We can do this despite the fact that now a y node may be matched with more than one x node by merging its neighbors into one x node (note that the neighbors of this merged x node still form an interval of the y-nodes). Let C_s denote the SCC of the node s in $\vec{G}$. An SCC of G which is disjoint from C_s is also an SCC of $\vec{G}\backslash s$. C_s, however, contains the union of zero or more SCCs of $\vec{G}\backslash s$. We wish to find these SCCs and merge them to obtain C_s. Each of these SCCs has the property that it can reach s and can be reached from s. For each SCC C we compute two flags, $reached\_from\_s[C]$ and $reaches\_s[C]$, and merge all components for which both flags are set to true into C_s.

We will use the following notation. For each SCC C of $\vec{G}\backslash s$, let $min\_y[C] = \min\{i|y_i \in C\}$ and $max\_y[C] = \max\{i|y_i \in C\}$ be the lowest and highest indices of y nodes in C. Moreover, let $reaches\_left[C] = \min\{\underline{D}_j|x_j \in C\}$ and $reaches\_right[C] = \max\{\overline{D}_j|x_j \in C\}$ be the minimum and maximum indices of y nodes that can be reached from C.

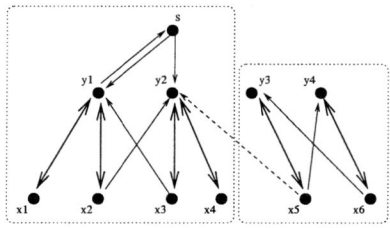

Fig. 4. The oriented intersection graph for our running example. It has two SCCs: $\{s, x_1, x_2, x_3, x_4, y_1, y_2\}$ and $\{x_5, x_6, y_3, y_4\}$. The dashed edge is inconsistent.

Lemma 8. *C can reach every y_i with reaches_left$[C] \leq i \leq$ reaches_right$[C]$ by one edge from an x node in C.*

Proof. The proof appears in [4]. It is simple and relies on the convexity.   □

Now we will explain how to determine whether s can reach a component C. If this is the case then there is a path Q from s to some node y_i in C. And hence, if we delete the first edge of Q, we obtain a path P from a node $y_{i'}$ to y_i in $\vec{G}\backslash s$. In the lemma below, we state that this implies the existence of path P' from $y_{i'}$ to y_i that traverses the SCCs of $\vec{G}\backslash s$ in monotonous manner, either from left to right (cf. Condition (1)) or from right to left (cf. Condition (2)):

Lemma 9. *If there is a path from y_{i_1} to y_{i_k} in $\vec{G}\backslash s$ then there is a path $P = (y_{i_1}, x_{j_1}) \circ (x_{j_1}, y_{i_2}) \circ \cdots \circ (x_{j_{k-1}}, y_{i_k})$ in $\vec{G}\backslash s$ such that if we let C_κ denote the component of y_{i_κ} for each $1 \leq \kappa \leq k$, then one of the following holds:*

$$\forall_{1 \leq \kappa < k}\ min\_y[C_\kappa] \leq min\_y[C_{\kappa+1}] \quad \text{right-monotony} \tag{1}$$

$$\forall_{1 \leq \kappa < k}\ max\_y[C_\kappa] \geq max\_y[C_{\kappa+1}] \quad \text{left-monotony} \tag{2}$$

Proof. If P visits more than one component, let κ be the smallest index such that $C_\kappa \neq C_{\kappa+1}$. Assume that Condition (1) holds for κ. If P does not fulfil Condition (1), then there are three components C_1, C_2, C_3 which are visited consecutively by P in that order such that $min\_y[C_1] < min\_y[C_2]$ and $min\_y[C_3] < min\_y[C_2]$. We will show that there is a path which skips C_2 and goes directly from C_1 to C_3.
If $min\_y[C_3] < min\_y[C_1] < min\_y[C_2]$ then by Lemma 8, C_2 can reach C_1 by a single edge, which closes a cycle that visits both of them. This means that $C_1 = C_2$, in contradiction to the assumption that they are distinct.
We therefore know that $min\_y[C_1] < min\_y[C_3] < min\_y[C_2]$. Then by Lemma 8, C_1 can reach C_3 by one edge. So we can construct a path from y_{i_1} to y_{i_k} which visits the same components as P except that it goes from C_1 directly to C_3 without going through C_2. Since this decreases the number of transitions between components along the path, we can obtain a monotonous path by a finite number of such modifications.
Similarly, if Condition (2) holds for κ then we can find a path that fulfils Condition (2) for all $1 \leq \kappa < k$. Assume that neither condition holds. Then

$min\_y[C_{\kappa+1}] < min\_y[C_{\kappa}]$ and $max\_y[C_{\kappa}] < max\_y[C_{\kappa+1}]$. By Lemma 8, $C_{\kappa+1}$ reaches back to C_{κ}, a contradiction.   □

The algorithm in Figure 5 performs a left to right scan and marks all the components of $\vec{G}\backslash s$ that can be reached from s via a right-monotonous path. In the initialization phase it marks all components that can be reached from s by a single edge and during the scan it marks each component that can be reached from a scanned marked component by one edge. The running time is $O(n')$.

---

forall SCCs C of $\vec{G}\backslash s$ **do** $reached\_from\_s[C] \leftarrow false$
for $i = 1$ to n' **do if** (s, y_i) exists **then** $reached\_from\_s[C[y_i]] \leftarrow$ true
(* Scan from left to right and find the maximum y's reached from s *)
$y\_reached \leftarrow 0$ (* Index of the rightmost y node that can be reached from s *)
for $i = 1$ to n' **do**
    $C \leftarrow C[y_i]$
    if $y\_reached \geq i$ **then** $reached\_from\_s[C] \leftarrow$ true
    if $reached\_from\_s[C]$ **then** $y\_reached \leftarrow \max\{y\_reached, reaches\_right[C]\}$
endfor

Fig. 5. Algorithm to mark SCCs that are reached from s via a right-monotonous path.

Lemma 10. *The algorithm in Figure 5 sets $reached\_from\_s[C]$ to true iff s can reach C by a right-monotonous path.*

Proof. It is easy to see that if a component becomes marked, then it can be reached from s. For the converse, let $P = (s, y_{i_1}) \circ \cdots \circ (y_{i_{k-1}}, x_{j_{k-1}}) \circ (x_{j_{k-1}}, y_{i_k})$ be a path such that P without its first edge is right-monotonous. We will show by induction on the length of P that after the i_k-th iteration, the component C_k of y_{i_k} is marked "reached from s".
For $|P| = 1$: $P = (s, y_{i_1})$ and the component of y_{i_1} is marked before the scan.
For $|P| > 1$: By the induction hypothesis, $reached\_from\_s[C_{k-1}]$ is set to true after iteration $min\_y[C_{k-1}]$ [3]. Since $x_{j_{k-1}}$ is in C_{k-1}, $reaches\_right[C_{k-1}] \geq i_k \geq min\_y[C_k]$. In iteration $min\_y[C_{k-1}]$, $y\_reached$ is set to at least $min\_y[C_k]$. By Lemma 9, we know that iteration $min\_y[C_k]$ does not preceed iteration $min\_y[C_{k-1}]$. Since the index $y\_reached$ can only increase, we get that in iteration $min\_y[C_k]$, C_k will be marked as reached from s.   □

A symmetric algorithm can be used to find the components that can be reached from s by a left-monotonous path. To find the components that can reach s, we can use the same approach: If we delete the last edge of a path in $\vec{G}$ from a node in C to s, we obtain a path in $\vec{G}\backslash s$. So we can mark all components that can reach s by two scans in time $O(n')$.

---

[3] We may assume w.l.o.g. that if P visits a component C then it also visits the node $y_{min\_y[C]}$.

5   Narrowing the Bounds of the x-Ranges

Let S denote the set of all solutions of the constraint, as defined in the introduction, and for $j = 1, \ldots, n$ let S_j be the projection of S onto the jth component. We will discuss how to compute the values $\overline{S}_1, \ldots, \overline{S}_n$ in time $O(n + n')$, a symmetric procedure can be used for the lower endpoints of the narrowed ranges.

Consider a node x_j and let C be its SCC in $\vec{G}$. By Lemma 2, a value $i \in D_j$ is contained in S_j iff $y_i \in C$. Thus $\overline{S}_j$ is the index of the rightmost y node in C that is connected to x_j. Suppose the y nodes $y_{i_1}, \ldots, y_{i_k}$ in C are sorted such that $i_1 < \cdots < i_k$. Then $\overline{S}_j = i_\kappa$ where $i_\kappa \le \overline{D}_j < i_{\kappa+1}$ (and $i_{k+1} = n' + 1$). So let us further assume that the x nodes $x_{j_1}, \ldots, x_{j_l}$ in C are sorted such that $\overline{D}_{j_1} \le \cdots \le \overline{D}_{j_l}$. Then we can determine $\overline{S}_j$ for every x_j in C by merging the sorted sequences $(i_1, \ldots, i_k)$ and $(\overline{D}_{j_1}, \ldots, \overline{D}_{j_l})$ in time $O(k + l)$.

We need to say how these sorted sequences are constructed. For the y's this can be done with bucketsort. We have a bucket for each component, and for $i = 1, \ldots, n'$, we append y_i to the bucket corresponding to its component. This takes time $O(n')$ and constructs the y-sequences for all SCCs of $\vec{G}$. Since we have a global sorting of the x's according to their upper range endpoints, we can use the same approach to sort them in time $O(n)$.

For the first SCC of our example we would merge the y sequence $(1, 2)$ with the x upper bounds $(2_{x_1}, 3_{x_2}, 3_{x_3})$ and narrow the domains of x_2 and x_3 from $[1, 3]$ to $[1, 2]$.

6   Narrowing the Bounds of the Count Variables

This section deals with the projections of S onto its components $S_{n+1}, \cdots, S_{n+n'}$. We show how to compute lower and upper bounds for the values in S_{n+i} for each $i = 1, \cdots, n'$. For the rest of this section we consider a fixed graph G. We assume that the generalized matching algorithm has computed the α_i and β_i values for G and terminated without reporting failure. Now we show that in any generalized matching, the number of x nodes matched to each y_i are in a certain range that we can compute in linear time.

Lemma 11. *Let M be a generalized matching and for $i = 1, \cdots, n'$ let $\mu_i = |M(\{y_i\})|$. Then for all i*

$$\max\left(L_i, n - \beta_{i-1} - \sum_{j=i+1}^{n'} \mu_j \right) \le \mu_i \le \min\left(U_i, n - \alpha_{i-1} - \sum_{j=i+1}^{n'} \mu_j \right) \quad (*)$$

Proof. By the choice of the μ's we have $|M(\{y_1, \cdots, y_{i-1}\})| = n - \sum_{j=i}^{n'} \mu_j$. By Lemmas 4, 5 we know that $\alpha_{i-1} \le |M(\{y_1, \cdots, y_{i-1}\})| \le \beta_{i-1}$.
Therefore $\alpha_{i-1} \le n - \sum_{j=i}^{n'} \mu_j \le \beta_{i-1}$ or $n - \beta_{i-1} \le \sum_{j=i}^{n'} \mu_j \le n - \alpha_{i-1}$.
And hence $n - \beta_{i-1} - \sum_{j=i+1}^{n'} \mu_j \le \mu_i \le n - \alpha_{i-1} - \sum_{j=i+1}^{n'} \mu_j$. $\square$

This motivates the following definition. We call a sequence $(\mu_s, \cdots, \mu_{n'})$ a *legal count choice* iff inequality (*) is satisfied for all i in $[s, n']$. The Lemma above implies that any generalized matching M in G induces the legal choice $(|M(y_1)|, \ldots, |M(y_{n'})|)$. This allows us to compute for any y_i a lower bound l_i and an upper bound u_i on $|M(y_i)|$. Unfortunately there exist examples where our bounds are not tight[4].

Apart from these bounds the algorithm below determines two count choices. The algorithm maintains the invariant that in iteration i both $(\kappa_i, \ldots, \kappa_{n'})$ and $(\lambda_i, \ldots, \lambda_{n'})$ are legal count choices such that for any legal count choice $(\mu_i, \ldots, \mu_{n'})$ we have $\sum_{j=i}^{n'} \kappa_j \leq \sum_{j=i}^{n'} \mu_j \leq \sum_{j=i}^{n'} \lambda_j$. As all sums that appear in the algorithm can be computed incrementally, the running time is $O(n')$.

for $i = n'$ **to** 1 **do**

$$l_i \leftarrow \max\left(L_i, n - \beta_{i-1} - \sum_{j=i+1}^{n'} \lambda_j\right); \; u_i \leftarrow \min\left(U_i, n - \alpha_{i-1} - \sum_{j=i+1}^{n'} \kappa_j\right)$$

$$\kappa_i \leftarrow \max\left(L_i, n - \beta_{i-1} - \sum_{j=i+1}^{n'} \kappa_j\right); \; \lambda_i \leftarrow \min\left(U_i, n - \alpha_{i-1} - \sum_{j=i+1}^{n'} \lambda_j\right)$$

endfor

We will now prove by induction on i that the algorithm computes the correct bounds for the count variables and that the invariant holds. For $i = n'$ Lemma 11 implies that $l_{n'}$ and $u_{n'}$ are lower and upper bounds. Since all sums are empty, we have $\kappa_{n'} = l_{n'}$ and $\lambda_{n'} = u_{n'}$, and hence, the claimed invariant holds.

For the induction step, we assume that our claim holds for $i + 1$ and deduce it for i. By the left-hand side of inequality (*), we see that the minimum legal value for μ_i is obtained if $\sum_{j=i+1}^{n'} \mu_j$ is set to its largest possible value. Applying the invariant for $i + 1$ this sum is maximized by the legal choice $(\lambda_{i+1}, \ldots, \lambda_{n'})$. So by Lemma 11, the algorithm computes a lower bound l_i. A similar argument holds for the upper bound u_i. By the definition of a legal choice, extending our two count choices by κ_i and λ_i respectively yields two legal choices again.

Fix a legal choice $(\mu_i, \ldots, \mu_{n'})$. What remains to prove are the two inequalities on the sum of the μ's.

$$\sum_{j=i}^{n'} \mu_j = \mu_i + \sum_{j=i+1}^{n'} \mu_j \overset{\text{L 11}}{\geq} \max\left(L_i, n - \beta_{i-1} - \sum_{j=i+1}^{n'} \mu_j\right) + \sum_{j=i+1}^{n'} \mu_j$$

$$= \max\left(L_i + \sum_{j=i+1}^{n'} \mu_j, n - \beta_{i-1}\right)$$

$$\overset{\text{IH}}{\geq} \max\left(L_i + \sum_{j=i+1}^{n'} \kappa_j, n - \beta_{i-1}\right)$$

$$= \max\left(L_i, n - \beta_{i-1} - \sum_{j=i+1}^{n'} \kappa_j\right) + \sum_{j=i+1}^{n'} \kappa_j$$

$$= \kappa_i + \sum_{j=i+1}^{n'} \kappa_j = \sum_{j=i}^{n'} \kappa_j$$

An analogous computation shows $\sum_{j=i}^{n'} \mu_j \leq \sum_{j=i}^{n'} \lambda_j$, so we can derive:

Lemma 12. *Suppose that $S \neq \emptyset$ and let $\ell_1, \cdots, \ell_{n'}$ and $u_1, \cdots, u_{n'}$ be the values computed by our algorithm. Then $\underline{S}_{n+i} \geq \ell_i$ and $\overline{S}_{n+i} \leq u_i$ holds for $i = 1, \cdots, n$.*

---

[4] Choosing $D_1 = [1, 3]$, $D_2 = [2, 2]$ and $E_1 = E_2 = E_3 = [0, 1]$ is such an example. The lower endpoint of E_2 will not be narrowed to 1 by our algorithm.

On our running example, the algorithm computes the values listed below:

i	l_i	u_i	κ_i	λ_i	$\sum_{j=i}^{n'} \kappa_i$	$\sum_{j=i}^{n'} \lambda_i$
4	1	1	1	1	1	1
3	1	1	1	1	2	2
2	1	2	1	2	3	4
1	2	3	3	2	6	6

The c-ranges are therefore narrowed to $E_1 = [\mathbf{2}, \mathbf{2}]$, $E_2 = [1, \mathbf{1}]$, $E_3 = [1, \mathbf{2}]$ and $E_4 = [0, \mathbf{1}]$, where the narrowed endpoints are typeset in bold.

7   Conclusion

We have designed a propagation algorithm for the Global Cardinality Constraint that achieves bound consistency for the assignment variables. We wish to point out that there are two possible implementations for the algorithm. One runs in time $O((n' + n) \log n)$, uses very simple data structures and performs well in practice. The other requires more elaborate data structures (for the offline-min computation) and achieves a running time of $O(n + n')$, plus the time required to sort the assignment variables by the endpoints of their ranges. In some cases the latter is asymptotically better.

In addition, we present an algorithm that narrows the bounds of the count variables, but it does not always achieve bounds consistency. So the following question remains open: Is there an efficient algorithm that achieves bound consistency for the count variables?

References

1. A. Aho, J. Hopcroft, and J. Ullman. *The Design and Analysis of Computer Algorithms*. Addison-Wesley, 1974.
2. H.N. Gabow and R.E. Tarjan. A Linear-Time Algorithm for a Special Case of Disjoint Set Union. *Journal of Computer and System Sciences*, 30(2):209–221, 1985.
3. L. R. Ford Jr. and D. R. Fulkerson. *Flows in Networks*. Princeton University Press, 1962.
4. I. Katriel and S. Thiel. Fast bound consistency for the global cardinality constraint. Research Report MPI-I-2003-1-013, Max-Planck-Institut für Informatik, Saarbrücken, Germany, 2003.
5. K. Mehlhorn and S. Thiel. Faster Algorithms for Bound-Consistency of the Sortedness and the Alldifferent Constraint. In *Proceedings of the 6th International Conference on Principles and Practice of Constraint Programming (CP 2000)*, volume 1894 of *LNCS*, pages 306–319, 2000.
6. J.-C. Régin. Generalized Arc-Consistency for Global Cardinality Constraint. In *Proceedings of the 13th National Conference on Artificial Intelligence (AAAI-96)*, pages 209–215, 1996.

Propagating N-Ary Rigid-Body Constraints

Ludwig Krippahl and Pedro Barahona

Dep. de Informática, Universidade Nova de Lisboa, 2859-516 Monte de Caparica, Portugal
{ludi,pb}@di.fct.unl.pt

Abstract. The paper presents an algorithm to propagate an n-ary constraint (with n greater than 2) specifying the relative positions of points in a three-dimensional rigid group. The variables to restrict are the positions (x, y, and z coordinates) of the points, and we assume the variable domains are cuboids, with the faces orthogonal to the coordinate axes. This algorithm is part of PSICO (Processing Structural Information with Constraint programming and Optimisation), a method we are developing to integrate experimental and theoretical data to solve protein structures [1,2]. We also present some preliminary results, and explain how this algorithm can be used to combine theoretical information such as secondary structure prediction or homology modelling with Nuclear Magnetic Resonance (NMR) data.

1 Introduction

Our motivation for developing this algorithm is the study of protein structure. Proteins play essential parts in living systems, and protein structure and function are important for modern biotechnology and pharmaceutical industries. Constant developments in molecular biology are shifting the emphasis of biochemical studies to structure and function; over-expression, isolation, and sequencing have become relatively straight-forward, and there is a large supply of material for structural studies.

Concurrently, improved understanding of metabolic pathways and determination of the complete genomes of some organisms have increased the demand for structural data on proteins, an important step towards metabolic engineering. The result is that protein structural studies are now a major component of biochemical research.

The algorithm we present here will help integrate structural information from different sources. As part of PSICO, it will provide an efficient solver for structural NMR data, but, more than that, it will allow PSICO to complement experimental data with theoretical predictions of secondary structures or homology models. We hope that this integration — the ability to use all the available data in a single solver, instead of modelling different parts separately — will be a useful feature for protein structure determination.

A protein consists of one or more chains of amino acids. The amino acids bind together in a condensation reaction that creates covalent bonds between them. These chains are flexible because the atoms can rotate around some covalent bonds, but most bonds are rigid, with fixed lengths and angles. We can imagine the protein as flexible chains of rigid groups containing a few atoms, as illustrated on Figure 1.

F. Rossi (Ed.): CP 2003, LNCS 2833, pp. 452–465, 2003.
© Springer-Verlag Berlin Heidelberg 2003

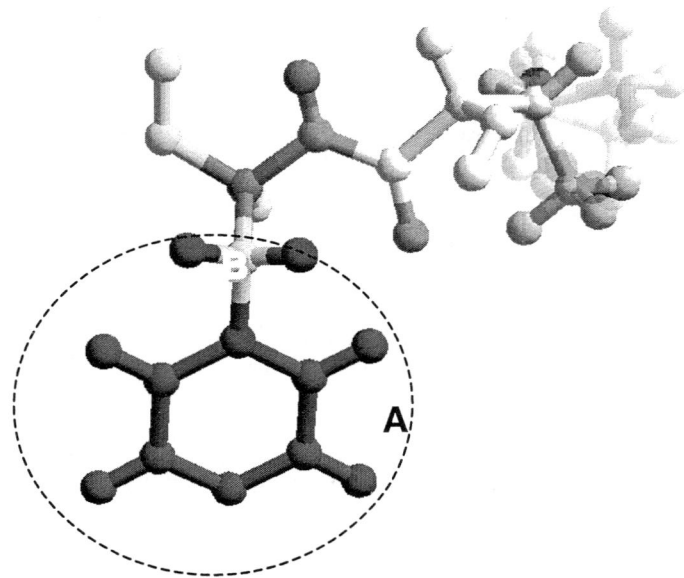

Fig. 1. Protein chains are sequences of rigid groups connected by bonds that can rotate. Different groups are shown in different shades of gray. The group of atoms inside the circle A is a rigid group that can rotate around atom B. At the right side of the picture, light gray shapes indicate alternative orientations of another rigid group, which in turn affects all other groups attached to it. In a protein, this chain could be many hundreds of atoms in length.

Although the amino acid sequence, and the structure of each amino acid, gives us a lot of information about the protein, it is not sufficient to specify the folding of the chain, and thus its three-dimensional structure.

There are two methods to determine protein structures from experimental data. The most used is X-Ray crystallography, in which an X-ray beam diffracts from a protein crystal. The resulting diffraction pattern gives the distribution of electron density in the protein, and from that, its structure.

Another important method is Nuclear Magnetic Resonance. This method probes the magnetic perturbations caused by the proximity of some atoms, using high intensity magnetic fields and radio waves. Its data can be used to generate a set of distance constraints between atoms, by assigning the perturbations measured to the correct atom pairs. Though limited to smaller proteins (around a few hundred amino acids), it has some advantages over X-Ray crystallography, because it doesn't require the formation of protein crystals, and it can be used in conditions similar to the physiological environment of the protein.

Constraint programming techniques have been applied to several biochemical problems, such as genome mapping [3] and theoretical studies on protein folding [4]. On the particular field of protein NMR spectroscopy, we know of attempts to apply CP to the problem of extracting the distance constraints from the experimental data [5,6], but none of the methods used to solve the actual structure, so far, take advantage of CP, generally relying on optimisation techniques, e.g. [7].

There are some algorithms available for propagating constraints on rigid structures, such as for qualitative determinations of possible movements [8] or for non-overlapping, convex, geometric figures [9]. However, these solutions are not adequate to our particular problem.

PSICO is being developed to apply CP techniques to the constraints generated by NMR data, and other structural information sources. The current propagation method in PSICO consists of enforcing arc-consistency on the network of all binary distance constraints in the group. The propagation algorithm we present here will make use of the information on the rigid structures that make up each amino acid to improve propagation in PSICO. These structures can range from groups of three atoms forming a fixed angle between two covalent bonds, to groups of dozens of atoms in some rigid prosthetic groups.

A potentially more useful application of the group propagation algorithm is to test a theoretical model against experimental data. It is often the case that proteins with similar sequences of amino acids also have similar structures. When determining the structure of one protein, it is useful to have a known similar structure to help assign constraints from the experimental data. The problem is how to know if one has chosen the correct homology model.

This is not a trivial problem, because the experimental constraints are seldom on the atoms the homology model restricts. For example, a homologous protein may give us an approximate idea of the folding of the backbone, while the experimental data gives us distance constraints for atoms in the side chains.

Finally, this algorithm can be extended to propagate constraints on torsion angles, the rotation angles between adjacent rigid groups. NMR data may provide constraints on these angles, so this is another potentially useful feature. Though this extension is still not developed, we shall elaborate a bit more on it at the end of the article.

Although our focus is on protein structure, the algorithm we present here is not exclusive for this use. Other possible applications could include antenna placement problems, computer-aided design, packing problems, or, in theory, any problem involving the constrained placement of rigid bodies. Some modifications may be necessary if the variable domains differ from the cuboid representations used in PSICO [1,2], but the basic principles described here should be applicable in general.

The paper is organised as follows. In section 2 we describe the group propagation method, and in section 3 we compare the group propagation algorithm with the current propagation method in PSICO, and show that it is more effective in reducing domains, and better at detecting inconsistencies between the domains and the constraints. Section 4 summarises the main results and discusses further improvements in our current agenda.

2 The Method

The algorithm we present here will be integrated into PSICO, and makes use of the cuboid domain representations we developed for that system and described in previous publications [1,2]. Summarising, a cuboid with faces orthogonal to the x, y, and z coordinate axes describes each atom domain, defining the region where the atom may be placed (the *Good* region). In addition, a set of non-overlapping cuboids, all included in this region, describes regions from where the atom must be excluded (*No-Good* regions). PSICO reduces these domains by propagation of distance constraints between atom pairs, enumeration, and bactracking until all domains are sufficiently small to define a protein structure (less than 2.5Å in length). The starting point for this process is the arbitrary placement of a set of atoms of known configuration, such as a small rigid group. This is possible because the position and orientation of the structure relative to the coordinate system is arbitrary, and irrelevant for the determination of the structure itself.

The algorithm presented here enables PSICO to propagate group constraints on the configuration of an arbitrary number of atoms, in addition to the binary distance constraints. The group constraint specifies that a set of atoms forms a rigid group, with three rotation and three translation degrees of freedom. By determining the possible placements of the group allowed by the domains of all atoms in the group, it is possible to restrict the domains of these atoms to those regions allowed by the possible placements of the group.

The group propagation algorithm considers only the Good region of each domain, because a) in practice, the No-Good regions are only useful to detect failures when enumeration has reduced the domains sufficiently to detect atomic overlaps, and b) processing an arbitrarily large set of No-Good regions in each domain would jeopardise the efficiency of the algorithm.

In essence, the group propagation algorithm consists of three nested loops that run through all orientations of the rigid group. For each orientation, the algorithm determines the domain boundaries of each atom from the limits that all domains impose on the translational freedom of the group, as shown in section 2.1. Without loss of generality, we shall consider the three rotation loops to correspond to rotations around the x, y, and z axes, from outer to inner loop. We shall designate these rotation angles by χ, φ, and ψ, respectively.

Though it is useful to imagine the algorithms as three nested loops of rotations around the three coordinate axes, the algorithm actually determines the domain limits analytically as a function of one rotation, as section 2.2 describes. Thus, the last rotation, around the z axis, is not an actual loop, but the analytical determination of the domain limits for the x and y coordinates. The domain limits in the z coordinate, being independent of the last rotation around the z axis, are determined analytically in the second loop, corresponding to the rotation around the y axis. This procedure is explained in section 2.3.

2.1 Domain Limits for a Fixed Orientation

Given a fixed orientation, it is simple to determine the limits for the translation of the rigid group. Figure 2 shows how this is done for a group of three atoms.

The range of the translation for the group is simply the intersection of the ranges allowed by all atoms. In this example, the horizontal displacement (left panel of Figure 2) is limited by the domain boundaries of atom B and the vertical displacement (right panel) is limited by the domains of atom A.

Denoting by w_c one of the coordinates of the center of the group (x, y or z), by w_j the same coordinate for atom j, and by w_{max} and w_{min} the upper and lower limits, respectively, for that coordinate of a domain (of atom j or of the center c), such limits are related by the following equations:

$$w_{max\,c} = Min_{j=1}^{n}(w_{max\,j} + (w_c - w_j)) \tag{1a}$$

$$w_{min\,c} = Max_{j=1}^{n}(w_{min\,j} + (w_c - w_j)) \tag{1b}$$

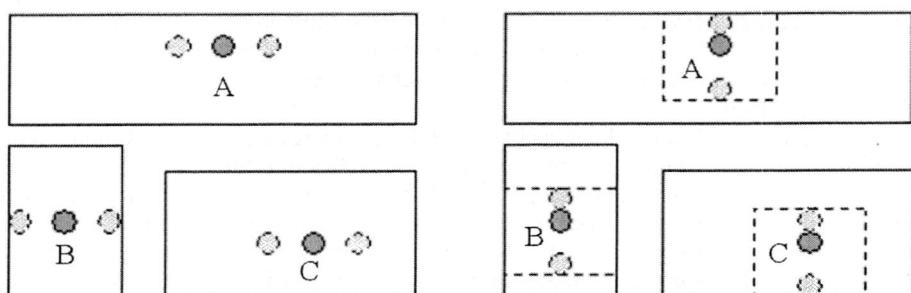

Fig. 2. The three atoms A, B, and C, form a rigid group (dark gray circles), and each atom is restricted to a rectangular domain. The left panel shows the limits for a horizontal translation, indicated in light gray circles, and the right panel shows the limits for a vertical translation. The dashed boxes on the right panel indicate the accessible regions for each atom with the group in this orientation.

Note that the absolute values of w_c and w_j are irrelevant; only the coordinate difference w_c-w_j is important, and is independent of translation. The center point is simply the pivot from which rotation is calculated. It can be the geometric center of the group, or any other point. The choice has impact only on some performance details, and not on the principles of the algorithm. In this paper, we shall consider it to be the geometric center of the group.

2.2 Domain Limits as a Function of a Single Rotation

Equations 1 assume a fixed orientation of the group, but we cannot make that assumption, since the group is free to rotate. Without loss of generality, we shall consider the case of the limits in the x and y coordinates as a function of a rotation around the z axis. Hence, the term $(w_j\text{-}w_c)$ in equation 1 may actually stand for the x-or y-components of the vector from atom j to the center of the group, or, in other words, the position of the center relative to atom j.

This vector is a function of the orientation of the group. Denoting by ψ the rotation around the z axis, by A the amplitude of the projection of the vector onto the xy plane (orthogonal to the rotation axis) and by α_j the angle of the vector y_c-y_j at ψ=0, then the terms w_c $-w_j$ for the x and y coordinates are given by

$$x_c - x_j = A_j \cos(\psi + \alpha) = A_j \sin(\psi + \alpha_j + \pi\!/_2) \tag{2a}$$

$$y_c - y_j = A_j \sin(\psi + \alpha) \tag{2b}$$

Figure 3 shows the case for the y-coordinate (the x-coordinate is shifted by 90°).

Though rotation freedom increases the complexity of the computation, it is necessary because our rigid group constraints only give information on the relative positions of the atoms in the group and not on the orientation or position of the group relative to other atoms or groups.

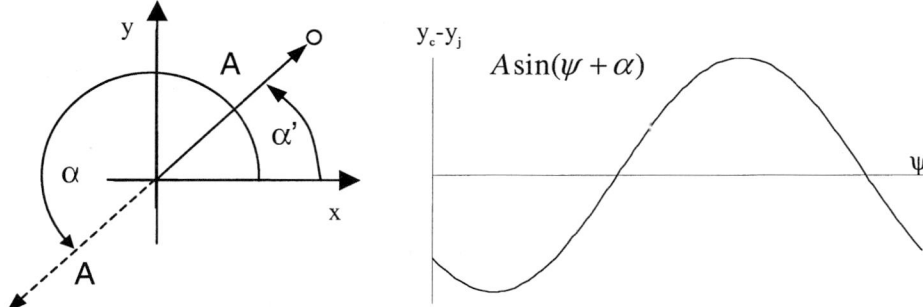

Fig. 3. The position of an atom relative to the center of the group as a function of the rotation angle ψ can be expressed as a sine function with amplitude A and phase α'. The position of the center relative to the atom is a similar curve, but with the phase shifted by 180° (α), giving the sine wave curve shown on the right.

Let us now recall the algorithm as outlined in the beginning of part 2. First, the orientation of the group around the x axis is fixed in an angle we designate χ. Next, the rotation around the y axis is fixed at angle φ. For each (χ;φ) pair, equations 2 can be used to describe the x and y coordinates for each atom as a function of the angle ψ, corresponding to the rotation around the z axis. An equation similar to equation 2 can also be used to describe the z coordinates of atom j (related to the centre of the group) as a function of the second rotation, φ, around the y axis.

With no loss of generality, we may replace y_c and y_j in equations 2 with L_c and L_j to denote, respectively, the domain limits of the center and of atom j in an arbitrary x, y, or z coordinate and by θ an arbitrary rotation angle (φ or ψ), and compute the contribution of each atom to the limits on the translation of the center of the group by means of Equation 3 below:

$$L_c = A_j \sin(\theta + \alpha_j) + L_j \tag{3}$$

Figure 4 shows two curves representing the limits on the movement of the center imposed by two different atoms.

The actual limits for the movement of the center for each orientation are the most restrictive limits (around gray areas on Figure 4). To calculate these we must calculate the intersection of two limits from different atoms:

$$A_i \sin(\theta + \alpha_i) + L_i = A_j \sin(\theta + \alpha_j) + L_j \Leftrightarrow \tag{4}$$

$$A\sin(\theta + \alpha) = L_j - L_i$$

The values for A and θ can be calculated using the formulae for the superposition of two sine waves of the same frequency, noting that the sign change for A_j when manipulating equation 4 is equivalent to changing the phase θ_j by π. Equation 5 calculates A and θ.

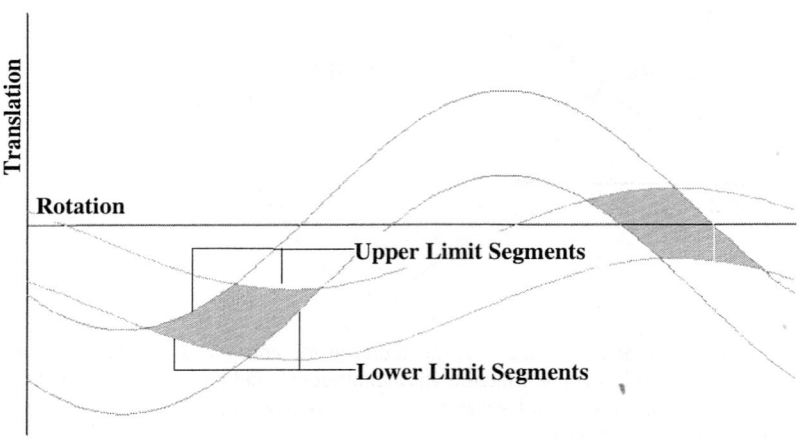

Fig. 4. Each atom constrains the translation of the group as a function of the domain of the atom and rotation of the group. This figure shows such constraints for two atoms along one coordinate axis for one rotation. The gray areas indicate the angles for which the two atom positions are compatible and the corresponding constraints on the translation of the whole group in this orientation.

$$\pm A = \sqrt{A_i^2 + A_j^2 + 2A_i A_j \cos(\alpha_j - \alpha_i + \pi)}$$

$$\tan \alpha = \frac{A_i \sin(\alpha_i) + A_j \sin(\alpha_j + \pi)}{A_i \cos(\alpha_i) + A_j \cos(\alpha_j + \pi)} \tag{5}$$

The intersection angles are thus:

$$\theta = \arcsin\left(\frac{L_j - L_i}{\pm A}\right) - \alpha \tag{6}$$

With equations 5 and 6 we can define the segments of the lines limiting the upper and lower bounds for the translation of the center. Each segment is the line between two interceptions, and is contributed by one atom. For the upper limit we choose the lowest segments corresponding to the upper limits of all atoms, and for the lower limit, the highest segments corresponding to the lower limits of the atoms. The allowed region for the center is thus the intersection of the regions allowed by the limits of each atom, as illustrated in Figure 4. Algorithm 1 shows the pseudo-code for CenterLimits.

Lu and Ld are lines formed by segments of the form of Equation 3. Functions UpperLimit and LowerLimit return the line defined in Equation 3, using respectively the upper and lower limit of the domain of the atom. Functions LowLine and HighLine intersect two lines and return, respectively, the set of the lowest or highest segments between intersections. The PossibleRegion procedure restricts the lines to the ranges of rotation angle where the upper line is greater than or equal to the lower line.

```
Lu=UpperLimit(Atom 1)
Ld=LowerLimit(Atom 1)
For n=2 to number of atoms do
        Lu=LowLine(UpperLimit(Atom n ),Lu)
        Ll=HighLine(LowerLimit(Atom n ),Ld)
PossibleRegion(Ld,Lu)
Return Ld, Lu
```

Algorithm 1. CenterLimits.

The CenterLimits algorithm returns two sets of segments; the upper and lower limits for the displacement of the center as a function of rotation. These sets of segments include only the possible regions, where the upper limit is equal to or higher than the lower limit, as shown in Figure 4. To calculate the limits for the displacement of each atom, it is necessary to add the function for the position of the atom relative to the center of the group. In other words, between the center and the atom there can be two vectors, one oriented from the atom to the center, the other from the center to the atom. We use the first to project the limits of each atom onto the displacement of the center, and then the second to project the limits of the center back onto the atom. This will give us a limited range of possible positions for the atom, which may be smaller than its domain, and so allow us to reduce this domain.

As shown in Figure 3, these vectors define sine wave lines that differ only in a phase difference of π. Deriving from equation 3:

$$L_c(\theta) = A_j \sin(\theta + \alpha_j) + L_j(\theta) \Leftrightarrow \qquad (7)$$

$$L_j(\theta) = A_j \sin(\theta + \alpha_j + \pi) + L_c(\theta)$$

We knew from Equation 3 that L_c would be a function of the rotation parameter. If there were only one atom, L_c would be independent of θ, because we would simply reverse the operation in Equation 3. However, with several atoms, L_j is the limit of the intersection of several possible regions, and can consist of several different segments, which can have different A and α parameters. So the term $A_j\sin(\theta+\alpha_j+\pi)$ must be added to each segment of $L_c(\theta)$, and $L_j(\theta)$ is also a list with the same number of segments. All these sums are superpositions of sine waves of the same frequency, so we can apply equation 5.

It is not necessary to do this for all atoms; we can ignore any atom that contributed to $L_c(\theta)$, because this implies the atom reached the limit of its domain, and so its domain cannot be reduced. It is just necessary to keep track of which atom contributed to which segment.

This solves the problem for the rotation around a single axis. However, it takes three axes to fully describe all possible orientations of the group. If we account for the additional rotations, the A and α terms in equation 4 become trigonometric functions of the other rotation parameters, which makes the system too complex for an efficient analytical solution.

The alternative is to use a discrete representation of the other rotation parameters, and interval algebra to account for the error introduced by this approach.

2.3 Full Rotation Search

As outlined in the beginning of part 2, the algorithm searches the possible rotations by fixing the angle of rotation around the x axis, then for each rotation value it searches the rotations around the y axis, and finally the z axis. Dividing the rotations into finite intervals, each orientation corresponds to an interval of angles, instead of just a single angle, and each coordinate to an interval of values.

For example, the x coordinate as a function of the rotation φ around the y axis is:

$$x(\varphi)_j = x_j \cos(\varphi) - z_j \sin(\varphi)$$

where x_j and z_j are the x and z coordinates for $\varphi = 0$. If we consider interval $[\varphi_a ; \varphi_b]$, then x will be in the interval $[x_a ; x_b]$, where

$$x_a = Min(x_j \cos(\varphi_a), x_j \cos(\varphi_b)) - Max(z_j \sin(\varphi_a), z_j \sin(\varphi_b))$$

$$x_b = Max(x_j \cos(\varphi_a), x_j \cos(\varphi_b)) - Min(z_j \sin(\varphi_a), z_j \sin(\varphi_b))$$

One thing to note is that the sine and cosine functions must be monotonous in the interval $[\varphi_a; \varphi_b]$. However, this is simple to guarantee; we just have to choose the partition of the rotation so that the step size is a sub-multiple of 90°. If x_j and z_j are themselves intervals too, the Min and Max functions will apply to their interval limits, following the rules for interval algebra.

Because of this approach, the equations derived in section 2.2 apply not to single coordinate values, but to intervals. Although the coordinates are in three dimensions, we need only consider the projection on the plane perpendicular to the rotation axis that provides the θ angle (θ corresponds to φ for the determination of the z limits as a function of the rotation around the y axis, or to ψ for the determination of the x and y limits as a function of the rotation around z axis). Let us assume, for example, that the rotation is around the z axis, and so the coordinates of one atom are $([x_a;x_b],[y_a;y_b])$. This is a rectangular region, as illustrated in Figure 5, whose corners are labeled A, B, C, and D. As figure 5 shows, these corners have different trajectories when the region is rotated.

What we need to find are two lines of the form of equation 3 which, by enclosing the trajectories of the corners, enclose the trajectories of all points in the region. Such lines are computed by allowing some slack δ to the trajectory of the central point of the region. The largest span is half the length of the diagonal of the rectangular region, hence the value of δ:

$$\delta = \frac{\sqrt{(x_b - x_a)^2 + (y_b - y_a)^2}}{2} \tag{8}$$

Figure 5 shows these lines, with δ added/subtracted from the upper/lower limit of the domain of the atom, thus ensuring that no values of the domain are lost.

To summarize, the algorithms searches the rotation space starting from the rotation around the x axis (χ), for each interval value of this rotation, the rotation around the y axis (φ), and for each (χ,φ) interval pair, the rotation around the z axis (ψ).

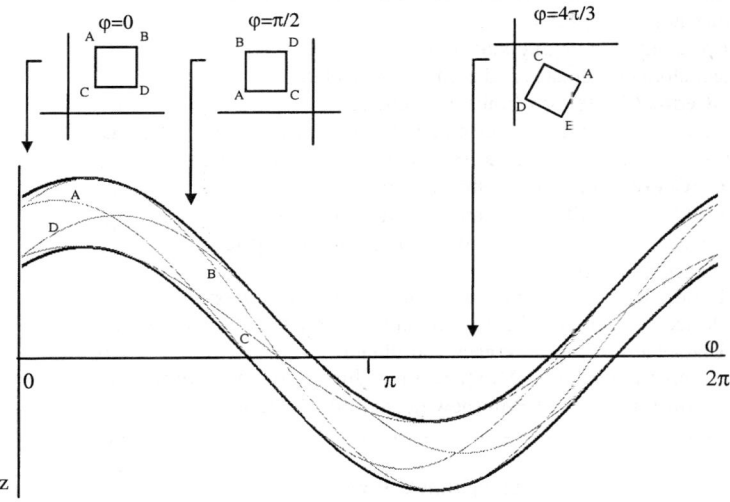

Fig. 5. The thick lines show the lines obtained by adding δ (top line) and subtracting δ (bottom line. The top panels show three orientations of the rectangle defined by the coordinate intervals. A, B, C, and D are the extreme points of the rectangle, and thin lines in the lower diagram show their trajectories as a function of the φ rotation parameter.

The x and y coordinates of each atom depend on all three rotation parameters, but the z coordinate depends only on the first two (χ and φ, respectively rotations around the x and y axes), being independent of ψ. This suggested Algorithm 2, Rotation-Search. The first rotation, χ, ranges from 0° to 180°, whereas ψ ranges from 0° to 360°. This is enough to represent all possible orientations of the atom group. For each step of the χ, RotationSearch calculates the domain of the center in the z direction using CenterLimits for rotation φ and the z limits of all atoms. This will often prune the φ rotation, and only those steps that are allowed by the z limits of the center will be considered in the calculation of the x and y limits.

For each (χ, φ) step, we have the center limits of x and y as a function of ψ, and the z limits as a function of φ, of which we only consider the segment referring to the current φ. All these segments are projected onto the atom domains to determine the possible range of each atom in each coordinate.

3   Results and Discussion

We compared this group constraint with arc-consistency on all binary distance constraints in the group. We generated each test group by placing each atom at random in a cube with a volume of 8 volume units times the number of atoms. To generate the upper limit of each initial domain we added to each coordinate of each point a uniformly distributed random variable ranging from zero to two units. We generated the lower limits by subtracting a random variable with the same distribution.

Initialize atom range limits
Search χ using discrete intervals. For each step do
  Project atom coordinates and z limits on yz plane
  ZL:=**CenterLimits** for z limits as a function φ
  Search allowed values of φ using discrete intervals. For each step, do:
    Project atom coordinates, x limits and y limits on xy plane
    XL:=**CenterLimits** for x limits as a function of ψ
    YL:=**CenterLimits** for y limits as a function of ψ
    Intercept XL and YL limits to determine allowed ψ values
    For each atom do
      Project XL,YL to atom domain and determine x, y extremes.
      Project φ interval of ZL to atom domain and determine z extremes
      Update atom ranges for each coordinate:
        Upper range limit =Max(new range limit, old range limit)
        Lower range limit=Min(new range limit, old range limit)

Algorithm 2. RotationSearch.

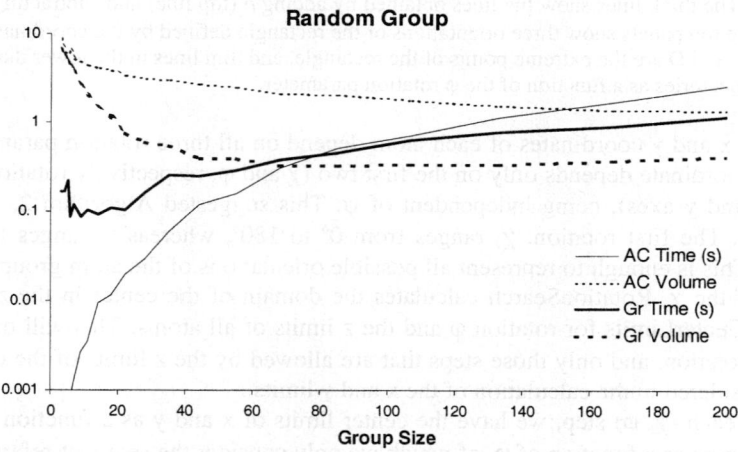

Fig. 6. Propagation times and final domain volumes for arc-consistency in binary distance constraints and group propagation for a randomly generated group. Times are in seconds for a PII at 300Mz running Windows. Volumes are arbitrary units.

For the propagation of binary distance constraints, we included the distance constraints between all pairs of points in the group ($\frac{1}{2}N^2$), and propagated all constraints to arc-consistency, as described in [1,2]. Though NMR data do not provide all constraints between all atoms, the purpose of this test was to compare the two propagation algorithms on rigid groups, in which all relative positions, and thus all pairwise distances are specified. In other cases, only the binary constraint propagation can apply. For the group propagation, we used 10° steps in the rotation searches.

Figure 6 shows the propagation times and the final domain volumes for both cases. Each point on the chart corresponds to the average of 30 independent runs. We can see that the group propagation algorithm is more effective than enforcing arc-consistency on a network of binary constraints, even using all constraints, except for very small groups. For small groups, less than 10-20 atoms, group propagation is only slightly more effective than arc-consistency on binary constraints. For groups of over 20, the final domains with group propagation are an order of magnitude greater than for arc-consistency of binary distance constraints.

The difference is even greater with more structured groups. Figure 7 shows the results of a similar experiment, but using a spiral structure with a radius of 1 unit, a step of 2 units per turn, and three atoms per turn. This approximates a α-Helix, a common structural motif in proteins, and which has 3.6 residues per turn and approximately the same dimensions in Ångstrom.

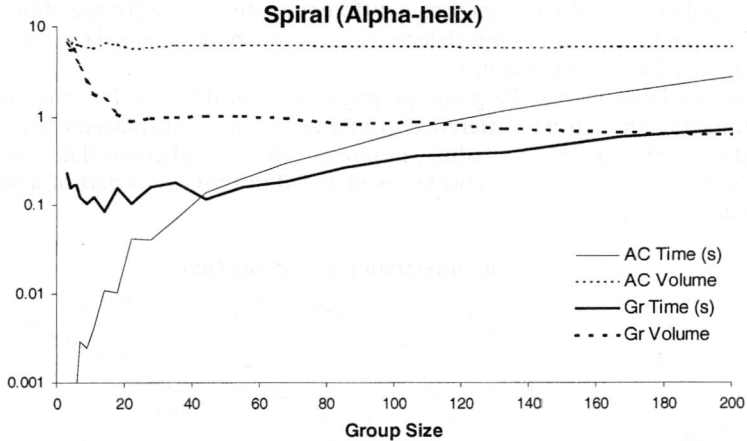

Fig. 7. Propagation times and final domain volumes for arc-consistency in binary distance constraints and group propagation for a spiral generated group, simulating an α-Helix structure. Times are in seconds for a PII at 300Mz running Windows. Volumes are arbitrary units.

This domain reduction has a significant time cost for smaller groups, although, for large groups, group propagation is both more effective and faster. The reason for this cost in smaller groups is that, with little or no domain reduction, there is also no pruning of the rotational search. The interesting feature is that, the more the domains can be reduced, the faster the group propagation algorithm completes the search. If we compare the average run times for small groups, AC on the binary constraints is about two orders of magnitude faster. But if we compare the minimum times, this difference reduces to one order of magnitude for the smallest groups, and with groups of 7 atoms, the minimum time for group propagation is already lower than the average time for AC on the binary constraints.

This inverse correlation between domain pruning and computation time suggests that heuristics can make group propagation very efficient. Rules like a time limit for the propagation or checking the pruning on the φ rotation by the z limits are simple and effective ways to use group propagation, because it is fastest when it is the most effective at reducing domains.

Another intended application of this algorithm is the integration of structural data from other sources, which can complement the experimental NMR constraints. These can be from secondary structure prediction (α-helices, β-sheets) or from homology modelling, for example, and can involve large rigid groups. As shown above, the group propagation algorithm is especially effective in these cases. But its use is not restricted to domain reduction; it is also useful for detecting inconsistencies, which is necessary to determine if the theoretical models assumed are compatible with the experimental data. To test this we generated random groups as described above, but then randomly changed the coordinates of the atoms used to generate the distance constraints and for the group propagation. Each x, y, and z coordinate was replaced by a uniformly distributed random value within a given distance of the original value. This simulates a situation where one set of constraints (e.g. from experimental data) reduced the domains to the current random configuration, and another constraint (e.g. from homology modelling) specifies a different configuration for the atoms. Figure 8 shows the percentage of failures detected as a function of this displacement parameter for groups of 20, 10, and 5 atoms.

These results show that the group propagation algorithm can detect inconsistencies more reliably. Though the difference in this test is in the displacement necessary to make the algorithms detect a failure, in practice this will also translate into detecting the failure sooner, when the algorithm is included in PSICO, as part of a propagation and enumeration cycle.

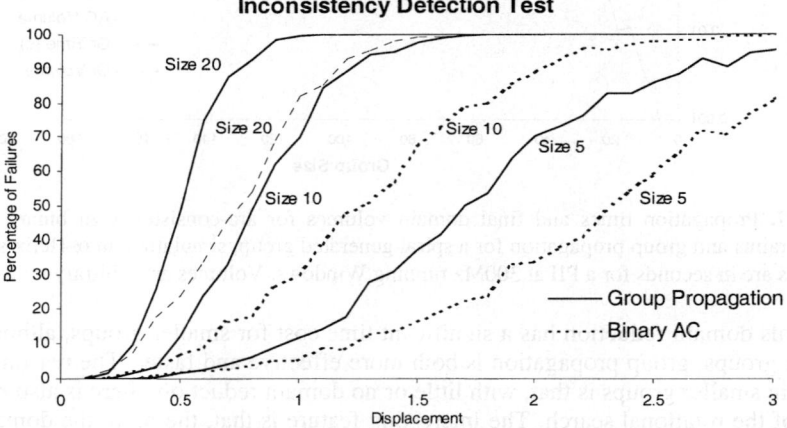

Fig. 8. Percentage of detected failures as a function of the maximum displacements of the atom coordinates. The figure shows three different group sizes (5, 10, and 20), comparing the binary arc-consistency algorithm implemented in PSICO with the group propagation described here.

This is a potentially useful feature because of the difficulty in interpreting NMR data. If PSICO can efficiently screen a database of homology candidates, fragments, secondary structure prediction (theoretical or even from the NMR data itself), this can help in interpreting the data.

We are still integrating the group propagation algorithm in PSICO, and have no experimental data on this feature. But the preliminary results indicate that the group propagation algorithm is very efficient at detecting inconsistencies, because if the rigid group cannot fit the domains, the rotation searches are always significantly pruned (often completely) and the algorithm, in this case, runs very quickly.

4   Conclusion and Future Work

We think our results show that this group propagation algorithm can increase the efficiency of protein structural NMR. Not only by speeding up the calculations, but also by helping in the data acquisition and interpretation by integrating theoretical models with the experimental data.

At the time of writing, we are extending the algorithm presented here to propagate constraints on torsion angles. Instead of having a single rigid group, this is a constraint on the relative positions of two rigid groups that are bound together by a rigid bond, and can rotate through a limited range of angles. This extension will give us the ability to process NMR data from a large set of proteins, and to test and develop a prototype application for the researchers in our Chemistry department.

This extension will involve a minor modification to the algorithm, only requiring an extra rotation search loop that will generate a sequence of rigid bodies by fixing the torsion angle, and use interval algebra to account for the discrete search, as the algorithm already does for the rotations.

Acknowledgements

This work was partly supported by grant PRAXIS XXI / BD / 19628 / 99, and project PROTEIN – POSI/33794/SRI/2000 granted by the Portuguese Foundation for Science and Technology, and carried out at CENTRIA: Center for Artificial Intelligence of UNL.

References

1. Krippahl, L., Barahona, P., PSICO: Solving Protein Structures with Constraint Programming and Optimisation, Constraints 2002, 7, 317-331
2. Krippahl, L., Barahona, P., *Applying Constraint Programming to Protein Structure Determination*, Principles and Practice of Constraint Programming, Springer Verlag, 1999 289-302
3. Revesz, P., Refining Restriction Enzyme Genome Maps, Constraints, V. 2, 361, 1997
4. Backofen, R, Constraint Techniques for Solving the Protein Structure Prediction Problem, CP98, Lecture Notes in Computer Science 1520, Springer-Verlag, 72-86
5. Leishman, S., Gray, PMD and Fothergill, JE, ASSASSIN: A Constraint Based Assignment System for Protein 2D Nuclear Magnetic Resonance, Applications and Innovations in Expert Systems II, (Proceedings of Expert Systems 94, Cambridge), ed. R.Milne and A.Montgomery, 263-280, December 1994
6. Zimmerman, D.E., Kulikowski C.A., Montelione G.T., A constraint reasoning system for automating sequence-specific resonance assignments from multidimensional protein NMR spectra. Ismb 1993;1:447-55
7. Güntert, P., Mumenthaler, C. & Wüthrich, K. (1997). Torsion angle dynamics for NMR structure calculation with the new program DYANA. J. Mol. Biol. 273, 283-298.
8. T. Stahovich, R. Davis, and H. Shrobe. Qualitative rigid-body mechanics. Artificial Intelligence, 119(1-2):19-60, 2000
9. N. Beldiceanu, Q. Guo, S.Thiel, Non-overlapping Constraints between Convex Polytopes, Lecture Notes in Computer Science, Vol. 2239:392, 2001.

Solving 'Still Life' with Soft Constraints and Bucket Elimination[*]

Javier Larrosa and Enric Morancho

Universitat Politecnica de Catalunya, Barcelona, Spain
larrosa@lsi.upc.es, enricm@ac.upc.es

Abstract. In this paper we study the applicability of *bucket elimination* (BE) to the problem of finding *still-life patterns*. Very recently, it has been tackled using *integer programming* and *constraint programming*, both of them being search-based methods. We show that BE, which is based on *dynamic programming*, provides an exponentially lower worst-case time complexity than search methods. Unfortunately, BE requires exponential space, which is a disadvantage over the polynomial space requirement of depth-first search.

With our experiments, we show that BE is quite competitive with search-based approaches. It clearly outperforms simple encodings and it is comparable with dedicated methods. While the best current search approach solves the $n = 14$ instance in about 6 cpu days, BE solves it in about 1 day. BE cannot solve the $n = 15$ instance due to space exhaustion (this instance is solved by search in 8 days). Finally, we show how BE can be adapted to exploit the problem symmetries, with which in several cases we outperform previous results in a relaxation of the problem which restrict solutions to symmetric patterns, only.

1 Introduction

The game of *life* was invented in the late 60s by John Horton Conway and was later popularized by Martin Gardner [6]. Given an infinite checkerboard, the only player places checkers on some of its squares. Each square is a *cell*. If there is a checker on it, the cell is *alive*, else it is *dead*. Each cell has eight *neighbors*: the eight cells that share one or two corners with it. The state of the board evolves iteratively according to three rules: (*i*) if a cell has exactly two living neighbors then its state remains the same in the next iteration, (*ii*) if a cell has exactly three living neighbors then it is alive in the next iteration and (*iii*) if a cell has fewer than two or more than three living neighbors, then it is dead in the next iteration.

While conceptually simple, the game has proven mathematically interesting and has attracted a lot of curiosity, as can be seen in,

home.interserv.com/~mniemiec/lifepage.htm

---

[*] The first author is supported by the REPLI project TIC-2002-04470-C03.

F. Rossi (Ed.): CP 2003, LNCS 2833, pp. 466–479, 2003.
© Springer-Verlag Berlin Heidelberg 2003

Maximum density stable patterns (also called *still lifes*) are board configurations with a maximal number of living cells which do not change along time. They can be seen as an academic simplification of a standard issue in discrete dynamic systems. [5] has shown that for the infinite board the maximum density is $1/2$. In this paper we are concerned with finite patterns. In particular, we consider $n \times n$ still lifes, for which no polynomial method is known. This problem has been recently included in the *CSPlib*[1] repository of challenging constraint satisfaction problems.

In [3] still life is solved using *integer programming* and *constraint programming*, both of them being search-based methods. Their best results were obtained with a hybrid approach which combines the two techniques and exploits the problem symmetries to reduce the search space. With their algorithm, they solved the $n = 15$ case in about 8 days of *cpu* with a modern computer. Another interesting work can be found in [11] where pure constraint programming techniques are used, and the problem is solved in its dual form. Although not explicitly mentioned, these two works use algorithms with worst-case time complexity $O(2^{(n^2)})$ and polynomial space.

In this paper we find still lifes using *dynamic programming*. We model the problem as a *weighted constraint satisfaction problem* (WCSP) [10, 2] and solve it with *bucket elimination* (BE) [4]. BE is a generic algorithm suitable for many automated reasoning and optimization problems. It is often overlooked due to its exponential space complexity. Here we show that for the still life problem it is highly competitive. In the theoretical side, we show that its time complexity is $\Theta(n^2 \times 2^{3n})$, which means an exponential improvement over search-based methods. Regarding space, the complexity is $\Theta(n \times 2^{2n})$. In the practical side we show that plain BE is much faster than basic search algorithms and comparable to sophisticated search methods. Our implementation of BE solves the $n = 14$ case in less than 30 hours. The $n = 15$ case cannot be solved with our computer due to space exhaustion. A nice feature of BE is that it can compute, with no extra cost, the number of optimal solutions. Thus, we report, for the first time, the number of still lifes up to $n = 14$.

An additional contribution of this paper is that we have adapted BE to exploit some of the problem symmetries, with which the speed is nearly doubled and the space requirement is halved (the $n = 14$ case is solved in about 15 hours, but we still could not solve the $n = 15$ case).

When n is too large to solve optimally with current methods, some authors [3, 11] find symmetric optimal solutions. We have also adapted BE to solve the problem subject to a vertical reflection symmetry and have solved the $n = 28$ case for the first time.

Although the space complexity seems to be a critical limitation of our method, it is not necessarily so. There are ways to trade space by time within the BE algorithm (see [7–9]), which give room to our approach to scale up and make it very promising. We discuss this in detail in Section 6.

---

[1] www.csplib.org

The structure of this paper is as follows: In Section 2 we give preliminary definitions. In Section 3 we show how the still life problem is modelled as a WCSP and solved with BE. In Section 4 we adapt BE to exploit problem symmetries. In Section 5 we modify BE to find symmetrical solutions. In Section 6 we highlight our ongoing work. Finally, Section 7 summarizes the conclusions of our work.

2   Preliminaries

A *Constraint satisfaction problem* (CSP) [12] is defined by a tuple (X, D, C), where $X = \{x_1, \ldots, x_n\}$ is a set of *variables* taking values from their finite *domains* ($D_i \in D$ is the domain of x_i). C is a set of *constraints*, which prohibit the assignment of some combinations of values. A constraint $c \in C$ is a *relation* over a subset of variables $var(c)$, called its *scope*. For each assignment t of all variables in $var(c)$, $t \in c$ iff t is allowed by the constraint. A *solution* to the CSP is an complete assignment that satisfies every constraint. Constraints can be given explicitly as tables of permitted tuples, or implicitly as mathematical expressions or computing procedures.

Weighted constraint satisfaction problems (WCSP) [2] and [10] augment the CSP model by letting the user express preferences among solutions. In WCSP, constraints are replaced by cost functions (also called *soft constraints*). Forbidden assignments receive cost ∞. Permitted assignments receive finite costs that express their degree of preference. The *valuation* of an assignment t is the sum of costs of all functions whose scope is assigned by t. A *solution* to the WCSP is a complete assignment with a finite valuation. The task of interest is to *find the solution with the lowest valuation*.

A WCSP instance is graphically depicted by means of its *interaction* or *constraint graph*, which has one node per variable and one edge connecting any two nodes whose variables appear in the same scope of some cost function.

Bucket elimination (BE) [4, 1] is a generic algorithm that can be used for WCSP solving. It is based upon two operators over functions. For the WCSP case they are:

- The *sum* of two functions f and g denoted $(f + g)$ is a new function with scope $var(f) \cup var(g)$ which returns for each tuple the sum of costs of f and g,

$$(f + g)(t) = f(t) + g(t)$$

- The *elimination* of variable x_i from f, denoted $f \Downarrow i$, is a new function with scope $var(f) - \{x_i\}$ which returns for each tuple t the minimum cost extension of t to x_i,

$$(f \Downarrow i)(t) = \min_{a \in D_i} \{f(t \cdot (x_i, a))\}$$

where $t \cdot (x_i, a)$ means the extension of t to the assignment of a to x_i. Observe that when f is a unary function (*i.e.*, arity one), eliminating the only variable in its scope produces a constant.

Example 1 Let $f(x_1, x_2) = x_1 + x_2$ and $g(x_1, x_3) = x_1 x_3$. The sum of f and g is $(f + g)(x_1, x_2, x_3) = x_1 + x_2 + x_1 x_3$. If domains are integers in the interval $[1..10]$, the elimination of x_1 from f is $(f \Downarrow 1))(x_2) = 1 + x_2$. The subsequent elimination of x_2, produces constant 2 (i.e, $((f \Downarrow 1) \Downarrow 2) = 2)$.

In the previous example, resulting functions were expressed intensionally for clarity reasons. Unfortunatelly, in general, the result of summing functions or eliminating variables cannot be expressed intensionally by algebraic expressions. Therefore, BE collects intermediate results extensionally in tables, which causes its high space complexity.

BE (Figure 1) uses an arbitrary variable ordering o that we assume, without loss of generality, lexicographical (i.e, $o = (x_1, x_2, \ldots, x_n)$). BE works in two phases. In the first phase (lines 1-5), the algorithm eliminates variables one by one, from last to first, according to o. In the second phase, the optimal assignment is computed processing variables from first to last. The elimination of variable x_i is done as follows: C is the set of current constraints. The algorithm stores the so called *bucket* of x_i, noted B_i, which contains all cost functions in C having x_i in their scope (Line 2). Next, BE computes a new function g_i by summing all functions in B_i and subsequently eliminating x_i (line 3). Then, C is updated by removing the functions in B_i and adding g_i (line 4). The new C does not contain x_i (all functions mentioning x_i were removed) but preserves the value of the optimal cost. The elimination of the last variable produces an empty-scope function (*i.e.*, a constant) which is the optimal cost of the problem. The second phase (lines 6-10) generates an optimal assignment of variables. It uses the set of buckets that were computed in the first phase. Starting from an empty assignment t (line 6), variables are assigned from first to last according to o. The optimal value for x_i is the best value regarding the extension of t with respect to the sum of functions in B_i (lines 8,9). We use the non standard notation $\text{argmin}_a\{f(a)\}$ to denote the value a producing minimum $f(a)$.

BE can also compute the number of optimal solutions with not additional overhead. More than that, *all* optimal solutions can be easily retrieved from the buckets computed during the process (see [4] for details).

The complexity of BE depends on the problem structure, as captured by its constraint graph G, and the ordering o. The *induced graph* of G relative to o, noted $G^*(o)$, is obtained by processing the nodes in reverse order of o. When considering node i, new edges are added in order to form a clique with all its adjacent nodes, appearing before i in the ordering o. Given a graph and an ordering of its nodes, the *width* of a node is the number of edges connecting it to nodes lower in the ordering. The *induced width of a graph* along ordering o, denoted $w^*(o)$, is the maximum width of nodes in the induced graph.

Theorem 1 *[4] The complexity of* BE *along ordering o is time $O(Q \times n \times d^{w^*(o)+1})$ and space $O(n \times d^{w^*(o)})$, where d is the largest domain size and Q is the cost of evaluating cost functions (usually assumed $O(1)$).*

function BE(X, D, C)
1. **for** $i = n$ **downto** 1 **do**
2. $B_i := \{f \in C | \ x_i \in var(f)\}$
3. $g_i := (\sum_{f \in B_i} f) \Downarrow i;$
4. $C := (C \cup \{g_i\}) - B_i;$
5. **endfor**
6. $t := \emptyset;$
7. **for** $i = 1$ **to** n **do**
8. $v := \text{argmin}_{a \in D_i}\{(\sum_{f \in B_i} f)(t \cdot (x_i, a))\}$
9. $t := t \cdot (x_i, v);$
10. **endfor**
11. **return**$(C, t);$
endfunction

Fig. 1. Bucket Elimination. (X, D, C) is the WCSP instance to be solved. The algorithm returns the optimal cost in C and one optimal assignment in t.

3   Finding Still Lifes with BE

3.1   Modelling Still Life as a WCSP

The *still life* problem consist of finding a $n \times n$ stable pattern of maximum density in the game of life, where all cells outside the pattern are assumed to be dead. Considering the rules of the game, it is clear that in stable patterns all *living cells must have exactly two or three living neighbors* in order to remain alive, and *dead cells must not have three living neighbors* in order to remain dead. Besides, *boundary rows and columns must not have more than two adjacent living cells*, since three consecutive cells would produce a new living cells outside the $n \times n$ region. Figure 2 (left) shows a 3×3 still life.

Still life can be easily modelled as a WCSP. We use a compact formulation with n variables, one for every row. Variable x_i is associated to the i-th row. Its domain D_i is the set of sequences of n bits. The j-th bit of value a, noted a_j, indicates the state of the j-th cell of the row. If a_j takes value 1 the corresponding cell is alive, else it is dead. Let a, b and c be domain values. We define $Z(a)$ as the number of zeroes in a. $S(a, b, c)$ is a boolean predicate satisfied iff all cells of b are stable cells being a the row above b and c the row below b ($S(a, b, c)$ is false if there is some unstable cell in b).

The problem has n cost functions f_i (with $i = 1, .., n$). For $i = 2, .., n - 1$, f_i is ternary, with scope $var(f_i) = \{x_{i-1}, x_i, x_{i+1}\}$. If the arguments represent an unstable configuration it returns ∞, else it returns the number of zeroes in the middle row. Formally,

$$f_i(a, b, c) = \begin{cases} \infty & : \quad \neg S(a, b, c) \\ \infty & : \quad a_1 = b_1 = c_1 = 1 \\ \infty & : \quad a_n = b_n = c_n = 1 \\ Z(b) & : \quad \text{otherwise} \end{cases}$$

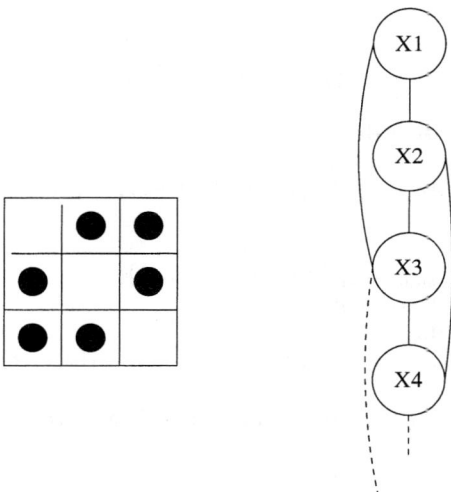

Fig. 2. *Left:* A 3×3 still life pattern. *Right:* Constraint graph of still life.

Functions f_1 and f_n are binary. They are equivalent to the ternary cost functions, but assuming dead cells above the top row and below the bottom row, respectively. The scope of f_1 is $\{x_1, x_2\}$ and it is defined as,

$$f_1(b, c) = \begin{cases} \infty & : \quad \neg S(\mathbf{0}, b, c) \\ Z(b) & : \quad \text{otherwise} \end{cases}$$

where $\mathbf{0}$ denotes the *all zeroes* string of bits. Similarly, the scope of f_n is $\{x_{n-1}, x_n\}$ and it is defined as,

$$f_n(a, b) = \begin{cases} \infty & : \quad \neg S(a, b, \mathbf{0}) \\ Z(b) & : \quad \text{otherwise} \end{cases}$$

Note that computing $f_i(a, b, c)$, $f_1(b, c)$ and $f_n(a, b)$ is $\Theta(n)$.

3.2   BE for Still Life

The constraint graph of our still life formulation is a sequence of size 3 cliques (Figure 2, right). The induced graph $G^*(o)$ with $o = (x_1, x_2, \ldots, x_n)$ does not have new edges (i.e, $G^*(o) = G$). Consequently, the induced width is $w^*(o) = 2$. Since domains have size 2^n, by Theorem 1, the complexity of BE is time $O(n^2 \times 2^{3n})$ and space $O(n \times 2^{2n})$.

The sequential structure of the constriant graph makes the implementation of BE very simple (see Figure 3). Sequences of bits of size n are represented by integers in the interval $[0..2^n - 1]$. In the first phase, we process variables from last to first. Buckets are implicitly computed. The bucket of x_n is $B_n = \{f_n, f_{n-1}\}$ (these are the only cost function having x_n in their scope). B_n is used

function BE(n)
1.   **for** $a, b \in [0..2^n - 1]$ **do**
2. $g_n(a, b) := \min_{c \in [0..2^n - 1]} \{f_{n-1}(a, b, c) + f_n(b, c)\}$;
3.   **endfor**
4.   **for** $i = n - 1$ **downto** 3 **do**
5.   **for** $a, b \in [0..2^n - 1]$ **do**
6. $g_i(a, b) := \min_{c \in [0..2^n - 1]} \{f_{i-1}(a, b, c) + g_{i+1}(b, c)\}$;
7.   **endfor**
8.   **endfor**
9. $(x_1, x_2) := \mathrm{argmin}_{a, b \in [0..2^n - 1]} \{g_3(a, b) + f_1(a, b)\}$;
10. $opt := g_3(x_1, x_2) + f_1(x_1, x_2)$;
11. **for** $i = 3$ **to** $n - 1$ **do**
12. $x_i := \mathrm{argmin}_{c \in [0..2^n - 1]} \{f_{i-1}(x_{i-2}, x_{i-1}, c) + g_{i+1}(x_{i-1}, c)\}$;
13. **endfor**
14. $x_n := \mathrm{argmin}_{c \in [0..2^n - 1]} \{f_{n-1}(x_{n-2}, x_{n-1}, c) + f_n(x_{n-1}, c)\}$;
15. **return**($opt, (x_1, x_2, \ldots, x_n)$);
endfunction

Fig. 3. Bucket Elimination for the still life problem. The algorithm returns the optimal value in opt and the optimal assignment in $(x_1, x_2, \ldots, x_n)$.

to compute a new binary cost function g_n with scope $\{x_{n-2}, x_{n-1}\}$ (lines 1-3). By construction, $g_n(a, b)$ is the cost of the best extention of $(x_{n-2} = a, x_{n-1} = b)$ to the eliminated variable x_n. The bucket of x_{n-1} is $B_{n-1} = \{g_n, f_{n-2}\}$. It is used to compute g_{n-1} with scope $\{x_{n-3}, x_{n-2}\}$ (lines 5-7, first iteration). $g_{n-1}(a, b)$ is the cost of the best extension of $(x_{n-3} = a, x_{n-2} = b)$ to the eliminated variables x_{n-1} and x_n. Subsequent iterations of the loop eliminate subsequent variables. In the last iteration variable x_3 is eliminated. When the algorithm reaches line 9, the current problem contains two cost functions: g_3, which contains the optimal extensions of each potential assignment of x_1 and x_2 to the rest of variables, and f_1. Instead of continuing the elimination of variables, we found it to be more efficient to solve the current problem with a brute-force exhaustive search (line 9). Variables x_1 and x_2 are assigned with their optimal values (line 9) and the optimal cost is assigned to opt (line 10).

In the second phase (lines 11-14), we process variables from first to last. We assign to each variable the best value according to its bucket and previously assigned variables.

It is easy to verify the complexity of the algorithm. Regarding space it is $\Theta(n \times 2^{2n})$, due to the space required to store functions g_i extensionally, which have 2^{2n} entries each. Regarding time, the critical part of the algorithm is the execution of lines 4-8. Line 6 has complexity $\Theta(n \times 2^n)$ (finding the minimum of 2^n alternatives, the computation of each one being $\Theta(n)$). It has to be executed $\Theta(n \times 2^{2n})$ times, which makes a global complexity of $\Theta(n^2 \times 2^{3n})$. Observe that the complexity of BE in the still life problem is an exponential improvement over search algorithms.

There is a simple average-case time optimization that we found very effective. Observe that lines 2 and 6 require the evaluation of $f_i(a, b, c)$ with a and b fixed and varying c. All values of c such that $f_i(a, b, c) = \infty$ are irrelevant because they cannot provide the minimum valuation. Let u_{ab} be the smallest value such that $f_i(a, b, u_{ab}) \neq \infty$. Clearly line 6 (similarly line 2) can be replaced by:

$$g_i(a, b) := \min_{c \in [u_{ab}..2^n - 1]} \{f_{i-1}(a, b, c) + g_{i+1}(b, c)\};$$

which in many cases reduces the interval size drastically. Since all f_i in the original problem are essentially equal (the only difference is their scope) value u_{ab} is common to all f_i (with $i = 2..n - 1$). For each a, b, we compute u_{ab} during a pre-process and store it in a table that is used to speed up every variable elimination. Note that this table has 2^{2n}. Thus, it does not affect the space complexity of the algorithm.

n	cost	n. sol.	BE	CP	IP	CP/IP-sym
5	16	1	0	0	1	0
6	18	48	0	1	23	0
7	28	2	0	10	7	0
8	36	1	1	189	65	2
9	43	76	4	> 1500	> 1500	51
10	54	3590	27	*	*	147
11	64	73	210	*	*	373
12	76	129126	1638	*	*	30360
13	90	1682	13788	*	*	30729
14	104	11	10^5	*	*	5×10^5
15	119	?	*	*	*	7×10^5

Fig. 4. Experimental results of four different algorithms on the still life problem. Times are in seconds.

3.3   Experimental Results

Table 4 reports the results that we obtained with a 1 Ghz Pentium III machine with 1 Gb of memory. From left to right, the first three columns report: problem size, solution cost (as the number of living cells) and number of optimal solutions (most of them have never been reported before). We count as different two solutions even if one can be transformed to the other through a problem symmetry. The fourth column reports the CPU time of our executions (BE) in seconds. For comparison purposes, the fifth, sixth and seventh columns show times obtained in [3] with basic constraint programming (CP), integer programming (IP), and a sophisticated hybrid algorithm (CP/IP-sym) which exploits the problem symmetries (see Section 4). In their experiments, they used a 650 Mhz Pentium III with 196 Mb of memory. Time comparison should be done with caution, because machines are different. Note as well that times in [3] were obtained using a commercial solver, while our times have been obtained with our *ad-hoc* implementation. On the one side, our implementation was made specifically for the

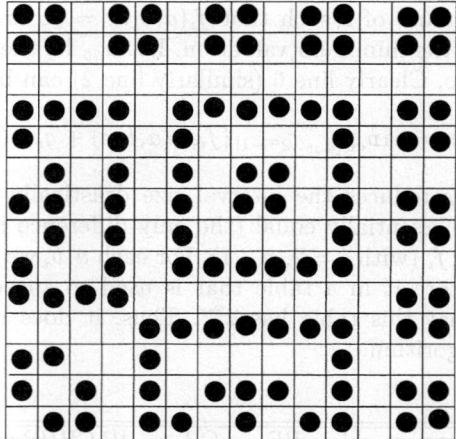

Fig. 5. A 14 × 14 still life pattern.

still life problem, which has the advantage of optimizing the use of space and specializing some parts of the code. On the other side, our implementation is a prototype, inplemented in a few weeks, which is in disadvantage with respect to commercial solvers, developed during months or years. Having said that, it can be observed that BE clearly outperforms basic CP and IP by orders of magnitude. While CP and IP algorithms cannot solve the problem beyond $n = 8$ in less than half an hour, BE can solve the $n = 12$ case subject to the same time limit. The $n = 14$ case is the largest instance that we could solve due to space exhaustion (see Figure 5). As a matter of fact, the original code could not be executed for the $n = 14$ case. We solved it by disabling the *counting solutions* feature which deallocates some memory. We computed the number of solutions in a different execution with a slower machine with more memory space. Comparing BE with the CP/IP hybrid we observe that both algorithms give very similar times (BE is faster, but within the same order of magnitude). Given the simplicity of the BE algorithm we consider it a very satisfactory result. An additional observation is that BE scales up very regularly, each execution requiring roughly eight times more time and four times more space than the previous, which is in clear accordance with the algorithm complexity.

4   Exploiting Problem Symmetries

Still life is a highly symmetric problem. For any stable pattern, it is possible to create an equivalent pattern by: (*i*) rotating the board by 90, 180 or 270 degrees, (*ii*) reflecting the board horizontally, vertically or along one diagonal or (*iii*) doing any combination of rotations and reflections. Search methods proposed in [3] and [11] exploit that fact by cutting off some search paths that only contain solutions that are symmetric of previously processed ones.

In the following we show how BE can also be adapted to take advantage of some of the symmetries.

Let's assume that n is an even number (the odd case is similar). Consider the algorithm of Figure 3 and assume that we stop the execution after the elimination of variable $x_{\frac{n}{2}+2}$. The elimination of $x_{\frac{n}{2}+2}$ produces $g_{\frac{n}{2}+2}$, with scope $\{x_{\frac{n}{2}}, x_{\frac{n}{2}+1}\}$. At this point supose that we change the order of elimination of the remaining variables to $x_1, x_2, \ldots, x_{\frac{n}{2}-1}$. The elimination x_1 produces a new function g_1 with scope $\{x_2, x_3\}$. Due to the 180 rotation symmetry it is the same to eliminate x_1 or rotate the board by 180 degrees and eliminate x_n. Therefore, for all a and b it holds that

$$g_1(a, b) = g_n(\bar{b}, \bar{a})$$

Where $\bar{a}$ (respectively, $\bar{b}$) is the reflection of value a (respectively, b). In addition, due to the vertical reflection symmetry we have that,

$$g_n(\bar{b}, \bar{a}) = g_n(b, a)$$

Therefore, it follows that,

$$g_1(a, b) = g_n(b, a)$$

In general, the elimination of variable x_i (with $1 \leq i \leq \frac{n}{2} - 1$) produces a new function g_i with scope $\{x_{i+1}, x_{i+2}\}$. Due to the problem symmetries, we have that,

$$g_i(a, b) = g_{n-i+1}(b, a)$$

Therefore, variables $x_1, x_2, \ldots, x_{\frac{n}{2}-1}$ do not have to be eliminated, because the effect of the elimination can be *inferred*. At this point, the current problem contains only two variables ($x_{\frac{n}{2}}$ and $x_{\frac{n}{2}+1}$) and one cost function between them $(g_{\frac{n}{2}+1}(x_{\frac{n}{2}}, x_{\frac{n}{2}+1}) + g_{\frac{n}{2}+1}(x_{\frac{n}{2}+1}, x_{\frac{n}{2}}))$. This problem can be solved by exhaustive exploration. It is clear that the savings from avoiding the elimination of half of the variables reduces the time and space requirements to one half.

The previous idea is illustrated by Algorithm BE-sym (Figure 6). In lines 1-6 the elimination of $x_n, x_{n-1}, \ldots, x_{\frac{n}{2}+2}$ is performed as in BE. In line 7, the optimal cost is computed where $g_{\frac{n}{2}+1}(x_{\frac{n}{2}}, x_{\frac{n}{2}+1})$ provides the effect of the performed elimination of $x_n, x_{n-1}, \ldots, x_{\frac{n}{2}+2}$ and the inferred elimination of $x_1, x_2, \ldots, x_{\frac{n}{2}-1}$. In line 8 the optimal assignment of $x_{\frac{n}{2}}$ and $x_{\frac{n}{2}+1}$ is computed. Lines 9-12 compute the optimal assignment of $x_n, x_{n-1}, \ldots, x_{\frac{n}{2}+2}$ as in the BE algorithm. Lines 13-16 compute the optimal assignment of $x_1, x_2, \ldots, x_{\frac{n}{2}-1}$. The optimal assignment of x_i without exploiting the simmetries would be,

$$x_i := \text{argmin}_{c \in [0..2^n-1]} \{f_{i+1}(c, x_{i+1}, x_{i+2}) + g_{i-1}(c, x_{i+1})\}$$

however, since $g_{i-1}(a, b) = g_{n-i}(b, a)$, it can be computed as,

$$x_i := \text{argmin}_{c \in [0..2^n-1]} \{f_{i+1}(c, x_{i+1}, x_{i+2}) + g_{n-i}(x_{i+1}, c)\}$$

Table 7 reports the results obtained with BE-sym. The first column tells the size of the problem. The second column indicates times obtained with BE-sym.

function BE-sym(n)

1.   **for** $a, b \in [0..2^n - 1]$ **do**
2. $g_n(a, b) := \min_{c \in [0..2^n - 1]} \{f_{n-1}(a, b, c) + f_n(b, c)\};$
3.   **for** $i = n - 1$ **downto** $n/2 + 2$ **do**
4.   **for** $a, b \in [0..2^n - 1]$ **do**
5. $g_i(a, b) := \min_{c \in [0..2^n - 1]} \{f_{i-1}(a, b, c) + g_{i+1}(b, c)\};$
6.   **endfor**
7. $opt := \min_{a, b \in [0..2^n - 1]} \{g_{\frac{n}{2}+2}(a, b) + g_{\frac{n}{2}+2}(b, a)\};$
8. $(x_{\frac{n}{2}}, x_{\frac{n}{2}+1}) := \text{argmin}_{a, b \in [0..2^n - 1]} \{g_{\frac{n}{2}+2}(a, b) + g_{\frac{n}{2}+2}(b, a)\};$
9.   **for** $i = \frac{n}{2} + 2$ **to** $n - 1$ **do**
10. $x_i := \text{argmin}_{c \in [0..2^n - 1]} \{f_{i-1}(x_{i-2}, x_{i-1}, c) + g_{i+1}(x_{i-1}, c)\};$
11. **endfor**
12. $x_n := \text{argmin}_{c \in [0..2^n - 1]} \{f_{n-1}(x_{n-2}, x_{n-1}, c) + f_n(x_{n-1}, c)\};$
13. **for** $i = \frac{n}{2} - 1$ **to** 2 **do**
14. $x_i := \text{argmin}_{c \in [0..2^n - 1]} \{f_{i+1}(c, x_{i+1}, x_{i+2}) + g_{n-i}(x_{i+1}, c)\};$
15. **endfor**
16. $x_1 := \text{argmin}_{c \in [0..2^n - 1]} \{f_2(c, x_2, x_3) + f_1(c, x_2)\};$
17. **return**($opt, (x_1, x_2, \ldots, x_n)$);
endfunction

Fig. 6. Bucket Elimination exploiting symmetries (assume n even).

n	BE-sym	BE	CP/IP-sym
9	2	4	51
10	14	27	147
11	120	210	373
12	813	1638	30360
13	7223	13788	30729
14	6×10^4	10^5	5×10^5
15	*	*	7×10^5

Fig. 7. Experimetal results of three algorithms on the still life problem.

To facilitate comparison, the third column reports results obtained with BE and the fourth column reports the best times obtained by [3] with their hybrid CP/IP algorithm which also exploits symmetries (again, be aware of the different machines). Comparing BE *vs.* BE-sym, the experiments confirm that BE-sym is twice as fast as BE. Although BE-sym requires less memory than BE, we still could not execute the $n = 15$ case. Comparing it with the CP/IP hybrid, it can be observed that BE-sym seems to be systematically faster.

5 Restricting to Symmetric Still Life

When n is too large to solve optimally with current methods, previous authors proposed finding symmetric optimal solutions. In [3] optimal horizontally symmetric solutions for $n = 18$ are found, and in [11] optimal 90 degrees rotational symmetric solutions for $n = 18$ are also found.

Fig. 8. A 28 × 28 symmetric still life. The optimal value is 406 living cells.

We followed the same approach and adapted BE to consider vertically symmetric patterns. With our formulation, changes are straightforward: we only need to reduce domains to symmetrical values. Lets assume that n is an even number (the odd case is similar). We represent symmetric sequences of bits of length n by considering the left side of the sequence (clearly, the symmetrical right part can be obtained by reversing the left part), which can be implemented as integers in the interval $[0..2^{\frac{n}{2}} - 1]$. It is easy to see that the complexity of BE is now time $\Theta(n^2 \times 2^{3n/2})$ and space $\Theta(n \times 2^n)$, which means that the size of problems that we can solve should be doubled. Observe that this problem has exactly the same symmetries as the original problem. Consequently, we can still use the BE-sym algorithm.

Figure 9 reports the results that we obtained with BE-sym. The first column contains the problem size (we only solved even values of n), the second column reports the optimal value as number of living cells, the third column reports the number of solutions and the fourth column reports CPU time obtained with the BE-sym algorithm. As predicted, we solve up to the $n = 28$ case (Figure 8). The $n = 30$ case could not be execute due to space exhaustion. These results improve significatively over the previous works of [3, 11].

n	opt. cost	n. sol.	BE-sym
10	52	133	0
12	76	8	0
14	104	1	0
16	136	3	0
18	170	4	10
20	208	1813	81
22	252	635	633
24	300	5363	4620
26	350	55246	37600
28	406	12718	1.7×10^5

Fig. 9. Experimental results on for finding vertical reflection symmetric still lifes with BE.

6 Future Work

We have shown that BE provides an efficient solver approach to the still life problem, although it has the fundamental limitation of its exponential space complexity which makes impossible with current computers to solve the problem beyond $n = 14$. Fortunately, some authors [7–9] suggest ways to overcome space exhaustion when executing BE. These approaches propose parameterized algorithms, where the parameter indicates the amount of space the user is willing to use. The algorithms dynamically switch to search each time BE cannot carry out the solving process. BE is resumed as soon as the space-costly part of the problem has been solved. We are currently exploring these ideas. Hopefully we will be reporting new results in the near future.

7 Conclusion

Bucket Elimination is often believed to be an algorithm of little practical interest due to its exponential space complexity. In this paper we showed that it is extremely competitive for the still life problem. We showed that it provides a much lower worst-case time complexity than search-based methods which makes it systematically faster in practice. The space complexity drawback comes to the fore where search methods fail due to their exponential time complexity. We reported some results, which we think are new: the number of optimal solutions up to $n = 14$ and the optimal cost and the number of solutions of vertically symmetric still lifes up to $n = 28$.

As far as we know, there is no previous work on how to adapt BE to exploit symmetries. We enhanced the performance of our BE implementation by considering some of the problem symmetries. We belive that it is a preliminary step towards a wider (although possibly limited) practical applicability of BE.

References

1. Bertele, U., Brioschi, F.: Nonserial Dynamic Programming. Academic Press, London, 1972.

2. Bistarelli, S., Montanari, U., Rossi, F.: Semiring-Based Constraint Satisfaction and Optimization. Journal of the ACM. **44(2)** (1997) 201–236.
3. Bosch, R., Trick, M.: Constraint programming and hybrid formulations for three life designs. Proceedings of the International Workshop on Integration of AI and OR Techniques in Constraint Programming for Combinatorial Optimization Problems, CP-AI-OR'02 (2002), 77–91.
4. Dechter, R.: Bucket elimination: A unifying framework for reasoning. Artificial Intelligence. **113** (1999) 41–85.
5. Elkies, N.D.: The still-life density problem and its generalisations. Voronoi's impact on modern science, Book 1 (1998) 228–253. Institute of Math. Kyiv.
6. Gardner, M.: The fantastic combinations of John Conway's new solitary game. Scientific American. **223** (1970) 120–123.
7. Larrosa, J., Dechter, R.: Boosting Search with Variable Elimination. In Proceedings of Principles and Practice of Constraint Programming, CP-2000 (Singapore, Singapore, 2000), 291–305.
8. Larrosa, J.: Boosting Search with Variable Elimination in Constraint Optimization and Constraint Satisfaction Problems. Constraints: an International Journal. To appear.
9. Dechter, R., El Fattah, Y.: Topological Parameters for Time-Space Tradeoff. Artificial Intelligence. To appear.
10. Schiex, T., Fargier, H., Verfaillie, G.: Valued Constraint Satisfaction Problems: hard and easy problems. In Proceedings of the 14th. International Join Conference on Artificial Intelligence, IJCAI-1995 (Montreal, Canada, 1995), 631–637.
11. Smith, B.: A dual graph translation of a problem in life. In Proceedings of Principles and Practice of Constraint Programming, CP-2002 (Ithaca, USA, 2002).
12. Tsang, E.: Foundations of Constraint Satisfaction. Academic Press, London, 1993.

Exploiting Multidirectionality
in Coarse-Grained Arc Consistency Algorithms

Christophe Lecoutre, Frédéric Boussemart, and Fred Hemery

CRIL (Centre de Recherche en Informatique de Lens)
CNRS FRE 2499
rue de l'université, SP 16
62307 Lens cedex, France
{lecoutre,boussemart,hemery}@cril.univ-artois.fr

Abstract. Arc consistency plays a central role in solving Constraint Satisfaction Problems. This is the reason why many algorithms have been proposed to establish it. Recently, an algorithm called AC2001 and AC3.1 has been independently presented by their authors. This algorithm which is considered as a refinement of the basic algorithm AC3 has the advantage of being simple and competitive. However, it does not take into account constraint bidirectionality as AC7 does. In this paper, we address this issue, and, in particular, introduce two new algorithms called AC3.2 and AC3.3 which benefit from good properties of both AC3 and AC7. Indeed, AC3.2 and AC3.3 are as easy to implement as AC3 and take advantage of bidirectionality as AC7 does. More precisely, AC3.2 is a general algorithm which partially exploits bidirectionality whereas AC3.3 is a binary algorithm which fully exploits bidirectionality. It turns out that, when Maintaining Arc Consistency during search, MAC3.2, due to a memorization effect, is more efficient than MAC3.3 both in terms of constraint checks and cpu time. Compared to MAC2001/3.1, our experimental results show that MAC3.2 saves about 50% of constraint checks and, on average, 15% of cpu time.

1 Introduction

Arc consistency plays a central role in solving Constraint Satisfaction Problems. Indeed, the MAC algorithm [10], i.e., the algorithm which maintains arc consistency during the search of a solution, is still considered as the most efficient generic approach to cope with large and hard problem instances [3]. Many algorithms have been proposed to establish arc consistency.

On the one hand, coarse-grained algorithms such as AC3 [8], AC2000 [5], AC2001 [5], AC3.1 [17] and $AC3_d$ [13] have been developed, the principle of which is to apply successive revisions of arcs, i.e., of pairs (C, X) composed of a constraint C and of a variable X belonging to the set of variables of C. These algorithms are easy to implement and efficient in practice.

On the other hand, fine-grained algorithms such as AC4 [9], AC6 [1] and AC7 [2] have been proposed, the principle of which is to apply successive revisions of "values", i.e., of triplets (C, X, a) composed of an arc (C, X) and of a value a belonging to the domain of X. These algorithms are more difficult to implement since it is necessary to

F. Rossi (Ed.): CP 2003, LNCS 2833, pp. 480–494, 2003.

manage heavy data structures. And even if, AC6 and AC7 are quite competitive with respect to coarse-grained algorithms in the context of a preprocessing stage, this is less obvious in the context of a search since maintaining these data structures can be penalizing.

Arc consistency algorithms can also be characterized by a certain number of desirable properties [2]. In particular, it is interesting to exploit constraint bidirectionality (called multidirectionality when constraints are not binary) in order to avoid useless constraint checks. Bidirectionality means that if a value b of the domain of a variable X_j supports (is compatible with) a value a of the domain of a variable X_i with respect to a binary constraint C defined on X_i and X_j then a of X_i also supports b of X_j. Hence, if a constraint check $C(a, b)$ is performed when looking for a support of a, there is no need to perform the same constraint check when looking for a support of b provided that the constraint check has been recorded as a success or a failure (positive and negative bidirectionality exploitation). Among all algorithms cited above, AC7 is the only one which fully takes into account bidirectionality. And, as far as we are aware, $AC3_d$ is the only coarse-grained algorithm that partially exploits bidirectionality (by using a so-called double-support domain heuristic).

In this paper, we address the issue of exploiting constraint bidirectionality with respect to coarse-grained algorithms. First, we introduce two new algorithms, called AC3.2 and AC3.3, which can be seen as improvements of AC2001/3.1. AC3.2 is a general algorithm, i.e., suitable to both binary and non-binary problems, which partially exploits positive bidirectionality whereas AC3.3 is a binary algorithm, i.e., only adapted to binary problems, which fully exploits positive bidirectionality. In both cases, integrating positive bidirectionality exploitation only requires a slight additional data structure.

Next, we show that AC2001/3.1, AC3.2, AC3.3 can all benefit from negative bidirectionality by concentrating the search of a support with respect to so-called candidates [4]. As a result, AC3.2 and AC3.3 benefit from good properties of both AC3 and AC7. Indeed, AC3.2 and AC3.3 are as easy to implement as AC3 and take advantage of bidirectionality as AC7 does (although AC3.3 is the only coarse-grained algorithm which fully takes into account bidirectionality).

Our experimentations show that, when arc consistency is used as a preprocessing, AC3.3 seems to be the most efficient algorithm. Compared to AC2001/3.1, AC3.3 saves about 25% of constraint checks and, on average, 15% of cpu time. However, it turns out that, when Maintaining Arc Consistency during search, MAC3.2, due to a memorization effect, is more efficient than MAC3.3 both in terms of constraint checks and cpu time. Compared to MAC2001/3.1, our experimental results show that MAC3.2 saves about 50% of constraint checks and, on average, 15% of cpu time.

2   Preliminaries

In this section, we briefly introduce some notations and definitions used hereafter.

Definition 1. *A constraint network is a pair* $(\mathscr{X}, \mathscr{C})$ *where:*

- $\mathscr{X} = \{X_1, \ldots, X_n\}$ *is a finite set of* n *variables such that each variable* X_i *has an associated domain* $dom(X_i)$ *denoting the set of values allowed for* X_i,

- $\mathscr{C} = \{C_1, \ldots, C_m\}$ *is a finite set of m constraints such that each constraint C_j has an associated relation $rel(C_j)$ denoting the set of tuples allowed for the variables $vars(C_j)$ involved in the constraint C_j.*

Without loss of generality, it is possible to assume that any set of variables $vars(C)$ associated with a constraint C is ordered. Then, we can get the position $pos(X, C)$ of a variable X in $vars(C)$ and the ith variable $var(i, C)$ in $vars(C)$. We shall say that a constraint C involves (or binds) a variable X if and only if X belongs to $vars(C)$. The arity of a constraint C is the number of variables involved in C, i.e., the number of variables in $vars(C)$.

A Constraint Satisfaction Problem (CSP) is the task of finding one (or more) solution for a constraint network. A solution is an assignment of values to all the variables such that all the constraints are satisfied. A solution guarantees the existence of a support in all constraints.

Definition 2. *Let C be a k-ary constraint, a k-tuple t is a list of k values indexed from 1 to $k = length(t)$ and denoted here $t[1], \ldots, t[k]$. A k-tuple t is:*

- *valid wrt C iff $\forall i \in 1..k, t[i] \in dom(var(i, C))$,*
- *allowed by C iff $t \in rel(C)$,*
- *a (current) support in C iff it is valid and allowed.*

A tuple t will be said to be a support of (X, a) in C when t is a support in C such that $t[pos(X, C)] = a$. Determining if a tuple is valid is called a validity check and determining if a tuple is allowed is called a constraint check. It is also important to note that, assuming a total order on domains, tuples can be ordered using a lexicographic order $\prec$.

To solve a CSP, a depth-first search algorithm with backtracking can be applied, where at each step of the search, a variable assignment is performed followed by a filtering process called constraint propagation. Usually, constraint propagation removes some values which can not occur in any solution. Modifying the domains of a given problem in order to get it arc consistent involves using constraint checks and, also, for some algorithms, validity checks. Constraint checks are required to find (new) supports whereas validity checks are used to determine if (old) supports are still valid.

Definition 3. *Let P be a CSP and (X, a) be a pair composed of a variable X of P and of a value $a \in dom(X)$. (X, a) is said to be consistent wrt a constraint C of P if either $X \notin vars(C)$ or there exists a support of (X, a) in C. (X, a) is said to be consistent wrt P iff (X, a) is consistent wrt all constraints of P. P is said to be arc consistent iff all pairs (X, a) are consistent wrt P.*

3 Properties of Arc Consistency Algorithms

In order to avoid useless constraint checks, arc consistency algorithms can exploit different properties. In this section, we present an adaptation of the desirable properties defined in [2].

Algorithm 1   AC3.X

1: $Q \leftarrow \{(C, X) \mid C \in \mathcal{C} \wedge X \in vars(C)\}$
2: init3.X()
3: **while** $Q \neq \emptyset$ **do**
4:      pick (C, X) in Q
5:      **if** revise3.X(C,X) **then**
6:          **if** $dom(X) = \emptyset$ **then** return FAILURE
7:          **else** $Q \leftarrow Q \cup \{(C', X') \mid X \in vars(C') \wedge X' \in vars(C') \wedge X \neq X' \wedge C \neq C'\}$
8:      **end if**
9: **end while**
10: return SUCCESS

In any arc consistency algorithm, a constraint check $C(t)$ is always performed with respect to a triplet (C, X, a) where C is a k-ary constraint, X a variable in $vars(C)$, a a value in $dom(X)$ and t a k-tuple. The following properties should be ideally verified by any arc consistency algorithm, given a triplet (C, X, a) and a tuple t.

- **positive unidirectionality** $C(t)$ is not checked if there exists a support t' of (X, a) in C already successfully checked wrt (C, X, a).
- **negative unidirectionality** $C(t)$ is not checked if it has already been unsuccessfully checked wrt (C, X, a).
- **positive multidirectionality** $C(t)$ is not checked if there exists a support t' of (X, a) in C already successfully checked wrt a triplet (C, Y, b) with $Y \neq X$.
- **negative multidirectionality** $C(t)$ is not checked if $C(t)$ has already been unsuccessfully checked wrt a triplet (C, Y, b) with $Y \neq X$.

Roughly speaking, above properties correspond to properties 1, 3a, 2 and 3b of [2].

4   AC3.X Algorithms

In this section, we present different algorithms which are based on AC3, and are consequently coarse-grained algorithms denoted AC3.X. First, we introduce the main procedure of all these algorithms and recall the AC2001/3.1 algorithm. Next, we propose two originals algorithms, called AC3.2 and AC3.3, which can be seen as improvements of AC2001/3.1. Note that the description of all below algorithms (except AC3.3) is given in the general case of non binary problems.

4.1   Main Procedure of AC3.X Algorithms

The structure of the AC3.X algorithms is identical to the one of the AC3 algorithm [8]. All these algorithms use a propagation set, denoted Q here, in order to hold all the arcs that need to be revised; the objective of the revision of an arc (C, X) being to remove the values of $dom(X)$ that have become inconsistent with respect to C.

Although we present, for the sake of simplicity, an arc-oriented propagation scheme, our implementation integrates a variable-oriented one since it turns out to be more efficient when using so-called revision ordering heuristics [6].

Algorithm 2   init3.1()

$\forall C \in \mathscr{C}, \forall X \in vars(C), \forall a \in dom(X)$
$\quad last[C, X, a] \leftarrow nil$

Algorithm 3   revise3.1(in C,X) : int

1: nbElements $\leftarrow$ | $dom(X)$ |
2: **for** each $a \in dom(X)$ **do**
3:    **if** $last[C, X, a]$ is valid **then** continue
4:    $seekNextSupport(C, X, a, last[C, X, a])$
5:    **if** $last[C, X, a] = nil$ **then** remove a from $dom(X)$
6: **end for**
7: return nbElements $\neq$ | $dom(X)$ |

Here is a quick description of the main procedure described by Algorithm 1. Initially, all arcs (C, X) are put in the set Q in order to be revised, and a call to *init3.X* allows the initialization of AC3.X specific data structures. Then, arcs are revised in turn, and when a revision is effective (at least a value has been removed), the set Q has to be updated.

4.2   AC2001/3.1

The same algorithm, seen as an extension of AC3, and called AC2001 by [5] and AC3.1 by [17] has been proposed independently by their authors. There is a simple but important difference between AC3 and AC2001/3.1. Indeed, when a support of a value has to be found, AC3 starts the search from scratch whereas AC2001/3.1 starts the search from a resumption point which corresponds to the last support found for this value. More precisely, AC2001/3.1 verifies positive and negative unidirectionality.

This less naive approach requires the introduction of a data structure, denoted *last*. This data structure is an array used to store the last support of any triplet (C, X, a) composed of an arc (C, X) and of a value a belonging to $dom(X)$. Initially, the structure *last* must be initialized to *nil* (see Algorithm 2). The revision (see Algorithm 3) involves testing for any value the validity of the last support (*nil* is not valid) and potentially looking for a new support.

Note that *seekNextSupport* (see Algorithm 4) modifies its parameter t with either the smallest support of (X, a) in C strictly greater than it or with *nil* (remember that a constraint check is denoted by $C(t)$). It calls the function *seekNextTuple* which modifies its parameter t with either the smallest valid tuple t' in C such that $t \prec t'$ and $t'[pos(X, C)] = a$ or with *nil*.

Algorithm 4   seekNextSupport(in C,X,a, in/out t)

1: **while** $t \neq nil$ **do**
2:    $seekNextTuple(C, X, a, t)$
3:    **if** $C(t)$ **then** break
4: **end while**

Algorithm 5 init3.2()

$\forall C \in \mathscr{C}, \forall X \in vars(C), \forall a \in dom(X)$
$\quad last[C, X, a] \leftarrow nil \; ; \; lastE[C, X, a] \leftarrow nil$

Algorithm 6 revise3.2(in C,X) : int

1: nbElements $\leftarrow \mid dom(X) \mid$
2: **for** each $a \in dom(X)$ **do**
3:     **if** $lastE[C, X, a]$ is valid **then** continue
4:     **if** $last[C, X, a]$ is valid **then** continue
5:     $seekNextSupport(C, X, a, last[C, X, a])$
6:     **if** $last[C, X, a] = nil$ **then** remove a from $dom(X)$
7:     **else**
8:       **for** each $Y \in vars(C) \mid Y \neq X$ **do**
9:        $b \leftarrow last[C, X, a][pos(Y, C)]$
10:       $lastE[C, Y, b] \leftarrow last[C, X, a]$
11:      **endfor**
12: **end for**
13: return nbElements $\neq \mid dom(X) \mid$

AC2001/3.1 has a space complexity of $O(md)$ and an optimal worst-case time complexity of $O(md^2)$ [5, 17] (even if we consider non binary constraints provided that we arbitrarily bound constraint arity).

4.3 AC3.2

To improve the behaviour of the AC2001/3.1 algorithm while keeping simplicity of the algorithm, it is possible to partially benefit from positive multidirectionality. In particular, when a support is found, it can be used not only for the value for which it was looking for but also for all values occurring in the support. To avoid dealing with heavy data structures, one simply records for any value the last extern support, i.e., a support that corresponds to the last support of another value.

For instance, let us consider a binary constraint C such that $vars(C) = \{X_i, X_j\}$. If a support (a, b) of (X_i, a) is found in C (when looking for a support of (X_i, a)), then it is also recorded as being the last extern support of (X_j, b) in C. If later, a support (c, b) of (X_i, c) is found in C, then the last extern support of (X_j, b) in C becomes (c, b).

This new algorithm requires the introduction of an additional data structure, denoted *lastE*. This data structure is an array used to store the last extern support of any triplet (C, X, a). Initially, the structure *lastE* must be initialized to *nil* (see Algorithm 5). The revision (see Algorithm 6) involves testing for any value the validity of the last extern support (line 3) and if, it fails, the validity of the last support (line 4). If neither are valid then a search of a new support is started, and if it succeeds, some extern supports are updated (lines 8 to 11).

AC3.2 keeps the time and space complexities of AC3.1. Indeed, in the worst case, the algorithm simply performs one extra test (line 3) and a bounded number of extra

---

Algorithm 7 init3.3()

$\forall C \in \mathscr{C}, \forall X \in vars(C), \forall a \in dom(X)$
   $last[C, X, a] \leftarrow nil$; $cpt[C, X, a] \leftarrow 0$

Algorithm 8 revise3.3(in $C_{i,j}$,X_i) : int

1: nbElements $\leftarrow$ | $dom(X_i)$ |
2: **for** each $a \in dom(X_i)$ **do**
3:    **if** $cpt[C_{i,j}, X_i, a] > 0$ **then** continue
4:    **if** $last[C_{i,j}, X_i, a]$ is valid **then** continue
5:    **if** $last[C_{i,j}, X_i, a] \neq nil$ **then**
6:      $cpt[C_{i,j}, X_j, last[C_{i,j}, X_i, a]] - -$
7:      $seekNextSupport(C_{i,j}, X_i, a, last[C_{i,j}, X_i, a])$
8:    **if** $last[C_{i,j}, X_i, a] = nil$ **then**
9:      remove a from $dom(X_i)$
10:     **for** each $C_{i,k} \in \mathscr{C} \mid k \neq j$ **do**
11:       **if** $last[C_{i,k}, X_i, a] \neq nil$ **then**
12:        $cpt[C_{i,k}, X_k, last[C_{i,k}, X_i, a]] - -$
13:     **else** $cpt[C_{i,j}, X_j, last[C_{i,j}, X_i, a]] + +$
14: **end for**
15: return nbElements $\neq$ | $dom(X_i)$ |

---

assignments (lines 8 to 11) for each value revision. And we only need an additional array to store the last extern supports.

4.4 AC3.3

AC3.2 only integrates a partial positive multidirectionality exploitation. For binary problems, it is possible to conceive a simple algorithm which fully exploits positive bidirectionality. This algorithm, which is called AC3.3, simply records for any value the number of its extern supports. Then, an array, denoted cpt is introduced in order to store the number of extern supports of any triplet (C, X, a).

After initializing these counters to 0 (see Algorithm 7), we have to carefully update them (see Algorithm 8), when a support is lost (line 6), a support is found (line 13) or a value is removed (lines 10 to 12). For the sake of simplicity, $last[C_{i,j}, X_i, a]$ will be considered as equivalent to $last[C_{i,j}, X_i, a][pos(X_j, C)]$. For instance, if (a, b) is the last support of (X_i, a) in $C_{i,j}$ then $last[C_{i,j}, X_i, a]$ will designate the value b instead of the pair (a, b). The correctness of AC3.3 is given by the following proposition (the proof of which is omitted here). As AC3.2, AC3.3 keeps the time and space complexities of AC2001/3.1.

Proposition 1. *The following invariant of the main loop of algorithm 8 holds:* $\forall C_{i,j} \in \mathscr{C}, \forall X_i \in vars(C_{i,j}), \forall a \in dom(X_i), cpt[C_{i,j}, X_i, a]$ *gives exactly the number of extern supports of* (X_i, a) *in* $C_{i,j}$.

Algorithm 9   seekCandidate(in C,X,a, in/out t, in k) : int

1: **for** k **from** $frontier$ **to** $length(t)$ **do**
2:    **if** $k = pos(C, X)$ **then** continue
3:    **if** $last[C, X, t[k]] = nil$ **then** continue
4:    $t' \leftarrow last[C, var(k, C), t[k]]$
5:    $s \leftarrow 1$
6:    **while** $s \leq length(t) \wedge t[s] = t'[s]$ **do** s++
7:    **if** $s = length(t) + 1$ **then** return SUPPORT
8:    **if** $t[s] > t'[s]$ **then** continue
9:    **if** $s < k$ **then** $k' \leftarrow seekNextTuple(C, X, a, t, k)$
10:    **else**
11:        $k' \leftarrow copy(C, t, t', s, pos(C, X))$
12:        **if** $k' = length(t) + 1$ **then** return SUPPORT
13:        **if** $k' = pos(C, X) \wedge t[k'] > t'[k']$ **then**
14:            reinitTupleAfter(C,X,a,t,k')
15:        **else** $k' \leftarrow seekNextTuple(C, X, a, t, k')$
16:    **end if**
17:    **if** $k' = -1$ **then** return NOTHING
18:    **else if** $k' - 1 < k$ **then** $k \leftarrow k' - 1$
19: **end for**
20: return CANDIDATE

---

5   Negative Multidirectionality Exploitation

In the previous section, we have focused our attention to positive multidirectionality. In this one, we show that AC2001/3.1, AC3.2, AC3.3 can all benefit from negative multidirectionality. New algorithms, denoted AC3.1*, AC3.2* and AC3.3*, are then obtained by replacing the call to the "standard" *seekNextSupport* function by a call to the *seekNextSupport** function described below.

The principle is to concentrate the search of a support with respect to so-called candidates [4]. A candidate is a tuple which has never been checked. Note that the presentation is quite technical as it is given for non binary constraints.

First, let us consider a function *seekCandidate* such that a call of the form *seekCandidate*(C, X, a, t, k) computes the smallest candidate t' valid w.r.t. C such that $t \preceq t'$ and $t'[pos(X, C)] = a$. Note that k is only given for optimization as it indicates that the $k - 1$ first values in t have been verified to be a possible prefix for a candidate. This function updates t with t' and returns one value among NOTHING, SUPPORT and CANDIDATE which respectively indicate that there are no more candidates, that the updated argument t is a support or simply a candidate. The difference between this function, described by Algorithm 9, and that of [4] is due to the fact that it can be called by an algorithm, such as AC2001/3.1 or AC3.2, which does not (fully) exploit positive multidirectionality. This is the reason why supports can be found when looking after candidates.

Three auxiliary procedures are called by *seekCandidate*:

- *seekNextTuple*(C, X, a, t, k) computes the smallest valid tuple t' in C such that $t \prec t', t'[pos(X, C)] = a$ and $\exists k' \leq k \mid t[k'] \neq t'[k']$. This function, similar to the one described in [4], updates t with t' and returns the smallest $k' \mid t[k'] \neq t'[k']$ or -1 if it does not exist.

- *reinitTupleAfter*(C, X, a, t, k) computes the smallest valid tuple t' in C such that $t \prec t'$, $t'[pos(X, C)] = a$ and $\forall i \in 1..k, t[i] = t'[i]$. This procedure updates t with t'.

- *copy*$(C, t, t', start, pivot)$ (see Algorithm 10) copies elements of t' in t from index *start* until an incompatibility is found at position *pivot* (line 3), an invalid value is found (line 5) or the end of the tuple (line 7).

Algorithm 10   copy(in C, in/out t, in t',start,pivot) : int

1: **for** i from start to length(t) **do**
2:    **if** $t[i] = t'[i]$ **then** continue
3:    **if** i = pivot **then** return i
4:    $t[i] \leftarrow t'[i]$
5:    **if** $t[i] \notin dom(var(i, C))$ **then** return i
6: **end for**
7: return length(t)+1

Due to the lack of space, we focus our analysis of this algorithm to original parts and report the reader, for a complementary description, to [4]. First, remark that $t' \leftarrow last[C, var(k, C), t[k]]$ can be equal to t and then be a candidate supporting (X, a) (line 7) since the tuple t is valid[1]. t' can also represent a support even if it is distinct of t provided that (X, a) is supported by t' and all values of t' are still valid (line 12). When (X, a) is not supported by t' or when there exists an invalid value in t', the copy is stopped at index k' and we have either to reinit values after k' or seek the next tuple with a different prefix of size k'.

Now that *seekCandidate* has been described, we can present the function *seekNext-Support*[*] that has to be called to exploit negative multidirectionality (and also a limited form a positive multidirectionality if it is called by AC2001/3.1 or AC3.2). This function (see Algorithm 11) is similar to the one in [4] but takes into account candidates detected as supports by *seekCandidate*.

6   Experiments

To prove the practical interest of the algorithms introduced in this paper, we have implemented them in Java [7] and performed some experiments (run on a PC Pentium IV 2,4GHz 512Mo under Linux) with respect to random, academic and real-world problems. Performances have been measured in terms of the number of constraint checks (#ccks), the number of validity checks (#vcks) and the cpu time in seconds (cpu). All coarse-grained algorithms have been implemented using a variable-oriented propagation scheme and the revision ordering heuristic dom^v which orders the variables in the

---

[1] Initially, t is valid, and after each turn of the main loop, either t is not modified or t is updated by a call to *setNextTuple* or *reinitTupleAfter* which both only yield valid tuples.

Algorithm 11   seekNextSupport*(in C,X,a, in/out t) : boolean

---

1: **if** $t = nil$ **then** $reinitTupleAfter(C, X, a, t, 0)$
2: **else** $seekNextTuple(C, X, a, t, length(t))$
3: $result \leftarrow seekCandidate(C, X, a, t, 1)$
4: **if** $result =$ NOTHING **then** return false
5: **if** $result =$ SUPPORT **then** return true
6: **while** true **do**
7:    **if** $C(t)$ **then** return true
8:    $k \leftarrow seekNextTuple(C, X, a, t, length(t))$
9:    **if** $k = -1$ **then** return false
10:    $result \leftarrow seekCandidate(C, X, a, t, k)$
11:    **if** $result =$ NOTHING **then** return false
12:    **if** $result =$ SUPPORT **then** return true
13: **end while**

---

propagation set by increasing current size of their domains (more details can be found in [6]). On the other hand, our implementation of AC7 integrates the two "standard" revision ordering heuristics *lifo* and *fifo*.

6.1   Stand-Alone Arc Consistency

First, we have considered stand alone arc consistency, i.e., the task of making arc consistent a constraint satisfaction problem. The first series of experiments that we have run corresponds to some random problems. In this paper, a class of random CSP instances will be characterized by a 5-tuple (n, d, m, k, t) where n is the number of variables, d the uniform domain size, m the number of k-ary constraints and t is either the number of not allowed tuples or the probability that a given tuple is not allowed.

Table 1. Stand alone arc consistency on random instances

		AC3	AC3.1	AC3.1*	AC3.2	AC3.2*	AC3.3	AC3.3*	AC7
P1	#ccks	99,968	99,968	97,967	94,012	93,984	94,012	93,984	93,994
	cpu	0.064	0.069	0.072	0.072	0.078	0.067	0.072	0.092
P2	#ccks	148,029	74,539	61,641	63,540	56,645	62,935	56,437	272,443
	cpu	0.087	0.048	0.046	0.044	0.043	0.045	0.045	0.266
P3	#ccks	2,351,578	587,505	504,941	478,135	446,188	470,177	442,867	506,340
	cpu	1.375	0.384	0.375	0.342	0.347	0.319	0.327	0.457
P4	#ccks	4,202,630	1,033,014	934,082	857,789	831,040	844,334	824,805	794,853
	cpu	2.490	0.701	0.704	0.636	0.661	0.627	0.652	0.614

We present the results, given in Table 1, about the random binary instances studied in [2, 5, 17]. More precisely, 4 classes, denoted here P1, P2, P3 and P4, have been experimented. P1=(150, 50, 500, 2, 1250) and P2=(150, 50, 500, 2, 2350) correspond to classes of under-constrained and over-constrained instances whereas P3=(150, 50, 500, 2, 2296) and P4=(50, 50, 1225, 2, 2188) correspond to classes of instances at the phase transition of arc consistency for sparse problems and for dense problems, respectively. For each class, 50 instances have been generated and the mean of cpu time, constraint checks and validity checks have been computed.

While all algorithms have close performances with respect to P1 and P2, one can notice that AC3.2, and especially AC3.3, clearly outperforms AC3.1 with respect to P3 and P4. On the other hand, the algorithms that exploit negative bidirectionality slightly reduce the number of constraint checks but, due to the overhead, not the cpu time.

Next, we have tested real-world instances, taken from the FullRLFAP archive[2], which contains instances of radio link frequency assignment problems. For stand alone arc consistency, we present the results, in Table 2, about two instances, respectively denoted SCEN#08 and SCEN#11, studied in [2, 13, 17].

Table 2. Stand alone arc consistency on RLFAP instances

		AC3	AC3.1	AC3.1*	AC3.2	AC3.2*	AC3.3	AC3.3*	AC7
SCEN	#ccks	46, 294	42, 223	35, 079	39, 795	34, 223	39, 713	34, 215	866, 382
#08	cpu	0.021	0.023	0.027	0.024	0.028	0.029	0.032	0.516
SCEN	#ccks	971, 893	971, 893	841, 225	671, 664	638, 932	671, 664	638, 932	638, 448
#11	cpu	0.226	0.247	0.272	0.225	0.243	0.206	0.232	0.376

For these instances, AC3.2 and AC3.3 are quite close. Both algorithms saves many constraint checks while not reducing cpu times compared to AC3 and AC3.1. Remark that the number of constraints checks required for SCEN#05 and SCEN#08 is far weaker than those presented by [2, 17]. This gap is mainly due to the introduction of our revision ordering heuristic [6]. A similar behaviour can be observed in [13].

The third problem that we have experimented is called Domino and is taken from [17]. The Domino problem corresponds to an undirected constraint graph with a cycle and a trigger constraint. Each instance, characterized by a pair (n, d) where n denotes the number of variables, the domains of which are $\{1, \ldots, d\}$, is such that there exists $n - 1$ equality constraints $X_i = X_{i+1}$ ($\forall i \in 1..n - 1$) and a trigger constraint $(X_1 = X_n + 1 \wedge X_1 < d) \vee (X_1 = X_n \wedge X_1 = d)$.

Table 3. Stand alone arc consistency on Domino instances

		AC3	AC3.1	AC3.1*	AC3.2	AC3.2*	AC3.3	AC3.3*	AC7
$n = 100$	#ccks	137.330M	5.970M	3.980M	3.980M	3.960M	3.980M	3.960M	2.029M
$d = 200$	cpu	22.799	1.259	1.417	0.951	1.055	1.009	1.089	0.802
$n = 100$	#ccks	459.011M	13.456M	8.970M	8.971M	8.926M	8.971M	8.926M	4.559M
$d = 300$	cpu	76.406	2.705	3.010	2.010	2.237	2.136	2.295	1.583

On Domino instances, AC3.2 and AC3.3 allow saving about 33% of constraint checks and about 20% of cpu time compared to AC3.1. AC3.2 is the fastest coarse-

[2] We thank the Centre d'Electronique de l'Armement (France).

Table 4. Maintaining arc consistency on random instances

		MAC3	MAC3.1	MAC3.1*	MAC3.2	MAC3.2*	MAC3.3	MAC3.3*	MAC7
A	#ccks	678, 547	441, 011	379, 966	212, 832	203, 995	361, 994	354, 709	522, 898
	#vcks	0	255, 119	255, 119	517, 056	517, 056	192, 606	192, 606	0
	cpu	0.422	0.411	0.406	0.318	0.327	0.460	0.487	0.923
B	#ccks	413, 987	279, 601	189, 628	145, 852	127, 128	−	−	426, 788
	#vcks	0	112, 551	112, 551	222, 671	222, 671	−	−	0
	cpu	0.250	0.225	0.209	0.167	0.171	−	−	0.660

Table 5. Maintaining arc consistency on random instances

		$MAC^s3.1$	$MAC^s3.1*$	$MAC^s3.2$	$MAC^s3.2*$	$MAC^s3.3$	$MAC^s3.3*$
A	#ccks	374, 190	318, 605	203, 989	193, 355	311, 094	303, 765
	#vcks	356, 732	356, 732	540, 728	540, 728	263, 548	263, 548
	cpu	0.476	0.481	0.365	0.373	0.539	0.553
B	#ccks	218, 929	142, 985	134, 792	110, 828	−	−
	#vcks	167, 684	167, 684	241, 715	241, 715	−	−
	cpu	0.237	0.225	0.183	0.185	−	−

grained algorithm with respect to this problem since AC3.2 seems to fully benefit from positive bidirectionality, and since its overhead is smaller than the one of AC3.3.

6.2   Maintaining Arc Consistency during Search

As it appears that one of the most efficient complete search algorithms is the algorithm which Maintains Arc Consistency during the search of a solution [10, 3], we have implemented all MAC versions of previous algorithms and experimented them. All our MAC algorithms integrate the *dom/futdeg* or *DD* [11] variable ordering heuristic.

Two classes of MAC algorithms have been developed for AC3.1, AC3.2 and AC3.3. Algorithms of the former class do not require any additional memory storage to manage the data structures, and hence, have a $O(md)$ space-complexity. As a result, some constraint checks are sacrificed since it is necessary to reinitialize the data structures *last* and *cpt* when backtracking. Algorithms of the latter class requires an additional memory storage to maintain the data structures, and hence, have a $O(md^2)$ space-complexity. We shall denote algorithms of this class MAC^s.

On the other hand, we have observed that it is worthwhile to leave unchanged the specific data structure *lastE* of AC3.2 while backtracking, having the benefit of a so-called memorization effect. It means that a (extern) support found at a given depth of the search has the opportunity to be still valid at a weaker depth of the search (after backtracking).

The performances of all algorithms have been compared with respect to three distinct problems. First, two classes of random instances from model RD of [16] denoted A and B have been experimented. A=$(25, 15, 150, 2, 90/256)$ and B=$(50, 5, 80, 3, 155/256)$ correspond to classes of instances at the phase transition of search for dense binary problems $(150/300 = 50\%)$ with low tightness $(90/256 = 35\%)$ and sparse ternary problems $(80/19600 \approx 0.40\%)$ with high tightness $(155/256 \approx 60\%)$, respectively. For each class, mean results are given for 50 generated instances.

Table 4 gives the results obtained when maintaining arc consistency with respect to A and B. MAC3.2 clearly outperforms MAC3, MAC3.1 and MAC3.3. The number of constraint checks achieved by MAC3.2 is two times less important than the number of constraint checks achieved by MAC3.1. The good behaviour of MAC3.2 results from its memorization effect. Indeed, many constraint checks have been replaced by validity checks: one can observe that the number of validity checks of MAC3.2 is two times more important than the number of validity checks of MAC3.3. As validity checks are cheap, and performed in constant time unlike constraint checks, MAC3.2 has a great advantage.

Table 5 gives the results for the MAC^s algorithms. Although some constraint checks are saved, the overhead of maintaining the data structures during the search is penalizing in terms of timing.

Next, we have experimented a combinatorial mathematics problem, called Golomb ruler, of the CSPLib benchmark library (http://4c.ucc.ie/~tw/csplib/). The satisfaction problem specification is the following: given two values l and m, does there exist a ruler of length l with m marks, i.e., a set of m integers $0 \leq a_1 < \ldots < a_m \leq l$ such that the $m(m - 1)/2$ differences $a_j - a_i, 1 \leq i < j \leq m$ are distinct. We have modeled this problem as a CSP by using ternary and binary constraints as described in [12]. The instance $(l, m) = (34, 8)$ corresponds to the maximum number of marks on a ruler of length 34.

Again, we observe the same phenomenon: MAC3.2 requires two times less constraint checks and two times more validity checks than MAC3.1. There is then a speed up of about 25%.

Table 6. Maintaining arc consistency on Golomb ruler instances

		MAC3	MAC3.1	MAC3.1*	MAC3.2	MAC3.2*	MAC7
$l = 34$	#ccks	10.677M	4.433M	3.334M	2.388M	2.129M	5.337M
$m = 8$	#vcks	0	1.297M	1.297M	2.390M	2.390M	0
	cpu	2.632	2.169	2.250	1.777	1.863	8.243
$l = 34$	#ccks	388.871M	208.674M	164.672M	87.691M	81.207M	303.586M
$m = 9$	#vcks	0	73.080M	73.080M	148.434M	148.434M	0
	cpu	95.508	108.452	111.867	81.150	85.202	485.369

Finally, the behaviour of the different MAC algorithms has been studied with respect to two real instances of the RLFAP archive. Whereas all algorithms are close in terms of CPU time with respect to GRAPH#14, MAC3.2 is the fastest with respect to the most difficult instance SCEN#11 (17, 001 visited nodes).

It is important to note the relative bad behaviour of MAC7. We believe that MAC7 could save more constraint checks by integrating some advanced revision ordering heuristics and could certainly save cpu time with a further optimized implementation.

Table 7. Maintaining arc consistency on RLFAP instances

		MAC3	MAC3.1	MAC3.1*	MAC3.2	MAC3.2*	MAC3.3	MAC3.3*	MAC7
SCEN	#ccks	137M	49.278M	44.193M	23.050M	21.622M	45.255M	43.935M	68M
#11	#vcks	0	53.675M	53.675M	89.842M	89.842M	47.504M	47.504M	0
	cpu	96.761	93.613	95.232	89.751	91.104	131.361	133.556	617
GRAPH	#ccks	2.944M	1.584M	1.333M	1.189M	1.115M	1.187M	1.115M	1.129M
#14	#vcks	0	0.712M	0.712M	1.034M	1.034M	0.638M	0.638M	0
	cpu	1.958	1.876	1.976	1.864	1.921	1.913	1.960	2.295

7   Conclusion

In this paper, we have introduced two new coarse-grained arc consistency algorithms. These algorithms, called AC3.2 and AC3.3, are extensions of AC2001/3.1. The positive form of multidirectionality is partially exploited by AC3.2 and fully exploited by AC3.3. As far as we are aware, $AC3_d$ was the only coarse-grained algorithm exploiting bidirectionality. However, unlike AC3.3 (and $AC3_d$), AC3.2 has the advantage to be adapted to non binary constraints.

Next, we have shown that the negative form of multidirectionality can be taken into account by AC3.1, AC3.2 and AC3.3, resulting in new algorithms denoted AC3.1*, AC3.2* and AC3.3*. As a result, AC3.3* is proved to fully exploit bidirectionality as AC7, a fine-grained algorithm, does.

The main differences between AC3.2/AC3.3 and AC7 are the following:

- AC3.2/AC3.3 are far more easier to implement (exploiting negative multidirectionality is immediate in the binary case) than AC7,
- AC7 does not perform useless validity checks (at the price of heavy data structures),
- AC3.2/AC3.3 perform revisions of arcs whereas AC7 performs revisions of "values".

With respect to the last item, we believe that it must be more difficult to enhance AC7 than AC3.2/3.3 by integrating a revision ordering heuristic [15,6] since the number of elements in the propagation set can be very important for AC7.

Some observations can be supported by our experimentations. When arc consistency is used as a preprocessing, AC3.3 seems to be the most efficient algorithm. Compared to AC2001/3.1, AC3.3 saves about 25% of constraint checks and, on average, 15% of cpu time. When arc consistency is maintained during the search, MAC3.2, due to a memorization effect, is more efficient than MAC3.3 both in terms of constraint checks and cpu time. Compared to MAC2001/3.1, our experimental results show that MAC3.2 saves about 50% of constraint checks and, on average, 15% of cpu time.

Finally, one could wonder if, MAC3.2 which seems to be the most efficient arc consistency algorithm in terms of constraint checks is also really the fastest algorithm. In [14], $MAC3_d$ is shown to be about 1.5 times faster than MAC2001 for difficult random problems. However, the version of MAC2001 used by [14] can be improved since it is simply equipped with the lexicographic revision ordering heuristic. In a related work [6], we have shown that using a variable-oriented variant of MAC2001 with a (not optimized) revision ordering heuristic based on the current domain size allows saving about

25% of cpu time. It is then very difficult to know which algorithm among MAC3$_d$ and MAC3.2 is the fastest without a direct confrontation. It is one perspective of this work.

Acknowledgements

This paper has been supported by the CNRS, the "programme TACT de la Région Nord/Pas-de-Calais" and by the "IUT de Lens".

References

1. C. Bessiere. Arc consistency and arc consistency again. *Artificial Intelligence*, 65:179–190, 1994.
2. C. Bessiere, E.C. Freuder, and J.C. Regin. Using constraint metaknowledge to reduce arc consistency computation. *Artificial Intelligence*, 107:125–148, 1999.
3. C. Bessiere and J.C. Regin. MAC and combined heuristics: two reasons to forsake FC (and CBJ?) on hard problems. In *Proceedings of CP'96*, pages 61–75, 1996.
4. C. Bessiere and J.C. Regin. Arc consistency for general constraint networks: preliminary results. In *Proceedings of IJCAI'97*, 1997.
5. C. Bessiere and J.C. Regin. Refining the basic constraint propagation algorithm. In *Proceedings of IJCAI'01*, pages 309–315, 2001.
6. C. Lecoutre, F. Boussemart, and F. Hemery. Revision ordering heuristics for the constraint satisfaction problem. In *submission*, 2003.
7. C. Lecoutre, F. Boussemart, F. Hemery, and S. Merchez. Abscon 2.0, a constraint programming platform. http://www.cril.univ-artois.fr/~lecoutre, September 2003.
8. A.K. Mackworth. Consistency in networks of relations. *Artificial Intelligence*, 8(1):118–126, 1977.
9. R. Mohr and T.C. Henderson. Arc and path consistency revisited. *Artificial Intelligence*, 28:225–233, 1986.
10. D. Sabin and E. freuder. Contradicting conventional wisdom in constraint satisfaction. In *Proceedings of the PPCPA'94*, Seattle WA, 1994.
11. B.M. Smith and S.A. Grant. Trying harder to fail first. In *Proceedings of ECAI'98*, pages 249–253, Brighton, UK, 1998.
12. B.M. Smith, K. Stergiou, and T Walsh. Modelling the Golomb ruler problem. Technical Report 1999.12, University of Leeds, 1999.
13. M.R.C. van Dongen. AC3$_d$ an efficient arc consistency algorithm with a low space complexity. In *Proceedings of CP'02*, pages 755–760, 2002.
14. M.R.C. van Dongen. Lightweight arc-consistency algorithms. Technical Report TR-01-2003, University college Cork, 2003.
15. R.J. Wallace and E.C. Freuder. Ordering heuristics for arc consistency algorithms. In *Proceedings of NCCAI'92*, pages 163–169, 1992.
16. K. Xu and W. Li. Many hard examples in exact phase transition. *Submitted*, 2002.
17. Y. Zhang and R.H.C. Yap. Making AC3 an optimal algorithm. In *Proceedings of IJCAI'01*, pages 316–321, Seattle WA, 2001.

Local-Search Techniques for Propositional Logic Extended with Cardinality Constraints

Lengning Liu and Mirosław Truszczyński

Department of Computer Science, University of Kentucky
Lexington, KY 40506-0046, USA

Abstract. We study local-search satisfiability solvers for propositional logic extended with cardinality atoms, that is, expressions that provide explicit ways to model constraints on cardinalities of sets. Adding cardinality atoms to the language of propositional logic facilitates modeling search problems and often results in concise encodings. We propose two "native" local-search solvers for theories in the extended language. We also describe techniques to reduce the problem to standard propositional satisfiability and allow us to use off-the-shelf SAT solvers. We study these methods experimentally. Our general finding is that native solvers designed specifically for the extended language perform better than indirect methods relying on SAT solvers.

1 Introduction

We propose and study local-search satisfiability solvers for an extension of propositional logic with explicit means to represent cardinality constraints.

In recent years, propositional logic has been attracting considerable attention as a general-purpose modeling and computing tool, well suited for solving search problems. For instance, to solve a graph k-coloring problem for an undirected graph G, we construct a propositional theory T so that its models encode k-colorings of G and there is a polynomial-time method to reconstruct a k-colorings of G from a model of T. Once we have such a theory T, we apply to it a satisfiability solver, find a model of T and reconstruct from the model the corresponding k-coloring of G.

Instances of many other search problems can be represented in a similar way as propositional theories and this modeling capability of the propositional logic has been known for a long time. However, it has been only recently that we saw a dramatic improvement in the performance of programs to compute models of propositional theories [12, 8, 14, 9, 10, 6]. These new programs can often handle theories consisting of hundreds of thousands, sometimes millions, of clauses. They demonstrate that propositional logic is not only a tool to represent problems but also a viable computational formalism.

The approach we outlined above has its limitations. The repertoire of operators available for building formulas to represent problem constraints is restricted to boolean connectives. Moreover, since satisfiability solvers usually require CNF theories as input, for the most part the only formulas one can use to express

F. Rossi (Ed.): CP 2003, LNCS 2833, pp. 495–509, 2003.

constraints are clauses. One effect of these restrictions is often very large size of CNF theories needed to represent even quite simple constraints and, consequently, poorer effectiveness of satisfiability solvers in computing answers to search problems. Researchers recognized this limitation of propositional logic. They proposed extensions to the basic language with the equivalence operator [7], with cardinality atoms [3,5] and with pseudo-boolean constraints [2,13,1, 4,11], and developed solvers capable of computing models for theories in the expanded syntax.

In this paper, we focus on an extension of propositional logic with *cardinality atoms*, as described in [5]. Specifically, a cardinality atom is an expression of the form kXm, where k and m are non-negative integers and X is a set of propositional atoms. Cardinality atoms offer a *direct* means to represent cardinality constraints on sets and help construct concise encodings of many search problems. We call this extension of the propositional logic the *propositional logic with cardinality constraints* and denote it by PL^{cc}.

To make the logic PL^{cc} into a computational mechanism, we need programs to compute models of PL^{cc} theories. One possible approach is to *compile cardinality atoms away*, replacing them with equivalent propositional-logic representations. After converting the resulting theories to CNF, we can use any off-the-shelf satisfiability solver to compute models. Another approach is to design solvers specifically tailored to the expanded syntax of the logic PL^{cc}. To the best of our knowledge, the first such solver was proposed in [3]. A more recent solver, *aspps*[1], was described in [5].

These two solvers are *complete* solvers. In this paper, we propose and study *local-search* satisfiability solvers that can handle the extended syntax of the logic PL^{cc}. In our work we built on ideas first used in *WSAT*, one of the most effective local-search satisfiability solvers for propositional logic [12][2]. In particular, as in *WSAT*, we proceed by executing a prespecified number of *tries*. Each try starts with a random truth assignment and consists of a sequence of local modification steps called *flips*. Each flip is determined by an atom selected from an *unsatisfied* clause. We base the choice of an atom on the value of its *break-count* (some measure of how much the corresponding flip increases the degree to which the clauses in the theory are violated). In *WSAT*, the break-count of an atom is the number of clauses that become unsatisfied when the truth value of the atom is flipped. In the presence of cardinality atoms, this simple measure does not lead to satisfactory algorithms and modifications are necessary.

In this paper, we propose two approaches. In the first of them, we change the definition of the *break-count*. To this end, we exploit the fact that cardinality atoms are only high-level shorthands for some special propositional theories and, as we already indicated earlier, can be *compiled* away. Let T be a PL^{cc} theory and let T' be its propositional-logic equivalent. We define the break-count of an atom a in T as the number of clauses *in the compiled theory T'* that become unsatisfied after we flip a. Important thing to note is that we do not need to compute T'

---

[1] The acronym for answer-set programming with propositional schemata.

[2] In the paper, we write *WSAT* instead of *WALKSAT* to shorten the notation.

explicitly in order to compute the break-count of a. It can be computed directly on the basis of T alone.

Our second approach keeps the concept of the break-count exactly as it is defined in $WSAT$ but changes the notion of a flip. This approach applies whenever a PL^{cc} theory T can be separated into two parts T_1 and T_2 so that: (1) T_2 consists of propositional clauses, (2) it is easy to construct random assignments that satisfy T_1, and (3) for every truth assignment satisfying T_1, (modified) flips executed on this assignment result in assignments that also satisfy T_1. In such cases, we can start a try by generating an initial truth assignment to satisfy all clauses in T_1, and then executing a sequence of (modified) flips, choosing atoms for flipping based on the number of clauses in T_2 (which are all standard propositional CNF clauses) that become unsatisfiable after the flip.

In the paper, we develop and implement both ideas. We study experimentally the performance of our algorithms on several search problems: the graph coloring problem, the vertex-cover problem and the open latin-square problem. We compare the performance of our algorithms to that of selected SAT solvers executed on CNF theories obtained from PL^{cc} theories by compiling away cardinality atoms.

2 Logic PL^{cc}

The language of the logic PL^{cc} is determined by the set At of *propositional atoms* and two special symbols $\perp$ and $\top$ that we always interpret as *false* and *true*, respectively. A *cardinality atom* (c-atom, for short) is an expression of the form kXm, where X is a set of propositional atoms, and k and m are non-negative integers. If $X = \{a_1, \ldots, a_n\}$, we will also write $k\{a_1, \ldots, a_n\}m$ to denote a c-atom kXm. One (but not both) of k and m may be missing. Intuitively, a c-atom kXm means: *at least k and no more than m of atoms in X are true.* If k (or m) is missing, the c-atom constrains the number of its propositional atoms that must be true only from above (only from below, respectively).

A *clause* is an expression of the form $\neg\alpha_1 \lor \ldots \lor \neg\alpha_r \lor \beta_1 \lor \ldots \lor \beta_s$, where each α_i, $1 \le i \le r$, and each β_j, $1 \le j \le s$, is a propositional atom or a c-atom. A *theory* of the logic PL^{cc} is any set of clauses[3].

An *interpretation* is an assignment of truth values $\mathbf{t}$ and $\mathbf{f}$ to atoms in At. An interpretation I *satisfies* an atom a if $I(a) = \mathbf{t}$. An interpretation I satisfies a c-atom $k\{a_1, \ldots, a_n\}m$ if $k \le |\{i\colon I(a_i) = \mathbf{t}\}| \le m$.

This notion of satisfiability extends in a standard way to clauses and theories. We will write interchangeably "is a model of" and "satisfies". We will also write $I \models E$, when I is a model of an atom, c-atom, clause or theory E.

We will now illustrate the use of the logic PL^{cc} as a modeling tool by presenting PL^{cc} theories that encode (1) the graph-coloring problem, (2) the graph vertex-cover problem, and (3) the open latin-square problem. We later use these theories as benchmarks in performance tests.

---

[3] It is easy to extend the language of PL^{cc} and introduce arbitrary formulas built of atoms and c-atoms by means of logical connectives. Since clausal theories, as in propositional logic, are most fundamental, we focus on clausal theories only.

In the first of these problems we are given a graph G with the set $V = \{1, \ldots, n\}$ of vertices and a set E of edges (unordered pairs of vertices). We are also given a set $C = \{1, \ldots, k\}$ of colors. The objective is to find an assignment of colors to vertices so that for every edge, its vertices get different colors. A PL^{cc} theory representing this problem is built of propositional atoms $c_{i,j}$, where $1 \leq i \leq n$, and $1 \leq j \leq k$. An intended meaning of an atom $c_{i,j}$ is that *vertex i gets color j*. We define the theory $col(G, k)$ to consist of the following clauses:

1. $1\{c_{i,1}, \ldots, c_{i,k}\}1$, for every i, $1 \leq i \leq n$. These clauses ensure that every vertex obtains *exactly one* color
2. $\neg c_{p,j} \vee \neg c_{r,j}$, for every edge $\{p, r\} \in E$ and for every color j. These clauses enforce the main colorability constraint.

It is easy to see that models of the theory $col(G, k)$ are indeed in one-to-one correspondence with k-colorings of G.

In a similar way, we construct a theory $vc(G, k)$ that represents the *vertex-cover* problem. Let G be an undirected graph with the set $V = \{1, \ldots, n\}$ of vertices and a set E of edges. Given G and a positive integer k, the objective is to find a set U of no more than k vertices, such that every edge has at least one of its vertices in U (such sets U are *vertex covers*). We build the theory $vc(G, k)$ of atoms in_i, $1 \leq i \leq n$, (intended meaning of in_i: vertex i is in a vertex cover) and define it to consist of the following clauses:

1. $\{in_1, \ldots, in_n\}k$. This clause guarantees that at most k vertices are chosen to a vertex cover
2. $in_p \vee in_r$, for every edge $\{p, r\} \in E$. These clauses enforce the main vertex cover constraint.

Again, it is evident that models of theory $vc(G, k)$ are in one-to-one correspondence with those vertex covers of G that have no more than k elements.

In the open latin-square problem, we are given an integer n and a collection D of triples (i, j, k), where i, j and k are integers from $\{1, \ldots, n\}$. The goal is to find an $n \times n$ array A such that all entries in A are integers from $\{1, \ldots, n\}$, no row and column of A contains two identical integers, and for every $(i, j, k) \in D$, $A(i, j) = k$. In other words, we are looking for a *latin square* of order n that extends the partial assignment specified by D. To represent this problem we construct a PL^{cc} theory $ls(n, D)$ consisting of the following clauses:

1. $a_{i,j,k}$, for every $(i, j, k) \in D$ (to represent the partial assignment D given as input)
2. $1\{a_{i,j,1}, \ldots, a_{i,j,n}\}1$, for every $i, j = 1, \ldots, n$ (to enforce that every entry receives exactly one value)
3. $\{a_{i,1,k}, \ldots, a_{i,n,k}\}1$, for every $i, k = 1, \ldots, n$ (in combination with (2) these clauses enforce that an integer k appears exactly once in a row i)
4. $\{a_{1,j,k}, \ldots, a_{n,j,k}\}1$, for every $j, k = 1, \ldots, n$ (in combination with (2) these clauses enforce that an integer k appears exactly once in a column j).

One can verify that models of the theory $ls(n, D)$ correspond to solutions to the open latin-square problem with input D.

The use of c-atoms in all these three examples results in concise representations of the corresponding problems. Clearly, we could eliminate c-atoms and
replace the constraints they represent by equivalent CNF theories. However, the
encodings become less direct, less concise and more complex.

3   Using SAT Solvers to Compute Models of PL^{cc} Theories

We will now discuss methods to find models of PL^{cc} theories by means of standard SAT solvers. A key idea is to compile away c-atoms by replacing them with
their propositional-logic descriptions. We will propose several ways to do so.

Let us consider a c-atom $C = k\{a_1, ..., a_n\}m$ and let us define a CNF theory
C' to consist of the following clauses:

1. $\neg a_{i_1} \vee ... \vee \neg a_{i_{m+1}}$, for any $m+1$ atoms $a_{i_1}, ..., a_{i_{m+1}}$ from $\{a_1, ..., a_n\}$ (there
   are $\binom{n}{m+1}$ such clauses); and
2. $a_{i_1} \vee ... \vee a_{i_{n-k+1}}$, for any $n-k+1$ atoms $a_{i_1}, ..., a_{i_{n-k+1}}$ in $\{a_1, ..., a_n\}$ (there
   are $\binom{n}{k-1}$ such clauses).

It is easy to see that the theory C' has the same models as the c-atom C.

Let T be a PL^{cc} theory. We denote by $compile\text{-}basic(T)$ the CNF theory
obtained from T by replacing every c-atom C with the conjunction of clauses
in C' and by applying distributivity to transform the resulting theory into the
CNF. This approach translates T into a theory in the same language but it is
practical only if k and m are small (do not exceed, say 2). Otherwise, the size of
the theory $compile\text{-}basic(T)$ quickly gets too large for SAT solvers to be effective.

Our next method to compile away c-atoms depends on counting. To simplify
the presentation, we will describe it in the case of a c-atom of the form kX but
it extends easily to the general case. We will assume that $k \geq 1$ (otherwise, kX
is true) and $k \leq |X|$ (otherwise kX is false).

Let us consider a PL^{cc} theory T and let us assume that T contains a c-
atom of the form $C = k\{a_1, \ldots, a_n\}$. We introduce new propositional atoms:
$b_{i,j}$, $i = 0, \ldots, n$; $j = 0, \ldots, k$. The intended role for $b_{i,j}$ is to represent the fact
that at least j atoms in $\{a_1, \ldots, a_i\}$ are true. Therefore, we define a theory C'
to consist of the following clauses:

1. $b_{0,j} \leftrightarrow \bot$, $j = 1, \ldots, k$,
2. $b_{i,0} \leftrightarrow \top$, $i = 0, \ldots, n$,
3. $b_{i,j} \leftrightarrow b_{i-1,j} \vee (b_{i-1,j-1} \wedge a_i)$, $i = 1, \ldots, n$, $j = 1, \ldots, k$.

Let I be an interpretation such that $I \models C'$. One can verify that $I \models b_{i,j}$ if
and only if $I \models j\{a_1, \ldots, a_i\}$. In particular, $I \models b_{n,k}$ if and only if $I \models C$.
Thus, if we replace C in T with $b_{n,k}$ and add to T the theory C' the resulting
theory has the same models (modulo new atoms) as T. By repeated application
of this procedure, we can eliminate all c-atoms from T. Moreover, if we represent
theories C' in CNF, the resulting theory will itself be in CNF. We will denote this
CNF theory as $compile\text{-}uc(T)$, where uc stands for *unary counting*. One can show

that the size of $compile\text{-}uc(T)$ is $O(R \times size(T))$, where R is the maximum of all integers appearing in T as lower or upper bounds in c-atoms. It follows that, in general, this translation leads to more concise theories than $compile\text{-}basic$. However, it does introduce new atoms.

The idea of counting can be pushed further. Namely, we can design a more concise translation than $compile\text{-}uc$ by following the idea of counting and by representing numbers in the binary system and by building theories to model binary counting and comparison. For a PL^{cc} theory T, we denote the result of applying this translation method to T by $compile\text{-}bc$ (bc stands for $binary$ $counting$). Due to space limitation we omit the details of this translation. We only note that the size of $compile\text{-}bc(T)$ is $O(size(T)\log_2(R+1))$, where R is the maximum of all integer bounds of c-atoms appearing in T.

4   Local-Search Algorithms for the Logic PL^{cc}

In this section we describe a local-search algorithm $Generic\text{-}WSAT^{cc}$ designed to test satisfiability of theories in the logic PL^{cc}. It follows a general pattern of $WSAT$ [12]. The algorithm executes $Max\text{-}Tries$ independent $tries$. Each try starts in a randomly generated truth assignment and consists of a sequence of up to $Max\text{-}Flips$ $flips$, that is, local changes to the current truth assignment. The algorithm terminates with a truth assignment that is a model of the input theory, or with no output at all (even though the input theory may in fact be satisfiable). We provide a detailed description of the algorithm $Generic\text{-}WSAT^{cc}$ in Figure 1.

We note that the procedure $Flip$ may, in general, depend on the input theory T. It is not the case in $WSAT$ and other similar algorithms but it is so in one of the algorithms we propose in the paper. Thus, we include T as one of the arguments of the procedure $Flip$.

We also note that in the algorithm, we use several parameters that, in our implementations, we enter from the command line. They are $Max\text{-}Tries$, $Max\text{-}Flips$ and p. All these parameters affect the performance of the program. We come back to this matter later in Section 5.

To obtain a concrete implementation of the algorithm $Generic\text{-}WSAT^{cc}$, we need to define $break\text{-}count(x)$ and to specify the notion of a $flip$. In this paper we follow two basic directions. In the first of them, we use a simple notion of a flip, that is, we always flip just one atom. We introduce, however, a more complex concept of the break-count, which we call the $virtual$ $break\text{-}count$. In the second approach, we use a simple notion of the break-count — the number of clauses that become unsatisfied — but introduce a more complex concept of a flip, which we call the $double\text{-}flip$.

To specify our first instantiation of the algorithm $Generic\text{-}WSAT^{cc}(T)$, we define the break-count of an atom x in T as the number of clauses in the CNF theory $compile\text{-}basic(T)$ that become unsatisfied after flipping x. The key idea is to observe that this number can be computed strictly on the basis of T, that is, $without$ actually constructing the theory $compile\text{-}basic(T)$. It is critical since

---

Figure 1 Algorithm *Generic-WSAT^{cc}(T)*

INPUT: T - a PL^{cc} theory
OUTPUT: σ - a satisfying assignment of T, or no output
BEGIN
1.   **For** $i \leftarrow 1$ **to** *Max-Tries*, **do**
2. $\sigma \leftarrow$ randomly generated truth assignment;
3.   **For** $j \leftarrow 1$ **to** *Max-Flips*, **do**
4.   **If** $\sigma \models T$ **then return** σ;
5. $C \leftarrow$ randomly selected unsatisfied clause;
6.   **For each** atom x **in** C, compute *break-count(x)*;
7.   **If** any of these atoms has break-count 0 **then**
8.   randomly choose an atom with break-count 0, call it a;
9.   **Else**
10.   with probability p, $a \leftarrow$ an atom x with minimum *break-count(x)*;
11.   with probability $1 - p$, $a \leftarrow$ a randomly chosen atom in C;
12.   **End If**
13. $\sigma \leftarrow Flip(T, \sigma, a)$;
14.   **End for** of j
15.   **End for** of i
END

---

the size of the theory *compile-basic(T)* is in general much larger than the size of T (sometimes even exponentially larger). We refer to this notion of the break-count as the *virtual* break-count as it is defined *not* with respect to an input PL^{cc} theory T but with respect to a "virtual" theory *compile-basic(T)*, which we do not explicitly construct.

Further, we define the procedure $Flip(\sigma, a)$ (it does not depend on T hence, we dropped T from the notation) so that, given a truth assignment σ and an atom a, it returns the truth assignment σ' obtained from σ by setting $\sigma'(a)$ to the dual value of $\sigma(a)$ and by keeping all other truth values in σ unchanged (this is the basic notion of the flip that is used in many local-search algorithms, in particular in *WSAT*). We call the resulting version of the the the algorithm *Generic-WSAT^{cc}(T)*, the *virtual break-count WSAT^{cc}* and denote it by *vb-WSAT^{cc}*.

The second instantiation of the algorithm *Generic-WSAT^{cc}* that we will discuss applies only to PL^{cc} theories of some special syntactic form. A PL^{cc} theory T is *simple*, if $T = T^{cc} \cup T^{cnf}$, where $T^{cc} \cap T^{cnf} = \emptyset$ and

1. T^{cc} consists of *unit* clauses $C_i = k_i X_i m_i$, $1 \leq i \leq p$, such that sets X_i are pairwise disjoint
2. T^{cnf} consists of propositional clauses
3. for every i, $1 \leq i \leq p$, $k_i < |X_i|$ and $m_i > 0$.

Condition (3) is not particularly restrictive. In particular, it excludes c-atoms kXm such that $k > |X|$, which are trivially false and can be simplified away from the theory, as well as those for which $k = |X|$, which forces all atoms in X to be true and again implies straightforward simplifications. The effect of the

---

Figure 2 Algorithm $Flip(T, \sigma, a)$

INPUT: T - a simple PL^{cc} theory $(T = T^{cc} \cup T^{cnf})$
              σ - current truth assignment
              a - an atom chosen to flip
OUTPUT: σ - updated σ after a is flipped
BEGIN
1.   **If** a occurs in a clause in T^{cc} and flipping a will break it **then**
2.   pick the best opposite atom, say b, in that clause w.r.t. break-count;
3. $\sigma(b) \leftarrow$ dual of $\sigma(b)$;
4.   **End if**
5. $\sigma(a) \leftarrow$ dual of $\sigma(a)$;
6.   **return** σ;
END

---

restriction $m > 0$ is similar; it eliminates c-atoms with $m = 0$, for which it must be that all atoms in X be false. We note that PL^{cc} theories we proposed as encodings of the graph-coloring and vertex-cover problems are simple; the theory encoding the latin-square problem is not.

In this section, we consider only simple PL^{cc} theories. Let us assume that we designed the procedure $Flip(T, \sigma, a)$ so that it has the following property:

(DF) if a truth assignment σ is a model of T^{cc} then $\sigma' = Flip(T, \sigma, a)$ is also a model of T^{cc}.

Let us consider a try starting with a truth assignment σ that satisfies all clauses in T^{cc}. If our procedure $Flip$ satisfies the property (DF), then all truth assignments that we will generate in this try satisfy all clauses in T^{cc}. It follows that the only clauses that can become unsatisfied during the try are the propositional clauses in T^{cnf}. Consequently, in order to compute the break-count of an atom, we only need to consider the CNF theory T^{cnf} and count how many clauses in T^{cnf} become unsatisfiable when we perform a flip.

Since all c-atoms in T^{cc} are pairwise disjoint, it is easy to generate random truth assignments that satisfy all these constraints. Thus, it is easy to generate a random starting truth assignment for a try. Moreover, it is also quite straightforward to design a procedure $Flip$ so that it satisfies property (DF). We will outline one such procedure now and provide for it a detailed pseudo-code description.

Let us assume that σ is a truth assignment that satisfies all clauses in T^{cc} and that we selected an atom a as the third argument for the procedure $Flip$. If flipping the value of a does not violate any unit clause in T^{cc}, the procedure $Flip(T, \sigma, a)$ returns the truth assignment obtained from σ by flipping the value of a. Otherwise, since the c-atoms forming the clauses in T^{cc} are pairwise disjoint, there is exactly one clause in T^{cc}, say kXm, that becomes unsatisfied when the value of a is flipped. In this case, clearly, $a \in X$.

We proceed now as follows. We find in X another atom, say b, whose truth value is opposite to that of a, and flip both a and b. That is, $Flip(T, \sigma, a)$ returns the truth assignment obtained from σ by flipping the values assigned to a and b

to their duals. Clearly, by performing this *double flip* we maintain the property that all clauses in T^{cc} are still satisfied. Indeed all clauses in T^{cc} other than kXm are not affected by the flips (these clauses contain neither a nor b) and kXm is satisfied because flipping a and b simply switches their truth values and, therefore, does not change the number of atoms in X that are true.

The only question is whether such an atom b can be found. The answer is indeed positive. If $\sigma(a) = \mathbf{t}$ and flipping a breaks clause kXm, we must have that the number of atoms that are true in X is equal to k. Since $|X| > k$, there is an atom in X that is false. The reasoning in the case when $\sigma(a) = \mathbf{f}$ is similar.

A pseudo-code for the procedure is given in Figure 2.

5   Experiments, Results and Discussion

We performed experimental studies of the effectiveness of our local-search algorithms in solving several difficult search problems. For the experiments we selected the graph-coloring problem, the vertex-cover problem and the latin-square problem. We discussed these problems in Section 2 and described PL^{cc} theories that encode them. To build PL^{cc} theories for testing, we randomly generate or otherwise select input instances to these search problems and instantiate the corresponding PL^{cc} encodings. For the graph-coloring and vertex-cover problems we obtain simple PL^{cc} theories and so all methods we discussed apply. The theories we obtain from the latin-square problem are not simple. Consequently, the algorithm $df\text{-}WSAT^{cc}$ does not apply but all other methods do.

Our primary goal is to demonstrate that our algorithms $vb\text{-}WSAT^{cc}$ and $df\text{-}WSAT^{cc}$ can compute models of *large* PL^{cc} theories and, consequently, are effective tools for solving search problems. To this end, we study the performance of these algorithms and compare it to the performance of methods that employ SAT solvers, specifically $WSAT$ and $zchaff$ [10]. We chose $WSAT$ since it is a local-search algorithm, as are $vb\text{-}WSAT^{cc}$ and $df\text{-}WSAT^{cc}$. We chose $zchaff$ since it is one of the most advanced *complete* methods. In order to use SAT solvers to compute models of PL^{cc} theories, we executed them on the CNF theories produced by procedures *compile-bc* and *compile-basic* (Section 3). We selected the method *compile-bc* as it results in most concise translations[4]. We selected the method *compile-basic* as it is arguably the most straightforward translation and it does not require auxiliary atoms.

For all local-search algorithms, including $WSAT$, we used the same values of *Max-Tries* and *Max-Flips*: 100 and 100000, respectively. The performance of local-search algorithms depends to a large degree on the on the value of the parameter p (noise). For each method and for each theory, we ran experiments to determine the value of p, for which the performance was best. All results we report here come from the best runs for each local-search method.

To assess the performance of solvers on families of test theories, we use the following measures.

---

[4] Our experiments with the translation *compile-uc* show that it performs worse. We believe it is due to larger size of theories it creates. We do not report these results here due to space limitations.

1. The average running time over all instances in a family
2. The success rate of a method: the ratio of the number of theories in a family, for which the method finds a solution, to the total number of instances in the family for which we were able to find a solution using *any* of the methods we tested (for all methods we set a limit of 2 hours of CPU time/instance).

The success rate is an important measure of the effectiveness of local-search techniques. It is not only important that they run fast but also that they are likely to find models when models exist.

We will now present and discuss the results of our experiments. We start with the coloring problem. We generated for testing five families $C_1, \ldots, C_5$, each consisting of 50 random graphs with 1000 vertices and 3850, 3860, 3870 3880 and 3890 edges, respectively. The problem was to find for these graphs a coloring with 4 colors (each of these graphs has a 4-coloring). We show the results in Table 1. Columns $vb\text{-}WSAT^{cc}$, $df\text{-}WSAT^{cc}$ show the performance results for our local-search algorithms run on PL^{cc} theories encoding the 4-colorability problem on the graphs in the families C_i, $1 \le i \le 5$. Columns $WSAT\text{-}bc$ and $zchaff\text{-}bc$ show the performance of the algorithms $WSAT$ and $zchaff$ on CNF theories obtained from the PL^{cc}-theories by the procedure *compile-bc*. Columns $WSAT\text{-}basic$ and $zchaff\text{-}basic$ show the performance of the algorithms $WSAT$ and $zchaff$ on CNF theories produced by the procedure *compile-basic* (since the bounds in c-atoms in the case of 4-coloring are equal to 1, there is no dramatic increase in the size when using the procedure *compile-basic*). The first number in each entry is the average running time in seconds, the second number — the percentage success rate. The results for local-search algorithms were obtained with the value of noise $p = 0.4$ (we found this value to work well for all the methods).

Table 1. Graph-coloring problem

Family	$vb\text{-}WSAT^{cc}$	$df\text{-}WSAT^{cc}$	$WSAT\text{-}bc$	$zchaff\text{-}bc$	$WSAT\text{-}basic$	$zchaff\text{-}basic$
C_1	39/96%	97/100%	27/0%	68/100%	29/100%	91/100%
C_2	40/98%	100/100%	27/0%	142/100%	29/100%	128/100%
C_3	41/100%	103/100%	27/0%	233/100%	30/98%	146/100%
C_4	41/100%	104/98%	28/0%	275/100%	30/96%	216/100%
C_5	42/96%	108/98%	28/0%	478/100%	30/96%	594/100%

In terms of the success rate, our algorithms achieve or come very close to perfect 100%, and are comparable or slightly better than the combination of *compile-basic* and $WSAT$. When comparing the running time, our algorithms are slower but only by a constant factor. The algorithm $vb\text{-}WSAT^{cc}$ is only about 0.3 times slower and the algorithm $df\text{-}WSAT^{cc}$ is about 3.5 times slower.

Next, we note that the combination *compile-bc* and $WSAT$ does not perform well at all. It fails to find a 4-coloring even for a single graph. We also observe that $zchaff$ performs well no matter which technique is used to eliminate c-atoms. It finds a 4-coloring for every graph that we tested. In terms of the running time there is no significant difference between its performance on theories obtained by *compile-bc* as opposed to *compile-basic*. However, *zchaff* is, in general, slower than *WSAT* and our local-search algorithms *vb-WSAT^{cc}* and *df-WSAT^{cc}*.

Finally, we note that our results suggest that our algorithms are less sensitive to the choice of a value for the noise parameter p. In Table 2 we show the performance results for our two algorithms and for the combination *compile-basic* and *WSAT* on theories obtained from the graphs in the family C_1 and for p assuming values 0.1, 0.2, 0.3 and 0.4.

Table 2. Coloring: sensitivity to the value of p

Noise	vb-WSAT^{cc}	df-WSAT^{cc}	WSAT-basic
$p = 0.1$	16%	100%	18%
$p = 0.2$	98%	100%	90%
$p = 0.3$	100%	100%	98%
$p = 0.4$	96%	100%	100%

We also tested our algorithms on graph-coloring instances that were used in the graph-coloring competition at the CP-2002 conference. We refer to http://mat.gsia.cmu.edu/COLORING02/ for details. We experimented with 63 instances available there. For each of these graphs, we identified the smallest number of colors that is known to suffice to color it. We then tested whether the algorithms *vb-WSAT^{cc}*, *WSAT* and *zchaff* (the latter two in combination with the procedure *compile-basic* to produce a CNF encoding) can find a coloring using that many colors. We found that the algorithms *df-WSAT^{cc}*, *WSAT* and *zchaff* (the latter two in combination with *compile-basic*) were very effective. Their success rate (the percentage of instances for which these methods could match the best known result) was 62%, 56% and 54%, respectively. In comparison, the best among the algorithms that participated in the competition, the algorithm MZ, has success rate of 40% only and the success rate of other algorithms does not exceed 30%.

For the vertex cover problem we randomly generated 50 graphs with 200 vertices and 400 edges. For $i = 103, \ldots, 107$, we constructed a family VC_i of PL^{cc} theories encoding, for graphs we generated, the problem of finding a vertex cover of cardinality at most i. For this problem, the translation *compile-basic* is not practical as translating just a single c-atom $\{in_1, \ldots, in_{200}\}i$ requires $\binom{200}{i+1}$ clauses and these numbers are astronomically large for $i = 103, \ldots, 107$. The translation *compile-bc* also does not perform well. Neither *WSAT* nor *zchaff* succeed in finding a solution to even a single instance (as always, within 2 hours of CPU time/instance). Thus, for the vertex-cover problem, we developed yet another CNF encoding, which we refer to as *ad-hoc*. This encoding worked well with *WSAT* but not with *zchaff*. We show the results in Table 3. For this problem, the value of noise $p = 0.1$ worked best for all local-search methods.

Our algorithms perform very well. They have the best running time (with *vb-WSAT^{cc}* being somewhat faster than *df-WSAT^{cc}*) and find solutions for all instances for which we were able to find solutions using these and other tech-

Table 3. Vertex-cover problem: graphs with 200 vertices and 400 edges

Family	vb-$WSAT^{cc}$	df-$WSAT^{cc}$	$WSAT$-bc	zchaff-bc	$WSAT$-ad-hoc	zchaff-ad-hoc
VC_{103}	117/100%	300/100%	11/0%	7200/0%	1696/100%	7200/0%
VC_{104}	86/100%	225/100%	11/0%	7200/0%	1400/100%	7200/0%
VC_{105}	69/100%	178/100%	11/0%	7200/0%	1191/100%	7200/0%
VC_{106}	29/100%	78/100%	11/0%	7200/0%	848/100%	7200/0%
VC_{107}	10/100%	27/100%	11/0%	7200/0%	671/100%	7200/0%

niques. In terms of the success rate $WSAT$, when run on *ad-hoc* translations, performed as well as our algorithms but was several (7 to 67, depending on the method and family) times slower.

As in the case of graph coloring, our algorithms again were less sensitive to the choice of the noise value p, as shown in Table 4 (the tests were run on the family VC_{103}).

Table 4. Vertex cover: sensitivity to the value of p

Noise	vb-$WSAT^{cc}$	df-$WSAT^{cc}$	$WSAT$-ad-hoc
$p = 0.1$	100%	100%	100%
$p = 0.2$	100%	100%	100%
$p = 0.3$	100%	100%	58%
$p = 0.4$	100%	100%	33%

We also experimented with the vertex-cover problem for graphs of an order of magnitude larger. We randomly generated 50 graphs, each with 2000 vertices and 4000 edges. For these graphs we constructed a family VC_{1035} consisting of 50 PL^{cc} theories, each encoding the problem of finding a vertex-cover of cardinality at most 1035 in the corresponding graph. With graphs of this size, all compilation methods produce large and complex CNF theories on which both $WSAT$ and *zchaff* fail to find even a single solution. Due to the use of c-atoms, the PL^{cc} theories are relatively small. Each consists of 2000 atoms and 4001 clauses and has a total of about 10,000 atom occurrences. Our algorithms vb-$WSAT^{cc}$ and df-$WSAT^{cc}$ run on each of the theories in under an hour and the algorithm df-$WSAT^{cc}$ finds a vertex cover of cardinality at most 1035 for 9 of them. The algorithm vb-$WSAT^{cc}$ is about two times faster but has worse success rate: finds solutions only in 7 instances.

The last test concerned the latin-square problem. We assumed $n = 30$ and randomly generated 50 instances of the problem, each specifying values for some 10 entries in the array. Out of these instances we constructed a family LS of the corresponding PL^{cc} theories. Since these PL^{cc} theories are not simple, we did not test the algorithm df-$WSAT^{cc}$ here. The results are shown in Table 5. For the local-search methods, we used the value of noise $p = 0.1$.

These results show that our algorithms are faster than the combination of $WSAT$ and *compile-basic* (*compile-bc* again does not work well with $WSAT$) and

Table 5. Open latin-square problem

vb-$WSAT^{cc}$	$WSAT$-bc	$zchaff$-bc	$WSAT$-$basic$	$zchaff$-$basic$
43/100%	0/0%	5/100%	250/84%	637/96%

have a better success rate. The fastest in this case is, however, the combination
of *zchaff* and *compile-bc*. The combination of *zchaff* and *compile-basic* works
worse and it is also slower than our algorithms.

6   Conclusions

Overall, our local-search algorithms vb-$WSAT^{cc}$ and df-$WSAT^{cc}$, designed explicitly for PL^{cc} theories, perform very well.

It is especially true in the presence of cardinality constraints with large
bounds where the ability to handle such constraints directly, without the need to
encode them as CNF theories, is essential. It makes it possible for our algorithms
to handle large instances of search problems that contain such constraints. We
considered one problem in this category, the vertex-cover problem, and demonstrated superior performance of our search algorithms over other techniques.
For large instances (we considered graphs with 2000 vertices and 4000 edges and
searched for vertex covers of cardinality 1035) SAT solvers are rendered ineffective by the size of CNF encodings and their complexity. Even for instances of
much smaller size (search for vertex covers of 103-107 elements in graphs with
200 vertices and 400 edges), our algorithms are many times faster and have a
better success rate than $WSAT$ (*zchaff* is still ineffective).

Also for PL^{cc} theories that contain only c-atoms of the form $1X1$, $X1$ and
$1X$, the ability to handle such constraints directly seems to be an advantage and
leads to good performance, especially in terms of the success rate. In the graph-
coloring and latin-square problems our algorithms consistently had comparable
or higher success rate than methods employing SAT solvers. In terms of time our
methods are certainly competitive. For the coloring problem, they were slower
than the method based on $WSAT$ and *compile-basic* but faster than all other
methods. For the latin-square problem, they were slower than the combination
of *zchaff* and *compile-bc* but again faster than other methods.

Finally, we note that our methods seem to be easier to use and more robust.
SAT-based method have a disadvantage that their performance strongly depends
on the selection of the method to compile away c-atoms and no method we
studied is consistently better than others. The problem of selecting the right
way to compile c-atoms away does not appear in the context of our algorithms.
Further, the performance of local-search methods, especially the success rate,
highly depends on the value of the noise parameter p. Our results show that
our algorithms are less sensitive to changes in p than those that employ $WSAT$,
which makes the task of selecting the value for p for our algorithms easier.

These results provide further support to a growing trend in satisfiability
research to extend the syntax of propositional logic by constructs to model high-

level constraints, and to design solvers that can handle this expanded syntax directly. In the expanded syntax, we obtain more concise representations of search problems. Moreover, these representations are more directly aligned with the inherent structure of the problem. Both factors, we believe, will lead to faster, more effective solvers.

In this paper, we focused on the logic PL^{cc}, an extension of propositional logic with c-atoms, that is, direct means to encode cardinality constraints. The specific contribution of the paper are two local-search algorithms $vb\text{-}WSAT^{cc}$ and $df\text{-}WSAT^{cc}$, tailored to the syntax of the the logic PL^{cc}. These algorithms rely on two ideas. The first of them is to regard a PL^{cc} theory as a compact encoding of a CNF theory modeling the same problem. One can now design local-search algorithms so that they work with a PL^{cc} theory but proceed as propositional SAT solvers would when run on the corresponding propositional encoding. We selected the procedure *compile-basic* to establish the correspondence between PL^{cc} theories and CNF encodings, as it does not require any new propositional variables and makes it easy to simulate propositional local-search solvers. We selected a particular propositional local-search method, $WSAT$, one of the best-performing local-search algorithms. Many other choices are possible. Whether they lead to more effective solvers is an open research problem.

The second idea is to change the notion of a flip. We applied it designing the algorithm $df\text{-}WSAT^{cc}$ for the class of simple PL^{cc} theories. However, this method applies whenever a PL^{cc} theory T can be partitioned into two parts T_1 and T_2 so that (1) it is easy to generate random truth assignments satisfying constraints in T_1, and (2) there is a notion of a flip that preserves satisfaction of constraints in the first part and allows one, in a sequence of such flips, to reach any point in the search space of truth assignments satisfying constraints in T_1. Identifying specific syntactic classes of PL^{cc} theories and the corresponding notions of a flip is also a promising research direction.

In our experiments we designed compilation techniques to allow us to use SAT solvers in searching for models of PL^{cc} theories. In general, approaches that rely on counting do not work well with $WSAT$, as they introduce too much structure into the theory. The translation *compile-basic* is the best match for $WSAT$ (whenever it does not lead to astronomically large theories). All methods seem to work well with *zchaff* at least in some of the cases we studied but none worked well for the vertex-cover problem. To design better techniques to eliminate c-atoms and to make the process of selecting an effective translation systematic rather than ad hoc is another interesting research direction.

Our work is related to [13] and [11], which describe local-search solvers for theories in propositional logic extended by pseudo-boolean constraints. However, the classes of formulas accepted by these two solvers and by ours are different. We use cardinality atoms as generalized "atomic" components of clauses while pseudoboolean constraints have to form unit clauses. On the other hand, pseudoboolean constraints are more general than cardinality atoms. At present, we are comparing the performance of all the solvers on the class of theories that are accepted by all solvers (which includes all theories considered here).

Acknowledgments

The authors are grateful to the reviewers for comments and pointers to papers on extensions of propositional logic by pseudoboolean constraints. This research was supported by the National Science Foundation under Grant No. 0097278.

References

1. F.A. Aloul, A. Ramani, I. Markov, and K. Sakallah. Pbs: a backtrack-search pseudo-boolean solver and optimizer. In *Proceedings of the Fifth International Symposium on Theory and Applications of Satisfiability*, pages 346 – 353, 2002.
2. P. Barth. A davis-putnam based elimination algorithm for linear pseudo-boolean optimization. Technical report, Max-Planck-Institut für Informatik, 1995. MPI-I-95-2-003.
3. B. Benhamou, L. Sais, , and P. Siegel. Two proof procedures for a cardinality based language in propositional calculus. In *Proceedings of STACS-94*, pages 71–82. 1994.
4. H.E. Dixon and M.L. Ginsberg. Inference methods for a pseudo-boolean satisfiability solver. In *The 18th National Conference on Artificial Intelligence (AAAI-2002)*, 2002.
5. D. East and M. Truszczyński. Propositional satisfiability in answer-set programming. In *Proceedings of Joint German/Austrian Conference on Artificial Intelligence, KI'2001*, volume 2174, pages 138–153. Lecture Notes in Artificial Intelligence, Springer Verlag, 2001. Full version submitted for publication (available at http://xxx.lanl.gov/abs/cs.LO/0211033).
6. E. Goldberg and Y. Novikov. Berkmin: a fast and robust sat-solver. In *DATE-2002*, pages 142–149. 2002.
7. C.M. Li. Integrating equivalency reasoning into davis-putnam procedure. In *Proccedings of the Seventeenth National Conference on Artificial Intelligence (AAAI-2000)*, pages 291–296, 2000.
8. C.M. Li and M. Anbulagan. Look-ahead versus look-back for satisfiability problems. In *Proceedings of the Third International Conference on Principles and Practice of Constraint Programming*, 1997.
9. J.P. Marques-Silva and K.A. Sakallah. GRASP: A new search algorithm for satisfiability. *IEEE Transactions on Computers*, 48:506–521, 1999.
10. M. Moskewicz, C. Madigan, Y. Zhao, L. Zhang, and S. Malik. Chaff: engineering an efficient SAT solver. In *Proceedings of the Design Automation Conference (DAC)*, 2001.
11. S.D. Prestwich. Randomised backtracking for linear pseudo-boolean constraint problems. In *Proceedings of the 4th International Workshop on Integration of AI and OR techniques in Constraint Programming for Combinatorial Optimisation Problems, CPAIOR-02*, pages 7–20, 2002.
12. B. Selman, H.A. Kautz, and B. Cohen. Noise strategies for improving local search. In *Proceedings of the Twelfth National Conference on Artificial Intelligence (AAAI-94)*, Seattle, USA, 1994.
13. J.P. Walser. Solving linear pseudo-boolean constraints with local search. In *Proceedings of the 11th Conference on Artificial Intelligence, AAAI-97*, pages 269–274. AAAI Press, 1997.
14. H. Zhang. SATO: an efficient propositional prover. In *Proceedings of the International Conference on Automated Deduction (CADE-97)*, pages 308–312, 1997. Lecture Notes in Artificial Intelligence, 1104.

Discrepancy-Based Additive Bounding
for the AllDifferent Constraint

Andrea Lodi[1], Michela Milano[1], and Louis-Martin Rousseau[2]

[1] D.E.I.S., Università di Bologna
Viale Risorgimento 2, 40136 Bologna, Italy
{alodi,mmilano}@deis.unibo.it
[2] Centre for Research on Transportation, Université de Montréal
CP 6128 Succ Centre-Ville Montréal, Canada, H3C 3J7
louism@crt.umontreal.ca

Abstract. In this paper we show how to exploit in Constraint Programming (CP) a well-known integer programming technique, the additive bounding procedure, when using Limited Discrepancy Search (LDS). LDS is an effective search strategy based on the concept of *discrepancy*, i.e., a branching decision which does not follow the suggestion of a given heuristic. The property of a node to have an associated discrepancy k can be modeled (and enforced) through a constraint, called *k-discrepancy constraint*. Our key result is the exploitation of the k-discrepancy constraint to improve the bound given by any relaxation of a combinatorial optimization problem by using the additive bounding idea. We believe that this simple idea can be effectively exploited to tighten relaxations in CP solvers and speed up the proof of optimality. The general use of additive bounding in conjunction with LDS has been presented in [14]. Here we focus on a particular case where the AllDifferent constraint is part of the CP model. In this case, the integration of additive bound in CP is particularly effective.

1 Introduction

It is widely recognized that integrating relaxations in *Constraint Programming* (CP) solvers leads to improved performance in optimization problems. In particular, relaxations can be used to obtain bounds on the objective function value, for cost-based filtering [11], and for guiding search (see, e.g., [7], [10] and [15] among others). This integration enables one to prune provably sub-optimal branches, thus performing optimality reasoning in CP. The efficiency of optimality reasoning depends largely on the quality of available bounds. If we have several bounding techniques for a given problem, we can simply select the tightest one. However, in this way we exploit only one relaxation structure.

The *Additive Bounding Procedure* (ABP) partially solves this problem. ABP is a general technique for computing accurate bounds for combinatorial problems. It has been proposed by Fischetti and Toth [8] and effectively applied to the Asymmetric Traveling Salesman Problem [9].

F. Rossi (Ed.): CP 2003, LNCS 2833, pp. 510–524, 2003.
© Springer-Verlag Berlin Heidelberg 2003

Roughly speaking, given a set of bounding procedures for a problem P, one can apply them in sequence in a way that the *information* provided by a procedure is used as an input for the next one. Then, the sum of the solution values of all the procedures is a valid bound for P. The only requirement is that each bounding procedure must provide a reduced cost vector used as cost vector by the next one, so that the sum of the solution values of all the procedures provides a valid bound for P.

In this paper we show how to exploit this remarkable technique when *Limited Discrepancy Search* (LDS) [13] and domain splitting are used. Given a heuristic that provides a ranking of values in the variables' domain, LDS is an effective search strategy that trusts the information provided. More precisely, a *discrepancy* is a branching decision which does not follow the suggestion of the heuristic. Thus, the LDS strategy explores the overall tree in such a way that sub-trees with lower discrepancy are considered first. LDS is currently available in many commercial CP solvers since it has proven to be effective in practice.

We have applied LDS together with domain splitting. At each node, a variable is selected and its domain partitioned in two parts according to a ranking given by the heuristic: the *good* domain part containing promising values (suggested by the heuristic) and the *bad* domain part (containing the remaining values). In the resulting search tree, the property of a leaf to have an associated discrepancy k can be modeled (and enforced) through a constraint, called k-*discrepancy constraint*. Its declarative semantics states that exactly k variables assume a value in their corresponding bad domain.

The idea to use the k-discrepancy constraint and additive bounding to accelerate the proof of optimality, has been proposed in [14]. This result can be applied in CP each time we use LDS and a relaxation of the problem providing reduced costs is available. Thus, the idea presented in [14] is very general and can be applied to a large variety of problems. In this paper, we focus on a particular application of this technique which indeed is less general, but more effective. The case considered is the use of the additive bounding procedure in LDS when the widely used AllDifferent constraint is contained in the CP model. In this case, the additive bound procedure can exploit the intrinsic IP model of the AllDifferent constraint and compute tighter bounds.

We present computational results both for the general approach proposed in [14] and for its specialized version proposed in this paper for the AllDifferent case. We show that the proof of optimality is in general much faster.

The remainder of the paper is organized as follows. In the next section some preliminaries on reduced costs, additive bounding and Limited Discrepancy Search are given. In section 3 the additive bounding technique is applied in the LDS context. Then, section 4 focuses on the specific AllDifferent case. Computational results are given in section 5 showing the effectiveness of the proposed approach. Finally, conclusions are drawn in section 6.

2   Preliminaries

2.1   Reduced Costs and Additive Bounding

The concept of reduced cost has been proved crucial for CP, as it allows cost based filtering [11], provides search heuristics [15] and enables one to improve bounds as it will be shown in this paper.

The reduced costs are computed as a result of the solution of a linear program. They come from duality theory and can be intuitively explained as follows. The solution of the linear program is computed, and each value $\bar{c}_i$ in the reduced cost vector can be seen as the cost which should be added to the optimal solution when the value of the corresponding variable x_i increases by one unit, i.e., variable x_i becomes part of the basis. An important point that should be taken into account is that in general reduced costs are not additive. Indeed, the overall effect of two or more variables simultaneously entering into the basis is not captured by the sum of their reduced costs.

The additive bounding procedure [8] is an interesting and effective technique for computing bounds for combinatorial optimization problems. Intuitively, an additive bounding procedure consists in solving a sequence of relaxations of a problem P each producing an improved bound. With no loss of generality, we consider here minimization problems.

More formally, we consider a problem P whose general form is:

$$\min z = c^T x \tag{1}$$
$$Ax \geq b \tag{2}$$
$$x \geq 0 \text{ integer} \tag{3}$$

where c is a cost vector, x is a solution vector, A a coefficient matrix and b the right-hand side vector. We suppose we have a set of bounding procedures $B_1, \ldots, B_{nr}$ for P. We denote as $B_i(c)$ the i-th bounding procedure when applied to an instance of problem P with cost vector c. For $k = 1, \ldots, nr$, the bounding procedure B_k returns a lower bound value LB_k and a reduced cost vector $\bar{c}^k$. This reduced cost vector is used to 'feed' the next bounding procedure B_{k+1}, i.e., $B_{k+1}(\bar{c}^k)$, as shown in Figure 1. The sum of the bounds $\sum_{k=1}^{nr} LB_k$ is a valid bound for problem P [8].

2.2   LDS and Its Variants

An important point which should be explained in the preliminary section concerns the search strategy that we are using and which is particularly interesting when connected with additive bounding.

In this paper we restrict our attention to binary trees explored through LDS. We assume that our heuristic ranks the values in the domain variables X_i $\forall i \in \{1, \ldots, n\}$ that are split in two sets: a set $\mathcal{G}_i$ containing the values in the domain which are likely to correspond to *good* solutions, and a set $\mathcal{B}_i$ for the values in the domain which are supposed to correspond to *bad* solutions. At each node,

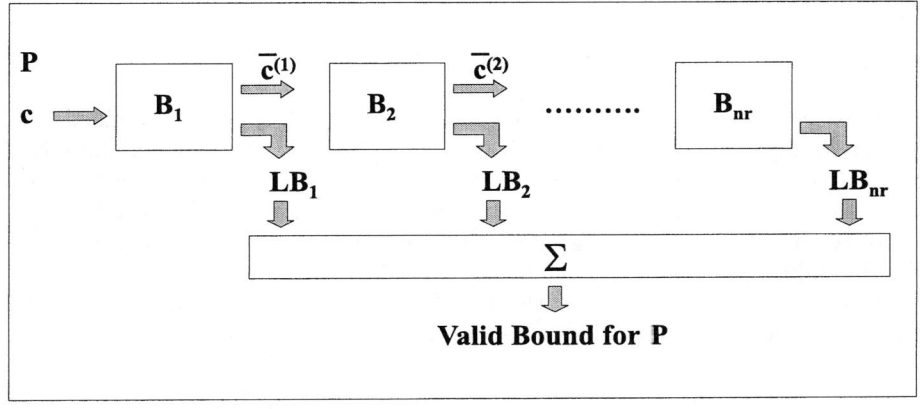

Fig. 1. Additive bounding scheme.

on the left branch we force the variable to range on the corresponding $\mathcal{G}_i$ and on the right branch on $\mathcal{B}_i$.

Then, the strategy we use is a two step search procedure: the first step concerns sub-problem generation where the variables are forced to range on one domain partition, while the second step concerns sub-problem solution. The tree is explored through an LDS. Thus, the first sub-problem generated has all variables ranging on the good domain part, then sub-problems are generated for increasing discrepancies. For discrepancy k we have k out of n variables that range on the bad domain part, while the remaining on the good one.

This search strategy, called *Decomposition-Based Search* (DBS), has been successfully applied to the Traveling Salesman Problem with Time Windows with a reduced costs based domain partitioning [15], and is theoretically and experimentally evaluated in [17].

3   Additive Bounding and DBS

Without loss of generality, we consider a minimization problem P defined on variables $X_1, \ldots, X_n$ whose domains are denoted as $D_1, \ldots, D_n$. Each time a relaxation is integrated in a CP solver, a mapping is needed that defines a correspondence between CP variables and relaxation variables. We consider here Linear Programming relaxations, and we consider that binary variables are mapped to CP domain values as follows. A classical mapping of CP variables into binary variables defines a variable x_{ij} such that:

$$x_{ij} \in \{0, 1\}, \forall i \in \{1, \ldots, n\}, \forall j \in D_i, \tag{4}$$
$$x_{ij} = 1 \leftrightarrow X_i = j. \tag{5}$$

Moreover, through this mapping a cost c_{ij} is associated to each x_{ij} variable, and we consider the following classical objective function:

$$\min z = \sum_{i=1}^{n} \sum_{j \in D_i} c_{ij} x_{ij}. \tag{6}$$

Finally, we suppose that a relaxation of problem P, say $R(P)$, defined with an Integer Linear Programming (ILP) model using the x variables, can be solved to optimality and returns: (i) a bound value LB, (ii) a vector of reduced costs $\bar{c}$, and (iii) an optimal solution x^* (which is, actually, not essential in the following).

Note that $R(P)$ is any relaxation and its solution procedure is used as the *first* bounding procedure of the additive bounding technique.

When the problem is solved through DBS we can add to the problem P a constraint, called k-discrepancy constraint:

$$\text{Discrepancy\_cst}([X_1, \ldots, X_n], [\mathcal{B}_1, \ldots, \mathcal{B}_n], k)$$

that holds iff k out of n variables range on the corresponding bad domain $\mathcal{B}$.

This constraint defined on CP variables can be expressed in terms of x variables by the following set of constraints:

$$\sum_{j \in \mathcal{B}_i} x_{ij} \leq 1 \quad \forall i \in \{1, \ldots, n\} \tag{7}$$

$$\sum_{i=1}^{n} \sum_{j \in \mathcal{B}_i} x_{ij} = k \tag{8}$$

$$x_{ij} \in \{0, 1\} \tag{9}$$

where constraints (7) express that at most one value in the *bad* set of each original variable X_i must be considered, while constraint (8) forces that exactly k of the constraints (7) must be tight.

Obviously, these constraints can be considered as *cutting planes* and added to the model of $R(P)$. In fact, taking into account constraints (7) and (8) in each node of the search tree would improve the lower bound obtained by only considering the constraints expressed by $R(P)$. However, if the relaxation $R(P)$ is solved through a special-purpose technique, it means that it has a special structure which is lost when the above constraints are added.

Thus, we are looking for a clean and general framework for improving the bound from $R(P)$ by taking into account constraints (7) and (8) and without a significant increase of the computational effort. This framework is indeed the additive bounding procedure, and this result is stated by the following theorem.

Theorem 1 (Lodi, Milano [14]).
We suppose that we have a relaxation $R(P)$ providing a lower bound LB and a reduced cost vector $\bar{c}$. Problem P':

$$\left\{ \min z' = \sum_{i=1}^{n} \sum_{j \in D_i} \bar{c}_{ij} x_{ij} \mid (7), (8), (9) \right\} \tag{10}$$

can be optimally solved in $O(n^2)$ time[1] and $LB' = LB + z'$ is a valid lower bound for problem P when a k-discrepancy constraint is imposed.

Proof: The optimal solution (i.e., z') of the above problem can be easily obtained through the following simple algorithm: (a) compute the smallest reduced cost $\min_{j \in D_i} \bar{c}_{ij}$ for each $i \in \{1, \ldots, n\}$; (b) sort the n obtained reduced costs; and (c) select the k smallest ones. The time complexity of phase (a) is trivially bounded by $O(n^2)$ being the most expensive one since phase (b) (resp., (c)) only requires $O(n \log n)$ (resp., $O(n)$).
Concerning the validity of the bound, it is trivially guaranteed by the additive argument since both $R(P)$ and the problem modeled by (6), (7), (8) and (9) are valid (disjunct) relaxations of P plus the k-discrepancy constraint. $\square$

As already pointed out, the above result is perfectly general and independent on the relaxation $R(P)$ considered, i.e., it can be used with any other global constraint. However, if the relaxation is the (continuous) *linear* one, it is not difficult to see that a better bound could be obtained by directly considering constraints (7) and (8) within the linear relaxation itself. On the other hand, the use of structured relaxations (thus, of special-purpose algorithms to solve them) is often appealing [12], and the additive operation when DBS is exploited provides a clean and efficient improvement.

It is worth mentioning that the additive procedure to improve the bound provided by a structured relaxation has been already tested in the specific context of the *Traveling Salesman Problem* [15] showing a satisfactory behavior.

Finally, before closing the section, we note that ABP is not the only way of taking into account constraints (7) and (8), i.e., branching constraints, without loosing the structure of a combinatorial relaxation. There are problem specific ways of doing this. For example, in the ATSP case branching on sub-tours can be efficiently handled by modifying accordingly the cost matrix (see, Carpaneto, Dell'Amico and Toth [1]). More generally, any kind of branching constraints can be dualized in Lagrangean fashion but this requires some kind of iterative optimization process, such as subgradient/bundle methods. However, ABP seems to be particularly suited in this context, since it is very simple and efficient to compute.

4   Application to the AllDifferent Constraint

It was shown in the previous section how to exploit additive bounding for improving a combinatorial relaxation in presence of a DBS constraint. In order to prove the effectiveness of this framework, we consider the general case of problems modeled using the *AllDifferent* constraint. It is well known that the ILP model of the *AllDifferent* is the classical linear *Assignment Problem* (AP, see, e.g., Dell'Amico and Martello [5]) provided the possible addition of dummy variables. Since the AP can be solved in polynomial time by special purpose

---

[1] This time bound is obtained assuming that $\max_i |D_i| \leq n$.

algorithms, using the AP as a combinatorial relaxation is particularly suited in this context.

The following is a general CP model of any problem containing the *AllDifferent* constraint and to which was added the discrepancy constraint needed to perform DBS:

$$\min \sum_{i \in N} C_{iX_i} \tag{11}$$

$$s.t. \ \text{AllDifferent}(X) \tag{12}$$

$$\text{AnySide\_cst}(X) \tag{13}$$

$$\text{Discrepancy\_cst}(X, \mathcal{B}, k) \tag{14}$$

$$X_i \in N \quad \forall i \in N \tag{15}$$

where $N = \{1, \ldots, n\}$.

Using the same mapping introduced in section 3, and for the sake of simplicity defining a graph $G = (N, A)$ where arc $(i, j) \in A$ if and only if $j \in D_i$, problem (11)-(15), denoted by P^{gen}, maps in the following ILP formulation:

$$z(P^{gen}) \ = \min \sum_{i \in N} \sum_{j \in N} c_{ij} \, x_{ij} \tag{16}$$

$$\text{subject to} \sum_{j \in N} x_{ij} = 1, \quad i \in N \tag{17}$$

$$\sum_{i \in N} x_{ij} = 1, \quad j \in N \tag{18}$$

$$\text{AnyLinearSide\_cst}(x) \tag{19}$$

$$\sum_{i \in N} \sum_{j \in \mathcal{B}_i} x_{ij} = k \tag{20}$$

$$x_{ij}\{0, 1\}, \quad \forall (i, j) \in A \tag{21}$$

where (7) is redundant due to (17) and (19) is an equivalent linear formulation of (13).

4.1   A First Approach

A first lower bound is easily deduced from P^{gen} as the relaxation of constraints (19) and (20) directly yield the formulation of the Assignment Problem. Since the AP can be efficiently and incrementally solved through the well-known *Hungarian Algorithm* (see, e.g., Carpaneto, Martello and Toth [2]), one would not like to change this structure even if one would like to take into account, at least partially, branching constraints.

In this context, we consider k-discrepancy (branching) constraints, and we use the output of the Hungarian Algorithm, $(z^*(\text{AP}), \bar{c})$, to define problem P' (10) whose optimal solution can be computed as follows:

(a) compute the smallest reduced cost $\min_{j \in N} \bar{c}_{ij} \; \forall i \in N$;
(b) sort the $|N|$ obtained reduced costs; and
(c) select the k smallest ones, say $\tilde{c}_1, \ldots, \tilde{c}_k$.

The improved bound is then $LB' = z^*(AP) + \sum_{h=1}^{k} \tilde{c}_h$ and the time complexity of this improvement is $O(n^2)$.

4.2   Better Exploiting the Structure

The method described in the previous section does not take into account the structure of the AP but only the fact that the AP can be solved through an algorithm that provides reduced costs. In fact, the structure of the AP can be efficiently exploited so as to improve the integration of k-discrepancy constraints. Formally, the following new relaxation, called k-*cardinality Assignment Problem* (k-AP), can be defined:

$$z(k\text{-AP}) \; = \min \sum_{i \in N} \sum_{j \in N} c_{ij} \, x_{ij} \tag{22}$$

$$\text{subject to} \sum_{j \in N} x_{ij} \leq 1, \qquad i \in N \tag{23}$$

$$\sum_{i \in N} x_{ij} \leq 1, \qquad j \in N \tag{24}$$

$$\sum_{i \in N} \sum_{j \in N} x_{ij} = k \tag{25}$$

$$x_{ij}\{0,1\}, \qquad \forall(i,j) \in A. \tag{26}$$

The k-AP is a relaxation of P^{gen} (16)-(21) where the constraint (19) has been removed, the degree constraints of both (17) and (18) are relaxed to the '$\leq$' form, and constraint (8) is relaxed to (25) by summing also on the variables x_{ij} such that $j \in \mathcal{G}_i$. The k-AP has been introduced by Dell'Amico and Martello [6], and can be solved in polynomial time by both primal and dual algorithms (see, Dell'Amico, Lodi and Martello [4]).

Since k-AP is another relaxation of the problems we obtain at each node of the branching tree by imposing a k-discrepancy constraint, we have now two combinatorial relaxations, and we can make them co-operate through the additive bounding procedure. Specifically, we decide to use the AP relaxation first, and then 'feed' the k-AP with the reduced cost vector $\bar{c}$. This procedure turns out to change the k-AP we defined before: since $\bar{c}_{ij} \geq 0$, $\forall(i,j) \in A$, then variables x_{ij} such that $i \in N$, $j \in \mathcal{G}_i$ can be disregarded (i.e., set to 0) because in the original k-discrepancy constraint (8) they are not considered. This induces a subgraph $G' = (N, A')$ where $A' = \{(i,j) | j \in \mathcal{B}_i\}$ and the definition of the following problem, k-AP', which is also a valid relaxation of P^{gen} when used as a second bound:

$$z(k\text{-AP}') \; = \min \sum_{(i,j) \in A'} \bar{c}_{ij} \, x_{ij} \tag{27}$$

$$\text{subject to} \sum_{(i,j)\in A'} x_{ij} \le 1, \quad i \in N \tag{28}$$

$$\sum_{(i,j)\in A'} x_{ij} \le 1, \quad j \in N \tag{29}$$

$$\sum_{(i,j)\in A'} x_{ij} = k \tag{30}$$

$$x_{ij}\{0,1\}, \quad \forall (i,j) \in A'. \tag{31}$$

The improved bound is then $LB' = z^*(\text{AP}) + z^*(k\text{-AP}')$. For clarity purpose we will now on refer to k-AP$'$ as simply k-AP.

5 Computational Experiments

In order to validate the ideas proposed in this paper, we need to define optimization problems which make use of the *AllDifferent* constraint. We propose to run experiments on two such problems, one being the very well know Traveling Salesman Problem (TSP) and the other a variant of the Assignment Problem (LAP)

5.1 Asymmetric Traveling Salesman Problem

The TSP and it asymmetric version (ATSP) are well known combinatorial optimization problems, and the CP models presented for this problem, except for 35 are generally variations of the following:

$$\min \sum_{i=1}^{n} C_{iX_i} \tag{32}$$

$$s.t. \ \text{AllDifferent}(X) \tag{33}$$

$$\text{NoSubTour\_cst}(X) \tag{34}$$

$$\text{Discrepancy\_cst}(X, \mathcal{B}, k) \tag{35}$$

$$X_i \in \{1, \dots, n\} \quad \forall i \in \{1, \dots, n\} \tag{36}$$

The X variables used in this model are successor variables, which means that X_i takes the value of the node directly visited after node i. The *AllDifferent* constraint (33) is used here to express conservation of flow in the network. Since the nature of the decision variables already enforces that each node has exactly one outgoing arc, we need only to make sure it also has exactly one ingoing arc. To do so, it is necessary to ensure that no two nodes have the same successor, which is the role of the *AllDifferent* constraint. The *NoSubTour_cst* constraint (34), taken from the work of Pesant *et al.* [16], enforces connectivity of the solution by preventing cycles which are not Hamiltonian. Constraint (35) is used to perform DBS by imposing that exactly k variables X take their values in their respective $\mathcal{B}$ sets. This problem maps into P^{gen} (16)-(21) by substituting (19) by the set of sub-tour elimination constraints equivalent to (34).

We are aware that many much more efficient methods have been devised to solve the ATSP, most of which based on Branch and Cut approaches. However, the aim of this work is to demonstrate that the proof of optimality of DBS can be improved by the use of additive bounding and not to show that DBS is a good approach to solve the ATSP.

The set of ATSP instances we used were based on the ones used in paper by Cirasella *et al.* [3]. They are 11 different classes of instances all presenting different cost structures[2].

5.2 Lower Assignment Problem

The Lower Assignment Problem (LAP) is a simple Assignment Problem enriched with an additional constraint imposing a lower bound on the objective. This problem, expressed by the following Constraint Programming model:

$$\min \sum_{i=1}^{n} C_{iX_i} \tag{37}$$

$$s.t. \ \sum_{i=1}^{n} C_{iX_i} \geq L \tag{38}$$

$$\text{AllDifferent}(X) \tag{39}$$

$$\text{Discrepancy\_cst}(X, \mathcal{B}, k) \tag{40}$$

$$X_i \in \{1, \dots, n\} \qquad \forall i \in \{1, \dots, n\} \tag{41}$$

Each assignment of a value j to a variable X_i incurs the cost C_{ij} and the objective functions (37) is the minimization of the sum of these costs over all variables. The lower bound on the objective in defined by (38), the *AllDifferent* constraint is expressed in (39), and the discrepancy based search is imposed by (40). This problems maps into P^{gen} (16)-(21) by substituting (19) by the linear equivalent of (38). It is easy to see that the LAP is NP-hard by standard reduction of the minimization version of the classical *subset-sum* problem.

This problem is very difficult to solve even for small instances. The complexity lies in the fact that the available lower bound (here the pure *AP* model) is arbitrarily loosen. If L is more than a few percent greater than the optimal solution of the *AP*, then the optimality gap becomes very hard to close. Furthermore, when L increases, the quality of the information provided by the *AP* bound (for instance to guide the search or to perform reduced cost based filtering ([11],[12])) decreases. This additional constraint (38) can thus be seen as an abstraction of any set of unstructured combinatorial constraints which make solutions near the lower bound infeasible and which cannot be treated by any special algorithm or global filtering constraint.

To generate instances of this problem we reused the ATSP instances described previously. In the original instances, the costs associated with diagonal entries

---

[2] The instances were created using the generator provided at
http://www.research.att.com/~dsj/chtsp/

of the matrix (C_{ii}) were set to 0 since these assignments are forbidden by the ATSP definition. We have to modify these entries and set them to ∞ in order to prevent the Assignment Problem optimal solution to be constituted only of self assignment $(X_i = i)$ and have an objective of value 0.

5.3   Implementation

The search strategies used to solve the problem are the typical branching schemes of Constraint Programming. The variables are dynamically ordered using the simple *first fail* criteria of increasing domain sizes. Once a variable is selected, it is fixed to the value of its domain which seems the most promising with respect to the objective function. For these applications, we have chosen the reduced costs as a quality criteria and we thus branch on the value j of D_i associated with the minimum reduced cost $\bar{c}_{ij}$. Reduced costs are also used to partition D_i into $\mathcal{G}_i$ and $\mathcal{B}_i$ for each X_i as discussed in section 5.5.

Since the relaxation provides reduced costs, we are also able to perform reduced cost filtering. This technique is employed to filter out values associated with sub-optimal solutions, which means eliminating all assignments whose reduced cost added to the current lower bound exceeds the upper bound. $LB + C'_{ij} > UB^3 \Rightarrow X_i \neq j, \ \forall i, j \in \{1, \ldots, n\}$.

For the LAP problem, the lower bound L set on the objective (in constraint (38)) is computed using the value of the Assignment Problem at the root node of the search tree. Values of L too close to the current value of lower bound make the problem too easy to solve (and not interesting) while too high values of L tend to generate very hard problems. For the present experimentation L was set to a value of 10% above the relaxation value, yielding difficult but solvable problems.

The Constraint Programming models were implemented using the ILOG Solver 5.2 library and all experimentations were performed on a Intel Mobile Pentium IV 1.8 GHz computer.

5.4   Method Comparison

To evaluate the performance of the Discrepancy Additive Bounding on the DBS, we compare three different approaches: a first approach using only the first AP bound (normal *DBS*), a simple implementation of the additive bound described in section 4.1 (*Count-RC*) and the more complex *k-Assignment* version of this bound detailed in section 4.2 (*k-AP*).

We considered 11 problem classes and generated 5 instances of each of them, for a total of 55 benchmark problems[4]. All problems are defined wiht $n = 25$ and all values reported in tables 1 and 2 are averaged on the number of problems solved by all methods. Problems that could not be solved by all methods are not accounted for in the given figures but reported separately in table 3.

---

[3] The upper bound is defined as the value of the best feasible solution -1 (for costs with ingeter values).

[4] Input data for problem generation is available on request.

Table 1. Comparison on ATSP.

Class	DBS				Count-RC				k-AP			
	nb	Time	BT	k	nb	Time	BT	k	nb	Time	BT	k
amat	5	0.3	346.4	21.0	5	0.1	138.2	1.0	5	0.1	138.2	1.0
coin	5	300.3	457495.0	26.0	5	90.9	197975.0	6.4	5	86.5	197067.6	5.8
crane	5	247.0	509641.4	26.0	5	127.5	365093.4	7.0	5	127.1	362161.4	5.8
disk	4	706.6	1243108.8	26.0	4	307.5	482212.0	6.8	4	225.6	470009.8	6.5
rect	3	690.6	966603.0	26.0	4	168.0	328863.7	7.7	4	153.6	314006.0	6.7
rtilt	3	564.7	689241.3	26.0	3	182.2	250469.3	9.3	3	167.1	224831.3	7.7
shop	5	4.3	6309.6	26.0	5	1.7	3472.0	3.8	5	1.7	3446.6	3.8
smat	5	4.8	5389.8	26.0	5	1.9	2723.8	4.4	5	1.8	2687.8	4.0
stilt	4	679.6	810107.0	26.0	4	165.3	207979.8	9.0	4	138.3	180666.0	7.8
super	5	0.4	753.8	16.0	5	0.1	247.2	1.0	5	0.1	247.2	1.0
tmat	5	0.6	839.4	16.0	5	0.1	200.6	1.4	5	0.1	200.6	1.4
tsmat	0	0	0	0	0	0	0	0	1	0	0	0

Table 2. Comparison on LAP with L set to 10% over AP optimal solution.

Class	DBS				Count-RC				k-AP			
	nb	Time	BT	k	nb	Time	BT	k	nb	Time	BT	k
amat	5	2.1	4499.2	26.0	5	0.6	1586.8	3.0	5	0.6	1565.4	2.6
coin	5	259.7	730824.0	26.0	5	68.3	214000.6	5.4	5	58.6	193188.6	5.0
crane	5	27.6	90946.6	26.0	5	10.3	39789.6	5.6	5	9.6	37780.2	4.8
disk	5	4.8	18247.8	26.0	5	2.9	12884.8	2.8	5	2.9	12884.8	2.8
rect	5	34.3	111333.6	26.0	5	12.8	45629.6	3.8	5	12.3	44735.4	3.6
rtilt	5	52.9	164368.8	26.0	5	18.2	61959.0	4.6	5	17.1	60556.8	4.4
shop	5	3.6	17324.4	26.0	5	3.6	17319.2	20.8	5	3.6	17314.0	15.6
smat	5	1.4	2969.2	26.0	5	0.4	1235.6	2.6	5	0.4	1233.6	2.6
stilt	5	19.7	56518.6	26.0	5	5.0	16792.8	4.8	5	4.6	16065.2	4.0
super	5	0.2	816.2	26.0	5	0.2	803.4	13.2	5	0.2	801.0	10.8
tmat	4	1548.9	4648922.8	26.0	4	954.9	2806462.8	10.3	4	612.6	1951198.5	7.5
tsmat	4	2426.7	8020314.8	26.0	4	1305.2	4277411.5	8.0	4	844.6	2908466.8	6.3

In the following tables we thus report the number of problems solved within a time limit of an hour (nb), the time (Time), number of backtracks (BT) and maximum number of discrepancy (k) needed to prove optimality.

Tables 1 and 2 clearly indicate that Discrepancy Additive Bounding, even in its simpler form, has a significant impact on the time and the number of backtracks needed to prove optimality. When considering all the problems, the Count-RC method reduces the time and size of the search tree needed to prove optimality from 46% to 66% as shown in table 4. The more sophisticated k-AP second bound, even though is more time consuming, achieves a reduction of 61% to 71% thus showing that taking advantage of a special structure (in this case the AllDifferent constraint) may be worth the effort.

If we compare the two k-discrepancy constraints we notice that the approach using the k-AP version generally needs fewer discrepancies (k) to prove optimal-

Table 3. ATSP Problems solved only by Discrepancy Additive Bounding.

Problem	Time	BT	k	Method
tsmat25.1	3290.61	4182262	9	*k-AP*
rect25.0	989.854	1385003	9	*Count-RC*
rect25.0	804.207	1142286	7	*k-AP*

Table 4. Reduction of the time and backtrack needed to prove optimality.

	Count-RC		*k-AP*	
Problem	Time	BT	Time	BT
ATSP	66%	59%	71%	61%
LAP	46%	46%	64%	62%

ity. This indicates that the lower bounds obtained by this method are higher, which not only allows to reduce the value of k but also allows a more effective pruning of the each subproblem search tree (which translates in a reduced number of backtracks.)

5.5   Additional Remarks

In this section we wish to make some remarks concerning issues of the general discrepancy-based solution process, which were not directly addressed in this paper.

Cardinality of the Good Set. As mentioned in [15], an important part of the Decomposition Based Search is clearly the separation of domains into $\mathcal{G}$ and $\mathcal{B}$ sets. To choose an efficient separation one must balance two conflicting objectives: the complexity of the sub-problems and the tightness of the additive bound. If the chosen $\mathcal{G}$ sets are relatively small then the sub-problems will have few values and will be easier to solve. However the reduced costs associated to the values in the $\mathcal{B}$ sets will also be lower yielding a weaker second bound and longer proof of optimality.

On the other hand, generating larger $\mathcal{G}$ sets would leave larger reduced costs in the $\mathcal{B}$ sets and increase the value of the discrepancy bound. Unfortunately, this would also make each sub-problem much harder to solve.

We have also noted that the difference in performance between counting the k minimum reduced costs and solving the k-AP tends to increase as the cardinality of $\mathcal{G}$ sets decreases, which is probably due to the presence of many small reduced costs in the $\mathcal{B}$ sets.

In this application, the $\mathcal{G}$ sets size were set to 20 % of the instance size (here 5 values). Moreover, all values which were less then 20% greater then the largest value in each $\mathcal{G}$ were also included into the $\mathcal{G}$, up to a maximum of 10 values (40% of the size). An ongoing work by VanHoeve and Milano [17] is dedicated to these issues and the analysis of Decomposition Based Search in general.

Application to Traditional LDS. The Discrepancy Based Additive Bounding presented in this paper can also be applied to the general LDS framework, when one counts one discrepancy for each left branch taken in search tree. Given all the values in the domains are ordered, that p_j^i is the position of value j in X_i's domain (first position being 0) and that x_{ij} takes value 1 when X_i is set to value j, the following equation can replace the discrepancy constraint (8).

$$\sum_{i \in N} \sum_{j \in B_i} p_j^i x_{ij} = k$$

Preliminary results are disappointing, again because they are too many small reduced costs (many of value 0) in the discrepancy branches. This means that, except for very high values of k, the discrepancy lower bound is either null or very small. Since traditional LDS can be compared to Decomposition Based Search where the cardinality of the $\mathcal{G}$ sets is 1 (see [17]), the preliminary tests performed confirm the issue raised in the previous remark.

6   Conclusion

In this paper we have demonstrated that the additive bounding procedure can be used to significantly accelerate the proof of optimality of Decomposition-Based Search. The case where the *AllDifferent* is an important part of the model has been studied and two different additive bounds where proposed and evaluated.

It is important to notice that the application of the additive bounding framework in the CP context is not limited to the interaction between a single global constraint and the search strategy. Indeed, ABP, as outlined in Figure 1, can be applied to a sequence of structured relaxations corresponding to several global constraints, plus, eventually, DBS or another suitable search strategy.

An extensive use of the additive bounding framework in CP and its application to real-world and complex problems for which Constraint Programming is an efficient solution method is the topic of future research.

Acknowledgements

Thanks are due to Matteo Fischetti, W.J. van Hoeve, and VanRanch for valuable comments and helpful discussions. Thanks are also due to anonymous referees for useful suggestions.

References

1. G. Carpaneto, M. Dell'Amico, P. Toth. Exact solution of large-scale asymmetric traveling salesman problems. *ACM Transactions on Mathematical Software*, 21:394–409, 1995.
2. G. Carpaneto, S. Martello, P. Toth. Algorithms and codes for the assignment problem. *Annals of Operations Research* 13, 193–223, 1988.

3. J. Cirasella, D.S. Johnson, L.A. McGeoch, W. Zhang. The asymmetric traveling salesman problem: algorithms, instance generators, and tests. In A.L. Buchsbaum and J. Snoeyink, editors, *Proceedings of ALENEX'01*, volume 2153 of *Lecture Notes in Computer Science*, pages 32–59. Springer-Verlag, Heidelberg, 2001.
4. M. Dell'Amico, A. Lodi, S. Martello. Efficient algorithms and codes for k-cardinality assignment problems. *Discrete Applied Mathematics* 110, 25–40, 2001.
5. M. Dell'Amico, S. Martello. Linear assignment. In F. Maffioli M. Dell'Amico and S. Martello, editors, *Annotated Bibliographies in Combinatorial Optimization*, pages 355–371. Wiley, 1997.
6. M. Dell'Amico, S. Martello. The k-cardinality Assignment Problem. *Discrete Applied Mathematics*, 76:103–121, 1997.
7. H. El Sakkout, M. Wallace. Probe backtrack search for minimal perturbation in dynamic scheduling. *Constraints*, 5:359–388, 2000.
8. M. Fischetti, P. Toth. An additive bounding procedure for combinatorial optimization problems. *Operations Research*, 37:319–328, 1989.
9. M. Fischetti, P. Toth. An additive bounding procedure for the asymmetric traveling salesman problem. *Mathematical Programming*, 53:173–197, 1992.
10. F. Focacci. Solving combinatorial optimization problems in constraint programming. PhD thesis, University of Ferrara, Italy, 2001.
11. F. Focacci, A. Lodi, M. Milano. Cost-based domain filtering. In J. Jaffar, editor, *Principle and Practice of Constraint Programming - CP 1999*, LNCS 1713, pages 189–203. Springer-Verlag, 1999.
12. F. Focacci, A. Lodi, M. Milano. Exploting relaxations in CP. In M. Milano, ed, *Constraint and Integer Programming combined*. Kluwer, to appear.
13. W. Harvey, M. Ginsberg. Limited discrepancy search. In *Proceedings of the 14th IJCAI*, pages 607–615, Morgan Kaufmann, 1995.
14. A. Lodi, M. Milano. Discrepancy-based additive bounding. *Proceedings of CP-AI-OR 2003*, pages 17–23, Montréal, Canada, 2003.
15. M. Milano, W.J. van Hoeve. Reduced cost-based ranking for generating promising subproblems. In P. Van Hentenryck, editor, *Principle and Practice of Constraint Programming - CP 2002*, LNCS 2470, pages 1–16. Springer-Verlag, 2002.
16. G. Pesant, M. Gendreau, J.-Y. Potvin, J.-M. Rousseau. An Exact Constraint Logic Programming Algorithm for the Traveling Salesman Problem with Time Windows. *Transportation Science*, 32:12–29, 1998.
17. W.J. van Hoeve, M. Milano. Decomposition-based search. A theoretical and experimental evaluation. *LIA Technical Report* LIA00203, University of Bologna, 2003.

A Synthesis of Constraint Satisfaction
and Constraint Solving

Michael J. Maher

Department of Computer Science
Loyola University Chicago
mjm@cs.luc.edu

Abstract. This paper offers a critique of the framework of Constraint Satisfaction Problems. While this framework has been successful in studying search techniques, and has inspired some constraint programming languages, it has some weaknesses that leave it not directly applicable to the study of complex constraints (including so-called global constraints) in constraint programming languages. In particular, it deals poorly with semantic relations whose consistency can be determined algorithmically. In this paper the philosophy of the CLP Scheme is applied to extend the CSP framework to a form more suitable for addressing complex constraints, where both constraint satisfaction and constraint solving have a role. Some rough principles for local consistency conditions in the extended framework are developed, and appropriate notions of local consistency are formulated. These can be used as a coarse measure of the degree of constraint propagation achieved by implementations of complex constraints.

1 Introduction

The study of constraint satisfaction problems (CSPs) has been remarkably successful. The CSP framework provides a flexible basis for formulating NP-complete problems, which can then be addressed by a wide range of methods. The study of systematic search in this framework has yielded techniques for performing search more efficiently and characterized classes of problems for which polynomial time is needed to find solutions.

However, the CSP framework also has some weaknesses. In particular, the framework assumes that data values come from a domain of uninterpreted constants where the only semantic relations are equality and its negation. This is in contrast to the use of many of the ideas from the study of CSPs in practice. Constraint programming systems routinely use interpreted values – such as integers – and semantic relations – such as ordering or arithmetic relations – to formulate and solve problems.

The complex constraints used in these systems – the global constraints [4] of CHIP [16], the hard constraints [28] of CLP($\Re$) [27], constraints in ILOG Solver [24], the demons written in CHIP or Solver, and predicates defined in Constraint Handling Rules [19], Claire [9], or Oz [37] – all exploit and infer semantic relations when solving problems. In some ways these complex constraints are the counterpart of constraints in the CSP framework, and searching for solutions of a query in these systems corresponds to search in CSPs. But there are several aspects of the CSP framework, as generally used, that are not appropriate for these applications.

F. Rossi (Ed.): CP 2003, LNCS 2833, pp. 525–539, 2003.

Traditional treatments of CSPs are not directly applicable to complex constraints because of assumptions and emphases that are not appropriate for complex constraints. In particular, most treatments:

1. consider only uninterpreted constants as values;
2. assume relations are finite and defined extensionally;
3. assume domains of variables are finite;
4. assume that there is only one constraint on a given set of variables;
5. almost exclusively study binary relations;
6. formulate notions of local consistency that focus on variables and the values that they may take, and do not address the possibility of other relations between variables;
7. assume branching in search is determined by the instantiation of variables by values.

As a consequence of the first two points, these treatments cannot include any constraint solving. There are several works that avoid a few of these assumptions (for example, [34, 15, 14]) but not to the extent that they are applicable to complex constraints.

The assumptions are often not justified in practice. Consider, for example, the *cumulative* constraint [1] which is widely used for problems of scheduling with scarce resources, and is representative of many complex constraints. This constraint

- applies to integers and lists of integers;
- represents an infinite relation;
- is not implemented extensionally but as a thread that reacts to the state of a constraint store;
- has arity 4.

Local consistency will be addressed in more detail later. However, it can be noted that in many situations arc consistency is inappropriate, for efficiency reasons. Consequently, many variants have been devised, including interval or bounds consistency [33] in finite domain systems, and hull consistency [7, 5] in solving non-linear real constraints.

Branching in search is often not performed by instantiating variables. In the conventional branch and bound implementation of integer programming (see, for example, [23]) branching is performed by imposing extra inequalities (for example $x \leq 5$ and $x \geq 6$). Interval techniques for the solution of non-linear equations over the real numbers use domain splitting (see, for example, [6]). Even in finite domain constraint programming, domain splitting is useful (see, for example, [33]).

The aim of this paper is to develop a suitable framework for addressing constraint programming search problems. In the next section, the CSP framework is extended to include semantic relations. It represents a synthesis of constraint satisfaction and constraint solving.

The remainder of the paper investigates local consistency in this extended framework. After outlining weaknesses of existing local consistency conditions for constraint programming search problems in Section 3, several are reformulated and generalized for the extended framework. In Section 4 the formulation of arc consistency in [32] is derived from the standard description, following the approach recommended in [31]. This sets the pattern for discussion and reformulation of node consistency (Section 5), pairwise and k-wise consistency (Section 6), and restricted path consistency (Section 8). A k-fold consistency is introduced in Section 7 as an extension of the reformulated arc consistency, and its relationship to other consistency conditions is shown.

Before going forward, a choice of terminology is needed, because the areas of constraint satisfaction and constraint solving use the word "constraint" differently. In constraint satisfaction, constraints are the uninterpreted relations that are the basis of the combinatorial problem to be solved. In constraint solving, constraints are the semantically-defined relations whose conjunctions can be solved (perhaps only partially) through algorithmic techniques. The distinction is not always straightforward in existing work, but in the framework proposed in this paper we will distinguish the two roles played by relations in these two areas. To avoid confusion, we will use "constraint" only to refer to semantic relations that are solved algorithmically in a constraint solver. Constraints in the sense of constraint satisfaction will be referred to as "properties". (Thus, in this terminology, CSPs do not involve constraints! Similarly, "global constraints" are not constraints; they are implementations of properties.)

2   Extending CSPs

This section proposes an extension of the CSP framework that addresses some of the weaknesses identified in the introduction. We begin by recalling the definition of a CSP in our modified terminology.

A *property* over a set of variables V is a pair $(\tilde{x}, \mathcal{P})$ where $\tilde{x}$ is a sequence of n variables in V and $\mathcal{P}$ is a relation of arity n. There is an implicit identification between the variables in the list and the columns/attributes of $\mathcal{P}$. Often this will be written as $\mathcal{P}(\tilde{x})$.

A *Constraint Satisfaction Problem (CSP)* is a 3-tuple $\langle Vars, Prop, D \rangle$ where $Vars$ is a set of variables, $Prop$ is a set of properties over $Vars$, and D maps each $x \in Vars$ to a finite set of constants (the domain of the variable). We can alternatively view D as a conjunction of unary relations, one for each $x \in Vars$. A binary CSP is a CSP where all properties are formed from binary relations. A solution to a CSP is a function s mapping each variable to a constant such that for every $x \in Vars$, $s(x) \in D(x)$, and for every $(\tilde{x}, \mathcal{P}) \in Prop$, $s(\tilde{x}) \in \mathcal{P}$.

To extend this framework we need to specify the semantic relations (constraints) that are admitted. Following the formulation in constraint logic programming [26], we specify these with a constraint domain.

A *signature* Σ is a set of function and relation symbols, each with an associated arity. We assume that the binary relation symbol $=$ is in Σ.

A *constraint domain* over a signature Σ is a pair $(\mathcal{D}, \mathcal{L})$ where $\mathcal{D}$ is a Σ-structure and $\mathcal{L}$ is a set of logical formulas over Σ and a set of variables. A *constraint* is a formula $c \in \mathcal{L}$. A *primitive constraint* c is a constraint of the form $r(t_1, \ldots, t_n)$ where r is a relation symbol and the t_i are terms. If $\tilde{x}$ is the free variables in c, we sometimes write $c(\tilde{x})$. Thus $\mathcal{L}$ specifies the syntax of constraints and $\mathcal{D}$ specifies their semantics. When we need to specify the subclass of constraints with free variables from a set V, we write $\mathcal{L}(V)$. We assume $=$ is interpreted as identity in $\mathcal{D}$ and that $\mathcal{L}$ is closed under variable renaming and conjunction[1]. The *conjunctive language generated by* a set S of constraints contains all constraints in S, and is closed under conjunction and variable renaming.

---

[1] In constraint logic programming it is convenient to also assume that $\mathcal{L}$ is closed under existential quantification, but that is not needed in this context.

Given a set of variables $Vars$ and a constraint domain $(\mathcal{D}, \mathcal{L})$, a *valuation* is a function $v : Vars \to \mathcal{D}$. A valuation on a subset of variables $\tilde{x}$ is the restriction of a valuation to $\tilde{x}$, denoted $v|_{\tilde{x}}$. The *complement* in a constraint c of a valuation v on $\tilde{x}$ is a formula equivalent to $c \wedge \neg \bigwedge_{x \in \tilde{x}} x = v(x)$. A valuation v satisfies a constraint $c(\tilde{x})$ if $c(v(\tilde{x}))$ evaluates to True in the structure $\mathcal{D}$. v satisfies a property $(\tilde{x}, \mathcal{P})$ if $v(\tilde{x}) \in \mathcal{P}$; if $v(\tilde{x}) = \tilde{a}$ we sometimes write this as $\mathcal{P}(\tilde{a})$.

We now extend the CSP framework, following the philosophy of the CLP scheme [25]. A problem is now parameterized by a constraint domain, and the variable domain D is replaced by an environment of constraints.

Definition 1. *An* Extended Constraint Satisfaction Problem (ECSP) *with signature* Σ *is a 4-tuple* $\langle (\mathcal{D}, \mathcal{L}), Vars, Prop, C \rangle$ *where* $(\mathcal{D}, \mathcal{L})$ *is a* Σ-*constraint domain,* $Vars$ *is a set of variables,* $Prop$ *is a set of properties over* $Vars$, *and* C *is a conjunction of constraints from* $\mathcal{L}(Vars)$, *called the* constraint environment.

A solution of the ECSP is a valuation v *that satisfies the constraints* C *and the properties in* $Prop$.

A CSP $\mathcal{C} = \langle Vars, Prop, D \rangle$ can be considered to be an ECSP $\mathcal{E}_{\mathcal{C}} = \langle (\mathcal{D}_{\mathcal{C}}, \mathcal{L}_{\mathcal{C}}), Vars, Prop, C \rangle$ where Σ contains all constants, and unary predicate symbols p_S for each subset S of constants; $\mathcal{L}_{\mathcal{C}}$ is the collection of conjunctions of unary predicates; $\mathcal{D}_{\mathcal{C}}$ is the structure with a domain consisting of the constants in Σ that interprets each $p_S(x)$ as the relation $x \in S$; and C is the conjunction $\bigwedge_{x \in Vars} p_{D(x)}(x)$.

ECSPs are able to represent a larger array of problems than CSPs, and represent them more naturally. In finite domain constraint programming, the primitive constraints restrict a variable to a finite interval of integers, variables range over integers and lists of integers, and properties are complex constraints such as *cumulative*, *alldifferent*, *element*, as well as arithmetic relations such as $x + y \leq z$.

The problem of finding solutions to non-linear equations over the reals [6] can be formulated as an ECSP, where the primitive constraints are floating point bounds on variables (for example, $x \leq f$, where f is a floating point number) over the real numbers, and the properties are the non-linear equations.

Similarly, the solving of finite set constraints [20] can be formulated as an ECSP, where the constraints are containment relations between a set variable and a set (for example, $S \subseteq \{a, b, c, d\}$), the set of values is the set of finite sets of constants (determined by Σ), and the properties represent relations between set variables, such as $S_1 \subseteq S_2$ or $S_1 \cap S_2 = S_3$.

The above examples involve unary primitive constraints, but constraints of greater arity are needed in applications like temporal reasoning (where there may be precedence constraints $x < y$), and to reflect languages like CLP($\Re$), where constraints may contain arbitrarily many variables. CLP($\Re$) queries are ECSPs where the constraints are linear arithmetic equations and inequalities over the real numbers, and the properties are non-linear equations and hard constraints like *pow(X, Y, Z)*.

In all these examples, the underlying values are infinite in number or have internal structure, the properties are not represented extensionally and generally are not binary, and there are semantic relations (constraints) that are central to the expression and solution of the problems. Although the CSP framework might theoretically be capable of representing these problems by treating constraints as properties, using possibly infinite relations to represent them, and admitting infinite domains for variables, such a representation would be far removed from the practice of solving these problems.

An ECSP, like a CSP, comes without any specific operational interpretation. However, an abstract execution model is a search tree where each node (except, possibly, the root) is an ECSP satisfying the invariant:

> the constraint environment is satisfiable and the ECSP satisfies a local consistency condition, or the constraint environment is unsatisfiable and the node has no children

Such an execution model requires a method for obtaining local consistency and a constraint solver to test satisfiability. Many constraint programs are constructed to generate constraints and properties in a first phase, and then search for solutions. The ECSP execution model reflects the second, search, phase. Constraint propagation achieved by implemented properties in that phase corresponds to achieving a form of local consistency in an ECSP. (For example, see [32].) Thus specific local consistency conditions, such as arc consistency, represent specific levels of constraint propagation.

The following lemma is used to prove later results. In the lemma, $\exists_{-\tilde{x}}$ denotes the existential quantification of all variables except $\tilde{x}$, and $\rightarrow$ denotes implication.

Lemma 1. *Let ψ and ϕ be formulas involving both properties and constraints, c and c' be constraints, and $\tilde{x}$ be a set of variables. Consider the following statements:*
(1) $(\psi \wedge \phi \wedge c) \rightarrow c'$ implies $(\phi \wedge c) \rightarrow c'$
(2) $(\phi \wedge c) \rightarrow \exists_{-\tilde{x}} (\psi \wedge \phi \wedge c)$

1. *If $vars(c') \subseteq \tilde{x}$ and (2) holds, then (1) holds.*
2. *If, for any valuation v on $\tilde{x}$, there is a constraint c_v that is the complement in c of v, and (1) holds for all c', then (2) holds.*

3 Local Consistency

There have been many different local consistency properties proposed over many years. Almost all are formulated – whether explicitly or implicitly – in terms of instantiations of variables and extensions of consistent instantiations[2].

For example, a large class of local consistency properties is as follows. A CSP is (i, j)-*consistent* [17] if any consistent instantiation of i variables can be extended to a further j variables. In particular, for binary CSPs[3], arc consistency is $(1, 1)$-consistency and path consistency is equivalent to $(2, 1)$-consistency.

While the idea of local consistency has been fruitful in improving systematic search as a method for solving CSPs, existing treatments are unsuitable in a number of respects as the basis for systematic search in constraint languages:

---

[2] A consistent instantiation of a set S of variables is an instantiation that satisfies all properties with all variables from S.

[3] Under the assumption that there is at most one property on a given pair of variables.

1. The presence of algorithmically solved constraints is not addressed.
2. Many forms of local consistency are formulated with binary properties in mind, although many properties arising in practice are not binary.
3. Most methods for maintaining local consistencies assume that tuples may be deleted from properties.
4. Almost all methods for maintaining local consistencies assume that values may be deleted from domains.
5. Many forms of local consistency emphasize the variables involved, rather than the relations. In particular, the concept of locality is almost always expressed solely in terms of variables.

The first point is inherent in the use of the CSP framework. The second is tied to the origins of constraint satisfaction, but it is clear that current practice involves non-binary properties, and encoding these as binary properties seems impractical. However several works have addressed the issue of generalizing local consistency conditions to properties of arbitrary arity. Generalized arc consistency [34] applies to properties of arbitrary arity, as does relational arc consistency [14]. Also in [14] are two generalizations of k-consistency that are independent of arity. In addition, pairwise consistency [2] and its extension to k-wise consistency [21], because they were defined originally in a database context, from the beginning were independent of arity, as are later extensions hyper-k-consistency [29] and ω-consistencies [36].

Many consistency conditions, such as path consistency, are enforced by modifying properties. Such an approach is very difficult if properties are not represented extensionally, and expensive in terms of space if they are represented extensionally. The latter point has led to further investigation of inverse consistencies [18], restricted path consistencies [8, 13] and singleton consistencies [12] that only modify variable domains. Since "global constraints" and related properties are represented as reactive threads of computation – and not extensionally – it is only such consistency conditions that show promise of applicability to constraint programming search problems.

However, even for these consistency conditions, enforcement algorithms assume that values can be deleted from variable domains. In general, in constraint programming, this assumption is invalid since many constraint programming systems do not provide constraints that can express arbitrary variable domains. This has led to several approximations of arc consistency where domains are replaced by intervals of integers [33], real numbers [7], or finite sets [20], and, more generally, approximation spaces [11]. [38] proposed a variety of interval consistencies, but that proposal does not consider the possbiility of constraints other than intervals, and cannot apply to languages like CLP($\Re$).

In reference to the fifth point, it is clear that both variables and properties are essential to the CSP framework. However, most local consistency conditions define locality in terms of variables. For example, (i, j)-consistency addresses various sub-problems (of the main problem) containing $i + j$ variables. As a consequence, many of these consistency conditions are defined in terms of extending a consistent instantiation for a set V of variables. Considering only consistent instantiations introduces the effect of an unknown number of unknown properties with variables from V when determining consistency. The (i, j)-consistencies and the relational consistencies of [14] are among those formulated this way, while the k-wise consistencies are not.

Such consistency conditions are practically impossible to achieve when implementing properties as reactive threads. To illustrate the difficulties, consider the implementation of the property $x + y = z$ over the constraint domain of finite integer intervals. It is possible that a given ECSP might also involve properties equivalent to $even(x)$ and $odd(x)$, where $even(x)$ (respectively $odd(x)$) is satisfied only if x is even (respectively, odd). If we wish to achieve $(2, 1)$-consistency then we need to obtain the following behavior:

- If $x + y = z$ is part of an ECSP involving properties equivalent to $even(x)$ and $odd(y)$, then the implementation of $x + y = z$ should restrict the possible values of z to odd numbers.
- If $x + y = z$ is part of an ECSP involving properties equivalent to $even(x)$ and $even(y)$, then the implementation of $x + y = z$ should restrict the possible values of z to even numbers.

Without these behaviors, a consistent instantiation for x and z might not be extendable to y. Clearly an implementation of $x + y = z$ must "know" what other properties are part of the ECSP if it is to guarantee $(2, 1)$-consistency. In an ECSP such as this, node consistency does not solve the problem; see Section 5. Thus, although $(2, 1)$-consistency is local in terms of variables, it is not local in terms of properties, and consequently it is difficult to achieve with reactive implementations of properties.

The remainder of this paper formulates local consistency conditions that address the above points. These conditions are: independent of arity; formulated in a manner independent of the particular kind of constraint, as closure requirements; and the locality of the conditions is based purely on properties, not on variables. In many cases they are generalizations of consistency conditions for CSPs. These are consistency conditions that have *prima facie* potential to reflect the behavior of implemented properties.

4   Arc Consistency

(Generalized) arc consistency of a property is often formulated as requiring that the instantiation of any variable by a value in the domain of the variable can be extended to an instantiation of all variables that satisfies the property.

Using logical notation, we can write this as

$$x \in D(x) \rightarrow \exists_{-x} (\mathcal{P} \wedge D)$$

where $\exists_{-x}$ denotes the existential quantification of all variables except x. If we adapt this definition to constraints, instead of variable domains, we obtain:

For every variable x,

$$\exists_{-x} c \rightarrow \exists_{-x} (P \wedge c)$$

This says that every value for x that is consistent with the constraint environment c can be extended to a solution of P and c.

Such a formulation is very close in spirit to the original definition, while generalizing from domains to general constraints, but it considers only one variable at a time. Consequently, the effect of c in this formulation is only to express unary (domain-like) constraints. We can interpret this formulation as saying that if any unary information is available in $P \wedge c$, it is already available in c.

This interpretation provides the basis for the further generalization of arc consistency to a form where variables are less important. We focus on the notion that certain information in $P \wedge c$ is contained wholly within c.

If we apply this idea too readily we reach a definition

$$c \to (P \wedge c)$$

which simply implies that P is irrelevant. We must restrict the information required to be embedded in c to certain types. We cannot do that directly with the above formulation, so we replace it with a weaker statement.

Definition 2. *A property P is* arc consistent *with a constraint c if, for every constraint c',*

$$(P \wedge c) \to c' \text{ implies } c \to c'$$

An ECSP $\langle (\mathcal{D}, \mathcal{L}), Vars, Prop, C \rangle$ is arc consistent *if every $P \in Prop$ is arc consistent with C.*

This relaxes the previous statement by restricting it to information expressible with constraints c'. It formulates the condition as a closure requirement on the constraint environment c. Such a formulation emphasizes that enforcing consistency involves expressing information implicit in the problem as explicit constraints.

This definition unifies several existing forms of local consistency, including generalized arc consistency, interval consistency and rule consistency for finite domain languages, and some forms of consistency used for floating point intervals over continuous domains. See [32] for more details. By restricting Definition 2 further, to particular classes of constraints, we can obtain a parameterized definition of arc consistency [32].

It might not be clear that the definition of arc consistency for ECSPs is equivalent to arc consistency for CSPs. However, using Lemma 1 where ψ is P, ϕ is $true$, and c is C, we have

Proposition 1. *Let C be a CSP and let $\mathcal{E}_C$ be the equivalent ECSP. Then C is generalized arc consistent iff $\mathcal{E}_C$ is arc consistent in the extended sense of Definition 2.*

The study of the $minimum$ property in [32] indicates that, in some cases, the definition of arc consistency might be too strong, because c' might involve variables not present in the property. Such a situation can make it difficult to implement the properties to achieve arc consistency. In such cases we can consider a slightly weaker form of arc consistency where c' is required to only contain variables appearing in P. The above proposition also holds for weak arc consistency.

Although arc consistency for ECSPs is a generalization of generalized arc consistency, and some forms of arc consistency (for example, interval consistency) are weaker[4]

---

[4] We say that a local consistency condition A is weaker than another condition B if every ECSP that satisfies B also satisfies A.

than generalized arc consistency, it is not true in general that generalized arc consistency is stronger than the extended form of arc consistency.

Example 1. Consider the property $\mathcal{P}(x, y, z)$ defined by

$\mathcal{P}$		
1	1	1
1	2	1
2	3	2
3	1	3

and the constraint environment c that states that x, y and z are in the interval 1..3. Then $\mathcal{P}$ is generalized arc consistent wrt the domains of the variables, but it is not arc consistent in the extended sense if the constraint language $\mathcal{L}$ contains equations. This because $\mathcal{P} \wedge c \rightarrow x = z$ but $c \not\rightarrow x = z$.

This situation arises because of the possibility of a constraint language that can express relations that cannot be expressed with domain constraints.

5   Node Consistency

Node consistency is the special case of generalized arc consistency where the property involved is unary. Thus it is already covered by the discussion in the previous section. The initial formulation is that

$$c \rightarrow \mathcal{P}$$

It is noteworthy that, in an ECSP, a unary property is not necessarily eliminable in the manner that it is in a CSP. The problem is that the property might not be representable by constraints. Consequently, under the above formulation, node consistency often cannot be achieved. For example, let $odd(x)$ refer to the property that holds for odd numbers between 0 and 100, and suppose the constraint language admits only interval constraints. Then the constraints are unable to represent the property.

On the other hand, the formulation as a closure requirement

$$(\mathcal{P} \wedge c) \rightarrow c' \text{ implies } c \rightarrow c'$$

concerns only information representable by constraints, and consequently this relaxed form of node consistency is achievable. Essentially c must contain the tightest outside approximation of $\mathcal{P} \wedge c$ by constraints. In the *odd* example, consistency is achieved when c is $1 \leq x \leq 99$.

Even so, there are situations where extended node consistency (and, more generally, arc consistency) is not attainable. For example, consider a constraint language over the real numbers permitting only rational bounds (for example, $x \leq \frac{1}{2}$), and the property $x \leq \sqrt{2}$. Since there is no least rational upper bound for $\sqrt{2}$, node consistency cannot be achieved for this property and constraint domain.

6 k-wise Consistency

A collection of properties is *pairwise consistent* [2] if, for every pair of properties $\mathcal{P}_1$ and $\mathcal{P}_2$ in the collection

$$(\exists_{-vars(\mathcal{P}_i)} \ \mathcal{P}_1 \wedge \mathcal{P}_2) \leftrightarrow \mathcal{P}_i \qquad\qquad \text{for } i = 1, 2$$

This condition means that $\mathcal{P}_1$ and $\mathcal{P}_2$ are essentially independent – that the presence of $\mathcal{P}_2$ does not eliminate any solutions of $\mathcal{P}_1$, and *vice versa*. It was proposed in the context of relational databases with no domains or constraints on variables. Adapting it for ECSPs (and CSPs), where we look for consistency with respect to the constraint environment C (respectively, the variable domains), we have, for $i = 1, 2$:

$$(\exists_{-vars(\mathcal{P}_i)} \ \mathcal{P}_1 \wedge \mathcal{P}_2 \wedge C) \leftrightarrow (\exists_{-vars(\mathcal{P}_i)} \ \mathcal{P}_i \wedge C)$$

which only requires that $\mathcal{P}_1$ and $\mathcal{P}_2$ are independent on solutions of C.

As with arc consistency, a relaxed formulation makes the closure requirement explicit:

For $i = 1, 2$ and constraints c' with $vars(c') \subseteq vars(\mathcal{P}_i)$

$$(\mathcal{P}_1 \wedge \mathcal{P}_2 \wedge C) \to c' \text{ implies } (\mathcal{P}_i \wedge C) \to c'$$

Pairwise consistency was generalized to k-wise consistency [21] which, after adapting it to CSPs and ECSPs, requires that for every subset $\{\mathcal{P}_1, \ldots, \mathcal{P}_k\}$ of properties in the collection and for $i = 1, \ldots, k$

$$(\exists_{-vars(\mathcal{P}_i)} \ \textstyle\bigwedge_{j=1}^{k} \mathcal{P}_j \wedge C) \leftrightarrow \exists_{-vars(\mathcal{P}_i)} \ (\mathcal{P}_i \wedge C)$$

After relaxation this definition becomes:

Definition 3. *An ECSP $\langle (\mathcal{D}, \mathcal{L}), Vars, Prop, C \rangle$ is k-wise consistent if, for every $\{\mathcal{P}_1, \mathcal{P}_2, \ldots, \mathcal{P}_k\} \subseteq Prop$ of size k, for $i = 1, \ldots, k$ and all constraints c' with $vars(c') \subseteq vars(\mathcal{P}_i)$*

$$(\textstyle\bigwedge_{j=1}^{k} \mathcal{P}_j \wedge C) \to c' \text{ implies } (\mathcal{P}_i \wedge C) \to c'$$

Obviously 1-wise consistency is trivial. Using Lemma 1 where ψ is $\bigwedge_{j=1}^{k} \mathcal{P}_j$ and ϕ is $\mathcal{P}_i$ we find that, for $k \geq 2$, this formulation of k-wise consistency is strictly weaker than the adapted formulation for CSPs.

Proposition 2. *Let C be a CSP and let $\mathcal{E}_C$ be the equivalent ECSP. If C is k-wise consistent then $\mathcal{E}_C$ is k-wise consistent in the extended sense above. But $\mathcal{E}_C$ might be k-wise consistent in the extended sense when C is not k-wise consistent, for $k \geq 2$.*

7 k-fold Consistency

The natural generalization of extended arc consistency is to consider more than one property at a time.

Definition 4. *An ECSP* $\langle(\mathcal{D}, \mathcal{L}), Vars, Prop, C\rangle$ *is* k-fold consistent *if, for every* $\{\mathcal{P}_1, \mathcal{P}_2, \ldots, \mathcal{P}_k\} \subseteq Prop$ *of size* k*, and every constraint* c'

$$\bigwedge_{i=1}^{k} \mathcal{P}_i \wedge C \to c' \text{ implies } C \to c'$$

Thus 1-fold consistency is extended arc consistency. As with arc consistency, we can also consider the weaker form, where each variable in c' also occurs in a property. k-fold consistency, like the previous local consistency conditions that we have discussed, defines locality purely in terms of properties, and not in terms of variables.

The finite domain constraint solvers discussed in [22] can be viewed as partial implementations of 2-fold consistency. Where one property is a linear equation involving at most 2 variables, substitution using the equation is used to improve propagation. Other pairs of properties may not achieve 2-fold consistency.

Proposition 3. *Let* $\mathcal{E}$ *be an ECSP containing at least* k *properties.*

If $\mathcal{E}$ *is* k-fold consistent, then $\mathcal{E}$ *is* $(k-1)$-fold consistent. However, the converse is not true. That is, $\mathcal{E}$ might be $(k-1)$-fold consistent, but not k-fold consistent.*

Thus k-fold consistency, for the various values of k, forms a hierarchy of local consistency conditions. This also holds for the weaker form where the variables of c' must occur in a property.

The *relational structure* of an ECSP $\mathcal{E} = \langle(\mathcal{D}, \mathcal{L}), Vars, Prop, C\rangle$ is a pair $\langle Vars, \{\tilde{x} \mid \mathcal{P}(\tilde{x}) \in Prop\}\rangle$. Let $\mathcal{E}$ be an ECSP and let $\langle Vars, \{\tilde{x}_1, \ldots, \tilde{x}_m\}\rangle$ be the relational structure of $\mathcal{E}$. Let $\tilde{x}_0 = Vars - \cup_{i=1}^{m}\tilde{x}_i$. We say that $\mathcal{E}$ has *lossless decomposition of constraints* if, for every constraint $c \in \mathcal{L}$,

$$c \leftrightarrow \bigwedge_{i=0}^{m} \exists_{-\tilde{x}_i} c$$

Lossless decomposition of constraints is similar to lossless joins and join dependencies in relational database theory [30]. As there, the relational structure is determined by properties (relations), but here the lossless decomposition applies to the constraint environment, rather than a universal relation.

It is straightforward to show that any conjunction of unary constraints has a lossless decomposition, independent of the relational structure. We use this fact and the next lemma to prove the following proposition.

Lemma 2. *Suppose a solvable ECSP* $\mathcal{E}$ *has lossless decomposition of constraints and is arc consistent and* k-wise consistent. Then $\mathcal{E}$ *is* k-fold consistent.

We now show that k-fold consistency is a stronger condition than k-wise consistency, but in a practical sense it is not much stronger.

Proposition 4. *Let* $\mathcal{E}$ *be an ECSP.*

1. *If* $\mathcal{E}$ *is* k-fold consistent then $\mathcal{E}$ *is* k-wise consistent.
2. *Suppose* $\mathcal{L}$ *is generated conjunctively from unary constraints. If* $\mathcal{E}$ *is* k-wise consistent and arc consistent then $\mathcal{E}$ *is* k-fold consistent.

In many settings of interest – CSPs, finite integer domains, finite sets, and interval approaches to continuous domains – the primitive constraints are unary and arc consistency is maintained. Thus, in these settings there is no practical difference between k-fold consistency and k-wise consistency. On the other hand, when addressing constraint solvers for non-unary constraints, as in CLP($\Re$) or in temporal reasoning, the two consistency conditions differ.

Example 2. Consider a linearly ordered set, where the only constraint relations are $<$ and $\leq$. For concreteness we choose the integers.

Consider the two properties $\mathcal{P}_1(x, y)$ and $\mathcal{P}_2(y, z)$ with relations defined as follows:

$\mathcal{P}_1$	
0	4
1	5
2	9

$\mathcal{P}_2$	
4	1
5	3
9	6

Consider an ECSP $\mathcal{E}$ where the properties are $\mathcal{P}_1$ and $\mathcal{P}_2$ and the constraint environment c is $0 \leq x \leq 2 \land 4 \leq y \leq 9 \land 1 \leq z \leq 6 \land x < y \land z < y$.

Then $\mathcal{E}$ is arc consistent, since neither property implies any stronger constraint. $\mathcal{E}$ is 2-wise consistent because $(\exists z\ \mathcal{P}_1 \land \mathcal{P}_2 \land c) \leftrightarrow (\exists z\ \mathcal{P}_1 \land c)$ and $(\exists x\ \mathcal{P}_1 \land \mathcal{P}_2 \land c) \leftrightarrow (\exists x\ \mathcal{P}_2 \land c)$. But $\mathcal{E}$ is not 2-fold consistent because $\mathcal{P}_1(x, y) \land \mathcal{P}_2(y, z) \to x < z$.

8   Restricted Consistencies

Enforcement of path consistency [35] requires, in general, that tuples be deleted from properties. Thus it is not of direct use, but we will need the definition later. Since path consistency is equivalent to (2,1)-consistency on a class of binary CSPs [35], a common definition of path consistency is that any solution of a property $\mathcal{P}$ can be extended to a solution of the two properties involving the variables of $\mathcal{P}$ and any one other variable:

For every tuple in every property $\mathcal{P}_0$ on variables x and y, and every variable z and corresponding properties $\mathcal{P}_1$ and $\mathcal{P}_2$

$$(\exists_{-x,y}\ \mathcal{P}_0(x, y) \land D) \to \exists_{-x,y}\ (\mathcal{P}_0(x, y) \land P_1(x, z) \land P_2(y, z) \land D)$$

There are many ways in which the idea of path consistency might be extended to properties of greater arity and to ECSPs. Here we will consider only one:

For all properties $\mathcal{P}_0(\tilde{x}), \mathcal{P}_1(\tilde{y}), \mathcal{P}_2(\tilde{z})$ such that $\tilde{x} \cap \tilde{y} \neq \emptyset, \tilde{x} \cap \tilde{z} \neq \emptyset$, and $(\tilde{y} \cap \tilde{z}) - \tilde{x} \neq \emptyset$:

$$(\exists_{-\tilde{x}}\ \mathcal{P}_0(\tilde{x}) \land C) \to \exists_{-\tilde{x}}\ (P_0(\tilde{x}) \land P_1(\tilde{y}) \land P_2(\tilde{z}) \land C)$$

Applying Lemma 1, we relax this to: for constraints c' with $vars(c') \subseteq \tilde{x}$,

$$P_0(\tilde{x}) \land P_1(\tilde{y}) \land P_2(\tilde{z}) \land C \to c'\ \text{implies}\ P_0(\tilde{x}) \land C \to c'$$

We can see immediately that path consistency is weaker than 3-wise consistency. It is not comparable in strength to pairwise consistency and 2-fold consistency, even in CSPs.

Restricted path consistency (RPC) [8] was designed to strengthen arc consistency towards path consistency on binary CSPs without requiring the deletion of tuples from properties. It does this by performing a path consistency check only when a discovery of inconsistency allows a value to be deleted from a variable domain. Reformulating this strengthening for arbitrary CSPs, it requires that for every property $\mathcal{P}_0(\tilde{x})$ and every value a in the domain of a variable $x \in \tilde{x}$, if there is only one tuple in $\mathcal{P}_0(\tilde{x})$ where x has the value a then a path consistency check should be applied to that tuple.

Obviously, the idea of a restricted consistency can be applied to any local consistency condition in place of path consistency. We now further generalize the formulation so that it can apply to ECSPs, and base it on an arbitrary X-consistency. We introduce a parameter $\mathcal{G}$ that describes the criteria for performing a X-consistency check on a property and the information derived should the check fail.

Definition 5. *Let $\mathcal{E} = \langle (\mathcal{D}, \mathcal{L}), Vars, Prop, C \rangle$ be an ECSP, let X-consistency be a consistency condition, and, for any property $\mathcal{P}$, let $\mathcal{G}(\mathcal{P}, C)$ be a set of pairs $\langle \phi, c \rangle$ where ϕ is a formula and c is a constraint.*

A property $\mathcal{P}_0 \in Prop$ is restricted X-consistent wrt $\mathcal{G}$ if, for every $\langle \phi, c \rangle \in \mathcal{G}(\mathcal{P}_0, C)$ such that

$$\mathcal{P}_0 \wedge \neg\phi \wedge C \rightarrow c \text{ and } \neg\phi \wedge C \not\rightarrow c$$

we have that the subrelation of $\mathcal{P}_0$ satisfying ϕ is X-consistent.

The ECSP $\mathcal{E}$ is restricted X-consistent wrt $\mathcal{G}$ if $\mathcal{E}$ is arc consistent and every property $\mathcal{P} \in Prop$ is restricted X-consistent wrt $\mathcal{G}$.

The definition can be interpreted as: if knowing $\neg\phi$ would enable us, using $\mathcal{P}_0$, to infer something new (c) then tuples of $\mathcal{P}_0$ satisfying ϕ should be X-consistent.

To retrieve the original definition of RPC – for the ECSP $\mathcal{E}_C$ corresponding to a CSP C – we can take X-consistency to be path consistency and define

$$\mathcal{G}(\mathcal{P}, C) = \{ \langle \tilde{x} = \tilde{a}, p_{D(x)-\{a\}}(x) \rangle \mid \mathcal{P}(\tilde{a}), \tilde{x} = \tilde{a} \rightarrow x = a, \exists! \tilde{x}\, \mathcal{P}(\tilde{x}) \wedge C \wedge x = a \}$$

where $\exists! z\, Q(z)$ denotes that there exists a unique value for z such that $Q(z)$ holds. In this case, $\tilde{x} = \tilde{a}$ is the formula ϕ defining the unique tuple of $\mathcal{P}$ where x has the value a and $p_{D(x)-\{a\}}(x)$ is the constraint c corresponding to the updated domain of x.

Proposition 5. *Let C be a binary CSP and let $\mathcal{E}_C$ be the equivalent ECSP. C is restricted-path consistent iff $\mathcal{E}_C$ is restricted-path consistent in the extended sense above. Furthermore, C is path consistent iff $\mathcal{E}_C$ is path consistent in the extended sense.*

The above definition also captures k-RPC [13] when ϕ is a disjunction of all k or fewer tuples of $\mathcal{P}_0$ with $x = a$. Since 2-fold consistency is incomparable in strength with path consistency, a variant of the above definition employing 2-fold instead of path consistency might be useful. 2-fold consistency has the advantage that only two properties are considered at one time. Thus, in general, we can usefully vary the restricted local consistency, as well as varying the degree of restrictedness through $\mathcal{G}$.

If X-consistency is formulated independent of arity, and is local with regard to properties, then restricted X-consistency also has these characteristics.

9   Conclusion

This paper has developed a synthesis of constraint satisfaction and constraint solving that is suitable for studying search problems that arise in constraint programming. The framework is an extension of the CSP framework. The paper also identified requirements for local consistency conditions to be useful for constraint programming, notably that locality should be based on properties. Although many local consistency conditions developed for CSPs are inappropriate for such problems, other have been identified, reformulated and generalized for the extended framework. In addition, a new local consistency condition, k-fold consistency, has been proposed.

These local consistency conditions can be used to measure the degree of propagation provided by implementations of properties. It appears that arc consistency is the strongest achievable consistency for independently-defined reactive implementations of properties, such as current "global constraints". However rewriting languages such as CHR [19], Claire [9], and ELAN [10], and techniques like communication among "global constraints" [3] have the potential to achieve stronger levels of consistency.

Acknowledgements

Thanks to Rina Dechter, Jeremy Franks, Mark Wallace, Toby Walsh and anonymous reviewers for discussions and suggestions that were helpful for this paper.

References

1. A. Aggoun & N. Beldiceanu, Extending CHIP to Solve Complex Scheduling and Packing Problems, In *Journées Francophones De Programmation Logique*, Lille, France, 1992.
2. C. Beeri, R. Fagin, D. Maier, M. Yannakakis, On the Desirability of Acyclic Database Schemes, *Journal of the ACM* 30(3): 479–513, 1983.
3. N. Beldiceanu, Global Constraints as Graph Properties on Structured Network of Elementary Constraints of the Same Type, SICS Technical Report T2000/01, 2000.
4. N. Beldiceanu & E. Contejean, Introducing Global Constraints in CHIP, *Mathematical Computer Modelling* 20 (12), 97–123, 1994.
5. F. Benhamou, F. Goualard, L. Granvilliers & J.-F. Puget, Revising Hull and Box Consistency, *International Conference on Logic Programming*, 230–244, 1999.
6. F. Benhamou, D.A. McAllester & P. Van Hentenryck, CLP(Intervals) Revisited, *International Symposium on Logic Programming*, 124–138, 1994.
7. F. Benhamou & W. J. Older, Applying Interval Arithmetic to Real, Integer, and Boolean Constraints. *Journal of Logic Programming* 32(1): 1–24, 1997.
8. P. Berlandier, Improving Domain Filtering using Restricted Path Consistency, *Proc. IEEE International Conference on Artificial Intelligence Applications (CAIA)*, 1995.
9. Y. Caseau, F. Josset, F. Laburthe, CLAIRE: Combining sets, search and rules to better express algorithms. *Theory and Practice of Logic Programming* 2(6): 769–805, 2002.
10. C. Castro, Building Constraint Satisfaction Problem Solvers Using Rewrite Rules and Strategies, *Fundamenta Informaticae* 34(3): 263–293, 1998.
11. A. Colmerauer, Solving the Multiplication Constraint in Several Approximation Spaces, *International Conference on Logic Programming*, 1, 2001.
12. R. Debruyne, C. Bessière, Some Practicable Filtering Techniques for the Constraint Satisfaction Problem, IJCAI (1) 1997: 412-417

13. R. Debruyne, C. Bessière, From Restricted Path Consistency to Max-Restricted Path Consistency, *Proc. Principles and Practice of Constraint Programming*, 312–326, 1997.
14. R. Dechter & P. van Beek, Local and Global Relational Consistency, *Theoretical Computer Science* 173(1): 283–308, 1997.
15. R. Dechter, I. Meiri & J. Pearl, Temporal Constraint Networks, *Artificial Intelligence*, 49, 61–95, 1991.
16. M. Dincbas, P. Van Hentenryck, H. Simonis, & A. Aggoun, The Constraint Logic Programming Language CHIP, *Proceedings of the 2nd. International Conference on Fifth Generation Computer Systems*, 249–264, 1988.
17. E.C. Freuder, A Sufficient Condition for Backtrack-Bounded Search, *Journal of the ACM* 32(4): 755–761, 1985.
18. E.C. Freuder & C.D. Elfe, Neighborhood Inverse Consistency Preprocessing, *Proc. AAAI/IAAI*, Vol. 1, 202–208, 1996.
19. T.W. Frühwirth, Theory and Practice of Constraint Handling Rules, *Journal of Logic Programming* 37(1-3): 95–138, 1998.
20. C. Gervet, Interval Propagation to Reason about Sets: Definition and Implementation of a Practical Language, *Constraints* 1(3): 191–244, 1997.
21. M. Gyssens, On the Complexity of Join Dependencies, *ACM Transactions on Database Systems* 11(1): 81–108, 1986.
22. W. Harvey, P.J. Stuckey, Constraint Representation for Propagation, *Proc. Conf. on Principles and Practice of Constraint Programming*, 235–249, 1998.
23. F.S. Hillier & G.J. Lieberman, *Introduction to Operations Research*, McGraw-Hill, 2001.
24. ILOG Inc., *ILOG Solver 4.2 User's Manual*, 1998.
25. J. Jaffar & J-L. Lassez, Constraint Logic Programming, *Proc. 14th ACM Symposium on Principles of Programming Languages*, 111–119, 1987.
26. J. Jaffar & M.J. Maher, Constraint Logic Programming: A Survey, *Journal of Logic Programming 19 & 20*, 503–581, 1994.
27. J. Jaffar, S. Michaylov, P. Stuckey & R.H.C. Yap, The CLP(ℜ) Language and System, *ACM Transactions on Programming Languages*, 14(3), 339–395, 1992.
28. J. Jaffar, S. Michaylov & R.H.C. Yap, A Methodology for Managing Hard Constraints in CLP Systems, *Proc. ACM-SIGPLAN Conference on Programming Language Design and Implementation*, 306–316, 1991.
29. P. Jégou, On the Consistency of General Constraint-Satisfaction Problems, *AAAI*, 114–119, 1993.
30. P.C. Kanellakis, Elements of Relational Database Theory, in: *Handbook of Theoretical Computer Science, Volume B: Formal Models and Sematics*, Elsevier, 1073–1156, 1990.
31. M.J. Maher, Adding Constraints to Logic-based Formalisms, in: *The Logic Programming Paradigm: a 25 Years Perspective*, K.R. Apt, V. Marek, M. Truszczynski and D.S. Warren (Eds.), Springer-Verlag, *Artificial Intelligence Series*, 313–331. 1999.
32. M.J. Maher, Propagation Completeness of Reactive Constraints, *Proc. International Conference on Logic Programming*, 148–162, 2002.
33. K. Marriott & P.J. Stuckey, *Programming with Constraints : An Introduction*, MIT Press, 1998.
34. R. Mohr & G. Masini, Good Old Discrete Relaxation, *Proc. ECAI*, 651–656, 1988.
35. U. Montanari, Networks of Constraints: Fundamental Properties and Applications to Picture Processing, *information Sciences* 7, 95–132, 1974.
36. W. Pang & S.D. Goodwin, Consistency in General CSPs, *PRICAI 2000*, 469–479, 2000.
37. P. Van Roy, P. Brand, D. Duchier, S. Haridi, M. Henz, C. Schulte, Logic programming in the context of multiparadigm programming: the Oz experience, *Theory and Practice of Logic Programming*, to appear.
38. T. Walsh, Relational Consistencies, APES Technical Report, APES-28-2001, 2001.

Maintaining Longest Paths Incrementally

Laurent Michel[1] and Pascal Van Hentenryck[2]

[1] University of Connecticut, Storrs, CT 06269-3155
[2] Brown University, Box 1910, Providence, RI 02912

Abstract. Modeling and programming tools for neighborhood search often support invariants, i.e., data structures specified declaratively and automatically maintained incrementally under changes. This paper considers invariants for longest paths in directed acyclic graphs, a fundamental abstraction for many applications. It presents bounded incremental algorithms for arc insertion and deletion which run in $O(\|\delta\|log\|\delta\|)$ and $O(|\delta\|)$ respectively, where $\|\delta\|$ is a measure of the change in the input and output. The paper also shows how to generalize the algorithm to various classes of multiple insertions/deletions encountered in scheduling applications. Preliminary experimental results show that the algorithms behave well in practice.

1 Introduction

The last decades have seen significant progress in the design and implementation of modeling and programming tools for combinatorial optimization. Historically, the major focus of that research has been on systematic search (e.g., constraint satisfaction and mathematical programming), but recent years have seen increased attention being devoted to local search and its variations (See, for instance, [6, 8, 10, 18, 20, 22]).

The design of modeling and programming tools for local search generally involves abstractions to express the neighborhood and to encapsulate incremental algorithms. Localizer [10] proposed the concept of invariants, which specifies, in a declarative fashion, data structures that are then maintained incrementally by the system. Invariants were used subsequently in [8, 21]. More recently, constraint-based approaches to local search (e.g., [3, 7, 11, 22]) were proposed, where constraints incrementally maintain properties such as their violation degrees. The Comet system [9] pushed this idea further and introduced the concept of differential objects, which can be viewed as the counterpart of global constraints for local search. Differentiable objects not only maintain properties incrementally, but also make it possible to evaluate the effects of various actions (or moves) on these properties (e.g., swapping the values of two variables), since such queries are often used to choose appropriate moves in local search algorithms. In general, differentiable objects capture combinatorial substructures of the application at hand and they were instrumental in finding novel, more efficient, algorithms for several combinatorial optimization problems [9, 12].

This paper was motivated by the study of differentiable objects for scheduling applications, where it is often critical to maintain longest paths in directed

F. Rossi (Ed.): CP 2003, LNCS 2833, pp. 540–554, 2003.

acyclic graphs (DAG) in order to evaluate the makespan or, more generally, earliest and latest completion times. These longest paths are then used in list or bidirectional scheduling (e.g. [5]), in insertion heuristics (e.g., [23]), as well as in neighborhood search (e.g., [1, 5, 13]). For instance, a key component of many of these algorithms is the ability to update the makespan after an insertion or to evaluate the impact of swapping two tasks on the makespan.

The main technical result of this paper are novel algorithms to maintain longest paths in directed acyclic graphs under arc insertions and deletions. The paper presents bounded incremental algorithms for these two operations which run in time $O(\|\delta\| log \|\delta\|)$ (insertion) and $O(|\delta|)$ (deletion), where $\|\delta\|$ represents the *size of the changes in the input and output*[1]. The results use the Bounded Incremental Computation (BIC) model of Ramalingam and Reps [15]. The BIC model differentiates more incremental algorithms than the traditional online computation model, which only analyzes algorithms in terms of the input size. The BIC model is particularly appropriate for heuristic and neighborhood search, where the change in the output is often small compared to the total input size. The paper also shows how to adapt these algorithms for important operations in scheduling and gives preliminary experimental results indicating the practicality of the algorithms.

The rest of the paper is structured as follows. Section 2 gives an overview of the BIC model. Section 3 discusses the intuition behind the algorithms. Sections 4 and 5 describe the algorithms in detail and give their correctness proofs. Section 6 presents generalizations to the algorithms, as well as their applications to scheduling. Section 7 gives some preliminary experimental results, Section 8 describes related work, while Section 9 concludes the paper.

2   Bounded Incremental Computation

At a high level of abstraction, incremental algorithms can be modelled as updating the output of a function subject to changes to its input. Let f be a function, x be an input, and ϵ be a change on x. An incremental algorithm receives x, $f(x)$, and ϵ as inputs and transforms $f(x)$ into $f(x + \epsilon)$, where $x + \epsilon$ denotes the result of applying change ϵ on input x. For instance, x may be a directed graph with a source, f may be a function which computes the length of the longest paths from the source to all vertices, and ϵ may be the insertion of an arc $a \to b$ or the removal of such an arc. In general, it is useful in incremental algorithms to maintain auxiliary information in order to compute $f(x + \epsilon)$. Provided that the auxiliary information is polynomially related in size to the output, the problem can then viewed as computing an enhanced function f' incrementally. As a consequence, we can safely ignore this issue without loss of generality and work directly with f'.

Various models for analyzing incremental algorithms have been proposed and they include online algorithms, amortized analysis (e.g., [19]), and *bounded incremental computation* (BIC) [15]. Many such models analyze the complexity

---

[1] We give more precise bounds later in the paper when the terminology is introduced.

of incremental algorithm in terms of the input size (e.g., $x + \epsilon$). *The BIC model, on the contrary, studies the behavior of incremental algorithms in terms of the changes in both the input and output.* As a consequence, the BIC model has a finer granularity and can differentiate algorithms that other models cannot. In addition, it is particularly appropriate in the context of neighborhood search, where most of the neighborhood generally remain unchanged from one iteration to the next. Analyzing incremental algorithms in terms of the neighborhood size is thus not very informative in general.

Since this paper assumes the BIC model, let us describe its main concepts more precisely. Let $\Delta(f, x, \epsilon)$ denote the change between $f(x)$ and $f(x + \epsilon)$ and let $\delta(f, x, \epsilon)$ denote $\epsilon + \Delta(f, x, \epsilon)$. For instance, in an incremental longest path algorithm, $\Delta(f, x, \epsilon)$ may represent the pairs (vertices,lenghts) which have changed when ϵ (e.g., an arc insertion) is performed. Since, in general, the function f and the change ϵ are clear from the context, we use Δ and δ for simplicity. The BIC model analyzes the performance of an algorithm in terms of $\|\delta\|$, i.e., a measure of the size of δ. The measure $\|\delta\|$ may actually be greater than $|\delta|$ for reasons that will become clear shortly, but it is, in general, closely related.

An incremental algorithm is *bounded* if, for all input x and all allowed change ϵ, its execution time depends only on δ, not the size of the entire input $x + \epsilon$. It is *unbounded* otherwise. Of course, many incremental algorithms are unbounded (e.g., graph reachability) and hence the existence of a bounded algorithm is a strong guarantee for incremental performance.

An example of bounded incremental algorithm is the shortest path algorithm of Ramalingam and Reps [15], which runs in $O(\|\delta\| \, log\|\delta\|)$ for arc insertions and deletions, when the arc weights are strictly positive. Here $\|\delta\|$ denotes the number of *affected vertices*, i.e., the vertices whose shortest paths have changed, and their adjacent arcs. It is natural to use $\|\delta\|$, and not $|\delta|$, since any algorithm would necessarily have to examine the adjacent vertices to an affected vertex in order to determine if they are affected as well. For graphs with bounded degrees (e.g., jobshop scheduling), this issue is of course moot.

This paper presents a bounded algorithm for incremental longest paths in a DAG. The algorithm takes $O(|\delta| \, log|\delta| + \|\delta\|)$ for an arc insertion and $O(\|\delta\|)$ for arc deletion. The paper also discusses several generalizations of this result, including the insertion/deletion of multiple arcs and the detection of cycles.

3   Intuition

We now give the high-level intuition behind the algorithms presented in this paper and we explain why some simple and natural ideas do not lead to bounded algorithms. We initially focus on graphs with strictly positive weights. This restriction is lifted in Section 6. Throughout the paper, we use directed acyclic graphs with a source s. Given a DAG $G = (V, A)$ and a vertex $v \in V$, we denote by $lp(G, v)$ the length of a longest path from the source of G to vertex v. The projection of a graph $G = (V, A)$ wrt its longest paths is the graph $G_{|l} = (V, A')$ where

```
1.    forall(v ∈ V) do
2.        degree(v) = |pred(G, v)|;
3.    Q = {v | degree(v) = 0};
4.    while Q ≠ ∅ do
5.        v = dequeue(Q);
6.        l(v) = max(w ∈ pred(G, v)) l(w) + d(w, v);
7.        forall w ∈ succ(G, v) do
8.            degree(w) = degree(w) − 1;
9.            if degree(w) = 0 then
10.               insert(Q, w);
```

Fig. 1. An Offline Algorithm for Longest Path in a DAG.

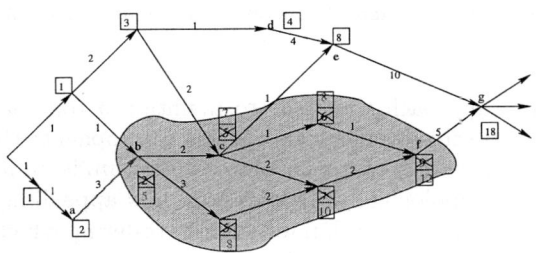

Fig. 2. The Affected Set of an Insertion.

$$A' = \{x \to y \mid lp(G, x) + d(x, y) = lp(G, y)\},$$

i.e., the subgraph consisting of all arcs belonging to longest paths.

Figure 1 presents an offline algorithm for longest paths in a DAG, which runs in $O(|V| + |E|)$ for a directed acyclic graph $G = (V, E)$. The key idea of the algorithm is to consider the vertices in topological order, which guarantees that, when a vertex is dequeued, its predecessors have the correct longest path values. Lines 1-2 compute the initial degree of the vertices and Line 3 inserts the source in the queue. Lines 4 and 5 dequeue a vertex and compute the length of its longest path from the source. Lines 7 to 9 decrease the degrees of the successors of v and insert them in the queue if all their predecessors have been updated, i.e., when their degrees is 0.

Consider now the problem of updating the longest paths after insertion of an arc $a \to b$. To obtain a bounded algorithm, it is necessary to consider affected vertices only, i.e., those vertices whose longest paths have changed. Figure 2 depicts such a situation. The affected vertices are shown in the grey area. Note that vertex g is not affected, although one of its predecessors is. The reason is that the new longest path coming from f is not longer than the longest path from e.

Since the batch algorithm works in terms of degrees, it would be ideal to apply the batch algorithm on the subgraph consisting of the affected vertices. Unfortunately, as vertex g indicates, computing the set of affected vertices requires the computation of longest paths.

procedure insertArc$(G, x \rightarrow y)$
begin
1. $G = G \cup \{x \rightarrow y\}$;
2.   **if** $l(x) + d(x,y) > l(y)$ **then**
3. $insert(Q, \langle l(y), y \rangle)$;
4.   **while** $Q \neq \emptyset$ **do**
5. $v = extractMin(Q)$;
6. $l(v) = max(x \in pred(G, v)) \, l(x) + d(x, v)$;
7.   **forall**$(w \in succ(G, v))$ **do**
8   **if** $l(v) + d(v, w) > l(w)$ **then**
9.   **if** $w \notin Q$ **then** $insert(Q, \langle l(w), w \rangle)$;
end

Fig. 3. A Preliminary Version of Procedure insertArc.

Another natural approach would be to maintain a topological ordering incrementally and to use this topological ordering to propagate the changes to the longest paths. The use of degrees in the offline algorithm is, in fact, a simple way to order the vertices topologically. This approach is appealling, since there exists a bounded incremental algorithm for priority ordering which can be used for that purpose [2]. Unfortunately, this simple idea does not lead to a bounded algorithm. Indeed, a change to the topological ordering does not necessarily entail a change to the longest paths, so that the incremental algorithm for topological ordering may consider non-affected vertices. For instance, if successive integers are used as topological numbers, the arc insertion $a \rightarrow b$ would change the topological number of g and its successors, although they are not affected vertices for the longest paths. Similar examples can of course be produced for other choices of topological numbers.

The key idea behind our insertion algorithm is the observation that the lengths of the longest paths in the graph G^- before the insertion are, in fact, a topological order for the affected vertices, since the longest path of a vertex is necessarily greater than the longest paths of its predecessors. As a consequence, it is possible to adapt the offline algorithm in order to propagate the changes to the longest paths using that topological ordering and to enqueue the successors of affected vertices when the lengths of their longest paths are increasing. Such an algorithm is shown in Figure 3. Let G^- be the graph G at call time. Line 2 tests whether the new arc $x \rightarrow y$ changes the longest path of its destination y. If it does, then y is inserted in the queue with $l(y)$, its longest path in G^-, as its key. The affected vertices are computed and processed in lines 5-9. Line 5 pops the vertex v with the smallest key and updates its longest paths. It then considers each successor w of v and inserts w in the queue if its longest paths increases and it is not in the queue already. The algorithm runs in time $O(|\delta| \, log|\delta| + \|\delta\|)$ using a priority queue. It only uses *insert* and *extractMin* on the queue (not *updateKey*, which updates a key in the queue) and each affected vertex enters the queue at most once.

The key idea behind deletion is rather different. The algorithm relies on the fact that the affected vertices can be identified without computing longest paths.

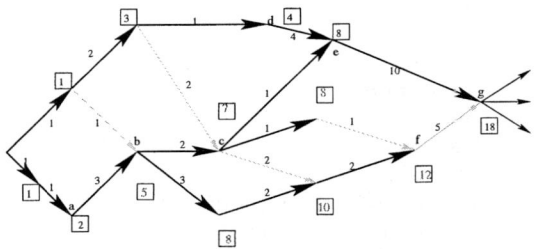

Fig. 4. The Longest Path Projection $G_{|l}$.

This is possible because it is sufficient to notice that the length of a longest path decreases: it is not necessary to know by how much. More precisely, arc deletion can be tought of as working on subgraphs $G_{|l}$ obtained by keeping only those arcs that belong to longest paths. If a vertex v is affected and w is one of its successors in $G_{|l}$, vertex w is affected if $v \to w$ is the only arc incident to w in $G_{|l}$. By proceeding this way, all affected vertices can be computed in $O(\|\delta\|)$. Figure 4 depicts the graph $G_{|l}$ from our previous example. Consider the deletion of $a \to b$ which obviously affects b. Its successor c is also affected, since it has only one incident arc in $G_{|l}$. On the other hand, vertex e is not affected since it has two incident arcs. Once the affected vertices are computed, arc deletion can proceed simply by applying the offline algorithm on the affected vertices. Of course, the above discussion indicates that $G_{|l}$ (or at least the degrees in $G_{|l}$) must be maintained incrementally. As we will see, maintaining $G_{|l}$ does not increase the complexity of the algorithms. The rest of the paper presents these algorithms in detail, together with the correctness proofs and some important generalizations. Once again, we focus on strictly positive weigths, this restriction being lifted in Section 6.

4   Insertion

Figure 5 depicts procedure `insertArc`. The main differences with the preliminary version presented earlier are lines 7-8 and 12-15, which maintain the projected graph. Lines 7-8 updates the projected graph for an affected vertex v, lines 12-13 adds an arc originating from an affected vertex to a non-affected vertex, while lines 14-15 handle the case of the inserted arc. We now prove the correctness of the algorithm. We first define formally the set of vertices affected by an arc insertion.

Definition 1 (Affected Vertices). *Let* $G = (V, A)$, $x \to y \notin A$, *and* $G' = (V, A \cup \{x \to y\})$. *The set of affected vertices by the insertion of* $x \to y$ *in* G *is defined as*

$$AffectedI(G, x \to y) = \{v \in V \mid lp(G', v) > lp(G, v)\}.$$

procedure insertArc$(G, x \to y)$
begin
1. $G = G \cup \{x \to y\}$;
2.   **if** $l(x) + d(x, y) > l(y)$ **then**
3. $insert(Q, \langle l(y), y \rangle)$;
4.   **while** $Q \neq \emptyset$ **do**
5. $v = extractMin(Q)$;
6. $l(v) = max(x \in pred(G, v))\ l(x) + d(x, v)$;
7. $G_l = G_l \setminus \{x \to v \mid x \to v \in G_l\}$;
8. $G_l = G_l \cup \{x \to v \mid x \in pred(G, v) \wedge l(x) + d(x, v) = l(v)\}$;
9.   **forall**$(w \in succ(G, v))$ **do**
10.   **if** $l(v) + d(v, w) > l(w)$ **then**
11.   **if** $w \notin Q$ **then** $insert(Q, \langle l(w), w \rangle)$;
12.   **else if** $l(v) + d(v, w) = l(w)$ **then**
13. $G_l = G_l \cup \{v \to w\}$;
14. **else if** $l(x) + d(x, y) = l(y)$ **then**
15. $G_l = G_l \cup \{x \to y\}$;
end

Fig. 5. Procedure insertArc.

In the following, we abuse notations and remove the arguments of *AffectedI* when they are clear from the context. The following proposition informally states that a vertex is affected only if one of its predecessors is affected.

Proposition 1. *Let* $G = (V, A)$, $x \to y \in A$, *and* $G' = (V, A \cup \{x \to y\})$. *Then,*

$$w \in AffectedI(G, x \to y) \Rightarrow \exists v \in pred(G', w) : lp(G', v) + d(v, w) > lp(G, w).$$

The proposition makes it natural to define a binary relation *affectI*.

Definition 2. *Let* $G = (V, A)$, $x \to y \notin A$, *and* $G' = (V, A \cup \{x \to y\})$. *The binary relation affectI is defined as*

$$affectI(v, w) \Leftrightarrow lp(G', v) + d(v, w) > lp(G, w) \wedge v \in pred(G', w).$$

We use affectI* to denote the transitive closure of affectI.

The following proposition characterizes the affected vertices.

Proposition 2. *Let* $G = (V, A)$, $x \to y \notin A$, $G' = (V, A \cup \{x \to y\})$, *and let* $v \in AffectedI(G, x \to y)$ $(v \neq y)$. *Then, affectI**(y, v) *holds, i.e., there exists a path of affected vertices from y to v.*

Definition 3 (Specification of insertArc**).** *Let* $G = (V, A)$ *be a DAG with strictly positive weights,* $x \to y \notin A$, *and* $G' = (V, A \cup \{x \to y\})$. *Procedure* insertArc$(G, x \to y)$ *satisfies the following specification:*

   Pre: $\forall v \in V : l(v) = lp(G, v) \wedge G_l = G_{|l}$.
   Post: $\forall v \in V : l(v) = lp(G', v) \wedge G_l = G'_{|l}$.

Theorem 1. *Procedure* `insertArc` *is correct and terminates.*

Proof. The proof relies on the observation that the algorithm partitions the affected vertices in three sets

$$P = \{x \in \mathit{AffectedI} \mid l(x) = lp(G', x)\};$$
$$Q = \{x \in \mathit{AffectedI} \mid \exists v \in P : v \to x \,\&\, x \notin P\};$$
$$R = \{x \in \mathit{AffectedI} \mid \exists v \in Q : \mathit{affectI}^*(v, x) \,\&\, x \notin P \cup Q\}$$

and that the following two invariants hold at line 4 in the algorithm

$$\mathit{AffectedI} = P \cup Q \cup R \qquad (1)$$
$$\forall v \in P, \forall x \in Q : lp(G, v) \leq lp(G, x). \quad (2)$$

Initially, $P = \emptyset$, $Q = \{y\}$, and $R = \mathit{AffectedI} \setminus \{y\}$, and the invariants hold by Proposition 2. Assume now that the invariants hold at iteration i. We show that lines 5-13 restore the invariant for iteration $i + 1$. Line 5 pops the vertex v with the smallest value $l(v) = lp(G, v)$ from Q. Since $lp(G, v) > lp(G, p)$ for all $p \in pred(G, v)$, all its affected predecessors must be in P by Invariant (2) and the fact that

$$\forall y \in succ(G, x) : lp(G, x) < lp(G, y).$$

As a consequence, line 6 correctly computes $l(v) = lp(G', v)$. Each successor w of v now belongs to $Q \cup R$ by Invariant (2) and lines 8-10 move these successors of v from R to Q, since $v \in P$ after line 6. Observe that no new vertices are added to the union $Q \cup R$ and hence Invariant (1) is restored. By selection of v and since $\forall y \in succ(G, x) : lp(G, x) < lp(G, y)$, Invariant (2) holds as well. On termination, Q is empty, which entails that R is empty, and hence $l(v) = lp(G', v)$ for all $v \in V$. The algorithm is also guaranteed to terminate, since the size of $Q \cup R$ strictly decreases at each iteration. It is easy to verify that G_l is also updated correctly, since it is recomputed for each affected vertex (lines 7-8) and since arcs to successors of affected vertices are inserted in lines 13 and 15.

5   Arc Deletion

Figures 6 and 7 depict the algorithms to compute the deletion of an arc $x \to y$. Function `computeAffected` in Figure 6 computes the set of affected vertices by a deletion. It starts with the deleted arc $x \to y$ and works on the projected graph. Each iteration dequeues an affected vertex and inserts its successors in the queue if they are affected. A successor w is affected if all its predecessors in the projected graph are affected. This is tested by removing from G_l all arcs $v \to w$, where v is affected. When a vertex has no predecessor in G_l, it is affected. Procedure `removeArc` in Figure 7 is the main routine. If the deletion of $x \to y$ affects y, the procedure computes the affected vertices using function `computeAffected`. It then initializes the degrees of all affected vertices using the affected vertices only. Indeed, the unaffected vertices can be considered as having been processed, since the lengths of their longest paths did not change. It then applies the traditional offline algorithm on the affected vertices. We now formalize the various concepts and give the correctness proofs.

function computeAffected(G_l, y)
begin
1. $Q = \{y\}$;
2. $A = \emptyset$;
3.   **while** $Q \neq \emptyset$ **do**
4. $u = dequeue(Q)$;
5. $A = A \cup \{u\}$;
6.   **forall**($v \in succ(G_l, u)$) **do**
7. $G_l = G_l \setminus \{u \rightarrow v\}$;
8.   **if** $pred(G_l, v) = \emptyset$ **then**
9. $insert(Q, v)$;
10. **return** A;
end

Fig. 6. Function computeAffected.

procedure removeArc($G, x \rightarrow y$)
begin
1. $G = G \setminus \{x \rightarrow y\}$;
2.   **if** $x \rightarrow y \in G_l$ **then**
3. $G_l = G_l \setminus \{x \rightarrow y\}$;
4.   **if** $pred(G_l, y) = \emptyset$ **then**
5, $Affected = \text{computeAffected}(G_l, y)$;
6.   **forall**($v \in Affected$) **do**
7. $degreelp(v) = |pred(G, v) \cap Affected|$;
8. $Q = \{v \in Affected \mid degreelp(v) = 0\}$;
9.   **while** $Q \neq \emptyset$ **do**
10. $v = dequeue(Q)$;
11. $l(v) = max(x \in pred(G, v))\, l(x) + d(x, v)$;
12. $G_l = G_l \cup \{x \rightarrow v \mid x \in pred(G, v) \wedge l(x) + d(x, v) = l(v)\}$;
13.   **forall**($w \in succ(G, v) \cap Affected$) **do**
14. $degreelp(w) = degreelp(w) - 1$;
15.   **if** $degreelp(w) = 0$ **then** $insert(Q, w)$;
end

Fig. 7. Procedure removeArc.

Definition 4 (Affected Vertices). *Let* $G = (V, A)$, $x \rightarrow y \in A$, *and* $G' = (V, A \setminus \{x \rightarrow y\})$. *The set of affected vertices by the deletion of* $x \rightarrow y$ *in* G *is defined as*

$$AffectedD(G, x \rightarrow y) = \{v \in V \mid lp(G', v) < lp(G, v)\}.$$

As before, we abuse notations and remove the arguments of *AffectedD* when they are clear from the context. We also denote by $x \rightarrow_l y$ an arc in $G_{|l}$ and by $x \rightarrow_l^* y$ the existence of a path from x to y in $G_{|l}$. The following proposition is the counterpart to Proposition 1 and states that a vertex is affected if and only if **all** its predecessors in the projected graph are affected.

Proposition 3. *Let $G = (V, A)$, $x \to y \in A$, $G' = (V, A \setminus \{x \to y\})$, and let $v \in V$ such that $v \neq y$. Vertex v is affected iff*

$$\forall p \in pred(G_{|l}) : p \in AffectedD(G, x \to y).$$

Proof. By definition, v is affected iff $lp(G', v) < lp(G, v)$ which is equivalent to $\forall p \in pred(G, v) : lp(G', p) + d(p, v) < lp(G, v)$. Since

$$\forall p \in pred(G, v) \setminus pred(G_{|l}, v) : lp(G, p) + d(p, v) < lp(G, v)$$

and since $lp(G', p) \leq lp(G, p)$, it follows that v is affected iff $\forall p \in pred(G_{|l}, v) :$ $lp(G', p) + d(p, v) < lp(G, v)$ which is equivalent to $\forall p \in pred(G_{|l}, v) : lp(G', p) < lp(G, p)$. The result follows.

Corollary 1. *Let $G = (V, A)$, $x \to y \in A$, $G' = (V, A \setminus \{x \to y\})$, and let $v \in V$ such that $v \neq y$. Vertex v is affected implies $y \to_l^* v$.*

Proof. Suppose that no such path exists. Then a longest path to v cannot go through y. By Proposition 3, the source must be affected, which is impossible.

Definition 5 (Specification of `computeAffected`). *Let $G = (V, A)$ be a DAG with strictly positive weights, $x \to y \in A$, $G' = (V, A \setminus \{x \to y\})$, and $lp(G', y) < lp(G, y)$. Procedure `computeAffected`$(G, x \to y)$ satisfies the specification:*

> *Pre: $G_l = G_{|l}$.*
> *Post: $G_l = G'_{|l} \setminus \{v \to w \mid v \in AffectedD\}$;*
>   *the function returns AffectedD.*

Theorem 2. *Procedure `computeAffected` is correct and terminates.*

Proof. The proof relies on the observation that the algorithm partitions the affected vertices in three sets A, Q, and R, satisfying the invariants

$$
\begin{align}
&v \in A \Rightarrow v \in AffectedD \tag{1} \\
&v \in Q \Rightarrow v \in AffectedD \tag{2} \\
&R = \{w \in AffectedD \setminus (A \cup Q) \mid \exists v \in Q : v \to_l^* v\} \tag{3} \\
&G_l = G_l \setminus \{v \to w \mid v \in A \cup Q\} \tag{4}.
\end{align}
$$

in line 3 of the algorithm. Initially, A is empty, $Q = \{y\}$, and the invariants hold by Corollary 1. By Invariant (2), lines 4 and 5 are correct. Moreover, if v is a successor of u and the test on line 8 succeeds, by Invariant (4), all predecessors of v must be in $A \cup Q$ and are affected. By Proposition 3, v is affected and line 9 is correct. Moreover, all other affected vertices are still reachable from vertices in Q. Indeed, if the only path to an affected vertex w not in $A \cup Q$ goes through u, i.e., $y \to_l \ldots \to_l u \to_l s \to_l \ldots \to_l w$, then s is in Q (because of lines 8-9) and $s \to_l^* w$. On termination, Q is empty and A is the set of affected vertices. The algorithm terminates, since $|Q \cup R|$ strictly decreases at each iteration.

Definition 6 (Specification of `removeArc`). *Let $G = (V, A)$ be a DAG with strictly positive weights, $x \to y \in A$, and $G' = (V, A \setminus \{x \to y\})$. Procedure `removeArc`$(G, x \to y)$ satisfies the specification:*

procedure propagateChanges(G,S)
begin
1. $Q = S$;
2. **while** $Q \neq \emptyset$ **do**
3. $v = extractMin(Q)$;
4. $l(v) = max(x \in pred(G,v))\, l(x) + d(x,v)$;
5.   **forall**$(w \in succ(G,v))$ **do**
6   **if** $l(v) + d(v,w) \neq l(w)$ **then**
7.   **if** $w \notin Q$ **then** $insert(Q, \langle l(w), w \rangle)$;
end

Fig. 8. Procedure propagateChanges.

> *Pre:* $\forall v \in V : l(v) = lp(G,v) \wedge G_l = G_{|l}$.
> *Post:* $\forall v \in V : l(v) = lp(G',v) \wedge G_l = G'_{|l}$.

Theorem 3. *Procedure* removeArc *is correct and terminates.*

Proof. The proof follows from Theorem 2 and the fact that the degrees for the non-affected vertices are initialized correctly.

6   Generalizations and Applications to Scheduling

Multiple Insertions/Deletions. It is easy to generalize the insertion algorithm to accommodate a set of arcs of the form $\{x \rightarrow y_1, \ldots, x \rightarrow y_n\}$. Indeed, since all these arcs have the same origin, the values $lp(G,v)$ are still a valid topological ordering for the affected vertices, since no new topological constraints are introduced between the affected vertices. Such multiple insertions are typical in list-scheduling and bidirectional search algorithms for jobshop scheduling [5]. This suggests that, as long as insertions/deletions do not change the topological ordering, adaptations of Procedure insertArc may be used.

Consider for instance changing (increasing or decreasing) the weights of a set of arcs of the form $\{x \rightarrow y_1, \ldots, x \rightarrow y_n\}$, i.e., changing $d(x,y_1), \ldots, d(x,y_n)$. Obviously, the lengths of longest paths $lp(G,v)$ provide a topological ordering of the graph, since the graph has not changed (only the weights). We can thus apply an algorithm similar to insertArc in order to propagate the changes to vertices in $\{y_1, \ldots, y_n\}$. The core of such an algorithm is depicted in Figure 8 and is essentially similar to insertArc. The main difference is in line 6, which tests whether the lengths have changed (i.e., have been increased or decreased). This procedure may be called with S initialized to those vertices in $\{y_1, \ldots, y_n\}$ which are affected.

A more complex use of multiple insertions/deletions arises in local search algorithms for jobshop or openshop scheduling. Here a typical move consists of swapping two vertices (or tasks) on a critical path which are executing on the same machine. Observe that swapping two such vertices is guaranteed not to create cycles [1] and that evaluating the impact of such moves on the makespan for a restricted set of vertices is the basic operation of the successful tabu-search

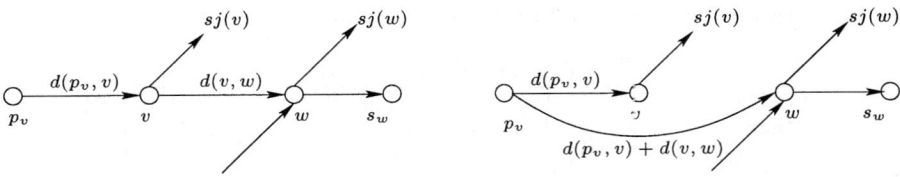

Fig. 9. Inverting Two Vertices on a Critical Path.

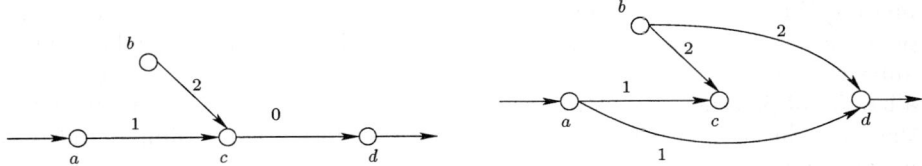

Fig. 10. A Graph with a Zero-Weight Arc and its Transformation.

algorithm of Nowicki [13]. The left side of Figure 9 depicts such a situation. In the figure, p_v, v, w, s_w are executed on the machine, and $s_j'(v)$ and $sj(w)$ represent the job successors of vertices v and w. Such a move seems rather complex. However, observe that we can add an arc $p_v \to w$ with weight $d(p_v, v) + d(v, w)$ in constant time, since no vertex is affected. We can now remove $v \to w$ in constant time since, again, no vertex is affected. Now the effect of swapping v and w on the makespan is achieved simply by modifying the weights of $p_v \to v$ and $p_v \to w$ appropriately. *As a consequence, algorithm* propagateChanges *gives us a bounded* $O(|\delta|log|\delta| + \|\delta\|)$ *incremental algorithm for evaluating changes to the makespan when swapping two critical vertices.* Of course, none of the above arc operations need to take place in practice. It is sufficient to apply propagateChanges on the affected vertices. Similar reasoning can be applied to many more situations, including moves in the neighborhood NB in [5] and arc additions in insertion algorithms [23] for scheduling. Observe also that our deletion algorithm supports multiple deletion naturally, since it only reasons on the projected graph.

Zero Weight Arcs. Our algorithm naturally generalizes to the case of zero-weight arcs. The difficulty here is that several vertices may have the same longest path lengths, although they are topologically ordered. Consider, for instance, the left side of Figure 10 which depicts parts of a DAG and assume that vertices c and d have the same longest path lengths and are affected (due to some of their predecessors). Vertices c and d are thus on the queue and d could be dequeued before c, although it comes after c in the topological ordering. This does not raise any major issue however. The intuition is to recognize that the arc $c \to d$ can be replaced by adding arcs $p \to d$ for each arc $p \to c$, and that this transformation, whose result is shown in on the right side of Figure 10, preserves the longest paths. After the transformation, observe that c and d are topologically independent and can be processed in any order.

Table 1. Experimental Evaluation of the Incremental Algorithms.

	abz7	abz8	abz9	la31	la32	la33	la34	la35
Offline	88.39	87.41	87.32	157.05	159.36	156.75	166.41	155.68
Incr	1.93	1.94	1.94	3.40	3.44	3.39	3.45	3.45
Incr(i+d+i)	2.75	2.88	2.70	5.00	4.95	4.78	5.00	4.97

Negative Weight Arcs. Negative weights can be handled by a similar transformation. When an arc $a \to b$ has a negative weight, it must be replaced by arcs of the form $p \to b$ for each predecessor p of a, whose weights must be reduced appropriately. In scheduling applications, these negative arcs represent a generalization of precedence constraints: they are not dynamic and generally shorter than the duration of the tasks. Hence the transformation is simple and only introduce a marginal increase in the size of the graph. Even if such insertions are dynamic, they correspond to cases which are well-handled by our algorithm, since they preserve the existing topological order of the affected vertices. The bookkeeping is however more tedious, since a more complex mapping between actual and virtual arcs must be maintained.

Cycle Detection. It is also easy to generalize our algorithm to detect cycles. Since procedure insertArc guarantees that a vertex can only be processed once, it suffices to mark the vertices popped from the queue. A cycle is detected if such a vertex is about to be reinserted in the queue.

7   Experimental Results

Table 1 reports some preliminary experimental results on the practicality of the algorithms. The only purpose of these experiments is to show that the algorithms can be implemented efficiently (i.e., the constants are not prohibitive) and may bring significant benefits. To validate this claim, we instrumented an implementation of bidirectional search so that each arc addition is propagated immediately. We then compared the behavior of a differentiable object with offline and incremental algorithms. Table 1 reports the results of running the resulting procedures on 10 longest paths simultaneously to minimize the impact of other parts of the procedure. Line offline depicts the offline implementation, line Incr gives the results of the incremental implementation, and line Incr(i+d+i) describes the results of the procedure testing deletion. In the instrumentation Incr(i+d+i), an arc addition is replaced by a sequence of three operations (addition,deletion,addition) of the same arcs. Of course, the differentiable object has no idea that it is being used in a bidirectional search procedure and cannot perform any optimization. The results show the significant benefits that may result from the incremental algorithm. For instance, la35 shows an improvement of a factor 48 for a graph of 300 tasks. Note also the excellent times Incr(i+d+i), where the times for the additional deletion and insertion are amortized by other parts of the bidirectional implementation.

8   Related Work

The bounded incremental computation (BID) model was formally introduced by Ramalingam and Reps [15]. However, it was used as early as 1982 (by Reps again [17]) to analyze algorithms for attribute grammars, as well as in several other papers, primarily in the programming language community. Ramalingam and Reps also proposed a bounded algorithm for maintaining shortest paths, which was the inspiration for this research. Their algorithms are adaptations of Dijkstra's shortest path algorithm, while ours are adaptations of topological sorting for longest paths. Their *insertArc* procedure runs in $O(|\delta|log|\delta| + \|\delta\|)$, but it needs a Fibonacci heap, since it updates elements of the queue. Their *deleteArc* procedure runs in $O(|\delta|log|\delta| + \|\delta\|)$, starts by computing the set of affected vertices using a projected subgraph, and uses the completement of the projected graph to initialize a Dijkstra-like second phase. Our deletion procedure runs in $O(\|\delta\|)$ and uses an offline algorithm (based on degrees) on the subgraph, once the affected vertices are computed. Reference [14] presents a grammar problem which can be viewed as a generalization of the shortest path problem. Using the transformations described earlier, it is possible to reduce longest paths to this problem, since longest paths give rise to superior functions. The resulting algorithm handles arbitrary multiple insertions/deletions. However, it runs in $O(\|\delta\|log\|\delta\|)$ and is more costly from a practical standpoint as well. Its additional complexity is not necessary for many applications. as we discussed earlier, where our simpler algorithms are significantly faster and should be preferred. Ramalingam [16] considers incremental feasibility of systems of difference constraints using incremental shortest path algorithms. These algorithms can be applied to incremental feasibility of temporal constraint networks [4].

9   Conclusion

This paper considered invariants for longest paths in directed acyclic graphs, a fundamental abstraction for programming tools supporting local search. It presented bounded incremental algorithms for arc insertion and deletion which run in $O(|\delta|log|\delta| + \|\delta\|)$ and $O(\|\delta\|)$ respectively, where $\|\delta\|$ is a measure of the change in the input and output. The algorithms were also shown to be practical experimentally and their generalizations to various scheduling applications were also discussed. There are several open issues raised by this research. On the one hand, it would be interesting to determine if there exists a $O(\|\delta\|)$ insertion algorithm, since the incremental algorithm has an additional log factor compared to the offline algorithm. On the other hand, it would be interesting to find out an algorithm that can handle negative weights without graph transformations.

Acknowledgments

Special thanks to G. Ramalingam and Tom Reps for clarifying the links between incremental priority orderings and longest paths. This work was partially supported by NSF ITRs DMI-0121495 and ACI-0121497.

References

1. E. Aarts, P. van Laarhoven, J. Lenstra, and N. Ulder. A computational study of local search algorithms for job shop scheduling. *ORSA Journal on Computing*, 6:113–125, 1994.
2. B. Alpern, R. Hoover, B. Rosen, P. Sweeney, and K. Zadeck. Incremental Evaluation of Computational Circuits. In *SODA-90*, 1990.
3. C. Codognet and D. Diaz. Yet Another Local Search Method for Constraint Solving. In *AAAI Fall Symposium on Using Uncertainty within Computation*, Cape Cod, MA., 2001.
4. R. Dechter, I. Meiri, and J. Pearl. Temporal constraint networks. In *KR-89*, 1989.
5. M. Dell'Amico and M. Trubian. Applying Tabu Search to the Job-Shop Scheduling Problem. *Annals of Operations Research*, 41:231–252, 1993.
6. L. Di Gaspero and A. Schaerf. *Optimization Software Class Libraries*, chapter Writing Local Search Algorithms Using EasyLocal++. Kluwer, 2002.
7. P. Galinier and J.-K. Hao. A General Approach for Constraint Solving by Local Search. In *CP-AI-OR'00*, Paderborn, Germany, March 2000.
8. F. Laburthe and Y. Caseau. SALSA: A Language for Search Algorithms. In *CP'98)*, Pisa, Italy, October 1998.
9. L. Michel and P. Van Hentenryck. A Constraint-Based Architecture for Local Search. In *OOPLSA'02*, Seattle, WA, November 1992.
10. L. Michel and P. Van Hentenryck. Localizer. *Constraints*, 5:41–82, 2000.
11. L. Michel and P. Van Hentenryck. Localizer++: An Open Library for Local Search. Technical Report CS-01-02, Brown University, 2001.
12. L. Michel and P. Van Hentenryck. A simple tabu search for warehouse location. *European Journal on Operations Research*, 2001. (to appear).
13. E. Nowicki and C. Smutnicki. A fast taboo search algorithm for the job shop problem. *Management Science*, 42(6):797–813, 1996.
14. G. Ramalingam and T. Reps. An incremental algorithm for a generalization of the shortest-path problem. *Journal of Algorithms*, 21:267–305, 1996.
15. G. Ramalingam and T. Reps. On the computational complexity of dynamic graph problems. *Theoretical Computer Science*, 158:233–277, 1996.
16. G. Ramalingam, J. Song, L. Joscovicz, and R. E. Miller. Solving difference constraints incrementally. *Algorithmica*, 23:261–275, 1999.
17. T. Reps. Optimal-Time Incremental Semantic Analysis for Syntax-Directed Editors. In *POPL-82*, 1982.
18. P. Shaw, B. De Backer, and V. Furnon. Improved local search for CP toolkits. *Annals of Operations Research*, 115:31–50, 2002.
19. R. Tarjan. Amortized Computational Complexity. *SIAM Journal of Algebraic Discrete Methods*, 6:306–318, 1985.
20. S. Voss and D. Woodruff. *Optimization Software Class Libraries*. Kluwer, 2002.
21. C. Voudouris, R. Dorne, D. Lesaint, and A. Liret. iOpt: A Software Toolkit for Heuristic Search Methods. In *CP'01*, Paphos, Cyprus, October 2001.
22. J. Walser. *Integer Optimization by Local Search*. Springer Verlag, 1998.
23. F. Werner and A. Winkler. Insertion techniques for the heuristic solution of the job-shop problem. *Discrete Applied Mathematics*, 58(2):191–211, 1995.

Resolution and Constraint Satisfaction

David G. Mitchell

Simon Fraser University
Burnaby, Canada

Abstract. We study two resolution-like refutation systems for finite-domain constraint satisfaction problems, and the efficiency of these and of common CSP algorithms. By comparing the relative strength of these systems, we show that for instances with domain size d, backtracking with 2-way branching is super-polynomially more powerful than back-tracking with d-way branching. We compare these systems with propositional resolution, and show that every family of CNF formulas which are hard for propositional resolution induces families of CSP instances that are hard for most of the standard CSP algorithms in the literature.

1 Introduction

Algorithms for constraint satisfaction problems (CSPs) are generally described in terms of a scheme which may be instantiated in many ways. For example, the usual backtracking algorithm does not prescribe how to choose which variable to branch on, leaving this detail up to implementers. Experimental studies of algorithms examine the relative performance of implementations with particular choices for these details, and on particular benchmark instances. Another approach is to consider the fundamental strengths or limitations of such algorithms. Here we study the relative power of various techniques measured by how efficiently they can refute a given unsatisfiable instance in the best circumstance — that is, with optimal strategies. We consider a number of standard CSP algorithms, and also two resolution-like proof systems which are useful for modeling the reasoning used in these algorithms.

Since refutations are the basis for our study, formally we restrict our attention to unsatisfiable instances, but our study is equally motivated by performance on satisfiable instances. For satisfiable instances backtracking with an optimal branching strategy will find a solution without backtracks. However, any poly-time computable branching strategy will make incorrect choices, necessitating showing unsatisfiability of restricted instances during search. Indeed, the only way a backtracking algorithm can generate a large search tree is if it does so while showing unsatisfiability in this sense.

We begin by recalling a familiar example from propositional logic. Consider a set ϕ of propositional clauses ϕ (henceforth simply called a formula). The lines of a resolution derivation from ϕ are clauses, and the resolution inference rule allows adding the line $A \vee B$ if we already have the lines $A \vee x$ and $B \vee \overline{x}$. A resolution derivation of the empty clause from ϕ is called a resolution refutation of ϕ. There

F. Rossi (Ed.): CP 2003, LNCS 2833, pp. 555–569, 2003.

is a refutation of ϕ if and only if ϕ is unsatisfiable. A derivation is tree-like if any derived line is used at most once to derive further lines. The smallest tree-like resolution refutation of a formula is of the same size as the search tree constructed by the backtracking algorithm (i.e., DLL) for SAT under an optimal branching strategy. Since there are formulas which have short refutations but no short tree-like refutations, we know that there are formulas which can be efficiently proven unsatisfiable by some algorithm, but require exponential time for DLL algorithms. The most effective current SAT solvers enhance DLL with "conflict clause learning", which provides more power than tree-like resolution but less power than un-restricted resolution. See [5] for initial steps in characterizing just how much power is gained.

1.1 CSP Refutations

Perhaps the most natural way to adapt the resolution idea to CSPs is to generalize the intuition of "exhausting the domain" of a variable. This leads to a system we call Nogood Resolution (**NG-RES** for short), because the lines of a refutation in this system are nogoods. A nogood for a CSP instance $\mathcal{I}$ is a disjunction of the form $(x_{i_1} \neq a_{i_1} \vee x_{i_2} \neq a_{i_2} \vee \ldots)$, where each x_i is a variable and each a_i a value from the domain. If the domain is $\{1, \ldots, d\}$, then from a collection of nogoods $\{(x \neq 1 \vee X_1), (x \neq 2 \vee X_2), \ldots (x \neq d \vee X_d)\}$, we may soundly infer $(X_1 \vee X_2 \vee \ldots \vee X_d)$, since every possible value for x is included in one of the disjunctions. For CSP instance $\mathcal{I}$ we take as axioms the set of nogoods corresponding to the partial assignments explicitly forbidden by constraints of $\mathcal{I}$, and there is an **NG-RES** derivation of the empty nogood from these if and only if $\mathcal{I}$ is unsatisfiable. **NG-RES** is equivalent to a system introduced in [1] and a special case of a general family of systems studied in [15].

NG-RES corresponds naturally to the usual backtracking algorithm for CSPs, which we denote **BT**. To solve instance $\mathcal{I}$, **BT** selects a variable x with domain $D = \{1, \ldots, d\}$, and for each $a \in D$ recursively tries to satisfy $\mathcal{I}$ restricted by setting $x = a$. Clearly $\mathcal{I}$ is unsatisfiable if and only if all d recursive calls fail. Now, consider a **BT** search tree T for unsatisfiable instance $\mathcal{I}$, and label each leaf of T with a nogood that is in the axioms for $\mathcal{I}$. Recursively label the internal nodes with derived nogoods, by labeling each node N with the result of applying the **NG-RES** derivation rule to the collection of nogoods labeling the children of N. A simple induction shows that the root of T is labeled with the empty nogood if and only if $\mathcal{I}$ is unsatisfiable. Moreover, the minimum number of lines in a tree-like **NG-RES** refutation of $\mathcal{I}$ is exactly the number of recursive calls made by **BT** under an optimal branching strategy.

We can compare the relative power of both algorithms and refutation proof systems in a uniform way as follows. For any two proof systems A and B, we say that A *dominates* B if for every instance $\mathcal{I}$ the smallest A-proof of $\mathcal{I}$ is no larger than the smallest B-proof of $\mathcal{I}$. We may also regard algorithms as proof systems as follows. For any complete CSP algorithm **A** and unsatisfiable instance $\mathcal{I}$, we view a trace of the execution of **A** on input $\mathcal{I}$ as an **A**-proof that $\mathcal{I}$ is unsatisfiable. Thus, we may say that **BT** dominates tree-like **NG-RES**, and vice versa — as refutation systems they have equivalent power.

Domination is a very strong but brittle property. We may easily find two proof systems are of essentially the same power but neither dominates the other. As a more robust measure, we say that A *p-simulates* B if we can always transform a B-proof of an instance $\mathcal{I}$ into a A-proof of $\mathcal{I}$ in polynomial time. As an example consider negative resolution, the restriction of propositional resolution in which, at each application of the resolution rule, one of the two clauses used must be negative (i.e., contain no positive literals). Certainly unrestricted resolution can p-simulate negative resolution, as every negative resolution refutation is also an unrestricted refutation. However, negative resolution cannot p-simulate unrestricted resolution. In particular, Goerdt [13] showed that there is an infinite family of formulas which have polynomially sized resolution refutations, but no negative refutations of size less than $n^{\Omega(logn)}$. We will later make us of these same instances in analyzing CSP algorithms.

The algorithms we will consider are backtracking-based algorithms, including the use of the following standard techniques: forward checking (**FC**), conflict-directed backtracking (**CBJ**), arc-consistency filtering (**AC**), k-consistency enforcement (K-**CON**) and nogood learning. We denote combinations of techniques with +, for example **BT+FC** denotes backtracking with forward checking. In general, by this notation we mean *any* complete algorithm definable by the given combination of methods. For example, by **BT+AC**, we denote the class of algorithms which amount to backtracking plus any use of arc-consistency filtering. Thus, **BT** which does not do any arc-consistency, and the algorithm **MAC** which is **BT** modified by doing complete arc consistency processing at every search node, are both included in **BT+AC**. **BT+CBJ** included backtracking plus any amount of back-jumping. The class of nogood learning schemes we capture is all restrictions of the general scheme described in [19], and called "backjump learning" in [12]. Here we denote this class Backjump Nogood Learning (**BNL**), and **BT+BNL** constitutes backtracking algorithms which use any strategy for storing "backjump nogoods". These are just the nogoods in the *NG-RES* refutation corresponding to **BT** as described above, which are also used in backjumping.

Baker [1] observes informally that (in our terminology) *NG-RES* dominates **BT**, **BT+CBJ**, and dynamic backtracking (**DBT**). Here we extend Baker's observations, showing that:

1. Tree-like *NG-RES* also dominates **BT+FC** and **BT+CBJ**.
2. *NG-RES* dominates, in addition to those algorithms that tree-like *NG-RES* dominates, the algorithms **BT+AC**, **BT+BNL** and **BT+K-CON**. In fact it dominates any combination of these.

The first point illustrates that **FC** and **CBJ** add no additional power to **BT**, in that everything they accomplish can be done by a good enough branching strategy. **FC** is a simple but useful mechanism to enforce certain properties of in the branching strategy. **CBJ** amounts to using a partial tree-search to decide which variable to branch on next, and then remembering the results of that search so that one branch does not have to be explored a second time. The second point gives us a method to characterize limitations of these methods, in that they can never refute an instance using fewer steps than an optimal **NG-RES** prover.

The main result in [1] implies that **BT**, **BT+CBJ** and **DBT** cannot p-simulate **NG-RES**. In particular, an infinite family of instances $\{\mathcal{I}_n\}$ is exhibited for which there are **NG-RES** proofs of size polynomial in n, but no **BT**, **BT+CBJ** or **DBT** proofs of size less than $n^{\Omega(\log n)}$, where n the number of variables. The instances $\{\mathcal{I}_n\}$ can be solved in polytime by algorithms which are efficient on instances with bounded induced width (or tree-width) [1], such as adaptive consistency [11] or **BT** with full backjump nogood learning [12].

Here, we exhibit an infinite family of instances **MPH**$_n$, that are hard for all the algorithms discussed so far, but are efficiently solved by making a "small" modification to the backtracking algorithm.

1.2   2-Way *vs* K-Way Branching

Most papers in the CSP literature on backtracking algorithms consider the version described above (**BT**), which might be described as backtracking with d-way branching, where d denotes the domain size. Another version, available in many commercial solvers such as Ilog and Eclipse, we call backtracking with 2-way branching, here be denoted **2BT**. In **2BT** we have mutable domains for variables. To solve $\mathcal{I}$, a variable x and a value a in the current domain of x are selected, and two recursive calls are made. The first is to solve $\mathcal{I}$ with x set to a, and the second with the value a removed from the domain of x. Clearly $\mathcal{I}$ is unsatisfiable if and only if both modified instances are unsatisfiable.

There are intuitive arguments in favour of both versions. The argument for superiority of 2-way branching is that, in the process of finding that there is no solution to $\mathcal{I}$ with $x = a$, we may have acquired information indicating that the best way to solve $\mathcal{I}$ is to branch on some variable other then x, rather than trying other values for x. The argument for preferring k-way branching is roughly that *a priori* it has a smaller space to search. If n is the number of variables, then k-way backtracking requires time at most $O(d^n)$. Allowing 2-way branching is essentially equivalent to transforming the CSP instance to a SAT instance with dn variables, wherein the only obvious upper bound is $2^{dn} >> d^n$.

It is easy to check that any strategy for k-way branching can be simulated by a 2-way branching strategy with no loss of efficiency. But can any 2-way branching strategy be efficiently simulated by some k-way strategy? We show that, at least when we allow enhanced versions involving some learning strategy the answer is no. In particular, we exhibit an infinite family of instances **MPH**$_n$ with the following properties:

1. **MPH**$_n$ has no **NG-RES** refutations of size smaller than $n^{\Omega(\log n)}$.
2. The k-way branching algorithm **BT**, with optimal branching strategy, and optimal use of **FC**, **AC**, **BCJ**, **K-CON**, and **BNL** cannot solve **MPH**$_n$ in fewer than $n^{\Omega(\log n)}$ steps.
3. The 2-way branching algorithm **2BT**, with a simple branching strategy, **AC**, and a simple and efficient **BNL** strategy, can solve **MPH**$_n$ in time $O(n^3)$.

Item 1 is obtained by showing that negative resolution efficiently simulates **NG-RES**, and applying Goerdt's result [13] that there are formulas $\mathbf{MPHP}_n$ which have no short negative refutations, but have short general refutations. Our CSP family is chosen so the CNF encoding of $\mathbf{MPH}_n$ is identical to $\mathbf{MPH}_n$, and the claim follows. Item 2 follows from 1 plus **NG-RES** simulations of the algorithms. For item 3, we exhibit such an algorthim.

1.3   *C-RES* and Hard Instances

If **NG-RES** cannot model the reasoning of CSP algorithms using 2-way branching, then we need a stronger proof system to do so. Such a system was suggested to us by de Kleer's study [10] showing a connection between CSP local consistency methods and propositional resolution. We call this system "Constraint Resolution", or **C-RES** for short. For a CSP instance $\mathcal{I}$, we let the axioms be the clauses of a CNF formula $\mathrm{CNF}(\mathcal{I})$ encoding $\mathcal{I}$, sometimes called the direct encoding of $\mathcal{I}$ [22]. A line in a **C-RES** proof of $\mathcal{I}$ is a clause over the variables of $\mathrm{CNF}(\mathcal{I})$, and indeed a **C-RES** refutation is just a resolution refutation of $\mathrm{CNF}(\mathcal{I})$. This system has been used or studied in [16, 17, 2, 3, 18]. In [16], it was shown that **C-RES** dominates **BT**, **BT+FC**, **BT+AC**, **BT+k-CON**, **BT+BNL** and **DBT**. In a little more detail:

1. Tree-like **C-RES** dominates both versions of backtracking, including those enhanced by **FC**, **AC**, and **CBJ**. Tree-like **C-RES** p-simulates any algorithm dominated or p-simulated by tree-like **NG-RES**.
2. **C-RES** dominates all algorithms dominated by tree-like **C-RES**, and all of these with the addition of **BNL** and K-**CON**.

We will show that **C-RES** p-simulates **NG-RES**; we have already pointed out that **NG-RES** cannot p-simulate **C-RES**. It is natural to ask what the relationship is between our versions of CSP resolution and propositional resolution. Not surprisingly, under natural translations between problem spaces **C-RES** is of essentially the same power as propositional resolution. This can be shown by simple simulation arguments.

There is a large and varied collection of instance families which are hard for both **C-RES** and **NG-RES**, in the sense that the smallest refutations of these instances are of exponential size. These instances must also require exponential time for the algorithms we consider. Hard instances based on simple pigeon-hole formulas were addressed in [16], and typical random CSP instances were shown hard in [17, 18, 23]. Random instances of k-colouring were shown hard in [2]. The simulations between **C-RES** and **RES** show that, corresponding to any family of k-CNF formulas which require exponential-sized resolution refutations, there is a k-ary boolean CSP family and also a binary CSP family with domain size k that require exponential-sized **C-RES** and **NG-RES** refutation.

1.4   Outline

The remainder is organized as follows. Section 2 provides definitions and gives an efficient **C-RES** simulation of **NG-RES**. Section 3 gives the separations between **NG-RES** and **C-RES**, and between **BT** and **2BT**. Section 4 discusses simulations between propositional resolution and **C-RES** and construction of hard instances for resolution-based CSP algorithms. Section 5 Gives **NG-RES** simulations of CSP algorithms. Finally, Section 6 briefly discusses some implications and future work.

2   Preliminaries

A CSP instance $\mathcal{I}$ is a tuple $\mathcal{I} = \langle X, D, C \rangle$. X is a set of variables, D a set of domains, one for each variable in X. We will consider only the case where all variables have the same domain, and call that domain D. This restriction is purely a matter of convenience, and has no bearing on our results. $C = \{C_1, C_2, \ldots, C_m\}$ is a set of constraints, where each $C_i = \langle S_i, R_i \rangle$ is a pair in which S_i is a tuple of variables from X, and R_i is relation over D of arity $|S_i|$. That is, $R_i \subset D^{|S_i|}$. Since we can denote the set of variables of $\mathcal{I}$ by vars($\mathcal{I}$) or even vars(C), we usually leave X implicit (i.e., we write $\mathcal{I} = \langle D, C \rangle$).

Let $\mathcal{I} = \langle D, C \rangle$ be a CSP instance. An *assignment* α for $\mathcal{I}$ is a function $\alpha : \text{vars}(C) \to D$ mapping each variable to a domain value. A *partial assignment* is an assignment which may be undefined at some variables: we denote that α is undefined at x by $\alpha(x) = \bot$. If α is an assignment and $S = \langle x_1, \ldots, x_k \rangle$ a tuple of variables, then we write $\alpha(S)$ to denote $\langle \alpha(x_1), \ldots, \alpha(x_k) \rangle$. An assignment α for $\mathcal{I}$ *satisfies* a constraint $\langle S, R \rangle$ if α is defined at every variable in S, and $\alpha(S) \in R$, and satisfies $\mathcal{I}$ if it satisfies every constraint in C. Assignment α *violates* a constraint $C = \langle S, R \rangle$ if α is defined at every variable in S, and $\alpha(S) \notin R$.

A (CSP) literal is an expression $x = a$, where x is a variable and a a domain element. We often write an assignment as a set of literals, i.e., $\alpha = \{x = a, y = b\}$ is the assignment with $\alpha(x) = a$, $\alpha(y) = b$ and $\alpha(z) = \bot$ for z different from x, y. We can then write $\alpha \subset \beta$ to indicate that β is defined at all variables α is, and possibly others. If α is an assignment for which $\alpha(x) = \bot$, then $\alpha; x = a$ is the assignment such that $\alpha; x = a(y) = \alpha(y)$ for $y \neq x$, and $\alpha; x = a(x) = a$.

2.1   Propositional Resolution and Proof Complexity

A literal is a propositional variable or its negation; A clause is a set of literals, written as a comma-separated sequence of literals within parentheses. A formula is a set of clauses. For a formula ϕ, we write vars(ϕ) for the set of variables appearing in ϕ. A truth assignment τ for ϕ is a function $\tau : \text{vars}(\phi) \to \{t, f\}$. For simplicity, we extend τ to negative literals so for $x \in \text{vars}(\phi)$, $\tau(\overline{x}) = t \leftrightarrow \tau(x) = f$. Assignment τ satisfies clause C if $\tau(p) = t$ for at least one literal in C, and satisfies ϕ if is satisfies every clause of ϕ.

The propositional *resolution rule* allows us to infer a clause (X, Y), where X and Y denote arbitrary sets of literals, from two clauses (X, x) and $(Y, \overline{x})$. We say that we *resolve* (X, x) and $(Y, \overline{x})$, on x, and that (X, Y) is the *resolvent*. A *resolution derivation* of a clause C from a set of clauses ϕ is a sequence $C_0, \ldots C_m$

of clauses, where each clause C_i is either an element of ϕ or is derived by the resolution rule from two clauses C_j, C_k, for $j, k < i$, and $C_m = C$. The derivation is of length or size m. A resolution derivation of the empty clause (denoted $\square$) from ϕ is called a *resolution refutation* of ϕ. We will denote this proof system by **RES**. **RES** is a sound and complete refutation system, meaning that there is a refutation of a formula ϕ if and only if ϕ is unsatisfiable. We will use "proof" and "refutation" interchangeably.

For any **RES** derivation π, the *graph of* π is the directed acyclic graph (DAG) $G_\pi \overset{def}{=} \langle V, E \rangle$ where V is the set of clauses of π and E is the set of ordered pairs (u, v) from V such that v is derived in π by resolving u with w, for some w in V. We will extend these notions to the other proof systems we use in the natural way. The restriction of proof system **P** to proofs whose graphs are trees is called tree-like **P**.

Intuitively, a proof is a string which can be efficiently inspected, after which the reader is convinced of some proposition. Adapting the formalization of a proof system from [9], we formally define a refutation system **P** for a CSP to be a poly-time function **P** whose range is the set of unsatisfiable CSP instances. A string π such that $\boldsymbol{P}(\pi) = \mathcal{I}$ is a **P**-proof of $\mathcal{I}$. An algorithm which computes the function **P** is a verifier for the proof system. For any proof system **P**, we define the **P**-complexity of an instance $\mathcal{I}$ to be the minimum size of any **P**-proof of $\mathcal{I}$, which we denote by $\boldsymbol{P}(\phi)$.

We may associate to any complete CSP algorithm **A** a refutation system **A**, where the trace of **A** on unsatisfiable instance $\mathcal{I}$ is a **A**-proof of $\mathcal{I}$. We say that a proof system **A** *dominates* proof system **B** if for every instance $\mathcal{I}$, $\boldsymbol{A}(\mathcal{I}) \leq \boldsymbol{B}(\mathcal{I})$. We say that proof system **A** p-simulates proof system **B** if there is a polynomial-time computable function f such that for every unsatisfiable instance $\mathcal{I}$ and every **A**-proof π of $\mathcal{I}$, $f(\pi)$ is a **B**-proof of $\mathcal{I}$.

2.2   Nogood Resolution

A *nogood* is a set of CSP literals in which no variable occurs in two literals. Note there is a 1-1 correspondence between partial assignments and nogoods. For clarity, we write $\eta(\alpha)$ for a nogood, where α is an assignment. The *initial nogoods* of an instance $\mathcal{I} = \langle D, C \rangle$ is the set

$$Init(\mathcal{I}) = \{\eta(\alpha) : \langle S, R \rangle \in C_\mathcal{I} \text{ and } S = vars(\alpha) \text{ and } \alpha(S) \notin R\}$$

The *nogood resolution rule* allows the following inference of a nogood from a set of nogoods, provided that the domain of x is $\{1, 2, \ldots d\}$:

$$\frac{\begin{array}{l}\eta(x{=}1,\ N_1)\\\eta(x{=}2,\ N_2)\\\quad\vdots\\\eta(x{=}d,\ N_k)\end{array}}{\eta(N_1, N_2, \ldots N_k)}\ x \in \{1, \ldots, d\}$$

A *nogood derivation* of a nogood N from a set of nogoods Γ for instance $\mathcal{I}$ with domain $A = \{1, 2, \ldots d\}$, is a sequence of nogoods, $N_0, \ldots N_m$, where each nogood N_i is either an element of Γ or is derived by the nogood resolution rule from a set of nogoods $N_{i_1}, N_{i_2}, \ldots, N_{i_k}$, where each $i_j < i$, and $N_m = N$. The derivation is of length or size m. A *nogood resolution refutation* of $\mathcal{I}$ is a nogood resolution derivation of the empty nogood $\eta() = \Box$ from the set of initial nogoods of $\mathcal{I}$. We denote the nogood resolution system by **NG-RES**. **NG-RES** is a sound and complete refutation system. That is, $\mathcal{I}$ has an **NG-RES** refutation if and only if $\mathcal{I}$ is unsatisfiable. Often, we will identify a CSP instance $\mathcal{I}$ with its set of initial nogoods $Init(\mathcal{I})$, together with its domain. We will henceforth always assume the domain is $D = [d] = \{1, \ldots, d\}$.

Example 1. Let G be a graph with vertices $\{a, b, c\}$ and edges $\{(a, b), (b, c), (a, c)\}$, and let $R_{\neq}$ be the binary relation on $\{1, 2\}$ such that let $R_{\neq}(x, y) \Leftrightarrow x \neq y$. Let $\mathcal{I}$ be the CSP instance $\mathcal{I} = \langle \{1, 2\}, \langle \langle a, b \rangle, R_{\neq} \rangle, \langle \langle b, c \rangle, R_{\neq} \rangle, \langle \langle a, c \rangle, R_{\neq} \rangle \rangle$. G is 2-colourable if and only if $\mathcal{I}$ is satisfiable. The set of initial nogoods of $\mathcal{I}$ is $\{\eta(a = 1, b = 1), \eta(a = 1, c = 1), \eta(b = 1, c = 1), \eta(a = 2, b = 2), \eta(a = 2, c = 2), \eta(b = 2, c = 2)\}$ and the following tree-like **NG-RES** refutation of $\mathcal{I}$ demonstrates that G is not 2-colourable.

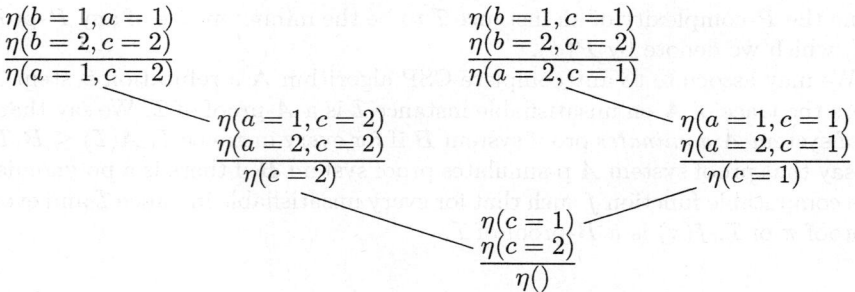

2.3 C-RES

For any CSP instance $\mathcal{I} = \langle D, C \rangle$, we define the associated formula CNF($\mathcal{I}$) as follows. For each CSP variable $x \in \text{vars}(\mathcal{I})$ we have d propositional variables, one for each value x may take. We write $x{:}a$ for the propositional variable intended to assert that CSP variable x is assigned value a. For each CSP variable x, CNF($\mathcal{I}$) has a *domain clause* asserting that x must take some value from A. For each constraint $C = \langle S, R \rangle$ of $\mathcal{I}$, and each partial assignment α defined at exactly the variables in S, if α violates C then CNF($\mathcal{I}$) has a *conflict clause* which forbids the corresponding assignment. There is a one-to-one correspondence between the conflict clauses in CNF($\mathcal{I}$) and the initial nogoods of $\mathcal{I}$. So the propositional formula associated with $\mathcal{I}$ is

$$\text{CNF}(\mathcal{I}) = \{\{v{:}a : a \in D\} : v \in \text{vars}(\mathcal{I})\} \cup \{\{\overline{x{:}a} : x = a \in \alpha\} : \eta(\alpha) \in Init(\mathcal{I})\}$$

CNF($\mathcal{I}$) is satisfiable if and only if $\mathcal{I}$ is satisfiable. Remark: It is natural to add clauses that enforce that a CSP variable be given *at most* one value, as well as those that say it need at least one. The presence of these clauses has no effect on our results, so we leave them out for simplicity.

We define a *constraint resolution refutation* (***C-RES*** refutation) for any CSP instance $\mathcal{I}$ to be a propositional resolution (***RES***) refutation of the formula $\text{CNF}(\mathcal{I})$. Soundness and refutational completeness of ***C-RES*** follow from the soundness and completeness of ***RES***, together with the correctness of $\text{CNF}(\mathcal{I})$.

2.4   Negative *C-RES* Simulation of *NG-RES*

Here we show how to efficiently simulate ***NG-RES*** with ***C-RES*** as follows.

Proposition 1. *For any n-variable CSP instance $\mathcal{I}$ with domain D,*

$$C\text{-}RES(\mathcal{I}) \leq |D|NG\text{-}RES(\mathcal{I}) + n.$$

Proof. Let π be an ***NG-RES*** refutation of $\mathcal{I}$. Define a mapping $\ulcorner\urcorner$ from nogoods to clauses such that, for any nogood N,

$$(x\!=\!a) \in N \iff \overline{x\!:\!a} \in \ulcorner N \urcorner.$$

Construct a ***C-RES*** refutation of $\mathcal{I}$ (i.e., a propositional resolution refutation of $\text{CNF}(\mathcal{I})$) as follows. First, modify π by replacing each nogood N of π with $\ulcorner N \urcorner$. Then, for each inference step, which now looks like this;

$$\frac{\begin{array}{c}(\overline{x\!:\!a_1}, X_1)\\(\overline{x\!:\!a_2}, X_2)\\ \vdots \\(\overline{x\!:\!a_k}, X_k)\end{array}}{(X_1, X_2\ldots, X_k)}$$

re-arrange the clauses together with the domain clause $(x\!:\!a_1, x\!:\!a_2, \ldots, x\!:\!a_k)$, to obtain the resolution derivation of Figure 1. The new construction is clearly a propositional resolution refutation, and since each leaf is an element of $\text{CNF}(\mathcal{I})$, it is a ***C-RES*** refutation of $\mathcal{I}$. Moreover, it is a *negative* resolution refutation, since the clauses corresponding to nogoods are all negative clauses. For each derived nogood N in π, the new refutation has $|D|$ derived clauses. There must also be one occurrence of each of the n domain clauses, giving the stated size bound.

3   Separating K-Way and 2-Way Branching

Theorem 1. *There is an infinite family of CSP instances* **MPH$_n$**, *one for each integer n, such that*

1. $C\text{-}RES(\mathbf{MPH_n}) = O(n^3)$,
2. $NG\text{-}RES(\mathbf{MPH_n}) = n^{\Omega(\log n)}$.

$$\frac{(x\!:\!a_1,\ x\!:\!a_2,\ \ldots,\ x\!:\!a_k) \qquad (\overline{x\!:\!a_1},\ X_1)}{(x\!:\!a_2,\ \ldots,\ x\!:\!a_k,\ X_1) \qquad\qquad (\overline{x\!:\!a_2},\ X_2)}$$
$$(x\!:\!a_3,\ \ldots,\ X_1,\ X_2)$$

$$\ddots$$

$$\frac{(x\!:\!a_k,\ X_1,\ \ldots,\ X_{k-1}) \qquad (\overline{x\!:\!a_k},\ X_k)}{(X_1,\ X_2\ldots,\ X_k)}$$

Fig. 1. *C-RES* simulation of an *NG-RES* step

We construct the family $\mathbf{MPH_n}$ as follows. Fix $n \in \mathbb{N}$ so that $m = \lfloor \log_2 n \rfloor$ is even. Let the domain be $D = [m] = \{1, \ldots m\}$. The variable set is $\mathrm{vars}(\mathbf{MPH_n}) = \{x_0, x_1, \ldots, x_{n-1}\}$. Define $R_{m,r} = \{\langle x, y \rangle : x, y \in [m], \text{ with } x, y \text{ not both } r\}$. The constraint set of $\mathbf{MPH_n}$ is

$$C_{\mathbf{MPH_n}} = \bigcup_{r \in [m]} \left\{ \langle \langle x_i, x_j \rangle, R_{m,r} \rangle : \begin{array}{l} k \in \{b2^r : 0 \le b < n/(2^r)\}, \\ k \le i < k + 2^{r-1}, \\ k + 2^{r-1} \le j < k + 2^r \end{array} \right\}$$

These instances are, more intuitively, as follows: We have n variables, each with domain of size $m = \log_2 n$. Variables x_1, x_2 may not both have value 1, x_3 and x_4 may not both be 1, x_5 and x_6 may not both be 1, etc. If any variable in $\{x_1, x_2\}$ has value 2, then no variable in $\{x_3, x_4\}$ may have value 2, and similarly for the pairs of sets $\{x_5, x_6\}, \{x_7, x_8\}$, etc. For value 3, the constraints are on pairs of sets of 4 variables, and so on. Finally, if any variable in $\{x_1, \ldots, x_{n/2}\}$ has value m, then no variable in $\{x_{(n/2)+1}, \ldots, x_n\}$ may, and *vice versa*.

Theorem 1, follows with only a little care from the proof of the main result in [13], where Goerdt defines an infinite family of CNF formulas, denoted $\mathbf{MPHP^n}$, and proves the following.

Theorem 2 (Goerdt [13]). *RES*$(\mathbf{MPHP^n}) = O(n^3)$, *but* *N-RES*$(\mathbf{MPHP^n})$ $= n^{\Omega(\log n)}$.

Proof. (Theorem 1) The formula $\mathrm{CNF}(\mathbf{MPH_n})$ associated to our CSP instance $\mathbf{MPH_n}$ is identical to the formula $\mathbf{MPHP^n}$ in [13]. The *C-RES* simulation we of *NG-RES* we give in proving Proposition 1 is a negative derivation, so it follows that $\mathbf{MPH_n}$ has no *NG-RES* refutations of size less than $n^{\Omega(\log n)}$. Trivially, $\mathbf{MPH_n}$ has size $O(n^3)$ *C-RES* refutations.

Theorem 3. *The family of CSP instances* $\mathbf{MPH_n}$ *satisfies*

1. $\mathbf{MPH_n}$ *cannot be solved with* **BT** *in less than* $n^{\Omega(\log n)}$ *time, even with an optimal branching strategy and optimal use of any or all of* **FC, AC, CBJ,** *K-*CON *and* **BNL,** *but*
2. $\mathbf{MPH_n}$ *can be solved in time* $O(n^3)$ *by* **2BT,** *using a simple branching strategy,* **AC,** *and a simple and efficient* **BNL** *learning scheme.*

Proof. Given Theorem 1, the lower bound requires only that **NG-RES** efficiently simulates the algorithms addressed. We give these simulations in Section 5. To show the upper bound, we exhibit such an algorithm.

It is important to understand that **AC**, for example, does exactly the same thing when used to enhance **BT** or **2BT**, but learning is fundamentally different. When learning while executing **BT**, we construct a nogood from a subset of the current partial assignment that **BT** is exploring, which it is now known cannot be extended to a satisfying assignment. While executing **2BT**, the current assignment involves both assignments of values to variables *and "non-assignments" of values to variables*. Thus, we must learn "generalized nogoods", in which we can include both claims of the form $x_i \neq a_i$ and claims of the form $x_j = a_j$.

The branching strategy for our algorithm is: Select a maximally constrained value amongst all variables and values, and set if first to maximize the number of values removed from other domains (that is, in the manner of fail-first). We assume **AC** is executed after every assignment made by **2BT**. The learning strategy is: Derive all back-jump clauses but record only those which are of size one or are strictly positive (whereas standard nogoods are strictly negative).

Let $S(n)$ denote the number of steps executed by the algorithm on $\mathbf{MPH_n}$. At the root, the algorithm chooses value d from some variable. Since the instance is symmetric with respect to variables, we may assume it is variable x_1. We set $x_1 = d$ and then run and arc consistency algorithm, which removes the value d from the domains of all variables $x_{1+n/2}, \ldots x_n$. The value d is now unconstrained in variables $x_2, \ldots x_{n/2}$ (since their only constraints are now satisfied). So, we are left with an instance of $\mathbf{MPH_{n/2}}$ on variables $x_{1+n/2}, \ldots x_n$, which we solve recursively in time $S(n/2)$. It is not hard to verify that in doing this the algorithm will learn the positive nogood that expresses $(x_{1+n/2} \vee \ldots \vee x_n)$.

Now we to search the other branch, beginning by setting $x_1 \neq d$. The most constrained values are now d in variables $x_2, \ldots x_{n/2}$. (We don't count learned nogoods for the branching heuristic, and because $x_1 \neq d$, each value d for variables $x_{1+n/2}, \ldots x_n$ now has one less constraint.) So we now branch on d for some x_i with $i \in \{2, \ldots n/2\}$. After setting $x_i = d$, arc consistency removes d from the domains of $x_{1+n/2}, \ldots x_n$, and falsifies the learned clause. Setting $x_i \neq d$, we repeat the same argument for value d of the remaining variables in $x_2, \ldots x_{n/2}$, and eventually obtain an instance of $\mathbf{MPH_{n/2}}$ on variables $x_1, \ldots x_{n/2}$. The total time (including allowing n^2 time to compute the branching heuristic), can be seen to be:

$$S(n) \leq 2S(n/1) + O(n^2) \leq O(n^3)$$

The algorithm also seems to run in $O(n^3)$ time with the slightly more natural branching strategy: branch the most constraint value of any variable with smallest domain. However, this version is less amenable to analysis.

4   *C-RES* *vs* *RES* and Hard Instances

The simplest transformation from k-SAT to CSP involves having the same set of variables, domain size 2, and a suitable k-ary constraint corresponding to each clause. We call this the *direct translation of k-SAT to CSP*. When we restrict the CSPs we consider to those which are the direct translation of CNF formulas, we find that **RES** and **C-RES** have almost the same power.

Proposition 2. *If Φ is a set of CNF formulas, and* **I** *is the set of CSP instances that are the direct translation of the instances of Φ to CSP, then*

$$\textbf{C-RES}(\textbf{I}) \geq \textbf{RES}(\Phi).$$

The CSP instances resulting from the direct translation from CNF formulas all have domain size 2, and have (some significant portion of) constraints of arity larger than 2. We give a second translation from SAT to CSP, which generates binary CSP instances with large domain size, and leaves resolution complexity unaltered. For simplicity, we restrict our attention to k-CNF formulas, in which every clause has the same number of literals.

For any k-CNF formula ϕ, we define the *binary translation of ϕ to CSP* to be the instance $\mathcal{I}$ constructed as follows. Let n be the number of variables and m the number of clauses of ϕ. The domain of $\mathcal{I}$ is $D = [k] = \{1, \ldots k\}$, The constraint set is constructed as follows. There is a variable x_i for each clause C_i of ϕ. For each pair of clauses C_i, C_j, such that there is a literal p in C_i and its negation $\bar{p}$ in C_j, there is a constraint $\langle \langle x_i, x_j \rangle, R_{i,j} \rangle$. The rth value in the domain of x_i is intended to correspond to the rth literal of C_i (under an arbitrary but fixed ordering). So if p is the rth literal in C_i, and $\bar{p}$ is the sth literal in C_j, then $\mathcal{I}$ must have the initial nogood $\eta(x_i = r, x_j = s)$. The constraint relations $R_{i,j}$ are chosen so that $\mathcal{I}$ has the initial nogoods on x_i and x_j.

Proposition 3. *For any k-CNF formula ϕ, if $\mathcal{I}$ is the binary translation of ϕ to CSP, then* **C-RES**$(\mathcal{I}) \geq$ **RES**(ϕ)

Thus, any set of CNF formulas for which exponential resolution lower bounds hold translates directly into two sets of CSP instances for which exponential **C-RES** and **NG-RES** lower bounds also hold. There are many examples of hard formulas in the literature, including [14, 20, 8, 21, 4, 6] among others.

5   Algorithm Simulations

Proposition 4. **BT** *is dominated by tree-like* **NG-RES**.

Proposition 5. **CBJ** *is dominated by tree-like* **NG-RES**.

Proof. Execute **BT** and simultaneously construct a tree-like **NG-RES** as described for **BT**, but with one subtlety. When assigning values to variable a, execute the recursive calls for each $a \in D$ in some order. After each returns, inspect the nogood obtained at the corresponding child node. If it does not mention the branching variable x, make no further recursive calls, label the current node with that same nogood, and immediately return "unsatisfiable". If it does mention x, continue with the next recursive call. If all d recursive calls are made, resolve together the d nogoods from the children as in **BT**. An easy induction shows that the set of variables in the conflict set computed in the usual description of conflict-directed backjumping is the same as the set of variables in the nogood derived at that corresponding node.

Proposition 6. BT+BNL *is dominated by* **NG-RES**.

Proof. (Sketch) The nogoods constructed by the caching schemes, as just described, are exactly those derived according to our scheme for constructing refutations corresponding to **BT** or **CBJ** executions, so we execute this nogood caching strategy merely by adding any chosen derived nogood to the cache.

Proposition 7. FC *is dominated by tree-like* **NG-RES**.

Proof. We simulate the domain reductions performed by **FC** as follows. For each variable x we maintain an array $C(x) = [\eta_1, \ldots, \eta_k]$. Initially, each η_i has the special value $\circ$. If the algorithm extends assignment α to $\alpha; x = a$, and as a result deletes the value b from the domain of variable y, then $\eta(x = a, y = b)$ is an initial nogood, and we set $C(x)[a] = \eta(x = a, y = b)$. (Upon backtracking, b is returned to the domain for y, and $C(x)[a]$ is reset to $\circ$.) If the domain of a variable x becomes empty, then the structure $C(x)$ contains a collection of nogoods $C(x) = [\eta(x = 1, \alpha_1), \ldots, \eta(x = i, \alpha_k)]$ which can be resolved on x producing $\eta(\alpha_1, \ldots, \alpha_k)$. It can then return immediately, no matter what the current branching variable is. At a node where we branch on x, and the domain of x has been reduced to $\{1, \ldots, r\}$ from $\{1, \ldots, r, \ldots, d\}$, the algorithm branches only on values $1, \ldots r$ for x. To derive the required nogood for this node, collect the nogoods returned by the r recursive calls, together with the $k - r$ nogoods stored in $C(x)$, and then apply the resolution rule.

5.1 k-Consistency

A CSP instance is called k-consistent if every partial assignment to $k-1$ variables that does not violate any constraint can be extended to any k^{th} variable without violating any constraint. Transforming an instance that is not k-consistent into an equivalent instance that is k-consistent is called k-consistency processing, or k-consistency enforcement. The "default" algorithm for doing this, which we denote **KC**, is as follows. For any assignment α for $k - 1$ variables, and any k^{th} variable y, test all assignments that extend α to y. If all violate some constraint, then α cannot be extended to a satisfying assignment. Modify $\mathcal{I}$ by (in our terms) adding $\eta(\alpha)$ to its set of initial nogoods.

Proposition 8. BT+K-CON *is dominated by* **NG-RES**.

Proof. If the conditions for k-consistency processing to add the size $k-1$ nogood $\eta(\alpha)$ are satisfied, then α does not violate any initial nogood of $\mathcal{I}$, but there is some k^{th} variable x with $\alpha(x) = \bot$ such that, for every value $a \in D$, the extension of α to $\alpha; x = a$ violates some initial nogood of $\mathcal{I}$. That is, for every $a \in D$, there is a initial nogood $\eta(\alpha; x = a)$. We may resolve all of these conflicts together on x, obtaining the new nogood $\eta(\alpha)$, and we are done.

Proposition 9. BT+AC, *when arc-consistency if computed by applying the* usual **Revise** *procedure, is dominated by* **NG-RES**.

Proof. Standard **AC** algorithms are based on repeated application the procedure called **Revise**, which takes a pair of variables and a value for the first variable, and removes that value from the domain of the first variable if there is no support for (no value consistent with it) it at the second variable. We model domain deletion done by **Revise** in essentially the same way we did for **FC**. If **Revise** deletes a value a from the domain of variable x, because there is no support for it at y, then for every value b in the domain of y there is an initial nogood $\eta(x = a, y = b)$. If the domain of y has not been reduced, we can resolve all of these together to obtain $\eta(x = a)$, modeling the removal of a from the domain of x. If the domain of y has have values removed, for example by previous arc-consistency processing, then for each value that was removed we have a collection of nogoods "hitting" that value, which were collected at the time it was removed. We can resolve all of these together to obtain a new nogood excluding $x = a$.

6   Discussion

The main conclusion about practical CSP algorithms is that, at least when learning is involved, 2-way branching may be substantially better than d-way branching, and should never be much worse. Since learning is essential in first-rate SAT solvers, we expect it will also soon be considered essential in first-rate CSP solvers. A fair experimental comparison of the two versions of backtracking is worth carrying out, but is not necessarily easy to design, as it requires understanding "corresponding" branching strategies.

The most obvious next step in this line of work is to improve the separation between **NG-RES** and **C-RES** (and thus between the two branching strategies) from super-polynomial to exponential. Recently the separation between negative resolution and unrestricted resolution has been improved from Goerdt's $n^{\log n}$ to $2^{n/\log n}$ [7]. The same separation almost certainly holds for **NG-RES** and **C-RES**, but the proof method does not carry over.

References

1. Andrew B. Baker. *Intelligent Backtracking on Constraint Satisfaction Problems: Experimental and Theoretical Results*. PhD thesis, University of Oregon, 1995.
2. P. Beame, J. Culberson, and D. Mitchell. The resolution complexity of random graph k-colourability. In preparation.
3. P. Beame, R. Impagliazzo, and A Sabharwal. Resolution complexity of independent sets in random graphs. In *Proc., 16th Annual Conference on Computational Complexity (CCC)*, pages 52–68, June 2001.
4. P. Beame, R. Karp, T. Pitassi, and M. Saks. On the complexity of unsatisfiability proofs for random k-CNF formulas. In *Proc. of the 30 Annual ACM Symp. on the Theory of Computing (STOC-98)*, pages 561–571, May 1998.

5. P. Beame, H. Kautz, and A. Sabharwal. Understanding the power of clause learning. In *Proc., Eighteenth Int'l. Joint Conferences on Artificial Intelligence (IJCAI-03)*, 2003. To appear.

6. E. Ben-Sasson and A. Wigderson. Short proofs are narrow: Resolution made simple. In *Proc. of the 31st Annual Symp. on the Theory of Computation. (STOC-99)*, pages 517–526, May 1999. (Also appears as ECCC report TR99-022).

7. J. Buresh-Oppenheim and T. Pitassi. The complexity of resolution refinements. In *Proc., Eighteenth Annual IEEE Symposium on Logic in Computer Science (LICS-03)*, pages 138–147, 2003.

8. V. Chvátal and E. Szemerédi. Many hard examples for resolution. *Journal of the ACM*, 35(4):759–768, 1988.

9. S. A. Cook and R. A. Reckhow. The relative efficiency of propositional proof systems. *J. Symbolic Logic*, 44(1):23–46, 1979.

10. J. De Kleer. A comparison of ATMS and CSP techniques. In *Proc. of the 11th Int'l. Joint Conf. on A. I. (IJCAI-89)*, pages 290–296, 1989.

11. R. Dechter. From local to global consistency. *Artificial Intelligence*, 55:87–107, 1992.

12. D. Frost and R. Dechter. Dead-end driven learning. In *Proc., Twelfth Nat. Conf. on Artificial Intelligence (AAAI-94)*, pages 294–300, 1994.

13. A. Goerdt. Unrestricted resolution versus N-resolution. *Theoretical Computer Science*, 93:159–167, 1992.

14. A. Haken. The intractability of resolution. *Theoretical Computer Science*, 39:297–308, 1985.

15. O. Kullmann. Upper and lower bounds on the complexity of generalized resolution and generalized constraint satisfaction problems. Manuscript, 2000.

16. D. G. Mitchell. Hard problems for CSP algorithms. In *Proc., 15th Nat. Conf. on Artificial Intelligence (AAAI-98)*, pages 398–405, 1998.

17. David G. Mitchell. Resolution complexity of random constraints. *Lecture Notes in Computer Science, LNCS 2470*, pages 295–309, 2002.

18. M. Molloy and M. Salavatipour. The resolution complexity of random constraint satisfaction problems. Submitted.

19. T. Schiex and G. Verfaillie. Nogood recording for static and dynamic csp. In *Proc. of the IJCAI-93/SIGMAN Workshop on Knowledge-based Production Planning, Scheduling and Control*, pages 305–316, August 1993.

20. A. Urquhart. Hard examples for resolution. *Journal of the ACM*, 34(1):209–219, January 1987.

21. A. Urquhart. Resolution proofs of matching principles. *Annals of Mathematics and Artificial Intelligence*, 2002. (To appear).

22. T. Walsh. SAT vs CSP. In *Proc. of the 6th Int'l. Conference on the Principles and Practice of Constraint Programming (CP-2000)*, pages 441–456, 2000.

23. K. Xu and W. Li. Exact phase transitions in random constraint satisfaction problems. *J. of Artificial Intelligence Research*, 12:93–103, 2000.

Generating High Quality Schedules
for a Spacecraft Memory Downlink Problem[*]

Angelo Oddi, Nicola Policella, Amedeo Cesta, and Gabriella Cortellessa

Planning & Scheduling Team
Institute for Cognitive Science and Technology
National Research Council of Italy
Viale K. Marx 15, I-00137 Rome, Italy
{oddi,policella,cesta,corte}@ip.rm.cnr.it
http://pst.ip.rm.cnr.it

Abstract. This work introduces a combinatorial optimization problem called MARS EXPRESS Memory Dumping Problem (MEX-MDP), which arises in the European Space Agency program MARS EXPRESS. It concerns the generation of high quality schedules for the spacecraft memory downlink problem. MEX-MDP is an *NP-hard* combinatorial problem characterized by several kinds of constraints, such as on-board memory capacity, limited communication windows over the downlink channel, deadlines and ready times on the observation activities. The contribution of this paper is twofold: on one hand it provides a CSP model of a real problem, and on the other it presents a set of metaheuristic strategies based on local and randomized search which are built around the *constraint-based* model of the problem. The algorithms are evaluated on a benchmark set distilled from ESA documentation and the results are compared against a lower bound of the objective function.

1 Introduction

Tackling hard optimization problems by means of *metaheuristic* strategies has became a pervasive technique not only in Constraint Programming, but also in many Artificial Intelligence research areas. In solving such problems, metaheuristics bridge the gaps between contrasting needs, such as anytime availability of a solution, bounded computational time and solution quality.

This paper describes, analyzes and models through the CSP paradigm a space mission planning problem within the ESA program MARS-EXPRESS which has launched a spacecraft toward Mars on June 2, 2003. This problem, referred to as the MARS EXPRESS Memory Dumping Problem (MEX-MDP), is aimed at synthesizing sequences of on-board memory dumps during the space probe's regular scientific activities around Mars. Any sequence of dump operations should satisfy a number of complex constraints such as limited availability of communication windows, maximal data rate in communication links, operation ready times and

---

[*] This work describes results obtained in the framework of a research study conducted for the European Space Agency (ESA-ESOC) under contract No.14709/00/D/IM.

F. Rossi (Ed.): CP 2003, LNCS 2833, pp. 570–584, 2003.

bounded on-board packet store capacities. The results we present are spawned from a study [1] aimed at demonstrating the effectiveness of Artificial Intelligence and constraint-based techniques in mission planning domains like MARS EXPRESS.

Space domains are very rich of challenging optimization problems. Similar problems to MEX-MDP arise also in satellite domains. Some of the previous works, see for example [2, 3], confirm the complexity of the domain constraints and show also how not all the best solutions are obtained by a single solving technique. Different needs —and, dually, different trade-offs between quality and computational times— are addressed by different algorithms or combinations of solving techniques in a *metaheuristic* schema. In a similar light, this work proposes a quite general constraint-based model for the on-board spacecraft memory scenario and a *portfolio* of heuristic strategies for MEX-MDP. These heuristic strategies, which are defined around the CSP formulation, join knowledge from different research areas such as Constraint Reasoning, Local Search and Randomized Algorithms [4, 5].

We will begin by describing the details of the MEX-MDP problem, and continue with an analysis of its complexity (Section 2). Section 3 contains the description of the CSP model, whereas Sections 4 and 5 describe and experimentally evaluate a *portfolio* of solving methods. We conclude with some comments about the results obtained, and more in general, about the experience described in this work.

2   The Mars Express Memory Dumping Problem

Inside the complex domain of a space mission like MARS-EXPRESS we have been concerned with the issue of data transmission to Earth. A space probe continuously produces a large amount of data from both scientific observations and house-keeping. Because MARS-EXPRESS is a single pointing probe, it points either to Mars (data production) or to Earth (data downlink). As a consequence data are first collected in the finite capacity on-board memory. The problem solving goal consists in synthesizing spacecraft operations for emptying as much as possible the on-board memory during downlink time intervals, in order to allow the spacecraft to save new information without losing previous data.

Different constraints are conflicting with the data preservation. Besides the communication channel availability there are different transmission rates to be taken into account. Additional constraints rise from the specific use of the on-board memory, which is subdivided into different memory banks (or packet stores), each of them having a finite capacity. For each piece of information produced inside the probe, a packet store is also defined in which such data should be stored. Different data are stored in a sequential way and the packet stores are managed cyclically. As a consequence, if the memory is full and new data becomes available, the stored data are lost.

We have formalized this problem as the Mars Express Memory Dumping Problem (MEX-MDP) whose different components are described in the rest of this section.

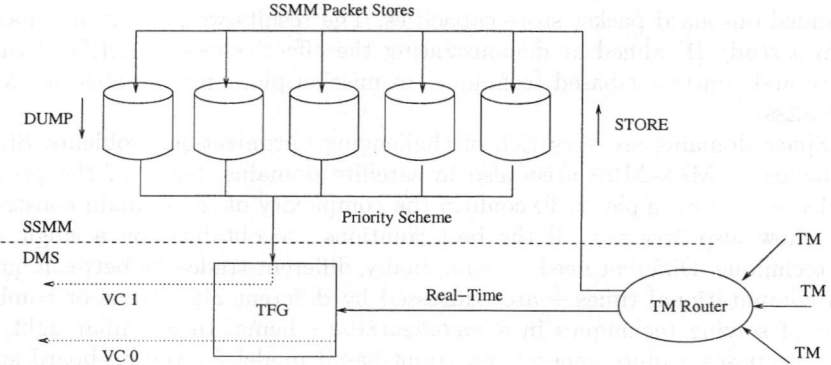

Fig. 1. On-board telemetry flow. Telemetry (TM) data produced on board are stored on the on board memory (SSMM) subdivided into packet stores. Memory stores are then downloaded with different dumps that transfer the data to the ground. The figure contains also the real-time communication path to Earth that is not considered in this study.

Problem Description. The basic ontological objects of the MEX-MDP domain are either *resources* or *activities*: resources represent domain subsystems able to give services; activities model tasks to be executed using resources over time. A set of *constraints* defines needed relationships between the two types of objects. Figure 1 shows a sketch of the MARS EXPRESS modules that are relevant to MEX-MDP. Three kinds of resources are present in MEX-MDP:

- *Packet Stores.* The on-board memory (Solid State Mass Memory or SSMM) is subdivided into a set of separated packet stores pk_i, i.e. they cannot exchange data among them. Each one has a fixed capacity c_i and a priority value p_i. Each packet store can be seen as a file of a given maximal size that is managed cyclically.
- *On-Board Payloads.* An on-board payload can be seen as a *finite state machine* in which each state has a different behavior in generating observation data. In particular, each possible state of the payload corresponds to a different generation data rate.
- *Communication Channels.* These resources are characterized by a set of separated communication windows identifying intervals of time for downlink. Each temporal window has a constant data rate[1].

Activities describe *how* the resources can be used. Three types are relevant in MEX-MDP: payload operations, memory dumps and continuous data streams. Each activity a_i has an associated execution interval, which is identified by its start time $s(a_i)$ and end time $e(a_i)$.

- *Payload Operations.* A payload operation por_i corresponds to a scientific observation. According to the MARS EXPRESS operational modalities each

---

[1] It will be 0 in case of no-transmission window.

observation generates an amount of data that is decomposed into different *store* operations, and distributed over the set of available packet stores.

- *Memory Dumps.* A memory dump operation md_i transfers a set of data from a packet store to a transfer device (Transfer Frame Generator - TFG). Those activities represent the transmission of the data through the communication channel.
- *Continuous Data Streams.* The particular case of the continuous data stream operations cds_i is such that $s(cds_i) = 0$ and $e(cds_i) = +\infty$. Each data stream is given a packet store. This activity represents a continuous generation of data with a fixed average data rate. We choose to model also a cds_i as a periodic sequence of store operations.

Each type of activity is characterized by a particular set of resource requirements and constraints. Given these basic domain entities, let us now define the MEX-MDP. A set of scientific observations, $POR = \{por_1, por_2, \ldots, por_n\}$ and a set of housekeeping productions, $CDS = \{cds_1, cds_2, \ldots, cds_m\}$, are both reduced to a set of store operations on the on-board memory. A *solution* to a MEX-MDP, is a set of dumping operations $S = \{md_1, md_2, \ldots, md_s\}$ such that:

- the whole set of data are "available" on ground within the considered temporal horizon $\mathcal{H} = [0, H]$.
- Each dump operation starts after the generation of the corresponding data. For each packet store, the data are moved through the communication channel according to a FIFO policy.
- Each dump activity, md_i, is executed within an assigned time window w_j which has a constant data rate r_j. Moreover, dump operations cannot reciprocally overlap.
- At each instant $t \in \mathcal{H}$, the amount of data stored in each packet store pk_i has to be less or equal to the packet store capacity c_i (i.e., overwriting is not allowed).

The additional goal is to find *high quality solutions* with respect to a set of evaluation parameters: a high quality plan delivers all the stored data as soon as possible according to a definite policy or objective function. A relevant piece of information to define an objective function is the *turnover time* of a payload operation por_i:

$$tt(por_i) = del(por_i) - e(por_i)$$

where $del(por_i)$ is the delivery time of por_i and $e(por_i)$ is its end time. Thus, we introduce as an objective function the *mean α-weighted turnover time MTT_α* of a solution S:

$$MTT_\alpha(S) = \frac{1}{n} \sum_{i=1}^{n} \alpha_i \, tt(por_i) \tag{1}$$

Given an instance of a MEX-MDP, an *optimal solution* with respect to a weight α is a solution S which *minimizes* the objective function $MTT_\alpha(S)$. Two weights

α have been found to be interesting, namely data priority and data volume generated by the observations (see [1] for a detailed description). The experimental evaluation in this paper considers the *Mean Turnover Time* (*MTT*) with $\alpha_i = 1$, $i = 1..n$.

Complexity Analysis. The MEX-MDP can be shown to be *NP-hard* by reduction from the problem[2] $1|chains; r_i; pmtn| \sum C_i$, i.e., a single-machine optimization scheduling problem where the goal is to minimize the sum of the activity completion times C_i [7]. There are n activities, each one having a ready time r_i and a duration p_i. Preemption (*pmtn*) is allowed, hence the execution of an activity a_i can be suspended and a new one can be resumed or started from scratch. Finally, among the set of activities, a partial order $\prec$, imposed by a set of precedence constraints, is defined[3] which partitions the set of activities into a set of separate *chains* of activities.

The problem $1|chains; r_i; pmtn| \sum C_i$ can be reduced to MEX-MDP considering: (1) each packet store with an infinite capacity; (2) the communication channel having a uniform data rate r over the total problem horizon; (3) an unbounded problem horizon; (4) each por_i stores data in a single packet store, and there is no pair of activities, por_i and por_j, which store data in the same packet store at the same time. These hypotheses allow to reduce $1|chains; r_i; pmtn| \sum C_i$ to MEX-MDP. In fact, the single-machine corresponds to the communication channel. Each activity a_i with duration p_i and ready time r_i, corresponds to a por_i which contains a single store activity with end-time r_i and size equal to the duration p_i multiplied by the channel data rate r. The number of packet stores is equal to the number of chains. Each *chain* of activities, corresponds to a set of activities in MEX-MDP which stores data in the same packet store and has the same temporal total order imposed by the chains (remember that each packet store is a FIFO buffer). Finally, we observe that the completion time C_i and the turnover time tt_i are equivalent objective functions. In fact, $C_i = tt_i + r_i$, hence a solution is optimal with respect to $\sum C_i$ if and only if it is optimal with respect to $\sum tt_i$.

The complexity of the MEX-MDP is a strong limitation to problem scalability for systematic solving methods in finding optimal (or near-optimal) solutions under tight temporal bounds on the computational time. For these reasons this work proposes a set of meta-heuristic strategies based on local and randomized search.

3   CSP Representation

A Constraint Satisfaction Problem, CSP, consists of a set of variables $X = \{X_1, X_2, \ldots, X_n\}$ each associated with a domain D_i of values, and a set of constraints $C = \{C_1, C_2, \ldots, C_m\}$ denoting the legal combinations of values for the

---

[2] Expressed in the $\alpha|\beta|\gamma$-notation of [6].
[3] Such that $a_i \prec a_j$ means a_j must start only after the end of a_i.

variables s.t. $C_i \subseteq D_1 \times D_2 \times \cdots \times D_n$ [8]. A solution consists of assigning to each variable one of its possible values so that all the constraints are satisfied. The resolution process can be seen as an iterative search procedure where the current (partial) solution is extended on each cycle by assigning a value to a new variable. As new decisions are made during this search, a set of "propagation rules" removes elements from domains D_i which cannot be contained in any feasible extension of the current partial solution. In general, it is not possible to remove all inconsistent values through propagation alone. Choices are made among possible values for some variables, giving rise to the need for variable and value ordering heuristics.

A CSP representation for a problem should focus on its important features. In the case of MEX-MDP, the following characteristics have been selected:

1. the temporal horizon $\mathcal{H} = [0, H]$,
2. the amount of data stored at the end time of each operation,
3. the channel communication windows,
4. the finite capacity c_i of each memory bank pk_i and its FIFO behavior.

It is worth noting that the FIFO behavior of the packet stores allows us to make an important simplification. In fact, it is possible to consider both the data in input and those in output to/from the memory as flows of data, neglecting the information about which operations those data refer to. In this way, given a generic time window over the communication channel, it is possible to split the problem into two levels of abstraction. A first one, where we just consider the constraints on the flows of data: for each generic dump window and each packet store the amount of residual data in the packet store should not exceed its capacity. And a second level, where a sequence of memory dump operations (generation of data packets) is generated over the communication link. In particular, we divide the temporal horizon $\mathcal{H}$ into a set of contiguous temporal windows $w_j = (t_{j-1}, t_j]$, with $j = 1 \ldots m$, according to the domain's *significant events*, that is: store operations and changes of transmission data rate. This partition allows us to consider temporal intervals, w_j, in which store operations do not happen (except for its upper bound t_j) and the data rate is constant.

As a consequence, the CSP decision variables are defined according to the set of windows w_j and to the different packet stores pk_i. We defined δ_{ij} as the amount of data dumped from the packet store pk_i within the window w_j. We also introduce: (1) d_{ij}, the amount of data stored[4] in pk_i at t_j, (2) l_{ij}, the amount of data[5] that pk_i can hold within w_j and (3) b_j, the maximal dumping capacity in the interval w_j. These represent the input of MEX-MDP.

A fundamental constraint captures the fact that for each window w_j the difference between the amount of generated data and the amount of dumped data cannot exceed l_{ij} the maximal imposed level in the window (*overwriting*).

---

[4] The variables $d_{i0} \leq c_i$ represent the initial level of data in the packet store pk_i.

[5] Defining $l_{ij} = c_i$ for $j < n$ and $l_{ij} = 0$ for $j = n$ we model that a solution has to download the whole set of spacecraft data.

Additionally, the dumped data cannot exceed the generated data (*overdumping*). We define the following inequalities as *conservative constraints*

$$\sum_{k=0}^{j} d_{ik} - \sum_{k=1}^{j} \delta_{ik} \leq l_{ij}$$

$$\sum_{k=0}^{j-1} d_{ik} - \sum_{k=1}^{j} \delta_{ik} \geq 0 \tag{2}$$

for $i = 1 \ldots n$ and $j = 1 \ldots m$. A second class of constraints considers the dumping capacity imposed by the communication channel. The following inequalities, called *downlink constraints*, state that for each window w_j it is not possible to dump more data than the available capacity b_j, $j = 1 \ldots m$,

$$0 \leq \sum_{i=1}^{n} \delta_{ij} \leq b_j \tag{3}$$

Each decision variable δ_{ij} has a potential interval of feasible values $[lb_{\delta_{ij}}, ub_{\delta_{ij}}]$ defined by its lower and upper bounds $lb_{\delta_{ij}}$ and $ub_{\delta_{ij}}$. For $i = 1 \ldots n$, $j = 1 \ldots m$:

$$lb_{\delta_{ij}} = \max\{0, \max\{0, \sum_{k=0}^{j} d_{ik} - l_{ij}\} - \max\{\sum_{k=1}^{j-1} b_k, \sum_{k=0}^{j-2} d_{ik}\}\} \tag{4}$$

$$ub_{\delta_{ij}} = \min\{b_j, \sum_{k=0}^{j-1} d_{ik} - \max\{0, \sum_{k=0}^{j-1} d_{ik} - l_{i(j-1)}\}\} \tag{5}$$

Equation (4) states that a lower bound of δ_{ij} is represented by the difference between the amount of data generated at t_j over the packet store capacity l_{ij} ($\sum_{k=0}^{j} d_{ik} - l_{ij}$) and the maximal amount of data which is "downloadable" by t_{j-1} ($\max\{\sum_{k=1}^{j-1} b_k, \sum_{k=0}^{j-2} d_{i,k}\}$). Whereas (5) claims that an upper bound of δ_{ij} is the minimal value between b_j and the maximal amount of data which is really "downloadable" within the window w_j ($\sum_{k=0}^{j-1} d_{ik} - \max\{0, \sum_{k=0}^{j-1} d_{ik} - l_{i(j-1)}\}$). Grounded on these constraints, a set of propagation rules (or domain filtering rules) are defined to further reduce the domain intervals $[lb_{\delta_{ij}}, ub_{\delta_{ij}}]$.

Domain Filtering Rules. Domain filtering rules are fundamental components of a CSP solver aimed at pruning the problem search space by removing inconsistent values in the decision variable domains.

On the basis of the conservative constraints, the following two rules update the bounds $lb_{\delta_{ij}}$ and $ub_{\delta_{ij}}$

$$lb_{\delta_{ij}} = max\{lb_{\delta_{ij}}, \sum_{k=0}^{j} d_{ik} - l_{ij} - \sum_{k=1, k \neq j}^{j} ub_{\delta_{ik}}\} \tag{6}$$

$$ub_{\delta_{ij}} = min\{ub_{\delta_{ij}}, \sum_{k=0}^{j} d_{ik} - \sum_{k=1, k\neq j}^{j} lb_{\delta_{ik}}\} \tag{7}$$

The intuition behind (6) is that the value $\sum_{k=0}^{j} d_{ik} - l_{ij} - \sum_{k=1, k\neq j}^{j} ub_{\delta_{ik}}$ is the minimal value for δ_{ij} in order to avoid overwriting in pk_i within w_j. In (7), $\sum_{k=0}^{j} d_{ik} - \sum_{k=1, k\neq j}^{j} lb_{\delta_{ik}}$ is the maximal value for δ_{ij} in order to avoid overdumping. A third rule, based on communication constraints, updates the values $ub_{\delta_{ij}}$.

$$ub_{\delta_{ij}} = min\{ub_{\delta_{ij}}, b_j - \sum_{k=1, k\neq i}^{n} lb_{\delta_{kj}}\} \tag{8}$$

In this case the basic intuition is that $b_j - \sum_{k=1, k\neq i}^{n} lb_{\delta_{kj}}$ represents the maximal value allowed for δ_{ij} on the basis of the other lower bounds $lb_{\delta_{ij}}$.

The application of the previous set of filtering rules generally updates the values $ub\delta_{ij}$ and $lb\delta_{ij}$. In particular, when the condition $lb\delta_{ij} \leq ub\delta_{ij}$ is violated for at least one window, the partial solution is *not consistent*. In Section 5 we will show how these rules effect our solving methods and we will highlight their importance to achieve a feasible solution.

4   Problem Solving

The further contribution of the paper is to propose a *portfolio* of heuristic strategies for MEX-MDP defined on the CSP formulation which joins knowledge from different research areas such as Constraint Reasoning, Local Search and Randomized Algorithms. One or more *meta-heuristic* strategies can be built on top of the set of basic solving components. In particular, we propose two basic solving strategies: a *greedy solver* and a *tabu search strategy* for improving an initial solution. Furthermore, these basic procedure are combined in three *meta-strategies*: (1) a serialization of greedy and tabu search; (2) an iterative sampling approach which uses a randomized version of the greedy procedure; (3) a serialization of iterative random sampling and tabu search.

A Greedy Solving Method. The basic greedy solving method uses two levels of abstraction for the MEX-MDP problem: (1) a first one called *data dump level*, where the horizon is partitioned into a set of windows $w_1, w_2, \ldots, w_m$, such that for each window w_j only the decision variables δ_{ij}, representing the amount of data to be dumped in the window, are considered; (2) a second level, called *packetization level*, where a sequence of memory dump operations is generated over the communication links according to the constraints imposed on each window w_j.

Data Dump Level. Figure 2 shows the algorithm *MakeConsistentDataDump()*. At first (Step 2) a propagation procedure is called. Such a procedure implements the propagation features described above and basically sets the domains

MakeConsistentDataDump:

Input: *mexmdp* instance
Output: a consistent assignment of the set of decision variables δ_{ij}

```
1.  {
2.     Propagation(mexmdp)
3.     j ← 1
4.     while (j ≤ m and Feasible(mexmdp)) {
5.        AssignDecisionVariablesΔ(j)
6.        Propagation(mexmdp)
7.        j ← j + 1
8.     }
9.  }
```

Fig. 2. Algorithm to generate a consistent assignment of the set of variables δ_{ij}.

$[lb\delta_{ij}, ub\delta_{ij}]$ of possible values for all the decision variables δ_{ij}. In addition, each time the algorithm performs a solving decision (Step 5), the *Propagation()* procedure is called again in order to further reduce the domains $[lb\delta_{ij}, ub\delta_{ij}]$ (Step 6).

The algorithm considers the set of windows $w_1, w_2, \ldots, w_m$ in increasing order of time, and for each window w_j, it considers the amount of data b_j that can be dumped within the window. Subsequently, by the sub-procedure *AssignDecisionVariablesΔ()*, it iteratively executes the following steps: selects a packet store (according to a given priority rule); computes an amount of data to be dumped from the selected packets store; updates the lower bound of the domain of the involved decision variable. For each window w_j the previous steps are executed until a dump capacity is available or a *failure* state occurs.

It is possible to implement different solving priority rules inside the step *AssignDecisionVariablesΔ()*. Two rules are currently used: CFF (Closest to Fill First) that selects the packet store with the highest percentage of data volume and HPF (Highest Priority First) which selects the packet store with the highest priority. In case that a subset of packet stores has the same priority, the packet store with the smallest store as outcome data is chosen.

It is worth noting that the greedy solver is based on the composition of effects between a dispatching strategy that takes decisions proceeding ahead in time and the propagation rules on the CSP representation that propagate decision effects forward and backward on the structure adjusting values according to problem constraints.

Packetization Level. The second step of the greedy procedure generates the final solution S, that is the sequence of memory dump operations. It works in analogous way to *MakeConsistentDataDump()* with the difference that no propagation function is called. In fact, when all the variables δ_{ij} are consistently assigned, it is possible to generate the sequence of data dumping operations without the risk of finding inconsistent states. Hence, the algorithm considers the set of windows $w_1, w_2, \ldots, w_m$ in increasing order of time, for each window

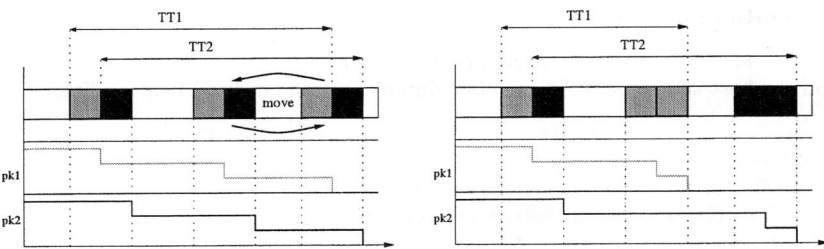

Fig. 3. An example of move.

w_j, considers the set of decision variables δ_{ij} (with $i = 1 \ldots n$) representing the assigned dumping capacity to each packet store i and generates a correspondent sequence of memory dumping operations (stream of data packets from the set of packet stores). Two alternative priority rules are currently used: SDF (Smallest to Dump First) which selects the packet store with the smallest value of the decision variable δ_{ij} and HPF (Highest Priority First) that selects the packet store with the highest priority.

A Tabu Search Strategy. Tabu search [9] is a well-known local search approach for solving hard combinatorial optimization problems. A tabu algorithm starts from an initial solution S_0. At each step it looks at the *neighborhood* of the current solution S_C, that is, a subset of solutions obtained from S_C by the application of a local transformation operator called *move*. Next the algorithm finds the solution S_N with the best value of a given objective function. S_N becomes the new current solution and the process is iterated until some termination conditions met and the best solution S* is returned. The search process is not allowed to turn back to solutions visited in the previous $MaxSt$ steps (cycles). For this purpose a *tabu list*, managed as a first-in-first-out queue, is defined with the last $MaxSt$ moves.

A tabu search strategy for solving a given optimization problem, requires the definition of some parameters (e.g., the tabu list length) and operators, in particular the *move* operator. For the sake of space we do not present a detailed description of the move here, but just give the intuition behind it by an example. Let us consider the MEX-MDP example in Fig. 3, there are two scientific observations, the grey and the black one, which respectively are stored in the packet store pk_1 and pk_2 and it is possible to dump data over the communication channel only within the periods containing the represented dumping activities. In the left-hand side of Fig. 3 a possible solution of the problem is shown, where both the level of data in the packet stores and the turnover times TT_1 and TT_2 are represented. After the application of the *move* operator[6] a new solution is obtained (shown in the right part). The new value of TT_1 improves the average turnover time.

---

[6] Basically it performs a swap of data packets over the communication link.

IterativeRandomSampling:

Input: *mexmdp* instance, termination conditions
Output: best sequence S^* of memory dumps over the communication links

```
1.  {
2.      S* ← ∅
3.      while (termination conditions not met) {
4.          S ← GreedyRandomSampling(mexmdp)
5.          UpdateBestSolution(S, S*)
6.      }
7.  }
```

Fig. 4. An algorithmic template for iterative sampling.

Meta-heuristic Strategies. Meta-heuristics are obtained by the application of two operators on the basic solving components: *random iteration*, a randomized version of a core solving procedure is iterated many times until some termination conditions are met; *serialization*, the output of one procedure becomes the input of the next one.

The *random iteration* is defined as the iterative random sampling strategy of Fig. 4 which samples the space of feasible solutions until a *termination condition* is met. Solutions are sampled by a randomized version of the greedy procedure (called *GreedyRandomSampling()*) which incrementally generates a solution or a failure. The overall process generates a stream of feasible solutions with different values of the objective function (together with a set of failures). When the procedure stops, the best solution is returned. It is worth noting that the integration of a propagation mechanism inside the random sampling has the main benefit of increasing the probability of finding feasible solutions during each iteration. This property is very useful when the optimization problem is formulated within a set of tight constraints, such that, the set of feasible solutions is *sparse* over the search space.

The procedure in Fig. 4 takes as input an instance of MEX-MDP problem (that is, a temporal horizon H, a set of store activities, a description of the communication links, and the set of packet stores) together with a set of *termination conditions*: for example a maximal number of iterations or a *cpu* time bound. The output of the algorithm is the best sequence S^* of memory dumps over the communication link consistent with all the domain constraints or a failure, in the case no iteration finds a feasible solution. The iterative sampling procedure is composed by these main steps: a random seed is generated and then used by the procedure *GreedyRandomSampling()*, after each random sampling, the best solution found so far is stored in S^*.

The next experimental section evaluates the iterative random sampling procedure together with two other strategies obtained by serialization: greedy and tabu search, iterative random sampling and tabu search.

5   Evaluation

An important step in the evaluation of a set of different solutions is to select a *touchstone*. Since it is not possible to easily obtain a reference set of optimal solutions for our MEX-MDP benchmark instances, we choose to analyze the performance of the solving procedures through a lower bound of the Mean Turnover Time. In particular, in order to find a representative lower bound we consider two relaxed formulation of MEX-MDP:

- first, we consider the relaxed version of the problem such that each packet store has an infinite capacity and there are no chain constraints among the activities. Under this hypothesis, the problem can be reduced to a classical optimization scheduling problem of minimizing the mean flow time (in our case called *MTT*) on a *single machine* (i.e., the communication channel) where *preemption* is allowed. For this problem a polynomial strategy which gives the optimal value is known[7],
- the second relaxed version of MEX-MDP considers that each packet store has a dedicated communication channel with identical characteristics to the original one. In this way any linear sequence of activities (chain) which stores data in a packet store has a dedicated channel for data dumping and the optimal solution can be easily computed in polynomial time.

Hence, we define the lower bound of MEX-MDP as the maximal value of the mean turnover times for the two relaxed formulations of the problem.

Experimental Results. During our study different benchmark sets have been generated based on the test data provided by the ESA mission planning experts. However, in this section we just present the results for one of these benchmark sets, which can be seen as the most critical with respect to, on one hand, the competition among the packet stores for the same channel bandwidth, and with respect to the limited capacity of the packet stores in comparison to the amount of generated data on the other. All the algorithms presented in this paper are implemented in Java 1.4.1 and the CPU times presented in the following tables are obtained on a Pentium III machine under Windows 98. A more complete experimentation and analysis can be found in [1]. In this section we consider only the Mean Turnover Time (MTT) and present five different types of result:

- the lower bound of the MTT values,
- the values generated by the greedy (one-pass) strategy with the best combinations between the two levels of priority rules (see Section 4),
- the values generated by the greedy strategy without the support of the domain filtering rules,
- the best MTT values obtained with the application of the iterative sampling optimization strategy (the number of iterations is set to 100),

---

[7] Shortest Remaining Processing Time (SRPT) [10].

Table 1. Each column represents percentage difference between the solution obtained with each approach and the lower bound.

pr. #	pr. size	greedy	no propagation	greedy+tabu	random sampling	rs+tabu
1	60	143,39	-	126,28	15,63	14,99
2	66	48,30	-	45,80	10,30	9,25
3	86	333,73	333,73	164,61	42,77	40,67
4	76	357,18	357,18	164,22	47,77	44,64
5	87	271,95	271,95	133,30	31,38	30,31
6	66	138,14	-	128,58	15,44	13,63
7	66	140,24	-	134,63	13,00	10,59
8	58	140,34	-	120,55	16,52	14,95
9	81	272,36	272,36	171,97	29,63	29,14
10	62	155,84	-	147,61	18,34	18,05
11	66	-	-	-	25,10	22,57
12	91	311,81	311,81	139,79	41,45	40,09
13	96	295,14	295,14	149,02	39,01	38,19
14	56	136,93	-	116,92	16,26	14,98
15	71	324,43	324,43	169,66	34,50	33,77
16	15	26,80	26,80	26,80	11,38	10,21
17	12	34,28	34,28	34,28	14,32	12,83

- the results of the application of the tabu search procedure[8] to the solutions obtained with the greedy algorithm and to the best solution found by the random sampling algorithm.

Table 1 presents the performance results for the solving procedures described in Section 4. Basically we evaluate and combine two types of metaheuristic strategies: improving an initial solution by local search and performing a broad random sampling of the search space. A third one is a combination of the previous two. The experimental data show how the tabu search procedure always improves an initial solution, even if we have different levels of improvement according to different methods used to construct the initial solution. When tabu search is applied to the iterative sampling solutions, indeed, the improvement is much less than what we obtain on the greedy solutions. That different behavior is justified by the fact that the iterative sampling approach is an effective solution method in itself for this kind of optimization problems. In fact, as it possible to see in Table 1, the solutions are quite close to the lower bound values. However, from these experiments we can draw an additional conclusion about the tabu search. Even if we have introduced a definition of move which is quite "natural" for the problem - we move data packets forwards and backwards in time (see Fig. 3) - the local search can easily get *stuck* in local minima. In other words, the structure of the search space is probably weakly (or not at all) connected with respect to the move definition. That is, due to the rich set of constraints of MEX-MDP, it is quite difficult (or impossible) to reach a near-optimal solution from a generic feasible solution through a sequence of move applications. This fact is confirmed by the CPU results reported in Table 2. As it is possible to see, the random sampling strategy shows the best trade-off between solution quality and CPU times compared to the tabu search performances. In fact, a broad random

---

[8] In particular, the tabu-list has a length set to 7 and the procedure stops when a maximal value of 100 neighborhoods are searched without solution improvement.

Table 2. CPU time (sec.).

pr. #	greedy	greedy+tabu	random sampling	rs+tabu
1	0,20	13,72	14,41	26,04
2	0,20	8,24	14,07	25,39
3	0,13	47,54	14,96	50,21
4	0,12	64,85	14,70	45,36
5	0,11	46,47	12,40	36,59
6	0,15	8,01	14,77	27,33
7	0,14	10,86	15,07	26,97
8	0,14	16,91	14,71	25,10
9	0,10	19,01	12,67	44,25
10	0,13	11,25	13,99	25,21
11	-	-	13,37	30,65
12	0,12	28,17	14,96	41,04
13	0,13	37,41	14,93	37,58
14	0,13	16,35	14,57	26,61
15	0,10	26,63	12,47	27,56
16	0,10	4,90	12,64	24,54
17	0,10	4,84	12,63	19,59

sampling strategy, as the one introduced in this work, is quite effective when the search decisions are correctly driven in the right direction by the propagation rules. This last aspect is underlined in Table 1 where the performance results of the greedy strategy without propagation rules are shown in the column labeled *no propagation*. The reader can see the main contribution of the deduction rules. Indeed, almost half of the problem instances are not solved because of the lack of propagation (for example, see the "-" reported for instances #1, #2 or #7). This proves the fundamental role of propagation rules: indeed, at each step they propagate the effects of current decisions on future ones, thus predicting unsuccessful decision branches.

6   Conclusions

This paper has presented a CSP approach to a real problem in the context of space missions. It is worth reminding that in MARS-EXPRESS the synthesis of memory dumping spacecraft operations is an activity which is decided manually by a human planner, for the entire life-cycle of the mission. In the study for MARS-EXPRESS we have formalized the problem as a MEX-MDP, and produced as set of algorithms grounded on a CSP representation. In addition, the algorithms described in this paper have been integrated in a decision support system that has been delivered to ESA in May 2002. The tool, called MEXAR [11], is an interactive system which allows the user to obtain solutions for MEX-MDP problems. In the process of doing so, the mission planner is given the opportunity to inspect different features of the solution. MEXAR is a CSP tool which basically solves difficult problems *for* the human planner, but maintaining the control over the strategic decisions in the hands of the user.

From the study the authors have derived an important experience in facing the realm of space missions, a working environment in which criticality is the name of the game. They have also drawn a number of directions for further research on MEX-MDP. At present the synthesis of different moves for the tabu search is being studied to obtain a more effective use of the neighborhood. This would enable both a reduction of the CPU time and the implementation of a full GRASP metaheuristic strategy.

Acknowledgements

This work could not have been possible without the support at ESA-ESOC of both the project officer Fabienne Delhaise and the MARS-EXPRESS mission planners Michel Denis, Pattam Jayaraman, Alan Moorhouse and Erhard Rabenau. We also would like to thank Prof. J.K. Lenstra for his useful notes about the complexity of the single-machine scheduling problem reported in Section 2.

References

1. Cesta, A., Oddi, A., Cortellessa, G., Policella, N.: Automating the Generation of Spacecraft Downlink Operations in MARS EXPRESS: Analysis, Algorithms and an Interactive Solution Aid. Technical Report MEXAR-TR-02-10 (Project Final Report), ISTC-CNR [PST], Italian National Research Council (2002)
2. Verfaillie, G., Lemaitre, M.: Selecting and Scheduling Observations for Agile Satellites: Some Lessons from the Constraint Reasoning Community Point of View. In: Principles and Practice of Constraint Programming - CP 2001 - LNCS 2239. (2001)
3. Bensana, E., Lemaitre, M., Verfaillie, G.: Earth Observation Satellite Management. Constraints: An international Journal, 4 (1999) 293–299
4. Resende, M., Ribeiro, C.: Greedy Randomized Adaptive Search Procedures. In Glover, F., Kochenberger, G., eds.: Handbook of Metaheuristics. Kluwer Academic Publishers (2002) 219–249
5. Motwani, S., Raghavan, P.: Randomized Algorithms. Cambrige University Press, New York, NY (1995)
6. Graham, R.L., Lawler, E.L., Lenstra, J.K., Rinnooy Kan, A.H.G.: Optimization and Approximation in Deterministic Sequencing and Scheduling: a Survey. Annals of Discrete Mathematics 4 (1979) 287–326
7. Lenstra, J.K.: Notes from Berkeley, July 11, 1980. Personal Communication (2002)
8. Tsang, E.: Foundation of Constraint Satisfaction. Academic Press, London and San Diego, CA (1993)
9. Glover, F., Laguna, M.: Tabu Search. Kluwer Academic Publishers, Boston (1997)
10. Lenstra, J.K., Rinnooy Kan, A.H.G., Brucker, P.: Complexity of Machine Scheduling Problems. Annals of Discrete Mathematics 1 (1977) 343–362
11. Cesta, A., Cortellessa, G., Oddi, A., Policella, N.: A CSP-based Interactive Decision Aid for Space Mission Planning. In: Proceedings of AI*IA '03. Lecture Notes in Artificial Intelligence, Springer (2003)

Symmetry Breaking Using Stabilizers

Jean-François Puget

ILOG, 9 avenue de Verdun, 94253 Gentilly, France
puget@ilog.fr

Abstract. The addition of symmetry breaking constraints is one of the most successful symmetry breaking technique for constraint satisfaction problems (CSP). In this paper we present STAB, a method that adds some symmetry breaking constraints during the search for solution. STAB adds constraints that are not yet broken by the current partial assignment. The computation of those additional constraints require the computation of graph isomorphism at each node. Graph isomorphism is not know to be NP complete, and in practice can be solved quite efficiently using an auxiliary CSP. The method is refined to be applied to matrix problems where rows and columns can be permuted. A theoretical comparison with previously published methods shows how to combine those methods together safely. An experimental comparison on a class of highly symmetrical combinatorial problems, namely BIBD shows that STAB is more than one order of magnitude more efficient than best published techniques so far.

1 Introduction

A symmetry for a CSP is a mapping of the CSP onto itself that preserves its structure as well as its solutions. Therefore, a symmetry map solutions to solutions. A symmetry also maps infeasible partial assignments into infeasible partial assignments. In this paper, we will only deal with complete tree search methods, such as MAC. If the problem is difficult, it may be the case that all symmetrical variants of every dead end encountered during the search must be explored before a solution can be found. Even if the problem is easy, all symmetrical variants of a solution are also solutions, and listing all of them may just be impossible in practice. Also, when optimizing, proving optimality may become impossible for the same reason. Those observations have triggered a lot of interest for the detection and removal of symmetries in the constraint programming community. Several methods to deal with symmetries have been published: adding symmetry breaking constraints S[13][3][6], using symmetry breaking heuristics[12], and using every completely generated sub tree as a no good to prevent the exploration of any symmetrical variants. The last approach either uses the addition of constraints during search (SBDS) [10][11][1], or the detection of dominance during search (SBDD)[9][5][14].

In this paper we will explore some refinements of the first kind of method. Our approach is to try to not add all the symmetry breaking constraints as in [3]

F. Rossi (Ed.): CP 2003, LNCS 2833, pp. 585–599, 2003.

at the start of the search for solution. Instead, during search, we add constraints that remove symmetries that are compatible with the current partial assignment.

The remainder of the paper is organized as following. Section 2 introduces the basic definitions used in the paper. It also discusses the relationship between adding symmetry breaking constraints and SBDD, including a possible combination. Section 3 introduces STAB, a method based on the computation of stabilizers of partial assignments. Section 4 describes how this technique can be efficiently realized for two dimensional matrix problems where rows and columns can be permuted. Section 5 describes an experimental evaluation on special matrix models known as BIBDs. Those results show that our new technique is more than one order of magnitude faster than any previously published method. Section 6 concludes the paper with a summary and a discussion of possible extensions.

2   Symmetry Breaking Techniques

Several definitions of symmetries exist in the literature, see for instance [11][14] [12][1]. The method presented here can be used with any of those definitions. We just need to know how a symmetry σ maps any partial assignment A into another partial assignment $\sigma(A)$. We will also only consider variable permutations.

2.1   Basic Notations

From now on we will consider a CSP $P = (V, D, C)$ where V is a n-vector of variables, D is a n-vector of domains, one for each variable, and C is a m-vector of constraints. The domains and the constraints are defined in the usual way. Together, domains and constraints define the set of solutions of the CSP.

In this section we will assume that the symmetry group G of the CSP is given. We will discuss how G can be generated in section 4. Let $|G|$ denote the size of G.

When the variables of the CSP can be represented as a $k \times l$ matrix such that any row or column permutation is a symmetry, we say that the CSP is a two dimensional *matrix model*. In such case, the size of the symmetry group is $|G| = k!l!$ elements. Problems in this class of CSP are quite common[6].

Let us define $I^n = \{1, \ldots, n\}$. Symmetries can be described in terms of permutations of I^k for some k[11]. Let S^n be the set of all permutations of the set I^n. A permutation in S^n is represented by an n-vector σ, with $\sigma[i]$ being the image of i under σ. If v is an n-vector and $\sigma \in S^n$, let $w = \sigma(v)$ denote the vector w obtained by permuting the coordinates of v according to σ, i.e.

$$w[\sigma[i]] = v[i], \text{ for all } i \in I^n$$

2.2   Canonical Solutions

In order to relate several symmetry breaking techniques, we will introduce a fixed variable ordering as well as a value ordering. Without loss of generality, we can assume that domains are subsets of I^k for some k, with the usual ordering on integers.

The ordering on domains can be extended to a lexicographic ordering on vectors. Let X be a $s-vector$ and Y a $t-vector$.

$X <_{Lex} Y$ if and only if there exists $i \in I^n$ such that
$\quad X[k] = Y[k]$, for all $k \in I^{i-1}$
$\quad (i = s$ and $s < t)$ or $X[i] < Y[i]$
$X \leq_{Lex} Y$ if and only if $X <_{Lex} Y$ or $X = Y$

Given a solution A for P, and a symmetry σ for P, $\sigma(A)$ is also a solution of A. We say that a solution is *canonical* if and only if it is smaller than all its symmetrical variants, i.e.

$$A \leq_{Lex} \sigma(A), \text{ for all } \sigma \in G$$

Symmetry breaking techniques' aim is to remove solutions without removing any canonical solutions.

2.3   Symmetry Breaking Constraints

Adding symmetry breaking constraints is one of the oldest method for reducing the number of symmetries of a CSP[13]. In [3], it is shown that any CSP can be turned into a CSP without symmetries by the addition of the following constraints to the CSP.

$$V \leq_{Lex} \sigma(V), \text{ for all } \sigma \in G \tag{1}$$

These symmetry breaking constraints remove all solutions but the canonical ones. Although very appealing, this technique is not scalable because of the potentially large size of the group G. Indeed, we exhibit in section 5 a problem with less than 450 variables that has more than 10^{90} symmetries.

In practice researchers have investigated the use of only some symmetry breaking constraints. For matrix models, it is useful to add the constraints (1) the permutations that swap two adjacent rows or that swap two adjacent columns. An equivalent (but simpler) set of constraints was proposed in[6]: a lexicographic constraint is stated between all pairs of consecutive rows, and also between all pairs of consecutive columns. We denote this set of constraints by Lex^2. It is also shown in [6] that although Lex^2 breaks many symmetries. it does not break all of them. Equivalently, the set of constraints stated by Lex^2 is not equivalent to the set of all constraints (1). We will provide further evidence for this in section 5.

2.4   Symmetry Breaking Search

The second approach we will discuss in the paper was introduced in [9][5] and further refined in [14]. We will refer to it as SBDD in the rest of the paper. It is based on a modification of the search tree. The idea is to prune sub trees that contain no canonical solutions.

Let T be the tree explored during the search for solution. We assume that T does not contain any inconsistent node. Therefore, the leaves of T are either solutions or nodes that cannot be consistently extended. Let us suppose we use fixed variable ordering and value ordering. Without loss of generality, we can assume that the variables are selected in the order $V[1], V[2], \ldots, V[n]$, and that the values are selected in increasing order. A node A at depth d in T is then a d-vector such that

$$A[i] \in D[i], \text{ for all } i \in I^d$$

Note that this departs from the usual definitions where A is called the partial assignment corresponding to the node. Every child of node A is obtained by extending the vector A by one additional element a. We denote this child by $\epsilon(A, a)$. The additional element a is the value assigned to the variable $V[d+1]$ in that child node. Nodes of T are explored in increasing lexicographic order: node A is explored before node B if and only if $A <_{Lex} B$.

SBDD then prunes search at every node that is symmetrical to a previously explored node. More precisely, SBDD explores the tree $T - sym(T)$, where,

$$sym(T) = \{A \in T \mid \exists \ \sigma \in G, \ B \in T \text{ such that } B = \sigma(A) \text{ and } B <_{Lex} A\}$$

It is proven in[14] that $sym(T)$ contains none of the canonical solutions of T. This means that SBDD will explore all the canonical solutions of T. In practice, SBDD requires at each node A the search for a symmetry σ and a previous node B such that $\sigma(B) \subseteq A$. The number of previously explored nodes can be exponential. However, the search for symmetries can be limited to d previously explored nodes where d is the depth of node A. For each pair A and B, the search for σ amounts to solve a sub graph isomorphism problem, which is known to be NP-complete. Although SBDD requires the solution of several NP-complete problems at each node, good results have been obtained on mid size problems. New results using SBDD are given in section 5.

2.5   SBDS

Symmetry Breaking During Search (SBDS)[10][1] is another technique that is worth mentioning here. Given a n vector X, let $pre(X, d)$ be the prefix of length d of X. Given a node $A \in T^d$ and one of its child $\epsilon(A, a)$, obtained by extending A by a value a, SBDS state the following constraint after exploring the sub tree rooted at $\epsilon(A, a)$.

$$pre(\sigma(V), d) = A \ \rightarrow \ \sigma(V)[d+1] \neq a$$

2.6   Combining Methods

If the same variable and value ordering are used, then it is valid to apply several symmetry breaking methods at the same time. Indeed, none of these methods remove canonical solutions. Therefore, any combination will keep canonical solutions. For instance, one may state the Lex^2 constraints and use SBDD at the same time for matrix models. This observation is also valid for the method we are going to present in the next section: this method can be combined with previous methods.

3 The STAB Method

In this section we will reuse the notations of the previous one. We will see in the end how to relax the requirement for a fixed variable and value ordering.

As said before, it is not possible in practice to state all the possible symmetry breaking constraints when the size of the symmetry group is too large. A natural idea is then to state only some of the symmetry breaking constraints, hoping that enough symmetries will be broken to yield good speedups in practice. For instance, Lex^2 only states a number of constraints linear in the size of the problem. Another possibility is not to state all the constraints at the root node, but to state some of them at each node of the search tree. This is for instance the basis for SBDS.

We suggest to state symmetry breaking constraints (1) only for symmetries that leave the partial assignment A at the current node unchanged:

$$stab(A) \ = \ \{\sigma \in G \mid \sigma(A) = A\}$$

This set is called the *stabilizer* of A, and it is a subgroup of G. Moreover, its size divides the size of G. In practice the size of the stabilizers is often much smaller than the size of G. Our method, then, amounts to add the following set of constraints at each node A.

$$V \ \leq_{Lex} \ \sigma(V), \text{ for all } \sigma \ \in \ stab(A) \tag{2}$$

These constraints remove all the solutions that are not canonical with respect to $stab(A)$ in the sub tree rooted at A.

Let us look at an example to explain how STAB works in more detail. For instance let us consider a 4×5 matrix model. For simplicity we will refer to the matrix of variable by V, i.e. we identify the vector of variables with its matrix representation:

$$
\begin{array}{ccccc}
x_1 & x_2 & x_3 & x_4 & x_5 \\
x_6 & x_7 & x_8 & x_9 & x_{10} \\
x_{11} & x_{12} & x_{13} & x_{14} & x_{15} \\
x_{16} & x_{17} & x_{18} & x_{19} & x_{20}
\end{array}
$$

Let us consider the partial assignment A where the first 10 variables, are assigned values in the following way.

$$
\begin{array}{ccccc}
0 & 0 & 0 & 1 & 1 \\
0 & 1 & 1 & 0 & 0
\end{array}
$$

Every symmetry for A is defined by a row permutation $\psi \in S^4$ and a column permutation $\phi \in S^5$ such that $A = A(\psi, \phi)$. We will see later how to compute these symmetries. They are listed below.

$$
\begin{aligned}
\sigma_1 &= (\psi_1, \phi_1), \quad \psi_1 = [1,2,3,4], \; \phi_1 = [1,2,3,4,5] \\
\sigma_2 &= (\psi_1, \phi_2), \quad \psi_1 = [1,2,3,4], \; \phi_2 = [1,3,2,4,5] \\
\sigma_3 &= (\psi_1, \phi_3), \quad \psi_1 = [1,2,3,4], \; \phi_3 = [1,2,3,5,4] \\
\sigma_4 &= (\psi_1, \phi_4), \quad \psi_1 = [1,2,3,4], \; \phi_4 = [1,3,2,5,4] \\
\sigma_5 &= (\psi_2, \phi_5), \quad \psi_2 = [2,1,3,4], \; \phi_5 = [1,4,5,2,3] \\
\sigma_6 &= (\psi_2, \phi_6), \quad \psi_2 = [2,1,3,4], \; \phi_6 = [1,4,5,3,2] \\
\sigma_7 &= (\psi_2, \phi_7), \quad \psi_2 = [2,1,3,4], \; \phi_7 = [1,5,4,2,3] \\
\sigma_8 &= (\psi_2, \phi_8), \quad \psi_2 = [2,1,3,4], \; \phi_8 = [1,5,4,3,2] \\
\sigma_9 &= (\psi_3, \phi_1), \quad \psi_3 = [1,2,4,3], \; \phi_1 = [1,2,3,4,5] \\
\sigma_{10} &= (\psi_3, \phi_2), \quad \psi_3 = [1,2,4,3], \; \phi_2 = [1,3,2,4,5] \\
\sigma_{11} &= (\psi_3, \phi_3), \quad \psi_3 = [1,2,4,3], \; \phi_3 = [1,2,3,5,4] \\
\sigma_{12} &= (\psi_3, \phi_4), \quad \psi_3 = [1,2,4,3], \; \phi_4 = [1,3,2,5,4] \\
\sigma_{13} &= (\psi_4, \phi_5), \quad \psi_4 = [2,1,4,3], \; \phi_5 = [1,4,5,2,3] \\
\sigma_{14} &= (\psi_4, \phi_6), \quad \psi_4 = [2,1,4,3], \; \phi_6 = [1,4,5,3,2] \\
\sigma_{15} &= (\psi_4, \phi_7), \quad \psi_4 = [2,1,4,3], \; \phi_7 = [1,5,4,2,3] \\
\sigma_{16} &= (\psi_4, \phi_8), \quad \psi_4 = [2,1,4,3], \; \phi_8 = [1,5,4,3,2]
\end{aligned}
$$

Then, we can state constraints (2) for each of these symmetries, except for the identity permutation. For instance, let us state the constraint for σ_6. The matrix $W = V(\psi_2, \phi_7)$ is defined by

$$ W[\psi_2(i), \phi_6(j)] = V[i,j] $$

This yields the matrix

$$
\begin{array}{ccccc}
x_6 & x_9 & x_{10} & x_8 & x_7 \\
x_1 & x_4 & x_5 & x_3 & x_2 \\
x_{11} & x_{14} & x_{15} & x_{13} & x_{12} \\
x_{16} & x_{19} & x_{20} & x_{18} & x_{17}
\end{array}
$$

The symmetry breaking constraint is then

$$ [x_1, x_2, x_3, x_4, x_5, x_6, x_7, x_8, x_9, x_{10}, x_{11}, x_{12}, x_{13}, x_{14}, x_{15}, x_{16}, x_{17}, x_{18}, x_{19}, x_{20}] $$
$$ \leq_{Lex} $$
$$ [x_6, x_9, x_{10}, x_8, x_7, x_1, x_4, x_5, x_3, x_2, x_{11}, x_{14}, x_{15}, x_{13}, x_{12}, x_{16}, x_{19}, x_{20}, x_{18}, x_{17}] $$

As the first 10 variables are bound, the constraint is

$$ [0,0,0,1,1,0,1,1,0,0, x_{11}, x_{12}, x_{13}, x_{14}, x_{15}, x_{16}, x_{17}, x_{18}, x_{19}, x_{20}] $$
$$ \leq_{Lex} $$
$$ [0,0,0,1,1,0,1,1,0,0, x_{11}, x_{14}, x_{15}, x_{13}, x_{12}, x_{16}, x_{19}, x_{20}, x_{18}, x_{17}] $$

As the two 20-vector have the same 10-vector prefix, the constraint can be simplified into:

$$[x_{11}, x_{12}, x_{13}, x_{14}, x_{15}, x_{16}, x_{17}, x_{18}, x_{19}, x_{20}] \leq_{Lex}$$
$$[x_{11}, x_{14}, x_{15}, x_{13}, x_{12}, x_{16}, x_{19}, x_{20}, x_{18}, x_{17}]$$

The prefixes are identical because we considered a symmetry in $stab(A)$.

Let us go back to the general case. The simplification based on identical prefixes is valid in general. Given the n-vector V, let $tail(V,$n-d$)$ be the vector obtained by removing the first d elements of V. If A is a d-vector then constraints (2) can be simplified into

$$tail(V, n-d) \leq_{Lex} \sigma(tail(V, n-d)), \text{ for all } \sigma \in stab(A) \tag{3}$$

This explains one advantage of using stabilizers: the symmetry breaking constraints are simpler. An even greater advantage is that the number of constraints (3) is much smaller than the number of constraints (1). Several simplifications and further improvements are possible.

A simple observation can be used to reduce the number of constraints that have to be added, without breaking less symmetries. Let us consider a node A and one of its children B. If a symmetry belongs to both $stab(A)$ and $stab(B)$, then we should not state the same constraint twice, i.e. we must not add it again in the node B. It happens for instance when $stab(B) \subseteq stab(A)$.

Another optimization is based on the fact that we use the same ordering for stating symmetry breaking constraints and for generating solutions. Therefore, as long as no backtracking has ever occured, the current partial assignment is minimal, and there is no need to state the constraints (3).

If two vectors of variables are lexicographically ordered, so are any of their prefixes. In other words, the vectors in a lexicographic constraint can be shortened, which yields a looser, but correct, symmetry breaking constraint. A direct application in our context is to limit the length of vectors appearing in a symmetry breaking constraint to a numbed that depends on the problem at hand.

The stabilizer for the root node is the full symmetry group. Hence a naive use of the method amounts to state all the constraints (1), which is not possible in practice. In practice, we can state a subset of the symmetry group, for instance the Lex^2 constraints for matrix models.

It is worth noting that STAB does not require the search tree to be explored in the lexicographic order used for stating the constraints. In fact, the order in which the variables and the values are generated can be arbitrary. Indeed, the definition of constraints (3) does not refer to the order in which the nodes of the tree are generated. We can then add them at each node of the tree, regardless of the order in which variables and values are tried. A similar observation for SBDD was made in [5], section 2.2.

4   An Efficient Realization of STAB for 2D Matrix Models

The example above shows how STAB can be applied to matrix models. The constraints (3) can be added at each node, as shown in the above example. However, by tailoring the search to the 2D matrix nature of the problem, further improvements can be made to STAB.

4.1   Using a Row by Row Variable Ordering

We will use the STAB method with all the optimization discused in the previous section. In particular, we will limit the length of the symmetry breaking constraints to one row length. In our example, the constraint stated for σ_6 is shortened to:

$$[x_{11}, x_{12}, x_{13}, x_{14}, x_{15}] \leq_{Lex} [x_{11}, x_{14}, x_{15}, x_{13}, x_{12}]$$

More generally, assume that the first r rows of variables have been assigned a value in node A. Let V_A be the matrix composed of the first r rows of V. Any permutation of the last $k - r$ rows of V is in $stab(A)$, because these rows are all identical w.r.t A. Therefore, the elements of $stab(A)$ can be obtained by the composition of any permutation of the last $k - r$ rows with a matrix permutation of V_A. There are $(k - r)!$ permutations of the last $k - r$ rows, therefore $|stab(A)| = (k - r)!|stab(V_A)|$.

However, by limiting the size of constraints to one row length, the number of constraints is reduced to $(k - r)|stab(V_A)|$. Indeed, any two permutations of the last $k - r$ rows that map the $r + 1$-th row to the same row yield identical symmetry breaking constraints. These symmetry breaking constraint state that row $r + 1$ is the smallest possible row given the symmetry group $stab(V_A)$.

4.2   Coping with the Root Node

Let us look again at what happens at the root node. The method above amounts to state that the first row is the smallest row given the symmetry group obtained by all the column permutations. Let S^b be the set of all column permutations, and let V_i be the i-th row of V. Then at the root node, STAB states the constraints:

$$V_1 \leq_{Lex} \phi(V_i), \text{ for all } i \in I^v, \ \phi \in S^b \tag{4}$$

The first of these constraints states that $V_1 \leq_{Lex} \phi(V_1)$ for all column permutation ϕ. This is equivalent to sort V_1 in increasing order:

Lemma 1. *Given a b-vector of variables V, and the full permutation group S^b, then the two following conditions are equivalent:*

$$V \leq_{Lex} \phi(V), \text{ for all } \phi \in S^b$$
$$V[i] \leq V[i + 1], \text{ for all } i \in I^{b-1}$$

Proof: Swapping any two consecutive columns where the elements of V_1 aren't in increasing order result in a smaller V_1.

The other constraints state that V_1 is lexicographically smaller than $\phi(V_i)$, for all column permutation ϕ. By the previous lemma, the smallest possible $\phi(V_i)$ is the vector $sort(V_i)$ obtained by sorting V_i in increasing order. Therefore, constraints (4) are equivalent to

$$V_1 \leq_{Lex} sort(V_i), \text{ for all } i \in I^v, \tag{5}$$

This can be further simplified by observing that we can use multiset ordering as explained in [8]. Note that STAB states a stronger constraint at the root node as it also states that V_1 is sorted in increasing order. Note also that when all the variables are $0 - 1$ variables using a multiset ordering among rows amounts to sort the sums of the rows.

4.3 Aggregating Identical Column

For matrix models, the complexity of symmetry breaking constraints can be further simplified, using an idea presented in the combinatorics community[4], although the latter does not use constraint programming. When all the variables are $0 - 1$ variables, then we can replace identical adjacent columns by their sum. Indeed, these columns can be freely permuted.

Let us look at our example. The idea is to replace each group of adjacent columns in V that are identical in A by their sum. The variable matrix then becomes $\Sigma_A(V)$

$$\begin{vmatrix} x_1 & (x_2 + x_3) & (x_4 + x_5) \\ x_6 & (x_7 + x_8) & (x_9 + x_{10}) \\ x_{11} & (x_{12} + x_{13}) & (x_{14} + x_{15}) \\ x_{16} & (x_{19} + x_{20}) & (x_{18} + x_{17}) \end{vmatrix}$$

and A matrix becomes $\Sigma_A(A)$,

$$\begin{vmatrix} 0 & 0 & 2 \\ 0 & 2 & 0 \end{vmatrix}$$

Its symmetry group is then

$$\sigma_{17} = (\psi_5, \phi_9), \ \psi_5 = [1, 2], \ \phi_9 = [1, 2, 3]$$
$$\sigma_{18} = (\psi_6, \phi_{10}, \ \psi_6 = [2, 1], \ \phi_{10} = [1, 3, 2]$$

Then for each of the above permutations, we state that row 3 is less than permuted rows 3 or permuted row 4. This yields three symmetry breaking constraint in our example, instead of fifteen when columns aren't aggregated:

$$[x_{11}, x_{12} + x_{13}, x_{14} + x_{15}] \leq_{Lex} [x_{11}, x_{14} + x_{15}, x_{13} + x_{12}]$$
$$[x_{11}, x_{12} + x_{13}, x_{14} + x_{15}] \leq_{Lex} [x_{16}, x_{17} + x_{18}, x_{19} + x_{20}]$$
$$[x_{11}, x_{12} + x_{13}, x_{14} + x_{15}] \leq_{Lex} [x_{16}, x_{19} + x_{20}, x_{17} + x_{18}]$$

4.4 Computing Stabilizers

There exists algorithms in the computation group theory that efficiently compute stabilizers if the symmetry group is given as input. These algorithms could be used to implement STAB in such case. We chosed to compute directly the stabilizers from the partial assignments A because we think that providing the symmetry group as input may be too complex for users. The method is explained with more details in [15].

We construct a labelled graph $g(A)$ whose nodes are the rows and the columns of A. There exists an arc between row i and column j with label $A[i, j]$. Then the symmetry group of this graph is the same as the stabilizer of A. Computing this stabilizer amounts to compute all the automorphisms of the graph $g(A)$. We can use an auxiliary CSP to perform this task.

Given a graph with labelled edges, we construct a CSP as follows. There is one variable y_i per node i. The domain of the variables are the set of nodes. There are two constraints. First of all, the variables are all different. Second, there is a constraint stating that neighbors are mapped onto neighbors. The rest of this section describes the second constraint into detail.

If i is a node, and a a label, let $\Gamma^a(i)$ be the set of nodes j such that there exists an arc labeled a whose ends are i and j. If $dom(y_i)$ is the domain of y_i, let $\Gamma^a(y_i)$ be,

$$\Gamma^a(y_i) = \bigcup_{j \in dom(y_i)} \Gamma^a(j)$$

Then the neighbor constraint says that

$$y_j \in \Gamma^a(y_i) \text{ for all } j \in \Gamma^a(i)$$

The propagation of this constraint is straightforward. The sets $\Gamma^a(y_i)$ are maintained incrementally. Whenever they are reduced, the above condition is used to reduce the domains of the variables y_j for each j neighbor of i.

This method is quite efficient for computing graph automorphisms. In the experiments described in section 5, the number of failed nodes explored when solving the auxiliary CSP is less than the number of automorphisms found. The time spent in the search for automorphisms ranges from 20 to 80 percents of the total running time.

5   Experimental Results

The evaluation of symmetry breaking techniques can be done in two ways, either by applying it to some specific real world problem, or by selecting a class of highly symmetrical problems. We have chosen the latter because it enables a direct comparison between competing techniques. Two classes of combinatorial problems have been traditionally used for comparing symmetry breaking techniques in the CP community, the social golfer problem, and balanced incomplete block designs (BIBD). Both are real world problems. We have selected BIBDs for our evaluation because all published work use the same CP model[6][12][11]. On the contrary, models for the social golfer problem differ in publications such as [14][5][6], which makes comparisons difficult to carry on.

A BIBD is defined as an arrangement of v points into b blocks such that each block contains exactly k distinct points, each point occurs in exactly r different blocks, and every two distinct points occur together in exactly λ blocks. An other way of defining a BIBD is in term of its *incidence matrix*, which is a binary matrix with v rows, b columns, r ones per row, k ones per column, and scalar product λ between any pair of distinct rows. A BIBD is fully specified by its parameters (v, k, λ), the other parameters can be computed using

$$r = \frac{\lambda(v-1)}{(k-1)}, \ b = \frac{\lambda v(v-1)}{k(k-1)}$$

A BIBD can be represented as a CSP with a v by b matrix model. Each variable in the matrix is a binary variable $m[i, j]$ with domain $\{0, 1\}$. There are three sets of constraints:

1. $\Sigma_{j \in I^b} \, m[i, j] \ = \ r$, for all $i \in I^v$
2. $\Sigma_{i \in I^v} \, m[i, j] \ = \ k$, for all $j \in I^b$
3. $\Sigma_{j \in I^b} \, m[i, j] m[i', j] \ = \ \lambda$, for all $i \in I^v, i' \in I^v, i < i'$

Any permutation of the rows or of the columns is a symmetry of the problem. The size of the symmetry group G is therefore $v!b!$

We use a static variable ordering: variables are selected row by row, then column by column. Values ordering is also fixed: 1 is tried first, then we try 0. This generates possible design in a decreasing lexicographic ordering. All the symmetry breaking techniques described above can be applied, provided we revert the lexicographic ordering.

As a first evaluation we compare STAB with the techniques $Lex^2[6]$, symmetry based heuristics[12], SBDS[11], and SBDD. To ensure a fair comparison, we have implemented the three methods Lex^2, SBDD and STAB with the same CP system (ILOG Solver) and the same implementation for lexicographic constraints[1]. Both STAB and SBDD methods are used in conjunction with Lex^2. We report running times to find the first solution in Table 1. We also give for each column, the CP technology used, the CPU type and speed in MHz in order to ease comparison. Note in particular that [12] used a much slower machine. We also report the running time ratios for our implementations in the last two columns. Means are computed with geometric means, which is much more reliable when averaging ratios. These results show that STAB is as efficient as our implementation of Lex^2. On the contrary, $SBDD$ is much slower.

We report the times for computing all solutions in Table 2. The running times are measured on a Pentium III 833 MHz laptop running Windows 2000 for the easy problems, and on a 1.4GHz Pentium mobile laptop for the problems after $(31, 6, 1)$. The problems are sorted by the time used by STAB. For each method, we report the running time and the number of solutions found. A "-" indicates that the running times were in excess of 10000 seconds. We also report information for the simultaneous use of STAB and SBDD (label "S+S"). That combination computes the same solutions as SBDD alone: the canonical solutions.

---

[1] Our implementation uses an algorithm different from the ones described in [7] and [2], but these algorithms could be used as well.

Table 1. Results when computing one solution.

| Problem | STAB | SBDD | LEX2 | LEX2[6] | [12] | $\frac{Lex^2}{STAB}$ | $\frac{SBDD}{STAB}$ |
| | Solver 5 | Solver 5 | Solver 5 | Solver 5 | | | |
$v\ k\ \lambda$	PIII 833	PIII 833	PIII 833	PIII 750	Ultra sparc 360		
8 4 6	0.03	1.5	0.07			2.3	50
7 3 10	0.04	0.04	0.03	11.4	2.4	0.8	1.0
6 3 10	0.04	1	0.04	1.7	0.8	1.0	25
6 3 12	0.08	2.2	0.05	4.6	1.5	0.6	28
12 6 5	0.08	37	0.14			1.8	463
13 4 2	0.09	0.04	0.03			0.3	0.4
9 3 9	0.1	3.3	0.09	8.4	14	0.9	33
9 3 10	0.12	4.7	0.1	8	14	0.8	39
11 5 4	0.13	18	0.15			1.2	138
16 6 3	0.13	25	0.12			0.9	192
16 4 1	0.14	1.9	0.05			0.4	14
10 3 6	0.15	11.8	0.13	111	5.3	0.9	79
19 9 4	0.22	78	1.7			7.7	355
12 3 4	0.23	33	1.1	249	5.1	4.8	143
10 3 8	0.25	30	0.24	1316	13	1.0	120
13 3 4	0.26	23	0.27	397	8.7	1.0	88
16 6 2	0.28	0.23	0.04			0.1	0.82
15 3 1	0.28	0.06	0.06		0.42	0.2	0.21
15 3 2	0.37	0.13	0.12	6.2	5.5	0.3	0.35
15 5 2	0.71	9.8	18.8			26.5	14
25 9 3	0.78	109	10			12.8	140
25 5 1	1.1	157	0.23			0.2	143
21 5 1	1.5	0.06	0.07			0.05	0.04
22 7 2	8.9	9.6	37			4.2	1.1
Mean						0.99	16

Table 2 shows that we are able to compute all solutions of the problems that have up to 1.10^{91} symmetries in a reasonable amount of time. This table also shows that SBDD is almost always slower than Lex^2, except for $(15, 3, 1)$ and $(21, 6, 2)$. However, SBDD eliminates all non canonical solutions, which is expensive. For instance, it computes only 80 solutions for $(15, 3, 1)$ instead of more than 32 millions found by Lex^2 on the same problem! The table further shows that STAB is about 15 times faster than Lex^2 (geometric mean) and even faster than SBDD. It also shows that combining STAB with SBDD improves SBDD by about 21 percents on average.

In [14], it was shown that running time of SBDD could be greatly improved if the symmetry checks were only performed on nodes close to the root of the tree. Similarly, we ran STAB with a threshold: stabilizer constraints were only added at nodes with a depth smaller than 70 percents of the maximal depth. We report results using this new method (label "PART") in Table 3 along the results for Lex^2 and $STAB$. We computed results for the BIBDs were STAB takes between 0.1 and 30 seconds, plus few others.

Table 2. Results when computing all solutions.

BIBD $v\ k\ \lambda$	num sym	Lex^2 soln	Lex^2 time	STAB soln	STAB time	$\frac{Lex^2}{STAB}$ time	SBDD soln	SBDD time	S+S time	$\frac{SBDD}{S+S}$ time
6 3 2	2.6e+9	1	0	1	0		1	0.01	0.01	1.0
7 3 1	2.6e+7	1	0	1	0.01	0.0	1	0	0	1.0
6 3 4	1.8e+21	21	0.02	4	0.01	2.0	4	0.32	0.25	1.3
9 3 1	1.7e+14	2	0.01	1	0.02	0.5	1	0.01	0.01	1.0
7 3 2	4.4e+14	12	0.01	7	0.02	0.5	4	0.1	0.1	1.0
8 4 3	3.5e+15	92	0.04	6	0.03	1.3	4	0.54	0.33	1.6
6 3 6	1.9e+35	134	0.13	7	0.04	3.3	6	2.2	1.7	1.3
11 5 2	1.6e+15	2	0.01	1	0.05	0.2	1	0.06	0.07	0.9
10 4 2	4.7e+18	38	0.05	4	0.05	1.0	3	0.83	0.36	2.3
7 3 3	2.6e+23	220	0.07	24	0.05	1.4	10	1.5	1.25	1.2
13 4 1	3.9e+19	2	0.03	1	0.07	0.4	1	0.03	0.07	0.4
6 3 8	5.9e+50	494	0.69	15	0.1	6.9	13	11.4	9.4	1.2
9 4 3	2.3e+21	2600	2.4	41	0.11	21.8	11	13.6	11.8	1.2
16 4 1	5.1e+31	12	0.21	1	0.14	1.5	1	2	2	1.0
7 3 4	1.5e+33	3209	1.17	116	0.17	6.9	35	19.4	16.5	1.2
6 3 10	2.2e+67	1366	2.7	26	0.24	11.3	19	45.1	38.4	1.2
9 3 2	2.2e+29	5987	1.4	344	0.5	2.8	36	28	20.5	1.4
16 6 2	4.3e+26	46	0.55	3	0.51	1.1	3	3	2.7	1.1
15 5 2	6.6e+31	0	17.8	0	0.67	26.6	0	9.8	7.9	1.2
13 3 1	2.5e+36	12800	13.6	21	0.68	20.0	2	11.3	6.6	1.7
7 3 5	5.2e+43	33304	15.1	542	0.76	19.9	109	155	142	1.1
15 7 3	1.7e+24	118	0.98	19	1	1.0	5	12.9	8.7	1.5
21 5 1	2.6e+39	12	0.52	1	1.7	0.3	1	0.47	1.9	0.2
25 5 1	4.1e+57	864	78	1	1.9	41.1	1	156	75	2.1
10 5 4	2.3e+22	8031	24.9	302	1.9	13.1	21	131	104	1.3
7 3 6	7.0e+54	250878	136	2334	3.3	41.2	418	1258	1176	1.1
22 7 2	1.2e+42	0	35	0	8.3	4.2	0	9.5	10.2	0.9
7 3 7	3.1e+66	1459585	966	8821	13.9	69.5	1508	8062	7632	1.1
8 4 6	1.2e+34	2058523	1282	17890	17	75.4	2310	11028	10046	1.1
19 9 4	1.4e+34	6520	1511	71	23	65.7	6	6411	5428	1.2
10 3 2	9.6e+38	724662	178	24563	25.6	7.0	960	2915	1845	1.6
31 6 1	6.7e+67	864	56	1	19.4	2.9	1	477	470	1.0
7 3 8	3.6e+78	6941124	2664	32038	25	106.6	5413	-	21302	
9 3 3	1.3e+47	14843772	1871	315531	76	24.6	22521	-	34077	
7 3 9	1.0e+91	38079394	13059	105955	98	133.3	-	-	-	
15 3 1	1.3e+52	32127296	13522	6782	128	105.6	80	4312	2522	1.7
21 6 2	1.6e+49	0	26654	0	337	79.1	0	-	9235	
13 4 2	2.5e+36	3664242	15139	83337	400	37.8	2461	-	18496	
11 5 4	4.5e+28	6142308	15734	106522	473	33.3	4393	-	83307	
12 6 5	5.4e+29		-	228146	3196		-		-	
25 9 3	2.4e+50		-	17016	9274		-		-	
16 6 3	1.3e+37		-	769482	14745		-		-	
Mean						14.6				1.21

Table 3. Partial symmetry breaking.

BIBD $v\ k\ \lambda$	Lex^2 soln	time	$STAB$ soln	time	PART soln	time	$\frac{Lex^2}{PART}$ time	$\frac{STAB}{PART}$ time
6 3 8	494	0.69	15	0.1	15	0.11	6.3	0.9
9 4 3	2600	2.4	41	0.11	45	0.1	24.0	1.1
16 4 1	12	0.21	1	0.14	1	0.12	1.8	1.2
7 3 4	3209	1.17	116	0.17	147	0.18	6.5	0.9
6 3 10	1366	2.7	26	0.24	26	0.24	11.3	1.0
9 3 2	5987	1.4	344	0.5	457	0.38	3.7	1.3
16 6 2	46	0.55	3	0.51	3	0.48	1.1	1.1
15 5 2	0	17.8	0	0.67	0	0.67	26.6	1.0
13 3 1	12800	13.6	21	0.68	24	0.33	41.2	2.1
7 3 5	33304	15.1	542	0.76	714	0.72	21.0	1.1
15 7 3	118	0.98	19	1	19	0.61	1.6	1.6
21 5 1	12	0.52	1	1.7	1	1.05	0.5	1.6
25 5 1	864	78	1	1.9	1	1.68	46.4	1.1
10 5 4	8031	24.9	302	1.9	302	1.5	16.6	1.3
7 3 6	250878	136	2334	3.3	3165	3.5	38.9	0.9
22 7 2	0	35	0	8.3	0	8.3	4.2	1.0
7 3 7	1459585	966	8821	13.9	11884	15.3	63.1	0.9
8 4 6	2058523	1282	17890	17	23252	18	71.2	0.9
19 9 4	6520	1511	71	23	71	23	65.7	1.0
10 3 2	724662	178	24563	25.6	28172	18	9.9	1.4
7 3 8	6941124	6569	32038	57	42888	65	101.1	0.9
9 3 3	14843772	4744	315531	182	418176	192	24.7	0.9
15 3 1	32127296	51784	6782	358	7154	157	329.8	2.3
Mean							14.4	1.17

The table 3 shows that STAB can be improved by about 17 percents using partial symmetry breaking. The resulting method is about 15 times faster than Lex^2 on these examples.

6   Conclusion

We presented a new method for symmetry breaking that adds constraints during search. These constraints break the symmetries that leave the current partial assignment unchanged. An efficient realization of this technique was presented for matrix models where variable symmetries are defined by rows and columns permutation. The new technique was related from a theoretical point of view to other techniques such as Lex^2 and SBDD. This theoretical analysis have shown how to safely combine these methods. Several improvements and optimizations for STAB were also discussed. A comprehensive test of experiments using BIBD problems have shown that our new technique is more than one order of magnitude faster than other methods. Moreover, STAB seemed much more scalable than any previous method, as it enabled to solve problems that are hopeless for other methods.

These results are encouraging and we plan to make a more general purpose implementation of STAB. More specifically we want to study its extension to symmetries involving value permutations. We also want to apply STAB to general CSPs, instead of only matrix models.

Acknowledgments

The author wants to thank anonymous referees for their constructive comments on previous versions of this paper, as well as Marie Puget for her thorough proof reading.

References

1. Backofen, R., Will, S.: Excluding Symmetries in Constraint Based Search. Proceedings of CP'99 (1999).
2. Carlsson, M., Beldiceanu, N. Revisiting the Lexicographic Ordering Constraint SICS Technical report T2002:17
3. Crawford, J., Ginsberg, M., Luks E.M., Roy, A. Symmetry Breaking Predicates for Search Problems. In proceedings of KR'96, 148-159.
4. Denny, P.C. Search and Enumeration Techniques for Incidence Structures. Tech report University of Auckland, (1998).
5. Fahle, T., Shamberger, S., Sellmann, M. Symmetry Breaking. Proceedings of CP01 (2001) 93-107.
6. P. Flener, A. M. Frisch, B. Hnich, Z. Kiziltan, I. Miguel, J. Pearson, T. Walsh. Breaking Row and Column Symmetries in Matrix Models. Proceedings of CP'02, pages 462-476, 2002
7. A. M. Frisch, B. Hnich, Z. Kiziltan, I. Miguel, T. Walsh Global Constraints for Lexicographic Orderings. In proceedings of CP'02, pp 93-108.
8. A. M. Frisch, C. Jefferson, I. Miguel. Constraints for Breaking More Row and Column Symmetries. Proceedings of CP'03.
9. Focacci, F., Milano, M.: Global Cut Framework for Removing Symmetries. Proceedings of CP'01 (2001) 75-92.
10. Gent, I.P., and Smith, B.M.: Symmetry Breaking During Search in Constraint Programming. Proceedings ECAI'2000, pp. 599-603
11. Gent, I.P., Harvey, W., and Kelsey, T.: Groups and Constraints: Symmetry Breaking during Search. Proceedings of CP'02, 415-430.
12. Meseguer, P., Torras, C.: Exploiting Symmetries Within Constraint Satisfaction Search. Art.Intell. **129** (1999) 133–163.
13. Puget, J.-F.: On the Satisfiability of Symmetrical Constraint Satisfaction Problems. Proceedings of ISMIS'93 (1993), 350–361.
14. Puget, J.-F.: Symmetry Breaking Revisited. Proceedings of CP'02, 446-461.
15. Puget, J.-F.: Using Constraint Programming to Compute Symmetries. Submitted.

An Efficient Bounds Consistency Algorithm for the Global Cardinality Constraint

Claude-Guy Quimper, Peter van Beek, Alejandro López-Ortiz,
Alexander Golynski, and Sayyed Bashir Sadjad

School of Computer Science
University of Waterloo
Waterloo, Canada

Abstract. Previous studies have demonstrated that designing special purpose constraint propagators can significantly improve the efficiency of a constraint programming approach. In this paper we present an efficient algorithm for bounds consistency propagation of the generalized cardinality constraint (*gcc*). Using a variety of benchmark and random problems, we show that on some problems our bounds consistency algorithm can dramatically outperform existing state-of-the-art commercial implementations of constraint propagators for the *gcc*. We also present a new algorithm for domain consistency propagation of the *gcc* which improves on the worst-case performance of the best previous algorithm for problems that occur often in applications.

1 Introduction

Many interesting problems can be modeled and solved using constraint programming. In this approach one models a problem by stating constraints on acceptable solutions, where a constraint is simply a relation among several unknowns or variables, each taking a value in a given domain. The problem is then usually solved by interleaving a backtracking search with a series of constraint propagation phases. In the constraint propagation phase, the constraints are used to prune the domains of the variables by ensuring that the values in their domains are locally consistent with the constraints.

Previous studies have demonstrated that designing special purpose constraint propagators for commonly occurring constraints can significantly improve the efficiency of a constraint programming approach (e.g., [9, 13]). In this paper we study constraint propagators for the global cardinality constraint (*gcc*). A *gcc* over a set of variables and values states that the number of variables instantiating to a value must be between a given upper and lower bound, where the bounds can be different for each value. This type of constraint commonly occurs in rostering, timetabling, sequencing, and scheduling applications (e.g., [1, 4, 11, 15]).

Two constraint propagation techniques for the *gcc* have been developed. Régin [10] gives an $O(n^2d)$ algorithm for domain consistency of the *gcc* (where n is the number of variables and d is the number of values) that is based on relating the *gcc* to flow theory. As well, a *gcc* can be rewritten as a collection of "atleast"

F. Rossi (Ed.): CP 2003, LNCS 2833, pp. 600–614, 2003.
© Springer-Verlag Berlin Heidelberg 2003

and "atmost" constraints, one for each value, and constraint propagation can be performed on the individual constraints [16]. However, on some problems the first technique suffers from its cubic run-time and the second technique suffers from its lack of pruning power. An alternative which has not yet been explored with the *gcc* is bounds consistency propagation, a weaker form of consistency than domain consistency. Bounds consistency propagation has already proven useful for the *alldifferent* constraint [7, 12], a specialization of the *gcc*.

In this paper we present an efficient algorithm for bounds consistency propagation of the *gcc*. The algorithm runs in time $O(t + n)$, where t is the time to sort the bounds of the domains of the variables and n is the number of variables. Using a variety of benchmark and random problems, we show that on some problems our bounds consistency algorithm can dramatically outperform existing state-of-the-art commercial implementations of constraint propagators for the *gcc*. We also present a new algorithm for domain consistency propagation of the *gcc* which improves on the worst-case performance of Régin's algorithm for problems that occur often in applications.

2   Background

A *constraint satisfaction problem* (CSP) consists of a set of n *variables*, $X = \{x_1, \ldots, x_n\}$; a set of d *values*, $D = \{v_1, \ldots, v_d\}$, where each variable $x_i \in X$ has an associated finite domain $dom(x_i) \subseteq D$ of possible values; and a collection of m *constraints*, $\{C_1, \ldots, C_m\}$. Each constraint C_i is a constraint over some set of variables, denoted by $vars(C_i)$. Given a constraint C, the notation $t \in C$ denotes a tuple t—an assignment of a value to each of the variables in $vars(C)$— that satisfies the constraint C. The notation $t[x]$ denotes the value assigned to variable x by the tuple t. A *solution* to a CSP is an assignment of a value to each variable that satisfies all of the constraints.

We assume in this paper that the domains are totally ordered. The minimum and maximum values in the domain $dom(x)$ of a variable x are denoted by $\min(dom(x))$ and $\max(dom(x))$, and the interval notation $[a, b]$ is used as a shorthand for the set of values $\{a, a+1, \ldots, b\}$.

CSPs are usually solved by interleaving a backtracking search with constraint propagation. The constraint propagation phase ensures that the values in the domains of the unassigned variables are "locally consistent" with the constraints.

Support Given a constraint C, a value $a \in dom(x)$ for a variable $x \in vars(C)$ is said to have: (i) a *domain support* in C if there exists a $t \in C$ such that $a = t[x]$ and $t[y] \in dom(y)$, for every $y \in vars(C)$; (ii) an *interval support* in C if there exists a $t \in C$ such that $a = t[x]$ and $t[y] \in [\min(dom(y)), \max(dom(y))]$, for every $y \in vars(C)$.

Local Consistency A constraint C is said to be: (i) *bounds consistent* if for each $x \in vars(C)$, each of the values $\min(dom(x))$ and $\max(dom(x))$ has an interval support in C; (ii) *domain consistent* if for each $x \in vars(C)$, each value $a \in dom(x)$ has a domain support in C.

A CSP can be made locally consistent by repeatedly removing unsupported values from the domains of its variables.

A *global cardinality constraint* (gcc) is a constraint which consists of a set of variables $X = \{x_1, \ldots, x_n\}$, a set of values $D = \{v_1, \ldots, v_d\}$, and for each $v \in D$ a pair $[l_v, u_v]$. A gcc is satisfied iff the number of times that a value $v \in D$ is assigned to the variables in X is at least l_v and at most u_v.

Example 1. Consider the CSP with six variables $x_1, \ldots, x_6$ with domains, $x_1 \in [2, 2]$, $x_2 \in [1, 2]$, $x_3 \in [2, 3]$, $x_4 \in [2, 3]$, $x_5 \in [1, 4]$, and $x_6 \in [3, 4]$ and a single global cardinality constraint $gcc(x_1, \ldots, x_6)$ with bounds on the occurrences of values, $l_1, l_2, l_3 = 1, l_4 = 2$ and $u_v = 3$, for all $v \in \{1, 2, 3, 4\}$. Enforcing bounds consistency on the constraint reduces the domains of the variables as follows: $x_1 \in [2, 2]$, $x_2 \in [1, 1]$, $x_3 \in [2, 3]$, $x_4 \in [2, 3]$, $x_5 \in [4, 4]$, and $x_6 \in [4, 4]$.

3 Local Consistency of the *gcc*

A *gcc* can be decomposed into two constraints: A *lower bound constraint* (lbc) which ensures that all values $v \in D$ are assigned to at least l_v variables, and an *upper bound constraint* (ubc) which ensures that all values $v \in D$ are assigned to at most u_v variables. We will show how to make both constraints locally (bounds or domain) consistent and prove that this is sufficient to make a *gcc* locally consistent.

3.1 The Upper Bound Constraint (*ubc*)

The *ubc* is a generalization of the well studied *alldifferent* constraint (in the *alldifferent* constraint $u_v = 1$, for each value v). Some previous algorithms for bounds consistency of the *alldifferent* constraint have been based on the concept of Hall intervals [3, 7, 8]. A Hall interval is an interval $H \subseteq D$ such that there are $|H|$ variables whose domains are contained in H. The definition of a Hall interval can be generalized to sets by using the notion of maximal capacity. Let $C(S)$, $S \subseteq D$, be the number of variables whose domains are contained in S. The maximal capacity $\lceil S \rceil$ of a set S is the maximum number of variables that can be assigned to the values in S; i.e., $\lceil S \rceil = \sum_{v \in S} u_v$.

Hall set A Hall set is a set $H \subseteq D$ such that there are $\lceil H \rceil$ variables whose domains are contained in H; i.e., H is a Hall set iff $C(H) = \lceil H \rceil$.

The values in a Hall set are fully consumed by the variables that form the Hall set and unavailable for all other variables. Clearly, a *ubc* is unsatisfiable if there is a set S such that $C(S) > \lceil S \rceil$. We show that the absence of such a set is a sufficient and necessary condition for a *ubc* to be satisfiable.

Lemma 1. *A ubc is satisfiable if and only if for any set $S \subseteq D$, $C(S) \leq \lceil S \rceil$.*

Proof. We reduce a *ubc* to an *alldifferent* constraint. We first duplicate u_v times each value v in the domain of a variable, using different labels to represent the same value. For example, the domain $\{1, 2\}$ with $u_1 = 3$ and $u_2 = 2$ is represented by $\{1a, 1b, 1c, 2a, 2b\}$. Clearly, this *alldifferent* constraint is satisfiable iff the *ubc* is satisfiable. In a *ubc*, the maximal capacity of a set S is given by $\lceil S \rceil$; in an *alldifferent* constraint, it is given by the cardinality $|S|$ of the set. Hall [3] proved that an *alldifferent* constraint is satisfiable iff for any set S, $C(S) \leq |S|$. Thus, the result holds also for a *ubc*. □

3.2 The Lower Bound Constraint (*lbc*)

Next we define some concepts that will be useful for constructing a propagator for the *lbc*. Let $I(S)$ be the number of variables whose domains intersect the set S. The minimal capacity $\lfloor S \rfloor$ of a set S is the minimum number of variables that must be assigned to the values in S; i.e., $\lfloor S \rfloor = \sum_{v \in S} l_i$.

Failure set A failure set is a set $F \subseteq D$ such that there are fewer variables whose domains intersect F than its minimal capacity; i.e., F is a failure set if $I(F) < \lfloor F \rfloor$.

Unstable set An unstable set is a set $U \subseteq D$ such that there are the same number of variables whose domains intersect U as its minimal capacity; i.e., U is an unstable set if $I(U) = \lfloor U \rfloor$.

Stable set A stable set is a set $S \subseteq D$ such that there are more variables whose domains are contained in S than its minimal capacity, and S does not intersect any failure or unstable sets; i.e., S is a stable set if $C(S) > \lfloor S \rfloor$, $S \cap U = \emptyset$ and $S \cap F = \emptyset$ for all unstable sets U and failure sets F.

These three sets are the main tools to understand how to make an *lbc* locally consistent. Failure sets determine if an *lbc* is satisfiable, unstable sets indicate where the domains have to be pruned, and stable sets indicate which domains do not have to be pruned because all of their values have supports.

Lemma 2. *An lbc is satisfiable if and only if it does not have a failure set.*

Proof. To satisfy an *lbc*, we must associate at least l_v different variables to each value $v \in D$ such that every variable is assigned a single value from its domain. For each value $v \in D$, we construct l_v identical sets T_v^i for $i = 1, \ldots, l_v$ that contain the indices of the variables that have v in their domain; i.e., $T_v^i = \{j \mid x_j \in X \land v \in dom(x_j)\}$. Let $\mathcal{T}$ be the set of all sets T_v^i. To satisfy the *lbc*, we must select one variable index from each set T_v^i such that all selected indices are different. The variables that are not selected can be instantiated to any arbitrary value in their domain. This problem is known as the complete set of distinct representatives problem and has been studied by Hall [3]. His main result states that for any family of sets, a complete set of distinct representatives exists if and only if the union of any k sets contains at least k elements. Formally the problem is solvable if and only if $|\bigcup_{t \in T} t| \geq |T|$ holds for any $T \subseteq \mathcal{T}$. Applying this theorem here, we have that an *lbc* is satisfiable if and only if for any set $S \subseteq D$ we have $I(S) \geq \lfloor S \rfloor$. Hence, the absence of a failure set is a necessary and sufficient condition for an *lbc* to be satisfiable. □

Lemma 3 shows that a value in a domain that intersects an unstable set has an interval/domain support only if the value also is in the unstable set.

Lemma 3. *A variable whose domain intersects an unstable set cannot be instantiated to a value outside of this set.*

Proof. Let U be an unstable set and x a variable whose domain intersects U. If x is instantiated to a value that does not belong to U then U becomes a failure set and the *lbc* is no longer satisfiable by Lemma 2. □

Lemma 4. *A variable whose domain is contained in a stable set can be instantiated to any value in its domain.*

Proof. By definition, a stable set S does not intersect any unstable or failure set. Thus, for any subset s of S, $I(s) > \lfloor s \rfloor$. If a variable whose domain is contained in S is assigned a value, the function $I(s)$ will decrease by at most one and therefore s will either stay a stable set or become an unstable set. In both cases, no failure set is created and the *lbc* is still satisfiable. □

A satisfiable *lbc* has several interesting properties: (i) the union of two unstable sets gives an unstable set, (ii) the union of two stable sets gives a stable set, and (iii) since stable and unstable sets are disjoint, there exists a stable set S and an unstable set U that forms a bipartition of D. The bipartition property implies that there are two types of variables: those whose domains are fully contained in a stable set and those whose domains intersect an unstable set.

3.3   An Iterative Algorithm for Local Consistency of the *gcc*

Suppose we have an algorithm $\mathcal{A}$ that makes a *ubc* locally consistent and suppose that we have an algorithm $\mathcal{B}$ that makes an *lbc* locally consistent. To make a *gcc* locally consistent we can decompose it, run $\mathcal{A}$ to prune the domains of the variables, and then run $\mathcal{B}$ to further prune the domains. Since the domains can potentially be pruned each time either algorithm is run, we alternatively run each algorithm until no more modifications occur. In principle, we might need to repeat this process a large number of times. Surprisingly, we prove that only one iteration is sufficient.

The outline of the proof is as follows. We first prove that if a *ubc* is satisfiable after running $\mathcal{A}$, the *ubc* is still satisfiable after running $\mathcal{B}$. We then prove that the *ubc* is still locally consistent after running $\mathcal{B}$.

Theorem 1. *If $\mathcal{B}$ is run after $\mathcal{A}$, $\mathcal{B}$ never creates a set s such that there are more variables whose domains are contained in s than its maximal capacity $\lceil s \rceil$.*

Proof. Suppose that algorithms $\mathcal{A}$ and $\mathcal{B}$ do not return a failure. Then there are no failure sets and there is an unstable set U and a stable set S that form a bipartition of D. Algorithm $\mathcal{B}$ does not modify the domains of the variables that belong to a stable set. Therefore we know that for all $s \subseteq S$ we have $C(s) \le \lceil s \rceil$ since the *ubc* is satisfiable according to $\mathcal{A}$.

We will show that for any set $E \subseteq U \cup S$ we have $C(E) \leq \lceil E \rceil$ and therefore the *ubc* is still satisfiable after running $\mathcal{B}$. Assume, by way of contradiction, there is a set E that exceeds its capacity; i.e., $C(E) > \lceil E \rceil$. We divide this set into two subsets: let $L = U \cap E$ be the unstable values in E and $F = S \cap E$ be the stable values in E. We also define $R = U - E$ as the unstable values that do not belong to E. We know that $\lceil F \rceil \geq C(F)$ since F is a subset of a stable set and we showed that the property holds for any such a set. We also know that R is not a failure set and U is an unstable set. Therefore we have $I(R) \geq \lfloor R \rfloor$ and $\lfloor L \rfloor + \lfloor R \rfloor = I(L \cup R)$.

$$\lceil F \rceil + \lfloor L \rfloor + \lfloor R \rfloor \leq \lceil F \rceil + \lceil L \rceil + \lfloor R \rfloor$$
$$\lceil F \rceil + I(L \cup R) < C(E) + \lfloor R \rfloor$$
$$\lceil F \rceil + I(L \cup R) < |\{x \in X \mid dom(x) \subseteq E \wedge dom(x) \nsubseteq F\}| + C(F) + \lfloor R \rfloor$$
$$\lceil F \rceil + I(L \cup R) < |\{x \in X \mid dom(x) \cap L \neq \emptyset \wedge dom(x) \cap R = \emptyset\}| + C(F) + \lfloor R \rfloor$$
$$\lceil F \rceil + I(R) < C(F) + \lfloor R \rfloor$$
$$\lceil F \rceil < C(F)$$

The last inequality is incompatible with the hypothesis hence the contradiction hypothesis cannot be true. Notice that the proof holds for both bounds and domain consistency. □

Theorem 2. *If $\mathcal{B}$ is run after $\mathcal{A}$, the* ubc *is still locally consistent after $\mathcal{B}$ is run.*

Proof. Suppose that $\mathcal{A}$ and $\mathcal{B}$ make the constraints locally consistent and neither returns a failure. To prove that the *ubc* is still locally consistent, we have to show that all variables are still consistent with all Hall sets. By a variable being consistent with a Hall set H we mean the following: for bounds consistency, the domain of the variable must have either both or neither bounds in H; and for domain consistency, the domain of the variable must be either fully included in or completely disjoint from H.

Since $\mathcal{B}$ did not return a failure, there is an unstable set U and a stable set S that form a bipartition of D. Let $H \subseteq D$ be a Hall set. We divide this Hall set into two subsets: $F = H \cap S$ contains the values of H that belong to a stable set and $L = H \cap U$ contains the values of H that belong to an unstable set. We also define $R = U - L$ as the unstable values that do not belong to H. Using these three sets, we will prove that all variables are consistent with H.

The unstable set U can be expressed as the union of L and R and therefore we have $\lfloor L \rfloor + \lfloor R \rfloor = I(L \cup R)$. Similarly, H is the union of F and L and implies $\lceil F \rceil + \lceil L \rceil = C(H) = |\{x \in X \mid dom(x) \subseteq H \wedge dom(x) \nsubseteq F\}| + C(F)$. Therefore,

$$\lceil F \rceil + \lfloor L \rfloor + \lfloor R \rfloor \leq \lceil F \rceil + \lceil L \rceil + \lfloor R \rfloor$$
$$\lceil F \rceil + I(L \cup R) \leq |\{x \in X \mid dom(x) \subseteq H \wedge dom(x) \nsubseteq F\}| + C(F) + \lfloor R \rfloor$$
$$\lceil F \rceil + I(L \cup R) \leq |\{x \in X \mid dom(x) \cap L \neq \emptyset \wedge dom(x) \cap R = \emptyset\}| + C(F) + \lfloor R \rfloor$$
$$\lceil F \rceil + I(R) \leq C(F) + \lfloor R \rfloor$$

By Theorem 1 we obtain $C(F) \leq \lceil F \rceil$ and since R is not a failure set, we have $I(R) \geq \lfloor R \rfloor$. Using these two inequalities, we find that R is an unstable set i.e. $I(R) = \lfloor R \rfloor$ and F is a Hall set i.e. $C(F) = \lceil F \rceil$. Using this observation, we now show that all variables whose domains are contained in S are consistent with H. The Hall set F is a subset of S and since algorithm $\mathcal{B}$ does not modify any variables whose domains are contained in S, algorithm $\mathcal{A}$ already identified F as a Hall set and made all variables consistent with it. Since the variables whose domains are contained in S were not modified by $\mathcal{B}$ they are still consistent with F. A variable whose domain intersects an unstable set like U and R must have both bounds in this set. Since $U = L \cup R$, a variable whose domain intersects U must have both bounds in either L or R and therefore be consistent with the Hall set H. Similarly, one can show the result also holds for domain consistency.

We have shown that any variable whose domain is either contained in S or intersects U is consistent with H. Thus all variables are consistent with any Hall set and the ubc is still locally consistent after running $\mathcal{B}$. □

Finally, we show that making the ubc and the lbc locally consistent is equivalent to making the gcc locally consistent.

Theorem 3. *A value $v \in dom(x)$ has a support in a gcc if and only if it has supports in the corresponding lbc and ubc.*

Proof. Clearly, if there is a tuple t that satisfies the gcc such that $t[x] = v$, this tuple also satisfies the lbc and the ubc. To prove the converse, we consider a value $v \in dom(x)$ that has a support in the lbc and a (possibly different) support in the ubc. We construct a tuple t such that $t[x] = v$ that satisfies the gcc and therefore prove that $v \in dom(x)$ also has a support in the gcc. We first instantiate the variable x to v. The lbc and ubc are still satisfiable since the value has a support in both constraints. We now show how to instantiate the other variables.

If there is an uninstantiated variable x whose domain does not intersect any unstable set and is not contained in any Hall set, then the domain of x is necessarily contained in a stable set. By Lemma 4 we can instantiate x to any value in its domain and keep the lbc satisfiable. We therefore choose a solution of the ubc and instantiate x to the same value as it is instantiated in the solution. This operation can create new unstable sets or new Hall sets but keeps both the lbc and the ubc satisfiable. For all variables that intersect an unstable set U, we choose a solution of the lbc and assign the variables to the same values as the solution. We perform the same operation for the variables whose domain is contained in a Hall set H using a solution of the ubc. There will be exactly l_v or u_v variables assigned to a value v depending if the value belongs to U or H, which in either case satisfies both the lbc and ubc. We repeat the above until all variables are instantiated. The constructed tuple t satisfies the lbc and the ubc simultaneously and therefore also satisfies the gcc. □

4   Bounds Consistency

We present algorithms for making a ubc and an lbc bounds consistent.

4.1   The Upper Bound Constraint (*ubc*)

Finding an algorithm that makes a *ubc* bounds consistent is relatively straightforward if we already know such an algorithm for the *alldifferent* constraint that uses the concept of Hall intervals. If there is a variable whose domain is $[a, b]$ and there is a Hall interval $[c, d]$ such that $c \leq a \leq d < b$ holds, the algorithm will update the domain of the variable to $[d + 1, b]$. The algorithm introduced in [7] detects Hall intervals by checking if there are $d - c + 1$ variables in an interval $[c, d]$. We can adapt this algorithm to a *ubc* without altering its complexity by finding a way to compute the maximal capacity of an interval in constant time. We use a partial sum data structure, implemented as an array A containing the partial sums of the maximal capacities $A[i] = \sum_{j=0}^{i} u_j$. The maximal capacity of an interval $I \subseteq D$ can be computed by subtracting two elements in A since we have $\lceil I \rceil = A[\max(I)] - A[\min(I) - 1]$. Initializing the array A takes $O(D)$ time to compute but this is done once and is reused for any future calls to the propagator. The algorithm time complexity is $O(t + |X|)$ where t is the time required for sorting the variable domains by lower and upper bounds.

4.2   The Lower Bound Constraint (*lbc*)

We now present an algorithm (see Figure 1) that shrinks the lower bounds of the variable domains received as input. The upper bounds can be updated symmetrically by a similar algorithm and consequently make the *lbc* bounds consistent.

The initialization step assigns to each value $v \in D$ exactly l_v empty *buckets* corresponding to the minimal capacity to be filled for v and setting a *failure flag* which indicates if v belongs to a failure set. The union-find data structure PS covers all values in D and contains potential stable sets. If the greatest element of a set $S \in PS$ is in a stable set then S is fully contained in this stable set. Stable sets are stored in the variable *Stable*.

Our algorithm processes each variable $x \in X$ in nondecreasing order by upper bound. Like the algorithm of Lipski *et al.* [6], it searches for the smallest value $v \in dom(x)$ that has an empty bucket and fills it in with a token. If $v > \min(dom(x))$ and v belongs to a stable set then the interval $I = [\min(dom(x)), v]$ is contained in this stable set. The algorithm regroups all values in I in its variable PS. If there are no empty buckets in $dom(x)$ then $\max(dom(x))$ belongs to a stable set and so do all the values that belong to the same set in PS.

The algorithm initially assumes that all values belong to a failure set. When processing variable x, an interval $I = [a, \max(dom(x))]$ with no empty buckets contains the domains of a least $\lfloor I \rfloor$ variables and thus cannot be a failure set. The algorithm unsets the failure flags for all values in I. If a value still has a failure flag set after processing all the variables then the *lbc* is unsatisfiable.

To shrink the domains, the algorithm stores in $NewMin[i]$ the smallest value $v \in dom(x_i)$ with a failure flag. If $dom(x_i)$ intersected an unstable set U, v would be the smallest value in $dom(x_i) \cap U$. If no values in $dom(x_i)$ have a failure flag, x_i belongs to a stable set and $NewMin[i]$ remains undefined. After processing all variables, the algorithm assigns the new lower bound $NewMin$ to the variables that are not contained in a stable set.

Let PS be a union-find data structure over the elements in D;
Let $Stable = \emptyset$;
for $v \in D$ **do**
$\quad$ associate l_v empty buckets to the value v;
$\quad$ **if** $l_v > 0$ **then** mark v as a *failure* element;
$D \leftarrow D \cup \{-\infty, \infty\}$;
associate ∞ buckets to the values $-\infty$ and ∞;
for $x_i \in X$ in nondecreasing order of $\max(dom(x_i))$ **do**
$\quad$ $a \leftarrow \min(dom(x_i))$; $b \leftarrow \max(dom(x_i))$;
$\quad$ $z \leftarrow \min(\{v \in D \mid v \geq a, a$ has an empty bucket$\})$;
$\quad$ **if** $z > a$ **then** union $(PS, a, a+1, \ldots, \min(b, z))$;
$\quad$ **if** $z > b$ **then**
$\quad\quad$ $S \leftarrow$findSet (PS, b);
$\quad\quad$ $Stable \leftarrow Stable \cup \{S\}$;
$\quad$ **else**
$\quad\quad$ add a token in one of the empty buckets of z;
$\quad\quad$ $z \leftarrow \min(\{v \in D \mid v \geq a, a$ has an empty bucket$\})$;
$\quad\quad$ $NewMin[i] \leftarrow \min(\{v \in D \mid v \geq a, v$ has a failure flag$\})$;
$\quad\quad$ **if** $z > b$ **then**
$\quad\quad\quad$ $j \leftarrow \max(\{v \in D \mid v \leq b, v$ has an empty bucket$\})$;
$\quad\quad\quad$ reset the *failure* flag for all elements in $(j, b]$;

if $|\{v \in D \mid v$ has a failure flag$\}| > 0$ **then** **return** *Failure*;
for $x_i \in X$ such that $\forall S \in Stable, dom(x_i) \not\subseteq S$ **do**
$\quad$ $dom(x_i) \leftarrow dom(x_i) - [\min(dom(x_i)), NewMin[i])$;
return *Success*;

Algorithm 1. Bounds consistency algorithm for the *lbc*

Example 2. Figure 1 shows a trace of the algorithm on the CSP introduced in Example 1. Initially, all buckets are empty and all values are marked with a failure flag. Figure 1 shows the data structures as the algorithm iterates through the variables. The circles represent the buckets, a letter f symbolizes a failure flag, and the state of the variables PS and $Stable$ are also represented by the sets of values. Upon completion of the algorithm, the new domains of the variables are: $x_1 \in [2, 2]$, $x_2 \in [1, 2]$, $x_3 \in [2, 3]$, $x_4 \in [2, 3]$, $x_5 \in [4, 4]$, and $x_6 \in [4, 4]$.

A naive implementation of our algorithm has time complexity $O(t + |X| |D|)$, where t is the complexity of sorting the intervals by upper bounds. Incremental and linear time sorting algorithms have time complexity less than $O(|X| \log |X|)$. We will show how to improve the complexity to $O(t + |X|)$.

To obtain a complexity independent of $|D|$, we consider the variables as semi-open intervals where $x_i = [a_i, b_i)$ and define the set D' as the union of the lower bounds a_i and the open upper bounds b_i of each variable. The size of D' is bounded by $2|X|$. Let c and d be two consecutive values in D' and let $I = (c, d]$ be a semi-open interval. We modify the algorithm to assign $\lfloor I \rfloor$ buckets to the value d using a partial sum data structure (see Section 4.1). We then run the

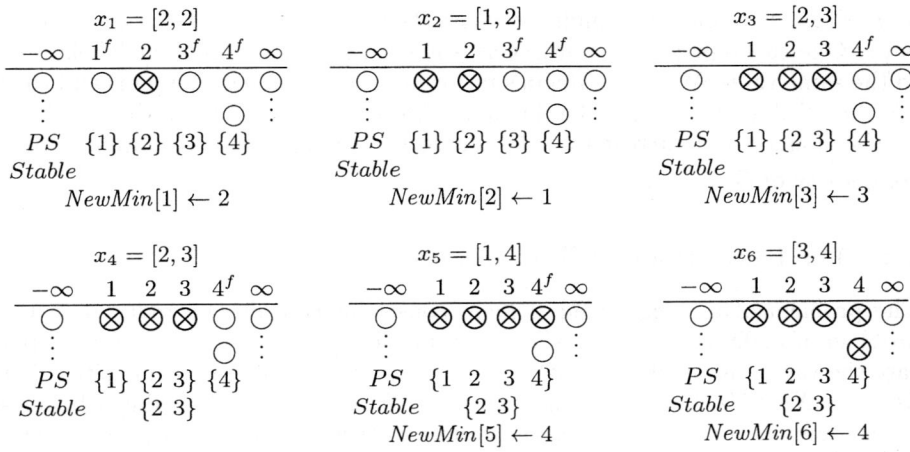

Fig. 1. Trace of Algorithm 1

algorithm as before using the set D' instead of D. This modification improves the time complexity to $O(t + |X|^2)$.

To get a linear complexity, we implement the buckets using a union-find data structure and an array of integers that stores the number of empty buckets a value v has. If all buckets of a value v are filled in, the algorithm merges the value v with the next element in D'. Requesting n times the next value having a free bucket is a linear time operation using the interval union-find data structure [2]. The algorithm takes $O(t + |X|)$ steps using the interval union-find for the failure flags, the stable sets *Stable*, and the potential stable sets *PS*.

Although the interval union-find data structure gives the best theoretical time complexity, we found that it did not result in the fastest code in practice in spite of our best efforts to optimize the code. In our experiments (see Section 6), we use instead the tree data structure described in [7] to obtain an algorithm with $O(t + |X| \log |X|)$ time complexity. This tree data structure even offers slightly better performance than the standard union-find data structure which runs in $O(t + |X|\alpha(|X|))$ where α is the inverse of Ackermann's function.

5   Domain Consistency

In this section we present a propagator that makes a *gcc* domain consistent. We will use Régin's propagator [9, 17] for the *alldifferent* constraint as a black box that has complexity $O(d|X|^{\frac{3}{2}})$, where d is the size of the largest domain of a variable, to make the *lbc* and *ubc* domain consistent.

5.1   The Upper Bound Constraint (*ubc*)

The problem of making a *ubc* domain consistent can be reduced to the problem of making an *alldifferent* constraint domain consistent. Consider the domain

$dom(x)$ of a variable x as a multiset where the multiplicity of a value $v \in dom(x)$ is u_v. One can represent a multiset as a normal set where different labels refer to the same value. We apply Régin's propagator with the new domains and then remove all duplicates from the domains. Since there are $|X|$ variables and the largest domain is bounded by $u|D|$ where $u = \max_{v \in D} u_v$, we obtain a time complexity of $O(u|D||X|^{\frac{3}{2}})$.

5.2 The Lower Bound Constraint (*lbc*)

The problem of making an *lbc* domain consistent can also be reduced to the problem of making an *alldifferent* constraint domain consistent. We first duplicate the values as we did in Section 5.1 according to the minimal capacities. Let M be a $|X| \times |D|$ binary matrix such that M_{ij} equals 1 if the value j belongs to the domain of the variable x_i and equals 0 otherwise. The transposed matrix M^T defines the dual problem. In a dual problem, the dual values D' represent the primal variables and the dual variables X' represent the primal values.

Theorem 4. *Solving the* alldifferent *problem on the dual problem solves the lower bound problem on the primal problem.*

Proof. Since we have duplicated some values in the domains of the variables, the minimal capacity of a set S is now equal to the size of the set; i.e., $\lfloor S \rfloor = |S|$. Let U be an unstable set in the primal problem. In the dual problem, the values in U are represented by variables. There are $|U|$ dual variables whose domains are contained in a set of $|U|$ dual values. Consequently, an unstable set in the primal corresponds to a Hall set in the dual. A propagator for the *alldifferent* problem removes from a domain the values contained in a Hall set only if the domain is not fully contained in the Hall set. If such a propagator is applied on the dual problem, it would remove from the domains that intersect an unstable set the values that do not belong to this unstable set. This operation is sufficient to make the primal domain consistent. The *alldifferent* propagator would also return a failure if the problem is unsolvable. A failure set in the primal corresponds to a set of values in the dual that contains more variables than values. Such a set makes the dual unsolvable and is detected by the *alldifferent* propagator.   □

We use Régin's propagator to solve the dual problem and then remove the duplicates from the domains of the variables. Since in the dual problem there are at most $l|D|$ variables and the largest domain is bounded by $|X|$, the total time complexity is $O(l^{1.5}|X||D|^{1.5})$ where $l = max_{v \in D} l_v$.

5.3 The Complete Algorithm for Domain Consistency of the *gcc*

The complete algorithm makes the *ubc* domain consistent and then makes the *lbc* domain consistent. The total time complexity is $O(u|X|^{1.5}|D| + l^{1.5}|X||D|^{1.5})$.

That the complexity depends on the number of values in D can make the filter inefficient for some problems. We identify two classes of problems that occur often in applications and where our algorithm offers a better complexity than existing algorithms. Our analysis assumes that the maximal capacity u_v is bounded by a constant for all values v. The first class consists of problems where the minimal capacity l_v is non-null. Since each value must be instantiated by at least one variable, we necessarily have $|D| \leq |X|$ for a solvable problem. In this case the algorithm runs in time $O(|D||X|^{1.5})$. The second class of problems is the one where the minimal capacity l_v is null for all values v. In this case we only need to make ubc domain consistent which can be done in time $O(|D||X|^{1.5})$. For either class, the complexity of the algorithm improves the previous best gcc propagator for domain consistency which runs in $O(|D||X|^2)$ [10].

6 Experimental Results

We implemented our new bounds consistency algorithm for the generalized cardinality constraint (denoted hereafter as BC) using the ILOG Solver C++ library, Version 4.2 [4][1]. Following a suggestion by Puget [8] adapted to the gcc, the range of applicability of BC can be extended by combining bounds consistency with the removal of a value when the number of times it has been assigned reaches its upper bound (denoted BC+). The ILOG Solver library already provides implementations of Régin's [10] domain consistency algorithm (denoted DC), and an algorithm (denoted CC) that enforces a level of consistency that is equivalent to enforcing domain consistency on individual cardinality constraints, where there is one cardinality constraint for each value [4, 16].

We compared the algorithms experimentally on various benchmark and random problems. All of the experiments were run on a 2.40 GHz Pentium 4 with 1 GB of main memory. Each reported runtime is the average of 10 runs except for random problems where 100 runs were performed. Unless otherwise noted, the minimum domain size variable ordering heuristic was used in the search.

We first consider problems introduced by Puget ([8]: denoted here as Pathological) that were "designed to show the worst case behavior" of algorithms for the *alldifferent* constraint. Here we adapt the problem to the gcc. A Pathological problem consists of a single gcc over $2n + 1$ variables with $dom(x_i) = [i - n, 0]$, $0 \leq i \leq n$, and $dom(x_i) = [0, i - n]$, $n+1 \leq i \leq 2n$ and each value must occur exactly once. The problems were solved using the lexicographic variable ordering. On these problems, our BC propagator offers a clear performance improvement over the other propagators (see Figure 2). Qualitatively similar results were obtained for a generalization of these problems where each value must occur exactly c times, where c is some small value.

We next consider instruction scheduling problems for multiple-issue pipelined processors. For these problems there are n variables, one for each instruction to be scheduled and latency constraints of the form $x_i \leq x_j + l$ where l is some small integer value, and one or more gcc's over all n variables (see [14] for more details on the problem). In our experiments, we used ten hard problems that were taken from the SPEC95 floating point, SPEC2000 floating point, and MediaBench

---

[1] The code discussed in this section is available on request from vanbeek@uwaterloo.ca

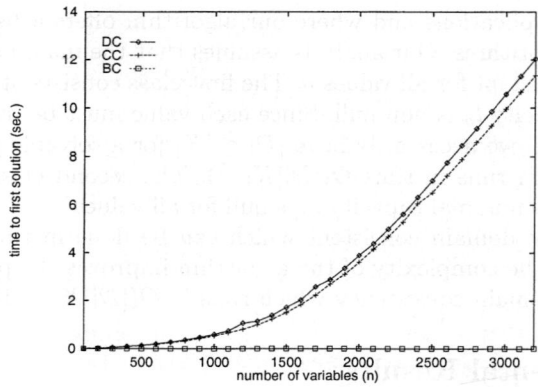

Fig. 2. Time (sec.) to first solution for Pathological problems

Table 1. Time (sec.) to optimal solution for instruction scheduling problems; (left) issue width = 2; (right) issue width = 2 + 2 = 4. A blank entry means the problem was not solved within a 10 minute time bound

n	CC	DC	BC	n	CC	DC	BC
69	0.01	0.12	0.00	69	0.00	0.07	0.00
70	0.00	0.07	0.00	70	0.01	0.07	0.00
111	0.03	0.75	0.01	111	0.03	0.44	0.01
211	0.51	9.24	0.07	211	0.56	7.16	0.11
214	0.60	9.29	0.09	214	0.61	7.85	0.13
216	2.67	124.07	0.31	216	2.78	89.61	0.48
220	5.09	285.91	0.52	220	2.90	98.15	0.57
690	1.34	493.15	1.67	690	2.17	307.20	2.81
856		471.16	3.84	856			
1006			8.70	1006	307.00		14.44

benchmarks. The issue width of a processor refers to how many instructions can be issued each clock cycle. In our experiments we used the representative cases of a processor with an issue width of two with two identical functional units, and an issue width of four with two floating point units and two integer units (see Table 1). Here, our BC propagator offers a clear performance improvement over the other propagators.

We next consider car sequencing problems (see [4]). For these problems there are n variables, n values, each configuration of five options is equally likely, and there are approximately $4n$ gcc's. Here, our BC+ propagator achieves almost the same pruning power as DC and becomes faster than the other propagators as n grows (see Table 2). We also consider sport league scheduling problems (see [15] and references therein). For these problems there are n^2 variables, n values, and $n/2$ gcc's. Here, our BC+ propagator is within 15% of the fastest propagator, DC, in terms of run-time and pruning power (see Table 3). The complexity or run-time of the CC and DC propagators depends on the number of domain values, whereas the BC/BC+ propagators do not. The car sequencing and sports league

Table 2. (left) Time (sec.) to first solution or to detect inconsistency for car sequencing problems; (right) number of backtracks (fails)

n	CC	DC	BC	BC+
10	0.07	0.07	0.09	0.09
15	3.40	3.88	5.39	4.12
20	20.65	30.05	30.95	21.83
25	131.27	203.23	163.97	118.57

n	CC	DC	BC	BC+
10	437	321	460	429
15	13,849	9,609	19,958	13,565
20	55,657	52,581	105,436	55,580
25	255,690	250,042	520,519	255,653

Table 3. (left) Time (sec.) to first solution for sports league scheduling problems; (right) number of backtracks (fails). A blank entry means the problem was not solved within a 10 minute time bound

n	CC	DC	BC	BC+
8	0.19	0.16	0.04	0.18
10	1.10	0.12	0.03	0.19
12	1.98	1.70	51.71	2.07
14	11.82	8.72		9.98

n	CC	DC	BC	BC+
8	1308	914	136	942
10	5767	428	54	689
12	6449	4399	149728	5356
14	33901	19584		22176

Table 4. Time (sec.) to first solution or to detect inconsistency for random problems where the bounds on number of occurrences of each value were (left) $[0, 2]$; (right) chosen uniformly at random from $\{[0, 1], [0, 2], [1, 1], [1, 2], [1, 3], [2, 2], [2, 3], [2, 4]\}$. A blank entry means some problems could not be solved within a 10 min. time bound

n	DC	BC
100		0.02 0.01
200		0.23 0.02
400		2.55 0.08
800		26.14 0.33
1600		266.80 1.24

		DC			BC	
n	$d/2$	d	$2d$	$d/2$	d	$2d$
100	0.00	0.01	0.33	0.00	0.00	0.00
200	0.00	0.07	4.81	0.00	0.01	0.01
400	0.01	0.60	74.88	0.00	0.03	0.04
800	0.03	4.58		0.01	0.15	0.16
1600	0.20	34.78		0.02	0.70	0.62

scheduling problems illustrate that the number of domain values does not have to be very large for this factor to lead to competitive run-times for our relatively unoptimized BC/BC+ propagators.

To systematically study the scaling behavior of the algorithm, we next consider random problems. The problems consisted of a single *gcc* over n variables and each variable had its initial domain set to $[a, b]$, where a and b, $a \leq b$, were chosen uniformly at random from $[1, d = n/2]$ (chosen so that a mixture of consistent and inconsistent problems would be generated). In these "pure" problems nearly all of the run-time is due to the *gcc* propagators, and one can clearly see the cubic behavior of the DC propagator and the nearly linear incremental behavior of the BC propagator (see Table 4). On these problems, CC (not shown) could not solve some of the smallest problems within a 10 minute time bound.

7   Conclusions

We presented an efficient algorithm for bounds consistency propagation of the *gcc* and showed its usefulness on a set of benchmark and random problems.

We also presented an algorithm for domain consistency propagation with an improved worst-case bound on problems that arise in practice.

Acknowledgments

The authors thank the participants of the constraint programming problem session at the University of Waterloo, Kent Wilken for providing the instruction scheduling problems used in our experiments and Irit Katriel and Sven Thiel [5] for trying out our algorithm. Alexander Golynski is partially supported by NSERC grant RGPIN8237.

References

1. Y. Caseau, P.-Y. Guillo, and E. Levenez. A deductive and object-oriented approach to a complex scheduling problem. In *Deductive and Object-Oriented Databases*, pages 67–80, 1993.
2. H. N. Gabow and R. E. Tarjan. A linear-time algorithm for a special case of disjoint set union. In *STOC-1983*, pages 246–251.
3. P. Hall. On representatives of subsets. *J. of the London Mathematical Society*, pages 26–30, 1935.
4. ILOG S. A. ILOG Solver 4.2 user's manual, 1998.
5. I. Katriel and S. Thiel. Fast bound consistency for the global cardinality constraint. In *CP-2003*.
6. W. Lipski and F. P. Preparata. Efficient algorithms for finding maximum matchings in convex bipartite graphs and related problems. In *Acta Informatica*, 15:329–346, 1981.
7. A. López-Ortiz, C.-G. Quimper, J. Tromp, and P. van Beek. A fast and simple algorithm for bounds consistency of the alldifferent constraint. In *IJCAI-2003*.
8. J.-F. Puget. A fast algorithm for the bound consistency of alldiff constraints. In *AAAI-1998*, pages 359–366.
9. J.-C. Régin. A filtering algorithm for constraints of difference in CSPs. In *AAAI-1994*, pages 362–367.
10. J.-C. Régin. Generalized arc consistency for global cardinality constraint. In *AAAI-1996*, pages 209–215.
11. J.-C. Régin and J.-F. Puget. A filtering algorithm for global sequencing constraints. In *CP-1997*, pages 32–46.
12. C. Schulte and P. J. Stuckey. When do bounds and domain propagation lead to the same search space. In *PPDP-2001*, pages 115–126.
13. K. Stergiou and T. Walsh. The difference all-difference makes. In *IJCAI-1999*, pages 414–419.
14. P. van Beek and K. Wilken. Fast optimal instruction scheduling for single-issue processors with arbitrary latencies. In *CP-2001*, pages 625–639.
15. P. Van Hentenryck, L. Michel, L. Perron, and J.-C. Régin. Constraint programming in OPL. In *PPDP-1999*, pages 98–116.
16. P. Van Hentenryck, H. Simonis, and M. Dincbas. Constraint satisfaction using constraint logic programming. *Artificial Intelligence*, 58:113–159, 1992.
17. W. J. van Hoeve. The alldifferent constraint: A survey. Unpublished manuscript, 2001.

Solving Existentially Quantified Constraints with One Equality and Arbitrarily Many Inequalities

Stefan Ratschan

Max-Planck-Institut für Informatik, Saarbrücken, Germany
stefan.ratschan@mpi-sb.mpg.de

Abstract. This paper contains the first algorithm that can solve disjunctions of constraints of the form $\exists y \in B \, [f = 0 \land g_1 \geq 0 \land \ldots \land g_k \geq 0]$ in free variables x, terminating for all cases when this results in a numerically well-posed problem. Here the only assumption on the terms $f, g_1, \ldots, g_n$ is the existence of a pruning function, as given by the usual constraint propagation algorithms or by interval evaluation. The paper discusses the application of an implementation of the resulting algorithm on problems from control engineering, parameter estimation, and computational geometry.

1 Introduction

Dealing with uncertainty is an important challenge for constraint programming. An important way of modeling bounded (in contrast to stochastic [30]) uncertainty uses the logical quantifiers $\forall$ and $\exists$—as illustrated by an over-60-paper-bibliography on applications of solving constraints with quantifiers [22]. However, the problem of solving real-number constraints with quantifiers is undecidable in general [29], and very hard for special cases [32, 7].

This paper is part of a research program on solving real-number constraints with quantifiers, with only the two restrictions of numerical well-posedness and existence of a pruning algorithm for the individual (atomic) constraints. The case we consider in this paper are constraints of the form $\exists y \in B \, [f = 0 \land g_1 \geq 0 \land \ldots \land g_n \geq 0]$ in free variables x, and disjunctions thereof. For example, this case is very important in parameter estimation [14]. For disproving such constraints or computing elements that are not in the solution set, one can use a method for solving constraint with quantifiers and no equality predicate symbols [26, 25]. However, proving such constraints or computing elements in its solution set introduces significant additional difficulties: First, the non-empty solution set of an equality might not contain any rational (or even real algebraic) number, as in the example $\exists x \, [\sin x = 0 \land x \geq 3 \land x \leq 4]$. Second, the branching step of the mentioned algorithms [26, 25] does not necessarily decrease the difficulty for such constraints. On the contrary—it can even produce a new, numerically ill-posed problem!

For the design of the algorithm introduced in this paper we use the following main objectives: First, it should terminate for all cases that are numerically

F. Rossi (Ed.): CP 2003, LNCS 2833, pp. 615–633, 2003.

well-posed. And second, computed positive and negative information should be mutually used within the algorithm.

We proceed by giving a criterion characterizing the numerical well-posedness of such constraints, extending the case [26] of just inequalities. Using this criterion we design an algorithm that is based on the usual branch-and-prune scheme extended with an additional checking step for proving the truth of the input constraint on a part of the free-variable space. Here, branching not only splits bounds on the free-variables, but can also split an existential quantifier into a disjunction of two existential quantifiers. If desired, the algorithm can also return witnesses in the case of a positive result. We have implemented the algorithm and applied it to problems in control engineering, parameter estimation, and computational geometry.

The paper is self-contained except for a few basic notions from analysis. Its structure is as follows: In Section 2 we introduce some basic notions; in Section 3 we present the main branch-prune-and-check algorithm; in Section 4 we give a characterization of the stability of such constraint; in Section 5 we discuss the pruning step, in Section 6 the branching step, in Section 7, the checking step; in Section 8 we apply the results to the main algorithm; in Section 9 we discuss an implementation of the algorithm and we apply it to simple application examples; in Section 10 we discuss related work; and in Section 11 we conclude the paper.

2   Preliminaries

In this paper we concentrate on a certain type of constraints:

Definition 1. *An* E-constraint *is a constraint of the form*

$$\exists y \in B_1 \, [f_1 = 0 \land g_{1,1} \geq 0 \land \ldots \land g_{1,k_1} \geq 0]$$
$$\lor \ldots \lor$$
$$\exists y \in B_n \, [f_n = 0 \land g_{n,1} \geq 0 \land \ldots \land g_{n,k_n} \geq 0], \text{ where}$$

- $B_1, \ldots, B_n$ *are boxes of the same dimension as the length of the variable vector* y, *and*
- $f_1, g_{1,1}, \ldots, g_{1,k_1}, \ldots, f_n, g_{n,1}, \ldots, g_{n,k_n}$ *are terms built from a fixed set of function symbols (e.g.,* $+$, $\cdot$, sin, cos, exp*) to which we give their usual meaning over the real numbers.*

Within this paper we call an E-constraint or any sub-constraint of an E-constraint a *constraint*. A bounded constraint is a pair consisting of a constraint ϕ in n free variables, and a box $B \subseteq \mathbb{R}^n$ (the *free-variable-bound*). A bounded constraint is true/false iff it is true/false for all elements of the bound. As usual in mathematics we will use the same notation to write down a term and the function it denotes. By "solving" we mean the following:

Definition 2. *Given a bounded E-constraint* (ϕ, B) *and* $\varepsilon \in \mathbb{R}^+$, *an* ε-solution *of* (ϕ, B) *is a pair* (T, F) *of sets of boxes such that*

- $\bigcup T \subseteq B, \bigcup F \subseteq B,$
- ϕ *is true on all elements of* $\bigcup T$,
- ϕ *is false on all elements of* $\bigcup F$, *and*
- *the volume of* $B \setminus \bigcup T \setminus \bigcup F$ *is smaller than* ε.

We will use a few basic notions from analysis such as continuity, intermediate value theorem, convergence of sequences. Furthermore, we say that a sequence of sets over $\mathbb{R}^n$ *converges* to a real vector $r \in \mathbb{R}^n$ iff all element sequences converge to r. In order to be able to use the convergence notion also for $n = 0$, we measure distance in $\mathbb{R}^0$ according to $d(x, y) = 0$ if $x = y$ and ∞, otherwise. We also say that a sequence $x_1, \ldots$ *eventually* fulfills a property P iff there is a k such that for all $i \geq k$, $P(x_i)$ holds. Finally, we define the *width of a box B (w(B))* to be the maximum of the width of its component intervals.

3   Overall Algorithm

One can extend numerical constraint satisfaction methods [8, 2] to constraints that contain quantifiers [23, 25]. This uses a branch-and-prune framework, where pruning tries to prove or disprove (parts of) the input constraints and if this fails, branching tries to decrease the difficulty by splitting one of the quantifiers into subproblems.

However, for constraints that contain equalities or disequalities this fails, because equalities have solution sets without volume, and disequalities have solution set complements without volume. For the example $\exists x \; [\sin x = 0 \land x \geq 3 \land x \leq 4]$ pruning will never compute a real number x fulfilling $\sin x = 0$ and so the method will never prove the whole constraint. In general, for E-constraints, pruning will disprove a false constraint (compute false elements) without problems. However, it fails in proving a true constraint (computing true elements). Note that formulating an equality by two inequalities will not help: this introduces an ill-posed problem because arbitrary perturbations of the inequalities will make any solution vanish.

In order to remedy this situation, we modify the according branch-and-prune algorithm, resulting in Algorithm 1. The main change consists of an additional checking step that tries to prove constraints. By letting pruning (for computing negative information) and checking (for computing positive information) work on the same constraints, one can take advantage of the results of the other.

Here we have the following sub-algorithm specifications:

Diff: Takes two sets of bounded constraints and returns a set of boxes such that their union is equal to the closure of the difference of the free-variable-bounds of the inputs.

Prune: Returns the input (a set of bounded constraints), with the free-variable bounds replaced by sub-boxes, such that the closure of the difference of the old and new bounds contains no solutions.

Check: Returns the input except for some true bounded constraints.

Algorithm 1 Solver

Input: (ϕ, B): a bounded E-constraint, $\varepsilon \in \mathbb{R}^+$

Output: T, F: an ε-solution of (ϕ, B)

    $C \leftarrow \{(\phi, B)\}$

    $C' \leftarrow C$; $C \leftarrow \mathrm{Prune}(C)$; $F \leftarrow F \cup \mathrm{Diff}(C', C)$

    $C' \leftarrow C$; $C \leftarrow \mathrm{Check}(C)$; $T \leftarrow T \cup \mathrm{Diff}(C', C)$

    while the volume of $\{B \mid (\phi, B) \in C\}$ is greater or equal ε **do**

        $C \leftarrow \mathrm{Branch}(C)$

        $C' \leftarrow C$; $C \leftarrow \mathrm{Prune}(C)$; $F \leftarrow F \cup \mathrm{Diff}(C', C)$

        $C' \leftarrow C$; $C \leftarrow \mathrm{Check}(C)$; $T \leftarrow T \cup \mathrm{Diff}(C', C)$

    end while

Branch: Splits a sub-constraint of the form $\exists x \in B$ ϕ into $\exists x \in B_1$ ϕ $\vee$ $\exists x \in B_2$ ϕ such that the union of B_1 and B_2 is B, and their intersection has zero volume, or splits a bounded constraint (ϕ, B) into (ϕ, B_1) and (ϕ, B_2), such that the union of B_1 and B_2 is B, and their intersection has zero volume.

Here we assume that in $\mathbb{R}^0$ the volume of the empty box is 0 and the volume of the non-empty box is ∞. In the algorithm, for closed inputs, the set C will never contain more than one element, and the algorithm terminates as soon as C becomes empty.

The reason, why such algorithms use a pruning step (instead of checking for false constraints also), is that often one can deduce information by pruning even when a checking step would fail. This allows us to keep the size of the problem small by avoiding branching. Based on the above specifications of the sub-algorithms, it is now easy to prove:

Theorem 1. *Algorithm 1 is correct.*

However, it is not clear when it will terminate. In the rest of the paper we will implement the sub-algorithms in such a way that we can prove termination in all cases that are numerically well-posed (in a sense that we will shortly define).

4   Stability of Constraints

Algorithms that involve rounding or approximation can only succeed on problems where this does not change the result in an essential way. Studying this phenomenon is one of the main tasks of the field of numerical analysis. In this section we undertake a similar endeavor for E-constraints. Readers who are interested only in algorithms for solving E-constraints and not in their detailed properties can skip this section.

Definition 3. *A constraint ϕ' is a result of a δ-perturbation of a constraint ϕ iff it results from ϕ by replacing the right-hand-side zeros of atomic constraints by terms denoting a continuous function (in both the free and quantified variables), whose co-domain is $[-\delta, \delta]$.*

Definition 4. *A closed E-constraint is stable iff there is a real number $\delta > 0$ such that all results of δ-perturbations have the same truth value.*

For example, the constraint $\exists x \in [-2, 2] \; x^2 = 0$ is unstable: although it is true, it becomes false under small perturbations. On the other hand, the constraint $\exists x \in [-2, 2] \; x^2 - 1 = 0$ is stable.

In the previous definition, perturbations by constants—as for the case of inequality constraints [26]—do not suffice for capturing the E-constraints that are solvable by numerical methods. For example, for functions f and g as in

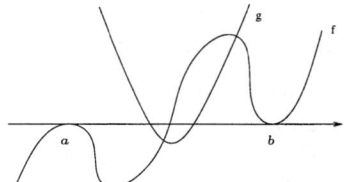

Fig. 1. Constant Perturbations Fail

Figure 1, the constraint $\exists x \; [f(x) = 0 \wedge g(x) \geq 0]$ would be stable and true, but the zero proving the existential quantifier jumps discontinuously between the zeros a and b. This obstructs the use of methods that involve rounding or approximation for such a problem.

Now, as in the case of inequality constraints [26], we introduce a number that replaces the discrete notion of truth of a constraint by a continuous one that is negative for false constraints, positive for true constraints, and such that the ease of proving this is proportional to its distance to zero. Similar to the notion of *condition number* in numerical analysis, this will allow us to study the difficulty of a problem (the essential difference being that, by using derivatives, condition numbers concentrate on local information, while we want to capture the problem globally).

The idea is, that for proving a constraint of the form $\exists y \in B \; [f = 0 \wedge g_1 \geq 0 \wedge \ldots \wedge g_k \geq 0]$, by Bolzano's intermediate value theorem, it suffices to prove that there is a path between two points within the quantification bound such that the inequalities $g_1 \geq 0 \wedge \ldots \wedge g_k \geq 0$ hold on the whole path, and the function f is non-positive at the beginning and non-negative at the end. We assume that the ease of proving an inequality between two real numbers is proportional to the distance of the two numbers; the ease of proving an inequality on all elements of a path is the minimal ease of proving the inequality on the path elements; and the ease of proving the whole E-constraint is proportional to the ease of performing the above on the easiest path:

Definition 5. *The degree of truth of a closed constraint $\exists y \in B \; [f = 0 \wedge g_1 \geq 0 \wedge \ldots \wedge g_n \geq 0]$ on a path $P \subseteq B$ between two points $p_1 \in B$ and $p_2 \in B$ is*

$$\min\{f(p_1), -f(p_2), \min_P g_1, \ldots, \min_P g_n\}$$

The degree of truth $\tau(\phi)$ of a closed E-constraint of the form $\exists \boldsymbol{y} \in B_1 \, \phi_1 \vee \ldots \vee \exists \boldsymbol{y} \in B_n \, \phi_n$ *is the maximum of the degree of truth of a sub-constraint* $\exists \boldsymbol{y} \in B_i \, \phi_i$ *over all paths in* B_i *and all* $i \in \{1, \ldots, n\}$.

Here we can deal with p_1 and p_2 in an asymmetric way, because the set of all paths contains for each path its reverse. Also we can use the maximum (instead of the supremum) over all paths because the degree of truth is a continuous function on the compact set of paths; therefore the supremum of the image of the degree of truth on the set of paths is attained on one path.

The degree of truth determines the truth of a sentence as follows:

Theorem 2. *For a closed E-constraint, positive degree of truth implies truth, a negative degree of truth implies falsehood.*

Proof. Assume that the degree of truth of a closed E-constraint is positive. This means that there is a sub-constraint of the form $\exists \boldsymbol{y} \in B \, [f = 0 \ \wedge \ g_1 \geq 0 \wedge \ldots \wedge g_n \geq 0]$ and a path $P \subseteq B$ with endpoints $p_1 \in B$ and $p_2 \in B$ such that $f(p_1)$ is positive and $f(p_2)$ is negative. Furthermore, $g_1, \ldots, g_n$ are positive on P. Therefore, by the Bolzano intermediate value theorem, the sub-constraint is true, and since this sub-constraint is part of a disjunction, the whole constraint is true.

Now assume that the degree of truth is negative and the constraint is true. The truth of the constraint implies that there is a sub-constraint of the form $\exists \boldsymbol{y} \in B \, [f = 0 \ \wedge \ g_1 \geq 0 \wedge \ldots \wedge g_n \geq 0]$ such that f has a zero in B, and $g_1, \ldots, g_n$ are greater or equal zero there. So the degree of truth of the path that just contains this zero is zero, implying that the total degree of truth is greater or equal zero—a contradiction. $\square$

For investigating the connection between degree of truth and stability, we use:

Lemma 1. *For every closed E-constraint ϕ and $\delta > 0$ there is a result of an δ-perturbation of ϕ whose degree of truth is larger/smaller than the one of ϕ.*

Proof.

- Increasing the degree of truth: Let $\exists \boldsymbol{y} \in B \, [f = 0 \ \wedge \ g_1 \geq 0 \wedge \ldots \wedge g_n \geq 0]$ be the sub-constraint and let P be the path on which the maximum is attained. We have to find a perturbation such that $\min\{f(p_1), -f(p_2), \min_P g_1, \ldots, \min_P g_n\}$ increases. This can be easily done by a perturbation that increases the degree of truth of each element of $\{f(p_1), -f(p_2), \min_P g_1, \ldots, \min_P g_n\}$ [1].
- Decreasing the degree of truth: We find a perturbation that decreases the degree of truth of every existentially quantified sub-constraint and every path. Let $\exists \boldsymbol{y} \in B \, [f = 0 \wedge g_1 \geq 0 \wedge \ldots \wedge g_n \geq 0]$ and let P be an arbitrary, but fixed path. Their degree of truth is $\min\{f(p_1), -f(p_2), \min_P g_1, \ldots, \min_P g_n\}$. For each of its elements one can easily find a perturbation that decreases it. $\square$

---

[1] For perturbing $f(p_1)$ and $f(p_2)$ independently we need perturbation by functions (instead of just constants) here, see Figure 1.

The degree of truth characterizes its stability as follows:

Theorem 3. *A closed E-constraint is stable iff its degree of truth is non-zero.*

Proof. ⇒: We assume a constraint with zero degree of truth and prove that it is unstable. This certainly holds because, by Lemma 1, a small perturbations will change the degree of truth, and by Theorem 2 this will also change the truth value.

⇐: Assume that the degree of truth is non-zero. Since the degree of truth depends continuously on perturbation, this implies that there is a $\delta > 0$, such that under all perturbations less than δ, the degree of truth does not change its sign. Hence, by Theorem 2, it also does not change its truth value. □

For false E-constraints, one can use a simpler characterization, that is compatible with the case of inequality constraints [23, 25].

Lemma 2. *The degree of truth of a false closed E-constraint of the form*

$$\exists \boldsymbol{y} \in B_1 \, [f_1 = 0 \wedge g_{1,1} \geq 0 \wedge \ldots \wedge g_{1,k_1} \geq 0]$$
$$\vee \ldots \vee$$
$$\exists \boldsymbol{y} \in B_n \, [f_n = 0 \wedge g_{n,1} \geq 0 \wedge \ldots \wedge g_{n,k_n} \geq 0]$$

is $\max_{i \in \{1 \ldots n\}} \sup_{\boldsymbol{y} \in B} \min\{f_i, -f_i, g_{i,1}, \ldots, g_{i,k_i}\}$.

Proof. We prove that for every $i \in \{1, \ldots, n\}$ the maximal path of the according disjunctive branch consists of just a point. Obviously this implies the lemma.

Since ϕ is false, by Theorem 2, $\tau(\phi)$ is non-positive, and so for every $i \in \{1, \ldots, n\}$ the degree of truth of every disjunctive branch on the maximal path P from p_1 to p_2 is non-positive.

Now there are three cases:

- There is a $j \in \{1, \ldots, k_i\}$ such that $\min\{f_i(p_1), -f_i(p_2), \min_P g_{i,1}, \ldots, \min_P g_{i,k_i}\}$ is $\min_P g_{i,j}$. In this case the minimum is attained on a certain point of P.
- The minimum of $\{f_i(p_1), -f_i(p_2), \min_P g_{i,1}, \ldots, \min_P g_{i,k_i}\}$ is $f_i(p_1)$: In this case, $-f_i(p_1)$ is not smaller than $f_i(p_1)$ and therefore the path just containing p_1 has the same degree of truth and therefore is also maximal.
- The minimum of $\{f_i(p_1), -f_i(p_2), \min_P g_{i,1}, \ldots, \min_P g_{i,k_i}\}$ is $-f_i(p_2)$: In this case, $f_i(p_2)$ is not smaller than $-f_i(p_2)$, and therefore the path just containing p_2 has the same degree of truth and therefore is also maximal. □

5 Pruning

In this section we develop the pruning step of Algorithm 1. Here we assume a pruning algorithm for atomic bounded constraints (i.e., bounded constraints where the first element is an equality or inequality) and extend it to E-constraints.

We start with introducing certain properties that we assume for atomic pruning. These properties refine the properties postulated for the notion of "narrowing operator" [3]. We will also use these properties later for implementing the branching and checking steps.

Note that branching can result in arbitrarily small boxes. So we have to use arbitrary precision arithmetic. However, the usual pruning techniques (for computing box-consistency [2], hull-consistency [8] etc.) are defined for fixed precision. So we add an additional precision parameter to the pruning function (a similar parameter is sometimes used to prevent slow convergence [10]).

The first property we assume is, that atomic pruning should result in a bounded constraint with the same constraint and a smaller bound (still we return a full bounded constraint instead of just a box because, when extending pruning to E-constraints, we will also allow changes of the constraint):

Property 1 (Contractance). For an atomic bounded constraint (ϕ, B) and positive real number p, $Prune_p(\phi, B) = (\phi', B')$ implies that $\phi = \phi'$ and $B' \subseteq B$.

It should only remove elements not in the solution set:

Property 2 (Correctness). For an atomic bounded constraint (ϕ, B) and positive real number p, $Prune_p(\phi, B) = (\phi', B')$ implies that the intersection of the solution set of ϕ with B is equal to the intersection of the solution set of ϕ' with B'.

Pruning is monotonic in the following sense:

Property 3 (Monotonicity). For an atomic constraint ϕ, boxes B_1 and B_2 such that $B_1 \supseteq B_2$ and positive real numbers p_1, p_2 such that $p_1 \leq p_2$, $Prune_{p_1}(\phi, B_1) = (\phi', B_1')$ and $Prune_{p_2}(\phi, B_2) = (\phi', B_2')$ implies $B_1' \supseteq B_2'$.

Pruning eventually succeeds for all well-posed inputs:

Property 4 (Convergence). For all atomic constraints ϕ and sequences of boxes $B_1, \ldots$ converging to a point at which ϕ is stably false, there is a natural number k and a real number p such that for all $k' \geq k$ and $p' \geq p$, $Prune_{p'}(\phi, B_{k'})$ has an empty bound.

Pruning results in borders on which it will succeed using the same precision:

Property 5 (Prunable Borders). For atomic ϕ, such that $Prune_p(\phi, B) = (\phi', B')$, for all new faces D of B' (i.e., faces of B' that are in the interior of B), $Prune_p(\phi, D) = (\phi, \emptyset)$.

This property has two purposes: First, it will allow the Diff function of Algorithm 1 to include the new borders into the result. And second, it will allow the checking step to compute the necessary information on the new borders using the current precision.

Pruning with a certain precision eventually reaches a fixpoint:

Property 6 (Fixed Point). For every positive real number p and infinite sequence $(\phi_1, B_1), \ldots$ of bounded constraints such that for every natural number i, B_{i+1} is the bound of $\text{Prune}_p(\phi_i, B_i)$, there is a k such that $B_k = B_{k+1} = \ldots$.

Now we can extend such a pruning algorithm to E-constraints as required by Algorithm 1. For this we accordingly adapt the case of constraints with quantifiers, as introduced in earlier papers [23, 25]:

- For a set C of E-constraints, $\text{Prune}(C) := \{\text{Prune}(\phi, B) \mid (\phi, B) \in C\}$
- $\text{Prune}(\phi_1 \vee \ldots \phi_n, B) := (\phi_1' \vee \ldots \vee \phi_n', B_1' \uplus \ldots \uplus B_n')$, where $(\phi_i', B_i') = \text{Prune}(\phi_i, B_i)$
- $\text{Prune}(\exists y \in B^{\boldsymbol{y}} \, \phi, B^{\boldsymbol{x}}) := (\exists y \in B^{\boldsymbol{y}'} \, \phi', B^{\boldsymbol{x}'})$,
  where $(\phi', B^{\boldsymbol{x}'} \times B^{\boldsymbol{y}'}) = \text{Prune}_{\text{prec}(B^{\boldsymbol{x}} \times B^{\boldsymbol{y}})}(\phi, B^{\boldsymbol{x}} \times B^{\boldsymbol{y}})$
- $\text{Prune}_p(\phi_1 \wedge \ldots \wedge \phi_k, B) := fix(\{\text{Prune}_p^i \mid 1 \le i \le k\})(\phi_1 \wedge \ldots \wedge \phi_k, B)$
- $\text{Prune}_p^i(\phi_1 \wedge \ldots \wedge \phi_k, B) := (\phi_1 \wedge \ldots \wedge \phi_i' \wedge \ldots \wedge \phi_k, B')$
  where $(\phi_i', B') := \text{Prune}_p(\phi_i, B)$

Here $\uplus$ denotes the smallest box containing the union of the argument boxes. The operator fix takes a set of functions and applies them to the second argument until a fixed point is reached (this fixed point exists by Property 6). The function prec() takes the Cartesian product of the bounds of the constraint and returns the desired precision. We only assume that this precision goes to infinity as the width of its argument goes to zero.

6   Safe Branching

In this section we study the branching step (i.e., either splitting a sub-constraint of the form $\exists x \in B \, \phi$ into $\exists x \in B_1 \, \phi \vee \exists x \in B_2 \, \phi$ such that the union of B_1 and B_2 is B, and their intersection has zero volume, or splitting a bounded constraint (ϕ, B) into (ϕ, B_1) and (ϕ, B_2), such that the union of B_1 and B_2 is B, and their intersection has zero volume). Here we have to ensure that this will allow pruning or checking to eventually succeed on the result. How can it happen that this fails? On the one hand, branching can introduce an unstable constraint (e.g., by replacing $\exists y \in [-1, 1] \, x = 0$ by $\exists y \in [-1, 0] \, x = 0 \vee \exists y \in [0, 1] \, x = 0$). On the other hand, it can fail to decrease the sizes of the free-variable and quantification bound appropriately.

In order to prevent the first possibility we ensure:

Definition 6. *Given a bounded constraint (ϕ, B) and a constraint ϕ' created from ϕ by branching at a quantifier, the branching is safe iff for all $\boldsymbol{x}_0 \in B$, ϕ' is stable at $\boldsymbol{x}_0$ if ϕ is stable at $\boldsymbol{x}_0$.*

One could easily ensure this by only branching the free-variable-bounds. However, then the second problem discussed above arises—the size of the quantification bound does not go to zero, and therefore pruning might never succeed to disprove a false constraint. So we have to analyze the problem in more detail.

Lemma 3. *Branching a quantification bound in a false E-constraint is safe.*

Proof. We prove that the degree of truth decreases by branching—by Theorems 2 and 3 this implies the lemma.

In each branch of the splitted sub-constraint the set of paths is a subset of the set of paths of the original constraint. Therefore the degree of truth of both paths decreases, and so also the degree of truth of the whole formula. $\square$

So we can branch the quantification bound of a false constraint without problems. Still we have to take care when branching true constraints. For now, we defer the problem by simply assuming that checking of true constraint will even succeed if the width of the quantification bound does not go to zero. Therefore, we only have to branch the quantification bound of false constraints, which according to Lemma 3 is no problem.

So we have to following situation:

- For stably false constraints, both the free-variable bound and the quantification bound size should go to zero.
- For stably true constraints, only the free-variable bound size should go to zero.

However, during the algorithm, we do not yet know whether a constraint is true! So we need a condition that can be checked more easily. The problem in the above example was that branching created a new boundary on the (lower-dimensional) solution set of the sub-constraint. We can avoid this as follows:

Theorem 4. *Branching a sub-constraint of the form $\exists y \in B^y\ \phi$ of an E-constraint with free-variable bound B^x into quantification bounds B_1^y and B_2^y is safe if $(\exists y \in B_1^y \cap B_2^y\ \phi, B^x)$ is false.*

Proof. Let $x_0 \in B^x$ be arbitrary, but fixed. Assume that the input is stable at x_0. We have two cases:

- The input is true at x_0. This means that the degree of truth is positive at x_0.
  If no path of positive degree of truth passes through the border $B_1^y \cap B_2^y$ then obviously the theorem holds.
  Now assume an arbitrary, but fixed path of positive degree of truth that passes through the border. This gives rise to a positive path in at least one resulting branch: Assume that the conjunction under the quantifier has the form $f = 0 \wedge g_1 \geq 0 \wedge \ldots \wedge g_n \geq 0$. Since the path has positive degree of truth, $g_1, \ldots, g_n$ are all positive on the path. This means that, on the border, f has to be non-zero, and so has opposite sign to one of the path end-points. Hence the branch containing this end-point has positive degree of truth, and therefore also the whole constraint.
- The input is false at x_0: Then, by Lemma 3, it remains false.

$\square$

Now we can use Theorem 4 in an algorithm for safe branching. How can we check the necessary condition? In the one-dimensional case we just have to check a single point, and by Property 4 it suffices to call Prune with the quantification bound replaced by the new border $B_1 \cap B_2$. However, in the higher-dimensional case, this will not succeed in branching the quantification bound of stably false constraints, as the width of this quantification bound does not go to zero. So we have to decompose B^y into parts such that the overall size goes to zero, and call Prune on all the parts.

Algorithm 2 Branching

Input: C: a set of bounded E-constraints

   $(\phi, B^x) \leftarrow$ an element of C with the free-variable bound of highest volume

   $\exists y \in B^y \ \phi' \leftarrow$ a sub-constraint of ϕ with quantification bound of highest volume

   $(B_1^y, B_2^y) \leftarrow$ bisection of B^y along the variable of maximal width

   $n \leftarrow \#(\exists y \in B^y \ \phi')^{\dim(B^y)-1}$

   $(B_1^y, \ldots, B_n^y) \leftarrow$ equal-sized decomposition of $B_1^y \cap B_2^y$ into n pieces

   if $w(B^y) > w(B^x)$ and for all $i \in \{1, \ldots, n\}$, Prune($\exists y \in B_i^y \ \phi', B^x) = \emptyset$ **then**

   return C with $\exists y \in B^y \ \phi'$ replaced by the result of branching B^y

   else

   return C with (ϕ, B^x) replaced by the result of branching B^x

   end if

The result is Algorithm 2. By $\#(\phi)$ we denote the number of times the algorithm already tried to branch the quantification bound of ϕ in earlier calls, but did not succeed (i.e., it took the else-branch of the if-statement). In the case of closed constraints, branching of the free-variable-bound will leave it unchanged.

By Theorem 4 the algorithm does safe branching. Does it also decrease the width of the bounds appropriately? For the free-variable bounds this is the case:

Theorem 5. *By repeatedly applying Algorithm 2 to a set of E-constraints, interleaved with any operation that removes elements from the set or decreases the width of their bounds, the width of all free-variable bounds in the set goes to zero.*

Proof. We prove that it cannot happen that a quantification bound is branched infinitely often without branching the free-variable bound. Certainly this holds, because eventually $w(B^y) > w(B^x)$ does not hold and the else branch is taken. □

Also the quantification bounds are branched as necessary:

Theorem 6. *By repeatedly applying Algorithm 2 to a set of E-constraints, interleaved with any operation that removes elements from the set or decreases the width of their bounds, the width of all quantification bound of stably false constraints goes to zero.*

Proof. Algorithm 2 cannot produce an infinite sequence of branchings of the free-variable bound because the precision of the if-statement-test goes to infinity.

Furthermore, it eventually branches each quantification bound, because of the maximal width choice.   □

7   Checking

In this section we show how to do the checking step within Algorithm 1. Here we compute some information for the atomic sub-constraints and propagate it to the whole constraint. For the latter (i.e., propagation) we could build upon the rules provided in an earlier paper [24]. However, in order to increase the readability of this paper, we use the formalism developed there only indirectly:

Obviously we can check a set of constraints by checking each of its elements. Furthermore we can check the disjunction of an E-constraint by just checking each of its branches. For proving a sub-constraint of the form $\exists y \in B^y \, [f = 0 \wedge g_1 \geq 0 \wedge \ldots \wedge g_k \geq 0]$ where the free variables range over a box B^x it suffices to find a subset $D \subseteq B^y$ such that all the inequality constraints hold on $B^x \times D$ and the equality constraint has at least one solution in D for each element of the free-variable-bound B^x (then the rules of Theorem 1 of that paper [24] show that the whole constraint holds).

We can prove the existence of a solution to an equality $f = 0$ in a set D by finding an element of D for which f is non-negative and an element for which f is non-positive. For this we can use pruning: If $(f < 0, B)$ is pruned to the empty free-variable bound then the sign of f on B is non-negative, and if $(f > 0, B)$ is pruned to the empty free-variable bound then the sign of f on B is non-positive. In a similar way we can use pruning for proving inequalities.

We search for such a set D by computing the sign of f on the Cartesian product of B^x with—in each direction—$\#(\exists y \in B^y \, [f = 0 \wedge g_1 \geq 0 \wedge \ldots \wedge g_k \geq 0]) + 2$ equally distributed sample points in B^y (including samples on the borders), but such that at least on each corner there is a sample (such as done in Figure 2 for $\#(\exists y \in B^y \, [f = 0 \wedge g_1 \geq 0 \wedge \ldots \wedge g_k \geq 0]) + 2 = 3$). For all this we use pruning with precision $\mathrm{prec}(B^x \times B^y)$.

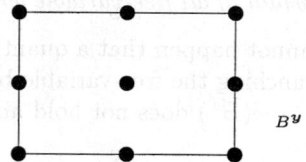

Fig. 2. Samples—coordinates corresponding to B^y

Furthermore we prove $g_1 \geq 0, \ldots, g_n \geq 0$ on the Cartesian product of B^x with boxes that contain a sample point on each corner, and no sample points elsewhere. If we can connect a positive and a negative sample point on a path where $g_1 \geq 0, \ldots, g_n \geq 0$ holds (as in Figure 3), then the constraint is proven. This can be easily done by considering a graph whose vertices are the samples

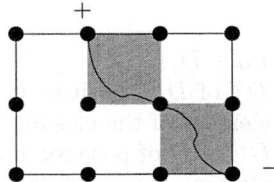

Fig. 3. Successful Check

and which has edges between all neighboring samples between which we have proven $g_1 \geq 0, \ldots, g_n \geq 0$. We want to find out whether there is a path between a positive and a negative vertex.

It is trivial to formalize the above informal algorithm description. Now, using Property 2 of pruning and Bolzano's intermediate value theorem, one can easily prove:

Theorem 7. *Checking is correct.*

Furthermore a witness for this correctness is given by the samples on which f is positive and negative, respectively, and a set of boxes that connects these samples and on which $g_1, \ldots, g_n$ are non-negative.

Checking is successful in the following sense:

Theorem 8. *For every sequence of bounded constraints of the form $(\exists \boldsymbol{y} \in B^{\boldsymbol{y}}$ $[f = 0 \ \wedge \ g_1 \geq 0 \wedge \ldots \wedge g_k \geq 0], B^{\boldsymbol{x}})$ that are stable and true for each element of the free-variable bound, and such that each element results from its predecessor as*

— one branch of branching, and
— pruning

checking eventually succeeds.

Proof. Every element of the sequence is stably true at each element of the free-variable-bound, and so by Theorems 2 and 3 also the degree of truth is positive at each element of the free-variable-bound. So there is an element $\boldsymbol{a}$ of the interior of the free-variable bound of all sequence elements, an element $\boldsymbol{b}$ of the interior of the quantification bound of all sequence elements, and a neighborhood D of $\boldsymbol{b}$ such that:

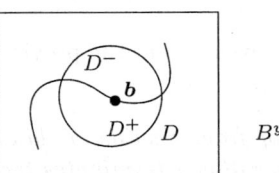

- f is zero at $\boldsymbol{a} \times \boldsymbol{b}$,
- $g_1, \ldots, g_n$ are positive on $\boldsymbol{a} \times D$,
- there is an open subset D^+ of D of positive volume such that f is positive on $\boldsymbol{a} \times D^+$, and $\boldsymbol{b}$ is an element of the closure of D^+, and
- there is an open subset D^- of D of positive volume such that f is negative on $\boldsymbol{a} \times D^-$, and $\boldsymbol{b}$ is an element of the closure of D^-.

Denote by $B_1^x, \ldots$ the sequence of free-variable bounds, and by $B_1^y, \ldots$ the sequence of quantification bounds. By Theorem 5, the width of the free-variable bound goes to zero ($\lim_{i \to \infty} w(B_i^x) = 0$), the width of the quantification bound not necessarily. We prove that checking will eventually succeed.

First we prove the success of finding a sample point on which f is positive. Observe that $D^+ \cap B_i^y$ always has positive volume since $\boldsymbol{b}$ is in the interior of B_i^y and is an element of the closure of D^+. So checking will eventually try infinitely many samples within this set. It remains to be proven that pruning eventually succeeds on one of them. Here we have two cases:

- The intersection of the border of B_i^y with D^+ eventually has positive volume on the border, and so we will eventually check a sample, and by Property 5, since this border has been created by pruning, pruning will be able to compute the sign at the sample using the current precision.
- Otherwise, for all i, D^+ has not more than singular intersection with the border of B_i^y: In this case, we can construct a sequence $D_1^y, \ldots$ of sub-boxes of the sequence of quantification bounds such that this sequence converges to an element of D^+. By Property 4, pruning with precision going to infinity eventually succeeds on the elementwise Cartesian product of that sequence with the corresponding free-variable bounds. Since the samples are equally distributed, for every element of the sequence $D_1^y, \ldots$ eventually a sample with higher precision will be created, and by Property 3 pruning will succeed on the Cartesian product of this sample with the corresponding free-variable bound.

In a similar way we can prove the success of finding a sample point on which f is negative.

These sample points are all within D, on which $g_1, \ldots, g_n$ are all positive. So, by Property 4, the positivity check will also eventually succeed.   □

8   Application to Overall Algorithm

Now we can use the results developed in the previous three sections in the main algorithm. As a result we get:

Theorem 9. *Using pruning from Section 5, branching from Section 6, and checking from Section 7, Algorithm 1 terminates for inputs for which the volume of the elements of B for which ϕ is not stable is zero.*

Proof.

- For bounded constraints converging to a point with positive degree of truth, by Theorem 8, eventually the check succeeds.
- For bounded constraints converging to a point with negative degree of truth eventually pruning succeeds: We have to prove that for all sequences of bounded constraints converging to a point with negative degree of truth, where one element results from the previous by pruning and branching (taking one element of the produced branches), eventually the free-variable-bound is the empty set.

  Let $\exists y \in B \ [f = 0 \land g_1 \geq 0 \land \ldots \land g_n \geq 0]$ be an arbitrary but fixed disjunctive branch of the constraint under consideration. By Lemma 2, its degree of truth is given by $\sup_{y \in B} \min\{f, -f, g_1, \ldots, g_n\}$. Let h be the element of $\{f, -f, g_1, \ldots, g_n\}$ on which the (negative) optimum is attained.

  Now, by Theorem 6 the width of the quantification bound goes to zero, and so by Property 4, Prune will eventually result in the empty set for h, disproving the constraint.

  □

9 Implementation and Applications

We have implemented a prototype of the algorithm in the programming language O'Caml (www.ocaml.org). We do not use more precision than available with machine-precision floating-point numbers. This suffices for all our examples. For pruning we use an extremely simple (and thus usually inefficient) algorithm for computing hull consistency based on the interval library smath [12, 11].

As there are no existing algorithms/implementations for the general problem studied in this paper, instead of a comparison, we illustrate the usefulness of our approach by discussing the application of the resulting solver to simple examples from control engineering, parameter estimation, and computational geometry.

In the first example, we consider a problem in control engineering [20]. Here one important tool to describe the behavior of a system is its *characteristic polynomial*. In the design process this polynomial is parametric, and the goal is to find values for these parameters such that the resulting polynomial has certain properties. For example, often one requires that the polynomial has a real root in a certain interval.

Now consider the characteristic polynomial $s(s + 1.71)(s + 100) + 6.63K = 0$ of the positioning system of a radio telescope antenna [20, p. 17ff, p. 295ff]. Here the parameter K denotes the gain of a certain amplifier. It needs to be set in such a way that the total system fulfill certain characteristics. We already know that, for the system to be stable, $0 < K < 2623$. Now we also want that the characteristic polynomial has a real root in $[-2.0, -0.5]$. This results in the constraint $\exists s \in [-2.0, -0.5] \ s(s + 1.71)(s + 100) + 6.63K = 0$ which the solver proves to be true for $K \in [0, 9.375]$ and false for $K > 11.25$. Very often, the design goal imposes additional constraints to the system. So we add the additional constraint $se^K \leq -1$. The solver reports the same solution as before.

The second example comes from the field of parameter estimation [31]. Here one has given a model of a system and some information coming from measurements on some of these variables. The goal is to deduce further information on the possible variable values.

We consider the following parameter estimation problem: Given a system model whose explicit solution (obtained from a differential equation) is $f(p_1, p_2, t) = 20e^{-p_1 t} - 8e^{-p_2 t}$ [15, 14, 18]. We have the information that f reaches zero some-when, but we only know that this happens between time 2 and 4. We want more information about the parameters p_1 and p_2. This results in the constraint $\exists t \in [2, 4]\ 20e^{-p_1 t} - 8e^{-p_2 t} = 0$ for which the implementation computes a strip of values for p_1 and p_2 as solutions.

The third example comes from computational geometry. Here, very often the situation arises that one wants to visualize high-dimensional non-linear objects. One method for doing this, is to project them into 2-dimensional space, resulting in constraints like $\exists z \in [-2, 2]\ [x^2 + y^2 + z^2 - 1 = 0 \wedge x^2 + y^2 - 0.5 \geq 0]$ to which we applied our solver, resulting in a 2-dimensional ring.

The run-times in all the above examples (for the precision 0.1) were under one second on an average Linux PC. However, for some bigger examples they increase rapidly. The main reason for this is that it often computes lots of sample points although pruning did not yet succeed in isolating a solution sufficiently enough.

10 Related Work

The main alternative to modeling uncertain variables by bounded quantification is stochastic [30]. For quantified constraints, despite of the undecidability of the general problem, several special cases could be solved:

- In the case without equality constraints, the atomic sub-constraints in general have solution sets with volume. Therefore, one can compute true elements by pruning the negation of the original constraints [26, 25, 1].
- In the case $k = 0$, that is, constraints of the form $\exists y \in B\ f = 0$, according to Bolzano's intermediate value theorem, one can reduce the problem to the previous case by reformulating it to $\exists y\ f \geq 0\ \wedge\ \exists y\ f \leq 0$. However, this method does not generalize to E-constraints, because here the solution set of the inequalities should connect the positive and negative elements of f.
- In the case $\exists y \in B_y\ [f = y \wedge g_1 \geq 0 \wedge \ldots \wedge g_n \geq 0]$, where f does not contain y, the equality holds a priori. One just has to make sure that it is contained in B_y and that it fulfills the inequalities, which can be checked by the usual interval methods. Note that in some cases one can isolate the variable y in such a way, but in general not! The case where some additional existentially quantified variables (but not the isolated one!) occur in f can be treated by additional splitting [14, p. 156].
- The case where all terms are polynomials, which is a classical research topic in computer algebra [29, 6, 13, 16].

- The case where the quantified variables fulfill certain structural restrictions (e.g., only occurring once) [28, 9, 33], or where primitive pruning operations suffice for solving [4].

Existence proofs for systems of equations, are usually done using variants of the interval Newton method. This fails for zeros that are well-posed, but not simple (e.g., the zero of $x^3 = 0$), and for very close zero clusters. These methods do not avoid splitting on solutions. Instead they usually use a method called ε-inflation which seems to succeed for simple zeros in practice, but whose general success is proven only for special cases [17, 27]. As shown by Neumaier [19, Chapter 5] one can alternatively construct a super-box of a presumed zero for which existence holds.

In general, existence proofs for non-simple, but still well-posed, zeros need techniques that do not rely on the derivative. A promising notion here is the topological degree [21, Chapter 6].

11   Conclusion

In this paper we have introduced the first known algorithm for solving a certain type of quantified constraint over the real numbers, and we have applied the algorithm to several application areas. In future work we will consider the following improvements of the method:

- heuristics for the number of computed samples, and the choice of branching,
- making the checking step incremental, by reusing the information computed in earlier steps, and
- replacing the checking operation by a dual pruning operation that removes elements from the free-variable-bound that provably belong to the solution set.

Our final goal is to be able to efficiently solve general well-posed quantified constraints.

Thanks to Laurent Granvilliers for interesting discussions on the topic and to Varadarajulu Reddy Pyda for help with the implementation of the solver.

References

1. F. Benhamou and F. Goualard. Universally quantified interval constraints. In *Proc. of the Sixth Intl. Conf. on Principles and Practice of Constraint Programming (CP'2000)*, number 1894 in LNCS, Singapore, 2000. Springer Verlag.
2. F. Benhamou, D. McAllester, and P. V. Hentenryck. CLP(Intervals) Revisited. In *International Symposium on Logic Programming*, pages 124–138, Ithaca, NY, USA, 1994. MIT Press.
3. F. Benhamou and W. J. Older. Applying interval arithmetic to real, integer and Boolean constraints. *Journal of Logic Programming*, 32(1):1–24, 1997.

4. L. Bordeaux and E. Monfroy. Beyond NP: Arc-consistency for quantified constraints. In P. V. Hentenryck, editor, *Proc. of Principles and Practice of Constraint Programming (CP 2002)*, number 2470 in LNCS. Springer, 2002.

5. B. F. Caviness and J. R. Johnson, editors. *Quantifier Elimination and Cylindrical Algebraic Decomposition*. Springer, Wien, 1998.

6. G. E. Collins. Quantifier elimination for the elementary theory of real closed fields by cylindrical algebraic decomposition. In Caviness and Johnson [5], pages 134–183.

7. J. H. Davenport and J. Heintz. Real quantifier elimination is doubly exponential. *Journal of Symbolic Computation*, 5:29–35, 1988.

8. E. Davis. Constraint propagation with interval labels. *Artificial Intelligence*, 32(3):281–331, 1987.

9. E. Gardeñes, M. Á. Sainz, L. Jorba, R. Calm, R. Estela, H. Mielgo, and A. Trepat. Modal intervals. *Reliable Computing*, 7(2):77–111, 2001.

10. L. Granvilliers. On the combination of interval constraint solvers. *Reliable Computing*, 7(6):467–483, 2001.

11. T. J. Hickey. smathlib.
http://interval.sourceforge.net/interval/C/smathlib/README.html.

12. T. J. Hickey, Q. Ju, and M. H. van Emden. Interval arithmetic: from principles to implementation. *Journal of the ACM*, 48(5):1038–1068, 2001.

13. H. Hong. *Improvements in CAD-based Quantifier Elimination*. PhD thesis, The Ohio State University, 1990.

14. L. Jaulin, M. Kieffer, O. Didrit, and E. Walter. *Applied Interval Analysis, with Examples in Parameter and State Estimation, Robust Control and Robotics*. Springer, Berlin, 2001.

15. L. Jaulin and E. Walter. Guaranteed nonlinear parameter estimation from bounded-error data via interval analysis. *Mathematics and Computers in Simulation*, 35(2):123–137, 1993.

16. R. Loos and V. Weispfenning. Applying linear quantifier elimination. *The Computer Journal*, 36(5):450–462, 1993.

17. G. Mayer. Epsilon-inflation in verification algorithms. *Journal of Computational and Applied Mathematics*, 60:147–169, 1994.

18. M. Milanese and A. Vicino. Estimation theory for nonlinear models and set membership uncertainty. *Automatica (Journal of IFAC)*, 27(2):403–408, 1991.

19. A. Neumaier. *Interval Methods for Systems of Equations*. Cambridge Univ. Press, Cambridge, 1990.

20. N. S. Nise. *Control Systems Engineering*. John Wiley & Sons, 3rd edition, 2000.

21. J. M. Ortega and W. C. Rheinboldt. *Iterative Solution of Nonlinear Equations*. Academic Press, 1970.

22. S. Ratschan. Applications of quantified constraint solving over the reals— bibliography. http://www.mpi-sb.mpg.de/~ratschan/appqcs.html, 2001.

23. S. Ratschan. Continuous first-order constraint satisfaction. In J. Calmet, B. Benhamou, O. Caprotti, L. Henocque, and V. Sorge, editors, *Artificial Intelligence, Automated Reasoning, and Symbolic Computation*, number 2385 in LNCS, pages 181–195. Springer, 2002.

24. S. Ratschan. Continuous first-order constraint satisfaction with equality and disequality constraints. In P. van Hentenryck, editor, *Proc. 8th International Conference on Principles and Practice of Constraint Programming*, number 2470 in LNCS, pages 680–685. Springer, 2002.

25. S. Ratschan. Efficient solving of quantified inequality constraints over the real numbers. http://www.mpi-sb.mpg.de/~ratschan/preprints.html, 2002. submitted for publication.

26. S. Ratschan. Quantified constraints under perturbations. *Journal of Symbolic Computation*, 33(4):493–505, 2002.

27. S. M. Rump. A note on epsilon-inflation. *Reliable Computing*, 4:371–375, 1998.

28. S. P. Shary. A new technique in systems analysis under interval uncertainty and ambiguity. *Reliable Computing*, 8:321–418, 2002.

29. A. Tarski. *A Decision Method for Elementary Algebra and Geometry*. Univ. of California Press, Berkeley, 1951. Also in [5].

30. T. Walsh. Stochastic constraint programming. In *Proc. of ECAI*, 2002.

31. E. Walter and L. Pronzato. *Identification of Parametric Models from Experimental Data*. Springer, 1997.

32. V. Weispfenning. The complexity of linear problems in fields. *Journal of Symbolic Computation*, 5(1–2):3–27, 1988.

33. N. Yorke-Smith and C. Gervet. On constraint problems with incomplete or erroneous data. In P. V. Hentenryck, editor, *Principles and Practice of Constraint Programming*, number 2470 in LNCS, pages 732–737, 2002.

Using Constraint Programming to Solve the Maximum Clique Problem

Jean-Charles Régin

ILOG Sophia Antipolis
Les Taissounières HB2
1681 route des Dolines
06560 Valbonne, France
regin@ilog.fr

Abstract. This paper aims to show that Constraint Programming can be an efficient technique to solve a well-known combinatorial optimization problem: the search for a maximum clique in a graph. A clique of a graph $G = (X, E)$ is a subset V of X, such that every two nodes in V are joined by an edge of E. The maximum clique problem consists of finding $\omega(G)$ the largest cardinality of a clique. We propose two new upper bounds of $\omega(G)$ and a new strategy to guide the search for an optimal solution. The interest of our approach is emphasized by the results we obtain for the DIMACS Benchmarks. Seven instances are solved for the first time and two better lower bounds for problems remaining open are found. Moreover, we show that the CP method we propose gives good results and quickly.

Introduction

Constraint Programming (CP) involves finding values for problem variables subject to constraints on which combinations are acceptable. One of the main principles of CP is that every constraint is associated with a filtering algorithm (also called a domain reduction algorithm) that removes some values that are inconsistent with the constraint. Then, the consequences of these deletions are studied thanks to a propagation mechanism that calls the filtering algorithms of the constraints until no more modification occurs. CP uses also a systematic search, like a branch-and-bound for instance, but this is not limited to this case, to find solutions.

In this paper, we aim to contradict some conventional wisdom of Constraint Programming. It is often considered that CP is not an efficient method to solve pure combinatorial optimization problems. By "pure problems", we mean problems in which only one kind of constraint is involved.

A clique of a graph $G = (X, E)$ is a subset V of X, such that every two nodes in V are joined by an edge of E. The maximum clique problem consists of finding $\omega(G)$ the largest cardinality of a clique. Finding a clique of size k is an NP-Hard problem. This problem is quite important because it appears in a lot of real world problems. Therefore almost all types of algorithms have been

F. Rossi (Ed.): CP 2003, LNCS 2833, pp. 634–648, 2003.

used to try to solve it. For more information the reader can consult the survey of Bomze, Budinich, Pardalos and Pelillo [3].

Fahle [7] has proposed to use CP techniques to solve this problem. The results he obtained were encouraging. Notably, he has been able to close some open problems. His model uses two constraints: one based on the degree, we will call it degreeCt, and one based on the search for an upper bound of the size of a maximum clique, we will call it UBMaxCliqueCt. These two constraints are defined on the set of nodes that are considered at every moment by the algorithm. Then a branch-and-bound algorithm is used to traverse the search space.

Fahle's algorithm tries to construct a clique as large as possible, by successively selecting a node and studying the **candidate set**, that is the set of nodes that can extend the clique currently under construction. After each selection of node, the filtering algorithms associated with the two constraints are triggered until no more modification of the candidate set occurs.

The filtering algorithm associated with degreeCT removes all nodes whose degree is too small to extend the current clique to a clique of size greater than the current objective value.

The filtering algorithm associated with UBMaxCliqueCt removes all nodes for which we know that they cannot belong to a clique of size greater than the current objective value. A non obvious bound is searched by computing an upper bound of the number of colors needed to color the subgraph induced by a node and its neighborhood such that two adjacent nodes have different colors.

The drawback of this filtering is the time required to compute such a bound, and also its systematic use. That is, a priori, we do not know whether the filtering algorithm will remove some values or not.

In this paper we propose to use another upper bound based on matching algorithm. The advantage of our method is that we can easily identify some cases for which the filtering algorithm will remove no value; and so we can avoid to call it.

Moreover, Fahle uses a common strategy to select the next node that will extend the current clique under construction. This strategy is based on the degree of the nodes and selects the one with the smallest value. We propose a different approach that can be viewed as an adaptation and a generalization of the Bron & Kerbosh's [4] ideas for enumerating the maximal cliques of a graph. This idea leads to a new filtering algorithm based on the study of the nodes that have already been tried. Our strategy is more complex but tends to find more quickly the cliques with a large size as it is shown by the results we obtain on the well-known DIMACS benchmarks.

The paper is organized as follows. First we present, new upper bounds for the maximum clique problem. Then, we introduce some new properties that are based on the ideas of the Bron & Kerbosh's algorithm. The strategy that exploits the previous ideas is detailed. After, we will give some results. Finally, we present some ideas about the definition of a maximum clique constraint and we conclude.

1   Preliminaries

1.1   Graph

A **graph** $G = (X, E)$ consists of a **node set** X and an **edge set** E, where every edge (u, v) is a pair of distinct nodes. u and v are the endpoints of (u, v). The complementary graph of a graph $G = (X, E)$ is the graph $\overline{G} = (X, F)$, where (x, y) is an edge of $\overline{G}$ if and only if $x \neq y$ and (x, y) is not an edge of G.

A **path** from node v_1 to node v_k in G is a list of nodes $[v_1, ..., v_k]$ such that (v_i, v_{i+1}) is an edge for $i \in [1..k-1]$. The path **contains** node v_i for $i \in [1..k]$ and arc (v_i, v_{i+1}) for $i \in [1..k-1]$. The path is a **cycle** if $k > 1$ and $v_1 = v_k$. The **length** of a path p, denoted by $length(p)$, is the number of arc it contains. $\Gamma(x)$ is the set of neighbors of x, that is the set of nodes y such that $(x, y) \in E$.

A **clique** of a graph $G = (X, E)$ is a subset V of X, such that every two nodes in V are joined by an edge of E. The **maximum clique problem** consist of finding $\omega(G)$ the largest cardinality of a clique. Given a node x, $\omega(G, x)$ denotes the size of the largest clique containing x.

A **independent set** of a graph $G = (X, E)$ is a subset S of X, such that every two nodes in V are not joined by an edge of E. The **maximum independent set** problem consist of finding $\alpha(G)$ the largest cardinality of an independent set.

A **vertex cover** of a graph $G = (X, E)$ is a subset V of X, such that every edge of E has an endpoint in V. The **minimum vertex cover** problem consist of finding $\nu(G)$ the smallest cardinality of a vertex cover.

A **matching** of a graph $G = (X, E)$ is a subset M of E, such that no two edges of M have a common node. The **maximum matching** problem consists of finding $\mu(G)$ the largest cardinality of a matching.

1.2   CP Algorithm for Solving Maximum Clique

Let $G = (X, E)$ be a graph. The idea is to start with a clique $C = \emptyset$, called the **current set**, and a **candidate set** equals to X. Then the algorithm successively selects nodes in the candidate set in order to increase the size of C. When a node x is added to C, all the nodes that are non adjacent to x are removed from the candidate set. The candidate set is also used for bounding. Algorithm 1 is a possible implementation. The algorithm must be called with $Current = \emptyset$, $Candidate = X$ and $K = \emptyset$, where K is the largest clique found so far. Function FILTERANDPROPAGATE returns false when we can prove that there is no clique whose cardinality is strictly greater than $|K|$ in the subgraph of G induced by $(Current \cup Candidate)$; otherwise it returns true. This function also aims to remove some values of $Candidate$ that cannot belong to a clique of size strictly greater than $|K|$ and containing $Current$. The simplest condition to remove a node y is to check whether $|\Gamma(y) \cap Candidate| + |Current| < |K|$

Every upper bound for the maximum clique problem is interesting in a CP approach, because we will use it to check whether a node can belong to a clique of a given size.

Algorithm 1: Basic Algorithm for searching for a maximum Clique

---

MAXIMUMCLIQUE($Current, Candidate, \textbf{io } K$)
while $Candidate \neq \emptyset$ **do**
  select x in Candidate and remove it
  save $Candidate$
  add x to $Current$
  remove from Candidate the nodes y s.t. $y \notin \Gamma(x)$
  if FILTERANDPROPAGATE($Current, Candidate, K$) **then**
    if $Candidate = \emptyset$ **then** $K \leftarrow Current$ // solution
    else MAXIMUMCLIQUE($Current, Candidate, K$)
  remove x from $Current$
  restore $Candidate$

Property 1 *Let $G = (X, E)$ be a graph and x a node, and K be a clique of G. If $\omega(G, x) < |K|$ then $\omega(G) = \omega(G - \{x\})$.*

Therefore any upper bound of $\omega(G, x)$ can be used to remove some nodes in the candidate set. A simple bound can be $|\Gamma(x) \cap Candidate| + |Current|$. That is, as proposed by [7], we can remove from the candidate set all the nodes such that $|\Gamma(x) \cap Candidate| + |Current| < |K|$. The deletion of a node modifies the neighborhood of its neighbors thus it can change the value of the upper bound of some other nodes, so the process is repeated until no more modifications occurs. Function FILTERANDPROPAGATE given by Algorithm 2 implements this idea.

Algorithm 2: Filtering algorithm and propagation

FILTERANDPROPAGATE($Current, Candidate, \textbf{io } K$)
do
  $continue \leftarrow false$
  for *each y in Candidate* **do**
    if $|\Gamma(y) \cap Candidate| + |Current| < |K|$ **then**
      remove y from $Candidate$
      if $|Candidate| + |Current| < |K|$ **then** return false
      $continue \leftarrow true$
while *continue*
return true

---

2   Upper Bounds for Clique

If we find better upper bounds for the size of the maximum clique involving a node then we will be able to improve function FILTERANDPROPAGATE and so to remove more values.

There are some relations between the maximum clique problem, the maximum independent set, the minimum vertex cover, and the maximum matching:

Property 2 *Let $G = (X, E)$ be a graph, then*
- $\omega(G) = \alpha(\overline{G})$
- $\alpha(G) = |X| - \nu(G)$
- $\omega(G) = |X| - \nu(\overline{G})$

proof: A maximum clique corresponds to an independent set in the complementary graph, hence $\omega(G) = \alpha(\overline{G})$. The subgraph induced by an independent set S does not contain any edge, thus every edge of G has an endpoint in $Y = X - S$, therefore Y is a vertex cover of G. Hence $S = X - Y$ and the largest set S is associated with the smallest set Y, so $\alpha(G) = |X| - \nu(G)$. Then, $\omega(G) = |X| - \nu(\overline{G})$ follows immediately.

Property 3 *Let $G = (X, E)$ be a graph, then*
$\nu(G) \geq \mu(G)$ *and the equality holds if G is bipartite.*

proof: Let V be any vertex cover of G. All the edges of a matching have no common nodes, thus at least one endpoint of every edge of the matching must be in V in order to cover this edge. Therefore $\nu(G) \geq \mu(G)$. The proof for the bipartite case can be found in [2].

From this property and the previous one we immediately deduce the well known property:

Property 4 $\omega(G) \leq |X| - \mu(\overline{G})$

This new upper bound could be used, but it has one drawback: $\overline{G}$ can be non-bipartite, and the algorithm to compute a maximum matching in a non-bipartite graph is complex. Thus we propose to use an original upper bound for $\omega(G)$, which is stronger and much more easy to compute. We need, first, to define the duplicated graph of a graph (See Figure 1.)

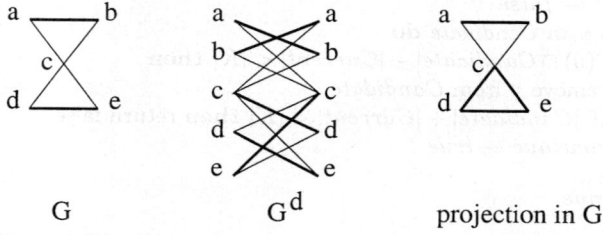

$$G \qquad\qquad G^d \qquad\qquad \text{projection in } G$$

Fig. 1. An example of a duplicated graph of a graph. The bold edges represent the edges of the matchings. The right graph is the projection of the matching of G^d in G. G is covered by an edge and a triangle, therefore $1 + 2$ nodes are necessary to cover all the edges and $\nu(G) \geq 3$.

Definition 1 *Let $G = (X, E)$ be a graph. The **duplicated graph** of G is the bipartite graph $G^d = (X, Y, F)$, such that Y is a copy of the nodes X, $c(u)$ is the*

*node of Y corresponding to the node u in X, and there is an edge $(u, c(v))$ in F
if and only if there is an edge (u, v) in E.*

Note that if $(u, v) \in E$ then $(v, u) \in E$.

Property 5 $\mu(G^d) \geq 2.\mu(G)$ *and there exist graphs G with $\mu(G^d) > 2.\mu(G)$*

proof: From a matching M of G we can create a set M' of edges of G^d as follows: for
each edge (u, v) in M we add the edges $(u, c(v))$ and $(v, c(u))$ to M'. M is matching
thus it involves $2.|M|$ nodes. By construction of M' and by definition of G^d, M' involves
$2.|M|$ nodes of X and $2.|M|$ nodes of Y. Therefore M' is matching of size $2.|M|$ and
$\mu(G^d) \geq 2.\mu(G)$. A triangle is an example of graph G with $\mu(G^d) = 3$ and $\mu(G) = 1$,
that is $\mu(G^d) > 2.\mu(G)$ (See also Figure 1.)

We define the projection of a matching of G^d in G:

Definition 2 *Let $G = (X, E)$ be a graph and M be a matching of G^d. Let E' by
the subset of E defined by $(u, v) \in E'$ if and only if either $(u, c(v))$ or $(v, c(u))$
belongs to M.*
*The **projection** of M in G is the subgraph of G induced by the subset E' of E.
We will denote it by $P(M, G)$.*

Figure 1 contains an example of projection.
We will denote by $edges(cc)$ the edge set of a connected component cc.

Property 6 *Let $G = (X, E)$ be a graph, M be a matching in G^d, $P(M, G)$ be
the projection of M in G, and CC be the set of the connected components of
$P(M, G)$. Then*

$$\nu(G) \geq \sum_{cc \in CC} \lceil \frac{|edges(cc)|}{2} \rceil$$

proof: Consider cc a connected component of $P(M, G)$. M is matching, so no node
of $P(M, G)$ can have a degree greater than 2. Therefore, cc is either an isolated node,
or a path, or a cycle. Hence, the number of nodes needed to cover the edges of cc is
$\lceil \frac{|edges(cc)|}{2} \rceil$. The connected components are node disjoint therefore the value associated with each component can be sum, and the property holds.

From this property we can also deduce a simpler property which is weaker
but interesting due to property 5.

Property 7 $\nu(G) \geq \lceil \frac{\mu(G^d)}{2} \rceil$

proof: Consider a matching M in G^d with $M = \mu(G^d)$, $P(M, G)$ the projection of
M in G, and cc a connected component of $P(M, G)$. As mentioned in the proof of
Property 6, cc is either an isolated node, or a path, or a cycle. Let $Medges(cc)$ be the
set of edges $(u, c(v))$ of M such that (u, v) belongs to cc. If cc is a path containing only
one edge then $|Medges(cc)| = 2$ and $\lceil \frac{|edges(cc)|}{2} \rceil = \lceil \frac{|Medges(cc)|}{2} \rceil$. In all the other cases
$|edges(cc)| = |Medges(cc)|$, and so $\lceil \frac{|edges(cc)|}{2} \rceil = \lceil \frac{|Medges(cc)|}{2} \rceil$. Moreover, by definition of the projection of M, for every edge $(u, c(v))$ of M there exists a connected com-
ponent cc containing $(u, c(v))$, then we have $\sum_{cc \in CC} \lceil \frac{|Medges(cc)|}{2} \rceil = \sum_{cc \in CC} \lceil \frac{|edges(cc)|}{2} \rceil$.

On the other hand $\sum \lceil \frac{i}{2} \rceil \geq \lceil \frac{\sum i}{2} \rceil$
thus we have:

$$\sum_{cc \in CC} \lceil \frac{|edges(cc)|}{2} \rceil = \sum_{cc \in CC} \lceil \frac{|Medges(cc)|}{2} \rceil \geq \lceil \frac{\sum_{cc \in CC} |Medges(cc)|}{2} \rceil \geq \lceil \frac{\mu(G^d)}{2} \rceil$$

And from Property 6 we deduce: $\nu(G) \geq \lceil \frac{\mu(G^d)}{2} \rceil$

Finally, from Property 2 we immediately have the property:

Property 8 $\omega(G) \leq |X| - \lceil \frac{\mu(\overline{G}^d)}{2} \rceil$

We decided to base our filtering algorithm on this property and not on Property 6 because with Property 8 we have a good test to know whether it can be interesting to check it. We just have to check whether $|X| - \lceil \frac{|X|}{2} \rceil$ is lower than the size of the clique currently computed. From our experiments, thanks to this test, only 5% of the matching that are computed are useless[1].

We have also implemented Property 6 but the gain is really small in term of eliminated nodes and more time is needed. We would like to stress on this point. CP involves a propagation mechanism, therefore, and especially for pure problems, the comparison of two properties is not simple because we have to take into account the propagation mechanism. Here, we have seen that the use of Property 8 and propagation gives equivalent result to the use of Property 6 with propagation, so we can eliminate the use of the second, if, of course, it required more time to be checked. Moreover, in practice, we can stop the computation of the maximum matching either when the current size of the matching is enough to conclude that we cannot find a clique with a largest size of the better found so far, or when we known that we will not be able to make such a deduction.

On the other hand, in practice there is an important difference between Property 4 and Property 8. It seems really worthwhile to improve the upper bound even by a small value, provided that we have an interesting test to avoid some useless computations.

Function FILTERANDPROPAGATE can be refined. Algorithm 3 gives its new code.

There is no need to explicitly create the subgraph in the function it is sufficient to traverse the nodes of $\Gamma(x) \cap Candidate$ and the matching can be computed by considering that an edge exists if two nodes are non adjacent. In the algorithm, we also apply this new test for the set $Candidate$ when a node is removed in order to know whether it is useless to continue the search.

3   Introduction of a Not Set

When enumerating all the maximal cliques of a graph, Bron and Kerbosh [4] have proposed to use a new set of nodes: a **not set** denoted by Not. This set

---

[1] More precisely, only 5% of nodes that satisfies this test (that is mark 1 in Algorithm 3) will not be removed by Algorithm 3 (that is by mark 2.)

Algorithm 3: Filtering algorithm and propagation: a new version

FILTERANDPROPAGATE($Current, Candidate, \textbf{io } K$)

do

    $continue \leftarrow false$

    for *each y in Candidate* **do**

        $N \leftarrow |\Gamma(y) \cap Candidate|$

        if $N + |Current| < |K|$ **then** remove y from $Candidate$

        else

1   **if** $N - \lceil \frac{N}{2} \rceil + |Current| < |K|$ **then**

                Let H be the subgraph of G induced by $\Gamma(x) \cap Candidate$

                compute $\mu(\overline{H}^d)$

                if $N - \lceil \frac{\mu(\overline{H}^d)}{2} \rceil + |Current| < |K|$ **then**

2   remove y from $Candidate$

        if $y \notin Candidate$ **then**

            Let H be the subgraph of G induced by $Candidate$

            compute $\mu(\overline{H}^d)$

            if $|Candidate| - \lceil \frac{\mu(\overline{H}^d)}{2} \rceil + |Current| < |K|$ **then** return false;

            $continue \leftarrow true$

while *continue*

return true

---

contains the nodes that have already been studied by the algorithm and that are linked to all the nodes of the *Current* set. We propose to adapt their idea to our case and to generalize it.

In order to clearly understand the meaning of the not set we propose to immediately adapt our algorithm (See Algorithm 4.) Function REMOVEFROMNOT(x) removes from *Not* the element that are not in $\Gamma(x)$.

The idea of Bron and Kerbosh corresponds to the following property:

Property 9 *If there is a node x in Not such that $Candidate \subseteq \Gamma(x)$ then the current branch of the search can be abandoned.*

proof: all cliques that we can find from the current set and from the candidate set will be a clique by adding x, therefore these cliques cannot be maximal.

This property can be refined when searching for the size of a maximum clique. A dominance property can be obtained:

Dominance Property 1 *If there is a node x in Not such that $|Candidate - \Gamma(x)| \leq 1$ then the current branch of the search can be abandoned.*

proof: We just have to consider the case $Candidate - \Gamma(x) = \{y\}$. There are two possible cliques: the cliques that contain y and the cliques that do not contain y. Consider any clique that does not contain y. In this case, this clique could also be found if y is removed from *Candidate* and therefore Property 9 can be applied. Consider any clique that contains y, then if we replace y by x we also obtain a clique because x is linked

---

Algorithm 4: Solving the maximum Clique problem: introduction of a not set

MAXIMUMCLIQUE(*Current, Candidate, Not,* **io** *K*)
while *Candidate* ≠ ∅ **do**
> select *x* in Candidate and remove it
> save *Candidate*
> save *Not*
> add *x* to *Current*
> remove from Candidate the nodes *y* s.t. *y* ∉ *Γ(x)*
> REMOVEFROMNOT(*x*)
> **if** FILTERANDPROPAGATE(*Current, Candidate, Not, K*) **then**
>> **if** *Candidate* = ∅ **then** *K* ← *Current* // solution
>> **else** MAXIMUMCLIQUE(*Current, Candidate, K*)
>
> restore *Not*
> remove *x* from *Current*
> add *x* to *Not*
> restore *Candidate*

---

to all the nodes except *y*, and the size of the clique is unchanged. And, this clique has already been found when *x* has been selected, hence we cannot improved the largest cardinality found so far.

This new property leads to a modification of our algorithm. In the Bron and Kerbosh's algorithm a node is removed from *Not* when the selected node is not linked to it. In our case, we slightly change this property: instead of removing a node *x* in *Not* when a selected node *y* is not linked to it, we can mark *x* if it is unmarked and remove *x* if it is already marked. Our property must be changed:

Dominance Property 2 *If there is a node x in Not such that x is not marked and |Candidate − Γ(x)| ≤ 1 then the current branch of the search can be abandoned.*
If there is a node x in Not such that x is marked and Candidate ⊆ Γ(x) then the current branch of the search can be abandoned.

Function REMOVEFROMNOT has to be accordingly modified. From this property we can define a new filtering algorithm:

Unfortunately, the cost of checking this property is high. In practice, it is not worthwhile to use it. We have preferred to use it in a different way. Instead of searching if the current neighborhood of every node of the candidate set is included in the neighborhood of every node in *Not*, we decided to limit our study to the node of not whose neighborhood contains almost all nodes of candidate. That is, for every node *x* of *Not* we compute the number of nodes of candidates that are linked to *x*. If this number is greater than |*Candidate*| − 2 we can immediately identify the nodes of the candidate set that must be selected or that must be removed. The strict application of Dominance Property 2 gives better results in terms of backtracks (around 10% less) than the restriction we propose. However, the latter approach is much more easy to implement and more efficient to compute, because we only need to compare the neighborhood of a node of Not with the candidate set and not with neighborhood of every node in the candidate set taken separately.

The final version of our algorithm is given by Algorithm 5.

Function FILTERINGFROMNOT uses the notion of mark or removes some nodes.

Algorithm 5: Filtering algorithm and propagation taken into account nodes of the not set

FILTERANDPROPAGATE($Current, Candidate,$ **io** K)

do

   do

      $continue \leftarrow false$

      for $each\ y\ in\ Candidate$ **do**

         $N \leftarrow |\Gamma(y) \cap Candidate|$

         if $N + |Current| < |K|$ **then** remove y from $Candidate$

         else

            if $N - \lceil \frac{N}{2} \rceil + |Current| < |K|$ **then**

               Let H be the subgraph of G induced by $\Gamma(x) \cap Candidate$

               compute $\mu(\overline{H}^d)$

               if $N - \lceil \frac{\mu(\overline{H}^d)}{2} \rceil + |Current| < |K|$ **then** remove y from $Candidate$

            if $y \notin Candidate$ **then**

               Let H be the subgraph of G induced by $Candidate$

               compute $\mu(\overline{H}^d)$

               if $|Candidate| - \lceil \frac{\mu(\overline{H}^d)}{2} \rceil + |Current| < |K|$ **then** return false; $continue \leftarrow true$

   while $continue$

   if $continue$ **then**

      $continue \leftarrow$ FILTERINGFROMNOT($Not, Candidate$)

while $continue$

return true

---

4 A New Search Strategy

As it has been shown by Bron and Kerbosh to enumerate the maximal cliques of a graph, it is interesting to select node such that Property 9 can be applied as soon as possible.

This means that when a node is added to Not, we identify first the node x in Not which has the largest number of neighbors in the candidate set. Then, we select for next node, a node y such that y is not linked to x

We have used exactly the same idea by considering in Not only the unmarked nodes. The ties have been broken by selecting the node y with the fewest number of neighbors in the candidate set, in order to have more chance to remove quickly y and then to be able to apply successfully Dominance Property 2.

When a node has not been removed, that is when the latest selection is successful; we select the node with the largest number of neighbors in the candidate set. This approach gives a better chance to find quickly cliques whose cardinality is huge. This is important for our approach because our filtering algorithm takes into account the size of the clique found so far.

4.1   Diving Technique

This technique is often used in conjunction with a MIP approach. It consists of searching whether of solution exists for every value of every variable. Each search for a solution is not complete. In other words, a greedy algorithm is used (that is no backtrack is allowed). Then, the new objective value is the best objective value found so far. The advantages of this approach is triple: its cost is low because the algorithm is polynomial, the minimum of the objective value can be improved, and an objective value can be quickly found whereas a depth first search strategy will need a lot of time to find it. In fact, a systematic search spends a lot of time to proved the local optimality of the current objective value; this proof is abandoned when a better value is found.

In our program, this technique is used after 10 minutes of computations. That is, we stop the current search, we apply the diving technique and the initial search continues with the objective value returned by the diving technique, which can be improved or not.

5   Experiments

We have used ILOG Solver to implement our algorithm and the well known DIMACS benchmark set for our tests [6].

All our experiments have been made on a Pentium IV mobile at 2Ghz with 512 Mo of memory.

The experiments have been stopped after 4 hours (that is 14,400 s) of computation, except for p_hat1000-2 because we saw after 14,400 s that the problem should be solved. In this case, 16,845 s are needed to close the problem.

The results are given in table entitled "Dimacs clique benchmarks".

All the problems having 400 nodes or less are solved. Notably, for the first time the brock400 series is now solved. Only, johnson32-2-4, prevent us from solving all the problems having 500 nodes or less.

All san series or sanr series are now solved.

7 problems have been closed for the first time: all the brock400 series, p_hat500-3, p_hat1000-2 and sanr200_0.9, which is solved in 150 s.

Two results are particularly remarkable: p_hat300-3 is solved in 40s, instead of 850s; and p_hat700-2 is solved in 255s instead of 2,086s.

Two lower bounds of the remaining open problems MANN_a45 (the optimal value is reached) and MANN_a81 have been improved.

			DIMACS CLIQUE BENCHMARKS								
		Wood			Östegard		Fahle			ILOG Solver		
Name	|K|	|K|	#select	time	|K|	time	|K|	#select	time	|K|	#select	time
brock200_1	21	21	379,810	53.68	21	18.10	21	66,042	92.37	21	93,795	10.72
brock200_2	12	12	2,594	0.26	12	0	12	437	0.31	12	2,185	0.29
brock200_3	15	15	24,113	2.57	15	0.15	15	2,332	2.23	15	7,821	0.86
brock200_4	17	17	52,332	6.20	17	0.33	17	8,779	8.18	17	23,037	2.13
brock400_1	27		fail			fail	≥ 24	fail		27	60,159,630	11,340.8
brock400_2	29		fail			fail	≥ 29	fail		29	36,843,872	7,910.6
brock400_3	31		fail			fail	≥ 24	fail		31	19,616,188	4,477.23
brock400_4	33		fail			fail	≥ 25	fail		33	32,457,068	6,051.77
brock800_1	23		fail			fail	≥ 21	fail		≥ 21	fail	
brock800_2	24		fail			fail	≥ 20	fail		≥ 20	fail	
brock800_3	25		fail			fail	≥ 20	fail		≥ 20	fail	
brock800_4	26		fail			fail	≥ 20	fail		≥ 20	fail	
c-fat200-1	12	12	8	0	12	0	12	5	0	12	3	0
c-fat200-2	24	24	7	0	24	0	24	5	0	24	3	0
c-fat200-5	58	58	27	0	58	2.6	58	5	0	58	3	0
c-fat500-1	14	14	13	0	14	0.02	14	3	0	14	3	0
c-fat500-10	126	126	1	0	126	0.02	126	5	0.02	126	3	0.04
c-fat500-2	26	26	23	0	26	0.03	26	5	0	26	3	0
c-fat500-5	64	64	23	0	64	3,480.21	64	5	0.02	64	3	0
hamming10-2	512	512	1	0	512	0.84	512	257	5.16	512	257	1.04
hamming10-4	≥ 40		fail			fail	≥ 32	fail		≥ 40	fail	
hamming6-2	32	32	1	0	32	0	32	17	0	32	17	0
hamming6-4	4	4	81	0	4	0	4	31	0	4	42	0
hamming8-2	128	128	1	0	128	0	128	65	0.07	128	65	0
hamming8-4	16	16	36,441	5.28	16	0.28	16	1,950	6.11	16	40,078	4.19
johnson16-2-4	8	8	256,099	13.05	8	0.09	8	126,460	7.91	8	250,505	3.80
johnson32-2-4	≥ 16		fail			fail	≥ 16	fail		≥ 16	fail	
johnson8-2-4	4	4	23	0	4	0	4	15	0	4	14	0
johnson8-4-4	14	14	115	0	14	0	14	39	0.03	14	140	0
keller4	11	11	12,829	1.23	11	0.17	11	1,771	2.53	11	7,871	0.5
keller5	27		fail			fail	≥ 25	fail		≥ 27	fail	
keller6	≥ 59		fail			fail	≥ 43	fail		≥ 54	fail	
MANN_a9	16	16	60	0	16	0	16	31	0	16	50	0
MANN_a27	126	126	47,264	46.95		fail	126	39,351	10,348.87	126	1,258,768	18.48
MANN_a45	345		fail			fail	≥ 331	fail		≥ 345	fail	
MANN_a81	≥ 1100		fail			fail	≥ 996	fail		≥ 1100	fail	
p_hat300-1	8	8	1,310	0.10	8	0	8	254	0.07	8	364	0.11
p_hat300-2	25	25	2,801	0.67	25	0.33	25	1,121	3.01	25	1,695	0.59
p_hat300-3	36		fail			fail	36	171,086	856.67	36	102,053	40.71
p_hat500-1	9	9	9.772	0.91	9	0.1	9	690	0.5	9	8,731	2.30
p_hat500-2	36	36	59,393	17.81	36	142.93	36	32,413	203.93	36	41,259	32.69
p_hat500-3	50		fail			fail	≥ 48	fail		50	10,986,526	12,744.7
p_hat700-1	11	11	25,805	2.69	11	0.22	11	2,195	2.67	11	25,653	6.01
p_hat700-2	44		fail			fail	44	188,823	2,086.63	44	259,775	255.79
p_hat700-3	≥ 62		fail			fail	≥ 54	fail		≥ 62	fail	
p_hat1000-1	10	10	179,082	18.88	10	1.95	10	19,430	16.43	10	69,582	27.80
p_hat1000-2	46		fail			fail	≥ 44	fail		46	14,735,370	16,845.7
p_hat1000-3	≥ 68		fail			fail	≥ 50	fail		≥ 66	fail	
p_hat1500-1	12		fail			fail	12	136,620	119.77	12	1,063,765	480.84
p_hat1500-2	≥ 65		fail			fail	≥ 52	fail		≥ 63	fail	
p_hat1500-3	≥ 94		fail			fail	≥ 56	fail		≥ 91	fail	
san1000	15	15	106,823	43.59	15	0.17	15	35,189	3044.09	15	256,529	102.80
san200_0.7_1	30	30	206	0.06	30	0.19	30	301	1.57	30	1,310	0.36
san200_0.7_2	18	18	195	0.03	18	0	18	394	0.66	18	3,824	0.37
san200_0.9_1	70	70	2,069	0.77	70	0.09	70	20,239	62.61	70	1,040	1.04
san200_0.9_2	60	60	211,889	70.13	60	1.43	60	309,378	1930.90	60	6,638	2.62
san200_0.9_3	44		fail			fail	44	32,327	194.96	44	758,545	182.70
san400_0.5_1	13	13	3,465	0.75	13	0	13	882	6.74	13	6,204	1.19
san400_0.7_1	40	40	38,989	13.25		fail	40	11,830	425.99	40	70,601	23.28
san400_0.7_2	30	30	1,591,030	415.12	30	168.7	30	26,818	159.72	30	249,836	67.53
san400_0.7_3	22		fail			fail	22	213,195	617.07	22	1,690,023	273.23
san400_0.9_1	100		fail			fail	100	291,195	7,219.55	100	984,133	1,700
sanr200_0.7	18	18	150,861	22.50	18	4.7	18	25,582	24.99	18	41,773	4.30
sanr200_0.9			fail			fail	≥ 41	fail		42	541,496	150.08
sanr400_0.5	13	13	233,381	22.55	13	2.21	13	32,883	23.09	13	164,276	17.12
sanr400_0.7			fail			fail	21	9,759,158	15,925	21	22,791,798	3,139.11

Our program reaches the best lower bounds found so far for 6 problems: p_hat700-3, johnson32-2-4, hamming10-4, keller5 (the optimal value is reached), MANN_a45 (the optimal value is reached), and MANN_a81.

Better lower bounds have been found by [1] for p_hat1500-2 (65) , and p_hat1500-3 (94); and by [8] for keller6 (59) and p_hat1000-3 (68).

We think that this method is not the good one to solve some problems: keller6, johnson32-2-4, hamming10-4. For the other open problems, we are more confident.

5.1   Comparison with Complete Methods

We compare our approach with 3 other algorithms:

• [11]: A branch-and-bound approach using fractionnal coloring and lower bound heuristic.

• [9]: this approach is similar to dynamic programming: solve the problem with one node, then with 2 nodes, and so on until reaching n. Each time the optimal value of the previous computations is used as a minimal value for the new problem.

• [7]: This is the first CP approach. Fahle proposes to consider two filtering: the first one consists of removing the nodes that have a degree which is too small to improve the current objective value, the second consists of computing an upper bound of the clique involving each vertex taken separately by using a well known heuristic algorithm for graph coloring. The strategy selects the node with the smallest degree.

We decided to use a normalization of the time of the other approaches, instead of re-program the algorithm, because we were able to compare the performance of our algorithm on several machines and then to obtain a time ratio that should be fair. Therefore we have used the following time ratio:

• The times given by Wood are divided by 15
• The times given by Östegard are divided by 3
• The times given by Fahle are divided by 1.5

We can resume the comparison with other complete method by the following table:

	Wood	Östegard	Fahle	ILOG Solver
number of solved problems	38	36	45	52
number of problems solved in less than 10 min.	38	35	38	44
number of best time	15	26	10	30
number of best lower bound for open problems	0	0	1	5

If we consider all the problems solved by Östegard in less than 10 minutes, then Östegard needs 345.88s for solving all these problems, whereas we need only 282.44s

Our approach is almost always better than the Fahle's one, only p_hat1500-1 is quickly solved by the Fahle's method.

5.2   Comparison with Heuristic Methods

Two heuristic methods give very interesting results for solving the maximum clique problem: QUALEX-MS [5] and the method proposed in [10].

For the set of benchmarks we consider, these two methods are able to reach the best bound known so far for 50 problems. In less than 1 minute QUALEX-MS found 48 best bounds.

Here are the results we obtain with our approach:

- Within a limit of 4 hours of computation, our method is able to reach the best bound for 58 problems (and for 52 the optimality is proved).
- In less than 10 minutes of computation, we are able to find 49 best bounds, whose 44 are proved to be optimal.
- Within a limit of 1 minute of computation, we can reach 41 best bounds, and prove that 37 are optimal.

These results show that our method is competitive in regards to the best heuristic methods, even when the computational time is limited.

5.3   Interest of the Diving Technique

The diving technique is used after 10 minutes of computations. This technique requires most of the time less than 10 s, except for some huge problems where 100 s are needed and for keller6 which needs one and half hour.

It improves the current objective value $|K|$ found so far by the search, for 4 problems:

• brock400_2: the current value is 24, and the diving technique gives 29. From this information the search is speed-up. Without the diving technique we need 9,163 s to solve the problem, whereas with it, we need only 7,910 s.

• keller6: the current value is 51, and the diving technique gives 54. This result is interesting because after 4 hours of computation the solver is not able to improve 51. Therefore the diving technique in itself gives a better result. This result cannot be improved in 4 hours of computation.

• p_hat1500-3: the current value is 89, and the diving technique gives 91. This value cannot be improved by further computations within the limit of 4 hours.

• san400_0.9_1: the current value is 92. The diving technique gives 100 which is the optimal value. With the diving technique 1,700 s are needed to solve the problem, instead of 2,900 s.

6   A Maximum Clique Constraint

We can imagine to have a constraint stating the a set of nodes of a graph must be a clique of size greater than a given integer K. For instance, this set of nodes can be represented by a set variable as presented in ILOG Solver. Then, the filtering algorithm associated with this constraint will aim to remove some values of this set variable. The current set will then be defined by the required elements of the set variable. Moreover, then a node will be required all its non-neighboor will be removed from the possible set. In this case Algorithm 3 can be used as a filtering algorithm.

Moreover, a *Not* set could also be used. For instance, it could be given at the definition, and the growing of this set could be managed. We can define a filtering algorithm involving this set by using Property 9. The dominance properties cannot be used because some solutions could be missed.

7 Conclusion

In this paper we have presented a CP approach to solve a famous combinatorial optimization problem. We have presented new upper bound for the maximum clique problem and adapted and generalized the ideas of Bron and Kerbosh to this problem. The results that we obtain are good: seven problems are closed and 2 lower bounds have been improved for problems remaining open. We have also discussed the possible definition of a maximum clique constraint and its association with a filtering algorithm based on the ones presented in this paper. We hope that our ideas will lead to new improvements of the CP approach. In order, to encourage these improvements we claim that our approach is, currently, one of the best methods to solve the Maximum Clique Problem.

References

1. E. Balas and W. Niehaus. Finding large cliques in arbitrary graphs by bipartite matching. In D. Johnson and M. Trick, editors, *DIMACS Series in Discrete Mathematics and Theoretical Computer Science*, volume 26, pages 29–52. American Mathematical Society, 1996.
2. C. Berge. *Graphe et Hypergraphes*. Dunod, Paris, 1970.
3. I. Bomze, M. Budinich, P. Pardalos, and M. Pelillo. The maximum clique problem. *Handbook of Combinatorial Optimization*, 4, 1999.
4. C. Bron and J. Kerbosh. Algorithm 457 : Finding all cliques of an undirected graph. *Communications of the ACM*, 16(9):575–577, 1973.
5. S. Busygin. A new trust region technique for the maximum weight clique problem. *Submitted to Special Issue of Discrete Applied Mathematics: Combinatorial Optimization*, 2002.
6. Dimacs. Dimacs clique benchmark instances.
   ftp://dimacs.rutgers.edu/pub/challenge/graph/benchmarks/clique, 1993.
7. Torsten Fahle. Simple and fast: Improving a branch-and-bound algorithm for maximum clique. In R. Möring and R. Raman, editors, *ESA 2002, 10th Annual European Symposium*, pages 485–498, 2002.
8. S. Homer and M. Peinado. Experiments with polynomial-time clique approximation algorithms on very large graphs. In D. Johnson and M. Trick, editors, *DIMACS Series in Discrete Mathematics and Theoretical Computer Science*, volume 26, pages 147–168. American Mathematical Society, 1996.
9. P Östegard. A fast algorithm for the maximum clique problem. *Discrete Applied Mathematics*, page to appear.
10. P. St-Louis, B. Gendron, and J. Ferland. A penalty-evaporation heuristic in a decomposition method for the maximum clique problem. In *Optimization Days*, Montreal, Canada, 2003.
11. D. Wood. An algorithm for finding maximum clique in a graph. *Operations Research Letters*, 21:211–217, 1997.

Greater Efficiency
for Conditional Constraint Satisfaction

Mihaela Sabin[1], Eugene C. Freuder[2], and Richard J. Wallace[2]

[1] Department of Mathematics and Computer Science
Rivier College, 420 Main Street, Nashua, NH 03060, USA
msabin@rivier.edu
[2] Cork Constraint Computation Center, Department of Computer Science
University College Cork, Cork, Ireland
{e.freuder,r.wallace}@4c.ucc.ie

Abstract. A conditional constraint satisfaction problem (CCSP) extends a standard constraint satisfaction problem (CPS) with a condition-based component that controls what variables participate in problem solutions. CCSPs adequately represent configuration and design problems in which selected subsets of variables, rather than the entire variable set, are relevant to final solutions. The only algorithm that is available for CCSP and operates directly on the original, unreformulated CCSP statement has been basic backtrack search. Reformulating CCSPs into standard CSPs has been proposed in order to bring the full arsenal of CSP algorithms to bear. One reformulation approach adds null values to variable domains and transforms CCSP constraints into CSP constraints. However, a complete null-based reformulation of CCSPs has not been available. In this paper we provide more advanced algorithms for CCSP and a full null-based reformulation into standard CSP. Thorough testing reveals that the advanced algorithms perform up to two orders of magnitude better than plain backtracking, but that realizing practical advantages from reformulation is problematic. The advanced algorithms extend forward checking and maintaining arc consistency to CCSPs. The null-based reformulation improves on the preliminary findings in [1] by removing the limitation on multiple activation, and by localizing changes. It identifies and addresses a difficulty presented by activity cycles.

1 Introduction

There are many important and complex tasks to which constraint satisfaction has been successfully applied. As a result, specialized constraint satisfaction problem (CSP) classes have emerged to cope more directly with specific characteristics of various application domains. Qualifiers such as partial, dynamic, hierarchical, composite, interval, mixed, and others characterize CSP specializations that have been studied in the last decade. The conditional constraint satisfaction is another specialization developed to cope with the special features of diagnosis and configuration problems.

F. Rossi (Ed.): CP 2003, LNCS 2833, pp. 649–663, 2003.

Conditional CSP extends standard CSP with a condition-based component that models dynamic changes of problem solutions with predefined conditions. The formalism has been introduced in [2] under the name of dynamic CSP. It integrates classical constraint satisfaction with a special type of constraint, *activity constraints*, responsible for selecting those variables that should participate in solutions. The formalism has been originally motivated by synthesis tasks such as product configuration, in which not all cataloged components are present in every single configured product. This class of dynamic CSPs is renamed *conditional constraint satisfaction problems (CCSPs)* [3] to (1) capture the nature of the control component that conditionally changes the initial model of the problem, and to (2) distinguish this class of problems from another class of dynamic CSPs that reuses problem solutions when problem changes over time [4–6].

Since its first formalization in 1990, conditional constraint satisfaction paradigm has been used for modeling not only configuration problems, but also diagnosis [7], design [1], and network management [8] problems. Despite increasing interest in the area of representing application problems as CCSPs, little progress has been made in the area of improving direct solving methods that operate on CCSP representations. In contrast with other CSP specializations, no standard CSP solving method, except for backtrack search [1], has been adapted to the conditional domain. The lack of specialized, direct solving methods is compounded by the fact that a benchmark test base for this type of problems is extremely limited [9, 10], although very much needed in experimental evaluations.

In this paper we present two advanced methods for solving CCSPs that use local consistency methods of forward checking and maintaining arc consistency. Solving methods find values for the set of active variables. These are obtained from the initial set of variables that are assigned values in every solution, and variables that are newly incorporated into the problem via activity constraints. The technical challenges encountered and overcome in extending forward checking and maintaining arc-consistency to CCSP are to: (1) keep track of variables' activity status as determined by consistency checking of activity constraints, (2) enforce chosen level of consistency when checking both compatibility and activity constraints, (3) in case of maintaining arc consistency, extend arc consistency with activation consistency along activity constraints.

The opportunity of importing efficient standard algorithms, whose behavior has been extensively tested, raises new challenges. Are there available similarly comprehensive experimental studies for evaluating CCSP solving? The reality of many application domains, such as configuration or diagnosis, is that either real-life problems data is not publicly available or problem examples are too simple. A practical approach that overcomes this difficulty and has proved very successful for benchmarking standard solving algorithms is to use randomly generated CSPs. This is the approach we consider in this paper to evaluate empirically the proposed algorithms. We extend a random standard CSP generation model [11] to produce random activity constraints, and use the model to implement a random conditional CSP generator. We generate large and diverse problem populations to conduct experimental studies that time algorithm execution, and count search operations specific to standard and conditional CSP solving. The testing reveals that the advanced algorithms perform up to two orders of magnitude better than plain backtracking.

An alternative approach to directly solving CCSP is to reformulate a CCSP into an equivalent standard CSP. This approach has the advantage of bringing to bear a mature constraint technology developed in the standard domain. The first reformulation of conditional CSP into standard CSP has been mentioned by Mittal and Falkenhainer [2], although they have not presented a full description of the transformation. They consider the addition of a special value, called "null", to the domains of all variables which are not initially active. A variable instantiation with "null" indicates that the variable does not participate in the problem solution. The feasibility of obtaining a null-based CSP reformulation of a CCSP has been examined in-depth by Gelle [1]. She develops a null-based reformulation algorithm that imposes the following limitation on CCSPs: non-initial variables are activated by at most one activity constraint. A transformation of multiple activations of the same variable has not been considered on the grounds of an additional limitation, i.e., the transformation does not preserve locality of change [1, 9].

We have developed an algorithm of null-based reformulation that removes these limitations. The algorithm (1) transforms multiple activations, and, (2) preserves locality of change by allowing a less restrictive local change than the one defined in [9]. Moreover, we have identified a new difficulty with null-based reformulation introduced by activity cycles. We have developed an alternative null-based reformulation algorithm that overcomes this difficulty at the cost of not preserving locality of change. We have evaluated experimentally the performance of solving the reformulated standard problem and compared it with results obtained from applying direct solving methods to the original problem. The findings show that the advanced solving methods are faster by one to two orders of magnitude than solving the equivalent, reformulated problem.

2 Conditional CSP: An Example

Before we recall the definition of the conditional CSP, we give an example of a simple product configuration task for which we develop a CCSP representation. The insights of the modeling exercise facilitate the introduction of the basic concepts of the CCSP framework. The example is a simplified version of an example introduced by [2] and specifies a car configuration task (Figure 1). The specifications include:

- required components, that participate in all final car configurations, with their values;
- optional components, that can be optionally selected according to certain configuration requirements, with their values;

- configuration requirements of compatibility, that restrict the values of the selected components according to product assembly requirements and promotional sales strategies;
- configuration requirements for selecting optional components, that express customer preferences and additional requirements with regard to assembling and selling the product.

Given the specified components and requirements, the task of configuration is to assign values to selected components in such a way that requirements pertinent to what is selected are satisfied. To obtain a CCSP representation of the car

---

Required components and their values
 - comfort package has luxury, deluxe, and standard values
 - frame has convertible and sedan values

Optional components and their values
 - sunroof has sr1 and sr2 values
 - air conditioner has ac1 and ac2 values

Configuration requirements of compatibility among component values
 1. standard comfort package is not compatible with ac2 air conditioner
 2. luxury comfort package is not compatible with ac1 air conditioner

Configuration requirements for selecting optional components
 1. luxury comfort package includes sunroof option
 2. luxury comfort package includes air conditioner option
 3. convertible frame excludes sunroof option

Fig. 1. A simple car configuration task example

configuration example, we identify problem variables, values, and constraints. We apply the following modeling guidelines and produce the CCSP representation in Figure 2.

- Configuration task components and their values correspond to problem *variables* and their associated *domains of values*. Required components, which are part of any configuration solution, are distinguished as *initial variables*. Initial variables have the property of being initially *active* or *included* in the problem search space. Optional components have their *activity status* initially undefined as they are not selected to either participate in, that is, be included, or to explicitly not participate in, or be excluded from, problem solutions.
- The requirements of component compatibility are modeled as *compatibility constraints*, which restrict the combinations of allowed values assigned to selected components.
- *activity constraints* change the initial variable set according to certain conditions. These conditions control which optional components get selected in a configuration, and which optional components are removed from a configuration.

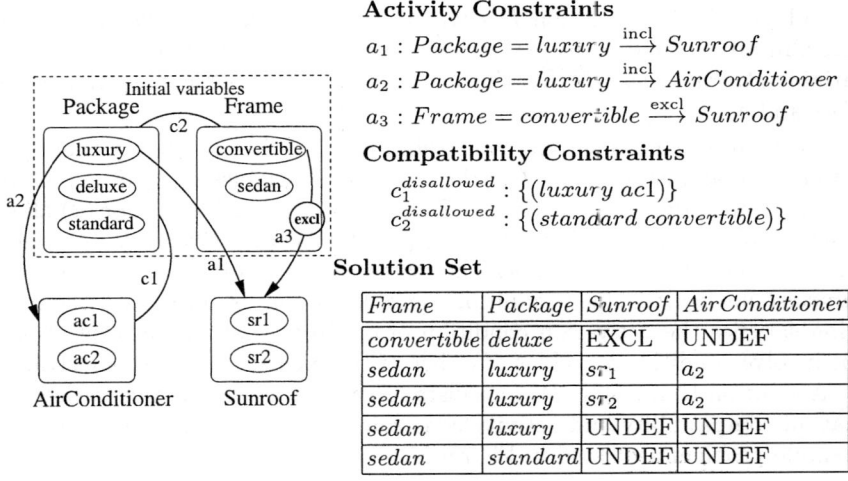

Activity Constraints

$a_1 : Package = luxury \xrightarrow{incl} Sunroof$

$a_2 : Package = luxury \xrightarrow{incl} AirConditioner$

$a_3 : Frame = convertible \xrightarrow{excl} Sunroof$

Compatibility Constraints

$c_1^{disallowed} : \{(luxury \; ac1)\}$

$c_2^{disallowed} : \{(standard \; convertible)\}$

Solution Set

Frame	Package	Sunroof	AirConditioner
convertible	deluxe	EXCL	UNDEF
sedan	luxury	sr_1	a_2
sedan	luxury	sr_2	a_2
sedan	luxury	UNDEF	UNDEF
sedan	standard	UNDEF	UNDEF

Fig. 2. Conditional CSP representation of the car configuration task example

This description of modeling a configuration task as a CCSP identifies five problem components. Thus, a conditional constraint satisfaction problem, $\mathcal{P} = \langle \mathcal{V}, \mathcal{D}, \mathcal{V_I}, \mathcal{C_C}, \mathcal{C_A} \rangle$, involves a set of variables, $\mathcal{V} = \{v_1 \ldots, v_n\}$, which, if active, can take on discrete values from their corresponding finite domains $\mathcal{D} = \{D_{v_1}, \ldots, D_{v_n}\}$, a non-empty set of initially active variables, called initial variables, $\mathcal{V_I}$, $\mathcal{V_I} \subseteq \mathcal{V}$, a set of compatibility constraints, $\mathcal{C_C}$, and a set of activity constraints, $\mathcal{C_A}$. All sets are finite.

The CCSP model in Figure 2 has four variables, two compatibility constraints $\{c_1, c_2\}$, and three activity constraints, $\{a_1, a_2, a_3\}$, of which a_1 and a_2 are inclusion activity constraints, and a_3 is an exclusion activity constraint. Two of the problem variables, *Package* and *Frame* are initial variables and, therefore, active. They participate in all solutions and define the initial search problem with which the solving process starts. The non-initial variables, *AirConditioner* and *Sunroof*, have their activity status initially undefined. Their participation in solutions is determined by activity constraints.

We say that a compatibility constraint c is consistent with an instantiation $\mathcal{I}$ of the constraint variables iff either not all constraint variables are active, or constraint variables are active and c satisfies $\mathcal{I}$. For example, the instantiation *Package = standard* and *Frame = convertible* trivially satisfies c_1 since the constraint variable *AirConditioner* is not active.

An inclusion activity constraint, $a : a_{cond} \xrightarrow{incl} v_t$, has an activation condition, a_{cond}, which is a regular constraint defined on a set of condition variables, and a target variable, v_t. We say that a is consistent with an instantiation $\mathcal{I}$ of the activation variables of a_{cond} iff either (1) not all condition variables are active, or $\mathcal{I}$ is inconsistent with a_{cond}, or (2) all condition variables are active, $\mathcal{I}$ satisfies a_{cond}, and v_t is active. The example's activity constraints of inclusion are

a_1 and a_2. The instantiation $Package = luxury$ makes $AirConditioner$ active according to a_1, and $Sunroof$ active according to a_2. In both cases, condition variable $Package$ is active and the instantiation satisfies the activation condition of a_1 and a_2.

Given an exclusion activity constraint, $a : a_{cond} \xrightarrow{\text{excl}} v_t$, we say that a is consistent with an instantiation $\mathcal{I}$ of the activation variables a_{cond} iff (1) either not all condition variables are active, or $\mathcal{I}$ is inconsistent with a_{cond}, or (2) all condition variables are active, $\mathcal{I}$ satisfies a_{cond}, and v_t is not active. a_3 is an example of an exclusion activity constraint. The instantiation $Frame = convertible$ makes $Sunroof$ not active, since condition variable $Frame$ is active and the instantiation satisfies the activation condition of a_3. Note that this instantiation does not involve condition variables of either of the inclusion activity constraints.

A solution to a CCSP $\mathcal{P}$ is an instantiation of a set of active variables such that all compatibility and activity constraints are satisfied. All solutions to the example problem are listed in Figure 2.

3   Solving Methods

The domain of standard CSPs benefits from a rich collection of thoroughly tested algorithms. In contrast, the study of conditional CSPs is still in its infancy with little research directed to specialized solving methods that operate directly on CCSP representations. Following the model of other CSP specializations, we develop adaptations of the most representative standard CSP methods for the conditional domain:

- modified backtrack search algorithm (CondBT) that handles both types of activity constraints,
- new forward checking algorithm (CondFC) that propagates compatibility constraints over active variables, and
- new maintaining arc-consistency algorithm (CondMAC) that propagates both compatibility and activity constraints.

In Section 4, the relative performance of the proposed methods is analyzed experimentally by using random CCSPs. We show that (1) the run-time complexity order in the standard domain holds in the conditional domain, i.e., CondBT < CondFC < CondMAC, and that (2) the advanced algorithms CondFC and CondMAC are faster by up to two orders of magnitude than CondBT. The full descriptions of the algorithms can be found in [12]. In the following we use a running example to describe the algorithms' behavior.

Backtrack search is the only algorithm that has been adapted for conditional constraint satisfaction [2, 1]. The proposed adaptation, however, handles only activity constraints of inclusion. Activity constraints of exclusion are reformulated as compatibility constraints [13]. We modify the algorithm, what we call CondBT, to handle both types of activity constraints as given in the original problem representation. Figure 3 shows the search tree for finding all solutions to the example problem in previous section. The algorithm maintains an agenda

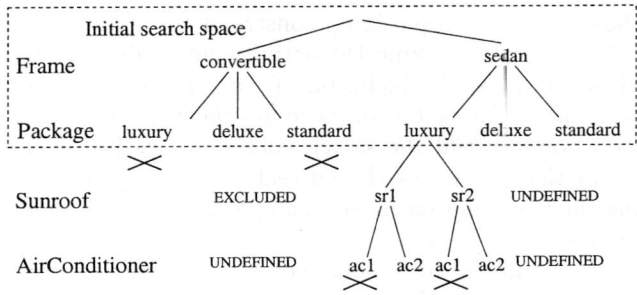

Fig. 3. CondBT search trace on the sample problem in Figure 2

of future variables, which await instantiation. Therefore, only active variables are stored in the agenda. The agenda's initial set is the set of the problem's initial variables. The algorithm's implementation uses recursion to traverse the search tree. For each active variable instantiation, the algorithm first checks the compatibility constraints and then the activity constraints. The backtrack search trace in Figure 3 has the initial search space defined by *Frame* and *Package*.

A compatibility constraint is checked only if it involves the current variable and previously instantiated variables, called past variables. Otherwise, no compatibility constraint check is performed. If the current instantiation is consistent with the value assignment of the past variables, the constraint is satisfied. For example, when search reaches the instantiation *Package = luxury*, with past variable *Frame = convertible*, both c_1 and c_2 are satisfied.

An activity constraint is checked only if its activation condition is defined on the current variable and past variables. Otherwise, the activity constraint is discarded and no check is performed. Checking the consistency of the activation condition has two possible outcomes: either (1) current instantiation violates the activation condition, in which case the constraint does not "trigger" or has no effect on the activity status of its target variable, or (2) activation condition holds, in which case its effect has to be determined. In the first case, the constraint is trivially satisfied. In the second case, the constraint satisfiability depends on matching the constraint type (of inclusion or exclusion) with the activity status of the target variable (included, excluded, or undefined). The constraint fails if an inclusion (or exclusion) activity constraint targets an already excluded (or included) variable. The constraint holds if the activity status of the target variable is consistent with the type of activation. The constraint also holds if the target variable's activity status is undefined. In this case, the activity constraint has the effect of setting the target's status to active (or included) or to excluded.

Let us consider that the current search point is *Frame = convertible*. Note that the activity status of *AirConditioner* and *Sunroof* is undefined. The only constraint checked at this point is the exclusion activity constraint a_3: its activation condition is satisfied, and the exclusion of *Sunroof* takes effect, that is, its activity status becomes excluded. The algorithm proceeds deeper in the tree by choosing the next future variable in the agenda, and instantiates *Package* with *luxury.* As shown before, compatibility constraint checking is successful and the algorithm continues with checking the activity constraints. Activity constraint a_1 is checked and it fails: the inclusion of *Sunroof* conflicts with its current activity status. *luxury* instantiation is found inconsistent, *luxury* is removed from *Package*'s domain, and the search goes sideways in the tree to the next value, *deluxe*, in the domain of the current variable. Constraint checking results in finding the first solution to the example problem: $Frame = convertible$, $Package = deluxe$.

Forward checking in the conditional context (CondFC) enforces look-ahead consistency [14] along compatibility constraints and prunes inconsistent values from the domains of future variables. When activity constraints come into play and newly activated variables are added to the set of future variables in the agenda, consistency propagation is reiterated to involve these variables as well: values which are inconsistent with the current partial solution are filtered from the newly active variables. In Figure 4 we use the same sample problem to trace CondFC execution. Let us consider that the current instantiation is $Package = luxury$. *Frame* has been assigned the value *sedan*, but the propagation of c_2 compatibility constraint did not find any inconsistent value in the domain of *Package*. When *luxury* is tried for *Package* the only applicable constraints are: a_1 includes *Sunroof* and a_2 includes *AirConditioner*. Both constraints are satisfied and the search space grows with these two variables. Forward checking prunes $ac1$ from the domain of *AirConditioner* by propagating c_1.

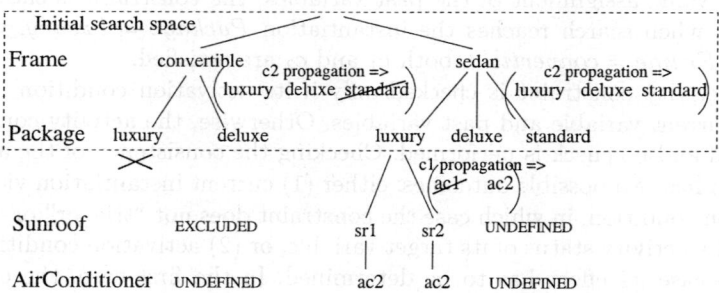

Fig. 4. CondFC search trace on the sample problem in Figure 2

The level of consistency enforced by CondFC can be extended to arc consistency over all future variables, which are both directly and indirectly connected via compatibility constraints to the current instantiation node in the search tree. Arc consistency processing has received constant attention in the research community since Mackworth' seminal paper on consistency in constraint networks [15]. Combining backtrack search with arc consistency has produced one of the most effective solving algorithm for binary standard CSPs, maintaining arc consistency (MAC) [16–19]. CondMAC is MAC's analog for binary conditional CSP. It uses arc consistency over binary compatibility constraints[1] and a new form of local consistency over binary activity constraints, called *activation consistency*.

---
[1] CondMAC implementation uses AC-4 arc consistency algorithm [20].

A modified version of the running example (Figure 5) is used to exemplify the execution of CondMAC. Prior to launching backtrack search, the agenda of initial variables is made arc consistent. The figure shows that there is only one compatibility constraint, c_2', which participates in the computation of the support counters associated with (and shown next to) the values of the initial variables. The support value of 0 for *hatchback* on c_2' indicates that *hatchback* is inconsistent with *Package*'s values and can be removed for *Frame*'s domain. Having completed this preliminary phase, in Figure 6 we show how local consistency is interleaved with backtrack search in CondMAC.

The improvement of CondMAC over CondFC consists of (1) making the newly included variables arc consistent along compatibility constraints and (2) propagating activity constraints to further remove condition values that contradict activity status of problem variables. When *convertible* is assigned to *Frame*, the other value left in its domain, *sedan*, is eliminated. Along the compatibility constraint c_2', *sedan* supports all three values at *Package*. Its elimination propagates via c_2' and support counters of *luxury*, *deluxe*, and *standard* are decremented. Consequently, *standard*'s support counter becomes 0, which shows its inconsistency with the partial solution *Frame* = *convertible*. The value is removed and no more arc consistency propagation takes place at this point. Following the checking of compatibility constraints, we check activity constraints whose condition variables are active. a_3 qualifies, it is satisfied, and *Sunroof* is marked as excluded from the search tree rooted at *Frame* = *convertible*. However, there is another activity constraint, a_1, whose condition involves future variable *Package*, and which conflicts with a_3. To maintain activation consistency over future variables, a_1's condition value, *luxury*, which is found inconsistent with *convertible*, is also removed from the domain of *Package*. All value removals due to enforcing activation consistency are propagated via arc consistency over compatibility constraints defined on future variables. In this example, removal of *luxury* propagates on c_2' and results in *convertible* losing one more support, down to 1 at this point. With this level of consistency achieved, search

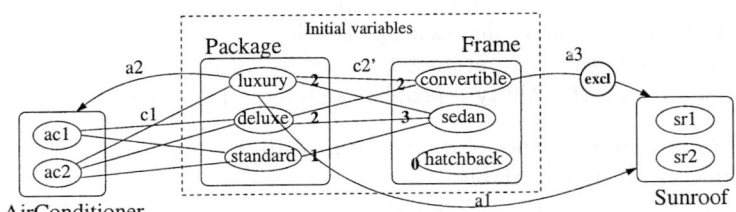

c_2' : {(*luxury convertible*)(*luxury sedan*)
        (*deluxe convertible*)(*deluxe sedan*)(*standard sedan*)}

Fig. 5. Modified version of sample problem: an additional value, *hatchback*, in *Frame*, and updated c_2', which leaves *hatchback* with no support at *Package*. Values participating in compatibility constraints have associated support counters

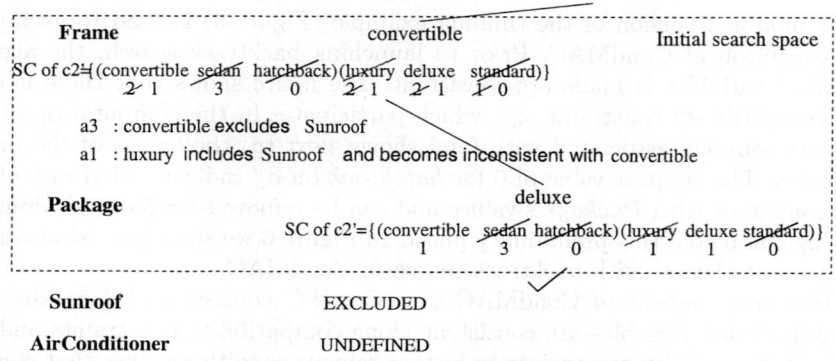

Fig. 6. CondMAC search trace on the sample problem in Example 5

continues with the instantiation of *Package* with the only value left in its do-main, *deluxe*. Applicable constraints (that is, c_2' only) are checked and satisfied, and the first solution to the problem is found.

4   Experimental Evaluation

In our experiments we use Freuder and Wallace's model of constant probabil-ity of inclusion for generating random CSPs [21, 11], extended with additional parameters that collect activity information, called *activity parameters*, for a specialized class of binary CCSPs. The class restricts both compatibility and ac-tivity constraints to binary constraints. Binary activity constraints are defined on a single condition variable, with an associated unary activation constraint, and the usual target variable. As a general practice, the most prevalent ex-perimental design for studying algorithm performance using random standard CSPs involves varying density and satisfiability parameters. In the context of random CCSPs, these parameters are the probability of generating compatibil-ity constraints, denoted d_c, and the probability of generating allowed pairs in a compatibility constraint, denoted s_c. Specific to CCSP, we are interested in generating combinations of parameter values for those activity parameters that control the amount of activity a problem exhibits. These parameters are:

- *density of activity*, denoted d_a, is the probability of generating a non-initial variable as a target variable.
- *satisfiability of activation*, denoted s_a, is the probability of generating a value in a domain as a condition value. The number of condition values in a domain measures the satisfiability of the activation condition defined on that domain.

The three algorithms for solving CCSPs, CondBT, CondFC, and CondMAC, were tested in experiments covering diverse populations of randomly generated problems. The algorithms' implementations handle binary constraints. This re-striction is imposed by the binary CondMAC algorithm and the binary random

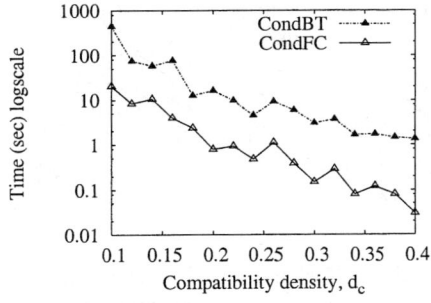

Test suite design: problem of 10 variables, with 8 values per domain, fixed satisfiability of compatibility, $s_c = 0.25$, density of activity, $d_a = 0.3$, and satisfiability of activation, $s_a = 0.3$. Compatibility density, d_c, varies in the range $[0.1 \ldots 0.4]$ in increments of 0.02. For each of the 16 (d_c, s_c, d_a, s_a) topological classes 100 instances were generated.

Fig. 7. CondBT and CondFC execution time for variable compatibility density, d_c

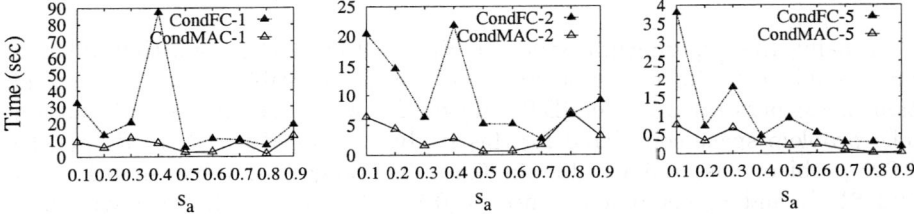

Fig. 8. CondFC and CondMAC execution time for variable satisfiability of activation, s_a and three values of density of activity: $d_a = 0.1$ (left), $d_a = 0.2$ (middle), and $d_a = 0.5$ (right). Fixed compatibility topology: $d_c = s_c = 0.2$

CCSPs used during testing. The experimental analysis has two types of studies. In the first category we measured execution time of each algorithm for finding minimum size solutions, that is, solutions that have a minimum number of variables that are assigned values. In the second category we run the algorithms to find all solutions, and we collected measures that are representative of algorithm effort: number of backtracks and compatibility checks as well as some new measurements specific to CCSP, such as number of condition checks, included and excluded variables, activity constraints that redundantly set variables' activity status, and activity constraints whose action conflict with variables' activity status.

Relative time performance of CondBT and CondFC is shown in Figure 7. We observe that CondFC runs one to two orders of magnitude faster than CondBT. Relative time performance of CondFC and CondMAC has been studied on a larger test suite that consists of 81 problem classes corresponding to all (d_a, s_a) activity parameter combinations, with d_a and s_a varying in the $[0.1 \ldots 0.9]$ range in 0.1 increments. Figure 9 shows time variation with s_a for three d_a values. Compatibility parameters are fixed: $d_c = s_c = 0.2$. There are 100 instances per problem class, each of 10 variables with domains of 10 values. The main result supported by the data is that CondMAC consistently outperforms CondFC.

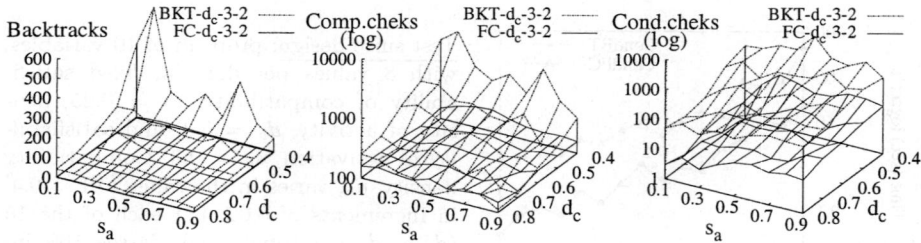

Fig. 9. Comparison between CondFC and CondFC effort measured as the number of backtracks (left), compatibility checks (middle), and condition checks (right). Variation of effort with density of compatibility, d_c, and satisfiability of activation, s_a. Fixed $s_c = 0.3$ and $d_a = 0.2$

Finally, the experimental study in Figure 9 evaluates algorithm efficiency measured by counting the number of backtracks, compatibility checks, and condition checks performed by CondBT and CondFC when searching for all solutions. The problem space considered for this study, as defined by (d_c, s_c, d_a, s_a), had 2,025 problem classes: 5 d_c values in $[0.4 \ldots 0.8]$ range, 5 s_c values in $[0.1 \ldots 0.4]$, and 81 d_a and s_a combined values in $[0.1 \ldots 0.9]$ range. Figure 9 synthesizes CondBT vs. CondFC comparison results for only 45 classes, with fixed $s_c = 0.3$ and $d_a = 0.2$. The study results show that CondFC outperforms CondBT on all measures and for all problem topologies. Similar to standard CSP solvers, all effort measures counted for CondBT and CondFC increase with problem satisfiability, s_c, and decrease with problem density, d_c. As problems exhibit more conditionality (larger d_a and s_a), CondBT and CondFC perform more condition checks, obviously, but fewer backtracks. CondFC is better than CondBT by one to two orders of magnitude on the number of backtracks and compatibility checks, and up to three orders of magnitude on the number of condition checks.

5 Reformulation

The prominence and maturity of the constraint satisfaction classical paradigm motivates our interest in reformulating the conditional CSP representation into a standard CSP. This reformulation requires the addition of a special value, called "null", to the domains of non-initial variables, and the transformation of compatibility and activity constraints into ordinary constraints [2, 1, 13, 9]. A null-based reformulation of conditional CSPs is presented and studied in depth in [1, 9]. However, this transformation is limited in the following key respects:

1. it does not transform multiple activations of the same variables,
2. it does not preserves locality of change: when the original problem changes with the addition of another activity constraint to a multiple activation cluster, which has already been reformulated, the reformulation cannot be updated locally,
3. it does not handle activity cycles.

To address these three limitations of the null-based reformulation, we have developed two alternative transformations. One removes the first two limitations; the other removes the third. Both algorithms synthesize non-binary ordinary constraints whose arity increases with the number of activity constraints in a multiple activation cluster or in an activity cycle.

Given the reformulation algorithms that overcome the limitations with multiple activations, locality of change, and activity cycles, we are interested in evaluating the relative efficiency of solving with standard methods the reformulated problem. The test suite we designed for this purpose has random conditional CSPs of 8 variables with domains of 6 values. The problems are organized in nine classes, each corresponding to a s_c value in $[0.1 \ldots 0.9]$. The other three problem generation parameters were fixed. Conditional CSPs were solved with CondMAC. Their non-binary null-based reformulations obtained with the reformulation algorithm that handles activity cycles, were first transformed into a binary constraint representations and then were solved with the MAC algorithm for binary CSPs. The execution time results are shown in Figure 10, on a normal scale (left) and logscale (right). We observe that solving binary null-based reformulations is much slower, up to two orders of magnitude, than solving original, conditional CSPs directly. Two conclusions can be drawn from these findings. First, greater efficiency in solving conditional CSPs lies with algorithms that operate on the original representation. Second, much has to be learned about what is specific to null-based reformulations and how standard methods can more efficiently exploit these representations.

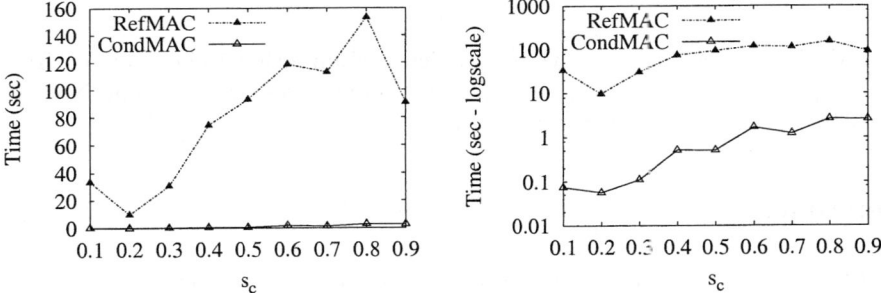

Fig. 10. Execution time of CondMAC and RefMAC - standard MAC for solving equivalent null-based, standard reformulations. Original conditional CSPs have 8 variables and 6-value domains. 100 problem instances per topological class: variable satisfiability of compatibility, s_c, in $[0.1 \ldots 0.9]$ and fixed $d_c = 0.15$, $d_a = s_a = 0.3$

6   Conclusion and Future Work

CCSPs are extensions to standard CSPs that have proved useful in representing configuration and diagnosis problems. In contrast to other CSP extensions, CCSP has not benefited from adaptations of efficient CSP solving algorithms to improve CCSP solving. Moreover, experimental analysis of the efficiency of available CCSP solvers has been extremely limited. In this paper we presented two advanced algorithms for CCSP that adapt forward checking and maintaining arc consistency to keep track of variables' activity status and to enforce local consistency along compatibility and activity constraints. We studied their efficiency experimentally and shown an improvement of up to two orders of magnitude over plain backtrack search. An alternative approach to directly solving CCSP is to reformulate it into an equivalent standard CSP. We studied a null-based reformulation of CCSPs, addressed its limitations, and provided experimental evidence that the proposed direct methods are more efficient.

We envision two directions for our future work. Real-life configuration and diagnosis problems are formulated as non-binary CCSPs. We want to generalize the current implementations of CondFC and CondMAC to handle non-binary constraints and take advantage of efficient non-binary local consistency algorithms [19, 22, 23]. In [1, 10] a reformulation method has been proposed that generates a set S of standard CSPs equivalent to the original CCSP. Conventional local consistency methods are then applied on intermediate problems generated along the way to producing S in order to reduce S and solve its members more efficiently with CSP solving algorithms. The method can be further improved with a hybrid approach that interleaves CSP solving, rather than just preliminary local consistency, with reformulation[2]. We are interested in a more comprehensive study of CCSP solving that will include this hybrid approach and facilitate new advances in solving and reformulating CCSPs.

Acknowledgments

This work has received support from Science Foundation Ireland under Grant 00/PI.1/C075, from the National Science Foundation under Grant No. IRI-9504316, and from Trilogy Software, Inc.

References

1. Gelle, E.: On the generation of locally consistent solution spaces. Ph.D. Thesis, Ecole Polytechnique Fédérale de Lausanne, Switzerland (1998)
2. Mittal, S., Falkenhainer, B.: Dynamic constraint satisfaction problems. In: Proceedings of the Eighth National Conference on Artificial Intelligence. (1990)
3. Sabin, M., Freuder, E.: Detecting and resolving inconsistency and redundancy in conditional constraint satisfaction problems. In: Web-published papers of the CP'98 Workshop on Constraint Problem Reformulation, Pisa, Italy (1998)
4. Dechter, R., Dechter, A.: Belief maintenance in dynamic constraint networks. In: Proceedings of AAAI-88. (1988) 37–42
5. Bessière, C.: Arc-consistency in dynamic constraint satisfaction problems. In: Proceedings of the 9th AAAI. (1991) 221–226

---

[2] E. Gelle, ABB Corporate Research Ltd., Switzerland, personal communication.

6. Verfaillie, G., Schiex, T.: Solution reuse in dynamic constraint satisfaction problems. In: Proceedings of the 12th AAAI, Seattle, WA (1994) 307–312
7. Sabin, D., Sabin, M., Russell, R., Freuder, E.: A constraint-based approach to diagnosing software problems in computer networks. In Montanari, U., ed.: Principles and Practice of Constraint Programming - CP'95, Lecture Notes of Computer Science 976, Springer Verlag (1995)
8. Sabin, M., Russell, R., Miftode, I.: Using constraint technology to diagnose errors in networks managed with spectrum. In: Proceedings of the IEEE Internationl Conference on Telecommunications, Bucharest, Romania (2001)
9. Soininen, T., Gelle, E., Niemelä, I.: A fixpoint definition for dynamic constraint satisfaction. Principles and Practice of Constraint Programming, CP'99 (1999)
10. Gelle, E., Faltings, B.: Solving mixed and conditional constraint satisfaction problems. Constraints 8 (2003) 107–141
11. Wallace, R.: Random CSP Generator. Constraint Computation Center, University of New Hampshire, Durham, NH, U.S.A. (1996) http://www.cs.unh.edu/ccc/code.html.
12. Sabin, M.: Solving and Reformulation of Conditional Constraint Satisfaction Problems. PhD thesis, University of New Hampshire, Durham, NH, U.S.A. (2003)
13. Haselböck, A.: Knowledge-based Configuration and Advanced Constraint Technologies. PhD thesis, Technical University of Vienna (1993)
14. Haralick, R., Elliott, G.: Increasing tree search efficiency for constraint satisfaction problems. Artificial Intelligence 14 (1980) 263–313
15. Mackworth, A.: Consistency in networks of relations. Artificial Intelligence 8 (1977)
16. Sabin, D., Freuder, E.: Contradicting conventional wisdom in constraint satisfaction. In Borning, A., ed.: Principles and Practice of Constraint Programming, Lecture Notes in Computer Science. Volume 874. Springer (1994) (PPCP'94: Second International Workshop, Orcas Island, Seattle, USA).
17. Grant, S., Smith, B.: The phase transition behavior of maintaining arc consistency. Technical Report 92.95, School of Computing, University of Leeds (1995) (A revised and shortened version appears in Proceedings ECAI'96, pp. 175-179, 1996).
18. Bessière, C., Régin, J.C.: MAC and combined heuristics: Two reasons to forsake FC (and CBJ?) on hard problems. In Freuder, E., ed.: Principles and Practice of Constraint Programming. Lecture Notes of Computer Science. Volume 1118., Springer (1996) 61–75 (CP'96: Second International Conference, Boston, MA, USA).
19. Bessière, C., Régin, J.C.: Arc consistency for general constraint networks: preliminary results. In: Proceedings IJCAI'97, Nagoya, Japan (1997) 398–404
20. Mohr, R., Henderson, T.: Arc and path consistency revisited. Aritificial Intelligence 28 (1986) 225–233
21. Freuder, E., Wallace, R.: Partial constraint satisfaction. Artificial Intelligence 58 (1992)
22. Bessière, C., Régin, J.C.: Refining the basic constraint propagation algorithm. In: Proceedings IJCAI'01, Seattle, WA (2001) 309–315
23. Bessière, C., Meseguer, P., Freuder, E., Larrosa, J.: On forward checking for non-binary constraint satisfaction. Artificial Intelligence 141 (2002) 205–224

Incremental Computation of Resource-Envelopes in Producer-Consumer Models

T.K. Satish Kumar

Knowledge Systems Laboratory
Stanford University
tksk@ksl.stanford.edu

Abstract. Interleaved planning and scheduling employs the idea of extending partial plans by regularly heeding to the scheduling constraints during search. One of the techniques used to analyze scheduling and resource consumption constraints is to compute the so-called *resource-envelopes*. These envelopes can then be used to derive effective heuristics to guide the search for good plans and/or dispatch given plans optimally. The key to the success of this approach however, is in being able to re-compute the envelopes incrementally as and when partial commitments are made. The resource-envelope problem in producer-consumer models is as follows: A directed graph $\mathcal{G} = \langle \mathcal{X}, \mathcal{E} \rangle$ has $\mathcal{X} = \{X_0, X_1 \ldots X_n\}$ as the set of nodes corresponding to events (X_0 is the "beginning of the world" node and is assumed to be set to 0) and $\mathcal{E}$ as the set of directed edges between them. A directed edge $e = \langle X_i, X_j \rangle$ in $\mathcal{E}$ is annotated with the simple temporal information $[LB(e), UB(e)]$ indicating that a consistent schedule must have X_j scheduled between $LB(e)$ and $UB(e)$ seconds after X_i is scheduled ($LB(e) \leq UB(e)$). Some nodes (events) correspond physically to production or consumption of resources and are annotated with a real number $r(X_i)$ indicating their levels of production or consumption of a given resource. Given a consistent schedule s for all the events, the total production (consumption) by time t is given by $P_s(t)$ $(C_s(t))$. The goal is to build the envelope functions $g(t) = max_{\{s \text{ is a consistent schedule}\}}(P_s(t) - C_s(t))$ and $h(t) = min_{\{s \text{ is a consistent schedule}\}}(P_s(t) - C_s(t))$. In this paper, we provide efficient incremental algorithms for the computation of $g(t)$ and $h(t)$, along with flexible consistent schedules that actually achieve them for any given time instant t.

1   Introduction

Interleaved planning and scheduling employs the idea of extending partial plans by regularly heeding to the scheduling constraints during search. One of the techniques used to analyze scheduling and resource consumption constraints in the context of the currently maintained partial plan is to compute the so-called resource-envelopes. These can then be used to guide the search for a good plan in a variety of ways (see [2] and [4]).

F. Rossi (Ed.): CP 2003, LNCS 2833, pp. 664–678, 2003.
© Springer-Verlag Berlin Heidelberg 2003

First, they provide sanity checks for early backtracking when it is possible to examine the envelopes and determine that no consistent schedule for the current set of constraints could possibly satisfy all the resource contentions. Second, they provide a heuristic value for estimating the *constrainedness* of a partial plan. Third, they provide a search termination criterion when it is possible to examine the envelopes and determine that any consistent schedule for the current set of constraints would be successful in satisfying the resource contentions. Fourth, they provide important subroutines for designing approximation algorithms in optimal dispatching/scheduling of plans.

The resource-envelope problem in producer-consumer models is as follows: A directed graph $\mathcal{G} = \langle \mathcal{X}, \mathcal{E} \rangle$ has $\mathcal{X} = \{X_0, X_1 \ldots X_n\}$ as the set of nodes corresponding to events (X_0 is the "beginning of the world" node and is assumed to be set to 0) and $\mathcal{E}$ as the set of directed edges between them. A directed edge $e = \langle X_i, X_j \rangle$ in $\mathcal{E}$ is annotated with the simple temporal information $[LB(e), UB(e)]$ indicating that a consistent schedule must have X_j scheduled between $LB(e)$ and $UB(e)$ seconds after X_i is scheduled ($LB(e) \leq UB(e)$). Some nodes (events) correspond physically to production or consumption of resources and are annotated with a real number $r(X_i)$ indicating their levels of production or consumption of a given resource. Given a consistent schedule s for all the events, the total production (consumption) by time t is given by $P_s(t)$ ($C_s(t)$). The goal is to build the envelope functions $g(t) = max_{\{s \text{ is a consistent schedule}\}}(P_s(t) - C_s(t))$ and $h(t) = min_{\{s \text{ is a consistent schedule}\}}(P_s(t) - C_s(t))$.

The producer-consumer model captures several realities associated with reasoning about actions and plans. A partial plan typically consists of a set of actions, a set of open conditions (sub-goals that still need to be achieved), a set of established causal links, a set of temporal constraints between various events that include the beginning and end points of actions, and a set of resource requirements associated with the execution of individual actions (see [6]). An action A can consume (produce) a resource in a variety of ways that includes: (1) A holding w_A amount of resource at the beginning of its execution and returning it at the end, (2) A holding w_A amount of the resource at the beginning of its execution and not returning it at the end, (3) A producing w_A amount of the resource at the end of its execution etc. All these can be expressed using the producer-consumer model and although continuous consumption and production of resources during execution of individual actions needs to be handled in a more general framework, the producer-consumer model is fairly expressive and the techniques that are shown in this paper to analyze them are illustrative of more complex resource production and consumption models.

Some attempts for computing the envelopes in producer-consumer models have been made in [2] and [4]. This paper improves upon them in a number of ways. First, the estimation of the envelopes provided in [2] is conservative, while it is tight in [4] and in the algorithms provided in this paper. Tightness in the estimates of $g(t)$ and $h(t)$ is extremely important because a tight bound can save us a potentially exponential amount of search through early backtracking and solution detection when compared to a looser bound. Tight bounds also provide better heuristic estimates for the *constrainedness* of a problem during search. Second, our algorithms are constructive in the sense that we can determine a flexible schedule s that actually achieves $g(t)$ or $h(t)$ for any given time instant t. This ensures good performance at bottleneck points (as argued in [3]) and is better than determining an arbitrary fixed schedule because flexible schedules tend to be robust in dealing with exogenous events and uncertainty of execution. Third, and most important, our algorithms are incremental—that is, they effectively reuse computation for determining the envelopes as and when search proceeds by making partial commitments and refining plans. Incremental computation is extremely important because the envelopes must be computed at every point in the search space and even a small saving in the complexity saves us an exponential amount of work. In the context of interleaved planning and execution monitoring for example, execution of a (partial) plan may not always result in the intended outcome and fast re-planning is necessary. Incremental computation of resource envelopes then becomes extremely important for an active management of planning and execution monitoring. We show that the incremental complexity of our algorithms is significantly lesser than re-computation from scratch—hence saving us a total amount of work that is proportional to this difference times the size of the search space. Fourth, we show how our algorithms can be adapted to reuse computation even within a single instance of the problem when envelopes need to be recalculated at discontinuities.

Throughout the paper, we will concentrate on (incremental) algorithms for computing the envelope function $g(t)$ only. The computation of $h(t)$ can be done in a directly analogous fashion by simply reversing the role of consumers and producers. This is because $h(t) = min_{\{s \text{ is a consistent schedule}\}}(P_s(t) - C_s(t)) = -max_{\{s \text{ is a consistent schedule}\}}(C_s(t) - P_s(t))$. We will assume that the temporal constraints specified in $\mathcal{E}$ are consistent[1] and will denote the set of all production events (all events $u \in \mathcal{X}$ such that $r(u) > 0$) by $\mathcal{P}$ and the set of all consumption events (all events $u \in \mathcal{X}$ such that $r(u) < 0$) by $\mathcal{C}$.

2   Computing the Envelopes

In this section, we provide efficient algorithms for computing the profile function $g(t)$ given an instance of the resource-envelope problem. Figure 1 shows the algorithm for computing $g(t)$ at a specified time instant t, along with a flexible consistent schedule s that actually achieves it. Figure 2 shows the algorithm for computing $g(t)$ for all t and Figure 3 shows a small example. A series of Lemmas are presented that prove the correctness of the algorithms. Central to the algorithms is the notion of a *distance graph* associated with a set of simple temporal constraints (see step 1 of Figure 1). An edge $\langle X_i, X_j \rangle$ in the distance graph is annotated with a real number w (instead of temporal bounds) and encodes the constraint $X_j - X_i \leq w$.

Lemma 1: A consistent schedule exists for $X_1, X_2 \ldots X_n$ in $\mathcal{G} = \langle \mathcal{X}, \mathcal{E} \rangle$ if and only if $\mathcal{D}(\mathcal{G})$ does not have any negative cycles (see step 1 of Figure 1).

---

[1] Any possible inconsistency is caught in higher level routines of a refinement planner.

ALGORITHM: UPPER-ENVELOPE-AT-T
INPUT: An instance of the resource-envelope problem, and a time instant t.
OUTPUT: $g(t)$ and a flexible consistent schedule s that achieves it.

1. Construct the distance graph $\mathcal{D}(\mathcal{G})$ on the nodes of $\mathcal{G}$ as follows:
   a. For every edge $e = \langle X_i, X_j \rangle$ in $\mathcal{E}$:
      i. Add the edge $\langle X_i, X_j \rangle$ annotated with $UB(e)$.
      ii. Add the edge $\langle X_j, X_i \rangle$ annotated with $-LB(e)$.
2. For every $X_p \in \mathcal{P}$ and $X_c \in C$:
   a. Compute the shortest distance from X_p to X_c in $\mathcal{D}(\mathcal{G})$ (denoted $dist(X_p, X_c)$).
   b. Construct a (directed) size-2 conflict between X_p and X_c (denoted $X_c \rightarrow X_p$)

      if and only if $dist(X_p, X_c) < 0$.
3. Build a directed graph $E(\mathcal{G})$ as follows:
   a. The nodes of $E(\mathcal{G})$ correspond to events in $\mathcal{P} \cup C$.
   b. The weight on X_i is set to $|r(X_i)|$.
   c. A directed edge $\langle X_p, X_c \rangle$ in $E(\mathcal{G})$ encodes a size-2 conflict $X_c \rightarrow X_p$.
4. Construct a graph $M(\mathcal{G})$ from $E(\mathcal{G})$ as follows:
   a. Remove a production node $X_p \in \mathcal{P}$ and all its adjacent edges if and only if $t + dist(X_p, X_0) < 0$.
   b. Remove a consumption node $X_c \in C$ and all its adjacent edges if and only

   if

      $dist(X_0, X_c) - t < 0$.
5. Compute $Q = \{u_1, u_2 \ldots u_k\}$ as the largest weighted independent set in $M(\mathcal{G})$.
6. **RETURN:**
   a. $g(t) = \sum_{y_i \in \mathcal{P}} |r(y_i)|(y_i \in Q) - \sum_{y_i \in C} |r(y_i)|(y_i \notin Q)$.
   b. $s = \mathcal{D}(\mathcal{G}) \cup \{\langle X_0, u_i \rangle$ annotated with t if $u_i \in \mathcal{P} \cap Q\} \cup \{\langle u_i, X_0 \rangle$ annotated with $-t$ if $u_i \in C \cap Q\}$.

END ALGORITHM

Fig. 1. Shows the computation of $g(t)$ for a given time instant t, along with a flexible consistent schedule s that achieves it.

Proof: If there is a negative cycle $X_{i_1}, X_{i_2} \ldots X_{i_k}$, the following are true of the constraints specified in $\mathcal{E}$: $X_{i_2} - X_{i_1} \leq w_1, X_{i_3} - X_{i_2} \leq w_2 \cdots X_{i_k} - X_{i_{k-1}} \leq w_{k-1}$, $X_{i_1} - X_{i_k} \leq w_k$. Summing over these inequalities, we have $0 \leq \sum_{i=1}^{k} w_i$. This is false since $\sum_{i=1}^{k} w_i$ is known to be negative. This means that there cannot exist any consistent schedule for $X_{i_1}, X_{i_2} \ldots X_{i_k}$. Conversely, if there are no negative cycles in $\mathcal{D}(\mathcal{G})$, then a consistent schedule exists for $X_1, X_2 \ldots X_n$, one of which is given by $X_i = d_{0i}$ where d_{0i} is the shortest distance from X_0 to X_i in $\mathcal{D}(\mathcal{G})$. Such a schedule satisfies all constraints in $\mathcal{D}(\mathcal{G})$. An edge $X_j - X_i \leq w_{ij}$ in $\mathcal{D}(\mathcal{G})$ is satisfied by $X_j = d_{0j}$ and $X_i = d_{0i}$ because $d_{0j} \leq w_{ij} + d_{0i}$ (since $w_{ij} + d_{0i}$ accounts for only one of the paths from X_0 to X_j).

Definition 1: A production event $p \in \mathcal{P}$ can contribute $+|r(p)|$ to the total production at time t, or not contribute at all. A consumption event $c \in C$ can contribute $-|r(c)|$ to the total production at time t, or not contribute at all. An event is said to be *p-active* if it contributes its maximum to the total production

---

ALGORITHM: UPPER-ENVELOPE-ALL-T
INPUT: An instance of the resource-envelope problem.
OUTPUT: $g(t)$ for all t.
  1. For all $X_p \in \mathcal{P}$:
    a. Insert $-dist(X_p, X_0)$ into list L.
  2. For all $X_c \in \mathcal{C}$:
    a. Insert $+dist(X_0, X_c)$ into list L.
  3. Sort L in ascending order $\langle d_1, d_2 \ldots d_{|L|} \rangle$.
  4. For $i = 1, 2 \ldots |L| - 1$:
    a. Compute $g(d_i) = $ UPPER-ENVELOPE-AT-T at time d_i.
    b. Set $g(t) = g(d_i)$ for all t in the interval $[d_i, d_{i+1})$.
  5. Set $g(t) = g(d_{|L|})$ for t in the interval $[d_{|L|}, +\infty)$.
  6. Set $g(t) = 0$ in the interval $(-\infty, d_1)$.
END ALGORITHM

Fig. 2. Shows the computation of $g(t)$ for all t.

by time t. This means that a production event p can be made *p-active* at time t if it is scheduled before (or at) t and a consumption event c can be made *p-active* at time t if it is scheduled after t.

Lemma 2: A schedule that achieves $g(t)$ at time t is also the one that maximizes $\sum_{y \in \mathcal{P} \cup \mathcal{C}} |r(y)| p\text{-}active(y, t)$.

Proof: We know that for any schedule s, $P_s(t) - C_s(t) = \sum_{p \in \mathcal{P}} |r(p)|(s(p) \leq t) - \sum_{c \in \mathcal{C}} |r(c)|(s(c) \leq t)$. Maximizing this is the same as maximizing $\sum_{c \in \mathcal{C}} |r(c)| + \sum_{p \in \mathcal{P}} |r(p)|(s(p) \leq t) - \sum_{c \in \mathcal{C}} |r(c)|(s(c) \leq t)$ because the additional term is independent of s. Combining the first and the third terms, we have $\sum_{p \in \mathcal{P}} |r(p)|(s(p) \leq t) + \sum_{c \in \mathcal{C}} |r(c)|(s(c) > t)$. The last two terms yield $\sum_{y \in \mathcal{P} \cup \mathcal{C}} |r(y)| p\text{-}active(y, t)$ as required.

Lemma 3: A production event $p \in \mathcal{P}$ can be made *p-active* at time t if the addition of the edge $\langle X_0, p \rangle$ annotated with t does not result in a negative cycle in $\mathcal{D}(\mathcal{G})$. A consumption event $c \in \mathcal{C}$ can be made *p-active* at time t if the addition of the edge $\langle c, X_0 \rangle$ annotated with $-t$ does not result in a negative cycle in $\mathcal{D}(\mathcal{G})$.

Proof: By definition, a production event p can be made *p-active* at time t if it is possible to schedule it before t. Retaining the semantics of the distance graph—that a constraint $X_b - X_a \leq w$ is specified as the edge $\langle X_a, X_b \rangle$ annotated with w—this corresponds to the addition of the edge $\langle X_0, p \rangle$ annotated with t to the distance graph without causing an inconsistency. Similarly, a consumption event c can be made *p-active* at time t if it is possible to schedule it after t, and this corresponds to the addition of the edge $\langle c, X_0 \rangle$ annotated with $-t$ without causing an inconsistency. The truth of the Lemma then follows from the fact that inconsistencies correspond to negative cycles as stated in Lemma 1.

Definition 2: A *conflict* is a set of events all of which cannot be made *p-active* simultaneously at a given time t. A *minimal conflict* is a conflict no proper subset of which is also a conflict.

Lemma 4: A set of events can be simultaneously made *p-active* at time t if there is no subset of them that constitutes a minimal conflict.

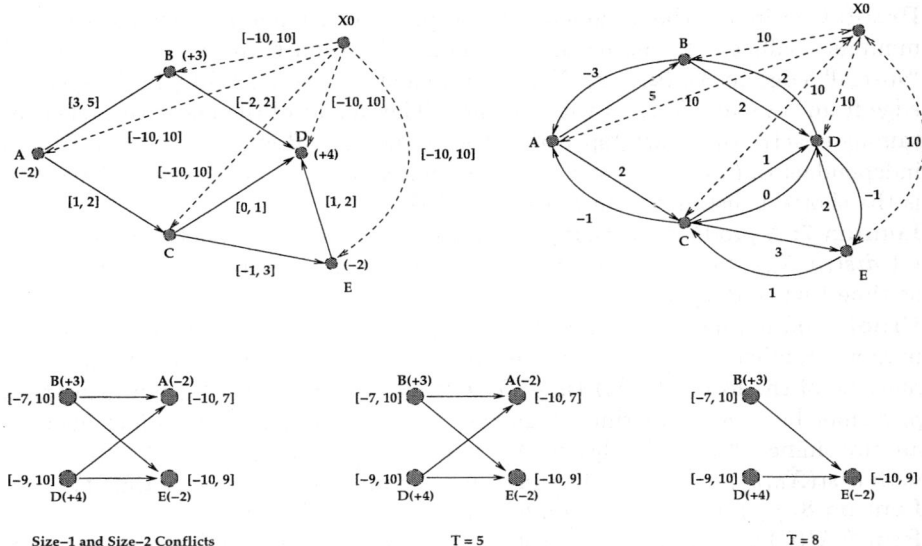

Fig. 3. Shows an instance of the resource-envelope problem cast as a bipartite matching problem. The top left diagram shows the original problem where nodes are annotated with their levels of production/consumption. The top right diagram shows the distance graph, and the bottom left diagram shows an encoding of the size-2 conflicts as a bipartite graph (the size-1 conflicts are represented using intervals annotating the nodes). The two other diagrams illustrate the change in the set of size-1 conflicts with t.

Proof: By definition of a conflict, a set of events can be simultaneously made *p-active* at time t, if and only if there is no subset of them that constitutes a conflict. Further, the truth of the Lemma follows from the fact that a set of events constitutes a conflict if and only if some subset of them constitutes a minimal conflict.

Lemma 5: The size of a minimal conflict is ≤ 2.

Proof: A set of production events $\{p_1, p_2 \ldots p_k\}$ and a set of consumption events $\{c_1, c_2 \ldots c_l\}$ can be attempted to be made simultaneously *p-active* at time t if for all p_i, we can add the edge $\langle X_0, p_i \rangle$ annotated with t, and for all c_j, we can add the edge $\langle c_j, X_0 \rangle$ annotated with $-t$, to the distance graph $\mathcal{D}(\mathcal{G})$ without creating a negative cycle. Let these edges be referred to as "special" edges and let $\mathcal{D}'(\mathcal{G})$ refer to the resulting distance graph. Knowing that $\mathcal{D}(\mathcal{G})$ does not have any negative cycles (because $\mathcal{E}$ is consistent), a negative cycle can occur in $\mathcal{D}'(\mathcal{G})$ only if it involves a "special" edge. Since all "special" edges have X_0 as an end point, a negative cycle must involve X_0. Further, since a fundamental cycle can have any node repeated at most once, at most 2 "special" edges can be present in a negative cycle in $\mathcal{D}'(\mathcal{G})$. Finally, since special edges correspond to *p-activation* of events, the size of a minimal conflict is ≤ 2.

Lemma 6: A size-2 conflict is independent of t.

Proof: Continuing the arguments in the proof of Lemma 5, when the size of a minimal conflict is 2, the negative cycle in $\mathcal{D}'(\mathcal{G})$ must involve an "incoming" "special" edge to X_0 (say $\langle c_j, X_0 \rangle$) with weight $-t$ and an "outgoing" "special" edge from X_0 (say $\langle X_0, p_i \rangle$) with weight t. The weight of the negative cycle containing exactly these two "special" edges is therefore $dist(p_i, c_j) + t - t$. This is independent of t and is negative if and only if $dist(p_i, c_j)$ is negative ($dist(p_i, c_j)$ is the shortest distance from p_i to c_j in $\mathcal{D}(\mathcal{G})$).

Lemma 7: A production event $p \in \mathcal{P}$ constitutes a size-1 conflict at time t when $t + dist(p, X_0) < 0$, and a consumption event $c \in \mathcal{C}$ constitutes a size-1 conflict at time t when $dist(X_0, c) - t < 0$.

Proof: Continuing the arguments in the proof of Lemma 5, when the size of a minimal conflict is 1 and it involves an "outgoing" "special" edge from X_0, it must be of the form $\langle X_0, p_i \rangle$ ($p_i \in \mathcal{P}$) with $dist(p_i, X_0) + t < 0$ (indicating that p_i cannot be *p-active* at time t). In the case that the minimal conflict involves an "incoming" "special" edge to X_0, it must be of the form $\langle c_j, X_0 \rangle$ ($c_j \in \mathcal{C}$) with $dist(X_0, c_j) - t < 0$ (indicating that c_j cannot be *p-active* at time t).

Lemma 8: $g(t)$ and s are as computed in step 6 of Figure 1.

Proof: $M(\mathcal{G})$ incorporates the deletion of all size-1 conflicts and the computation of an independent set incorporates the absence of all size-2 conflicts. The computation of the largest weighted independent set in $M(\mathcal{G})$ therefore takes care of all minimal conflicts and targets the maximum possible *p-activity* at time t. Step 6(a) measures the total production corresponding to this *p-activity* and the required flexible consistent schedule s (computed in step 6(b)) corresponds to the addition of edges required to *p-activate* the qualifying events.

Lemma 9: $g(t)$ is piecewise constant and changes only at a polynomial number of time points.

Proof: By Lemma 8, $g(t)$ is the weight of the largest weighted independent set in the graph $M(\mathcal{G})$. Since $M(\mathcal{G})$ is computed from $E(\mathcal{G})$ by deleting all size-1 conflicts at time t, the number of times $g(t)$ changes is equal to the number of times the set of size-1 conflicts changes in $M(\mathcal{G})$. Since $dist(X_0, c)$ ($c \in \mathcal{C}$) and $-dist(p, X_0)$ ($p \in \mathcal{P}$) respectively mark the membership of a consumption event c and a production event p in this set, the potential number of transition points for the piecewise constant function $g(t)$ is $O(|\mathcal{P}| + |\mathcal{C}|)$.

The complexity of the steps in Figure 1 that are independent of t (and can therefore be done just once) is dominated by the computation of shortest paths in the presence of negative cost edges using the Bellman-Ford algorithm. This is equal to $O(|\mathcal{X}||\mathcal{E}||\mathcal{P}||\mathcal{C}|)$. The time-dependent complexity is dominated by the computation of *maxflow* in a bipartite graph and is equal to $O((|\mathcal{P}|+|\mathcal{C}|)^{2.5})$. The complexity of the algorithm in Figure 2 is therefore equal to $O(|\mathcal{X}||\mathcal{E}||\mathcal{P}||\mathcal{C}| + (|\mathcal{P}| + |\mathcal{C}|)^{3.5})$.

3   Maximum Weighted Independent Set Computation

In this section, we present a polynomial-time algorithm for the computation of the largest weighted independent set in a bipartite graph (see Figure 4). A series

ALGORITHM: MAX-WT-IND-SET
INPUT: A bipartite graph $B = \langle P, C, E \rangle$ with $p_i \in P$ having weight $|r(p_i)|$ and $c_i \in C$ having weight $|r(c_i)|$.
OUTPUT: Maximum weighted independent set I^* in B.
  1. Construct a directed graph $D = \langle U, Y \rangle$ as follows:
     a. $U = P \cup C \cup \{S, T\}$.
     b. For all $p_i \in P$: Y contains the edge $S \rightarrow p_i$ with capacity $|r(p_i)|$.
     c. For all $c_j \in C$: Y contains the edge $c_j \rightarrow T$ with capacity $|r(c_j)|$.
     d. For all $\langle p_i, c_j \rangle \in E$: Y contains the edge $p_i \rightarrow c_j$ of infinite capacity.
  2. Compute a *maxflow* F (with residual graph R_F) in D from S to T.
  3. Compute $H = \{\langle S, p_i \rangle | p_i \in P$ and p_i is unreachable from S in $R_F\} \cup \{\langle c_i, T \rangle |$ $c_i \in C$ and c_i is reachable from S in $R_F\}$.
  4. Compute $V = \{p_i | \langle S, p_i \rangle \in H\} \cup \{c_i | \langle c_i, T \rangle \in H\}$.
  5. RETURN: $I^* = P \cup C \backslash V$.
END ALGORITHM

Fig. 4. Shows the algorithm for computing the maximum weighted independent set in a bipartite graph.

of Lemmas are presented that prove the correctness of the algorithm (see [1]). To keep the proofs of these Lemmas simple, we first deal with the case when all nodes have unit weight (imagine setting $|r(p_i)|$ and $|r(c_i)|$ to 1 in steps 1(b) and 1(c) of Figure 4). We then provide a single concluding Lemma that generalizes the correctness of the algorithm to the weighted version as required. We make use of the standard result that when all edges have integral capacities in an instance of the *maxflow* problem, a *maxflow* with integral amount of flow on all edges can be efficiently computed (see [1]).

Definition 3: A *matching* M in a bipartite graph B is a set of edges that do not share a common end-point. The *size of a matching* (denoted $|M|$) is the number of edges in it, and a *maximum matching* (denoted M^*) is a matching of maximum size. A *vertex cover* V in B is a set of nodes such that at least one end point of every edge is in it. A *minimum vertex cover* is one such that the total weight on all the nodes is minimized.

Lemma 10: If M^* is the maximum matching in B, then $|M^*| = F$.

Proof: For an integral flow, there cannot exist two edges of the form $\langle p_i, c_{j_1} \rangle$ and $\langle p_i, c_{j_2} \rangle$ both with non-zero flows. This is because the edge $\langle S, p_i \rangle$ has unit capacity and the flow has to be conserved at p_i. Similarly, there cannot exist two edges of the form $\langle p_{i_1}, c_j \rangle$ and $\langle p_{i_2}, c_j \rangle$ both with non-zero flows because $\langle c_j, T \rangle$ is of unit capacity. Therefore, an integral flow in D defines a matching in B of the same size and a *maxflow* F in D defines a maximum matching M^* in B of the same size, hence making $|M^*| = F$.

Lemma 11: If V^* is the minimum vertex cover in B, then $|V^*| \geq |M^*|$.

Proof: For any edge in M^*, at least one of its end points must be in V^*. Also, since no two edges in M^* share a common end point, they cannot be covered by the same element in V^*. This means that $|V^*| \geq |M^*|$.

Lemma 12: $|V| = F$ (F is the *maxflow* in D and V is the vertex cover for B constructed in step 4 of Figure 4).

Proof: From the construction of V, $p_i \in P$ is in V if and only if $\langle S, p_i \rangle$ is in H and $c_j \in C$ is in V if and only if $\langle c_j, T \rangle$ is in H. This means that $|V| = |H|$. Since H is formed out of considering all edges that have one end reachable from S and the other unreachable in R_F, it constitutes a *minimum cut* between S and T in D. From the *maxflow-mincut* Theorem, $|H| = F$, and hence $|V| = F$ as required.

Lemma 13: For the bipartite graph B, if V^* is the minimum vertex cover, then $|V| = |V^*|$ (where V is the vertex cover constructed for B in step 4 of Figure 4).

Proof: From the above Lemmas, we have that $|V| = F$, $|V^*| \geq |M^*|$ and $|M^*| = F$. This means that $|V^*| \geq |V|$. Since V^* is the optimal vertex cover by definition, we have that $|V| = |V^*|$ and is the required minimum vertex cover.

Lemma 14: If I^* is the largest independent set, then $|I^*| + |V^*| = |P \cup C|$. Moreover, $P \cup C \backslash V$ is an optimal independent set.

Proof: Consider any vertex cover U. $P \cup C \backslash U$ does not contain any two nodes of the form $p_i \in P$ and $c_j \in C$ such that there is an edge $\langle p_i, c_j \rangle$ between them. This means that $P \cup C \backslash U$ is an independent set. Also, since $P \cup C \backslash U$ and U form a partition of $P \cup C$, we have that $|P \cup C \backslash U| + |U| = |P \cup C|$. When U is the minimum vertex cover V^* we have that $|I^*| + |V^*| = |P \cup C|$. Finally since V computed in step 4 of Figure 4 is optimal (Lemma 13), we have that $P \cup C \backslash V$ is the required largest independent set in B.

Lemma 15: The algorithm presented in Figure 4 works for arbitrary positive weights $|r(y_i)| > 0$.

Proof: From the foregoing Lemmas, we know that the algorithm works for unit weights—i.e. $|r(y_i)| = 1$ for $y_i \in P \cup C$. Now suppose that the weights were positive integers (still not the general case). Conceptually, a new bipartite graph can be constructed where node y_i (in $P \cup C$) with weight $|r(y_i)|$ is replicated $|r(y_i)|$ times—each of unit weight and independent of each other. An edge $p_i \rightarrow c_j$ entails all copies of p_i (denoted $p'_{i_1}, p'_{i_2} \ldots p'_{i_{|r(p_i)|}}$) to have an edge to all copies of c_j (denoted $c'_{j_1}, c'_{j_2} \ldots c'_{j_{|r(c_j)|}}$). The staged *maxflow* in D will then have all copies of y_i behaving identically. Also since all edges of the form $\langle p'_{i_k}, c'_{j_l} \rangle$ have infinite capacity, we can replace the group of edges $\langle S, p'_{i_1} \rangle, \langle S, p'_{i_2} \rangle \ldots \langle S, p'_{i_{|r(y_i)|}} \rangle$ (each of unit capacity) with a single edge $\langle S, p_i \rangle$ of capacity $|r(p_i)|$, and similarly replace all edges of the form $\langle c'_{j_1}, T \rangle, \langle c'_{j_2}, T \rangle \ldots \langle c'_{j_{|r(c_j)|}}, T \rangle$ (each of unit capacity) with a single edge $\langle c_j, T \rangle$ of capacity $|r(c_j)|$. All intermediate edges are of infinite capacity and are defined (as previously) using the idea of directed size-2 conflicts. Now consider the most general case where $|r(y_i)|$ is positive but need not be an integer. In such a case, the idea is to conceptually scale all the weights by a uniform factor L to convert all of them to integers. We can then find the largest independent set using the scaled weights and since uniform scaling does not affect the largest weighted independent set, the same computed set can then be used after scaling down the weights by L. Computationally however, the idea of scaling is not reflected anywhere except in the fact that the weights $r(y_i)$ can be used as they are to define capacities on the edges in D.

4   Incremental Computation

A refinement planner proceeds by refining and extending partial plans. The refinement operators used to extend partial plans include the addition of new actions to satisfy open conditions or sub-goals, and the addition of new temporal constraints to resolve threats between actions (see [6]). Because the resource-envelopes need to be computed at each stage to guide the search for a good plan, incremental computation becomes extremely important. In general, there are two places where incremental computation can be leveraged: (1) in the computation of the envelopes across points of discontinuity (for the same set of events and constraints), and (2) in the computation of the envelopes as and when new events and constraints (reflecting the refinement of partial plans) are added. The second case is more general and we deal with it directly.

4.1   Incremental *maxflow* in Bipartite Graphs

Because the computation of the envelopes involves computing the *maxflow* in bipartite graphs, we will first show how to make this incremental—i.e., we will show how we can reuse the computation for one instance of the *maxflow* problem on bipartite graphs into solving another instance. The complexity of this incremental algorithm is analyzed in terms of the parameters that characterize the difference between the two instances.

We will denote a staged *maxflow* problem in bipartite graphs by $\langle P, C, E, S, T \rangle$. Here, P is the set of production events, C is the set of consumption events, E is the set of edges between P and C (each of them assumed to be of infinite capacity as is indeed so in the context of computing envelopes), and S and T are respectively the source and terminal nodes. The incremental *maxflow* problem is then to solve $\langle P, C, E, S, T \rangle$ given the solution for $\langle P', C', E', S, T \rangle$.

Figure 5 shows the incremental computation of *maxflow* for $\langle P, C, E, S, T \rangle$ using the residual graph carried over from the computation of *maxflow* for $\langle P', C', E', S, T \rangle$. Figure 6 illustrates the working of this algorithm on a small example. Central to the algorithm is the exploitation of the fact that the complexity of solving a *maxflow* problem can be characterized both by the topology of the graph (like it is easier in bipartite graphs than in general) and the value of the *maxflow* itself (independent of the topology). The algorithm makes use of calls to *maxflow* on changed instances of the problem (steps 6 and 9 in Figure 5) which are assumed to be solved directly using greedy flow augmentation methods within a complexity of $O(m|f^*|)$ ($|f^*|$ is the value of the *maxflow* and m is the number of edges in the graph) (see [1]). These changed instances are assured of having a "small" $|f^*|$, hence making the complexity of the algorithm much better than re-computation from scratch. A series of Lemmas are presented that establish the correctness of the algorithm.

Lemma 16: A feasible flow F for $\langle P_{new}, C_{new}, D_{new}, S, T \rangle$ is also feasible for $\langle P, C, E, S, T \rangle$ if its associated residual graph R_F has residual capacity 0 on all edges of the form $\{\langle u, v \rangle | u \in C' \backslash C \text{ or } v \in P' \backslash P\}$ (see Figure 5).

ALGORITHM: INCR-MAX-FLOW
INPUT: $\langle R', f', M' \rangle$ for $\langle P', C', E', S, T \rangle$, and a new instance $\langle P, C, E, S, T \rangle$.
OUTPUT: $\langle R, f, M \rangle$ for $\langle P, C, E, S, T \rangle$.

01. Create a bipartite graph $\langle P_{new}, C_{new}, D_{new} \rangle$ such that:
    a. $P_{new} = P \cup P'$.
    b. $C_{new} = C \cup C'$.
    c. $D_{new} = \{\langle S, u \rangle$ with capacity $|r(u)|$ s.t. $u \in P \backslash P'\} \cup \{\langle v, T \rangle$ with capacity $|r(v)|$ s.t. $v \in C \backslash C'\} \cup \{\langle u, v \rangle$ with infinite capacity s.t. $u \in P \backslash P'$ or $v \in C \backslash C'$
    and $\langle u, v \rangle \in E\} \cup \{\langle u, v \rangle$ with capacity $R'(\langle u, v \rangle) | \langle u, v \rangle$ is an edge in $R'\}$.
02. For all edges $\langle u, v \rangle$ in D_{new}:
    a. Set $f_{back}(\langle u, v \rangle) = R'(\langle u, v \rangle)$, if $u \in C' \backslash C$ or $v \in P' \backslash P$.
    b. Set $f_{back}(\langle u, v \rangle) = 0$, otherwise.
03. For all edges $\langle u, v \rangle$ in D_{new}:
    a. Set $R_{back}(\langle u, v \rangle) = 0$, if $\{u, v\} \cap (C' \backslash C \cup P' \backslash P) \neq \{\}$.
    b. Set $R_{back}(\langle u, v \rangle) = R'(\langle u, v \rangle)$, otherwise.
04. For all nodes u in $P_{new} \cup C_{new}$:
    a. Set $ex(u) = \sum_{\langle v, u \rangle \in D_{new}} f_{back}(\langle v, u \rangle) - \sum_{\langle u, v \rangle \in D_{new}} f_{back}(\langle u, v \rangle)$.
05. Create a directed graph G_{morph} from R_{back} as follows:
    a. Add new nodes S' and T'.
    b. For all nodes $u \in P_{new} \cup C_{new}$:
        i. If $ex(u) > 0$, add the edge $\langle S', u \rangle$ with capacity $ex(u)$.
        ii. If $ex(u) < 0$, add the edge $\langle u, T' \rangle$ with capacity $-ex(u)$.
    c. Add edges $\langle S, T \rangle$ and $\langle T, S \rangle$ of infinite capacities.
06. Solve for $\langle R_{cons}, f_{cons}, M_{cons} \rangle = maxflow$ on G_{morph} from S' to T'.
07. For all edges $e \in D_{new}$:
    a. Set $f_{legal}(e) = f_{cons}(e) + f_{back}(e)$.
08. Create a graph G_{final} from R_{cons} as follows:
    a. Remove S' and T'.
    b. Remove all edges of the form $\langle u, v \rangle$ where $\{u, v\} \cap \{S', T'\} \neq \{\}$.
    c. Remove the edges $\langle S, T \rangle$ and $\langle T, S \rangle$.
09. Solve for $\langle R_{final}, f_{final}, M_{final} \rangle = maxflow$ on G_{final} from S to T.
10. Build a graph R_{return} from R_{final} by removing all nodes u and their associated
    edges when $u \in P' \backslash P \cup C' \backslash C$.
11. For all edges $\langle u, v \rangle$ in $E \cup \{\langle S, u \rangle$ s.t. $u \in P\} \cup \{\langle v, T \rangle$ s.t. $v \in C\}$:
    a. Set $f_{return}(\langle u, v \rangle) = R_{return}(\langle v, u \rangle)$.
12. Set $M_{return} = \sum_{u \in P} f_{return}(\langle S, u \rangle)$.
13. RETURN: $\langle R_{return}, f_{return}, M_{return} \rangle$.
END ALGORITHM

Fig. 5. Shows the algorithm for incremental *maxflow* in bipartite graphs. The idea is to reverse the flow on edges that are not present in the new instance by first computing the amount by which such a reverse flow would violate the conservation constraints at intermediate nodes. After the excess at each node is measured, a *maxflow* is staged between two auxiliary nodes S' and T' to regain conservation consistency. A subsequent maximization phase is carried out that respects this consistency. R, f and M are respectively used to denote the residual graph, the maximum flow vector and the value of the maximum flow.

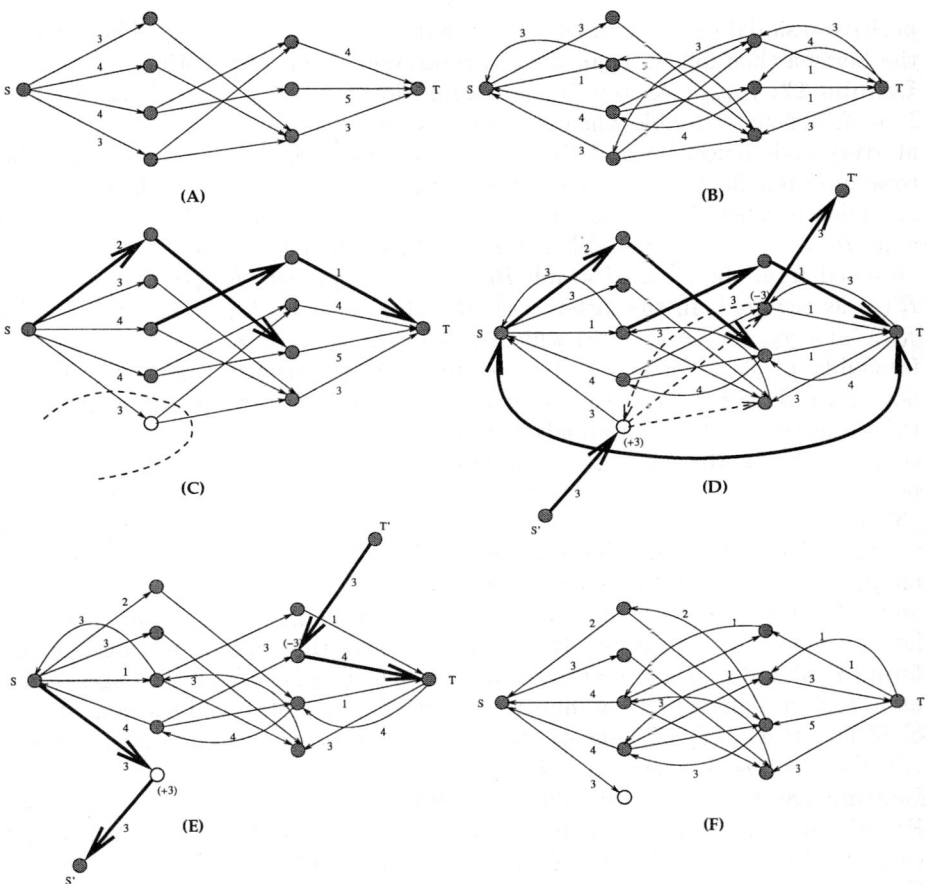

Fig. 6. Illustrates an example for the working of the algorithm in Figure 5 (all edges not explicitly annotated with their capacities are assumed to be of infinite capacities). (A) shows the staged *maxflow* on a bipartite graph with two extra nodes S and T, which are also the source and terminal nodes for the *maxflow* respectively. A *maxflow* computation on this problem results in a residual graph as shown in (B). (C) shows a slightly different problem compared to that in (A). The dark lines indicate the addition of extra elements and the dotted lines indicate deletions. The idea is to solve this instance by making use of the residual graph in (B). (D) illustrates the idea of reversing the flow on illegal edges by computing the excess at each node and deleting the illegal edges as indicated by the dotted lines. (E) indicates the result of a *maxflow* computation between S' and T' to regain feasibility. Finally, (F) shows the computation of a *maxflow* between S and T without pushing back any flow on the illegal edges, as required.

Proof: A feasible flow for $\langle P_{new}, C_{new}, D_{new}, S, T \rangle$ is also so for $\langle P, C, E, S, T \rangle$ if no flow is pushed through any of the edges in D_{new} that are not present in $\langle P, C, E, S, T \rangle$. If there were such an edge, then it must have been of the form $\langle u, v \rangle$ with $u \in P' \backslash P$ or $v \in C' \backslash C$, and its utilization would create a positive residual capacity in the opposite direction—viz. in $\langle v, u \rangle$. The truth of the Lemma then follows from the contrapositive of this implication.

Lemma 17: f_{legal} (see step 7) is a feasible flow for $\langle P_{new}, C_{new}, D_{new}, S, T \rangle$.

Proof: A flow is feasible when (1) all capacity constraints are satisfied, and (2) at every node (except S and T) conservation constraints are preserved—i.e. the total incoming flow to that node = total outgoing flow from that node. Condition (1) holds because $f_{back}(e)$ is set to either $R'(e)$ or 0 (see step 2). In the former case, $R_{back}(e)$ is set to 0 and hence $f_{cons}(e)$ (which is a feasible flow for G_{morph} obtained from the residual graph R_{back}) is 0. Together, $f_{back}(e) + f_{cons}(e) \leq R'(e)$ as required. In the latter case, $R_{back}(e)$ is set to $R'(e)$ (see step 3) and $f_{cons}(e) + f_{back}(e) = f_{cons}(e)$ which we know is $\leq R_{back}(e) = R'(e)$ (from the feasibility of f_{cons} for G_{morph}) as required. Now consider condition (2). The flow f_{back} does not heed to conservation constraints, but we will prove that the projection of f_{cons} on all edges except those that involve S' or T', exactly compensates for this. Step 4(a) first accounts for the excess at every node—viz. net inflow − net outflow. Now suppose that f_{cons} saturated all edges of the form $\langle S', u \rangle$ and $\langle v, T' \rangle$. Then by construction, the net inflow (w.r.t. f_{cons}) to a node u with positive excess = net outflow = $ex(u)$. Now if we take the projection of f_{cons} on all edges except those that involve S' or T', we have that the net inflow = 0 and net outflow = $ex(u)$, exactly compensating for $f_{back}(e)$. A similar argument holds when $ex(u)$ is negative. It is easy to observe that in fact, all edges of the form $\langle S', u \rangle$ and $\langle v, T' \rangle$ are saturated after step 6. This is because the edges $\langle S, T \rangle$ and $\langle T, S \rangle$ are made to be of infinite capacities in step 5(c), and the consistency of R' for $\langle P', C', E', S, T \rangle$ ensures that $R'(\langle u, S \rangle) \geq |ex(u)|$ when $ex(u) > 0$ and $R'(\langle T, v \rangle) \geq |ex(v)|$ when $ex(v) < 0$.

Lemma 18: f_{legal} is a feasible flow for $\langle P, C, E, S, T \rangle$.

Proof: From the above two Lemmas, it suffices to prove that R_{cons} has residual capacity 0 on all edges of the form $\{\langle u, v \rangle | u \in C' \backslash C$ or $v \in P' \backslash P\}$. Since all these edges and those of the form $\{\langle v, u \rangle | u \in C' \backslash C$ or $v \in P' \backslash P\}$ are made to have capacity 0 before computing f_{legal} (step 3), the final residual capacity on these edges remains 0 as required.

Lemma 19: G_{final} is the residual graph for f_{legal} on $\langle P, C, E, S, T \rangle$ (see step 8 in Figure 5).

Proof: Since f_{cons} works on G_{morph} (derived from R_{back}) directly, the projection of R_{cons} on all edges that do not involve S' or T' (viz. G_{final}) is the residual graph for $f_{cons} + f_{back} = f_{legal}$ on $\langle P, C, E, S, T \rangle$.

Lemma 20: R_{return} is the required residual graph for $\langle P, C, E, S, T \rangle$.

Proof: From the previous Lemma, G_{final} is the residual graph for f_{legal}. f_{legal} is just a legal flow and is not necessarily the *maxflow*. Step 9 ensures that any further flow that can be augmented between S and T is indeed done so by maintaining the legality constraints of using a capacity of 0 for all edges of the form $\langle u, v \rangle$ or $\langle v, u \rangle$ with $u \in C' \backslash C$ or $v \in P' \backslash P$ (step 3). R_{return} is then the required residual graph for $\langle P, C, E, S, T \rangle$ given that it is the projection of R_{final} on $\{S, T\} \cup P \cup C$ (the legal nodes in the new instance).

ALGORITHM: INCR-SHRT-PATHS
INPUT: D' and Π' for $\mathcal{G}' =$ $\langle \mathcal{X}', \mathcal{E}', \mathcal{P}', \mathcal{C}' \rangle$, and a new instance $\mathcal{G} =$ $\langle \mathcal{X}, \mathcal{E}, \mathcal{P}, \mathcal{C} \rangle$, with $\mathcal{X}' \subseteq \mathcal{X}$, $\mathcal{E}' \subseteq \mathcal{E}$, $\mathcal{P}' \subseteq \mathcal{P}$, and $\mathcal{C}' \subseteq \mathcal{C}$.
RESULT: D and Π for $\mathcal{G}$.
  1. For all $i \in \mathcal{X}$ and $p \in \mathcal{P} \cup \{X_0\}$:
    a. Set $d_{p,i} = d'_{p,i}$.
    b. Set $\pi_{p,i} = \pi'_{p,i}$.
  2. For each edge $\langle u, v \rangle \in \mathcal{E} \backslash \mathcal{E}'$:
    a. RELAX-EDGE$(u, v, \mathcal{P}')$.
  3. For each edge $\langle u, v \rangle \in \mathcal{E}$:
    a. RELAX-EDGE$(u, v, \mathcal{P} \backslash \mathcal{P}')$.
END ALGORITHM
	ALGORITHM: RELAX-EDGE
	INPUT: edge $\langle u, v \rangle$ and a set of production events P.
	RESULT: modifications in D and Π.
	  1. If $P = \{\}$ RETURN.
	  2. For all $p \in P$:
	    a. If $d_{p,v} > d_{p,u} + weight(\langle u, v \rangle)$:
	      i. $d_{p,v} = d_{p,u} + weight(\langle u, v \rangle)$.
	      ii. $\pi_{p,v} = u$.
	    b. Else:
	      i. Remove p from P.
	  3. For all edges $\langle v, y \rangle$:
	    a. RELAX-EDGE(v, y, P).
	END ALGORITHM

Fig. 7. Shows the incremental computation of shortest paths required for posing new bipartite matching problems as and when search proceeds. $d_{p,i}$ is the current best estimate of the shortest path from node p to node i, and $\pi_{p,i}$ is the predecessor node of i in the shortest path from p to i. D and Π are the corresponding 2D arrays.

Lemma 21: f_{return} and M_{return} are the required maximum flow and its value correspondingly.

Proof: Given that R_{return} is the required residual graph, the flow on any edge $\langle u, v \rangle$ is given by the residual capacity in the opposite direction and is computed in step 11. Similarly, M_{return} is the sum of the flows on all edges outgoing from S, and is computed in step 12.

The complexity of the incremental *maxflow* algorithm in Figure 5 is dominated by steps 6 and 9. Step 6 has a complexity of $O(m|f_{cons}|)$ and step 9 has a complexity of $O(m|f_{final}|)$. By construction, $|f_{cons}| \leq \sum_{\{y_i \in P' \backslash P \cup C' \backslash C\}} |r(y_i)|$ and $|f_{final}| \leq \sum_{\{y_i \in P \backslash P' \cup C \backslash C'\}} |r(y_i)|$. When the computation of the resource envelopes needs to be done frequently, the sets $P \backslash P'$, $P' \backslash P$, $C \backslash C'$ and $C' \backslash C$ are very small, and the complexity of the algorithm is only about $O(m)$. This is significantly lesser than the complexity of recomputing the envelopes from scratch—viz. $O(n^{2.5})$. The total amount of work that we save is therefore equal to this difference (at each step) times the size of the search space (which is usually exponential).

4.2   Incremental Shortest Path Computation

All other incremental computation required to be done to pose a new bipartite *maxflow* problem as and when search proceeds by making partial commitments, can be done using algorithms similar to the Bellman-Ford algorithm for computing shortest path distances. Figure 7 illustrates this computation. Because of its similarity to the standard Bellman-Ford algorithm (see [1]), we do not provide a rigorous proof of its correctness in this paper. At any stage, the set of size-1 conflicts is given by all $p \in \mathcal{P}$ such that $d_{p,X_0} < -t$, and all $c \in \mathcal{C}$ such that $d_{X_0,c} < t$. The set of size-2 conflicts is given by all $c \to p$ such that $d_{p,c} < 0$.

The complexity of the incremental shortest path computation is $O(|\mathcal{E}\backslash\mathcal{E}'||\mathcal{E}||\mathcal{P}'| + |\mathcal{P}\backslash\mathcal{P}'||\mathcal{E}|^2)$. When the computation of the resource envelopes needs to be done frequently, the sets $\mathcal{P}\backslash\mathcal{P}'$ and $\mathcal{E}\backslash\mathcal{E}'$ are very small, and the complexity of the algorithm is only about $O(|\mathcal{E}|^2)$. This is significantly lesser than the complexity of recomputing the shortest path distances from scratch—viz. $O(|\mathcal{P}||\mathcal{E}|^2)$. The total amount of work that we save is therefore equal to this difference (at each step) times the size of the search space (which is usually exponential).

5   Conclusions and Future Work

We described efficient algorithms for the incremental computation of resource envelopes in producer-consumer models. This is important in all contexts where the computation of resource envelopes can potentially be used to guide the search for a good plan. In the context of interleaved planning and scheduling, a refinement planner proceeds by making partial commitments and the resource envelopes need to be recomputed at each point in the search space. In the context of interleaved planning and execution monitoring, execution of a plan may not always result in the intended outcome and fast re-planning is necessary. Incremental computation of resource envelopes then becomes extremely important for an active management of planning and execution monitoring. The algorithms presented in this paper are also constructive in that they yield flexible consistent schedules that actually achieve $g(t)$ or $h(t)$ for any given time point. This ensures both good performance at bottleneck points (as argued in [3]) and robustness with respect to exogenous events and uncertainty of execution.

We are also currently working on interesting approximation algorithms for optimal plan scheduling that use the resource envelope computation as an important subroutine. Future work will also pursue empirical verification of using resource envelopes within the general framework of interleaved planning and scheduling, and interleaved planning and execution monitoring.

References

1. Cormen T. H., Leiserson, C. E. and Rivest, R. L. Introduction to Algorithms. *Cambridge, MA, 1990.*
2. Laborie P. Algorithms for Propagating Resource Constraints in AI Planning and Scheduling: Existing Approaches and New Results. *ECP 2001.*
3. Muscettola N. On the Utility of Bottleneck Reasoning for Scheduling. *AAAI 1994.*
4. Muscettola N. Computing the Envelope for Stepwise-Constant Resource Allocations. *CP 2002.*
5. Smith D., Frank J. and Jonsson A. Bridging the Gap Between Planning and Scheduling. *Knowledge Engineering Review 15:1, 2000.*
6. Nguyen X. and Kambhampati S. Reviving Partial Order Planning. *IJCAI-2001.*

Approximated Consistency
for Knapsack Constraints*

Meinolf Sellmann

Cornell University
Department of Computer Science
4130 Upson Hall
Ithaca, NY 14853
sello@cs.cornell.edu

Abstract. While global constraints give a broader view on the entire problem and therefore allow more effective constraint propagation, the development of efficient generalized arc-consistency (GAC) algorithms for global constraints is frequently prevented by the fact that the associated decision problems are NP-hard. A prominent example for this is the Knapsack Constraint. On the other hand, there exist approximation algorithms for many NP-hard problems. By introducing the concept of approximated consistency for a special class of global constraints, so-called optimization constraints, we show how existing approximation algorithms can be exploited for the development of efficient filtering algorithms for Knapsack Constraints. As our main result, we show how ϵ-GAC for Knapsack and Bounded Knapsack Constraints can be achieved in time $O(n \log n + \frac{n}{\epsilon^2})$ or $O(n \log n + \frac{n}{\epsilon^3})$, respectively.

Keywords: global constraints, optimization constraints, cost-based filtering, relaxed consistency, approximation algorithms

1 Introduction

When dealing with discrete optimization problems, it is of utmost importance to obtain a global view on the problem that allows to assess what solution quality can still be achieved in a given subtree. To obtain a more global view, in constraint programming it has been suggested to incorporate so-called *optimization constraints* that link the objective function with some other constraints of the problem [2, 4, 6]. For many optimization constraints, efficient filtering algorithms have been developed (see [3, 11, 13, 14] for examples). However, frequently no polynomial time bounded generalized arc-consistency (GAC [1, 7]) algorithm can be developed for optimization constraints, because it is NP-hard to decide whether a *feasible and improving* solution still exists after a variable takes a specific value. We find ourselves in the same unsatisfactory situation when dealing with Knapsack Constraints that are defined as follows:

---

* This work was supported by the Intelligent Information Systems Institute, Cornell University (AFOSR grant F49620-01-1-0076).

F. Rossi (Ed.): CP 2003, LNCS 2833, pp. 679–693, 2003.

Definition 1. *Let* $n, w_1, \ldots, w_n, C, p_1, \ldots, p_n, B \in \mathbb{N}$. B *denotes the objective value to be exceeded,* C *the capacity of the knapsack,* n *the number of items, and* w_i *the weight of item* i *with profit* p_i $\forall 1 \leq i \leq n$. *Given* n *binary variables* $X_1, \ldots, X_n$, *we define:*

— *The* Knapsack Problem *consists in maximizing*

$$\sum_{i \leq n} p_i X_i \quad \text{s.t.} \quad \sum_{i \leq n} w_i X_i \leq C.$$

— *A* Knapsack Constraint $KP(X_1, \ldots, X_n, w_1, \ldots, w_n, C, p_1, \ldots, p_n, B)$ *is true, iff*

$$\sum_{i \leq n} w_i X_i \leq C \quad \text{and} \quad \sum_{i \leq n} p_i X_i > B.$$

To achieve GAC for a Knapsack Constraint, we have to eliminate all items (i.e. remove value 1 from the corresponding domain) that cannot be part of any feasible solution with profit greater than B, and we have to permanently include all items (i.e. remove value 0 from the corresponding domain) that are included in all feasible solutions with profit greater than B. However, since the Knapsack Problem (KP) is NP-hard, so is the problem of achieving GAC for Knapsack Constraints.

Two alternative filtering algorithms for Knapsack Constraints have been proposed in the literature. In [15], Trick develops a pseudo-polynomial time GAC algorithm for Subset-Sum Constraints. These constraints are special Knapsack Constraints where profit and weight of each item are equal. The algorithm uses a dynamic programming scheme for solving the Subset-Sum Problem to optimality and then exploits the information gathered for domain filtering. Addressing the general case where weights and profits can be chosen arbitrarily, Fahle and Sellmann [3] propose to drop the requirement that GAC must be achieved for the Knapsack Constraint. Instead, they introduce a notion of *relaxed consistency* for optimization constraints and use bounds based on linear programming relaxations for polynomial time domain filtering.

While the latter approach is more appealing with respect to the worst-case running time of the filtering procedure, the effectiveness of the algorithm is highly determined by the quality of the bounds that are used. In [3], different filtering algorithms are presented that are based on previously developed integer programming bounds for KP. While these bounds might often be rather tight in practice, their relative error could be arbitrarily close to a factor of 2.

Our aim is to provide filtering algorithms for Knapsack Constraints that are based on bounds with guaranteed accuracy. To achieve this goal, we exploit existing *approximation algorithms* for the Knapsack Problem. With the term "approximation algorithm" we refer to an algorithm that computes a solution to a problem with guaranteed accuracy in polynomial time. A family of approximation algorithms that, for each $\epsilon > 0$, provides an algorithm that computes a solution with relative error at most ϵ and that runs in time polynomial in the input length and in $1/\epsilon$, is called a *fully polynomial time approximation scheme*

(FPTAS). We will show how existing FPTAS for the Knapsack Problem can be used for cost-based filtering with respect to bounds of arbitrary accuracy, whereby the ϵ-parameter allows us to trade time for filtering effectiveness.

The remaining presentation is organized as follows: In Section 2, we review the literature on approximation algorithms for KP. Then in Section 3, we define the notion of approximated consistency for optimization constraints. Finally, in Sections 4 and 5, we develop efficient filtering algorithms for Knapsack Constraints and Bounded Knapsack Constraints.

2 Knapsack Approximation

To obtain provably tight bounds on the Knapsack Problem, we can use the existing polynomial time bounded approximation algorithms that solve the KP with arbitrary relative precision $\epsilon > 0$. The best currently known FPTAS for KP runs in time $O(n \log \frac{1}{\epsilon} + \frac{1}{\epsilon^{2+2\delta}})$, where $\delta = \frac{\alpha}{1+\alpha}$, with $\alpha \in O(C)$ [9]. This result strengthens and is based on the research presented in [5, 8, 12]. We briefly review the main ideas presented in [5] that we will use as a basis for the filtering algorithms that we develop later.

When reviewing the GAC algorithm for Subset-Sum Constraints in [15], we were already reminded that there exist pseudo-polynomial time algorithms for KP that are based on dynamic programming. One of these algorithms is pseudo-polynomial in the optimal objective value P^*: We set up a matrix M with $2P_0+1$ rows and $n + 1$ columns (both starting with index 0), where P_0 is such that $P_0 \leq P^* \leq 2P_0$ [1]. Now, in $M_{q,k}$ we store the minimum knapsack capacity that is needed to achieve exactly profit q when using only items in $\{1, \ldots, k\}$. Clearly, $M_{0,k} = 0 \; \forall k$, and $M_{q,0} = \infty \; \forall q > 0$, and the following recursion equation holds:

$$M_{q,k} = \min\{M_{q,k-1}, M_{q-p_k,k-1} + w_k\}. \tag{1}$$

By filling the matrix M row by row from left to right and examining the greatest value q such that $M_{q,n} \leq C$, we can solve the KP in time $O(nP^*)$. Now, we can reduce the running time by scaling down the profit values. We set $\overline{p}_i := \lfloor \frac{p_i}{K} \rfloor$ for some scaling factor $K \geq 1$ and get a running time in $O(n\overline{P^*}) = O(n\frac{P^*}{K})$. It is easy to show that we achieve an ϵ-approximate solution for the original problem when we set $K := \frac{\epsilon P_0}{n}$, where P_0 is the value of a 2-approximate solution as before [2]. Consequently, we can compute an ϵ-approximate solution to KP in time $O(\frac{n^2}{\epsilon} \frac{P^*}{P_0}) = O(\frac{n^2}{\epsilon})$.

The running time can be further reduced in n by partitioning the items into two sets: the set L of *large* items that contains all items with a profit value greater than some threshold value $T \geq 1$, and the set S of *small* items that contains all items i with profit $p_i \leq T$. We approximate the large item KP by scaling the profit vector and applying the dynamic programming scheme in (1).

---

[1] The value P_0 can be computed in linear time [8].

[2] Actually, we set $K := \max\{\frac{\epsilon P_0}{n}, 1\}$ of course, but here and in the following we assume that the scaling factor K is always greater or equal 1 without further mentioning it.

As a result, for each scaled profit value $0 \leq q \leq \lfloor \frac{2P_0}{K} \rfloor$, we get the minimum knapsack capacity $M_{q,|L|}$ that is needed to achieve profit q in the scaled large item KP. Now, for all q, we try to fill the remaining capacity $C - M_{q,|L|}$ with small items. We do this by inserting the small items in order of decreasing efficiency $\frac{p_i}{w_i}$ until we reach the first item that exhausts the remaining capacity. We denote the profit that is added by the small items with $\phi(C - M_{q,|L|})$. When we take, out of all the $\lfloor \frac{2P_0}{K} \rfloor + 1$ different knapsacks that were computed, the solution with maximum value $Kq + \phi(C - M_{q,|L|})$, it can be shown that the relative error that we make is bounded by $\frac{K}{T} + \frac{T}{P^*}$. Therefore, we achieve an ϵ-approximation by setting $K := \frac{\epsilon^2 P_0}{4}$ and $T := \frac{\epsilon P_0}{2}$ [8]. In order to perform the filling process of the remaining capacities with small items, we can sort the small items according to their efficiency first. Then, the entire algorithm requires time

$$O(n \log n + \frac{P^*}{K}n) = O(n \log n + \frac{4n}{\epsilon^2}\frac{P^*}{P_0}) = O(n \log n + \frac{n}{\epsilon^2}).$$

As stated before, the FPTAS can be strengthened further to give a worst-case running time that is linear in n for any given constant approximation accuracy $\epsilon > 0$. However, the filtering algorithm that we develop later will make use of efficiency and profit orderings. It therefore requires time $\Omega(n \log n)$ anyway, which is why we make no further effort here to base our filtering algorithm on more sophisticated versions of the general procedure as sketched above.

3   Approximated Consistency

Our aim now is to exploit the existing approximation algorithms in order to provide efficient filtering algorithms for Knapsack Constraints. As stated before, we cannot hope to achieve GAC for Knapsack Constraints in polynomial time. Therefore, we introduce a new measure for the consistency of an optimization constraint.

Definition 2. *Given $n \in \mathbb{N}$, let $X_1, \ldots, X_n$ denote some variables with finite domains $D_1 := D(X_1), \ldots, D_n := D(X_n)$. Furthermore, given a constraint $\zeta : D_1 \times \cdots \times D_n \to \{0,1\}$, and an objective function $P : D_1 \times \cdots \times D_n \to \mathbb{N}$, let $x_i \in D_i \, \forall \, 1 \leq i \leq n$.*

- *Let $B \in \mathbb{Q}$ denote a lower bound on the objective P to be maximized. Then, a function $\vartheta_{\zeta,P}[B] : D_1 \times \cdots \times D_n \to \{0,1\}$ with $\vartheta_{\zeta,P}[B](x_1, \ldots, x_n) = 1$ iff $\zeta(x_1, \ldots, x_n) = 1$ and $P(x_1, \ldots, x_n) > B$ is called maximization constraint.*
- *Given a maximization constraint $\vartheta_{\zeta,P}[B]$ and some $\epsilon \geq 0$, we say that $\vartheta_{\zeta,P}[B]$ is ϵ-GAC, iff for all $1 \leq i \leq n$ and $x_i \in D_i$ there exist $x_j \in D_j$ for all $j \neq i$ such that $\vartheta_{\zeta,P}[B - \epsilon P^*](x_1, \ldots, x_n) = 1$, whereby $P^* = \max\{P(y_1, \ldots, y_n) \mid y_i \in D_i, \zeta(y_1, \ldots, y_n) = 1\}$.*

Clearly, the Knapsack Constraint is a maximization constraint. Note that our notion of ϵ-GAC generalizes the notion of generalized arc-consistency in the sense that GAC is equivalent to 0-GAC. To achieve a state of approximated consistency for a Knapsack Constraint, we must ensure that

1. all items that cannot be part of any feasible solution that achieves a profit greater than $B - \epsilon P^*$ have to be deleted (i.e. the value 1 must be removed from the corresponding domain), and

2. all items that are included in all feasible solutions with profit greater than $B - \epsilon P^*$ have to be permanently inserted into the knapsack (i.e. value 0 has to be removed from the corresponding domain).

That is, in contrast to GAC for a maximization constraint, we do not enforce that all domain values are filtered that cannot be used in any improving solution, but at least we want to remove all values for which the performance drops too far below the critical objective value.

4   Cost-Based Filtering for Knapsack Constraints

A simple way to achieve a state of approximated consistency for the Knapsack Constraint is to use the algorithm in [9] for probing. This filtering algorithm then runs in time $O(n^2 \log \frac{1}{\epsilon} + \frac{n}{\epsilon^{2+2\delta}})$ with $\delta \to 1$ as $C \to \infty$. In this section, we develop a more sophisticated ϵ-GAC algorithm that runs in time $O(n \log n + \frac{n}{\epsilon^2})$.

4.1   Generalized Arc-Consistency for Knapsack Constraints

The basis of our algorithm is the approximation algorithm described in Section 2. We start by giving a GAC algorithm for the Knapsack Constraint that is based on the dynamic programming scheme in (1). The idea of our algorithm is similar to that described in [15]. We define a weighted, directed, and acyclic graph $G = (V, E, v)$ by setting

- $V_M := \{M_{q,k} \mid 0 \le q \le 2P_0, 0 \le k \le n\}$.
- $V := V_M \cup \{t\}$.
- $E_0 := \{(M_{q,k-1}, M_{q,k}) \mid k \ge 1, M_{q,k} \in V_M\}$.
- $E_1 := \{(M_{q-p_k,k-1}, M_{q,k}) \mid k \ge 1, q \ge p_k, M_{q,k} \in V_M\}$.
- $E_t := \{(M_{q,n}, t) \mid q > B, M_{q,n} \in V_M\}$.
- $E := E_0 \cup E_1 \cup E_t$.
- $v(e) := 0$ for all $e \in E_0 \cup E_t$.
- $v(M_{q-p_k,k-1}, M_{q,k}) := w_k$ for all $(M_{q-p_k,k-1}, M_{q,k}) \in E_1$.

We consider the graph G because there is a one-to-one correspondence between paths from $M_{0,0}$ to t and variable instantiations that yield a profit greater than B. Moreover, the length of such a path is exactly the weight of the corresponding instantiation. Therefore, every path from $M_{0,0}$ to t with length lower or equal C defines a feasible, improving solution. Vice versa, every feasible, improving solution also defines a path from $M_{0,0}$ to t with length lower or equal C.

   The algorithm proceeds as follows: We perform a shortest-path computation on G and get the shortest-path distances from $M_{0,0}$ to all other nodes as a byproduct. If the minimum distance from $M_{0,0}$ to t is greater than C, then there exists no feasible, improving solution, and we can backtrack.

Otherwise, following an idea presented in [6], we now reduce G by eliminating all arcs that cannot be part of any path from $M_{0,0}$ to t with length lower or equal C. We can do this efficiently by computing the shortest-path distances to t. Then:

- Remove all edges $(M_{q,k-1}, M_{q,k}) \in E_0$ for which

$$length(M_{0,0}, M_{q,k-1}) + length(M_{q,k}, t) > C.$$

- Remove all edges $(M_{q-p_k,k-1}, M_{q,k}) \in E_1$ for which

$$length(M_{0,0}, M_{q-p_k,k-1}) + w_k + length(M_{q,k}, t) > C.$$

Denote the reduced arc sets with E_0^R and E_1^R, respectively. To perform cost-based filtering, we now examine all items $1 \leq k \leq n$ sequentially. Item k is removed from the knapsack (i.e., value 1 is filtered from the domain D_k), iff there exists no q such that there is an arc in E_1^R that ends in $M_{q,k}$. Analogously, item k is added to the knapsack (i.e., value 0 is filtered from the domain D_k), iff there exists no q such that there is an arc in E_0^R that ends in $M_{q,k}$.

The algorithm sketched above is correct and achieves a state of generalized arc-consistency:

- **Correctness:** Assume our algorithm removes value 0 (or value 1) from some domain D_k. Then, there exists no path from $M_{0,0}$ to t in G with length lower or equal C such that an arc $(M_{q,k-1}, M_{q,k}) \in E_0$ (or an arc $(M_{q-p_k}, M_{q,k}) \in E_1$, respectively) is visited. Therefore, there also exists no feasible and improving solution such that $X_k = 0$ ($X_k = 1$).
- **GAC:** Assume that, when setting $X_k := 0$ (or $X_k := 1$), there exists no extension to a full instantiation of the variables that is feasible with respect to the Knapsack Constraint. Then, there exists no feasible and improving solution with $X_k = 0$ (or $X_k = 1$). Consequently, there also exists no path from $M_{0,0}$ to t in G with length lower or equal C that visits an arc $(M_{q,k-1}, M_{q,k}) \in E_0$ (or an arc $(M_{q-p_k}, M_{q,k}) \in E_1$, respectively).

Regarding the time complexity: since shortest-path computations on directed acyclic graphs can be performed in linear time, the algorithm requires time proportional to the size of G. Now, the out-degree of each node in G is bounded by 2. Therefore, the algorithm needs time $O(|V| + |E|) = O(|V|) = O(|V_M|) = O(|M|) = O(nP^*)$.

An example is given in Figure 1(a). We consider a Knapsack Constraint with four variables $X_1, \ldots, X_4$ with profits $p^T = (50, 40, 30, 20)$ and weights $w^T = (3, 3, 4, 5)$. The knapsack's capacity is $C = 10$, and the profit value to be exceeded is supposed to be $B = 81$. We see that the value 0 can be removed from the domains of the variables X_1 and X_2, because in the reduced arc set there are no horizontal arcs left that end in their corresponding columns. Likewise, value 1 can be removed from D_4. All remaining values cannot be filtered, because the solutions $X = (1, 1, 1, 0)$ and $X = (1, 1, 0, 0)$ are both feasible and they improve upon the value of the incumbent solution.

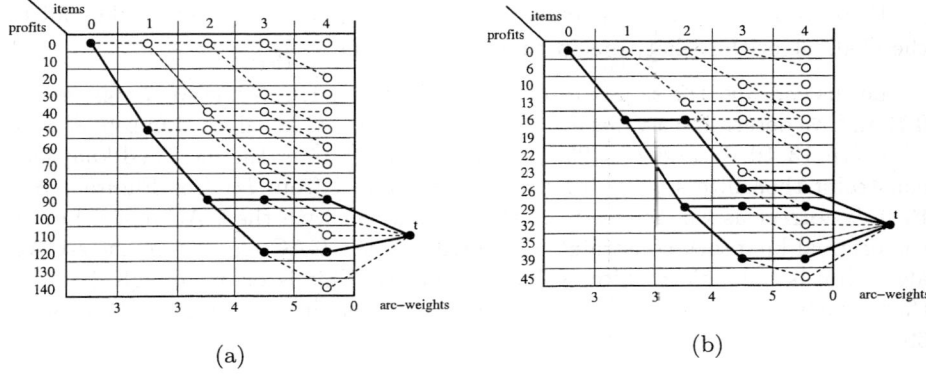

Fig. 1. Both figures show the graph G that is defined for the GAC algorithm. We assume that all arcs are directed from left to right, whereby the arrows are omitted to improve the readability. The matrix structure that is given corresponds to the dynamic programming schema M, whereby we do not show most cells, nodes and arcs that cannot be reached from $M_{0,0}$, again in order to improve the readability. The node-labels are defined by their row and column number, the sink node t is marked separately. The value of non-horizontal arcs that cross a vertical line is given under that line, horizontal arcs have weight 0. Hollow nodes and dashed arcs mark those nodes and arcs that are removed by the GAC algorithm, because there exists no path from $M_{0,0}$ to t with weight lower or equal C that visits them.

4.2   Scaling of Profits

We achieve a polynomial time algorithm for approximated consistency by scaling the profit space and applying the previous algorithm on the scaled problem. We set $K := \frac{\epsilon P_0}{n}$, $\overline{p}_i := \lfloor \frac{p_i}{K} \rfloor$ for all $1 \le i \le n$, and $\overline{B} := \frac{B - \epsilon P_0}{K}$, and we apply the GAC algorithm in Section 4.1 on the Knapsack Constraint $KP(X_1, \ldots, X_n, w_1, \ldots, w_n, C, \overline{p}_1, \ldots, \overline{p}_n, \overline{B})$.

This procedure is correct and achieves a state of ϵ-GAC:

- **Correctness:** Assume a value $b \in \{0, 1\}$ is removed from some domain D_k by the GAC algorithm on $KP(X_1, \ldots, X_n, w, C, \overline{p}, \overline{B})$. Then, for the optimal feasible solution $\overline{x}$ with $\overline{x}_k = b$ it holds:

$$\overline{p}^T \overline{x} \le \overline{B} = \frac{B - \epsilon P_0}{K}.$$

With x^*, we denote the optimal feasible solution to the unscaled problem with side constraint $X_k = b$. It follows

$$p^T x^* - \epsilon P_0 = p^T x^* - Kn \le K \overline{p}^T x^* \le K \overline{p}^T \overline{x} \le B - \epsilon P_0,$$

and therefore $p^T x^* \le B$. Thus, it is justified to remove b from D_k.

- **ϵ-GAC:** Let $k \in \{1, \ldots, n\}$, $b \in \{0, 1\}$, define $\overline{x}$ and x^* as before, and assume $p^T x^* \le B - \epsilon P^*$. Then,

$$\overline{p}^T \overline{x} \le \frac{p^T \overline{x}}{K} \le \frac{p^T x^*}{K} \le \frac{B - \epsilon P^*}{K} \le \frac{B - \epsilon P_0}{K} = \overline{B}.$$

Consequently, value b is removed from D_k.

Regarding the time complexity: Clearly, the dominating step is the call to the GAC algorithm that runs in time $O(n\frac{P^*}{K}) = O(\frac{n^2}{\epsilon}\frac{P^*}{P_0}) = O(\frac{n^2}{\epsilon})$.

Let us consider the same example as in Section 4.1. Assume we are given $\epsilon = 0.1$, and we determine a value $P_0 = 120$. Then, the ϵ-GAC algorithm sets $K = 3$, $\overline{p}^T = (16, 13, 10, 6)$, and $\overline{B} = 23$. The GAC algorithm for the modified knapsack constraint then filters value 0 from D_1 and value 1 from D_4 (see Figure 1(b)). Both is correct as we can see from the comparison with the GAC algorithm on the original knapsack constraint. In contrast to the GAC algorithm, the ϵ-GAC algorithm is not able to filter value 0 from D_2. This is okay, though, because there exists a feasible solution $X = (1, 0, 1, 0)$ that has profit $50 + 30 = 80 > 69 = 81 - 120/10 = B - \epsilon P_0$.

4.3   Separation of Items

So far we have not achieved any gains over the brute-force probing method that utilizes the best known approximation scheme for Knapsack Problems. For any given constant approximation guarantee $\epsilon > 0$, both algorithms require time quadratic in n. We try to improve on this by separating the items in the style of [5]. We set $K := \frac{\epsilon^2 P_0}{8}$, $T := \frac{\epsilon P_0}{2}$, and define

$$S := \{j_1, \ldots, j_{|S|}\} := \{1 \leq i \leq n \mid p_i \leq T\},$$

whereby we assume that the items in S are ordered with respect to decreasing efficiency, i.e. $\frac{p_{j_l}}{w_{j_l}} \geq \frac{p_{j_{l+1}}}{w_{j_{l+1}}}$ for all $1 \leq l < |S|$. Further, let

$$L := \{i_1, \ldots, i_{|L|}\} := \{1 \leq i \leq n \mid p_i > T\}$$

and set $\overline{B} := B - \epsilon P_0$, and $\overline{p}_k := \lfloor \frac{p_{i_k}}{K} \rfloor$ for all $1 \leq k \leq |L|$. Similar to Section 4.1, we define a weighted, directed, and acyclic graph $G = (V, E, v)$ by setting:

- $V_M := \{M_{q,k} \mid 0 \leq q \leq \lfloor \frac{2P_0}{K} \rfloor, 0 \leq k \leq |L|\}$.
- $V := V_M \cup \{t\}$.
- $E_0 := \{(M_{q,k-1}, M_{q,k}) \mid k \geq 1, M_{q,k} \in V_M\}$.
- $E_1 := \{(M_{q-\overline{p}_k,k-1}, M_{q,k}) \mid k \geq 1, q \geq \overline{p}_k, M_{q,k} \in V_M\}$.
- $E_t := \{(M_{q,|L|}, t) \mid M_{q,|L|} \in V_M\}$.
- $E := E_0 \cup E_1 \cup E_t$.
- $v(e) := 0$ for all $e \in E_0$.
- $v(M_{q-\overline{p}_k,k-1}, M_{q,k}) := w_{i_k}$ for all $(M_{q-\overline{p}_k,k-1}, M_{q,k}) \in E_1$.

To complete the definition, we still need to weight the remaining arcs in E_t. We do this be setting

$$v(M_{q,|L|}, t) := \min\{\sum_{l=1}^{s} w_{j_l} \mid s \leq |S|, \sum_{l=1}^{s} p_{j_l} > \overline{B} - Kq\}$$

for all $0 \leq q \leq \lfloor \frac{2P_0}{K} \rfloor$, whereby we define $\min \emptyset := \infty$.

Again, we observe a correspondence between paths from $M_{0,0}$ to t in G and possible knapsack instantiations. While all combinations of large items are possible, the selection of small items is restricted to collections of items with highest efficiency. Note also that the length of a path from $M_{0,0}$ to t, if it is lower than infinity, gives the weight of the corresponding solution $\overline{x}$. Then, when we denote with u_S the small item part and with u_L the large item part of a vector u, it holds:

$$p^T\overline{x} \geq K\overline{p}_L^T\overline{x}_L + p_S^T\overline{x}_S > \overline{B}.$$

Therefore, any path from $M_{0,0}$ to t with weight lower or equal C defines a feasible solution with profit greater $\overline{B}$.

Given $\epsilon > 0$, we propose to use Algorithm 1 to achieve ϵ-GAC for the Knapsack Constraint $KP(X_1, \ldots, X_n, w, C, p, B)$.

1: Sort the items according to decreasing efficiency and compute a profit ordering of the items.

2: Compute P_0 such that for the optimal solution P^* it holds: $P_0 \leq P^* \leq 2P_0$. Then, set $\overline{B} := B - \epsilon P_0$, $K := \frac{\epsilon^2 P_0}{8}$, and $T := \frac{\epsilon P_0}{2}$.

3: Set up the graph $G = (V, E, v)$ as defined above and compute the shortest-path distances $length(M_{0,0}, s)$ for all $s \in V$.

4: If $length(M_{0,0}, t) > C$, then set $D_k := \emptyset$ for all $1 \leq k \leq n$ and return.

5: Compute the shortest-path distances $length(s, t)$ for all $s \in V$.

6: Remove all arcs from E_0 and E_1 that cannot be part of any path from $M_{0,0}$ to t with length lower or equal C. Denote the reduced arc sets with E_0^R and E_1^R, respectively.

7: For all items $k \in L$ and $b \in \{0, 1\}$, remove b from D_k iff for all $M_{q,k} \in V_M$ there exists no arc in E_b^R that ends in $M_{q,k}$.

8: For all $0 \leq q \leq \lfloor \frac{2P_0}{K} \rfloor$, iterate over all items $k = j_r \in S$ in order of increasing profit and compute

$$v(q, k, 0) := \min\{\textstyle\sum_{l \leq s, l \neq r} w_{j_l} \mid s \leq |S|, \textstyle\sum_{l \leq s, l \neq r} p_{j_l} > \overline{B} - Kq\}$$
$$v(q, k, 1) := \min\{w_k + \textstyle\sum_{l \leq s, l \neq r} w_{j_l} \mid s \leq |S|, p_k + \textstyle\sum_{l \leq s, l \neq r} p_{j_l} > \overline{B} - Kq\}.$$

9: For all $k \in S$, remove $b \in \{0, 1\}$ from D_k iff for all $0 \leq q \leq \lfloor \frac{2P_0}{K} \rfloor$

$$length(M_{0,0}, M_{q,|L|}) + v(q, k, b) > C.$$

10: Return.

Algorithm 1: ϵ-GAC Knapsack Filtering Algorithm.

Theorem 1. *Algorithm 1 is correct and achieves ϵ-GAC.*

Proof. Define

$$f(x) := K\overline{p}_L^T x_L + p_S^T x_S,$$

and for all $k \in \{1, \ldots, n\}$ and $b \in \{0, 1\}$ set

$$F_{k,b} := \{y \in \{0, 1\}^n \mid w^T y \leq C, \, y_k = b\}, \text{ and}$$

$$A_{k,b} := \{y \in F_{k,b} \mid \forall l < |S|, \, j_l \neq k \neq j_{l+1} : \, y_{j_l} = 0 \Rightarrow y_{j_{l+1}} = 0\}.$$

Without formal proof, it is easy to see that our filtering procedure removes a value $b \in \{0, 1\}$ from some domain D_k (no matter whether $k \in L$ or $k \in S$) iff $f(x) \leq \overline{B}$ for all $x \in A_{k,b}$.

- **Correctness:** Assume a value $b \in \{0,1\}$ is removed from some domain D_k. Denote with $\overline{x}$ a vector in $A_{k,b}$ that achieves a maximum profit, i.e.:

$$f(\overline{x}) := \max\{f(x) \mid x \in A_{k,b}\} \leq B - \epsilon P_0.$$

Now, let $x^* \in F_{k,b}$ denote any feasible knapsack solution with $x_k^* = b$. Then, since $\sum_{i \in L} x_i^* \leq \frac{p_L^T x_L^*}{T}$, it holds:

$$p^T x^* = p_L^T x_L^* + p_S^T x_S^* < K(\overline{p}_L^T x_L^* + \frac{p_L^T x_L^*}{T}) + p_S^T x_S^*. \tag{2}$$

Further, we know that

$$f(\overline{x}) \geq f((x_L^*, \overline{x}_S)) = K\overline{p}_L^T x_L^* + p_S^T \overline{x}_S^T. \tag{3}$$

Subtracting inequality (3) from inequality (2) yields:

$$p^T x^* - f(\overline{x}) < \frac{K}{T} p_L^T x_L^* + p_S^T (x_S^* - \overline{x}_S) \leq \frac{K}{T} 2 P_0 + T = \epsilon P_0.$$

Consequently,

$$p^T x^* - \epsilon P_0 \leq f(\overline{x}) \leq B - \epsilon P_0,$$

and therefore $p^T x^* \leq B$. Thus, value b is correctly filtered from D_k.
- **ϵ-GAC:** Assume there exist $b \in \{0,1\}$ and $k \in \{1,\dots,n\}$ such that for all $x \in F_{k,b}$: $p^T x \leq B - \epsilon P_0$. Then, for all $\overline{x} \in A_{k,b}$ it holds that

$$f(\overline{x}) = K\overline{p}_L^T \overline{x}_L + p_S^T \overline{x}_S \leq p^T \overline{x} \leq B - \epsilon P_0 = \overline{B}.$$

Therefore, b is removed from D_k.

$\square$

Regarding the time complexity: Step 1 takes time $O(n \log n)$, and step 2 then can easily be performed in linear time (see [5]). The computations in steps 3–7 can be performed in time $O(E) = O(n\frac{2P_0}{K}) = O(\frac{n}{\epsilon^2})$ (compare with Section 4.1). Since we are considering the items in S in order of increasing profit, by using the same analysis as in [3], we can show that the computations in step 8 can be performed in time $O(2n\frac{2P_0}{K}) = O(\frac{n}{\epsilon^2})$. Step 9 finally takes time $O(2n\frac{2P_0}{K}) = O(\frac{n}{\epsilon^2})$. Note that step 1 needs to be carried out only once when the filtering algorithm is called several times with changing domains D_k. It follows:

Theorem 2. *For a Knapsack Constraint $KP(X_1, \dots, X_n, w, C, p, B)$, and for all $\epsilon > 0$, ϵ-GAC can be achieved in time $O(n \log n + \frac{n}{\epsilon^2})$. For $\Omega(\log n)$ different calls to the filtering routine with changing domains $D_k \subseteq \{0,1\}$, the algorithm runs in amortized time $O(\frac{n}{\epsilon^2})$ per call.*

One may ask why our filtering algorithm is not based on the best known approximation algorithm in [9], but uses the rather old approximation schema in [5]. While the slightly different separation of items in [9] and the advanced scaling scheme in [8] could easily be integrated in our algorithm, for us they do not result in an improved running time. The reason for this is twofold: First, when filtering the items in the small item set in step 8, we make extensive use of efficiency and profit orderings, and their computation takes time $\Theta(n \log n)$ anyway. Second, the advanced scaling scheme in [8] is proposed in order to reduce the number of large items that need to be considered to find an optimal approximation. However, we cannot reduce the number of large items with respect to optimality considerations, because we are looking for *improving* solutions, but not necessarily for *optimal* ones. Therefore, when filtering the large items in steps 3–7, we need to consider all of them, no matter which scaling scheme is used.

Regarding the practicability of our algorithm, for very large n and really small ϵ, there is clearly a problem with respect to the memory requirements. While in the previously developed FPTAS it is sufficient to store only one column of the matrix M at a time, we require to store the entire graph G. Therefore, the memory needed is in $\Theta(\frac{n}{\epsilon^2})$. The asymptotic constants can be reduced, however, by using an ϵ-approximate solution P_1 instead of the 2-approximation P_0 and setting $K := \frac{\epsilon^2 P_1}{4}$. Then, the size of M can be bounded by $\frac{4n}{(1-\epsilon)\epsilon^2}$ (instead of $\frac{16n}{\epsilon^2}$), and we can show that, for all $\frac{1}{2} > \epsilon > 0$, we achieve ϵ-GAC in time $O(n \log n + \frac{n}{\epsilon^2})$.

5   Approximated Consistency for Bounded Knapsack Constraints

To model more realistic problems, we now would like to rid ourselves of the restriction that all variables must have binary domains. We can generalize the results obtained by considering bounded knapsack constraints where each variable is associated with a domain $D_k = \{0, \ldots, u_k\}$:

Definition 3. *Let* $n, w_1, \ldots, w_n, C, p_1, \ldots, p_n, B, u_1, \ldots, u_n \in \mathbb{N}$. B *denotes the value of the incumbent solution,* C *the capacity of the knapsack,* n *the number of items, and* w_i *the weight of item* i *with profit* p_i $\forall 1 \leq i \leq n$. *Given* n *variables* $X_1, \ldots, X_n$ *that can take values in* $D_k = \{0, \ldots, u_k\}$ *for all* $1 \leq k \leq n$, *we define the* Bounded Knapsack Constraint *as follows:*
$$BKP(X_1, \ldots, X_n, w_1, \ldots, w_n, C, p_1, \ldots, p_n, B) \text{ is true iff}$$
$$\sum_{i \leq n} w_i X_i \leq C \quad \text{and} \quad \sum_{i \leq n} p_i X_i > B.$$

Note that, even though in the definition we require the variables to have domains that start at 0, this is no real restriction, because if some X_k is required to take values in $\{l_k, \ldots, u_k\}$, we can simply set $B' := B - l_k p_k$, $C' := C - l_k w_k$, and $D'_k := \{0, \ldots, u_k - l_k\}$ and consider $BKP(X_1, \ldots, X'_k, \ldots, X_n, w, C', p, B')$, whereby now the variable X'_k takes values in D'_k.

Generally, to approximate the Bounded (or even the Unbounded) Knapsack Problem, we can follow the same procedure as described in Section 2. To cope with the large items, it has been suggested to introduce multiple copies for each of them. And, in order to compute the profit gained by the small items, it was proposed to sort the items according to their efficiency and then to try to add u_k copies of the current item until we reach the first item where this is not possible anymore. Then, it is easy to compute the number of copies of this item that can still be introduced without exceeding the knapsack's capacity.

With respect to cost-based filtering, we also try to follow the procedure given in Algorithm 1 very closely. However, the suggestions on how to treat large and small items cannot easily be adapted. First of all, when introducing multiple copies of the large items, the best we can hope for is the information that a variable cannot take values greater than 0 anymore; or likewise, that a variable must take its maximum value. However, we can never get a result that reduces the domains of a variable without setting it to its minimum or maximum value automatically. This effect is of course due to the fact that all copies of an item are symmetric to each other. This means, if for one of the copies it is found that it has to (or must not, respectively) be included in the knapsack, this automatically holds for all other copies, too.

The other problem that we are facing regards the small items. A simple adoption of the procedure given in Section 4 also gives us some trouble to determine how many copies of an item we can afford to remove from (or to insert in, respectively) our knapsack without losing too much profit. In what follows, we address both problems and show how to tackle them efficiently.

5.1   Filtering of Large Items

Let us start by considering the set of large items. Instead of adding u_k copies for each item, we suggest to add a polynomial number of arcs to the graph defined in Section 4.2. First, we observe that, for any large item $k \in L$, u_k can be bounded from above, because: $u_k \frac{\epsilon P_0}{2} = u_k T \leq u_k p_k \leq 2P_0$, and therefore, $u_k \leq \frac{4}{\epsilon}$.

Then, we recall that the edge set was partitioned into the sets E_0, E_1, and E_t. The last set contains all arcs that end in the sink node t, whereas the first two sets were used to model the choice between insertion and not-insertion of an item. In the same manner, we can introduce additional arc sets $E_2, \ldots, E_u$ that model the insertion of multiple copies of an item, whereby $u := \max\{u_{i_k} \mid 1 \leq k \leq |L|\} \leq \frac{4}{\epsilon}$. Formally, we define:

$$E_l := \{(M_{q-l\overline{p}_k, k-1}, M_{q,k}) \mid k \geq 1, \; u_{i_k} \geq l, \; q \geq l\overline{p}_k, M_{q,k} \in V_M\} \quad \forall \, 2 \leq l \leq u.$$

The newly added arcs are weighted by setting

$$v(M_{q-l\overline{p}_k, k-1}, M_{q,k}) := l w_{i_k} \quad \forall \, (M_{q-l\overline{p}_k, k-1}, M_{q,k}) \in E_l, \; 2 \leq l \leq u.$$

With this setting, we are able to consider all possible instantiations to large item variables by conducting shortest-path computations in G. To perform cost-based filtering, we reduce the graph again in the usual way and check whether there exist $1 \leq k \leq |L|$ and $0 \leq l \leq u$ such that E_l^R does not contain arcs anymore that end in some node $M_{q,k} \in V$.

With respect to the worst case running time, we lose a factor of $\frac{1}{\epsilon}$ because now $|E| \in O(\frac{1}{\epsilon}|V|)$. Therefore, the filtering of the large items now takes time $O(\frac{n}{\epsilon^3})$.

5.2 Filtering of Small Items

Now let us consider the items in the set S. Recall from Algorithm 1 (steps 8 and 9) that, in order to filter values for small items, for all $0 \leq q \leq \frac{2P_0}{K}$ we have to find out whether we can still close the profit-gap between Kq and $\overline{B}$ with the help of the remaining available capacity $C - length(M_{0,0}, M_{q,|L|})$ when a certain variable takes a specific value. If we use the same approach as presented in Algorithm 1, for bounded knapsack constraints this requires time $\Theta(n \max\{u_k \mid k \in S\})$. Now, in contrast to the large items, the small item's domains cannot tightly be bounded from above. Therefore, this procedure has pseudo-polynomial/exponential running time.

We can do much better though, and we can even rid ourselves from the necessity to compute a profit ordering of the items: Assume all items in S (for simplicity, let us assume $S = \{1, \ldots, n\}$) are ordered with respect to decreasing efficiency $e_i := \frac{p_i}{w_i}$ for all $1 \leq i \leq n$. We consider the items sequentially. Denote the current item with k. If there is still capacity in the current knapsack X (recall from Section 4.2 that we need to consider a sequence of knapsacks) left, we insert u_k copies of item k. Let s^X denote the first item where this is not possible anymore. Then, we add as many copies of s^X as is still possible; the number of copies of s^X that are inserted is denoted with c_s^X. Furthermore, we denote the value that the small items achieve in this way by $\phi^X(C^X)$, whereby C^X denotes the current knapsack's capacity. Likewise, we denote with $\phi_s^X(W)$ the capacity that the *remaining* items can achieve (whereby at most $u_{s^X} - c_s^X$ copies of item s^X are allowed) by exploiting some given capacity W in the same manner as described for ϕ^X. Now, denote with $R^X := (u_{s^X} - c_s^X)w_{s^X} + \sum_{i>s^X}^n u_i w_i$ the total weight of the remaining items. Then, for a given profit value B^X that has to be exceeded by the small items, and for all $1 \leq k < s^X$, we define

$$\Delta_k^X := \max\{W \leq R^X \mid \phi^X(C^X) + \phi_s^X(W) \geq B^X + 1 + We_k\}.$$

With this setting, Δ_k^X reflects the total weight of an item k that we can afford to lose while still achieving a total profit of at least $B^X + 1$. Note that this total weight is allowed to exceed the actual weight of all copies of an item k, which is exactly $u_k w_k$. Now, assume $\Delta_k^X \geq u_k w_k$. Then, for all item $k < s^X$ in the current knapsack X, we can afford to use no copy of item k at all, and therefore, no reduction of the domain D_k can take place. However, if $\Delta_k^X < u_k w_k$ for some $k < s^X$, then we cannot afford to lose more than $\frac{\Delta_k^X}{w_k}$ copies of item k. Then, we set $D_k^X := \left\{ \left\lceil \frac{u_k w_k - \Delta_k^X}{w_k} \right\rceil, \ldots, u_k \right\}$.

Likewise, for all $k > s^X$, we define

$$\Gamma_k^X := \max\{W \leq C^X \mid \phi^X(C^X - W) \geq B^X + 1 - We_k\},$$

and, if $\Gamma_k^X < u_k w_k$, we set $D_k^X := \left\{ 0, \ldots, \left\lfloor \frac{\Gamma_k^X}{w_k} \right\rfloor \right\}$.

The important observation is, that there is some monotonicity among the Δ_k^X and Γ_k^X. Since the items are ordered with respect to decreasing efficiency, it holds

$$\Delta_{k+1}^X \geq \Delta_k^X \quad \forall\, 1 \leq k < s^X \qquad \text{and} \qquad \Gamma_{k+1}^X \geq \Gamma_k^X \quad \forall\, s^X < k \leq n.$$

Therefore, by using a similar routine to that described in [3], once an efficiency ordering of the items is known, the computation of the different D_k^X can be done in time $O(n)$. To complete the computation, eventually we determine the minimal $D_{s^X}^X$ separately, which can also be done easily in time $O(n)$ once the efficiency ordering of the items is known.

After having computed D_k^X for all $1 \leq k \leq n$ and for all small item knapsacks X that need to be considered, we can finally set

$$D_k := \bigcup_X D_k^X.$$

Since there are $O(\frac{1}{\epsilon^2})$ knapsacks that need to be considered, the entire filtering process for the small items takes time $O(n \log n + \frac{n}{\epsilon^2})$.

Putting the results for the large and the small items together, we have shown

Theorem 3. *For a Bounded Knapsack Constraint $BKP(X_1, \ldots, X_n, w, C, p, B)$, and for all $\epsilon > 0$, ϵ-GAC can be achieved in time $O(n \log n + \frac{n}{\epsilon^3})$. For $\Omega(\log n)$ different calls to the filtering routine with changing domains of the form $D_k = \{l_k, \ldots, u_k\}$, the algorithm runs in amortized time $O(\frac{n}{\epsilon^3})$ per call.*

6   Conclusion and Future Work

Since achieving a state of generalized arc-consistency for many global constraints is an NP-hard task, we introduced the notion of approximated consistency for optimization constraints. This notion allows to determine the filtering power of a propagation algorithm by the guaranteed approximation quality of the bounds that are used. Most importantly, by trading time for effectiveness, the ϵ-parameter allows to tune the filtering algorithm with respect to the specific constraint optimization problem that has to be solved.

For Knapsack Constraints, we have shown how existing approximation algorithms for the Knapsack Problem can be exploited for the development of efficient filtering algorithms. We presented an algorithm that achieves ϵ-GAC for Knapsack Constraints. For all constant $\epsilon > 0$, that algorithm runs in linear time for $\Omega(\log n)$ different calls with changing variable domains. It therefore improves clearly upon the filtering algorithms developed in [3]. Moreover, we developed an extension of our algorithm that can cope with Bounded Knapsack Constraints and that achieves ϵ-GAC in amortized time $O(\frac{n}{\epsilon^3})$.

The filtering algorithms described in this paper are currently being implemented. We shall soon be able to evaluate their practical performance and to perform experiments that give an insight regarding good choices of the approximation accuracy. Since we can smoothly vary the filtering effectiveness, we hope that these experiments will eventually establish a better understanding of the frequently observed duality between inference and search.

References

1. K. R. Apt. The Rough Guide to Constraint Propagation. *5th International Conference on Principles and Practice of Constraint Programming (CP)*, LNCS 1713:1–23, 1999.
2. T. Fahle, U. Junker, S.E. Karisch, N. Kohl, M. Sellmann, B. Vaaben. Constraint programming based column generation for crew assignment. *Journal of Heuristics*, 8(1):59-81, 2002.
3. T. Fahle, M. Sellmann. Cost-Based Filtering for the Constrained Knapsack Problem. *Annals of Operations Research*, 115:73–93, 2002.
4. F. Focacci, A. Lodi, M. Milano. Cost-Based Domain Filtering. *Principles and Practice of Constraint Programming (CP)* Springer LNCS 1713:189–203, 1999.
5. O.H. Ibarra, C.E. Kim. Fast Approximation Algorithms for the Knapsack and Sum of Subset Problems. *Journal of the ACM*, 22(4):463–468, 1975.
6. U. Junker, S.E. Karisch, N. Kohl, B. Vaaben, T. Fahle, M. Sellmann. A Framework for Constraint programming based column generation. *Principles and Practice of Constraint Programming (CP)*, Springer LNCS 1713:261–274, 1999.
7. V. Kumar. Algorithms for Constraints Satisfaction problems: A Survey. *The AI Magazine, by the AAAI*, 13:32-44, 1992.
8. E.L. Lawler. Fast Approximation Algorithm for Knapsack Problems. *Proceedings of the 18th Annual Symposium on Foundations of Computer Science*, pp. 206–213, 1977.
9. Y. Liu. On the Fully Polynomial Approximation Algorithm for the 0-1 Knapsack Problem. *Theory of Computing Systems*, 35:559-564, 2002.
10. J.-C. Régin. A filtering algorithm for constraints of difference in CSPs. *12th National Conference on Artificial Intelligence*, AAAI, pp. 362–367, 1994.
11. J.-C. Régin. Cost-Based Arc Consistency for Global Cardinality Constraints. *Constraints*, 7(3-4):387–405, 2002.
12. S. Sahni. Approximate algorithms for the 0/1 Knapsack Problem. *Journal of the ACM*, 22(1):115–124, 1975.
13. M. Sellmann. An Arc-Consistency Algorithm for the Weighted All Different Constraint. *8th International Conference on Principles and Practice of Constraint Programming (CP)*, LNCS 2470:744–749, 2002.
14. M. Sellmann, T.Fahle. Coupling Variable Fixing Algorithms for the Automatic Recording Problem. *Annual European Symposium on Algorithms (ESA)*, Springer LNCS 2161: 134–145, 2001.
15. M. Trick. A Dynamic Programming Approach for Consistency and Propagation for Knapsack Constraints. *3rd International Workshop on Integration of AI and OR Techniques in Constraint Programming for Combinatorial Optimization Problems (CP-AI-OR)*, pp. 113–124, 2001.

Cost-Based Filtering for Shorter Path Constraints*

Meinolf Sellmann

Cornell University
Department of Computer Science
4130 Upson Hall
Ithaca, NY 14853
sello@cs.cornell.edu

Abstract. Many real world problems, e.g. in personnel scheduling and transportation planning, can be modeled naturally as Constrained Shortest Path Problems (CSPPs), i.e., as Shortest Path Problems with additional constraints. A well studied problem in this class is the Resource Constrained Shortest Path Problem. Reduction techniques are vital ingredients of solvers for the CSPP, that is frequently NP-hard, depending on the nature of the additional constraints. Viewed as heuristics, until today these techniques have not been studied theoretically with respect to their efficiency, i.e., with respect to the relation of filtering power and running time. Using the concepts of Constraint Programming, we provide a theoretical study of cost-based filtering for shorter path constraints on acyclic, on undirected and on directed graphs that do not contain negative cycles.

Keywords: constrained shortest paths, problem reduction, optimization constraints, relaxed consistency

1 Introduction

Real world problems can frequently be modeled as Shortest Path Problems with additional constraints. The best known Constrained Shortest Path Problem (CSPP) is probably the *Resource Constrained Shortest Path Problem* [1, 3, 6, 14, 16] that consists in the combination of a Shortest Path Problem and capacity constraints on a set of resources. Even on directed acyclic graphs (DAGs), for non-negative objective functions and for only one resource that problem is known to be NP-hard [13].

Standard applications for the Resource Constrained Shortest Path Problem are route planning in traffic networks and quality of service routing [29, 21]. The Crew Scheduling Problem is another example of a real world problem where CSPPs are used in many successful approaches: In a column generation process, CSPPs have to be solved to generate columns, which correspond to individual lines of work in this context [7, 30].

Generally, CSPPs appear very often as subproblems in column generation approaches. Examples range from route guidance [15] and duty scheduling in public transit [4] up to the scheduling of switching engines [19]. In [17], a general framework for constraint programming based column generation was developed that formalizes the use of optimization constraints in this context.

---

* This work was supported by the Intelligent Information Systems Institute, Cornell University (AFOSR grant F49620-01-1-0076).

F. Rossi (Ed.): CP 2003, LNCS 2833, pp. 694–708, 2003.

To solve Constrained Shortest Path Problems, state of the art solvers compute lower and upper bounds on the problem and then close the duality gap. The latter task is carried out by an enumeration procedure such as a tree search [3], dynamic programming [20] or a k-shortest path algorithm [14]. Particularly in a tree search, but also in the other approaches the tightening of (sub-)problems is vital for an effective gap closing procedure. And therefore, it is essential for the overall performance and the practical success of the entire approach.

The first tightening strategy that was proposed goes back to a work done by Aneja et al. [1] for problem reduction of the Resource Constrained Shortest Path Problem. The basic idea consists in identifying nodes and arcs that cannot be visited by any path that obeys the given resource restrictions. The same method can also be used to identify nodes and arcs that cannot be visited by any improving path, which gives a first cost-based filtering algorithm for the problem. Dumitrescu and Boland [6] proposed a repeated problem reduction procedure that has shown to be very successful for hard constrained problems. Beasley and Christofides [3] have shown how a tighter global, Lagrangian relaxation based bound can be used for the elimination of nodes and arcs.

Apparently, none of these heuristics has been classified with respect to its filtering abilities. Moreover, the reduction techniques used all focus on the removal of nodes and arcs, but those arcs and nodes that must be visited by all paths of a certain quality remain undetected. However, with respect to the additional constraints of the CSPP this information can be very valuable as it may prove useful for an additional simplification of the problem.

Constraint Programming theory provides means for the state of consistency that a domain filtering algorithm achieves. In [8], we extended the notion of generalized arc-consistency (GAC) to the concept of *relaxed consistency* for optimization constraints. It allows to measure and compare heuristic filtering algorithms not only with respect to their running time, but also to their filtering power that is determined by the quality of the relaxation used. With respect to shorter path constraints, we study the complexity of achieving GAC. Since the problem is NP-hard in the general case, we introduce shortest-path relaxations and develop and compare different filtering algorithms for different graph classes.

Particularly, in Section 2, we review the notion of relaxed consistency, and in Section 3, we define shorter path constraints formally. In Section 4, we investigate the problem of achieving GAC for a shorter path constraint on undirected graphs, where it is shown to be NP-hard. We introduce a shortest-path relaxation and formulate a linear time algorithm that achieves a state of relaxed consistency. Finally, in Section 5, we develop cost-based filtering algorithms for shorter path constraints on directed acyclic and general directed graphs with non-negative costs or graphs that at least do not contain negative weight cycles.

2   Definitions and General Observations

Within a tree search, during the course of optimization we compute a sequence of feasible solutions. We refer to the best known feasible solution as the *incumbent solution*.

Obviously, once we have found a solution of a certain quality, we are searching for improving solutions only. Thus, we impose a restriction on the objective. That restriction in combination with other side-constraints of the original problem forms an *optimization constraint* [7, 10, 11, 17, 22], which is the core concept that we will be using throughout this paper. It was developed by a community that has been working on the integration of constraint programming (CP) and operations research (OR) in recent years. Though never explicitly stated as constraints, in the OR world optimization constraints are frequently used for bound computations and variable fixing. From a CP perspective, they can be viewed as *global constraints* that link the objective with some other constraints of the problem:

Given $n \in \mathbb{N}$, let $X_1, \ldots, X_n$ denote variables with finite domains $D_1 := D(X_1)$, $\ldots, D_n := D(X_n)$. Further, given a constraint $\zeta : D_1 \times \cdots \times D_n \to \{0, 1\}$, and an objective function $Z : D_1 \times \cdots \times D_n \to \mathbb{Q}$, let $x_i \in D_i \ \forall \ 1 \le i \le n$.

Definition 1. *Let $B \in \mathbb{Q}$ denote an upper bound on the objective Z to be minimized.*
A function $\vartheta_{\zeta,Z}[B] : D_1 \times \cdots \times D_n \to \{0, 1\}$ with $\vartheta_{\zeta,Z}[B](x_1, \ldots, x_n) = 1$ iff $\zeta(x_1, \ldots, x_n) = 1$ and $Z(x_1, \ldots, x_n) < B$ is called minimization *or, more generally,* optimization constraint.

The purpose of optimization constraints is twofold: first, they can be used for pruning by computing a lower bound on the objective, which is the common idea in branch and bound algorithms. Second, they may also be used to remove those values from variable domains that cannot be part of any improving solution, which may be viewed as a generalization of the variable fixing technique (for problems containing binary variables only, variable fixing and domain filtering are of course the same).

2.1 On the Complexity of Cost-Based Domain Filtering Problems

In order to achieve generalized arc-consistency (GAC) [2, 18] of an optimization constraint, we have to find and remove all assignments that cannot be extended to an *improving* solution that is *feasible* with respect to ζ. That is, if ζ is the only constraint of a combinatorial optimization problem (we call that optimization problem and the optimization constraint *corresponding to* or *associated with* each other), a GAC algorithm allows us to compute improving solutions in a backtrack-free search. Consequently, if the original problem is NP-hard, so is the problem of achieving GAC for the corresponding optimization constraint. As an example, consider e.g. the Knapsack Problem [8].

If the optimization problem associated with an optimization constraint is polynomial, then the problem of achieving GAC may also be polynomial. For example, consider the AllDifferent constraint with costs. The corresponding optimization problem is the Weighted Bipartite Matching Problem (WBMP) for which there exists a polynomial time algorithm. Now, since the removal of an edge or two nodes (when the edge between the nodes is chosen to be part of the matching) does not change the structure of the problem (i.e., the subproblem is again a WBMP), achieving GAC for the AllDifferent with costs can obviously be done in polynomial time [24, 25].

The situation may change, however, if the problem structure is not preserved when a variable is forced to take a specific value. Consider a Shortest Path Problem in an arbitrary network, where we use a binary variable for each edge (whereby a value 1 means that the edge is chosen to be on the path, and a value 0 represents that the edge is not on the path). The problem of finding a shortest path is of course solvable in polynomial time. However, if we are to compute the set of edges that must or cannot be part of any simple path that does not exceed a certain length, we are facing an NP-hard problem, which is easy to see by reduction to the Two Vertex Disjoint Paths Problem [9].

2.2 Degrees of Consistency

The discussion shows that we cannot always hope for an efficient cost-based domain filtering algorithm that achieves GAC. Therefore, we may consider to develop less effective but polynomial time bounded filtering algorithms that may only achieve a weaker degree of consistency.

Regarding cost-based filtering, an idea that has been developed in OR to perform variable fixing on linear integer problems is the *reduced cost filtering* method: when solving the continuous relaxation bound on a linear combinatorial optimization problem with the help of a general LP solver (such as the simplex algorithm or interior point methods), we get dual information and reduced cost data for free. That data can be used to compute a lower bound on the loss of performance that we have to accept when adding a new constraint of the form $X = x$ (usually this is done by performing one dual simplex re-optimization step). And of course, if the loss is too large, we can deduce that x must be removed from the domain of X. In [8], we strengthened and generalized the basic idea by coupling optimization constraints and relaxations:

Definition 2. *Given a minimization constraint* $\vartheta_{\zeta,Z}[B] : D_1 \times \cdots \times D_n \to \{0,1\}$, *let* $\Delta := D_1 \times \cdots \times D_n$. *Further, denote with* 2^Δ *the set of all subsets of* Δ, *and let* $L : 2^\Delta \to \mathbb{Q}$ *such that for all* $M_i \subseteq D_i$, $1 \le i \le n$,

$$L(M_1 \times \cdots \times M_n) \le \min\{Z(x_1,\ldots,x_n) \mid \zeta(x_1,\ldots,x_n) = 1, \ x_i \in M_i, \ 1 \le i \le n\},$$

where $\min \emptyset = \infty$. *We call* L *a relaxation of* $\vartheta_{\zeta,Z}$ *and say that* $\vartheta_{\zeta,Z}[B]$ *is relaxed* L-*consistent, iff for any given* $1 \le i \le n$ *and* $x_i \in D_i$, $L(D_1 \times \cdots \times \{x_i\} \times \cdots \times D_n) < B$.

As one would expect, the definition states that relaxed L-consistency can the easier be achieved the weaker the relaxation L is. For $L \equiv -\infty$, there is no work to do to achieve relaxed L-consistency, whereas GAC is enforced when $L(M_1 \times \cdots \times M_n) = \min\{Z(x_1,\ldots,x_n) \mid \zeta(x_1,\ldots,x_n) = 1, \ x_i \in M_i, \ 1 \le i \le n\}$. That is, the choice of L determines the degree of domain filtering.

In practice, L is usually chosen as a fairly tight bound that can still be computed quickly. For example, linear programming relaxations can be used, as it was done in [8]. Generally, within a tree search there is a trade-off between the time spent per search node and the total number of search nodes. Thus, the favorable choice of the accuracy of the relaxation is always subject to the optimization problem at hand. We introduced the concept of relaxed consistency because it allows to compare domain filtering algorithms not only with respect to the running time but also with respect to the degree of consistency they achieve.

3   Shorter Path Constraints

Definition 3. *Denote with $G = (V, E, c)$ a weighted (directed or undirected) graph with $||c||_\infty \in O(poly(|E|, |V|))$* [1], *and let $h \in \mathbb{N}$.*

- *A sequence of nodes $P = (i_1, \ldots, i_h) \in V^h$ with $(i_f, i_{f+1}) \in E$ for all $1 \leq f < h$ is called a* path *from i_1 to i_h in G.*
- *A path P is called* simple *iff P visits every node at most once. For all $i, j \in V$, denote with $\pi(i, j)$ the set of all simple paths from i to j.*
- *For all paths P, nodes $i \in V$ and edges $(i, j) \in E$, we write $i \in P$ or $(i, j) \in P$ iff P visits node i or the edge (i, j), respectively. For a set of nodes or edges S, we write $S \subseteq P$, iff $s \in P$ for all $s \in S$. Correspondingly, we write $P \subseteq S$ iff $s \in S$ for all $s \in P$.*
- *The cost of a path $P = (i_1, \ldots, i_h)$ is defined as $cost(P) := \sum_{1 \leq j < h} c_{i_j i_{j+1}}$. Accordingly, for any set $S \subseteq E$ we define $cost(S) := \sum_{(i,j) \in S} c_{ij}$.*

Definition 4. *Let $G = (V, E, c)$ denote a (directed or undirected) graph with $n = |V|$ and $m = |E|$, a designated source $v_1 \in V$ and sink $v_n \in V$, and arc costs $c_{ij} \in \mathbb{Z}$. Further, assume we are given binary variables $X_1, \ldots, X_m$, and an objective bound $B \in \mathbb{Z}$.*

- *A constraint $SPC(X_1, \ldots, X_m, G, v_1, v_n, B)$ that is true, iff*
  1. *the set $\{e_i \mid X_i = 1\} \subseteq E$ determines a simple path in the graph G from the source v_1 to the sink v_n, and*
  2. *the cost of the path defined by the instantiation of X is lower than B*
  is called a shorter path constraint.
- *We call every simple path in G from source to sink with costs less than B* admissible.

Obviously, the shorter path constraint is an optimization constraint. Now, to ease the notation, for the remainder of this section we assume that a shorter path constraint is associated with a set variable $Y \subseteq E$ that represents the set of edges e_i for which $X_i = 1$. The (current) domains of the variables X will be represented by two sets: the set of *possible members* $pos(Y)$, and the set of *required members* $req(Y)$ of Y. In the subtree of the search rooted at the current choice point, we require $req(Y) \subseteq Y \subseteq pos(Y)$. That is, $req(Y)$ represents the set of variables for which it has been set $X_i = 1$, and the set $E \setminus pos(Y)$ represents the set of variables for which it has been decided to set $X_i = 0$ already. Then, in the current choice point, we have to search for admissible paths P such that $req(Y) \subseteq P \subseteq pos(Y)$. Note that we use the set variable Y only to ease the presentation. It has no impact on the implementation that is assumed to use only the variables X. Especially, the didactic use of a set variable has no impact on the state of GAC that we try to achieve [2]. To achieve GAC of a shorter path constraint, we must ensure:

---

[1] This is the common *similarity assumption* that states that the largest cost is bounded by some polynomial in $|E|$ and $|V|$.

[2] Note that we could also model the shorter path constraint with a set variable instead of m binary variables. Then, GAC for the binary model corresponds to bound-consistency in the set model.

- For all $e \in pos(Y)$, there exists an admissible path P with $req(Y) \cup \{e\} \subseteq P \subseteq pos(Y)$, and
- for all $e \notin req(Y)$, there exists an admissible path with $req(Y) \subseteq P \subseteq pos(Y) \setminus \{e\}$.

That is, we have to find the set of all edges that must or cannot be part of all/any paths with length lower than B.

Obviously, whether there exists an admissible path at all can be decided by applying a shortest path algorithm. However, to decide whether there exists a simple path that visits a set of edges is already an NP-hard task which can be shown by a simple reduction to the Two Vertex Disjoint Path Problem. Consequently, the problem of achieving GAC for the general shorter path constraint is also NP-hard.

4 Shortest Path Problems on Undirected Graphs

First, we consider shorter path constraints on undirected graphs with non-negative edge weights. Obviously, on the existence of an admissible path can be decided by applying a shortest path algorithm. However, it is easy to see that to decide whether there exists a simple path that visits a set of edges is an NP-hard task. Therefore, in the following we develop a cost-based filtering algorithm that achieves relaxed consistency rather than generalized arc-consistency. In order to introduce the relaxation we want to use, we start with

Definition 5. *Denote with $G = (V, E, c)$ a weighted (directed or undirected) graph.*

- *A path P is called a k-simple path in G iff for all $j \in V$ the path P visits j at most k times. Note that a 1-simple path is a simple path in G.*
- *With $P(i, j) \in \pi(i, j)$ we refer to a shortest path from i to j (with respect to c). Then, to ease the notation, we set $c(i, j) := cost(P(i, j))$.*
- *Given a shorter path constraint, a k-simple path P from v_1 to v_n is called a k-admissible path iff $cost(P) < B$.*

Note that, in a graph with non-negative edge weights, a shortest admissible path is also a shortest 2-admissible path. Now, instead of checking for admissible paths only, we consider the following shortest path relaxation (see Definition 2): Denote with $D(Y)$ the domain of Y represented as the pair of sets $(req(Y), pos(Y))$. We set $H := \{P \mid P \in \pi(v_1, v_n) \text{ with } P \subseteq pos(Y)\}$ and $F_f := \{P \mid P \text{ is a 2-simple path from } v_1 \text{ to } v_n \text{ with } f \in P\}$ for all $f \in E$. Then, we define

$$L_1(D(Y)) := \max\{ \min\{cost(P) \mid P \in H\}, \\ \max_{f \in req(Y)}\{\min\{cost(P) \mid P \in F_f\}\}\}.$$

Lemma 1. *L_1 is a shortest path relaxation.*

Proof: According to Definition 2, we have to show that

$$L_1(D(Y)) \leq \min\{cost(P) \mid P \in \pi(v_1, v_n), req(Y) \subseteq P \subseteq pos(Y)\}.$$

Let $P \in \pi(v_1, v_n)$ denote a shortest path in G with $req(Y) \subseteq P \subseteq pos(Y)$. Obviously, it holds that $P \in H$ and $P \in F_f$ for all $f \in req(Y)$. And therefore, $L_1(D(Y)) \leq cost(P)$.

□

The big advantage of the above relaxation is that it allows to be checked for consistency very easily, as we shall see below. Note, however, that L_1 does not require that the 2-admissible paths must visit all nodes in $req(Y)$ simultaneously. Of course, this weakens the relaxation. In practice, we can reduce the negative effects by improving the probability that a 2-admissible path visits the edges in $req(Y)$: we set $c_{ij} := 0$ for all $\{i, j\} \in req(Y)$ and subtract $cost(req(Y))$ from B.

According to the definition, a shorter path constraint is relaxed L_1-consistent, iff

1. for all $f \in pos(Y)$, there exists a 2-admissible path $P \in F_f$, and
2. for all $f \notin req(Y)$, there exists an admissible path $P \in H$ with $f \notin P$.

In the following two sections, we show how relaxed L_1-consistency can be achieved efficiently.

4.1 Removing Edges from the Possible Set

First, for all edges in E, we have to check whether there exists a 2-admissible path in G that visits an edge $\{i, j\} \in E$. We observe that the shortest 2-simple path from v_1 to v_n that visits $\{i, j\}$ is either $(P(v_1, i), P(j, v_n))$ with costs $c(v_1, i) + c_{ij} + c(j, v_n)$ or $(P(v_1, j), P(i, v_n))$ with costs $c(v_1, j) + c_{ij} + c(i, v_n)$. Therefore, to check whether an edge has to be removed from $pos(Y)$ with respect to the relaxation L_1 it is sufficient to know the shortest-path distances from the source and to the sink of all nodes. Both values can be computed for all nodes by only two shortest-path computations in G in time $O(m + n \log n)$ by using Dijkstra's algorithm in combination with Fibonacci heaps [12]. In a random access machine (RAM) model, shortest paths on undirected graphs can be computed in time $O(m + n)$ when using the algorithm of Thorup (see [28] and the recent extension of Pettie and Ramachandran in [23]). Thus, the set of edges that has to be removed from $pos(Y)$ to achieve relaxed L_1-consistency can be computed in time $O(m + n \log n)$, and in time $O(m + n)$ on a RAM.

4.2 Adding Edges to the Required Set

After having removed all edges from G that cannot be part of any 2-admissible path, the edges that must be visited by all such paths can be characterized by

Theorem 1. *Assume that all edges in G are part of at least one 2-admissible path. Then, an edge $\{r, s\} \in E$ must be visited by all admissible paths, iff $\{r, s\} \in P(v_1, v_n)$, and $\{r, s\}$ is a bridge in G* [3].

We can prove the above theorem with the help of the following two lemmas:

Lemma 2. *Assume that all edges in G are part of at least one 2-admissible path. Let $\{r, s\} \in E$ denote an edge that must be visited by all admissible paths and that can be removed from G without disconnecting v_1 and v_n. Then, there exists an edge $\{k, l\} \in E$ such that*

---

[3] A bridge is an edge whose removal disconnects the graph.

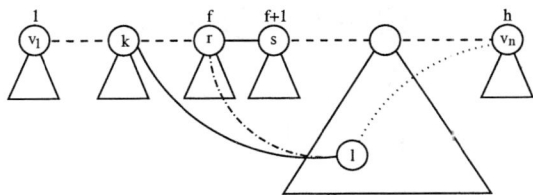

Fig. 1. The figure schematically shows an edge $\{k,l\} \in E$ that must exist according to Lemma 2. Solid lines mark edges in E, dashed lines parts of the shortest path between v_1 and v_n. The dotted line between l and v_n indicates that there exists a path between the two nodes that does not visit the edge $\{r,s\}$. The dashed lines between l and r indicate that the shortest path from l to v_n visits node r. The numbers on top of the nodes give their corresponding DFS numbers, and triangles mark DFS subtrees.

1. $\exists\, P \in \pi(v_1, v_n) : \{k,l\} \in P$ and $\{r,s\} \notin P$,
2. k is a shortest-path predecessor of r, and
3. $\{r,s\} \in P(l, v_n)$.

Proof: (See Fig. 1.) Assume we compute a shortest path $P = (i_1, \ldots, i_h) \in \pi(v_1, v_n)$. Then, $i_1 = v_1, i_h = v_n$ and $i_f = r, i_{f+1} = s$ for some $1 \le f < h$. Next, we change the graph representation of G such that $\{i_g, i_{g+1}\}$ is the first outgoing edge of node i_g for all $1 \le g < h$. For all nodes $j \in V$, denote with $d_j \in \{1, \ldots, n\}$ the ordering in which the nodes are first visited by a depth first search using the modified graph representation of G. Then, $d_{i_g} = g$ for all $1 \le g \le h$. Since the removal of $\{r,s\}$ does not disconnect v_1 and v_n, there exists a forward edge $\{k,l\} \in E$ with $d_k < f$ and $d_l > f+1$. This implies the Statements 1 and 2.

It remains to show that $\{r,s\} \in P(l, v_n)$. By assumption, there exists a 2-admissible path R through the edge $\{k,l\}$. There are two possibilities: either R visits node k or node l first, which corresponds to:

a) $c(v_1, k) + c_{kl} + c(l, v_n) < B$, or
b) R visits l before k and $c(v_1, l) + c_{kl} + c(k, v_n) < B$.

In the first case, because $\{r,s\} \notin P(v_1, k)$ and $\{r,s\}$ must be visited by all admissible paths, it holds that $\{r,s\} \in P(l, v_n)$, and we are done.

So let us consider the second case. Let $Q \in \pi(v_1, l)$ denote a shortest path from v_1 to l with $\{r,s\} \notin Q$. Without loss of generality we may assume that k and l are chosen such that $\{k,l\} \in Q$. We observe that $\{r,s\} \in P(v_1, l)$, because otherwise this implies that $\{k,l\} \in Q = P(v_1, l)$. But then the 2-admissible path visits node k before node l. Now, because k is a shortest-path predecessor of r and $\{r,s\} \in P(v_1, l)$, it holds that $k \in P(v_1, l)$. And then,

$$
\begin{aligned}
c(v_1, k) + c_{kl} + c(l, v_n) &\le c(v_1, k) + c_{kl} + c(l, k) + c(k, v_n) \\
&= c(v_1, k) + c(k, l) + c_{kl} + c(k, v_n) \\
&= c(v_1, l) + c_{kl} + c(k, v_n) \\
&< B,
\end{aligned}
$$

which reduces this case to (a). $\qquad\square$

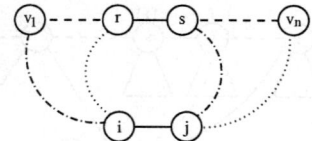

Fig. 2. The figure schematically shows an edge $\{i, j\} \in E$ that must exist according to Lemma 3. Solid lines mark edges in E, dashed lines mark parts of the shortest path between v_1 and v_n. Dashed lines indicate parts of the shortest path from v_1 to a node, dotted lines parts of the shortest path from a node to v_n. The proof of Theorem 1 shows that the path $(P(v_1, r), P(r, i), P(j, s), P(s, v_n))$ is two admissible and does not visit the edge $\{r, s\}$.

Lemma 3. *Assume that all edges in G are part of at least one 2-admissible path. Let $\{r, s\} \in E$ denote an edge that must be visited by all admissible paths and that can be removed from G without disconnecting v_1 and v_n. Then, there exists an edge $\{i, j\} \in E$ such that $\{r, s\} \in P(i, v_n)$ and $\{r, s\} \notin P(j, v_n)$, and $\{r, s\} \notin P(v_1, i)$ and $\{r, s\} \in P(v_1, j)$.*

Proof: (see Fig. 2.) Denote with $\{k, l\} \in E$ an edge as in Lemma 2. Then, there exists a path $P \in \pi(l, v_n)$ with $\{r, s\} \notin P$ and $\{r, s\} \in P(l, v_n)$.

1. Due to $\{r, s\} \notin P(v_n, v_n)$, there exists an edge $\{i, j\} \in P$ such that $\{r, s\} \in P(i, v_n)$ and $\{r, s\} \notin P(j, v_n)$.
2. By assumption, there is a 2-admissible path that visits j. Since $\{r, s\} \notin P(j, v_n)$, it follows that $\{r, s\} \in P(v_1, j)$, because $\{r, s\}$ must be visited by all admissible paths. Finally, assume that $\{r, s\} \in P(v_1, i)$. Then, the shortest path visiting node i has costs

$$c(v_1, r) + c_{rs} + c(s, i) + c(i, r) + c_{rs} + c(s, v_n).$$

But the path from v_1 via r, i and s to v_n has costs

$$c(v_1, r) + c(r, i) + c(i, s) + c(s, v_n),$$

which is lower or equal to the cost of the shortest path visiting i. This implies that it is a shortest path visiting node i, too. But it does not visit some edges with zero costs. Particularly, it does not visit the edge $\{r, s\}$. Therefore, we may assume that $\{r, s\} \notin P(v_1, i)$.

□

Proof of Theorem 1:

$\Leftarrow$ Let $\{r, s\}$ be a bridge on the shortest path $P \in \pi(v_1, v_n)$. Then, the removal of $\{r, s\}$ disconnects the graph G. Since the node pairs (v_1, r) and (s, v_n) are still connected, the removal of $\{r, s\}$ also disconnects v_1 and v_n. Thus, for all $P \in \pi(v_1, v_n)$, it holds that $\{r, s\} \in P$. Therefore, also all admissible paths must visit $\{r, s\}$.

$\Rightarrow$ Obviously, if there exists any admissible path, then $P(v_1, v_n)$ is admissible, too. Thus, $\{r, s\} \in P(v_1, v_n)$. Now assume that the removal of $\{r, s\}$ does not disconnect v_1 and v_n. Then, according to Lemma 3, there exists an edge $\{i, j\} \in E$ such that

$\{r, s\} \in P(i, v_n)$, $\{r, s\} \notin P(j, v_n)$, $\{r, s\} \notin P(v_1, i)$ and $\{r, s\} \in P(v_1, j)$. By assumption, there exists a 2-admissible path R visiting $\{i, j\}$. Without loss of generality we may assume that R visits node i before node j, because

$$
\begin{aligned}
c(v_1, j) + c_{ij} + c(i, v_n) &= c(v_1, r) + c_{rs} + c(s, j) + c_{ij} \\
&\quad + c(i, r) + c_{rs} + c(s, v_n) \\
&\geq c(v_1, r) + c(r, i) + c_{ij} + c(j, s) + c(s, v_n) \\
&\geq c(v_1, i) + c_{ij} + c(j, v_n).
\end{aligned}
$$

But this implies that $\{r, s\} \notin R$, which is a contradiction to the assumption that every admissible path must visit $\{r, s\}$.

$\square$

Using Theorem 1, after having removed all edges that cannot be part of any 2-admissible path, we can compute all edges that must be visited by all admissible paths in time $O(m + n)$: first, we compute a shortest path $P \in \pi(v_1, v_n)$ and mark all edges on this path. Then, we compute all bridges in G (which can easily be done in linear time, see [5]) and check which ones are visited by P. It follows:

Corollary 1. *On undirected graphs with non-negative edge weights, relaxed L_1-consistency of a shorter path constraint can be achieved in time $O(m + n \log n)$, and in time $O(m + n)$ on a RAM.*

5   Shortest Path Problems on Directed Graphs

On acyclic graphs, it is easy to see that arc-consistency can be achieved in linear time by computing shortest-path distances from the source and to the sink, and be determining bridges in the undirected version of the graph after the removal of arcs.

So let us consider general directed graphs with non-negative arc weights. In the end of this section, we will also give two theorems that we can prove for graphs that may contain negative arc weights but no negative cycles.

As for undirected graphs, achieving arc-consistency for shorter path constraints in general directed networks is NP-hard. Regarding the removal of arcs from the possible set, relaxed L_1-consistency on directed graphs with non-negative arc weights can be achieved in the same way as on undirected graphs. However, with respect to arcs that must be visited by all admissible paths, the situation is even more complicated. Recall the result from Section 4: After having removed the infeasible edges, in undirected graphs the edges that have to be required are exactly the ones on the shortest path that must be visited by *all* paths from v_1 to v_n.

Unfortunately, this classification does not hold for directed graphs as can be seen in Figure 3. Thus, for all arcs $(i, j) \in P(v_1, v_n)$, we have to recompute the shortest-path value when removing (i, j) from E, which may require $n - 1$ shortest-path computations in the worst case. It follows:

Theorem 2. *On directed graphs with non-negative arc weights, relaxed L_1-consistency can be achieved in time $O(n(m + n \log n))$.*

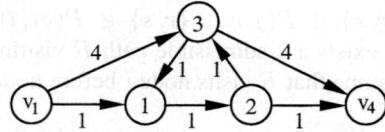

Fig. 3. A directed graph with non-negative arc weights. Assume we are given an upper bound $B = 8$. All arcs in the graph are part of an admissible path with costs lower than B. And every admissible path with costs lower than B must visit the arc $(1, 2)$. However, there exists a path $(v_1, 3, v_4)$ that does not visit this arc.

Since the computation time of the algorithm sketched in the above may not be efficient enough to be of profit when being applied in a tree search, in the following we consider another shortest path relaxation. Let $T \subseteq E$ denote a shortest-path tree in G rooted at v_1. Without loss of generality, we may assume that every node in G can be reached from v_1. Obviously, when $e \in E$ is removed from T, the nodes in V are partitioned into two sets: the set $v_1 \in S_e \subset V$ of nodes that are still connected with v_1 in $T \setminus \{e\}$, and the complement of S_e in V, S_e^C (see Fig. 4).

Obviously, $S_e^C \neq \emptyset$ iff $e \in T$. We set

$$J := \{P \mid P \text{ is a 2-simple path from } v_1 \text{ to } v_n \text{ with}$$
$$P \subseteq pos(Y) \text{ or, if } e \in P \setminus pos(Y), \text{ then there}$$
$$\text{exists an arc } (i, j) \in P \setminus T \text{ such that}$$
$$i \in S_e \text{ and } j \in S_e^C\}.$$

And we define

$$L_2(D(Y)) := \max\{ \min\{cost(P) \mid P \in J\},$$
$$\max_{f \in req(Y)}\{\min\{cost(P) \mid P \in F_f\}\}.$$

To understand the above shortest path relaxation better, we make the following observations:

- Obviously, because $H \subseteq J$, L_2 is dominated by L_1, i.e., $L_2 \leq L_1$. And therefore, L_2 is also a shortest path relaxation.
- The difference between relaxations L_1 and L_2 only consists in the set J that is used instead of H to determine the arcs that have to be required to achieve a state of relaxed consistency. In contrast to H, the set J also contains paths P that are not simple and that may visit arcs $e \notin pos(Y)$. However, if $e \in P \setminus pos(Y)$, then we enforce that P must also visit another arc $(i, j) \notin T$ that connects S_e with S_e^C. This implies $e \in T$, as otherwise $S_e^C = \emptyset$. Moreover, it holds that $cost(P) \geq \min\{c(v_1, i) + c_{ij} + c(j, v_n) \mid (i, j) \in (S_e \times S_e^C) \setminus T\}$.
- Like L_1, also L_2 does not force the 2-admissible paths to visit the nodes in $req(Y)$ simultaneously. Again we can improve the effectiveness of the filtering algorithm by setting $c_{ij} := 0$ for all $(i, j) \in req(Y)$ and by subtracting $cost(req(Y))$ from B.
- A shorter path constraint is relaxed L_2-consistent, iff
  1. for all $f \in pos(Y)$, there exists a 2-admissible path $P \in F_f$, and
  2. for all $f \notin req(Y)$, there exists a 2-admissible path $P \in J$ with $f \notin P$, or there exists an arc $e \in P \setminus T$ such that $e \in S_f \times S_f^C$.

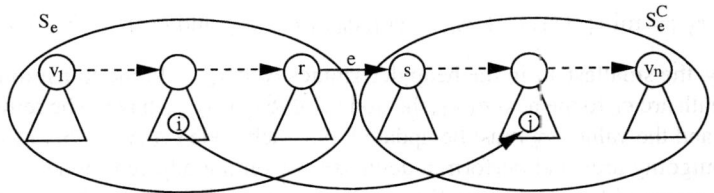

Fig. 4. The figure schematically shows a shortest-path tree T rooted at v_1. Solid lines denote arcs in G, dashed lines mark parts of the shortest path $P(v_1, v_n)$ from v_1 to v_n. The triangles symbolize shortest-path subtrees. For an edge $e = (r, s) \in P(v_1, v_n)$, the nodes in V are partitioned into two non-empty sets S_e and S_e^C. If e is removed from the graph, the shortest path from v_1 to v_n must visit an edge $(i, j) \in (S_e \times S_e^C) \setminus T$.

We have seen that the relaxation L_2 is dominated by L_1. Nevertheless, we can show that cost-based filtering that achieves relaxed L_2-consistency is still at least as strong as ordinary reduced cost filtering:

Lemma 4. *If a shorter path constraint is relaxed L_2-consistent, reduced cost filtering is ineffective[4].*

5.1 Relaxed L_2-Consistency

As relaxations L_1 and L_2 do not differ with respect to the definition of F_f, $f \in E$, to remove arcs from $pos(Y)$ we can simply follow the procedure sketched in Section 4.

Regarding the identification of arcs that have to be added to $req(Y)$ so as to achieve relaxed L_2-consistency, for all $e \in pos(Y) \setminus req(Y)$ we have to compute the cost of the shortest 2-simple path P from v_1 to v_n such that $e \notin P$ or such that there exists an edge $(i, j) \in P \setminus T$ with $(i, j) \in S_e \times S_e^C$, where T is a shortest-path tree in G rooted at v_1.

First, we compute the shortest paths from v_1 to v_n and v_n to v_1 in the reverse of G in time $O(m + n \log n)$. As a byproduct, we get $T \subseteq E$ and shortest-path distances $c(v_1, i), c(i, v_n)$ for all $i \in V$. If $c(v_1, v_n) \geq B$, the current choice point is inconsistent, and we can backtrack. Otherwise, candidates to be added to $req(Y)$ are only the arcs $e \in P(v_1, v_n)$. Since $v_1 \in S_e$ and $v_n \in S_e^C$, the shortest 2-simple path P from v_1 to v_n with $e \notin P$ must contain an arc $(i, j) \in S_e \times S_e^C$. And since $T \cap S_e \times S_e^C = \{e\}$, we have that $(i, j) \notin T$. Therefore, it is sufficient to compute, for all $e \in P(v_1, v_n)$, the costs of the shortest 2-simple path P from v_1 to v_n that contains some $(i, j) \in (S_e \times S_e^C) \setminus T$.

Let $P(v_1, v_n) = (r_1, r_2, \ldots, r_h, r_{h+1})$, $h \in \mathbb{N}$, $r_1 = v_1$ and $r_{h+1} = v_n$, and denote with $(e_1, \ldots, e_h)$ the sequence of arcs that $P(v_1, v_n)$ visits, whereby $e_k = (r_k, r_{k+1})$ for all $1 \leq k \leq h$. Further, for all $1 \leq k \leq h$, denote with Q_k a shortest 2-simple path from v_1 to v_n with $(i, j) \in Q_k$ for some $(i, j) \in (S_{e_k} \times S_{e_k}^C) \setminus T$. Then,

$$cost(Q_k) = \min\{c(v_1, i) + c_{i,j} + c(j, v_n) \mid (i, j) \in (S_{e_k} \times S_{e_k}^C) \setminus T\}.$$

A brute force approach requires time $\Theta(nm)$ to determine these values. However, we can do better when we compute the values $cost(Q_k)$ for all $1 \leq k \leq h$ sequentially. Note that $S_{e_1} \subseteq \cdots \subseteq S_{e_h}$ and $S_{e_h}^C \subseteq \cdots \subseteq S_{e_1}^C$. We keep the nodes j in the current set $S_{e_k}^C$ in a min-heap, whereby the associated value of j in the heap is defined as

---

[4] The proof is omitted due to space restrictions. A full version of the paper can be found in [26].

$$x_j := \min\{c(v_1, i) + c_{i,j} + c(j, v_n) \mid i \in S_{e_k} \text{ and } (i, j) \in E \setminus T\}.$$

Obviously, the smallest x_j in the heap determines $cost(Q_k)$. In the transition from one shortest-path arc e_k to the next e_{k+1}, the nodes $i \in S_{e_k} \setminus S_{e_{k+1}}$ have to be removed from the heap, and the values x_j must be updated. For each node $i \in S_{e_k} \setminus S_{e_k+1}$, we iterate over all outgoing arcs and perform a *decrease-key* on the adjacent nodes if necessary. Then, i is removed from the heap. Since every node in V leaves the heap at most once and never re-enters it, for all $1 \leq k \leq h$ this procedure requires at most m *decrease-key* operations and n *delete-min* operations. Therefore, when using a Fibonacci heap, the values $cost(Q_k)$ for all $1 \leq k \leq h$ can be determined in time $O(m + n \log n)$. Then, e_k is added to $req(Y)$ iff $cost(Q_k) \geq B$. It follows

Theorem 3. *On directed graphs with non-negative arc weights, relaxed L_2-consistency of a shorter path constraint can be achieved in time $O(m + n \log n)$.*

Finally, we would like to note that the results can be extended for directed graphs with no negative cycles (see [26] for proofs):

Theorem 4. *On directed graphs without negative cycles, relaxed L_1-consistency of a shorter path constraint can be achieved in time $O(n(m + n \log n))$.*

Theorem 5. *On directed graphs without negative cycles, relaxed L_2-consistency of a shorter path constraint can be achieved in time $O(nm)$. For $\Omega(\log n)$ calls to the filtering procedure with changing variable domains, relaxed L_2-consistency can be achieved in amortized time $O(m + n \log n)$.*

6   Conclusion

We summarize the results that we achieved (see Table 1): On arbitrary directed and on undirected graphs, achieving GAC is an NP-hard task. Therefore, we introduced the notion of relaxed consistency and developed two shortest path relaxations L_1 and L_2. Both relaxations are based on the class of 2-simple paths. We showed that L_1 dominates L_2, and cost-based filtering based on L_2 is superior to reduced cost filtering. On undirected graphs with non-negative edge weights, relaxed L_1-consistency (and therefore also relaxed L_2-consistency) can be achieved in time $O(m + n \log n)$ and in time $O(m + n)$ on a RAM. On DAGs, generalized arc-consistency can be achieved in linear time. On general directed graphs with non-negative arc weights, relaxed L_1-consistency can be obtained in time $O(n(m + n \log n))$, and a state of relaxed L_2-consistency can be achieved in time $O(m + n \log n)$. Finally, in the presence of negative arc weights, we achieve relaxed L_1-consistency in time $O(n(m + n \log n))$, and L_2-consistency in time $O(nm)$ or $O(m + n \log n)$ for $\Omega(n)$ calls of the filtering algorithm with changing variable domains.

Note that these results are superior to the heuristics in [1], since we can also identify arcs that must be visited, which is a valuable information with respect to other constraints that may be present. With respect to the idea of an iterated reduction procedure as suggested in [6], we may assume that this is given by embedding the cost-based filtering algorithms in a CP solver. Regarding the tightening of lower bounds with respect to

Table 1. The table gives an overview of the findings in this paper.

Graph Type	Degree of Consistency			
	GAC	L_1	L_2	RedCost
undirected, $c \geq 0$	NP-hard	$O(m + n \log n), [RAM]O(m + n)$		
DAG	$O(m + n)$			
directed, $c \geq 0$	NP-hard	$O(n(m + n \log n))$	$O(m + n \log n)$	
directed, no negative cycles	NP-hard	$O(n(m + n \log n))$	O(nm) amort.$[\Omega(n)]$: $O(m + n \log n)$	

other linear constraints, e.g. as proposed in [3] for the Resource Constrained Shortest Path Problem, we refer the reader to the concept of CP-based Lagrangian relaxation presented in [27]. Finally, note that the algorithms we developed are all practicable and easy to implement (except of course the linear time shortest path algorithm on undirected graphs). Therefore, we expect this work to be relevant for many applications and practical approaches in the field of discrete optimization.

References

1. Y. Aneja, V. Aggarwal, K. Nair. Shortest chain subject to side conditions. *Networks*, 13:295-302, 1983.
2. K. R. Apt. The Rough Guide to Constraint Propagation. *Principles and Practice of Constraint Programming (CP)*, Springer LNCS 1713:1–23, 1999.
3. J. Beasley, N. Christofides. An Algorithm for the Resource Constrained Shortest Path Problem. *Networks*, 19:379-394, 1989.
4. R. Borndoerfer, A. Loebel. Scheduling duties by adaptive column generation. *Technical Report*, Konrad-Zuse-Zentrum fuer Informationstechink Berlin ZIB-01-02, 2001.
5. T.H. Cormen, C.E. Leiserson, R.L. Rivest. Introduction to Algorithms. *The MIT Press*, 1993.
6. I. Dumitrescu, N. Boland. The weight-constrained shortest path problem: preprocessing, scaling and dynamic programming algorithms with numerical comparisons. *International Symposium on Mathematical Programming (ISMP)*, 2000.
7. T. Fahle, U. Junker, S.E. Karisch, N. Kohl, M. Sellmann, B. Vaaben. Constraint programming based column generation for crew assignment. *Journal of Heuristics*, 8(1):59-81, 2002.
8. T. Fahle, M. Sellmann. Cost-Based Filtering for the Constrained Knapsack Problem. *Annals of Operations Research*, 115:73–93, 2002.
9. S. Fortune, J. Hopcroft, J. Wyllie. The directed subgraph homeomorphism problem. *Theoretical Computer Science*, 10(2):111–121, 1980.
10. F. Focacci, A. Lodi, M. Milano. Cost-Based Domain Filtering. *Principles and Practice of Constraint Programming (CP)* Springer LNCS 1713:189–203, 1999.
11. F. Focacci, A. Lodi, M. Milano. Cutting Planes in Constraint Programming: An Hybrid Approach. *CP-AI-OR'00*, Paderborn Center for Parallel Computing, Technical Report tr-001-2000:45–51, 2000.
12. M. L. Fredmann, R. E. Tarjan. Fibonacci heaps and their uses in improved network optimization algorithms. *Journal of the ACM* 34:596–615, 1987.
13. M. R. Garey, D. S. Johnson. Computers and Intractability, A Guide to the Theory of NP-Completeness. *Freeman*, San Francisco, 1979.
14. G. Handler, I. Zang. A Dual Algorithm for the Restricted Shortest Path Problem. *Networks*, 10:293-310, 1980.

15. O. Jahn, R. Moehring, A. Schulz. Optimal routing of traffic flows with length restrictions in networks with congestion. *Technical Report*, TU Berlin 658-1999, 1999.

16. H. Joksch. The Shortest Route Problem with Constraints. *Journal of Mathematical Analysis and Application*, 14:191-197, 1966.

17. U. Junker, S.E. Karisch, N. Kohl, B. Vaaben, T. Fahle, M. Sellmann. A Framework for Constraint programming based column generation. *Principles and Practice of Constraint Programming (CP)*, Springer LNCS 1713:261–274, 1999.

18. V. Kumar. Algorithms for Constraints Satisfaction problems: A Survey. *The AI Magazine, by the AAAI*, 13:32-44, 1992.

19. M. Luebbecke, U. Zimmermann. Computer aided scheduling of switching engines. *CASPT*, 2000.

20. K. Mehlhorn, M. Ziegelmann. Resource Constrained Shortest Paths. *Proc. 8th European Symposium on Algorithms (ESA)*, Springer LNCS 1879:326-337, 2000.

21. A. Orda. Routing with end to end QoS guarantees in broadband networks. *Conference on Computer Communications (Infocom)*, IEEE, 27-34, 1998.

22. G. Ottosson, E.S. Thorsteinsson. Linear Relaxation and Reduced-Cost Based Propagation of Continuous Variable Subscripts. *CP-AI-OR'00*, Paderborn Center for Parallel Computing, Technical Report tr-001-2000:129–138, 2000.

23. S. Pettie, V. Ramachandran. Computing undirected shortest paths using comparisons and additions. *ACM-SIAM Symposium on Discrete Algorithms*, January 2002.

24. J.C. Régin. Arc Consistency for Global Cardinality Constraints with Costs. *Principles and Practice of Constraint Programming (CP)*, Springer LNCS 1713:390–404, 1999.

25. M. Sellmann. An Arc-Consistency Algorithm for the Weighted All Different Constraint. *Principles and Practice of Constraint Programming (CP)*, Springer LNCS 2470:744–749, 2002.

26. M. Sellmann. Reduction Techniques in Constraint Programming and Combinatorial Optimization. *PhD Thesis*, University of Paderborn, Germany, http://www.upb.de/cs/sello/diss.ps, 2002.

27. M. Sellmann and T.Fahle. Coupling Variable Fixing Algorithms for the Automatic Recording Problem. *Annual European Symposium on Algorithms (ESA)*, Springer LNCS 2161: 134–145, 2001.

28. M. Thorup. Undirected single source shortest paths in linear time. *Annual Symposium on Foundations of Computer Science (FOCS)*, IEEE, 12–21, 1997.

29. G. Xue. Primal-dual algorithms for computing weight-constrained shortest paths and weight-constrained minimum spanning trees. *International Performance, Computing, and Communications Conference (IPCCC)*, IEEE, 271-277, 2000.

30. T. H. Yunes, A. V. Moura, C. C. Souza. A hybrid approach for solving large crew scheduling problems. *International Workshop on Practical Aspects of Declarative Languages (PADL)*, Springer LNCS 1753:293-307, 2000.

Bounded Backtracking for the Valued Constraint Satisfaction Problems

Cyril Terrioux and Philippe Jégou

LSIS - Université d'Aix-Marseille 3
Avenue Escadrille Normandie-Niemen
13397 Marseille Cedex 20, France
{cyril.terrioux,philippe.jegou}@univ.u-3mrs.fr

Abstract. We propose a new method for solving Valued Constraint Satisfaction Problems based both on backtracking techniques - branch and bound - and the notion of tree-decomposition of valued constraint networks. This mixed method aims to benefit from the practical efficiency of enumerative algorithms while providing a warranty of a bounded time complexity. Indeed the time complexity of our method is $O(d^{w^+ +1})$ with w^+ an approximation of the tree-width of the constraint network and d the maximum size of domains.

Such a complexity is obtained by exploiting optimal bounds on the sub-problems defined from the tree-decomposition. These bounds associated to some partial assignments are called *"structural valued goods"*. Recording and exploiting these goods may allow our method to save some time and space with respect to ones required by classical dynamic programming methods. Finally, this method is a natural extension of the BTD algorithm [1] proposed in the classical CSP framework.

1 Introduction

The CSP formalism (Constraint Satisfaction Problem) offers a powerful framework for representing and solving efficiently many problems. In particular, many academic or real problems can be formulated in this framework which allows the expression of NP-complete problems. However, in this formalism, we can't express some notions like possibility or preference because the constraints are either satisfied or violated. In other words, there is no graduation in violation. To avoid this drawback, many extensions of the CSP formalism have been proposed (for instance [2–4]). In this paper, we focus on the valued CSP formalism (VCSP [4]) which allows the violations of some constraints by associating a cost (called a *valuation*) to each violated constraint. Solving the problem then consists in finding a complete assignment which optimizes a given criterion about the cost of constraint violations. Generally, we are interested by finding a complete assignment which minimizes the cost of all the violations. So, thanks to the VCSP framework, we can express optimization problems.

The basic method for solving VCSP is the Branch and Bound algorithm. Many improvements have been proposed from the CSP framework [4–8]. On

F. Rossi (Ed.): CP 2003, LNCS 2833, pp. 709–723, 2003.

the other hand, some methods based on dynamic programming ([9, 10]) often provide good results on such problems.

In this article, we propose a new enumerative method for solving VCSPs. This method, called BTD_{val}, is a natural generalization of the BTD method [1] defined in the classical CSP framework. Such a generalization requires the extension of the theoretical frame used for BTD and the classical CSPs. Nevertheless, like BTD, BTD_{val} relies on backtracking techniques (branch and bound) and the notion of tree-decomposition of valued constraint graphs. Such an hybrid method aims to benefit from the advantage of the two approaches, namely the practical efficiency of enumerative algorithms and the time complexity bounds of structural decomposition methods. Thanks to the tree-decomposition notion, BTD_{val} divides the initial problem into several subproblems. Then, it solves each subproblem and records the optimal valuation of each subproblem. These optimal valuations associated with some assignments are called *structural valued goods*. Structural valued goods are then exploited in order to solve each subproblem only once, what allows BTD_{val} to provide time complexity bounds better than ones of classical enumerative methods. Indeed, the time complexity of BTD_{val} is $O(ns^2 m \log(d).d^{w^+ + 1})$ while the space complexity is $O(nsd^s)$ with $w^+ + 1$ an approximation of the tree-width of the constraint graph, s the size of the biggest minimal separator, n the number of variables and d the size of the largest domain. These bounds only depend on the used tree-decomposition (i.e. on some structural parameters). In [1], experimental results show that on classical CSPs, BTD clearly outperforms an approach founded on dynamic programming like Tree-Clustering [11, 12]. So, for VCSPs, we can hope that this behaviour will be confirmed in practice.

The paper is organized as follows. Section 2 introduces the main definitions about the VCSP formalism. Section 3 is devoted to the tree-decomposition notion. Then, section 4 describes the method we propose and present some theoretical results. Finally, in section 5, we discuss about some related works, before concluding in section 6.

2   Valued CSPs

A *constraint satisfaction problem* (CSP) is defined by a quadruplet (X, D, C, R). X is a set $\{x_1, \ldots, x_n\}$ of n variables. Each variable x_i takes its values in the finite domain d_{x_i} from D. Variables are subject to constraints from C. Each constraint c is defined as a set $\{x_{c_1}, \ldots, x_{c_k}\}$ of variables. A relation r_c (from R) is associated with each constraint c such that r_c represents the set of allowed tuples over $d_{x_{c_1}} \times \cdots \times d_{x_{c_k}}$. Given $Y \subseteq X$ such that $Y = \{x_1, \ldots, x_k\}$, an *assignment* of variables from Y is a tuple $\mathcal{A} = (v_1, \ldots, v_k)$ from $d_{x_1} \times \cdots \times d_{x_k}$. A constraint c is said *satisfied* by $\mathcal{A}$ if $c \subseteq Y, (v_1, \ldots, v_k)[c] \in r_c$, *violated* otherwise. We note the assignment $(v_1, \ldots, v_k)$ in the more meaningful form $(x_1 \leftarrow v_1, \ldots, x_k \leftarrow v_k)$.

Definition 1 ([4]) *A **valuation structure** is a 5-tuple $(E, \preceq, \oplus, \bot, \top)$ with E a set of valuations which is totally ordered by $\preceq$ with a minimum element* noted $\perp$ and a maximum element noted $\top$. $\oplus$ is a monotonous, commutative, associative closed binary operation on E such that $\perp$ is an identity element and $\top$ an absorbing element.

The elements of E express different levels of violation. $\perp$ characterizes the satisfaction of a constraint and $\top$ an unacceptable violation. $\oplus$ allows to combine (aggregate) several valuations. Note that, in some cases, it can have some additional properties like idempotency or strict monotonicity. Thanks to the valuation structure, one can formally define the notion of valued CSP [4]:

Definition 2 *A valued CSP (VCSP) $\mathcal{P} = (X, D, C, R, S, \phi)$ consists of a classical CSP (X, D, C, R) with a valuation structure $S = (E, \preceq, \oplus, \perp, \top)$ and an application ϕ from C to E which associates a valuation to each constraint of C. A VCSP is called **binary** if each constraint of C involves at most two variables.*

The valuation of an assignment $\mathcal{A}$ on X is obtained by aggregating the valuations of the constraints violated by $\mathcal{A}$:

Definition 3 *Let $\mathcal{P}$ be a VCSP and $\mathcal{A}$ an assignment on X. The **valuation** of $\mathcal{A}$ with respect to $\mathcal{P}$ is defined by $\mathcal{V}_{\mathcal{P}}(\mathcal{A}) = \bigoplus\limits_{c \in C | \mathcal{A}\ violates\ c} \phi(c)$.*

Given an instance $\mathcal{P}$, the VCSP problem consists in finding an assignment on X with a minimum valuation according to $\preceq$. This optimal valuation is called the *VCSP valuation* and is denoted $\alpha_{\mathcal{P}}^*$. Determining the valuation of a VCSP is an NP-hard problem. For instance, let us consider the VCSP whose constraint graph is presented in figure 1(a). We suppose that each domain d_x is equal to $\{1, 2, 3\}$ and each constraint c_{xy} means "$x < y$" if the letter represented by x precedes one represented by y in the alphabetical order (for example c_{AB} represents the constraint $A < B$). We exploit the valuation structure $S = (\overline{\mathbb{N}}, <, +, 0, +\infty)$. For each constraint c, the associated valuation is 1. For this VCSP, we obtain $\alpha_{\mathcal{P}}^* = 2$. $(A \leftarrow 1, B \leftarrow 1, C \leftarrow 2, D \leftarrow 2, E \leftarrow 3, F \leftarrow 2, G \leftarrow 2, H \leftarrow 3, I \leftarrow 3, J \leftarrow 3)$ is the best assignment. It violates the constraints c_{AB} and c_{CF}. The assignment valuation notion can be extended to partial assignments:

Definition 4 *Let $\mathcal{P}$ be a VCSP and $\mathcal{A}$ an assignment on $Y \subset X$. The **local valuation** of $\mathcal{A}$ with respect to $\mathcal{P}$ is defined by $v_{\mathcal{P}}(\mathcal{A}) = \bigoplus\limits_{c \in C | c \subseteq Y\ and\ \mathcal{A}\ violates\ c} \phi(c)$.*

The following property establishes the link between the valuation of a complete assignment and the local valuation:

Property 1 *Let $\mathcal{P}$ be a VCSP, $\mathcal{A}$ an assignment on X and $\mathcal{B} \subseteq \mathcal{A}$. $v_{\mathcal{P}}(\mathcal{B}) \preceq v_{\mathcal{P}}(\mathcal{A}) = \mathcal{V}_{\mathcal{P}}(\mathcal{A})$.*

So the local valuation can provide a lower bound of the global valuation. The main interest of the local valuation consists in its computation which can be achieved incrementally.

The basic method for solving VCSPs is the branch and bound algorithm (noted BB). This enumerative method exploits the local valuation of the current assignment as a lower bound and the valuation of the best known solution as a upper bound. If the lower bound doesn't exceed the upper one, it extends the current assignment by assigning a new variable. Otherwise, it backtracks to the last assigned variable and then it tries to assign a new value to this variable. If all the values have been tried, it backtracks again. Many improved methods have been proposed from the classical CSP framework like valued Forward-Checking (noted vFC [4]), Nogood Recording [5], ... The use of the arc-consistency notion has been studied too ([6–8]). On the other hand, some methods based on dynamic programming, like the Russian Dolls Search (noted RDS) or the structural method proposed by Koster [10], often provide good results. These methods divide the problem into different subproblems and solve the initial problem by exploiting some informations recorded during the resolution of each subproblem.

3   Tree-Decomposition

The only guarantees which can exist in terms of theoretical complexity before solving a problem are offered by structural decomposition methods. These methods proceed by isolating the parts intrinsically exponential (i.e. intractable in polynomial theoretical time) to induce a second step which guarantees a polynomial time of resolution. These methods generally exploit topological properties of the constraint graph and are based on the notion of tree-decomposition of graphs as defined below by Robertson and Seymour [13].

Definition 5 ([13]) *Let $G = (X, E)$ be a graph. A **tree-decomposition** of G is a pair $(\mathcal{C}, \mathcal{T})$ with $\mathcal{T} = (I, F)$ a tree and $\mathcal{C} = \{\mathcal{C}_i : i \in I\}$ a family of subsets of X, such that each cluster $\mathcal{C}_i$ is a node of $\mathcal{T}$ and verifies:*

1. *$\cup_{i \in I} \mathcal{C}_i = X$,*
2. *for all edge $\{x, y\} \in E$, there exists $i \in I$ with $\{x, y\} \subseteq \mathcal{C}_i$, and*
3. *for all $i, j, k \in I$, if k is in a path from i to j in $\mathcal{T}$, then $\mathcal{C}_i \cap \mathcal{C}_j \subseteq \mathcal{C}_k$*

The width of a tree-decomposition $(\mathcal{C}, \mathcal{T})$ is equal to $max_{i \in I}|\mathcal{C}_i| - 1$. The tree-width of G is the minimal width over all the tree-decompositions of G.

For the reader who isn't familiar with these notions, note that the above definition refers to a tree $\mathcal{T} = (I, F)$ where F is a set of edges which is required to satisfy the part (3) of this definition.

Even if finding an optimal tree-decomposition is an NP-Hard problem [14], many works have been developed in this direction [15], which often exploit equivalent definitions of this notion, including one based on an algorithmic approach related to *triangulated* graphs. The link between triangulated graphs and tree-decomposition is obvious. Indeed, given a triangulated graph, the set of maximal cliques $\mathcal{C} = \{\mathcal{C}_1, \mathcal{C}_2, \ldots, \mathcal{C}_k\}$ of (X, E) corresponds to the family of subsets associated with a tree-decomposition. As any graph $G = (X, E)$ is not necessarily triangulated, a tree-decomposition can be approximated by a triangulation of

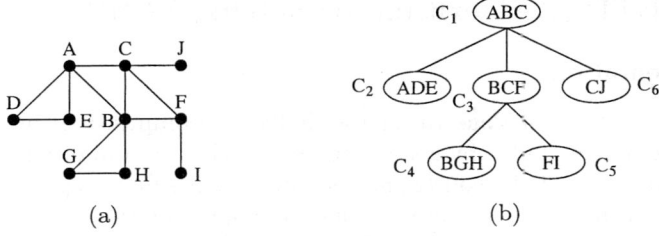

Fig. 1. (a) A constraint graph on 10 variables. (b) A tree-decomposition of this constraint graph.

G which computes a triangulated graph G'. The width of G' is equal to the maximal size of cliques minus one in the resulting graph G'. The tree-width of G is then equal to the minimal width over all triangulations.

The graph in figure 1(a) is already triangulated. The maximum size of cliques is three and the tree-width of this graph is two. In figure 1(b), a tree whose nodes correspond to maximal cliques of the triangulated graph is a possible tree-decomposition for the graph of figure 1(a). So, we get $\mathcal{C}_1 = \{A, B, C\}$, $\mathcal{C}_2 = \{A, D, E\}$, $\mathcal{C}_3 = \{B, C, F\}$, $\mathcal{C}_4 = \{B, G, H\}$, $\mathcal{C}_5 = \{F, I\}$ and $\mathcal{C}_6 = \{C, J\}$.

The notion of tree-decomposition is exploited in the classical CSPs framework by many structural decomposition methods (see [16] for a survey about such methods and a theoretical comparison). These methods have the advantage of providing the best known bounds for the theoretical time complexity. For instance, the CSP decomposition method called *Tree-Clustering* [11, 12] is generally presented using an approximation of an optimal triangulation. It has a time complexity in $O(m.d^{w^+ +1})$ with $w^+ + 1$ the size of the biggest cluster ($w^+ + 1 \leq n$). However, the space complexity is in $O(n.s.d^s)$ with s the maximal size of minimal separators (i.e. the size $s \leq w^+$ of the biggest intersection between two clusters). Finally, note that for every decomposition which induces a value w^+, we have $w \leq w^+$ with w the tree-width of the initial constraint graph.

The BTD method [1] solves classical CSPs by using the tree-decomposition notion jointly with backtracking techniques. Then, it benefits from a practical efficiency (thanks to enumerative techniques) while providing time complexity bounds equivalent to ones of structural decomposition methods (thanks to the tree-decomposition notion). Its time and space complexities are then similar to Tree-Clustering's ones. However, in practice, BTD obtains better results than Tree-Clustering while performing either as good as classical enumerative methods or better.

In the VCSP framework, the dynamic programming approach proposed by Koster [10] also exploits a tree-decomposition. It has a time complexity in $O(nd^{3(w^+ +1)})$ and a space complexity in $O(d^{w^+ +1})$. In the both frameworks, the required space can make the structural methods unusable in practice.

In the next section, we present an enumerative method for solving VCSPs which, by exploiting a tree-decomposition, provides complexity bounds similar to ones given above.

4 The BTD$_{val}$ Algorithm for Solving VCSPs

4.1 Presentation

Like BTD, BTD$_{val}$ (for Backtracking with Tree-Decomposition) proceeds by an enumerative search guided by a static pre-established partial order induced by a tree-decomposition of the constraint network. So, the first step of BTD$_{val}$ consists in computing a tree-decomposition or an approximation of a tree-decomposition. The obtained partial order allows to exploit some structural properties of the graph, during the search, in order to prune some branches of the search tree. Hence, BTD$_{val}$ differs from other techniques in the following points:

- the variable assignment order is induced by a tree-decomposition of the constraint graph,
- some subproblems won't be visited again if it we have computed yet their optimal valuation (notion of *structural valued good*).

Although our method is called BTD$_{val}$ for Backtracking with Tree-Decomposition, we will see later that the enumerative search can be based on BB or vFC.

4.2 Theoretical Foundations

In the following, let us consider an instance $\mathcal{P} = (X, D, C, R, S, \phi)$ and a tree-decomposition $(\mathcal{C}, \mathcal{T})$ (or an approximation) of the constraint graph (X, C). We assume that the elements of $\mathcal{C} = \{\mathcal{C}_i : i \in I\}$ are indexed with respect to the notion of *compatible numbering*:

Definition 6 *A numbering on $\mathcal{C}$ compatible with a prefix numbering of $\mathcal{T} = (I, F)$ with $\mathcal{C}_1$ the root is called* **compatible numbering** $N_{\mathcal{C}}$.

Remark that in the previous definition, $\mathcal{T} = (I, F)$ is a tree (according to definition 5) with I the set of indices and F the set of edges. For example, figure 1(b) presents a compatible numbering on $\mathcal{C}$. We note $Desc(\mathcal{C}_j)$ the set of variables belonging to the union of the descendants $\mathcal{C}_k$ of $\mathcal{C}_j$ in the tree rooted in $\mathcal{C}_j$, $\mathcal{C}_j$ included. For instance, $Desc(\mathcal{C}_3) = \mathcal{C}_3 \cup \mathcal{C}_4 \cup \mathcal{C}_5 = \{B, C, F, G, H, I\}$. Note that the numbering $N_{\mathcal{C}}$ defines a partial variable ordering that permits to get an enumeration order on the variables of $\mathcal{P}$:

Definition 7 *A* **compatible enumeration order** *is an order $\preceq_X$ on the variables of X such that $\forall x, y \in X, x \preceq_X y$ if $\exists \mathcal{C}_i \ni x, \forall \mathcal{C}_j \ni y, i \leq j$.*

For example, the alphabetical order $A, B, \ldots, I, J$ is a compatible enumeration order. The tree-decomposition with the numbering $N_{\mathcal{C}}$ permits to partition the constraint set.

Definition 8 *Let $\mathcal{C}_i$ be a cluster. The set $E_{\mathcal{P}, \mathcal{C}_i}$ of* **proper constraints** *of cluster $\mathcal{C}_i$ is defined by $E_{\mathcal{P}, \mathcal{C}_i} = \{c \in C | c \subseteq \mathcal{C}_i \text{ and } c \not\subseteq \mathcal{C}_{p(i)}\}$ with $\mathcal{C}_{p(i)}$ the parent cluster of $\mathcal{C}_i$.*

The set $E_{\mathcal{P},\mathcal{C}_i}$ contains each constraint $c_{xy} = \{x,y\}$ with x and y two variables of $\mathcal{C}_i$ such that x and y don't belong both to $\mathcal{C}_{p(i)}$ the parent cluster of $\mathcal{C}_i$. For instance, if we consider the problem described in figure 1, we obtain $E_{\mathcal{P},\mathcal{C}_1} = \{c_{AB}, c_{AC}, c_{BC}\}$, $E_{\mathcal{P},\mathcal{C}_2} = \{c_{AD}, c_{AE}, c_{DE}\}$, $E_{\mathcal{P},\mathcal{C}_3} = \{c_{BF}, c_{CF}\}$, $E_{\mathcal{P},\mathcal{C}_4} = \{c_{BG}, c_{BH}, c_{GH}\}$, $E_{\mathcal{P},\mathcal{C}_5} = \{c_{FI}\}$ and $E_{\mathcal{P},\mathcal{C}_6} = \{c_{CJ}\}$.

Property 2 *The sets $(E_{\mathcal{P},\mathcal{C}_i})_i$ form a partition of C.*

Proof: First, we are going to show that $\bigcup\limits_{\mathcal{C}_i \subseteq X} E_{\mathcal{P},\mathcal{C}_i} = C$.

As $\bigcup\limits_{\mathcal{C}_i \subseteq X} E_{\mathcal{P},\mathcal{C}_i} \subset C$ is obvious, we have to prove $\bigcup\limits_{\mathcal{C}_i \subseteq X} E_{\mathcal{P},\mathcal{C}_i} \supset C$.

Let $c \in C$. According to definition 5, there exists at less a cluster $\mathcal{C}_i$ such that $c \subseteq \mathcal{C}_i$. In particular, we necessarily have $c \subseteq \mathcal{C}_k$ where $k = \min\{i | c \subseteq \mathcal{C}_i\}$ and $c \not\subseteq \mathcal{C}_{p(k)}$. Therefore, $c \in E_{\mathcal{P},\mathcal{C}_k}$. So we obtain $\bigcup\limits_{\mathcal{C}_i \subseteq X} E_{\mathcal{P},\mathcal{C}_i} \supset C$ and then

$$\bigcup\limits_{\mathcal{C}_i \subseteq X} E_{\mathcal{P},\mathcal{C}_i} = C$$

Now we have to prove that $\forall \mathcal{C}_i, \mathcal{C}_j, \; E_{\mathcal{P},\mathcal{C}_i} \cap E_{\mathcal{P},\mathcal{C}_j} = \emptyset$.
Assume that there exists two clusters $\mathcal{C}_i$ and $\mathcal{C}_j$ such that $E_{\mathcal{P},\mathcal{C}_i} \cap E_{\mathcal{P},\mathcal{C}_j} \neq \emptyset$. Let $c \in E_{\mathcal{P},\mathcal{C}_i} \cap E_{\mathcal{P},\mathcal{C}_j}$. According to definition 8, we have $c \subseteq \mathcal{C}_i \cap \mathcal{C}_j$.
Then, according to definition 5, there exists a path between $\mathcal{C}_i$ and $\mathcal{C}_j$ such that if $\mathcal{C}_k$ belongs to this path, $\mathcal{C}_i \cap \mathcal{C}_j \subseteq \mathcal{C}_k$. The parent cluster of $\mathcal{C}_i$ or $\mathcal{C}_j$'s one clearly belongs to this path. Therefore $c \subseteq \mathcal{C}_{p(i)}$ or $c \subseteq \mathcal{C}_{p(j)}$. So we obtain a contradiction since $c \in E_{\mathcal{P},\mathcal{C}_i}$ and $c \in E_{\mathcal{P},\mathcal{C}_j}$. So $\forall i, j, \; E_{\mathcal{P},\mathcal{C}_i} \cap E_{\mathcal{P},\mathcal{C}_j} = \emptyset$

Hence, the sets $(E_{\mathcal{P},\mathcal{C}_i})_i$ form a partition of C. $\square$

Note that this property becomes fundamental when $\oplus$ isn't idempotent. Indeed, in such a case, we must be careful not to take into account a constraint several times. Exploiting the sets $E_{\mathcal{P},\mathcal{C}_i}$ prevents such a problem from occurring and so ensures that BTD_{val} safely computes the valuation of assignments. Then, we can define the notion of induced VCSP:

Definition 9 *Let $\mathcal{C}_i$ and $\mathcal{C}_j$ be two clusters with $\mathcal{C}_j$ a son of $\mathcal{C}_i$. Let $\mathcal{A}$ be an assignment on $\mathcal{C}_i \cap \mathcal{C}_j$. $\mathcal{P}_{\mathcal{A},\mathcal{C}_i/\mathcal{C}_j} = (X_{\mathcal{P}_{\mathcal{A},\mathcal{C}_i/\mathcal{C}_j}}, D_{\mathcal{P}_{\mathcal{A},\mathcal{C}_i/\mathcal{C}_j}}, C_{\mathcal{F}_{\mathcal{A},\mathcal{C}_i/\mathcal{C}_j}}, R_{\mathcal{P}_{\mathcal{A},\mathcal{C}_i/\mathcal{C}_j}}, S, \phi)$ is the **VCSP induced by** $\mathcal{A}$ on the descent of $\mathcal{C}_i$ rooted in $\mathcal{C}_j$ (i.e. on $\mathcal{C}_j$ and its descendants) with:*

- $X_{\mathcal{P}_{\mathcal{A},\mathcal{C}_i/\mathcal{C}_j}} = Desc(\mathcal{C}_j)$,
- $D_{\mathcal{P}_{\mathcal{A},\mathcal{C}_i/\mathcal{C}_j}} = \{d_{x,\mathcal{P}_{\mathcal{A},\mathcal{C}_i/\mathcal{C}_j}} = \{\mathcal{A}[x]\} | x \in \mathcal{C}_i \cap \mathcal{C}_j\} \cup \{d_{x,\mathcal{P}_{\mathcal{A},\mathcal{C}_i/\mathcal{C}_j}} = d_x | x \in Desc(\mathcal{C}_j) \backslash (\mathcal{C}_i \cap \mathcal{C}_j)\}$,
- $C_{\mathcal{P}_{\mathcal{A},\mathcal{C}_i/\mathcal{C}_j}} = E_{\mathcal{P},\mathcal{C}_j} \cup \bigcup\limits_{\mathcal{C}_d \text{ descendant of } \mathcal{C}_j} E_{\mathcal{P},\mathcal{C}_d}$,
- $R_{\mathcal{P}_{\mathcal{A},\mathcal{C}_i/\mathcal{C}_j}} = \{r_c \cap \prod\limits_{x \in c} d_{x,\mathcal{P}_{\mathcal{A},\mathcal{C}_i/\mathcal{C}_j}} \mid c \in C_{\mathcal{P}_{\mathcal{A},\mathcal{C}_i/\mathcal{C}_j}} \text{ and } r_c \in R\}$.

The induced VCSP $\mathcal{P}_{\mathcal{A},\mathcal{C}_i/\mathcal{C}_j}$ corresponds to the VCSP $\mathcal{P}$ restricted to the subproblem rooted in $\mathcal{C}_j$ such that the domain of each variable x in $\mathcal{C}_i \cap \mathcal{C}_j$ is reduced to the value assigned to x in $\mathcal{A}$. That is, we consider the subproblem whose variables are ones of $\mathcal{C}_j$ and its descendants. As for the constraint set of $\mathcal{P}_{\mathcal{A},\mathcal{C}_i/\mathcal{C}_j}$, it only contains the constraints which exclusively appear in $\mathcal{C}_j$ and its descendants. For instance, given the assignment $\mathcal{A} = (B \leftarrow 2, C \leftarrow 2)$ on $\mathcal{C}_1 \cap \mathcal{C}_3$, let us consider $\mathcal{P}_{\mathcal{A},\mathcal{C}_1/\mathcal{C}_3}$ the VCSP induced by $\mathcal{A}$ on the descent of $\mathcal{C}_1$ rooted in $\mathcal{C}_3$. We have $X_{\mathcal{P}_{\mathcal{A},\mathcal{C}_1/\mathcal{C}_3}} = \{B, C, F, G, H, I\}$, $d_B = d_C = \{2\}$, $d_F = d_G = d_H = d_I = \{1, 2, 3\}$ and $C_{\mathcal{P}_{\mathcal{A},\mathcal{C}_1/\mathcal{C}_3}} = \{c_{BF}, c_{CF}, c_{BG}, c_{BH}, c_{GH}, c_{FI}\}$. Note that the constraint c_{BC} doesn't belong to the constraint set of $\mathcal{P}_{\mathcal{A},\mathcal{C}_1/\mathcal{C}_3}$ because it isn't a proper constraint of $\mathcal{C}_3$ ($c_{BC} \subseteq \mathcal{C}_1$ and $\mathcal{C}_1 = \mathcal{C}_{p(3)}$). Now, from the sets $E_{\mathcal{P},\mathcal{C}_i}$, we can introduce the notion of local valuation for a cluster:

Definition 10 *Given a cluster $\mathcal{C}_i$ and an assignment $\mathcal{A}$ on $Y \subset X$ with $Y \cap \mathcal{C}_i \neq \emptyset$. The **local valuation for the cluster** $\mathcal{C}_i$ of the assignment $\mathcal{A}$ with respect to $\mathcal{P}$ (noted $v_{\mathcal{P},\mathcal{C}_i}(\mathcal{A})$) is the local valuation of $\mathcal{A}$ restricted to the constraints of $E_{\mathcal{P},\mathcal{C}_i}$, that is to say $v_{\mathcal{P},\mathcal{C}_i}(\mathcal{A}) = \displaystyle\bigoplus_{\substack{c \in E_{\mathcal{P},\mathcal{C}_i} | c \subseteq Y \\ and\ \mathcal{A}\ violates\ c}} \phi(c)$*

In other words, the valuation local for a cluster $\mathcal{C}_i$ only takes into account the constraints proper to $\mathcal{C}_i$. Remark that the local valuation for a cluster can be computed incrementally. This valuation presents many interesting properties. First, its computation only depends on the variables of the considered cluster.

Property 3 *Let $\mathcal{C}_i$ be a cluster and $\mathcal{A}$ an assignment on $Y \subseteq X$ such that $\mathcal{C}_i \subseteq Y$. $v_{\mathcal{P},\mathcal{C}_i}(\mathcal{A}) = v_{\mathcal{P},\mathcal{C}_i}(\mathcal{A}[\mathcal{C}_i])$*

Proof:

$$v_{\mathcal{P},\mathcal{C}_i}(\mathcal{A}) = \bigoplus_{\substack{c \in E_{\mathcal{P},\mathcal{C}_i} | c \subseteq Y \\ and\ \mathcal{A}\ violates\ c}} \phi(c) = \bigoplus_{\substack{c \in E_{\mathcal{P},\mathcal{C}_i} | c \subseteq Y \cap \mathcal{C}_i \\ and\ \mathcal{A}\ violates\ c}} \phi(c)$$

$$= \bigoplus_{\substack{c \in E_{\mathcal{P},\mathcal{C}_i} | c \subseteq Y \cap \mathcal{C}_i \\ and\ \mathcal{A}[\mathcal{C}_i]\ violates\ c}} \phi(c) = v_{\mathcal{P},\mathcal{C}_i}(\mathcal{A}[\mathcal{C}_i]) \quad \square$$

Then, the aggregation of local valuations for a cluster allows us to compute the valuation of a complete assignment.

Property 4 *Let $\mathcal{A}$ be an assignment on X.*
$$\mathcal{V}_{\mathcal{P}}(\mathcal{A}) = \bigoplus_{\mathcal{C}_i \subseteq X} v_{\mathcal{P},\mathcal{C}_i}(\mathcal{A})$$

Proof: Since the sets $(E_{\mathcal{P},\mathcal{C}_i})_i$ form a partition of C (property 2), each constraint of C is taken into account only once. So, $\mathcal{V}_{\mathcal{P}}(\mathcal{A}) = \bigoplus_{\mathcal{C}_i \subseteq X} v_{\mathcal{P},\mathcal{C}_i}(\mathcal{A})$. $\square$

It follows from these two properties that we can compute the valuation of a complete assignment $\mathcal{A}$ by exploiting only the local valuation for each cluster $\mathcal{C}_i$ of the assignment $\mathcal{A}[\mathcal{C}_i]$. Finally, the next property ensures that the local valuation for a cluster $\mathcal{C}_j$ of an assignment $\mathcal{B}$ with respect to $\mathcal{P}$ is preserved if we considered an induced subproblem which contains $\mathcal{C}_j$.

Property 5 *Let C_i and C_j two clusters with C_j a descendant of C_i. Let A be an assignment on $C_i \cap C_{p(i)}$ and $P' = P_{A,C_{p(i)}/C_i}$. If B is an assignment on C_j such that $B[C_j \cap C_i \cap C_{p(i)}] = A[C_j \cap C_i \cap C_{p(i)}]$, $v_{P,C_j}(B) = v_{P',C_j}(B)$.*

Proof: as $E_{P,C_j} = E_{P',C_j}$ $v_{P,C_j}(B) = v_{P',C_j}(B)$. □

Now, we are able to define the notion of structural valued good.

Definition 11 *Let C_i and C_j two clusters with C_j a son of C_i. A **structural valued good** of C_i with respect to C_j is a pair (A, v) with A an assignment on $C_i \cap C_j$ and v the optimal valuation of the VCSP $P_{A,C_i/C_j}$.*

For instance, if we consider the assignment $A = (B \leftarrow 2, C \leftarrow 2)$ on $C_1 \cap C_3$, we obtain the good $(A, 2)$ since the best assignment on $Desc(C_3)$ is $(B \leftarrow 2, C \leftarrow 2, F \leftarrow 3, G \leftarrow 3, H \leftarrow 3, I \leftarrow 3)$. Note that this assignment violates the constraints c_{BC}, c_{GH} and c_{FI}, but c_{BC} is discarded (since $c_{BC} \notin E_{P,C_3}$).

Given an assignment A on C_i, the following theorem expresses that we can compute the valuation of the best assignment B on $Desc(C_i)$ with $B[C_i] = A$ by exploiting the optimal valuation of each subproblem rooted in a son C_f of C_i and induced by $A[C_i \cap C_f]$. Note that the optimal valuation of each subproblem is provided either by solving the considered subproblem or by exploiting a structural valued good. Finally, remark that this optimal valuation can be computed independently of ones of other subproblems.

Theorem 1 *Let C_i be a cluster, A an assignment on C_i and $P' = P_{A[C_i \cap C_{p(i)}],C_{p(i)}/C_i}$.*

$$\min_{\substack{B|X_B = Desc(C_i) \\ and\ B[C_i] = A}} v_{P'}(B) = v_{P,C_i}(A) \oplus \bigoplus_{C_f\ son\ of\ C_i} \alpha^*_{P_{A[C_i \cap C_f]},C_i/C_f}$$

The proof of this theorem requires the following lemma:

Lemma 1 *Let C_i be a cluster and A an assignment on C_i. Let $P' = P_{A[C_i \cap C_{p(i)}],C_{p(i)}/C_i}$.*

$$Let\ \lambda = \min_{\substack{B|X_B = Desc(C_i) \\ and\ B[C_i] = A}} \left(\bigoplus_{C_j \in Sons(C_i)} \left[\bigoplus_{C_k \subseteq Desc(C_j)} v_{P',C_k}(B) \right] \right).$$

$$Let\ \lambda' = \bigoplus_{C_j \in Sons(C_i)} \left(\min_{\substack{B|X_B = Desc(C_j) \cup C_i \\ and\ B[C_i] = A}} \left[\bigoplus_{C_k \subseteq Desc(C_j)} v_{P',C_k}(B) \right] \right).$$

We have $\lambda = \lambda'$.

Proof (lemma 1):

For each C_j son of C_i, we note $\lambda_{C_j} = \min_{\substack{B|X_B = Desc(C_j) \cup C_i \\ and\ B[C_i] = A}} \left[\bigoplus_{C_k \subseteq Desc(C_j)} v_{P',C_k}(B) \right]$. We

then have $\lambda' = \bigoplus_{C_j \in Sons(C_i)} \lambda_{C_j}$.

For each $\mathcal{C}_j$ son of $\mathcal{C}_i$, there exists an assignment $\mathcal{B}_{\mathcal{C}_j}$ on $Desc(\mathcal{C}_j) \cup \mathcal{C}_i$ such that $\mathcal{B}_{\mathcal{C}_j}[\mathcal{C}_i] = \mathcal{A}$ and $\lambda_{\mathcal{C}_j} = \bigoplus\limits_{\mathcal{C}_k \subseteq Desc(\mathcal{C}_j)} v_{\mathcal{P}', \mathcal{C}_k}(\mathcal{B}_{\mathcal{C}_j})$. Likewise, there is an assignment

$\mathcal{B}_\lambda$ on $Desc(\mathcal{C}_i)$ such that $\mathcal{B}_\lambda[\mathcal{C}_i] = \mathcal{A}$ and $\lambda = \bigoplus\limits_{\mathcal{C}_j \in Sons(\mathcal{C}_i)} \left[\bigoplus\limits_{\mathcal{C}_k \subseteq Desc(\mathcal{C}_j)} v_{\mathcal{P}', \mathcal{C}_k}(\mathcal{B}_\lambda) \right]$.

We want to prove that for each son $\mathcal{C}_j$ of $\mathcal{C}_i$, we have

$$\bigoplus\limits_{\mathcal{C}_k \subseteq Desc(\mathcal{C}_j)} v_{\mathcal{P}', \mathcal{C}_k}(\mathcal{B}_\lambda[Desc(\mathcal{C}_j) \cup \mathcal{C}_i]) = \lambda_{\mathcal{C}_j}.$$

Assume there exists a son $\mathcal{C}_s$ of $\mathcal{C}_i$ such that

$$\bigoplus\limits_{\mathcal{C}_k \subseteq Desc(\mathcal{C}_s)} v_{\mathcal{P}', \mathcal{C}_k}(\mathcal{B}_\lambda[Desc(\mathcal{C}_s) \cup \mathcal{C}_i]) \neq \lambda_{\mathcal{C}_s}.$$

By definition of $\lambda_{\mathcal{C}_s}$, $\lambda_{\mathcal{C}_s} \prec \bigoplus\limits_{\mathcal{C}_k \subseteq Desc(\mathcal{C}_s)} v_{\mathcal{P}', \mathcal{C}_k}(\mathcal{B}_\lambda[Desc(\mathcal{C}_s) \cup \mathcal{C}_i])$

$= \bigoplus\limits_{\mathcal{C}_k \subseteq Desc(\mathcal{C}_s)} v_{\mathcal{P}', \mathcal{C}_k}(\mathcal{B}_\lambda)$

Let $\mathcal{B}'$ be an assignment on $Desc(\mathcal{C}_i)$ such that $\mathcal{B}'[\mathcal{C}_i] = \mathcal{A}$ and $\forall \mathcal{C}_j \in Sons(\mathcal{C}_i)$, $\mathcal{B}'[Desc(\mathcal{C}_j) \cup \mathcal{C}_i] = \mathcal{B}_{\mathcal{C}_j}$. Such an assignment exists since $\forall \mathcal{C}_j, \mathcal{C}_{j'} \in Sons(\mathcal{C}_i)$, $Desc(\mathcal{C}_j) \cap Desc(\mathcal{C}_{j'}) \subseteq \mathcal{C}_i$.

Furthermore, we have $\lambda_{\mathcal{C}_s} = \bigoplus\limits_{\mathcal{C}_k \subseteq Desc(\mathcal{C}_s)} v_{\mathcal{P}', \mathcal{C}_k}(\mathcal{B}'[Desc(\mathcal{C}_s) \cup \mathcal{C}_i])$.

So, $\bigoplus\limits_{\mathcal{C}_j \in Sons(\mathcal{C}_i)} \left[\bigoplus\limits_{\mathcal{C}_k \subseteq Desc(\mathcal{C}_j)} v_{\mathcal{P}', \mathcal{C}_k}(\mathcal{B}') \right] = \bigoplus\limits_{\mathcal{C}_j \in Sons(\mathcal{C}_i)} \lambda_{\mathcal{C}_j} = \lambda'$

$\lambda' = \lambda_{\mathcal{C}_s} \oplus \bigoplus\limits_{\mathcal{C}_j \in Sons(\mathcal{C}_i) \setminus \{\mathcal{C}_s\}} \lambda_{\mathcal{C}_j}$

$\prec \bigoplus\limits_{\mathcal{C}_k \subseteq Desc(\mathcal{C}_s)} v_{\mathcal{P}', \mathcal{C}_k}(\mathcal{B}_\lambda[Desc(\mathcal{C}_s) \cup \mathcal{C}_i])$

$\oplus \bigoplus\limits_{\mathcal{C}_j \in Sons(\mathcal{C}_i) \setminus \{\mathcal{C}_s\}} \left[\bigoplus\limits_{\mathcal{C}_k \subseteq Desc(\mathcal{C}_j)} v_{\mathcal{P}', \mathcal{C}_k}(\mathcal{B}_\lambda[Desc(\mathcal{C}_j) \cup \mathcal{C}_i]) \right]$

$\prec \bigoplus\limits_{\mathcal{C}_k \subseteq Desc(\mathcal{C}_s)} v_{\mathcal{P}', \mathcal{C}_k}(\mathcal{B}_\lambda) \oplus \bigoplus\limits_{\mathcal{C}_j \in Sons(\mathcal{C}_i) \setminus \{\mathcal{C}_s\}} \left[\bigoplus\limits_{\mathcal{C}_k \subseteq Desc(\mathcal{C}_j)} v_{\mathcal{P}', \mathcal{C}_k}(\mathcal{B}_\lambda) \right] = \lambda$

Hence, we obtain a contradiction with the definition of λ. So, for each son $\mathcal{C}_j$ of $\mathcal{C}_i$, $\bigoplus\limits_{\mathcal{C}_k \subseteq Desc(\mathcal{C}_j)} v_{\mathcal{P}', \mathcal{C}_k}(\mathcal{B}_\lambda[Desc(\mathcal{C}_j) \cup \mathcal{C}_i]) = \lambda_{\mathcal{C}_j}$. It ensues that $\lambda = \lambda'$. $\square$

Proof (theorem 1):
We note $M = \min\limits_{\substack{\mathcal{B} \mid X_\mathcal{B} = Desc(\mathcal{C}_i) \\ \text{and } \mathcal{B}[\mathcal{C}_i] = \mathcal{A}}} v_{\mathcal{P}'}(\mathcal{B})$.

$M \underset{\text{property 1}}{=} \min\limits_{\substack{\mathcal{B} \mid X_\mathcal{B} = Desc(\mathcal{C}_i) \\ \text{and } \mathcal{B}[\mathcal{C}_i] = \mathcal{A}}} \mathcal{V}_{\mathcal{P}'}(\mathcal{B})$.

$\underset{\text{property 4}}{=} \min\limits_{\substack{\mathcal{B} \mid X_\mathcal{B} = Desc(\mathcal{C}_i) \\ \text{and } \mathcal{B}[\mathcal{C}_i] = \mathcal{A}}} \left(\bigoplus\limits_{\mathcal{C}_j \subseteq Desc(\mathcal{C}_i)} v_{\mathcal{P}', \mathcal{C}_j}(\mathcal{B}) \right)$

$$= \min_{\substack{\mathcal{B}|X_{\mathcal{B}}=Desc(\mathcal{C}_i) \\ and\ \mathcal{B}[\mathcal{C}_i]=\mathcal{A}}} \left(v_{\mathcal{P}',\mathcal{C}_i}(\mathcal{B}) \oplus \bigoplus_{\substack{\mathcal{C}_j|j\neq i, \\ \mathcal{C}_j\subseteq Desc(\mathcal{C}_i)}} v_{\mathcal{P}',\mathcal{C}_j}(\mathcal{B}) \right)$$

$$\underset{property\ 3}{=} \min_{\substack{\mathcal{B}|X_{\mathcal{B}}=Desc(\mathcal{C}_i) \\ and\ \mathcal{B}[\mathcal{C}_i]=\mathcal{A}}} \left(v_{\mathcal{P}',\mathcal{C}_i}(\mathcal{B}[\mathcal{C}_i]) \oplus \bigoplus_{\substack{\mathcal{C}_j|j\neq i, \\ \mathcal{C}_j\subseteq Desc(\mathcal{C}_i)}} v_{\mathcal{P}',\mathcal{C}_j}(\mathcal{B}) \right)$$

For every assignment $\mathcal{B}$ such that $X_{\mathcal{B}} = Desc(\mathcal{C}_i)$ and $\mathcal{B}[\mathcal{C}_i] = \mathcal{A}$, we have $v_{\mathcal{P}',\mathcal{C}_i}(\mathcal{B}[\mathcal{C}_i]) = v_{\mathcal{P}',\mathcal{C}_i}(\mathcal{A})$. As $v_{\mathcal{P}',\mathcal{C}_i}(\mathcal{A})$ is a constant, we have:

$$M = v_{\mathcal{P}',\mathcal{C}_i}(\mathcal{A}) \oplus \min_{\substack{\mathcal{B}|X_{\mathcal{B}}=Desc(\mathcal{C}_i) \\ and\ \mathcal{B}[\mathcal{C}_i]=\mathcal{A}}} \left(\bigoplus_{\substack{\mathcal{C}_j|j\neq i, \\ \mathcal{C}_j\subseteq Desc(\mathcal{C}_i)}} v_{\mathcal{P}',\mathcal{C}_j}(\mathcal{B}) \right)$$

$$= v_{\mathcal{P}',\mathcal{C}_i}(\mathcal{A}) \oplus \min_{\substack{\mathcal{B}|X_{\mathcal{B}}=Desc(\mathcal{C}_i) \\ and\ \mathcal{B}[\mathcal{C}_i]=\mathcal{A}}} \left(\bigoplus_{\mathcal{C}_j\in Sons(\mathcal{C}_i)} \left[\bigoplus_{\mathcal{C}_k\subseteq Desc(\mathcal{C}_j)} v_{\mathcal{P}',\mathcal{C}_k}(\mathcal{B}) \right] \right)$$

$$\underset{lemma\ 1}{=} v_{\mathcal{P}',\mathcal{C}_i}(\mathcal{A}) \oplus \bigoplus_{\mathcal{C}_j\in Sons(\mathcal{C}_i)} \left(\min_{\substack{\mathcal{B}|X_{\mathcal{B}}=Desc(\mathcal{C}_j)\cup\mathcal{C}_i \\ and\ \mathcal{B}[\mathcal{C}_i]=\mathcal{A}}} \left[\bigoplus_{\mathcal{C}_k\subseteq Desc(\mathcal{C}_j)} v_{\mathcal{P}',\mathcal{C}_k}(\mathcal{B}) \right] \right)$$

$$M = v_{\mathcal{P}',\mathcal{C}_i}(\mathcal{A}) \oplus \bigoplus_{\mathcal{C}_j\in Sons(\mathcal{C}_i)} \left(\min_{\substack{\mathcal{B}|X_{\mathcal{B}}=Desc(\mathcal{C}_j)\ and \\ \mathcal{B}[\mathcal{C}_i\cap\mathcal{C}_j]=\mathcal{A}[\mathcal{C}_i\cap\mathcal{C}_j]}} \left[\bigoplus_{\mathcal{C}_k\subseteq Desc(\mathcal{C}_j)} v_{\mathcal{P}',\mathcal{C}_k}(\mathcal{B}) \right] \right)$$

$$\underset{property\ 5}{=} v_{\mathcal{P},\mathcal{C}_i}(\mathcal{A}) \oplus \bigoplus_{\mathcal{C}_j\in Sons(\mathcal{C}_i)} \left(\min_{\substack{\mathcal{B}|X_{\mathcal{B}}=Desc(\mathcal{C}_j)\ and \\ \mathcal{B}[\mathcal{C}_i\cap\mathcal{C}_j]=\mathcal{A}[\mathcal{C}_i\cap\mathcal{C}_j]}} \left[\bigoplus_{\mathcal{C}_k\subseteq Desc(\mathcal{C}_j)} v_{\mathcal{P},\mathcal{C}_k}(\mathcal{B}) \right] \right)$$

$$\underset{property\ 4}{=} v_{\mathcal{P},\mathcal{C}_i}(\mathcal{A}) \oplus \bigoplus_{\mathcal{C}_j\in Sons(\mathcal{C}_i)} \left(\min_{\substack{\mathcal{B}|X_{\mathcal{B}}=Desc(\mathcal{C}_j) \\ and\ \mathcal{B}[\mathcal{C}_i\cap\mathcal{C}_j]=\mathcal{A}[\mathcal{C}_i\cap\mathcal{C}_j]}} V_{\mathcal{P}_{\mathcal{A}[\mathcal{C}_i\cap\mathcal{C}_j],\mathcal{C}_i/\mathcal{C}_j}}(\mathcal{B}) \right)$$

$$= v_{\mathcal{P},\mathcal{C}_i}(\mathcal{A}) \oplus \bigoplus_{\mathcal{C}_j\ son\ of\ \mathcal{C}_i} \alpha^*_{\mathcal{P}_{\mathcal{A}[\mathcal{C}_i\cap\mathcal{C}_j],\mathcal{C}_i/\mathcal{C}_j}} \qquad \square$$

From theorem 1, we deduce the following corollary. This corollary establishes the link between the optimal valuation of a subproblem rooted in $\mathcal{C}_i$ and the optimal valuation of each subproblem rooted in a son $\mathcal{C}_j$ of $\mathcal{C}_i$.

Corollary 1 *Let $\mathcal{C}_i$ be a cluster and $\mathcal{A}$ an assignment on $\mathcal{C}_i \cap \mathcal{C}_{p(i)}$.*

$$\alpha^*_{\mathcal{P}_{\mathcal{A},\mathcal{C}_{p(i)}/\mathcal{C}_i}} = \min_{\substack{\mathcal{B}|X_{\mathcal{B}}=\mathcal{C}_i\ and \\ \mathcal{B}[\mathcal{C}_i\cap\mathcal{C}_{p(i)}]=\mathcal{A}}} \left(v_{\mathcal{P},\mathcal{C}_i}(\mathcal{B}) \oplus \bigoplus_{\mathcal{C}_j\ son\ of\ \mathcal{C}_i} \alpha^*_{\mathcal{P}_{\mathcal{B}[\mathcal{C}_i\cap\mathcal{C}_j],\mathcal{C}_i/\mathcal{C}_j}} \right)$$

4.3   The BTD$_{val}$ Algorithm

The BTD$_{val}$ method is based on the BB algorithm (note that we can also base it on vFC). It explores the search space by exploiting a compatible order, which begins with the variables of the root cluster $\mathcal{C}_1$. Inside a cluster $\mathcal{C}_i$, it proceeds

classically like BB by assigning a value to a variable, by maintaining and comparing upper and lower bounds and by backtracking if a lower bound is greater than
(or equal to) the corresponding upper bound. However, unlike BB, BTD_{val} uses
two kinds of bounds: local bounds and global ones. The local bounds only take
into account the subproblem rooted in C_i (namely the induced VCSP $\mathcal{P}_{\mathcal{A},C_{p(i)}/C_i}$
with $\mathcal{A}$ the current assignment on $C_i \cap C_{p(i)}$). The local lower bound corresponds
to the valuation of the current assignment on $Desc(C_i)$, that is to say, the local
valuation of the current assignment with respect to $\mathcal{P}_{\mathcal{A},C_{p(i)}/C_i}$. The local upper bound is then defined by the valuation of the best known assignment $\mathcal{B}$ on
$Desc(C_i)$ such that $\mathcal{B}[C_i \cap C_{p(i)}] = \mathcal{A}$. In other words, it's the valuation of the
best known solution for $\mathcal{P}_{\mathcal{A},C_{p(i)}/C_i}$. The global bounds are similar to BB's ones,
that is to say the local valuation of the current assignment for the lower bound
and the valuation of the best known solution for the upper one.

When every variable in C_i is assigned, if each lower bound is less than the
corresponding upper bound, BTD_{val} keeps on the search with the first son of
C_i (if there is one). More generally, let us consider a son C_j of C_i. Given the
current assignment $\mathcal{A}$ on C_i, BTD_{val} checks whether the assignment $\mathcal{A}[C_i \cap C_j]$
corresponds to a valued structural good:

- if so, BTD_{val} aggregates the valuation associated to this valued good with
  each lower bound.
- else, it extends $\mathcal{A}$ on $Desc(C_j)$ in order to compute the valuation v of the
  best assignment $\mathcal{B}$ such that $\mathcal{B}[C_i \cap C_j] = \mathcal{A}[C_i \cap C_j]$. Then, it aggregates v
  with each lower bound and it records the valued good $(\mathcal{A}[C_i \cap C_j], v)$.

If, after having proceeded the son C_j, the two lower bounds don't exceed their
respective upper bound, BTD_{val} keeps on the search with the next son of C_i. Remark that by exploiting the structural valued goods, BTD_{val} doesn't solve again
some subproblems. So the variables of these subproblems aren't assigned again.
Hence we call such a phenomenon a *forward-jump* (by analogy with backjump).
For instance, suppose that we use the alphabetical order as variable order and
that, after assigning the variable F in C_3, we exploit a good on $C_3 \cap C_4$. Then,
we try to assign I without exploring again $Desc(C_4)$. If every son has been proceeded and each lower bound doesn't exceed its corresponding upper bound,
then a better solution for $\mathcal{P}_{\mathcal{A},C_{p(i)}/C_i}$ has been found. Finally, if a failure occurs,
BTD_{val} tries to modify the current assignment on C_i.

In fact, due to the structural valued good definition, the global lower bound
is defined by the valuation of the best extension of $\mathcal{A}$ on every cluster which
precedes the current cluster in the used compatible enumeration. It's the same
for the local lower bound, but we only consider the clusters belonging to the
descent of the current cluster. Remark that we consider an extension of $\mathcal{A}$, and
not $\mathcal{A}$, because $\mathcal{A}$ only contains the variables belonging to a cluster located on
the path between the root cluster and the current cluster. Finally note that the
global upper bound is the same as BB's one, unlike the global lower bound which
is better than BB's one.

Figure 2 describes the BTD_{val} algorithm. Given an assignment $\mathcal{A}$ and a cluster $\mathcal{C}_i$, BTD_{val} looks for the best assignment $\mathcal{B}$ on $Desc(\mathcal{C}_i)$ such that $\mathcal{A}[\mathcal{C}_i \backslash V_{\mathcal{C}_i}] = \mathcal{B}[\mathcal{C}_i \backslash V_{\mathcal{C}_i}]$ and $v_{\mathcal{P}_{\mathcal{A}[\mathcal{C}_i \cap \mathcal{C}_{p(i)}], \mathcal{C}_{p(i)}/\mathcal{C}_i}}(\mathcal{B}) \prec \alpha_{\mathcal{C}_i}$, where:

- $V_{\mathcal{C}_i}$ is the set of unassigned variables in $\mathcal{C}_i$,
- $\alpha_{\mathcal{C}_1}$ is the valuation of the best known solution,
- l_{tot} is the valuation of the best extension $\mathcal{A}'$ of $\mathcal{A}$ on all the clusters which precede $\mathcal{C}_i$ according to the compatible numbering $(l_{tot} = v_{\mathcal{P}}(\mathcal{A}') \prec \alpha_{\mathcal{C}_1})$,
- $\alpha_{\mathcal{C}_i}$ is the valuation of the best known assignment $\mathcal{B}'$ on $Desc(\mathcal{C}_i)$ such that $\mathcal{A}[\mathcal{C}_i \cap \mathcal{C}_{p(i)}] = \mathcal{B}'[\mathcal{C}_i \cap \mathcal{C}_{p(i)}]$
- $l_{\mathcal{C}_i} = v_{\mathcal{P}, \mathcal{C}_i}(\mathcal{A}) \prec \alpha_{\mathcal{C}_i}$.

If BTD_{val} finds such an assignment, it returns its valuation, otherwise it returns a valuation greater than (or equal to) $\alpha_{\mathcal{C}_i}$. The initial call is $BTD_{val}(\emptyset, \mathcal{C}_1, \mathcal{C}_1, \perp, \top, \perp, \top)$.

Theorem 2 *BTD_{val} is sound, complete and terminates.*

$BTD_{val}(\mathcal{A}, \mathcal{C}_i, V_{\mathcal{C}_i}, l_{tot}, \alpha_{\mathcal{C}_1}, l_{\mathcal{C}_i}, \alpha_{\mathcal{C}_i})$
1. **If** $V_{\mathcal{C}_i} = \emptyset$
2. **Then**
3.   **If** $Sons(\mathcal{C}_i) = \emptyset$ **Then** Return $l_{\mathcal{C}_i}$
4.   **Else**
5. $F \leftarrow Sons(\mathcal{C}_i)$
6. $\alpha \leftarrow \perp$
7.   **While** $F \neq \emptyset$ **and** $\alpha \oplus l_{tot} \prec \alpha_{\mathcal{C}_1}$ **and** $\alpha \oplus l_{\mathcal{C}_i} \prec \alpha_{\mathcal{C}_i}$ **Do**
8.   Choose $\mathcal{C}_j$ in F
9. $F \leftarrow F \backslash \{\mathcal{C}_j\}$
10.   **If** $(\mathcal{A}[\mathcal{C}_j \cap \mathcal{C}_i], v)$ is a good of $\mathcal{C}_i/\mathcal{C}_j$ in G **Then** $\alpha \leftarrow \alpha \oplus v$
11.   **Else**
12. $v \leftarrow BTD_{val}(\mathcal{A}, \mathcal{C}_j, \mathcal{C}_j \backslash (\mathcal{C}_j \cap \mathcal{C}_i), l_{tot} \oplus \alpha, \alpha_{\mathcal{C}_1}, \perp, \alpha_{\mathcal{C}_i})$
13. $\alpha \leftarrow \alpha \oplus v$
14.   Record the good $(\mathcal{A}[\mathcal{C}_j \cap \mathcal{C}_i], v)$ of $\mathcal{C}_i/\mathcal{C}_j$ in G
15.   **EndIf**
16.   **EndWhile**
17.   Return $\alpha \oplus l_{\mathcal{C}_i}$
18.   **EndIf**
19. **Else**
20.   Choose $x \in V_{\mathcal{C}_i}$
21. $d \leftarrow d_x$
22.   **While** $d \neq \emptyset$ **and** $l_{tot} \prec \alpha_{\mathcal{C}_1}$ **and** $l_{\mathcal{C}_i} \prec \alpha_{\mathcal{C}_i}$ **Do**
23.   Choose a in d
24. $d \leftarrow d \backslash \{a\}$
25. $L \leftarrow \{c = \{x, y\} \in E_{\mathcal{P}, \mathcal{C}_i} | y \notin V_{\mathcal{C}_i}\}$
26. $l_a \leftarrow \perp$
27.   **While** $L \neq \emptyset$ **and** $l_{tot} \oplus l_a \prec \alpha_{\mathcal{C}_1}$ **and** $l_{\mathcal{C}_i} \oplus l_a \prec \alpha_{\mathcal{C}_i}$ **Do**
28.   Choose c in L
29. $L \leftarrow L \backslash \{c\}$
30.   **If** c violates $\mathcal{A} \cup \{x \leftarrow a\}$ **Then** $l_a \leftarrow l_a \oplus \phi(c)$
31.   **EndWhile**
32.   **If** $l_{tot} \oplus l_a \prec \alpha_{\mathcal{C}_1}$ **and** $l_{\mathcal{C}_i} \oplus l_a \prec \alpha_{\mathcal{C}_i}$
33.   **Then** $\alpha_{\mathcal{C}_i} \leftarrow \min(\alpha_{\mathcal{C}_i}, BTD_{val}(\mathcal{A} \cup \{x \leftarrow a\}, \mathcal{C}_i, V_{\mathcal{C}_i} \backslash \{x\}, l_{tot} \oplus l_a, \alpha_{\mathcal{C}_1}, l_{\mathcal{C}_i} \oplus l_a, \alpha_{\mathcal{C}_i}))$
34.   **EndIf**
35.   **EndWhile**
36.   Return $\alpha_{\mathcal{C}_i}$
37. **EndIf**

Fig. 2. The BTD_{val} algorithm.

Finally, we provide the time and space complexities of BTD_{val}. We suppose that a tree-decomposition (or an approximation) has been computed. Therefore the parameters used in the next theorem are related to this decomposition. BTD_{val} obtains complexities similar to Tree-Clustering's ones:

Theorem 3 BTD_{val} has a time complexity in $O(n.s^2.m.\log(d).d^{w^++1})$ and a space complexity in $O(n.s.d^s)$ with $w^+ + 1$ the size of the biggest C_k and s the size of the biggest intersection $C_i \cap C_j$ where C_j is a son of C_i.

5   Related Works

BTD_{val} is mostly based on tree-decomposition. So, works like Tree-Clustering and its improvements [11, 12] or the dynamic programming approach of Koster [10] are close to our approach. BTD_{val} can be considered as an hybrid approach realizing a tradeoff between practical time and space complexity. In [12], Dechter and El Fattah present a time-space tradeoff scheme. This scheme allows them to propose a spectrum of algorithms such that tree-clustering and cycle-cutset conditioning (linear for space complexity) are two extremes in this spectrum. Another interesting idea in their work is the possibility to modify the size of separators to minimize space. This idea can also be exploited in BTD_{val}.

BTD_{val} presents a better time complexity than the dynamic programming approach of Koster. Then, BTD_{val} differs from this approach in computing a tree-decomposition (or an approximation of a tree-decomposition). BTD_{val} exploits a triangulation of the constraint graph, while the dynamic programming approach uses a heuristic method and network flow techniques. Furthermore, Koster proposes several pretreatments. In particular, one of these pretreatments allows to reduce the size of the constraint graph, which may also reduce the time complexity. So adding such pretreatments may be useful for our approach.

BTD_{val} is close to a method like the russian dolls search [9]. Indeed, in order to find the optimal valuation of a VCSP, BTD_{val} solves many subproblems according a pre-established compatible order. The BTD_{val}'s clusters have a role similar to one of variables in RDS. Nevertheless, the two methods exploit differently the optimal valuations of subproblems. Like BTD_{val}, the method Tree-RDS [17] (a variant of RDS) takes advantage of the constraint graph in order to determine whether some problems are independent or not. However, if the independence of subproblems is used similarly, the Tree-RDS's subproblems differ conceptually from BTD_{val}'s ones. It's the same for the adaptation [18] of the algorithm Pseudo-Tree Search and its combination with a variant of RDS.

6   Conclusion

In this paper, we have defined a new method (called BTD_{val}) for solving valued CSPs. This method can actually be based on BB or on vFC. Thanks to the notion of structural valued goods we have introduced, BTD_{val} obtains complexity bounds similar to (or better than) the best known ones. Indeed, the time complexity of BTD_{val} is $O(ns^2m\log(d).d^{w^++1})$ with $w^+ + 1$ the size of the biggest cluster while the space complexity is $O(nsd^s)$ with s the size of the biggest intersection between two clusters. Now, an experimental study is required to assess the practical interest of our approach.

Among the possible extensions of this work, we must base our algorithm on more efficient methods like the russian dolls search or algorithms which use directional arc-consistency [19–21]. Using such methods seems natural since BTD_{val} exploits a compatible enumeration order.

References

1. P. Jégou and C. Terrioux. Hybrid backtracking bounded by tree-decomposition of constraint networks. *Artificial Intelligence*, 146:43–75, 2003.
2. E. Freuder and R. Wallace. Partial constraint satisfaction. *Artificial Intelligence*, 58:21–70, 1992.
3. S. Bistarelli, U. Montanari, and F. Rossi. Constraint solving over semirings. In *Proc. of the 14th IJCAI*, pages 624–630, 1995.
4. T. Schiex, H. Fargier, and G. Verfaillie. Valued Constraint Satisfaction Problems: hard and easy problems. In *Proc. of the 14th IJCAI*, pages 631–637, 1995.
5. P. Dago and G. Verfaillie. Nogood Recording for Valued Constraint Satisfaction Problems. In *Proc. of ICTAI 96*, pages 132–139, 1996.
6. J. Larrosa, P. Meseguer, and T. Schiex. Maintaining reversible DAC for Max-CSP. *Artificial Intelligence*, 107(1):149–163, 1999.
7. T. Schiex. Une comparaison des cohérences d'arc dans les Max-CSP. In *Actes des JNPC'2002*, pages 209–223, 2002. In french.
8. J. Larrosa. On arc and node consistency. In *Proc. of AAAI*, 2002.
9. G. Verfaillie, M. Lemaître, and T. Schiex. Russian Doll Search for Solving Constraint Optimization Problems. In *Proc. of the 14th AAAI*, pages 181–187, 1996.
10. A. Koster. *Frequency Assignment - Models and Algorithms*. PhD thesis, University of Maastricht, November 1999.
11. R. Dechter and J. Pearl. Tree-Clustering for Constraint Networks. *Artificial Intelligence*, 38:353–366, 1989.
12. R. Dechter and Y. El Fattah. Topological Parameters for Time-Space Tradeoff. *Artificial Intelligence*, 125:93–118, 2001.
13. N. Robertson and P.D. Seymour. Graph minors II : Algorithmic aspects of tree-width. *Algorithms*, 7:309–322, 1986.
14. S. Arnborg, D. Corneil, and A. Proskuroswki. Complexity of finding embedding in a k-tree. *SIAM Journal of Discrete Mathematics*, 8:277–284, 1987.
15. A. Becker and D. Geiger. A sufficiently fast algorithm for finding close to optimal clique trees. *Artificial Intelligence*, 125:3–17, 2001.
16. G. Gottlob, N. Leone, and F. Scarcello. A Comparison of Structural CSP Decomposition Methods. *Artificial Intelligence*, 124:343–282, 2000.
17. P. Meseguer and M. Sánchez. Tree-based Russian Doll Search. In *Proc. of Workshop on soft constraint*. CP'2000, 2000.
18. J. Larrosa, P. Meseguer, and M. Sánchez. Pseudo-Tree Search with Soft Constraints. In *Proc. of the 15th ECAI*, pages 131–135, 2002.
19. R. Wallace. Directed arc consistency preprocessing. In *Proc. of the ECAI-94 Workshop on Constraint Processing, LNCS 923*, pages 121–137, 1994.
20. R. Wallace. Enhancements of Branch and Bound Methods for the Maximal Constraint Satisfaction Problem. In *Proc. of AAAI*, pages 188–195, 1996.
21. J. Larrosa and P. Meseguer. Exploiting the use of DAC in Max-CSP. In *Proc. of the 2nd CP*, pages 308–322, 1996.

Consistency and Propagation with Multiset Constraints: A Formal Viewpoint

Toby Walsh*

Cork Constraint Computation Center, University College Cork, Ireland
tw@4c.ucc.ie

Abstract. We study from a formal perspective the consistency and propagation of constraints involving multiset variables. That is, variables whose values are multisets. These help us model problems more naturally and can, for example, prevent introducing unnecessary symmetry into a model. We identify a number of different representations for multiset variables and compare them. We then propose a definition of local consistency for constraints involving multiset, set and integer variables. This definition is a generalization of the notion of bounds consistency for integer variables. We show how this local consistency property can be enforced by means of some simple inference rules which tighten bounds on the variables. We also study a number of global constraints on set and multiset variables. Surprisingly, unlike finite domain variables, the decomposition of global constraints over set or multiset variables often does not hinder constraint propagation.

1 Introduction

Set variables have been incorporated into most of the major constraint solvers (see, for example, [1,2]). It is therefore surprising that few constraint solvers permit multiset variables. The one exception is ILOG's Configurator. However, little is known from a theoretical perspective about such variables. The aim of this paper is to correct this imbalance, to study formal notions of consistency and propagation for multiset variables, and to discuss how they can be implemented. Many problems naturally involve multisets. Consider the template design problem [3] (prob002 in CSPLib) in which we assign designs to printing templates. As there are a fixed number of slots on each template, we can model this problem with a variable for each slot, whose value is the design in this slot. However, slots on a template are indistinguishable. This model therefore introduces an unnecessary symmetry, namely the permutations of the slots. A "better" model would remove this symmetry by having a variable for each template, whose value is the multiset of designs assigned to that template. It is a multiset, not a set, as the designs on a template can be repeated.

The paper is structured as follows. We start with the formal background (Section 2). We then compare different ways to represent multiset variables (Section

---

* The author is supported by the Science Foundation Ireland. He wishes to thank the members of the 4C lab, the APES research group, and Chris Jefferson.

F. Rossi (Ed.): CP 2003, LNCS 2833, pp. 724–738, 2003.

3) and define a notion of local consistency for multiset variables (Section 4). We identify a number of primitive multiset constraints (Section 5) and show how to enforce this local consistency property on such constraints (Section 6). We also study a number of global multiset constraints (Section 7). We then give some experimental results comparing different representations of multiset variables (Section 8). Finally we describe related work (Section 9) and end with conclusions (Section 10).

2   Formal Background

A constraint satisfaction problem consists of a set of variables, each with some domain of values, and a set of constraints specifying allowed values for subsets of variables. A solution is an assignment of values to the variables satisfying the constraints. To find such solutions, we can explore partial assignments enforcing a local consistency like generalized arc-consistency (GAC). A constraint is GAC iff, when a variable in the constraint is assigned a value, compatible values exist for all the other variables in the constraint. GAC reduces to arc-consistency (AC) for binary constraints. A constraint is bounds consistent iff, when a variable in the constraint is assigned its maximum or minimum value, there exist compatible values for all the other variables in the constraint.

We will also need vectors, sets and multisets. A vector is an ordered list of elements, written $\langle m_0, \ldots, m_n \rangle$. A set is an unordered list of elements without repetition, written $\{m_0, \ldots, m_n\}$. A multiset is an unordered list of elements in which repetition is allowed, written $\{\!\{m_0, \ldots, m_n\}\!\}$. We assume that the elements of vectors, sets and multisets are integers drawn from a finite domain. Basic operations on sets generalize to similar operations on multisets. We let $occ(m, X)$ be the number of occurrences of m in the multiset X. Multiset union, addition, intersection, difference, equality and inclusion are defined by the follow identities: $occ(m, X \cup Y) = max(occ(m, X), occ(m, Y))$, $occ(m, X \uplus Y) = occ(m, X) + occ(m, Y)$, $occ(m, X \cap Y) = min(occ(m, X), occ(m, Y))$, $occ(m, X - Y) = max(0, occ(m, X) - occ(m, Y))$, $X = Y$ iff $occ(m, X) = occ(m, Y)$ for all m, and $X \subseteq Y$ iff $occ(m, X) \leq occ(m, Y)$ for all m. Finally, we write $|X|$ for the cardinality of the set or multiset X.

3   Representing Multisets

A naive method to represent a multiset variable is a finite domain variable whose values are all the possible multisets. However, this will be computationally intractable as the number of possible multisets is exponential.

3.1   Bounds Representation

A better representation for multiset variables is a generalization of the upper and lower bounds used for set variables in [1, 4]. For each multiset variable, we maintain two multisets: a least upper and a greatest lower bound. The least upper bound is the smallest multiset containing all those values that can be in the multiset, whilst the greatest lower bound is the largest multiset containing all those values that must be in the multiset. We write $lub(X)$ and $glb(X)$ for the least upper and greatest lower bound respectively. This representation is compact but is unable to represent all forms of disjunction. Consider, for example, a multiset variable X with two possible multiset values: $\{\!\{0\}\!\}$ or $\{\!\{1\}\!\}$. To represent this, we would need $lub(X) = \{\!\{0, 1\}\!\}$ and $glb(X) = \{\!\{\}\!\}$. However, this representation also permits X to take the multiset values $\{\!\{\}\!\}$ and $\{\!\{0, 1\}\!\}$.

3.2   Occurrence Representation

Set variables can be represented by their characteristic function (a vector of Boolean variables, each of which indicates whether a particular value is in the set or not). A straightforward generalization to multisets is the occurrence vector. Each multiset variable X can be represented by a vector $\langle X_0, \ldots, X_n \rangle$ of integer variables with $X_i = occ(i, X)$. This representation is also compact but again cannot represent all forms of disjunction. Consider again the example of a multiset variable X with two possible multiset values: $\{\!\{0\}\!\}$ or $\{\!\{1\}\!\}$. To represent this, we would need an occurrence vector with $X_0 = \{0, 1\}$ (that is, the value 0 can occur zero times or once) and $X_1 = \{0, 1\}$ (that is, the value 1 can occur zero times or once). Like the bounds representation, this also permits X to take the multiset values $\{\!\{\}\!\}$ and $\{\!\{0, 1\}\!\}$.

3.3   Fixed Cardinality

Set or multiset variables of a fixed cardinality are common in a number of problems. For example, the template design problem can be modelled as finding a multiset of designs of fixed cardinality for each template. In such situations, we can represent each of the members of the set or multiset with a variable whose values are the possible set or multiset elements. This may appear to introduce symmetry into the problem (via permutations of these variables). This is not the case as we will post constraints on these variables which ignore their permutation. This representation is again compact but again carries the penalty of not being able to represent all forms of disjunction. Consider, for example, a multiset variable X of cardinality 3 with two possible multiset values: $\{\!\{0, 0, 0\}\!\}$ or $\{\!\{1, 1, 1\}\!\}$. To represent this, we would need three variables: $X_1 = \{0, 1\}$, $X_2 = \{0, 1\}$ and $X_3 = \{0, 1\}$. Each finite domain variable represents one of the possible elements of the multiset. However, this representation also permits X to take the multiset values: $\{\!\{0, 0, 1\}\!\}$, and $\{\!\{0, 1, 1\}\!\}$. If the set or multiset variables are not of a fixed cardinality but there are upper bounds on their maximum cardinality, we can use a similar representation but introduce an additional value which represents no value being assigned to a particular variable.

3.4   Nested Sets and Multisets

We may want to find a set of sets or multisets, or a multiset of sets or multisets. For example, in the template design problem we actually want to find a set of templates, each of which is a multiset of designs. To model such problems, we can introduce set or multiset variables, whose elements themselves are sets or multisets. How do our different representations cope with such variables? The bounds representation handles such cases easily. The least upper and greatest lower bounds are now (multi)sets of (multi)sets. The occurrence representation is more problematic as we have to index over a potential exponential number of sets or multisets. This will require exponential space in general. By comparison, the fixed cardinality representation handles such cases easily. We introduce a variable for each element of the set or multiset, and each of these variables is itself a set or multiset variable.

3.5   Expressivity

We can compare the expressivity of these different representations. We say that one representation is **as expressive as** another if it can represent the same multiset values, **more expressive** if it is as expressive and there are multiset values that it can represent that the other cannot, and **incomparable** if neither representation is as expressive as the other.

Theorem 1 *The occurrence representation is more expressive than the bounds representation. The fixed cardinality representation is incomparable to both the bounds and the occurrence representation.*

Proof: Clearly the occurrence representation is as expressive as the bounds. Consider a multiset variable X with two values: $\{\!\{\}\!\}$ or $\{\!\{0,0\}\!\}$. This can be represented exactly with the occurrence variable $X_0 = \{0,2\}$. By comparison, a bounds representation would need $lub(X) = \{\!\{0,0\}\!\}$ and $glb(X) = \{\!\{\}\!\}$, and this permits the additional value $\{\!\{0\}\!\}$.

Consider a multiset variable X of cardinality 2 with six values: $\{\!\{0,1\}\!\}$, $\{\!\{0,2\}\!\}$, $\{\!\{0,3\}\!\}$, $\{\!\{1,1\}\!\}$, $\{\!\{1,2\}\!\}$, or $\{\!\{1,3\}\!\}$. The fixed cardinality representation can represent this exactly with two finite domain variables $X_1 = \{0,1\}$ and $X_2 = \{1,2,3\}$. Both the bounds and the occurrence representations of this would also permit the additional value $\{\!\{2,3\}\!\}$. On the other hand, consider a multiset variable X of cardinality 2 with three values: $\{\!\{0,1\}\!\}$, $\{\!\{0,2\}\!\}$, or $\{\!\{1,2\}\!\}$. In the bounds representation, we need $lub(X) = \{\!\{0,1,2\}\!\}$ and $glb(X) = \{\!\{\}\!\}$. The only two element multisets between these bounds are exactly $\{\!\{0,1\}\!\}$, $\{\!\{0,2\}\!\}$, or $\{\!\{1,2\}\!\}$ as required. Similarly with an occurrence representation, we need $X_0 = X_1 = X_2 = \{0,1\}$. The only two element multisets between these bounds are again the required ones. A fixed cardinality representation cannot, on the other hand, represent this exactly. We would need two finite domain variables with, say, $X_1 = \{0,1\}$ and $X_2 = \{1,2\}$. These would permit X to take the additional value $\{\!\{1,1\}\!\}$. ♣

Note that if we restrict the occurrence representation to maintain just bounds on the number of occurrences of a value in the multiset then we obtain a representation that is as expressive as the original multiset bounds representation.

4   Local Consistency

We now propose a new definition of local consistency that works with constraints involving multiset, set and/or integer variables. We want a definition of local consistency over multiset, set and integer variables since constraints often have a mixture of such variables. For example, channelling between the bounds and occurrence representation of multiset variables uses constraints of the form $X_m = occ(m, X)$, where X_m is an integer variable representing the number of occurrences of the value m, and X is a multiset variable. Cardinality and membership constraints can also involve both multiset, set and integer variables.

Given a constraint C over the variables $X_1, \ldots, X_n$, we write $sol(X_i)$ for the values for X_i which can be extended to the other variables. That is,

$$sol(X_i) = \{d_i \mid C(d_1, \ldots, d_n) \wedge \forall j \, . \, int(X_j) \to glb(X_j) \leq d_j \leq lub(X_j) \, \wedge$$
$$\forall j \, . \, (mset(X_j) \vee set(X_j)) \to glb(X_j) \subseteq d_j \subseteq lub(X_j)\}$$

Where $mset(X)$, $set(X)$ and $int(X)$ test for multiset, set or integer variables, and $glb(X_j)$ and $lub(X_j)$ are the bounds on X_j (defined below).

We say that a constraint $C(X_1, \ldots, X_n)$ is **BC** iff:

For each multiset or set variable, X_j in the constraint, $sol(X_j) \neq \{\}$ and:

$$lub(X_j) = \bigcup_{m \in sol(X_j)} m \quad \text{and} \quad glb(X_j) = \bigcap_{m \in sol(X_j)} m$$

And for each integer variable, X_i in the constraint, $sol(X_i) \neq \{\}$ and:

$$lub(X_i) = max(\{d \in sol(X_i)\}) \quad \text{and} \quad glb(X_i) = min(\{d \in sol(X_i)\})$$

This definition of local consistency might look rather expensive, being defined over the set of *all* solutions. However, this set merely identifies *support* for particular values in the set or multiset. When using BC to filter, we will identify values which occur in no solutions and so can be pruned. Thus, we will not be finding all solutions but merely identifying those values that occur in no solutions (i.e. lack support). The following theorem justifies why BC can be called "bounds consistency".

Theorem 2 *BC is equivalent to bounds consistency applied to the occurrence representation.*

Proof: Suppose that a constraint is BC. Consider any integer variable X in this constraint. Then, the value $lub(X)$ for X can be extended to some solution. That is, it has support. Similarly the value $glb(X)$ for X can be extended to some other solution. That is, it also has support. Hence X is bounds consistent. On the other hand, consider any multiset variable X in the constraint. We can construct an equivalent occurrence representation. Suppose $m_{\max} = occ(m, lub(X))$ and $m_{\min} = occ(m, glb(X))$. Then we let the variable X_m in the occurrence vector have a domain $[m_{\min}, m_{\max}]$. Consider $X_m = m_{\max}$. Then, from the definition of

BC and the generalized multiset union operator, there must be a satisfying solution to the constraint in which $occ(m, X) = m_{\max}$. If there are several, we choose one non-deterministically. This solution is support for the bounds consistency of this integer variable in the occurrence representation. A similar argument holds for $X_m = m_{\min}$, and for any set variable. Hence, BC implies bounds consistency of the occurrence representation. The proof reverses directly. ♣

This theorem might appear to offer an easy and effective route to prune values from multiset variables: encode the problem into constraints on occurrence variables and use "off the shelf" bounds consistency algorithms. However, the occurrence representation greatly increases the number of variables in the problem. For example, suppose we have a constraint like $X \neq Y$ where X and Y are multiset variables. This maps into a large disjunctive constraint in the occurrence representation over $2d$ integer variables where d is the maximum possible cardinality of the two multisets. It is therefore worth developing specialized propagation algorithms that exploit the semantics of set or multiset constraints. Such algorithms can work on either a bounds or an occurrence representation. In the next two sections, we show how to define such algorithms by means of some simple inference rules. Note that a degenerate version of this last theorem is that BC on a constraint containing just integer variables is equivalent to bounds consistency on these variables. Some other properties also follow immediately from this result.

Theorem 3 *If a set of constraints are satisfiable, there are unique least upper and greatest lower bounds for each variable that makes the constraints BC.*

Proof: Immediate from the last result, and the fact that bounds consistency on integer variables returns an unique answer. ♣

5   Multiset Constraints

What sort of constraints can be posted on multiset variables? We assume constraints on multisets and set variables are defined as follows. A constraint is of the form $X \subseteq Y$, $X \subset Y$, $X = Y$, $X \neq Y$, $|X| = N$, $occ(N, X) = m$ or $occ(m, X) = N$ where X and Y are set or multiset expressions, N is an integer variable, and m is an integer. A set of multiset expression is, in turn, either a ground set or multiset, a set or multiset variable, or an expression of the form $X \cup Y$, $X \uplus Y$, $X \cap Y$, or $X - Y$ where X and Y are again set or multiset expressions. To make constraint propagation easier, we decompose constraints into a flattened normal form in which constraints are at most ternary and only of the form: $X \subseteq Y$, $X = Y \cup Z$, $X = Y \uplus Z$, $X = Y \cap Z$, $X = Y - Z$, $X \neq Y$, $|X| = N$, $occ(N, X) = m$ or $occ(m, X) = N$ where X and Y are either set or multiset variables or ground sets or multisets, N is an integer variable, and m is an integer. This decomposition takes any nested set or multiset expression and replaces it by a new equality constraint. For example, $(X \cup Y) \subseteq Z$ is normalized to give $XY = X \cup Y$ and $XY \subseteq Z$ where XY is a new multiset variable. A similar decomposition of set constraints was used in [4]. In general, such decomposition hinders constraint propagation.

Theorem 4 *BC on a set of constraints is strictly stronger than BC on the equivalent set of constraints decomposed into normal form.*

Proof: Clearly it is as strong. For strictness, we consider each type of multiset or set constraint in turn. For a set not-equals constraint, consider $X \cup (Y \cap Z) \neq (X \cup Y) \cap (X \cup Z)$ with $X = Y = Z = \{\} :: \{0\}$. BC determines that this constraint has no solution. But in the decomposition, with $YZ = Y \cap Z$, $XYZ = X \cup YZ$, $XY = X \cup Y$, $XZ = X \cup Z$, $XYXZ = XY \cap XZ$ and $XYZ \neq XYXZ$, the domains $X = Y = Z = YZ = XYZ = XY = XZ = XYXZ = \{\} :: \{0\}$ make the dec omposed constraints BC. Similar arguments hold for the other types of constraints. ♣

Under the simple restriction that there are no repeated occurrences of variables, decomposition does not hinder constraint propagation.

Theorem 5 *BC on a set of constraints, none of which contains a repeated occurrence of variables, is equivalent to BC on the equivalent set of constraints decomposed into a normal form.*

Proof: The proof uses induction on the number of auxiliary variables introduced and the structure of the multiset expressions which they replace, followed by extensive case analysis. Consider, for example, the multiset constraint $X - Y \subset Z$ and the decomposition: $XY = X - Y$, $XY \subset Z$. Suppose each of the decomposed constraints is BC but the original undecomposed constraint is not BC. There are six possible cases. In the first, $glb(X)$ is too small and we can add at least one value m to it. This is only possible if m is a member of $glb(Y)$ or of $glb(Z)$. In either case, the original pair of decomposed constraints could not be BC. The other five cases are similar. ♣

6   Enforcing Local Consistency

We now give some simple constraint propagation rules that enforce BC on multiset constraints in normal form. The equivalent inference rules for set constraints can be obtained by treating the operators in the rules as set and not multiset operations. Similarly, for mixed constraints involving both set and multiset variables, we need merely treat operators as appropriate set or multiset operations. Each rule tightens an upper and/or lower bound on a variable. The rules therefore terminate either with domains at a fixed point or by flagging failure. The rules can be applied in any order, though some orders may be quicker than others (especially when the constraints cannot be made BC). Similar rules for set variables are given in [4].

Multiset Inclusion Rules:

$$\frac{X \subseteq Y}{glb(X) \cup glb(Y) \subseteq Y}$$

$$\frac{X \subseteq Y}{X \subseteq lub(X) \cap lub(Y)}$$

Multiset Equality Rules:

$$\frac{X = Y \cup Z}{glb(X) \cup (glb(Y) \cup glb(Z)) \subseteq X \subseteq lub(X) \cap (lub(Y) \cup lub(Z))}$$

$$\frac{X = Y \cup Z}{Y \subseteq lub(Y) \cap lub(X)}$$

$$\frac{X = Y \cup Z}{Z \subseteq lub(Z) \cap lub(X)}$$

$$\frac{X = Y \uplus Z}{glb(X) \cup (glb(Y) \uplus glb(Z)) \subseteq X \subseteq lub(X) \cap (lub(Y) \uplus lub(Z))}$$

$$\frac{X = Y \uplus Z}{glb(Y) \cup (glb(X) - lub(Z)) \subseteq Y \subseteq lub(Y) \cap (lub(X) - glb(Z))}$$

$$\frac{X = Y \uplus Z}{glb(Z) \cup (glb(X) - lub(Y)) \subseteq Z \subseteq lub(Z) \cap (lub(X) - glb(Y))}$$

$$\frac{X = Y \cap Z}{glb(X) \cup (glb(Y) \cap glb(Z)) \subseteq X \subseteq lub(X) \cap (lub(Y) \cap lub(Z))}$$

$$\frac{X = Y \cap Z}{glb(Y) \cup glb(X) \subseteq Y}$$

$$\frac{X = Y \cap Z}{glb(Z) \cup glb(X) \subseteq Z}$$

$$\frac{X = Y - Z}{glb(X) \cup (glb(Y) - lub(Z)) \subseteq X \subseteq lub(X) \cap (lub(Y) - glb(Z))}$$

$$\frac{X = Y - Z}{glb(Y) \cup (glb(X) \uplus glb(Z)) \subseteq Y \subseteq lub(Y) \cap (lub(X) \uplus lub(Z))}$$

$$\frac{X = Y - Z}{glb(Z) \cup (glb(Y) - lub(X)) \subseteq Z \subseteq lub(Z) \cap (lub(Y) - glb(X))}$$

Multiset Inequality Rules:

$$\frac{X \neq Y, glb(Y) = lub(Y) = glb(X), |lub(X)| = |glb(X)| + 1}{X = lub(X)}$$

$$\frac{X \neq Y, glb(Y) = lub(Y) = lub(X), |lub(X)| = |glb(X)| + 1}{X = glb(X)}$$

$$\frac{X \neq Y, glb(X) = lub(X) = glb(Y), |lub(Y)| = |glb(Y)| + 1}{Y = lub(Y)}$$

$$\frac{X \neq Y, glb(X) = lub(X) = lub(Y), |lub(Y)| = |glb(Y)| + 1}{Y = glb(Y)}$$

Multiset Cardinality Rules:

$$\frac{|X| = N}{max(min(N), |glb(X)|)) \leq N \leq min(max(N), |lub(X)|)}$$

$$\frac{|X| = N, min(N) = max(N) = |glb(X)|}{X = glb(X)}$$

$$\frac{|X| = N, min(N) = max(N) = |lub(X)|}{X = lub(X)}$$

Multiset Membership Rules:

$$\frac{occ(N, X) = m, occ(min(N), glb(X)) > m}{N > min(N)}$$

$$\frac{occ(N, X) = m, occ(min(N), lub(X)) < m}{N > min(N)}$$

$$\frac{occ(N, X) = m, occ(max(N), glb(X)) > m}{N < max(N)}$$

$$\frac{occ(N, X) = m, occ(max(N), lub(X)) < m}{N < max(N)}$$

$$\frac{occ(N, X) = m, max(N) = min(N)}{glb(X) \cup \underbrace{\{N, \ldots, N\}}_{m \text{ times}} \subseteq X \subseteq lub(X) - \underbrace{\{N, \ldots \ldots, N\}}_{max(0, occ(N, lub(X)) - m)}}$$

$$\frac{occ(m, X) = N}{max(min(N), occ(m, glb(X))) \leq N \leq min(max(N), occ(m, lub(X)))}$$

$$\frac{occ(m, X) = N}{glb(X) \cup \underbrace{\{m, \ldots \ldots, m\}}_{min(N) \text{ times}} \subseteq X \subseteq lub(X) - \underbrace{\{m, \ldots \ldots, m\}}_{max(0, occ(m, lub(X)) - max(N))}}$$

Failure Rules: Each of the inference rules given so far tightens the bounds for a variable. We fail whenever this rules out all possible values for the variable. The following additional inference rules also lead to failure:

$$\frac{X \subseteq Y, glb(X) \not\subseteq lub(Y)}{Fail}$$

$$\frac{X = Y \cup Z, glb(X) \not\subseteq lub(Y) \cup lub(Z)}{Fail}$$

$$\frac{X = Y \cup Z, glb(Y) \cup glb(Z) \not\subseteq lub(X)}{Fail}$$

$$\frac{X = Y \uplus Z, glb(X) \not\subseteq lub(Y) \uplus lub(Z)}{Fail}$$

$$\frac{X = Y \uplus Z, glb(Y) \uplus glb(Z) \not\subseteq lub(X)}{Fail}$$

$$\frac{X = Y \cap Z, glb(X) \not\subseteq lub(Y) \cap lub(Z)}{Fail}$$

$$\frac{X = Y \cap Z, glb(Y) \cap glb(Z) \not\subseteq lub(X)}{Fail}$$

$$\frac{X = Y - Z, glb(X) \not\subseteq lub(Y) - glb(Z)}{Fail}$$

$$\frac{X = Y - Z, glb(Y) - lub(Z) \not\subseteq lub(X)}{Fail}$$

$$\frac{X \neq Y, glb(X) = lub(X) = glb(Y) = lub(Y)}{Fail}$$

$$\frac{|X| = N, max(N) < |glb(X)|)}{Fail}$$

$$\frac{|X| = N, |lub(X)| < min(N)}{Fail}$$

$$\frac{occ(N, X) = m, \forall y \, . \, occ(y, lub(X)) < m \ \lor \ m < occ(y, glb(X))}{Fail}$$

$$\frac{occ(m, X) = N, max(N) < occ(m, glb(X))}{Fail}$$

$$\frac{occ(m, X) = N, occ(m, lub(X)) < min(N)}{Fail}$$

Properties. It is easy to see that the application of these rules terminates either with domains that are at a fixed point or with failure. Indeed, these rules terminate either with the unique BC domains or, if the problem cannot be made BC, fail, in both cases independent of the order of application of the rules.

Theorem 6 *If a set of constraints in normal form can be made BC, these inference rules reach an unique fixed point in which domains are BC. If the constraints cannot be made BC, the inference rules terminate with failure. Both take at most $O(enm^2)$ time where e is the number of constraints, n is the number of variables and m is the maximum cardinality of the multiset variables.*

Proof: (Outline) Each inference rule tightens the upper and lower bounds of a variable or flags failure. The rules must therefore reach a fixed point or fail.

Suppose that we reach some fixed point applying these rules to a set of constraints in normal form. The proof uses case analysis on the type of constraint. Consider, for example, a constraint of the form $X = Y \cup Z$. We consider each of the multiset variables in turn and show that their domains are BC. For the variable X, as the inference rule tightening X's upper and lower bound is at a fixed point, it must be the case that $glb(Y) \cup glb(Z) \subseteq glb(X)$, $lub(X) \subseteq lub(Y) \cup lub(Z)$ and $glb(X) \subseteq lub(X)$. The assignment $X = glb(X)$, $Y = lub(Y) \cap glb(X)$ and $Z = lub(Z) \cap glb(X)$ will satisfy the constraint $X = Y \cup Z$ and the conditions that $glb(Y) \subseteq Y \subseteq lub(Y)$ and $glb(Z) \subseteq Z \subseteq lub(Z)$. Similarly, the assignment $X = lub(X)$, $Y = lub(Y) \cap lub(X)$ and $Z = lub(Z) \cap lub(X)$ will satisfy the constraint $X = Y \cup Z$ and the conditions that $glb(Y) \subseteq Y \subseteq lub(Y)$ and $glb(Z) \subseteq Z \subseteq lub(Z)$. Hence X's domain is BC. Similar arguments hold for the domains of Y and Z, as well as for the other types of constraints. Hence, if the rules terminate at a fixed point, the resulting domains are BC.

We now prove that, if the domains in the problem can be made BC, the rules terminate at this fixed point. Consider a problem that can be made BC, and its unique BC domains. The proof again uses extensive case analysis on the type of constraint. Consider, for instance, the constraint $X = Y \cup Z$ and the BC domains for X, Y and Z. To prove that the rules terminate at this fixed point, we assume that an inference rule can still narrow a domain or flag failure. There are five cases corresponding to the five different inference rules associated with this constraint. In the first, the inference rule narrows the least upper bound of Y by removing one or more values. Suppose one of these removed values is m. Let X_m, Y_m and Z_m be the number of occurrences of m in X, Y and Z respectively. As m is pruned by this inference rule, $max(Y_m) > max(X_m)$. The original multiset variables are not therefore BC (which is a contradiction). Hence, there can be no value m removed and this inference rule is at a fixed point if the domains are BC. Similar arguments hold for the other 4 inference rules.

These rules therefore terminate at a fixed point iff the resulting domains are BC. As the rules must terminate either at a fixed point or by flagging failure, it follows that the rules flag failure iff the problem cannot be made BC. As each rule tightens the bounds on a multiset, set or finite domain occurrence variable, the worst case is when the rules tighten each bound by just one element at a time. We may therefore have to apply $O(nm)$ rules. To find which rule applies, we may have to go through each of the e constraints in turn. Associated with each type of constraint, a fixed number of rules can be tried. The cost of applying the inference rules is thus at most $O(enm)$ multiplied by the cost of applying a single inference rule. This last cost is dominated by the $O(m)$ cost to test (dis)equality or inclusion, and the $O(m)$ cost to perform one of the basic operations like union or difference. Hence, the total cost is $O(enm^2)$ in the worst case. ♣

7   Global Constraints

An important aspect of constraint programming is global (or non-binary) constraints [5, 6]. Such constraints capture common patterns and often come with efficient and effective propagation algorithms. An important question about such constraints is whether decomposition hurts. Consider a global constraint on finite domain variables like the all-different constraint [5]. This can be decomposed into binary not-equals constraints, but this decomposition hinders constraint propagation. For instance, GAC on an all-different constraint is strictly stronger than arc-consistency (AC) on the decomposed binary not-equals constraints [7]. We therefore have to develop a specialized propagation algorithm to achieve GAC on an all-different constraint. Surprisingly, the decomposition of global constraints involving set or multiset variableos often does *not* hinder constraint propagation. This is good news. We can provide global constraints on set and multiset variables to help users compactly specify models. However, we do not need to develop complex algorithms for reasoning about them as is the case with finite domain variables. We can simply decompose such global constraints into primitive constraints and use the inference rules given in the last section. In the rest of this section, we give results to show that decomposition on the occurrence representation often does not hinder GAC, and that decomposition on the occurrence or bounds representation does not hinder BC.

Disjoint Constraint. The constraint $disjoint([X_1, \ldots, X_n])$ ensures that the multiset variables are pairwise disjoint. This global constraint can be decomposed into the binary constraints: $X_i \cap X_j = \{\!\{\}\!\}$ for all $i \neq j$. Such decomposition does not hinder constraint propagation.

Theorem 7 *GAC (resp. BC) on a disjoint constraint is equivalent to AC (resp. BC) on the binary decomposition.*

Proof: Clearly GAC (resp. BC) on a disjoint constraint is as strong as AC (resp. BC) on the decomposition. To show the reverse, suppose that the binary decomposition is AC (resp. BC). If the disjoint constraint is not GAC or BC then there must be at least two multiset variables, X_i and X_j with a value m in common. That is, $X_{im} \geq 1$ and $X_{jm} \geq 1$. However, in such a situation, the decomposed constraint $\min(X_{im}, X_{jm}) = 0$ would neither be AC nor BC. ♣

Partition Constraint. The constraint $partition([X_1, \ldots, X_n], X)$ ensures that the multiset variables, X_i are pairwise disjoint and union together to give X. By introducing new auxiliary variables, it can be decomposed into binary and union constraints of the form: $X_i \cap X_j = \{\!\{\}\!\}$ for all $i \neq j$, and $X_1 \cup \ldots \cup X_n = X$. Decomposition again causes no loss in pruning.

Theorem 8 *GAC (resp. BC) on a partition constraint is equivalent to GAC (resp. BC) on the decomposition.*

Proof: Clearly GAC (resp. BC) on a partition constraint is as strong as GAC (resp. BC) on the decomposition. To show the reverse, by Theorem 7, we need focus just on the union constraints. Suppose that the decomposition is GAC (resp. BC). If the partition constraint is not GAC or BC then there must be one value m that does not occur frequently enough in the upper bounds of the multiset variables. But, in this case, the decomposed constraint (which is equivalent to $\sum_{i=1}^{n} X_{im} = X_m$) would neither be GAC nor BC. ♣

This result continues to hold even if the union constraint is decomposed into the set of ternary union constraints by introducing new auxiliary variables: $X_1 \cup X_2 = X_{12}, X_{12} \cup X_3 = X_{13}, \ldots, X_{1n-1} \cup X_n = X$. We can also consider the non-empty partition constraint which also ensures that each multiset variable is not empty. Decomposition now hinders constraint propagation.

Theorem 9 *GAC (resp. BC) on a non-empty partition constraint is strictly stronger than GAC (resp. BC) on the decomposition.*

Proof. Clearly it is as strong. For strictness, consider 3 multiset variables with $glb(X_1) = glb(X_2) = glb(X_3) = \{\!\{\}\!\}$, $lub(X_1) = lub(X_2) = \{\!\{1,2\}\!\}$ and $lub(X_3) = \{\!\{1,2,3\}\!\}$. The decomposition is both GAC and BC. However, enforcing GAC or BC on the non-empty partition constraint gives $glb(X_3) = lub(X_3) = \{\!\{3\}\!\}$. ♣

Distinct Constraint. Consider the constraint $distinct([X_1, \ldots, X_n])$ which ensures that all the multisets are distinct from each other. This decomposes into pairwise not equals constraints: $X_i \neq X_j$ for all $i \neq j$. Decomposition in this case hinders constraint propagation.

Theorem 10 *GAC (resp. BC) on a distinct constraint is strictly stronger than AC (resp. BC) on the decomposition.*

Proof: Clearly it is as strong. For strictness, consider a distinct constraint on 3 multiset variables with $glb(X_1) = glb(X_2) = \{\!\{\}\!\}$, $lub(X_1) = lub(X_2) = \{\!\{0\}\!\}$, $glb(X_3) = \{\!\{0\}\!\}$, and $lub(X_3) = \{\!\{0,0\}\!\}$. The decomposition is both AC and BC. But enforcing GAC or BC on the distinct constraint gives $glb(X_3) = lub(X_3) = \{\!\{0,0\}\!\}$. ♣

8   Experimental Results

Our preliminary experiments show that the choice of representation for multiset variabls can make a large difference even on relatively easy problems. Table 1 shows results for the template design problem (prob002 in CSPLib). The model is relatively easy to solve when the multiset variables are represented via the occurrence representation. However, despite the fact that the multiset variables in this problem represent the contents of each template and these are of fixed size, the model is difficult to solve when the multiset variables are represented via the fixed cardinality representation.

When constraint programming with multiset variables, a number of issues arise which we are currently exploring. For example, which of the different representations for multiset variables is best? Is it simply enough to find the representation in which the constraints are "easy" to express? When do we go for multiple representations with channelling between them? We also need to develop new variable and value ordering heuristics for multiset variables. The fail first principle for variable ordering translates into: *branch on the multiset variable X in which* $|lub(X) - glb(X)|$ *is smallest.* However, when we have both set, multiset and integer variables, we need heuristics to choose between them. We must also decide what sort of branching decision to make. For example, do we branch on the number of occurrences or try to split the difference between lower and upper bounds?

9   Related Work

ILOG's Configurator has an `IlcBagPort` variable to model the multiset of components connected to a particular component. This uses an occurrence representation for the multisets, as well as integer variables for the cardinality of the

Table 1. Solutions to the template design problem modelled using multiset variables. The objective is the production run length. Multiset variables are represented with either the occurrence or fixed cardinality representations. The objective is the production run length. All solutions are optimal for the given number of templates. Runtimes are for OPL Studio 3.5.1 on a Pentium III 1.2 GHz with 512 MB of RAM running Windows XP. Entries marked "*" are not solved within 3 hours.

Problem	Number of templates	Objective value	Goal	Occurrence rep		Fixed card rep	
				fails	runtime/sec	fails	runtime/sec
cat food	1	550	find	8	0.00	371	0.03
			prove	0	0.00	389	0.03
	2	418	find	1173	0.12	3397750	502.40
			prove	5708	0.43	*	*
	3	409	find	48721	5.63	*	*
			prove	*	*	*	*
herbs	1	115	find	142	0.01	*	*
			prove	31	0.00	*	*
	2	96	find	54	0.01	*	*
			prove	132788714	10386.20	*	*

multiset and for the number of values in the multiset. The only multiset constraints that appear to be supported are equality, inclusion and their negations. The domain of a set or multiset variable can include the `IlcWildCard` value, representing any possible extension of the set or multiset. It would be interesting to study the theoretical properties of this extension.

Set variables have been integrated into the ECLIPSE constraint logic programming language using a bounds representation [4]. Our definition of bounds consistency generalizes the local consistency property given in [4] for set variables. For example, a subset constraint $S_1 \subseteq S_2$ is *locally consistent* iff $glb(S_1) \subseteq glb(S_2)$ and $lub(S_1) \subseteq lub(S_2)$, whilst a cardinality constraint $l \le |S_1| \le u$ is *locally consistent* iff $l \le |glb(S_1)|$ and $|lub(S)| \le u$. Another advantage of our definition is that it works with any type of constraint, and is not restricted to those types of constraint considered in [4].

Theorem 11 *A subset constraint $S_1 \subseteq S_2$ is locally consistent iff it is BC. A cardinality constraint $l \le |S_1| \le u$ is locally consistent iff it is BC.*

Proof: Suppose $S_1 \subseteq S_2$ is BC and $lub(S_1) \not\subseteq lub(S_2)$. Then there must be $a \in lub(S_1)$ with $a \notin lub(S_2)$. Hence there exists $S \in sol(S_1)$ with $a \in S$, but for all $S \in sol(S_2)$ there is no $a \in S$. The value S for S_1 cannot then have support in the constraint $S_1 \subseteq S_2$. Hence $lub(S_1) \subseteq lub(S_2)$. By an analogous argument, $glb(S_1) \subseteq glb(S_2)$. The proof reverses easily.

Suppose $l \le |S_1| \le u$ is BC. Then for $S \in sol(S_1)$, $l \le |S|$. Hence $l \le |glb(S)|$. By an analogous argument, $|lub(S_1)| \le u$. The proof reverses easily. ♣

The constraint logic programming language {Log} provides sets and multisets as basic types [8]. Sets and multisets are axiomatically defined and solved using a mixture of unification and rewriting. However, computational efficiency is not a major goal as {Log} is more concerned with expressivity, e.g. being able to represent and reason about partially specified and nested sets. Our goals, however, are more computational. We wish to augment constraint solving with efficient constraint propagation techniques for dealing with multiset variables. Some other systems like CLPS [9] also build sets into their unification procedure but are again more concerned with expressivity than efficiency.

10   Future Work and Conclusions

We have formally studied the role of multiset variables in constraint programming. We identified a number of different representations for multiset variables and compared them. We proposed a definition of local consistency for constraints involving multiset, set or integer variables. This definition is a generalization of the notion of bounds consistency for integer variables. We showed how this local consistency property can be enforced by means of some simple inference rules which tighten bounds on the variables. We also studied a number of global constraints on set and multiset variables. Surprisingly, unlike finite domain variables, the decomposition of global constraints over set or multiset variables often does not hinder constraint propagation.

References

1. Gervet, C. Conjunto: constraint logic programming with finite set domains. In Bruynooghe, M., ed.: Proc. of the 1994 Int. Symp. on Logic Programming, MIT Press (1994) 339–358
2. Müller, T., Müller, M. Finite set constraints in Oz. In Bry, F., Freitag, B., Seipel, D., eds.: 13th Logic Programming Workshop, TU München (1997) 104–115
3. Proll, L., Smith, B. Integer linear programming and constraint programming approaches to a template design problem. INFORMS Journal on Computing, **10** (1998) 265–275
4. Gervet, C. Interval Propagation to Reason about Sets: Definition and Implementation of a Practical Language. Constraints **1** (1997) 191–244
5. Régin, J. A filtering algorithm for constraints of difference in CSPs. In Proc. of the 12th National Conference on AI, American Association for AI (1994) 362–367
6. Beldiceanu, N. Global constraints as graph properties on a structured network of elementary constraints of the same type. In Proc. of 6th Int. Conf. on Principles and Practice of Constraint Programming (CP2000), Springer (2000) 52–66
7. Gent, I., Stergiou, K., Walsh, T. Decomposable constraints. Artificial Intelligence **123** (2000) 133–156
8. Dovier, A., Piazza, C., Pontelli, E., Rossi, G. Set and constraint logic programming. ACM Trans. on Programming Languages and Systems **22** (2000) 861–931
9. Legeard, B., Legros, E. Short overview of the CLPS system. In Proc. of 3rd Int. Symp. on Programming Language Implementation and Logic Programming, Springer-Verlag (1991) 431–433 LNCS 528.

Pruning while Sweeping over Task Intervals

Armin Wolf

Fraunhofer FIRST, Kekuléstraße 7, D-12489 Berlin, Germany

Abstract. Overload checking, forbidden regions, edge finding, and not-first/not-last detection are well-known propagation rules to prune the start times of tasks which have to be processed without any interruption and overlapping on an exclusively available resource, i.e. machine. We show that these rules are correct and that "sweeping" over task intervals is an efficient and sufficient technique to achieve maximal pruning with respect to all these propagation rules. All the presented algorithms have quadratic time and linear space complexity with respect to the number of tasks. To our knowledge, this is the first presentation where the correctness of all these rules is proved and where it is shown and proved that the combination of these algorithms achieves the same pruning of the start times achieved by other algorithms with cubic time and quadratic space complexity.

1 Introduction

Recent publications [4, 5] have shown that "sweeping" originated and used widely in computational geometry [11] is also an efficient pruning technique when adapted and applied to finite domain constraint solving problems.

This paper presents different kinds of sweeping over "task intervals" (cf. [7]) to apply the well-known pruning rules efficiently for non-preemptive one-machine constraint problems: overload checking, forbidden regions, edge finding, and not-first/not-last detection (e.g. (re-)presented in [3, 4]).

In detail, the main contributions of the paper are:

- The correctness proofs of all the presented pruning rules (see Section 3–6).
- The proofs that the consideration of (generalised) task intervals instead of arbitrary subsets of tasks is sufficient to yield maximal pruning with these rules (see Section 3–6), reducing time complexity from exponential to quadratic.
- The proof that the combination of edge finding and forbidden regions, both with quadratic time and linear space complexity, results in the same pruning as the processing over task intervals presented in [7] having cubic time and quadratic space complexity (see Section 5, especially Theorem 2).
- The presentation of high-efficient pruning algorithms resulting from these theoretical results, all based on sweeping over task intervals (see Section 7).
- Experimental results made with these algorithms on some well-known job-shop scheduling benchmark problems (see Section 8).

F. Rossi (Ed.): CP 2003, LNCS 2833, pp. 739–753, 2003.

2   The Non-preemptive One-Machine Constraint Problem

Informally, the non-preemptive one-machine constraint problem is the problem of finding a serialisation of non-interruptible tasks to be processed on a single machine such that they are not overlapping. More formally, the problem is defined as follows:

Definition 1. *A task t is a non-interruptible activity having a non-empty set of potential start times S_t, i.e. a finite integer set which is the domain of its variable start time. Furthermore, a task t has a fixed duration $d(t)$, i.e. a positive integer value[1].*

Given a finite set of tasks $T = \{t_0, \ldots, t_n\}$ with at least two elements ($n > 0$), the problem is to find a solution, i.e. some start times $s(t_0) \in S_{t_0}, \ldots, s(t_n) \in S_{t_n}$ such that either $s(t_i) + d(t_i) \leq s(t_j)$ or $s(t_j) + d(t_j) \leq s(t_i)$ holds for $0 \leq i < j \leq n$ — or equivalent, that there is a permutation $\delta : \{0, \ldots, n\} \to \{0, \ldots, n\}$ satisfying $s(t_{\delta(i-1)}) + d(t_{\delta(i-1)}) \leq s(t_{\delta(i)})$ for $i = 1, \ldots, n$. Both conditions force a total order on the set of tasks T.

Thus, a non-preemptive one-machine constraint problem is determined by a set of tasks T which is solvable if there is such a solution and unsolvable, otherwise[2].

Assuming that the (average) size of all sets of potential start times is m, the determination of some/all solutions has in general an exponential time complexity of $O(m^n)$. To reduce this complexity, Constraint Programming (CP) uses *constraint propagation*, i.e. the iteration over algorithms pruning the variables' domains such that within a reasonable time some – ideal all – values are eliminated that are not part of any solution. Considering the non-preemptive one-machine constraint problem, we know from complexity theory that there is no efficient propagation that prunes the tasks' start times ideally. However, there are several pruning rules, i.e. overload checking, forbidden regions, edge finding and not-first/not-last detection that prune the tasks' start times considerably in the non-preemptive one-machine constraint problem in polynomial time and space.

In the following, we only consider non-preemptive one-machine constraint problems. Thus, it is always implicitly assumed that a set of tasks T with at least two elements is given such that each task $t \in T$ has a well-defined set of start times S_t and a well-defined duration $d(t)$. For each task $t \in T$ a feasible start time $s(t) \in S_t$, i.e. a solution, has to be determined.

Furthermore, we identify for each task $t \in T$ its *earliest start time* $est(t)$ and its *latest completion time* $lct(t)$. Given the actual set of start times S_t of a task $t \in T$ it holds $est(t) \leq \min(S_t)$ and $lct(t) \geq \max(S_t) + d(t)$.

For any task t the primed set of potential start times S'_t identifies an update of this set, i.e. the effect of any pruning operation resulting in a subset of S_t.

---

[1] A generalisation with sets of potential durations that may be zero is possible, too.
[2] Empty or singleton sets of tasks determine trivial problems.

Given a non-empty subset of tasks $M \subseteq T$ we define:

$$d(M) := \sum_{t \in M} d(t) \qquad est(M) := \min_{t \in M}(est(t)) \qquad lct(M) := \max_{t \in M}(lct(t)) \; .$$

In the following we focus on "special" subsets of tasks called *task intervals*:

Definition 2. *Given a set of tasks* $T = \{t_0, \ldots, t_n\}$ *then for each* $i \in \{0, \ldots, n\}$ *and for each* $j \in \{0, \ldots, n\}$ *with* $est(t_i) \leq lct(t_j)$ *we define the* task interval

$$[t_i, t_j] := \{t \in T \mid est(t_i) \leq est(t) \wedge lct(t) \leq lct(t_j)\} \; .$$

3   Overload Checking

A necessary condition for the solubility of a non-preemptive one-machine constraint problem determined by a non-empty set of tasks $T = \{t_0, \ldots, t_n\}$ is that each set of tasks $M \subseteq T$ is not overloaded, i.e. the "slack" $lct(M) - est(M) - d(M)$ is non-negative:

Proposition 1. *A non-preemptive one-machine constraint problem determined by a set of tasks* T *is unsolvable, if there is a non-empty set of tasks* $M \subseteq T$ *such that* $lct(M) - est(M) < d(M)$.

Proof. Let $M = \{t_{i_0}, \ldots, t_{i_k}\}$ be a non-empty subset of $T = \{t_0, \ldots, t_n\}$ such that $lct(M) - est(M) < d(M)$ holds. Now, we assume that there is a solution of the non-preemptive one-machine constraint problem determined by T, i.e. there are $s(t_0) \in S_{t_0}, \ldots, s(t_n) \in S_{t_n}$ such that after an appropriate renaming of the tasks $s(t_{i-1}) + d(t_{i-1}) \leq s(t_i)$ for $i = 1, \ldots, n$ holds, especially

$$s(t_{i_{j-1}}) + d(t_{i_{j-1}}) \leq s(t_{i_j}) \quad \text{for } j = 1, \ldots, k.$$

Obviously, it follows that $s(t_{i_k}) \geq s(t_{i_0}) + \sum_{j=0}^{k-1} d(t_{i_j})$. Thus, by definition it holds $lct(t_{i_k}) \geq s(t_{i_k}) + d(t_{i_k}) \geq s(t_{i_0}) + d(M) \geq est(M) + d(M) > lct(M)$ contradicting $lct(t_{i_k}) \leq lct(M)$. Consequently, the assumption is wrong, i.e. there is no solution of the considered constraint problem. □

A naive overload checking of all $2^{n+1} - 1$ non-empty subsets of T is not necessary. It is sufficient to consider the at most $(n+1)^2$ well-defined task intervals $[t_i, t_j]$ $(i, j \in \{0, \ldots, n\})$:

Proposition 2. *Given a non-empty set of tasks* $M \subseteq \{t_0, \ldots, t_n\}$ *such that* $lct(M) - est(M) < d(M)$. *Then, there is a well-defined task interval* $[t_i, t_j]$ *with* $i, j \in \{0, \ldots, n\}$ *such that* $lct([t_i, t_j]) - est([t_i, t_j]) < d([t_i, t_j])$ *holds.*

Proof. We choose a task $t_i \in M$ such that $est(t_i) = est(M)$ and a task $t_j \in M$ such that $lct(t_j) = lct(M)$ holds. Obviously, $M \subseteq [t_i, t_j]$ and $d([t_i, t_j]) \geq d(M)$ holds. By definition, it follows immediately that $lct([t_i, t_j]) - est([t_i, t_j]) = lct(M) - est(M) < d(M) \leq d([t_i, t_j])$ holds. □

4   Forbidden Regions

Consider a non-preemptive one-machine constraint problem determined by a set of tasks T. A *forbidden region* of a task $t \in T$ is an integer interval I such that for any start time $s(t) \in I$ it is impossible to schedule another task $r \in T \setminus \{t\}$ either before or after the task t: The application of the pruning rule

$$\forall t \in T \, \forall r \in T \setminus \{t\} \; : \; lct(r) - d(r) - d(t) + 1 \leq est(r) + d(r) - 1$$
$$\Rightarrow s(t) \notin [lct(r) - d(r) - d(t) + 1, est(r) + d(r) - 1] \qquad (1)$$
$$\text{i.e. } S'_t = S_t \setminus [lct(r) - d(r) - d(t) + 1, est(r) + d(r) - 1]$$

determines the *forbidden regions* of each task $t \in T$ locally with respect to another task $r \in T \setminus \{t\}$. The updating of the start times of the task t (cf. S'_t) will prune the search space of all feasible schedules correctly:

Proposition 3. *Given a non-preemptive one-machine constraint problem determined by a set of tasks T and two different tasks $t \in T$, $r \in T \setminus \{t\}$. Further, let $lct(r) - d(r) - d(t) + 1 \leq est(r) + d(r) - 1$. Then, there is no solution of the given constraint problem with $s(t) \in [lct(r) - d(r) - d(t) + 1, est(r) + d(r) - 1]$.*

Proof. Assuming that there is a solution of the given constraint problem with $s(t) \in [lct(r) - d(r) - d(t) + 1, est(r) + d(r) - 1]$ then the task r is either scheduled before the task t or after it. If r is before t it holds $s(r) + d(r) \leq s(t) \leq est(r) + d(r) - 1$ contradicting $s(r) \geq est(r)$. If r is after t it holds $s(t) + d(t) \leq s(r)$ or equivalently: $lct(r) - d(r) - d(t) + 1 \leq s(t) \leq s(r) - d(t)$ contradicting $lct(r) - d(r) \geq s(r)$. Thus, the assumption is wrong, i.e. there is no solution of the given constraint problem with $s(t) \in [lct(r) - d(r) - d(t) + 1, est(r) + d(r) - 1]$. $\square$

A naive consideration for all $(n + 1)n$ pairs of different tasks $r \neq t$ is not necessary for any pruning. If the intervals from their earliest start times to their latest completion times minus one are disjoint, the forbidden regions $F_{t,r} := [lct(r) - d(r) - d(t) + 1, est(r) + d(r) - 1]$ and $F_{r,t} := [lct(t) - d(r) - d(r) + 1, est(t) + d(t) - 1]$ (if existing, i.e. $i \leq j$ in $[i, j]$) are neither pruning the potential start times of these two tasks nor the search space:

Lemma 1. *Let two tasks r and t be given with*

$$[est(r), lct(r) - 1] \cap [est(t), lct(t) - 1] = \emptyset \quad then \quad F_{t,r} \cap S_t = F_{r,t} \cap S_r = \emptyset \; .$$

Proof. Without any loss of generality, we assume that $lct(r) \leq est(t)$ holds (otherwise rename r and t). It follows that $est(r) + d(r) \leq est(t)$ holds. Thus, $F_{t,r} \cap S_t = \emptyset$ holds. Furthermore, it follows that $lct(t) - d(t) \geq lct(r)$. Thus, $lct(t) - d(t) - d(r) \geq lct(r) - d(r)$ follows, i.e. $F_{r,t} \cap S_r = \emptyset$ holds, too. $\square$

5   Edge Finding

Considering a non-preemptive one-machine constraint problem determined by a set of tasks T. *Edge finding* [1, 6] checks whether a task $t \in T$ must be after respective before all the tasks in a non-empty set of tasks $M \subseteq T \setminus \{t\}$. With respect to recent publications on constraint-based scheduling [2, 3], "... the following rules capture the 'essence' of the edge finding bounding technique:"

$$\forall t \in T \, \forall M \subseteq T \setminus \{t\}, M \neq \emptyset \; : \; lct(M) - est(M \cup \{t\}) < d(M) + d(t)$$

$$\Rightarrow s(t) \geq \max_{\emptyset \neq N \subseteq M} (est(N) + d(N)) \quad \text{i.e.} \tag{2}$$

$$S'_t = S_t \cap [\max_{\emptyset \neq N \subseteq M} (est(N) + d(N)), +\infty)$$

$$\forall t \in T \, \forall M \subseteq T \setminus \{t\}, M \neq \emptyset \; : \; lct(M \cup \{t\}) - est(M) < d(M) + d(t)$$

$$\Rightarrow s(t) + d(t) \leq \min_{\emptyset \neq N \subseteq M} (lct(N) - d(N)) \quad \text{i.e.} \tag{3}$$

$$S'_t = S_t \cap (-\infty, \min_{\emptyset \neq N \subseteq M} (lct(N) - d(N)) - d(t)].$$

Whenever the pruning rule (2) applies, i.e. there is a task $t \in T$ and a non-empty set of tasks $M \subseteq T \setminus \{t\}$ such that $lct(M) - est(M \cup \{t\}) < d(M) + d(t)$, the value

$$\alpha(t) := \max_{\emptyset \neq N \subseteq M \subseteq T \setminus \{t\}} \{est(N) + d(N) \mid lct(M) - est(M \cup \{t\}) < d(M) + d(t)\}$$

is well-defined and the updating $S'_t = S_t \cap [\alpha(t), +\infty)$ will prune the search space of all feasible schedules correctly:

Proposition 4. *Given a non-preemptive one-machine constraint problem determined by a set of tasks T and a task $t \in T$ such that $\alpha(t)$ is well-defined. Then, for all solutions of the given constraint problem it holds $s(t) \geq \alpha(t)$.*

Proof. Assuming that there is a solution of the given problem with $s(t) < \alpha(t)$, it follows that there are sets of tasks N', M' with $\emptyset \neq N' \subseteq M' \subseteq T \setminus \{t\}$ such that $lct(M') - est(M' \cup \{t\}) < d(M') + d(t)$ and $\alpha(t) = est(N') + d(N')$ holds.

The total order determined by the solution defines an according numbering on the tasks in M'; i.e. let $M' = \{r_0, \ldots, r_m\}$ such that $s(r_{i-1}) + d(r_{i-1}) \leq s(r_i)$ holds for $i = 1, \ldots, m$. From $s(t) < est(N') + d(N')$ it follows that there is at least one task $r \in N'$ where $N' = \{r_{i_0}, \ldots, r_{i_k}\} \subseteq M'$ which is after the task t, i.e. $s(t) + d(t) \leq s(r)$. Otherwise, it would hold that $s(r_{i_j}) + d(r_{i_j}) \leq s(t)$ for $j = 0, \ldots, k$ and thus $est(N') + d(N') \leq s(r_{i_0}) + \sum_{j=0}^{k} d(r_{i_j}) \leq s(r_{i_k}) + d(r_{i_k}) \leq s(t)$.

From the existence of such a task $r \in M'$ it follows that $s(r_m) + d(r_m) - \min(s(r_0), s(t)) \geq d(M') + d(t)$ holds and thus $lct(M') - est(M' \cup \{t\}) \geq d(M') + d(t)$ because by definition we know that $lct(M') \geq s(r_m) + d(r_m)$ and $est(M' \cup \{t\}) \leq \min(s(r_0), s(t))$. This contradicts $lct(M') - est(M' \cup \{t\}) < d(M') + d(t)$. Thus the assumption is wrong, i.e. there is no solution with $s(t) < \alpha(t)$. $\square$

With respect to the task t a naive consideration of all $2^n - 1$ non-empty subsets of $T \setminus \{t\}$ and all of its subsets for any pruning based on the pruning rule (2) is not necessary. It is sufficient to consider at most $(n + 1)^2$ well-defined task intervals $[t_i, t_j]$ with $t_i, t_j \in [t_i, t_j]$:

Theorem 1. *Given a non-preemptive one-machine constraint problem determined by a set of tasks T and a task $t \in T$ such that $\alpha(t)$ is well-defined, i.e. there are two sets of tasks N' and M' with $\emptyset \neq N' \subseteq M' \subseteq T \setminus \{t\}$ such that:*

$$lct(M') - est(M' \cup \{t\}) < d(M') + d(t) \quad and \quad \alpha(t) = est(N') + d(N') .$$

Now, if there is no overloading (cf. Section 3), i.e. for each non-empty set of tasks $M \subseteq T$ it holds $lct(M) - est(M) \geq d(M)$ then there are well-defined task intervals $[v, w]$ and $[u, w]$ with $u, v, w \in T$ such that $lct(w) < lct(t)$, $N' \subseteq [v, w]$, $M' \subseteq [u, w]$, $[v, w] \subseteq [u, w] \subseteq T \setminus \{t\}$, and

$$lct([u, w]) - est([u, w] \cup \{t\}) < d([u, w]) + d(t) \qquad (4)$$
$$\alpha(t) = est([v, w]) + d([v, w]) . \qquad (5)$$

Proof. Assuming that $lct(t) \leq lct(M')$ holds, it follows immediately (from non-overloading) that $lct(M') - est(M' \cup \{t\}) = lct(M' \cup \{t\}) - est(M' \cup \{t\}) \geq d(M' \cup \{t\}) = d(M') + d(t)$, contradicting the precondition. Thus, $lct(t) > lct(M')$ holds.

Let $u, w \in M'$ such that $est(u) = est(M')$ and $lct(w) = lct(M')$. Obviously, it holds $lct(w) < lct(t)$, $M' \subseteq [u, w]$, $t \notin [u, w]$, and $est([u, w] \cup \{t\}) = est(M' \cup \{t\}) = \min(est(u), est(t))$. Additionally, it holds $d(M') \leq d([u, w])$ because $M' \subseteq [u, w]$. Consequently, the condition (4) holds.

Let $v \in N'$ such that $est(v) = est(N')$. Obviously, it holds $N' \subseteq [v, w] \subseteq [u, w]$ and thus $d([v, w]) \geq d(N')$ and $est(N') + d(N') \leq est([v, w]) + d([v, w])$. Considering the choice of N', i.e. $est(N') + d(N')$ is maximal, it holds that $d(N') = d([v, w])$. Consequently, the condition (5) holds. □

Symmetrical statements are also valid for the pruning rule (3). Due to lack of space, their formulations and proofs are omitted.

Considering [7], two other propagation rules are applicable whenever a task t is detected to be after/before a task interval M not containing t: These rules are based on the knowledge that each task $r \in M$ must be before/after the task t, i.e. it must be completed before the latest start time respective begin after the earliest completion time of the task t. However, a naive application of these rules for pruning the start times requires the consideration of $O(n)$ tasks in $O(n^2)$ task intervals, resulting in a time complexity of $O(n^3)$.

In the following we show that the pruning resulting from the application of these rules is covered by the pruning performed by the forbidden regions rules (see Section 4) which has a time complexity of $O(n^2)$.

Theorem 2. *Given a non-preemptive one-machine constraint problem determined by a set of tasks T. After applying the pruning rules (2) and (3) let $est(t) := \min(S_t)$ and $lct(t) := \max(S_t) + d(t)$ for each task $t \in T$. Then, after the application of the pruning rule (1) it holds:*

$$\forall t \in T \, \forall M \subseteq T \setminus \{t\}, M \neq \emptyset \; : \; lct(M) - est(M \cup \{t\}) < d(M) + d(t)$$
$$\Rightarrow \forall r \in M : s(r) + d(r) \leq lct(t) - d(t) \qquad (6)$$
$$\forall t \in T \, \forall M \subseteq T \setminus \{t\}, M \neq \emptyset \; : \; lct(M \cup \{t\}) - est(M) < d(M) + d(t)$$
$$\Rightarrow \forall r \in M : s(r) \geq est(t) + d(t) \qquad (7)$$

Proof. Let a task $t \in T$ and a non-empty set of tasks $M \in T \setminus \{t\}$ be given such that $lct(M) - est(M \cup \{t\}) < d(M) + d(t)$ holds. We assume that $s(r) + d(r) > lct(t) - d(t)$ holds for an arbitrary task $r \in M$. Thus, with $lct(r) \geq s(r) + d(r) > lct(t) - d(t)$ it holds $lct(M) > lct(t) - d(t)$ because $r \in M$.

Further, we assume that $est(t) + d(t) \leq lct(M)$ holds. By the definition of $est(t)$, especially after the application of the pruning rule (2), it holds that $est(t) \geq est(M) + d(M)$. It follows immediately that $est(M) + d(M) + d(t) \leq est(t) + d(t) \leq lct(M)$ holds and thus $d(M) + d(t) \leq lct(M) - est(M) \leq lct(M) - est(M \cup \{t\})$ because $est(M) \geq est(M \cup \{t\})$ holds by definition. This contradicts the precondition, i.e. $est(t) + d(t) > lct(M)$ holds.

Combining both results, the interval $[lct(t) - d(t) - d(r) + 1, est(t) + d(t) - 1]$ is the non-empty forbidden region of the task r with respect to t containing at least $lct(M)$ (cf. Figure 1). Remembering our assumption, it holds that $s(r) \geq est(t) + d(t) > lct(M)$. This contradicts $lct(M) \geq lct(r) \geq s(r) + d(r) \geq s(r)$. Thus the assumption is wrong, i.e. it holds $s(r) + d(r) \leq lct(t) - d(t)$ for each task $r \in M$ (cf. the rule (6)).

Let a task $t' \in T$ and a non-empty set of tasks $M' \in T \setminus \{t'\}$ be given such that $lct(M' \cup \{t'\}) - est(M') < d(M') + d(t')$ holds. Accordingly, it is provable that $s(r') \geq est(t') + d(t')$ holds for each task $r' \in M'$ (cf. the rule (7)). $\square$

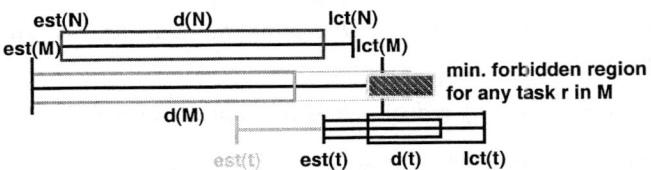

Fig. 1. After edge finding the forbidden region rule prunes the latest start times of all tasks $r \in M$ sufficiently.

Concluding the presented results, it is sufficient to prune the forbidden regions after edge finding to perform the same pruning as proposed in [7] in $O(n^2)$ time instead of $O(n^3)$.

6   Not-First/Not-Last-Detection

We prove the correctness of the *not-first/not-last* detection rules proposed in [3]. Furthermore, we show that the consideration of generalised task intervals is sufficient for the exclusion of infeasible start times performed by these rules which are formulated for arbitrary sets of tasks.

6.1   The Not-First Detection Rule

Consider a non-preemptive one-machine constraint problem determined by a set of tasks T. The *not-first* rule checks whether a task $t \in T$ cannot be before all the tasks in a non-empty set of tasks $M \subseteq T \setminus \{t\}$. If t is not before all these tasks it must be after at least one task $r \in M$:

$$\forall t \in T \, \forall M \subseteq T \setminus \{t\}, M \neq \emptyset \; : \; lct(M) - est(t) < d(M) + d(t)$$
$$\Rightarrow s(t) \geq \min_{r \in M}(est(r) + d(r)) \quad \text{i.e.} \tag{8}$$
$$S'_t = S_t \cap [\min_{r \in M}(est(r) + d(r)), +\infty) \; .$$

Whenever this rule applies, i.e. there is a task $t \in T$ and a non-empty set of tasks $M \subseteq T \setminus \{t\}$ such that $lct(M) - est(t) < d(M) + d(t)$ holds, the value

$$\alpha(t) := \max_{\emptyset \neq M \subseteq T \setminus \{t\}} (\min_{r \in M}(\{est(r) + d(r) \mid lct(M) - est(t) < d(M) + d(t)\}))$$

is well-defined and the updating $S'_t = S_t \cap [\alpha(t), +\infty)$ will prune the search space of all feasible schedules correctly:

Proposition 5. *Given a non-preemptive one-machine constraint problem determined by a set of tasks T and a task $t \in T$ such that $\alpha(t)$ is well-defined. Then, for all solutions of the given constraint problem it holds $s(t) \geq \alpha(t)$.*

Proof. Assuming that there is a solution of the given constraint problem with $s(t) < \alpha(t)$ it follows that there is a non-empty set of tasks $M' \subseteq T \setminus \{t\}$ such that $lct(M') - est(t) < d(M') + d(t)$ and $\alpha(t) = \min_{r \in M'}(est(r) + d(r))$ holds.

Furthermore, there is a task $r' \in M'$ having minimal earliest completion time which defines $\alpha(t)$:

$$est(r') + d(r') \leq est(r) + d(r) \quad \forall r \in M' \; \text{ and } \; \alpha(t) = est(r') + d(r') \; .$$

The total order determined by the solution defines an according numbering on the tasks in M'; i.e. let $M' = \{r_0, \ldots, r_m\}$ such that $s(r_{i-1}) + d(r_{i-1}) \leq s(r_i)$ holds for $i = 1, \ldots, m$. From $s(t) < est(r') + d(r')$ it follows that each task $r_i \in M'$ is after the task t, i.e. $s(r_i) \geq s(t) + d(t)$ for $i = 0, \ldots, m$. Otherwise, it would hold that $s(t) \geq s(r) + d(r)$ for a task $r \in M'$ and thus $s(t) \geq est(r') + d(r')$ because $est(r') + d(r')$ is the earliest completion time of all tasks in M'.

It follows that $s(r_m) + d(r_m) - s(t) \geq d(M') + d(t)$ holds and thus $lct(M') - est(t) \geq d(M') + d(t)$. This contradicts $lct(M') - est(t) < d(M') + d(t)$. Thus the assumption is wrong, i.e. there is no solution with $s(t) < \alpha(t)$. $\qquad \square$

With respect to the task t a naive consideration of all $2^n - 1$ non-empty subsets of $T \setminus \{t\}$ and all of its members for any pruning based on the detection rule (8) is not necessary. It is sufficient to consider at most $(n+1)^2$ generalised task intervals $]t_i, t_j]$ with $t_i, t_j \in \,]t_i, t_j]$:

Theorem 3. *Given a non-preemptive one-machine constraint problem determined by a set of tasks T and a task $t \in T$ such that $\alpha(t)$ is well-defined, i.e. there is a non-empty set of tasks $M' \subseteq T \setminus \{t\}$ and a task $r' \in M'$ such that:*

$$lct(M') - est(t) < d(M') + d(t)$$
$$est(r') + d(r') = \alpha(t) = \min_{r \in M'}(est(r) + d(r)) \; .$$

Then, there is a task $s \in M'$ such that for the generalised task interval

$$]r', s] := \{u \in T \mid est(r') + d(r') \leq est(u) + d(u) \wedge lct(u) \leq lct(s)\}$$

it holds $M' \subseteq]r', s] \setminus \{t\}$ and $lct(]r', s] \setminus \{t\}) - est(t) < d(]r', s] \setminus \{t\}) + d(t)$, i.e. the generalised task interval $]r', s]$ triggers the pruning rule (8).

Proof. Choose a task $s \in M'$ such that $lct(s) = lct(M')$ holds and let an arbitrary task $v \in M'$ be given. By the definition of M' it holds that $v \neq t$. By the definition of r' and the choice of s it holds that $est(r') + d(r') \leq est(v) + d(v)$ and $lct(v) \leq lct(s)$, thus $v \in]r', s] \setminus \{t\}$ and consequently $M' \subseteq]r', s] \setminus \{t\}$.

By definition it holds $lct(]r', s] \setminus \{t\}) = lct(s) = lct(M')$ and thus $lct(]r', s] \setminus \{t\}) - est(t) = lct(M') - est(t)$. Further, it holds $d(M') + d(t) \leq d(]r', s] \setminus \{t\}) + d(t)$ because $M' \subseteq]r', s] \setminus \{t\}$ holds. Consequently, $lct(]r', s] \setminus \{t\}) - est(t) = lct(M') - est(t) < d(M') + d(t) \leq d(]r', s] \setminus \{t\}) + d(t)$ is proven. □

6.2   The Not-Last Detection Rule

Consider a non-preemptive one-machine constraint problem determined by a set of tasks T. The *not-last* rule checks whether a task $t \in T$ cannot be after all the tasks in a non-empty set of tasks $M \subseteq T \setminus \{t\}$. If t is not after all these tasks it must be before at least one task $r \in M$:

$$\forall t \in T \ \forall M \subseteq T \setminus \{t\}, M \neq \emptyset \ : \ lct(t) - est(M) < d(M) + d(t)$$
$$\Rightarrow s(t) + d(t) \leq \max_{r \in M}(lct(r) - d(r)) \quad \text{i.e.} \qquad (9)$$
$$S'_t = S_t \cap (-\infty, \max_{r \in M}(lct(r) - d(r)) - d(t)] \ .$$

This rule is symmetrical to the not-first rule (8). Thus, symmetrical statements are valid, too[3].

7   Sweeping over Task Intervals

Sweeping means iterating over chronological ordered events and performing some event-driven actions. In our case, these events are the boundaries of well-defined (generalised) task intervals: the chronological ordered earliest start and latest completion times of a set of tasks T determining a non-preemptive one-machine constraint problem (cf. Figure 2). During the iteration, information is gathered in a data structure called the *sweep line* which is in our case an initial empty sequence of already considered tasks, i.e. we "swept" over.

Therefore, for each task $t \in T$ an event is generated for its actual earliest start time $est(t) := \min(S_t)$ and another event for its actual latest completion time $lct(t) := \max(S_t) + d(t)$. Then, all events are sorted in ascending order such that for any two tasks $s, t \in T$ with $est(s) = lct(t)$ it holds that $est(s)$ is before $lct(t)$ within this order.

---

[3] Again, due to lack of space, their formulations and proofs are omitted.

7.1   Forbidden Regions while Sweeping

For the detection and pruning of forbidden regions, it is assumed that the tasks in T are numbered $t_0, \ldots, t_n$ with respect to the ascending order of their earliest start times, i.e. $est(t_0) \leq \cdots \leq est(t_n)$. Then, we are sweeping forward, i.e. in ascending order, over the sorted events:

If the next event is $est(t_j)$ $(0 \leq j \leq n)$ then

– append t_j at the end of the sweep line.

If the next event is $lct(t_j)$ $(0 \leq j \leq n)$ then

– iterate forward over the tasks $t_{l_0}, \ldots, t_{l_k}$ in the sweep line – for $i = l_0, \ldots, l_k$:
  - if $i \neq j$ and $lct(t_i) - d(t_i) - d(t_j) + 1 \leq est(t_i) + d(t_i) - 1$ then
    let $S_{t_j} := S_{t_j} \setminus [lct(t_i) - d(t_i) - d(t_j) + 1, est(t_i) + d(t_i) - 1]$.
  - if $i \neq j$ and $lct(t_j) - d(t_j) - d(t_i) + 1 \leq est(t_j) + d(t_j) - 1$ then
    let $S_{t_i} := S_{t_i} \setminus [lct(t_j) - d(t_j) - d(t_i) + 1, est(t_j) + d(t_j) - 1]$.
  - remove t_j from the sweep line.

The algorithm works as follows: During the forward iteration over the sweep line, all tasks $t_i \neq t_j$ with $est(t_i) \leq lct(t_j) \leq lct(t_i)$ are considered. If there is a forbidden region of t_j with respect to t_i or vice versa, then the precondition of the pruning rule (1) is satisfied and the correspondent start times are pruned accordingly. Considering Lemma 1, the algorithm performs all the pruning possible with the pruning rule (1). Furthermore, the performed pruning is at least as strong as the disjunctive propagation proposed in [3].

Given n tasks the time complexity of this algorithm is $O(n^2)$: $O(n \log n)$ for sorting the $2n$ events, iteration over these $2n$ events and consideration of at most n tasks for each event. Obviously, the space complexity is $O(n)$.

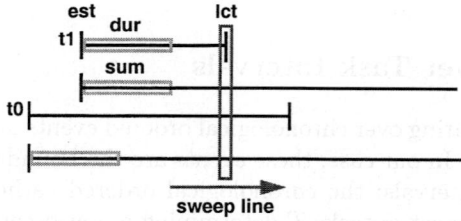

Fig. 2. Sweeping over task intervals.

7.2   Overload Checking and Edge-Finding while Sweeping

To perform pruning based on the edge finding rule (2) while sweeping over task intervals, it is assumed that the tasks in T are numbered $t_0, \ldots, t_n$ with respect to the ascending order of their earliest start times, i.e. $est(t_0) \leq \cdots \leq est(t_n)$. Then, we are sweeping forward, i.e. in ascending order, over the sorted events:

If the next event is $est(t_j)$ $(0 \leq j \leq n)$ then

- append t_j at the end of the sweep line and set $\sigma_j := 0$.

If the next event is $lct(t_j)$ $(0 \leq j \leq n)$ then

- if there are $k+1$ tasks in the sweep line then let $\delta_{k+1} := -\infty$
- iterate backward over the tasks $t_0, \ldots, t_k$ in the sweep line – for $i = k, \ldots, 0$:
  - if $est(t_j) \geq est(t_i)$ then
    * let $\sigma_i := \sigma_i + d(t_j)$,
    * let $\delta_i := \max(\delta_{i+1}, est(t_i) + \sigma_i)$,
    * if $\delta_i > lct(t_j)$ then there is no feasible schedule; exit.
- iterate forward over the tasks $t_0, \ldots, t_k$ in the sweep line – for $i = 0, \ldots, k$:
  - if $\sigma_i > 0$ then let $\delta_{k+1} := \max(\delta_{k+1}, est(t_i) + \sigma_i)$.
  - if $lct(t_i) > lct(t_j)$ then
    * if $est(t_i) + \sigma_i + d(t_i) > lct(t_j)$ then let $S_{t_i} := S_{t_i} \cap [\delta_i, +\infty)$.
    * if $\delta_{k+1} + d(t_i) > lct(t_j)$ then let $S_{t_i} := S_{t_i} \cap [\delta_0, +\infty)$.

The algorithm works as follows: During the backward iteration over the sweep line for $i = k, \ldots, 0$, some approximations of the durations $d([t_i, t_j]) \geq \sigma_i$ are calculated for all non-empty task-intervals $[t_i, t_j]$. However, sweeping over all talks guarantees that there are always tasks t'_j such that $lct(t'_j) = lct(t_j)$ and $d([t_i, t_j]) = d([t_i, t'_j]) = \sigma_i$. Further, $\delta_i \leq \max(\{est(t_l) + d[t_l, t_j] \mid [t_l, t_j] \neq \emptyset, l \in \{k, \ldots, i\}\})$ are calculated. If $\delta_i > lct(t_j)$ holds then there is an overloading: $d[t_i, t_j] \geq \delta_i - est(t_i) > lct(t_j) - est(t_i)$ holds. The algorithm stops accordingly.

During the forward iteration over the sweep line for $i = 0, \ldots, k$ the approximation $\delta_{k+1} \leq \max(\{est(t_l) + d[t_l, t_j] \mid [t_l, t_j] \neq \emptyset, l \in \{0, \ldots, i\}\})$ is calculated which is further used to check whether the precondition of the pruning rule (2) is satisfied. Now, if the necessary condition $lct(t_i) > lct(t_j)$ for an optimal pruning is satisfied (cf. Theorem 1), two cases are distinguished:

If $est(t_i) + \sigma_i + d(t_i) > lct(t_j)$ holds, then $lct([t_i, t_j]) - est([t_i, t_j] \cup \{t_i\}) \leq lct(t_j) - est(t_i) < \sigma_i + d(t_i) \leq d[t_i, t_j] + d(t_i)$ holds, too. Thus, the precondition of the rule (2) is satisfied, i.e. the start time is pruned with $\delta_i \leq \max(\{est(t_l) + d[t_l, t_j] \mid \emptyset \neq [t_l, t_j] \subseteq [t_i, t_j]\}$.

If $\delta_{k+1} + d(t_i) > lct(t_j)$ holds, then $lct([t_l, t_j]) - est([t_l, t_j] \cup \{t_i\}) \leq lct(t_j) - est(t_l) < \delta_{k+1} - est(t_l) + d(t_i) \leq d([t_l, t_j]) + d(t_i)$ holds for an $l \in \{0, \ldots, i\}$ because $est(t_l) \leq est(t_i)$. Furthermore, $lct([t_0, t_j]) - est([t_0, t_j] \cup \{t_i\}) \leq lct(t_j) - est(t_l) < \delta_{k+1} - est(t_l) + d(t_i) \leq d([t_l, t_j]) + d(t_i)$ holds because $est(t_0) \leq est(t_l)$ by construction of the sweep line. Thus, the precondition of the rule (2) is satisfied with respect to the task interval $[t_0, t_j]$), i.e. the start time is pruned with $\delta_0 \leq \max(\{est(t_l) + d[t_l, t_j] \mid \emptyset \neq [t_l, t_j] \subseteq [t_0, t_j]\}$.

In both cases, sweeping over all talks guarantees that there are always tasks t'_j such that $lct(t_j) = lct(t'_j)$ and $\delta_i = \max(\{est(t_l) + d[t_l, t'_j] \mid \emptyset \neq [t_l, t'_j] \subseteq [t_i, t'_j]\}) = \max(\{est(t_l) + d[t_l, t_j] \mid \emptyset \neq [t_l, t_j] \subseteq [t_i, t_j]\})$ holds during the consideration of t'_j, i.e. maximal pruning with respect to $[t_i, t_j]$ is performed.

The correctness of the given algorithm follows directly from Theorem 1 because overload checking (see Section 3, especially Proposition 2) is integrated.

Furthermore, the algorithm performs all the pruning possible with the rule (2): For each task $t \in T$ and each non-empty set of tasks $M \subseteq T \setminus \{t\}$ with $est(t) > lct(M)$ the application of the rule (2) performs no further pruning: In fact the precondition of the rule is satisfied because $lct(M) - est(t) < 0$ holds, however, $est(N) + d(N) \leq lct(N) \leq lct(M) < est(t) \leq s(t)$ holds for each non-empty set of tasks $N \subseteq M$, if there is no overloading.

The given algorithm is a refinement of the algorithm given in [3]: Only the necessary tasks (which are in the sweep line) are considered.

Due to lack of space, the analogous algorithm to perform pruning based on the edge finding rule (3) while sweeping over task intervals is omitted[4].

Given n tasks the time complexity of edge finding is $O(n^2)$: $O(n \log n)$ for sorting the $2n$ events, iteration over these $2n$ events and consideration of at most n tasks for each event. Obviously, the space complexity is $O(n)$.

7.3   Not-First/Not-Last-Detection while Sweeping

To perform pruning based on the not-first rule (8) while sweeping over task intervals, it is assumed that the tasks in T are numbered $t_0, \ldots, t_n$ with respect to the descending order of their latest completion times, i.e. $lct(t_0) \geq \cdots \geq lct(t_n)$. Then, we are sweeping backward, i.e. in descending order, over the sorted events:

if the next event is $lct(t_j)$ $(0 \leq j \leq n)$ then

 – append t_j at the end of the sweep line.

if the next event is $est(t_j)$ $(0 \leq j \leq n)$ then

 – if there are $k+1$ tasks in the sweep line then let $\sigma_{k+1} := 0$ and $\delta_{k+1} := +\infty$
 – iterate backward over the tasks $t_0, \ldots, t_k$ in the sweep line – for $i = k, \ldots, 0$:
   • if $est(t_i) + d(t_i) \geq est(t_j) + d(t_j)$ then let $\sigma_i := \sigma_{i+1} + d(t_i)$
     else let $\sigma_i := \sigma_{i+1}$.
   • if $\sigma_i > 0$ then let $\delta_i := \min(\delta_{i+1}, lct(t_i) - \sigma(t_i))$ else let $\delta_i := \delta_{i+1}$.
 – iterate forward over the tasks $t_0, \ldots, t_k$ in the sweep line – for $i = 0, \ldots, k$:
   • if $est(t_i) + d(t_i) < est(t_j) + d(t_j)$ then
     * if $est(t_i) + d(t_i) > \delta_0$ then let $S_{t_i} := S_{t_i} \cap [est(t_j) + d(t_j), +\infty)$.
   • else if either $est(t_i) + d(t_i) > \delta_{i+1}$ or $est(t_i) > \delta_0$ then
     let $S_{t_i} := S_{t_i} \cap [est(t_j) + d(t_j), +\infty)$.

The algorithm works as follows: During the backward iteration over the sweep line for $i = k, \ldots, 0$, the durations $\sigma_i := d(\,]t_j, t_i] \setminus \{t_{i-1}, \ldots, t_0\})$ are calculated for all the tasks t_i in the sweep line, i.e. for all well-defined generalised task intervals $]t_j, t_k] \subseteq \cdots \subseteq]t_j, t_0]$. Furthermore, for $i = k, \ldots, 0$ the values $\delta_i := \min(\{lct(t_l) - d(\,]t_j, t_l] \setminus \{t_{i-1}, \ldots, t_0\}) \mid]t_j, t_l] \neq \emptyset, l \in \{i, \ldots, k\}\})$ are calculated. These values are used to check whether the precondition of the not-first rule is satisfied during the forward iteration over the sweep line: If $est(t_i) + d(t_i) < est(t_j) + d(t_j)$ holds then $t_i \notin]t_j, t_l]$ holds for $l = k, \ldots, 0$. If further $est(t_i) +$

---

[4] The necessary adaptations are left to the interested reader.

$d(t_i) > \delta_0$ then $est(t_i) + d(t_i) > lct(t_l) - d(\,]t_j, t_l] \setminus \{t_{l-1}, \ldots, t_0\})$ respective $lct(t_l) - est(t_i) < d(\,]t_j, t_l] \setminus \{t_{l-1}, \ldots, t_0\}) + d(t_i)$ holds for the smallest $l \in \{k, \ldots, 0\}$ with $lct(t_l) < lct(t_{l-1})$. Thus, $d(\,]t_j, t_l] \setminus \{t_{l-1}, \ldots, t_0\}) = d(\,]t_j, t_l]) = d(\,]t_j, t_l] \setminus \{t_i\})$ is valid.

Otherwise, if $est(t_i) + d(t_i) \leq est(t_j) + d(t_j)$ and $est(t_i) + d(i) > \delta_{i+1}$ then $est(t_i) + d(t_i) > lct(t_l) - d(\,]t_j, t_l] \setminus \{t_{l-1}, \ldots, t_0\})$ respective $lct(t_l) - est(t_i) < d(\,]t_j, t_l] \setminus \{t_{l-1}, \ldots, t_0\}) + d(t_i)$ holds for the smallest $l \in \{k, \ldots, i+1\}$ with that $lct(t_l) < lct(t_{l-1}) \leq lct(t_i)$, i.e. $t_i \notin]t_j, t_l]$. Thus, $d(\,]t_j, t_l] \setminus \{t_{l-1}, \ldots, t_0\}) = d(\,]t_j, t_l]) = d(\,]t_j, t_l] \setminus \{t_i\})$ is valid.

Finally, if $est(t_i) + d(t_i) \leq est(t_j) + d(t_j)$ and $est(t_i) + d(i) \leq \delta_{i+1}$ but $est(t_i) > \delta_0$ then $est(t_i) > lct(t_l) - d(\,]t_j, t_l] \setminus \{t_{l-1}, \ldots, t_0\})$ respective $lct(t_l) - est(t_i) < d(\,]t_j, t_l] \setminus \{t_{l-1}, \ldots, t_0\})$ holds for the smallest $l \in \{i+2, \ldots, 0\}$ with $lct(t_i) \leq lct(t_l) < lct(t_{l-1})$, i.e. $t_i \in]t_j, t_l]$. Thus, $d(\,]t_j, t_l] \setminus \{t_{l-1}, \ldots, t_0\}) = d(\,]t_j, t_l]) = d(\,]t_j, t_l] \setminus \{t_i\}) + d(t_i)$ is valid.

In all three cases the precondition of the rule (8) is satisfied and the start times of t_i are pruned accordingly.

The correctness of the given algorithm follows immediately from Theorem 3. Furthermore, the algorithm performs all the pruning possible with the rule (8): For each task $t \in T$ and each non-empty set of tasks $M \subseteq T \setminus \{t\}$ with $lct(t) < est(M)$ the pruning rule (8) is not applicable because the precondition of the rule is not satisfied: it holds $est(t) + d(t) \leq lct(t) < est(M) + d(M)$.

The given algorithm is a refinement of the algorithm given in [3]: Only the necessary tasks (which are in the sweep line) are considered.

Due to lack of space, the analogous algorithm to perform pruning based on the not-last rule (9) is omitted[5].

Given n tasks the time complexity of not-first/not-last is $O(n^2)$: $O(n \log n)$ for sorting the $2n$ events, iteration over these $2n$ events and consideration of at most n tasks for each event. Obviously, the space complexity is $O(n)$.

8   Experimental Results

For runtime and performance comparisons we implemented the disjunctive constraint propagation as recommended in [3] (Section 2.1.2.). This propagation technique is realized by two nested loops iterating over the tasks. We also implemented the pruning algorithms presented in Section 7 considering Theorem 2. All implementations are integrated in our own constraint programming engine called firstcs realized in pure Java[6]. We applied both – disjunctive constraint propagation and sweeping over task intervals – on some classical job-shop scheduling benchmark problems from abz5–abz9 [9], ft06–ft10 [8], la01–la40 [10], orb01–orb10 [1], swv01–20 [12], and yn1–yn4 [13]. We measured the maximal makespans where the insolubility of the problems are detected by pruning without any search (columns 2 and 4). The experiments were performed on a PC Pentium 4

---

[5]   Again, the necessary adaptations are left to the interested reader.

[6]   A detailed presentation of firstcs is in the pipeline.

with 2.8 GHz running Microsoft Windows XP Professional and Java 1.4.0. Furthermore, for each benchmark we compared the reduction of all domains at the better approximation of the lower bound of the make-span. This is the greater value of both maximal make-spans where inconsistencies are detected plus one, i.e. 854 for the ft10 problem. The results are presented in the following table:

benchmark problem	disjunctive constraint propagation		sweeping over task intervals		domain reduction [%]	
	max. make-span	time [msecs.]	max. make-span	time [msecs.]	disjunctive	sweeping
abz5	999	31	1102	62	68.17	71.39
abz6	831	31	854	62	67.39	69.07
abz7	637	47	650	93	54.79	64.82
abz8	565	47	596	78	61.81	69.06
abz9	605	47	616	109	58.55	60.24
ft06	52	31	52	46	62.11	64.00
ft10	795	31	853	78	57.20	64.39
ft20	1163	31	1163	47	18.35	18.55
la01	665	16	665	31	37.36	40.95
la02	654	16	654	31	35.06	35.77
la10	957	31	957	31	23.68	23.73
la20	835	31	849	62	63.32	64.92
la40	1068	31	1169	62	63.73	67.06
orb01	927	31	928	47	55.58	57.12
orb02	732	16	799	62	63.19	63.28
orb10	867	16	898	47	59.14	67.30
swv01	1365	31	1365	46	33.24	33.48
swv02	1474	31	1474	62	31.56	31.84
swv10	1559	32	1568	94	48.39	48.69
swv20	2822	47	2822	78	15.97	16.00
yn1	736	78	771	140	75.12	75.95
yn2	749	79	818	140	70.68	74.08
yn3	738	78	792	93	72.17	75.30
yn4	817	62	870	94	68.18	69.17

These results show that sweeping over task intervals is slower but performs equal or better than disjunctive propagation with respect to the considered benchmark set and their lower bounds. For instance, the approximation of the lower bound of the make-span of the ft10 problem found with disjunctive constraint propagation is 796. However, sweeping performs a much better approximation: 854. Even the consideration of the pruning at the better approximation (see the last two columns) shows that sweeping yields a better reduction of the domains of the tasks' start times. For example, the domains of the start times of the ft10 problem, that are initial the integer intervals from 0 to 854 minus the task's duration are reduced by 64.39%. This is much better than the reduction of 57.20% resulting from disjunctive propagation.

Finally, the experiments have shown that the application of all presented pruning rules are not idempotent, i.e. there are problems in the considered benchmark set, where the re-application of the rules performs a further pruning of the potential start times. We therefore iterated over the algorithms presented in Section 7 until a fix-point was reached.

9   Conclusion

In this paper, a survey of all well-known pruning rules for non-preemptive one-machine constraint problems are re-considered. These rules are theoretically examined and new, more efficient algorithms based on sweeping over task intervals are deduced from the theoretical results: all pruning is possible with quadratic time and linear space complexity. Last but not least, the algorithms are successfully applied to well-known benchmark problems yielding some encouraging results. However, the experiments also shows that more pruning requires more calculations, i.e. run-time. Thus for practical applications, we decided to introduce switches to activate or deactivate the pruning algorithms separately.

References

1. David Applegate and William Cook. A computational study of the job-shop scheduling problem. *ORSA Journal on Computing*, 27(3):149–156, 1991.
2. Philippe Baptiste. *A Theoretical and Experimental Study of Resource Constraint Propagation*. PhD thesis, Université de Technologie de Compiègne, UMR CNRS 6599 Heudiasyc, 1998.
3. Philippe Baptiste, Claude le Pape, and Wim Nuijten. *Constraint-Based Scheduling*. Number 39 in International Series in Operations Research & Management Science. Kluwer Academic Publishers, 2001.
4. Nicolas Beldiceanu and Mats Carlsson. Sweep as a generic pruning technique applied to the non-overlapping rectangles constraint. In Toby Walsh, editor, *Proceedings of the 7th International Conference on Principles and Practice of Constraint Programming - CP2001*, number 2239 in Lecture Notes in Computer Science, pages 377–391. Springer Verlag, 2001.
5. Nicolas Beldiceanu and Mats Carlsson. A new multi-resource cumulatives constraint with negative heights. In Pascal van Hentenryck, editor, *Proceedings of the 8th International Conference on Principles and Practice of Constraint Programming - CP2002*, number 2470 in Lecture Notes in Computer Science, pages 63–79. Springer Verlag, 2002.
6. J. Carlier and E. Pinson. An algorithm for solving the job-shop problem. *Management Science*, (2):164–176, 1989.
7. Yves Caseau and François Laburthe. Improved CLP scheduling with task intervals. In Pascal van Hentenryck, editor, *Proceedings of the Eleventh International Conference on Logic Programming, ICLP'94*, pages 369–383. MIT Press, 1994.
8. G. L. Thompson H. Fisher. Probabilistic learning combinations of local job-shop scheduling rules. In G. L. Thompson J. F. Muth, editor, *Industrial Scheduling*, pages 225–251. Prentice Hall, Englewood Cliffs, New Jersey, 1963.
9. E. Balas J. Adams and D. Zawack. The shifting bottleneck procedure for job shop scheduling. *Management Science*, 34:391–401, 1988.
10. S. Lawrence. Resource constrained project scheduling: an experimental investigation of heuristic scheduling techniques (supplement). Technical report, Graduate School of Industrial Administration, Carnegie-Mellon University, Pittsburgh, Pennsylvania, 1984.
11. Franco P. Preparata and Michael Ian Shamos. *Computational Geometry, An Introduction*. Texts and Monographs in Computer Science. Springer Verlag, 1985.
12. R. Vaccari R.H. Storer, S.D. Wu. New search spaces for sequencing instances with application to job shop scheduling. *Management Science*, pages 1495–1509, 1992.
13. T. Yamada and R. Nakano. A genetic algorithm applicable to large-scale job-shop instances. In R. Manner and B. Manderick, editors, *Parallel instance solving from nature 2*, pages 281–290. North-Holland, Amsterdam, 1992.

Improving Backtrack Search for Solving the TCSP

Lin Xu and Berthe Y. Choueiry

Constraint Systems Laboratory
Department of Computer Science and Engineering
University of Nebraska-Lincoln University of Nebraska-Lincoln, Lincoln NE
{lxu,choueiry}@cse.unl.edu

Abstract. In this paper, we address the task of finding the minimal network of a Temporal Constraint Satisfaction Problem (TCSP). We report the integration of three approaches to improve the performance of the exponential-time backtrack search (BT-TCSP) proposed by Dechter et al. [6] for this purpose. The first approach consists of using a new efficient algorithm ($\triangle$STP) [21] for solving the Simple Temporal Problem (STP), an operation that must be executed at each node expansion during BT-TCSP. The second approach improves BT-TCSP itself by exploiting the topology of the temporal network. This is accomplished in three ways: finding and exploiting articulation points (AP), checking the graph for new cycles (NewCyc), and using a new heuristic for edge ordering (EdgeOrd). The third approach is a filtering algorithm, $\triangle$AC, which is used as a preprocessing step to BT-TCSP, and which significantly reduces the size of the TCSP [22]. In addition to introducing two new techniques, NewCyc and EdgeOrd, this paper discusses an extensive evaluation of the merits of the above three approaches. Our experiments on randomly generated problems demonstrate significant improvements in the number of nodes visited, constraint checks, and CPU time.

1 Background and Motivation

A Simple Temporal Problem (STP) is defined by a graph $G = (V, E, I)$ where V is a set of vertices i representing time points p_i; E is a set of directed edges $e_{i,j}$ representing constraints between two time points p_i and p_j; and I is a set of constraint labels for the edges, see Fig. 1 (left). A constraint label $I_{i,j}$ of edge $e_{i,j}$ is an interval $[a, b]$, $a, b \in \mathbb{R}$,

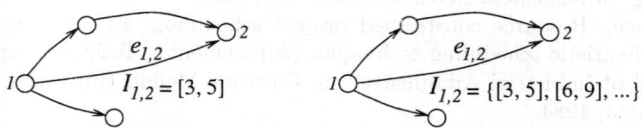

Fig. 1. *Left:* STP. *Right:* TCSP.

and denotes a constraint of bounded difference $a \leq (p_j - p_i) \leq b$. Note that $I_{i,j} = [a, b]$ $\Leftrightarrow I_{j,i} = [-b, -a]$. A Temporal Constraint Satisfaction Problem (TCSP) is defined by a similar graph $G = (V, E, I)$, where each edge label $I_{i,j} = \{l_{ij}^{(1)}, l_{ij}^{(2)}, \ldots, l_{ij}^{(k)}\}$ is a *set* of disjoint intervals denoting a disjunction of constraints of bounded differences between i

F. Rossi (Ed.): CP 2003, LNCS 2833, pp. 754–768, 2003.

and j, see Fig. 1 (right). We assume that the intervals in a label are disjoint and ordered in a canonical way. The following is a typical example:

> *Tom has class at 8:00 a.m. He can either make breakfast for himself (10-15 minutes), or get something to eat from a local store (less than 5 minutes). After breakfast (5-10 minutes), he goes to school either by car (20-30 minutes) or by bus (at least 45 minutes). Today, Tom gets up between 7:30 a.m. and 7:40 a.m.*

We wish to answer queries such as: "Can Tom arrive at school in time for class?", "Is it possible for Tom to take the bus?", "If Tom wanted to save money by making breakfast for himself and taking the bus, when should he get up?", and so on. This temporal problem can be represented as a temporal graph.

Let p_0 be a reference time-point (e.g., 6:00 am), p_1 the time point Tom gets up, p_2 the time point he starts his breakfast, p_3 the time point he finishes it, and p_4 the time point he arrives at the school. Fig. 2 shows the temporal graph of this TCSP.

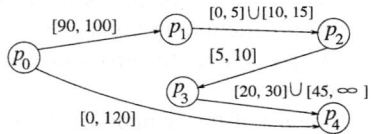

Fig. 2. A TCSP example.

Dechter [5] described a backtrack search procedure (BT-TCSP) for solving a TCSP, which is an NP-hard problem. To this end, the TCSP is expressed as a 'meta' Constraint Satisfaction Problem (meta-CSP). The variables of the meta-CSP are the edges $e_{i,j}$ of G. Their number depends on the density of the temporal graph. The domain of a variable $e_{i,j}$ is its label, $I_{i,j} = \{l_{ij}^{(1)}, l_{ij}^{(2)}, \ldots, l_{ij}^{(k)}\}$. A partial solution is a set $\{(e_{ij}, l_{ij}^{(h)})\}$ of variable-value pairs (vvps) that form a consistent STP, *which is a global constraint*. A complete solution is a consistent STP in which all the edges of G appear. The minimal network of the TCSP is the union of *all* complete solutions. Each node in the tree generated by BT-TCSP is an STP P' that has E' edges, a subset of the edges of the original network ($E' \subseteq E$), each labeled with a unique interval from its domain. When P' is consistent, the node is expanded by adding to P' an edge from $(E - E')$ labeled with an interval from its domain. This yields a new STP that is checked again for consistency. Fig. 3 illustrates the tree corresponding to the example of Fig. 2, where edges are considered in their lexicographical order.

In this paper, we combine the following techniques to improve the performance of BT-TCSP, and demonstrate their effectiveness on randomly generated problems:

1. Every node in the tree is an STP that needs to be solved before the search can proceed. Hence, the performance of a TCSP solver depends critically on that of the STP solver. We compare for the first time the performance of various known STP solvers, including a new one, $\triangle$STP, that we proposed in [21]. We show that it outperforms all others. Note that the performance of the STP solver does not affect the number of nodes visited in BT-TCSP.

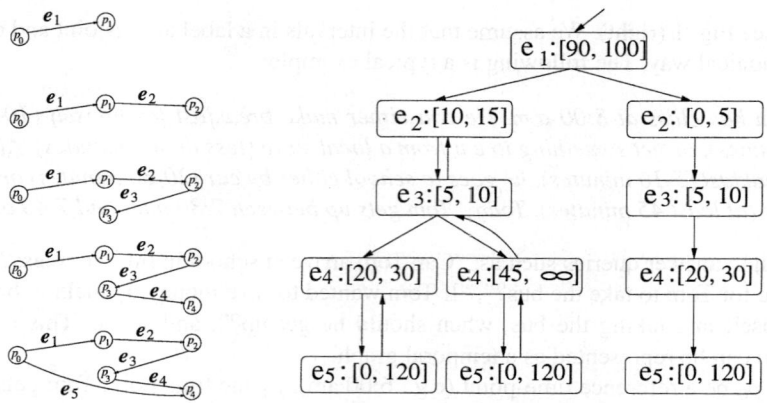

Fig. 3. The search tree for the example of Fig. 2.

2. One well-known technique to improve the performance of a CSP is to decompose it into sub-problems using its articulation points [9, 11, 6], and to solve the sub-problems independently. We provide for the first time an empirical evaluation of the effectiveness of this technique.

3. Further exploiting the topology of the temporal network, we show how to avoid running an STP-solver by checking for the existence of new cycles (NewCyc) in the network as edges are added along a given path in the tree. In the example of Fig. 3, the first four consistency checks are unnecessary because there are no cycles in the respective networks and the corresponding STPs are always consistent.

4. Another way to improve the performance of BT-TCSP is to find a good variable-ordering heuristic for the search. This corresponds to a sequencing of E, the edges of G, as they are added along a given path in the tree. A good sequence reduces unnecessary backtracking and also the number of constraint checks. We introduce a new ordering heuristic (EdgeOrd) that exploits the adjacency of existing triangles in the graph to determine the ordering of their edges in the tree.

5. We reduce the domains of the variables of the meta-CSP by using the efficient filtering algorithm, $\triangle$AC, described in [22].

The contributions of this paper can be summarized as follows:

1. A new technique for saving constraint checks (NewCyc) and a new ordering heuristic (EdgeOrd).

2. The combination of the above listed techniques (i.e., an STP-solver, AP, NewCyc, EdgeOrd, and $\triangle$AC) to find all the solutions of the TCSP.

3. Empirical evaluation and analysis of the effectiveness of these techniques and their combinations to demonstrate their significance.

This paper is structured as follows. Section 2 reviews the STP-solvers used. Section 3 discusses the three improvements exploiting the topology of the temporal network. Section 4 summarizes a filtering algorithm used as a preprocessing step. Section 5 describes our experiments and observations. Finally, Section 6 concludes this paper.

2   Algorithms for Solving the STP

TCSP is **NP**-hard and is solved with backtrack search. Every node expansion in the search tree needs to check the consistency of an STP. Thus a good STP solver is critical for solving the TCSP. We test the following STP solvers: Directed Path Consistency DPC [7], Partial Path Consistency PPC [2], and Triangle-STP $\triangle$STP [21].

2.1   Solving the STP Using Directional Path Consistency (DPC)

A basic algorithm to solve an STP is the Floyd-Warshall algorithm (F-W), which computes all-pairs shortest-paths in a distance graph [4]. F-W guarantees consistency, minimality, and decomposability and has a complexity of $\Theta(n^3)$. Montanari showed that F-W is a special case of the Path Consistency (PC) algorithm [15]. Dechter et al. propose the Directed-Path Consistency (DPC) algorithm [7]. This algorithm is never more costly than F-W, runs in $O(n^3)$, and can determine the consistency of an STP in $O(n(W^*(d))^2)$, where $W^*(d)$ is the induced width of the graph along a given ordering d. DPC determines the consistency of the STP, but does not necessarily yield the minimal and decomposable network. Since only the consistency of an STP matters during BT-TCSP, we use DPC instead of F-W because of its lower cost.

2.2   Solving the STP Using Partial Path Consistency (PPC)

Bliek and Sam-Haroud introduced Partial Path-Consistency (PPC), an algorithm applicable to general CSPs (and not restricted to temporal networks) [2]. PPC works on a triangulated graph, unlike the PC algorithm which requires a complete graph. Further, Bliek and Sam-Haroud showed that when the constraints are *convex*, the PC algorithm (operating on the complete graph) and the PPC algorithm (operating on the triangulated graph) yield equivalent results: the same labeling for the edges common to both graphs and the minimality and decomposability of the STP. PPC never requires more constraint checks than PC, which is advantageous when the (triangulated) graph is sparse. This is particularly attractive in BT-TCSP, which requires solving an STP at each node.

PPC requires that the graph be triangulated, which may result in new edges being added to the graph. We triangulate the temporal network using the algorithm devised in [17]. We represent the new edges as universal constraints in the original constraint graph and set their label to $(-\infty, \infty)$.

In the tree generated by BT-TCSP, each node represents an STP whose graph adds exactly one edge to the graph of the parent of the node (and must be triangulated to be used by PPC). Assuming a static ordering in the tree, the total number of graphs that appear along any given complete path is exactly equal to the number of edges in the original problem. Further, all nodes at a given level of the search tree have the same graph (only the edge labelings may vary). Thus, under static ordering, the number of possible graphs considered during the BT-TCSP process is exactly equal to the total number of edges in the temporal network.

We test two methods for accessing the triangulations of the STPs given a static variable ordering, Fig. 4. In the first method, *Plan A*, we pre-compute all the STPs needed in search, triangulate them, and store their triangulations for use during search.

All-triangulated-subgraphs (G_0, d)	Induced-subgraphs (G_t, G_i)
$G \leftarrow$ nil	$E_t \leftarrow$ edges of G_t
TriSubGs $\leftarrow$ nil	$N_i \leftarrow$ all nodes $\in G_i$
$E_0 \leftarrow$ all edges in G_0 using ordering d	$E_i \leftarrow$ nil
For $e \in E_0$ **do**	**Forall** $e_{i,j} \in E_t$
Push(e, G)	**When** $i \in N_i$ and $j \in N_i$
Push(**Triangulate**(G), *TriSubGs*)	**Then** Push($e_{i,j}$, E_i)
Return Reverse(*TriSubGs*)	**Return** E_i

Fig. 4. *Left:* List of triangulated subgraphs given an ordering. *Right:* Inducing a subgraph from the triangulated original graph.

In the second method, *Plan B*, we triangulate the entire network only once. We then induce from the triangulated graph the subgraph whose vertices form the STP under consideration. Since the original graph is triangulated, each induced subgraph is also triangulated.

- *Plan A*: Given a variable ordering d, the list of the graphs considered during BT-TCSP is generated as shown in Fig. 4 (left). Push adds an item to a list, Reverse reverses a list, and **Triangulate** triangulates a graph. We use the ith element of TriSubGs list as the triangulated subgraph for the node at the ith level of the tree.
- *Plan B:* Here we compute the triangulated graph only once and induce from it the subgraph needed at every step. Fig. 4 (right) shows the algorithm where G_t is the triangulated graph of the original network and G_i is the subgraph considered at level $1 \leq i \leq |E|$ in the search. Note that this technique may end up considering denser graphs than necessary, which increases the cost of solving the STP.

Our experimental results show that *Plan A* always outperforms *Plan B* in terms of the number of constraint checks and CPU time. Note that neither of these two plans affects the number of backtracks (the number of nodes visited) in BT-TCSP.

2.3   △STP Algorithm Used with TCSP Algorithm

△STP algorithm yields the same minimal network as F-W and PPC. It uses the idea of triangulation and considers the temporal graph as composed of triangles instead of edges. Constraint propagation is 'triangle-based' rather than 'edge-based.' As a finer version of PPC, △STP can find the minimal network with less cost than F-W and PPC. When density is low, △STP is even cheaper than DPC, which does not guarantee the minimal network. Similar to PPC, the pre-requisite condition for △STP is to first triangulate the temporal graph. We have introduced two plans to obtain triangulated subgraphs in the previous subsection. We will use *Plan A* for its lower cost in practice.

When solving a TCSP with search, the STP examined at each node in the search tree is a subgraph of the original TCSP. Since the STPs we need to check always have lower density than the original TCSP, the outstanding performance of △STP under low density makes it even more attractive to use for solving the TCSP.

3 Exploiting the Topology of the Constraint Network

We propose three topology-based techniques to enhance the performance of search. While the first technique is applied *prior* to search to decompose the problem into independent components, the last two are intertwined with the search process.

3.1 Decomposition Using Articulation Points

The existence of articulation points in the graph of the temporal network can be used to decompose the network into its biconnected components, which can be solved independently. Finding the articulation points can be done in $O(|E|)$ [4]. This method provides an upper bound to the search effort in the size of the largest biconnected component [11]. It can effectively reduce the number of constraint checks in BT-TCSP and the number of nodes visited in its tree. A solution to the entire network is a combination of any of the solutions of the biconnected components. The total number of solutions is: $S = \prod_{i=1}^{n} s_i$, where s_i is the number of solutions for component i. This conjunctive decomposition of the temporal network [12] allows us to solve the sub-problems in parallel, as in a multi-agent system. Articulation points usually appear only when the density is low or when the TCSP has a special topology. Note that even in the absence of articulation points, we could 'induce' such decompositions by removing some edges of the graph, in a manner similar to the cycle-cutset method of Dechter and Pearl [8]. We have implemented the mechanism for finding and using existing articulation points but not yet explored how to induce their existence.

3.2 New Cycle Check

The inconsistency of an STP is detected by the existence of a negative cycle in its distance graph. When the graph of an STP has no cycles, the STP is necessarily consistent.

Proposition 1. *A tree-structured constraint network is necessarily globally consistent.*

Note that is a stronger result than using the tree-structure of the constraint graph, which requires ensuring 2-consistency [10]. In BT-TCSP, nodes are expanded by adding one edge at a time. When the addition of a new edge does not yield a new cycle in the graph, a consistent STP remains consistent regardless of the labeling chosen for the new edge. We exploit this observation to save unnecessary consistency checks.

Corollary 1. *When the addition of an edge to a globally consistent STP yields no new cycles, the resulting STP is globally consistent.*

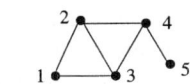

Fig. 5. Simple constraint graph.

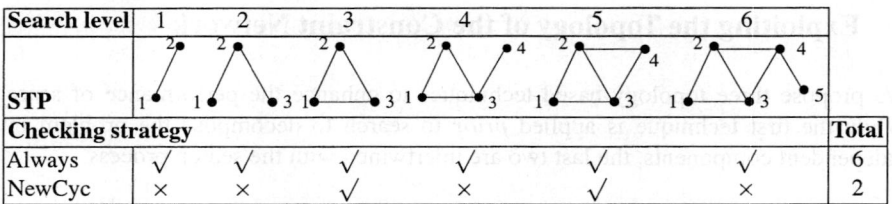

Search level	1	2	3	4	5	6	
STP							
Checking strategy							**Total**
Always	✓	✓	✓	✓	✓	✓	6
NewCyc	×	×	✓	×	✓	×	2

Fig. 6. Comparison of STP checks using the new-cycle check heuristic.

Consider the example of Fig. 5. Suppose that search adopts the following ordering of the edges: $e_{1,2}$, $e_{2,3}$, $e_{1,3}$, $e_{3,4}$, $e_{2,4}$, and $e_{4,5}$. Fig. 6 shows the configurations of the STPs checked for consistency at each level in the search.

Along a given path, as the tree generated by search is being explored in a depth-first manner, two strategies can be adopted at a given level: (1) Always check the STP for consistency, and (2) check the consistency of the STP only when a new cycle has been added to the network. At levels 1 and 2, no cycles exist in the graph, and the STP is necessarily consistent, Fig. 6. At levels 4 and 6, no new cycles have been added to the graph of levels 3 and 5 respectively, and the corresponding STPs remain necessarily consistent regardless of their labeling. As illustrated above, checking for new cycles saves us unnecessary operations. Further, when the addition of a new edge yields a new cycle, two biconnected components of the previous level are necessarily merged into a new biconnected component at the current level. We need to check *only* the consistency of the newly formed biconnected component, and we can safely ignore the rest of the temporal network. This allows us to localize the effort of consistency checking to the necessary part of the network.

Corollary 2. *When the addition of an edge to a globally consistent STP yields a new cycle, the resulting STP is globally consistent if and only if the newly formed biconnected component is a consistent STP.*

The application of this new heuristic, NewCyc, significantly enhances the performance of solving the meta-CSP with search. To apply it, we need to identify, between two levels of the search tree, (1) that a new cycle has been introduced and (2) the two biconnected components that were merged as a result. This is done by running the $O(|E|)$ algorithm for finding articulation points at each level, checking whether the number of biconnected components was reduced between two levels, and identifying the component to be checked as that containing the new edge.

3.3   Ordering Heuristic for the Meta-CSP

Variable ordering is an effective heuristic for improving the performance of search. In general, it is governed by the 'fail first principle.' The shallower the node pruned in the tree, the larger the pruned subtree, and the larger the cost savings. For the meta-CSP, a node is pruned when it corresponds to an inconsistent STP. Thus, the ordering of the edges (which are the variables of the meta-CSP) affects how quickly an inconsistent STP is found and also the effectiveness of constraint propagation in the STP.

As stated in Corollary 1, along a given path, no inconsistency may occur between one level and the next unless at least one new cycle is formed in the temporal graph. Consequently, a reasonable ordering heuristic is to first consider those edges that form triangles with edges existing in the STP. This may allow us to uncover inconsistencies as early as possible. It also increases the effectiveness of backtracking, because it is more likely to undo an inconsistency by changing the labeling of an edge in the same triangle as the one that yielded the inconsistency than that of a random edge. Our new edge-ordering heuristic orders the edges of the temporal graph in such a way that the network is expanded triangle by triangle 'around' the existing edges. The algorithm, given in Fig. 7, returns the list of edges in the order to be used by the search. It uses basic operations on lists. Append concatenates two lists in the order provided. Pop removes and returns the first item in a list. It requires that each edge be associated with the number

---

EdgeOrd (G)
$E_0 \leftarrow$ all edges of G
$E \leftarrow$ nil
While E_0 **do**
$\quad e_{i,j} \leftarrow$ Edge of E_0 appearing in the largest number of triangles in E_0
$\quad E \leftarrow$ Append $(E, \{e_{i,j}\})$
$\quad Q \leftarrow$ nil
$\quad$ **While** $e_{i,j}$ **do**
$\quad\quad$ **Forall** k such that ijk is a subgraph of G **do**
$\quad\quad\quad Q \leftarrow$ Append $(Q, \{e_{i,k}, e_{j,k}\}),\ \ E \leftarrow$ Append $(E, \{e_{i,k}, e_{j,k}\})$
$\quad\quad\quad E_0 \leftarrow E_0 \setminus \{e_{i,j}, e_{i,k}, e_{j,k}\}, \quad\quad e_{i,j} \leftarrow$ Pop(Q)
Return E

Fig. 7. Edge ordering heuristic.

of triangles in which it appears in G, which is bounded by $(n-1)$, where n is the number of nodes in G (i.e., the time points). We obtain these numbers as a by-product of the implementation of the triangulation algorithm.

Based on the topology of the network, we choose the edge that participates in the largest number of triangles and schedule the edges of those triangles for a priority instantiation during the search. Fig. 8 illustrates the first steps of the application of the algorithm starting from edge I. First, the triangles in which edge I participates are explored. From there, we reapply iteratively the same process to each of the edges explored, i.e. edges II, III, and IV, gradually covering all the edges in the biconnected component. The modification of the label of any these edges propagates through these triangles. Thus, inconsistencies and deadends are likely to be more quickly detected during search, and backtrack remains locally contained.

We can show that this process stops when all the edges in the biconnected component have been visited. Then EdgeOrd restarts from an unvisited edge from the original graph and repeats the process until all edges of the original network have been visited. The function returns a list in which the edges that are in a given biconnected component appear in sequence. As a result, this ordering heuristic implicitly enables search to

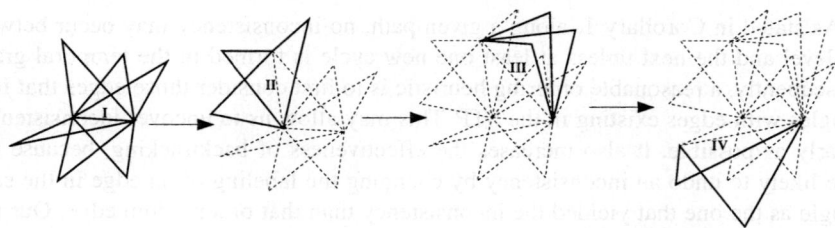

Fig. 8. Illustrating the exploration of the edges of a graph by the edge ordering heuristic.

examine the biconnected components of the graph in isolation, and thus decompose the graph automatically. The advantages of this mechanism are:

1. *Localized backtracking*: Neighboring levels in the search tree are likely to correspond to edges that form a triangle and thus are topologically related. When it encounters a deadend, search will backtrack to an edge that is more likely the culprit than another edge taken randomly from the graph.
2. *Automatic decomposition of the graph into its biconnected components*: This ordering heuristic implicitly guarantees that articulation points in the graph (if any), are exploited, as if the network was decomposed into its biconnected components without using the special algorithm necessary for this purpose (see Section 3.1).

We believe, but still need to show, that these features make EdgeOrd a more effective heuristic than a dynamic variable-ordering heuristic based only on domain size.

4 △Arc-Consistency

When solving a CSP, it is common to run a domain filtering mechanism (such as arc-consistency, AC) as a preprocessing step to search, and to interleave search with a lookahead strategy (such as forward-checking, FC [13]). Consistency checking may reduce the domain of the variables, thus reducing the size of the CSP and the search effort.

The size of the meta-CSP is exponential in the size of the TCSP. If k is the number of intervals in the label of an edge in the TCSP, $|E|$ is the number of edges, and n is the number of nodes where $|E| \leq \frac{n(n-1)}{2}$, the size of the meta-CSP is in $O(k^{|E|})$. Thus it is important to explore mechanisms to reduce the size of the meta-CSP by removing 'inconsistent' intervals from the edge labels. The only constraint in the meta-CSP is a *global* constraint that requires all variable-value pairs of the meta-CSP to form a consistent STP. Thus, for the meta-CSP, AC is the generalized arc-consistency of this unique constraint, which is NP-hard [22]. In [22], we introduce the concept of △Arc-Consistency as an approximation of the generalized arc-consistency of the meta-CSP. We also introduce an efficient algorithm, △AC, that implements △Arc-Consistency. This algorithm ensures that for every interval $l_{ij}^{(x)}$ in the domain of a meta-CSP variable $e_{i,j}$ there exist an interval $l_{ik}^{(y)}$ in the domain of the meta-CSP variable $e_{i,k}$ and an interval $l_{kj}^{(z)}$ in the domain of the meta-CSP variable $e_{k,j}$ such that $l_{ij}^{(x)} \cap (l_{ik}^{(y)} \circ l_{kj}^{(z)}) \neq \emptyset$, where $\cap$ is interval intersection and ∘ is interval composition [5]. We establish that the complexity of △AC is $O(degree(G) \times |E| \times k^3) = O(n|E|k^3)$. The value of △AC lies in the data structures it uses, reminiscent of AC-4 [14] and AC-2001 [1], to save significantly the number of constraint checks[1]. We have not yet used △AC in a lookahead strategy, but plan to do so in the future.

5   Experimental Results

Fig. 9 shows the TCSP solvers we tested, with and without pre-processing by △AC.

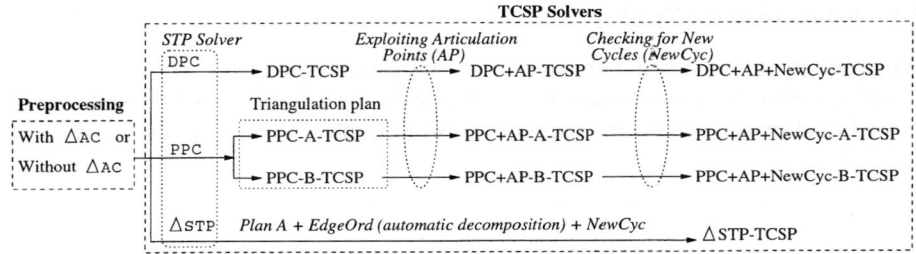

Fig. 9. TCSP solvers tested.

The STP solvers we used are DPC, PPC, and △STP all as described in Section 2. The network is triangulated only prior to PPC and △STP. We combined these STP solvers with the techniques proposed in Section 3 (i.e., AP, NewCyc, and EdgeOrd). Since we have not yet implemented a lookahead strategy, all the TCSP solvers tested use a static variable ordering. By default, and except for △STP-TCSP (where we use EdgeOrd), it is a lexicographical ordering of the lexicographically sorted tuples naming the edges by their two endpoints. We compared the performance of the TCSP solvers in terms of the number of nodes visited NV, constraint checks CC, and CPU time. Since all CPU time curves have almost exactly the same shapes as the CC curves, *they are omitted to save space but are all available upon request.* We carried out our tests on randomly generated, (guaranteed) connected problems. Our generator, described in [22], guarantees that at least 80% of these problems have at least one solution. The TCSP instances generated have the following characteristics: $n = 8$, k randomly chosen between 1 and 5, density of the temporal network ($d = \frac{|E|-|E_{min}|}{|E_{max}|-|E_{min}|}$) varies in [0.02, 0.1] with a step of 0.02 and in [0.2, 0.9] with a step of 0.1. The number of variables in the meta-CSP, for which we find *all solutions*, varies from 7 to 26. The size of the meta-CSP varies on average between 1.6×10^5 and 5.2×10^{15}. We averaged the results of over 100 samples. The goal of our experiments was to study the *effects* on the various solvers of the improvements we proposed[2] (i.e., △STP, AP, NewCyc, EdgeOrd, △AC), and to establish their effectiveness. An extensive comparison of the the performance of the various STP solvers can be found in [21].

---

[1] We are investigating an improvement that may establish its optimality.

[2] Note that although decomposition according to articulation points is a well-known technique, to the best of our knowledge, it has not been yet assessed experimentally.

Section 5.1 discusses the number of solutions of the problems tested. Naturally, all solvers find the same solutions. Section 5.2 shows the effect of our techniques on the shape of the tree by measuring the number of nodes visited. Section 5.3 shows the effect of our techniques on the various TCSP solvers (i.e., DPC, PPC, and $\triangle$STP) on the number of constraint checks. In Sections 5.2 and 5.3 we also show how filtering the meta-CSP with $\triangle$AC dramatically improves the performance of search. The effect of this preprocessing is clearly visible in comparisons of the scale of the vertical axis of the charts without and after preprocessing. While the benefits of this filtering algorithm are discussed in [22], we confirm here that it is useful in every TCSP solver we tested.

5.1   Solutions to the TCSP

When density is low, there are few constraints, any partial solution is likely to be extended to a global solution, and there are many solutions to the meta-CSP as is seen in Fig. 10. Indeed, under low density, the temporal network (which is guaranteed connected by

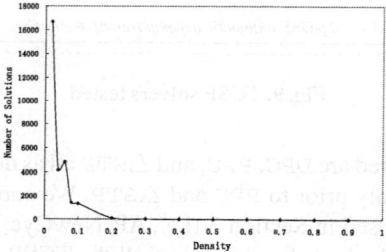

Fig. 10. The number of solutions of the meta-CSP.

construction) has almost no cycles. Thus, almost any combination of intervals in the label of the edges is a solution to the meta-CSP (see Proposition 1). The number of solutions quickly drops as density rises. When $d=0.9$, there are only one or two solutions, one of which is guaranteed by construction.

5.2   Effects on the Size of the Search Tree

The effects of AP and EdgeOrd on the 'shape' of the tree can be assessed by the number of nodes visited NV by search. They are shown in Fig. 11.

Note that the effects of NewCyc on the various STP solvers (i.e., DPC, PPC, and $\triangle$STP) are irrelevant to this measurement. Indeed, they aim at reducing the cost of checking the consistency of the STP at a node in the tree once search has effectively reached the node. The '*' in the legend of Fig. 11 indicates that these results hold for all STP solvers tested. Fig. 11 shows that AP reduces significantly NV when density is low. When density is high, almost no articulation point exists, hence AP does not impact NV. The effect of EdgeOrd is quite dramatic across all values for density because it allows BT-TCSP to quickly identify dead-ends, as a good ordering heuristic is supposed to do. Moreover, and thanks to $\triangle$AC, we start to notice the existence of a phase transition

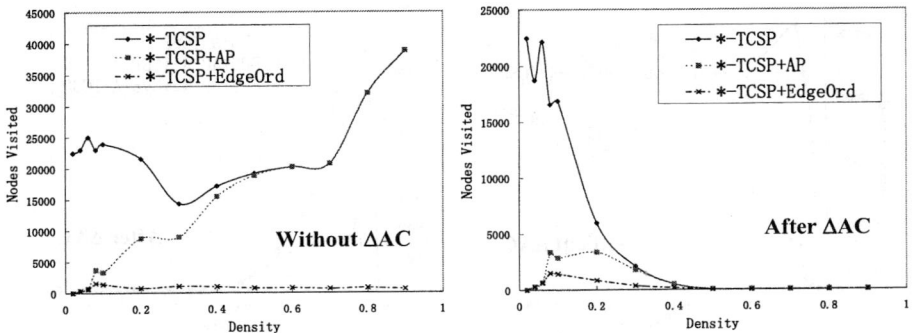

Fig. 11. Nodes visited by BT-TCSP. Left: without preprocessing. Right: after filtering with $\triangle$AC.

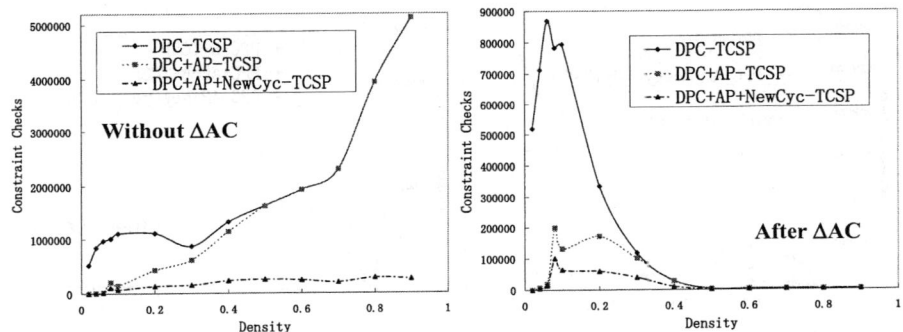

Fig. 12. Constraint checks for *DPC-TCSP*.

that appears around $d = 0.1$ and becomes increasingly visible as we move toward more effective TCSP solvers.

5.3   Effects on the Number of Constraints Checks (Same as CPU Time)

Here we discuss the effects of our techniques on the various TCSP solvers: DPC, PPC, and $\triangle$STP. We show the benefits of AP and NewCyc on DPC (Fig. 12). We show the benefits of AP, NewCyc on PPC for both *Plan A* (Fig. 13) and *Plan B* (Fig. 14) Finally, we show the benefits of EdgeOrd and NewCyc under *Plan A* on $\triangle$STP (Fig. 15).

Exploiting Articulation Points: For DPC (Fig 12) and PPC (Fig. 13 and 14), AP is again particularly effective for low density graphs but useless for high density ones.

New Cycle Check: NewCyc dramatically reduces CC across all density values (even though it has no effect on the number of nodes visited, as stated in Section 5.2).

Triangulation Plans: The triangulation of an STP during search, required for PPC solver, is carried out according to *Plan A* (Fig. 13) and *Plan B* (Fig. 14) of Section 2.2. By comparing the scale of the vertical axis of these two figures, we conclude that *Plan A*

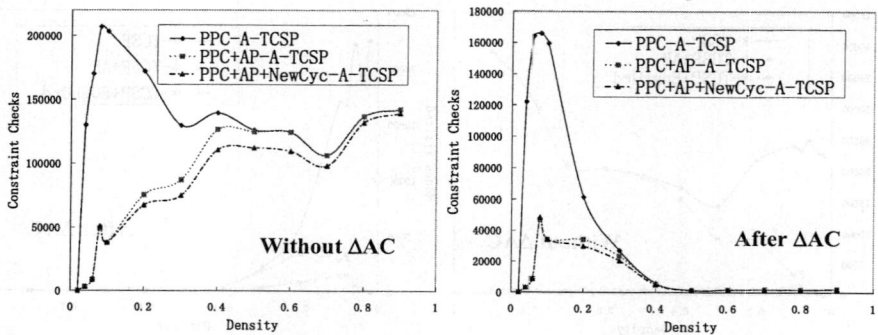

Fig. 13. Constraint checks for *PPC-TPCS* using Plan A.

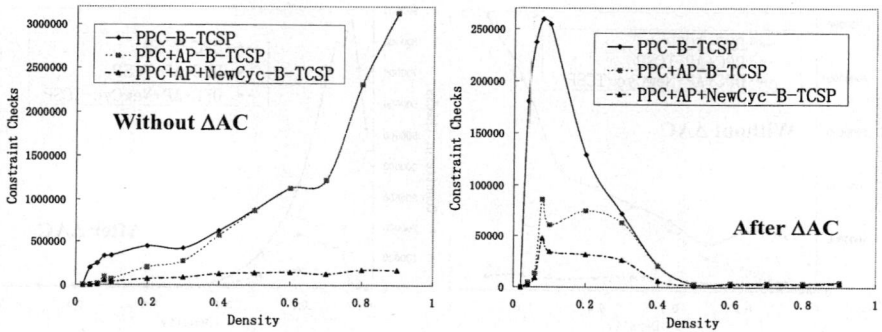

Fig. 14. Constraint checks for *PPC-TCSP* using Plan B.

is superior to *Plan B*. This can be explained as follows. *Plan A* triangulates, before search, all the networks that will be checked for consistency during search (there are exactly $|E|$ such graphs). *Plan B* finds the triangulation of an STP at a given node during search by inducing a subgraph from the triangulated original STP. Hence, *Plan B* triangulates the network only once, while *Plan A* carries out as many triangulation operations as the number of edges in the network (and levels in the search). However, the induced subgraphs in *Plan B* end up much denser than the ones used by *Plan A*, thus requiring more effort from PPC, the STP solver. Further, the fact that *Plan A* yields no denser graphs than *Plan B* becomes an even more desirable feature when TCSP is dense. This explains the significant differences in behavior between *Plan A* and *Plan B* under high density TCSPs.

The Winning Combination: In [21] we compared the performances of F-W, DPC, PPC, and △STP for solving an STP. We found that DPC, PPC, and △STP consistently outperform F-W, the Floyd-Warshall algorithm. Further, △STP consistently outperforms PPC. Indeed, the former is a finer version of the latter. Importantly, when the density of the temporal graph is below 0.4, △STP (which guarantees minimality) outperforms DPC (which does not). For sensibly high densities, we found DPC to be more effective. Since in the search for solving the meta-CSP we consider subgraphs of the original network,

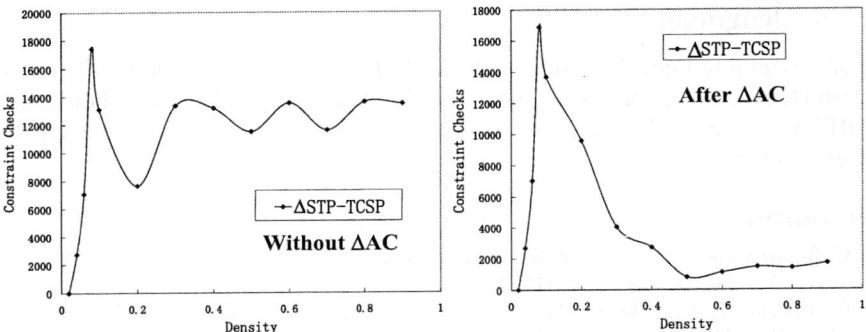

Fig. 15. Constraint checks for $\triangle$STP-TCSP.

the networks at the different levels of the tree are more likely to be sparse than dense. This shows that even when the TCSP is dense, $\triangle$STP is a good choice for the STP solver. Hence, among the techniques tested, the best combination one could use to solve a TCSP is the one we called $\triangle$STP-TCSP (Fig. 9). Indeed $\triangle$STP outperforms all TCSP solvers including the one based on DPC (compare Fig. 12 and 15).

6   Conclusions

At the beginning of our investigations, the best mechanism known to date for solving the meta-CSP[3] was one based on DPC. We introduced $\triangle$STP, enhanced it with NewCyc and EdgeOrd, and showed empirically that it results in dramatic improvements. Indeed, in comparison to the original DPC, the best combination of our techniques reduces the number of constraint checks by a factor of 500 (median) and 40,000 (average) and that of CPU by a factor of 320 (median) and 1,200 (average).

Further, we showed that our techniques uncover the existence of a phase-transition-like phenomenon for solving the TCSP as the density of the network varies[4]. This is most visible with $\triangle$STP-TCSP. This observation calls for more detailed investigations in this direction. As directions for future research, we plan to:

1. Exploit $\triangle$AC in a lookahead strategy for solving the meta-TCSP. And,
2. Evaluate empirically how to improve BT-TCSP with dynamic bundling [3].

Beyond the TCSP, $\triangle$STP is directly applicable for solving the disjunctive temporal problem (DTP) with backtrack search [19, 16, 20], but requires triangulating the STP incrementally at each node in the tree. We believe that NewCyc is also applicable as long as the constraint added applies to two points that are not yet constrained in the current path in the tree. These directions require further investigation and evaluation.

---

[3] Note that we do not include in our comparison algorithms that tighten these intervals in the labels of the edges. Those may not terminate in the general case and are prohibitively expensive in the integral case [18].

[4] Schwalb and Dechter [18] report a similar phenomenon when varying the number of variables and the tightness of the constraints.

Acknowledgments

We are grateful to Eddie Schwalb and Rina Dechter for various pointers to TCSPs and to Deb Derrick for editorial help. This work is supported by a NASA-Nebraska grant, CAREER Award #0133568 from the National Science Foundation, and a gift from Honeywell Laboratories.

References

1. C. Bessière and J.-C. Régin. Refining the Basic Constraint Propagation Algorithm. In *Proc. of the 17th IJCAI*, pages 309–315, 2001.
2. C. Bliek and D. Sam-Haroud. Path Consistency for Triangulated Constraint Graphs. In *Proc. of the 16th IJCAI*, pages 456–461, 1999.
3. B.Y. Choueiry and A.M. Davis. Dynamic Bundling: Less Effort for More Solutions. In Koenig and Holte, editors, *5th International Symposium on Abstraction, Reformulation and Approximation (SARA 2002)*, vol 2371 of *LNAI*, pages 64–82. Springer Verlag, 2002.
4. T.H. Cormen, C.E. Leiserson, and R.L. Rivest. *Introduction to Algorithms*. McGraw-Hill Book Co & MIT Press, 2001.
5. R. Dechter. *Constraint Programming*. Morgan Kaufmann, 2003.
6. R. Dechter, I. Meiri, and J. Pearl. Temporal Constraint Networks. *Artificial Intelligence*, 49:61–95, 1991.
7. R. Dechter and J. Pearl. Network-Based Heuristics for Constraint-Satisfaction Problems. *Artificial Intelligence*, 34:1–38, 1987.
8. R. Dechter and J. Pearl. The Cycle-Cutset Method for improving Search Performance in AI Applications. In *Third IEEE Conference on AI Applications*, pages 224–230, 1987.
9. S. Even. *Graph Algorithm*. Computer Science Press, 1979.
10. E.C. Freuder. A Sufficient Condition for Backtrack-Free Search. *JACM*, 29 (1):24–32, 1982.
11. E.C. Freuder. A Sufficient Condition for Backtrack-Bounded Search. *JACM*, 32 (4):755–761, 1985.
12. E.C. Freuder and P.D. Hubbe. A Disjunctive Decomposition Control Schema for Constraint Satisfaction. In Vijay Saraswat and Pascal Van Hentenryck, editors, *Principles and Practice of Constraint Programming*, pages 319–335. MIT Press, 1995.
13. R.M. Haralick and G.L. Elliott. Increasing Tree Search Efficiency for Constraint Satisfaction Problems. *Artificial Intelligence*, 14:263–313, 1980.
14. R. Mohr and T.C. Henderson. Arc and Path Consistency Revisited. *Artificial Intelligence*, 28:225–233, 1986.
15. U. Montanari. Networks of Constraints: Fundamental Properties and Application to Picture Processing. *Information Sciences*, 7:95–132, 1974.
16. A. Oddi and A. Cesta. Incremental Forward Checking for the Disjunctive Temporal Problem. In *Proc. of the 14th ECAI*, 2000.
17. U. Kjærulff. Triangulation of Graphs - Algorithms Giving Small Total State Space. Research Report R-90-09, Aalborg University, Denmark, 1990.
18. E. Schwalb and R. Dechter. Processing Disjunctions in Temporal Constraint Networks. *Artificial Intelligence*, 93:29–61, 1997.
19. K. Stergiou and M. Koubarakis. Backtracking Algorithms for Disjunctions of Temporal Constraints. *Artificial Intelligence*, 12- (1):81–117, 2000.
20. I. Tsamardinos and M.E. Pollack. Efficient Solution Techniques for Disjunctive Temporal Reasoning Problems. *Artificial Intelligence*, 2003. In press.
21. L. Xu and B.Y. Choueiry. A New Efficient Algorithm for Solving the Simple Temporal Problem. In *Proc. of the 10th TIME-ICTL*, 2003. IEEE Computer Society Press.
22. L. Xu and B.Y. Choueiry. An Approximation of Generalized Arc-Consistency for TCSPs. In *Working notes of the Workshop on Spatial and Temporal Reasoning (IJCAI 03)*, 2003.

Certainty Closure

A Framework for Reliable Constraint Reasoning with Uncertainty

Neil Yorke-Smith and Carmen Gervet

IC–Parc, Imperial College London, SW7 2AZ, UK
{nys,cg6}@icparc.ic.ac.uk

Abstract. Constraint problems with incomplete or erroneous data are often simplified to tractable deterministic models, or modified using error correction methods, with the aim of seeking a solution. However, this can lead us to solve the wrong problem because of the approximations made. Such an outcome is of little help to a user who expects the right problem to be tackled and reliable information returned. The *certainty closure* framework we present aims to provide the user with reliable insight by: (1) enclosing the uncertainty using what is known for sure about the data, to guarantee that the true problem is contained in the model so described, (2) deriving a closure, a set of possible solutions to the uncertain constraint problem. In this paper we first demonstrate the benefits of reliable constraint reasoning on two different case studies, and then generalise our approaches into a formal framework.

1 Motivation

Data uncertainties are inherent in real-world Large Scale Combinatorial Optimisation problems (LSCOs). The uncertainty can be due to the dynamic and unpredictable nature of the commercial world, but also due to the information available to those modelling the problem. In this paper we are concerned with the latter form of uncertainty, which can arise when the data is not fully known or is even erroneous.

Our work is motivated by practical issues we faced when addressing two real-world applications: energy trading [10] and network traffic analysis [11]. In both applications the data information is incomplete or erroneous. In the energy trading problem, the demand and cost profiles had evolved due to market privatisation; thus the existing simulation or stochastic models did not help address the actual problem, since no valid data trends were available. Further, the obsolete data was inconsistent with the constraint model. In the network traffic analysis problem, the overwhelming amount of information forced us to use partial data. Further, due to practical measurement difficulties (e.g. unrecorded packet loss), the data acquired in the problem was frequently erroneous.

When addressing the energy trading problem, we understood that the customer did not need nor want a solution to an approximation of his problem, but rather a guarantee that the model built was reliable, and that from it informed decisions could be made. Informally, a model and solution are *reliable* with respect to the state of the world if they accurately reflect the true problem and its possible solutions. The uncertain data is represented using what is known for sure about it, without any approximation, and no potential solutions are excluded. Our goal was to build such a model and to provide

F. Rossi (Ed.): CP 2003, LNCS 2833, pp. 769–783, 2003.

effective insight into the set of possible solutions. It became clear that further research was necessary to extend the potential of constraint programming to meet this goal.

Indeed, in the face of data uncertainty, existing CP approaches come from quite a different perspective. Models and methods have been proposed to tackle incomplete and dynamic data by seeking robust solutions to the problem, i.e. solutions that hold under the maximum number of possible states of the world [8]; or by reasoning upon probabilistic data distributions [5, 21]. These approaches are suited for applications where data trends are available and realistic, or where robustness is sought after: for example, dynamic scheduling problems. However, they are less suited for the reliable reasoning our motivational problems demand.

In this paper we focus on uncertainty due to incomplete or erroneous data. With the aim of providing the user with reliable insight, our threefold objective is:

1. To create a reliable model of the LSCO, i.e. remove approximations about the data and enclose the true problem in the model.
2. To compute the *full closure*, i.e. the set of all possible solutions to the model; or a subset of it as the user specifies. By possible, we mean a solution that holds for at least one realisation of the data.
3. To propose two resolution forms to solve uncertain CSPs, and give instances over specific constraint classes.

In Sect. 2, we first show on two different uncertain LSCOs how we can attain such an objective in practice. We then generalise the case studies as instances of the certainty closure framework, in Sect. 3 and 4. The framework, based on the CSP formalism, allows us to reason about uncertain problems by modelling explicitly what is known about the uncertain data in terms of an *uncertain constraint satisfaction problem* (UCSP). We define a UCSP and its full closure. Then, we formally describe two resolution forms that can derive closures in a practical way, and we give examples of the forms for various classes of UCSPs. In Sect. 5 we review and contrast with related work, and finally we conclude in Sect. 6.

2   Case Studies

Despite the presence of incompleteness or errors, we assume that those modelling the problem do have some definite knowledge about the data. We use this knowledge to enclose the uncertainty within an interval or a set of values. We assume further that knowledge about the data is only refined (e.g. to a subset of the initial possible values). Since the closure excludes no possible solution, we guarantee that the true solution lies in the closure whatever the state of the world. However, the closure might comprise of a large set of solutions. A key issue therefore is how informative it is in practice, and how complex it is to derive and represent.

In this section we investigate the practical benefits of reliable constraint reasoning by considering two quite different case studies which address real-world problems. The first case study is the network traffic analysis problem introduced earlier; the second is a planning problem in the aerospace domain. In both, an uncertain CSP is presented, together with a solution operator used to derive the closures. Both problems were modelled and solved using the ECL^{i}PS^e CLP platform [13].

2.1 Network Traffic Analysis

The network traffic analysis problem poses a diagnosis question. The problem is: for a known network with incomplete and possibly erroneous traffic measurements at routers, determine guaranteed bounds for each end-to-end traffic flow. The true problem must be satisfiable, because the network exists and is executing. The complexity lies in adequately handling the data, in guaranteeing that the right problem is being solved, and in seeking tight bounds. We illustrate our approach on an example fragment of a network.

Initial Model. Consider the fragment of a network shown in Fig. 1. Four nodes, corresponding to routers and designated A–D, are shown, together with the bidirectional traffic flow on each link. Each router makes decisions on how to direct traffic it receives, based on a routing algorithm.

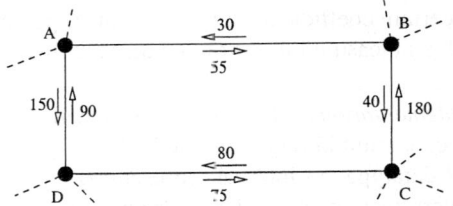

Fig. 1. Traffic flow in a network fragment

The network was initially modelled as a classical CSP, as follows. The variables correspond to the traffic flow between any two end-points, and their domains are the non-negative reals: $V_{ij} \in \mathbb{R}^+$ is the volume of traffic entering the network at node i and leaving it at node j. The constraints form a linear flow model. They state that the volume of traffic through each link in each direction is the sum of the traffic entering the link in that direction. There is also an upper bound (here, 64) on the flows that use only a single link, such as V_{AB} or V_{AD}.

The traffic volume data is collected by reading router tables at each node over a given time interval (e.g. 20 minutes). As a result, the data information obtained is erroneous. On the link D→C, for example, the flow might measure as 70 at D and as 80 at C, whereas the true value, equal at both nodes, is presumably somewhere in between. A common approach therefore is to use the median value.

Another source of uncertainty comes from traffic routing. In 90% of cases, the traffic is known to be split equally when two paths are of equal cost (from the perspective of the routing algorithm). In our running example we consider this to be the case for flows between any two non-consecutive nodes, e.g. from A to C. To simplify the model, it was first assumed that the traffic is split equally in all such cases. For example, on the link A→D the traffic flow constraint generated is:

$$A \rightarrow D \qquad\qquad V_{AD} + 0.5V_{AC} + 0.5V_{ED} = 150 \qquad\qquad (1)$$

The generated CSP model was unsatisfiable. Thus a data correction procedure (minimising deviation on the link traffic volumes) was employed in order to reach a satisfiable, deterministic model. The resulting model was solved using the most suitable techniques; in this case standard Linear Programming (LP). Maximum and minimum bounds were derived for each flow variable V_i by solving two linear programs, with objectives max V_i and min V_i respectively.

Certainty Closure Approach. The first approach amalgamated data uncertainty and constraint satisfiability issues. Our aim was to investigate whether the approach was leading to the true problem, and hence whether the bounds obtained were reliable. We therefore removed the approximations made: we represented the uncertain flow measurements explicitly, and we modelled the splitting of traffic, actually known to be anywhere between 30–70%. We modelled the problem as an uncertain CSP. For example, on the link A→D we have the following constraint (in which $[\underline{a}, \overline{a}]$ denotes an interval):

$$\text{A→D} \qquad V_{AD} + [0.3, 0.7]V_{AC} + [0.3, 0.7]V_{BD} = [135, 160] \qquad (2)$$

Uncertain coefficients thus represent (i) percentage of traffic going through each route, and (ii) measured flow volume on each link.

Implementation and Solving. We modelled and solved the problem using the `ic` interval constraint library from the ECL^{i}PS^e platform [13]. The library provides a *bounded real* datatype: an interval representing an unknown real value; and interval constraint solvers over numerical constraint systems of arbitrary combinations of integer and bounded real variables. Using `ic`, we can model constraints such as (2) simply by: V_{AD} + 0.3__0.7 V_{AC} + 0.3__0.7 V_{BD} = 135__160.

To calculate the closure, we first tried to solve the uncertain CSP as is, using interval and quantified CSP methods (e.g. [4, 15]). The methods proved costly or unsuited to producing tight bounds when compared with the presented method. We then considered a transformation of the uncertain model to an equivalent certain CSP, in order to benefit from existing resolution methods for standard CSPs. We defined a transform operator and proved its correctness using methods from interval linear programming [7]. A full description of the transformation can be found in [22].

Hereafter, we illustrate the transform in the three variable case for simplicity. Let V_1, V_2 and V_3 be variables with domains in $\mathbb{R}^+$. Then the constraints have the form c: $a_1 V_1 + a_2 V_2 + a_3 V_3 \leq a_4$, where $a_i = [\underline{a_i}, \overline{a_i}]$ are real, closed intervals. Each uncertain flow constraint c can be transformed into a certain constraint $\tau(c)$ as follows:

$$\tau(c) = \begin{cases} \underline{a_1}V_1 + \underline{a_2}V_2 + \underline{a_3}V_3 \leq \overline{a_4} & \text{if } \underline{a_3} \geq 0 \\ \underline{a_1}V_1 + \underline{a_2}V_2 + \overline{a_3}V_3 \leq \underline{a_4} & \text{if } 0 \in a_3 \\ \overline{a_1}V_1 + \overline{a_2}V_2 + \overline{a_3}V_3 \leq \underline{a_4} & \text{if } \overline{a_3} < 0 \end{cases} \qquad (3)$$

By convexity, it suffices to operate on the bounds of the data values. The transformation operates only on linear inequalities. Thus as a prelude to the transform, each equality constraint is replaced by a pair of inequalities; the decision variables remain unchanged. For example, the constraint (2) above is transformed to:

$$(V_{AD} + 0.3V_{AC} + 0.3V_{BD} \leq 160) \wedge (V_{AD} + 0.3V_{AC} + 0.3V_{BD} \geq 160) \qquad (4)$$

The resulting model, like the initial model, describes a standard LP problem. Thus we can solve it using the same method, but now we obtain guaranteed bounds. For the example above, we obtain the following intervals, which represent the projection of the closure onto the variable domains: $V_{AC} \in [0, 150]$, $V_{AD} \in [30, 64]$, $V_{BD} \in [0, 133]$, $V_{BA} \in [0, 20]$, $V_{DC} \in [0, 40]$, $V_{DB} \in [32, 200]$, $V_{CA} \in [0, 133]$, $V_{CB} \in [17, 64]$ (omitting the four single-link flows in the clockwise direction).

Outcome. Compared to the initial approach to the problem, the certainty closure has lead to more reliable quantitative results and to improved understanding of the relationship between network topology and traffic flow. For instance, if the closure is empty, we can infer that the problem is unsatisfiable due to the constraint network and not due to the data: since no approximation is considered but the data enclosure. Treating the data adequately reveals the true reasons for unsatisfiability.

2.2   Planning for Aerospace Equipment

The second case study arises in the aerospace domain, where future systems will be expected to achieve more complex missions with less human intervention [20]. The system must continuously operate in a changing, ill-known environment; command complicated equipment; and simultaneously fulfill mission goals and satisfy system requirements, e.g. timeliness and safety. On the whole, however, existing aerospace component design does not integrate uncertainty into autonomous planning functions [20].

Fig. 2 shows an example automaton, representing the behaviour of a thruster subsystem (a satellite 'engine'). The goal is to achieve a certain thrust performance in a given time window, while maintaining the internal temperature within given limits. Temperature, however, evolves in an ill-known way according to the heating (thrust) and cooling states. We model the thruster as a non-deterministic finite state automaton (FSA) where temperatures are attached to transitions and states of the automaton. The data uncertainty concerns the temperature increments, which are subject to both measurement errors and incomplete information. We associate with the automaton the following constraint model.

Model. Our constraint model is again an uncertain CSP. Here it is simplified for the sake of clarity; a full description is found in [23]. The variables are all finite domain integers. A path in the automaton is specified by transition and timing variables. The transitions $S_i \in [0, N]$ are a sequence of states, where S_0 is the initial state. The timings $T_i \in \mathbb{N}$ specify the duration spent in each state. We write $i \in [0, H]$ to index the states on the path, and $j \in [0, N]$ for the value of the jth state: i.e. $j = S_i$. Associated with the path are edge boolean variables $E_j \in \{0, 1\}$, which specify whether an edge is ever taken on the path. Finally, the temperature is modelled with variables $\Theta_i \in [0, 100]$, and the uncertain temperature increments with coefficients $\Delta_j \in [-100, 100]$.

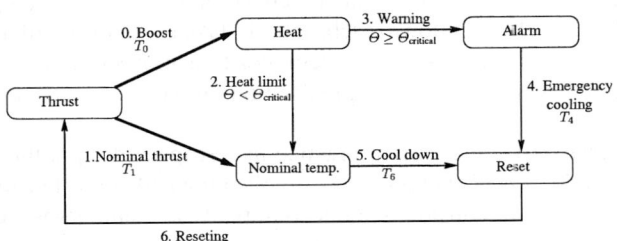

Fig. 2. Discrete automaton representing the behaviour of a thruster sub-system. The temperature increments are uncertain in the two thrusting states and in the two cooling states.

The main constraints are of three types. The first two types are certain. Constraint (5) states flow conservation on the edge variables. For example, for state 5: $E_1 + E_2 = E_6$. Constraint (6) is an example of a constraint modelling a contingent event. Here it is the event that the temperature exceeds the warning threshold, whereupon if in state 0 we must move to state 3. The final type of constraint describes the evolution of the temperature, and is thus uncertain. For this automaton, (7) models a linear recursion.

$$\sum_{k \in e^+(j)} E_k = \sum_{k \in e^-(j)} E_k \qquad \forall j \in [0, N] \qquad (5)$$

$$\Theta_j \geq \Theta_{\text{critical}} \implies S_{i+1} = j + 3 \qquad \forall j \text{ corresponding to state 0} \qquad (6)$$

$$\Theta_{i+1} = E_j \times (\Theta_i + T_i \Delta_j) \qquad \forall i \in [0, H] \qquad (7)$$

Solving. The need to guarantee safe behaviour even in the worst case means that seeking a single plan, however optimality is measured, is inadequate for our problem[1]. Therefore, we chose to compute a *covering set closure* of feasible plans: a set containing at least one plan for every feasible realisation. Ideally this set should be of minimal size, because a smaller set in general is more compact to represent.

Given the heterogeneous nature of the constraints, we found no natural transformation from the UCSP to an equivalent CSP. We describe in [23] different enumeration methods to compute a covering set closure. For space reasons, we will outline the most efficient: enumeration using a decomposition method. The idea is to first derive a feasible plan for a given realisation, and then decompose the remainder of the UCSP by removing from future consideration all realisations covered by this plan. This decomposition method is based on the conditional decision method for mixed CSPs with full observability [8]. It uses a technique called *sub-domain subproblem extraction* [9]. Given a feasible plan (a solution), the extraction technique decomposes the set of realisations into a disjunction of two sets: one containing precisely the realisations covered by the plan. The decomposition approach is tractable because the data is discrete, and each constraint contains at most one uncertain coefficient.

To give the intuition of the approach, consider the UCSP with just one uncertain constraint: $Y = X + T \cdot \Delta$, where variables $X, Y, T \in \{0, 100\}$ and $\Delta \in \{-50, 50\}$ is an uncertain coefficient. We can find a covering set closure as follows. For each possible value δ of Δ, form the *realised CSP* P_δ, and solve it to find a consistent tuple for (X, Y, T). For example, if $\delta = 20$, the realised CSP is $Y = X + T \cdot 20$, and a consistent tuple is $(10, 70, 3)$. A naive approach would require us to: (i) generate each realised CSP P_δ, (ii) seek a solution to each, and (iii) take the union of all the solutions to derive a covering set closure. The use of decomposition allows us to consider a smaller number of realised CSPs, by eliminating realisations already covered as we progress.

Outcome. Contrasted to some current practice in aerospace design, the certainty closure approach enables a new expressiveness in planning and control of low-level components, by allowing us to consider the uncertainty. As a result, aerospace component behaviour can be adapted in a more reliable way to its environment, and so the behaviour and performance guarantees sought by aerospace designers can be reinforced.

---

[1] Unless it holds under all realisations, or unless we rely on online plan repair.

3   Uncertain CSP and Its Closures

The two case studies indicate the practical value and potential benefits of reliable reasoning. We now define the certainty closure framework to provide a comprehensive and generic approach to reliable reasoning under uncertain data. After some preliminaries, we define the concepts of an uncertain CSP and its closures.

3.1   Preliminaries

We consider the CSP formalism since it has the generality we desire to model LSCO problems. Recall that a classical CSP is a tuple $\langle \mathcal{V}, \mathcal{D}, \mathcal{C} \rangle$, where $\mathcal{V}$ is a finite set of variables, $\mathcal{D}$ is the set of corresponding domains, and $\mathcal{C} = \{c_1, \ldots, c_m\}$ is a finite set of constraints. A solution is a complete consistent value assignment. We represent a CSP by a conjunction of its constraints $\bigwedge_i c_i$ (as opposed to the set of its allowed tuples). Similarly, we represent a solution or set of solutions to a CSP by a conjunction of constraints. These constraints should be from a simple class, e.g. unary equalities.

Recall that, with respect to a given computation domain, a constraint domain specifies the syntax and semantics of permitted constraints. It specifies the constants, functions and constraint relations. The constants we will refer to as *coefficients*. A coefficient may be *certain* (its value is known) or *uncertain* (value not known). In a classical CSP, all the coefficients are certain. We assume the user has some knowledge of the possible values for the coefficients, or bounds on their range. Call the set of possible values of a coefficient λ_i its *uncertainty set*, denoted U_i. We say an *uncertain constraint* is one in which some coefficients are uncertain. Note the coefficients in an uncertain constraint are still constants; merely their exact values are unknown. For example, if the coefficient λ_1 has uncertainty set $U_1 = \{2, 3, 4\}$, the constraint $X > \lambda_1$ is uncertain.

Regarding the data, following Ben-Tal and Nemirovski [3], a *data realisation* is a fixing of the coefficients to values; in related literature, the terms *possible world* and *context space* are also used. The notation $\widehat{\cdot}$ will denote certainty. For an uncertain CSP P, we will say that any certain CSP $\widehat{P}$, corresponding to a data realisation of the coefficients of P, is a *realised* CSP, and write $\widehat{P} \in P$. Each uncertain constraint is made certain by a realisation, thus $\widehat{P} = \langle \mathcal{V}, \mathcal{D}, \widehat{\mathcal{C}} \rangle$, where $\widehat{\mathcal{C}} \in \mathcal{C}$ denotes a set of *realised* constraints. In the same way, a realisation of a constraint c will be denoted $\hat{c} \in c$. It is worth noting that an uncertain constraint can have many realisations, as many as the size of the Cartesian product of the uncertainty sets involved.

3.2   Uncertain Constraint Satisfaction Problem

A UCSP is a simple extension to a classical CSP with an explicit description of the data:

Definition 1 (UCSP). *An* uncertain constraint satisfaction problem $\langle \mathcal{V}, \mathcal{D}, \Lambda, \mathcal{U}, \mathcal{C} \rangle$ *is a classical CSP* $\langle \mathcal{V}, \mathcal{D}, \mathcal{C} \rangle$ *in which some of the constraints may be uncertain. The finite set of coefficients is denoted by Λ, and the set of corresponding uncertainty sets by $\mathcal{U}$.*

In this paper we assume the coefficients are either all discrete or all continuous. We also assume the coefficients are independent. The uncertainty set $\mathcal{U}$ is then the

Cartesian product of the uncertainty sets of the coefficients, i.e. the Cartesian product of their possible values. Other than this, there is no requirement as to the nature of the data or the representation of $\mathcal{U}$.

Example 1. The constraints for the network traffic analysis problem form a UCSP with the uncertainty specified by real intervals. Similarly, the constraints for the aerospace planning problem form a UCSP with the uncertainty specified by finite sets. □

For a certain CSP $\widehat{P}$, recall that its complete solution set (or space) is the set of all solutions to $\widehat{P}$, which we will denote $\mathcal{S}_{\widehat{P}}$. The extension of this concept to UCSPs will play a key role. In line with our aim of reliable reasoning, we define the complete solution set $\mathcal{S}_P$ of a UCSP P as the set of all solutions supported by *at least one* realisation.

3.3 Closures of a UCSP

A *closure* is the resolution to a UCSP model. Depending on his application, the user might be interested in different types of closures. We distinguish several types of closures by the properties they hold. For example, a *covering set* is a set of solutions that contains at least one solution (not necessarily all solutions) for each realisation. A *most robust solution* is a solution that is supported by the greatest number of realisations. The *full* closure of a UCSP P is the set of all solutions such that each is supported by at least one realisation, i.e. the complete solution space $\mathcal{S}_P$. A closure in general is a subset of the complete solution space:

Definition 2 (Closure). *Let P be a UCSP $\langle \mathcal{V}, \mathcal{D}, \Lambda, \mathcal{U}, \mathcal{C} \rangle$. We say that a subset of the complete solution space $\mathcal{S}_P$ is a closure for P. If the closure is the entire solution space, we say it is the* full *closure, denoted* $\mathrm{Cl}(P)$.

Let s denote a solution satisfying a realised CSP $\langle \mathcal{V}, \mathcal{D}, \widehat{\mathcal{C}} \rangle$ and $\langle s \rangle$ be a conjunction of constraints describing s. Then we can write the full closure of P as the constraint:

$$\mathrm{Cl}(P) = \bigvee_{\widehat{\mathcal{C}} \in \mathcal{C}} \ \bigvee_{s \text{ satisfies } \widehat{\mathcal{C}}} \langle s \rangle \qquad\qquad (\star)$$

Example 2. Let X and Y be temperature variables with integer domains $[1, 5]$ over the following constraints: $c_1 : X > \lambda_1$, $c_2 : |X - Y| = \lambda_2$, and $c_3 : Y - \lambda_1 \neq 1$. Let λ_1 and λ_2, which represent temperature increments, have uncertainty sets $U_1 = \{2, 3, 4\}$ and $U_2 = 2$ respectively. The full closure is $(X, Y) \in \{(3, 1), (3, 5), (4, 2), (5, 3)\}$; a covering set closure of minimal size is $(X, Y) \in \{(3, 1), (5, 3)\}$, since this solution set covers all three realisations. □

The different closures form a lattice under inclusion. A simple hierarchy of closures is shown in Fig. 3. The full closure is the top, and the empty closure (the empty set) the bottom. The observation that the different closures fall into a lattice hierarchy allows us to study how they relate to one another.

For example, consider the UCSP depicted in Fig. 4. The full closure at the top of the lattice hierarchy is the set $\top = \{a, b, c, d, e\}$. The most robust solution is b; and there are two covering sets of minimal cardinality, $\{a, b\}$ and $\{b, c\}$.

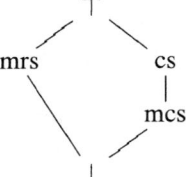

$$
\begin{array}{c|ccc}
\widehat{P_1} & a & b & d \\
\widehat{P_2} & a & c & \\
\widehat{P_3} & b & & e \\
\widehat{P_4} & b & c &
\end{array}
$$

Fig. 3. Simple hierarchy of closures. At the top of the lattice is the full closure, at the bottom the empty closure. Illustrated in the middle are a covering set (cs), a minimal covering set (mcs), and the most robust solution (mrs)

Fig. 4. Realised CSPs (denoted $\widehat{P_1}$–$\widehat{P_4}$) and their feasible solutions (denoted a–e)

4   Resolution Forms

A UCSP adds expressive power and flexibility to a CSP but, depending on the closure demanded, is harder to solve. Indeed, the complexity of deriving a closure from an UCSP is in the worst case that of finding at least one solution to a realised CSP, times the size of the Cartesian product of all the uncertainty sets[2]. Thus we cannot expect to derive the full closure, for example, by a generic practical approach, unless we restrict to a modest number of uncertain coefficients or accept approximation. Rather, we will look at two resolution forms — two possibilities to move from a UCSP to a closure — and we will instantiate the resolution forms to specific constraint domains. Where possible, we would like to exploit existing methods for CSP solving. Each case study in Sect. 2 is an instances of one of the resolution forms.

The first resolution form is to transform the UCSP: we find and then solve an equivalent certain CSP. The set of all its solutions is the closure to the UCSP. The second form, enumeration, applies when there are a finite number of realisations. Each realisation gives rise to a certain CSP, which we solve, and the closure is then the union of all the solutions to the satisfiable CSPs. We show how this approach relates to methods for handling disjunctions.

4.1   Comparing Uncertain and Certain Constraints

For both resolution forms, we reason about uncertain constraints in terms of certain constraints. This section describes the algebraic structure over which we perform the reasoning. The central idea is that uncertain constraints form a lattice:

Proposition 3 (Constraint lattice). *Let $\mathbb{C}$ be the set of all constraints, certain and uncertain, that can arise with respect to a computation domain. With conjunction and disjunction as meet and join, $\mathbb{C}$ is a distributive lattice. With logical implication of constraints, $\mathbb{C}$ has a natural partial order. Let $\widehat{\mathbb{C}} \subset \mathbb{C}$ be the subset of certain constraints; then $\widehat{\mathbb{C}}$ forms a sublattice of $\mathbb{C}$.* □

---

[2] UCSP solving is a highly specialised case of quantifier elimination (i.e. computing an equivalent, quantifier-free version of a first-order formula), which is known as an exceedingly difficult problem in the general case [15].

The conjunction, disjunction and implication operations, defined as usual for certain constraints (i.e. on $\widehat{\mathbb{C}}$), need to be extended to $\mathbb{C}$. For space reasons, we will only present the extension of the implication operation. In line with our aim for reliable reasoning, we say that an assignment satisfies an uncertain constraint if it satisfies *at least one* realisation. Hence implication is defined by: if every assignment that holds under some realisation of c_1 also holds under some realisation of c_2 (not necessarily the same), then c_1 implies c_2.

Recall that any UCSP can be represented by the conjunction of its constraints. Prop. 3 tells us this conjunction is an element of a suitable constraint lattice. More-over, since solutions to a CSP can also be represented by a conjunction of constraints, every closure of a UCSP can likewise be described as an element of $\mathbb{C}$. Depending on the constraint class, this element may be a disjunction. For example, the full closure $\mathrm{Cl}(P)$ is described by the constraint ($\bigstar$). A well-chosen representation of a closure is crucial in any practical application.

As a consequence, firstly and importantly, mappings from $\mathbb{C}$ to itself can encapsulate the solving process. Reliable solutions in the certainty closure framework will be guaranteed by properties of the mappings. Secondly, knowledge refinement can be seen in terms of a *subsumed-by* order on solutions. Should we learn more about the data, the revised closure will be subsumed by the old. We say that a constraint c_2 *subsumes* a constraint c_1 if the complete solution set of c_2 contains that of c_1:

Definition 4 (Order). *Recall the subsumed-by partial order on $\widehat{\mathbb{C}}$, defined by Tsang [17][3]. Let $\preceq$ be an extension of the order to $\mathbb{C}$ such that $c_2 \in \mathbb{C}$ subsumes $c_1 \in \mathbb{C}$, written $c_1 \preceq c_2$, if and only if $\mathrm{Cl}(c_2)$ subsumes $\mathrm{Cl}(c_1)$.*

This partial order is well-defined because $\mathrm{Cl}(c)$ is always a certain constraint. It is compatible with and extends the natural order that arises from constraint implication.

Along with the lattice $\mathbb{C}$, we need a notion of equivalence to be able to compare the solution sets of UCSPs (which we seek) and CSPs (which we use to describe a closure). The subsumed-by relation of Def. 4 provides this notion.

Example 3. Consider constraints $c_1: X > \{2, 3, 4\}$ and $\hat{c}_1: X > 2$. c_1 and $\hat{c}_1$ are equivalent under $\preceq$: they describe the same set of possible values for X. Note that $\hat{c}_1$ is precisely the full closure of c_1. □

4.2 Solution Operators

Recall that a classical CSP is solved by propagation and search: one calculates the fixed-point of some local consistency operators and (if necessary) explores the search space. Since we wish to consider both discrete and continuous CSPs, we encapsulate fully solving a CSP by a *solution operator*. The specific methods used to solve CSPs are not relevant: the essential point is to guarantee that the inferences are correct.

We define a solution operator as a map from $\widehat{\mathbb{C}}$ to itself that provides the conjunction of a set of solutions to a CSP $\widehat{P}$. The conjunction may be empty, indeed must be if $\widehat{P}$ is inconsistent. A *complete* solution operator is one that yields the set of all solutions.

---

[3] Intuitively, $\hat{c}_1 \in \widehat{\mathbb{C}}$ is *subsumed-by* $\hat{c}_2 \in \widehat{\mathbb{C}}$ if for every satisfying tuple t_1 to $\hat{c}_1$ there exists a satisfying tuple t_2 to $\hat{c}_2$ such that t_1 is a projection of t_2.

Definition 5 (Solution operator). *Let $\widehat{P}$ be a certain CSP. Let $\phi : \widehat{\mathbb{C}} \to \widehat{\mathbb{C}}$ be a map such that $\phi(\mathcal{C})$ describes a set of solutions to the CSP. If ϕ obeys:*

1.	*Contraction*	*The final state is a subset of the initial state: $\phi(\mathcal{C}) \preceq \mathcal{C}$*
2.	*Monotone*	*Subsumed-by order respected: $\mathcal{C}_1 \preceq \mathcal{C}_2 \implies \phi(\mathcal{C}_1) \preceq \phi(\mathcal{C}_2)$*
3.	*Idempotence*	*Further application of ϕ yields no further solutions*

Then we say that ϕ is a solution operator[4]. *If further $\phi(\mathcal{C})$ describes the set of all solutions to $\widehat{P}$, we say ϕ is* complete *for $\widehat{P}$.*

Example 4. Consider a solution operator for finite domain CSPs. Let ϕ_1 be the map that corresponds to naive backtrack search. If we insist that the whole search tree be explored, then ϕ_1 will give all solutions; this makes it complete.   □

Similarly, a solution operator for uncertain CSPs is a map that yields a closure when given a UCSP P. A *complete* uncertain solution operator is one that yields the full closure $\mathrm{Cl}(P)$. Formally, it is defined as a mapping from $\mathbb{C}$ to $\widehat{\mathbb{C}}$:

Definition 6 (Uncertain solution operator). *Let P be a UCSP. An* uncertain solution operator *is a map $\rho : \mathbb{C} \to \widehat{\mathbb{C}}$ such that $\rho(\mathcal{C}) \subseteq \mathrm{Cl}(P)$. An uncertain solution operator ρ must obey the contraction, monotone and idempotence properties. If further $\rho(\mathcal{C}) = \mathrm{Cl}(P)$, we say ρ is* complete *for P.*

This definition is stated in a simple way because it builds on the results of Sect. 4.1; the concept of a solution operator thus transfers naturally to UCSPs. Transformation to an equivalent certain CSP is one way to build an uncertain solution operator; enumeration is another. In the following sections we describe both resolution forms.

4.3 Solving an Equivalent CSP

The issues related to this approach are twofold: finding a CSP equivalent to the UCSP, i.e. one whose set of all solutions coincides with the sought closure to the original problem; and then solving it efficiently. We achieve the first part by seeking a transformation operator from UCSP to CSP which satisfies certain properties, for the second part we can use any existing technique appropriate to the computation domain at hand.

Unless she specifies otherwise, by default we suppose the user desires the full closure, since it excludes no possible solution. For reasons of space, we now concentrate the discussion to the case. The equivalent CSP is found using a CET:

Definition 7 (Certain Equivalence Transform). *A map $\tau : \mathbb{C} \to \widehat{\mathbb{C}}$ is a certain equivalence transform if it: (1) preserves certainty, i.e. $\tau(\hat{c}) = \hat{c} \;\; \forall \hat{c} \in \widehat{\mathbb{C}}$; (2) is a closure operator, i.e. is increasing, monotone and idempotent; and (3) distributes over meet.*

Preservation of certainty and the closure properties ensure that a certain constraint system is found. The third property governs the behaviour on conjunctions of constraints. Together, the properties which characterise a CET allow us to guarantee correctness of the uncertain solution operator. In other words, they ensure that the complete

---

[4] Note the equivalents in other theoretical frameworks, e.g. Apt's reduction functions [1].

solution set of the equivalent CSP contains the full closure to the original problem. Further, if the solution sets are equivalent, then τ is a *tight* CET. If τ is a non-tight CET, we obtain only an outer approximation to the closure. There is often value in such an approximation, if suitably close, since correctness is retained.

Prop. 8 sums up the result: an uncertain solution operator ρ can be defined as a composition of a tight CET τ and a solution operator ϕ. The proof is omitted.

Proposition 8 (Closure by transformation). *Let P be a UCSP. If τ is a tight CET and ϕ is a solution operator complete for $\tau(\mathcal{C})$, then $\rho = \phi \circ \tau$ is an uncertain solution operator, complete for P.*   □

Example 5. Recall how resolution by transformation was applied to the network traffic analysis problem. In Sect. 2.1 we gave a simplified form (3) of the CET τ used. It can be shown to be tight and to have the properties of Def. 7. Our use of LP as the solution operator ϕ likewise obeys the properties expected in Def. 5. Hence by Proposition 8, the certainty closure framework derives an enclosure guaranteed to be reliable.   □

4.4   Enumerating Realised CSPs

Depending on the constraint class, it might not always be possible to find a CET. A second means to derive closures is by enumeration. As an essentially exhaustive technique, enumeration requires operationally there be only finitely-many, $M < \infty$, realisations of the data. We generate and solve each realised CSP, forming the closure from the solutions to all the good realisations. Contrasted with transformation, the cost of enumerating and solving M possibly similar CSPs grows with M, which can be exponential in the size of the UCSP. This said, in a given computation domain, it may be possible to exploit knowledge of the structure of the realised problems (e.g. [16, Chapter 6]).

Example 6. Consider a UCSP with three variables: $X, Y, T \in \mathbb{N}$, and constraints of the form: $Y = X + T \cdot \Delta$, where $\Delta \in \mathbb{Z}$ is an uncertain coefficient. In Sect. 2.2 we showed how to derive by enumeration a covering set closure for this class of UCSPs.   □

4.5   Approximation

In practice it might be desirable to approximate the closure, either because the user seeks a different representation, or because the complexity of deriving or representing the closure to the UCSP is too high. Approximation must not impair correctness, i.e. omit elements of a closure (since it would no longer be a reliable resolution of a UCSP model), but may forgo tightness, i.e. include non-elements of the closure. We must balance complexity and closeness of the approximation.

For example, in the network traffic analysis problem, since the user's interest is to determine safe operating capacities, he will be satisfied by reliable intervals for the traffic flow variables. Thus we can give a tight outer box approximation. This means we need not calculate a general convex polytope, which could be computationally expensive, but a simpler shape, an axis-parallel hyperbox.

4.6   Instances of Resolution Forms

The choice of the resolution form is driven by the constraint class, variable domains and nature of the uncertain data. We give some instances of the resolution forms for four classes of UCSPs $\langle \mathcal{V}, \mathcal{D}, \Lambda, \mathcal{U}, \mathcal{C} \rangle$. We sketch how existing solution methods can be leveraged to provide practical algorithms for deriving closures in each class.

Transformation for UCSPs with $\mathcal{D} = \mathbb{R}^m$, $\mathcal{U} = \mathbb{R}^\ell$ and $\mathcal{C} = \{n\text{-ary linear constraints}\}$.
When the variable domains are nonnegative, i.e. $\mathcal{D} = (\mathbb{R}^+)^m$, the UCSP P is an instance of a *positive orthant interval linear system*. The CET we saw in Sect. 2.1 transforms P into an equivalent linear problem, solvable in polynomial time by LP.

A generalisation in operational research is to semi-definite problems[5] with uncertain data coefficients. In particular, for the class of UCSPs with ellipsoidal data and linear constraints, the CET transforms the UCSP to an equivalent conic quadratic problem, solvable in polynomial time by interior point methods [3].

Enumeration for UCSPs with $\mathcal{D} = \mathbb{R}^m$, $\mathcal{U} = \mathbb{R}^\ell$ and $\mathcal{C} = \{n\text{-ary negatable constraints}\}$.
If reals are finitely represented (e.g. as in floating point arithmetic), enumeration is applicable to continuous data. In the field of interval constraint solving, several works seek complete, sound solution sets in the presence of universally quantified variables. At present, the constraints must be able to be negated (which excludes equalities). The combination of numerical constraint propagation and search can be thought of as a non-naive enumeration. In [4], an exact method for a single uncertain coefficient is given; in [15], an approximate method for many coefficients.

Transformation and Enumeration for UCSPs with $\mathcal{D} = \mathbb{Z}^m$, $\mathcal{U} = \mathbb{Z}^\ell$ and $\mathcal{C} = \{basic constraints\}$. Over finite domains, consider the classes of basic constraints as defined in [18]. A system of uncertain monotone constraints (e.g. binary inequalities) can be transformed by a CET similar to (3) in Sect. 2.1. The constraints of the resulting CSP are monotone, and their complete solution set can be found in linear time by computing the 2D integer hull [12]. For other types of basic constraints, enumeration is available.

Enumeration for UCSPs with $\mathcal{D} = \mathbb{Z}^m$, $\mathcal{U} = \mathbb{Z}^\ell$. CSP algorithms have been extended to derive robust solutions for mixed CSPs [8]. These algorithms can be adapted for the discrete data case of UCSPs over finite domains, as Sect. 2.2 illustrated.

If we consider a UCSP P as a disjunction of its realised CSPs, $\bigvee_i \widehat{P}_i$, then $\mathrm{Cl}(P)$ is a constraint implied by the disjunction. Specifically, in *constructive disjunction* one eliminates all domain values not supported in at least one of the disjuncts (i.e. not supported by at least one realisation) [19]. However, because each $\widehat{P}_i$ is itself a conjunction, the constraints in P would have to be of simple form if the algorithms of constructive disjunction are to be applied. In a similar way, *generalised propagation* can be thought of as reasoning on a disjunction to infer a constraint that describes all solutions [14]. Depending, again, on the complexity of the constraints, the *topological branch and bound* algorithm [14] can be used to derive the full closure to P by enumeration.

---

[5] That is, optimisation problems with semi-definite constraint matrix.

5   Related Work

Existing generic approaches to uncertain data in CP propose models and methods for robust solutions to the problem. The *mixed CSP* framework [8] of Fargier et. al., defined for discrete data and variables, seeks a solution that holds under the most possible realisations of the data[6]; the *stochastic CSP* framework [21] of Walsh attaches a probability distribution to parameters and seeks a solution that maximises expectation. The purpose of computing robust solutions is to ensure that whatever the real world situation, the solution holds under most cases. Robust solutions are semantically ideal for dynamic changes but inadequate for handling data errors where one is certainly not looking for a solution that satisfies as many erroneous models as possible.

In dealing with unsatisfiability, the potential data issue is not considered in CP. The approach most widely used consists of reasoning at the constraint level: when the model is unsatisfiable, the usual interpretation is that the problem is over-constrained. Thus, most of the research has focused on relaxing constraints and setting priorities (e.g. [6]).

Besides work on quantified constraints over the reals [4], we are not aware of any work in CP aimed at building reliable solution sets in the presence of uncertain data. The closest parallels are the meta-solution reasoning of generalised propagation [14] and constructive disjunction [19].

While our work is defined with CP modelling in mind, in concept it is more closely related to work in control theory and operational research on continuous problems. In particular, *convex modelling* (of which interval analysis over the reals is a simple instance) is used to obtain a closure guaranteed to contain the true solution [2, 3, 7].

6   Discussion and Future Work

In this paper we have investigated how the successes of CP can be extended to real-world problems with data uncertainty. We introduced the certainty closure as a generic framework to allow the modelling of incomplete and erroneous data, both discrete and continuous. It guarantees reliable reasoning in that, whatever the true value of the data, the solution to the corresponding realised CSP is contained within the full closure.

A formal framework does not suffice unless its application to real LSCOs is practical. We derive a reliable solution set by solving standard CSPs, to make use of the most appropriate specific resolution techniques for the problem at hand. We have demonstrated the use of the framework by showing the benefits of reliable constraint reasoning on case studies from network traffic analysis and aerospace planning.

Most models with data uncertainty presently assume independence of the data (e.g. [8, 21]). For the certainty closure, assuming independence retains correctness but loses tightness. Future work will include study of how to extend the framework to account for dependency. We also wish to study new instances of the resolution forms for different

---

[6] If we restrict to finite domains and discrete data, a UCSP $\langle \mathcal{V}, \mathcal{D}, \Lambda, \mathcal{U}, \mathcal{C} \rangle$ can be viewed as a *mixed CSP* $\langle \Lambda, L, \mathcal{V}, \mathcal{D}, \mathcal{K}, \mathcal{C} \rangle$ with $\mathcal{U}$ being the complete solution set of the CSP $\langle \Lambda, L, \mathcal{K} \rangle$ induced by the parameters. However, as we discussed, the objectives (and algorithms, in general) of the two frameworks are quite different.

uncertain constraint classes. In particular we will consider the hybrid case where the data uncertainty is both discrete and continuous.

Acknowledgements

The authors thank P. Brisset, C. Guettier, S. Ratschan, M. Wallace, and the participants of the UICS'02 workshop for their discussions; and the reviewers for their recommendations. This work was partially supported by the EPSRC under grant GR/N64373/01.

References

1. K. R. Apt. The essence of constraint propagation. *TCS*, 221(1–2), 1999.
2. Y. Ben-Haim and I. Elishakoff. *Convex Models of Uncertainty in Applied Mechanics*. Elsevier Science Publishers, Amsterdam, 1990.
3. A. Ben-Tal and A. Nemirovski. Robust convex optimization. *Mathematics of Operations Research*, 23, 1998.
4. F. Benhamou and F. Goualard. Universally quantified interval constraints. In *CP-2000*.
5. T. Benoist, E. Bourreau, Y. Caseau, and B. Rottembourg. Towards stochastic constraint programming: A study of online multi-choice knapsack with deadlines. In *Proc. of CP'01*.
6. S. Bistarelli, H. Fargier, U. Montanari, F. Rossi, T. Schiex, and G. Verfaillie. Semiring-based CSPs and valued CSPs: Basic properties and comparison. In *LNCS 1106*. 1996.
7. J. W. Chinneck and K. Ramadan. Linear programming with interval coefficients. *J. Operational Research Society*, 51(2), 2000.
8. H. Fargier, J. Lang, and T. Schiex. Mixed constraint satisfaction: A framework for decision problems under incomplete knowledge. In *Proc. of AAAI-96*, pages 175–180, 1996.
9. E. Freuder and P. Hubbe. Extracting constraint satisfaction subproblems. In *Proc. of IJCAI-95*, pages 548–557, 1995.
10. C. Gervet, Y. Caseau, and D. Montaut. On refining ill-defined constraint problems: A case study in iterative prototyping. In *Proc. of PACLP'99*, pages 255–275, 1999.
11. C. Gervet and R. Rodošek. RiskWise-2 problem definition. IC–Parc Internal Report, 2000.
12. W. Harvey. Computing two-dimensional integer hulls. *SIAM J. Computing*, 28(6), 1999.
13. IC–Parc. *ECL^{i}PS^e User Manual Version 5.6*, June 2003.
14. T. Le Provost and M. Wallace. Generalized constraint propagation over the CLP scheme. *J. Logic Programming*, 16(3), 1993.
15. S. Ratschan. Continuous first-order constraint satisfaction. In *LNCS 2385*, 2002.
16. I. Tsamardinos. *Constraint-Based Temporal Reasoning Algorithms with Applications to Planning*. Ph.D. Thesis, University of Pittsburgh, 2001.
17. E. Tsang. *Foundations of Constraint Satisfaction*. Academic Press, London, 1993.
18. P. Van Hentenryck, Y. Deville, and C.-M. Teng. A generic arc-consistency algorithm and its specializations. *Artificial Intelligence*, 57(2–3), 1992.
19. P. Van Hentenryck, V. Saraswat, and Y. Deville. Design, implementation, and evaluation of the constraint language cc(FD). In *LNCS 910*, 1994.
20. G. Verfaillie. What kind of planning and scheduling tools for the future autonomous spacecraft? In *Proc. ESA Workshop on On-Board Autonomy*, 2001.
21. T. Walsh. Stochastic constraint programming. In *Proc. of AAAI'01 Fall Symposium on Using Uncertainty within Computation*, pages 129–135, 2001.
22. N. Yorke-Smith and C. Gervet. Data uncertainty in constraint programming: A non-probabilistic approach. In *Proc. of Using Uncertainty within Computation*, 2001.
23. N. Yorke-Smith and C. Guettier. Towards automatic robust planning for the discrete commanding of aerospace equipment. In *Proc. of IEEE ISIC'03*, Oct. 2003. To appear.

clp(pdf(y)): Constraints for Probabilistic Reasoning in Logic Programming

Nicos Angelopoulos

Department of Computer Science, York University, York, YO10 5DD, UK
nicos@cs.york.ac.uk

Abstract. We argue that the clp(X) framework is a suitable vehicle for extending logic programming (LP) with probabilistic reasoning. This paper presents such a generic framework, clp(pdf(Y)), and proposes two promising instances. The first provides a seamless integration of Bayesian Networks, while the second defines distributions over variables and employs conditional constraints over predicates. The generic methodology is based on attaching probability distributions over finite domains. We illustrate computational benefits of this approach by comparing program performances with a clp(fd) program on a cryptographic problem.

1 Introduction

LP has been an integral part of symbolic problem solving. Its success with crisp reasoning makes its extension to deal with statistical reasoning an appealing proposition. To this direction, a number of approaches, which enhance LP with the ability to reason under uncertainty, have been suggested. These have been mainly based on Probability Theory. Invariably, a probabilistic measure, or interval, is attached to LP clauses or specialised facts.

Such approaches are either based on Markov process principles [9, 4, 7] and subordinate probabilistic reasoning to logical reasoning, or based on Bayesian principles and subordinate the later form of reasoning to the former. In most approaches, the use of a single clause to express both kinds of knowledge, leads to an asymmetric symbiosis. In this paper we present an extension based on constraint LP (CLP) principles. The use of techniques developed in the clp(X) framework avoids overloading the clausal representation. In particular, we introduce a generic formalism clp(pfd(Y)) which uses finite domains as basic objects on which probability distributions can be attached. Furthermore, the store is extended to hold probabilistic information such as conditional constraints and probabilistic evidence. Uncertain and crisp reasoning is integrated further, by considering predicates containing probabilistic variables as statistical events in an intuitive probability space.

Preliminaries. Our notation follows [5]. Predicates, or atomic formulae, are of the form $r(t, A)$, r is a predicate name and t with A are first-order terms (t a constant and A a logical variable). We extend first-order terms to also include probabilistic variables. Names for logical and probabilistic variables start with

F. Rossi (Ed.): CP 2003, LNCS 2833, pp. 784–788, 2003.
© Springer-Verlag Berlin Heidelberg 2003

a capital letter. A logic program, $\mathcal{P}$, is a set of definite clauses. A substitution θ, e.g. $\{A/a\}$, is a set of variables to term pairs. Applying θ to a formula will replace every occurrence of a variable in θ with its associated term, e.g. $\theta r(t, A)$ is equivalent to $r(t, a)$. Store $\mathcal{S}$ is a set of constraints. We use $P_{\mathcal{S}}(E)$ to denote the probability of E in the context of $\mathcal{P}$ and $\mathcal{S}$. Queries are of the form $?E_1, E_2, \ldots$ where each E_i is a predicate. $?E_1, \ldots$ succeeds iff $\mathcal{P} \cup \mathcal{S} \vdash E_1 \wedge E_2 \wedge \ldots$ ($\vdash$ is the derives operator and $\wedge$ the logical *and*). Each successful derivation often provides a substitution θ, denoting that $\mathcal{P} \cup \mathcal{S} \vdash \theta(E_1 \wedge \ldots)$. We take $\mathcal{P} \cup \mathcal{S} \vdash \neg Q$ to be equivalent to $\mathcal{P} \cup \mathcal{S} \nvdash Q$. Note that in this case there is no associated θ.

2   Framework and Instances

In clp(pfd(Y)) a probabilistic variable V is introduced to the store with an associated finite domain and a function operating over subsets of this domain. The constraint store can, in addition to clp(fd) constraints, hold probabilistic information about such variables. In a clp(pfd(Y)) store $\mathcal{S}$, probabilistic inference computes $\psi_{\mathcal{S}}(V) = \{(v_1, \pi_1), (v_2, \pi_2), \ldots, (v_n, \pi_n)\}$. Each v_i is an element of V's finite domain and the π_is should define a probability distributions, i.e. $0 \leq \pi_i \leq 1$ and $\sum_i \pi_i = 1$. We let $P_{\mathcal{S}}(V = v_i)$ be the probability attached to element v_i under store $\mathcal{S}$. By definition $P_{\mathcal{S}}(V = v_i) = \pi_i$.

In probability theory an event is a subset of the space of all possible outputs for an experiment. Treating the assignment of all possible values to probabilistic variables as our space of possible outcomes, we can view predicates containing such variables as events in this space. The main intuition is that the probability assigned to events is proportional to the space covered by combinations leading to successful derivations.

Let $pvars(E)$ be the vector of probabilistic variables in predicate E, $\mathcal{P}$ be the program defining E and $\mathcal{S}$ a constraint store. We use $\mathcal{E}_i$ to index the variables in $pvars(E)$. Also let e be a vector collecting one element from the finite domain of each variable in $pvars(E)$ and $P_{\mathcal{S}}(\mathcal{E}_i = e_i)$ the probability attached to value e_i of variable $\mathcal{E}_i$ as defined above. E/e denotes predicate E with its probabilistic variables replaced by their respective elements in e. The probability of predicate E with respect to store $\mathcal{S}$ and program $\mathcal{P}$ is

$$P_{\mathcal{S}}(E) = P(E \mid \mathcal{P} \cup \mathcal{S}) = \sum_{\substack{\forall e \\ \mathcal{P} \cup \mathcal{S} \vdash E/e}} P_{\mathcal{S}}(E/e) = \sum_{\substack{\forall e \\ \mathcal{P} \cup \mathcal{S} \vdash E/e}} \prod_i P_{\mathcal{S}}(\mathcal{E}_i = e_i)$$

For example, for program $\mathcal{P}_1$:   lucky(iv, hd). lucky(v, hd). lucky(vi, hd). and store $\mathcal{S}_1$ with variables D and C, with $\psi_{\mathcal{S}_1}(D) = \{(i, 1/6), (ii, 1/6), (iii, 1/6), (iv, 1/6), (v, 1/6), (vi, 1/6)\}$ and $\psi_{\mathcal{S}_1}(C) = \{(hd, 1/2), (tl, 1/2)\}$. The probability of a lucky combination is $P_{\mathcal{S}_1}(lucky(D, C)) = 1/4$.

The benefit of regarding predicates containing constraint variables as events is threefold. Firstly the seamless integration of crisp and uncertain reasoning. Secondly the provision of a time point marking prior to posterior distribution transitions. Thirdly the algorithmic separation of crisp and uncertain inference, leading to accountability of resource usage. In comparison to clp(fd) its probabilistic extension provides additional information about the elements in its domain. One important way in which this information can be exploited is during labelling. In clp(pfd(Y)) backtrackable predicate **label**(*V, Select, ElPrb, PrbSum*) can be used to instantiate a probabilistic variable (*V*) to an element of its finite domain and *ElPrb* to the element's probability. The order is dictated by *Select* and *PrbSum* keeps the sum of the *ElPrb* encountered so far.

To fully instantiate clp(pfd(Y)) there are three choices to be made: (i) the kind of probabilistic information provided when declaring a probabilistic variable; (ii) the constraints that can be added to the store and (iii) the algorithms for probabilistic inference, which use (i) and (ii) to derive probability distributions for the variables.

clp(pfd(bn)). The framework can be instantiated to a language that introduces Bayesian Networks, BNs [6], reasoning to LP. The importance of such integration has been highlighted in [8] and [3]. The first work embedded BNs to abductive horn clauses. In [3] probability distributions are declared over skolem functions and the emphasis is on machine learning tasks, rather than on probabilistic reasoning. BNs are propositional in that only assignment events ($X = x$ for variable X and value x) are considered. Also, the relationships between variables are widely viewed in a causality context. The basic premise of a BN is that it represents the full probabilistic knowledge of a field. Evidence about particular cases is weighted against the accumulated knowledge. What is sought, is the probabilities of events which explain the evidence. Consider the example BN

	A = y	A = n
B = y	0.80	0.10
B = n	0.20	0.90

	A = y	A = n
C = y	0.60	0.90
C = n	0.40	0.10

Marginal distributions are calculated from the potentials (conditional or joint distribution tables) and the probability of specific cases based on relevant evidence entered in the network. The existence of evidence about C may result to changes in the distribution of B and vice versa. The direction in which BNs use conditional probability is determined by the presence of evidence.

In clp(pfd(bn)) probabilistic variables correspond to nodes in a BN and are introduced with their full conditional probability tables. A variable V with parent nodes the list of variables *Parents* and conditional table *Table* is introduced to the store with *cpt*(*V, Parents, Table*). In the example BN, variables are declared as $cpt(A, [], [y, n])$, $cpt(B, [A], [(y, y, .8), (y, n, .2), (n, y, .1), (n, n, .9)])$
and $cpt(C, [A], [(y, y, .6), (y, n, .4), (n, y, .9), (n, n, .1)])$

BN algorithms weight currently available evidence, when computing the posterior distributions of variables. In the example, evidence might suggest that the distribution of A is $\{(y, .8), (n, .2)\}$. Using this and $P(C|A)$ we can derive $P(C)$. In this case $P(C) = \{(y, .66), (n, .34)\}$. In clp(pfd(bn)) evidence are stored in the constraint store. The example evidence is added by *evidence*$(A, [(y, .8), (n, .2)])$. The important factor, in using the store for holding current evidence, is that the introduction of evidence to the store provides a convenient time transition point. The inference algorithms employed in clp(pfd(bn)) are those of probability or belief updating in BNs (see [6]). In BNs the most important predicate is = and inference computes probability of specific values. In our framework this is equivalent to finding the distribution of a probabilistic variable.

clp(pfd(c)). Another instantiation for clp(pfd(Y)) is to clp(pfd(c)) (see [1] for more details). This uses functions over domains to designate basic probabilistic behaviour and conditional constraints for dividing the constraint store into probabilistic fragments. We term this instantiation clp(pfd(c)) in recognition of the important role the conditional constraint plays. A probabilistic variable has two parts: (i) a *finite domain*, which at each stage holds the collection of possible values that can be assigned to the variable and (ii) a *probability assigning function* which is used to assign probabilities to the elements of the domain. The probability function declares the basic statistical behaviour of the variable.

Let Fd be a list of distinct objects representing a finite domain, ϕ_V be a probability function defined over all sublists of Fd and $Args$ a list of ground terms. Probabilistic variables are declared with $V \sim \phi_V(Fd, Args)$. For a subset T of Fd ($T \subseteq Fd$) the result of $\phi_V(T, Args)$ is a list of pairs, each pair coupling an element of T to its associated probability. Each element of T should be given a value and the sum of all given values should be one. $Args$ parameterise aspects of ϕ_V and if it is the empty list we shorten $\phi_V(Set, [])$ to $\phi_V(Set)$. We will use this shorter form when ϕ_V is applied, since $Args$ only play a role in variable declarations. We will also drop the subscript from ϕ_V when the context clearly identifies a particular V. In relation to the ψ notation, the following holds for empty store $\emptyset$: $\phi_V(Fd) = \psi_\emptyset(V)$.

For example, $Heat \sim finite\_geometric([l, m, h], 2)$ declares a finite geometric distribution for variable $Heat$. In this case the deterioration factor is 2. The distribution in the absence of other information is $\psi_\emptyset(Heat) = \{(l, 4/7)(m, 2/7), (h, 1/7)\}$. A distinct feature of clp(pfd(c)) is that the two constituents of a probabilistic variable are kept separate. As a result, the variable is still capable of participating in finite domain constraints, thus it is orthogonal to clp(fd) while sharing information, and also probabilistic functions capture statistical behaviour of variables in a manner which is, to a large extent, independent of specific domain values. Adding clp(fd) constraint $Heat \neq m$ to the store, changes the distribution of $Heat$ to $\{(l, 2/3), (h, 1/3)\}$.

The probabilistic information added to the store is the conditional constraint. Its main intuition is that of defining probability subspaces in which we know that certain events hold. Conditional C is of the form: $D_1 : \pi_1 \oplus \ldots \oplus D_m : \pi_m \mid Q$. Each D_i is a predicate and all should share a single probabilistic variable V. Q is a predicate not containing V, and $0 \leq \pi_i \leq 1, \sum_i \pi_i = 1$. V's distribution is altered as a result of C being added to the store, see [1]. The distribution of V according to conditional C, $P_{\{C\}}(V = v)$, is computed by considering all subspaces ($1 \leq j \leq i$) and by applying ϕ_V within each subspace. clp(pfd(c)) instantiates the proposed framework as follows. Probabilistic information at declaration time is given by ϕ_V, which describes the probabilistic behaviour of the variable after all finite domain pruning. Conditionals add probabilistic information to the store. This information partitions the space to weighted subspaces within which differ-

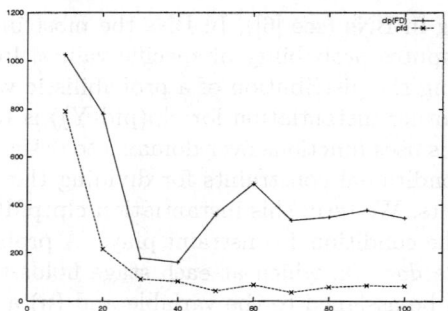

Fig. 1. clp(pfd(c)) versus clp(fd) timings comparison.

ent events hold. Inference uses these partitions and the application of functions to compute updated probability distributions for the conditioned variables.

3   Comparative Example

To illustrate benefits from the additional information in clp(pfd(Y)) when compared to clp(fd) we juxtapose performances of respective programs for a simple Caesar encoding scheme. The two programs are identical bar: (i) distribution over domains in clp(pfd(c)) based on the formula $\frac{|freq(E_i)-freq(D_i)|}{\sum_k |freq(E_i)-freq(D_k)|}$ for E_i an encoded letter, D_i a dictionary letter and $freq()$ their respective frequencies and (ii) labelling in clp(pfd(c)) uses a best-first algorithm. Execution times for ten random sets at points in the range of 10-100 words drawn from a dictionary are shown in Fig. 1. Both programs run on the SICStus engine. One was written in clp(fd) [2] and one in a meta-interpreted implementation of clp(pfd(c)) (see http://www.cs.york.ac.uk/~nicos/sware/pfds/).

References

1. N. Angelopoulos. *Probabilistic Finite Domains*. PhD thesis, Department of Computing Science, City University, London, UK, 2001.
2. M. Carlsson, G. Ottosson, and B. Carlson. An open-ended finite domain constraint solver. In *Progr. Languages: Implem., Logics, and Programs*, 1997.
3. V. S. Costa, D. Page, and J. Cussens. CLP($\mathcal{BN}$) constraint logic programming for probabilistic knowledge, 2002. Personal communication, unpublished work.
4. J. Cussens. Stochastic logic programs: Sampling, inference and applications. In *16th Conference on Uncertainty in AI (UAI-2000)*, pages 115–122, 2000.
5. C. J. Hogger. *Essentials of Logic Programming*. OUP, Oxford, 1990.
6. F. V. Jensen. *Bayesian Networks and Decision Graphs*. Springer, 2001.
7. Y. Kameya and T. Sato. Efficient learning with tabulation for parameterized logic programs. In *CL2000*, pages 269–294, July 2000.
8. D. Poole. Probabilistic horn abduction and bayesian networks. *AI*, 64:81–129.
9. S. Riezler. *Probabilistic Constraint Logic Programming*. PhD thesis, Neuphilologische Fakultät, Universität Tübingen, Germany, 1998.

To Be or Not to Be ... a Global Constraint*

Christian Bessière[1] and Pascal Van Hentenryck[2]

[1] LIRMM-CNRS, 161 rue Ada, 34392 Montpellier Cedex 5, France
bessiere@lirmm.fr
[2] Brown University, P.O. Box 1910, Providence, RI 02912
pvh@cs.brown.edu

Abstract. Constraint propagation is widely recognized as a fundamental reasoning component in constraint programming. In the last decade, the concept of "global constraint" has attracted significant attention, since it is critical to achieve reasonable pruning, and efficiency, in many applications. However, even if the name "global constraint" carries a strong intuition in itself, there is no formal definition of this important concept. This paper proposes various notions of globality in order to understand this concept more thoroughly.

1 Introduction

Constraint technology is widely used to solve a large scope of combinatorial problems arising in various application fields such as resource allocation, hardware verification, diagnosis, scheduling, etc. Progresses in constraint technology usually come from two close subareas traditionally named 'constraint reasoning' (or CSP), and 'constraint programming' (or CP). Thanks to common events such as the CP conference series, these two communities became closer and closer, and their border became more fuzzy. Nevertheless, scientists from these two subfields often have different cultural origins, vocabulary, and ways of approaching theoretical and practical issues. An example that illustrates such differences appeared during the CP'02 conference, held at Ithaca NY. CP'02 featured a tutorial, whose title was "global constraints". This tutorial gave rise to a heated debate, not because of its content, but rather because nobody seemed to agree on the definition of "global constraint".

This paper tries to characterize the concept of "global constraint" formally. We understand that proposing a definition for a concept already widely used is difficult and inevitably controversial. We also understand that other definitions may be proposed and that our definitions represent our own biases. However, we believe that this endeavour can only increase our understanding of global constraints and thus benefits the community as a whole. In particular, we believe that our definitions, which build on well-known concepts, isolate some fundamental intuitions in the folklore of the communities, and are consistent with the "practice of constraint programming". In the worst case, these definitions will be a first step toward a fundamental understanding of this important concept.

---

* [1] contains a long version of this short paper.

F. Rossi (Ed.): CP 2003, LNCS 2833, pp. 789–794, 2003.
© Springer-Verlag Berlin Heidelberg 2003

The starting point of this paper is the recognition that a constraint C is often called "global" when "processing" C as a whole gives better results than "processing" any conjunction of constraints that is "semantically equivalent" to C. Thus, the concept of globality goes beyond "semantic equivalence" and seems to include operational and algorithmic concepts. Consider the well-known example of the *alldiff* constraint: *alldiff*$(x_1, \ldots, x_k)$ holds when all the x_i's are given different values. This constraint can easily be represented by a clique of binary inequalities on the x_i's. Hence, it may not be considered "global", since it can be decomposed into more primitive constraints. However, performing arc consistency on the clique does not usually prune as many values as performing arc consistency directly on the *alldiff* constraint. Hence, the *alldiff* constraint can be considered "global" wrt the filtering property, which is clearly one important criterion for "globality" in constraint programming. More generally, this paper distinguishes between semantic globality (expressiveness), operational globality (quality of filtering), and algorithmic globality (computational efficiency of the filtering).

The paper also addresses the issue of globality both from a CSP and CP standpoint. The CSP standpoint does not restrict the constraint language and gives considerable freedom in the choice of domains and constraints. But the CSP standpoint must harness this freedom and imposes a natural, but strong, restriction on the nature of globality. As a result, the CSP standpoint is best seen as a theory of globality for conjunctive constraints. The CP standpoint takes the dual approach and restricts the language under consideration. As a consequence, it makes it possible to encompass complex rewritings in the definition of globality.

2 Background

Constraints are defined in a slightly unusual way in order to make them independent from the constraint network in which they appear.

Definition 1 (Constraint). *A constraint (or **relation**) R of arity k is a set of sequences of k components. A component can be any entity/object in the world.*

Example 1. The constraint *alldiff* of arity k is defined by the set of all the sequences of k different components. If $k = 3$, *alldiff* is $\{(2, 3, 1), (cow, car, cup), \ldots\}$.

We now define the notion of constraint instance, which is traditionally called "constraint" in the CSP community. It links a constraint with its variables and their domains.

Definition 2 (Constraint Instance). *An **instance** c of a constraint R is a triple (X_c, D_c, R_c), where X_c is an ordered set $(x_1, \ldots, x_{|X_c|})$ of variables, $D_c = (D_c(x_1), \ldots, D_c(x_{|X_c|}))$ is an ordered set representing the domains of these variables. The set $R \cap D_c(x_1) \times \cdots \times D_c(x_{|X_c|})$ is denoted by sol(c).*

Example 2. The instance of the constraint *alldiff* posted on the three variables x_1, x_2, and x_3 of respective domains $\{a, b\}, \{a, b\}$, and $\{a, b, c, d\}$ allows the solutions (a, b, c), $(a, b, d), (b, a, c)$, and (b, a, d) for the variables x_1, x_2, x_3.

Definition 3 (Constraint Network). *A finite* **constraint network** N *is defined as a triplet* (X_N, D_N, C_N) *where* $X_N = \{x_1, \ldots, x_n\}$ *is a set of n* **variables**, $D_N = \{D_N(x_1), \ldots, D_N(x_n)\}$ *is a set of finite* **domains**, *and* C_N *is a set of* **constraint instances** *such that* $\forall c \in C_N : X_c \subseteq X_N, \forall x \in X_c : D_c(x) = D_N(x)$. *Finally, the set of constraint networks is denoted by* $\mathcal{N}$.

We now introduce the concept of constraint decomposition, which is fundamental in characterizing global constraints.

Definition 4 (Constraint Decomposition). *A constraint network* N *is a* **decomposition** *of a constraint instance* c *if* $X_N = X_c$, $D_N = D_c$, $\forall e \in C, |X_e| < |X_c|$, $R_e = R_c[X_e]$, *and* $sol(N) = sol(c)$.

Example 3. Let $N = (X, D, C)$ be the network defined by $X = \{x_1, x_2, x_3\}$, where $D(x_1) = \{a, b\}, D(x_2) = \{a, b\}, D(x_3) = \{a, b, c, d\}$, and $C = \{c_{12}, c_{13}, c_{23}\}$, where c_{12}, c_{13}, c_{23} are the binary inequality $\neq$ posted on (x_1, x_2), (x_1, x_3), and (x_2, x_3). N is a decomposition of the *alldiff* instance posted on (x_1, x_2, x_3) in Example 2.

A constraint decomposition scheme is simply a function which decomposes the instances of a constraint. This concept simplifies subsequent definitions.

Definition 5 (Constraint Decomposition Scheme). *Let* R *be a constraint and let* $\mathcal{C}$ *be the set of instances of* R. *A* **constraint decomposition scheme** *for* R *is a function* $\delta : \mathcal{C} \to \mathcal{N}$ *such that* $\delta(c)$ *is a constraint decomposition of* c.

3   Global Constraints

We now propose three notions of globality: semantic globality, operational globality, and algorithmic globality. Semantic globality is the stronger notion (i.e., it implies the two others) but it does not completely capture what is generally understood as "global" (at least, in our opinion). Operational globality, which considers the quality of the filtering, implies algorithmic globality.

Definition 6 (Semantic Globality). *A constraint* R *is* **semantically global** *if there exists no constraint decomposition scheme for* R.

Operational globality considers both a constraint R and a consistency notion Φ. The constraint is said to be "global" if there exists no decomposition scheme for which the consistency notion removes as many local inconsistencies as on the original constraint. This concept is important because it compares the pruning of the constraint and its decompositions wrt a consistency notion. (In the following, $\Phi(N)$ denotes the closure of the network N wrt to Φ.)

Definition 7 (Operational Globality). *A constraint* R *is* **operationally** Φ**-global** *if there exists no constraint decomposition scheme* δ *for* R *such that* $D_{\Phi(c)} = D_{\Phi(\delta(c))}$ *for all instances* c *of* R.

Example 4. The *alldiff* constraint is operationally AC-global. Examples 2 and 3 show an instance of a constraint for which there exists no decomposition on which arc consistency performs the same amount of filtering.

When a constraint R is not operationally global wrt a local consistency Φ, this means that, from a pruning standpoint, there is no advantage in using R in a problem formulation on which Φ is the consistency notion used. However, it can be argued that it is still beneficial to consider R wrt Φ if this provides complexity advantages. This justifies algorithmic globality (see [1]). We present its definition in the section on languages, where it is easier to introduce.

4   Constraint Programming Languages

Constraint languages raise interesting issues because they have a fixed vocabulary for expressing constraints and domains. In addition, constraint languages have specific encodings of constraints and domains, which makes it easier to discuss some complexity notions which are necessarily more abstract in the CSP community.

Definition 8 (Constraint Language). *A constraint language L is a triplet (L^C, L^D, L^ϵ) where L^C is the set of constraints supported in L, L^D is the set of domains supported in L, and L^ϵ is an encoding scheme which specifies how constraints and domains are represented in L. For simplicity, we often use $L(R)$ and $L(d)$ to denote $L^\epsilon(R)$ and $L^\epsilon(d)$. We also use $\|L(R)\|$ and $\|L(d)\|$ to represent the size of the encoding of a constraint R and of a domain d in L.*

We now define which constraint networks can be expressed in a language. The extension of decomposition and decomposition schemes definitions follow immediately.

Definition 9 (Language Embedding). *Let L be a constraint language and N be a constraint network. N is **embedded** in L if $\forall d \in D_N : d \in L^D$ and $\forall c \in C_N : R_c \in L^C$. If N is embedded in L, $L(N)$ denotes its encoding in L. The size of the encoding $L(N)$, denoted by $\|L(N)\|$, is defined as*

$$\sum_{c \in C_N} \|L(R_c)\| \; + \sum_{x \in X_N} \|L(D_N(x))\|.$$

Definition 10 (Language Decomposition). *Let L be a constraint language, c be a constraint instance, and N be a network. N is a **L-decomposition** of c if $X_N = X_c$, $D_N = D_c$, $c \notin C_N$, $sol(N) = sol(c)$, and N is embedded in L.*

4.1   Globality in Languages

We are now in position to define globality in the context of constraint languages. The first two notions, semantic globality and operational globality, are direct generalizations of the CSP case. Algorithmic globality is defined in terms of the size of the encodings, which captures the fact that domains and constraints are encoded, sometimes very efficiently, in constraint languages.

Definition 11 (Algorithmic Globality in a Language). *Assume that a consistency notion Φ can be enforced in time $O(f(\|L(c)\|))$ and space $O(g(\|L(c)\|))$ on all instances c of a constraint R. R is **algorithmically Φ-global** wrt L if there exists no L-decomposition scheme δ for R such that, for all instances c of R,*

1. *$D_{\Phi(c)} = D_{\Phi(\delta(c))}$;*
2. *Φ can be enforced in time $O(f(\|L(c)\|))$ and space $O(g'(\|L(c)\|))$ on $L(\delta(c))$;*
3. *$\|L(\delta(c))\|$ is $O(g(\|L(c)\|))$.*

The first two conditions are natural: the decomposition should preserve the pruning (1) and the complexity bounds (2). The third condition imposes a bound on the space complexity on the decompositions. This condition is critical to reflect the actual space complexity of the decomposition, since the consistency algorithm receives $\delta(c)$ as an input.

4.2   Strong Globality

Constraint programmers, or implementations of constraint programming systems, often rewrite complex constraints in terms of simpler ones by introducing new variables. This section generalizes the concepts to accommodate this important technique.

Definition 12 (Constraint Rewriting). *A constraint network N is a **rewriting** of a constraint instance c if $X_c \subseteq X_N$, $D_N[X_c] = D_c$, $c \notin C_N$, and $sol(N)[X_c] = sol(c)$.*

Example 5. Let $y = 4 \cdot x$ be a constraint instance on the variables x and y having domains $D_x = D_y = 1..10$. The constraint network involving x, y, and the additional variable z with $D_z = 1..10$, on which we post the constraint instances $z = 2 \cdot x$ and $y = 2 \cdot z$ is a rewriting of $y = 4 \cdot x$.

A language rewriting (*L-rewriting*) is simply a constraint rewriting which can be embedded in the language. The notions of strong globality are direct generalizations of the notions of globality, where L-decompositions are replaced by L-rewritings.

5   Illustrations

Example 6 (The Sum Constraint). Consider the language L containing constraints of the form $x_1 + x_2 = y$ and the $(n+1)$-ary *sum* constraint $\sum_{i \in 1..n} x_i = y$, $n > 2$. *sum* does not allow any decomposition scheme. There is no way to represent it with smaller arity constraints on the same variables. Hence it is semantically global (and thus operationally and algorithmically global). But *sum* is not strongly semantically global wrt L. Indeed, it can be rewritten by adding $n - 2$ additional variables z_j that represent the sum of the j first x_i's in the following way: $x_1 + x_2 = z_2, z_2 + x_3 = z_3, \ldots, z_{n-1} + x_n = y$. It is not strongly operationally AC-global wrt L, since arc consistency on the rewriting removes the same values in the original variable domains as the original constraint. But the *sum* constraint is strongly algorithmically AC-global wrt L. Indeed, on the one hand, in order to enforce arc consistency on the rewriting, the domain sizes on the intermediary variables may become exponential in the sizes of the original domains (either in the rewriting or during the consistency algorithm). (If $D_{x_1} = \{0, 10, 20, \ldots, 90\}$ and $D_{x_2} = \{0, 1, 2, \ldots, 9\}$, $x_1 + x_2$ takes values in $\{0, 1, \ldots, 99\}$.) On the other hand, there exists an AC algorithm which runs on sum in linear space wrt the initial domains and in time $O(s^n)$, where s is the size of the largest domain. Interestingly, the sum constraint is not strongly algorithmically BC-global, since only intervals are needed to compute bound consistency.

Acknowledgements

We would like to thank A. Aggoun, F. Benhamou, and E. Bourreau for the discussions we had on this topic.

References

1. C. Bessière and P. Van Hentenryck. To be or not to be ... a global constraint. Technical Report 03050, LIRMM – University of Montpellier II, Montpellier, France, June 2003. (available at http://www.lirmm.fr/~bessiere/).

Constraint Programming
for Modelling and Solving Modal Satisfiability

Sebastian Brand[1], Rosella Gennari[2], and Maarten de Rijke[3]

[1] CWI, Amsterdam, The Netherlands
sebastian.brand@cwi.nl
[2] ITC-irst, Trento, Italy
gennari@irst.itc.it
[3] Language and Inference Technology Group, ILLC
University of Amsterdam, The Netherlands
mdr@science.uva.nl

Abstract. We explore to what extent and how efficiently constraint programming can be used in the context of automated reasoning for modal logics. We encode modal satisfiability problems as constraint satisfaction problems with non-boolean domains, together with suitable constraints. Experiments show that the approach is very promising.

1 Introduction

In various branches of artificial intelligence, modal and modal-like formalisms are used for reasoning about relational structures [3], such as transition systems. Recently, there have been increased efforts to develop algorithms for solving the satisfiability problem for modal logic. Some implementations use special purpose algorithms for modal logic, such as DLP [11], FaCT [7], RACER [5], *SAT [12], while others exploit existing tools or provers for either first-order (MSPASS [9]) or propositional logic (KSAT [4], KBDD [10]) through some encoding.

We follow the latter approach: we model and solve the modal satisfiability problem via Constraint Programming (CP). We build on the fact that a modal formula is satisfiable in the basic logic K only if it is so on a tree-like model [2, 1]. This property allows us to stratify K-satisfiability problems into "layers" of propositional satisfiability problems. In [1] this layering was encoded into a translation from modal into first-order logic. We build on the schema for KSAT [4], following the intuitions in [1]. We encode modal input formula into layers of finite constraint satisfaction problems (CSPs) with additional non-Boolean values; we show that *any complete constraint solver* for finite CSPs can be used to solve them (and, hence, to determine modal satisfiability).

Our aim in this paper is to explore to what extent and how efficiently CP can be used in the context of automated reasoning for modal logics. To the best of our knowledge, our work constitutes the first attempt in this direction. The novelty of the paper is two-fold: first, *encoding* modal satisfiability problems as CSPs with enlarged domains; and second, *solving* such CSPs by means of suitable propagation algorithms in a CP environment.

F. Rossi (Ed.): CP 2003, LNCS 2833, pp. 795–800, 2003.

We turn to modal logic matters in Section 2. In Section 3 we report on an experimental assessment and comparison. We conclude in Section 4.

2   Modal Logic and CSPs

Modal Logic. We focus on the basic mono-modal logic K, even though our results can easily be generalized to a multi-modal version. Let P be a finite set of propositional variables. K-formulas are produced by the rule $\phi ::= p \mid \neg\phi \mid \phi \wedge \phi \mid \phi \vee \phi \mid \Box\phi$, where $p \in P$. A formula is *boxed* if it is of the form $\Box\phi$.

A *modal model* is a triple $\mathcal{M} = (W, R, V)$ where W is a non-empty set (the model's domain), R is a binary relation on W, and $V : P \to 2^W$ is a valuation, assigning subsets of W to proposition letters. *Satisfaction* of a formula ϕ at a state w in a model $\mathcal{M}$ ($\mathcal{M}, w \models \phi$) is defined by induction on ϕ: $\mathcal{M}, w \models p$ if $w \in V(p)$; $\mathcal{M}, w \models \neg\phi$ iff $\mathcal{M}, w \not\models \phi$; $\mathcal{M}, w \models \phi \wedge \psi$ iff $\mathcal{M}, w \models \phi$ and $\mathcal{M}, w \models \psi$; and $\mathcal{M}, w \models \Box\phi$ iff for all v such that Rwv, $\mathcal{M}, v \models \phi$. A formula ϕ is *satisfiable* if for some model $\mathcal{M}$ and state w in $\mathcal{M}$ we have that $\mathcal{M}, w \models \phi$. K-*satisfiability* is the following problem: given a mono-modal formula ϕ, is ϕ satisfiable?

A *tree model* is a model $\mathcal{M} = (W, R, V)$ such that (W, R) is a tree. K-formulas satisfy the *tree model property*: they are satisfiable only if they are satisfiable at the root of a tree model; see [3, Chapter 2] for details.

Let ψ be a modal formula on P. A ψ subformula of the form $p \in P$ or $\Box\psi'$ is a *layer-0 variable* (of ψ). A formula ϕ is a *layer-0 proposition* (of ψ) iff it is a layer-0 variable of ψ or its negation, the conjunction or disjunction of layer-0 propositions of ψ. In general, a *layer-$(i+1)$ variable* θ (of ψ) is a subformula of ψ of the form θ' where $\Box\theta'$ is a layer-i proposition. A *layer-$(i+1)$ proposition* (of ψ) is a layer-$(i+1)$ variable of ψ or its negation, a conjunction or disjunction of layer-$(i+1)$ propositions of ψ.

```
μ := ∅;
Propositions := stack_init([ψ]);
while not stack_empty(Propositions) do
   ψ := stack_pop(Propositions);
   sat(ψ, μ);        % return μ ≠ ∅ else backtrack
   Θ := ⋀ {θ : □θ = 1 in μ} ;
   for each □ν = 0 in μ do
      Propositions := stack_push(¬ν ∧ Θ, Propositions);
```

The k_sat Schema. The algorithm schema k_sat on the right-hand side, on which KSAT [4] is based, determines the satisfiability of formulas in K: the sat procedure determines the satisfiability of ψ as a proposition by returning a propositional assignment, if no exists backtracking takes place. Thus, the modal search space is explored layer by layer, in a depth-first manner.

The KCSP Algorithm. Our next aim is to devise a modal decision procedure based on the k_sat schema, with CSP algorithms as the underlying propositional solver.

Definition. Let ϕ be a modal formula and X the set of all layer-0 variables in ϕ. Consider ϕ as a layer-0 proposition with variables in X; then the *CSP of the modal formula* ϕ is the CSP of the layer-0 proposition ϕ. Let us denote the CSP of the modal formula ϕ with $CSP(\phi)$.

We instantiate *sat* with a complete constraint solver for finite CSPs in k_sat and transform ψ into $CSP(\psi)$ before passing it on to the constraint solver; the result is the KCSP *algorithm*.

KCSP is a decision procedure due to the fact that k_sat is so if *sat* returns a Boolean assignment whenever the input formula is satisfiable, otherwise the empty assignment; see [4].

Theorem (Total Correctness of KCSP**).** KCSP *is a decision procedure for* ***K***-*satisfiability.*

The solver adopted as *sat* in our implementation of KCSP is backtracking search interleaved with constraint propagation for generalized arc-consistency. Furthermore, the input formula is transformed into conjunctive normal form.

3   Experimental Assessment and Optimisations of KCSP

We provide an empirical evaluation of KCSP, using the Heuerding and Schwendimann (HS) test set [6] that was used at the TANCS'98 comparison of systems for non-classical logics [13]. The HS test set consists of classes of formulas for ***K***, which are either provably false (labelled with p) or satisfiable (labelled with n). One tests formulas from each class, starting with the easiest instance, until the satisfiability status of a formula can not be determined within 100 seconds. The result from this class will then be a parameter (ranging from 0 to 21) of the largest formula that can be solved within the time limit. It is important to note that the formula size is exponential in this parameter. A linear speed-up in processor or program speed does not change in essence the benchmark results.

Optimisations and Analysis. We implemented the KCSP algorithm in the Constraint Logic Programming (CLP) system ECL^{i}PS^e, version 5.5. We ran our experiments on an AMD Athlon Processor (1 GHz), with 512MB RAM, under Red Hat Linux 7.1. The HS formulas used in the experiments and the code for KCSP are at available at http://www.cwi.nl/~sbrand/Research/kcsp/.

We turn to a brief discussion of our optimisations and their impact. To get partial Boolean assignments in KCSP so that the reasoning on the boxed formulas is "delayed" (and possibly never done), we ensure that propositional variables have as domains $\{0, 1\}$, while boxed formulas have as domains $\{0, 1, 2\}$, where 2 describes "irrelevance". We add constraints to obtain a partial assignment with a small number of boxed formulas "switched on" (i.e., with a value $\neq 2$). We call these the *(assignment-) minimising constraints*. We also add heuristics to reduce the size of the KCSP search tree: the value 2 is preferred for boxed formulas, and among them for positively occurring ones. Additionally, the instantiation ordering of boxed formulas is along their increasing modal depth, that is, shallow boxed formulas are assigned first.

Minimising constraints make a substantial difference, especially in the case of the so-called *branch* formulas within the HS test set: KCSP with total assignments can only solve the first two formulas in *branch_p*, whereas KCSP with minimising constraints solves all of them in less than 2 seconds; a similar result holds for *branch_n* — see also the comparison table below.

Another optimization concerns disjunctive information. In the KCSP algorithm, formulas are transformed in CNF form before being converted into CSPs; in particular, every time 0 is assigned to a formula $\neg\Box\psi$, the subformula $\neg\psi$ is first transformed in CNF and then into CSP form. This CNF-conversion is not an efficient choice; it can be avoided by treating $\neg\psi$ as a disjunctive constraint $\neg\psi = \bigvee_{i=1}^{n} \phi_i$. The clauses ϕ_i are reified by means of link variables L_i, which are constrained to contain at least one that is set to true. Avoiding CNF conversion by means of disjunctive constraints has a substantial effect; e.g., $ph_n(4)$ — an instance of the pigeon-hole problem — is now solved in a few seconds but with CNF conversion KCSP halts due to a lack of memory.

Next, we added constraints for factoring. Consider a subformula $\Box\psi$ of ϕ, the input KCSP; suppose that $\Box\psi$ occurs several times in ϕ, positively and negatively; then, in the KCSP algorithm, each occurrence at position i is encoded as a different variable in the corresponding CSP, say x_i. To avoid this, we add a constraint $C_{\Box\psi}$ on the CSP variables for $\Box\psi$ which states that no two variables x_i, x_k (representing $\Box\psi$) exist with $x_i = 0$ and $x_k = 1$. This form of factoring is beneficial for formulas with the same boxed subformula occurring repeatedly.

Finally, we added simplifications. These take place only once, upon reading the formula. We use standard simplification rules for propositional formulas, at all layers, in a bottom-up fashion. Simplification makes an important different in the case of the *lin* formulas in the HS test set.

	branch		d4		dum		grz		lin		path		ph		poly		t4p	
	n	p	n	p	n	p	n	p	n	p	n	p	n	p	n	p	n	p
KSATC	8	8	5	8	>	11	>	17	3	>	8	4	5	5	12	13	18	10
KCSP	13	>	6	9	19	12	>	13	>	>	11	4	4	4	15	10	7	10

Results and a Comparison. The table on the right-hand side displays a comparison of KSATC with KCSP in which all the optimisations above are switched on; from now on we refer to this as KCSP. The results for KSATC are taken from [8]; there KSATC was run on the Heuerding and Schwendimann test set, on a 350 MHz PentiumII with 128 MB of main memory. In the table, we write $>$ when all 21 formulas in the test set are solved within 100 CPU seconds, else we write the number of the most difficult formula decided within the time out. For some classes, KCSP clearly outperforms KSATC, for some it is the other way around, and for yet others the differences do not seem significant. E.g., KCSP is superior in the case of *lin* and *branch* formulas; *branch_n* is often considered to be the hardest "truly modal test class" for current modal theorem provers; thus adding constraints to limit the number of boxed formulas to reason on, while still exploring the truly propositional search space, seems to be a winning idea in this case. In the case of $t4$, KSATC is superior to KCSP; notice, however, that KSATC features a number of optimisations for early *modal* pruning that we have not (yet) added to KCSP.

4   Finale

We have described a method for modeling and solving modal satisfiability problems using a constraint-based approach. Guided by the tree model property for modal logic, the method works by stratifying modal satisfiability problems into sequences of propositional satisfiability problems, each of which is encoded as a non-Boolean CSP. Our implementation, KCSP, is competitive with the best modal-theorem provers on the hardest "truly modal class" in the Heuerding and Schwendimann test set, namely *branch*. An important advantage of KCSP is that encoding optimisations (e.g., for factoring or partial assignments) can be done very elegantly and compactly in our constraint-based setting.

Our ongoing and future work focuses on: CNF-free modelling, modal learning heuristics, the use of stronger forms of constraint propagation, and an extension of our CSP-based approach to more expressive modal-like logics.

Acknowledgments

We thank our referees for their useful comments. Maarten de Rijke was supported by grants from the Netherlands Organization for Scientific Research (NWO), under project numbers 612-13-001, 365-20-005, 612.069.006, 612.000.106, 220-80-001, and 612.000.207.

References

1. C. Areces, R. Gennari, J. Heguiabehere, and M. de Rijke. Tree-based Heuristics in Modal Theorem Proving. In *Proc. ECAI 2000*, pages 199–203. IOS Press, 2000.
2. P. Blackburn and M. De Rijke. Zooming in, zooming out. *Journal of Logic, Language and Information*, 6:5–31, 1997.
3. P. Blackburn, M. De Rijke, and Y. Venema. *Modal Logic*. Cambridge University Press, 2001.
4. F. Giunchiglia and R. Sebastiani. Building Decision Procedures for Modal Logics from Propositional Decision Procedures. The Case Study of Modal $K(m)$. *Information and Computation*, 162(1–2):158–178, 2000.
5. V. Haarslev and R. Möller. RACER. URL: http://kogs-www.informatik.uni-hamburg.de/~race/, September 2002.
6. A. Heuerding and S. Schwendimann. A Benchmark Method for the Propositional Modal Logics K, KT, $S4$. Technical Report IAM-96-015, University of Bern, 1996.
7. I. Horrocks. FaCT. URL: http://www.cs.man.ac.uk/~horrocks/FaCT/, September 2002.

8. I. Horrocks, P.F. Patel-Schneider, and R. Sebastiani. An Analysis of Empirical Testing for Modal Decision Procedures. *Logic J. of the IGPL*, 8(3):293–323, 2000.
9. MSPASS V 1.0.0t.1.2.a. URL: http://www.cs.man.ac.uk/~schmidt/mspass, February 23, 2001.
10. G. Pan, U. Sattler, and M. Y. Vardi. BDD-Based Decision Procedures for *K*. In *Proceedings of CADE 2002*, pages 16–30. Springer LINK, 2002.
11. P.F. Patel-Schneider. DLP. URL: http://www.bell-labs.com.user/pfps/dlp/, September 2002.
12. A. Tacchella. *SAT System Description. In *Collected Papers from the International Description Logics Workshop 1999, CEUR*, 1999.
13. TANCS: Tableaux Non-Classical Systems Comparison. URL: http://www.dis.uniroma1.it/~tancs, January 17, 2000.

Distributed Forward Checking[*]

Ismel Brito and Pedro Meseguer

Institut d'Investigació en Intel.ligència Artificial
Consejo Superior de Investigaciones Científicas
Campus UAB, 08193 Bellaterra, Spain
{ismel,pedro}@iiia.csic.es

Abstract. A reason to distribute constraint satisfaction is privacy: agents may not want to share their values, and they may wish to keep constraints as private as possible. In this paper, we present the *Distributed Forward Checking* algorithm, a natural successor of Asynchronous Backtracking, where some privacy is achieved on agent values. Regarding constraints, we introduce the *Partially Known Constraints* model, which allow a constraint between two agents to be not completely known by any of them. With these elements, we obtain new solving algorithms that enforce privacy and maintain completeness. Empirical results are provided.

1 Introduction

A distributed CSP (DisCSP) is a CSP where variables, domains and constraints are distributed among agents. The variable-based DisCSP model assumes that each variable belongs to one agent and constraints are shared between agents. Following this approach, Yokoo et al. proposed the asynchronous backtracking (ABT) algorithm [4], using a total ordering among agents. Privacy ideally requires that agents should not share their values, and constraints among agents should be kept as private as possible. The ABT algorithm, usually taken as reference, does not satisfy these requirements because (i) agents share their values with other agents, and (ii) a constraint is totally known by all agents involved.

In this work, we propose a new solving approach that considers the above privacy requirements. First, we present a new algorithm, *Distributed Forward Checking ($DisFC$)*, based on ABT, that implements the following idea: instead of an agent sending its value to other agents, it sends the effects that its value has on other agents' domains. This idea reproduces *Forward Checking* pruning on future domains [3]. Second, we introduce the *Partially Known Constraints* (PKC) model, where a constraint between two agents is replaced by two new constraints, each known by one agent and unknown by the other.

Differently from the centralized case, $DisFC$ does not improve ABT efficiency, since the ability to accumulate pruning on future domains is lost (it is an asynchronous algorithm). However, $DisFC$ is able to achieve some privacy

---

[*] This research is supported by the REPLI project TIC-2002-04470-C03-03.

F. Rossi (Ed.): CP 2003, LNCS 2833, pp. 801–806, 2003.

on values and constraints. In this context, it is worth mentioning the approach [5], that achieves a high level of privacy using encryption. $DisFC$ is a simpler approach that achieves a lower level of privacy without using encryption.

2   Privacy

Assuming binary DisCSP, with ABT solving there are two main privacy issues,

1. Values. Agents exchange the values of their variables when notifying their assignments to other agents or when performing backtracking.
2. Constraints. An interagent constraint C_{ij} is known by the agents owning its related variables, that is, C_{ij} is known by agents i and j.

However, this approach might be inappropriate for those applications for which privacy is the main reason to be solved in a distributed form. In that case, agents may desire to hide the actual values of their variables from other agents, considered as potential competitors. For the same reasons, the information contained in the problem constraints may be considered reserved, and agents could not be willing to share it with other agents.

Regarding values, in ABT values exchanged are used with two purposes:

1. Consistency. The notification that a variable of a higher priority agent has taken a new value allows receiver to change its own assignment in order to make it consistent with the higher priority agent.
2. Detecting obsolescence. The agent view of each agent is composed by the values that it believes that are assigned to variables in higher priority agents. The agent view is used to detect obsolete backtracking messages.

Regarding constraints, ABT assumes that a constraint C_{ij} is *totally known* by the agents i and j [4]. In fact, it is required that $rel(C_{ij})$ is totally known by one agent only. We define the *Totally Known Constraints* (TKC) model when the scope $var(C_{ij})$ of each constraint is known by every related agent, but the relation $rel(C_{ij})$ is known by one agent only. It is clear that ABT follows the TKC model. In addition, we introduce the *Partially Known Constraints* (PKC) model of a DisCSP as follows. A constraint C_{ij} is only partially known by its related agents. From C_{ij}, agent i knows the constraint $C_{i(j)}$ with agent j as,

$$var(C_{i(j)}) = \{x_i, (x_j)\} \qquad rel(C_{ij}) \subseteq rel(C_{i(j)})$$

where (x_j) in $var(C_{i(j)})$ means that agent i knows little about the other variable of the constraint. From constraint C_{ij}, agent j knows the constraint $C_{(i)j}$,

$$var(C_{(i)j}) = \{(x_i), x_j\} \qquad rel(C_{ij}) \subseteq rel(C_{(i)j})$$

It is required that,

$$rel(C_{ij}) = rel(C_{i(j)}) \cap rel(C_{(i)j})$$

How to develop the PKC model of any problem is currently an open question. However, this idea can be directly applied to some problems which can naturally formulate their constraints in this way. For instance, the n-pieces m-chessboard problem (Section 4), consists of locating n chess pieces on a $m \times m$ chessboard such that they do not attack each other. If each piece knows the identity of every other piece below in the ordering, it follows the TKC model. If pieces do not know any other piece, the problem can be formulated using the PKC model.

3   Distributed Forward Checking

The main feature of centralized Forward Checking (FC) [3] is the pruning of future domains when the current variable is assigned. Applying this idea to ABT, we obtain the *Distributed Forward Checking* ($DisFC$) algorithm, that works as follows. When a variable x_i is assigned, instead of sending its value to the agent j connected by the constraint C_{ij}, it sends to j the part of D_j compatible with its value. Variable x_j will choose a new value consistent with x_i, from the received filtered domain, but without knowing x_i's value.

To detect obsolete information, when x_j receives a *Back* message including x_i, ABT requires that x_j should know the current value of x_i. Instead of the current value, we propose to use the sequence number of x_i, defined as follows. Each variable keeps a sequence number that starts from 1 (or some random value), and increases monotonically each time the variable changes its value. It acts as a unique identifier for each value of the variable, so for privacy purposes it can safely replace the actual value. Messages notifying a new value replace the actual value by the sequence number of the sender variable. The agent view is composed by the sequence numbers the agent believes are hold by variables in higher priority agents. Consistently, nogoods contain variables and their sequence numbers, in substitution of the actual values.

Combining these two strategies, sending filtered domains to other agent variables and replacing the own value by its sequence number, allows one agent to exchange enough information with other agents to reach a global consistent solution (or proving that no solution exists) without revealing its own assignment at any time. And this can be done under the two models of constraints, totally and partially known constraints.

3.1   DisFC with Totally Known Constraints

$DisFC$ under the TKC model ($DisFC$-TKC) requires that each constraint C_{ij} is totally known by the highest priority agent in its scope. For simplicity of presentation, we assume that $DisFC$-TKC is based on ABT_0 [1], a version of ABT where all possible links that ABT may add during search are added in a preprocessing step, before the search begins. $DisFC$-TKC can be easily adapted to other algorithms of the ABT family.

Like ABT, $DisFC$-TKC requires constraints to be directed and a compatible total order among agents. Basically, $DisFC$-TKC considers two types of messages: *Info* and *Back*. An *Info* message informs receiver that sender has changed its value. It includes the sequence number of the value taken by sender, and the subset of receiver values which are compatible with the current assignment of sender. A *Back* message, which is sent from lower to higher priority agents, contains the *nogood* found by the sender and requests receiver to change its value.

The $DisFC\text{-}TKC$ algorithm has three differences with ABT_0,

1. Consistency. A constraint C_{ij} is checked by the higher priority agent when sending the filtered domain to the lower priority agent.
2. Selecting a Value. When agent i receives an *Info* message, it also updates the nogood store, adding one nogood for each domain value not included in the filtered domain of the *Info* message. Then, a new value (if current value is no longer valid) is selected. The new value have to be compatible with the nogood store and with at least one value in domains of variables constrained with i with lower priority.
3. Detecting obsolescence. Sequence numbers act as representative for values assigned to variables. In that way, agents can detect obsolete information.

$DisFC\text{-}TKC$ inherits the correctness and completeness properties of ABT_0.

3.2   DisFC with Partially Known Constraints

In the PKC model, each constraint C_{ij} is replaced by two constraints $C_{i(j)}$ and $C_{(i)j}$, each known by the agents i and j respectively. $DisFC$ under PKC model ($DisFC\text{-}PKC$) performs a loop with two phases. Each phase is as follows,

- Phase I. Constraints are directed forming a DAG, and a compatible total order of agents is selected. Then, a solution is found with respect to the constraints $C_{i(j)}$, where i has higher priority than j. If no solution is found, the process stops.
- Phase II. The solution of Phase I is checked against constraints $C_{(i)j}$. If they are satisfied, this solution is a true solution and the process stops. Otherwise, one or several nogoods are generated and search is resumed on Phase I.

Regarding unsolvable instances, Phase I will eventually detect that there is no solution, after possibly several loop iterations involving Phase II execution.

Phase I is performed as explained in Section 3.1, wrt the $C_{i(j)}$ constraints. The innovative part is Phase II, specifically checking $C_{(i)j}$ and reacting if this check is negative. This is done as follows. Since in $DisFC$ a constraint is checked by the high priority agent, and j is the only agent knowing $C_{(i)j}$, j must have a higher priority than i. This is obtained by reversing the direction of each constraint in the directed constraint graph of Phase I. Given that the reverse of a DAG is also a DAG, this transformation has no effect on the solving capacities of $DisFC$. Once directed constraints are reversed, the high priority agent j informs the lower one i of its filtered domain wrt x_j value. If the value of x_i is allowed by $C_{(i)j}$ x_i does nothing. Otherwise, x_i sends a *Back* message to x_j with a nogood that considers incompatible the current values of x_i and x_j (this is done using their respective sequence numbers). When x_j receives a *Back* message, x_j records the nogood in the nogood store and does nothing.

After sending all *Info* and *Back* messages, quiescence is detected, and directed constraints are reversed again. Then, Phase I is resumed. From the end of previous Phase I, the only agents that have changed their memory are the receivers of a *Back* message in Phase II. They include a nogood that discard their current value. But now these agents are low priority agents, so they have to change their values to find a consistent assignment. In this way, nogoods found in Phase II are used in Phase I to escape from incompatible assignments.

The main loop starts performing Phase I. If a solution has been found, the directed constraint graph is reversed, Phase II is performed and the directed constraint graph is reversed again. The loop ends when the empty nogood has been produced (the problem is unsolvable), or when Phase II generates no *Back* messages (the solution of Phase I satisfies the constraints of Phase II).

4   Experimental Results

DisFC-TKC and *DisFC-PKC* have been tested on a simulated environment under GNU/Linux operating system. These algorithms have been compared on two different problems: *n*-pieces *m*-chessboard and binary random DisCSP.

The *n*-pieces *m*-chessboard problem consists of locating n chess pieces on a $m \times m$ chessboard, where no pieces attacks any other. We have tested two soluble instances of this problem. The first instance has 9 pieces, 3 queens, 2 castles, 2 bishops and 2 knights, to be placed on a 8×8 chessboard. The second instance has 11 pieces, 3 queens, 3 castles, 2 bishops and 3 knights, to be located in a 10×10 chessboard. Under the TKC model, each piece knows the identity of the pieces below it in the ordering. Under the PKC model, no piece knows the identity of any other piece.

A binary random DisCSP class is characterized by $\langle n, d, p_1, p_2 \rangle$, where n is the number of variables, d the number of values per variable, p_1 the network *connectivity* defined as the ratio of existing constraints, and p_2 the constraint *tightness* defined as the ratio of forbidden value pairs. Using this model, we have tested random instances of 16 agents and 8 values per agent with low connectivity ($p_1 = 0.2$). In the PKC model, every forbidden tuple of C_{ij} is associated with $C_{i(j)}$ or with $C_{(i)j}$ but not both.

In both problems, the search cost is evaluated using the number of *Info* messages, *Back* messages, the total number of messages exchanged and the number of constraint checks. As we expected, *DisFC-PKC* –which offers higher privacy– requires more computational and communication effort. This is the price one has to pay to keep some privacy on values and constraints.

References

1. Bessiere C., Brito I., Maestre A., Meseguer P. The Asynchronous Backtracking Family. Submitted for publication, 2003.
2. Bessiere C., Maestre A., Meseguer P. Distributed Dynamic Backtracking. In Distributed Constraint Reasoning Workshop, IJCAI-01, Seattle, USA, 2001.
3. Haralick R., Elliot G. Increasing Tree Search Efficiency for Constraint Satisfaction Problems. Artificial Intelligence **14** (1980) 263–313.
4. Yokoo M., Durfee E., Ishida T., Kuwabara K. The Distributed Constraint Satisfaction Problem: Formalization and Algorithms. IEEE Trans. Knowledge and Data Engineering **10** (1998) 673–685.
5. Yokoo M., Suzuki K., Hirayama K. Secure Distributed Constraint Satisfaction: Reaching Agreement without Revealing Private Information. In Proc. of the 8th. CP, 2002.

A New Class of Binary CSPs for which Arc-Consistency Is a Decision Procedure

David A. Cohen

Computer Science Department
Royal Holloway, University of London, UK

Abstract. In this report weintroduce a new hybrid class for which arc-consistency is a decision procedure.
This new hybrid class includes infinitely many instances whose tractability is not assured by any tractable language or structural restriction, and strongly motivates the search for a unifying principle for the tractable constraint classes decided by arc-consistency.

1 Introduction

The class of Constraint Satisfaction Problems (CSPs) is NP-hard However, there are certain restrictions that make it tractable. These tractable classes have a polynomial decision procedure.

In this report we concentrate on those classes of constraint satisfaction problem instances for which arc-consistency ($k = 2$) is a decision procedure. We will define a new hybrid class of binary constraint problem instances with a non-Boolean domain for which arc-consistency is a decision procedure.

A constraint satisfaction problem instance (CSP) consists of a set of variables which have to be assigned values from some domain. The set of allowed values is restricted for certain subsets of the variables.

Definition 1. *A **CSP**, is a triple $\langle V, D, C \rangle$, where:*

- *V is a finite set of **variables**;*
- *D is a finite set called the **domain** of P;*
- *C is a set of **constraints**. Each constraint $c \in C$ is a pair $c = \langle \sigma, \rho \rangle$ where $\sigma = \langle v_1, \ldots, v_k \rangle$ is a list of variables from V, called the constraint **scope**, and ρ is a subset of D^k called the constraint **relation**.*

*A **solution** to $P = \langle V, D, C \rangle$ is an assignment s of a value in D to each variable v such that, for every constraint $\langle \sigma, \rho \rangle$, the projection of s onto σ is contained in ρ. The set of solutions to P is denoted $\mathrm{Sol}(P)$.*

The general CSP (decision) problem is NP-complete [6] Naturally we want to identify subproblems for which polynomial algorithms exist.

Most tractability results rely on restricting either the structure, or the underlying language of the problem instances. We now define these concepts.

F. Rossi (Ed.): CP 2003, LNCS 2833, pp. 807–811, 2003.

Definition 2. *The **structure** [5] of $P = \langle V, D, C \rangle$ is a hypergraph $\langle V, E \rangle$ whose vertexes V are the set of variables of P, and whose hyperedges E are the sets defined by the scopes of the constraints of P. That is:*

$$E = \{\{x_1, \ldots, x_k\} \mid \exists \langle \langle x_1, \ldots, x_k \rangle, \rho \rangle \in C, \}$$

*A **constraint language** is a set of relations. The **language** [6] of $P = \langle V, D, C \rangle$ is the set, Γ_P, of constraint relations occurring in P. That is:*

$$\Gamma_P = \{\rho \mid \exists \langle \sigma, \rho \rangle \in C\}$$

Lastly, we need to define what we mean when we say a CSP is arc-consistent.

Definition 3. *Let $P = \langle V, D, C \rangle$ be a CSP instance.*

*For any subset $W \subseteq V$ the **restriction** of P to W, denoted P_W^* is the instance with variables W and domain D, where the constraints are obtained from the constraints of P by eliminating all the constraints with scope not contained in W. That is, $P_W^* = \langle W, D, C' \rangle$ where $\langle \sigma, \rho \rangle \in C'$ if and only if $\langle \sigma, \rho \rangle \in C, \sigma \subseteq W$.*

*We say that P is (j, k)-**consistent** $(0 \leq j \leq k)$ [3] if, for any sets of variables W, W' with $W \subseteq W' \subseteq V$, containing at most j and k variables respectively, any solution to P_W^* can be extended to a solution to $P_{W'}^*$.*

*A problem is **arc-consistent** if it is $(1, 2)$-consistent.*

For every CSP, P, there is a unique CSP[1], $\mathcal{A}(P)$ which is arc-consistent and has the same set of solutions as P. The problem of determining $\mathcal{A}(P)$ for any P is polynomial [1].

2 When Arc-Consistency Is Enough

Sometimes establishing arc-consistency results in domain wipe-out. By this we mean that $\mathcal{A}(P)$ has some variable with an empty unary constraint. In this case it is clear that P cannot be solved.

We say that arc-consistency is a decision procedure for a class $\mathcal{C}$ of CSPs if every CSP in $\mathcal{C}$ either has a solution or arc-consistency results in domain wipe-out. Such a class is clearly tractable.

We have a characterisation of those structures for which arc-consistency is a decision procedure. We also have a characterisation of those languages for which there is some $k > 1$ for which $(1, k)$-consistency is a decision procedure.

Theorem 1. *Let $\mathcal{H}$ be a class of hypergraphs. The class of CSPs whose structure is in $\mathcal{H}$ has arc-consistency as a decision procedure exactly when all the dual graphs are trees.*

The result about $(1, k)$-consistency [3] requires a definition.

---

[1] We assume an explicit representation of constraints as a set of allowed labellings. For the uniqueness of $\mathcal{A}(P)$ we assume that we merge unary constraints.

Definition 4. *Let ϕ be a function from D^k to D. We say that a relation τ over D is* **closed** *under ϕ if, whenever we take k (not necessarily distinct) rows of τ and apply ϕ to them componentwise, we get a row of τ.*

A **set function** *on D is any function from the set of subsets of D to D. A set function ϕ naturally generates a k-ary function ϕ_k for each k where $\phi_k(x_1, \ldots, x_k) = \phi(\{x_1, \ldots, x_k\})$. A relation τ is closed under the set function ϕ when it is closed under each such ϕ_k.*

A constraint language Γ is closed under a function ϕ when each $\tau \in \Gamma$ is closed under ϕ.

Theorem 2. *[3] Let Γ be a constraint language. There is some $k > 1$ for which establishing $(1, k)$-consistency is a decision procedure for $CSP(\Gamma)$ exactly when Γ is closed under a set function.*

3   A Hybrid Case

In order to define our new hybrid class we need the notion of the complement of the microstructure of a CSP. This is a hypergraph and is defined as follows.

Definition 5. *The* **complement of the microstructure** *of the CSP, $P = \langle V, D, C \rangle$, denoted $\overline{\mathcal{M}}(P)$, is a hypergraph $\langle W, F \rangle$.*

The vertex set W is the set of all (variable, domain value) pairs for P.

The hyperedges of F are of two types.

Let $s = \{\langle v_1, d_1 \rangle, \ldots, \langle v_r, d_r \rangle\}$ be a set of vertexes of W. Suppose that there is some r-ary constraint $\langle \sigma, \rho \rangle$ where $\sigma = \langle v_1, \ldots, v_r \rangle$ and $\langle d_1, \ldots, d_r \rangle \notin \rho$. Then s is a hyperedge of F.

Alternatively, let $s = \{\langle v, d_1 \rangle, \langle v, d_2 \rangle\}$ be a pair of vertexes of W corresponding to two assignments to some variable v. In this case also, s is a hyperedge of F.

That is:

$$W = \bigcup_{v \in V} \{v\} \times D(v)$$
$$F = \{\{\langle v, d \rangle, \langle v, e \rangle\} \mid d \neq e\} \cup$$
$$\{\{\langle v_1, d_1 \rangle, \ldots, \langle v_r, d_r \rangle\} \mid \exists \langle \langle v_1, \ldots, v_r \rangle, \rho \rangle \in C, \langle d_1, \ldots, d_r \rangle \notin \rho\}$$

It is clear that solutions to P correspond exactly to independent sets in $\overline{\mathcal{M}}(P)$ containing $|V|$ vertexes. In this paper we will only be interested in the complements of the microstructure of binary CSPs. It is worth noting that the complement of the microstructure of a binary CSP is a graph.

Definition 6. *Let P be a CSP. We say that P is* **triangulated** *if it is binary and $\overline{\mathcal{M}}(P)$ is triangulated.*

Let G be a graph and $<$ be an ordering of the vertexes of G. We say that $<$ is an **elimination ordering** *if, for any vertex v of G, the set of vertexes that are smaller than, and connected to, v form a clique.*

*A **maximal cardinality ordering** of the vertexes of G is constructed in* $|V|$ *steps as follows. At step 1, choose any vertex* v_1. *At step i, for* $i < |V|$ *we have chosen* $v_1, \ldots, v_{i-1}$. *Now choose for* v_i *any vertex that is connected to the largest set of previously numbered vertexes. We order* $v_i < v_j$ *if* $i < j$.

We can prove the following.

Theorem 3. *The class of triangulated CSPs is tractable, and arc-consistency is a decision procedure.*

Proof. Proof omitted for brevity. The proof relies on the fact that a maximal cardinality ordering of a triangulated graph is an elimination ordering [7], and that it is tractable to determine whether a graph is triangulated [8].

We end this section by describing the language of all triangulated CSPs.

Definition 7. *Let* ρ *be a binary relation. The **Boolean configuration** for* $\langle a, b, c, d \rangle$ *of* ρ *is the induced relation on* $\langle a, b \rangle \times \langle c, d \rangle$.
    The two configurations $\{\langle a, c \rangle, \langle b, d \rangle\}$ *and* $\{\langle a, d \rangle, \langle b, c \rangle\}$, *are called **permutations**.*

Lemma 1. *Let* Γ *be the language of triangulated CSPs. The relation* ρ *is in* Γ *if and only if it has no Boolean configurations that are permutations.*

Proof. Straightforward, omitted for brevity

4   When Arc-Consistency Is a Decision Procedure

In this section we will compare the class of triangulated CSPs with other known classes for which arc-consistency is a decision procedure.

Definition 8. *Two CSP instances are **renamably equivalent** if one may be transformed into the other by renaming the variables and the domain elements.*
    A tractable class of instances S *is **subsumed** by another class* T *if all but finitely many instances of* S *are renamably equivalent to CSPs in* T.
    *Two tractable classes are **incomparable** if neither subsumes the other.*

Lemma 2. *The equals relation occurs in no triangulated CSP.*

Proof. Follows directly from Lemma 1.

Proposition 1. *The language,* Γ, *of the class of triangulated CSPs is NP-complete.*

Proof. Omitted for brevity. Relies on the (triangulated) binary relations $X_D = \{\rho_a \mid a \in D\}$ where ρ_a allows all tuples *except* $\langle a, a \rangle$, and a reduction from graph colourability.

Proposition 2. *Triangulated CSPs are not structurally tractable.*

Proof. Any CSP where every relation is the "allows everything" relation is triangulated. This includes a CSP with every structure,

Theorem 4. *The class of triangulated CSPs is incomparable with any structural or relational class decided by arc-consistency.*

Proof. Follows directly from Proposition 1, Proposition 2, Theorem 1, Theorem 2, and Lemma 2

We have shown that triangulated CSPs are indeed a hybrid class. In order to show that they are a novel class decided by arc-consistency we have to show that they are not subsumed by any known hybrid class.

There are two families of hybrid classes decided by arc-consistency. The first comes from the satisfiability community and includes examples such as the extended Horn class [2]. Clearly none of these Boolean classes can subsume triangulated CSPs which are in general, non-Boolean.

The other family is the approximately max-closed class [4]. These are the instances where some (independent) permutation of each domain can make them max-closed. A case by case analysis of the known tractable approximately max-closed classes shows that triangulated CSPs are incomparable with any of them.

5 Discussion

In this paper we have identified a new class of CSP instances decided by arc-consistency. The apparent similarity between the algorithms for solving ACI based instances, tree-structured instances and triangulated instances suggests that there may a single reason underlying the tractability of these three classes.

References

1. C. Bessiére. Arc-consistency and arc-consistency again. *Artificial Intelligence*, 65(1):179–190, 1994.
2. V. Chandru and J.N. Hooker. Extended Horn sets in propositional logic. *Journal of the ACM*, 38:205–221, 1991.
3. V. Dalmau and J. Pearson. Closure functions and width 1 problems. In J. Jaffar, editor, *Principles and Practice of Constraint Programming—CP'99*, volume 1713 of *Lecture Notes in Computer Science*, pages 159–173. Springer-Verlag, 1999.
4. M.J. Green and D.A. Cohen. Tractability by approximating constraint languages. Technical Report CSD-TR-03-01, Department of Computer Science, Royal Holloway, University of London, Egham, Surrey, UK, 2003.
5. M. Gyssens, P.G. Jeavons, and D.A. Cohen. Decomposing constraint satisfaction problems using database techniques. *Artificial Intelligence*, 66(1):57–89, 1994.
6. P.G. Jeavons, D.A. Cohen, and M. Gyssens. Closure properties of constraints. *Journal of the ACM*, 44:527–548, 1997.
7. D.J. Rose. Triangulated graphs and the elimination process. *Journal of Mathematical Analysis and Applications*, 32:597–609, 1970.
8. Robert E. Tarjan and Mihalis Yannakakis. Simple linear-time algorithms to test chordality of graphs, test acyclicity of hypergraphs, and selectively reduce acyclic hypergraphs. *SIAM Journal on Computing*, 13(3):566–579, 1984.

Semi-automatic Modeling by Constraint Acquisition[*][**]

Remi Coletta[1], Christian Bessière[1], Barry O'Sullivan[2],
Eugene C. Freuder[2], Sarah O'Connell[2], and Joel Quinqueton[1]

[1] LIRMM-CNRS (UMR 5506), 161 rue Ada 34392 Montpellier Cedex 5, France
{coletta,bessiere,jq}@lirmm.fr
[2] Cork Constraint Computation Centre
Department of Computer Science, University College Cork, Ireland
{b.osullivan,e.freuder,s.oconnell}@4c.ucc.ie

Abstract. Constraint programming is a technology which is now widely used to solve combinatorial problems in industrial applications. However, using it requires considerable knowledge and expertise in the field of constraint reasoning. This paper introduces a framework for automatically learning constraint networks from sets of instances that are either acceptable solutions or non-desirable assignments of the problem we would like to express. Such an approach has the potential to be of assistance to a novice who is trying to articulate her constraints. By restricting the language of constraints used to build the network, this could also assist an expert to develop an efficient model of a given problem.

1 Introduction

Over the last 30 years, considerable progress has been made in the field of Constraint Programming (CP). However, the use of CP still remains limited to specialists in the field. Modelling a problem in the constraint formalism requires significant expertise in constraint programming. Indeed, humans usually find it difficult to articulate their constraints. While the human user can recognize examples of where their constraints should be satisfied or violated, they cannot articulate the constraints themselves. However, by presenting examples of what is acceptable, the human user can be assisted in developing a model of the set of constraints she is trying to articulate. This can be regarded as an instance of constraint acquisition. One of the goals of our work is to assist the, possibly novice, human user by providing semi-automatic methods for acquiring the user's constraints.

Furthermore, even if the user has sufficient experience in CP to encode her problem, a poor model can negate the utility of a good solver based on state-of-the-art filtering techniques. For example, in order to provide support for modelling, some solvers provide facilities for defining constraints extensionally (i.e., by enumerating the set of allowed tuples). Such facilities considerably extend the expressiveness and ease-of-use of the

[*] [1] contains a long version of this paper.
[**] The collaboration between LIRMM and the Cork Constraint Computation Centre is supported by a Ulysses Travel Grant from Enterprise Ireland, the Royal Irish Academy and CNRS (Grant Number FR/2003/022). This work has also received support from Science Foundation Ireland under Grant 00/PI.1/C075.

F. Rossi (Ed.): CP 2003, LNCS 2833, pp. 812–816, 2003.
© Springer-Verlag Berlin Heidelberg 2003

constraints language, thus facilitating the definition of complex relationships between variables. However, a disadvantage of modelling constraints extensionally is that the constraints lose any useful semantics they may have which can have a negative impact on the inference and propagation capabilities of a solver. Therefore, another goal of our work is to facilitate the expert user who wishes to reformulate her problem (or a part of it that is suspected of slowing down the resolution). Given sets of accepted/forbidden instantiations of the (sub)problem (that can be generated automatically on the initial formulation), the expert will be able, for instance, to test whether an optimised constraint library associated with her solver is able to model the (sub)problem in a way which lends itself to being efficiently solved.

However, constraint acquisition is not only important in an interactive situation involving a human user. Often we may wish to acquire a constraint model from a large set of data. For example, given a large database of tuples defining buyer behaviour in a variety of markets, for a variety of buyer profiles, for a variety of products, we may wish to acquire a constraint network which describes the data in this database. While the nature of the interaction with the source of training data is different, the constraint acquisition problem is fundamentally the same.

Our contribution is an algorithm (named CONACQ), that extends version space machine learning techniques [3] to deal with the specificity of learning constraints. It takes solutions (positive instances) and non solutions (negative instances), called a training set, as input, and generates a (set of) constraint network(s) consistent with the training set. Using version spaces we can maintain the whole set of possible 'target' networks during the learning process. This set is represented by the tightest (specific bound) and loosest (general bound) networks consistent with the training data. We adapted the classical version space technique to maintain a reasonably low space complexity by representing the general bound as a set of clauses. In the following, we just give an overview of the learning framework, and discuss preliminary experiments and the issues they raise. A comprehensive description of the CONACQ algorithm can be found in [1].

2   The Fundamental Problem

As a starting point, we assume that the user knows the set of variables of her problem and their domains of possible values. She is also assumed to be able to provide or classify both positive (a solution) and negative (non-solution) examples. Therefore, the available data are the set $\mathcal{X}$ of the variables of the problem, their domains $\mathcal{D}$, a subset E^+ of the solutions of the problem, and a set E^- of non-solutions.

In addition, from the 'assisting the expert' perspective, the aim is to encode the problem efficiently, using only efficient constraint relations between these variables; i.e. a library of constraints with efficient propagation features is assumed to be known. Indications can also be given revealing the possible location of the constraints, by defining variables between which constraints must be found (learned), or by restricting ourselves to binary constraints only. These semantical and structural limitations define the inductive bias:

Definition 1 (Bias). *Given a set $\mathcal{X}$ of variables and the set $\mathcal{D}$ of their domains, a bias $\mathcal{B}$ on $(\mathcal{X}, \mathcal{D})$ is a sequence $(B_1, \ldots, B_m)$ of local biases, where a local bias B_i is defined* *by a sequence* $var(B_i) \subseteq \mathcal{X}$ *of variables, and a set* $L(B_i)$ *of possible relations on* $var(B_i)$.

The set $L(B_i)$ of relations allowed on a set of variables $var(B_i)$ can be any library of constraints of arity $|var(B_i)|$.

Definition 2 (Membership of a Bias). *Given a set $\mathcal{X}$ of variables and the set $\mathcal{D}$ of their domains, a sequence of constraints $\mathcal{C} = (C_1, \ldots, C_m)$ belongs to the bias $\mathcal{B} = (B_1, \ldots, B_m)$ on $(\mathcal{X}, \mathcal{D})$ if $\forall C_i \in \mathcal{C}, var(C_i) = var(B_i)$ and $rel(C_i) \in L(B_i)$. We note $\mathcal{C} \in \mathcal{B}$.*

The problem consists in looking for a sequence of constraints $\mathcal{C}$ belonging to a given bias $\mathcal{B}$, and whose solution set is a superset of E^+ containing no element of E^-.

Definition 3 (Constraint Acquisition Problem). *Given a set of variables $\mathcal{X}$, their domains $\mathcal{D}$, two sets E^+ and E^- of instances on $\mathcal{X}$, and a bias $\mathcal{B}$ on $(\mathcal{X}, \mathcal{D})$, the constraint acquisition problem consists in finding a sequence of constraints $\mathcal{C}$ such that:*

$\mathcal{C} \in \mathcal{B}$,
$\forall e^- \in E^-, e^-$ *is a non solution of* $(\mathcal{X}, \mathcal{D}, \mathcal{C})$, *and,*
$\forall e^+ \in E^+, e^+$ *is a solution of* $(\mathcal{X}, \mathcal{D}, \mathcal{C})$.

If the sets E^+ and E^-, called the *training data*, are provided by an interaction with the user, then the acquisition problem can be regarded as the modelling phase for the user's problem. Otherwise, it can be regarded as an assistance to the expert for an automatic reformulation of her problem.

As stated in the introduction, a version space does not only provide one consistent hypothesis, but all constraint sequences belonging to a bias that are consistent with the training data:

Definition 4 (Version Space). *Given $(\mathcal{X}, \mathcal{D})$ a set of variables and their domains, E^+ and E^- two training data sets, and $\mathcal{B}$ a bias on $(\mathcal{X}, \mathcal{D})$, the version space is the set:*

$$V = \{\mathcal{C} \in \mathcal{B}/E^+ \subseteq Sol(\mathcal{X}, \mathcal{D}, \mathcal{C}), E^- \cap Sol(\mathcal{X}, \mathcal{D}, \mathcal{C}) = \emptyset\}$$

3   Experiments and Observations

We report here on some preliminary experiments to evaluate the learning capabilities of our approach. Rather than focusing on techniques for minimising the number of interactions, our focus here is on studying a number of properties of the CONACQ algorithm which provide motivation for our research agenda.

We performed experiments with a simulated teacher, which plays the role of the user, and a simulated learner. The teacher has the knowledge of a randomly generated (target) network, represented by the triple $< 50, 8, C >$, defining a problem involving 50 variables with domains $\{1, ..8\}$, and a number C of constraints. Each constraint is randomly chosen from the bias $\{<, =, >, \leq, \neq, \geq\}$. The teacher provides the learner with solutions and non solutions. The learner acquires a version space for the problem using the CONACQ algorithm [1].

Table 1. Effect of the timing of the introduction of positive instances

Introduction date for positives	0 (a)	50 (b)	90 (c)
Computing time (in sec.)	3.3	5.1	8.6
$log(|V|)$	2,234	2,234	2,234

Table 2. Effect of the partial instances

Nb of variables involved in instances of E^-	50	10	5	2
$log(|V|)$	2,234	2,233	2,225	2,144
$|K|$ (10^4 meta-variables)	7.6	6.1	3.2	0

3.1 Experiment 1: Effect of the Order of the Instances

In this following experiment, we assess aspects of the runtime characteristics of the CONACQ algorithm. In particular, we study computing time and the size of the version space while varying the order in which examples are presented. Instances from a set E of size 100 are given by the teacher to the learner based on a $< 50, 8, 50 >$ network. The set E contains 10 positive and 90 negative instances.

Table 1 presents the time needed by the learner to acquire the version space, V, for the example set while varying the arrival time of the 10 positive instances. The positive instances were presented at the beginning (a), middle (b), and end (c) of the interaction between teacher and learner.

We observe that *"the sooner, the better"* seems to be the good strategy for the introduction of positive instances. Indeed, the specific bound rises quickly with positive instances, reducing the size of the version space. Because of that, the CPU time needed is also reduced when positive instances arrive at the beginning. But we can see that the final size of the version space is not affected by the order of the instances. This is due to the commutativity property of version spaces.

3.2 Experiment 2: Partial Instances

In some cases, the user can reject an instance while justifying it by a negative sub-instance. For example, in a real-estate setting the customer (teacher) might reject an apartment citing the reason that *"this living-room is too small for me"*. The estate agent (learner) knows that the violation is due to the variables defining the living room, which can being very helpful for handling negative examples. The usefulness of such justified rejections can be measured by providing our learner with partial instances. In the following experiment (Table 2), the teacher provides the learner with 90 partial negative instances (after 10 complete positive ones) in the training data. We consider partial instances involving 2, 5, 10 variables, and report the size of the version space and of the set of clauses K (effective space used to represent the general bound) after 100 instances have been given.

We observe that partial instances speed up the process of convergence of the version space. The smaller are these partial instances, the more helpful they are. This opens a promising way of helping the learning process: asking the user to justify why she rejects some instances can assist in reducing the length of the dialog with the teacher. This is a critical issue if we are learning in an interactive setting from a human user.

4   Aspects of Our Research Agenda

In this paper we have presented an approach to acquiring models of constraint satisfaction problems from examples. There is significant scope for research in this area. Here we give some insights into some aspects of our research in this area.

Standard version space learning algorithms are senstive to noise in the training data and, as a consequence, are brittle to false positives and negatives provided to the algorithm. However, some recent work from the machine learning community gives us a basis for making our approach more robust to such errors [2].

Another issue for which we did not show experiments because of space limitations, is that of implicit constraints and redundancy. An implicit constraint is one that does not belong to a network but that could be detected by inference. For example, if we have $X_1 = X_2$ and $X_2 = X_3$ in a network $\mathcal{N}$, the constraint $X_1 = X_3$ is an implicit constraint for $\mathcal{N}$. The general phenomenon of constraints that can be inferred by other constraints can prevent the version space from converging to the smallest possible one. Applying some levels of local consistency seems to be a promising approach for improving the reduction of the version space, by adding implicit constraints to the learned network. When we will deal with partial instances, this will have some interesting implications, such as the effect that the order in which examples are provided has on the representability of a particular problem in the given constraint language.

Finally, we considering the effect that various models of interaction can have on the speed with which we can learn the target problem, particularly from the perspective of minimising the number of interactions with the user. Some preliminary results have already been reported on this issue [4, 5].

References

1. R. Coletta, C. Bessiere, B. O'Sullivan, E.C. Freuder, S. O'Connell, and J. Quinqueton. Semi-automatic modeling by constraint acquisition. Technical Report 03051, LIRMM – University of Montpellier II, Montpellier, France, June 2003. (available at http://www.lirmm.fr/~bessiere/).
2. F.A. Marginean. Soft learning: A bridge between data mining and machine learning. In *Proceedings of the 4th International Conference on Recent Advances in Soft Computing (RASC-2002)*, pages 108–115, December 2002.
3. Tom Mitchell. Generalization as search. *Artificial Intelligence*, 18(2):203–226, 1982.
4. S. O'Connell, B. O'Sullivan, and E.C. Freuder. Strategies for interactive constraint acquisition. In *Proceedings of the CP-2002 Workshop on User-Interaction in Constraint Satisfaction*, pages 62–76, September 2002.
5. B. O'Sullivan, S. O'Connell, and E.C. Freuder. Interactive constraint acquisition for concurrent engineering. In *Proceedings of the 7th International Conference on Concurrent Enterprising – ICE-2003*, 2003.

Structured vs. Unstructured Large Neighborhood Search: A Case Study on Job-Shop Scheduling Problems with Earliness and Tardiness Costs

Emilie Danna[1,2] and Laurent Perron[1]

[1] ILOG. 9, rue de Verdun. 94253 Gentilly Cedex, France
[2] Laboratoire d'Informatique d'Avignon. CRNS - FRE 2487. 339, chemin des Meinajariès. Agroparc, BP 1228. 84911 Avignon Cedex 9, France
{edanna,lperron}@ilog.fr

1 Introduction

Large Neighborhood Search (LNS) [8] is a local search paradigm based on two main ideas to define and search large neighborhoods. The first key idea of LNS is to define its neighborhoods by fixing a part of an existing solution. The elements of the solution that are fixed are usually explicit or implicit variables of the model. For example, in a scheduling model, one may choose to fix the values of the start times of each activity (explicit variables) or one may add additional constraints that force one activity to be scheduled before another (implicit disjunctive variables). The rest of the variables are *released*: they are free to change values. The neighborhood is hence defined by all possible extensions of the fixed partial solution. Because a number of variables are released at a time, the neighborhoods defined are usually large, larger than typical local search neighborhoods.

Because of their size, the so-defined neighborhoods require a powerful algorithm to be explored; one cannot rely on enumeration or simple heuristics. The second key idea of LNS is to use some form of tree search, constraint programming (CP) or mixed integer programming (MIP) to search its neighborhoods, *i.e.*, to solve its sub-problems. The tree search is most often truncated with a possibly adaptive time limit, node limit or discrepancy limit.

The large size of the neighborhoods and the powerful algorithm used to solve sub-problems provide LNS with inherent diversification and intensification properties, respectively. Therefore the essential question in LNS, even more than in a typical local search algorithm, is how to define the neighborhoods, that is which variables to choose and fix together. The rule to define a promising neighborhood is to free simultaneously *related* variables. First, the problem might be so constrained that, even when freeing a number of randomly chosen variables, there might exist no other extension of the so-defined partial solution than the current solution. It is therefore essential to free related variables because they allow each other to change values. Next, the essence of LNS is to compute more complex moves that yield a new solution further away from the current solution

F. Rossi (Ed.): CP 2003, LNCS 2833, pp. 817–821, 2003.

than when exploring smaller neighborhoods. This provides diversification and this allows us to solve difficult core sub-problems. But LNS will succeed only if the neighborhood it defines corresponds to a sub-problem that is not a concatenation of smaller and independent sub-problems but a consistent core problem in itself. One hopes indeed that the gain obtained by simultaneously computing new values for the released variables will be greater than the gain obtained by changing the value of each variable independently. It is therefore essential to free related variables because they allow each other to take more meanigful values.

In the literature, choosing related variables is most often achieved by taking advantage of the known *high level structure* of the specific problem at hand. Recently, a new algorithm called *Relaxation Induced Neighborhood Search* (RINS) [5] was introduced: it is a form of LNS that only relies on the continuous relaxation of the MIP model of the problem to define its neighborhood. It can be used on any MIP model without any other input than the model itself. Unlike all previous LNS algorithms, it is therefore *unstructured*.

The aim of this paper is to compare relaxation induced neighborhood search and a structured large neighborhood search approach tailored to a particular and difficult problem. On the one hand, we want to evaluate how powerful LNS approaches are — structured or unstructured. On the other hand, we want to investigate how a generic approach like RINS compares to a domain-dependent approach. We have chosen for these aims the job-shop scheduling problem with earliness and tardiness costs. The exact problem description and a state of the art are given in a more detailed version of this paper [4].

2   Unstructured LNS in Mixed Integer Programming

We use the classical MIP model of Applegate and Cook [1] based on the disjunctive variables that state if a job is scheduled before or after another job on a given machine.

In order to find better integer solutions, we use the generic MIP heuristic Relaxation Induced Neighborhood Search (RINS) [5]. RINS is based on the intuition that decisions (*i.e.*, instantiations of variables) common to the incumbent (which is integral but not optimal) and the continuous relaxation (which is optimal but not integral) form a partial solution that is likely to be extended towards a complete solution that achieves integrality and reaches or comes near to optimality. Therefore, it focuses attention on those variables that differ in the continuous relaxation and in the incumbent, which are intuitively the ones that appear to merit further attention. Our RINS algorithm is thus simple. At every f node of the global branch-and-cut tree, the variables that have the same value in the incumbent and in the current continuous relaxation are fixed and a sub-MIP is solved on the remaining variables with a node limit nl. Parameters f and nl can be set to a wide range of values without degrading performances. We use $f = 100$, $nl = 1000$.

3   Structured LNS in Constraint Programming

Our structured LNS algorithm develops as follows. At each LNS iteration, a neighborhood of the current solution is first built, according to one randomly chosen scheme among the five kinds of neighborhood described thereafter. The rank of all activities not included in this neighborhood is then fixed and the remaining activities are ranked with a dedicated CP algorithm. The start times of all activities are last assigned with an LP-based algorithm [3].

We have implemented five structured neighborhoods. The *random* neighborhood is completely unstructured and generic. It releases randomly chosen activities. The *resource based* neighborhood releases all activities on given resources. The *random time window* neighborhood releases activities scheduled within different time windows on different resources; there is no correlation between the time windows selected for different resources. The *consecutive pair* neighborhood releases pairs of consecutive activities, *i.e.* that are scheduled on the same resource one after the other in the current solution. These very simple neighborhoods can be applied directly to any scheduling problem with unary resources and extended easily to resources with capacity greater than one. Note that they rely heavily on randomness in their definition. Our last structured neighborhood is dedicated to the earliness/tardiness ojective function. We select two jobs p and q that are not scheduled on time in the current solution and release each activity of job p and q, plus some other activities scheduled after or before each in the current solution, depending on whether the corresponding job is early or late. The aim is to allow the corresponding job to be pushed left or right in order to decrease its tardiness or its earliness cost.

4   Computational Results

The unstructured LNS approach **uLNS** presented in Section 2 uses a modified version of CPLEX 8.1. The structured LNS approach **sLNS** presented in Section 3 uses ILOG Solver 5.3, ILOG Scheduler 5.3 and ILOG CPLEX 8.1. All experiments were done on a 1.5GHz Pentium IV system.

The first benchmark [2] consists of 90 randomly generated problems, divided in three sets depending on the value of the *looseness* parameter (see [6] for a discussion on the influence of this parameter). For all problems with looseness 1.3 and 1.5, **sLNS** and **uLNS** find (and prove for the latter) the optimal solutions very easily. We concentrate therefore on the more difficult 30 1.0-looseness problems for which we now report the sum of the cost of the solutions obtained and the GMR (geometric mean of the ratio: cost of the solution obtained/cost of the best known upper bound). We also report results obtained on the same test system with the same time limit by other algorithms: default CPLEX on the basic model of **uLNS**, a simple constraint programming approach (default CP) [2], CRS-All [2] and HLS [3][1]. The *best* column gives the best known upper bounds, that were found either by one of our algorithms or by CRS-All. The *LB* column

---

[1] HLS results were obtained on a 4 to 5 times slower computer.

gives the lower bound obtained by our MIP-based approach. Note that our unstructured LNS approach embbeded in constraint programming is an incomplete method, it neither provides lower bounds nor optimality proofs.

	uLNS	sLNS	Default CPLEX	Default CP [2]	CRS-ALL [2]	HLS [3]	best	LB
GMR	3.35	1.43	18.59	26.56	10.60	13.98		
SUM	156,001	52,307	654,290	1,060,634	885,546	478,181	36,459	11,407

The second benchmark [7] has been used in several studies of scheduling with genetic algorithms (GA). We compare our results otained in two hours on our test system to the best results obtained by various GAs as reported in [9][2]. For each algorithm, we provide the GMR over the whole set (GMR 12) and over the five largest instances (GMR 5) that are still open.

	uLNS	sLNS	GA-best
GMR 12	1.08	1.07	1.41
GMR 5	1.21	1.16	1.21

5   Conclusion

In this paper we have shown that large neighborhood search is a powerful paradigm to solve hard combinatorial problems. Both our approaches of structured and unstructured LNS have proved to be effective and robust — outperforming a variety of existing algorithms on two benchmarks for the job-shop scheduling problem with earliness and tardiness costs. Note in particular that our structured LNS embedded in constraint programming dramatically improves on pure constraint programming by defining a specific neighborhood that exploits the structure of the earliness/tardiness objective. This allows to attack successfully a sum objective, on which constraint propagation was traditionnally very weak.

Our structured and unstructured LNS approaches yield competitive results on every benchmark, each approach outperforming the other on some benchmarks and vice versa. We propose four elements to explain the difference of performance between the two approaches. The first is how neighborhoods are defined, using explicitly the high level structure of the problem or not. The second is how the neighborhoods are explored, using constraint programming or branch-and-cut. The third explanation we propose is that RINS defines neighborhoods in a deterministic manner, whereas our structured LNS approach relies heavily on randomization. This allows to diversify the search in a simple yet effective way. Finally, our fourth explanation is that our unstructured LNS approach not only consists in RINS but also in exploring a global branch-and-cut tree as when solving any MIP. Therefore not the whole computation time is devoted to finding upper bounds, but a significant part of the time is spent in branching and solving continuous relaxations at each node of the global branch-and-cut

---

[2] The time limit used by the genetic algorithms is not mentioned.

tree. In turn, this allows to compute lower bounds and to produce optimality proofs, which is not possible with our structured LNS approach.

It should finally be noted that none of our approaches is totally generic. This is obvious for structured LNS: its neighborhoods depend heavily on the specific problem at hand. Though less apparent, this is also true for RINS. RINS uses not other input than the MIP model itself, and hence is generic to any MIP. But the improvement of our results with successive versions of our MIP model [4] show that tightening the MIP model is a important element of the unstructured LNS strategy. For RINS, the problem-specific part of the work is the definition of the MIP model instead of the definition of the tailored neighborhoods as in structured LNS.

Acknowledgments

The authors wish the express their heartfelt thanks to Philippe Refalo who provided the LP-based time placement code used in the structured LNS approach. We would like also to thank Claude Le Pape for his support and his deep thinking that helped us with this work.

References

1. D. Applegate and W. Cook. A computational study of the job-shop scheduling problem. *ORSA Journal on Computing*, 3(2):149–156, 1991.
2. J. C. Beck and P. Refalo. A hybrid approach to scheduling with earliness and tardiness costs. In *Proceedings of the Third International Workshop on Integration of AI and OR Techniques in Constraint Programming for Combinatorial Optimisation Problems (CP-AI-OR'01)*, pages 175–188, 2001.
3. J. C. Beck and P. Refalo. Combining local search and linear programming to solve earliness/tardiness scheduling problems. In *Proceedings of the Fourth International Workshop on Integration of AI and OR Techniques in Constraint Programming for Combinatorial Optimisation Problems (CP-AI-OR'02)*, pages 221–235, 2002.
4. E. Danna and L. Perron. Structured vs. unstructured large neighborhood search: A case study on job-shop scheduling problems with earliness and tardiness costs. Technical Report 03-005, ILOG, 2003.
5. E. Danna, E. Rothberg, and C. Le Pape. Exploring relaxation induced neighborhoods to improve MIP solutions. Technical Report 03-004, ILOG, 2003.
6. E. Danna, E. Rothberg, and C. Le Pape. Integrating mixed integer programming and local search: A case study on job-shop scheduling problems. In *Proceedings of the Fifth International Workshop on Integration of AI and OR Techniques in Constraint Programming for Combinatorial Optimisation Problems (CP-AI-OR'03)*, 2003.
7. T. Morton and D. Pentico. *Heuristic Scheduling Systems*. John Wiley and Sons, 1993.
8. P. Shaw. Using constraint programming and local search methods to solve vehicle routing problems. In M. Maher and J.-F. Puget, editors, *Proceeding of CP '98*, pages 417–431. Springer-Verlag, 1998.
9. M. Vasquez and L. Whitley. A comparison of genetic algorithms for the dynamic job shop scheduling problem. In *Proceedings of the Genetic and Evolutionary Computation Conference (GECCO-2000)*, pages 1011–1018, 2000.

Using the Breakout Algorithm
to Identify Hard and Unsolvable Subproblems

Carlos Eisenberg and Boi Faltings

Artificial Intelligence Laboratory (LIA)
Swiss Federal Institute of Technology (EPFL)
IN-Ecublens, 1015 Lausanne, Switzerland
{eisenberg,faltings}@lia.di.epfl.ch
http://liawww.epfl.ch/

Abstract. Local search algorithms have been very successful for solving constraint satisfaction problems (CSP). However, a major weakness has been that local search is unable to detect unsolvability and is thus not suitable for highly constrained or overconstrained problems. In this paper, we present a scheme where a local search algorithm, the breakout algorithm, is used to identify hard or unsolvable subproblems and to derive a variable ordering that places the hardest subproblems first.

1 Introduction

The breakout algorithm is an efficient, local search algorithm for solving Constraint Satisfaction Problems (CSPs). The roots of the algorithm go back to Minton et al. ([4]) and Morris ([5]).

The strengths of the breakout algorithm are simplicity, robustness, low memory requirement and high efficiency for solving underconstrained problems. These properties are extremely useful when dealing with large scale constraint satisfaction problems. The major weak point of the breakout algorithm is its incompleteness: it cannot guarantee termination, even when a solution exists, and it will not terminate when no solution exists. In this paper we present a hybrid algorithm where we combine an incomplete, local search algorithm, the breakout algorithm, with a systematic, complete search algorithm, backtracking. By combining the breakout algorithm with backtracking, we compensate its weaknesses: incompleteness and difficulty to deal with tightly- and overconstrained problems. Moreover, we discover that the combination of the two algorithms leads to synergies. By using the weight information that is generated during the local search process, we can locate and order particularly hard or unsolvable subproblems. These can guide the complete search process such that variables of the hardest subproblems come first, providing a powerful fail-first heuristic for systematic search. The scheme is also useful for generating explanations of unsolvability. The longer version of this paper can be found at [2].

F. Rossi (Ed.): CP 2003, LNCS 2833, pp. 822–826, 2003.
© Springer-Verlag Berlin Heidelberg 2003

2   Preliminaries

2.1   Definitions

Definition 1 (Constraint Satisfaction Problem P). *A finite, binary constraint satisfaction problem is a tuple $P =< X, D, C >$ where:*

- *$X = \{x_1, .., x_n\}$ is a set of n variables,*
- *$D = \{d_1(x_1), .., d_n(x_n)\}$ is a set of n domains, and*
- *$C = \{c_1, .., c_p\}$ is a set of p constraints, where each constraint $c_l(x_i, x_j)$ involves two variables x_i and x_j.*

A solution of P is a variable value assignment where all constraints are satisfied.

Definition 2 (Subproblem P_k). *A subproblem P_k of a problem P with k variables is defined as a tuple $P_k =< X_{P_k} \subseteq X, D_{P_k} \subseteq D, C_{P_k} \subseteq C >$ with the additional constraint that C_{P_k} contains all and only constraints between variables in X_{P_k}. We define the size of a subproblem $size(P_k)$ as the number of constraints $|C_{P_k}|$.*

Definition 3 (Unsolvable Subproblems). *A subproblem P_k is unsolvable if there is no value assignment to variables in X_{P_k} that satisfies all constraints in C_{P_k}. An unsolvable subproblem P_k is minimal if it becomes solvable by removing any one of its variables.*

The breakout algorithm ([5]) is a further development of the min-conflicts algorithm ([4]) and is the basis for our work. In the breakout algorithm, every constraint has an associated weight that is used to escape from local non solution minima:

Definition 4 (Constraint Weight w). *Each constraint is assigned a weight $w(c(x_i, x_j))$ or in short $w_{i,j}$. All weights are positive integer numbers and are set to 1 initially.*

Conflict minimization consists of choosing a variable and a new value that reduces as much as possible the conflicts in the current state. If no improvement is possible, the algorithm is in a local minimum. In this case, the algorithm increases the weight of each violated constraint by 1, and again attempts to compute the possible improvements. For the breakout algorithm, we can observe the following:

Lemma 1. *After m breakout iterations, the sum of the constraint weights $w_{sum} = \sum_{c(x_i, x_j) \in C_{P_k}} w_{i,j}$ of an unsolvable subproblem P_k with $|C_{P_k}| = q$ constraints must be greater than or equal to $m + q$.*

Proof. If a subproblem is unsolvable, then in every breakout step, one or more of the subproblem constraints must be violated and the corresponding constraint weight is increased. The lower bound for w_{sum} can be derived by assuming that in every iteration only one constraint is violated. In this case the weight sum must be equal to $m + q$.

Thus, if after m iterations the breakout algorithm has not found a solution, and we suspect that the problem contains an unsolvable subproblem with 3 constraints, then we only have to consider subproblems whose weight sum is at least $m + 3$. If we apply this constraint in the problem of Figure 1, we find that the constraints of w1, w9, w10, whose sum is 103, are the only three constraints that satisfy the sum constraint and indeed describe an unsolvable subproblem of size 3, colouring a graph of 3 nodes with only 2 colours.

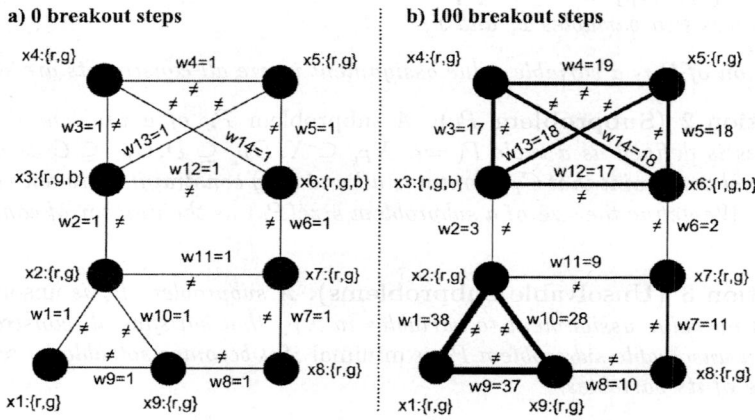

Fig. 1. The weight graph of an unsolvable graph colouring problem containing three unsolvable subproblems of size 3 (x_1, x_2, x_9), 4 (x_3, x_4, x_5, x_6) and 5 (x_1, x_2, x_7, x_8, x_9), after 0 and 100 breakout steps.

3   The Scheme and Hybrid Solver BOBT

The observed properties of the breakout algorithm inspired us to use the constraint weight information, which is generated by the breakout algorithm, for localizing the critical problem variables and thus hard or unsolvable subproblems. This idea is based on the observation that the constraint weights are also violation counters, which are incremented whenever the search is in a local minimum. Increasing the weights only in local minimum states is an advantage; in this state the noise level, generated by constraints not belonging to a hard or unsolvable subproblem is the lowest. We are now going to present a hybrid scheme where we first apply the breakout algorithm, and then switch to backtrack search when no solution has been found after a given iteration limit.

When the local search method does not find a solution, we terminate and sort the variables according to the constraint weights and the graph structure. Intuitively, variables which cause the greatest conflict and thus describe the hardest part of the problem will therefore be located at the top of the ordered variable list. The subsequent complete search method will then consider those first.

The hybrid solver BOBT, Algorithm 1, begins by searching for a solution using the standard breakout method. If after a bounded number of breakout iterations, the local search process has not found a solution, the process is aborted and the constraints are sorted according to their weights. Constraints with a high weight are most likely to belong to an unsolvable subproblem. Therefore, the constraint with the highest weight is selected and its variables make up the first candidate subproblem P.

The algorithm then iterates the following steps. First, it attempts to solve the subproblem P by a systematic backtrack search. If the search finds a solution, then either it has found a solution to the original problem and returns it, or the subproblem is extended by the variable x_i such that the sum of the weights of all constraints connecting x_i to P is highest. If not, then the algorithm has found an unsolvable subproblem, calls the function *musp* to determine its minimal version, and returns it. Function musp is derived from the fo-search algorithm described in [3].

```
 1: function BOBT(X, D, C, maxbreak)
 2: (S, W) ← breakout(< X, D, C >, ∞, maxbreak)
 3: if S is a solution then
 4:    return(solvable, S)
 5: else
 6:    P ← vars(argmax_{c∈C}(w(c))
 7:    loop
 8:       S ← backtrack − search(P, D, C)
 9:       if S is a solution then
10:          if S = X then
11:             return(solvable, S)
12:          else
13:             P ← P ∪ {argmax_{x_i∈X\P} Σ_{c(x_i,x_j),x_j∈P} w(c)}
14:       else
15:          musp ← musp(P, D, C)
16:          return (unsolvable, musp)
```

Algorithm 1: Hybrid solver BOBT: returns either a solution or a minimal unsolvable subproblem.

4   Experiments and Results

For evaluating the presented scheme we generated a large set of 10,000 random graph 3-colouring problems according to the method described in [Davenport et.al. 1995]. The problem graphs that we generate consist of 30 variables with a connectivity of 2-6. The ratio of the solvable to the unsolvable problems is 1:1.

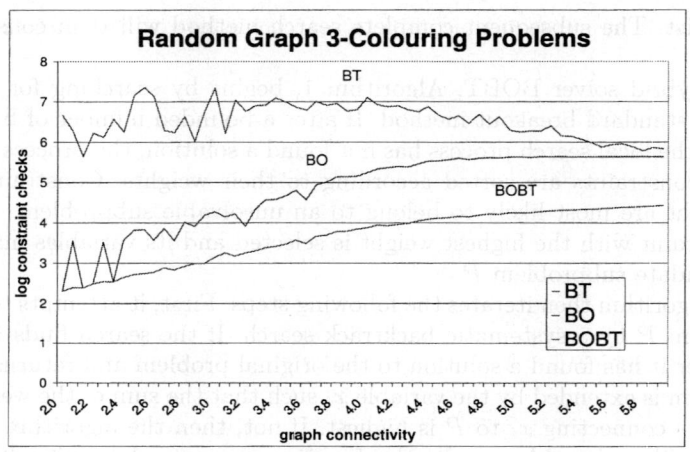

Fig. 2. Number of constraint checks on a logarithmic scale for solving 10,000 randomly generated, 30 node graph 3-colouring problems with BT, BO and BOBT.

Figure 2 shows the results of the experiments. We draw the number of constraint checks on a logarithmic scale for BT, BO and BOBT as function of the problem connectivity.

We observe that the hybrid algorithm BOBT clearly outperforms BT and BO for all connectivity values. Analyzing the execution of the hybrid algorithm, we notice that BO finds the most solutions for underconstrained problems, while for tightly constrained problems BT finds more solutions.

References

1. A. Davenport and E. P. K.Tsang. An empirical investigation into the exceptionally hard problems. Technical Report CSM-239, Department of Computer Science, University of Essex, U.K., 1995.
2. C. Eisenberg and B. Faltings. Using the Breakout Algorithm to Identify Hard and Unsolvable Subproblems. Technical Report IC-2003-46,Swiss Federal Institute of Technology (EPFL), Switzerland, 2003.
   http://ic2.epfl.ch/publications/documents/IC_TECH_REPORT_200346.pdf
3. B. Faltings and S. Macho-Gonzalez. Open Constraint Satisfaction. Proc. of the 8th International Conference on Principles and Practice of Constraints Programming, 2002.
4. S. Minton, M. Johnston, A. Philips and P. Laird. Minimizing Conflicts: A Heuristic Repair Method for Constraint Satisfaction and Scheduling Problems. Artificial Intelligence, Vol. 58, P. 161-205, 1992.
5. P. Morris. The breakout method for escaping from local minima. Proc. of the 11th National Conf. on Artificial Intelligence (Washington, DC), 1993, pp. 40–45.

Toy(FD): Sketch of Operational Semantics

Antonio J. Fernández[1], Teresa Hortalá-González[2], and Fernando Sáenz-Pérez[2]

[1] Dept. de Lenguajes y Ciencias de la Computación, Univ. de Málaga, Spain[*]
afdez@lcc.uma.es
[2] Dept. Sistemas Informáticos y Programación, Univ. Complutense de Madrid
{teresa,fernan}@sip.ucm.es

1 Introduction

In [2] we proposed the integration of finite domain (FD) constraints into the functional logic programming language TOY and, as result, presented the language TOY(FD). We showed that TOY(FD) integrates the best features of existing functional and logic languages into FD constraint solving. This paper describes a sketch (due to space limitations) of the TOY(FD) operational semantics that consists of a novel combination of lazy evaluation and FD constraint solving.

2 Denotational Semantics

Types. We assume a countable set $\mathcal{T}Var$ of *type variables* α, β, ... and a countable ranked alphabet $TC = \bigcup_{n \in \mathbb{N}} TC^n$ of *type constructors* $C \in TC^n$. Types $\tau \in Type$ have the syntax $\tau ::= \alpha \mid C \ \tau_1 \ldots \tau_n \mid \tau \to \tau' \mid (\tau_1, \ldots, \tau_n)$, $C \ \overline{\tau}_n$ abbreviates $C \ \tau_1 \ldots \tau_n$, "$\to$" associates to the right, $\overline{\tau}_n \to \tau$ abbreviates $\tau_1 \to \cdots \to \tau_n \to \tau$ and $(\tau_1, \ldots, \tau_n)$ denotes n-tuples. A type without any occurrence of "$\to$" is called a *datatype*. A *polymorphic signature* over TC is a triple $\Sigma = \langle TC, \ DC, \ FS \rangle$, where $DC = \bigcup_{n \in \mathbb{N}} DC^n$ and $FS = \bigcup_{n \in \mathbb{N}} FS^n$ are ranked sets of *data constructors* resp. *defined function symbols*. Each n-ary $c \in DC^n$ comes with a principal type declaration $c :: \overline{\tau}_n \to C \ \overline{\alpha}_k$, where $n, k \geq 0, \alpha_1, \ldots, \alpha_k$ are pairwise different, τ_i are datatypes, and the set of type variables occurring in τ_i is included in $\{\alpha_1, \ldots, \alpha_k\}$ for all $1 \leq i \leq n$. Every n-ary $f \in FS^n$ comes with a principal type declaration $f :: \overline{\tau}_n \to \tau$, where τ_i, τ are arbitrary types. In practice, each TOY(FD) program P has a signature which corresponds to the type declarations occurring in P. In the sequel, we always assume a given signature Σ, often not made explicit in the notation and write $\Sigma_\bot$ for the result of extending Σ with a new data constructor $\bot :: \alpha$, intended to represent an undefined value belonging to every type. As notational conventions, in the rest of the paper, we use $c, d \in DC$, $f, g \in FS$ and $h \in DC \cup FS$.

Patterns and Expressions. We assume a countable set Var of (data) variables $X, Y, \ldots$ disjoint from $\mathcal{T}Var$ and Σ. *Partial expressions* have the syntax

---

[*] This author has been partially supported by the projects TIC2001-2705-C03-02, and TIC2002-04498-C05-02 funded by both the Spanish Ministry of Science and Technology and FEDER.

F. Rossi (Ed.): CP 2003, LNCS 2833, pp. 827–831, 2003.

$e ::= \perp \ \mid X \mid h \mid e\,e' \mid (e_1, \ldots, e_n)$ where $X \in \mathit{Var}$, $h \in DC \cup FS$ and
e, e' and e_i (for $1 \leq i \leq n$) are partial expressions ($e \in \mathit{Exp}_\perp$). Expressions
of the form $e\,e'$ stand for the application of expression e (acting as a function)
to expression e' (acting as an argument), while expressions $(e_1, \ldots, e_n)$ represent tuples with n components. An expression e is *non-primitive*, and we write
non–primitive(e), iff it contains no function symbol. *Partial patterns* are built
as $t ::= \perp \mid X \mid c\ t_1 \ldots t_l \mid f\ t_1 \ldots t_m$ where $X \in \mathit{Var}$, $c \in DC^k$, $0 \leq l \leq$
k, $f \in FS^n$, $0 \leq m < n$ and t_i's are partial patterns ($t \in \mathit{Pat}_\perp \subset \mathit{Exp}_\perp$). Expressions and patterns without any occurrence of $\perp$ are called *total*. The sets of
total expressions and patterns are denoted, respectively, by Exp and Pat.

Functions and FD Constraints. Each function $f \in FS^n$ is defined by a set of
conditional rules of the form $f\ t_1 \ldots t_n = r \ \Leftarrow \psi_1, \ldots, \psi_k$, where $(t_1 \ldots t_n)$ form
a tuple of linear (i.e., with no repeated variable) *patterns*, r is an *expression* and
ψ_j can be either a *joinability statement* of the form $e == e'$, or a *disequality
statement* of the form $e\,/=\,e'$, with $e, e' \in \mathit{Exp}$, or a Boolean function. Rules
have a conditional reading: $f\ t_1 \ldots t_n$ can be reduced to r if all the conditions
ψ_i are satisfied ($1 \leq i \leq k$). FD constraints are defined as functions and their
complete definitions were shown in [2] and are available in [3]. In this paper,
$FS_{FD} \subset FS^n$ denotes the set of FD constraints that return a Boolean value.

Substitutions. A *substitution* is a mapping $\theta : \mathit{Var} \rightarrow \mathit{Pat}$ with a unique
extension $\hat{\theta} : \mathit{Exp} \rightarrow \mathit{Exp}$, which is also denoted as θ. Let Subst denote the set of
all substitutions and let the set of all the *partial substitutions* $\theta : \mathit{Var} \rightarrow \mathit{Pat}_\perp$
denote $\mathit{Subst}_\perp$, and defined analogously. We define the *domain* $dom(\theta)$ as the
set of all variables X s.t. $\theta(X) \neq X$. By convention, we write $e\theta$ instead of $\theta(e)$,
and $\theta\sigma$ for the composition of θ and σ, such that $e(\theta\sigma) = (e\theta)\sigma$ for any e.

Finite Domains. A *finite domain* (FD) is a mapping $\delta : \mathit{Var} \rightarrow \wp(\mathit{Integer})$,
where $\wp(\mathit{Integer})$ denotes the powerset of integers. The set of all FDs is denoted
as $\mathcal{FD}$. Also δ is *inconsistent* (resp.*consistent*), and write *inconsistent*(δ) (resp.
consistent(δ)), if there exists (resp. does not exist) X such that $\delta(X) = \emptyset$.

Programs. A program defines a set of functions where each $f \in FS^n$ has an
associated principal type $\tau_1 \rightarrow \ldots \rightarrow \tau_m \rightarrow \tau$ (with τ not containing $\rightarrow$).
As usual in functional programming, types are inferred and, optionally, can be
declared in the program.

3   Operational Semantics

This section presents part (due to space limitations) of the operational semantics
of TOY(FD) that deals with higher order (HO) programming by translating HO
expressions into first order, and consists of a novel combination of lazy narrowing
and constraint solving. $\psi_1, \ldots, \psi_n$ is a goal whose variables have an existential
reading. Solving a goal means obtaining conditions (a mixture of substitutions
and finite domains) over their variables to ensure the satisfiability of the initial
goal.

  Notational conventions. Let $e, e' \in \mathit{Exp}$; by $[e]_\mu$, $e[\mu \leftarrow e']$ and $e[\forall \mu \in I.\mu \leftarrow X_\mu]$, we respectively mean the sub-expression of e at position μ, the expression resulting from replacing $[e]_\mu$ in e by e', and the expression resulting from replacing, for each $\mu \in I$ with $I \in \wp(Integer)$, $[e]_\mu$ in e by a fresh variable X_μ. If $e \equiv f\ e_1 \ldots e_n$ and $f \in FS^n$, $NonPri_e \equiv \{j \mid non\text{--}primitive(e_j) \wedge 1 \le j \le n\}$ is the set identifying the positions of all the non-primitive arguments in e.

Let $\mathcal{P}$ be a TOY(FD) program with a signature $\Sigma = \langle TC, DC, FS \rangle$. There is a natural notion of model of rules and programs, for which it can be proved that every semantically non-ambiguous TOY(FD) program $\mathcal{P}$ has a least model $\mathcal{I}_\mathcal{P}$ [4]. Then, a *solution wrt.* $\mathcal{P}$ for a goal ψ is a substitution σ such that σ satisfies ψ in $\mathcal{I}_\mathcal{P}$ ($\sigma \models_{\mathcal{I}_\mathcal{P}} \psi$). We also say that σ satisfies $\exists \overline{U} \psi$ if there is σ' which satisfies ψ and coincides with σ over $dom(\sigma) - U$.

In the following, by $\mid \psi \mid$, *the shell of* ψ, we denote the result of replacing in ψ all the outermost sub-expressions of the form $f\ e_1 \ldots e_n$ by $\perp$. Following the schema in [1], we say a goal ψ is *semantically finished* wrt. σ if σ is a solution of $\mid \psi \mid$ wrt. $\mathcal{P}$ and by simplicity we also write $\sigma \models_{\mathcal{I}_\mathcal{P}} \psi$. The words *semantically finished* are used to express ψ may still contain non-primitive sub-expressions but their values are irrelevant to the fact that σ is a solution of the goal.

We consider configurations $\langle e, \sigma, \delta \rangle_{C_a}$ where $e \in Exp$, $\sigma \in Subst$, $\delta \in \mathcal{FD}$ and C_a is a set of primitive FD constraints (i.e., with no function symbol in the arguments). The initial state to solve a goal ψ is $\langle \psi, \epsilon, \mathcal{E} \rangle_\emptyset$ where ϵ denotes the empty substitution and $\delta(X) = Integer$ for any integer variable X in Var. Next table shows some important rules of the TOY(FD) operational semantics.

NON-SATISFACTION

$$\frac{inconsistent(\delta) \vee \sigma \not\models_{\mathcal{I}_\mathcal{P}} e}{\langle e, \sigma, \delta \rangle_{C_a} \mapsto \text{ termination with failure}}$$

SOLUTION

$$\frac{consistent(\delta) \wedge \sigma \models_{\mathcal{I}_\mathcal{P}} e}{\langle e, \sigma, \delta \rangle_{C_a} \mapsto \text{ termination with solution } \sigma}$$

ONE-STEP NARROWING

$$\frac{[e]_\mu \equiv f\ e_1 \ldots e_n,\ f \in FS^n - FS_{FD}^n,\ \sigma' = \{X_1 \mapsto e_1, \ldots, X_n \mapsto e_n\},}{\langle e, \sigma, \delta \rangle_{C_a} \mapsto \langle e[\mu \leftarrow r\sigma'] \wedge \psi\sigma', \sigma, \delta \rangle_{C_a}}$$

$f\ X_1 \ldots X_n = r \Leftarrow \psi$ is a variant rule for f in FS with fresh variables $\overline{X} \cup \overline{Y}$

FD CONSTRAINT SOLVING

$$\frac{[e]_\mu = (g\ e_1 \ldots e_n),\ g \in FS_{FD},\ C_{FD} \equiv [e]_\mu[\forall j \in NonPri_{[e]_\mu}.j \leftarrow X_j]}{C_a' = C_a \cup C_{FD},\ C_{FD} \rightsquigarrow_\delta^{C_a'} \delta'}{\langle e, \sigma, \delta \rangle_{C_a} \mapsto \langle e[\mu \leftarrow true] \bigwedge \{X_j == e_j \mid j \in NonPri_{[e]_\mu}\}, \sigma, \delta' \rangle_{C_a'}}$$

The *non-satisfaction* and *solution* rules check for termination returning a failure or a solution, respectively. The *lazy computation mechanism* is based mainly in the rule *one-step narrowing* that basically rewrites a goal by taking into account the demanded positions [4].

We note that, due to space limitations, we do not provide correctness proof and also that the semantics described here is a simplification of the operational semantics of TOY(FD) (observe for example that it generates reductions that are actually not performed, because of variable sharing, and also that we do not show the rule that considers pattern matching in the function arguments).

TOY(FD) also integrates a solving mechanism for FD constraints that is mainly based in the rule *FD constraint solving* in which it is assumed the existence of a mechanism $C_{FD} \leadsto_\delta^{C_a} \delta'$ to define the resolution of a FD constraint C_{FD} under the initial conditions imposed by both the finite domain δ and the constraints in C_a. The resolution gives place to a new (possibly inconsistent) finite domain δ' that replaces the original δ in the transition process among configurations. Observe that only primitive constraints are sent to the FD constraint solver. This is because non-primitive constraints are first translated to primitive ones by replacing the non-primitive arguments by new fresh variables before executing constraint solving and by registering new bindings in forms of equality constraints between the non-primitive arguments and the new variables. This last step is reflected in the addition of the sub-goal $X_j == e_j$, with X_j as fresh variable, corresponding to each non-primitive argument e_j in the original constraint $[e]_\mu$. Note also that this allows for HO computations possibly to be done on the arguments $e_1, \ldots, e_n$.

Upon termination and finding a solution, the final state is $\langle \phi, \sigma, \delta \rangle$ with δ consistent and σ satisfying ϕ in $\mathcal{I}_\mathcal{P}$. Termination and correctness of constraint solving is responsibility of the constraint solving mechanism $\leadsto_\delta^{C_a}$.

4   An Example: Imposing Infinite Lists of Constraints

TOY(FD) provides lazy evaluation (i.e., *call-by-need*) that means that the arguments (to functions) are evaluated to the required extent in contrast to *eager or strict evaluation* in which arguments are evaluated before the call (i.e., *call-by-value*). This aspect of TOY(FD) increases the possibilities of constraint solving by, for example, using infinite list of constraints. Consider the (well-known) magic series problem [6] and the following TOY (FD) functions[1]:

```
generateFD :: int -> [int]
generateFD N = [X | generateFD N] <== domain [X] 0 (N-1)

constrain :: [int] -> [int] -> int -> [int] -> bool
constrain [] A B [] = true
constrain [X|Xs] L I [I|S2] = true <== count I L (#=)  X,
                                       constrain Xs L  I+1 S2
lazymagic :: int -> [int]
lazymagic N = L <== take N (generateFD N) == L, constrain L L 0 Cs,
                    sum L (#=) N, scalar_product Cs L (#=) N, labeling [ff] L

magicfrom :: int -> [[int]]
magicfrom N = [lazymagic N | magicfrom (N+1)]
```

The function `lazymagic/1` uses the predefined FD constraints `count/4` (via `constrain/4`), `sum/3`, `scalar_product/4`, `#=/2` and `labeling/2` and the

---

[1] Lists follows the syntax of Prolog lists and Variables start with uppercase, whereas the remaining symbols start with lowercase.

primitive function `take:: int -> [A] -> [A]` defined such that `take N L` returns the list with the first N elements of L. `generateFD/1` imposes an infinite list of membership constraints (i.e., `domain/3`) by generating an infinite list of variables ranging in the interval [0,N-1] for some N. The N-magic serial is calculated by lazy evaluation by solving the goal `lazymagic N`, for some natural N. However, observe that an eager evaluation would not terminate as it tries to evaluate first the second argument in `take N (generateFD N) == L` yielding to an infinite list. Also, `magicfrom/1` generates an infinite list of N-magic series from a number N, and, again by lazy evaluation, it is possible to return answers; for example, the goal `take 3 (magicfrom 7) == L` returns in L a 3-element list containing, respectively, the solution to the problems of 7, 8, and 9-magic series.

5   Conclusions

We have presented a sketch of the operational semantics of TOY(FD), a functional logic programming language with support for FD constraint solving. This semantics consists of a novel combination of laziness and constraint solving in such a way that both remain independent; the advantage is that termination and correctness of lazy evaluation is left to the functional logic language that acts as host language whereas the same properties for constraint solving are responsability of a FD constraint solver connected to the host language. The system TOY(FD) is available in [3].

Note that we focus on the integration of finite domains into a functional-logic language, a proposal quite different from the language Oz [5], which combines FD constraints and functions.

References

1. P. Arenas, A. Gil, and F. López-Fraguas. Combining lazy narrowing with disequality constraints. In *6th International Symposium on Programming Languages Implementation and Logic Programming (PLILP'94)*, number 844 in LNCS, pages 385–399, Madrid, Spain, 1994. Springer-Verlag.
2. A. J. Fernández, M. T. Hortalá-González, and F. Sáenz-Pérez. Solving combinatorial problems with a constraint functional logic language. In P. Wadler and V. Dahl, editors, *Practical Aspects of Declarative Languages (PADL'2003)*, number 2562 in LNCS, pages 320–338, New Orleans, Louisiana, USA, 2003. Springer-Verlag.
3. A. J. Fernández, T. Hortalá-González, and F. Sáenz-Pérez. TOY(FD): User manual, latest version. http://www.lcc.uma.es/~afdez/cflpfd/index.html, 2002.
4. F. López-Fraguas. *Programación funcional y lógica con restricciones*. PhD thesis, Universidad Complutense de Madrid, Departamento de Informática y Automática, Septiembre 1994.
5. G. Smolka. The Oz programming model. In J. Van Leeuwen, editor, *Computer Science Today*, number 1000 in LNCS, pages 324–343, Berlin, 1995. Springer-Verlag.
6. P. Van Hentenryck. *Constraint satisfaction in logic programming*. The MIT Press, Cambridge, MA, 1989.

Scheduling in the Face
of Uncertain Resource Consumption and Utility

Jeremy Frank and Richard Dearden*

Computational Sciences Division
NASA Ames Research Center, MS 269-2
Moffett Field, CA 94035
{frank,dearden}@email.arc.nasa.gov

Abstract. We discuss the problem of scheduling tasks that consume uncertain amounts of a resource with known capacity and where the tasks have uncertain utility. In these circumstances, we would like to find schedules that exceed a lower bound on the expected utility when executed. We show that the problems are $\mathcal{NP}$-complete, and present some results that characterize the behavior of some simple heuristics over a variety of problem classes.

1 Introduction

In this paper we discuss scheduling problems in which the resource consumption and the utility of the task are given only as probability distributions. Due to the uncertainty of the resource consumption, some scheduled tasks may not actually be performed when a schedule is executed. If we assume that we have accurate knowledge of the distribution of resource consumption and job utility, we can compute the *expected* utility of a schedule by accounting for both the uncertain resource consumption and utility. We can then find a schedule that maximizes the expected utility, or find a schedule whose expected utility exceeds a lower bound.

Traditionally, constraint reasoning approaches have been applied to scheduling problems with known resource consumption and temporal constraints; this has led to "global" resource constraints such as those described in [1, 2]. These techniques must be extended to handle problems with uncertain resource consumption and utility, where the goal is to find schedules that exceed a utility bound. While these problems are similar in spirit to bin-packing problems, Monte Carlo integration is required to convolve arbitrary probability distributions over resource availability. This introduces challenges in the application of constraint reasoning approaches to solve the problems.

2 Theory

We first introduce some notation. Let X be a set of events, and let R be a set of resources. Let r^{max} be the capacity of $r \in R$; thus, at all times, the amount of

---

* Research Institute for Advanced Computer Science

F. Rossi (Ed.): CP 2003, LNCS 2833, pp. 832–836, 2003.

available resource is bounded between 0 and r^{max}. Let $I_r(z)$ be the probability distribution over the initial amount of available resource r. Define $C_{x,r}(z)$ as the probability distribution over the change in availability of resource r after executing x. We assume that all resource consumption probabilities are independent. Define $U_x(w)$ as the probability distribution over the utility received from executing x. Finally, let $T = \tau_i(x, y)$ be a set of binary metric temporal constraints over pairs of events x, y. We will denote a schedule by π and the jth event in a schedule by π_j. We then define $A_{\pi,r,j}(z)$ as the probability distribution over the availability of resource r after the *successful* execution of the first j events of π. For convenience, we define $A_{\pi,r,0}(z) \equiv I_r(z)$. We can now define the probability that event j successfully executes, conditioned on the successful execution of the previous $j - 1$ jobs:

$$S(\pi, r, j) = \int_0^{r^{max}} A_{\pi,r,j-1}(z) * C_{\pi_j,r}(z) dz \tag{1}$$

This formula says that event π_j fails if it attempts to allocate more resource than r has available after the successful execution of the first $j - 1$ events of π, and succeeds otherwise. We can now write the following recurrence for $A_{\pi,r,j}(z)$:

$$A_{\pi,r,j}(z) = \frac{A_{\pi,r,j-1}(z) * C_{\pi_j,r}(z)}{S(\pi, r, j)} \tag{2}$$

Note that the probability distribution $A_{\pi,r,j}(z)$ is permitted to be nonzero between 0 and r^{max}, and must be 0 elsewhere. We are now in a position to write the expected value of a schedule π. If there are n events in π, then the probability of successfully executing only the first i events of schedule π is given by

$$X(\pi, i) = (1 - S(\pi, r, i + 1)) \prod_{j=1}^i S(\pi, r, j) \tag{3}$$

(where we define $S(\pi, r, n + 1) = 0$). The expected utility of these i events is $\sum_{j=1}^i E(U(\pi_j))$. So the expected utility of the schedule π is given by

$$E(\pi) = \sum_{i=1}^n X(\pi, i) \left(\sum_{j=1}^i E(U(\pi_j)) \right) \tag{4}$$

The task is to find a schedule whose expected utility exceeds a bound B.

Initially, we will assume that there is only one resource r with maximum capacity r^{max}. We will also assume without loss of generality that the probability that there is less than 0 resource initially available is 0. Finally, we will assume that $C_{r,j}(z) > 0$ only when $z < 0$. We will call this problem the *Uncertain Consumable Resource Scheduling Problem* (UCRSP).

Theorem 1. *UCRSP is in $\mathcal{NP}$.*

Proof. Suppose that the UCRSP has no temporal constraints. First, note we only need to convolve a linear number of distributions and compute a linear number of event utilities to compute the schedule utility. The multiplications and sums in the formula presented above are all polynomial time operations. All that remains is showing that the convolution operation is a polynomial time operation. In the worst case, we can do each convolution using Monte Carlo Integration, which takes constant time for a fixed error [3]. We can add temporal constraints back to the UCRSP and preserve $\mathcal{NP}$-completeness. The only additional machinery needed is to observe that we can validate the temporal constraints in polynomial time using the results of Dechter, Meiri and Pearl [4].

Theorem 2. *UCRSP is $\mathcal{NP}$-Hard.*

Proof. We will reduce the Knapsack problem to UCRSP. A Knapsack item $j = (s, u)$ where s is the size and u is the utility. Thus, we map j to a UCRSP event j with $C_{r,j}(s) = 1$ and $U_j(u) = 1$). The initial amount of resource r in the UCRSP is the bound on the Knapsack size R. The utility bound of the Knapsack is mapped to the expected utility bound of our problem. There are no temporal constraints in the resulting UCRSP. This mapping requires only linear time. Now consider a schedule π that satisfies the expected utility bound of the UCRSP. Any schedule can be mapped into a partition of jobs by the following linear time procedure: while there is still any resource available, add π_j to the Knapsack. If adding π_j violates the resource constraint, pi_k for $k \geq j$ are not in the Knapsack. Thus, the set of Knapsack items obeys the Knapsack constraint. Further, by construction of the UCRSP, each event j that contributes utility is guaranteed to contribute all of is utility, since all such events execute with probability 1. It is clear from the simplicity of this mapping that the (expected) utility of the schedule is the value of a solution to the Knapsack. Thus, a solution to the UCRSP is a solution to the Knapsack problem. Thus, UCRSP is $\mathcal{NP}$-Hard.

Corollary 1. *UCRSP is $\mathcal{NP}$-Complete.*

Finally, we observe that scaling the UCRSP up to multiple resources does not increase the difficulty of the problem. Suppose there are q resources. The probability of successfully executing only the first i events of schedule π is now given by

$$X(\pi, i) = \left(\sum_{k=1}^{q} (1 - S(\pi, k, i+1)) \right) \left(\prod_{k=1}^{q} \prod_{j=1}^{i} S(\pi, k, j) \right) \tag{5}$$

We briefly describe some relaxations of the above two problems. We first note that if we eliminate the uncertainty in the resource consumption but preserve the uncertainty in the utility, we see that finding schedules that satisfy an expected utility bound is trivially reducible to the Knapsack problem. We also note that if we allow a schedule to consist of ordered *sets* of otherwise unordered events that UCRSP is no longer $\mathcal{NP}$-hard. The reason is that all permutations of each set must be analyzed to find out what the expected value of the totally ordered schedules and to check for compliance with the bound B.

3   Practice

We devised three heuristics to choose among unscheduled events: maximize the expected partial schedule utility (E), minimize the expected resource consumption of the job (R), and minimize the probability of job failure given the current partial schedule (S). To test the performance of the heuristics we performed a number of experiments on relatively simple, random domains. We considered problems with between ten and 20 jobs to be scheduled, and with approximately half that many constraints. Each of the jobs had a Gaussian distribution for the quantity of resources it consumed, with a range of values for the means. We considered problems in which the resource consumption means had uniformly low variance, uniformly high variance, and random variance, and we varied the resource limit between ten percent and 50 percent of the expected resource requirement for all the jobs. For each setting of these parameters, we generated 100 problems, and ran each of the heuristics on each problem.

We evaluated the heuristics by using them greedily to select a single valid schedule. We then computed the expected value of that schedule as shown in Equation 4. The performance of the three heuristics was consistent over all sizes of problems and resource limits, so we show the results for a single setting of those parameters in Table 1. In this case, the problems had 20 jobs, ten constraints, mean resource usages for the jobs uniformly distributed between ten and 50, job utilities uniformly distributed between one and ten, and a resource limit of 60 (ten percent of the expected resources required by all the jobs). We were particularly interested in the effects on the algorithms of changing the variance of the resource usage of the jobs, so we present results for three different resource usages.

As the left-hand columns of Table 1 show, the E heuristic (choose the job that maximizes the expected utility of the schedule built so far) considerably outperforms the other two on essentially all these problems. The only exception is on a few very small problems on which both E and R are finding optimal, or very close to optimal schedules. We expected the E heuristic to perform poorly when most job's resource consumption and utility are positively correlated. We performed additional experiments on such problems, but it still outperforms R and S. When job resource consumption and utility are anti-correlated R actually performed slightly better than E, but these results are not statistically significant. In fact, both heuristics produce very similar schedules for these problems, and appear to perform very close to optimal (on small problems we have computed the optimal for).

One problem with using the E heuristic is that it takes approximately 15 times as long to find a schedule as the other two, due to the complexity of the Monte Carlo estimate of the value of the whole schedule at each step. One approximation is to ignore the condition that previous jobs succeeded, and instead

836   Jeremy Frank and Richard Dearden

Table 1. (Left) Performance of the three heuristics on "uncorrelated" problems with 20 jobs, 10 constraints, and a resource limit of 60. (Right) Performance of the three heuristics on problems with correlated and anti-correlated resource usage and utility.

Job Variance	Heuristic	Mean	Variance	Problem Type	Heuristic	Mean	Variance
	E	20.35	26.20		E	13.88	32.88
0.1–1.0	R	18.52	33.92	Uncorr.	E*	16.07	26.75
	S	17.53	32.45		R	11.71	45.39
	E	13.88	32.88		E	10.08	0.07
0.1–0.2	R	11.71	45.39	Corr.	E*	8.01	0.78
	S	11.18	26.55		R	7.22	0.57
	E	13.91	37.71		E	27.74	50.03
0.8–1.0	R	11.72	44.91	AntiCor.	E*	23.64	51.16
	S	11.63	43.91		R	27.7364	50.04

use the probability that the schedule up to a particular job will complete in the given amount of resources. This is easily computed for Gaussian resource usage distributions as it it simply the sum of the usages for the jobs, which is itself a Gaussian. However, it overestimates the value of each schedule. The right-hand columns of Table 1 shows results on the same set of problems using this approximation, again only for the low variance case.

The approximation actually beats E for the uncorrelated problems by a statistically significant amount. Our intuition is jobs that use few resources gain more from the approximation than large jobs, so the approximation favours small jobs at the beginning of the schedule, which is good for cases such as this with tight resource bounds. The approximation performs comparably to R, and is in fact worse on anti-correlated problems. The computation time is still somewhat larger (a factor of around 2) for the approximation, which suggests that there is relatively little advantage to using the approximation over using R for many problems.

References

1. Muscettola, N.: Computing the envelope for stepwise-constant resource allocations. Proceedings of the 9th International Conference on the Principles and Practices of Constraint Programming (2002)
2. Beldiceanu, N., Carlsson, M.: A new multi-resource *cumulatives* constraint with negative heights. Proceedings of the 8th International Conference on the Principles and Practices of Constraint Programming (2002)
3. Hammersley, J.M., Handscomb, D.C.: Monte Carlo Methods. J. Wiley (1964)
4. Dechter, R., Meiri, I., Pearl, J.: Temporal constraint networks. Artificial Intelligence **49** (1991) 61–94

Supertree Construction with Constraint Programming

Ian P. Gent[1], Patrick Prosser[2], Barbara M. Smith[3], and Wu Wei[2]

[1] School of Computer Science, University of St. Andrews, Scotland
ipg@dcs.st-and.ac.uk
[2] Department of Computing Science, University of Glasgow, Scotland
pat@dcs.gla.ac.uk
[3] School of Computing and Engineering, University of Huddersfield, England
b.m.smith@hud.ac.uk

1 Introduction

A central goal of systematics is the construction of a *tree of life*, where the tree represents the relationship between all living things. The leaf nodes of the tree correspond to species and the internal nodes to hypothesized species, assumed to be extinct, where species have diverged. One problem that biologists face is to assemble a *supertree* from many smaller trees that have overlapping leaf sets. Polytime algorithms have been proposed for this problem [3, 5]. We present a simple constraint encoding of this problem. This is based on the observation that any rooted tree can be considered as being min-ultrametric when we label interior nodes with their depth in that tree. That is, any path from the root to a leaf corresponds to a strictly increasing sequence. Our encoding takes a radically different approach to solving these problems, and represents a new perspective.

2 Species Trees and Supertrees

In a fully resolved (i.e. bifurcating) species tree each internal node has degree 3, with the exception of the root. Consequently a fully resolved species tree with n leaf nodes has $n-1$ internal nodes. In Figure 1 we have three species, namely a, b, and c. Species a and b are more closely related to one another than they are to c. More specifically, we say that *the most recent common ancestor of a and b is greater than the most recent common ancestor of a and c (equally b and c)*, where the most recent common ancestor of two leaf nodes a and b is the internal node furthest from the root that has a and b as descendants. We compare most recent common ancestors by measuring their distance from the root. That is,

$$mrca(a, b) > mrca(a, c) \tag{1}$$
$$mrca(a, b) > mrca(b, c) \tag{2}$$
$$mrca(a, c) = mrca(b, c) \tag{3}$$

Note, that in Figure 1 we have labeled the two interior nodes. Generally, interior nodes are anonymous and we introduce this labeling only to explain the equations

F. Rossi (Ed.): CP 2003, LNCS 2833, pp. 837–841, 2003.

above. We see that the most recent common ancestor of a and b is interior node Y, i.e. $mrca(a, b) = Y$. Furthermore, $mrca(a, b) = mrca(b, a) = Y$ (i.e. the relation is symmetric) and from equation (3) $mrca(a, c) = mrca(b, c) = X$. From equation (1) we have $mrca(a, b) > mrca(a, c)$ (i.e. $Y > X$) and $mrca(a, b) > mrca(b, c)$ (i.e. yet again $Y > X$ from equation (2)).

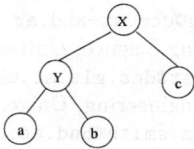

Fig. 1. A species tree, where species a and b are more closely related to each other than they are to species c. This small tree can also be represented as the rooted triple $((a, b), c)$.

Species trees are frequently presented as a collection of rooted triples, of the form $((a, b), c)$ meaning that $mrca(a, b) > mrca(a, c)$, $mrca(a, b) > mrca(b, c)$, and $mrca(a, c) = mrca(b, c)$. The *BreakUp* algorithm of [3] takes as input a species tree and delivers as a result a set of rooted triples that define that tree. The *OneTree* algorithm [3, 1] takes these triples as input and produces a supertree, if one exists. In Figure 2 two trees are combined to produce a supertree. First, the two initial trees are broken up into rooted triples using the *BreakUp* algorithm. These triples are then passed to *OneTree* along with the set of species $\{a, b, c, d, e, f, g\}$, and a supertree (f,((d,e),((c,(a,b)),g))) is produced. Note that there are 9 possible supertrees that respect those triples [6]. The *OneTree* algorithm is of complexity $O(m.n)$ where we have n leaf nodes and m triples.

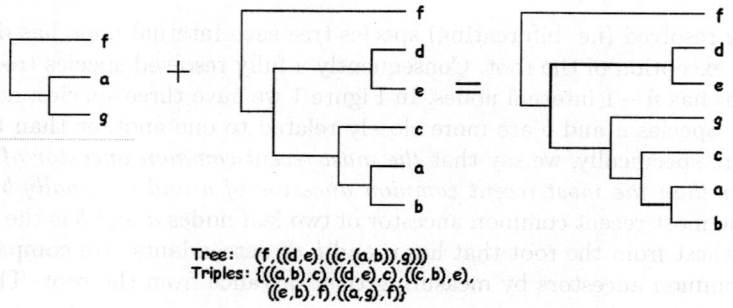

Tree: (f,((d,e),((c,(a,b)),g)))
Triples: {((a,b),c),((d,e),c),((c,b),e),
          ((e,b),f),((a,g),f)}

Fig. 2. *OneTree* applied to the two trees (f,(a,g)) and (f,((d,e),(c,(a,b)))), giving the supertree (f,((d,e),((c,(a,b)),g))). *OneTree* takes as input the set of rooted triples $R = \{((a, g), f), ((a, b), c), ((d, e), c), ((c, b), e), ((e, b), f)\}$ and the set of species $S = \{a, b, c, d, e, f, g\}$.

Definition 1. *An* **ultrametric tree** T *is a rooted tree with n uniquely labeled leaves and interior nodes labeled with values (real or integer) such that any path from the root to a leaf node constitutes a strictly* decreasing *sequence. In a* **min-ultrametric tree** *interior nodes are labeled with values such that any path from root to a leaf is a strictly* increasing *sequence [2].*

An ultrametric tree can be represented by an ultrametric matrix D, and an ultrametric matrix can be represented by an ultrametric tree.

Definition 2. *Let D be an $n \times n$ symmetric matrix. D is an* **ultrametric matrix** *if there are at most $n-1$ distinct values within D, and for any three indices i, j, and k there is a tie for the maximum of $D_{i,j}$, $D_{i,k}$, and $D_{j,k}$.*

In Figure 3 we have an ultrametric matrix D and the corresponding ultrametric tree T (these figures are taken from [2] page 450). Looking at the tree and matrix we see that the most recent common ancestor of A and D is labeled with the value 5, and the most recent common ancestor of E and B is labeled with value 8. The leaf nodes might be considered as species, and the values on the interior nodes the number (let's say) of millions of years that have passed since species diverged (i.e. species D diverged from species E 5 million years ago). An ultrametric tree can be constructed from an ultrametric matrix in time $O(n^2)$ [2].

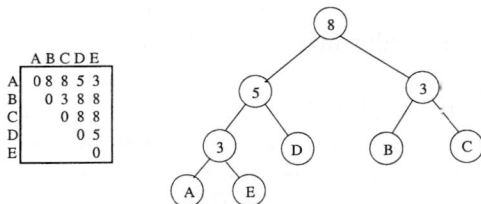

Fig. 3. The ultrametric matrix D and its ultrametric tree T.

2.1   The Min-ultrametric Constraint

We now present a constraint encoding which provides a unique representation of trees up to symmetry of either renaming of internal nodes, or swapping of left and right subtrees at any node. We encode the *depth of* the most recent common ancestors in the tree. We have a $n \times n$ two dimensional array D of constrained integer variables. Each variable $D_{i,j}$ takes a value in the range 0 to $n-1$. Since the array is symmetric, $D_{i,j} = D_{j,i}$, for all i and j, and we arbitrarily set the diagonal $D_{i,i} = 0$. The value assigned to $D_{i,j}$ represents the depth of the most recent common ancestor of leaf nodes i and j. To encode the constraints on D, we first associate the integers 1 to n with the species and start with the constraint for the triple $((a,b),c)$.

$$triple(a,b,c) \equiv [(D_{a,c} = D_{b,c}) \wedge (D_{a,b} > D_{b,c}) \wedge (D_{a,b} > D_{a,c})] \qquad (4)$$

This encodes the equations (1), (2), and (3). We can then guarantee that D is a min-ultrametric matrix by demanding that:

$$\forall a \in \{1..n-2\}. \ \forall b \in \{a+1..n-1\}. \ \forall c \in \{b+1..n\}$$
$$(triple(a,b,c) \vee triple(b,c,a) \vee triple(c,a,b)) \tag{5}$$

i.e. one of these triples holds for every combination of three species a, b, and c. This successfully encodes that the minimum value of the three variables $D_{a,b}$, $D_{b,c}$, $D_{c,a}$ is shared by two of them and not the third, the defining property of a min-ultrametric matrix where the resultant tree is bifurcating. This can also be viewed from a geometric perspective. We can consider the indices a, b and c as being vertices of a triangle, and the matrix elements $D_{a,b}$, $D_{a,c}$ and $D_{b,c}$ as being the length of the edges of that triangle. Triangles are forced to be isosceles, and equilateral triangles are disallowed.

We need to insist that the values in a row of D do not contain any gaps. That is, in the resultant tree any path from the root to a leaf node will be an increasing sequence, and that sequence will have no numeric gaps. We do this by introducing arrays of constrained integer variables to count the number of occurrences of each integer in each row of D. We then demand that if the count for i is zero, then the count for $i+1$ is also zero. Equivalently, if i occurs in a row, and i is greater than 0, then $i-1$ occurs in that row also, i.e.

$$\forall \ a \ \forall \ b \ [(D_{a,b} = i \ \wedge \ i > 0) \rightarrow \exists \ c \ (D_{a,c} = i-1)] \tag{6}$$

With this encoding, any consistent instantiation of the variables in D is min-ultrametric and has a min-ultrametric tree. The number of possible such instantiations is $\frac{(2n-2)!}{2^{n-1}(n-1)!}$ [4].

Given a set of rooted triples R we can then post each triple as a constraint on the array D. For a triple $((i,j),k) \in R$ we post the constraint $triple(i,j,k)$ from equation (4) above. This breaks the three disjunctive constraints already posted between these three variables in (5) above. Consequently, a consistent instantiation of the variables in D will correspond to a species tree that respects the triples in R. Given that consistent instantiation of D we can then process D to construct the tree, using the algorithm in [2]. Therefore, our constraint encoding achieves the same net result as the *OneTree* algorithm, and trivially extends to the enumeration of all species trees (i.e. performing the same function as *AllTrees* [3]). To generate all trees we allow our solving procedure to backtrack whenever it finds a solution, and to continue on to the next solution.

Our encoding only produces bifurcating trees, whereas *OneTree* may produce trees with interior nodes with more than two children. This happens when the triples do not fully define the tree, whereas the constraint encoding automatically forces a resolution. We can relax our constraints to allow this. The disjunctive constraints posted across the matrix D can be relaxed as follows:

$$relTriple(a,b,c) \equiv [(D_{a,c} = D_{b,c}) \ \wedge \ (D_{a,b} \geq D_{b,c}) \ \wedge \ (D_{a,b} \geq D_{a,c})] \tag{7}$$

In equation (5) replace $triple(a,b,c)$ with our relaxed constraint $relTriple(a,b,c)$. From a geometric perspective, for any three vertices a, b, c, by default we allow

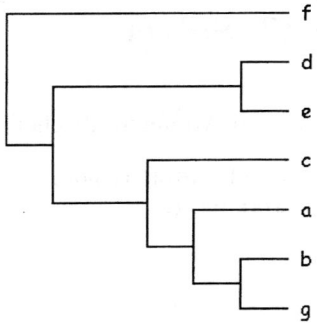

	a	b	c	d	e	f	g
a	0	4	3	2	2	1	4
b	4	0	3	2	2	1	5
c	3	3	0	2	2	1	3
d	2	2	2	0	3	1	2
e	2	2	2	3	0	1	2
f	1	1	1	1	1	0	1
g	4	5	3	2	2	1	0

Fig. 4. The min-ultrametric matrix and tree produced from the rooted triples $\{((a, g), f), ((a, b), c), ((d, e), c), ((c, b), e), ((e, b), f)\}$. Note that there are again 9 possible solutions [6]. This tree is comparable to that given in Figure 2.

triangles to be isosceles or equilateral. Our constraint encoding requires $O(n^2)$ variables, each with a domain of size n, and $O(n^3)$ ternary constraints. Figure 4 shows the species tree with its ultrametric matrix, resulting from the constraint encoding of the trees in Figure 2.

3   Conclusion and Future Work

We have presented a new method for building supertrees. This is based on the observations that any tree can be considered min-ultrametric when we label interior nodes with their depth in that tree, and any min-ultrametric matrix has a corresponding min-ultrametric tree. This then leads us to an encoding of the decision problem as a constraint satisfaction problem. This can be extended to deal with unresolved triples as well as over-constrained problems. We also expect that our encoding can be made more efficient.

References

1. D. Bryant and M. Steel. Extension Operations on Sets of Leaf-labeled Trees. *Advances in Applied Mathematics*, 16:425–453, 1995.
2. Dan Gusfield. *Algorithms on Strings, Trees, and Sequences.* Cambridge University Press, 1997.
3. Meei Pyng Ng and Nicholas C. Wormald. Reconstruction of rooted trees from subtrees. *Discrete Applied Mathematics*, 69:19–31, 1996.
4. E. Schröder. Vier combinatorische probleme. *Zeit. für Math. Phys.*, 15:361–376, 1870.
5. Charles Semple and Mike Steel. A supertree method for rooted trees. *Discrete Applied Mathematics*, 105:147–158, 2000.
6. Joseph L. Thorley. Cladistic information, leaf stability and supertree construction. *PhD Thesis, University of Bristol, Department of Biological Sciences*, 2000.

(In)Effectiveness of Look-Ahead Techniques in a Modern SAT Solver

Enrico Giunchiglia, Marco Maratea, and Armando Tacchella

DIST, Università di Genova, Viale Causa, 13 – 16145 Genova, Italy
{enrico,marco,tac}@mrg.dist.unige.it

Abstract. In this paper[1] we investigate the effect of adding a failed literal detection method to the traditional unit clause propagation method in the look-ahead component of a modern SAT solver. Our investigation points out that, in all the SAT instances that we have tried, failed literal detection is bound to be ineffective, even assuming it has no overhead.

1 Introduction

In the last couple of years, we have seen a tremendous boost in the performances of SAT solvers, such boost mostly due to Chaff [1]. Chaff owes its efficiency to four components: (*i*) efficient data structures, (*ii*) an innovative look-back method, (*iii*) an effective heuristic, and (*iv*) low-level optimizations of the code. zChaff (Chaff latest incarnation) was the best among the complete SAT solvers on industrial and hand-made benchmarks in the SAT 2002 competition [2]. Thus, when we speak of modern SAT solvers, we have in mind a "Chaff-like" engine.

In this paper we investigate the effect of adding a failed literal detection method to the traditional unit clause propagation method in the look-ahead component of a modern SAT solver. Failed literal detection was first introduced in POSIT [3], used extensively, e.g., in SATZ [4] and RelSAT [5], and similar techniques led to positive results on real-world instances in [6]. Our analysis is mostly experimental and has been performed using our solver Simo modified to incorporate ideas (*i*) - (*iii*) above. We have run our experiments using several challenging real-world benchmarks. On the basis of the collected data, we conclude that enhanced look-ahead based on failed literal detection does not pay off in modern SAT solvers. Further, we show that even assuming we had an oracle answering whether a literal will fail, or an oracle giving us the list of literals which will fail, enhanced look-ahead is not effective.

Throughout the paper, we will assume that the reader is familiar with the topics of Boolean satisfiability and satisfiability search algorithms for Boolean formulas in conjunctive normal form (for an extensive coverage of these topics see, e.g., [7]).

---

[1] This work is partially supported by MIUR, ASI, and by a grant from the Intel Corporation.

F. Rossi (Ed.): CP 2003, LNCS 2833, pp. 842–846, 2003.

```
DLL-SOLVE()                          FAILED-PROPAGATE()
 1 do                                 1 for each oper. atom a
 2   r ← LOOK-AHEAD()                 2   r ← UNIT-PROPAGATE(a)
 3   if r = T then                    3   LOOK-BACK()
 4     r ← HEURISTIC()                4   if r = F then
 5   else                            5     r ← UNIT-PROPAGATE( ¬a)
 6     r ← LOOK-BACK()               6     if r = F then return F
 7 while r = U                        7   else
 8 return r                          8     r ← UNIT-PROPAGATE( ¬a)
                                     9     LOOK-BACK()
LOOK-AHEAD()                        10     if r = F
 1 r ← UNIT-PROPAGATE(NIL)          11       UNIT-PROPAGATE( a)
 2 if r = F then                    12 return T
 3   return F
 4 else
 5   return FAILED-PROPAGATE()
```

Fig. 1. Overview of Simo.

2   (In)Effectiveness of Failed Literal Detection

For the lack of space, the description of the solvers and the benchmarks used for our experimental analysis is limited to a quick overview (see [8] for more details). We use two versions of Simo: the default configuration and Simo-Fp, i.e., Simo enhanced with failed literal detection as described in Fig. 1. LOOK-AHEAD, Fig. 1 (bottom-left) discriminates the two versions: in Simo, lines 2-5 of LOOK-AHEAD are replaced with the instruction "**return** r"; in Simo-Fp, the implementation of LOOK-AHEAD is exactly as detailed in Fig. 1. The test set consists of 483 real world instances. The benchmarks have been selected considering classical SAT problems and instances submitted to the SAT 2002 competition [2]. All the experiments have been run on two identical Pentium IV 1.8 Ghz, with 512MB of RAM running Linux RedHat 8.0.

2.1   Introducing Oracles in Simo-Fp

We can think of three oracle-based versions of Simo-Fp, that we call Simo-Fp(TO), Simo-Fp(FO), and Simo-Fp(FRO). In particular, we assume to have in Simo-Fp(TO), an oracle testing whether a literal will fail, thus saving the time necessary to try the literals which will not be failed; in Simo-Fp(FO), an oracle returning the sequence of literals which will fail in Simo-Fp, thus saving also the time necessary to scan the list of open literals; in Simo-Fp(FRO), an oracle returning the sequence of literals which will fail in Simo-Fp and their reasons, thus saving also the time necessary to calculate the reasons of the failed literals.

Since the oracles cannot be implemented in practice with a single-pass algorithm, we need to calculate the performance of the oracle-based versions using the experimental data of Simo-Fp. In order to accomplish this, we introduce four

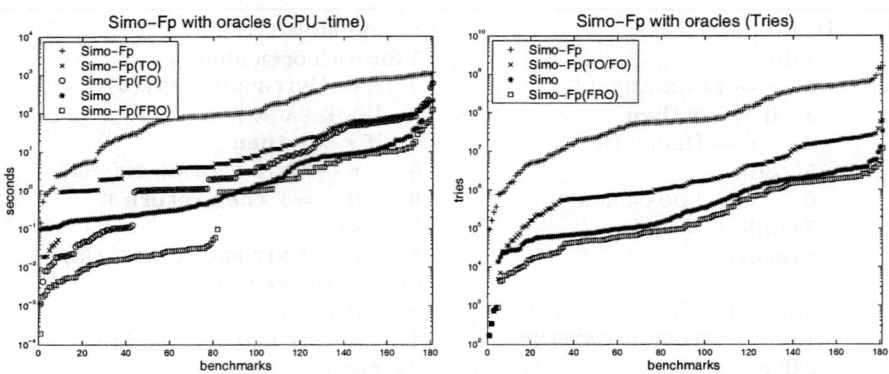

Fig. 2. Simo, Simo-Fp and Simo-Fp(*), considering CPU time (left) and tries (right).

CPU time counters inside FAILED-PROPAGATE (line numbers refer to FAILED-PROPAGATE in Fig. 1): Total time (T_f) is the sum of the run times of each call to FAILED-PROPAGATE; time spent on failed (T_s) is the sum of the run times spent to perform literal propagations when the literals are failed (lines 2-5 and lines 8-11, when the tests on lines 4 and 10 are successful, respectively); time wasted on failed (T_w) is the same as above, but when the literals are not failed (lines 2-3 and lines 8-9, when the tests on lines 4 and 10 are not successful, respectively); time spent on reason (T_r) is the sum of the run times spent to calculate the reason of each failed literal when the literal is failed (lines 2-3 and lines 8-9 when the tests on lines 4 and 10 are successful, respectively). Let T be the CPU time of Simo-Fp, and $T(*)$ be the CPU time of Simo-Fp(*). The performance of the oracle-based algorithms can be calculated as follows: $T(\text{TO}) = T - T_w$, $T(\text{FO}) = T - T_f + T_s$, and $T(\text{FRO}) = T - T_f + T_s - T_r$.

To calculate the tries of the oracle-based versions of Simo-Fp we introduce four more counters (still with reference to FAILED-PROPAGATE in Fig. 1): total tries (N_f) is the sum of the tries performed in each call to FAILED-PROPAGATE; tries spent on failed (N_s) is the sum of the tries spent to perform literal propagations when the literals are failed (the tries performed by UNIT-PROPAGATE in lines 2,5 or 8,11 when the literal is failed); tries wasted on failed (N_w) is the same as above, but when the literals are not failed (the tries performed by UNIT-PROPAGATE in lines 2 or 8 when the literal is not failed); tries spent on reason (N_r) is the sum of the tries spent to calculate the reason of each failed literal when the literal is failed (the tries performed by UNIT-PROPAGATE in lines 2 or 8 when the literal is failed). Let N be the number of tries performed by Simo-Fp, and $N(*)$ the number of tries performed by Simo-Fp(*). The number of tries performed by the oracle-based algorithms can be calculated as follows: $N(\text{TO/FO}) = N - N_w$ and $N(\text{FRO}) = N - N_f + N_s - N_r$. Notice that $N(\text{TO}) = N(\text{FO})$, so we do not need two distinct measures for the tries of Simo-Fp(TO) and Simo-Fp(FO).

Table 1. Simo, Simo-Fp and Simo-Fp(*) Tries arranged by benchmark family.

Benchmarks					Simo Tries (x1000)			
Family	Sat	Tot	At#	Cl#	Plain	Fp	Fp(FRO)	Fp(TO/FO)
Beijing-1996	8	8	8,226	53,390	1,151	4,475,504	113	5,141
bmc	14	30	10,466	52,995	95,253	5,006,227	33,669	290,623
des	7	7	3,285	20,539	3,073	85,967	786	13,554
fev	0	3	1,324	3,819	1,636	168,740	786	2,814
fpga	10	30	32,612	194,786	10,326	960,441	9,232	48,375
fvp-unsat.2.0	0	5	1,468	15,206	8370	1,047,241	5,438	52,900
mediator	2	2	561.50	12,086	3,689	22,472	1,289	12,833
miters	3	12	2,261	6,119	27,398	2,505,136	23,478	72,405
sss-sat.1.0	79	79	5,022	51,043	75,227	17,553,074	56,333	601,287
vliw-sat.1.1	5	5	20,780	284,509	242	2,657,969	127	8,374

2.2   Simo vs. Simo-Fp(*)

In the following, we use *tries* as a CPU independent performance measure, instead of branches. The number of tries is the number of times that a literal is assigned a value, for whatever reason, be it a choice of the heuristic, a unit literal, a failed literal, or a tentative assignment performed during FAILED-PROPAGATE. Considering the oracles presented in the previous subsection, we compare Simo and Simo-Fp with the data of Simo-Fp(TO), Simo-Fp(FO), and Simo-Fp(FRO). For all such real and oracle-based versions of Simo, the distributions of the run time and the number of tries are summarized in Fig. 2. The x-axis in both plots is an ordinal in the range (0-180), and the y-axis is, respectively, CPU seconds in Fig. 2 (left) and number of branches in Fig. 2 (right). The total number of problems visualized is 181 out of 483 since we discarded (*i*) instances in which either Simo or Simo-Fp exceeded the time out, and (*ii*) instances in which the run time of Simo was less than 0.1 seconds. Both plots in Fig. 2 are obtained by ordering the results of Simo and Simo-Fp independently and in ascending order.

By looking at Fig. 2 we can immediately conclude that aggressive failed literal detection is bound to be ineffective, both in terms of run time and, more interestingly, also in terms of search space explored. The only version of Simo-Fp that can barely compete with Simo is Simo-Fp(FRO), the version of Simo-Fp embodying the most powerful oracle presented in Sub. 2.1. In spite of its power, the number of tries performed by Simo-Fp(FRO) is, on average, only about 80% of the number of tries performed by Simo. As we can deduce from the plots, Simo-Fp performances are influenced by two major factors: (*i*) the time (and the tries) spent to check whether a given literal is failed or not, and (*ii*) the time (and the tries) spent to calculate the reasons of failed literals. By looking at Fig. 2 (right) we can see two order-of-magnitude gaps in the number of tries: one between Simo-Fp and Simo-Fp(TO/FO), which confirms point (*i*), and one between Simo-Fp(TO/FO) and Simo-Fp(FRO), which confirms point (*ii*).

To complete our experimental analysis, we need to confirm that the cumulative results of Fig. 2 are true also of each single family, i.e., there are no compensation effects among different families of benchmarks. In Table 1 we present the data regarding Simo, Simo-Fp and the oracle-based versions of Simo-Fp. Each row of the Table contains data about a single family of benchmarks. For each family we report: the number of benchmarks left in the family after instances have been filtered out as described in Sub. 2.2 (column Tot); the number of satisfiable instances (column Sat); the average number of atoms and clauses (columns At# and Cl#, respectively); the total number of tries performed by Simo, Simo-Fp, Simo-Fp(TO/FO) and Simo-Fp(FRO) divided by 1,000. Notice that clauses and atoms statistics have been rounded to 1, and tries statistics have been rounded to 1,000. Although we cannot show here the complete data, compensation effects are absent also when looking at single instances in each family. In other words, there is no single instance in our test set on which Simo-Fp(TO/FO) performs less tries than Simo or Simo-Fp(FRO), while on all the instances Simo-Fp(FRO) performs less tries than Simo.

3   Conclusions

In this paper we have presented strong empirical evidence that enhanced look-ahead based on failed literal detection does not pay off in modern SAT solvers, at least in the case of real-world problems. In particular we showed that (i) the number of tries performed by Simo-Fp is, on average, about three orders of magnitude bigger than the number of tries performed by Simo; (ii) the number of tries performed by Simo-Fp(TO/FO) is, on average, about one order of magnitude bigger than the number of tries performed by Simo; (iii) the number of tries performed by Simo-Fp(FRO) is, on average, only about 80% of the number of tries performed by Simo.

References

1. M. W. Moskewicz, C. F. Madigan, Y. Zhao, L. Zhang, and S. Malik. Chaff: Engineering an Efficient SAT Solver. In *Proc. of DAC*, 2001.
2. L. Simon, D. Le Berre, and E. A. Hirsch. The SAT2002 Competition.
3. J. W. Freeman. *Improvements to propositional satisfiability search algorithms*. PhD thesis, University of Pennsylvania, 1995.
4. C. M. Li and Anbulagan. Heuristics Based on Unit Propagation for Satisfiability Problems. In *Proc. of IJCAI*, pages 366–371. Morgan-Kauffmann, 1997.
5. R. J. Bayardo, Jr. and R. C. Schrag. Using CSP Look-Back Techniques to Solve Real-World SAT instances. In *Proc. of AAAI*, pages 203–208. AAAI Press, 1997.
6. F. Bacchus. Enhancing Davis Putnam with Extended Binary Clause Reasoning. In *Proc. of AAAI*. AAAI Press, 2001.
7. J. Gu, P. W. Purdom, J. Franco, and B. W. Wah. Algorithms for the Satisfiability (SAT) Problem: A Survey. In *Satisfiability Problem: Theory and Applications*, DIMACS Series in Discrete Mathematics and Theoretical Computer Science, pages 19–153. AMS, 1997.
8. E. Giunchiglia, M. Maratea, and A. Tacchella. (In)Effectiveness of Look-Ahead Techniques in a Modern SAT Solver, 2003. Technical report available at http://www.mrg.dist.unige.it/~tac/Reports/failed.ps.

Reduce and Assign: A Constraint Logic Programming and Local Search Integration Framework to Solve Combinatorial Search Problems

Nuno Gomes, Zita Vale, and Carlos Ramos

GECAD – Knowledge Engineering and Decision Support Research Group
Polytechnic Institute of Porto / Institute of Engineering, Portugal
{ngomes,zav}@dee.isep.ipp.pt, csr@dei.isep.ipp.pt

Abstract. Since the early 90's that Constraint Logic Programming (CLP) has been used to solve Combinatorial Search Problems. Generally, CLP has a good performance with highly constrained problems, but it lacks a "global perspective" of the search space, making the search for the optimal solution more difficult when the problems becomes larger and less constrained. On the other hand, Local Search Methods explore the search space directly through an "intelligent" construction of solution neighbourhoods, turning these methods suitable for solving less constrained and large search spaces problems. The aim of this paper is to present a hybridisation framework that allows combining Local Search methods with Constraint Logic Programming. The first results demonstrate that while maintaining the CLP strengths it is possible to overcome their weaknesses and improve its search efficiency.

1 Introduction

One of the final objectives of many areas like *Operations Research*, *Artificial Intelligence* or *Mathematical Programming* has been to solve real world problems like Scheduling, Planning, Transportation, Assignment, just to name few. These problems are usually classified as *Combinatorial Optimization Problems* and have been solved using several traditional approaches. One of the most successful was CLP [1]. CLP combines the declarativeness of logic programming with constraint solving techniques from Mathematical Programming, Operations Research, and others. Generally, CLP has a very good behaviour for highly constrained problems, but it lacks a "*global perspective*" of the search space, which makes the search of the optimal solution more difficult for large and less constrained ones. On the other hand, Local Search Methods explore directly the search space through the "*intelligent*" construction of solution *neighbourhoods*, which makes these methods suitable for solving problems less constrained and with large search spaces. The aim of this paper is to present a hybridisation framework that allows combining Local Search methods with Constraint Logic Programming, in order to overcome their weaknesses and maintain their strengths.

F. Rossi (Ed.): CP 2003, LNCS 2833, pp. 847–852, 2003.

The basic idea of this framework consists of using Local Search to dynamically select promising areas of the search space and then use CLP to find the local optimum for the selected areas. The idea is better explained in section 3.

2   Other Integration Approaches

Since the appearance of the first CLP systems in the late 80s, we could see the first signs of hybridization. Revising history, we can distinguish 3 main paths for integration.

The first and probably the most explored one is the hybridization of CLP with *Linear Programming*, where several integration schemes were tried. These schemes usually differ in the way the problem is decomposed and the model is built. Some examples can be found in [2],[3],[4]. The second path, which is more relevant for this work, is the hybridization of CLP with LS methods. Some approaches try to integrate CLP techniques in LS methods, in order to improve the neighbourhood exploration or selection like in [5]. On other approaches, conceptually closer to our approach, the problem is modeled using CLP and then a combination of CLP and LS is used to perform the search as in [6]. Finally in the third path the followers try to hybridize CLP with *Artificial Neural Networks*. A scheme for this integration can be seen in [7], and was named *GENET*. The framework presented on this work is general, in the sense that it lies mainly on the second path but allows the inclusion of ideas from the first or third path.

3   Solving Combinatorial Problems by Reduce and Assign

Reduce and Assign is a general framework that allows the hybridisation of LS Algorithms, with CLP. The framework has two components. One, named *LS_comp,* is responsible for exploring the global search space selecting smaller search spaces areas that constitute a unique sub-problem. The other, named *CP_comp* is responsible for solving each of the sub-problems. Similarly to traditional LS methods the LS_comp executes local moves through neighbourhoods. The difference is that the neighbourhood is not a set of feasible solutions obtained from a transformation of an initial solution, but is one, or a set, of sub-search spaces obtained from a transformation of an initial sub-search space. The LS_comp can be represented by the function $LS\_comp(D,l): S_D \rightarrow Ss_D$, where D is the initial set of variables domain and l is a parameter indicating the size of the sub-search space Ss_D. Any sub-search space is obtained through variables domain reduction, so it can be represented by a new set of constraints that prune the non-wanted domain values. The LS_comp function has a parameter that defines the size of the sub-search space. This parameter is fundamental for search efficiency. Generally it balances the search effort between each of the components. In the limit, if the parameter is equal to 1 we only have Local Search (the sub-search space only allows 1 assignment), else if the parameter is equal to the number of domain values we only have CLP search and the solution returned by the CLP component is always a global optimum (the number of possible assignments is equal to the Cartesian product of the variable domains). Ideally the optimal l value is the smaller that allows the CLP component to find the optimal global solution.

The CP_comp component is responsible for solving the new sub-problem and can be represented by the function $CP\_comp(X,D,C,o_p,C'):(X,D)\to s'$, where C' is a new set of constraints representing a new sub-search space and o_p the optimisation function. The result returned by the component is the local optimal solution if it exists, or *"no"* if not. Naturally, the solution has a cost with respect to the optimisation function. The answer of the CLP component is returned to the LS component that, based on it, selects a new neighbour (sub-domain). In order to avoid being trapped in local optima any traditional strategy can be implemented.

4   Illustrating Example – Guided Constraint Search Applied to Maintenance Scheduling of Electric Generating Units

In this section we present an instance of our framework named *Guided Constraint Search* (GCS) applied to the *Maintenance Scheduling of Electric Generating Units (MSEGU)*. Due to the lack of space the presentation will be summarized, we recommend the reading of [8] for a more detailed description. The main objective of the MSEGU problem consists of determining, for each predicted maintenance task, a specific start time in the scheduling horizon (e.g. an year), while satisfying the system constraints and maintaining system reliability. This objective should be accomplished while a function is optimized (e.g. the sum of operation and maintenance costs is minimized).

4.1   Guided Constraint Search Algorithm

In order to solve the problem we propose for the LS component a function based on ideas from *Guided Local Search* [9]. Similarly, we define a *useful (useless)* function, *penalties* and *costs*. However, we differ from GLS on the way we use these values.

The basic element of the LS_comp is an *inutility function*. This function defines for each possible variable assignment $a(x_i)$, or in other words, for each pair variable/value (x_i,v_j) a quantity that indicates if the corresponding value should be included, or not, in a given sub-search space S_{S_D}. The inutility function is defined by $I_{ij} = CO_{ij} + Bc_{ij}*p_{ij}$, where I is the inutility value; CO is an initial heuristic cost; Bc is the best solution cost that includes the pair and p is the penalty parameter. Initially p and Bc are initialized, for all possible variable assignments, respectively the value 1 and the problem upper cost bound. CO can be used to express some heuristics that give the possible best initial values. On each iteration the CLP component is used to solve a new Sub-search space problem defined by LS component. This sub-search is defined by selecting for each variable domain the l values with the smallest inutility. Based on the returned solution, if existing, the used pairs inutility function parameters are updated, depending if they belong to a new best solution, or not. Specifically, the penalty parameter is incremented by one unit for the pairs that do not belong to the best solution. For the other pairs, the penalty remains the same being the Bc parameter updated to the new best cost. Naturally, if no better solution is found, all the pairs see their penalty increased. This update procedure accomplishes two objectives. First, the probability of certain (possible best) pairs being chosen is progressively increased as they belong to good solutions (convergence of the search). Second, the search is diversified because the penalty of the pairs that do not belong to new best solutions is increased. The key to the effectiveness of GCS is the equilibrium between penalizing "bad" pairs variable/values and not penalizing "good" ones.

Any CLP component has a search procedure that is based on a variable and value selection heuristic. We have used two different search procedures. One results from the work in [10]. We named it *Branch and Bound* procedure with *Smallest* variable selection heuristic and *Smallest* value selection heuristic (BBSS). The other results from the work in [11], and we called it as *Branch and Bound* procedure with Smallest Inutility variable and value selection heuristic (BBSI).

4.2   Experimental Results

In order to evaluate the different search procedures and respective variants we have used data from the Portuguese Electric Power Generation Company (EDP). The method was implemented using *ECLiPSe* [12] system, running on an AMD at 650Mhz, with 128Mb of memory, using WIN98. Note that this method has not any stochastic component. Consequently, we only need to run the program once for each parameter set.

Prior to test the algorithm's performance we conducted some experiences in order to test the l and st parameters influence. Due to a lack of space, we do not show the results but we concluded that l should not take small nor high values. We also concluded that as smaller are st values more difficult is to find the optimal solution, and that, as higher is the st value more time is needed to find the optimal solution. The right st value grows with the size of the problem. Based on these tests, we can empirically say that a good l value is in the interval $[\,{}^1\!/_4 T, {}^1\!/_2 T]$, and $st > 10 + 2*T$ seconds.

In order to verify the efficiency of the method we used the results obtained in [13]. The results presented on the paper report several evolutionary techniques applications (e.g. Simulated Annealing, Tabu Search, Memetic Algorithms, etc) to 3 different size problems. They also indicate the number of what they call combination and order constraints. We applied the two variations of the method to 3 same sized, number and type of constrains problems. Table 1 shows the results of the methods described above compared to a pure CLP approach of [10], named CBB+S+SV+Mc and 3 of the methods used in [13], namely *Simulated Annealing* (SA), *Tabu Search* (TS) and

Memetic Algorithm with a Tabu Search Operator (MA(TS)). The used data is the same of [10] but different from [13]. We do not indicate the cost of our method neither of [10] because it has no interest for the comparison, regarding that data is different. Instead, we indicate between parentheses the value of the l and time parameter. Times shown are in *minutes:seconds* format and for the 3 stochastic methods. The average cost for 40 runs is indicated between parentheses. Considering that problems with the same size and structure are equally demanding in terms of computation time we can say that the proposed methods perform better than the CBB+S+SV+Mc and, for problem 2 and 3, better than the MA(TS) that is the best method of [13].

Table 1. Results of the GCS method applied to 3 instances of the MSEGU problem

Problem	1	2	3
SA	0:03	0:18	0:46
TS	0:10	0:59	3:08
MA(TS)	1:12	6:34	25:29
CBB+S+SV+Mc	1:40	8:22	48:26
BBSS	1:26 (l=8;	4:46 (l=13;	20:23 (l=15;
BBSI	1:34 (l=8;	5:12 (l=13;	18:12 (l=15;

5 Conclusions and Future Work

This paper presents "Reduce and Assign" a hybrid framework that allows the integration of Constraint Logic Programming with Local Search Methods. The basic idea consists of using Local Search to explore the global search space and CLP to find local optimum solutions for a given sub-search space. In order to validate the framework we presented one possible instance named of Guided Constraint Search. The comparison of the results with other approaches for both the instances allow us to conclude that the framework is more efficient than pure CLP approaches and even very competitive in relation to other non CLP based approaches. We demonstrated that the framework is sufficiently flexible to allow the integration of different Local Search methods as also the integration of several techniques in the CLP search procedure. For the future we address to lines of research, one is the integration of other Local Search procedures, as for example *Tabu Search*, and the other the improvement of the CLP component by the integration of different methods and techniques. In this last topic the authors have done already some work, namely with the integration of Linear Programming methods in the CLP component. First results were very encouraging. Finally, we intend to test the presented instances together with those we are working on in different type of optimization problems.

References

1. Jaffar J. and Lassez J., Constraint Logic Programming, Proceedings 14th ACM Symposium on Principles of Programming Languages, Munich, Germany, pp. 111-119, 1987.
2. Harjunkoski I., Jain V., G. I., Hybrid mixed-integer/constraint logic programming strategies for solving scheduling and combinatorial optimization problems, Computers and Chemical Engineering, vol. 24, pp. 337-343, 2000.
3. Bockmayr A. and Kasper T., Branch-and-Infer: A unifying framework for integer and finite domain constraint programming, INFORMS J. Computing, vol. 10, pp. 287-300, 1998.
4. Thorsteinsson E., "Branch-and-Check: A Hybrid Framework Integrating Mixed Integer Programming and Constraint Logic Programming, (CP2001), Cyprus, 2001.
5. Codognet P. and Diaz D., Yet Another Local Search Method for Constraint Solving, Stochastic Algorithms: Foundations and Applications, (SAGA), 2001.
6. Nareyek A., Using Global Constraints for Local Search, Constraint Programming and Large Scale Discrete Optimization, DIMACS Volume 57, 9-28, 2001.
7. Eugene C., Rina D., Matthew L., Bart S., and Tsang E, Systematic Versus Stochastic Constraint Satisfaction, {IJCAI}, pp. 2027-2032, 1995.
8. Gomes N., Vale Z., and Ramos C., Hybrid Constraint Algorithm for the Maintenance Scheduling of Electric Power Units, (ISAP2003), Greece, 2003.
9. Voudouris C. and Tsang, E. P. K., University of Essex, UK, CSM-247, Aug 1995.
10. 10.Gomes N. and Vale Z., Constraint Based Maintenance Scheduling of Electric Power Units, Power and Energy Systems (PES2003), Palm Springs, California, USA, pp. 55-61, 2003.
11. Gomes N. and Vale Z., "Guided Constraint Search," ISEP, IS2343, 2002.
12. Mark Wallace, Two Problems - Two Solutions: One System - ECLiPSe, in IEE Colloquium on Advanced Software Technologies for Scheduling, 1993.
13. Burke E, S. A., Hybrid Evolutionary Techniques for the Maintenance Scheduling Problem IEEE Transactions on Power Systems, vol. 15, pp. 122-128, 2000.

A Canonicity Test for Configuration

Stephane Grandcolas, Laurent Henocque, and Nicolas Prcovic

Laboratoire des Sciences de l'Information et des Systèmes
LSIS (UMR CNRS 6168)
Campus Scientifique de Saint Jérôme
Avenue Escadrille Normandie Niemen
13397 Marseille Cedex 20

Abstract. Configuring consists in simulating the realization of a complex product from a catalog of component parts, using known relations between types, and picking values for object attributes. An inherent difficulty in solving configuration problems is the existence of many isomorphisms among interpretations. We describe a formalism independent approach to improve the detection of isomorphisms by configurators, which does not require to adapt the problem model. We exploit the properties of a structural subset of configuration problems, which canonical solutions can be produced or tested at low cost by an algorithm, possibly used as a symmetry breaking constraint.

1   Introduction

Configuring consists in simulating the constrained realization of a complex product from a catalog of component parts (e.g. processors, hard disks in a PC), using known relations between types (motherboards can connect up to four processors), and instantiating object attributes (selecting the ram size, bus speed, ...). The industrial need for configuration applications is ancient [4], and has triggered the development of many configuration applications.

One difficulty with configuration problems is that isomorphisms naturally arise from the fact that many constraints are universally quantified [3, 6, 5]. We propose a general approach for the elimination of structural isomorphisms in configuration problems, which generalizes existing methods (the interchangeability of "unused" objects, as well as the use of cardinality counters) while not requiring to adapt the configuration model, and extends a strategy successfully applied to finite model search [1]. After describing the formalism used throughout the paper and *structural sub-problems* (section 2), we define *T-trees* and their canonical representatives (section 3). Finally we propose an algorithm to test the canonicity of configurations (section 4), and conclude in section 5. Proofs, bibliographic details and combinatorial comparisons can be found in [2].

2   Configuration Problems, and Structural Sub-problems

A configuration problem describes a generic product, in the form of declarative statements (rules or axioms) about product well-formedness. Valid configuration

F. Rossi (Ed.): CP 2003, LNCS 2833, pp. 853–857, 2003.

model instances (called *configurations*) involve objects and their relationships, notably *types* (unary relations involved in taxonomies) and binary *composition* relations (an object is a component of at most one composite). We isolate configuration sub-problems called *structural problems*, that are built from the composition relations, the related types and the structural constraints alone, and study their isomorphisms. For simplicity, we abstract from any configuration formalism, and consider a totally ordered set O of objects (we normally use $O = \{1, 2, \ldots\}$), a totally ordered set T_C of type symbols (unary relations) and a totally ordered set R_C of composition relation symbols (binary relations). We note $\prec_O$, $\prec_{T_C}$ and $\prec_{R_C}$ the corresponding total orders.

Definition 1 (syntax). *A structural problem, is a tuple (t, T_C, R_C, C), where $t \in T_C$ is the root configuration type, and C is a set of structural constraints applied to the elements of T_C and R_C.*

Definition 2 (semantics). *An* instance *of a structural problem (t, T_C, R_C, C) is an interpretation I of t and of the elements of T_C and R_C, over the set O of objects. If an interpretation satisfies the constraints in C, it is a* solution *(or* model*) of the structural problem.*

In the spirit of usual finite model semantics, T_C members are interpreted by elements of $\mathcal{P}(O)$, and R_C members by elements of $\mathcal{P}(O \times O)$ (relations). We use the term *configuration* to denote a structural problem model .

Definition 3 (root, composite, component). *A configuration, solution of a structural problem (t, T_C, R_C, C), can be described by the set U of interpretations of all the elements of R_C. If R_U denotes the union of the relations in U ($R_U = \bigcup_{rel \in U} rel$), and R_t denotes its transitive closure, then we have:*

1. *$\exists! \, root \in O$ called* root of the configuration[1] *for which $\forall o \in O \,\, (o, root) \notin R_U$,*
2. *$\forall o \in O$ s.t. $o \neq root$, $\exists! \, c \in O$ s.t. $(c, o) \in R_U$;*
   we call c the composite *of o and o a* component *of c,*
3. *$\forall o \in O$ s.t. $o \neq root$, $(root, o) \in R_t$.*

Definition 4. *We note $U(r)$ the relation interpreting the relational symbol $r \in R_C$ in U. Two configurations U and U' are* isomorphic *if and only if there exists a permutation θ over the set O, such that $\forall r \in R_c, \theta(U)(r) = U'(r)$*

3   Coding Configurations: T-Trees

Because composition relations bind component objects to at most one composite object, configurations can naturally be represented by trees where nodes are labeled by objects of O, edges are labeled by the component side type of the corresponding relation, and child nodes are sorted first by their type according to $\prec_{T_C}$, then by their label according to $\prec_O$. Figure 1 shows that object numbers are redundant. We thus introduce *T-trees* (illustrated in figure 2):

---

[1] Root unicity does not restrict generality.

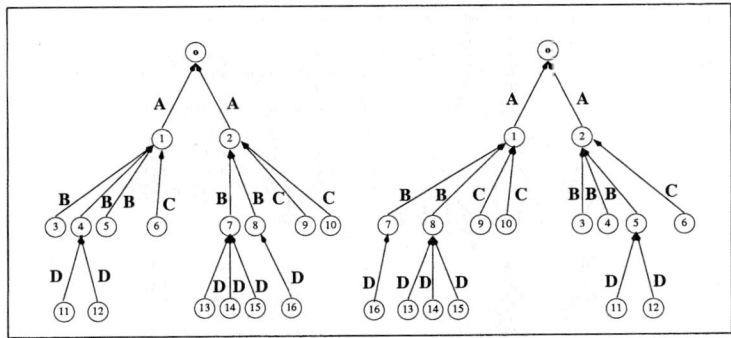

Fig. 1. Two isomorphic configuration trees.

Definition 5 (T-tree). *A T-tree is a finite and non empty ordered tree where nodes are labeled by types and children are ordered according to $\prec_{T_C}$. We note $(T, \langle c_1, \ldots c_k \rangle)$ the T-tree with sub-trees $c_1, \ldots c_k$ and root label T.*

Proposition 1. *Let A_1 be a configuration tree, C_1 the corresponding T-tree , and A_2 the configuration tree rebuilt from C_1. Then A_1 and A_2 are isomorphic.*

Configuration trees and T-trees being trees, they are iscmorphic, equal, superposable, under the same assumptions as standard trees.

Proposition 2. *Two configurations are isomorphic iff their corresponding T-trees are isomorphic (two T-trees are isomorphic if there exists a set of permutations of their lists of subtrees that makes them identical).*

As a means of isolating a canonical representative of each equivalence class of T-trees, we define a total order over T-trees. We note $nct(T)$ (number of component types) the number of types T_i having T as composite type for a relation in R_C. The types T_i ($1 \leq i \leq nct(T)$) are numbered on each node according to $\prec_{T_C}$. If C is a T-tree, we call *T-list* and we note $T_i(C)$ the list of its children having T_i as a root label. $|T_i(C)|$ is the number of T-trees of the T-list $T_i(C)$. We note $\langle a_i \rangle_1^n$ the list $\langle a_1, a_2, ..., a_n \rangle$. Many ways exist to lexicographically compare trees. We use two orders $\preccurlyeq$ and $\ll$:

Definition 6 (The relations $\preccurlyeq$, $\preccurlyeq_{lex}$, $\ll$ and $\ll_{lex}$).
We define the following four relations: $\preccurlyeq$ compares T-trees with roots of the same type T, $\preccurlyeq_{lex}$ is its lexicographic generalization to T-lists, $\ll$ compares two T-lists of same type T_i, and $\ll_{lex}$ is its lexicographic generalization to lists $\langle T_i(C) \rangle_1^{nct(T)}$. These four order relations recursively define as follows:

- $\forall T \in T_C \; : \; (T, \langle \rangle) \preccurlyeq (T, \langle \rangle)$.
- $\forall C, \; C' \neq (T, \langle \rangle): C \preccurlyeq C' \iff \langle T_i(C) \rangle_1^{nct(T)} \ll_{lex} \langle T_i(C') \rangle_1^{nct(T)}$.
- $\forall C, \; C' \neq (T, \langle \rangle), \; \forall i: T_i(C) \ll T_i(C') \iff$
  $|T_i(C)| < |T_i(C')| \lor |T_i(C)| = |T_i(C')| \land T_i(C) \preccurlyeq_{lex} T_i(C')$.

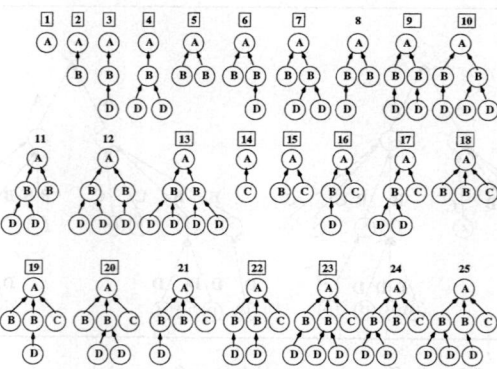

Fig. 2. The first 26 T-trees ordered by $\preccurlyeq$ for a sample problem. The $\preccurlyeq$-minimal representatives are framed.

Each T-tree is built from a root of type T and a list of T-lists of sub-trees. A proof that $\preccurlyeq$, $\preccurlyeq_{lex}$, $\ll$ and $\ll_{lex}$ are total orders can be found in [2].

Definition 7 (Canonicity of a T-tree). *A T-tree C is canonical iff it has no child or if $\forall i$, $T_i(C)$ is sorted by $\preccurlyeq$ and $\forall c \in T_i(C)$, c itself is canonical.*

Proposition 3. *A T-tree is the $\preccurlyeq$-minimal representative of its equivalence class (wrt. T-tree isomorphism) iff it is canonical.*

The search space of a (structural) configuration problem can be described by a state graph $G = (V, E)$ where the nodes in V correspond to valid (solution) T-trees and the edges correspond to *unit extensions* (adding a single terminal node to a T-tree). The goal of a constructive search procedure is to find a path in G starting from the tree $(t, \langle\rangle)$ (t is the type of the root object) and reaching a T-tree which respect all the problem constraints.

Proposition 4. *Let G be the state graph of a configuration problem. Its subgraph G_c corresponding to the only canonical T-trees is connex.*

It immediately follows that any configuration procedure that discards the non canonical structural configurations remains complete.

4   Algorithms

A test of canonicity straightforwardly follows from the definition of canonicity. It is defined by two functions: *Canonical* and *Less* listed in pseudo code by the figure 3. We note $ct(T)$ the list of component types of T, sorted according to $\prec_{T_C}$, and by extension, as the labels of nodes of a T-tree are types, we generalize these notations to $ct(C)$ for a given T-tree C. The worst case complexity of **Less** is $\Theta(n)$, n being the number of nodes of the smallest T-tree. *Canonical* is of complexity $\Theta(n \log n)$.

function **Canonical**(C)	function **Less**(C, C')
{*returns True iff C is canonical*}	{*Returns* True *iff* $C \preceq C'$}
begin	**begin**
if C is a leaf **then return** True	**if** C is a leaf **then return** True
Let $ct(C) = (T_1, \ldots, T_k)$	**if** C' is a leaf **then return** False
for $i := 1$ to k **do**	Let $ct(C) = (T_1, \ldots, T_k)$
Let $(a_1, \ldots a_l)$ be the list $T_i(C)$	**for** $i := 1$ to k **do**
for $j := 1$ to l **do**	Let $(a^i_1, \ldots, a^i_{l_a})$ be the list $T_i(C)$,
if **not**(Canonical(a_j)) **then**	Let $(b^i_1, \ldots, b^i_{l_b})$ be the list $T_i(C')$
return False	**if** $(l_a < l_b)$ **then return** True
for $j := 1$ to $l - 1$ **do**	**if** $(l_a > l_b)$ **then return** False
if **not**(Less(a_j, a_{j+1})) **then**	**for** $j := 1$ to l_a **do**
return False	**if** (Less(a^i_j, b^i_j) =False) **then**
return True	**return** False
end function	**return** True
	end function

Fig. 3. The functions *Canonical* and *Less.*

5 Conclusion

This work greatly extends the possibilities of dealing with configuration isomorphisms, until today limited either to the detection of the interchangeability of all yet unused individuals of each type or to the use of counters of non configurable object counters (as in the ILOG software products[3]). We have shown that the isomorphisms stemming from the properties of a sub-problem called the structural problem, can be efficiently and totally tackled, by using low cost amortizable algorithm.

References

1. Gilles Audemard and Laurent Henocque. The extended least number heuristic. In Rajeev Goré, Alexander Leitsch, and Tobias Nipkow, editors, *Proceedings of the First International Joint Conference, IJCAR, Sienne, Italie*, volume 2083 of *Lecture Notes in Computer Science*, pages 427–442. Springer, June 2001.
2. Stephane Grandcolas, Laurent Henocque, and Nicolas Prcovic. Pruning isomorphic structural sub-problems in configuration. Technical report, LSIS (UMR CNRS 6168), Marseille, France, June 2003. Available from the CoRR archive at http://arXiv.org/abs/cs/0306135.
3. Daniel Mailharro. A classification and constraint-based framework for configuration. *AI in Engineering, Design and Manufacturing, (12)*, pages 383–397, 1998.
4. John P. McDermott. R1: A rule-based configurer of computer systems. *Artificial Intelligence*, 19:39–88, 1982.
5. Juha Tiihonen, Timo Soininen, Ilkka Niemela, and Reijo Sulonen. Empirical testing of a weight constraint rule based configurator. In *Proceedings of the Configuration Workshop, 15th European Conference on Artificial Intelligence*, pages 17–22, Lyon, France, 2002.
6. Rainer Weigel, Boi Faltings, and Marc Torrens. Interchangeability for case adaptation in configuration problems. In *Workshop on Case-Based Reasoning Integrations (AAAI-98)*, volume Technical Report WS-98-15, pages 166–171, Madison, Wisconsin, USA, July 1998. AAAI Press.

Improved Algorithms
for Max-restricted Path Consistency[*]

Fabrizio Grandoni and Giuseppe F. Italiano

Dipartimento di Informatica, Sistemi e Produzione
Università di Roma "Tor Vergata"
Via del Politecnico 1
00133 Roma, Italy
{grandoni,italiano}@disp.uniroma2.it

Abstract. A binary constraints network consists of a set of n variables, defined on domains of size at most d, and a set of e binary constraints. The binary constraint satisfaction problem consists in finding a solution for a binary constraints network, that is an instantiation of all the variables which satisfies all the constraints. A value a in the domain of variable x is inconsistent if there is no solution which assigns a to x. Many filtering techniques have been proposed to filter out inconsistent values from the domains. Most of them are based on enforcing a given kind of local consistency. One of the most important such consistencies is max-restricted path consistency. The fastest algorithm to enforce max-restricted path consistency has a $O(end^3)$ time complexity and a $O(end)$ space complexity. In this paper we present two improved algorithms for the same problem. The first still has a $O(end^3)$ time complexity, but it reduces the space usage to $O(ed)$. The second improves the time complexity to $O(end^{2.575})$, and has a $O(end^2)$ space complexity.

1 Introduction

Constraint programming is a declarative programming paradigm which allows to naturally formulate computational problems [10]. A computational problem is formulated as a *constraint satisfaction problem*, which consists in deciding whether there is an instantiation of a set of variables, defined on finite domains, which satisfies a set of constraints. Any such instantiation is a *solution* for the *constraints network*. The task of the constraint programming system is to find a solution (or alternatively all the solutions, or the "best" one). Any constraint satisfaction problem can be reduced [11] to an equivalent *binary constraint satisfaction problem*, that is a constraint satisfaction problem where each constraint involves only a pair of variables.

A value a in the domain of variable x is *inconsistent* if there is no solution which assigns a to x. Inconsistent values can be filtered out from the domains

---

[*] This work has been partially supported by the IST Programme of the EU under contract n. IST-1999-14.186 (ALCOM-FT), by the Italian Ministry of University and Research (Project "ALINWEB: Algorithmics for Internet and the Web").

F. Rossi (Ed.): CP 2003, LNCS 2833, pp. 858–862, 2003.

without loosing any solution. Since the binary constraint satisfaction problem is NP-complete, there is no hope that all the inconsistent values can be detected in polynomial time. For this reason, local consistency properties have been studied, which allow to "quickly" remove a subset of the inconsistent values.

Some of the most important such consistencies are *arc consistency* [1, 9], *path inverse consistency* [3, 6, 7] and *ℓ inverse consistency* [6, 7].

In [4], a new and promising local consistency property has been proposed: the *max-restricted path consistency*. Computational experiments give evidence that max-restricted path consistency offers a particularly good compromise between computational cost and pruning efficiency [5]. Debruyne and Bessiere [4] developed the fastest known filtering algorithm based on max-restricted path consistency, denoted by `max-RPC-1`, which has a $O(end^3)$ time complexity and a $O(end)$ space complexity, where n is the number of variables, e is the number of binary constraints and d is the size of the largest domains.

In this paper we present a new algorithm for the same task, which we denote by `max-RPC-2`, with the same time complexity as `max-RFC-1`, but with a smaller space complexity, that is $O(ed)$.

As a second contribution of this paper, we shortly describe a variant of `max-RPC-2` of $O(end^{2.575})$ time complexity and $O(end^2)$ space complexity. This algorithm makes use of fast matrix multiplication.

The remainder of this paper is organized as follows. In Section 2 we introduce some preliminaries. In Section 3 we present Algorithm `max-RPC-2`. In Section 4 we shortly describe how to reduce the time complexity via fast matrix multiplication.

2 Preliminaries

A *binary constraints network* is a triple $(\mathcal{X}, \mathcal{D}, \mathcal{C})$, where $\mathcal{X} = \{x_1, x_2 \ldots x_n\}$ is a set of n variables, $\mathcal{D} = \{D_1, D_2 \ldots D_n\}$ is a set of n domains of cardinality at most d, and $\mathcal{C} = \{C_{\{i_1, j_1\}}, C_{\{i_2, j_2\}} \ldots C_{\{i_e, j_e\}}\}$ is a set cf e binary constraints. Variable x_i is defined over domain D_i. By a_i we denote an element of D_i. For simplicity and without lost of generality, we assume that all the values in the domains are distinct. We moreover assume that the domains are ordered (the order can be fixed arbitrarily). A *value assignment* is a pair (x_i, a_i), whose meaning is that we assign the value a_i to variable x_i. An *instantiation* is a set of value assignments, one for each variable. A *binary constraint* $C_{\{i,j\}}$ describes which assignments of values to the variables x_i and x_j are mutually compatible. The constraint $C_{\{i,j\}}$ can be represented extensively through a 0-1 matrix $A_{i,j}$ which we interpret in the following way: $A_{i,j}[a_i, a_j] = 1$ if and only if the pair of value assignments (x_i, a_i) and (x_j, a_j) satisfy the constraint $C_{\{i,j\}}$. Notice that there may be pairs of variables x_i and x_j for which there is no constraint $C_{\{i,j\}}$ in $\mathcal{C}$. In that case all the assignments of values to x_i and x_j are mutually compatible. A *solution* is an instantiation which satisfies all the constraints. The *binary constraint satisfaction problem* consists in deciding whether a binary constraints network admits a solution.

A value a_i is *inconsistent* if there is no solution which assigns a_i to variable x_i. A value a_i is *max-restricted path consistent* if it has a *path-consistent support* on each variable x_j such that $C_{\{i,j\}} \in C$. A path-consistent support for a_i on x_j is a value $a_j \in D_j$ such that $A_{i,j}[a_i, a_j] = 1$ and the pair $\{a_i, a_j\}$ has at least one *witness* on each variable x_k such that $C_{\{i,k\}}$ and $C_{\{j,k\}}$ belong to C. A witness for $\{a_i, a_j\}$ on x_k is a value $a_k \in D_k$ such that $A_{i,k}[a_i, a_k] = A_{j,k}[a_j, a_k] = 1$.

A *subdomain* $\mathcal{D}'$ of $\mathcal{D}$ is a set $\{D'_1, D'_2 \ldots D'_n\}$ such that, for any $i \in \{1, 2 \ldots n\}$, $D'_i \subseteq D_i$. The *order* of $\mathcal{D}'$ is the sum of the cardinalities of the domains D'_i. A subdomain $\mathcal{D}'$ is max-restricted path consistent if, for any $i \in \{1, 2 \ldots n\}$, D'_i is non-empty and all the values $a'_i \in D'_i$ are max-restricted path consistent. By $\mathcal{D}_{\text{max-RPC}}$ we denote the max-restricted path consistent subdomain of $\mathcal{D}$ of maximum order (if any).

3   Max-restricted Path Consistency in Less Space

The fastest known filtering algorithm based on max-restricted path consistency, `max-RPC-1` [4], has a $O(end^3)$ time complexity and a $O(end)$ space complexity. In this section we present a new algorithm for the same problem, which we denote by `max-RPC-2`, with the same time complexity as `max-RPC-1` but with a smaller space complexity, that is $O(ed)$.

Let $(\mathcal{X}, \mathcal{D}, \mathcal{C})$ be a binary constraints network. Our algorithm removes non-max-restricted path consistent values from the domains one by one, until a domain becomes empty or all the remaining values are max-restricted path consistent.

The algorithm uses two kinds of data structures. A set `DelSet` of integers and a set S_a of values for each value a. The set `DelSet` is used to keep trace of the domains from which a value has been removed. Whenever we remove a value a_i, we store i in `DelSet`. The set S_{a_i} is used to store the last path-consistent support a_j found for a_i on variable x_j, for any x_j such that $C_{\{i,j\}} \in C$.

The algorithm consists of two main steps: an initialization step and a propagation step. In the initialization step we consider each value a_i and we check if it is max-restricted path consistent. If not, we remove a_i from D_i and we add i to `DelSet`. Otherwise we store the path-consistent supports found for a_i in S_{a_i}.

In the propagation step we have to propagate efficiently the effects of deletions. In fact, the deletion of one value can induce as a side effect the deletion of other values (which were previously recognized as max-restricted path consistent). There are substantially two kinds of such situations. The first case is when we delete the unique path-consistent support a_j for the value a_i on the variable x_j. The second is when we remove the unique witness a_j on variable x_j for the pair $\{a_i, a_k\}$, where a_k is the unique path-consistent support for a_i on variable x_k. In both cases the value a_i is not max-restricted path consistent.

Thus in the propagation step, until `DelSet` is not empty, we extract an integer j from `DelSet` and we proceed as follows. We consider any value a_i, with $C_{\{i,j\}} \in C$, and we check if a_i is not max-restricted path consistent because of one of the two situations described above. In particular, we first check if the last path-consistent support a_j found for a_i on x_j (which is stored in S_{a_i}), still belongs to D_j. If not, we search for a new path-consistent support for a_i on x_j, and we update S_{a_i} accordingly. If such path-consistent support does not exist, a_i is removed and i is added to DelSet. Then, if a_i has not been removed in the previous step, for any variable x_k such that $C_{\{i,k\}}$ and $C_{\{j,k\}}$ belong to $\mathcal{C}$, we consider the last path-consistent support a_k found for a_i on x_k (which is stored in S_{a_i}). We check if the pair $\{a_i, a_k\}$ has a witness on variable x_j (by simply considering all the values in D_j). If not, we search for a new path-consistent support for a_i on x_k, and we update S_{a_i} accordingly. If such path-consistent support does not exist, a_i is removed and i is added to DelSet. In both cases, when we search for a new path-consistent support, we follow the order on the corresponding domain. This way we make sure that the same potential path-consistent support is checked at most once.

Theorem 1. *Let $(\mathcal{X}, \mathcal{D}, \mathcal{C})$ be a binary constraints network, with n variables, defined on domains of size at most d, and e constraints. Algorithm* max–RPC–2 *computes $\mathcal{D}_{max\text{-}RPC}$ or determines that it does not exist in* $\mathrm{O}(ed)$ *space and* $\mathrm{O}(end^3)$ *time.*

Proof (Sketch). Without loss of generality, we assume $e = \Omega(n)$. Moreover we indicate with e_i the number of domains D_j such that $C_{\{i,j\}} \in \mathcal{C}$. The set DelSet requires $\mathrm{O}(n)$ space. For each a_i, the set S_{a_i} takes $\mathrm{O}(e_i)$ space. Then the space complexity of max–RPC–2 is $\mathrm{O}(n + \sum_{i=1}^{k} e_i d) = \mathrm{O}(ed)$.

The time complexity is bounded by the cost of searching for witnesses (which is required for both searching for new path-consistent supports and for checking previously detected ones). Searching for a witness costs $\mathrm{O}(d)$. Then checking a potential path-consistent support a_j for a value a_i on variable x_j costs $\mathrm{O}(e_j + e_i d) = \mathrm{O}(n + e_i d)$. Value a_i has $\mathrm{O}(d)$ potential path-consistent supports on each of the $\mathrm{O}(e_i)$ variables x_j such that $C_{\{i,j\}} \in \mathcal{C}$. No potential path-consistent support is checked more than once. Thus the total cost to search for new path-consistent supports is $\mathrm{O}\left(\sum_{i=1}^{n} e_i d^2(n + e_i d)\right) = \mathrm{O}(end^3)$. Whenever a deletion occurs into a domain D_j, we have to search for a witness on x_j for all the pairs of values $\{a_i, a_k\}$ where a_k is the current path-consistent support for a_i on x_k, and $C_{\{i,j\}}$, $C_{\{i,k\}}$ and $C_{\{j,k\}}$ belong to $\mathcal{C}$. The number of such pairs is $\mathrm{O}(e_j^2 d)$, and we can detect them in $\mathrm{O}((e_i + e_j)d) = \mathrm{O}((n + e_j)d)$ steps. Each check costs $\mathrm{O}(d)$. Since domain D_j is interested by $\mathrm{O}(d)$ deletions, the total cost of these checks is $\mathrm{O}\left(\sum_{j=1}^{n} d^2(nd + e_j^2 d)\right) = \mathrm{O}(end^3)$. Thus the time complexity of max–RPC–2 is $\mathrm{O}(end^3)$. $\qquad\square$

Notice that Algorithm max–RPC–2 may check the same potential witness for a given pair of values more than once: since these redundant checks are relatively infrequent, they do not affect the total time complexity. Algorithm max–RPC–1 instead, avoids redundancies by storing (in $\mathrm{O}(end)$ space) all the witnesses found: this way, the space complexity is increased without reducing asymptotically the time complexity.

4   Max-restricted Path Consistency in Less Time

The first author [7] developed a fast path inverse consistency based filtering algorithm, based on fast matrix multiplication. A similar technique can be applied to max-restricted path consistency. In particular, given a triple of variables x_i, x_j, x_k, there is a decremental procedure to maintain the number of witnesses for each pair of the kind $\{a_i, a_j\}$ on x_k, during deletions of values in D_k, which has a $O(d^{2.376})$ initialization cost, a $O(d^{0.575})$ query cost and a $O(d^{1.575})$ amortized updating cost per deletion. Using this procedure, one can develop a variant of Algorithm max-RPC-2, of $O(end^{2.575})$ time complexity and $O(end^2)$ space complexity. For reasons of space, we cannot enter into details.

References

1. C. Bessière. Arc-consistency and arc-consistency again. *Artificial Intelligence*, pages 179–190, 1994.
2. D. Coppersmith and S. Winograd. Matrix multiplication via arithmetic progressions. *Journal of Symbolic Computation*, 9(3):251–280, 1990.
3. R. Debruyne. A property of path inverse consistency leading to an optimal PIC algorithm. In *ECAI-00, Berlin, Germany*, pages 88–92, 2000.
4. R. Debruyne and C. Bessière. From restricted path consistency to max-restricted path consistency. In *Principles and Practice of Constraint Programming*, pages 312–326, 1997.
5. R. Debruyne and C. Bessière. Domain filtering consistencies. *Journal of Artificial Intelligence Research*, (14):205–230, may 2001.
6. E. C. Freuder and C. D. Elfe. Neighborhood inverse consistency preprocessing. In *AAAI/IAAI, Vol. 1*, pages 202–208, 1996.
7. F. Grandoni. Incrementally maintaining the number of l-cliques. Technical Report MPI-I-2002-1-002, Max-Planck-Institut für Informatik, Saarbrücken, 2002.
8. X. Huang and V. Pan. Fast rectangular matrix multiplication and applications. *J. Complexity*, 14(2):257–299, 1998.
9. A. K. Mackworth. Consistency in networks of relations. *Artificial Intelligence*, 8:99–118, 1977.
10. K. Marriott and P. J. Stuckey. *Programming with constraints: an introduction*. MIT Press, Cambridge, MA, 1998.
11. U. Montanari. Networks of constraints: Fundamental properties and applications to picture processing. *Information Sciences*, 7:95–132, 1974.

CP-IP Techniques for the Bid Evaluation in Combinatorial Auctions

Alessio Guerri and Michela Milano

DEIS, University of Bologna
Viale Risorgimento 2
40136 Bologna, Italy
{aguerri,mmilano}@deis.unibo.it

Abstract. Combinatorial auctions are an important e-commerce application where bidders can bid on combinations of items. The problem of selecting the best bids that cover all items, i.e., the Winner Determination Problem (WDP), is NP-hard. In this paper we consider the time constrained variant of this problem, that is the Bid Evaluation Problem (BEP) where temporal windows and precedence constraints are associated to each task in the bid. We propose different algorithms based on CP, IP and a hybrid approach based on both of them. We show that even the simplest pure CP based approach outperforms the only existing approach. We selected a set of algorithms which do not dominate each other. We identified a set of instance-dependent structural features that enable to select the best class of algorithms to apply. This is the first step toward an automatic algorithm selection in algorithm portfolios.

1 Introduction

Business to business e-commerce applications are becoming more and more popular. Among them, auctions are a way of allocating items among autonomous and self-interested agents. Items are not limited to goods, but can represent also resources and services.

In this paper we consider *combinatorial auctions*, see [4]. Among M items, bidders can bid on combinations of items, and associate a price for each combination. The auctioneer should solve the Winner Determination Problem (WDP), i.e., he should choose the best bids that cover all items at a minimum cost or maximum revenue. This problem is NP-hard.

A variant of this problem is the so called Bid Evaluation Problem (BEP) for coordinated tasks. When the auctioneer should, for example, buy a set of services, he should also consider temporal constraints. Therefore, items in the bid are associated to a temporal window, a duration, and are linked by precedence constraints. In this case, beside the WDP, the auctioneer should maintain feasibility of the temporal constraints. To our knowledge, the only system that tackles this problem is MAGNET (Multi-Agent Negotiation testbed) [1] and it is based on Integer Programming and Simulated Annealing.

F. Rossi (Ed.): CP 2003, LNCS 2833, pp. 863–867, 2003.

Surprisingly, Constraint Programming (CP) has been very rarely used to solve either the WDP or the BEP, while we think CP can be successfully used as an effective tool for modelling and solving problems related to combinatorial auctions. In particular, CP can be effective when additional constraints are introduced.

In this paper, we propose different algorithms for the BEP: two variants of a pure CP algorithm, one based on Limited Discrepancy Search (LDS) and one on Depth First Search (DFS); two approaches based on pure IP and two hybrid approaches merging CP and IP, one based on LDS and one on DFS. We show that even the simplest approach we developed, based on pure CP, outperforms the one presented in MAGNET[1]. We evaluated all algorithms and discovered that those based on DFS are always dominated by the others. Among the remaining algorithms none of the them dominates all the others, so we tried to select among the set of instance-dependent structural features proposed in [3] the ones that allow to select the best algorithm. An interesting result achieved is that the standard deviation of the Clustering Coefficient provides a clear indication if to use an IP or a CP based algorithm.

2 Bid Evaluation Problem: Model and Algorithms

We have different variants of combinatorial auctions. In this paper, we consider **single unit reverse auctions**, where the auctioneer wants to buy a set M of distinguishable items (services) minimizing the cost.

Each bidder j $(j = 1..n)$ posts one or more bids. A bid is represented as $B_j = (S_j, Est_j, Lst_j, D_j, p_j)$ where a set $S_j \subseteq M$ of services is proposed to be sold at the price p_j. Est_j and Lst_j are lists of earliest and latest starting time of the services in S_j and D_j their duration.

The BEP can be seen as a variant of the WDP where a set of temporal constraints define the feasibility of the assignments computed by the WDP.

We implemented four algorithms, plus two variants based on DFS and LDS, to solve the BEP. Two algorithms are based on the IP model: the first (referred in tables to as IP) is a traditional complete solver implementing Branch and Bound based on linear relaxation, while the second (referred in tables to as LR+IP) is an incomplete approach that solves the linear relaxation of the problem, then ranks the variables according to their shadow price, and finally solves the IP problem considering only the first $p\%$ variables, where p is a parameter to be experimentally tuned.

One algorithm is based on a pure CP model (referred in tables to as CP). Starting from the same model, one variant explores the search tree with DFS and one with LDS. In both cases, the heuristic used to select the variable value is the bid-price divided by bid-size, that is $p_i/|S_i|$. The last approach, referred to as LR+CP in tables, performs an indeed quite loose but effective integration. Starting from a CP model, we solve a linear relaxation at the root node and we

---

[1] This software has been kindly provided by the authors J. Collins and M. Gini.

order values based on shadow prices. Again we have two variants, one based on DFS and one on LDS.

3 Comparing CP and MAGNET

We first compared the pure CP algorithms we developed and MAGNET [1] on instances generated using MAGNET itself. We ran our experiments on a 2.4Ghz Intel Pentium 4 with 512Mb RAM. We considered four kinds of MAGNET instances with a number of tasks between 5 and 20 and bids between 15 and 400.

For each instance set we used our CP algorithms, MAGNET implementing Simulated Annealing (referred to as SA in figures) and, when possible, MAGNET using Integer Programming (M-IP).

In the first two sets of experiments (5 tasks and 15 bids and 10 tasks and 35 bids), the M-IP approach always finds the optimal solution, while in the third (10 tasks and 100 bids) it does not provide the optimal solution within 15 minutes. In the first set also SA provides the optimal solution, while, in the second set, it provides the optimal solution only in the 60% of the cases. In the third set of experiments it never provides the optimal solution. Our CP approaches always finds the optimal solution in all instance sets. Mean search time for the first three sets are depicted in Figure 1, where for each group values are normalized w.r.t. mean value over all algorithms.

As concern the fourth instance set (20 tasks and 400 bids) none of the approaches find the optimal solution within 15 minutes, but solutions found found by the CP based approaches are, on average, 30% better than those produced by MAGNET. Moreover, the time to produce the best solution is in general considerably lower than 15 minutes and our algorithms always outperform MAGNET. The relative quality of SA with respect to LDS and DFS is also depicted in Figure 2 where we show the trend of the solution quality for hard instances with SA, DFS and LDS. M-IP approach did not find any solution.

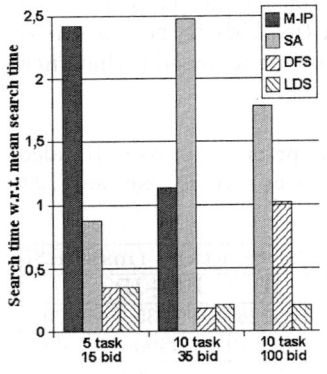

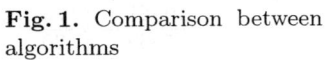

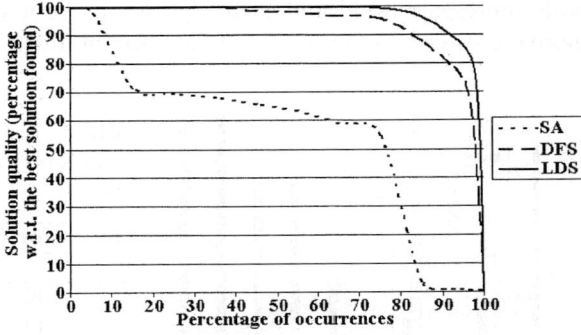

Fig. 1. Comparison between algorithms

Fig. 2. Comparison between algorithms on instances with 20 tasks and 400 bids

4 Experimental Results of CP, IP and Hybrid Approaches

In this section, we provide results on instances generated using both MAGNET and CATS, a suite for generating realistic auction instances [2]. CATS instances are more realistic, enabling to set an higher bid-size and bid-size variability. We generated problems with 10, 15, 20 and 30 tasks, with a number of bids growing from 40 up to 1000 and with a variable tasks-per-bid values.

In Figure 3 we present results for all algorithms described in section 2 except for those using DFS since they are always outperformed by those using LDS. Each group in the histogram represents a different instance set, having the mean tasks-per-bid value expressed in x-axis. Y-axis values represent, for each group, mean search time normalized w.r.t. mean over all algorithms. Some instances are best solved by CP-based approaches (namely CP and LR+CP), while others by IP approaches (namely IP and LR+IP), depending on the number of tasks-per-bid (see Section 5 for a deeper analysis).

Finally, we ran experiments on hardest problems, with 30 tasks, 1000 bids and a growing tasks-per-bid value. We found that only the IP-based approach provided results. In Table 1 we show the mean search time for both complete and incomplete IP solver (i.e., IP and LR+IP). For the incomplete approach, the percentage of variables considered is reported in the last column. Only in the first 3 instance sets it was possible to prove optimality over all instances.

5 Problem Structure Analysis

In this section, we are interested in identifying a set of instance-dependent parameters that help in determining the best algorithm to solve the instance itself. From tables in previous section, we noticed that tasks-per-bid parameter roughly influences algorithms' quality. Here we are interested in more precise parameter.

Starting from the notable classification in [3], we extracted from each instance the 25 features described in the paper. We refer to the bid graph, where each node represents a bid and each edge stands between two bids if there is one or more constraints containing that bids. An interesting result achieved is that there

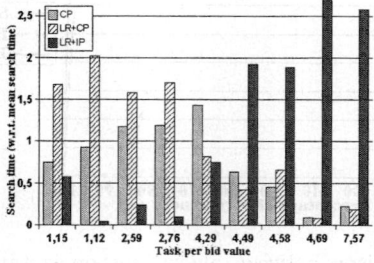

Fig. 3. Comparison between algorithms

Table 1. Comparison between IP algorithms on instances with 30 tasks and 1000 bids

Tasks for Bid	Search time (ms)		CR%
	IP	LR+IP	
1.40	36328	1235	70
2.49	242281	3500	45
3.34	900000	6975	25
4.62	-	19681	25
6.52	-	25969	30

is a correspondence between the standard deviation of the Clustering Coefficient (SDCC) in the bid graph and the experimental results. SDCC is a measure of the *local cliqueness*. Typically, in our instances this value ranges from 0.02 e 0.2, and each time it is greater than 0.09, the IP-based approach is preferable to the CP-based one. It is worth noting the fact that, if SDCC is close to 0.09 both approaches have satisfactory behaviors. For the instances considered it is a *systematic* result, but, unfortunately, for larger instances this feature extraction takes too much time. Therefore, we looked for a similar but easier-to-compute parameter. We observed that there is a correspondence between SDCC and the Edge Density (ED) in the bid graph. ED can range from 0 to 1, and we observed that it is in inverse proportion with SDCC.

We have identified three significant ranges for the ED: if $ED < 0.5$, SDCC is always greater than 0.09 (thus the IP-based approach is preferable); if $ED > 0.75$, SDCC is always lower than 0.09 (thus the CP-based approach is preferable); if $0.5 < ED < 0.75$, we do not have a clear indication of SDCC and therefore on the preferable approach. In this case, we recompute ED allowing multiple edges between the nodes (when more than one constraint is present among them). If new ED is significantly greater than the previous one, the CP-based approach is to be preferred; otherwise, if it remains quite unchanged, the best approach is IP.

If the IP approach is the technique of choice, we can use either the complete approach or the incomplete one named LR+IP. So we have to tune the percentage of variables to be considered. We did not find a systematic correspondence between those choices and any feature we calculated, but from the L_1 and L_∞ norms of the integer slack vector we can often find out a good superior boundary to the percentage of variables to be considered using IP approach. These norms are in a way a measure of how fractional is the linear relaxation solution; we noticed that, in general, the higher the norms, the higher the percentage of variables to include to obtain the best solution.

Acknowledgement

This work was supported by the SOCS project, funded by the CEC, contract IST-2001-32530. We would like to thank Andrea Lodi and Andrea Roli for useful discussion. In addition, we warmly thank Maria Gini and John Collins for providing the MAGNET software and for their assistance in using it.

We also thank anonymous reviewers for useful comments.

References

1. J. Collins and M. Gini, An integer programming formulation of the bid evaluation problem for coordinated tasks, *Mathematics of E-Commerce*, Springer-Verlag.
2. K. Leyton-Brown, M. Pearson and Y. Shoham, Towards an Universal Test Suite for Combinatorial Auction Algorithms, *Proc. EC00*, 2000.
3. K. Leyton-Brown, E. Nudelman and Y. Shoham, Learning the Empirical Hardness of Optimization Problems: The Case of Combinatorial Auctions, *Proc CP02*, 2002.
4. T. Sandholm, Algorithm for optimal winner determination in combinatorial auction, *AI*, Vol 135, 2002.

A Two-Level Search Strategy for Packing Unequal Circles into a Circle Container

Wen Qi Huang[1], Yu Li[2], Bernard Jurkowiak[2], Chu Min Li[2], and Ru Chu Xu[1]

[1] HuaZhong Univ. of Science and Technology Wuhan 430074, China
{wqhuang,Xu}@hust.edu.cn
[2] LaRIA, Université de Picardie Jules Verne, 5 Rue du Moulin Neuf, 80000 Amiens, France
{yli,jurkowia,cli}@laria.u-picardie.fr

Abstract. We propose a two-level search strategy to solve a two dimensional circle packing problem. At the first level, a good enough packing algorithm called $A1.0$ uses a simple heuristic to select the next circle to be packed. This algorithm is itself used at the second level to select the next circle to be packed. The resulted packing procedure called $A1.5$ considerably improves the performance of the algorithm in the first level, as shown by experimental results. We also apply the approach to solve other CSPs and obtain interesting results.

1 Introduction

Given a set of n circles of different radii $r_1, ..., r_n$ and a circle container, the two dimensional (2D) circle packing problem consists in finding the minimal radius r_0 of the container so that all the n circles can be packed into the container without overlap. If we find an efficient algorithm to solve this problem for a fixed circle container, we can solve the original problem by using some search strategies (e.g. dichotomous search) to reach the minimal radius of the container.

No significant published research appears to exist addressing this problem, except [2]. On the contrary, a lot of algorithms are proposed in the literature for packing equal circles into a circle container (see e.g. [4, 3]).

In this paper we propose a greedy approach called two-level search strategy to solve this problem.

2 The Two-Level Search Strategy

Consider a 2D Cartesian coordinate system. The coordinate of the center of the container is (0,0) and the coordinate of the center of the ith circle center is denoted by (x, y). We call *configuration* a pattern (layout) where m (≥ 2) circles have been already placed inside the container without overlap, and $n - m$ circles remain to be packed into the container.

A *legal action* (i, x, y) is the placement of circle i inside the container at position (x, y) so that circle i does not overlap any other circle and is tangent with 2 circles in the container (note that one of the 2 circles may be the container itself). There may be several legal actions for circle i.

F. Rossi (Ed.): CP 2003, LNCS 2833, pp. 868–872, 2003.
© Springer-Verlag Berlin Heidelberg 2003

Let (i, x, y) be a legal action, u and v be the two circles in the container and tangent with circle i if i is placed at (x, y). The degree λ of this action is defined as $\lambda = (1 - \frac{d_{min}}{r_i})$, where d_{min} is the minimal distance from circle i to other circles in the container (excluding u and v but including the container) and r_i is the radius of the circle i.

$$d_{min} = \min_{j \in \mathcal{M}, j \neq u, j \neq v} (|\sqrt{(x - x_j)^2 + (y - y_j)^2} - r_j| - r_i)$$

where $\mathcal{M}$ is the set of circles already placed inside the container (note that the container is itself included in $\mathcal{M}$).

Procedure *CirclePacking(I)*
Begin
  for *k:=1* to *n-1* **do**
    for *l:=k+1* to *n* **do**
      Generate an initial configuration C using circles *k* and *l*;
      Generate the legal action list $\mathcal{L}$;
      if (CirclePackingCore(C, $\mathcal{L}$) returns a successful
        configuration)
      then stop with success;
  Stop with failure;
End.

Procedure *CirclePackingCore(C, $\mathcal{L}$)*
Begin
  while (there are legal actions in $\mathcal{L}$) **do**
    Compute the benefit of each legal action
    Select the legal action *(i, x, y)* with the maximum benefit;
    Modify C by placing circle *i* at *(x, y)*;
    Modify $\mathcal{L}$;
  Return C;
End.

Fig. 1. A generic circle packing algorithm

Our packing procedures *A1.0* and *A1.0Core* are respectively *CirclePacking* and *CirclePackingCore* shown in figure 1. At every iteration, *A1.0Core* places the circle with the largest λ and re-calculate the degree of all existing legal actions. If all circles are placed in the container without overlap, *A1.0Core* stops with success. If none of the circles outside the container can be placed into container without overlap ($\mathcal{L}$ is empty), it stops with failure.

However, given a configuration, *A1.0* only looks at the relation between the circles already inside the container and the circle to be packed. It doesn't examine the relation between the circles outside the container.

In order to more globally evaluate the benefit of a legal action and to overcome the limit of *A1.0*, we compute the benefit of a legal action using *A1.0Core* itself in the *CirclePackingCore* procedure to obtain our main packing algorithm called *A1.5*, the *CirclePackingCore* procedure becoming *A1.5Core* in this case.

In other words, *A1.5Core* is *CirclePackingCore* calling the subprocedure *BenefitA1.5* shown in Figure 2 to compute the benefit of legal actions.

Procedure *BenefitA*1.5(*i*, *x*, *y*, *C*, *L*)
Begin
  let *C'* and *L'* be copies of *C* and *L*;
  Modify *C'* by placing circle *i* at *(x,y)* and modify *L'*;
  C' =A1.0*Core* (*C'* , *L'*) ;
  if (*C'* is successful) **then** return *C'*; **else** return *density*(*C'*);
End.

Fig. 2. Subprocedure of Algorithm *A*1.5 for computing the benefit of a legal action

Given a copy C' of the current configuration C and a legal action (i, x, y), *BenefitA1.5* begins by placing the circle i in the container at (x, y) and calls *A1.0Core* to reach a final configuration. If *A1.0Core* stops with success then *BenefitA1.5* returns a successful configuration, otherwise *BenefitA1.5* returns *the density* (the ratio of the total surfaces of the circles inside the container to the surface of the container) of a failure configuration as the benefit of the legal action (i, x, y). In this manner, *A1.5* evaluates all existing legal actions and chooses the best.

Roughly speaking, under the current configuration, *the first level of the strategy* consists in choosing the best action (i, x, y) by using a simple heuristic. *The second level* uses the first level itself to select the next legal action. We call this approach *two-level search strategy*.

3   Experimental Results

A1.0 and *A1.5* are implemented in C and executed on an Athlon XP2000+ CPU under Linux system.

Given a set of circles we respectively use *A1.0* and *A1.5* to find the minimum container radius (r_{min}) so that the set of circles can be packed into the container without overlap.

Table 1 shows the minimum container radius of the two hard instances illustrated in figures 3 and 4 found by *A1.0* and *A1.5*. It is clear that *A1.5* is substantially more powerful. The resolution of other instances in our experimentation using *A1.0* and *A1.5* exactly gives the same conclusion. *A1.5* is also substantially better than the approach presented in [2].

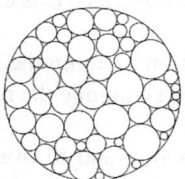

Fig. 3. Instance 1
$(n = 50, r_{min} = 380.00)$

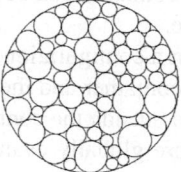

Fig. 4. Instance 2 $(n = 60, r_{min} = 522.93)$

Table 1. Minimum container radius found by *A1.0* and *A1.5* and runtime (in seconds) used by *A1.0* and *A1.5* to find the successful configuration with the container radius r_{min}

Instance	A1.0		A1.5		Instance	A1.0		A1.5	
	r_{min}	time	r_{min}	time		r_{min}	time	r_{min}	time
1	381.05	2712s	380.00	5396s	2	527.57	4216s	522.93	6615s

4   Solving CSPs with the Two-Level Search Strategy: First Results

Constraint Satisfaction Problems (CSPs) involve the assignment of values to variables subject to a set of constraints.

Formally, a CSP is defined by a triplet (X, D, C) where X is a set of n variables $\{X_1, X_2, \ldots, X_n\}$, D is a set of n finite domains $\{D_1, D_2, \ldots, D_n\}$ with each D_i is a set of possible values $\{v_{i1}, \ldots, v_{ik_i}\}$ for X_i, and C is a set of m constraints between variables $\{C_1, C_2, \ldots, C_m\}$. A solution is an assignment of values to all variables such that all constraints are satisfied.

The circle packing problem can be considered as a CSP : X is the set of circles to be packed into the circle container, D_i is the set of all legal actions associated with circle i and C is the set of constraints saying that all circles should be placed in the container without overlap.

Consequently assigning a value (i, x, y) to X_i means the execution of the legal action (i, x, y) placing a circle i at position (x, y). A1.0 is just a search procedure where the benefit of an assignment $X_i = (i, x, y)$ for every unassigned variable X_i and every $(i, x, y) \in D_i$ is defined by degree $\lambda\S$. A1.5 is similar except that the benefit of an assignment is evaluated using *A1.0*.

More generally, the two-level search strategy can be used to solve satisfiable CSPs or Max-CSP. The key issue is the definition of the benefit of a variable assignment $X_i = v$. At the first level, we use the value $0 - c$ as the benefit of $X_i = v$, where c is the total number of values in the domain of other unassigned variables conflicting with $X_i = v$. At the second level, the search procedure at the first level is itself used to evaluate the benefit of $X_i = v$, i.e., after assigning v to X_i, the search procedure at the first level runs until a final configuration, where either all variables are assigned, or the domain of each unassigned variable is empty. We use the number of assigned variables in the final configuration as the benefit of $X_i = v$.

Intuitively, we should choose an assignment to leave as many rooms as possible to other unassigned variables. Our current heuristic at the first level is very simple but not precise enough. However, with a quick implementation, this heuristic already gives us the first interesting results to solve Round Robin and n-queens problems. These two well-known CSPs appear to be quite hard for backtracking methods.

In the n-queens problem, one has to place n queens on a $n \times n$ chessboard so that no two queens attack each other. Although specific methods are known to solve this problem easily, it has been used extensively to test constraint satisfaction algorithms.

As in a backtracking approach, we define n variables with domain $\{1, 2, \cdots, n\}$, one for each queen to be placed. Intuitively, queen X_i is to be placed in some column in ith row. We then define constraints stating that there are no two queens in any column or diagonal.

The search procedure at the first level solves some n-queens instances, but it is the search procedure at the second level that solves this problem up to 600 queens in less than 10 hours on a Athlon XP2000+ PC.

In the n teams (n even) Round Robin scheduling problem, one has to place the $(n-1)n/2$ meetings (all teams meet each other exactly once) on a $n/2$ row and $n-1$ column matrix, such that every team occurs exactly once in each column and no more than twice in each row. See [1] for a formal definition of this problem.

The Round Robin problem is challenging for integer programming or standard constraint satisfaction techniques, because of its explosive combinatorics. Linear programming is not able to find a solution for $n \geq 14$. Using the powerful C++ constraint programming library ILOG SOLVER, Gomes et al. [1] built a deterministic backtrack-style CSP engine able to find a solution for $n = 14$. Then the CSP engine has been reinforced by randomization with restart in choosing branching variables to find a solution for $n = 16$ in 1.4 hours and for $n = 18$ in 22 hours. Note that Gomes et al.'s results in [1] for this problem were among the best until 1999.

We use $(n-1)n/2$ variables, one for each meeting. At the first level, no solution is found even for $n = 6$. However, we are able to solve this problem at the second level for n up to 18 in one hour.

5   Conclusion

We have proposed a new heuristic and a two-level search strategy, from which an effective algorithm called *A1.5* is designed for packing unequal circles into a circle container. At the first level *A1.0* uses the new heuristic to select the next legal action. Then at the second level *A1.5* uses *A1.0* itself to select the next legal action. Experimental results show the effectiveness of this strategy.

The two-level search strategy can also be used to solve other CSPs. The first results obtained using simple heuristics are very encouraging. We are searching for new and more precise heuristics.

References

1. Gomes C.P., Selman B., Kautz H. *Boosting Combinatorial Search Through Randomization*, In proceedings of AAAI'98, 1998.
2. Huang W.Q., Li Y. Xu R.C., *Local Search Based on a Physical Model for Solving a Circle Packing Problem,* In proceedings of the 4th Metaheuristics International Conference (MIC'2001), Porto, Portugal, July 16-20, 2001.
3. Melissen H., *Densest packing of eleven congruent circles in a circle*, Geom. Dedicata 50 (1994) 15-25.
4. Reis G.E., *Dense packing of equal circles within a circle*, Math. Mag. 48 (1975) 33-37.

Unrestricted Nogood Recording in CSP Search

George Katsirelos and Fahiem Bacchus

Department of Computer Science, University Of Toronto*
Toronto, Ontario, Canada
{gkatsi,fbacchus}@cs.toronto.edu

Abstract. Recently spectacular improvements in the performance of SAT solvers have been achieved through nogood recording (clause learning). In the CSP literature, on the other hand, nogood recording remains a fairly minor technique for improving backtracking algorithms. In this paper we demonstrate how recent nogood recording techniques from SAT can be generalized to CSPs. The result is a significant enhancement over current nogood recording techniques used in CSPs. We also report on some preliminary empirical results which indicate that generalized nogood recording can have a significant performance benefit.

1   Introduction

A number of works have investigated nogood recording as a technique for improving backtracking search, e.g., [FD94] (a longer version of this paper, [KB03], contains many more details, as well as a more detailed list of citations). Abstractly, a nogood is an easily checkable condition that can be used to test the nodes of a backtracking search tree. If the condition is true, then there can be no solution to the CSP below that node, otherwise the node remains plausible. Nogoods are discovered as we explore nodes in the backtracking tree. These nogoods capture the reason various nodes of the tree failed to yield a solution. By recording these reasons we can test nodes subsequently visited by the search, backtracking immediately if the node satisfies any previously recorded nogood.

Although it is well known that nogood recording can offer benefits in CSPs, it remains an underutilized algorithmic technique in the field. For example, the main commercial solvers offer no support for nogood recording. Furthermore, the nogood recording techniques in the CSP literature are significantly less general than the more modern techniques utilized in SAT solvers. First, the CSP literature (even recent work like [JDB00]) has only explored the recording of restricted types of nogoods that contain only literals with the same sign. This means that no extra reasoning, e.g., unit propagation, is possible over the nogood database. Second, due to this restriction, alternate ways of learning nogoods from conflicts, e.g., the 1-UIP technique used in Zchaff [MMZ+01], cannot be supported. Instead, the recorded nogoods are always subsets of the decisions made on the way to the conflict. Third, heuristics based on the most recently learned nogoods have not been examined. And fourth, the CSP literature has concentrated on techniques that restrict the number and/or size of the nogoods that can be recorded, e.g., using relevance or length bounded nogood recording [BM96].

---

* This research was supported by the Canadian Government through their NSERC program.

F. Rossi (Ed.): CP 2003, LNCS 2833, pp. 873–877, 2003.

All of these nogood recording techniques are prominent components of modern SAT solvers, and they have yielded spectacular improvements in SAT solver performance. In this paper we demonstrate how all of these improved techniques can be generalized to CSPs, and report on some preliminary empirical results based on an implementation of these techniques. Our empirical results indicate that these more sophisticated techniques for utilizing nogood recording can sometimes have a significant benefit—e.g., allowing us to solve some previously unsolved problems. However, the results also indicate that further tuning of these techniques might be needed for them to attain their full potential with CSPs.

2 Nogoods in Backtracking Search

Definitions: A CSP consists of a set of variables $\{V_1, \ldots, V_k\}$, a domain of values for each variable, and a set of constraints, each constraint being a boolean valued function over a subset of the variables that maps each assignment of values to these variables to TRUE/FALSE. If its value is TRUE, we say that this particular assignment of values *satisfies* the constraint. A solution to the CSP is an assignment of a value to each variable such that every constraint is satisfied by this set of assignments.

The standard notion of nogood, as explored in the CSP literature, is *a set of assignments that cannot be extended to a solution of the problem*. Each node in the backtracking tree is defined by the set of assignments made so far, with all descendant nodes extending this set of assignments. Hence, if a node covers a nogood, i.e., includes all of the assignments in the nogood, all nodes in the subtree below it must also cover the nogood, and none of them can be a solution.

Nogoods are the CSP equivalent of clauses learned by SAT solvers. To see this consider the simplest SAT encoding of a CSP [Wal00] in which each possible assignment of a variable, $V \leftarrow a$ becomes a proposition asserting that V has been assigned that value. The constraints of the CSP are then encoded as clauses over this set of propositional symbols. In addition, the constraint that each variable must be assigned one and only value, implicit in the CSP encoding, is also encoded as a set of clauses. Under this direct encoding, a nogood $V_1 \leftarrow a_1, \ldots, V_i \leftarrow a_i$ is equivalent to the clause $(V_1 \nleftarrow a_1, \ldots V_i \nleftarrow a_i)$. That is, at least one of the assignments (literals) in the nogood must be false. Viewing the nogood as a conjunction (rather than a disjunctive clause), when one of its assignments becomes false the nogood is falsified the nogood becomes inactive. Similarly, when one of its assignments becomes true, we can *reduce* the nogood (implicitly) removing that assignment. Finally, when the nogood has been reduced to a single assignment (become unit), we can *force* this last one assignment to be false (an assignment $V \leftarrow a$ is forced to be false by pruning a from the domain of V).

Using Nogoods: Nogood recording can be accomplished in any algorithm that maintains the reasons for each pruned value [Bac00]. These reasons can be stored in a global array: if the reason for pruning $V \leftarrow a$ is NG, then $NoGood[V, a] = NG$. Whenever all the values of a variable V are eliminated through search or propagation, a new nogood is discover and recorded: $NG = \bigcup \{NoGood[V, d] - (V, d) : d \in Domain[V]\}$.

To use the recorded nogoods, the nogood store is checked for unit nogoods after making an assignment, before constraint propagation. Standard nogoods can only be reduced by assignments, so checking at this stage is sufficient. For every nogood NG that has been made unit by the assignment, we force its remaining untrue assignment to false, by pruning the corresponding value and setting NG as the reason for that pruning. Prunings due to a set of assignments violating a constraint use the assignments to the constraint's scope as the reason for the pruning[1].

3   Utilizing SAT Techniques for Nogoods

SAT solvers gain much mileage from the fact that their store of recorded clauses can generate long chains of unit propagations, quickly simplifying the problem. Standard nogoods as described above do not support such chains of unit propagation—all the literals in standard nogoods have the same sign so no chaining is possible.

The solution is to record nogoods containing literals of both signs: assignments and non-assignments. With this we obtain propagation in the nogood store. For example, let $NG_1 = \{V_1 \not\leftarrow a, V_2 \not\leftarrow c, V_3 \leftarrow d\}$, and $NG_2 = \{V_1 \not\leftarrow b, V_3 \not\leftarrow d, V_4 \leftarrow c\}$; say the search makes the assignment $V_1 \leftarrow c$; and the value c is pruned from the domain of V_2. $V_1 \leftarrow c$ implies that $V_1 \not\leftarrow a$ and $V_1 \not\leftarrow b$ both become true. The pruning of c means that $V_2 \not\leftarrow c$ becomes true. Thus NG_1 is reduced to the unit nogood $\{V_3 \leftarrow d\}$, which prunes d from the domain of V_3. This then causes NG_2 to become the unit $\{V_4 \leftarrow c\}$, resulting in c being pruned from the domain of V_4.

Recording Generalized Nogoods: To understand how general nogoods can be recorded during search, it is useful to consider why it is that the unioning of nogoods is a valid way of producing a new nogood. Implicit in the CSP representation is a "must have a value" nogood, $M = \{V \not\leftarrow x_1, \ldots, V \not\leftarrow x_d\}$. When we have a nogood $NG_i = \{V \leftarrow x_i, R_i\}$ for each of V's values, we can resolve each NG_i against M. The final result will be $\{R_1, \ldots, R_d\}$.

To discover generalized nogoods, we replace the above procedure with one that incrementally unwinds the "must have a value" nogood, always replacing the chronologically most recent assignment by the reason (nogood) associated with it. Eventually, we have a nogood whose most recent assignment is the choice assignment in its level. We can then backtrack to that level, and store the nogood. The key is that during this incremental unwinding process some of the non-assignments in the "must have a value" nogood persist.

Unique Implication Point (UIP):   An alternative to completely unwinding the "must-have-a-value" nogood is to stop when exactly one assignment remains at the current level. That assignment is called a unique implication point [ZMMM01]. Nogoods computed via UIPs can be quite different from those computed via the standard technique. We have experimented with both techniques for nogood recording.

Non-binary Domain Processing   The SAT encoding of a CSP contains clauses to enforce the constraint that each variable must have one and only one value. These clauses

---

[1] In the case of prunings due to GAC propagation the reason (nogood) for the pruning can be composed from the nogoods of the values pruned from the other variables in the constraint's scope.

(nogoods) could be added to the nogood store prior to search, but it is more efficient (and effective) to account for the implicit presence of these clauses by special processing of the nogoods. There are three cases that can be processed in this way. First, whenever a variable V is assigned a value a all assignments $V \leftarrow x$ for $x \neq a$ become false. Second, if a nogood contains an assignment to a variable we can remove all non-assignments to the same variable prior to storing the nogood (the assignment subsumes the non-assignments). Third, if a nogood is reduced to a collection of non-assignments to the same variable, we can immediately prune all other values from the variable's domain. It can be noted that the last two cases cannot be captured by simply unit propagating the implicit "must have a value" and "only-one-value" nogoods.

Heuristics Based on Recently Recorded Nogoods: The recorded nogoods can be used to rank the unassigned variables by the frequency with which they appear in recently recorded nogoods. The Variable Decay heuristic utilized in SAT solvers uses this technique to encourage the tree search to produce short clauses. We have experimented with such a heuristic, but to date have not found an effective version of it in the context of CSPs. Nevertheless, there is increasing evidence that heuristic guidance can be the most effective of the nogood recording techniques utilized in SAT solvers. Hence, we are continuing our investigations in this area.

Recording Large Numbers of Nogoods: SAT solvers utilize lazy data structures (watch literals) to optimize the management and propagation of large numbers of large nogoods. With these techniques previous restrictions on nogood recording utilized in CSP algorithms can be removed, and instead large databases of nogoods can be efficiently managed.

4   Empirical Results

We have implemented unrestricted nogood recording, with standard nogoods as well as generalized nogoods. We have also implemented UIP processing which can be used with generalized nogoods. All experiments were performed on a Pentium-4 2.2 GHz machine, with 4GB of RAM, and times are reported in CPU seconds.

We report on one set experiments containing 100 instances of hard crossword puzzles, presented in [BCSvB01], Beacham et al.. Beacham et al. identified EAC (extensional arc consistency) as the best algorithm. In our experiments we compared their implementation of EAC against various nogood recording algorithms based on FCCBJ: *FCCBJ+RB* (3rd order relevance bounded recording of standard nogoods), *FCCBJ+S* (unrestricted recording of standard nogoods), *FCCBJ+G* (unrestricted recording of generalized nogoods) and *FCUIP* (unrestricted recording of generalized nogoods that result from UIP reasoning). In Table 1 we report on the instances that were unsolvable by at least one of the algorithms. The rest were easily solvable by all, with no major time differences.

We see that relevance bounded nogood recording is not very effective, always being slower than the rest of the algorithms, and solving fewer problems. FCCBJ+S presents a clear improvement. Recording generalized nogoods with UIP reasoning in some cases can pay off, but more tuning is needed to obtain maximal benefit from this technique.

Table 1. Crossword puzzles with FC-based algorithms

	EAC		FCCBJ+RB		FCCBJ+S		FCCBJ+G		FCCBJ+UIP	
Problem	Time	Nodes	Time	Nodes	Time	Nodes	Time	Nodes	Time	Nodes
UK-21.04	20.36	447	817.36	5924008	1491.22	1170356	-	-	5312.95	824067
UK-23.06	84.72	1306	-	-	5203.07	2994762	-	-	1028.48	835313
UK-23.10	210.54	1834	177.06	1236956	134.59	415718	2199.28	710566	-	-
words-15.01	-	-	-	-	5395.93	2423058	-	-	1122.5	655479
words-15.10	2.29	265	-	-	5752.77	3702947	-	-	-	-
words-19.03	502.12	21096	-	-	156.56	526797	-	-	490.26	482251
words-19.04	10.58	580	-	-	15.46	118325	43.47	124524	30.53	97721
words-21.01	-	-	-	-	3921.84	5056685	-	-	1266.06	1207743
words-21.06	4.35	484	-	-	45.11	168548	350.27	287223	31.94	75443
words-23.03	-	-	-	-	144.57	672178	5006	1902648	1959.23	1400760
words-23.04	207.16	3783	-	-	14715.87	6194196	-	-	-	-
words-23.08	-	-	-	-	-	-	-	-	4529.65	1817350
words-23.09	269.79	9933	-	-	-	-	-	-	-	-

5 Conclusion

We have developed methods for importing current clause learning techniques from SAT into CSPs. These techniques do allow us to solve some previously unsolved problems, but more work remains to obtain to maximal potential from these techniques in the CSP context.

References

[Bac00]   Fahiem Bacchus. Extending forward checking. In *International Conference on Principles and Practice of Constraint Programming*, number 1894 in Lecture Notes in Computer Science, pages 35–51. Springer-Verlag, New York, 2000.

[BCSvB01] Adam Beacham, Xinguang Chen, Jonathan Sillito, and Peter van Beek. Constraint programming lessons learned from crossword puzzles. In *Proceedings of the 14th Canadian Conference on Artificial Intelligence*, pages 78–87, 2001.

[BM96]   R. J. Bayardo Jr and D. P. Miranker. A complexity analysis of space-bounded learning algorithms for the constraint satisfaction problem. In *Proceedings of the Thirteenth National Conference on Artificial Intelligence*, pages 298–304, Portland, Oregon, 1996.

[FD94]   Daniel Frost and Rina Dechter. Dead-end driven learning. In *Proceedings of the AAAI National Conference*, pages 294–300, 1994.

[JDB00]   Narendra Jussien, Romuald Debruyne, and Patrice Boizumault. Maintaining arc-consistency within dynamic backtracking. In *International Conference on Principles and Practice of Constraint Programming*, number 1894 in Lecture Notes in Computer Science, pages 249–261. Springer-Verlag, New York, 2000.

[KB03]   George Katsirelos and Fahiem Bacchus. Unrestricted nogood recording in csp search. availble at www.cs.toronto.edu/~gkatsi/publications.html, 2003.

[MMZ+01]   M. Moskewicz, C. Madigan, Y. Zhao, L. Zhang, and S. Malik. Chaff: Engineering an efficient sat solver. In *Proc. of the Design Automation Conference (DAC)*, 2001.

[Wal00]   Toby Walsh. Sat v csp. In *International Conference on Principles and Practice of Constraint Programming*, number 1894 in Lecture Notes in Computer Science, pages 441–456. Springer-Verlag, New York, 2000.

[ZMMM01]   L. Zhang, C. Madigan, M. Moskewicz, and S. Malik. Efficient conflict driven learning in a boolean satisfiability solver. In *Proceedings of IEEE/ACM International Conference on Computer Design (ICCAD)*, pages 279–285, 2001.

Constraints over Ontologies

François Laburthe

Bouygues e-lab
1 avenue Eugène Freyssinet
78061 St Quentin en Yvelines cedex, France
flaburthe@bouygues.com

Abstract. This paper presents a new constraint domain, where variables can be assigned values that are organised in a tree hierarchy. The introduction of this new constraint domain is motivated by applications for the configuration of product and services, for instance, in the context of e-commerce. The paper proposes a small constraint language, based on comparisons and the use of monotonic functions. An approximation of domains as convex sets is detailed and propagation rules for achieving bound-consistency on the constraints are reviewed. This new constraint domain is general, and the author hopes that it will be a useful tool not only for solving configuration problems but also for promoting constraint technology in new application domains related to content classification or the semantic web.

1 Modelling Problems with Hierarchical Values

The theory of Constraint Programming has been developed in full generality, independently of value domains: constraint programmers can state problems where the variables are unknowns who should take their values among (integer, real) numbers, Booleans, predefined enumerations or even richer structures such as subsets from a known finite set, bags or trees. In practice, CP systems often seldom support constraints over anything other than integers, reals and finite sets. We introduce a new type of domains, where all values that a variable may take are organized into an hierarchy. Such hierarchies are often called ontologies or thesauri in AI (see for instance the seminal work of Gruber [Gr 93]). They can be encountered for instance, with class hierarchies describing product types, with domains modelled at different scales (think of geographical data, such as zipcodes) or, with keywords from a thesaurus that are used to index a set of documents.

Constraint over hierarchies have been studied in the context of typing systems (see for instance [CF 03] that adresses the case of a much richer structure, e.g. infinite quasi –lattices). To our knowledge, they have however, never been used in constraint prorgramming for modelling purposes.

2 The Constraint Language

The constraint language is defined from four constituents:
- Concepts are the constant values (from a predefined finite set). They are noted *a*, *b, c, d, ...*

F. Rossi (Ed.): CP 2003, LNCS 2833, pp. 878–882, 2003.

- Concepts are partitioned into a set of ontologies. The set of concepts forming an ontology is structured by a *refines* relation Its directed graph is a tree spanning the ontology, and rooted in a particular concept called the root of the ontology. The transitive closure of the *refines* relation is a partial order called the subsumption relation and denoted *subsumes*. For each ontology O, its root a is the maximal element of the subsumption relation.
- Ontology variables are unknowns, denoted $x, y, z,...$ that may be bound to any concept from one given ontology. The original domain from a variable is a given ontology. Integer variables shall also be considered and be denoted $t, u, ...$
- Constraints are expressions involving variables and constants. They are denoted $C, D, E...$ and can be formed from the following constructs.
    o Unary comparisons :

    $$C \equiv \quad x \leq a \qquad \text{where } a \text{ is a concept from the ontology of } x$$
    $$C \equiv \quad a \leq x \qquad \text{where } a \text{ is a concept from the ontology of } x$$

    o Binary comparisons :

    $$C \equiv \quad x \leq y \qquad \text{where } x, y \text{ are defined on the same ontology}$$

    o Functions:

    $$C \equiv \quad f(x) = t \qquad \text{where } f \text{ is a monotonic function}$$

The semantic of the constraints is straightforward. Comparisons $x \leq y$ are satisfied for all instantiations $(x = a, y = b)$ such that b *subsumes* a. Monotonic functions are mappings from an ontology O onto the integers such that for all pairs of concepts $a, b \in O$, $(a\ subsumes\ b) \Rightarrow (f(b) \leq f(a))$ (increasing functions) or $(a\ subsumes\ b) \Rightarrow (f(a) \leq f(b))$ (decreasing functions). Increasing functions tend to describe the extent of a concept, measuring how it covers a domain (the broader the concept, the higher the measure). Examples of increasing functions include the area or population for geographic concepts, or the probability of occurrence of a class of keywords in a corpus of data. Decreasing functions tend to describe the quantity of information of a concept (the narrower the concept, the higher the measure). Examples of decreasing functions include node depth in the ontology, inverse frequency measures or entropy measures. Note that such functions are called "graded functions" in the case of set constraints, in the *Conjunto* system [Ge 97].

3   Convex Sets and Domain Management

This section describes how constraint propagation over ontology domains is performed using convex approximations for the domains. The situation is analogue to the case of arithmetic constraints, propagated over interval domains.

Definition: Given an ontology O, a subset S of O is **convex** if and only if
   For all triplets $a, b, c \in O$, $(a \leq b \leq c \land a \in S \land c \in S) \Rightarrow b \in S$

Definition: Given a concept a from an ontology O, the **lower cone** and **upper cone** of a, denoted $a\!\downarrow$ and $a\!\uparrow$ are defined as
   $$a\!\downarrow = \{b \in O \mid b \leq a\}$$
   $$a\!\uparrow = \{b \in O \mid b \geq a\}$$

Definition: Let O be an ontology and S a subset of O; let (m_i) be its minimal elements, and (M_j) its maximal elements. The **convex envelope** $env(S)$ is defined as

$$env(S) = \bigcup_i (m_i\uparrow) \cap \bigcup_j (M_j\downarrow)$$

Proposition: Each subset S of an ontology is included in its envelope, $S \subseteq env(S)$; moreover, the equality $S = env(S)$ holds if and only S is convex.

In the special case of trees-shaped partial orders, the number of minimal elements in a set tends to be large. Thus, we use a compact representation.

Definition: Given an ontology O, and concepts $a_1, \ldots, a_n$ and $b_1, \ldots, b_m$ from O (with $n \geq 1$, $m \geq 0$), a **lower cone expression** S is defined as

$$S = a_1\downarrow \cup \ldots \cup a_n\downarrow \setminus (b_1\downarrow \cup \ldots \cup b_m\downarrow)$$

Proposition: The convex sets of an ontology are exactly its cone expressions.

Definition: The **normal form of a convex set** is the cone expression with a minimal number n of a_i and a minimal number m of b_j. We denote $l(S)$ the size of its normal form (ie. $O(n + m)$) for a convex set S.

Each convex set S can either be represented by its convex envelope $S = \bigcup_i (m_i\uparrow) \cap \bigcup_j (M_j\downarrow)$ or by its lower cone expression $S = a_1\downarrow \cup \ldots \cup a_n\downarrow \setminus (b_1\downarrow \cup \ldots \cup b_m\downarrow)$. The upper limit of both expressions coincides: the set of a_j is identical to the set of M_j.

Algorithm: The intersection of two convex sets S and T is computed in $O(l(S).l(T))$.
Let $S = a_1\downarrow \cup \ldots \cup a_n\downarrow \setminus (b_1\downarrow \cup \ldots \cup b_m\downarrow)$
       $T = c_1\downarrow \cup \ldots \cup c_p\downarrow \setminus (d_1\downarrow \cup \ldots \cup d_q\downarrow)$

The intersection $S \cap T = \bigcup_{i,j} (a_i\downarrow \cap c_j\downarrow) \setminus (b_1\downarrow \cup \ldots \cup b_m\downarrow \cup d_1\downarrow \cup \ldots \cup d_q\downarrow)$
Where $(a_i\downarrow \cap c_j\downarrow) =$ $a_i\downarrow$ if $a_i \leq c_j$,
                        $c_j\downarrow$ if $a_i \leq c_j$ and
                        $\varnothing$ otherwise (if a_i and c_j are incomparable).

Domains can be a priori arbitrary sets of nodes from a common ontology. These sets are approximated by their convex envelope: the data structure used for storing domains can store only convex sets. The data structure directly implements a lower cone expression. For a given convex set which lower cone representation is $S = a_1\downarrow \cup \ldots \cup a_n\downarrow \setminus (b_1\downarrow \cup \ldots \cup b_m\downarrow)$, the data structure stores the set of a_i, the set of b_j, and, for each b_j, the unique i such that $b_j \leq a_i$ (a useful information to cache for computing with lower cone expressions).

Note that such an approximation is similar to the interval approximations that are done for domains of numerical variables (discrete or continuous). Constraints are propagated not up to arc-consistency (as one would not be able to store "holes" that make the domain non-convex). Instead, constraints are propagated up-to the equivalent of bound consistency.

Definition: A constraint C involving ontology variables is called bound consistent if and only for each variable x involved in C, with domain

$$domain(x) = \bigcup_i (mx_i\uparrow) \cap \bigcup_j (Mx_j\downarrow)$$

each maximal value from the domain Mx_j and each minimal value mx_i has a support in the Cartesian product of the domains for all variables involved in C.

As usual, propagating the constraints comes to reducing the domains until all constraints are bound consistent [Apt 97][Ben 94].

4   Constraint Propagation

This section proposes propagation rules for the constraint language that has been presented above. The reader should however not be abused by the apparent simplicity of the rule expressions: computations are more complex than in the integer case, as computing the intersections of two ontology convex subsets requires more computations than computing the intersection of two numerical intervals. In the remainder, we shall denote by h the height of the ontology, by δ its degree and by n its overall size. Moreover, t will denote an integer variable with domain $[inf(t), sup(t)]$ and x and y will denote two variables with the following domains

$$domain(x) = \cup_i(mx_i\uparrow) \cap \cup_j (Mx_j\downarrow)$$
$$domain(y) = \cup_k(my_k\uparrow) \cap \cup_l (My_l\downarrow)$$

4.1   Propagating Comparisons

The constraint $x \leq a$ is propagated with the following rule:
$$domain(x) \leftarrow domain(x) \cap a\downarrow$$

The complexity of the rule is $O(l(domain(x)))$.

The constraint $a \geq x$ is propagated with the rule
$$domain(x) \leftarrow domain(x) \cap a\uparrow$$

The complexity of the rule is $O(l(domain(x)) . h.\delta)$ (as $l(a\uparrow) \leq h . \delta$, see [La 03]).

The constraint $x \leq y$ is propagated with the following two rules:
$$domain(x) \leftarrow domain(x) \cap \cup_l (My_l\downarrow)$$
$$domain(y) \leftarrow domain(y) \cap \cup_i(mx_i\uparrow)$$

The complexity of the first rule is $O(l(domain(x)) . l(domain(y)))$. The complexity of the second one is $O(l(domain(x)) . l(domain(y)) . h . \delta)$, see [La 03]).

4.2   Propagating Monotonic Functions

The constraint $f(x) = t$ (f increasing) is propagated with the following four rules:

$$sup(t) \leftarrow min(sup(t), Max_j (f(Mx_j)))$$
$$inf(t) \leftarrow max(inf(t), Min_i (f(mx_i)))$$
while $\exists\ Mx_j$ maximal in $domain(x)$ s.t. $f(Mx_j) > sup(t)$
$$domain(x) \leftarrow domain(x) \cap (O \setminus Mx_j\uparrow)$$

$$\text{while } \exists \, mx_i \text{ minimal in } domain(x) \text{ s.t. } f(mx_j) < inf(t)$$
$$domain(x) \leftarrow domain(x) \cap (O \setminus mx_i\!\downarrow)$$

The complexity of the first rule is $O(l(domain(x)))$, as is the complexity of one iteration of the third rule. Rules 2 and 4 are more expensive, as they require iterating over the set of minimal elements mx_i of $domain(x)$ for evaluating f. Their complexity is thus $O(n)$. Their complexity can be improved to $O(l(domain(x)) \cdot h \cdot \delta)$ using preprocessing to compute $g(d) = min(f(c) \mid c \in d\!\downarrow)$ on each node d. (see [La 03]).

5   Conclusions

This paper introduces a new domain for constraint programming where the possible values for a variable are a finite set of items ("concepts") organized in a tree ("ontology") structured by a partial order relation ("subsumption"). This new domain is directly motivated from constraint-based configuration where one needs to model the very kind of objects in the solution through domain variables. The authors have the intuition and preliminary evidence that such domains can also be useful for other applications related to content indexing, semantic annotations to data, or the capture of user wishes.

A simple constraint language is provided, mostly based on comparisons and monotonic functions. An encoding of domains based on the approximation of sets of values by their convex envelope is proposed. Propagation rules for the constraint language relying on the convex approximation are also proposed. The propagation framework is thus based on a calculus of interesections of convex subsets of the domain, rewriting convex sets into a dedicated normal form (cone expressions).

References

[Apt 97]   K. Apt, From chaotic iteration to constraint propagation, Proc. ICALP'97, Lecture Notes in Computer Science n°1297, p. 36-55, Springer, 1997.

[Ben 94]   F. Benhamou, Interval Constraint Logic Programming, Proc. CP 94: p. 1-21, 1994.

[CF 03]   E. Coquery, F. Fages, Subtyping constraints in quasi-lattices, INRIA 2003.

[Gr 93]   T.R. Gruber, A Translation approach to portable ontology specifications, Knowledge Acquisition, 5(2):199-220, 1993.

[Ge 97]   C. Gervet, Interval propagation to reason about sets: definition and implementation of a practical language, Constraints 1 (3): 191-244, Kluwer, 1997.

[La 03]   F. Laburthe, Constraints over ontologies, Bouygues research report 2003-02, 2003.

Using Constraints for Exploring Catalogs

François Laburthe and Yves Caseau

Bouygues e-lab, 1 av. Eugène Freyssinet
78061 St Quentin en Yvelines Cedex, France
flaburthe@bouygues.com, ycaseau@bouyguestelecom.fr

Abstract. Searching objects within a catalog is a problem of increasing importance, as the general public has access to increasing volumes of data.
Constraint programming has addressed the case of searching databases of complex products that can be customized and build from components, through constraint-based configurators. We address the issue of searching objects within
catalogs of simpler items for which no logic description is available. We propose to embed constraint technology in a search assistant supporting dynamic
and concise dialogs based on the exchange of constraint formulations between
the client and the server. At each iteration, the server analyses the data available
in the catalog, computes abstractions, cluster decompositions and relaxations in
order to provide the user with alternative for either explicitly focusing the
search (adding constraints to the user's wish) or enlarging it (relaxing, to some
extent, a subset of the user's constraints).
This cooperative system is currently used for Intranets, customer relationship
management systems and e-commerce websites.

1 Introduction

As users in the general public and in professional environments have increasing access to large repositories of data, the issue of searching objects within catalogs gains
importance. Most sites are powered with search engines helping users to find what
they wants. Such engines can be either only content-based, using string matching
algorithms to find the documents, and statistical analysis to sort them by relevance, or
logic-based, implementing a configuration process: user state their requirements in an
input form, and the configurator updates the form with implied features (propagation), or new input criteria (generative constraint programming).

Our research focuses on the intermediate case where the database is more structured than a document repository (the objects are more than plain textual content,
some of their characteristics are described in a database), but no logical formulation
of the configuration task is available. This case is representative of Intranets, digital
marketplaces, auction and classified ads sites

In the spirit of cooperative answering systems [GGM92], the server assists the user
in his exploration, by providing him with relevant answers to his queries. Instead of
trying to guess the user's preferences (as recommender systems do), the method im-

F. Rossi (Ed.): CP 2003, LNCS 2833, pp. 883–888, 2003.

plements some of the natural ideas from human sales dialogs where the user is being explained the structure of the catalog (with a gross idea of the available objects). This method extends the work on intensional answers to database queries [Mot 94], and its application to interactive data retrieval systems [OY 95].

This method is implemented in a system (*Wishbone*) In contrast with standard approaches using constraint technology, computations do not rely exclusively upon algorithms for propagation and search, but upon algorithms for abstraction, clustering, relaxation and simplification. The method is data-driven as all the constraint management done by the engine is relative to a given state of the catalog (the database): the engine takes advantage of a Galois connection between constraints and sets of objects from the catalog in order to compute solution sets to constraints, analyze these sets and abstract them back in terms of constraints.

2 Powering Websites with Human-Inspired Search Dialogs

When searching for a product over the Internet (a used car to buy, an apartment to rent, …), users must answer questions from the sites (by means of input forms, or sets of hyperlinks to choose from). The experience turns painful when:
-   either no items match the user's request and he is asked him to formulate another one, without further help.
-   or too many answers match the user's question and he is asked to enter additional criteria, again without any help.

We propose to incorporate some of the logic from the salesclerk into the search dialog with the service, by building dynamic dialogs, where:
-   the user first states his initial need by partially filling a form,
-   he is answered with a gross estimate of the results matching his need (number of items, common properties of those items),
-   if many items are available for his need, he is proposed a choice between a few groups of items. Those groups are built dynamically, from the actual data available for the client's request so that the decomposition amounts to a "reasonable" alternative. The user may answer the server's question (select one group from the alternative) or ask for another discriminate criterion.
-   if no items are available for his need, he is proposed a choice between various explicit ways of turning his request into a feasible one.

In both cases (refinement and relaxation alternatives), the user is informed, for each branch, of the consequences of selecting it (with the number of matching results and a set of common properties of these results).

The user states his request by means of constraints; the server returns information on the available objects also by means of constraints. The dialog can thus be described as a process where both parties, the client and the server, synthesize a wish that both matches the user expectation and the possibilities from the data at hand. The wish is passed back and forth between the client and the server that both add information to it. The dialog converges from a vague wish into one with only a few solutions (available items from the catalog). For lack of space, the theory and algorithms of the method are only sketched in this paper, we refer the reader to [LC 03] for more details.

3   Exchanging Constraint Models

We start by introducing useful notations. *Catalogs* contain *objects*; *objects* are instances of *classes* and *classes* are organized in a single inheritance *hierarchy*. The descendents of a class c is the set of classes inheriting from c. We denote by $o:c$ the fact that object o is an instance of class c. Each class extends the structure of its superclass by adding new *slots*. We call *range* of a slot the type of values that it contains. *Slots* may have different ranges: *boolean, string, number, date* and all classes c (such slots contain instances of classes d that are descendents from c). Last, $o.s$ reads the value in the slot s of the object o.

3.1   The Syntax of the Constraint Language

Constraints use *paths* to access object features, potentially through sub-objects.

Definition: a path is defined by a support class c from the class hierarchy, and a sequence of k slots $s_1, ..., s_k$ $(k \geq 0)$ such that for all $i, 1 \leq i \leq k$, s_i is of type $d_i \rightarrow r_i$, with d_i (the domain of slot s_i), a descendent of the class r_{i-1} (the range of the previous slot s_{i-1}, or by convention, the support class $c=r_0$). The path p is written $c::[s_1, ..., s_k]$.
   A path is applicable to an object if and only if each slot can be recursively followed from the root object. When a path $p = c::[s_1, ..., s_k]$ is applicable to an object x, its application returns a set of values (accessible through the chain of slots)

Definition a constraint is defined by a path p, an operator *op* and operands $a_1,...,a_n$. It is written $C(p, op, a_1)$, $C(p, op, [a_1,...,a_n])$ or $C(p, op, [a_1,...,a_k], [a_{k+1},...,a_n])$.

   The supported operators in the constraint language are the following:
   -   $\leq, \geq$ (unary) and *inrange* (binary) for paths of range *number* or *date*
   -   $=$ (unary), for paths of range *number, Boolean, date* or *string*
   -   *inset* (n-ary), for paths of range *string*
   -   *oftype* (n-ary), for paths of range *object*

3.2   The Semantics of the Constraint Language

Constraints are evaluated on objects by applying the path and checking the formula.

Definition: given a constraint $C(p, op, [a_1,...,a_n])$ and an object x such that *applies(p,x)*, the evaluation operator *eval* is defined as follows:

$$eval(C(p, \geq, a), x) = \text{true} \qquad \Leftrightarrow \exists y \in applies(p,x) \mid y \geq a$$

$$eval(C(p, \leq, a), x) = true \qquad \Leftrightarrow \exists\, y \in applies(p,x) \mid y \leq a$$
$$eval(C(p, =, a), x) = true \qquad \Leftrightarrow \exists\, y \in applies(p,x) \mid y = a$$
$$eval(C(p, inrange, [a, b]), x) = true \Leftrightarrow \exists\, y \in applies(p,x) \mid a \leq y \leq b$$
$$eval(C(p, inset, [a_1,...,a_n]), x) = true \ \Leftrightarrow \exists\, y \in applies(p,x) \mid y \in \{a_1,...,a_n\}$$
$$eval(C(p, oftype, [c_1,...,c_n],[d_1,...,d_p]), x) = true$$
$$\Leftrightarrow \exists\, y \in applies(p,x) \mid (y{:}e \wedge (\exists\, i, 1{\leq}i \leq n, e \leq c_i) \wedge$$
$$(\forall\, j, 1{\leq}j \leq p, \neg(e \leq d_j)))$$

Definition: a wish w is defined by a support class c and a set of constraints $[C^1,...,C^k]$ whose paths are pair-wise different but all have c as support. The wish is denoted by $w= (c, [C^1,...,C^k])$. For some $x{:}d$ such that $d \leq c$, w can be evaluated with:

$$eval(w, x) = true \Leftrightarrow \forall\, j, 1{\leq}j \leq k,\ eval(C^j,x) = true$$

Definition: Computing solutions to a wish $w=(c, [C^1,...,C^k])$ is called _filtering_ and its application is denoted by ϕ

$$\phi(w) = \{x \mid x{:}d,\ d \leq c \wedge eval(w,x)=true\}$$

4 Constraint-Based Abstraction

Abstraction is the inverse step of filtering: instead of finding a (the largest) set of instances satisfying a wish, one finds the (most precise) wish satisfied by a set of instances. We denote this task by α (note that if the constraint language was made of arbitrary linear inequalities over numerical slots, α would amount to the computation of the convex envelope).

Definition: $\alpha(S)$ is the maximal wish satisfied by all objects in S.

Proposition: Objects and wishes are related through α and ϕ by a Galois connection, a structure studied in abstract interpretation [CC 77] (see [LC 03] for details). Abstraction is used as a wish strengthening mechanism, in order to warn the user about implied constraints of his wishes. For all wishes w, the wish $\alpha(\phi(w))$ (which is tighter as $\alpha(\phi(w)) \leq w$ but has the same solution set as $\phi(\alpha(\phi(w)))=\phi(w))$ is computed and returned to the user. He is thus aware of features that are common to all solutions to his current request.

Note that this Galois connection between formulas and sets of objets is commonly used with concept lattices for information retrieval [GMA 98].

5 Constraint-Based Clustering

Clustering is used in order to separate a set of instances into several subsets. The server transforms the user's wish w into an alternative among a few (say, three) tighter wishes w_1, w_2, w_3 such that $\phi(w)= \phi(w_1) \cup \phi(w_2) \cup \phi(w_3)$. With one click, the user will refine w into one of the sub-wishes w_i; the objective of this separation is thus twofold :

-   *Quick convergence.* Entropy reduction principles are used in order for the dialog to converge quickly towards solutions.
-   *Tight information.* The formulation of each sub-wish should be as tight as possible, in order for the user to easily accept or refuse branches, based on their description. Ssince the clusters cannot be any subset of instances, but must be expressed as solutions to a sub-wish, the very syntax of the wish (its operands) also accounts in the quality of the decomposition.

6 Constraint-Based Relaxation

A fuzzy evaluation function *feval* is introduced for the constraint language in order to distinguish objects that slighlty violate a constraint from objects that significantly do. Thus, for an infeasible constraint C, one can sort all candidate objects (inheriting from the support class) x by decreasing values of *feval(C,x)*. For a small integer k, let $x_1, ..., x_k$ be those k best fuzzy matches. The wish $\alpha(x_1, ..., x_k)$ has at least k solutions, and it is a relaxation of constraint C. This is the basis for wish relaxation.

When an infeasible wish $w=(c, [C^1,....,C^n])$ is submitted, the engine looks for ways of relaxing the wish into a feasible one and returns an alternative where each branch w_i is a wish made of a set of constraints kept as such from w, a set of relaxed constraints (constraints that are somewhat looser than their counterpart in w), and constraints from w that are ignored (absent from the w_i branch). The algorithm (see [LC03]) builds an alternative such that, in each branch w_i, the set of constraints kept from w is maximal (keeping one more constraint from w would make that branch infeasible). It goes in two steps: first, generating maximal subsets of hard constraints, then, using each subset of hard constraints to build a relaxation w_i for the alternative. It ensures that at most n w_i are proposed, and that each constraint of the original wish that is feasible appears as a hard constraint in at least one of the w_i.

7 Conclusions

This paper has presented a method and a cooperative system for searching items in a catalog. The system supports nicer dialogs between the user and the system, where the very information that is exchanged is more meaningful and more concise. Dialogs are based on a constraint language; and the server handles constraint with a variety of methods such as abstraction, clustering, relaxation and simplification. This approach complements constraint-based configuration: configurators use logic-based algorithms (propagation and search) to guide the search through complex catalogs, we use data-driven algorithms (abstraction and clustering) to navigate through simpler ones.

References

[CC 77]   P. Cousot, R. Cousot. Abstract Interpretation: a Unified Lattice Model for Static Analysis of Programs by Construction or Approximation of Fixpoints, POPL 1977.

[GGM92]   T. Gaasterland, P. Godfrey, J. Mincker, An overview of cooperative answering, Journal of Intelligent Information Systems, Kluwer, 1(2) 123-157, 1992.

[GMA 98]   R. Godin, R. Missaoui, A. April, Experimental comparison of navigation in a Galois lattice with conventional information retrieval methods, International Journal of Man-Machine Studies 38, 747-767, 1998.

[LC 03]   F. Laburthe, Y. Caseau. On the use of constraints for exploring catalogs Bouygues research report 2003-01, 2003.

[Mot 94]   A. Motro, Intensional answers to database queries IEEE transactions on Knowledge and Data Engineering 6(3) 444-454, 1994.

[OY 95]   J. Ozawa, K. Yamada, Discovery of Global Knowledge in a database for cooperative answering, Proc. IEEE Int. Conference on fuzzy systems, 849-854, 1995.

Intermediate (Learned) Consistencies

Arnaud Lallouet, Andreï Legtchenko,
Thi-Bich-Hanh Dao, and AbdelAli Ed-Dbali

Université d'Orléans – LIFO
BP 6759 – F-45067 Orléans – France

Abstract. What makes a good consistency? Depending on the constraint, it may be a good pruning power or a low computational cost. By using machine learning techniques (search in an hypothesis space and clustering), we propose to define new automatically generated solvers which form a sequence of consistencies intermediate between bound- and arc-consistency.

Introduction. Since their introduction, CSP consistencies have been recognized as one of the most powerful tool to strengthen search mechanisms. Since then, their considerable pruning power has motivated a lot of efforts to find new consistencies and to improve the algorithms to compute them. Consistencies can be partially ordered according to their pruning power. However, this pruning power should be put into balance with the complexity of enforcing them. For example, path-consistency is often not worth it: its pruning power is great, but the price to pay is high. Similarly, on many useful CSPs, bound-consistency is faster than arc-consistency even if it does not remove values from the middle of variable domains.

Very often, the programmer has the choice only between bound- and arc-consistency. But he or she has often little clue about which one to choose. Recently, it has been shown that consistencies can be built automatically using machine learning techniques. In [2], a consistency weaker than bound-consistency but as close to it as possible was constructed. In this paper, we present an method to automatically build approximations of arc-consistency. Actually, the method builds a full range of comparable consistencies for a given constraint. These *intermediate consistencies* are located between bound- and arc-consistency.

This set of consistencies is provided by a new solver learning method based on a clustering of the constraint's tuples, a sampling of the search space and a repair technique able to fix a too weak operator. We call this consistency *multibound-consistency*. The pruning power and the computational cost of such a consistency is directly related to the number of allowed clusters. The programmer can finely tune the ratio between filtering and search by choosing a level of consistency in this set instead of just bound- and arc-consistency. The tests show that on semi-regular constraints, the best performance is obtained for an intermediate consistency which is able to perform the most important part of the work of arc-consistency while saving enough tests to be faster.

F. Rossi (Ed.): CP 2003, LNCS 2833, pp. 889–893, 2003.

Consistencies. Let V be a set of variables and $D = (D_X)_{X \in V}$ their (finite) domains. For $W \subseteq V$, we denote by D^W the set of tuples on W, namely $\Pi_{X \in W} D_X$. A *constraint* c is a pair (W, T) where: $W \subseteq V$ is denoted by $var(c)$ and $T \subseteq D^W$ is denoted by $sol(c)$. A *CSP* is a set of constraints. For $W \subseteq V$, a search state consists in a set of yet possible values for each variable: $s_W = (s_X)_{X \in W}$ such that s_X is a subset of D_X. The search space is $S_W = \Pi_{X \in W} \mathcal{P}(D_X)$. *Singleton* states comprises a single value for each variable, and hence represents a single tuple. A tuple is promoted to a singleton search state by the operator $\lceil \ \rceil$: for $t \in D^W$, let $\lceil t \rceil = (\{t_X\})_{X \in W} \in S_W$ and for $E \subseteq D^W$, let $\lceil E \rceil = \{\lceil t \rceil \mid t \in E\} \subseteq S_W$. Conversely, a search state is converted into the set of tuples it represents by taking its cartesian product Π : for $s \in S_W$, $\Pi s = \Pi_{X \in W} s_X \subseteq D^W$. We denote by $Sing_W$ the set $\lceil D^W \rceil$ of singleton search states. By definition, $\lceil D^W \rceil \subseteq S_W$. In this paper, we call *consistency* for a constraint c an operator f on S_W having some properties. We denote by $Fix(f)$ the set of its fixpoints. In order for an operator to be related to a constraint, we need to ensure that it is contracting and that no solution tuple could be rejected anywhere in the search space. An operator having such property is called a *preconsistency*:

Definition 1 (Preconsistency). *An operator* $f : S_W \to S_W$ *is a preconsistency for* $c = (W, T)$ *if:*

- *f is monotonic, i.e.* $\forall s, s' \in S_W, s \subseteq s' \Rightarrow f(s) \subseteq f(s')$.
- *f is contracting, i.e.* $\forall s \in S_W, f(s) \subseteq s$.
- *f is correct, i.e.* $\forall s \in S_W, \Pi s \cap sol(c) \subseteq \Pi f(s) \cap sol(c)$.

The last property means that if a state contains a solution tuple, this one will not be eliminated by consistency.

An operator on S_W is *associated* to a constraint $c = (W, T)$ if its singleton fixpoints represent the constraint's solution tuples T, i.e. if $Fix(f) \cap Sing_W = \lceil sol(c) \rceil$. This property is also called *singleton completeness*.

Definition 2 (Consistency). *An operator* f *is a* consistency *for* c *if it is associated to* c *and it is a preconsistency for* c.

Consistency operators can be easily scheduled by a chaotic iteration algorithm [1]. By the singleton completeness property, the consistency check for a candidate tuple can be done by the propagation mechanism itself. Let us now define some consistencies associated to a constraint c:

- ID_c is a family of contracting operators such that any $id_c \in ID_c$ verify: $\forall s \in S_W \setminus Sing_W, id_c(s) = s$ and $\forall s \in Sing_W, s \in \lceil sol(c) \rceil \Leftrightarrow id_c(s) = s$. In particular, on non-solution singleton states, id_c reduces at least one variable's domain to $\emptyset$. The non-uniqueness of id_c comes from the fact that all search states s such that $\Pi s = \emptyset$ represent the empty set of solution for a constraint. In the following, we denote by id_c any member of ID_c.
- ac_c is the well-known arc-consistency operator defined by $\forall s \in S_W, ac_c(s) = s'$ with $\forall X \in W, s'_X = s_X \cap sol(c)|_X$.

Bound-consistency can also be defined in this framework.

Intermediate Consistencies. Consistencies are compared by considering their pruning power, which is described by the following ordering: let f and f' be two operators on S_W and let $E \subseteq S_W$. We say that f is *more precise* than f' on E, denoted by $f \sqsubseteq_E f'$ if $\forall s \in E, f(s) \subseteq f'(s)$. If $E = S_W$, we simply write $f \subseteq f'$. For example, it is well-known that $ac_c \subseteq bc_c$. The consistency ac_c is the most precise consistency for c. The following notion of approximation compares consistencies for the same constraint:

Definition 3 (Approximation). *Let f and f' be two consistencies on S_W for a constraint c. The consistency f' approximates f if $f \subseteq f'$ and $f' \sqsubseteq_{sing_W} f$.*

For example, bc_c is an approximation of ac_c. Consistencies which are approximations of ac_c or even bc_c are what we call *intermediate consistencies*. They define the same constraint but perform different prunings along the search space. We define formally the *pruning power* of a preconsistency f from the number of extra tuples maintained by f with respect to arc-consistency over the whole search space. Since $ac_c \subseteq f$, it is enough to assume that f is a preconsistency: the *pruning power* of f is given by $P(f) = \dfrac{1}{1 + \dfrac{\sum_{s \in S_W}(|\Pi f(s)| - |\Pi ac_c(s)|)}{|S_W|}}$. In this formula, the big sum is a kind of distance between f and arc-consistency which measure the number of tuples "missed" by f and which are removed by arc-consistency. Thus, ac_c has a pruning power of 1, and $P(bc_c) \leq 1$. The pruning power defines a total ordering on consistencies. The pruning power of a consistency must be put into balance with the computational cost needed to enforce it: the *complexity* of f, denoted by $C(f)$ is the sum of the number of operations necessary to compute f on every $s \in S_W$. To be meaningful, it is of course needed to agree on the basic operations allowed to compute the consistencies. Note that the complexity is evaluated on the whole search space and is not a function of the size of the data or arity. The next idea of *quality* is to relate the pruning power of a consistency to the complexity of its evaluation measured by the number of operations necessary to enforce it: the quality of f is $Q(f) = P(f)/C(f)$.

Learning Consistencies. In order to build a consistency, we need to define an hypothesis space in which search is performed. Let d be a distance between two operators and let $\mathcal{L}$ be a language in which the operators are expressed. The problem of learning an operator for a consistency $cons_c$ amounts in finding a term $l_0 \in \mathcal{L}$ such that $l_0 = \min_{l \in \mathcal{L}} d(cons_c, l)$. But only minimizing this distance does not ensure that the learned operator is actually an approximation of $cons_c$. We must also ensure the correctness $cons_c \subseteq l$. Hence the learning problem is stated as follows:

$$\begin{array}{ll} \text{minimize} & d(cons_c, l) \\ \text{subject to} & \forall s \in S_W, cons_c(s) \subseteq l(s) \subseteq s \end{array}$$

The correctness of the algorithm is ensured by construction. Following machine learning vocabulary, $cons_c$ represents the *example* space and $\mathcal{L}$ the *hypothesis* space.

Repair. Building directly a consistency is difficult because the expression of such a consistency may not be possible in the language in which the operators are expressed. It may also be possible but at the price of using very long and tricky expressions. In the chaotic iteration framework, we can build a consistency by combining the mutual strengths of several operators. We learn a preconsistency instead of a consistency because enforcing correction on the whole search space and at the same time singleton completeness is difficult. A full consistency can be reconstituted by combining the consistency id_c which is associated to c with the learned preconsistency.

Sampling Method.   One of the biggest problem encountered in the search of a good operator is that the correctness constraints have to be verified along the whole search space S_W. Fortunately, monotonic operators have an other interesting property, they preserve the solution tuples of their associated constraint across the search space:

Proposition 4. *Let f be a monotonic and contracting operator such that $\lceil sol(c) \rceil \subseteq Fix(f)$. Then f is a preconsistency for c.*

By this proposition, if we can ensure that the constructed operator is monotonic, it is sufficient to be correct with respect to the singleton solution states $\lceil sol(c) \rceil$. Actually, good operators are very quickly obtained and only less than a hundred samples are enough. This allows to apply the method on real-world constraints. For example, a constraint of arity of 5 with a domain size of 100 values yields, only for bound-consistency, a search space of size 3.10^{18} which could not be handled without this method.

Clustering and Multibound-Consistency.   The idea is to isolate disjunctive chunks of the constraint and to apply bound consistency on each chunk. We call this consistency *multibound-consistency*. A constraint is cut off into pieces by a clustering algorithm. A clustering of c is a set of constraints $CL = \{c_1 = (W, T_1), \ldots, c_n = (W, T_n)\}$ such that $\{T_1, \ldots, T_n\}$ form a partition of T. We use the agglomerative complete-link clustering algorithm [3]. The consistency obtained consists in applying the bound-consistency on each separate cluster:

Definition 5 (Multibound-consistency). *Let c be a constraint and CL be a clustering of c. Let bc_{cl} be the bound-consistency for a constraint cl. The multibound-consistency is defined by the operator:*

$$\forall s \in S_W, \quad mb_c(s) = s \cap \bigcup_{cl \in CL} bc_{cl}(s)$$

Note that when each cluster only holds one tuple, we get arc-consistency, and when all tuples are in a single cluster, we get bound-consistency. Since the clustering wraps some holes, it is needed to compose the learned operator with id_c in order to get a consistency. The multibound-consistency operator is obviously monotonic. The programmer can measure the quality parameter to get an information about the behavior of the learned consistency on average or find a different measure which fits better to his/her problem.

Examples.   For all examples, we have compared multibound-consistency as computed by our clustering algorithm to Gnu-Prolog table constraint `fd_relation` which computes arc-consistency.

Robot Vision.   In this example, a 100×100 map is filled with 1945 points representing obstacles. This map constraint is intersected randomly 5000 times with a constraint representing the vision angle of a robot ($90°$ angle oriented from right to left). The solutions are the obstacles visible by the robot. The multibound-consistency is learned for this constraint and the maximal quality is obtained for around 230 clusters, far less than the 620 clusters necessary to get arc-consistency. The maximum speed-up with respect to `fd_relation` is 6.84 for this map.

Square Map.   On this example, the map is a simple square of size 10×10 with 10 holes. On this constraint, one cluster is enough and bound-consistency is close to the optimal.

Crosswords.   Crossword compilation can be done by considering that "being a 3-letter word" is a constraint described by the allowed 3-letter words taken in a dictionary (here we use 48 random words). The test consists in building a 3×3 grid with a central hole. In this constraint, tuples are located sparsely at random places, making the clustering ineffective. The maximal quality is thus obtained around arc-consistency and we do not get any speed-up.

A last remark concerns the universality of this approach. We strongly believe that no single method can account for every constraint. Features like density, proximity or shape can affect very seriously the suitability of a particular representation. Most important, the quality we define gives an *average* measure of the consistency quality and the constraint may be used in a specific way in an actual CSP. More experiments are needed in order to determine which approximation to use according to the problem family or to dynamically tune the ratio pruning/search during search.

Summary.   In this paper, we propose a new consistency generation method which allows to build a full range of consistencies between bound- and arc-consistency. These consistencies can be compared both by their pruning power and by their computational complexity. This allows to optimize the ratio pruning/complexity to find the optimal consistency for a constraint. A full version of this paper can be found in [4].

Acknowledgements.   We would like to thank Daniel Diez for his kind support on the internals of Gnu-Prolog, Slim Abdennadher, Lionel Martin and the rest of the Solar Team. This project is supported by French CNRS grant 2JE095.

References

1. K. R. Apt. The essence of constraint propagation. *Theoretical Computer Science*, 221(1-2):179–210, 1999.
2. Thi-Bich-Hanh Dao, Arnaud Lallouet, Andrei Legtchenko, and Lionel Martin. Indexical-based solver learning. In Pascal van Hentenryck, editor, *International Conference on Principles and Practice of Constraint Programming*, volume 2470 of *LNCS*, pages 541–555, Ithaca, NY, USA, Sept. 7 - 13 2002. Springer.
3. A. K. Jain, M. N. Murty, and P. J. Flynn. Data clustering: a review. *ACM Computing Surveys*, 31(3):264–323, 1999.
4. Arnaud Lallouet, Andreï Legtchenko, Thi-Bich-Hanh Dao, and AbdelAli Ed-Dbali. Intermediate (learned) consistencies. Research Report RR-LIFO-2003-04, LIFO, Laboratoire d'Informatique Fondamentale d'Orléans, 2003.

Semi-independent Partitioning:
A Method for Bounding the Solution to COP's

David Larkin

University of California, Irvine

Abstract. In this paper we introduce a new method for bounding the solution to constraint optimization problems called semi-independent partitioning. We show that our method is a strict generalization of the mini buckets algorithm [1]. We demonstrate empirically that another specialization of SIP, called greedy SIP, generally produces a better answer than mini buckets in much less time.

1 Introduction

In this paper we introduce a new method for approximating the solution to constraint optimization problems [5]. These problems are NP-hard in general, but have many practical applications. State of the art methods for solving them [3, 6, 8, 7] rely upon branch and bound search with a heuristic to compute a lower bound on the quality of the best solution that can be found by extending the partial assignment associated with the current node.

Our algorithm, called semi-independent partitioning, computes a lower bound on the best solution of a COP, with the solution quality and running time being controlled by a complexity parameter i. We will show that SIP is a generalization of the mini buckets algorithm [1, 4]. We will present empirical results showing that an alternative instantiation of SIP, greedy SIP, generally computes a much better lower bound than MB in less time.

This paper is divided into several parts. Following this introduction, we introduce basic concepts in Section 2. Then in Section 3 we introduce the semi-independent partitioning algorithm and compare it with mini buckets. In Section 4 we summarize the results of an experimental comparison, and in Section 5 we conclude.

2 Basic Concepts

A set of constraints C defined on finite-domain variables X is a set of functions $C = \{C_1, C_2, ..., C_m\}$, where C_i is defined on a subset of X, S_i, called its scope. The size of the scope is called the constraint arity. C_i maps allowed tuples to 0 and disallowed tuples to 1. The cost of an assignment to X is the number of constraints it does not satisfy, or $\sum_{\{c \in C\}} c$, where c is evaluated on the assignment. The cost of the optimum solution then is $\min_X \sum_{\{c \in C\}} c$. The MAX-CSP problem is to find this quantity. It is NP-hard in general.

F. Rossi (Ed.): CP 2003, LNCS 2833, pp. 894–898, 2003.
© Springer-Verlag Berlin Heidelberg 2003

C can be associated with a binary graph $G = (X, E)$ called the constraint graph. An edge $\{x, y\}$ is in E if and only if there exists a constraint c in C whose scope includes both x and y. The induced width w^* of C's graph is defined in reference to an ordering of the variables in X or absolutely. In reference to an ordering, it is calculated by removing the variables from the graph from last to first, connecting all neighbors of a node when it is removed. The maximum number of neighbors any node has when it is deleted is the induced width. The absolute induced width is the minimum induced width over all orderings. Finding the absolute induced width is NP-hard, but orderings with good induced width can be found with heuristics. The min-degree heuristic, for example, orders the vertices from last to first, at each point choosing the variable with minimum degree in the graph, then removing it and connecting its neighbors. More material on the induced width measure can be found in [2].

Given a variable $x \in X$, and set of constraints $C_x \subseteq C$ defined on $X' \subseteq X$ which all mention x in their scopes, the operation of projecting x out of C_x computes a new function $g = \min_x \sum_{\{c \in C_x\}} c$ which is defined on $X' - x$. It occupies $O(\exp(|X'| - 1))$ space and the time complexity of computing it is the same. Variable elimination [2] is an exact algorithm for MAX-CSP whose complexity is exponential in the induced width of the graph along an elimination ordering. It simplifies a problem C by repeatedly applying projection operations to eliminate variables from last to first. Variable x is eliminated from C by collecting all the constraints C_x that mention x and replacing them with the function g that results from projecting x out. The desired quantity $\min_X \sum_{\{c \in C\}} c$ is the result of projecting out all the variables in X one by one. Its correctness follows from the fact that $\min_X \sum_{\{c \in C\}} c = \min_{X-x} \left(\sum_{\{c \in C - C_x\}} c + \min_x \sum_{\{c' \in C_x\}} c' \right) = \min_{X-x} \sum_{\{c \in C - C_x\}} c + g$.

3   The Semi-independent Partitioning Algorithm

In this section we introduce the semi-independent partitioning algorithm. First in subsection 3.1 we introduce the algorithm in its most general form, which allows any number of specific solution strategies. Then in subsection 3.2 we describe a specialization which uses a greedy strategy. In subsection 3.3 we show that mini buckets is another specialization.

3.1   General Semi-independent Partitioning

Let C be a set of constraints defined on variables X, and let i be a complexity bound. Our problem is to find a good lower bound on the cost of the optimal solution $\min_X \sum_{\{c \in C\}} c$ with $O(|C||X| \exp(i))$ time and space complexity.

The exact method variable elimination, described in Section 2, can be used if an ordering of C's graph can be found with $w^* \leq i$. However in general $w^* > i$ and this is not possible, and in any case finding an optimum ordering is an NP-hard problem.

We can partition a set of constraints C defined on X into subsets C_1 and C_2, where $C_1 \cup C_2 = C$ and $C_1 \cap C_2 = \emptyset$, and the induced width of C_1 is bounded by i. Variable elimination can be applied to completely or partially solve C_1, resulting in the value of its optimum solution or a function giving the cost of the optimum extension of any assignment to its scope variables. Formally, if Y is the set of variables we wish to eliminate from C_1, then $\min_X \sum_{\{c \in C\}} c = \min_X \sum_{\{c \in C_1\}} c + \sum_{\{c' \in C_2\}} c' \geq \min_{X-Y}(\min_Y \sum_{\{c \in C_1\}} c) + (\min_Y \sum_{\{c' \in C_2\}} c') = \min_X g + \sum_{\{c' \in C_2\}} c'$, where $g = (\min_Y \sum_{\{c \in C_1\}} c)$ is the solution of C_1 that is derived by variable elimination.

Algorithm `General SIP`
Input: `Constraints` C`, complexity limit` i`, partitioning method` S`.`
Output: `Lower bound on the solution of` C`.`
`While` $w^*(C) > i$ `according to a heuristic ordering...`

1. `Select` $C_1 \subseteq C$ `s. t.` $w^*(C_1) \leq i$ `with` S`, let` $C_2 = C - C_1$`.`
2. `Let` S `choose a set` Y `of variables to eliminate from` C_1 `with v. e.`
3. `Set` $g = \min_Y \sum_{\{c \in C_1\}} c$`, let` $C = g \cup C_2$`.`

`Return the solution of` C `found with variable elimination.`

Fig. 1. The General SIP Algorithm

Pseudo-code for general SIP is given Figure 1. Each invocation of variable elimination costs $O(|X| \exp(i))$. Assuming at least two constraints are eliminated each time, and that no more than one new function is generated, then the total running time is $O(|C||X| \exp(i))$.

3.2 Greedy SIP

Up until now we have not specified how general SIP is to partition the constraints or decide what variables to eliminate. In this subsection we describe an instantiation of general SIP, called greedy SIP, which offers a practical strategy.

The basic problem is to partition a set of constraints C into C_1 and C_2, such that an ordering of C_1 can be found with induced width bounded by i. Greedy SIP's method is to greedily try to add constraints from C into C_1, maintaining at all times a heuristic ordering of C_1 with bounded induced width, and refusing to add a constraint to C_1 if that makes its heuristic ordering exceed the limit. The partitioning is completed when one attempt has been made to add every constraint in C. The set of variables Y to be eliminated is simply all but the first i variables in the final heuristic ordering.

For example, consider the problem shown in Figure 2. The i bound is 2, and the initial problem C is the clique of size 6 in the upper left corner. We will use the min-degree heuristic ordering. A greedy partitioning is shown in the upper right corner, where C_1 is to the left of the $\cup$ and C_2 is to the right. A min-degree

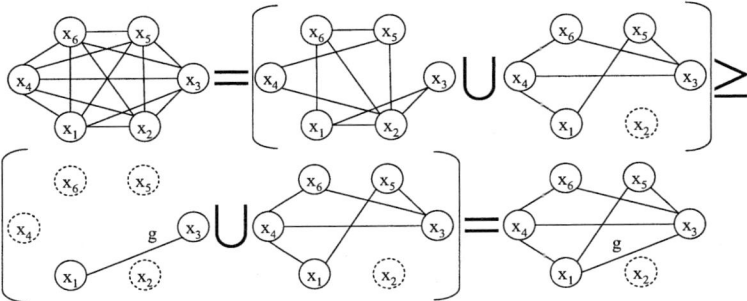

Fig. 2. Example of Greedy SIP

ordering of C_1 is x_3, x_1, x_2, x_6, x_5, x_4, which has induced width 2. Note that if we try to add any other edge from C_2 to C_1, the induced width of the min degree ordering will exceed the limit. For example, if we add (x_1, x_5) to C_1, the min degree ordering has induced width 3.

Now greedy SIP will eliminate all but the first 2 variables x_3 and x_1 from C_1. The result is shown in the lower left corner. C is then set to the function g defined on x_1 and x_3 joined with C_2, as shown on the lower right. Since a min degree ordering of C now has induced width 2, variable elimination can be applied to finish the problem.

3.3 Mini Buckets

In this subsection we describe mini buckets [1, 4] as another specialization of general SIP.

Mini buckets always maintains a variable to eliminate, x. When it partitions a set of constraints C with complexity bound i, it selects a subset B_x of C called x's *bucket*, which is the set of all constraints in C mentioning x. Then it selects a maximal subset of M_x of B_x called a *mini bucket*, such that the total number of variables appearing in M_x is not more than $i + 1$, and no other member of B_x can be added without destroying this property. M_x is chosen to be C_1 and C_2 becomes $C - M_x$. M_x is ordered arbitrarily, except that the bucket variable x is placed at the end of the ordering and it is selected as the only variable to eliminate. Doing this creates a function g of arity i which does not mention x. C is then set to $g \cup C_2$ and the process continues. If B_x is empty, then a new variable x' is selected to be eliminated next. The algorithm halts when all variables have been eliminated.

4   Empirical Results

To compare MB and greedy SIP, we tested them on random binary MAX-CSP problems with 55 variables and domain size 4. Every constraint had a 40 percent chance of being present. All constraints randomly disallowed half of the possible value pairs and allowed the other half. We averaged the results of 25 experiments for each value of i from 6 to 9. The results are summarized in Figure 3. For all settings of i, greedy SIP achieved a significantly better lower bound in less time than MB. For example, at $i = 6$ SIP computed an average lower bound of 67.5 in 12 seconds. Even at $i = 9$ MB was not quite as accurate, computing a lower bound of 64.1 in 1020 seconds.

	$i = 6$		$i = 7$		$i = 8$		$i = 9$	
	MB	SIP	MB	SIP	MB	SIP	MB	SIP
Lower Bound	41.9	67.5	49.7	77.4	57.1	84	64.1	90.5
Time	19s	12s	72s	39s	272s	136s	1020s	485s
Max. Memory	1.1M	0.2M	3.7M	0.6M	12M	2.2M	42M	9M

Fig. 3. Empirical results (average $w^* = 39$)

5   Conclusion

In this paper, we introduced a new algorithm for computing lower bounds on the quality of the best solution of a MAX-CSP problem. We compared it empirically with the mini buckets method, showing that it performed significantly better.

For future work, of course it would be of interest to directly evaluate the efficiency of our method as a heuristic for branch and bound search to find an exact optimum. Since our method, unlike mini buckets, does not follow a natural static variable ordering, it would have to be called dynamically at every node.

References

1. Rina Dechter. Mini-buckets: A general scheme for generating approximations in automated reasoning. In *IJCAI*, 1997.
2. Rina Dechter. Bucket elimination: A unifying framework for reasoning. *Artificial Intelligence*, October 1999.
3. Rina Dechter, Kalev Kask, and Javier Larrosa. A general scheme for multiple lower bound computation in constraint optimization. In *Proc. of the Conf. on Principles and Practice of Constraint Programming*, 2001.
4. Rina Dechter and Irina Rish. A scheme for approximating probabilistic inference. In *Proc. of the Conf. on Uncertainty in Artificial Intelligence*, 1997.
5. E. Freuder and R. Wallace. Partial constraint satisfaction. *Artificial Intelligence*, 58:21–70, 1992. Unobtained.
6. Kalev Kask and Rina Dechter. A general scheme for automatic generation of search heuristics from specification dependencies. *Artificial Intelligence*, 129:91–131, 2001.
7. J. Larrosa, P. Meseguer, and T. Schiex. Maintaining reversible DAC for Max-CSP. *Artificial Intelligence*, 107:149–163, 1999.
8. Javier Larrosa and Pedro Meseguer. Partition-based lower bound for Max-CSP. In *Principles and Practice of Constraint Programming*, pages 305–315, 1999.

Boosting as a Metaphor for Algorithm Design

Kevin Leyton-Brown, Eugene Nudelman,
Galen Andrew, Jim McFadden, and Yoav Shoham

Stanford University, Stanford CA 94305[*]
{kevinlb,eugnud,galand,jmcf,shoham}@cs.stanford.edu

1 Introduction

Although some algorithms are better than others on average, there is rarely a best algorithm for a given problem. Instead, different algorithms often perform well on different problem instances. Not surprisingly, this phenomenon is most pronounced among algorithms for solving $\mathcal{NP}$-hard problems, when runtimes are highly variable from instance to instance. When algorithms exhibit high runtime variance, one is faced with the problem of deciding which algorithm to use for each particular instance; in 1976 Rice dubbed this the "algorithm selection problem" [8]. More recent work on this problem includes [5,4].

Our previous work [7] demonstrates that statistical regression can be used to learn surprisingly accurate models of an algorithm's runtime. In a recent extended abstract [6] we discussed the use of these runtime models for algorithm selection, and also for the automated tuning of instance generators. This companion paper extends these ideas, describing new techniques for making algorithm portfolios more practical and for making benchmarks harder. As in [7, 6], we evaluate our techniques in a case study on the combinatorial auction winner determination problem (WDP)—an $\mathcal{NP}$-hard combinatorial optimization problem formally equivalent to weighted set packing. We consider three algorithms for solving WDP: ILOG's CPLEX package; GL (Gonen-Lehmann) [3], a simple branch-and-bound algorithm with CPLEX's LP solver as its heuristic; and CASS [2], a more complex branch-and-bound algorithm with a non-LP heuristic.

What does it mean to see boosting as a metaphor for algorithm design? Boosting is a machine learning paradigm [9] based on two insights: (1) poor classifiers can be combined to form an accurate ensemble when the classifiers' areas of effectiveness are sufficiently uncorrelated; (2) new classifiers should be trained on problems on which the current aggregate classifier performs poorly. We argue that algorithm design should be informed by two analogous ideas: (1) algorithms with high average running times can be combined to form an algorithm portfolio with low average running time when the algorithms' easy inputs are sufficiently uncorrelated; (2) new algorithm design should focus on problems on which the current algorithm *portfolio* spends most of its time.

---

[*] Thanks to Ryan Porter, Carla Gomes and Bart Selman for helpful discussions. This work was supported by DARPA grant F30602-00-2-0598, the Intelligent Information Systems Institute at Cornell, and a Stanford Graduate Fellowship.

F. Rossi (Ed.): CP 2003, LNCS 2833, pp. 899–903, 2003.

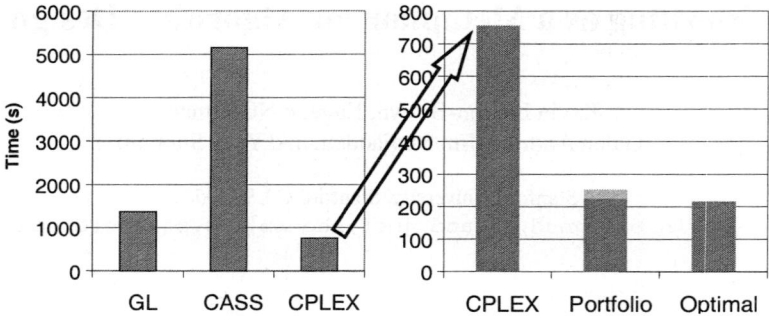

Fig. 1. Algorithm and Portfolio Runtimes

2 Making Algorithm Portfolios Practical

We have demonstrated that algorithm portfolios can offer significant speedups over winner-take-all algorithm selection (see Fig. 1, reproduced from [6]). It is thus worthwhile to consider modifications to the methodology that make it more useful in practice.

2.1 Transforming the Response Variable

Average runtime is an obvious measure of portfolio performance if one's goal is to minimize computation time over a large number of instances. Since our models minimize root mean squared error, they appropriately penalize 20 seconds of error equally on instances that take 1 second or 10 hours to run. However, another reasonable goal may be to select an algorithm well on every instance regardless of its hardness; in this case, relative error is more appropriate. Let r_i^p and r_i^* be the portfolio's runtime and the optimal runtime respectively on instance i, and n be the number of instances. One measure that gives an insight into the portfolio's relative error is *percent optimal*: $\frac{1}{n}\#\{i|r_i^p = r_i^*\}$. Another measure of relative error is *average percent suboptimal*: $\frac{1}{n}\sum_i \frac{r_i^p - r_i^*}{r_i^*}$.

Taking a logarithm of runtime is a simple way to equalize the importance of relative error on easy and hard instances. Thus, models that predict a log of runtime help to improve the average percent suboptimal, albeit at some expense in terms of the portfolio's average runtime. Other transformations achieve different tradeoffs. In Figure 2 (overleaf) we show three different functions; linear (identity) and log are the extreme values; clearly, many functions can fall in between. The functions are normalized by their maximum value, since this does not affect regression, but allows us to better visualize their effect. In our case study (section 2.4) we found that the cube root function was particularly effective.

2.2 Smart Feature Computation

Feature values must be computed before the portfolio can choose an algorithm to run. We expect that portfolios will be most useful when they combine several exponential-time algorithms having high runtime variance, and that fast polynomial-time features should be sufficient for most models. Nevertheless, on some instances the computation of individual features may take substantially longer than one cr even all algorithms would take to run. In such cases it would be desirable to perform algorithm selection without spending as much time computing features, even at the expense of some accuracy in choosing the fastest algorithm—if an instance is easy for all algorithms, we can tolerate a much greater prediction error. We partition the features into sets ordered by time complexity, $S_1, \ldots, S_l$, with $i > j$ implying that each feature in S_i takes significantly longer to compute than each feature in S_j. The portfolio can start by computing the easiest features, and iteratively compute the next set only if the expected benefit to selection exceeds the cost of computation. More precisely:

1. For each set S_j learn or provide a model $c(S_j)$ that estimates time required to compute it. Often, this could be a simple average time scaled by input size.
2. Divide the training examples into two sets. Using the first set, train models $M_1^i \ldots M_l^i$, with M_k^i predicting algorithm i's runtime using features in $\bigcup_{j=1}^k S_j$. Note that M_l^i is the same as the model for algorithm i in our basic portfolio methodology. Let M_k be a portfolio which selects $\operatorname{argmin}_i M_k^i$.
3. Using the second training set, learn models $D_1 \ldots D_{l-1}$, with D_k predicting the difference in runtime between the algorithms selected by M_k and M_{k+1} based on S_k. The second set must be used to avoid training the difference models on data to which the runtime models were fit.

Given an instance x, the portfolio now works as follows:

4. For $j = 1$ to l
   (a) Compute features in S_j
   (b) If $D_j[x] > c(S_{j+1})[x]$, continue.
   (c) Otherwise, return with the algorithm predicted to be fastest according to M_j.

2.3   Capping Runs

The methodology of [7] requires gathering runtime data for every algorithm on every problem instance in the training set. While the time cost of this step is fundamentally unavoidable for our approach, gathering perfect data for every instance can take an unreasonably long time. When algorithm a_1 is usually much slower than a_2 but in some cases dramatically outperforms a_2, a perfect model of a_1's runtime on hard instances may not be needed for discrimination. The process of gathering data can be made much easier by capping the runtime of each algorithm and recording these runs as having terminated at the captime. This is safe if the captime is chosen so that it is (almost) always significantly greater than the minimum of the algorithms' runtimes; if not, it might still be preferable to sacrifice some predictive accuracy for dramatically reduced model-building time. Note that if one algorithm is capped, it can be dangerous (particularly without a log transformation) to gather data for another algorithm without capping at the same time, because the portfolio could inappropriately select the algorithm with the smaller captime.

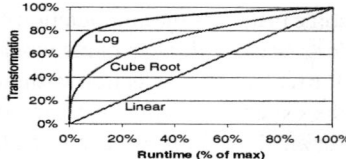

Fig. 2. Transformation

	Average Runtime	% Optimal	Average % Suboptimal
(Optimal)	216.4 s	100	0
Log	236.5 s	97	9
Cuberoot	225.6 s	89	17
Linear	225.1 s	81	1284

Fig. 3. Portfolio Results

2.4   Case Study Results

Table 3 shows the effect of our response variable transformations on average runtime, percent optimal and average percent suboptimal. The first row has results that would be obtained by a perfect portfolio. As discussed in section 2.1, the linear (identity) transformation yields the best average runtime, while the log function leads to better algorithm selection. We tried several transformation functions between linear and log. Here we only show the best, cube root: it has nearly the same average runtime performance as linear, but also made choices nearly as accurately as log. Notice that the three models shown here are not equally accurate on our dataset (they are non-linear transformations of each other). The effect of the transformations is to shift model accuracy to achieve different tradeoffs. That fact that all of these models achieve good portfolio performance illustrates the robustness of our portfolio results with respect to model accuracy.

When using smart feature computation described in section 2.2, on our test set the average feature computation took 27 seconds instead of 48, while the selected algorithm took only an average of 1 second longer to run. This result becomes quite significant for easy instances.

3   Inducing Hard Distributions

Once we have decided to select among existing algorithms using a portfolio approach, it is necessary to reexamine the way we design and evaluate algorithms. Since the purpose of designing new algorithms is to reduce the time that it will take to solve problems, designers of new algorithms should aim to complement an existing portfolio. First, it is essential to choose a distribution D that reflects the problems that will be encountered in practice. Let H_f be a model of portfolio runtime based on instance features, constructed as the minimum of the models that constitute the portfolio. By normalizing, we can reinterpret this model as a density function h_f. Given a portfolio, the greatest opportunity for improvement is on instances that are hard for that portfolio, common in D, or both. More precisely, the importance of a region of problem space is proportional to the amount of time the current portfolio spends working on instances in that region (formally, importance is measured by $D \cdot h_f$). This is analogous to the principle from boosting that new classifiers should be trained on instances that are hard for the existing ensemble, in the proportion that they occur in the original training set.

Sampling from $D \cdot h_f$ is problematic, since D may be non-analytic (an instance generator), while h_f depends on features and so can only be evaluated after an instance has been created. One way to handle this is rejection sampling [1]: generate problems from D and keep them with probability proportional to h_f. (In fact, the technique described below is approximate rejection sampling, which saves us from having to normalize H_f

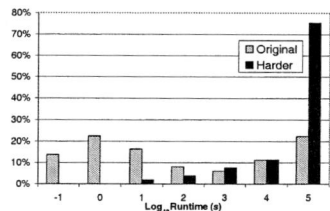

Fig. 4. Inducing Harder Distributions

and always outputs an instance after a constant number of samples.) This method works best when another distribution is available to guide the sampling process toward hard instances. Test distributions usually have some tunable parameters $\overrightarrow{p}$, and although the hardness of instances generated with the same parameter values can vary widely, $\overrightarrow{p}$ will often be somewhat predictive of hardness. We can generate instances from $D \cdot h_f$ in the following way:

1. Create a hardness model H_p with features $\overrightarrow{p}$, and normalize it to create a pdf, h_p.
2. Generate a large number of instances from $D \cdot h_p$.
3. Construct a distribution over instances by assigning each instance s probability proportional to $\frac{H_f(s)}{h_p(s)}$, and select an instance by sampling from this distribution.

Note, that if h_p is helpful, hard instances from $D \cdot h_f$ will be encountered quickly. Even in the worst case where h_p directs the search away from hard instances, we'll still sample from the correct distribution, since the weights are divided by $h_p(s)$.

Figure 4 shows the results of applying this procedure to our dataset. Since our runtimes were capped, the induced distribution doesn't generate any instances that are orders of magnitude harder than previous instances. In [6] we showed that this can also be achieved, making extremely easy distributions between 50 and 100 times harder.

References

1. A. Doucet, N. de Freitas, and N. Gordon(ed.). *Sequential Monte Carlo Methods in Practice.* Springer-Verlag, 2001.
2. Y. Fujishima, K. Leyton-Brown, and Y. Shoham. Taming the computational complexity of combinatorial auctions: Optimal and approximate approaches. In *IJCAI*, 1999.
3. R. Gonen and D. Lehmann. Linear programming helps solving large multi-unit combinatorial auctions, April 2001. TR-2001-8, Leibniz Center for Research in Computer Science.
4. E. Horvitz, Y. Ruan, C. Gomes, H. Kautz, B. Selman, and M. Chickering. A Bayesian approach to tackling hard computational problems. In *UAI*, 2001.
5. M. Lagoudakis and M. Littman. Algorithm selection using reinforcement learning. In *ICML*, 2000.
6. K. Leyton-Brown, E. Nudelman, G. Andrew, J. McFadden, and Y. Shoham. A portfolio approach to algorithm selection. In *IJCAI*, 2003.
7. K. Leyton-Brown, E. Nudelman, and Y. Shoham. Learning the empirical hardness of optimization problems: The case of combinatorial auctions. In *CP*, 2002.
8. J. R. Rice. The algorithm selection problem. *Advances in Computers*, 15:65–118, 1976.
9. R. Schapire. The strength of weak learnability. *Machine Learning*, 5:197–227, 1990.

An Efficient Filtering Algorithm
for Disjunction of Constraints

Olivier Lhomme

ILOG
1681, route des Dolines
F-06560 Valbonne
olhomme@ilog.fr

1 Introduction

Disjunctions of constraints frequently appear in applications of constraint programming. In this paper, we propose a new filtering algorithm for the disjunctions of constraints. It performs the same domain reductions as constructive disjunction [1,2], but is more efficient.

The paper is organized as follows. In Section 2 we give background on constraint networks. Section 3 reviews the existing approaches of dealing with disjunctions of constraints. Then, we present a new algorithm to achieve arc consistency on a disjunction of constraints (Section 4).

2 Background

Constraint Network. A (*constraint network*) $\mathcal{N} = (X, \mathcal{D}, \mathcal{C})$ is defined as a set of n *variables* $X = \{x_1, \ldots, x_n\}$, a set of *domains* $\mathcal{D} = \{D(x_1), \ldots, D(x_n)\}$ where $D(x_i)$ is the finite set of possible *values* for variable x_i, and a set $\mathcal{C}$ of *constraints* between variables. Let $<_d$ be a total ordering on $D(x_i), \forall x_i \in X$.

Constraint. A constraint C on the ordered set of variables $X(C) = (x_{i_1}, \ldots, x_{i_r})$ is a subset of the Cartesian product $D(x_{i_1}) \times \cdots \times D(x_{i_r})$ that specifies the *allowed* combinations of values for the variables $x_{i_1}, \ldots, x_{i_r}$.

Tuple. An instantiation of the variables in $X(C)$ is called a *tuple* on $X(C)$. The value of variable x in a tuple τ is denoted by $\tau[x]$. By extension, if V is a subset of $X(C)$, $\tau[V]$ denotes the values of the variables of V in the tuple τ. A tuple τ on $X(C)$ is *valid* iff $\forall x \in X(C), \tau[x] \in D(x)$.

Support. Let $\mathcal{N} = (X, \mathcal{D}, \mathcal{C})$ be a constraint network, and let C be a constraint in $\mathcal{C}$. A value a for a variable x is often denoted by (x, a). Let $a \in D(x)$ be a value, let τ be a valid tuple on $X(C)$, such that $a = \tau[x]$. τ is called a *support* for (x, a) on C iff it is allowed by C.

Arc Consistency. Let $\mathcal{N} = (X, \mathcal{D}, \mathcal{C})$ be a constraint network, C a constraint in $\mathcal{C}$. A value $a \in D(x)$ is *consistent with* C iff $x \notin X(C)$, or $\exists \tau$ such that τ is a support for (x, a) on C. C is *arc consistent* iff $\forall x \in X(C), D(x) \neq \emptyset$ and $\forall a \in D(x)$, a is consistent with C.

F. Rossi (Ed.): CP 2003, LNCS 2833, pp. 904–908, 2003.
© Springer-Verlag Berlin Heidelberg 2003

3   Disjunction of Constraints: Existing Approaches

This section reviews two existing approaches of dealing with the disjunction of constraints: the "standard implementation" and the constructive disjunction.

The standard implementation for the constraint $or(c_1, c_2)$ consists in applying the following propagation rules: (1) if c_1 is false on the current domains then add(c_2) to the solver; (2) if c_2 is false on the current domains then add(c_1) to the solver. A side-effect of such a propagation rule is that, as long as both constraints can be true, the or constraint will not be able to prune anything. Indeed, using the standard propagation rule does not ensure arc-consistency for the variables in the disjunction.

Example 1 *Let x be a variable and its domain be $D(x) = \{1, 2, 3\}$. Let us consider the constraint $or(x = 1, x = 2)$. It is easy to see that the value 3 is not possible for x. Nevertheless, the above propagation rule will not be able to prune the value 3 since the two constraints $x = 1$ and $x = 2$ can be true.*

Another approach to implement the or constraint is the use of *constructive disjunction* [1, 2]. The idea is to propagate independently each term of the disjunction. The domains of the variables are the union of their domains in the different branches of the disjunction. In our example, we have: $constraint(x = 1) \longrightarrow D_1(x) = \{1\}$, and: $constraint(x = 2) \longrightarrow D_2(x) = \{2\}$. Then the union of $D_1(x)$ and $D_2(x)$ can be computed: $\{1\} \cup \{2\} = \{1, 2\}$. Thus $D(x)$ can be reduced to $D_1(x) \cup D_2(x) = \{1, 2\}$.

Whereas the standard propagation rule for the or constraint in general leads to a simple generate-and-test behavior, with no pruning at all, the constructive disjunction performs a very good pruning of the domains. In fact it is easy to show the following proposition:

Proposition 1 *Let C_1 and C_k be k constraints whose filtering algorithms achieve arc-consistency. Then constructive disjunction applied on $or(C_1, ..., C_k)$ achieves arc-consistency.*

Proof: *Consider a variable x whose domain after reduction is $D(x)$. The domain $D(x)$ is, by definition, the union of the domains of x in the different branches $D(x) = D_1(x) \cup ... \cup D_k(x)$. Thus if value a is in $D(x)$ it is also in one domain $D_i(x)$ at least. In the branch i, we know that C_i is arc-consistent. Thus (x, a) is arc-consistent in the branch i. For a disjunction, to be consistent, it suffices that one branch is consistent, thus (x, a) is arc-consistent for $or(C_1, ..., C_k)$.*

Constructive disjunction thus performs an optimal reduction of the domains. Nevertheless, the constructive disjunction is not so often used in constraint programming applications. The main reason of such a limited use of constructive disjunction seems to be that it is much more expensive in term of CPU time than the standard filtering for disjunction, and, even if its pruning may be much stronger, constructive disjunction does not always pay off [2].

4   A New Filtering Algorithm
for the Disjunction of Constraints

In that section, we introduce a filtering algorithm for **or** constraint that performs
the same pruning as constructive disjunction, and thus achieves arc-consistency,
but which is much more efficient. The idea is to seek supports only when needed.
This is not the case in constructive disjunction which may compute useless supports, as we will now show in the following example:

Example 2 *Let x, y, z be three variables, let their respective domains be $D(x) =
[1, 1000], D(y) = [1, 2], D(z) = [1, 1000]$, and let C be the constraint $or(x = y, y =
z)$. The tuple $\{(x, 1), (y, 1)\}$ is a support for the constraint $x = y$. That is to say,
when $x = 1$ and $y = 1$, the constraint $x = y$ is true, and thus C is true, even
if the constraint $y = z$ is false. In other terms, for any value v of z in $D(z)$,
the tuple $\{(x, 1), (y, 1), (z, v)\}$ is a support on the constraint C. Symetrically,
$\{(y, 2), (z, 2)\}$ is a support on the constraint $y = z$, and thus $\{(x, v), (y, 2), (z, 2)\}$
is a support on C for every value $v \in D(x)$. Indeed, the two above support checks
are sufficient to prove arc-consistency of the constraint C.*

*If one wants to use constructive disjunction to prove arc-consistency of C, it
will first compute arc-consistency for constraint $x = y$, and then for constraint
$y = z$, doing at least 1000 constraints checks for each constraint.*

The example 2 should have given to the reader the intuition of the new
filtering algorithm for the **or** constraint. Proposition 2 formalizes that intuition.

Proposition 2 *Let C be the constraint $or(C_1, C_2)$. Let V_1 be the variables of C_1
that are not in C_2, let V_2 be the variables of C_2 that are not in C_1, and let V_3 be
the variables that are shared by C_1 and C_2. That is: $V_1 = X(C_1) - X(C_2), V_2 =
X(C_2) - X(C_1), V_3 = X(C_1) \cap X(C_2)$.*

- *Let τ_1 be a support on C_1. Let τ be a tuple on C such that:*
    1. *$\tau[X(C_1)] = \tau_1[X(C_1)]$*
    2. *for all variable z in V_2, $\tau[z] \in D(z)$.*
    Then τ is a support on C.
- *Let τ_2 be a support on C_2. Let τ be a tuple on C such that:*
    1. *$\tau[X(C_2)] = \tau_2[X(C_2)]$*
    2. *for all variable x in V_1, $\tau[x] \in D(x)$.*
    Then τ is a support on C.

Proof: *we give the proof for the first assertion, the other one is symetric. The
values of variables in $X(C_1)$ are in the domains since τ_1 is a support and thus
is valid. Then, in τ, the values of variables $X(C_1)$ are in the domains. As, by
construction the values of variables V_2 in τ are also in the domains, we know
that τ is valid. As τ makes the constraint C_1 true, the constraint $or(C_1, C_2)$ is
true, and thus τ is an allowed tuple, hence it is a support.*

*Then, a support τ on C can be simply derived from a support τ_1 on C_1 (resp.
τ_2 on C_2). It suffices to complete τ_1 (resp. τ_2) by adding values for the variables
in V_2 (resp. V_1): any value in their domains can be taken.*

Corollary 1 *A first corollary is that, for the variables that are in V_3, it suffices to find one support per value, either in C_1 or in C_2.*

Indeed, corollary 1 uses for the meta-constraint level the principle of lazy support that was introduced in AC-6 [3].

Corollary 2 *A second corollary is that if a support τ_1 on C_1 is found, we can derive directly a support on C for **all the values** (z, b) where z is a variable in V_2 and $b \in D(z)$. Thus, τ_1 plays the role of a generic support for the variables in V_2, and there is no reason to waste time in searching individual supports in C_2 for the variables in V_2. (A symetric argument holds for a support in C_2 and variables in V_1.)*

The filtering algorithm in Figure 1 simply applies those principles. Once we know there exists a support of (x, a) on C, it is clearly a waste of time to try to find another one.

```
procedure globalOrFiltering(C₁, C₂)
    τ₁ = getAnySupport(C₁)
    if τ₁ = nil
        replace this constraint by C₂
        return
    τ₂ = getAnySupport(C₂)
    if τ₂ = nil
        replace this constraint by C₁
        return
    For each variable x in V₃
        For each value a in D(x)
            τ = getSupport(C₁, (x, a))
            if τ = nil
                τ = getSupport(C₂, (x, a));
                if τ = nil
                    remove a from D(x)
```

Fig. 1. A global filtering algorithm for or(C_1, C_2)

Description of the Algorithm. The algorithm first computes any support for C_1, thanks to the method getAnySupport(C_1) which is supposed to exist. If such a support can be found, then it is a generic support for every variable in V_2. If none exists, then C_1 is false; thus C_2 must be true, it is added to the constraint solver (and the constraint or(C_1, C_2) can be removed from the constraint solver). A similar generic support is sought for C_2.

Then the algorithm has to find a support for each value of each variable in V_3. It suffices to find one support of this pair variable/value in C_1 or in C_2. If none exists, the value can be removed from the domain of the variable. The method getSupport($C, (x, a)$) is supposed to exist for each constraint C_1 and C_2.

The following proposition is a direct consequence of the proposition 2:

Proposition 3 *The filtering agorithm globalOr achieves arc-consistency for the constraint* $or(C_1, C_2)$.

Following the GAC-schema [4], two important characteristics for arc-consistency algorithms are: (1) *incrementality* of arc-consistency maintenance during search; (2) taking into account *multidirectionality* of supports (i.e., a support for a given pair variable/value is also a support for every pairs variable/value that compose the support). The algorithm of Figure 1 can be easily extended to take into account incrementality (by storing supports) and multidirectionnality.

Complexity of the Algorithm. Let us assume a general model with p constraints in disjunction $or(C_1, C_2, ..., C_p)$. Assume that: (1) there are $k > 0$ variables that are shared in the p constraints; (2) all the variables have d values in their domains; (3) all the constraints have the same arity r; (4) we do not take into account multidirectionnality of support in our complexity analysis.

Constructive disjunction will find $p * r * d$ supports. The globalOr filtering algorithm will find $k * d$ supports. As $k \leq r$, globalOr save at least a factor of p in CPU time. The gain may be much larger, for example, if there are two variables that are shared by 100 constraints whose arity is 10, and with domains of size 20: there are 40 supports to find in one case and 20000 in the other case.

5 Conclusion

We have proposed in that paper an algorithm that achieves arc-consistency over disjunctions of constraints. It is always better than constructive disjunction in efficiency for the same pruning. It improves constructive disjunction in the same way AC-6 [3] improved AC-4 [5]. Furthermore the approach can be applied to all meta constraints on cardinality like: atmost (or at least) p constraints are true among q.

References

1. Van Hentenryck, P., Saraswat, V., Deville, Y.: Design, implementation, and evaluation of the constraint language cc(FD). In Podelski, A., ed.: Constraint Programming: Basics and Trends. LNCS 910. Springer (1995) (Châtillon-sur-Seine Spring School, France, May 1994).
2. Würtz, J., Müller, T.: Constructive disjunction revisited. In Görz, G., Hölldobler, S., eds.: 20th German Annual Conference on Artificial Intelligence. Volume 1137., Dresden, Germany, Springer-Verlag (1996) 377–386
3. Bessière, C.: Arc-consistency and arc-consistency again. Artificial Intelligence **65** (1994) 179–190
4. Bessière, C., Régin, J.C.: Arc consistency for general constraints networks: preliminary results. In: IJCAI'97, Nagoya (1997) 398–404
5. Mohr, R., Henderson, T.C.: Arc and path consistency revisited. Artificial Intelligence **28** (1986) 225–233

INCOP: An Open Library
for INcomplete Combinatorial OPtimization

Bertrand Neveu and Gilles Trombettoni

Projet COPRIN, CERMICS-I3S-INRIA
Route des lucioles, BP 93, 06902 Sophia Antipolis France
{Bertrand.Neveu,Gilles.Trombettoni}@sophia.inria.fr

Abstract. We present a new library, INCOP, which provides incomplete algorithms for optimizing combinatorial problems. This library offers local search methods such as simulated annealing, tabu search as well as a population based method, Go With the Winners. Several problems have been encoded, including Constraint Satisfaction Problems, graph coloring, frequency assignment.

INCOP is an open C++ library. The user can easily add new algorithms and encode new problems. The neighborhood management has been carefully studied. First, an original parameterized move selection allows us to easily implement most of the existing meta-heuristics. Second, different levels of incrementality can be specified for the configuration cost computation, which highly improves efficiency.

INCOP has shown great performances on well-known benchmarks. The challenging `flat300_28` graph coloring instance has been colored in 30 colors for the first time by a standard Metropolis algorithm.

1 Introduction

Discrete optimization problems can be solved by two majors types of methods, complete and incomplete ones. Complete algorithms are based on a tree search with a Branch and Bound schema. Several commercial software tools propose such methods. When an optimization problem can be modeled by linear constraints and a linear criterion, MIP packages can be used. Otherwise, constraint programming tools, such as `IlogSolver` or `Chip`, can be used.

When the search space becomes too large, these systematic search techniques are often outperformed by incomplete methods, that cannot prove the optimality of a solution, but often give rapidly a good solution. The most common incomplete methods are based on local search which tries to make local changes to *one* configuration for improving its cost. Other incomplete methods explore the search space by managing a population of configurations.

To efficiently implement complete algorithms requires a great effort and therefore commercial tools have been built and are successfully used. Conversely, it is easier to implement an incomplete method and no important effort has been made to build a commercial tool. `IlogSolver` has recently added a local search module, but it is included in the whole library and cannot be used separately.

F. Rossi (Ed.): CP 2003, LNCS 2833, pp. 909–913, 2003.
© Springer-Verlag Berlin Heidelberg 2003

This lack of tool has recently led many researchers to build their own incomplete search method libraries [12]. We can cite iOpt [14] by British Telecom, SCOOP [10] by SINTEF, Localizer++ [6] at Brown University, Hotframe [13] at University of Braunschweig, Discropt [11] at State University of New York. Philippe Galinier and Jin-Kao Hao [4] also proposed a framework for local search.

However, at the moment, all these libraries are not free or not available. We have found only one free library available on the Web: EasyLocal++, at University of Udine [2], that implements local search methods.

Initially, we wanted to test a new population-based method and compare it with local search methods in the same implementation. In that purpose, we decided to provide a free library, implementing the main local search meta-heuristics and efficient population-based methods.

2   Architecture

We have chosen an object oriented design and implemented the library in C++, using virtual methods and data structures provided by the STL. The main classes are: OpProblem, Algorithm, Configuration, Move , NeighborhoodSearch, Metaheuristic. It is then not difficult to define new meta-heuritics, new neighborhoods or new problems by defining subclasses.

The most popular local search metaheuristics are implemented such as Hill Climbing, GSAT, Simulated Annealing, Tabu Search. For adding a new meta-heuristic, one has to define a subclass of Metaheuristic, with its data, an acceptance condition of a candidate move and a executebeforemove method for updating the meta-heuristic data (like the temperature of simulated annealing or the tabu list) before executing a move.

A configuration is represented by a fixed set of integer variables, with a priori known domains of values. Important combinatorial optimization problems, as traveling salesman problems (TSP) can be encoded in this framework. Constraint Satisfaction Problems (CSP) are transformed into MAX-CSP optimization problems for which the number of violated constraints (or more generally a criterion computed on these violations) is minimized. We have implemented several CSPs, including graph coloring and frequency assignment problems.

Adding a New Problem. The criterion to be optimized is specific to a given problem. Three methods compute this criterion. config_evaluation evaluates the cost of an initial configuration; move_evaluation performs the incremental evaluation of a move; update_conflicts updates the conflicts data structure of a configuration when a move is executed.

3   Contributions

This section details original features of INCOP. First, the incremental configuration cost computations offered by our library improve efficiency. Second, efficient population-based algorithms can be used to tackle the most difficult instances. Third, an original parameterized move selection can lead to easily create new variants of local search algorithms.

3.1 Incrementality

The contribution of any variable value to the evaluation of a configuration cost is the number of constraints violated by this value (considering the current value of the other variables). Since this evaluation is performed very often, it is crucial to rapidly evaluate the impact of a move on the whole configuration cost. We provide 3 manners to manage the conflicts, implemented by 3 classes.

1. In `CSPconfiguration`, the conflicts are not stored: one needs to compute the number of constraints violated by the old and the new values.
2. In `IncrCSPconfiguration`, the contribution of the current value is stored in `conflicts`; we need to compute only the contribution of the new value.
3. In `FullincrCSPconfiguration`, all the contributions of all possible values are stored in `conflicts`; the evaluation of a move is immediate.

The incremental evaluations are performed by the two following methods: `move_evaluation` is called when a move is tested, and `update_conflicts` when a move is performed. With full incrementality, the computation effort is mainly done in `update_conflicts`. It is fruitful when a lot of moves must be tested before accepting one. When the problem is sparse as in most of graph coloring instances, the updating is not costly. It only concerns the values of the few variables linked by a constraint with the currently changed variable. Full incrementality can save an order of magnitude in computing time. The memory required is also reasonable for coloring problems: the size of the conflict data structure is $N \times D$, where N is the number of nodes and D the number of colors.

3.2 Go with the Winners Algorithms

The population-based algorithms implemented in `INCOP` are variants of the Go With the Winners algorithm [3]. Several configurations are handled simultaneously. Every configuration, named particle, performs a random walk and, periodically, the worst particles are redistributed on the best ones. To ensure improvements in the population, a threshold is lowered during the search and no move passing above the threshold is allowed.

The hybridization with local search is straightforward: instead of performing a random walk, every particle performs a local search. `GWW-grw` [9], a hybridization of `GWW` with a simple walk algorithm, has given very good results.

3.3 Selection of a Move

An atomic step in local search algorithms is the way neighbors of the current configuration are tested. An original generic move selection, a kind of candidate list strategy [5], has been embedded in `INCOP`. First, the method `is_feasible` gives a feasibility condition for the move. For instance, in `GWW` algorithms, the configuration cost must stay under the current threshold. In order to finely tune the intensification effort of the search, 3 parameters are used:

Table 1. Results on graph coloring benchmarks. The best results of known algorithms are reported in the left side (number of colors, time); the results with INCOP in the right side (number of colors, number of conflicts (average on 10 trials), cpu time (average on 10 trials), success rate, algorithm and neighborhood used.

	nb-col	time	nb-col	conflicts	time	success	algo	neighb.
le450_15c	15	min	15	0	1.1 min	10/10	GWW-grw	var-conflict
le450_15d	15	min	15	1.4	1 min	5/10	GWW-grw	var-conflict
le450_25c	25	min	25	1.5	55 min	1/10	Metropolis	var-conflict
le450_25d	25	min	25	1.3	58 min	1/10	Metropolis	var-conflict
flat300_28	31	h	31	0.3	4 min	9/10	Metropolis	min-conflict
flat300_28	31	h	30	1.6	1.6 h	5/10	Metropolis	min-conflict

Table 2. Results on CELAR frequency assignment benchmarks. The results of the best known algorithms are in the left side; the results with INCOP in the right side.

	bound	best found	bound (average)	time	succes	algo
celar6	3389	min	3389 (3405.7)	9 min	4/10	GWW-grw
celar7	343592	min	343596 (343657)	4.5 h	1/10	GWW-grw
celar8	262	min	262 (267.4)	33 min	2/10	GWW-grw

1. We first test Min_neighbors neighbors in order to select the *best* one.
2. If none has been accepted by the meta-heuristics, we test other neighbors until *one* is accepted or a sample of Max_neighbors is exhausted.
3. Finally, if no neighbor among these Max_neighbors has been accepted, the No_acceptation parameter indicates how to select a configuration: either the best feasible or any feasible among the Max_neighbors visited neighbors.

These parameters allow us to implement many different classical behaviors as searching the best neighbor in the entire neighborhood or the first acceptable neighbor in a sample of K neighbors.

4   Experiments

We have performed experiments on difficult instances mainly issued from two categories of problems encoded as weighted MAX-CSPs: difficult graph coloring instances proposed in the DIMACS challenge, and CELAR frequency assignment problems[1]. All the tests have been performed on a PentiumIII 935 Mhz.

4.1   Graph Coloring Instances

Incomplete algorithms succeeded in coloring flat300_28 in 31 colors [8].We colored it in 31 colors in a few minutes and in 30 colors in 1.6 hour using a Metropolis algorithm (i.e., simulated annealing with constant temperature [1]) and a neighborhood implementing the Min-conflicts heuristics [7].

---

[1] Thanks to the "Centre d'ELectronique de l'ARmement".

4.2 CELAR Frequency Assignment Instances

The constraints are of the form $|x_i - x_j| = \delta$ or $|x_i - x_j| > \delta$. The objective function is a weighted sum of violated constraints.

5 Conclusion

This paper has presented a new C++ library for incomplete combinatorial optimization. We have implemented several local search, and original and efficient population-based algorithms. A great effort has been done for the neighborhood management. An important issue is the incrementality in move evaluations. We have obtained it by maintaining a conflict data structure. Finally, we hope that our parameterized move selection process will improve existing meta-heuristics.

We think that no incomplete algorithm can efficiently solve all the problems. So it is important to test rapidly different algorithms, different neighborhoods. Such a library permits it and we have obtained good results for CELAR frequency assignment problems with GWW-grw and for graph coloring problems with GWW-grw or Metropolis, with a min-conflict or a var-conflict neighborhood. We have, for the first time, colored flat300_28 with 30 colors.

References

1. D. T. Connolly. An improved annealing scheme for the QAP. *European Journal of Operational Research*, (46):93–100, 1990.
2. L. DiGaspero and A. Schaerf. Easylocal++ : An object oriented framework for flexible design of local search algorithms. Technical Report UDMI/13, Universita degli Studie di Udine, 2000.
3. Tassos Dimitriou and Russell Impagliazzo. Towards an analysis of local optimization algorithms. In *Proc. STOC*, 1996.
4. Philippe Galinier and Jin-Kao Hao. Hybrid evolutionary algorithms for graph coloring. *Journal of Combinatorial Optimization*, 3(4):379–397, 1999.
5. F. Glover and M.Laguna. *Tabu Search*. Kluwer Academic Publishers, 1997.
6. L. Michel and P. Van Hentenryck. Localizer++ : An open library for local search. Technical Report CS-01-02, Brown University, 2001.
7. S. Minton, M. Johnston, A. Philips, and P. Laird. Minimizing conflict: a heuristic repair method for constraint satisfaction and scheduling problems. *Artificial Intelligence*, 58:161–205, 1992.
8. C. Morgenstern. Distributed coloration neighborhood search. In D. Johnson and M. Trick, editors, *Cliques, Coloring, and Satisfiability*, volume 26 of *dimacs*, pages 335–357. American Mathematical Society, 1996.
9. Bertrand Neveu and Gilles Trombettoni. When local search goes with the winners. In *Proc. of CPAIOR'03 workshop*, 2003.
10. P. K. Nielsen. *SCOOP 2.0 Reference Manual*. SINTEF Report 42A98001, 1998.
11. V. Phan and S. Skiena. Coloring graphs with a general heuristic search engine. In *Computational Symposium of Graph Coloring and Generalizations*, 2002.
12. S. Voß and D. Woodruff. *Optimization Software Class Libraries*. Kluwer, 2002.
13. S. Voß and D.L. Woodruff. Hotframe: A heuristic optimization framework. [12], pages 81–154.
14. C. Voudouris and R.Dorne. Integrating heuristic search and one-way constraints in the iOpt toolkit. [12], pages 177–192.

A Composition Algorithm for Very Hard Graph 3-Colorability Instances[*]

Seiichi Nishihara, Kazunori Mizuno, and Kohsuke Nishihara

Institute of Information Sciences and Electronics, University of Tsukuba
Tsukuba, Ibaraki 305-8573, Japan
nishihara@is.tsukuba.ac.jp
mizuno@algor.is.tsukuba.ac.jp
pml01582@mail1.accsnet.ne.jp

1 Introduction

Graph colorability (COL) is a constraint satisfaction problem, which has been studied in the context of computational complexity and combinatorial search algorithms. It is also interesting as subjects of heuristics [2]. Many research reports discuss the complexity of COL [2–4, 8–10]. Examples of possible candidates of order parameters that explain the mechanism making COLs very hard include the 3-paths [10], the minimal unsolvable subproblems [8], and the frozen developments [4]. Instead of generate-and-test approaches, we propose a constructive approach producing 3-colorablity problems (3COLs) that are exceptionally hard for usual backtracking algorithms adopting Brélaz heuristics and for Smallk coloring program [1]. Instances generated by our procedure (1) are 4-critical, (2) include no near-4-cliques(n4c's; 4-cliques with 1 edge removed) as subgraphs, and (3) have the degree of every node limited to 3 or 4: quasi-regular.

2 Graph 3-Colorability and 4-Critical Graphs

Let $G = (V, E)$ be a graph to be colored, where V and E corresponds to the set of vertices and edges. Let $n = | V |$ and $m = | E |$. An edge $(i, j) \in E$ has the constraint that prohibits assigning the same color to vertices, i and j. Phenomena similar to physical phase transitions are generally observed in COLs, where search cost follows an easy-hard-easy pattern as a function of constraint density, or $\gamma(= 2m/n)$. The region where median search cost becomes the most time-consuming lies very close to the cross-over point, at which half the instances are solvable and half unsolvable (primary PT). An interesting region also exists at a slightly lower constraint density than that of primary PT, in which exceptionally hard instances (EHIs) [5] tend to occur, although most are solved easily (secondary PT).

[*] This research was supported in part by the Ministry of Education, Culture, Sports, Science and Technology of Japan, Grant-in-Aid for Scientific Research (B)(2), No. 14380134, 2002–2005.

F. Rossi (Ed.): CP 2003, LNCS 2833, pp. 914–919, 2003.
© Springer-Verlag Berlin Heidelberg 2003

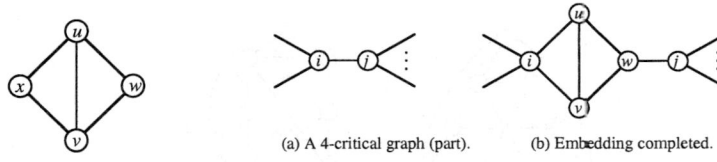

Fig. 1. An n4c.   **Fig. 2.** Embedding operator embed_$K_4(i, j)$.

A hard non 3-colorable graph necessarily contains large 4-critical subgraphs [4,8], i.e., non 3-colorable but any proper subgraph is 3-colorable. K_4, 4-clique, is the smallest 4-critical graph because removing an arbitrary edge from it makes a 3-colorable graph, which we call an n4c (Fig. 1) [4]. The n4c contains an interesting constraint, constraint(x, w), that claims the colors for x and w must be the same. Let Fig. 2(a) be part of a 4-critical graph, where the degree of vertex i, deg(i), is 3. Introduce an operation, embed_ $K_4(i, j)$, where an n4c is added in place of edge (i, j) merging i and x and connecting j and w [1]. Starting with K_4 as the initial graph, arbitrarily large 4-critical instances are constructed by repeating embed_$K_4(i, j)$ recursively to meet the many known conditions EHIs may have to satisfy [4, 7, 8, 10].

3   Composition Algorithm for EHI without n4c's

Because embed_$K_4(i, j)$ always leaves an n4c in the graph, we can find at any stage of graph construction at least 1 n4c, which is the footprint where the latest embedding operation was executed. By repeating collapse. i.e., inverse operation of embed_$K_4(i, j)$, the given graph straightforwardly is reduced to a single K_4 that is unsolvable. To overcome this drawback, we introduce a set of original n4c-free 4-critical graphs independent of each other in that no graph is a subgraph of any other. We found 7 such graphs by trial and error (Fig. 3), in which each graph is termed MUG$_{nt}$, where MUG stands for "minimal unsolvable graph," n means the number of vertices included, and t is used to identify the type if necessary. Let us naturally extend the embedding operation to embed_MUG$_{nt}(i, j)$. These operations are the same as Hajós' join construction [6] except that both vertices to be merged should have the degree of 3.

Proposition 1 *When embed_MUG$_{nt}(i, j)$ is applied to a 4-critical graph, the result remains 4-critical.*

Proposition 2 *Quasi-regularity is maintained by embed_MUG$_{nt}$ operation where nt is 9, 10, 11a, 11b, or 12c.*

Proposition 3 *Let the graph to embed contain, m edges and $n = n_3 + n_4 + n_5$ vertices, where n_i is the number of vertices with degree i. The numbers of vertices*

---

[1] Note that 4-criticality is maintained because the constraint, constraint(i, w), remains after embedding while u and v are not adjacent to other vertices.

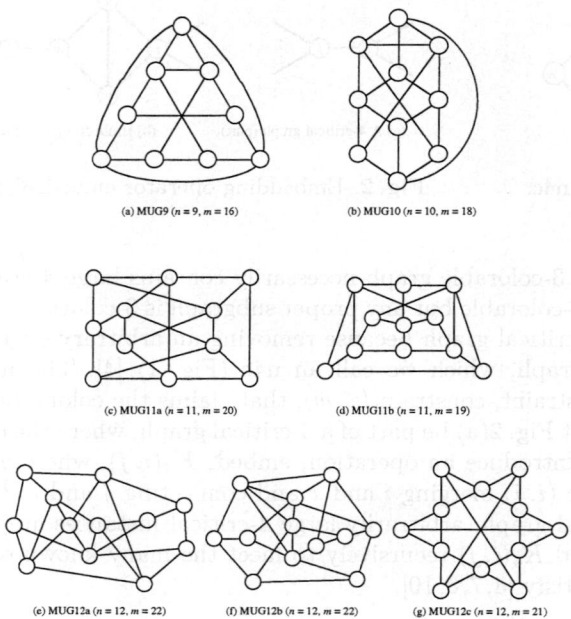

(a) MUG9 ($n = 9, m = 16$)   (b) MUG10 ($n = 10, m = 18$)

(c) MUG11a ($n = 11, m = 20$)   (d) MUG11b ($n = 11, m = 19$)

(e) MUG12a ($n = 12, m = 22$)   (f) MUG12b ($n = 12, m = 22$)   (g) MUG12c ($n = 12, m = 21$)

Fig. 3. 4-critical n4c-free graphs.

with degrees 3,4,5 increase by $n_3 - 2, n_4 + 1, n_5$. The total number of vertices increases by $n - 1$, and edges by $m - 1$.

Starting with a 4-critical graph, we construct arbitrarily large 4-critical graphs, i.e., including an arbitrary number of vertices, by repeating embedding. Fig. 4 gives the procedure "graph-generator(k)" which repeats embedding operations k times randomly. When we start with 1 of 7 graphs (Fig. 3), we produce graphs contain no n4c's. Further, if a quasi-regular graph is assigned initially to G_{init} at (1) in Fig. 4, and both MUG12a and MUG12b are excluded from candidates at (2), then the graph-generator produces quasi-regular graphs.

4   Experiments and Discussion

We test the difficulty of 3COL instances generated by "graph-generator(k)" where all graphs except for MUG12a and MUG12b are used to generate quasi-regular graphs. For 8 cases from $k = 5$ to $k = 12$, 100 instances are generated for each case, i.e., a total of 800 generated instances. These instances are applied to the backtracking algorithm with Brélaz heuristics and the Smallk coloring program. In the Brélaz algorithm, only 500 instances from $k = 5$ to $k = 9$ are used for testing. These algorithms are implemented in C on a PC with 1 GHz of Pentium III and 512 Mbytes of RAM. Fig. 5 gives results for search costs

procedure graph-generator(k)
begin
    input an initial graph G_{init};   (1)
    $G := G_{init}$;
    for $w := 1$ **to** k **do**
        choose randomly an edge$(i,j) \in E(G)$ where $\deg(i) \leq 3$;
        choose randomly MUG_{nt}, (nt =9, 10, 11a, 11b, 12a, 12b, or 12c);   (2)
        embed_$MUG_{nt}(i,j)$;
    end for;
end.
procedure embed_$MUG_{nt}(i,j)$
begin
    choose randomly an edge $(x,y) \in E(MUG_{nt})$ where $\deg(x) \leq 3$;
    remove edges (i,j) and (x,y);
    add an edge (j,y);
    merge x with i;
end.

Fig. 4. 3COL instance generator.

and CPU time, where "average line" shows the variation in average search cost and CPU time for each k as a function of the average number of vertices for each k. Smallk is more sophisticated than the Brélaz algorithm, but both search cost and CPU time clearly exhibit exponential growth[2]. We also conduct experiments on randomly generated instances. For 33 cases from $\gamma = 3.0$ to $\gamma = 5.0$ at the intervals of 0.2 in $n = 100$, 200, and 300, 10,000 instances are randomly generated for each cases, i.e., a total of 3.3 million generated instances, each of which is solved using Smallk. In the Brélaz algorithm, only 1.1 million instances with $n = 100$ are used. It is obvious that the hardness of our instance set cannot be compared with that of the huge set of random instances (Fig. 6)[3].

Experiments confirmed that our method stably produces EHIs whose computational cost is of an exponential order of n. Researchers adopting generate-and-test approaches found that conditions under which EHIs tend to occur are as follows: (1) Their constraint density is near the secondary PT region [7], (2) the smallest minimal unsolvable subproblem is very large compared to the instance size [8], and (3) their structure is homogeneous, i.e., quasi-regular [10]. It seems reasonable that instances produced by our method meet all these conditions. Because our instances contain no n4c's, most frozen pairs [4] are hidden from the surface, which makes our instances hard to solve even for sophisticated algorithms such as Smallk. We still do not know theoretically why our instances become EHIs. The ultimate question may be whether our instances are inher-

---

[2] As long as we see results of Culberson and Gent in [4], our instances seem to be much harder than their threshold graphs, although the complexity of their graphs also exhibit exponential growth.

[3] In Smallk, it is only 2.6 *sec.* and 103 *sec.* to determine the colorability of each hardest random instance with *200* and *300* vertices at $\gamma = 4.8$, whereas it requires more than 500 *sec.* on average in solving our instances with even *100* vertices or so in Fig. 5.

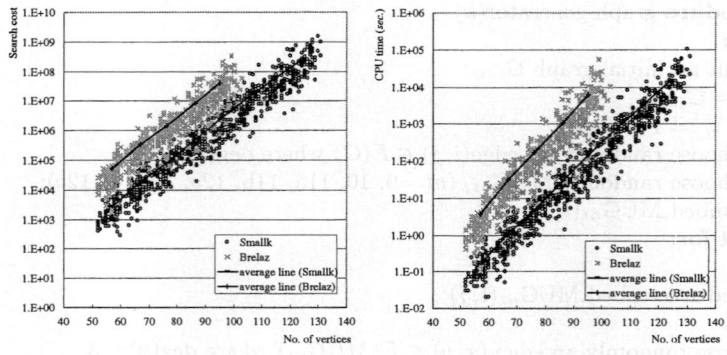

Fig. 5. Experimental results on 3COL instances generated by our procedure.

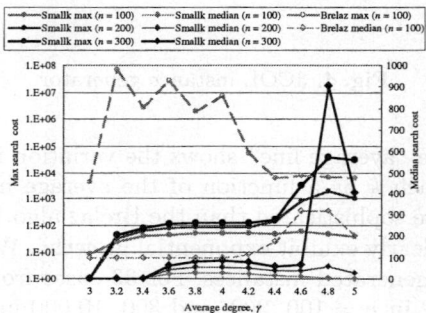

Fig. 6. Experimental results on randomly generated instances.

ently hard for any search algorithms. Let us move on to an issue probably related to heuristics. Fig. 3 introduces only 7 n4c-free MUGs independent of each other. Although we surmise that the number of such graphs is infinite, we still do not know how to generate them systematically. The method for producing such graphs may be necessary for hiding the structural weakness of an instance so that no clever heuristics can find and exploit it.

5   Conclusions

We have proposed a constructive algorithm to generate EHIs of 3COL, which recursively repeat self-embedding operations of MUGs. The EHIs generated are 4-critical and contain no n4c's, to hide a structural weakness that heuristics would be able to exploit. Using Brélaz heuristics and Smallk, we showed that the complexity of 3COL instances generated by our algorithm is an exponential order of the number of vertices. We plan to develop a systematic method to arbitrarily produce many MUGs independent of each other to construct hard instances, and to clarify whether heuristics exist that cope with these instances.

References

1. *Overview of the Smallk Graph Coloring Program*, 2000.
   http://www.cs.ualberta.ca/ joe/Coloring/Colorsrc/smallk.html.
2. D. Brélaz. New Methods to Color the Vertices of a Graph. *Comm. ACM*, 22(4), 1979.
3. P. Cheeseman, B. Kanefsky, and W. M. Taylor. Where Really Hard Problems Are. In *Proc. 12th IJCAI*, 1991.
4. J. Culberson and I. Gent. Frozen development in graph coloring. *Theor. Computer Sci.*, 265, 2001.
5. S. A. Grant and B. M. Smith. Modelling Exceptionally Hard Constraint Satisfaction Problems. In *Proc. CP97*, 1997.
6. D. Hanson, G. C. Robinson, and B.Toft. Remarks on the Graph Colour Theorem of Hajós. *Congressus Numerantium*, 55, 1986.
7. T. Hogg and C. P. Williams. The hardest constraint problems: a double phase transition. *Artif. Inell.*, 69, 1994.
8. D. L. Mammen and T. Hogg. A New Look at Easy-Hard-Easy Pattern of Combinatorial Search Difficulty. *Jour. Artif. Intell. Research*, 7, 1997.
9. K. Mizuno and S. Nishihara. Toward Ordered Generation of Exceptionally Hard Instances for Graph 3-Colorability. In *Computational Symposium on Graph Coloring and its Generalizations(COLOR02), Ithaca, N.Y., Sept.*, 2002.
10. D. R. Vlasie. Systematic Generation of Very Hard Cases for Graph 3-Colorability. In *Proc. 7th IEEE ICTAI*, 1995.

Efficient Representation of Discrete Sets
for Constraint Programming

Shuji Ohnishi, Hiroaki Tasaka, and Naoyuki Tamura

The Graduate School of Science and Technology, Kobe University
shuji@kurt.scitec.kobe-u.ac.jp
tasaka@trombone.cs.scitec.kobe-u.ac.jp
tamura@kobe-u.ac.jp

Abstract. In constraint solving for finite domains, efficient set representation is an important issue. In this paper we propose an enhancement of Erwig's *diet* representation called the *enhanced diet*, which represents a finite domain as an AVL tree of intervals. In addition to element insertion and deletion, we show that the domain splitting used for constraints such as $X \leq Y$ can be done in $O(\log m)$ steps by adopting Crane's Algorithm, where m is the number of intervals, not the number of elements.

1 Introduction

In constraint solvers for finite domains, such as ILOG Solver [1], JSolver [2], B-Prolog [3], clp(FD) [4] and others, variables are associated with finite domains and constraint propagation is done by set operations on those finite domains. Efficient set representation is therefore an important issue for implementation of constraint systems.

There have been several ways to represent finite domains, especially concerning subsets of integers. Bit vectors and hash maps are complete and efficient in set operations, but unsuitable for large sets. Single-interval representation (that is, a finite domain as a pair of lower and upper bound values) is efficient in space and in set operations. However, this representation is incomplete. Representing a domain as a (chained) list or an array of intervals is complete and efficient in space, but set operations on them are inefficient. For example, the complexity of element deletion is $O(m)$, where m represents the number of intervals.

Another way is the use of the *diet* (the *discrete interval encoding tree*) [5] proposed by Erwig, which represents a subset of integers as a binary tree of intervals. The diet is complete and efficient in space. Insertion and deletion for elements on the diet take only $O(\log m)$ steps. However, diets are simple, not necessarily balanced, binary trees. Therefore, the worst-case complexities of these operations are still $O(m)$ as interval lists.

In this paper we describe an enhancement of the diet called the *enhanced diet* which represents a subset of integers as an *AVL tree* of intervals. In the enhanced diet, element insertion and deletion take only $O(\log m)$ steps for both average and worst-case scenarios. Though we consider for simplicity only the case for

F. Rossi (Ed.): CP 2003, LNCS 2833, pp. 920–924, 2003.

integer sets, the methods we present can be applied to any domains with a total order and a predecessor and a successor functions.

We take the following notations: a closed interval $[a, b]$ represents a set $\{i \in \mathbf{Z} \mid a \le i \le b\}$, and we denote by m the number of (maximal closed) intervals. For example, a set $D = \{1, 2, 3, 6, 9, 10, 11, 12\}$ can be represented as a set of intervals $\{[1, 3], [6, 6], [9, 12]\}$ and $m = 3$ for D.

2   The Diet

Martin Erwig has proposed a set representation called the *diet* (the *discrete interval encoding tree*) [5]. The idea is to represent a set as a binary tree of intervals. Figures 1(a) and (b) show a binary tree representation and a diet representation of a set $\{1, 2, 3, 7, 8, 9, 10, 11, 12, 13, 14, 19, 20\}$ respectively. An important property of the diet is that between each two distinct intervals of a diet there is a gap of at least one element, i.e. for any diet its intervals neither overlap nor touch. An example of invalid diets is shown in Fig. 1(c): it is invalid for an interval [7, 10] touches another interval [11, 14].

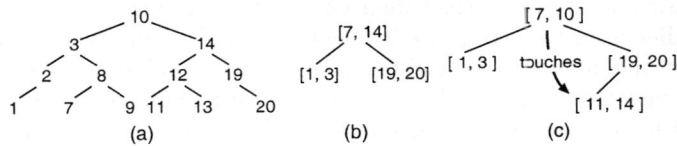

(a)   (b)   (c)

Fig. 1. (a)A Binary Tree, (b)a Diet and (c)an Illegal Diet.

The diet is complete and efficient in space. Erwig has presented algorithms of insertion and deletion for elements on the diet and shown that they take only $O(\log m)$ steps. However, diets are simple, not necessarily balanced, binary trees. Therefore, the worst-case complexities of these operations are still $O(m)$. Moreover, operations other than insertion or deletion have not been shown.

3   Enhancement of the Diet for Constraint Satisfaction

In this section we describe an implementation of the diet as AVL tree for improving the worst-case complexities of deletion and other operations. We call the diet which we have extended the *enhanced diet*. We also describe a specialization of the enhanced diet to speed up constraint solving and the algorithm of domain splitting used for constraints such as $X \le Y$.

3.1   Data Structure of the Enhanced Diet

In Erwig's original diet, each node has only its interval and left and right children, since they are not balanced and used only for insertion and deletion. To implement the diet as AVL tree and to efficiently perform more complicated set operations on them, we need more information.

First, a node of AVL tree has its height value. Second, in constraint solving, the minimum and the maximum values of domains are often used. As enhanced diets are (balanced) binary trees, getting the minimum or maximum value takes $O(\log m)$ steps. Third, the cardinalities of domains are used in constraint solving when choosing the next variable to be instantiated. One of the most common strategies is to choose the variable bound to the domain of the smallest cardinality (*first-fail* principle). Since you need visit all the nodes to calculate the cardinality, it takes $O(m)$ steps.

Consequently, each node of enhanced diets we have defined has the following values other than its interval and children: (1) its height, (2) the minimum and maximum values, and (3) the cardinality. Since each node has these auxiliary values, it takes only $O(1)$ steps to get them from an enhanced diet.

3.2   Set Operations on the Enhanced Diet

For we have chosen AVL tree as the implementation of the enhanced diet, our algorithms are based in part on [6].

The basic operations for the enhanced diet as AVL tree are: (1) making a new enhanced diet from two existing enhanced diets and an interval as the new root node, where the difference in heights between the two enhanced diets equals zero or one; (2) inserting an interval node into an existing enhanced diet; (3) deleting an interval node from an existing enhanced diet; and (4) extracting a leftmost or rightmost interval node from an existing enhanced diet. Operations (2), (3) and (4) are performed as in usual AVL tree. In operation (1), the parameters of the new root node are calculated as in Fig. 2.

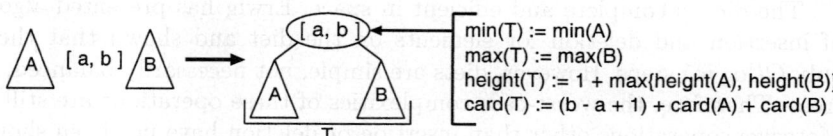

Fig. 2. Making a New Enhanced Diet from Two Existing Enhanced Diets.

The algorithms of element insertion and deletion for diets have been proposed by Erwig and one can easily apply them to enhanced diets. Since enhanced diets are balanced, element insertion and deletion take $O(\log m)$ steps for both average and worst-case scenarios.

Concatenation is a kind of union, which makes a new enhanced diet $T = T_1 \cup T_2$ from two existing enhanced diets T_1 and T_2, where $max(T_1) < min(T_2)$ or $max(T_2) < min(T_1)$. This is used as an auxiliary operation for the domain-splitting operation and others. A fast algorithm of concatenating two AVL trees was proposed by Clark A. Crane and its description can be found in [6]. Figure 3 describes Crane's concatenation algorithm. Suppose we want to concatenate two AVL trees T_1 and T_2 such that $max(T_1) < min(T_2)$ and $height(T_1) \geq$

$height(T_2)$. The other cases are similar. First go down the right links of T_1 until reaching a subtree D such that $height(D) - height(T_2) \le 1$. Then extract the rightmost node d from D, calling it the juncture node, and let D' be the resulting tree. Then make a new AVL tree from d, D', and T_2 as its root node, left subtree and right subtree respectively. Then reconstruct subtrees upward as if the new node d had just been inserted. Crane proved this concatenation algorithm for AVL tree takes $O(\log n)$ steps, when the original (higher) tree contains n nodes.

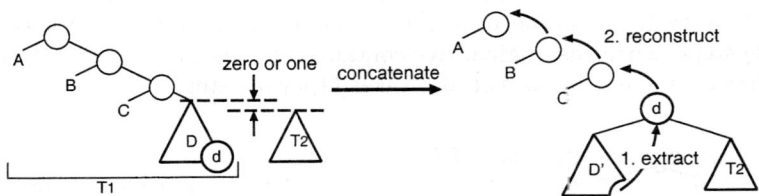

Fig. 3. Concatenation of Two AVL Trees.

Crane's algorithm is not perfect for enhanced diets when they touch each other. Let $T_1 = \{[1, 3], [5, 10]\}$ and $T_2 = \{[11, 15], [20, 35]\}$, then concatenating the two enhanced diets by Crane's algorithm would produce an invalid enhanced diet $\{[1, 3], [5, 10], [11, 15], [20, 35]\}$, not a valid one $\{[1, 3], [5, 15], [20, 35]\}$.

Figure 4 shows how to cope with these cases. If T_1 touches T_2, i.e. $max(T_1) + 1 = min(T_2)$, then not only extract the rightmost interval node J_1 from T_1 but also extract the leftmost interval node J_2 from T_2, and make the juncture node J_3 whose lower bound is that of J_1 and upper bound is that of J_2. Then concatenate T_1' and T_2' with J_3 as the juncture node. Reconstruction is performed as is in Crane's original algorithm. This algorithm takes $O(\log m)$ steps as Crane's original algorithm for AVL tree.

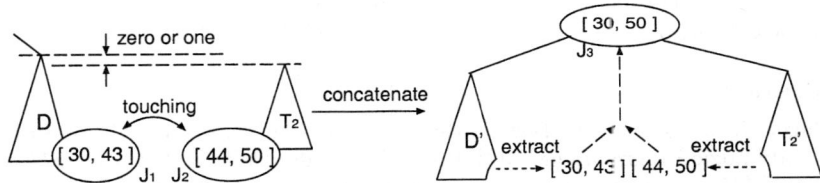

Fig. 4. Concatenation of Two Touching Enhanced Diets.

Domain-splitting operation is used for constraints such as $X \le Y$. It makes a new domain D' from an existing domain D and a given value d such that $D' = \{x \in D \mid x \ge d\}$ or $D' = \{x \in D \mid x \le d\}$. This problem is also solved by Crane for AVL trees. His AVL-splitting algorithm can be applied to enhanced diets with slight changes: in the enhanced diet, each node represents an interval, not a single value. Figure 5 shows how our splitting algorithm based on Crane's algorithm is performed. A_i's and B_i's represent subtrees and P_i's represent interval nodes. In this example, we want to make a new enhanced diet which has values contained in the original enhanced diet and less than or equal to a given cutting value 57. The path to the node which contains the cutting value is something like in the figure. We wish to construct an enhanced diet that contains the nodes of A_1, P_1, A_2, P_2, A_3, P_3, A_4, and [50, 57]. This construction can be done by a sequence of concatenations: first insert [50, 57] into A_4 and let A_4' be the resulting enhanced diet, then concatenate A_4' and A_3 with P_3 as their juncture node, then concatenate A_3' and A_2 with P_2, and finally concatenate A_2' and A_1 with P_1. Crane proved his splitting algorithm for AVL tree takes $O(\log n)$ steps, when the original tree contains n nodes, and our slightly changed algorithm for the enhanced diet also takes $O(\log m)$ steps.

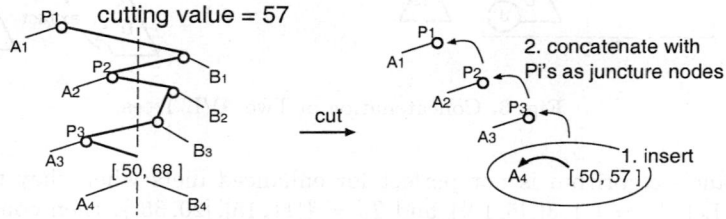

Fig. 5. Domain Splitting (Less than or Equal to).

4   Conclusion

In this paper we proposed a set representation called the *enhanced diet*, which represents a subset of integers as a *balanced* binary search tree of intervals. The enhanced diet is complete and can represent large sets efficiently in space. Element insertion and deletion on the enhanced diet take $O(\log m)$ steps for both average and worst-case scenarios. The domain splitting used for constraints such as $X \leq Y$ can also be done in $O(\log m)$ steps by adopting Crane's algorithm. Future work will involve combining the enhanced diet and bit vectors.

References

1. Puget, J.F., Leconte, M.: Beyond the glass box: Constraints as objects. In Lloyd, J., ed.: Logic Programming. MIT Press, Cambridge, MA, (1995) 513–527
2. Wai, A.: Constraint programming in Java with JSolver. The Proceedings of The Practical Application of Constraints Technologies and Logic Programming (PA-CLP99) (1999)
3. Zhou, N., Nagasawa, I.: An efficient finite-domain constraint solver in Beta-Prolog. Journal of Japanese Society for Artificial Intelligence **9** (1994) 275–282
4. Codognet, P., Diaz, D.: Compiling constraints in clp(FD). Journal of Logic Programming **27** (1996) 185–226
5. Erwig, M.: Diets for fat sets. Journal of Functional Programming **8** (1998) 627–632
6. Knuth, D.E.: The Art of Computer Programming, Volume 3: Sorting and Searching. 2nd edn. Addison Wesley Longman, Reading, Massachusetts (1998)

Applying Interchangeability Techniques to the Distributed Breakout Algorithm

Adrian Petcu and Boi Faltings

Ecole Politechnique Federale de Lausanne (EPFL), CH-1015 Lausanne (Switzerland)
{adrian.petcu,boi.faltings}@epfl.ch
http://liawww.epfl.ch

Abstract. This paper presents two methods for improving the performance of the Distributed Breakout Algorithm using the notion of interchangeability. In particular, we use neighborhood *partial* and *full* interchangeability techniques to keep conflicts localized and avoid spreading them to neighboring areas.
Our experiments on distributed sensor networks show that such techniques can significantly reduce the number of cycles required to solve the problems (therefore also reduce communication and time requirements), especially on difficult problems. Moreover, the improved algorithms are able to solve a higher proportion of the test problems.

1 Introduction

Distributed Constraint Satisfaction (DisCSP) is a powerful paradigm applicable for a wide range of coordination and problem solving tasks in distributed artificial intelligence.

Among the distributed algorithms that were developed for this kind of problems ([4]), the Distributed Breakout Algorithm (DBA) received quite some interest (e.g. [9]) because of a number of properties that this algorithm exhibits (simple, efficient, low overhead, linear memory requirements, good anytime characteristics).

DBA is an extension of the original centralized Breakout Algorithm ([8]). This algorithm is a local search method, with an innovative technique for escaping from local minima: the constraints have weights, which are dynamically increased to force the agents to adjust their values while in a local minimum. During the execution of the algorithm, each agent proposes improvements to the current state by changing it's variable value such that the cost of violated constraints is decreased as much as possible.

While having the interesting properties that we enumerated above, local search algorithms also have a common problem: choosing indiscriminately between the possible values of the local variable (only considering the cost of the immediate constraint violations) can lead to "chain-reactions" (one conflict originating in one part of the constraint graph needlessly propagates throughout the whole graph, only to (hopefully) be resolved in a completely different part of the graph).

F. Rossi (Ed.): CP 2003, LNCS 2833, pp. 925–929, 2003.
© Springer-Verlag Berlin Heidelberg 2003

We analyzed these phenomena, and drew the conclusion that using interchangeability techniques, one can determine what values from the local domain will not cause such conflict propagations, and use one of those values as the next variable assignment. In this way, we look for a "local resolution" to all conflicts, in the sense that we keep them contained as much as possible, and only involve "external parties" when there is no other way.

We discovered that techniques based on interchangeability [3] (both *neighborhood partial* and *full interchangeability* [1]) can improve the performance of this algorithm.

2   Preamble

2.1   Problem Description and Formalization

The distributed sensor network problem ([2]) consists of a sensor field composed of n sensors, and m targets to be tracked. Each sensor has its own visibility *range*. The sensors can communicate among themselves, but not necessarily every sensor with every other sensor.

Some restrictions apply: 3 sensors have to be assigned to each target, and they must be able to communicate among themselves; each sensor can only track one target at a time.

In our approach, one agent corresponds to a target; each agent has 3 local variables (the sensors to be assigned to each target), and the domain of each variable is the set of sensors that can track the respective target.

There are two types of constraints: *intra-agent constraints* (the variables belonging to one agent must be assigned to different sensors, and the sensors assigned to one agent must have a communication link between themselves) , and *inter-agent constraints* (no 2 variables from any 2 agents can be assigned the same value - a sensor can track a single target).

2.2   Interchangeability Background

The concept of interchangeability informally means equivalence between values of a CSP variable:

- *Neighborhood Interchangeability (NI)*: 2 values a and b of a variable V_i are NI if they are equivalent for every constraint involving V_i;
- *Neighborhood Partial Interchangeability (NPI)*: a weaker form of NI, defined for a subset of values from the local domain with respect to a set of neighbors, where the impact of the change of the local variable is limited to the reference set of neighbors.

2.3   Breakout Algorithm

In the distributed version of this algorithm, agents communicate through *ok?* and *improve* messages: an *ok?* message is used to send the current variable value, and an *improve* message is used to send possible improvement in the evaluation of variable value. When receiving *ok?* messages from all neighbors, an agent calculates the evaluation of the current variable value and its possible maximal improvement and sends them to neighbors via *improve* messages. When receiving *improve* messages from all neighbors, an agent compares them with its own improvement. If there is a greater improvement than its own, the agent will not do anything. If there is no possible improvement (all are 0), the agent will increase the weights of the violated constraints. If its improvement is the greatest, the agent will change its variable to the value giving the maximal improvement.

Note that ties in improvement comparison are broken deterministically by comparing agent identifiers. After this step, the agents send *ok?* messages to their neighbors. When no more constraints are violated, the problem is solved.

3   Algorithms

Due to lack of space, we will present here only a high-level overview of the algorithms that we developed.

NI-DBA: the idea is that if we find the NI-sets for the local variables, we can safely assign values from those sets, being certain this won't cause any conflicts with the neighboring agents. The NI-sets are determined during the pre-processing phase, based on the domains of the neighbors, and are used at runtime like this: if an agent has a conflict with a neighbor, it will search for an improvement in it's local domain *giving preference to the values from the NI-set*. This avoids any future conflicts with any neighbor.

NPI-DBA: the NPI-sets are computed at runtime, w.r.t. the set of the neighbors that we already have conflicts with. When searching for a local improvement, we *give preference to the values from the NPI-sets*, thus not risking to cause future conflicts with neighbors that are not already involved, therefore keeping conflicts contained.

4   Evaluation

We made our evaluations in these settings: a sensor grid with 400 sensors in total, and randomly generated *solvable* problems with 40, 60, 80, 100, 110, 115, 120, 125 and 130 simultaneous targets (meaning three times as many variables). The sensor grid was the same for all the problems, and the targets were placed randomly, such that the problems were still solvable.

We collected these results: problem solved/not solved (a problem is declared unsolved after the number of cycles reaches a threshold of 50000 cycles), and solving effort (time spent and number of cycles required).

For small numbers of targets, all the algorithms performed well; the differences increased with the problem difficulty, and peaked at 130 targets (most difficult problems), where NPI-DBA solved more than 70% of the problems, whereas Standard-DBA solved less than 50% (see Figure 1) Both the average

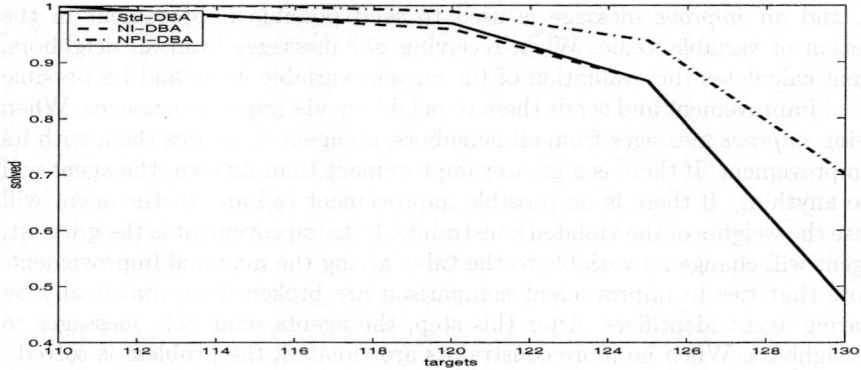

Fig. 1. Percentage of solved problems.

number of rounds and the solving time for standard DBA are bigger than those for NPI-DBA, and close to the ones of NI-DBA.

We see in Figure 2 that for difficult problems, the number of required rounds for NPI-DBA is about 40% smaller than the one of Standard DBA. A similar diagram for the time is available, but not included here.

We developed a visual interface that allows us to monitor the solving process, thus giving us clear indications that using the strategies based on NI/NPI greatly inhibits the propagation of conflicts around the constraint graph.

The initialization of the variables was pseudo-random (identical for all the algorithms), in order to keep the algorithms comparable, and see the improvements that the *search strategy* brings. Initialization with values from the NI-sets yields even larger improvements, leading us to believe that both the "informed" initialization of the variables and the subsequent search strategy play a role in the performance of the algorithm.

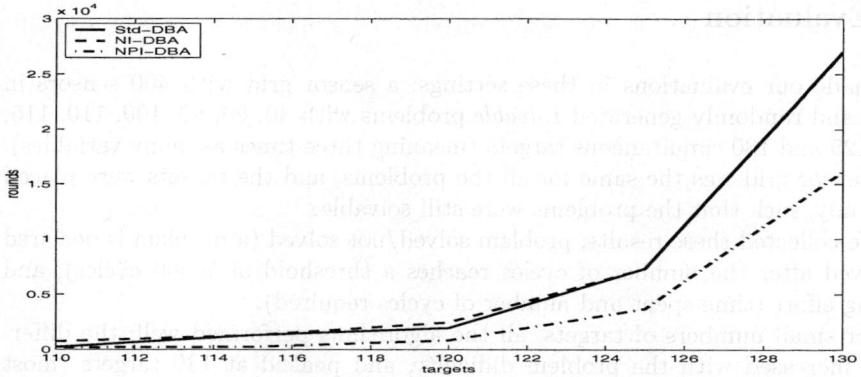

Fig. 2. Average no. of rounds spent on each problem size.

Overall, our results have shown that NPI-DBA is much better than NI-DBA. This is due to the fact that in dense problems, there is usually little or no NI at all, whereas NPI, being a weaker form of NI is still computable.

5   Conclusions and Future Work

The techniques presented here can be easily generalized beyond inequality constraints and resource allocation problems (in that case, the NI and NPI sets are more difficult to compute: simple disjunction between sets is not enough anymore, and discrimination trees [3] and joint discrimination trees [1] must be used).

NPI-DBA clearly outperforms standard DBA for difficult problems, and NI-DBA shows comparable performance. Further speedups weer obtained with "informed" initializations, based on the NI data available after the preprocessing phase.

Further improvements could also be obtained by allowing multiple simultaneous changes of the local variables at each step, and by trying a hierarchical approach, where certain agents are delegated as "local authorities" for solving a particularly difficult local problem. It would be interesting to study in more detail the scalability of these algorithms.

References

1. Berthe Y. Choueiry and Guevara Noubir: *On the Computation of Local Interchangeability in Discrete Constraint Satisfaction Problems*. In Proceedings of AAAI 1998, Madison, Wisconsin, USA
2. Carla Gomes, Cesar Fernandez, Ramon Bejar and Bhaskar Krishnamachari *Communication and Computation in DisCSP Algorithms*. In Proceedings of CP-2002, Ithaca, New York, USA
3. Eugene C. Freuder *'Eliminating interchangeable values in Constraint Satisfaction Problems'* In Proceedings of AAAI 1991, p 227-231, 1991, Anaheim, California, USA
4. Makoto Yokoo *The Distributed Constraint Satisfaction Problem: Formalization and Algorithms*. IEEE Transactions on Knowledge and Data Engineering 10(5), 673-685, 1998
5. Makoto Yokoo and Katsutoshi Hirayama *'Algorithms for distributed constraint satisfaction: A review'* In Proceedings of Autonomous Agents and Multi-agent Systems 2000, Barcelona, Catalonia, Spain
6. Makoto Yokoo and Katsutoshi Hirayama *Distributed Breakout Algorithm for Solving Distributed Constraint Satisfaction Problems*. In Proceedings of the Second International Conference on Multiagent Systems 1996, Kyoto, Japan
7. Nicoleta Neagu and Boi Faltings *Exploiting Interchangeabilities for Case Adaptation* In Proceedings of ICCBR'01, Vancouver, British Columbia, Canada
8. Paul Morris *The breakout method for escaping from local minima*. In Proceedings of the Eleventh National Conference on Artificial Intelligence, pp 40-45, 1993, Washington, D.C., USA
9. Weixiong Zhang and Lars Wittenburg *Distributed Breakout Revisited*. In Proceedings of AAAI 2002, Edmonton, Alberta, Canada

Symmetry Breaking in Graceful Graphs

Karen E. Petrie and Barbara M. Smith

School of Computing & Engineering, University of Huddersfield, UK
{k.e.petrie,b.m.smith}@hud.ac.uk

1 Introduction

Symmetry occurs frequently in Constraint Satisfaction Problems (CSPs). For instance, in 3-colouring the nodes of a graph, a CSP model that assigns a specific colour to each node has sets of equivalent solutions in which the three colours are permuted. Symmetry in CSPs can cause wasted search, because the search for solutions may repeatedly visit partial assignments symmetric to ones already considered. If a partial assignment does not lead to a solution, neither will any symmetrically equivalent assignment. When searching for all solutions, for every solution found, all the symmetrically equivalent solutions will also be found.

To avoid this wasted effort, the search algorithm can be modified so that search never visits assignments symmetric to those already considered. One such approach is Symmetry Breaking During Search (described in [7]). On backtracking to a choice point, having explored the subtree resulting from the assignment of a value to a variable, say $var = val$, the search will explore the subtree in which $var \neq val$. SBDS adds constraints to ensure that in this subtree, no assignment is considered that is symmetrically equivalent to one already met.

SBDS requires a function for each symmetry in the problem describing its effect on the assignment of a value to a variable. To allow SBDS to be used in highly symmetric CSPs, Gent et al. [5] linked SBDS (in ECL^{i}PS^e) with GAP (Groups, Algorithms and Programming) [4], a system for computational group theory. GAP-SBDS allows the symmetry group, rather than its individual elements, to be described. Symmetry can then be handled more efficiently than in SBDS, since the elements of the group are not explicitly created. On the other hand, GAP-SBDS has the overhead of the communication between ECL^{i}PS^e and GAP. Furthermore, the symmetry-breaking constraints posted on backtracking are constructed dynamically rather than being pre-defined in the symmetry functions as in SBDS.

Symmetry Breaking via Dominance Detection (SBDD) [1,2] checks every node in the search tree to see if it is dominated by a symmetric equivalent of a subtree already explored, and if so prunes this branch. Gent et al. [6] have developed GAP-SBDD, a generic version of SBDD that uses the symmetry group of the problem and links SBDD (in ECL^{i}PS^e) with GAP. At each node in the search tree ECL^{i}PS^e calls GAP to check for dominance. If the node is not dominated, GAP sometimes identifies variable/value pairs that can be deleted from domains; this information is returned to ECL^{i}PS^e. Gent et al. compared GAP-SBDD with GAP-SBDS applied to BIBDs and showed that GAP-SBDD could

F. Rossi (Ed.): CP 2003, LNCS 2833, pp. 930–934, 2003.
© Springer-Verlag Berlin Heidelberg 2003

solve much larger problems, and was faster than GAP-SBDS on the smaller problems which both could solve.

In this paper, we compare SBDS, GAP-SBDS and GAP-SBDD on a class of graph labelling problems. Constraint programming has proved valuable for solving these problems, and eliminating symmetry has led to many new results. Some are presented here; more can be found in a longer version of the paper [9] and at http://scom.hud.ac.uk/scombms/Graceful.

2   Graceful Graphs

A labelling f of the nodes of a graph with q edges is *graceful* if f assigns each node a unique label from $\{0, 1, ..., q\}$ and when each edge xy is labelled with $|f(x) - f(y)|$, the edge labels are all different. Figure 1 shows an example. Gallian [3] surveys graceful graphs, i.e. graphs with a graceful labelling, and lists the graphs whose status is known.

The problem of finding a graceful labelling of a graph can be expressed as a CSP. A possible model, used by Lustig & Puget [8] to find a graceful labelling of $K_4 \times P_2$ (see section 3), has a variable for each node, $x_1, x_2, ..., x_n$, each with domain $\{0, 1, ..., q\}$ and a variable for each edge, $d_1, d_2, ..., d_q$, each with domain $\{1, 2, ..., q\}$. The constraints of the problem are: if edge k joins nodes i and j then $d_k = |x_i - x_j|$; $x_1, x_2, ..., x_n$ are all different; and $d_1, d_2, ..., d_q$ are all different. We treat the allDifferent constraint on the node variables as a set of binary $\neq$ constraints, whereas for the edge variables we use the highest level of propagation provided for the allDifferent constraint in ECL^{i}PS^e. We assign values to the node variables only and use lexicographic variable ordering.

There are two sources of symmetry in the CSP: first, symmetry in the graph. For instance, if the graph is a clique, any permutation of the node labels in a graceful labelling is also graceful, and if the graph is a path, P_n, the node labels can be reversed. Second, we can replace the value of every node variable x_i by its complement $q - x_i$. We can also combine each graph symmetry with the complement symmetry. For instance, the graceful labelling $(0, 3, 1, 2)$ of P_4 has three symmetric equivalents: $(2, 1, 3, 0)$; $(3, 0, 2, 1)$; $(1, 2, 0, 3)$.

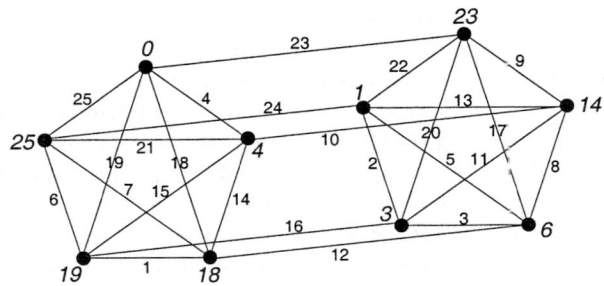

Fig. 1. The unique graceful labelling of $K_5 \times P_2$.

3 $K_m \times P_2$ Graphs

$K_5 \times P_2$, shown in Figure 1, consists of two copies of K_5, with corresponding vertices in the two cliques forming the vertices of a path P_2. The symmetries of $K_5 \times P_2$ are, first, any permutation of the 5-cliques which acts on both in the same way. For instance, if the nodes of the first clique are numbered 1 to 5 and those of the second 6 to 10, we can transpose nodes 1 and 2 and simultaneously 6 and 7. Second, inter-clique symmetry: all the node labels in the first clique can be interchanged with the labels of the adjacent nodes in the second. These can also be combined with each other and with the complement symmetry. Hence, the size of the symmetry group is 5! $\times$ 2 $\times$ 2, or 480. We can eliminate all the symmetry using SBDS, GAP-SBDS or GAP-SBDD; or some of the symmetry can be eliminated instead by adding a constraint to the CSP. We devised several different strategies to use in our comparison:

A: Eliminate all the symmetry (i.e. the full symmetry group of 480 elements).

B: Eliminate only the graph symmetry, and not the complement symmetry (a subgroup of size 240): at worst this will double the number of solutions.

C: Ignoring the complement symmetry, eliminate the inter-clique symmetry by adding a constraint to the CSP that the node labelled 0 is in the first clique. This leaves only the clique permutations (120 elements).

D: In SBDS, use a constraint to break the inter-clique symmetry (as in C). The remaining symmetry allows all permutations of the subsets $\{x_1, x_6\}$, $\{x_2, x_7\}$, $\{x_3, x_8\}$, $\{x_4, x_9\}$ and $\{x_5, x_{10}\}$. This is a generalisation of symmetry due to indistinguishable variables and can be eliminated by just the ten transpositions of the subsets. For instance, one transposition swaps x_1 with x_2 and x_6 with x_7. Strategy D is not possible in GAP-SBDS or GAP-SBDD, because the subset of transpositions is not a group.

These strategies for dealing with symmetry in three instances of the class $K_m \times P_2$ using SBDS, GAP-SBDS and GAP-SBDD are compared in Table 1. GAP-SBDS and GAP-SBDD require the symmetry group of the problem as input. We extended both to simplify this task. Similar GAP code was used to output the symmetry functions required for SBDS from a set of group generators.

There are 4 non-isomorphic graceful labellings of $K_3 \times P_2$ and 15 of $K_4 \times P_2$. $K_5 \times P_2$ has a unique graceful labelling (shown in Figure 1). $K_4 \times P_2$ was shown to be graceful by Lustig & Puget [8] but the number of non-isomorphic graceful labellings and the gracefulness of $K_5 \times P_2$ were not previously known.

We find all graceful labellings, partly because when finding just one solution, symmetry does not always cause wasted effort. However, finding a graceful labelling of $K_5 \times P_2$ with no symmetry breaking takes 30,010 backtracks and 1830 sec., much longer than SBDS, GAP-SBDS or GAP-SBDD take to both find the solution *and* prove that it is unique, when breaking all the symmetry.

In strategy A, SBDS does less search than GAP-SBDS; this seems to be due to lazy evaluation in GAP-SBDS, to delay imposing constraints. However, SBDS is fastest when the number of symmetry functions is smallest (strategy D): increasing the number of symmetry functions severely affects its runtime, even when the number of backtracks is greatly reduced. The speed of GAP-SBDS, on

Table 1. Comparison of different levels of symmetry breaking using SBDS, GAP-SBDS or GAP-SBDD for finding all graceful labellings of $K_m \times P_2$, for $m = 3, 4, 5$. 'bt' is the number of backtracks. The running time is on a 1.6GHz Pentium 4, running ECL^iPS^e.

	$K_3 \times P_2$						$K_4 \times P_2$						$K_5 \times P_2$					
	SBDS		GAP-SBDS		GAP-SBDD		SBDS		GAP-SBDS		GAP-SBDD		SBDS		GAP-SBDS		GAP-SBDD	
	bt	sec.	bt	sec.	bt	sec.	bt	sec.	bt	sec.	bt	sec.	bt	sec.	bt	sec.	bt	sec.
A	6	0.25	9	0.54	22	0.69	147	12.9	165	8.3	496	20.6	4172	1356	4390	382	17977	1310
B	16	0.24	16	0.59	50	1.33	369	13.1	369	14.3	1276	53.6	9889	929	9889	793	51623	3910
C	16	0.21	16	0.58	24	0.63	369	11.0	369	14.1	473	16.5	9889	659	9889	783	11710	859
D	16	0.2	-	-	-	-	369	10.6	-	-	-	-	9889	629	-	-	-	-

the other hand, is much less affected by the number of symmetries, and its best strategy is to break all the symmetry and hence benefit from the reduction in search. For a small number of symmetries (e.g. strategy C) SBDS is faster than GAP-SBDS, since it avoids the overhead of interacting with GAP.

On these problems, GAP-SBDD performs very poorly in comparison to GAP-SBDS. From detailed examination of the search trees, this is because the search variables of the CSP are the node variables, whereas the edge variables cause most constraint propagation. In GAP-SBDD, GAP returns just a boolean to indicate whether the current node is dominated or not, and possibly a list of values to remove from the domains of specified search variables. This successfully breaks the symmetry and prunes the search tree, but provides no information that can propagate to the non-search variables, in this case the edge variables. On the other hand, GAP-SBDS breaks symmetry by posting constraints on backtracking, and these can propagate in the same way as any other constraint.

Because GAP returns limited information to ECL^iPS^e, GAP-SBDD can solve much larger problems than GAP-SBDS, as found by Gent *et al.* in their BIBD experiments [6]. Our results have shown the disadvantage of this reduced communication. CSP models in which only some of the variables are used for search, but constraint propagation over the full set of variables is crucial to solving the problem quickly, are not unusual. It is an important finding that GAP-SBDD performs badly on such a model.

4   Conclusions

We have carried out an experimental investigation of symmetry breaking in graceful graph problems. We have compared three techniques which break symmetry during search, namely SBDS, GAP-SBDS and GAP-SBDD. Experiments with the $K_m \times P_2$ graceful graph problems have confirmed that GAP-SBDS outperforms SBDS when the symmetry group is large. However, for problems with small numbers of symmetries, SBDS will be the better choice.

The limited earlier comparisons of GAP-SBDD and GAP-SBDS suggested that GAP-SBDD can handle much larger symmetry groups than GAP-SBDS. However, we have shown that GAP-SBDD is much worse than GAP-SBDS at solving the graceful graphs problems. We traced its difficulty to a feature of the CSP model: much of the constraint propagation involves non-search variables. Since this happens frequently in CSP models developed by expert modellers, it is a significant drawback to GAP-SBDD.

With good symmetry breaking, constraint programming is a valuable tool for finding graceful labellings of symmetric graphs or proving that they are not graceful. This investigation has produced several new results, and those for $K_m \times P_n$ graphs are included in the latest version of Gallian's survey [3].

Acknowledgments

The authors are members of the APES group (see http://www.dcs.st-and.ac.uk/~apes) and would like to thank the other members, especially Ian Gent for his encouragement and interest. Tom Kelsey and Steve Linton have been very helpful in discussing the implementation of GAP-SBDD. We are also very grateful to Warwick Harvey for his help, including continuing advice and technical assistance with ECL^{i}PS^e. This work was supported by EPSRC grant GR/R29673.

References

1. T. Fahle, S. Schamberger, and M. Sellmann. Symmetry Breaking. In T. Walsh, editor, *Principles and Practice of Constraint Programming - CP 2001*, LNCS 2239, pages 225–239. Springer, 2001.
2. F. Focacci and M. Milano. Global Cut Framework for Removing Symmetries. In T. Walsh, editor, *Principles and Practice of Constraint Programming - CP 2001*, LNCS 2239, pages 77–92. Springer, 2001.
3. J. A. Gallian. A Dynamic Survey of Graph Labeling. *The Electronic Journal of Combinatorics*, (DS6), 2002. http://www.combinatorics.org/Surveys.
4. The GAP Group. *GAP – Groups, Algorithms, and Programming, Version 4.3*, 2002. http://www.gap-system.org.
5. I. P. Gent, W. Harvey, and T. Kelsey. Groups and Constraints: Symmetry Breaking during Search. In P. van Hentenryck, editor, *Principles and Practice of Constraint Programming - CP 2002*, LNCS 2470, pages 415–430. Springer, 2002.
6. I. P. Gent, W. Harvey, T. Kelsey, and S. Linton. Generic SBDD using Computational Group Theory. In F. Rossi, editor, *Principles and Practice of Constraint Programming - CP 2003*, LNCS. Springer, 2003.
7. I. P. Gent and B. M. Smith. Symmetry Breaking During Search in Constraint Programming. In W. Horn, editor, *Proceedings ECAI'2000*, pages 599–603, 2000.
8. I. J. Lustig and J.-F. Puget. Program Does Not Equal Program: Constraint Programming and Its Relationship to Mathematical Programming. *INTERFACES*, 31(6):29–53, 2001.
9. K. E. Petrie and B. M. Smith. Symmetry Breaking in Graceful Graphs. Technical Report APES-56a-2003, APES Research Group, June 2003. Available from http://www.dcs.st-and.ac.uk/~apes/apesreports.html.

Tree Local Search

Nicolas Prcovic

Laboratoire des Sciences de l'Information et des Systèmes (UMR CNRS 6168)
Campus Scientifique de Saint Jérôme, Avenue Escadrile Normandie Niemen
13397 MARSEILLE Cedex 20, France

Abstract. This paper presents Tree Local Search (TLS), a generic algorithm that hybridizes tree and local search methods. It has the following properties: it can filter all its instantiations and allows to freely select the variable whose value changes in case of failure. The primitive version of TLS can be regarded as a Hill-Climbing method that handles filtered instantiations. An extended version generalizes the Backtracking and Min-Conflicts algorithms.

1   Introduction

Tree search (TS) and local search (LS) are two general search approaches for solving CSPs that were often opposed. Roughly, TS tries to prove that a problem is unsatisfiable: almost all the mechanisms associated to TS (filtering, variable ordering) look for a failure as quickly as possible. Hence, finding a solution is only the consequence of the impossibility to prove the unsatisfiability. On the other hand, LS has the only goal to find a solution as quickly as possible without caring about systematicity and completeness. It is obvious that a TS must be used when it is expected that a problem has no solution. Conversely, LS is supposed to be more efficient than TS on problems with many solutions. Now, it is not easy to decide the two approaches when dealing with hard problems with very few solutions. The nature of these problems requires to combine driving quickly the search toward a solution while discarding the unsatisfiable parts of the search space. This is why many propositions to integrate LS satisfiability mechanisms and TS unsatisfiability mechanisms to design hybrid algorithms were experimented until today. According to us, even if the existing hybrid algorithms have practical interests, they are often lacking theoretical foundations. What principles should we follow when designing hybrid algorithms?

2   The Tightest Coupling Property

In the following, we call *variable assignment* the assignment of one variable, *total instantiation* an instantiation of all the variables of the problem, *partial instantiation* an instantiation of a (non-strict) subset of the variables and *terminal instantiation* a partial instantiation which last variable assignment permitted to determine that no solution of the problem can contain this instantiation. A terminal instantiation corresponds to a failure detected by a tree search algorithm.

F. Rossi (Ed.): CP 2003, LNCS 2833, pp. 935–939, 2003.

The two fundamental differences between TS and LS are (1) the type of instantiation (terminal or total) they handle and (2) the way that they generate a successor of the current instantiation. LS has the advantage to be able to change the value of any variable for reaching a solution as quickly as possible. TS can only change the last variable(s) chosen to extend the instantiation. On the other hand, LS only handles total instantiations so its search space size is the product of the domain sizes. TS only handles partial instantiations. Each time a partial instantiation is extended by a variable assignment, it is checked or filtered to determine if it can be extended to obtain a solution. If not, a great number of total instantiations can be eliminated at the same time. The maximum set of instantiations that can be generated by TS can really be smaller than the one of LS. The hybridation of TS and LS has a simple goal: take advantage of both (1) filtering and (2) free selection of the variable whose value changes. Now, how should these two properties be integrated into one algorithm? The tighter the coupling, the more potential has the search to fully exploit the advantages of both TS and LS all along the search. It seems impossible to achieve a tighter coupling between TS and LS than enforcing filtering and free variable selection on every partial instantiation. Actually, as it always seems preferable to extend a consistent partial instantiation than to change the value of one variable already assigned, changing the value of a variable is only needed for terminal instantiations.

Definition 1. *A search algorithm has the* tightest coupling property *if: (1) it filters all its partial instantiations and (2) it allows to freely select the variable whose value changes when a terminal instantiation is generated.*

3   Tree Local Search

As far as we know, no existing hybrid algorithm has the tightest coupling property. We now present a new algorithm that fullfills this property. It is based on Limited Discrepancy Search[1] (LDS), which has a similar property: LDS filters all the instantiations and it can be used to generate the neighborhood of an instantiation.

We call *most promising instantiation*, a total instantiation where all the variables are assigned to the first value selected by the heuristic. It can be regarded as the extension of the current instantiation by assigning the first selected value of their domain to the remaining variables. As the authors of [1] noticed, LDS iteration 1 allows to generate all the instantiations differing by one value from the most promising instantiation. If iteration 1 of ILDS is run without checking the constraints before all the variables are assigned, the set of total instantiations that are generated is equal to the neighborhood (in the common sense used in LS) of the most promising instantiation. To simulate a LS, it suffices to select the best neighbor (e.g., the one that satisfies the greater number of constraints) and make it become the most promising instantiation. This is enforced by changing the value ordering heuristic so that it chooses the values of the best neighbor first. In practice, the domains of the variables are statically ordered before the resolution. When the best neighbor is found, all its values are moved to the first position of the domains (and the other values are shifted to the right). So, we can see that Min-Conflicts[2] (MC) can be simulated by a tree search algorithm that performs successive LDS iteration 1 with domain reordering.

If the constraints are checked each time a partial instantiation is extended during LDS iteration 1, the neighborhood has a different nature but the principle remains the same. The neighborhood is composed of terminal instantiations whose all variable assignments but one belong to the most promising instantiation. The criterion that determines the best neighbor depends on the way the constraints are checked. If the contraints are checked like BT, that is, by checking the compatibility between the last variable assignment and the previous ones, only one variable assignment is the source of conflicts. A first obvious criterion is to select the neighbor that has the greater number of variable assignments: the more variable assignments, the more compatible assignments and the most likely may these assignments take part to a solution. If the constraints are checked through a filtering (e.g. Forward-Checking, MAC), in addition to the number of variable assignment criterion, it is possible to consider the sizes of domains that have not been emptied so as to select a neighbor.

In figure 1 is defined Tree Local Search (TLS), a generic tree search algorithm that performs a Hill-Climbing search while filtering partial instantiations. We call TLS-BT a specific TLS that does no filtering but only checks the compatibility between the last variable assignment and the previous ones, like in the simple Backtracking algorithm (BT)(see figure 2).

4   Extensions of TLS

Even if TLS has the tightest coupling property, it remains rudimentary. It must be seen as the core of an algorithm that requires to be extended and completed to be efficient in practice. We are going to define a generalization of TLS-BT, called TLS-BT(i,k), such that TLS-BT, BT and MC are particular cases of it. To achieve this, we extend the notion of neighborhood so that it captures the one of BT and then we extend the notion of terminal instantiation so that it captures the one of MC.

Definition 2. *Neighborhood of order i*
Let $N(s)$ be the neighborhood of a total instantiation s. $N(s)$ represents all the total instantiations that differs from s by one variable assignment. The extended neighborhood of order i is defined by $N_0(s) = \{s\}$ and $N_{i+1}(s) = \bigcup_{s' \in N_i(s)} N(s')$.

$N_i(s)$ represents all the total instantiations that differs from s by at most i variable assignments. Notice that $N_1(s) = N(s)$ and $N_n(s)$ is the set of all possible total instantiations, when n is the number of variables. The notion of extended neighborhood already appears in [3], where the Variable Neighborhood Search (VNS) is presented. The main idea of VNS is to extend the neighborhood if a local optimum is reached.

```
TLS:
1   min ← ∞;
2   LOOP
3       s ← LDS-iteration1(∅)
4       IF f(s) = 0 THEN return s
5       IF f(s) < min THEN min = f(s)
6                          reorder-domains(s)
7                   ELSE return FAILURE
```

```
LDS-iteration1(s):
1   IF all the variables are assigned THEN return s
2   ELSE
3       s_min ← s; S ← list-of-extentions(s)
4       FOR z ← 1 TO |S|
5           IF NOT inconsistent(S[z]) AND discrepancies(S[z]) ≤ 1 THEN
6               s ← LDS-iteration1(S[z])
7               IF f(s) = 0 THEN RETURN s
8               IF f(s) < f(s_min) THEN s_min ← s
9       RETURN s_min
```

Fig. 1. The Tree Local Search algorithm. The function f evaluates the proximity of terminal instantiations to a solution. When $f(s) = 0$, s is a solution. f may be the count of violated constraints. The function list-of-extentions(s) returns all the possible extensions of a partial instantiation s by choosing a value to assign to the next variable. This function may also filter the domains if a filtering mechanism is wanted in the algorithm. The function inconsistent(s) may just check the compatibility of the last assignment with previous one or check if a domain is empty (if filtering is integrated).

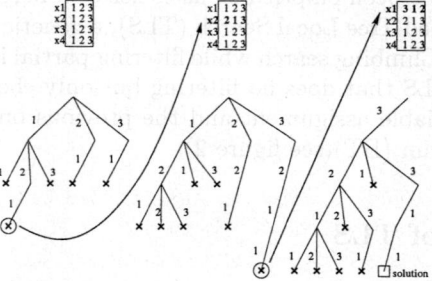

Fig. 2. TLS-BT running on a CSP with 4 variables and domain size equal to 3. The criterion for selecting the best neighbor is the number of assigned variables.

The notion of neighborhood of order i is directly extended to terminal instantiations: the neighborhood of order i of a terminal instantiation s is the set of terminal instantiations generated by the iteration i of LDS (when the values of s are the first of their ordered domains). To obtain an algorithm that generalizes both TLS-BT and BT, it suffices to replace iteration 1 by iteration i, where i is a parameter set before the algorithm is run. If we call this algorithm TLS-BT(i) then we have TLS-BT(1) = TLS-BT and TLS-BT(n) = BT.

We now extend the notion of terminal instantiation so as to find a generalization of TLS-BT and MC. The main difference between these two algorithms is the type of instantiation they handle. We must find an instantiation type more general than the total instantiation type and the terminal instantiation type.

Definition 3. *k-inconsitency. A partial instantiation is said* k-inconsistent *if the number of constraints it violates is greater or equals to* k.

In that context, we call *terminal instantiation* a partial instantiation whose last variable assignment made k-inconsistent or a total instantiation that is not a solution. By replacing the inconsistency check of BT by a k-inconsistency check, we obtain an algorithm generalizing TLS-BT and MC. Instead of backtracking as soon as a constraint is violated, it waits until at least k constraints are violated by the partial instantiation. When setting k to 1, we fall back to TLS-BT. When setting k to $\frac{n(n-1)}{2}$, the maximal number of constraints in a binary CSP with n variables, we fall back to MC. To generalize TLS-BT and MC, in addition to applying a k-inconsistency check, the criterion to compare terminal instantiations must be adapted. The number of violated constraints must be taken into consideration. The criterion of comparison that we propose is the following. A terminal instantiation is better than another one if it has assigned more variables or if it has assigned as much variables but has violated fewer constraints. This criterion is more general than the ones of TLS-BT and MC. If $k = 1$, k-inconsistency is just the usual inconsistency because an instantiation is terminal as soon as it violates one constraint. If $k = \frac{n(n-1)}{2}$, only total instantiations may be k-inconsistent, so the instantiation can only be selected thanks to the number of violated constraints, just like with MC. By integrating both the extended neighborhood of order i and the k-inconsistency check into TLS-BT, we obtain the TLS-BT(i,k) algorithm that generalizes TLS-BT, BT and MC.

5 Conclusion and Perspectives

The primitive procedure of TLS has been generalized to obtain TLS-BT(i,k), so as to generalize also Min-Conflicts and Backtracking, the basic search methods of local search and tree search. Tuning the parameters i and k makes TLS-BT(i,k) smoothly increase or decrease the size and the composition of the instantiation neighborhoods. As a more general algorithm than BT and MC, appropriate settings of TLS-BT(i,k) guarantees an efficiency at least as good as BT or MC. The nature of TLS-BT(i,k) should allow to extend it easilly to generalize efficient widely-used local search and tree search algorithms such as Forward-Checking, MAC, VNS, Tabu Search and many others. TLS has the potential to integrate the latest refinements of filtering procedures and mechanisms for escaping a local optimum. Future experiments on such more sophisticated variants of TLS will show how they compete with the best search methods.

References

1. W. D. Harvey and M. L. Ginsberg. Limited Discrepancy Search. In *Proceedings of 14th International Joint Conference on Artificial Intelligence*, pages 607–613, 1995.
2. S. Minton, M. Johnston, A. Philips, and P. Laird. Minimizing conflicts: a heuristic repair method for constraint satisfaction and scheduling problems. *Artificial Intelligence*, 58:160–205, 1992.
3. N. Mladenovic and P. Hansen. Variable neighborhood search. *Computers and Operation Research*, 24:1097–1100, 1997.

A SAT-Based Approach
to Multiple Sequence Alignment

Steven Prestwich[1], Des Higgins[2], and Orla O'Sullivan[2]

[1] Cork Constraint Computation Centre
[2] Department of Biochemistry,
University College, Cork, Ireland

Abstract. Multiple sequence alignment is a central problem in Bioinformatics. A known integer programming approach is to apply branch-and-cut to exponentially large graph-theoretic models. This paper describes a new integer program formulation that generates models small enough to be passed to generic solvers. The formulation is a hybrid relating the sparse alignment graph with a compact encoding of the alignment matrix via channelling constraints. Alignments obtained with a SAT-based local search algorithm are competitive with those of state-of-the-art algorithms, though execution times are much longer.

1   Background

Multiple sequence alignment (MSA) is a central problem in Bioinformatics and is known to be NP-complete [3]. Given a number of sequences of symbols from an alphabet, the aim is to align them while maximizing some function. Gaps may be introduced between symbols, and in some MSA formulations the objective function includes a measure of the number and length of gaps. A common data structure is the *alignment matrix* which contains one sequence per row, including gaps; aligned symbols occur in the same column.

Numerous heuristic methods have been proposed for multiple alignment, of which by far the most widely used is *progressive alignment*. This involves clustering the sequences first to give a guide tree and then building up the alignment gradually, following the branching order in the guide tree. This is very fast even for hundreds of sequences, and the most widely used software is the well-known ClustalW package [11]. The T-Coffee package [8] also uses a progressive heuristic but has been shown to be more accurate than ClustalW, at the expense of extra computing time. There are also several methods based on optimising the WSP (weighted sums of pairs) objective function which use Genetic Algorithms [7] or iteration [2]. These vary in the extent to which they are practical for more than a few sequences or in the quality of the optimisation.

Dynamic programming [6] has been used for MSA problems but is known to scale poorly to more than a few sequences. More successful is the *Complete Maximum Weight Trace* (CMWT) formulation in which the symbols are viewed as vertices in an *alignment graph* $G = (V, E)$ (actually an *extended* graph that includes edges between adjacent symbols in each sequence). Each vertex is a position i in sequence j, which we shall denote by (i, j). Each edge connects two vertices from different sequences. Each edge

F. Rossi (Ed.): CP 2003, LNCS 2833, pp. 940–944, 2003.

$e \in E$ has a *weight* w_e representing the usefulness of aligning its two symbols. An alignment *realises* an edge if it aligns its two symbols, and the aim is to maximize the sum of the weights of the realised edges. The set of realised edges is a *trace* if certain constraints are satisfied, and an alignment matrix can always be constructed from a trace.

The CMWT generates large models which can be reduced by using the *Sparse Maximum Weight Trace* (MWT) formulation. This restricts attention to a carefully chosen subgraph, defining only those edges that are used in pairwise alignments of high quality. Besides reducing the size of the models, the MWT provides an opportunity to input biological knowledge via the choice of subgraph. The usual way of ensuring that the realised edges form a valid trace is to enumerate all *critical mixed cycles* in the graph, adding a constraint to prohibit each cycle [1, 4, 10] (other constraints may also be added). The MWT and related formulations have natural integer linear program (ILP) models. The number of constraints is exponential in the size $|E|$ of the graph [1] but these are not passed en masse to a solver. Instead a branch-and-cut approach is used, generating violated constraints as required in order to derive cutting planes. Generating the relevant constraints is known as the *separation problem* and can be done in polynomial time.

We explore an alternative ILP approach to the MSA. Instead of accessing an exponentially large model in polynomial time, we use a model with a polynomial number of constraints that can be passed to a generic solver. To avoid the use of cycle constraints we model the alignment matrix directly, and relate it to the sparse alignment graph by channelling constraints. Instead of applying branch-and-cut we transform the model to pseudo-Boolean form and pass it to a SAT-based local search algorithm.

2   A Hybrid 0/1 Model

As in the MWT define a binary variable v_e for each edge $e \in E$. The problem is then to maximize $\sum_{e \in E} w_e v_e$ subject to constraints ensuring the construction of an alignment matrix. The matrix has n rows (one per sequence) and c columns where $c \geq \max_j(l_j)$ and l_j is the length of sequence j. We allow each sequence position to be placed anywhere in the corresponding row of the matrix, subject to constraints. We denote an edge $e \in E$ between (i, j) and (i', j') by $e = ((i, j), (i', j'))$ where $j < j'$ by convention. A matrix entry with no sequence position placed in it implicitly contains a gap. The symbols are not explicitly modelled, only the way in which sequence positions are mapped to matrix columns. Let $b = \lceil \log_2 c \rceil$ so that the c matrix columns can be represented using b bits. Define 0/1 variables p_{ijk} where $1 \leq j \leq n$, $1 \leq i \leq l_j$ and $1 \leq k \leq b$. Then $1 + \sum_{k=1}^{b} 2^{k-1} p_{ijk}$ denotes the matrix column of symbol (i, j). There are two sets of constraints. To ensure that sequence positions are placed in the alignment matrix in an ordered way, add *ordering constraints* $\sum_{k=1}^{b} 2^{k-1}(p_{ijk} - p_{i'jk}) \geq i - i'$ where $1 \leq j \leq n$ and $1 \leq i' < i \leq l_j$. To relate the p_{ijk} and v_e variables add *channelling constraints*

$$(v_e = 1) \rightarrow \left(\sum_{k=1}^{b} 2^{k-1} p_{ijk} = \sum_{k=1}^{b} 2^{k-1} p_{i'j'k} \right)$$

where $e = ((i, j), (i', j')) \in E$, which can be implemented by the linear constraints $p_{ijk} - p_{i'j'k} + v_e \leq 1$ and $p_{i'j'k} - p_{ijk} + v_e \leq 1$ where $1 \leq k \leq b$ and $e =$

$((i, j), (i', j')) \in E$. A motivation for the model was to avoid the exponential number of constraints in the MWT, and it can be shown that it has space complexity $O(nm^2 \log m)$.

3   Experiments

We reduce an MSA optimisation problem to a series of CSPs, each with a cost constraint $\sum_{e \in E} w_e v_e > W$ for some integer lower bound W. The CSPs have increasing values of W, each being the weight of the previous solution, and the initial bound W_0 is 0. Each CSP is solved by transforming it to linear pseudo-Boolean form, which contains only constraints $\sum_i w_i l_i \geq d$ where the weights w_i and the constant d are positive integers, and the literals l are either variables v or their negations $\bar{v} = 1 - v$. The interest of this form is that it is only a slight extension of SAT, and many SAT algorithms generalise easily to it. We apply the Saturn hybrid local search algorithm, which was generalised in [9] and gave good results on block design and sports scheduling problems. Saturn uses each solution as a starting point for the next CSP, by reassigning as many variables as possible (under a random variable ordering, without violating any constraints). On solving the final CSP an alignment matrix is constructed, then post-processed by applying simple transformations to reduce the number of columns used.

We take MSA instances from the HOMSTRAD [5] database of protein alignments. We generate sparse alignment graphs using T-Coffee with default settings. It takes every pair of sequences and outputs weighted pairs of symbols, aligning each pair of sequences using dynamic programming and recording all of the pairs of aligned symbols. The weights are simply the percent identity of the parent sequences for each pair. We measure the accuracy of our results by counting the percentage of columns in the alignment matrix that are identical with reference alignments, which are automatically derived by comparing the 3-dimensional structures of the proteins. These alignments are not guaranteed to be optimal but are of high quality. This is a measure commonly used by working biologists; though trace weight is the measure being optimised, there is only an approximate correspondence between weight and alignment quality, partly because of some arbitrariness in the weights assigned to the alignment graph edges.

We first applied Saturn to four fairly small problems: ChtBD is a family of chitin binding domains which are structural proteins in plant cells, hla consists of a group of histocompatibility proteins involved in the immune system, TIG contains a group of glucanotransferases which are involved in metabolism, and ch is a family of calponin homology domain proteins which are involved in actin binding in the cell. These have between 4 and 6 similar sequences of between 43 and 178 residues, apart from ch which has 4 very dissimilar sequences. In each case Saturn finds the same solutions as ClustalW and T-Coffee in a few minutes, except for ch where it finds a less optimal solution.

Next we applied Saturn to two larger problems. Firstly the mmp problem is a family of matrix metalloproteineases which are important proteins in the cytoskeleton of the cell. It has 6 sequences, 55% identical to each other, and an average length of 164 residues. The model has 6723 v_e variables, 7872 p_{ijk} variables, 80311 ordering constraints and 107569 channelling constraints. The alignment found by Saturn is 95.5% correct, equalling that found by T-Coffee, while ClustalW's alignment is 92.4% correct. Secondly the oxidored_q6 problem is a family of NADH ubiquinone oxidoreductases,

```
---KHRPSVVWLHNAECTGCTEAAIRTIKPYIDALILDTISLDYQETIMAAAGETSEAAL
---KKRPSVVYLHNAECTGCSESVLRTVDPYVDELILDVISMDYHETLMAGAGHAVEEAL
----SRPSVVYLHAAECTGCSEALLRTYQPFIDTLILDTISLDYHETIMAAAGEAAEEAL
LMGPRRPSVVYLHNAECTGCSESVLRAFEPYIDTLILDTLSLDYHETIMAAAGDAAEEAL
----KKAPVIWVQGQGCTGCSVSLLNAVHPRIKEILLDVISLEFHPTVMASEGEMALAHM

HEALEGKDG-YYLVVEGGLPTIDGGQWGMVAG-------HPMIETCKKAAAKAKGIICIG
HEAIKGD---FVCVIEGGIPMGDGGYWGKVGG-------RNMYDICAEVAPKAKAVIAIG
QAAVNGPDG-FICLVEGAIPTGMDNKYGYIAG-------HTMYDICKNILPKAKAVVSIG
EQAVNSPHG-FIAVVEGGIPTAANGIYGKVAN-------HTMLDICSRILPKAQAVIAYG
YEIAEKFNGNFFLLVEGAIPTAKEGRYCIVGEAKAHHHEVTMMELIRDLAPKSLATVAVG

TCSPYGGVQKAKPNPSQAKGVSEAL---G--VKTINIPGCPPNPINFVGAVVHVLT----
TCATYGGVQAAKPNPTGTVGVNEALGKLG--VKAINIAGCPPNPMNFVGTVVHLLT----
TCACYGGIQAAKPNPTAAKGINDCYADLG--VKAINVPGCPPNPLNMVGTLVAFLK----
TCATFGGVQAAKPNPTGAKGVNDALKHLG--VKAINIAGCPPNPYNLVGTIVYYLKN---
TCSAYGGIPAAEGNVTGSKSVRDFFADEKIEKLLVNVPGCPPHPDWMVGTLVAAWSHVLN

K---GIPDLDENGRPKLFYGELVHDNCPRLPHFEASEFAPSFDSEEAKKGFCLYELGCKG
K---GMPELDKQGRPVMFFGETVHDNCPRLKHFEAGEFATSFGSPEAKKGYCLYELGCKG
G---QKIELDEVGRPVMFFGQSVHDLCERRKHFDAGEFAPSFNSEEARKGWCLYDVGCKG
K---AAPELDSLNRPTMFFGQTVHEQCPRLPHFDAGEFAPSFESEEARKGWCLYELGCKG
PTEHPLPELDDDGRPLLFFGDNIHENCPYLDKYDNSEFAETFTK-----PGCKAELGCKG

PVTYNNCPKVLFNQ-VNWPVQAGHPCLGCSEPDFWDTMTPFYEQG
PDTYNNCPKQLFNQ-VNWPVQAGHPCIACSEPNFWDLYSPFYSA-
PETYNNCPKVLFNE-TNWPVAAGHPCIGCSEPNFWDDMTPFYQN-
PVTMNNCPKIKFNQ-TNWPVDAGHPCIGCSEPDFWDAMTPFYQN-
PSTYADCAKRRWNNGINWCVEN-AVCIGCVEPDFPDGKSPFYVAE
```

Fig. 1. Saturn alignment for the oxidored_q6 problem.

which are enzymatic proteins involved in the Citric Acid Cycle in the cell. This has 5 sequences, 57% identical to each other, and an average length of 265 residues. The model has 4563 v_e variables, 11934 p_{ijk} variables, 175237 ordering constraints and 82135 channelling constraints. The alignment found by Saturn is shown in Figure 1. It is 98.7% correct, ClustalW's is 97.3%, and T-Coffee's 95.5%. Thus on these problems the pseudo-Boolean approach is competitive with ClustalW and T-Coffee in terms of solution quality. It is far slower, taking tens of minutes as opposed to seconds or less, but these are promising first results. In future work we hope to improve the results by generalising Saturn to handle non-binary domains, to avoid the use of binary representations for matrix columns.

Acknowledgment

This work was supported in part by the Boole Centre for Research in Informatics, University College, Cork, Ireland, and from Science Foundation Ireland under Grant

00/PI.1/C075. Orla O'Sullivan was paid from a Basic Research grant from Enterprise Ireland to D. Higgins.

References

1. E. Althaus, A. Caprara, H.-P. Lenhof, K. Reinert. Multiple Sequence Alignment With Arbitrary Gap Costs: Computing an Optimal Solution Using Polyhedral Combinatorics. *Bioinformatics* Suppl 2:S4–S16.
2. O. Gotoh. Significant Improvement in Accuracy of Multiple Protein Sequence Alignments by Iterative Refinement as Assessed by Reference to Structural Alignments. *Journal of Molecular Biology* vol. 264, 1996, pp. 823–838.
3. J. D. Kececioglu. Exact and Approximation Algorithms for DNA Sequence Reconstruction. PhD thesis, University of Arizona, 1991.
4. J. D. Kececioglu, H.-P. Lenhof, K. Mehlhorn, P. Mutzel, K. Reinert, M. Vingron. A Polyhedral Approach to Sequence Alignment Problems. *Discrete Applied Mathematics* vol. 104, 2000, pp. 143–186.
5. K. Mizuguchi, C. M. Deane, T. L. Blundell, J. P. Overington. HOMSTRAD: A Database of Protein Structure Alignments for Homologous Families. *Protein Science* vol. 7, 1998, pp. 2469–2471.
6. S. B. Needleman, C. D. Wunsch. A General Method Applicable to the Search of Similarities in the Amino Acid Sequences of Two Proteins. *Journal of Molecular Biology* vol. 48, 1970, pp. 443–453.
7. C. Notredame, D. G. Higgins. SAGA: Sequence Alignment by Genetic Algorithm. *Nucleic Acids Research* vol. 2, 1996, pp. 1515–1524.
8. C. Notredame, D. G. Higgins, J. Heringa. T-COFFEE: A Novel Method for Fast and Accurate Multiple Sequence Alignment. *Journal of Molecular Biology* vol. 302, 2000, pp. 205–217.
9. S. D. Prestwich. Randomised Backtracking for Linear Pseudo-Boolean Constraint Problems. *Fourth International Workshop on Integration of AI and OR techniques in Constraint Programming for Combinatorial Optimisation Problems*, le Croisic, France, 2002, pp. 7–20.
10. K. Reinert, H.-P. Lenhof, P. Mutzel, K. Mehlhorn, J. Kececioglu. A Branch-and-Cut Algorithm for Multiple Sequence Alignment. *First Annual International Conference on Computational Molecular Biology*, 1997, pp. 241–249.
11. J. D. Thompson, D. G. Higgins, T. J. Gibson. CLUSTAL W: Improving the Sensitivity of Progressive Multiple Sequence Alignment Through Sequence Weighting, Position-Specific Gap Penalties and Weight Matrix Choice. *Nucleic Acids Research* vol. 22, 1994, pp. 4673–80.

Maintaining Dominance Consistency

Igor Razgon and Amnon Meisels

Department of Computer Science
Ben-Gurion University of the Negev
Beer-Sheva, 84-105, Israel
{irazgon,am}@cs.bgu.ac.il

Abstract. A new type of local consistency is presented. The local consistency is based on pruning "by analogy" and can be associated with symmetry breaking via dominance detection and interchangeability methods. We present an algorithm for achieving the local consistency and show how it can be combined with forward checking.

1 Introduction

The paper presents a new type of local consistency. Algorithms that achieve the local consistency use pruning "by analogy". The idea of pruning can be associated with symmetry breaking via dominance detection [1,2] and interchangeability methods [3,4].

Every node of the search tree can be associated with a constraint network (CN). The present paper demonstrates possibility of pruning when a part of the CN associated with the current node is equal to a part of the CN associated with some dead-end. The result of the pruning is either rejection of the current node of the search tree or filtering of domains of the CN associated with the node.

We introduce a concept of k-dominance ($k \geq 0$). If a CN X_1 is k-dominated by an unsolvable CN X_2, X_1 is either unsolvable (if $k = 0$) or additional constraints of arity k can be imposed on X_1 (if $k > 0$). Next, the notion of k-dominance consistency is introduced. A CN X is k-dominance consistent with a set S of unsolvable CNs, if it is not i-dominated ($0 \leq i \leq k$) by any CN of S.

The present paper concentrates on 1-dominance consistency. The reason is that achieving 1-dominance consistency allows direct filtering of domains following the unary constraints imposed. On other side, constraints of arity two and more are not added, therefore the structure of the processed CN is not changed.

The rest of the paper is organized as follows. Section 2 provides the necessary background. Section 3 defines k-dominance consistency and provides an algorithm for achieving 1-dominance consistency. Section 4 provides methods for maintaining 1-dominance consistency combined with Forward Checking (FC). Section 5 briefly describes experimental evaluations.

2 Preliminaries

Definition 1. *A binary constraint network (CN) is a triple (Z,D,C), where Z is a set of variables, D is a set of domains, C is a set of binary constraints. For*

F. Rossi (Ed.): CP 2003, LNCS 2833, pp. 945–949, 2003.

every variable $v \in Z$, $D_v \in D$ *contains the set of values, that can be assigned to* v. *For every pair of variables* v, u, $C_{v,u} \in C$ *is a subset of the Cartesian product of* D_v *and* D_u *that contains all compatible pairs of assignments of variables* u *and* v [1].

Let X be a CN. Then $Z(X)$ is the set of variables of X, $D(X)$ is the set of domains of all variables of X and $C(X)$ is the set of constraints of X. The domain of v is denoted by $D(X)_v$ and the constraint between variables v and u is $C(X)_{v,u}$. To emphasize that val is a value of the domain of a variable V, denote it by $val(V)$. If a variable V is assigned with a value $val(V)$, the assignment is denoted by $\langle V, val \rangle$.

Definition 2. *Let X be a CN. A set of assignments*
$P = \{\langle V_1, val_1 \rangle, \langle V_2, val_2 \rangle, \ldots, \langle V_m, val_m \rangle\}$ *to different variables of $Z(X)$ is a partial solution of X if for every i, k, $1 \le i, k \le m$, $(\langle V_i, val_i \rangle, \langle V_k, val_k \rangle)$ satisfies* $C(X)_{V_i, V_k}$.

Let P be a partial solution, then $Vars(P)$ denotes the set of variables assigned in P, for every $V \in Vars(P)$, $P(V)$ denotes the assignment of V in P.

Given a CN X. To solve CSP is to find a partial solution that assigns all the variables of $Z(X)$.

Definition 3. *Let X be a CN. A nogood of X is a partial solution of X that cannot be extended into a solution of X.*

Definition 4. *Let X be a CN. Let Var be a subset of $Z(X)$. The projection of X to Var is a CN X' such that $Z(X') = Var$, for every $V \in Z(X')$, $D(X')_V = D(X)_V$, $C(X') = C(X)$. The projection of X to Var is denoted by X^{Var}.*

3   Dominance Consistency

Definition 5. *X' is a subnetwork of a CN X if the following conditions hold: $Z(X') \subseteq Z(X)$, for every $v \in Z(X')$ $D(X')_v \subseteq D(X)_v$, a pair of assignments satisfies $C(X')$ if and only if it satisfies $C(X)$.*

Definition 6. *Two CNs X_1 and X_2 are coordinated if for every $V, V' \in Z(X_1) \cap Z(X_2)$ and for every $val \in D(V)_{X_1} \cap D(V)_{X_2}$ and every $val' \in D(V')_{X_1} \cap D(V')_{X_2}$, $\langle V, val \rangle$ and $\langle V', val' \rangle$ are compatible in X_1 if and only if they are compatible in X_2.*

Let us now define the concept of k-dominance consistency.

Definition 7. *Let X_1 and X_2 be 2 coordinated CNs, such that $Z(X_2) \subseteq Z(X_1)$, and there are k variables of $Z(X_1) \cap Z(X_2)$ whose domains in X_1 are not contained in their domains in X_2 (variables distinguishing X_1 from X_2). We say that X_1 is k-dominated by X_2.*

---

[1] It is assumed that constraints are symmetric, that is $C_{v,u} = C_{u,v}$ for every pair of variables u and v.

Definition 8. *Let X be a CN. Let $F = \{X_1, \ldots, X_l\}$ be a set of unsolvable CNs coordinated with X such that for every $X_i \in F$, $Z(X_i) \subseteq Z(X)$. We call F a filtering set of X.*

Definition 9. *Let X be a CN, and let F be a filtering set of X. X is k-dominance consistent with F if for any i, $0 \leq i \leq k$, X is not i-dominated by any CN of F. If X is not k-dominance consistent with F, we say that X is k-dominated by F.*

Special cases of k-dominance consistency are 0 and 1-dominance consistencies. If a CN X is 0-dominated by a filtering set F, then X is unsolvable. If X is 1-dominated by F then it is possible to filter domains of X without loosing a solution. The process of filtering domains in this manner can be termed achieving 1-dominance consistency. Algorithm 1 describes a simple procedure for achieving 1-dominance consistency.

Algorithm 1 ACHIEVING 1-DOMINANCE CONSISTENCY

1: **repeat**
2:    **for** every $X_i \in F$ **do**
3:       **if** X is dominated by X_i **then**
4:          Report the unsolvability of X
5:          Stop
6:       **end if**
7:       **if** X is 1-dominated by X_i **then**
8:          Let V be the variable distinguishing X from X_i
9:          $D(X)_V \leftarrow D(X)_V \setminus D(X_i)_V$
10:          **if** The domain of V is empty **then**
11:             Report the unsolvability of X
12:             Stop
13:          **end if**
14:       **end if**
15:    **end for**
16: **until** No value is removed from any domain during the last iteration

---

4   Maintaining 1-Dominance Consistency for Forward Checking

Definition 10. *Let P be a partial solution of a CN X. The subnetwork X_P of X induced by P is defined as follows. $Z(X_P) = Z(X) \setminus Vars(P)$. For every $v \in Z(X_P)$, $D(X_P)_v$ contains the set of all values of $D(X)_v$ that are compatible with assignments in P of all variables of $Vars(P) \cap Z(X)$.*

The execution of forward checking (FC) can be represented as a sequence of states. Every state contains the *current partial solution* and the *current CN*. Let

P be the current partial solution at some state of FC while processing a CN X. Then the current CN equals X_P.

FC immediately rejects P if X_P contains a variable with the empty domain. Otherwise, FC tries to extend P. We propose a combination of FC with maintaining of 1-dominance consistency. The combination is called FC-DC. For every visited P such that X_P is not empty, FC-DC constructs a filtering set FS. Then 1-dominance consistency of X_P with FS is achieved. Performing 1-dominance consistency, FC-DC can filter domains of the current CN or even reject P. Algorithm 2 presents a procedure for construction of FS.

Algorithm 2 CONSTRUCTION OF A FILTERING SET

1: $FS \leftarrow \emptyset$
2: **for** every $V \in Vars(P)$ **do**
3:    Let P' be a subset of P containing variables assigned before V
4:    Let P'' be a subset of P containing variables assigned after V
5:    **for** every $val(V)$ eliminated from the current domain of V **do**
6:       **if** $val(V)$ is compatible with all assignments of P' and P'' **then**
7:          $X' \leftarrow X_{P' \cup \{\langle V, val \rangle\}}$
8:          $X'' \leftarrow X'_{P''}$
9:          $FS \leftarrow FS \cup \{X''\}$
10:       **end if**
11:    **end for**
12: **end for**

The filtering set generated by Algorithm 2 contains CNs induced by a set of nogoods of X. The set of nogoods is obtained using values eliminated from current domains of assigned variables. Given an assigned variable V. A set P' generated in line 3 of the algorithm is the subset of the current partial solution containing all variables assigned before V. Then for every $val(V)$ eliminated from the current domain of V, if $val(V)$ is compatible with all assignments of P' then $P' \cup \{\langle V, val \rangle\}$ is a nogood. Therefore, a CN X' generated in line 7 of the algorithm is unsolvable. However, X' still cannot be inserted into FS as X' can contain variables that are not in X_P. Obtaining X'', the algorithm removes these redundant variables.

Proposition 1. *Let X be a CN and let $FS = \{X_1, \ldots, X_m\}$ be a filtering set of X. Let $FS' = \{X'_1, \ldots, X'_m\}$ be a set of constraints such that X'_i is an unsolvable projection of X_i. Then FS' is a filtering set of X. Moreover, if X is 1-dominated by FS then it is 1-dominated by FS'.*

Proposition 1 suggests that replacing in Algorithm 2 the CN X' by its unsolvable projection increases the filtering ability of maintaining 1-dominance consistency.

We describe a procedure that constructs for $val(V)$ a set S of variables such that $(X')^S$ is unsolvable. We call S a responsibility set of $val(V)$. The set is constructed at the moment when $val(V)$ is being eliminated from the current domain of V. If V is unassigned and $val(V)$ is incompatible with the last assignment of the current partial solution then S is empty. Otherwise, $\langle V, val \rangle$ is itself the last assignment of the current partial solution. In this case, there must be an unassigned variable V' with the empty current domain. Let $S_1 \ldots S_l$ be the responsibility sets associated with the eliminated values of V'. Then S is set to $\bigcup_i S_i$.

Note that if at least one value of V' was deleted because achieving of 1-dominance consistency, the method cannot be applied and S is set to $Vars(X')$.

The method for obtaining responsibility sets is strongly related to the reasoning reusing method proposed by T.Schiex [5]. Instead of acquiring a set of constraints responsible for elimination of a value, we take the set of unassigned variables participating in these constraints.

5   Preliminary Evaluations

The proposed method of local consistency maintenance was evaluated on a set of CNs generated randomly given their density p_1 and tightness p_2. All CNs contained 25 variables and every variable had the domain of size 5. For every value of p_1 we took the value of p_2 that is close to the phase transition region.

We compared the pure FC with FC computing responsibility sets and maintaining 1-dominance consistency (FCR-DC). FCR-DC visits less nodes than FC for all tried values of p_1. FCR-DC performs better than FC in the number of consistency checks for $0.1 \leq p_1 \leq 0.5$ (even in orders of magnitude better for $p_1 = 0.1$). For $p_1 > 0.5$, FCR-DC performs more consistency checks than FC.

References

1. T. Fahle, S. Schamberger, and M. Sellmann. Symmetry breaking. In *CP2001*, pages 93–108. Springer, November 2001.
2. F. Focacci and M. Milano. Global cut framework for removing symmetries. In *CP2001*, pages 93–108. Springer, November 2001.
3. E.C. Freuder. Eliminating interchangeable values in constraint satisfaction problems. In *AAAI 91*, pages 227–233, 1991.
4. A. Haselbock. Exploiting interchangeabilities in constraint satisfaction problems. In *IJCAI 93*, pages 282–287, 1993.
5. T. Schiex and G. Verfaillie. Two approaches to the solution maintenance problem in dynamic constraint satisfaction problems, 1993.

Terminating Decision Algorithms Optimally

Tuomas Sandholm

Computer Science Department
Carnegie Mellon University
Pittsburgh PA 15213
sandholm@cs.cmu.edu

Abstract. Incomplete decision algorithms can often solve larger problem instances than complete ones. The drawback is that one does not know whether the algorithm will finish soon, later, or never. This paper presents a general decision-theoretic method for optimally terminating such algorithms. The stopping policy is computed based on a prior probability of the answer, a payoff model describing the value that different probability estimates would provide at different times, and the algorithm's run-time distribution. We present a linear-time algorithm for determining the optimal stopping policy given a finite cap on the number of algorithm steps. To increase accuracy, the initial satisfiability probability and the run-time distribution are conditioned on features of the instance. The expectation of the result at each future time step is computed using Bayesian updating. We then extend the framework to settings where no exogenous cap is given on the number of algorithm steps. The method also provides a normative basis for algorithm selection. Finally, our method can be used to terminate and/or select complete algorithms optimally as well[1],[2].

1 Introduction

Decision problems are problems where the answer is either yes (Y) or no (N). Such problems are central to computer science and ubiquitous in the world. A *decision algorithm* is an algorithm that determines the answer to such a problem. A *complete decision algorithm* is a decision algorithm that always gives the answer in finite time. An *incomplete decision algorithm* never finishes if the answer is N, and may or may not finish if the answer is Y. So, if such an algorithm finishes, the answer is Y.

Incomplete algorithms are important because they can often solve significantly larger problem instances than complete algorithms. Commonly the user of an incomplete algorithm initiates its execution, and after a while gets tired of waiting for a solution. She may be tempted to terminate the algorithm. At the same time she knows that the algorithm might finish, and that this might occur even in the very next step. Should she terminate the algorithm?

This paper presents a method for optimally determining when the algorithm should be terminated if it has not found a solution. The key observation is that

---

[1] A short, very tentative version of this paper appeared in a workshop [3].
[2] This material is based upon work supported by the NSF under CAREER Award IRI-9703122, Grant IIS-9800994, ITR IIS-0081246, and ITR IIS-0121678.

F. Rossi (Ed.): CP 2003, LNCS 2833, pp. 950–955, 2003.
© Springer-Verlag Berlin Heidelberg 2003

incomplete algorithms are iterative refinement algorithms and approximation algorithms in that over time they implicitly refine a probability estimate that a solution exists. Let us define the following symbols:

$SOL_t =$"Solution found by time t" (so, if a solution is found at time t, then $SOL_{t'} = 1$ for all $t' \geq t$), and

$NOSOL_t =$"No solution found by time t".

The iterative refinement algorithm emerges when we realize that the probability of the answer being Y decreases with the number of steps that the algorithm has executed (unless the algorithm halts which guarantees that the answer is Y). This probability, $p(Y|NOSOL_t)$, can be computed using a statistical performance profile, $p(SOL_t|Y)$, of the algorithm, i.e., the probability of finding a solution by time t given that a solution exists. The performance profile can be constructed from prior runs of the algorithm as we will describe.

2   Method for Terminating Decision Algorithms

This section presents a method for optimally terminating an incomplete decision algorithm. The incomplete algorithm is used to update the probability estimate of the answer being Y. Based on a run-time distribution of the algorithm, an agent can anticipate how this estimate will change as more time is allocated to the algorithm. The agent can also anticipate its expected payoff in the real world given that it will act based on the probability estimate available at the time of action (the probability will be 1 if the algorithm happens to find a solution). Using this information, the agent can calculate the optimal time to terminate the algorithm.

Terminating optimally seems difficult because all of the following concerns have to be taken into account:

- Further computation adds value because it can cause the algorithm to find a solution. This is nontrivial to analyze because the probability of finding a solution at a given future time step changes based on how many unsuccessful steps the algorithm has executed. For example, at step 0, step 905 may look unprofitable while at step 708, step 905 may well look profitable. Alternatively, at step 0, step 905 may look profitable while at step 708, step 905 may look unprofitable.
- Further computation adds value because it refines the probability that a solution exists even if the algorithm does not terminate. The probability that a solution exists decreases as the algorithm takes unsuccessful steps.
- As this probability estimate gets refined, it can be used to make future termination/continuation decisions. Therefore, these decisions can be made with better information than what is available at the outset. The fact that such new information is valuable due to this reason is yet another motivation to execute the algorithm further.
- The payoff from a given probability estimate that a solution exists (this probability is 1 if a solution has been found) decreases with time because the agent misses the opportunities of using the answer earlier in the agent's choice of what to do in the world.
- Further computation adds to the computational cost.
- If the deliberation controller has let the algorithm execute past the optimal termination time, it can be optimal to let it execute even further since the losses incurred so far have become sunk cost.
- In some cases, the agent's expected payoff is maximized by never terminating the algorithm (unless the algorithm finishes, i.e., determines that the answer is Y).

It turns out that all of these factors can be soundly taken into account. The method that we present does this in a Bayesian framework and leads to an optimal termination decision. Specifically, the problem is that of finding an optimal policy for the deliberation controller, i.e., deciding what the agent should do in each of the max nodes in Figure 1.

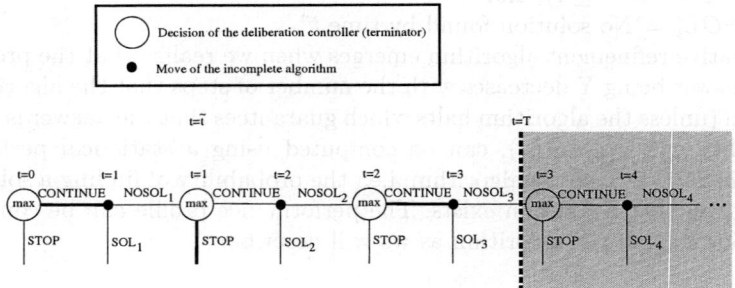

Fig. 1. Deliberation controller's decision tree. The bold lines show an example policy where the deliberation controller will terminate the algorithm at time $t = \tilde{t} = 1$ if the algorithm has not found a solution.

2.1 Conditional Performance Profiles: Probability Updates Using a Run-Time Distribution

To determine when to terminate, the deliberation controller needs to know how the probability of finding a solution by any given time changes based on how many steps the algorithm has executed so far without finding a solution. Let τ_1 and τ_2 be arbitrary times such that $\tau_1 \leq \tau_2$. We are interested in determining the quantity $p(SOL_{\tau_2}|NOSOL_{\tau_1})$. Trivially,

$$p(SOL_{\tau_2}|NOSOL_{\tau_1}) = 1 - p(NOSOL_{\tau_2}|NOSOL_{\tau_1}) \tag{1}$$

The right hand side can be solved using the definition of conditional probability:

$$p(NOSOL_{\tau_2}|NOSOL_{\tau_1}) = \frac{p(NOSOL_{\tau_2} \wedge NOSOL_{\tau_1})}{p(NOSOL_{\tau_1})} \tag{2}$$

Because $p(NOSOL_{\tau_2} \wedge NOSOL_{\tau_1}) = p(NOSOL_{\tau_2})$, this can be simplified to

$$p(NOSOL_{\tau_2}|NOSOL_{\tau_1}) = \frac{p(NOSOL_{\tau_2})}{p(NOSOL_{\tau_1})} \tag{3}$$

which can be solved using

$$p(NOSOL_t) = p(Y)p(NOSOL_t|Y) + p(N)p(NOSOL_t|N) \tag{4}$$

Using the fact that $p(N) = 1 - p(Y)$ and the fact that the algorithm never finishes if no solution exists, i.e., $p(NOSOL_t|N) = 1$, the above equation can be rewritten:

$$p(NOSOL_t) = p(Y)p(NOSOL_t|Y) + 1 - p(Y) \tag{5}$$

The termination algorithm also needs to know the chance that the answer is Y given that no solution has been found by step t. This can be determined using Bayes rule:

$$p(Y|NOSOL_t) = \frac{p(Y)p(NOSOL_t|Y)}{p(Y)p(NOSOL_t|Y) + p(N)p(NOSOL_t|N)}$$

$$= \frac{p(Y)p(NOSOL_t|Y)}{p(Y)p(NOSOL_t|Y) + p(N)}$$

$$= \frac{p(Y)p(NOSOL_t|Y)}{p(Y)p(NOSOL_t|Y) + 1 - p(Y)} \tag{6}$$

where
$$p(NOSOL_t|Y) = 1 - p(SOL_t|Y) \tag{7}$$

So, the agent can compute both $p(SOL_{T_2}|NOSOL_{T_1})$ and $p(Y|NOSOL_t)$ in constant time if it knows $p(Y)$ and $p(SOL_t|Y)$. The quantity $p(Y)$ is simply the agent's prior probability that the answer is Y, i.e., the agent's belief before it has executed any steps of the algorithm. In the extended version at www.cs.cmu.edu/~sandholm/util_term.extended.pdf we present an example that demonstrates how $p(Y)$ can be obtained using features of the problem instance that are quick to measure. The quantity $p(SOL_t|Y)$ can be determined empirically off-line by running the algorithm on instances (similar to the instance that needs to be solved in the on-line situation) whose answer is Y, and seeing on what fraction of them the algorithm has found a solution by time t. Alternatively, $p(SOL_t|Y)$ could be determined from an analytical model of the run-time distribution.

2.2   The Payoff Model

To determine when to terminate, the deliberation controller also needs to know how the agent would use the information that the algorithm provides in the real world. This depends on the application. However, for the purposes of the termination decision, this information can be represented in a domain independent way using a payoff function. Let us denote by $\pi_{world}(x, p_Y, t)$ the agents real-world payoff if the actual outcome is x, $x \in \{Y, N\}$, the agent's estimate—after running the algorithm for t steps—of the answer being Y is p_Y, and the agent acts according to this estimate at time t (or later if the agent finds that more beneficial). The agent's choice of a real-world action depends on p_Y and t, but the real-world payoff, π_{world}, of that action depends on the true posteriori x and when the action is taken, t. In the extended version of this paper we present an example application and illustrate how the π_{world} function can be constructed.

The agent's payoff, $\pi(x, p_Y, t)$, takes into account both the real-world payoff, $\pi_{world}(x, p_Y, t)$, and the computation cost. If they are independent, we can write

$$\pi(x, p_Y, t) = \pi_{world}(x, p_Y, t) - h(t) \tag{8}$$

where $h(t)$ is the computation cost. If there is a fixed unit cost of computation, c_{comp}, then $h(t) = c_{comp} \cdot t$. Our termination method applies to general π: it does not assume that the computation cost is independent of the real-world payoff.

2.3   Algorithm for Computing an Optimal Termination Policy

Put together, the inputs to the algorithm that computes the optimal termination policy are 1) the prior probability that a solution exists, $p(Y)$, 2) the run-time distribution in the form of $p(SOL_t|Y)$, and 3) the payoff model, $\pi(x, p_Y, t)$.

Conceptually, the stop/continue decisions are solved starting from the end of the decision tree (Fig. 1), and moving toward the root. For now, say that the tree ends at step T (we relax this assumption of an exogenous upper bound on the optimal termination time in the extended version of this paper). This does not mean that the algorithm is terminated at step T. This section describes how the termination time, $\tilde{t}$, is computed ($\tilde{t} \leq T$).

For every decision node of the tree, the expected payoff from stopping is computed, and so is the expected payoff from continuing. The expected payoff from continuing at node t depends on the solution that was acquired for node $t+1$. At a node, the deliberation controller should terminate the algorithm if and only if the expected payoff from stopping is higher than that of continuing. The pseudocode below computes this optimal termination policy. The function $v(t)$ solves the expected value of the subtree rooted at the deliberation controller's decision node t. The policy can be solved by making the call $v(0)$. The optimal decision for each decision node, t, is stored in $decision[t]$, and the time when the deliberation controller should first terminate the algorithm is stored in $\tilde{t}$ [3].

Algorithm 1 (Compute an optimal termination policy)

function $v(t)$
*   if $t = 0$*
* $p_{SOL} = 0$ /* Chance that a solution was found in this step */*
* $\pi_{SOL} = 0$ /* Payoff of that solution */*
*   else*
* $p_{SOL} = p(SOL_t|NOSOL_{t-1})$*
* $\pi_{SOL} = \pi(1,1,t)$*
* $p_Y = p(Y|NOSOL_t)$*
* $E[\pi|STOP] = p_{SOL} \cdot \pi_{SOL} + (1 - p_{SOL})(p_Y \cdot \pi(1,p_Y,t) + (1 - p_Y) \cdot \pi(0,p_Y,t))$*
*   if $t = T$ /* End of the tree */*
* $decision[t] = STOP; \tilde{t} = t;$ return $E[\pi|STOP]$ /* recursion bottoms here */*
*   else*
* $E[\pi|CONTINUE] = p_{SOL} \cdot \pi_{SOL} + (1 - p_{SOL}) \cdot v(t+1)$ /* recursion */*
*   if $E[\pi|STOP] \geq E[\pi|CONTINUE]$*
* $decision[t] = STOP; \tilde{t} = t;$ return $E[\pi|STOP]$*
*   else*
* $decision[t] = CONTINUE;$ return $E[\pi|CONTINUE]$*

Algorithm 1 runs in $O(T)$ time and space. The values $p(SOL_t| NOSOL_{t-1})$ and $p(Y|NOSOL_t)$ are computed in constant time from the inputs $p(Y)$ and $p(SOL_t|Y)$ using the formulas derived in Section 2.1.

3 Other Results

An extended version of this paper is available at www.cs.cmu.edu/~sandholm/util_term.extended.pdf. It presents an example application of how the method can be used (in the context of a manufacturing planning problem converted to 3SAT), how the payoff model $\pi(x, p_Y, t)$ can be derived, how the prior $p(Y)$ can be constructed (using statistical information and features of the problem instance), and how the run-time distribution $p(SOL_t|Y)$ can be constructed

---

[3] In classical stopping problems, at every time step after the first optimal stopping point it is better to stop. Here that is not the case. The algorithm determines a set of stopping points (t s.t. $decision[t] = STOP$) which need not be consecutive. These points state when to terminate the incomplete algorithm even if, for some reason, it was not terminated at the first optimal stopping point.

from runs of the algorithm. It also discusses ways how the method can be used when an exogenous upper bound T on the optimal run-time is not given, and presents example settings where it is best to never terminate the algorithm. Finally, it discusses related research (e.g., [2, 1]), and presents more elaborate conclusions and directions for future research.

References

1. H. Hoos and T. Stützle. Evaluating Las Vegas algorithms—pitfalls and remedies. *Proceedings of the Uncertainty in Artificial Intelligence Conference (UAI)*, 1998.
2. E. Horvitz and A. Klein. Reasoning, metareasoning, and mathematical truth: Studies of theorem proving under limited resources. *UAI*, 1995.
3. T. Sandholm and V. Lesser. Utility-based termination of anytime algorithms. *ECAI Workshop on Decision Theory for DAI Applications*, p. 88–99, Amsterdam, 1994.

Scene Reconstruction Based on Constraints: Details on the Equation System Decomposition

Gilles Trombettoni[1] and Marta Wilczkowiak[2]

[1] COPRIN Project, I3S-INRIA-CERMICS, 2004 route des lucioles
06902 Sophia Antipolis cedex, B.P. 93, France
trombe@sophia.inria.fr
[2] MOVI Project, INRIA Rhône-Alpes, 655 avenue
de l'Europe, Montbonnot, 38334 Saint Ismier cedex, France
Marta.Wilczkowiak@inrialpes.fr

Abstract. We present a new approach to 3D scene modeling based on geometrical constraints. Contrary to most of the existing methods, we obtain 3D scene models that respect the given constraints *exactly*. Our tool can describe a large variety of linear and non-linear constraints in a flexible way.

Our approach is based on a dictionary of so-called *r-methods*, based on theorems in geometry, which can solve a subset of geometrical constraints in a very efficient way. Two fast and complete graph-based algorithms are proposed to find a reduced parameterization of a scene, and to decompose the equation system in a sequence of r-methods.

1   Introduction

Reconstruction of accurate and photorealistic 3D models is one of the most challenging tasks in Computer Vision. In this paper, we address the problem of image-based reconstruction of a scene respecting a set of geometrical constraints. Defining geometrical constraints between scene primitives and incorporating them into the reconstruction system helps to stabilize the calibration, improves the quality of the model and limits the number of required images.

A common approach consists in incorporating the constraints into the optimization process. These methods however are often costly. Furthermore, they guarantee neither the convergence nor the (exact) constraint satisfaction.

Our model acquisition approach is detailed in [7]. It is divided into three main phases: initialization, constraint planning and optimization.

Initialization. In addition to 2D images, geometric objects and constraints must be defined. The 3D model is represented by **points, lines** and **planes.** They are subject to linear and non–linear constraints such as **distance, incidence, parallelism** and **orthogonality.**

An initial reconstruction is provided by a quasi-linear approach exploiting projections and geometrical constraints [6]. After this phase, all the variables (camera and model parameters) have an initial value.

F. Rossi (Ed.): CP 2003, LNCS 2833, pp. 956–961, 2003.

Constraint Planning. Our model reconstruction system requires a set of **r-methods** which allows us to decompose the whole equation system into small subsystems. An r-method [5] is a predefined routine used to solve a subset of geometric constraints. An *r-method* computes the coordinates of *output objects* based on the current value of *input object* coordinates, and satisfies the underlying constraints between input and output objects. For example, an r-method computes the parameters of a line based on the current position of two points incident to this line.

Several r-method patterns have been incorporated in a dictionary used by our system. They correspond to standard theorems of geometry. The constraint planning is divided into two steps:

1. *R-method addition phase:* Add *automatically* in the equation graph all the r-methods corresponding to r-method patterns present in the dictionary.
2. *Planning phase:* Perform GPDOF [5][1] on the enriched equation graph. GPDOF produces a set of **input parameters** and a sequence of r-methods (called *plan*) to be executed one by one. Input parameters are a subset of the variables describing the scene such that, when a value is given to them, there exists a finite set of solutions for the system satisfying the constraints.

Model Optimization. The optimization process[2] only adjusts the input parameters. Every time the cost function is computed (inside the numerical algorithm), the r-methods in the plan are executed, producing a new value for the other variables such that all the constraints are satisfied. The detailed process can be found in [7].

1.1 Contribution

Many works have focused on incorporating geometrical constraints for camera calibration and 3D reconstruction including [3, 2]. The reader will refer to [7] for more details on the existing approaches which often require costly computations or do not guarantee to provide a solution. The approach presented in this paper overcomes these drawbacks. It is complete, fast and can be used to model nonlinear constraints like distances, angles and distance/angle ratios.

This paper focus on the constraint planning process (Section 2) and shows experimental results in Section 3.

2 Constraint Planning

This section details the algorithms necessary for the constraint planning.

2.1 Automatic Addition of R-Methods

The automatic addition of r-methods is essentially based on a simple subgraph isomorphism algorithm performed on the constraint graph. When a subgraph matches an entry in the dictionary, the corresponding r-methods are added to the equation graph. Two steps are performed:

[1] GPDOF stands for General Propagation of Degrees of Freedom.

[2] based on a standard numerical algorithm and minimizing the *reprojection errors*.

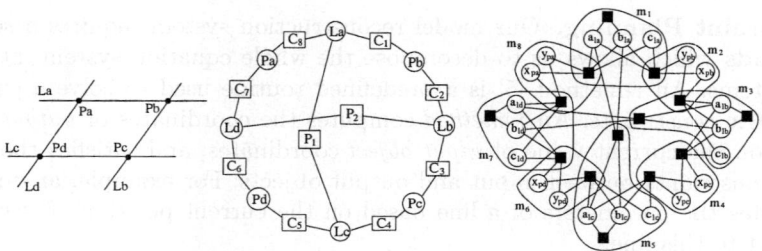

Fig. 1. Left: A didactic 2D scene describing a parallelogram in terms of lines, points, incidence constraints and parallelism constraints. **Center:** The corresponding constraint graph. It contains 4 points P_a,...,P_d, 4 lines L_a,...,L_d, 8 incidence constraints C_1,...,C_8 and 2 parallelism constraints P_1, P_2. **Right:** The enriched equation graph after automatic addition of r-methods. Equations are represented by rectangles and variables by circles. An r-method is represented by a hyper-arc including equations and output variables. Only 8 of the 16 r-methods are depicted for the sake of clarity. These r-methods match one of the three following patterns: line incident to two points (e.g., r-methods m_1 and m_7); point at the intersection of two known lines (m_2, m_4, m_6, m_8); line passing through a known point and parallel to another line (m_3, m_5)..

-1-. The first step explores all the connected subgraphs with size at most a small value k equal to the maximum number of nodes (objects+constraints) implied in any r-method of the dictionary, e.g., 7 in our tool. Starting from every single node, the subgraphs are built by incrementally adding a neighbor node to the current connected subgraph until the size k is reached. This depth first search algorithm is a simplification of the algorithmic scheme presented in [1]. The key idea allowing the algorithm to explore a *tree* of subgraphs is to consider at each step only a specific subset of selected neighbors, depending on a unique numbering of the nodes [1].

In practice, the time complexity of this algorithm is linear in the actual number of connected subgraphs of size less than k (which is $O(n^k)$). It is acceptable for small values of k and sparse graphs.

-2-. For every found subgraph, a second procedure compares it with the subgraph patterns in our dictionary implemented as a hash table, which eliminates most of the subgraphs. A final comparison is made by a combinatorial process [3] inspired by the solving process of CSPs (BT). In short, objects in the subgraph are reordered to be matched with objects in a subgraph pattern. If the subgraph matches, the corresponding r-methods are added to the equation graph.

2.2   The GPDOF Algorithm

GPDOF [5] works on an enriched equation graph. It computes a sequence of r-methods to be executed for satisfying all the equations. GPDOF solves this combinatorial problem in polynomial-time and is quasi-linear in practice. It performs

---

[3] Deciding whether two graphs are *isomorphic* is still an open problem.

the three following steps until no more equation remains in the equation graph G (success) or no more free r-method is available (failure)[4]:

1. select a **free** r-method m [5],
2. remove from G the equations and the output variables of m,
3. create all the *submethods* of a r-method m_i that share equations or output variables with m.

A plan can be obtained by reversing the selection order: the first selected r-method will be executed last. The first two steps above define the standard PDOF local propagation algorithm [4] on which GPDOF is based (PDOF accepts only r-methods solving *one* equation.) Selecting iteratively free r-methods ensures that no loop is created in the plan.

It turns out that, when r-methods can solve several equations, there is no guarantee that PDOF finds a plan, even if one exists. This highlights the notion of *submethod* which renders GPDOF complete. In short, the notion of submethod explains that a partially removed r-method remains available for a future selection. The reader will refer to [5] to get a more detailed information.

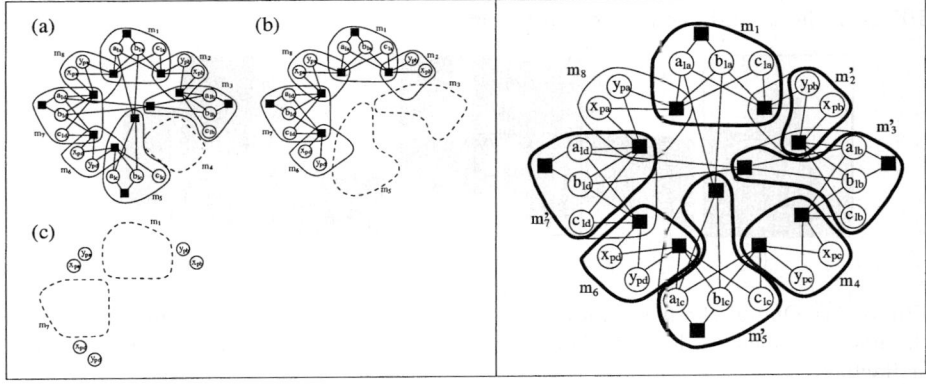

Fig. 2. Two possible planning phases performed by GPDOF on the didactic scene.
Left: At the beginning, r-methods m_2, m_4, m_6, m_8 are free, so that one of them is selected, e.g., m_4. **(a)** This selection implies the removal of the equations and the output variables of m_4 from the equation graph. **(b)** This frees r-methods m_3 and m_5 which are selected and removed next in any order. **(c)** The r-methods m_1 and m_7 are then free and can be selected. The process ends since no more constraint remains in the equation graph. The obtained plan is the sequence $(m_1, m_7, m_3, m_5, m_4)$.
Right: GPDOF may also select first m_6 which is free. The third step of GPDOF then creates the submethod m_5' of m_5 and the submethod m_7' of m_7. The process continues and selects m_4, m_5', m_1, m_2', m_3', and finally m_7'. Selected r-methods (m_1, m_4, m_6) and submethods (m_2', m_3', m_5', m_7') are represented by thick hyper-arcs. .

---

[4] In this case, one obtains an incomplete plan which solves only a subpart of the equations (geometric constraints) and more parameters are adjusted by optimization.

[5] Output variables of a free r-method appear in no "external" equations.

2.3   Determining the Input Parameters

The input parameters modified by the numerical optimization simply consist of the variables which are output by no r-method in the plan. This yields the 6 coordinates of points P_a, P_b, P_d for the plan illustrated in Fig. 2-left- or the 2 coordinates of point P_a for the plan illustrated in Fig. 2-right-. Due to the selection of submethods, the values of variables in a second set of parameters are read a first time (recall that every variable has an initial value) and computed later by r-methods, e.g., the coordinates of P_b are in this set (Fig. 2-right-). The other variables are only modified by r-method execution. This subtlety cannot be explained here due to a lack of space.

3   Results

We have used our approach to build a model of a church (see Figure 3). Five images architectural plans (distances) were used. The scene includes 137 constraints (including 10 distances), 251 equations, 119 objects, 427 variables. The time for the constraint planning (2 min. on a Pentium IV 2GHz) is dominated by the exploration of the connected subgraphs. 2213 r-methods have been added automatically. The execution time of GPDOF is negligible. The plan was built of 107 r-methods and is executed in 55 ms.

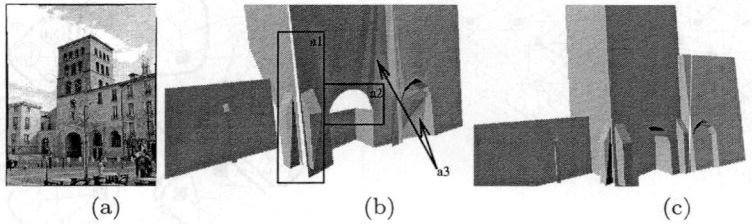

(a)   (b)   (c)

Fig. 3. (a)–One of the five photos used for the reconstruction; (b)–Some artifacts of the unconstrained model. (c)–The constrained model after optimization corrects the artifacts.

Acknowlegments

Thanks to D. Chancel for the architectural drawings. Thanks to E. Boyer, D. Daney, C. Jermann, B. Neveu and P. Sturm for useful discussions.

References

1. David Avis and Komei Fukuda. Reverse Search Enumeration. *Discrete Applied Mathematics*, 6:21–46, 1996.
2. Didier Bondyfalat, Bernard Mourrain, and Theodore Papadopoulo. An application of automatic theorem proving in computer vision. In *Automated Deduction in Geometry*, pages 207–231, 1998.

3. P.E. Debevec, C.J. Taylor, and J. Malik. Modeling and rendering architecture from photographs: a hybrid geometry-and image-based approach. In SIGGRAPH '96, *New Orleans*, August 1996.

4. Ivan Sutherland. *Sketchpad: A Man-Machine Graphical Communication System.* PhD thesis, Department of Electrical Engineering, MIT, 1963.

5. Gilles Trombettoni. A Polynomial Time Local Propagation Algorithm for General Dataflow Constraint Problems. In *Proc. Constraint Programming CP'98, LNCS 1520 (Springer Verlag)*, pages 432–446, 1998.

6. M. Wilczkowiak, P. Sturm, and E. Boyer. The analysis of ambiguous solutions in linear systems and its application to computer vision. In *To Appear in Proceedings of the 14th British Machine Vision Conference, Norwich, England*, September 2003.

7. M. Wilczkowiak, G. Trombettoni, C. Jermann, P. Sturm, and E. Boyer. Scene reconstruction based on constraint decomposition techniques. In *Proceedings of the 9th International Conference on Computer Vision*, 2003.

A New Approach
to Solving SAT-Encoded Binary CSPs*

Carlos Ansótegui

Computer Science Department, Universitat de Lleida, Spain

We investigate the use of many-valued clausal forms as an intermediate formalism between CSP and SAT for solving combinatorial problems. In this research programme, we have recently designed and implemented a complete many-valued SAT solver called Mv-Satz [1], which builds on the popular Boolean solver Satz, and conducted an experimental investigation that provides evidence that Mv-Satz outperforms Satz and zChaff on a number of problems.

We present here the results we have obtained when solving SAT-encoded random binary CSPs that were generated using the so-called model B. In the table we show the experimental results for zChaff, Satz, and Mv-Satz using the *direct* and *support* SAT encodings. For each solver we provide the mean and median time (in seconds) needed to solve sets of 100 instances. Observe that Mv-Satz outperforms Satz up to one order of magnitude, and zChaff up to two orders of magnitude.

parameters		zChaff		Satz		Mv-Satz	
$\langle n, d, p_1, p_2 \rangle$	encoding	mean	median	mean	median	mean	median
$\langle 15, 25, 80/105, 283/625 \rangle$	direct	95	116	35	36	11	13
	support	20	23	157	216	72	84
$\langle 15, 30, 80/105, 424/900 \rangle$	direct	488	598	100	91	26	25
	support	73	72	503	606	175	199
$\langle 25, 15, 198/300, 65/225 \rangle$	direct	1118	1102	177	176	30	31
	support	508	422	549	607	188	203
$\langle 25, 20, 198/300, 126/400 \rangle$	direct	16588	12963	1374	1303	187	181
	support	8820	5836	6185	5590	1057	1135
$\langle 35, 15, 305/595, 60/225 \rangle$	direct	67826	40610	6807	6518	637	653
	support	60271	42036	7412	7334	1896	1880
$\langle 45, 10, 415/990, 22/100 \rangle$	direct	6217	4492	919	875	140	135
	support	5577	4122	418	415	322	301
$\langle 70, 6, 1050/2415, 4/36 \rangle$	direct	10231	8183	129	125	65	58
	support	17341	13983	164	153	142	129
$\langle 100, 4, 2000/4950, 1/16 \rangle$	direct	1774	1862	5	5	5	5
	support	2492	2375	17	16	18	18

References

[1] C. Ansótegui, J. Larrubia, C. M. Li, and F. Manyà. Mv-Satz: A SAT solver for many-valued clausal forms. In *4th International Conference Journées de L'Informatique Messine, JIM-2003, Metz, France*, 2003.

* Research partially supported by project CICYT TIC2001-1577-C03-03 funded by the *Ministerio de Ciencia y Tecnología*.

FeReRA: A Multi-agent Approach to Constraint Satisfaction

Muhammed Basharu

School of Computing, The Robert Gordon University, St. Andrew Street
Aberdeen, AB25 1HG, U.K.
mb@comp.rgu.ac.uk

This work introduces the FeReRA (Feedback, Reinforcement, and Reactive Agents) algorithm, an extension to the ERA framework [3]. ERA (Environment, Reactive Rules, and Agents) introduced a non-deterministic, self-organising, multi-agent approach to solving Constraint Satisfaction Problems (CSP) whereby a problem is broken up into smaller sub-problems and each sub-problem is to be solved by an independent agent. Each agent inhabits a local environment which represents the domain of its respective variables, and will try to find solutions to its sub-problem by seeking positions in the environment that translates to consistent value assignments for the variables in the sub-problem. ERA's key strength is that it is capable of finding solutions to CSPs without much computational overhead. Its Achilles' heel, however, is its inconsistent performance resulting from inbuilt random behaviours which are relied on to escape local optimums. To overcome this weakness, FeReRA extends ERA by replacing the random decisions with a deterministic feedback mechanism that helps the algorithm to decide which agents are to make non-improving moves necessary to take it out of a local optimum. This feedback process is structure dependent, and it takes into account the cumulative effects of individual agents' behaviours on the global state of the system. This is in contrast with the approaches taken in similar work [2][4], where emphasis is placed on individual agents detecting and escaping quasi-local minimums . Preliminary results from experiments on graph colouring instances are as follows: First, on critically constrained instances, the time taken to find solutions on average was equal or better with FeReRA compared to ERA. Secondly, on over constrained instances the quality of solutions found was consistent with FeReRA and was on average better or equal to ERA's performance. An extended version of this abstract is available at [1].

References

1. Basharu M.B., FeReRA: A Multi-agent approach to constraint satisfaction *available at http://www.comp.rgu.ac.uk/staff/mb/*
2. Fabiunke M. and Kock G., A connectionist method to solve job shop problems. *Cybernetics and Systems: An International Journal* 31(5) pp. 491-506, 2000.
3. Liu J., Han J. and Tang Y.Y., Multi-agent oriented constraint satisfaction *Artificial Intelligence* 136(1) pp. 101-144, 2002.
4. Yokoo M. and Hirayama K., Distributed breakout algorithm for solving distributed constraint satisfaction problems. In *Proceedings of the Second International Conference on Multi-Agent Systems,* pp. 401-408, MIT Press, 1996.

F. Rossi (Ed.): CP 2003, LNCS 2833, p. 963, 2003.
© Springer-Verlag Berlin Heidelberg 2003

Semantic Decomposition
for Solving Distance Constraints

Heikel Batnini and Michel Rueher

University of Nice - INRIA Sophia-Antipolis - I3S - CERMICS
{Heikel.Batnini,Michel.Rueher}@sophia.inria.fr

Numerical constraint problems occurs in numerous applications. Consistency techniques on finite domains have been adapted to handle continuous CSP(e.g. 2B-consistency, kB-consistency[1], Box-consistency[2], ...). Roughly speaking, these local filtering methods compute an external approximation of the solution space. That is to say, intervals the bounds of which are local consistents. Thus, this external approximation still contains a huge number of local inconsistent values. Splitting techniques are often used to isolate individual solutions. However, these techniques are ineffective when the domain contains continuous subspaces of solutions. Moreover, they do not take advantage of the semantic of the constraints for splitting the intervals.

We introduce here a pruning technique, called LDF(Local Decomposition Filtering)[3], for solving systems of distance equations. This method is based on a local decomposition of the domains which is guided by the properties of the distance constraints(convexity and monotonicity). More precisely, the domains of the coordinates of two points involved in a constraint c is decomposed using the properties of c(see figure 1). The canonical form of the distance equations($X^2 + Y^2 - D^2 = 0$) identifies the monotonous and convex parts on $\mathbb{R}^+ \times \mathbb{R}^+$, $\mathbb{R}^+ \times \mathbb{R}^-$, $\mathbb{R}^- \times \mathbb{R}^+$ and $\mathbb{R}^- \times \mathbb{R}^-$.

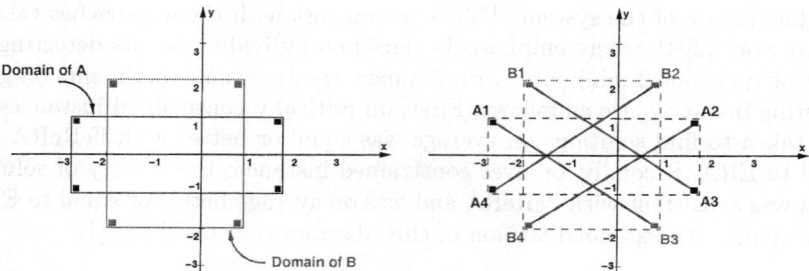

Fig. 1. Consider constraint $(x_A - x_B)^2 + (y_A - y_B)^2 = D^2$ with $D \in [4.95, 5]$. Left picture shows the domains of the points A and B after 2B-consistency filtering. Right picture shows the four subdomains of A and B and the micro-structure computed by LDF.

[1] O. Lhomme. *Consistency techniques for numerical CSPs*. Proceedings of the 13th IJCAI. Chambéry, France, August 28 -September 3, 1993. Morgan Kaufmann, p232-238.
[2] P. Van Hentenryck, D. McAllester, and D. Kapur. *Solving Polynomial Systems Using a Branch and Prune Approach*. SIAM Journal on Numerical Analysis , 34(2), p797-827, April 1997.
[3] H. Batnini and M.Rueher. *Filtrage local par décomposition de CSP continus*. JNPC'03. 9eme Journées Nationales pour la résolution de Problemes NP-Complets. p39-51. Juin 2003. Amiens. France.

F. Rossi (Ed.): CP 2003, LNCS 2833, pp. 964–965, 2003.
© Springer-Verlag Berlin Heidelberg 2003

This decomposition is propagated on the other variables by the way of a local consistency algorithm. A graph of intervals is updated by a specific projection procedure which connects the consistent pairs of subdomains. We prove that the global reduction of the domains is at least equivalent with that carried out by *2B-consistency*. The structure of the resulting graph can be compared to an arc-consistant finite CSP. Thus, classical searching algorithms can be used to identify potential subspaces of solutions.

The first results on academic examples are promising. Further work concerns experimentations on real problems (robotics and theory of the mechanisms) as well as the extension of this approach to other systems of non-linear constraints.

Using Constraint Programming and Simulation for Execution Monitoring and On-Line Rescheduling with Uncertainty

Julien Bidot

[1] ILOG S. A., 9, rue de Verdun, B. P. 85
94253 Gentilly Cedex, France
jbidot@ilog.fr
[2] L. G. P. /ENIT, 47, av. d'Azereix, B. P. 1629
65016 Tarbes Cedex, France

Modern scheduling techniques must take into account incomplete information and/or potential changes in the environment, i.e. uncertainty. The central issue is to design robust scheduling techniques, aimed at guaranteeing the feasibility and the quality of the executed schedule. Several ways to get a more robust schedule have already been investigated. One way among others is to keep one and only one fixed schedule to execute, but reschedule when it appears the quality of the currently executing schedule degrades. This approach is relevant as far as rescheduling is fast enough w.r.t. the scheduling execution, i.e. when the dynamics of the system are low. The problem we tackle is on-line rescheduling with temporal uncertainty: activity durations are uncertain and activity end times must be observed during execution. In this paper we assume we have a representation of the uncertainty on each activity duration in the form of probability distributions which are used in the simulation of schedule execution. We use the simulations to monitor the execution of the schedule and in particular to estimate the quality of the schedule and the end times of the activities. Given an initial schedule, execution starts and we must decide when to reschedule. We propose and explore a non-monotonic technique where each time we reschedule we can completely change the existing schedule except for those activities that have already started or finished execution. This paper addresses the basis on which the decision to reschedule is made by investigating three simple measures of the data provided by simulation that are called the rescheduling criteria. We have chosen to use constraint programming for scheduling the initial problem and rescheduling when necessary. We illustrate our approach on job-shop problems with uncertain durations. The first experimental results are promising since on-line rescheduling improves schedule quality with a little additional computational effort whatever the rescheduling criterion used. In addition, these techniques can easily be extended to solve more complex problems and simulation permits us to quickly obtain good approximations whatever type of uncertainties and probability distributions are considered. Future work will focus on developing these scheduling methods to better tune the different parameters and implementing a monotonic approach where a partial schedule is built until some horizon and never questioned.

F. Rossi (Ed.): CP 2003, LNCS 2833, p. 966, 2003.
© Springer-Verlag Berlin Heidelberg 2003

On the Enhancement
of the Informed Backtracking Algorithm

Jlifi Boutheina[1] and Khaled Ghéd:ra[2]

[1] UR. SOI²E, ISG, Tunis University
Boutheina.jlifi@insat.rnu.tn
[2] UR. SOI²E, ISG, Tunis University, ENSI, 2010 Campus Manouba, Tunisia
Khaled.ghedira@isg.rnu.tn

This paper addresses Constraint Satisfaction Problems (CSP), known to be NP-complete, by a repair-based algorithm referred to as informed backtracking (IBt). The method consists in taking an initial complete but inconsistent assignment and incrementally repairing constraint violations until a solution is achieved. It is guided by a simple ordering heuristic for repairing constraint violations: the Min-conflict-heuristic. This latter selects a variable that is currently participating in a constraint violation, and chooses a new value that minimises the number of outstanding constraint violations.

Although its advantages when compared with the simple backtracking, its efficiency can be improved by enriching it with other simple methods. The approach attempts to combine the forward checking algorithm (FC) with the IBt in order to prevent future conflicts by checking the constraints between the current variable and the future variables. The new algorithm (IBtFC) allows branches of the search tree that will lead to failure to be pruned earlier than with IBt.

To show the advantages of this approach, experimental comparisons between IBt and IBtFC are given. Our experiments are performed on binary CSP-samples randomly generated. This generation is guided by classical CSP parameters. In order to have a quick and clear comparison of the relative performance of the two approaches, we compute ratios of (IBt) and (IBtFC) performance using the Run time, and constraint checks as follows:

CPU-ratio = IBt-Run-time/ IBtFC -Run-time

Cchecks-ratio = IBt- Cchecks/ IBtFC -Cchecks

From the CPU time point of view, IBtFC requires up to three times less for the most strongly tight and , even for the most weakly constrained set of examples. Moreover it requires up to two times less for the over-constrained set of examples. It follows that, when we are considering Cchecks-ratio, we have significant related results that confirm the efficiency of our approach.

As perspectives, we intend to compare our algorithm with other ones (for instance, MAC). Some heuristics, such as variable scheduling, known to be efficient in CSP field have also to be adapted in order to improve the approach's efficiency.

F. Rossi (Ed.): CP 2003, LNCS 2833, p. 967, 2003.
© Springer-Verlag Berlin Heidelberg 2003

Extending CLP with Metaheuristics

Ole Boysen

Fraunhofer FIRST, Kekuléstraße 7, 12489 Berlin, Germany
boysen@first.fhg.de

Modern Constraint Logic Programming (CLP) systems have a number of approved features like their declarative programming language, the incorporation of sophisticated search space pruning and propagation algorithms as well as deterministic complete search algorithms. But for very complex, large-scale combinatorial optimization problems as they occur in the real world, CLP often fails to deliver high quality solutions. This is the application area where metaheuristics are often reported to reach dominant results. Consequently, considerable effort has been directed to combine the constraint programming and metaheuristic search paradigms and exploit their respective superior features.

To take advantage of both paradigms, we propose the integration of metaheuristics into an existing CLP system. We define an interface which encodes the declarative problem specification given to it by the CLP system as a general CSP. This involves mapping the given constraints and associated variables with their domains. Since metaheuristics do not enforce constraints explicitly we transform the constraint system into a penalty function which counts the number of violated constraints and weights those by their "degree" of violation. Thus, by minimizing the penalty function a metaheuristic implicitly tries to respect the constraints. In contrast, variable domains are enforced directly, since heuristics are restricted to select values from within the given variable domains. After search, the metaheuristic returns a complete assignment of all variables to values which may or may not be feasible with respect to the constraint system.

Experiments with a Tabu Search (TS) metaheuristic have shown that additional problem knowledge beyond the given CSP is required for efficient application of metaheuristics: For instance, TS requires carefully designed operators for each problem, e.g. neighborhood and tabu list operators. Also, excessive use of equality constraints causes inefficiencies which can be corrected by use of propagators inside the metaheuristics. These kinds of additional information are communicated to the metaheuristics by adding pseudo constraints to the constraint system which have no effect on the CLP system itself but improve the efficiency of the metaheuristics drastically.

The presented approach of extending a CLP system with metaheuristics has several benefits: The CLP system remains fully functional while the metaheuristics work from the same declarative problem specification. The metaheuristics can be applied to any (sub-)problem of the CLP desired but also can solve extended problems. As tools for optimization metaheuristics can additionally take optimization goals into account and also allow non-linear constraints which both are easily implemented and integrated in form of pseudo constraints. The interaction between both systems can be freely defined and imposes no restrictions on them.

F. Rossi (Ed.): CP 2003, LNCS 2833, p. 968, 2003.
© Springer-Verlag Berlin Heidelberg 2003

Self Configuring
Constraint Programming Systems*

Tom Carchrae

Cork Constraint Computation Centre, Department of Computer Science
University College Cork, Cork, Ireland
carchrae@4c.ucc.ie

It could be argued that the widespread use of constraint programming (CP) tools is not being hampered so much by the efficiency of the tools, as much as it is by the limited number of experts available to install and configure such systems. It remains a 'black-art' as to what combination of techniques will result in a system which is not only able to solve the problem, but does so in a manner which is appropriate for the application. To this end, we attempt to tackle this problem by creating a system that takes a basic problem description and considers the objectives of an application to create a *self-configured* system. Further, in the event that system performance starts to decline, we will revisit the original configuration and the system will *self-tune* to deal with changes in the use of the application.

We are inspired by the approach taken by many consultants when creating an application. A problem description is given, using a specification language, which describes the logic of the application and what constitutes an acceptable solution to the problem. The description is usually combined with some sample data to create a set of problem instances. In addition to this, the consultant is given some objectives which state how the system will be used and what constitutes acceptable performance. Often the main strategy used by humans is to build a prototype, evaluate it based on the objectives, and then to adjust the prototype iteratively until it reaches an acceptable state. These trials and tribulations are a process which guides the consultant to a specific configuration which is able to tackle the problem. It is rare that a complex system is built on the first iteration unless it matches some very similar project the consultant has worked on in the past.

Our approach is not to try and automate the process of acquiring the description or objectives (which is a complex problem in its own right) but rather to automate the trials and tribulations step by giving a machine the ability to build prototypes and evaluate them. Even if the machine is capable of a modest number of ways to restructure the application, then it should be possible to gain an advantage in two main ways. There is the advantage of the technology being accessible to someone who is not trained in CP. A further and potentially more valuable benefit is that a human consultant's effort on a project is typically governed by time and cost restrictions. An automated system may be able to outperform this effort and yield a better tailored application for the problem.

* This work has received support from Science Foundation Ireland under Grant 00/PI.1/C075.

F. Rossi (Ed.): CP 2003, LNCS 2833, p. 969, 2003.

Interactive Tradeoff Generation*

Moyra Duggan, Barry O'Sullivan, and Eugene C. Freuder

Cork Constraint Computation Centre
Department of Computer Science, University College Cork, Ireland
{m.duggan,b.osullivan,e.freuder}@4c.ucc.ie

The central idea in this work is that it is possible to assist users satisfy a set of inconsistent preferences by generating tradeoffs [1]. For example, during an interactive configuration session when we reach a point where our desires cannot be met we consider tradeoffs between our preferences.

We model tradeoffs as additional constraints and have begun to study the issues involved in generating and evaluating them. Our work attempts to address important but ill-defined questions like "what is a good tradeoff?" in a formal and experimental manner. There is a large body of work in constraint-based configuration. We make further contributions toward the development of techniques that learn user preferences and use these to assist users achieve satisfactory configurations. We utilize the n-queens configuration problem, with the addition of user-generated preference constraints and system-generated trade-off constraints. During an interactive session with the configurator, the user may specify a preference constraint which causes an inconsistency. At this point our configurator attempts to recommend a set of appropriate "tradeoff" constraints to the user from which she can select one before continuing to develop a solution for the configuration problem. Tradeoffs are modelled as binary constraints. Modelling tradeoffs as binary constraints is useful, particularly since standard constraint processing algorithms can be used to reason over them.

One of our primary objectives is to assist the user achieve a viable solution that she will find acceptable in as few tradeoffs as possible [1]. However in the case of an inconsistency it may be necessary to revisit previously accepted tradeoffs because an acceptable tradeoff cannot be found. Our aim is to adapt existing backtracking algorithms for interactive tradeoff generation to help us revisit previously accepted tradeoffs. The idea of generating tradeoffs that best satisfy user preferences is a simple one and the ability of configurators to generate tradeoffs to users during interactive configuration is valuable. Our current work is concerned with (a) finding efficient methods for computing tradeoffs, and (b) efficiently revisiting previously accepted tradeoffs when the need arises.

References

1. Eugene C. Freuder and Barry O'Sullivan. Generating tradeoffs for interative constraint-based configuration. In Toby Walsh, editor, *Proceedings of the Seventh International Conference on Principles and Practice of Constraint Programming*, pages 590–594, November 2001.

* This work has received support from Enterprise Ireland under their Basic Research Grant Scheme (Grant Number SC/02/289). This work has also been supported by Science Foundation Ireland under Grant 00/PI.1/C075.

F. Rossi (Ed.): CP 2003, LNCS 2833, p. 970, 2003.

Introducing ESRA, a Relational Language for Modelling Combinatorial Problems (Abstract)[*]

Pierre Flener, Justin Pearson, and Magnus Ågren[**]

Department of Information Technology
Uppsala University, Box 337, S – 751 05 Uppsala, Sweden
{pierref,justin,agren}@it.uu.se

Current-generation constraint programming languages are considered by many, especially in industry, to be too low-level, difficult, and large. In order to unleash the proven powers of constraint technology and make it available to a wider range of people, a higher-level, simpler, and smaller modelling notation is needed.

In our opinion, even recent commercial languages such as OPL[1] do not go far enough in that direction. Many common modelling patterns have not been captured in special constructs. They have to be painstakingly spelled out each time, at a high risk for errors, often using low-level devices such as reification.

Sets recently started appearing as modelling devices in some constraint programming languages. However, relations have not received much attention yet, except the particular case of a total function via the concept of an array.

We claim that a suitable first-order relational calculus is a good basis for a high-level ADT-based constraint modelling language. It gives rise to very natural and easy-to-maintain models of combinatorial problems. We do not aim at providing a complete language, as long as it is capable of modelling a large number of problems. More important is a small language with orthogonal constructs.

Due to this, we present our new modeling language, called ESRA[2], and in order to demonstrate its expressiveness, we present a model for the BIBD[3] problem:

dom $Varieties, Blocks$
cst $r, k, \lambda \in \mathbb{N}$
var $BIBD : Varieties \ {}^r\times^k \ Blocks$
solve $\forall(v_1 \neq v_2 \in Varieties) \ \mathrm{count}(\lambda)(i \in Blocks \mid BIBD(v_1, i) \wedge BIBD(v_2, i))$

The declaration of the decision variable $BIBD$, a relation in $Varieties \times Blocks$, immediately takes care of the constraints that each block is to be of size k and that each variety is to be in r blocks. The only remaining constraint, that each distinct pair of varieties is to be in the same block exactly λ times, is taken care of using the count quantifier, a generalisation of existential quantification.

---

[*] This work is partially supported by grant 221-99-369 of VR the Swedish Research Council.

[**] The authors' names are ordered according to the Swedish alphabet.

[1] P. Van Hentenryck. *The* OPL *Optimization Programming Language*. MIT Press, 1999.

[2] P. Flener, J. Pearson, and M. Ågren. *The Syntax, Semantics, and Type System of* ESRA. At http://www.it.uu.se/research/group/astra, April 2003.

[3] See problem 28 at http://www.csplib.org for more information.

F. Rossi (Ed.): CP 2003, LNCS 2833, p. 971, 2003.

Abstracting Constraints Using Constraints*

James Gibbons

Cork Constraint Computation Centre
Department of Computer Science
University College, Cork
Ireland
j.gibbons@4c.ucc.ie

Abstraction is a process where problems are modified in some way to make them easier to solve. For our purposes, we look at abstraction as adding constraints in such a manner as to reduce the number of solutions, or removing constraints in order to make more solutions valid. It is a form of simplification, where certain details of a problem are ignored, or temporarily cast aside, in order to make the problem less difficult to solve. The central idea in this paper is to use constraints in order find candidate abstractions of a problem, making the abstraction process quicker, easier, and more efficient.

When abstracting a problem, one of the most important points is deciding on which elements of the problem to abstract. Making the right choices in this respect is crucial and can mean the difference between finding a near optimal solution, an acceptable solution, or, in the worst case, no solution to the abstracted problem.

The process of abstraction begins with taking a subject problem P, and generating a candidate abstraction, using CP-based techniques. We use this abstracted problem, AP, the basis for creating the abstracted model of P, which is P^*. Naturally, there are some side effects to the changes made. The problem we will have created is not the problem we were asked to solve, and we may have to changed the characteristics of the original problem in some way.

We then solve the abstract problem, giving us a solution. This solution however, is not automatically a valid solution to the original problem, P. We must concretize this solution, in order to make it an acceptable solution to the original problem. Depending on the problem involved, this may be a very difficult and time consuming task or it may be completely trivial.

Applying abstraction to constraint programming is an area that has been examined, although in the area of using constraints to actually generate the abstractions, there does not appear to be any work. Indeed much of the work seems to concentrate in the abstractions themselves, rather than the process by which they were created.

Here we present the idea of using the power of constraints to find valid abstractions and to choose the best option available for abstraction. We intend to further examine the issue of abstraction using constraints as it is potentially very useful for solving larger problems.

* This work has been supported by Science Foundation Ireland under Grant 00/PI.1/C075 and ILOG, SA.

Sensitivity Analysis in CSPs*

Diarmuid Glynn

Cork Constraint Computation Centre, UCC.
dglynn@4c.ucc.ie

When modeling real-world problems, we cannot always be sure about the nature of our problem, nor be certain that it is immune to change. In job-shop scheduling, machines can break down, tasks may take longer in reality than in our model, and the market prices for the various commodities may change. Clearly, it would be beneficial if our CSP model could be analysed, so that we could be aware of the effects of various changes on our solution. An analysis may also furnish information useful in itself, such as that a particular machine is not needed.

It is important to decide on what exactly constitutes sensitivity analysis in CSPs. We have limited ourselves to studying the effects of:

- adding/removing a constraint
- adding/removing a value from the domain of a variable
- altering the objective function in an optimisation CSP
- altering the values of constants

We propose a method of sensitivity analysis which utilises techniques already available in integer linear programming[1]. A CSP is first converted into an ILP using a direct encoding, and then this new ILP has the sensitivity analysis outlined in [1] applied to it.

We have shown that the ILP sensitivity analysis allows us to detect redundant constraints in our CSP. Further, if the CSP has a linear optimisation function, we can predict the effect of perturbations of constants within the optimisation function on a given optimal solution.

In future, we hope to develop more direct methods for sensitivity analysis.

References

1. M. Dawande and J. N. Hooker. Inference-based sensitivity analysis for mixed integer/linear programming. Technical report, Pittsburgh, PA, 1996.

* Research supported by IRCSET and Science Foundation Ireland. I would like to thank the members of the APES group, especially my supervisors, Brahim Hnich and Toby Walsh.

F. Rossi (Ed.): CP 2003, LNCS 2833, p. 973, 2003.

Solution Stability
in Constraint Satisfaction Problems*

Emmanuel Hebrard

Cork Constraint Computation Centre, UCC.
e.hebrard@4c.ucc.ie

Solution stability is the ability of a new solution to share as many values as possible with the original if a break arises. Whenever large changes to a solution introduces additional expense or reorganisation, stability is valuable. Stability also facilitate the search for a new solution. *Supermodels* are solutions of SAT formulas which are stable to change [MGR98]. We propose the following extention of the definition of supermodels to the CSP framework:

A solution S to a CSP is (a, b)-super solution iff the loss of the values of at most a variables in S can be repaired by assigning other values to these variables, and modifying the assignment of at most b other variables.

Intuitively, for a given number of breaks (loss of values), only a small number of repairs (reassignments) is required. A necessary but not a sufficient condition for the existence of a supermodel is the absence of backbone variables. A *backbone variable* is a variable that takes the same value in all solutions. The presence of a backbone variable in a SAT problem makes it impossible to find any (a, b)-supermodels as that particular variable has no alternative. To solve the *super constraint satisfaction problem*, we propose to apply methods derived from local consistency, that we call *super consistency*. These methods lead to an efficient algorithm for $a = 1$ and $b = 0$. One key point is that a value need at least *two* supports to belong to a super solution instead of one. Indeed, if any value of a solution has only one support, then this support is in the solution as well. Therefore its loss would have as consequence the loss of the former value. Observe, however, that those two supports haven't the same function. By definition, only one of them will be in the solution. Based on this, we propose an algorithm that not only separates consistent from inconsistent values, but marks the values as:

- inconsistent
- consistent, but only as a "repair" (*repair value*)
- consistent, with two supports on each neighbor (*super value*)

The algorithm branches only on the later, super values.

References

[MGR98] A. Parkes, M. Ginsberg and A. Roy. Supermodels and robustness. In *Procedding AAAI-98*, pages 334–339, 1998.

* Supported by the Science Foundation Ireland. I would like to thank the members of the APES group, especially my supervisors, Brahim Hnich and Toby Walsh.

F. Rossi (Ed.): CP 2003, LNCS 2833, p. 974, 2003.

distn: An Euclidean Distance Global Constraint

Michael Heusch

[1] PLATON, THALES Research and Technology, France
[2] IRIN, Université de Nantes
michael.heusch@irin.univ-nantes.fr

Abstract. We present a global constraint that maintains the Euclidean distance between n points.

Euclidean Distance constraints appear in many application domains of CP, such as molecular conformation, robotics or facility location. Solving problems involving many distance constraints is a difficult task, and several solutions have been proposed in [1–3]. The method of "active areas" introduced in the Circle Packing problem [4] enables us to build the propagation algorithm of a global constraint that maintains the Euclidean distance between n points.

The declarative semantics of the constraint we propose are

$$distn(rel, [Z_1, \dots, Z_n], D) \tag{1}$$

where rel is one of $\{\leq, \geq, =\}$, the Z_i are pairs of "location domain variables" (X_i, Y_i) and D is a positive "distance domain variable". The constraint (1) holds if

$$\forall z_i \in Z_i, \ \forall j, \ \exists z_j \in Z_j \ / \ distance(z_i, z_j) \ rel \ D$$

This provides the user with a modeling tool, and the first benchmarks have shown its propagation algorithm outperforms the classical consistency algorithms found both in discrete and continuous constraint solvers. Moreover, the involved algorithm can be extended to take a matrix defining the distance relations as input. The algorithm has been integrated into a continuous constraint solver, and its extension to three dimensions and comparison with [1–3] are in preparation.

References

1. Heikel Batnini and Michel Rueher. Semantic decomposition for solving distance constraints. In *Proc. of CP-03*, Kinsale, County Cork, Ireland, 2002.
2. Ludwig Krippahl and Pedro Barahona. PSICO: solving protein structures with constraint programming and optimization. *Constraints*, 7(3-4):317–331, 2002.
3. Yahia Lebbah, Michel Rueher, and Claude Michel. A global filtering algorithm for handling systems of quadratic equations and inequations. In *Proc. of CP-02*, Ithaca, NY, USA, 2002.
4. Míhaly C. Markót. An interval method to validate optimal solutions of the "packing circles in a unit square" problems. *Central European Journal of Operational Research*, 8:63–78, 2000.

F. Rossi (Ed.): CP 2003, LNCS 2833, p. 975, 2003.

Algorithmic Mechanism Design and Constraints*

Alan Holland and Barry O'Sullivan

Cork Constraint Computation Centre
Department of Computer Science, University College Cork, Ireland
{a.holland,b.osullivan}@cs.ucc.ie

Ensuring truthfulness amongst self-interested agents who are bidding against one another in an auction is computationally expensive. The Vickrey-Clarke-Groves (VCG) mechanism guarantees that each of the agent's dominant strategy is to tell the truth, but it requires solving $n + 1$ optimisation problems for n agents. The objective of our work is to use constraints in conjunction with Operations Research to make truthful mechanisms computationally feasible. Eliciting truthful responses from self-interested agents has been previously studied in game theory and economics. A class of VCG mechanisms have been developed whereby the dominant strategy for any agent is to tell the truth, meaning that rational agents maximise their utility by truthfully revealing their preferences.

It has been shown that if non-optimal solutions are found to the optimisation problems that determine the prices paid in VCG mechanisms, then the mechanism is no longer guaranteed to be truthful [2]. This is a major drawback because it precludes the use of various polynomial-time heuristics and approximation algorithms that can provide good or near optimal solutions very quickly to NP-complete problems such as combinatorial auctions.

CP algorithms can borrow techniques from OR to minimise the punitive computational burden when ensuring truthfulness. Using propagation and inference techniques, CP can aid the search when the conditions for solutions are complicated by additional constraints. We shall conduct an empirical study of the benefits of using CP for task scheduling in a grid environment within a pricing mechanism framework. We also plan to investigate the suitability of DCSP as an underlying infrastructure for Distributed Algorithmic Mechanism Design [1]. Our main aim is to show that constraint technology, when allied with OR algorithms, can make truthfulness more computationally feasible and improve flexibility.

References

1. Joan Feigenbaum and Scott Shenker. Distributed algorithmic mechanism design: Recent results and future directions. In *Proceedings of the 6th International Workshop on Discrete Algorithms and Methods for Mobile Computing and Communications*, pages 1–13, New York, 2002. ACM Press.
2. Noam Nisan and Amir Ronen. Computationally feasible VCG mechanisms. In *ACM Conference on Electronic Commerce*, pages 242–252, 2000.

* This research is funded by Enterprise Ireland through their Research Innovation Fund (Grant Number RIF-2001-317).

F. Rossi (Ed.): CP 2003, LNCS 2833, p. 976, 2003.

Preference Constraints: New Global Soft Constraints Dedicated to Preference Binary Relations

Rémy-Robert Joseph[1], Peter Chan[2], Michael Hiroux[1,2], and Georges Weil[1,2]

[1] Université Joseph Fourier-Grenoble 1, Laboratoire IMAG/TIMC, Equipe SIC
Institut Albert Bonniot, 38706 La Tronche, France
[2] Equitime S.A., Grand sablon, 4 Avenue de l'Obiou 38700 La Tronche, France
Remy.Joseph@imag.fr

The privileged preference representation used for combinatorial problems has been the objective function. It is almost exclusively used at every aggregation levels of a hierarchical preference model, and has remarkable structural properties as transitivity and completeness. These properties are often judged too restrictive, because some important aggregation concepts are incomplete by definition, as efficiency and equity. Moreover, preferences are not necessarily transitive because of uncertainty. For all these reasons, we decided to enlarge objective function-based combinatorial problems toward weaker structured preference concepts: preference binary relations.

Given a set of solutions S, a *preference binary relation* $\succcurlyeq$ of an individual on S can be interpreted as a mapping from $S \times S$ to the set of *fundamental attitudes* $FA = \{$indifferent, better, worse, incomparable$\}$. The power set of FA minus the empty set and FA is called the *set of attitudes* $PR(FA)$. When S is an explicit solutions set, preference binary relation is explicitly represented. But in an implicit solutions set environment as for constraint-based problems (S is then a Cartesian product) this way of modelling is inadequate. We propose a new soft constraint called preference constraint, dedicated to preference binary relations on constraints systems. So, the *preference constraint*, noted $\{c_\succcurlyeq[\alpha, x]\}_{\alpha, x}$, describing the preference binary relation $\succcurlyeq$, is the set of constraints $\{c_\succcurlyeq[\alpha, x], \forall (\alpha, x) \in PR(FA) \times \mathcal{D}_v\}$ on the variable set V, with $\mathcal{D}_v$ the Cartesian product of domains $D(v)$ for all $v \in V$. Each constraint $c_\succcurlyeq[\alpha, x]$ is parameterized by a solution x and an attitude α, and its feasible set is made up of solutions $y \in \mathcal{D}_v$ such that $y \, \alpha_\succcurlyeq \, x$, with $\alpha_\succcurlyeq$ indicating the attitude α of the preference binary relation $\succcurlyeq$. In a digraph context, the feasible set describes the neighborhood of x in the solution set according to the binary relation $\alpha_\succcurlyeq$.

Preference constraints offer great flexibility for preferences elicitation: Complex evaluation models of solutions involve several viewpoints from several individuals, which are methodically synthesized with various aggregations rules in order to obtain a single collective preference binary relation. In this kind of hierarchical preference model, each aggregation rule is represented by one preference constraint defined recursively. Consequently, the instance of a constraint-based combinatorial problem can be defined as a couple $(CS, \{c_\succcurlyeq[\alpha, x]\}_{\alpha, x})$, called *preference-based constraint system*, where $CS = (V, D, C)$ is a constraint system describing the set of solutions, and $\{c_\succcurlyeq[\alpha, x]\}_{\alpha, x}$ is a recursively-defined preference constraint. To tackle real world problems, each preference constraint is designed as a global constraint parameterized by α and x. We present algorithms based on Branch-and-Bound and discuss an initial implementation solving the nurse scheduling problem with encouraging results.

F. Rossi (Ed.): CP 2003, LNCS 2833, p. 977, 2003.
© Springer-Verlag Berlin Heidelberg 2003

Optimising the Representation and Evaluation
of Semiring Combination Constraints*

Jerome Kelleher and Barry O'Sullivan

Cork Constraint Computation Centre
Department of Computer Science, University College Cork, Ireland
{j.kelleher,b.osullivan}@4c.ucc.ie

Classical constraint satisfaction problems (CSPs) provide an expressive formalism for modeling and solving many real-world problems. However, classical CSPs prove to be restrictive in any situation where uncertainty, fuzziness, probability, optimisation or partial satisfaction are intrinsic. Soft constraints alleviate many of the restrictions which classical constraint satisfaction impose. In particular, soft constraints provide a basis for capturing notions such as vagueness, uncertainty and cost in the CSP model.

The semiring framework [1–4] for generalised constraint satisfaction is based upon the central observation that a semiring (a set together with two binary operators which satisfy certain properties) is all that is needed to describe many constraint satisfaction paradigms. The semiring set provides the levels of consistency, which can be interpreted as cost, degrees of preference, probabilities or any other criteria consistent with the requirements of the framework. The two operations then allow us to combine constraints ($\times$) and to compare ($+$) consistency levels from this set.

In this work we demonstrate a time and space efficient method for representing and evaluating c-semiring combination constraints. We show how combination constraints can be represented intentionally in a time and space efficient manner. We then utilise a basic property of the definition of a c-semiring to allow us to perform a generalised lazy evaluation of combination constraints that can be applied transparently to all instances of the framework. We evaluate the performance implications of the cumulative effect of this run-time optimisation, demonstrating the utility and generality of this approach.

References

1. S. Bistarelli. *Soft Constraint Solving and programming: a general framework.* PhD thesis, Dipartimento di Informatica, Università di Pisa, Italy, Mar 2001. TD-2/01.
2. S. Bistarelli, U. Montanari, and F. Rossi. Constraint Solving over Semirings. In *Proc. IJCAI-95*, San Francisco, CA, USA, 1995.
3. S. Bistarelli, U. Montanari, and F. Rossi. Semiring-based Constraint Solving and Optimization. *Journal of the ACM*, 44(2):201–236, Mar 1997.
4. S. Bistarelli, U. Montanari, and F. Rossi. Soft concurrent constraint programming. In *Proc. ESOP, Grenoble, France*, volume 2305 of *LNCS*. Springer, 2002.

* This work has received support from Enterprise Ireland under their Basic Research Grant Scheme (Grant Number SC/02/289).

Symmetry Breaking Ordering Constraints*

Zeynep Kiziltan

Department of Information Science
Uppsala University, Box 513, SE-751 20, Uppsala, Sweden
Zeynep.Kiziltan@dis.uu.se

An important class of symmetries in constraint programming arises in matrices of decision variables (we assume 2 dimensional matrices without loss of generality) where rows and columns represent indistinguishable objects and are therefore symmetric. We can permute any two rows as well as two columns of a matrix with row and column symmetry without affecting any (partial) assignments. An $n \times m$ matrix with row and column symmetry has $n!m!$ symmetries, which increase super-exponentially thus it can be very expensive to visit all the symmetric branches of the search tree. In order to break such symmetries effectively, we investigate ordering constraints that can be posted on matrices without removing feasible solutions.

To break row symmetry, we can enforce that the rows are lexicographically ordered. To break row and column symmetries, we can insist that the rows and columns are both lexicographically ordered. We can also treat each row as a multiset and enforce that the rows are multiset ordered. Unlike lexicographic ordering, multiset ordering the rows is invariant to column permutation. Multiset ordering is incomparable to lexicographic ordering. To break row and column symmetries, we can insist that the rows and columns are both multiset ordered. Alternatively, we can enforce multiset ordering in one dimension and lexicographic ordering in the order. To easily pose, and effectively and efficiently propagate the ordering constraints, we have devised global constraints for lexicographic and multiset orderings.

If the search strategy pushes search in a different direction than that of the ordering constraints, the search tree enlarges. This conflict can be overcome by incorporating more inference into the the ordering constraints by combining together the problem and the ordering constraints. We therefore introduce a new global constraint on 0/1 variables that combines together the lexicographic ordering constraint with two sum constraints. Such constraints frequently occur together in problems involving capacity or partitioning that are modelled with symmetric matrices of decision variables.

Experimental results confirm the effectiveness and the efficiency of the global constraints, as well as the value of the ordering constraints in breaking row and column symmetries effectively.

---

* I am very grateful to Toby Walsh for his excellent supervision of this work. Many thanks to Brahim Hnich, Alan Frisch, and Ian Miguel for their comments and fruitful discussions. This research received support from VR grant 221-99-369 and SFI. Zeynep Kiziltan. *Symmetry Breaking Ordering Constraints*. PhD thesis, Uppsala University. Due to be submitted late 2003.

F. Rossi (Ed.): CP 2003, LNCS 2833, p. 979, 2003.

Observation of Constraint Programs*

Ludovic Langevine

INRIA Rocquencourt, BP 105, 78153 Le Chesnay Cedex, France
Ludovic.Langevine@inria.fr

Constraint programming still lacks the suitable debugging tools and techniques. When a program gives incorrect results or when its performances are disappointing, the developer gets very little support from his programming environment to find out the problem. Specific tools are needed to ease this debugging stage.

Debugging tools use data that are retrieved during the execution. This basic information can be taken out from an execution trace generated by a tracer embedded in the solver. Thus, a traditional tracer, that provides a rich enough trace, is a powerful front-end to new debugging tools. The difficult task of instrumenting the solver is made only once.

We have defined a *generic trace* for constraint solvers over finite domains [1]. The genericity of the trace is twofold: it can feed a large variety of tools and it can reflect the behavior of several constraint programming platforms. The goal of the generic trace is to ease the definition of debugging tools independently of the platforms. We claim that most of the functioning a user wants to observe can be captured by this trace. This trace reflects the interesting aspects of the execution while hiding solver specific issues.

Real-life constraint programs can generate a huge amount of trace data. To limit the volume of the trace, the tracer has to generate only the subset of the trace that is relevant for a given debugging tool. Thus, the tracer has to implement a *lazy generation* of the trace: the tool must be able to configure the subset of the trace to be generated and to ask the tracer to modify it dynamically to fit its needs.

A first "lazy" tracer has already been developed for the GNU-Prolog platform. It implements a refinement of the generic trace model. A first experimental assessment has shown the efficiency of this tracer. A further step would be to connect the tracer to visualization tools.

References

1. P. Deransart, M. Ducassé, and L. Langevine. A generic trace model for finite domain solvers. In Barry O'Sullivan, editor, *Proc. of UICS'02, a CP conference workshop*, Cornell University (USA), Aug 2002.

---

* This work is partly supported by OADymPPaC, a French RNTL project. My work is directed by Pierre Deransart and Mireille Ducassé.

F. Rossi (Ed.): CP 2003, LNCS 2833, p. 980, 2003.

Search Programming

Wojciech Legierski

Institute of Automatic Control, Silesian Technical University, Akademicka 16
44-100 Gliwice, Poland
wlegierski@ia.polsl.gliwice.pl
http://www.ia.polsl.gliwice.pl/~wlegiers

Programming search seems to be major factor of adapting constraint programming paradigm for large-scale real-world application such as timetabling problem. Presented work tries to use explicit search implemented in Mozart/Oz, what allows to create complicated, custom-tailored distribution strategy and search method. Well-known first-fail distribution strategy was not sufficient, because timetabling problem with room allocation is consider and there are two finite domain variables connected with course. Choosing proper course rather than variable is consider and decision is made due several factors.

For resolving soft constraining method of value assessment was used. The assessment of the value corresponds to the fulfillment of the soft constraint. If a value does not fulfill the soft constraint its assessment is increased corresponding to the weight of that constraint. Some of hard and soft constraints was introduced during distribution for reducing complexity of computations.

Often in sophisticated combinatory problems occurs thrashing, repeated failure due to the same reason and redundant work. Method of counting fails and researching was introduced, which bases on counting which course is making fail during search and using it in course selection. Next if solution is not found in some limit time, search is restarted and number of fails from previous searches are taken into account in selecting course. It leads to effect, that variables that cause thrashing are schedule at the beginning. This method is also used with relaxing bound for removing value with too high assessment - technique for increasing constraint propagation that accelerate finding feasible and good solution.

Improving solution by standard branch and bound did not give good results because distribution is design to find good solution right away and branch and bound is systematic method that make a lot of redundant work. Described approach tries not to resign from constraint propagation and uses advantages of the local search paradigm to optimize timetable. After finding solution course, that causes the highest cost, is relaxed together with courses depending on it. All other courses have the same start time. Search is made only on relaxed courses and is treated as neighborhood move. If it produces better solution, it is kept. The tabu list is added not to relax always the same courses.

The presented approach allows generating feasible and good solutions for real high-school and university department timetabling data. Future work consists on using better local search techniques for optimization[1].

---

[1] A part of the research has been supported by the Foundation for Polish Science.

F. Rossi (Ed.): CP 2003, LNCS 2833, p. 981, 2003.

Exploiting Microstructure in CSPs*

Chavalit Likitvivatanavong

Cork Constraint Computation Centre, University College Cork, Ireland
chavalit@4c.ucc.ie

The general aim of my research involves a new perspective on the study of standard CSP notions. In this view, a typical unit in the CSP paradigm can be seen as a combination of smaller units. An operation can be considered as a composition of smaller operations. Here I describe two such studies.

The first research concerns interchangeability of values in a CSP domain. The main idea is based on treating each value as a combination of smaller sub-values. Identical fragments from other values can then be merged together. Since the new domain contains no two values having overlapping set of microstructure support, it is expected that the amount of duplicate effort during search would be reduced. Preliminary experiment in [1] confirms the hypothesis. An example of the idea is shown in Figure 1.

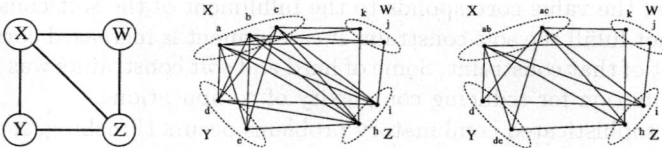

Fig. 1. From left to right: A CSP involving four variables, its microstructure, and the transformed CSP after merging identical sub-values.

The second research direction deals with the process of variable instantiation. Departing from the normal viewpoint, we see a variable instantiation as a removal of domain values; removing all but one value from a variable domain is equivalent to the usual instantiation. This non-standard perception allows us to treat variable instantiation as a successive process of value removal. It has the following advantage: during search when a conflict is encountered, instead of looking at particular variable assignments as the cause we try to narrow down the "culprit", a set of values whose removal leads to that conflict. Any assignment of a value not in the culprit set will lead to the same dead-end, since assigning it amounts to the deletion of all other values including the culprit set. Consequently, each value not included in the culprit set can not be part of a solution and can be immediately ruled out.

References

1. James Bowen and Chavalit Likitvivatanavong. Splitting the atom: A new approach to neighbourhood interchangeability in constraint satisfaction problems. In *Proceedings of IJCAI'03*, Acapulco, Mexico, 2003.

* This work has received support from Science Foundation Ireland under Grant 00/PI.1/C075

Using Case-Based Reasoning to Write Constraint Programs*

James Little, Cormac Gebruers, Derek Bridge, and Eugene C. Freuder

Cork Constraint Computation Centre
Computer Science Department
University College Cork

'Constraint programming' (CP) is a powerful tool for problem solving. However, to obtain maximum benefit from CP, programmers require significant knowledge and experience. We describe a new approach where Case-Based Reasoning is used to help write good constraint programs. Our approach provides the potential for the full range of CBR advantages to be brought to bear on the task of automating constraint programming:

- Experts can provide knowledge conveniently in the form of cases
- Expertise can be naturally provided in a modular, incremental fashion
- Solution methods can be matched with problem characteristics for efficient execution
- Cases can be automatically adapted to cover unforeseen situations
- Adaptations can be generalised and added to the case base to implement a form of learning from experience

Case-Based Reasoning is a problem-solving methodology based on reusing experience gained in previous problem-solving episodes. In CBR, a new problem is not generally solved by reasoning 'from scratch' but by retrieving stored solutions to similar previously-solved problems, and transferring and adapting these solutions to the new problem. To use CBR to write constraint programs thus requires the identification of problem characteristics (*viz.* a problem representation) that enables us to say that two problems are 'similar'. We can then reuse an effective solution strategy from one constraint program on new, but similar, problems. A key advantage of using CBR is the ability to predict a rich combination of programming choices simultaneously i.e. choice of Variable Ordering Heuristic *and* Value Ordering Heuristic *and* constraint representation.

Apart from their experience, the constraint programmer's main methodology for writing good programs is empirical experimentation. An alternative way of achieving efficient constraint programs is by shifting part of the knowledge burden required from the developer to the machine. Our methodology, O'Casey, makes it possible to encapsulate into cases both the expertise and findings of case studies, and examples of effective constraint programs written by experts. O'Casey can also utilise abstract specifications to generate programs but with less of a knowledge burden on the programmer than existing systems.

* This work has received support from Science Foundation Ireland under Grant 00/PI.1/C075

F. Rossi (Ed.): CP 2003, LNCS 2833, p. 983, 2003.
© Springer-Verlag Berlin Heidelberg 2003

Reformulation Techniques
for a Class of Permutation Problems

Toni Mancini

Dipartimento di Informatica e Sistemistica, Università di Roma "La Sapienza"
tmancini@dis.uniroma1.it

The long-term goal of our research is to provide syntactic criteria for the automatic reformulation of combinatorial and constraint problems specifications, in order to improve solver efficiency. Our current investigations focus on the selection of constraints that can be safely "delayed" and solved afterwards, yet guaranteeing that every solution of the reformulated spec can be reconduced, via the application of the delayed constraints, to a solution of the original one. A consequence of this approach is that the set of solutions is enlarged, thus hopefully obtaining a speed-up in the solving process.

In this paper we focus on reformulation techniques for the subclass of *permutation problems* characterized by constraints that bind an element of the permutation either to the next or the previous one. A paradigmatic example is the *Hamiltonian circuit* (HC) of a graph problem, which aims to find a permutation of the graph nodes (i.e., a bijective mapping from the n nodes to the integer range $[1..n]$) s.t. every node is linked to its successor, and the last to the first one. Another example is the *permutation flow-shop scheduling* problem. In this context, we identify the Injective constraint (Inj) as *safe-delay*. By ignoring it and slightly changing the other constraints, we obtain possible reformulations of the original problems. As an example, for HC, removing (Inj) results in clusters of nodes that can be visited in an arbitrary way (thus, identifying only a partial order among them). To guarantee that every solution of the reformulated problem can be reconduced to a solution of the original one, the adjacency constraint has to be extended to nodes with the same order number, thus forcing clusters to be cliques. In this way, we allow abstraction from the level of nodes to the level of clusters, by first identifying cliques, and then solving the HC problem on the abstract graph. Further elaborations of the above idea are possible, leading to two additional reformulations of the original problem which result to abstract graphs with less edges. As a consequence, they seem more efficiently evaluable wrt the original spec, especially for negative instances, for particular classes of solvers (e.g., SAT based ones). As for the planned work, we aim to extend the experimentation through the use of state-of-the-art solvers for CP, e.g., OPL.

From a methodological point of view, it is important to emphasize that our goal is not to provide a new and more efficient algorithm for solving a particular problem, but to show that consistent speed-ups can be achieved by a mere and syntactically-based reformulation of a pure declarative spec, which can be in principle performed automatically by the system in a preprocessing stage.

Acknowledgments. The author is grateful to his advisor, Prof. Marco Cadoli, for guiding, supporting, and encouraging his research activity.

F. Rossi (Ed.): CP 2003, LNCS 2833, p. 984, 2003.
© Springer-Verlag Berlin Heidelberg 2003

NuSBDS:
An Easy to Use Symmetry Breaking System

Iain McDonald*

School of Computer Science, University of St Andrews
Fife, Scotland
iain@dcs.st-and.ac.uk

Over the past few years we have seen a marked increase in the interest of symmetry breaking in constraint programming. Many new techniques have been introduced to deal with the problems that symmetrical CSPs create. Previous methods of symmetry breaking such as SBDS [1] and SBDD [2,3] require an explicit list of the symmetries of a CSP, or a dominance checker, respectively. Also, the GHK-SBDS method [4] of breaking symmetry requires the user to supply a generator set of a group representing the symmetries of the CSP.

In all cases, some effort is needed by the constraint programmer to describe the symmetries of their problem. This is a barrier that needs to be broken if we are to see symmetry breaking used by the constraint community in general.

We present an implementation that breaks this barrier: NuSBDS, which has been designed to allow the average constraint programmer to break symmetry in their CSPs quickly and easily. NuSBDS is a C++ library that works with ILOG Solver 5.x and is based on the GHK-SBDS method of symmetry breaking. It has an additional layer of code which allows the constraint programmer to list the types of symmetry that exist in their CSPs easily by stating the name of a macro. Multiple macros can be used to describe many complex groups of symmetry while the user need not know any group theory. Consult [5] for a more detailed explanation with examples of how to use NuSBDS.

References

1. Ian Gent and Barbara Smith. Symmetry breaking in constraint programming. In W. Horn, editor, *Proceedings of ECAI-2000*, pages 599–603. IOS Press, 2000.
2. Torsten Fahle, Stefan Schamberger, and Meinolf Sellman. Symmetry breaking. In Toby Walsh, editor, *Principles and Practice of Constraint Programming - CP2001*, pages 93–107. Springer-Verlag, 2001.
3. Filippo Focacci and Michaela Milano. Global cut framework for removing symmetries. In Toby Walsh, editor, *Principles and Practice of Constraint Programming - CP2001*, pages 77–92. Springer-Verlag, 2001.
4. Ian Gent, Warwick Harvey, and Tom Kelsey. Groups and constraints: Symmetry breaking during search. In P Van Hentenryck, editor, *Principles and Practice of Constraint Programming*, pages 415–430. Springer-Verlag, 2002.
5. Iain McDonald. NuSBDS: An easy to use Symmetry Breaking System. Technical Report APES-61-2003, APES Research Group, July 2003.

* I would like to thank all the members of the APES research group for their help. I would also like to thank the EPSRC for funding my research.

F. Rossi (Ed.): CP 2003, LNCS 2833, p. 985, 2003.

Interactivity in Constraint Programming

Tomáš Müller

Charles University, Department of Theoretical Computer Science
Malostranske namesti 2/25, Prague, Czech Republic
muller@kti.mff.cuni.cz

During the last few years, thanks to the faster, smaller, cheaper personal computers and well-developed, user friendly software, the interactive behaviour is more and more requested. In this paper, we will discuss what impacts the interactivity can have on CSP.

Interactivity manifests itself in several ways. At first, the possibility to influence the problem solving process seems to be the most important. Such capability can give the users a very powerful tool to tackle with difficulties that are sometimes very hard to solve for an automated solver. The solver has to be able to handle somehow modified solution and to continue solving the problem. The generated solution should not differ much from the previous one (what the user modified), because the user has to be able to follow up the changes. If the solver gives a completely different solution, the system will be useless.

Another, also very important property is the visualisation of results - not only some feasible, final solutions, but also some incomplete and even inconsistent solutions, generated during the search or when feasible results cannot be found in some reasonable time. The user should understand where the problems are and why a feasible or better solution was not found.

The capability to help the user make some decisions is also very interesting. The system can for example generate and evaluate some hints, like what to change and how (e.g. what constraint to weaken). There can also be more sophisticated advices, like what impact will some change have on the difference from the previous solution, what next changes will such modification cause, what has to be changed next.

There are several ongoing approaches, for example minimization of the number of differences between the previous and the new solution desired on an altered problem (e.g. minimal perturbation problem in [1,3]). Another approach tries to response very quickly after each single user interaction (e.g. by a local search based technique working on feasible partial solutions [2]).

References

1. [1] R. Barták, T. Müller, H. Rudová. *Minimal Perturbation Problem – A Formal View*. In Proceedings of the ERCIM Workshop on Constraints, Budapest, 2003
2. [2] T. Müller and R. Barták. *Interactive Timetabling: Concepts, Techniques, and Practical Results*. In Proceedings to PATAT'02 Conference, Gent, 2002.
3. [3] El. Sakkout and M Wallace. *Probe Backtrack Search for Minimal Perturbation in Dynamic Scheduling*, Constraints, Special Issue on Industrial Constraint-Directed Scheduling, Vol 5 No 4, 2000

F. Rossi (Ed.): CP 2003, LNCS 2833, pp. 986, 2003.
© Springer-Verlag Berlin Heidelberg 2003

Identifying Inconsistent CSPs by Relaxation

Tomas Nordlander[1], Ken Brown[2], and Derek Sleeman[1]

[1]Dept of Computing Science, University of Aberdeen Scotland, UK
{tnordlan,sleeman}@csd.abdn.ac.uk
[2]Cork Constraint Computation Centre, Dept of Computer Science, UCC, Ireland
k.brown@cs.ucc.ie

MUSKRAT (Multistrategy Knowledge Refinement and Acquisition Toolbox) [1] aims to unify problem solving, knowledge acquisition and knowledge-base refinement in a single computational framework. Given a set of Knowledge Bases (KBs) and Problem Solvers (PSs), the MUSKRAT-Advisor investigates whether the available KBs will fulfil the requirements of the selected PS for a given problem. We would like to reject impossible combinations of KBs and PSs quickly. We propose to represent combinations of KBs and PSs as CSPs. If a CSP is not consistent, then the combination does not fulfil the requirements. The problem then becomes one of quickly identifying inconsistent CSPs. To do this, we propose to relax the CSPs: if we can prove that the relaxed version is inconsistent then we know that the original CSP is also inconsistent. It is not obvious that solving relaxed CSPs is any easier. In fact, phase transition research (e.g. [2]) seems to indicate the opposite when the original CSP is inconsistent. We have experimented with randomly generated CSPs [3], where the tightness of the constraints in a problem varies uniformly. We have shown that careful selection of the constraints to relax can save up to 70% of the search time. We have also investigated practical heuristics for relaxing CSPs. Experiments show that the simple strategy of removing constraints of low tightness is effective, allowing us to save up to 30% of the time on inconsistent problems without introducing new solutions.

In the constraints area, future work will look at extending this approach to more realistic CSPs. The focus will be on scheduling problems, which are likely to involve non-binary and global constraints, and constraint graphs with particular properties (e.g. [4]). We will also investigate more theoretical CSP concepts, including higher consistency levels and problem hardness. Success in this research will allow us to apply constraint satisfaction and relaxation techniques to the problem of knowledge base reuse.

References

1. S. White and D. Sleeman, A Constraint-Based Approach to the Description & Detection of Fitness-for-Purpose, ETAI, vol. 4, pp. 155-183, 2000.
2. P. Prosser, Binary constraint satisfaction problems: Some are harder than others, Proceedings ECAI-94 (11th European Conference on Artificial Intelligence), 1994, pp. 95-99.
3. T. Nordlander, K. Brown and D. Sleeman, Identifying Inconsistent CSPs by Relaxation, TR0304, University of Aberdeen, 2003.
4. T. Walsh, Search on high degree graphs, IJCAI-2001, 2001, pp. 266-274.

F. Rossi (Ed.): CP 2003, LNCS 2833, pp. 987, 2003.
© Springer-Verlag Berlin Heidelberg 2003

Useful Explanations*

Barry O'Callaghan, Eugene C. Freuder, and Barry O'Sullivan

Cork Constraint Computation Centre
Department of Computer Science, University College Cork, Ireland
{b.ocallaghan,e.freuder,b.osullivan}@4c.ucc.ie

Explanations for failure in constraint satisfaction tend to focus on blame. However, in an interactive context we also require explanations that are "useful" in the sense that they provide the basis for assisting the user move forward in search. In particular, when the user is faced with a dead-end, a subset of the assigned variables for which there exists an alternative assignment that permits moving forward should be found. This set of variables can be regarded as a *Useful Explanation*.

Several methods exist which can be used to compute explanations, such as PaLM [1] and QUICKXPLAIN [2], and through the use of dependency records [3, 4]. However, these approaches tend to find the reason that caused the problem, rather than advising the user what she can do to eliminate it.

By comparison, Useful Explanations focus solely on helping a user to make progress in an interactive environment. Useful Explanations concentrate on answering one question, namely *"what can I do to restore one or more values to a variable domain which has been wiped out?"*. By focusing on which assignments should be "fixed" the user can be helped to overcome inconsistency and to continue selecting values for the remaining variables in the problem. Useful Explanations are especially beneficial in interactive contexts in which users attempt to solve a constraint satisfaction problem (CSP), by assigning values to variables in turn, e.g. in e-commerce configuration.

Our current work focuses on developing efficient algorithms for computing Useful Explanations, developing metrics for evaluating the quality of explanations and investigating to what extent current blame-based explanation techniques compute explanations which are useful. In particular, we are interested in techniques which generate explanations which are guaranteed to be useful.

References

1. N. Jussien and V. Barichard. The PaLM system: explanation-based constraint programming. In *Proceedings of the CP-2000 TRICS Workshop*, pages 118–133, September 2000.
2. U. Junker. QUICKXPLAIN: Conflict detection for arbitrary constraint propagation algorithms. In *IJCAI'01 Workshop on Modelling and Solving problems with constraints*, 2001.
3. J. Bowen. Using dependency records to generate design coordination advice in a constraint-based approach to concurrent engineering. *Computers in Industry*, 22(1):191–199, 1997.
4. E. C. Freuder, C. Likitvivatanavong, and R. Wallace. Deriving Explanations and Implications for Constraint Satisfaction Problems. In *Proceedings of CP-2001*, pages 585–589, November 2001.

---

* This research is funded by Enterprise Ireland through their Research Innovation Fund (Grant Number RIF-2001-317). This work has also received support from Science Foundation Ireland under Grant 00/PI.1/C075.

F. Rossi (Ed.): CP 2003, LNCS 2833, p. 988, 2003.

Teacher and Learner Profiles
for Constraint Acquisition*

Sarah O'Connell, Barry O'Sullivan, and Eugene C. Freuder

Cork Constraint Computation Centre
Department of Computer Science, University College Cork, Ireland
{s.oconnell,b.osullivan,e.freuder}@4c.ucc.ie

In many practical applications users often find it difficult to articulate their constraints [1]. We have begun studying the issues involved in interactively acquiring constraints and have already made a number of novel contributions [3]. We view interactive constraint acquisition as the process of learning constraints from examples [2, 4] and focus on the role the user has to play during an interactive session. If we consider our user as a teacher, it may be possible that there are things that our teacher can do to provide "better" examples even without being able to precisely articulate the target concept. We have compared a number of teacher profiles and demonstrate that the ability of the teacher (the user) and the ability of the learner (constraint acquisition system) has an impact on the acquisition process.

We have found that while good query generation strategies, adopted by the learner, and good teachers can work well separately, when coupled their combined power is greatly increased. However, we have observed that while a teacher of average ability results in longer dialogs with the learner than the ideal teacher, the number of examples required to acquire the target constraint can often be of comparable magnitude. If we regard examples as being expensive, since they may be difficult to find, and responding to queries as being cheap, there is an interesting tradeoff to be considered between the cost of being a good teacher and the length of the dialog between the teacher and the learner. This raises a number of fundamental questions which we are currently studying.

Our current work focuses on acquiring multiple constraints from teachers of differing abilities using acquisition systems based on different query generation strategies. The insights gained here inform our research agenda in the area of interactive constraint acquisition.

References

1. Eugene C. Freuder and Richard J. Wallace. Suggestion strategies for constraint-based match-maker agents. In *Proceedings of CP98*, pages 192–204, October 1998.
2. Tom Mitchell. Generalization as search. *Artificial Intelligence*, 18(2):203–226, 1982.
3. Sarah O'Connell, Barry O'Sullivan, and Eugene C. Freuder. A study of query generation strategies for interactive constraint acquisition. In *Applications and Science in Soft Computing*, Advances in Soft Computing Series. Springer Verlag, 2003.
4. Claude Sammut and Ranan Banerji. Learning concepts by asking questions. In Ryszard S. Michalski, Jamie G. Carbonell, and Tom M. Mitchell, editors, *Machine Learning : An Artificial Intelligence Approach*, volume 2, chapter 7, pages 187–191. Morgan Kaufmann, 1986.

* This work has been supported by Science Foundation Ireland under Grant 00/PI.1/C075.

Comparison of Symmetry Breaking Methods

Karen E. Petrie

School of Computing & Engineering
University of Huddersfield
Huddersfield HD1 3DH, UK
k.e.petrie@hud.ac.uk

Constraint satisfaction problems (CSPs) are often highly symmetric. Given any solution, there are others which are equivalent in terms of the underlying problem being solved. Constraint programmers use symmetry breaking methods to exclude all but one in each equivalence class of solutions.

A common way to achieve this is to add constraints to the CSP. Ideally, the new constraints should only be satisfied by one assignment in any symmetrically equivalent class. An alternative is to adapt the search algorithm so that constraints are added during search. Symmetry breaking during search (SBDS) [1][3] works by taking a list of symmetry functions, provided by the programmer, and placing related constraints at branching points during search. In recent years Gent *et. al.*[2] have linked SBDS (in ECL^{i}PS^e) with a computational group theory package called GAP. Individual symmetries in a CSP correspond to elements in a group, so GAP-SBDS allows the symmetry group rather than the individual symmetries to be described. It is possible to combine both SBDS and GAP-SBDS with symmetry breaking constraints, as long as we ensure that each symmetrical equivalence class is only eliminated once.

The design and implementation of various symmetry breaking methods has lead to the need for investigations into which method should be used in different situations, and when a combination is needed. We have developed a framework for the design of such tests. In general, it is vital to choose an appropriate problem and consider the model and search heuristics. The problem should be one where you can easily vary the type and numbers of symmetries, as well as break the symmetry group down to subgroups; this gives a full suite to run comparisons over. The model and the search heuristic should be as simple as possible so as not to mask any differences in the symmetry methods, but it must be efficient enough to allow many test cases to be run in reasonable time. These decisions can be made by the use of a case study.

References

1. R. Backofen and S. Will. Excluding symmetries in constraint-based search. In *Principles and Practice of Constraint Programming*, pages 73–87, 1999.
2. I. P. Gent, W. Harvey, and T. Kelsey. Groups and Constraints: Symmetry Breaking During Search. In *Principles and Practice of Constraint Programming*, pages 415–430, 2002.
3. I. P. Gent and B. M. Smith. Symmetry breaking in constraint programming. In *Proceddings of ECAI-2002*, pages 599–603. IOS press, 2000.

F. Rossi (Ed.): CP 2003, LNCS 2833, p. 990, 2003.
© Springer-Verlag Berlin Heidelberg 2003

Improved Branch and Bound Algorithms for Max-2-SAT and Weighted Max-2-SAT*

Jordi Planes

Department of Computer Science, Universitat de Lleida, Spain
jordi@eup.udl.es

We developed novel branch and bound algorithms for solving Max-SAT and weighted Max-SAT, which are variants of the algorithm of Borchers & Furman (BFA) [1]. We improved BFA by (i) defining a lower bound of better quality, and (ii) incorporating a new variable selection heuristic.

The lower bound of BFA is the number of clauses not satisfied by the current partial assignment, but BFA does not incorporate any underestimation of the number of clauses that become unsatisfied if the current partial assignment is extended into a complete assignment. We incorporate that underestimation by taking into account the inconsistencies between past and future variables. Our first algorithms is BFA+UND; i.e., a new version of BFA that incorporates our lower bound.

The variable selection heuristic of BFA is MOMS (i.e., it selects a variable among those that appear more often in clauses of minimum size). We also used the Two-Sided Jeroslow-Wang rule (JW) [2] instead of MOMS in order to take into account the occurrences of variables in clauses which are not of minimum size. Our second algorithms is BFA+UND+JW; i.e., a new version of BFA that incorporates our lower bound with JW as variable selection heuristic.

We next show some experimental results comparing BFA, BFA+UND, and BFA+UND+JW. The left (right) plot shows the behaviour of the algorithms on 50-variable randomly generated (weighted) Max-2-SAT instances. Observe that our algorithms decreases the time needed to solve an instance up to two orders of magnitude.

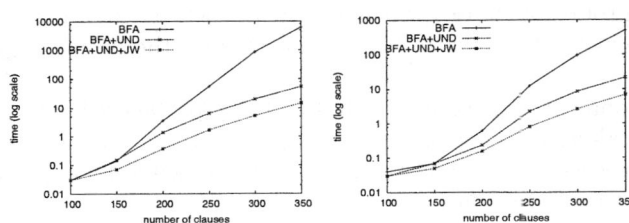

[1] B. Borchers and J. Furman. A two-phase exact algorithm for MAX-SAT and weighted MAX-SAT problems. *Journal of Combinatorial Optimization*, 2:299–306, 1999.

[2] R. G. Jeroslow and J. Wang. Solving propositional satisfiability problems. *Annals of Mathematics and Artificial Intelligence*, 1:167–187, 1990.

* This Research was partially supported by the project CICYT TIC2001-1577-C03-03 funded by the Spanish *Ministerio de Ciencia y Tecnología*.

Search for Mathematical Objects*

Colin Quirke

Boole Centre for Research in Informatics
Department of Computer Science
University College Cork, Ireland
cquirke@4c.ucc.ie

Abstract. Many open problems exist in mathematics. Many of these problems are combinatorial in nature and can theoretically be solved using search algorithms. Existing search algorithms are unable to cope with the large solution space and model size of many of these problems. We propose to solve these problems by modifying existing search algorithms and developing new algorithms to cope with the challanges that these problems offer.

The aim of this work is to apply recent advances in search technology to mathematical problems. In particular we aim to discover new mathematical objects which are imprecisely known: For example Ramsey numbers, zero-sum square matrices, and low-autocorrelation binary sequences. Systematic backtrack search can be used for proofs of nonexistence while stochastic search can be used to find solutions quickly. We hope to solve open questions in mathematics, and to exploit mathmatical insights to design new search algorithms.

In order to address these, and other open problems in combinatorial mathematics, we are limited by existing techniques. Many of these problems produce models which are too large for existing techniques to deal with. Some work has already been done on lifted search engines which allow SAT clauses to be expressed intentionally for sets of variables [1]. This allows large models to be expressed as groups of clauses which are then generated when they are needed. We itend to extend this work to make it suitable for the problems which we are interested in.

The development of new approaches to these problems is likely to find application to real-world problems. For example, techniques for handling the very large models necessary for Ramsey numbers are immediately applicable to other large combinatorial problems.

References

1. A. Parkes. *Lifted Search Engines for Satisfiability*. PhD thesis, University of Oregon, 1991.

---

* This research is funded by the Boole Center for Research in Informatics, UCC

F. Rossi (Ed.): CP 2003, LNCS 2833, p. 992, 2003.

Explanations for Global Constraints

Guillaume Rochart[*]

[1] Département Informatique de l'École des Mines de Nantes
4, rue Alfred Kastler - B.P. 20722 – F-44307 Nantes Cedex 3
[2] Institut de Recherche en Informatique de Nantes – Université de Nantes
2, rue de la Houssinière - BP 92208 – F-44322 Nantes Cedex 3
`grochart@emn.fr`

Numerous industrial problems can be modelled as constraint satisfaction problems: scheduling, call centers, television spots, etc. Constraint programming offers high-level modelling and reusable techniques for solving such problems. In order to provide efficient solvers and to better meet user needs, global constraints are often used. They model complex constraints over numerous variables: for instance, `gcc`, `alldiff` or `stretch`.

Explanation-based algorithms like dynamic backtracking, its extension mac-dbt or decision-repair have now proven their efficiency. However, the production of precise (thus useful) explanations is quite hard with global constraints. The aim of our work is to show that investing in sophisticated algorithms to provide precise explanations for global constraints is a good thing: solvers become more efficient.

An explanation contains enough information to justify a state or a decision (throwing a contradiction, reducing a domain...): it is composed of the constraints and the choices made during the search which are sufficient to justify such an inference. Although computing explanations for basic constraints is easy, using explanations with global constraints is quite more difficult. Indeed, it may be hard or even infeasible to make explanations about the filtering inferences without using internal data structures.

We compute here such explanations thanks to identifying explanations for all depending computations within global constraints. For instance, in the case of the `stretch` constraint, explanations should be identified for all the bounds of stretch. Regarding the `flow` constraint which allows to check wether there exists a flow in a network satisfying capacity constraints, we prove that a minimal cut can be used to justify the maximal flow in such a network. In both cases, these explanations can then be directly used in order to justify each decision taken in the pruning algorithm. The next step is to work on a generic framework for computing explanations for global constraints.

Our propositions were tested in order to show that precise explanations are really useful for improving problem solving. Experiments show good results in term of both number of nodes and computation times. Explanations for global constraints open new fields: solver cooperation, documentation, analysis, debugging, etc.

---

[*] This work is partially founded by Bouygues e-lab.

F. Rossi (Ed.): CP 2003, LNCS 2833, p. 993, 2003.

Watching Clauses
in Quantified Boolean Formulae

Andrew G.D. Rowley

University of St. Andrews, Fife, Scotland
agdr@dcs.st-and.ac.uk

The introduction of watched literals[1], a lazy data structure for satisfiability (SAT) search algorithms, has resulted in great improvements in the run-time of SAT solvers. Watched literals keeps track of two literals remaining in a clause so as to detect when a clause becomes unit or empty. Watched literals is non-trivial to implement in QBF search. Quantified Boolean Formulae (QBFs) are SAT formulae with some variables universally quantified. This changes the semantics of unit and false clauses. The issue of watching literals in QBF is addressed in [2].

In this paper, I show that the use of lazy data structures need not be restricted to literals in clauses. In SAT, the detection of pure literals and deleted variables appears to be unimportant[3], and so watched literals has so far been the only implemented lazy data structure. In search for QBF satisfiability, this is not the case; the detection of universal pure literals in particular is critical. This is because a universal pure literal is set false, and so removes the universal from clauses. These clauses could then lead to further unit propagation.

To detect a pure literal, one must know the number of literals of each sign of a variable that exist in the problem. An easy way in which to do this is to keep a list of which clauses a variable occurs in an which sign the literal of the variable has in those clauses. If the positive and negative occurences are kept separate, detecting pure literals becomes trivial. The watched method improves upon this by keeping one positive and one negative watched "c-literal" per variable. If either is ever remove d and no other can be found to take its place, the variable is detected as having a pure literal.

In an experimental comparison, the watched clause method outperformed the standard method by up to 8825 times on some problems, and never performed worse. The watched clause method is not restricted to QBF and implementation in SAT may prove the effectiveness of pure literals in SAT.

References

1. Moskewicz, M., Madigan, C., Zhao, Y., Zhang, L., Malik, S.: Chaff: Engineering an Efficient SAT Solver. In: DAC. (2001)
2. Gent, I., Giunchiglia, E., Narizzano, M., Rowley, A., Tacchella, A.: Efficient data structures for QBF solvers. In: SAT. (2003)
3. Zhang, L., Malik, S.: The quest for efficient Boolean satisfiability solvers. In: CADE. (2002) 295–313

F. Rossi (Ed.): CP 2003, LNCS 2833, p. 994, 2003.
© Springer-Verlag Berlin Heidelberg 2003

Distributed Constraint-Based Railway Simulation

Hans Schlenker

Fraunhofer FIRST, Kekuléstraße 7, 12489 Berlin, Germany
hans.schlenker@first.fraunhofer.de

In Railway Simulation, given timetables have to be checked against various criteria, mainly correctness and robustness. Most existing approaches use classical centralized simulation techniques. This work goes beyond that in two main aspects: I use Constraint Satisfaction to get rid of dead lock problems and the simulation is done distributed. This should make it possible to solve a Railway Simulation problem, never solved before in its complexity: the German railway network. In all existing simulation approaches, physical systems are described in terms of states and (mostly discrete) events. In Constraint-Based Simulation, we use a modeling that is completely different to classical approaches: The system to be simulated is described as one complex Constraint Satisfaction Problem (CSP). This CSP is solved using state-of-the-art propagation and search techniques. In our application, the railway network is mapped into an abstract discrete model: It is partitioned into blocks, while each real track section may be cut in more than one block. A block is then the atomical exclusion unit: In no event, one block may be occupied by more than one train at the same time. The way of a train through the network is divided into parts such that each part refers to exactly one block and the concatenation of all parts makes up the whole way of the train from its source to its destination. Assigning start and duration times to each part wrt. its block then gives directly a solution to the simulation problem. The big advantage of this approach is that deadlock situations are detected very early: constraint propagation does this for us. Distributed Railway Simulation (DRS) is Railway Simulation in a distributed manner: The simulation problem is cut into several pieces, which are simulated in several nodes. We currently decompose the problem wrt. space: The network is partitioned such that the number of parts fits the number of available computing nodes while the number of cut railway lines is minimized. A meta-algorithm conducts the distributed simulation process: (1) Decompose problem (2) Start simulators (3) Distribute problem parts (4) Main loop: (4a) Let parts be simulated (4b) Try merging parts; where necessary to fit solutions: re-do simulation of parts (5) Merge partial results into global result. The algorithm may or may not be synchronized. In non-synchronized mode, each node simulates its part, communicates the entering and leaving trains to its neighbours, and immediately recomputes the part in case some neighbour has sent appropriate changes. In synchronized mode, the node, after having finished its part, waits until all other nodes have completed their work and restarts afterwards. The main advantage of the synchronized mode is that it makes the overall computation deterministic. The non-synchronized mode is non-deterministic, but has a higher degree of concurrency.

F. Rossi (Ed.): CP 2003, LNCS 2833, p. 995, 2003.
© Springer-Verlag Berlin Heidelberg 2003

Dynamic Step Size Adjustment
in Iterative Deepening Search

Daniel Sheridan

University of Edinburgh, Kings Buildings, Edinburgh, UK
djsheridan@sms.ed.ac.uk

If an iterative deepening search (IDS) procedure has the property that solutions at a given iteration are also found at later iterations, it is possible to skip iterations without loss of correctness. We examine the conditions required for skipping to be worthwhile and give an algorithm for dynamically adapting the skipping to the behaviour of the search procedure.

We consider the problem f with solution π, written $\pi \models f$. If a solution is found during IDS at depth i, we write $\pi \models_i f$. We write $T(f, i)$ for the time taken for the ith iteration. We make the following simplifying assumptions:

- If f has a solution, this solution may be found by iterative deepening search to some depth k: $\pi \models f \rightarrow \exists k \cdot \pi \models_k f$
- If f has a solution at depth i then it is solvable at all greater depths: $\pi \models_i f \rightarrow \forall j \geq i, \pi \models_j f$
- $T(f, i)$ is monotonically increasing with i: $\forall j \geq i, T(f, j) \geq T(f, i)$

To decide on the size of a step to be taken, we consider the circumstances under which a particular step size will save time overall. Suppose we are currently at depth i during the IDS. It is preferable to solve $\pi \models_{i+\Delta} f$ next rather than the sequence $\forall_{j=i..n} \pi \models_j f$ iff $i + \Delta > n$ and $T(f, i+\Delta) < \sum_{j=i+1}^n T(f, j)$. The point of comparison, n, is chosen by a simple heuristic found in testing to be sufficient: the first solution of f is equally likely to lie at any depth $k, 0 \leq k < \infty$, so we take $n = i + \lceil \frac{\Delta}{2} \rceil$.

To construct the algorithm, we approximate $T(f, i)$ as an exponential ba^i, which is appropriate for many possible applications including bounded model checking. We determine the a and b using standard statistical methods on the past behaviour of the search, and hence choose a maximum Δ which satisfies the conditions above. This gives us the following algorithm:

- Initialise: $a, b \leftarrow \infty$, current depth $i \leftarrow 0$, list of past behaviour $B \leftarrow []$
- Until a solution is found, loop:
  - Solve $\pi \models_i f$, recording the time taken in t
  - Append the pair $\langle i, t \rangle$ to B
  - Use best-fit on B to estimate a and b
  - Choose Δ such that $ba^{i+\Delta} < \sum_{j=i+1}^{i+\lceil \frac{\Delta}{2} \rceil} ba^j$
  - $i \leftarrow i + \Delta$

Our preliminary experimental evaluation demonstrates the efficacy of this method on bounded model checking problems; however, other iterative-deepening-style problems must be tried in order to determine the generality of the heuristic chosen.

F. Rossi (Ed.): CP 2003, LNCS 2833, p. 996, 2003.

Learning Good Variable Orderings

Paula Sturdy

School of Computing and Engineering, University of Huddersfield, UK
p.sturdy@hud.ac.uk

Variable ordering heuristics try to reduce the cost of searching for a solution to a constraint satisfaction problem (CSP). On real problems that have non-binary and non-uniform constraints it is harder to make a good choice of variable ordering: surprisingly little is known about when and why variable ordering heuristics perform well. In an attempt to address this problem we present initial problem-specific investigations into variable orderings. The problem selected was the graceful labelling of the graph $2C_4 + K_1$ shown in figure 1.

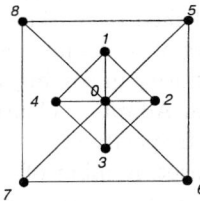

Fig. 1. The 'double wheel' graph $2C_4 + K_1$.

This problem is described by Petrie and Smith [1]. Their initial model specified a static variable ordering informed by the behaviour of what are already known to be good heuristics such as smallest remaining domain. Whilst good results were obtained, in terms of the total number of backtracks to find all solutions, other static variable orderings are significantly better. These observations led to this more thorough investigation: more detail can be found in [2].

It is usually expected that the length of the search depends greatly on the selection of the first variable: in fact, our results show for this problem that it is possible to obtain good results with *any* choice of first variable. This suggests that choosing a good initial order for the variables as the basis for either a static or dynamic variable ordering heuristic may be less straightforward, at least for some problems, than hitherto thought.

References

1. K. E. Petrie and B. M. Smith. Symmetry Breaking in Graceful Graphs. In F. Rossi, editor, *Principles and Practice of Constraint Programming - CP2003*, LNCS. Springer, 2003.
2. P. Sturdy. Learning Good Variable Orderings. Technical Report APES-64-2003, APES Research Group, July 2003. Available from
http://www.dcs.st-and.ac.uk/~apes/apesreports.html

F. Rossi (Ed.): CP 2003, LNCS 2833, p. 997, 2003.
© Springer-Verlag Berlin Heidelberg 2003

An Adaptive Controller for Real-Time Resolution of the Vehicle Routing Problem

Ann Tighe, Finlay Smith, and Gerard Lyons

Dept of Information Technology
National University of Ireland, Galway
{Ann.Tighe,Finlay.Smith,Gerard.Lyons}@nuigalway.ie

The Vehicle Routing Problem (VRP) is a mathematical model that closely approximates the real-world problems freight companies must deal with on a daily basis. Given the dynamic nature of these problems, VRP can have different levels of constraints and consequently many varied solving techniques. Different constraints on the VRP such as time constraints or the number of vehicles in a fleet, has brought about a need for tailor-made algorithms. Many hybrid techniques to solve the VRP have been established [1–3]. The success of these multiple strategy procedures on different types of problems and the underlining evidence that no one method has shown superiority in solving various versions of this problem has led to the investigation of an Adaptive Controller for resolving the VRP.

This Adaptive Controller will specify strategies for each particular problem using details such as size of dataset, number of constraint, and tightness of constraints. It can utilise a collection of constraint programming and metaheuristic methods to solve a VRP. This controller guides the selection of suitable techniques for any variation of the problem, based upon experience and general examination of the dataset. The system will therefore learn to choose or combine the most suitable procedures for each particular problem.

V-LAB combines different technologies to create a multi-agent software system that will facilitate companies competing for extra work convenient to their individual schedule. This system will be an appropriate testing ground for the Adaptive Controller. Here a wide range of VRPs will be generated, from small problems with minor constraints, to large sophisticated problems with an abundance of constraints. This work is funded through Enterprise Ireland's Advanced Technologies Research Programme.

References

1. B. Backer, V.Furnon, P. Kilby, P. Prosser, and P. Shaw. Solving vehicle routing problems using constraint programming and metaheuristics. *Journal of Heuristics*, 6:501–523, 2000.
2. P. Cowling, G. Kendall, and E. Soubeiga. Hyperheuristics: A tool for rapid prototyping in scheduling and optimisation. *2nd European Workshop on Evolutionary Computation in Combinatorial Optimization (EvoCOP2002)*, 2279:1–10, April 2002.
3. K. Tan, L. Lee, and K. Ou. Artificial intelligence heuristics in solving vehicle routing problems with time window constraints. *Engineering Applications of Artificial Intelligence*, 14:825–837, 2001.

F. Rossi (Ed.): CP 2003, LNCS 2833, p. 998, 2003.
© Springer-Verlag Berlin Heidelberg 2003

α-Dynamic Controllability of Simple Temporal Problems with Preferences and Uncertainty

Kristen Brent Venable

University of Padova
kvenable@math.unipd.it

Abstract. We define Simple Temporal Problems with Preferences and Uncertainty to handle at, the same time, soft temporal preferences and uncontrollable events. We extend the notion of Dynamic Controllability to this new class of temporal problems and give two algorithms that, given an STPPU in input, respectively check if the property holds and find the highest preference level at which it holds.

Research on temporal reasoning, once exposed to the difficulties of real-life problems, can be found lacking both expressiveness and flexibility. To address the lack of expressiveness in standard Simple Temporal Problems, the *Simple Temporal Problems with Preferences* (STPP) framework merge STPs with semiring-based soft constraints [1]. To address the lack of flexibility in execution of standard STPs, [2] introduced *Simple Temporal Problems under Uncertainty* (STPUs). While durations are given by intervals, timepoints are decided by the agent (requirement) or decided by 'nature' (contingent). We define STPPUs (STPs with Preferences and Uncertainty) a natural unifying model, where there are requirement and contingent time points, and constraints consist of intervals and preference functions that map the elements of the intervals into preferences. A STPU is *dynamically controllable* if there is a online execution strategy that depends only on observed timepoints in the past and that can always be extended to a complete schedule whatever may happen in the future. We extend DC to STPPUs defining α-Dynamic Controllability. An STPPU is α-DC if there is a schedule that satisfies DC and it has an associated preference of at least α. We propose an algorithm that checks α-DC of an STPPU by testing the DC of the STPU obtained considering, on each constraint, the subinterval mapped in a preference $\geq \alpha$. We also propose an algorithm that performs a binary search of the highest preference level α_{max} at which α-DC holds.

References

1. F. Rossi, A. Sperduti, K.B. Venable, L. Khatib, P. Morris, and R. Morris. Learning and solving soft temporal constraints: An experimental study. In *Proc. of CP'02*, pages 249–263, Ithaca, NY, 2002.
2. Thierry Vidal and Hélène Fargier. Handling contingency in temporal constraint networks: From consistency to controllabilities. *Journal of Experimental and Theoretical Artificial Intelligence*, 11(1):23–45, 1999.

F. Rossi (Ed.): CP 2003, LNCS 2833, p. 999, 2003.

Computing Explanations
for Global Scheduling Constraints

Petr Vilím

Charles University, Faculty of Mathematics and Physics
Malostranské náměstí 2/25, Praha 1, Czech Republic
vilim@kti.mff.cuni.cz

Abstract. Integration of explanations into a CSP solver is a technique
addressing difficult question *"why my problem has no solution"*. Besides
providing some sort of answer to the user, explanations can be used for
debugging, solving dynamic problems and in advanced search algorithms.
Explanations work pretty well with simple constraints. However, in order
to use explanations together with a global constraint, its filtering algorithm (*i.e.* propagation) has to be enhanced to be explanation-aware.
In my work I focus on such a technique for classical scheduling filtering
algorithms like edge-finding and not-first/not-last.

When working with explanations ([2]), whenever a filtering algorithm reduces
a domain of a variable, an explanation for this reduction have to be generated
and recorded on a stack. The explanation is a set of terms (*i.e.* just propagated
constraint and current domains of involved variables) which justify the reduction.
When a search comes to a dead end, explanations can be used to find a subset
of problem, which is unfeasible. This subset can be very useful for a user. Also,
advanced search techniques can use this information to reduce a search space
(see e.g. [3]).

There are two main dificulties when adapting a filtering algorithm to generate
explanations: to find the actual explanation and to not slow the algorithm down
too much. In case of edge-finding ([4] and not-first/not-last [1], I found such an
algorithms with time complexity $O(n^2)$.

References

1. Baptiste, P., Le Pape, C.: Edge-Finding Constraint Propagation Algorithms for
   Disjunctive and Cumulative Scheduling. In proceedings of the Fifteenth Workshop
   of the U.K. Planning Special Interest Group (1996)
2. Narendra Jussien: e-constraints: explanation-based Constraint Programming. CP01
   Workshop on User-Interaction in Constraint Satisfaction, 2001
3. Christelle Guéret and Narendra Jussien and Christian Prins: Using intelligent backtracking to improve branch and bound methods: an application to Open-Shop problems, European Journal of Operational Research, 2000
4. Paul Martin and David B. Shmoys: A New Approach to Computing Optimal Schedules for the Job-Shop Scheduling Problem. Proceedings of the 5th International
   Conference on Integer Programming and Combinatorial Optimization, IPCO'96

F. Rossi (Ed.): CP 2003, LNCS 2833, p. 1000, 2003.

Restart Strategies: Analysis and Simulation

Huayue Wu and Peter van Beek

School of Computer Science, University of Waterloo, Canada
{hwu,vanbeek}@uwaterloo.ca

Randomized restart is an effective technique for eliminating heavy-tails and improving the performance of backtrack algorithms [1]. Different restart strategies use different cutoff schedules and some of the better studied ones include a fixed-cutoff strategy and Luby et al.'s universal strategy [2]. However, these strategies are more of theoretical interest and in practice Walsh's geometric strategy seems to offer more tangible benefits [3]. Our two focuses are to firstly provide some theoretical results on the geometric strategy and secondly to establish an empirical method for studying the different strategies in a more systematic and efficient manner.

We show that the geometric strategy has tail probability of the form $e^{-\log^2 t}$ and thus establish the effectiveness of the strategy in removing heavy-tails. The mean and variance of the geometric strategy are both finite, and instead of relating these quantities to that of the optimal fixed-cutoff strategy we express them in terms of the strategy parameters (geometric factor and scaling factor). We believe this approach better describes the dynamics of performance change and may be more useful for strategy tuning. For general cases where the exponent of the geometric sequence is some polynomial function of degree m we obtain a tail probability of the form $e^{-(\log t)^{1+\frac{1}{m}}}$.

Our empirical studies adopt a fast simulation based approach suitable for observing general patterns. Given the original run-time distributions, heavy-tail parameters, and strategy parameters as input, we numerically construct the run-time distributions of the restart strategies. The means and variances can be plotted against the input parameters and compared within and across strategy families. Among other results, we confirm that skewness in the original distribution is desirable. We also find that the best strategy in each family is the one that most closely resembles the optimal fixed-cutoff strategy. Lastly, plateaus are sometimes observed in the parameter space of geometric strategies, which may be a robustness feature useful in strategy design. Generally, we found that there is no one best strategy, but there are non-trivial patterns and biases that deserve more in-depth study.

References

1. C.P. Gomes, B. Selman, N. Crato, and H. Kautz. Heavy-tailed phenomenon in satis- fiability and constraint satisfaction problems. *J. of Auto. Reas.*, 24:67–100, 2000.
2. M. Luby, A. Sinclair, and D. Zuckerman. Optimal speedup of Las Vegas algorithms. *Information Processing Letters*, 47:173–180, 1993.
3. T. Walsh. Search in a small world. In *Proceedings of IJCAI-99*, pages 1172–1177.

F. Rossi (Ed.): CP 2003, LNCS 2833, p. 1001, 2003.
© Springer-Verlag Berlin Heidelberg 2003

OpenSolver: A Coordination-Enabled Abstract Branch-and-Prune Tree Search Engine

Peter Zoeteweij

CWI, P.O. Box 94079, 1090 GB AMSTERDAM, The Netherlands
P.Zoeteweij@cwi.nl

Coordination programming deals with building complex software systems from largely autonomous component systems. Cooperative constraint solving (see for example [1]), which is widely recognized as a means to improve efficiency of constraint solving, is an area that may benefit from techniques developed in coordination programming, because the solvers that we want to combine are generally autonomous applications that have diverse interfaces.

OpenSolver is an experimental constraint solver that has been designed with solver cooperation in mind. As a result, it allows for easy coordination. It implements a branch-and-prune tree search solving algorithm that is abstract in the sense that the actual functionality is determined by software plug-ins in a number of predefined categories, corresponding to different aspects of this solving algorithm. A special category of plug-ins covers the *coordination layer* of the solver. Through a plug-in in this category, the execution of the solving algorithm can be controlled, and data can be shared with other solvers.

The main categories of functional plug-ins are domain types for CSP variables, domain reduction functions (DRF's) that perform the actual pruning, schedulers that control the application of the DRF's, branching strategies that expand the search tree, and several categories corresponding to different aspects of a strategy for traversing the search tree.

OpenSolver is the basis for implementing DICE (DIstributed Constraint Environment) [2], a framework for cooperative constraint solving where it plays the role of a component solver, and of a wrapper that allows other solvers to be coordinated through it. For this purpose, a coordination layer plug-in is being developed through which OpenSolver instances can participate in a distributed constraint propagation algorithm, and in parallel search. These are the main modes of solver cooperation supported by DICE. Other possible coordination layer plug-ins are a user interface that drives a single OpenSolver as a stand-alone configurable constraint solver, and interfaces for nested search, through which an OpenSolver can be used as a DRF, or as a branching strategy plug-in.

References

1. E. Monfroy, F. Arbab. Constraints Solving as the Coordination of Inference Engines, in Omicini, Zambonelli, Klusch, Tolksdorf (eds.) *Coordination of Internet Agents: Models, Technologies and Applications*, pp. 399–419, Springer Verlag, 2001.
2. P. Zoeteweij. Coordination-Based Distributed Constraint Solving in DICE. In Brajendra Panda (ed.) *Proceedings of the 2003 ACM Symposium on Applied Computing*, pp. 360–366.

F. Rossi (Ed.): CP 2003, LNCS 2833, p. 1002, 2003.
© Springer-Verlag Berlin Heidelberg 2003

Author Index

Lecture Notes in Computer Science

For information about Vols. 1–2746
please contact your bookseller or Springer-Verlag